Sixth
Edition

BOND MARKETS, ANALYSIS, AND STRATEGIES

Frank J. Fabozzi, CFA

Adjunct Professor of Finance and Becton Fellow
School of Management
Yale University

UPPER SADDLE RIVER, NEW JERSEY 07458

Library of Congress Cataloging-in-Publication Data

Fabozzi, Frank J.
  Bond markets, analysis and strategies / Frank J. Fabozzi.—6th ed.
    p. cm.
  ISBN 0-13-198643-0
  1. Bonds.   2. Investment analysis.   3. Portfolio management.   4. Bond market.
  I. Title.

HG4651.F28 2006
332.63'23—dc22

2006041617

AVP/Executive Editor: David Alexander
VP/Editorial Director: Jeff Shelstad
Manager, Product Development:
  Pamela Hersperger
Editorial Assistant: Michael Dittamo
Media Project Manager: Peter Snell
AVP/Executive Marketing Manager:
  Sharon Koch
Marketing Assistant: Patrick Barbera
Associate Director, Production Editorial:
  Judy Leale
Senior Managing Editor: Cynthia Regan
Senior Production Editor: Carol Samet
Permissions Coordinator: Charles Morris
Associate Director, Manufacturing:
  Vinnie Scelta

Manufacturing Buyer: Michelle Klein
Design/Composition Manager:
  Christy Mahon
Cover Design: Kiwi Design
Cover Illustration/Photo: Peter Gridley/
  Taxi/Getty Images, Inc.
Manager, Cover Visual Research &
  Permissions: Karen Sanatar
Composition: GGS Book Services
Full-Service Project Management:
  GGS Book Services
Printer/Binder:
  RRDonnelley-Harrisonburg
Typeface: 10/12 Times Ten Roman

Credits and acknowledgments borrowed from other sources and reproduced, with permission, in this textbook appear on appropriate page within the text.

Pearson Education LTD.
Pearson Education Singapore, Pte. Ltd
Pearson Education, Canada, Ltd
Pearson Education–Japan

Pearson Education Australia PTY, Limited
Pearson Education North Asia Ltd
Pearson Educación de Mexico, S.A. de C.V.
Pearson Education Malaysia, Pte. Ltd

10 9 8 7 6 5 4 3 2 1
ISBN: 0-13-198643-0

To the memory of two wonderful mothers,
Josephine Fabozzi and Patricia Marie Hieber

Brief Contents

Preface   **xv**

Chapter 1   Introduction   1
Chapter 2   Pricing of Bonds   13
Chapter 3   Measuring Yield   34
Chapter 4   Bond Price Volatility   58
Chapter 5   Factors Affecting Bond Yields and the Term Structure of
             Interest Rates   94
Chapter 6   Treasury and Agency Securities Markets   127
Chapter 7   Corporate Debt Instruments   155
Chapter 8   Municipal Securities   187
Chapter 9   Non-U.S. Bonds   206
Chapter 10   Residential Mortgage Loans   225
Chapter 11   Mortgage Pass-Through Securities   243
Chapter 12   Collateralized Mortgage Obligations and Stripped
             Mortgage-Backed Securities   273
Chapter 13   Commercial Mortgage-Backed Securities   304
Chapter 14   Asset-Backed Securities   328
Chapter 15   Collateralized Debt Obligations   348
Chapter 16   Interest-Rate Models   362
Chapter 17   Analysis of Bonds with Embedded Options   377
Chapter 18   Analysis of Residential Mortgage-Backed
             Securities   407
Chapter 19   Analysis of Convertible Bonds   432
Chapter 20   Corporate Bond Credit Analysis   444
Chapter 21   Credit Risk Modeling   493
Chapter 22   Active Bond Portfolio Management Strategies   510
Chapter 23   Indexing   550
Chapter 24   Liability Funding Strategies   560
Chapter 25   Bond Performance Measurement and Evaluation   592
Chapter 26   Interest-Rate Futures Contracts   609
Chapter 27   Interest-Rate Options   640
Chapter 28   Interest-Rate Swaps and Agreements   683
Chapter 29   Credit Derivatives   719

Index   741

Contents

Preface   **xv**

CHAPTER 1   Introduction   1

Sectors of the U.S. Bond Market   2

Overview of Bond Features   3

Risks Associated with Investing in Bonds   6

Secondary Market for Bonds   9

Financial Innovation and the Bond Market   10

Overview of the Book   11

CHAPTER 2   Pricing of Bonds   13

Review of Time Value of Money   13

Pricing a Bond   20

Complications   28

Pricing Floating-Rate and Inverse-Floating-Rate
Securities   29

Price Quotes and Accrued Interest   31

Summary   32

CHAPTER 3   Measuring Yield   34

Computing the Yield or Internal Rate of Return on Any
Investment   35

Conventional Yield Measures   38

Potential Sources of a Bond's Dollar Return   46

Total Return   49

Applications of the Total Return
(Horizon Analysis)   54

Calculating Yield Changes   54

Summary   55

CHAPTER 4   Bond Price Volatility   58

Review of the Price-Yield Relationship for
Option-Free Bonds   59

Price Volatility Characteristics of
Option-Free Bonds   60

Measures of Bond Price Volatility   62

Convexity   73

Additional Concerns When Using Duration   83

Don't Think of Duration as a Measure
of Time   83

Approximating a Bond's Duration and Convexity
Measure   84

Measuring a Bond Portfolio's Responsiveness
to Nonparallel Changes in Interest
Rates   86

Summary   89

**CHAPTER 5   Factors Affecting Bond Yields and the Term
Structure of Interest Rates   94**

Base Interest Rate   95

Risk Premium   96

Term Structure of Interest Rates   101

Summary   122

**CHAPTER 6   Treasury and Agency Securities
Markets   127**

Treasury Securities   127

Stripped Treasury Securities   146

Federal Agency Securities   147

Summary   153

CHAPTER 7   Corporate Debt Instruments   155

Corporate Bonds   156

Medium-Term Notes   174

Commercial Paper   177

Bankruptcy and Creditor Rights   182

Summary   184

CHAPTER 8   Municipal Securities   187

Types and Features of Municipal
Securities   188

Municipal Money Market Products   195

Municipal Derivative Securities   196

Credit Risk   199

Risks Associated with Investing in Municipal
Securities   200

Yields on Municipal Bonds   201

Municipal Bond Market   202

The Taxable Municipal Bond Market   203

Summary   204

CHAPTER 9   Non-U.S. Bonds   206

Classification of Global Bond Markets   207

Foreign Exchange Risk and Bond Returns   209

Eurobond Market   210

Non–U.S. Government Bond Markets   214

The Pfandbriefe Market   221

Emerging Market Bonds   221

Summary   222

CHAPTER 10 Residential Mortgage Loans   225

What Is a Mortgage?   226

Participants in the Mortgage Market   226

Alternative Mortgage Instruments   229

Nonconforming Mortgages   235

Risks Associated with Investing in Mortgages   236

Summary   241

CHAPTER 11 Mortgage Pass-Through Securities   243

Cash Flow Characteristics   244

WAC and WAM   244

Agency Pass-Throughs   245

Nonagency Pass-Throughs   246

Prepayment Conventions and Cash Flow   248

Factors Affecting Prepayments and
Prepayment Modeling   256

Cash Flow for Nonagency Pass-Throughs   263

Cash Flow Yield   265

Prepayment Risk and Asset/Liability Management   267

Secondary Market Trading   269

Summary   270

**CHAPTER 12 Collateralized Mortgage Obligations and
Stripped Mortgage-Backed Securities   273**

Collateralized Mortgage Obligations   274

Stripped Mortgage-Backed Securities   298

Summary   300

**CHAPTER 13 Commercial Mortgage-Backed
Securities   304**

Commercial Mortgage Loans   305

Commercial Mortgage-Backed Securities   307

Summary   326

CHAPTER 14 Asset-Backed Securities   328

Creation of an ABS   329

Collateral Type and Securitization Structure   337

Credit Risks Associated with Investing in ABS   338

Review of Several Major Types of ABS   341

Summary   345

CHAPTER 15 Collateralized Debt Obligations   348

Structure of a CDO   349

Arbitrage Transactions   350

Cash Flow Transactions   353

Market Value Transactions   356

Synthetic CDOs   358

Summary   359

CHAPTER 16 Interest-Rate Models   362

Mathematical Description of One-Factor Interest-Rate
Models   363

Arbitrage-Free Versus Equilibrium Models   366

Empirical Evidence on Interest-Rate Changes 369

Selecting an Interest-Rate Model 371

Estimating Interest-Rate Volatility Using
Historical Data 372

Summary 375

**CHAPTER 17 Analysis of Bonds with Embedded
Options 377**

Drawbacks of Traditional Yield Spread Analysis 378

Static Spread: An Alternative to Yield Spread 378

Callable Bonds and Their Investment
Characteristics 383

Components of a Bond with an Embedded
Option 386

Valuation Model 387

Option-Adjusted Spread 400

Effective Duration and Convexity 401

Summary 403

**CHAPTER 18 Analysis of Residential Mortgage-Backed
Securities 407**

Static Cash Flow Yield Methodology 408

Monte Carlo Simulation Methodology 417

Total Return Analysis 427

Summary 428

CHAPTER 19 Analysis of Convertible Bonds 432

Convertible Bond Provisions 432

Minimum Value of a Convertible Bond 434

Market Conversion Price 435

Current Income of Convertible Bond
Versus Stock 436

Downside Risk with a Convertible Bond 437

Investment Characteristics of a Convertible Bond 438

Pros and Cons of Investing in a Convertible Bond 438

Types of Investors in Convertible Bonds 440

Options Approach 441

Summary 442

CHAPTER 20 Corporate Bond Credit Analysis   444

Overview of Corporate Bond Credit Analysis   445

Analysis of Business Risk   447

Corporate Governance Risk   450

Financial Risk   453

Corporate Bond Credit Analysis and
    Equity Analysis   456

Summary   457

Appendix A   459

Appendix B   489

CHAPTER 21 Credit Risk Modeling   493

Difficulties in Credit Risk Modeling   494

Overview of Credit Risk Modeling   495

Credit Ratings Versus Credit Risk Models   496

Structural Models   496

Reduced-Form Models   504

Incomplete Information Models   507

Summary   508

**CHAPTER 22 Active Bond Portfolio Management
    Strategies   510**

Overview of the Investment Management
    Process   511

Tracking Error and Bond Portfolio Strategies   514

Active Portfolio Strategies   522

The Use of Leverage   539

Summary   545

CHAPTER 23 Indexing   550

Objective of and Motivation for Bond Indexing   551

Factors to Consider in Selecting an Index   552

Bond Indexes   553

Indexing Methodologies   554

Logistical Problems in Implementing an Indexing
    Strategy   556

Enhanced Indexing   557

Summary   558

CHAPTER 24 Liability Funding Strategies   560

General Principles of Asset/Liability
    Management   561

Immunization of a Portfolio to Satisfy a
    Single Liability   566

Structuring a Portfolio to Satisfy Multiple
    Liabilities   581

Extensions of Liability Funding Strategies   584

Combining Active and Immunization Strategies   585

Summary   586

**CHAPTER 25 Bond Performance Measurement and
                    Evaluation   592**

Requirements for a Bond Performance and Attribution
    Analysis Process   593

Performance Measurement   593

Performance Attribution Analysis   600

Summary   605

CHAPTER 26 Interest-Rate Futures Contracts   609

Mechanics of Futures Trading   610

Futures Versus Forward Contracts   612

Risk and Return Characteristics of Futures
    Contracts   613

Currently Traded Interest-Rate Futures Contracts   613

Pricing and Arbitrage in the Interest-Rate Futures
    Market   622

Bond Portfolio Management Applications   630

Summary   637

CHAPTER 27 Interest-Rate Options   640

Options Defined   641

Differences Between an Option and a Futures
    Contract   641

Types of Interest-Rate Options   641

Intrinsic Value and Time Value of an Option   644

Profit and Loss Profiles for Simple Naked Option
    Strategies   646

Put–Call Parity Relationship and Equivalent
    Positions   658

Option Price   660

Models for Pricing Options   661

Sensitivity of Option Price to Change in Factors   669

Hedge Strategies   673

Summary   678

CHAPTER 28 Interest-Rate Swaps and Agreements   683

Interest-Rate Swaps   684

Interest-Rate Agreements (Caps and Floors)   708

Summary   715

CHAPTER 29 Credit Derivatives   719

Types of Credit Risk   720

Categorization of Credit Derivatives   721

ISDA Documentation   721

Asset Swaps   723

Total Return Swaps   725

Credit Default Swaps   727

Credit Spread Options   733

Credit Spread Forwards   735

Structured Credit Products   736

Summary   737

Index   741

Preface

The first edition *of Bond Markets, Analysis, and Strategies* was published in 1989. The objective was to provide coverage of the products, analytical techniques for valuing bonds and quantifying their exposure to changes in interest rates, and portfolio strategies for achieving a client's objectives. In the four editions subsequently published and in the current edition, the coverage of each of these areas has been updated. In the product area, the updating has been primarily for the latest developments in mortgage-backed securities and asset-backed securities. The updating of analytical techniques has been in interest rate and credit risk modeling. Strategies for accomplishing investment objectives, particularly employing credit default swaps, have been updated in each edition.

Each edition has benefited from the feedback of readers and instructors using the book at universities and training programs. Many discussions with portfolio managers and analysts, as well as my experiences serving on the board of directors of several funds and consulting assignments, have been invaluable in improving the content of the book. Moreover, my fixed income course at Yale's School of Management and various presentations to institutional investor groups throughout the world provided me with the testing ground for new material.

I am confident that the sixth edition continues the tradition of providing up-to-date information about the bond market and the tools for managing bond portfolios.

NEW TO THIS EDITION

- Three New Chapters
  - "Interest Rate Models" (Chapter 16)
  - "Corporate Bond Credit Analysis" (Chapter 20)
  - "Credit Risk Modeling" (Chapter 21)
- Extensive Revisions
  - "Asset-Backed Securities" (Chapter 14)
  - "Mortgage Pass-Through Securities" (Chapter 11) includes expanded coverage on prepayment modeling
  - "Credit Derivatives" (Chapter 29) includes expanded coverage on single-name credit default swaps and credit default swap indexes
- Two New Appendices
  - "Corporate Bond Credit Analysis" (Chapter 20) features an appendix from Wachovia Securities that will benefit students who want to see how credit analysis is tackled in the real-world rather than presenting a mere crunching of numbers.

FOR INSTRUCTORS

The following supplements are available to adopting instructors. For detailed descriptions, please visit www.prenhall.com/fabozzi.

Instructor's Resource Center (IRC)
Register. Redeem. Login.

The Instructor's Resource Center (IRC) at www.prenhall.com/irc is where instructors can access a variety of print, media, and presentation resources available with this text in downloadable, digital format. For most texts, resources are also available for course management platforms, such as Blackboard, WebCT, and CourseCompass.

It gets better

Once you register, you will not have any additional forms to fill out or multiple usernames and passwords to remember to access new titles and/or editions. As a registered faculty member, you can login directly to download resource files and receive immediate access and instructions for installing course management content to your campus server.

Need help?

Our dedicated technical support team is ready to assist instructors with questions about the media supplements that accompany this text. Visit: http://247.prenhall.com for answers to frequently asked questions and toll-free, user-support phone numbers.

Electronic Instructor's Manual with Solutions
Visit the IRC for this great resource.

ACKNOWLEDGMENTS

I am grateful to Oren Cheyette and Alex Levin for reviewing and commenting on Chapter 16 and Tim Backshall for reviewing and commenting on Chapter 21. Some material in Chapter 20 draws from my work with Jane Howe.

I thank Wachovia Securities for allowing me to include as Appendix A to Chapter 20 the research report coauthored by Eric Sell and Stephanie Renegar, and Martin Fridson for allowing me to include as Appendix B to the same chapter the "Rich/Cheap" recommendation from his weekly publication *Leverage World*. Donald Smith (Boston University) pointed out an error in the valuation of interest rate caps and floors in the previous edition. I thank him for taking the time to point out the error and providing the correct methodology.

I am indebted to the following individuals who shared with me their views on various topics covered in this book: Mark Anson (British Telecommunications Pension Scheme and Hermes Pensions Management Ltd.), William Berliner (Countrywide Securities), Anand Bhattacharya (Countrywide Securities), John Carlson (Fidelity Management and Research), Moorad Choudry (KBC Financial Products), Dwight Churchill (Fidelity Management and Research), Sylvan Feldstein (Guardian Life), Michael Ferri (George Mason University), Sergio Focardi (The Intertek Group), Laurie Goodman (UBS), David Horowitz (Morgan Stanley), Frank Jones (San Jose

State University), Andrew Kalotay (Andrew Kalotay Associates), Dragomir Krgin (Morgan Stanley), Martin Leibowitz (Morgan Stanley), Jack Malvey (Lehman Brothers), Steven Mann (University of South Carolina), Lionel Martellini (EDHEC), Jan Mayle (TIPS), William McLelland, Christian Menn (Cornell University), Ed Murphy (Merchants Mutual Insurance), Wesley Phoa (The Capital Group Companies), Mark Pitts (White Oak Capital Management), Philippe Priaulet (HSBC and University of Evry Val d'Essonne), Scott Richard (Morgan Stanley), Ron Ryan (Ryan ALM), Richard Wilson, David Yuen (Franklin Advisors), Paul Zhao (TIAA-CREF), and Yu Zhu (China Europe International Business School and Fore Research & Management).

I also received extremely helpful comments from a number of colleagues using the text in an academic setting. These individuals helped me refine previous editions, and I am sincerely appreciative of their suggestions. They are:

Şenay Ağca, George Washington University
Michael J. Alderson, St. Louis University
John Edmunds, Babson College
R. Philip Giles, Columbia University
Martin Haugh, Columbia University
Deborah Lucas, Northwestern University
Davinder K. Malhotra, Philadelphia University
John H. Spitzer, University of Iowa
Joel M. Vanden, Dartmouth College
Russell R. Wermers, University of Colorado at Boulder
Xiaoqing Eleanor Xu, Seton Hall University

FEEDBACK

The author and product team would appreciate hearing from you! Let us know what you think about this textbook by writing to college_finance@prenhall.com. Please include "Feedback about Fabozzi 6e" in the subject line.

If you have questions related to this product, please contact our customer service department online at *www.247.prenhall.com*.

CHAPTER 1

INTRODUCTION

After reading this chapter you will understand:

■ the fundamental features of bonds

■ the types of issuers

■ the importance of the term to maturity of a bond

■ floating-rate and inverse-floating-rate securities

■ what is meant by a bond with an embedded option and the effect of an embedded option on a bond's cash flow

■ the various types of embedded options

■ convertible bonds

■ the types of risks faced by investors in fixed-income securities

■ the secondary market for bonds

■ the various ways of classifying financial innovation

A bond is a debt instrument requiring the **issuer** (also called the **debtor** or **borrower**) to repay to the lender/investor the amount borrowed plus interest over a specified period of time. A typical ("plain vanilla") bond issued in the United States specifies (1) a fixed date when the amount borrowed (the principal) is due and (2) the contractual amount of interest, which typically is paid every six months. The date on which the principal is required to be repaid is called the **maturity date**. Assuming that the issuer does not default or redeem the issue prior to the maturity date, an investor holding a bond until the maturity date is assured of a known cash flow pattern.

For a variety of reasons to be discussed later in this chapter, the 1980s and 1990s saw the development of a wide range of bond structures. In the residential mortgage market particularly, new types of mortgage designs were introduced. The practice of pooling of individual mortgages to form mortgage pass-through securities grew dramatically. Using the basic instruments in the mortgage market (mortgages and mortgage pass-through securities), issuers created derivative mortgage instruments such as collateralized mortgage obligations and stripped mortgage-backed securities that met specific investment needs of a broadening range of institutional investors.

SECTORS OF THE U.S. BOND MARKET

The U.S. bond market is the largest bond market in the world. The market is divided into six sectors: U.S. Treasury sector, agency sector,[1] municipal sector, corporate sector, asset-backed securities sector, and mortgage sector. The **Treasury sector** includes securities issued by the U.S. government. These securities include Treasury bills, notes, and bonds. The U.S. Treasury is the largest issuer of securities in the world. This sector plays a key role in the valuation of securities and the determination of interest rates throughout the world.

The **agency sector** includes securities issued by federally related institutions and government-sponsored enterprises. The distinction between these issuers is described in Chapter 6. The securities issued are not backed by any collateral and are referred to as **agency debenture securities**. This sector is the smallest sector of the bond market.

The **municipal sector** is where state and local governments and their authorities raise funds. The two major sectors within the municipal sector are the general obligation sector and the revenue sector. Bonds issued in the municipal sector typically are exempt from federal income taxes. Consequently, the municipal sector is commonly referred to as the **tax-exempt sector**.

The **corporate sector** includes securities issued by U.S. corporations and non-U.S. corporations issued in the United States. Issuers in the corporate sector issue bonds, medium-term notes, structured notes, and commercial paper. The corporate sector is divided into the investment grade and noninvestment grade sectors. In some broad-based bond market indexes described later in this book, the corporate sector is referred to as the "credit sector."

An alternative to the corporate sector where a corporate issuer can raise funds is the **asset-backed securities sector**. In this sector, a corporate issuer pools loans or receivables and uses the pool of assets as collateral for the issuance of a security. The various types of asset-backed securities are described in Chapter 14.

The mortgage sector is the sector where securities are backed by mortgage loans. These are loans obtained by borrowers in order to purchase residential property or to purchase commercial property (i.e., income-producing property). The mortgage sector is thus divided into the **residential mortgage sector** and the **commercial mortgage sector**. Organizations that have classified bond sectors have defined the residential mortgage sector in different ways. For example, the organizations that have created bond indexes include in the residential mortgage sector only mortgage-backed securities issued by a federally related institution or a government-sponsored enterprise. Residential

---

[1] In later chapters we will see how organizations that create bond market indexes provide a more detailed breakdown of the sectors.

mortgage-backed securities issued by corporate entities are often classified as asset-backed securities. Residential mortgage loans and mortgage-backed securities are the subject of Chapters 11 and 12. Commercial mortgages and commercial mortgage-backed securities are described in Chapter 13.

Non-U.S. bond markets include the Eurobond market and other national bond markets. We discuss these markets in Chapter 9.

OVERVIEW OF BOND FEATURES

In this section we provide an overview of some important features of bonds. A more detailed treatment of these features is presented in later chapters. The bond **indenture** is the contract between the issuer and the bondholder, which sets forth all the obligations of the issuer.

Type of Issuer
A key feature of a bond is the nature of the issuer. There are three issuers of bonds: the federal government and its agencies, municipal governments, and corporations (domestic and foreign). Within the municipal and corporate bond markets, there is a wide range of issuers, each with different abilities to satisfy their contractual obligation to lenders.

Term to Maturity
The term to maturity of a bond is the number of years over which the issuer has promised to meet the conditions of the obligation. The maturity of a bond refers to the date that the debt will cease to exist, at which time the issuer will redeem the bond by paying the outstanding principal. The practice in the bond market, however, is to refer to the **term to maturity** of a bond as simply its **maturity** or **term**. As we explain subsequently, there may be provisions in the indenture that allow either the issuer or bondholder to alter a bond's term to maturity.

Generally, bonds with a maturity of between one and five years are considered **short term**. Bonds with a maturity between 5 and 12 years are viewed as **intermediate-term**, and **long-term** bonds are those with a maturity of more than 12 years.

There are three reasons why the term to maturity of a bond is important. The most obvious is that it indicates the time period over which the holder of the bond can expect to receive the coupon payments and the number of years before the principal will be paid in full. The second reason that term to maturity is important is that the yield on a bond depends on it. As explained in Chapter 5, the shape of the yield curve determines how term to maturity affects the yield. Finally, the price of a bond will fluctuate over its life as yields in the market change. As demonstrated in Chapter 4, the volatility of a bond's price is dependent on its maturity. More specifically, with all other factors constant, the longer the maturity of a bond, the greater the price volatility resulting from a change in market yields.

Principal and Coupon Rate
The **principal value** (or simply **principal**) of a bond is the amount that the issuer agrees to repay the bondholder at the maturity date. This amount is also referred to as the **redemption value**, **maturity value**, **par value**, or **face value**.

The **coupon rate**, also called the **nominal rate**, is the interest rate that the issuer agrees to pay each year. The annual amount of the interest payment made to owners during the term of the bond is called the **coupon**. The coupon rate multiplied by the principal of the bond provides the dollar amount of the coupon. For example, a bond with an 8% coupon rate and a principal of $1,000 will pay annual interest of $80. In the United States and Japan, the usual practice is for the issuer to pay the coupon in two semiannual installments. For bonds issued in certain European bond markets, coupon payments are made only once per year.

Note that all bonds make periodic coupon payments, except for one type that makes none. The holder of a **zero-coupon bond** realizes interest by buying the bond substantially below its principal value. Interest is then paid at the maturity date, with the exact amount being the difference between the principal value and the price paid for the bond. The reason behind the issuance of zero-coupon bonds is explained in Chapter 3.

Floating-rate bonds are issues where the coupon rate resets periodically (the coupon reset date) based on a formula. The formula, referred to as the **coupon reset formula**, has the following general form:

$$\text{reference rate} + \text{quoted margin}$$

The quoted margin is the additional amount that the issuer agrees to pay above the reference rate. For example, suppose that the reference rate is the 1-month London interbank offered rate (LIBOR), an interest rate that we discuss in later chapters. Suppose that the quoted margin is 150 basis points. Then the **coupon reset formula** is:

$$\text{1-month LIBOR} + 150 \text{ basis points}$$

So, if 1-month LIBOR on the coupon reset date is 3.5%, the coupon rate is reset for that period at 5.0% (3.5% plus 150 basis points).

The reference rate for most floating-rate securities is an interest rate or an interest rate index. There are some issues where this is not the case. Instead, the reference rate is some financial index such as the return on the Standard & Poor's 500 or a nonfinancial index such as the price of a commodity. Through financial engineering, issuers have been able to structure floating-rate securities with almost any reference rate. In several countries, there are bonds whose coupon reset formula is tied to an inflation index.

While the coupon on floating-rate bonds benchmarked off an interest rate benchmark typically rises as the benchmark rises and falls as the benchmark falls, there are issues whose coupon interest rate moves in the opposite direction from the change in interest rates. Such issues are called **inverse-floating-rate bonds** or **inverse floaters**.

In the 1980s, new structures in the high-yield (junk bond) sector of the corporate bond market provided variations in the way in which coupon payments are made. One reason is that a leveraged buyout (LBO) or a recapitalization financed with high-yield bonds, with consequent heavy interest payment burdens, placed severe cash flow constraints on the corporation. To reduce this burden, firms involved in LBOs and recapitalizations issued **deferred-coupon bonds** that let the issuer avoid using cash to make interest payments for a specified number of years. There are three types of deferred-coupon structures: (1) deferred-interest bonds, (2) step-up bonds, and (3) payment-in-kind bonds. Another high-yield bond structure requires that the issuer reset the coupon rate so that the bond will trade at a predetermined price. High-yield bond structures are discussed in Chapter 7.

In addition to indicating the coupon payments that the investor should expect to receive over the term of the bond, the coupon rate also indicates the degree to which the bond's price will be affected by changes in interest rates. As illustrated in Chapter 4, all other factors constant, the higher the coupon rate, the less the price will change in response to a change in interest rates.

Amortization Feature

The principal repayment of a bond issue can call for either (1) the total principal to be repaid at maturity or (2) the principal repaid over the life of the bond. In the latter case, there is a schedule of principal repayments. This schedule is called an **amortization schedule**. Loans that have this feature are automobile loans and home mortgage loans.

As we will see in later chapters, there are securities that are created from loans that have an amortization schedule. These securities will then have a schedule of periodic principal repayments. Such securities are referred to as **amortizing securities**. Securities that do not have a schedule of periodic principal repayment are called **nonamortizing securities**.

For amortizing securities, investors do not talk in terms of a bond's maturity. This is because the stated maturity of such securities only identifies when the final principal payment will be made. The repayment of the principal is being made over time. For amortizing securities, a measure called the **weighted average life** or simply **average life** of a security is computed. This calculation will be explained later when we cover the two major types of amortizing securities, mortgage-backed securities and asset-backed securities.

Embedded Options

It is common for a bond issue to include a provision in the indenture that gives either the bondholder and/or the issuer an option to take some action against the other party. The most common type of option embedded in a bond is a **call provision**. This provision grants the issuer the right to retire the debt, fully or partially, before the scheduled maturity date. Inclusion of a call feature benefits bond issuers by allowing them to replace an old bond issue with a lower-interest cost issue if interest rates in the market decline. A call provision effectively allows the issuer to alter the maturity of a bond. For reasons explained in the next section, a call provision is detrimental to the bondholder's interests.

The right to call an obligation is also included in most loans and therefore in all securities created from such loans. This is because the borrower typically has the right to pay off a loan at any time, in whole or in part, prior to the stated maturity date of the loan. That is, the borrower has the right to alter the amortization schedule for amortizing securities.

An issue may also include a provision that allows the bondholder to change the maturity of a bond. An issue with a **put provision** included in the indenture grants the bondholder the right to sell the issue back to the issuer at par value on designated dates. Here the advantage to the investor is that if interest rates rise after the issue date, thereby reducing a bond's price, the investor can force the issuer to redeem the bond at par value.

A **convertible bond** is an issue giving the bondholder the right to exchange the bond for a specified number of shares of common stock. Such a feature allows the bondholder to take advantage of favorable movements in the price of the issuer's common stock. An **exchangeable bond** allows the bondholder to exchange the issue for a specified number of common stock shares of a corporation different from the issuer of the bond. These bonds are discussed and analyzed in Chapter 19.

Some issues allow either the issuer or the bondholder the right to select the currency in which a cash flow will be paid. This option effectively gives the party with the right to choose the currency the opportunity to benefit from a favorable exchange rate movement. Such issues are described in Chapter 9.

The presence of embedded options makes the valuation of bonds complex. It requires investors to have an understanding of the basic principles of options, a topic covered in Chapter 17 for callable and putable bonds and Chapter 18 for mortgage-backed securities and asset-backed securities. The valuation of bonds with embedded options frequently is complicated further by the presence of several options within a given issue. For example, an issue may include a call provision, a put provision, and a conversion provision, all of which have varying significance in different situations.

RISKS ASSOCIATED WITH INVESTING IN BONDS

Bonds may expose an investor to one or more of the following risks: (1) interest-rate risk, (2) reinvestment risk, (3) call risk, (4) credit risk, (5) inflation risk, (6) exchange-rate risk, (7) liquidity risk, (8) volatility risk, and (9) risk risk. While each of these risks is discussed further in later chapters, we describe them briefly in the following sections. In later chapters, other risks, such as yield curve risk, event risk, and tax risk, are also introduced.

Interest-Rate Risk
The price of a typical bond will change in the opposite direction from a change in interest rates: As interest rates rise, the price of a bond will fall; as interest rates fall, the price of a bond will rise. This property is illustrated in Chapter 2. If an investor has to sell a bond prior to the maturity date, an increase in interest rates will mean the realization of a capital loss (i.e., selling the bond below the purchase price). This risk is referred to as **interest-rate risk** or **market risk**. This risk is by far the major risk faced by an investor in the bond market.

As noted earlier, the actual degree of sensitivity of a bond's price to changes in market interest rates depends on various characteristics of the issue, such as coupon and maturity. It will also depend on any options embedded in the issue (e.g., call and put provisions), because, as we explain in later chapters, these options are also affected by interest-rate movements.

Reinvestment Income or Reinvestment Risk
As explained in Chapter 3, calculation of the yield of a bond assumes that the cash flows received are reinvested. The additional income from such reinvestment, sometimes called **interest-on-interest**, depends on the prevailing interest-rate levels at the time of reinvestment, as well as on the reinvestment strategy. Variability in the reinvestment rate of a given strategy because of changes in market interest rates is called

reinvestment risk. This risk is that the interest rate at which interim cash flows can be reinvested will fall. Reinvestment risk is greater for longer holding periods, as well as for bonds with large, early cash flows, such as high-coupon bonds. This risk is analyzed in more detail in Chapter 3.

It should be noted that interest-rate risk and reinvestment risk have offsetting effects. That is, interest-rate risk is the risk that interest rates will rise, thereby reducing a bond's price. In contrast, reinvestment risk is the risk that interest rates will fall. A strategy based on these offsetting effects is called immunization, a topic covered in Chapter 24.

Call Risk

As explained earlier, bonds may include a provision that allows the issuer to retire or "call" all or part of the issue before the maturity date. The issuer usually retains this right in order to have flexibility to refinance the bond in the future if the market interest rate drops below the coupon rate.

From the investor's perspective, there are three disadvantages to call provisions. First, the cash flow pattern of a callable bond is not known with certainty. Second, because the issuer will call the bonds when interest rates have dropped, the investor is exposed to reinvestment risk (i.e., the investor will have to reinvest the proceeds when the bond is called at relatively lower interest rates). Finally, the capital appreciation potential of a bond will be reduced because the price of a callable bond may not rise much above the price at which the issuer will call the bond.[2]

Even though the investor is usually compensated for taking call risk by means of a lower price or a higher yield, it is not easy to determine if this compensation is sufficient. In any case the returns from a bond with call risk can be dramatically different from those obtainable from an otherwise comparable noncallable bond. The magnitude of this risk depends on various parameters of the call provision, as well as on market conditions. Call risk is so pervasive in bond portfolio management that many market participants consider it second only to interest-rate risk in importance. Techniques for analyzing callable bonds are presented in Chapter 17.

Credit Risk

It is common to define **credit risk** as the risk that the issuer of a bond will fail to satisfy the terms of the obligation with respect to the timely payment of interest and repayment of the amount borrowed. This form of credit risk is called **default risk**. Market participants gauge the default risk of an issue by looking at the **default rating** or **credit rating** assigned to a bond issue by one of the three rating companies—Standard & Poor's, Moody's, and Fitch. We will discuss the rating systems used by these rating companies (also referred to as rating agencies) in Chapter 7 and the factors that they consider in assigning ratings in Chapter 20.

There are risks other than default that are associated with investing in bonds that are also components of credit risk. Even in the absence of default, an investor is concerned that the market value of a bond issue will decline in value and/or the relative price performance of a bond issue will be worse than that of other bond issues, which the investor is compared against. The yield on a bond issue is made up of two components: (1) the yield

---

[2]The reason for this is explained in Chapter 17.

on a similar maturity Treasury issue and (2) a premium to compensate for the risks associated with the bond issue that do not exist in a Treasury issue—referred to as a spread. The part of the risk premium or spread attributable to default risk is called the **credit spread**.

The price performance of a non-Treasury debt obligation and its return over some investment horizon will depend on how the credit spread of a bond issue changes. If the credit spread increases—investors say that the spread has "widened"—the market price of the bond issue will decline. The risk that a bond issue will decline due to an increase in the credit spread is called **credit spread risk**. This risk exists for an individual bond issue, bond issues in a particular industry or economic sector, and for all bond issues in the economy not issued by the U.S. Treasury.

Once a credit rating is assigned to a bond issue, a rating agency monitors the credit quality of the issuer and can change a credit rating. An improvement in the credit quality of an issue or issuer is rewarded with a better credit rating, referred to as an **upgrade**; a deterioration in the credit quality of an issue or issuer is penalized by the assignment of an inferior credit rating, referred to as a **downgrade**. An unanticipated downgrading of an issue or issuer increases the credit spread sought by the market, resulting in a decline in the price of the issue or the issuer's debt obligation. This risk is referred to as **downgrade risk**.

Consequently, credit risk consists of three types of risk: default risk, credit spread risk, and downgrade risk.

Inflation Risk

Inflation risk or **purchasing-power risk** arises because of the variation in the value of cash flows from a security due to inflation, as measured in terms of purchasing power. For example, if investors purchase a bond on which they can realize a coupon rate of 7% but the rate of inflation is 8%, the purchasing power of the cash flow actually has declined. For all but floating-rate bonds, an investor is exposed to inflation risk because the interest rate the issuer promises to make is fixed for the life of the issue. To the extent that interest rates reflect the expected inflation rate, floating-rate bonds have a lower level of inflation risk.

Exchange-Rate Risk

From the perspective of a U.S. investor, a non–dollar-denominated bond (i.e., a bond whose payments occur in a foreign currency) has unknown U.S. dollar cash flows. The dollar cash flows are dependent on the exchange rate at the time the payments are received. For example, suppose that an investor purchases a bond whose payments are in Japanese yen. If the yen depreciates relative to the U.S. dollar, fewer dollars will be received. The risk of this occurring is referred to as **exchange-rate** or **currency risk**. Of course, should the yen appreciate relative to the U.S. dollar, the investor will benefit by receiving more dollars.

Liquidity Risk

Liquidity or **marketability risk** depends on the ease with which an issue can be sold at or near its value. The primary measure of liquidity is the size of the spread between the bid price and the ask price quoted by a dealer. The wider the dealer spread, the more the liquidity risk. For individual investors who plan to hold a bond until it matures and have the ability to do so, liquidity risk is unimportant. In contrast, institutional investors must market their positions to market periodically. **Marking a position to market**, or simply **marking to market**, means that the portfolio manager must periodically determine the market value of each bond in the portfolio. To get prices that reflect market value, the bonds must trade with enough frequency.

Volatility Risk

As explained in Chapter 17 the price of a bond with certain types of embedded options depends on the level of interest rates and factors that influence the value of the embedded option. One of these factors is the expected volatility of interest rates. Specifically, the value of an option rises when expected interest-rate volatility increases. In the case of a bond that is callable, or a mortgage-backed security, in which the investor has granted the borrower an option, the price of the security falls, because the investor has given away a more valuable option. The risk that a change in volatility will affect the price of a bond adversely is called **volatility risk**.

Risk Risk

There have been new and innovative structures introduced into the bond market. Unfortunately, the risk/return characteristics of these securities are not always understood by money managers. **Risk risk** is defined as not knowing what the risk of a security is. When financial calamities are reported in the press, it is not uncommon to hear a money manager or a board member of the affected organization say "we didn't know this could happen." Although a money manager or a board member may not be able to predict the future, there is no reason why the potential outcome of an investment or investment strategy is not known in advance.

There are two ways to mitigate or eliminate risk risk. The first approach is to keep up with the literature on the state-of-the-art methodologies for analyzing securities. Your reading of this book is a step in that direction. The second approach is to avoid securities that are not clearly understood. Unfortunately, it is investments in more complex securities that offer opportunities for return enhancement. This brings us back to the first approach.

SECONDARY MARKET FOR BONDS

The secondary market is the market where securities that have been issued previously are traded. Secondary trading of common stock occurs at several trading locations in the United States: centralized exchanges and the over-the-counter (OTC) market. Centralized exchanges include the major national stock exchanges (New York Stock Exchange and American Stock Exchange) and regional stock exchanges, which are organized and somewhat regulated markets in specific geographic locations. The OTC market is a geographically dispersed group of market makers linked to one another via telecommunication systems. The dominant OTC market for stocks in the United States is the Nasdaq. In addition, there are two other types of secondary markets for common stock: electronic communication networks and crossing networks.[3]

---

[3]Electronic Communication networks (ECNs) are privately owned broker-dealers that operate as market participants with the Nasdaq system. Crossing networks are systems developed to allow institutional investors to cross orders—that is, match buyers and sellers directly—typically via computer.

The secondary markets in bonds in the United States and throughout the world are quite different from those in stocks.[4] The secondary bond markets are not centralized exchanges but are OTC markets, which are a network of noncentralized (often called fragmented) market makers, each of which provide "bids" and "offers" (in general, "quotes") for each of the issues in which they participate. Thus, an investor's buy or sell is conducted with an individual market maker at his quoted price, which does not emanate from any centralized organization, such as an exchange.

FINANCIAL INNOVATION AND THE BOND MARKET

Since the 1960s, there has been a surge of significant financial innovations, many of them in the bond market. Observers of financial markets have categorized these innovations in different ways. For example, the Economic Council of Canada classifies financial innovations into three broad categories:[5]

- **Market-broadening instruments**, which augment the liquidity of markets and the availability of funds by attracting new investors and offering new opportunities for borrowers.
- **Risk-management instruments**, which reallocate financial risks to those who are less averse to them, or who have offsetting exposure, and who are presumably better able to shoulder them.
- **Arbitraging instruments and processes**, which enable investors and borrowers to take advantage of differences in costs and returns between markets, and which reflect differences in the perception of risk as well as in information, taxation, and regulation.

Another classification system of financial innovations based on more specific functions has been suggested by the Bank for International Settlements: **price-risk-transferring innovations**, **credit-risk-transferring instruments**, **liquidity-generating innovations**, **credit-generating instruments**, and **equity-generating instruments**.[6] Price-risk-transferring innovations are those that provide market participants with more efficient means for dealing with price or exchange-rate risk. Credit-risk-transferring instruments reallocate the risk of default. Liquidity-generating innovations do three things: (1) they increase the liquidity of the market, (2) they allow borrowers to draw upon new sources of funds, and (3) they allow market participants to circumvent capital constraints imposed by regulations. Credit- and equity-generating innovations increase the amount of debt funds available to borrowers and increase the capital base of financial and nonfinancial institutions, respectively.

Stephen Ross suggests two classes of financial innovation: (1) new financial products (financial assets and derivative instruments) better suited to the circumstances of the time (e.g., to inflation and volatile interest rates) and to the markets in which they trade and (2) strategies that primarily use these financial products.[7]

---

[4]Some corporate bonds, however, are listed on the NYSE (traded in the NYSE's so-called "bond room").
[5]*Globalization and Canada's Financial Markets* (Ottawa, Ontario, Canada: Supply and Services Canada, 1989), p. 32.
[6]Bank for International Settlements, *Recent Innovations in International Banking* (Basel: BIS, April 1986).
[7]Stephen A. Ross, "Institutional Markets, Financial Marketing, and Financial Innovation," *Journal of Finance*, July 1989, p. 541.

One of the objectives of this book is to explain the financial innovations that are taking place in the bond market. As you read the chapters on various bond sectors and various bond portfolio strategies, be sure you understand the factors behind the innovations.

OVERVIEW OF THE BOOK

The next four chapters set forth the basic analytical framework necessary to understand the pricing of bonds and their investment characteristics. How the price of a bond is determined is explained in Chapter 2. The various measures of a bond's potential return are illustrated and evaluated critically in Chapter 3, which is followed by an explanation of the price-volatility characteristics of bonds in Chapter 4. The factors that affect the yield of a bond are explained in Chapter 5, and the important role of the term structure of interest rates (i.e., the relationship between maturity and yield) is introduced.

In Chapters 6 through 15 the various sectors of the debt market are described. As Treasury securities provide the benchmark against which all bonds are valued, it is imperative to have a thorough understanding of the Treasury market. Treasury securities, Treasury derivative securities (zero-coupon Treasury securities or "stripped" Treasury securities), and federal agency securities are introduced in Chapter 6. In Chapters 7, 8, and 9 the investment characteristics and special features of U.S. corporate debt, municipal securities, and non–U.S. bonds, respectively, are explained.

Chapters 10, 11, and 12 focus on residential mortgage-backed securities. The various types of residential mortgage instruments are described in Chapter 10. Residential mortgage pass-through securities are discussed in Chapter 11 and derivative mortgage-backed securities (collateralized mortgage obligations and stripped mortgage-backed securities) in Chapter 12. Chapter 13 covers commercial mortgages and commercial mortgage-backed securities. Asset-backed securities and a relatively new debt instrument, collateralized debt obligations, are covered in Chapters 14 and 15, respectively.

In the next four chapters, methodologies for valuing bonds are explained. Chapter 16 provides the basics of interest rate modeling. The lattice method for valuing bonds with embedded options is explained in Chapter 17, and the Monte Carlo simulation model for mortgage-backed securities and asset-backed securities backed by residential loans is explained in Chapter 18. A byproduct of these valuation models is the option-adjusted spread. The analysis of convertible bonds is covered in Chapter 19.

Chapters 20 and 21 deal with corporate bond credit risk. Chapter 20 describes traditional credit analysis. Chapter 21 provides the basics of credit risk modeling, describing the two major models: structural models and reduced-form models.

Portfolio strategies are discussed in Chapters 22–25. Chapter 22 explains the objectives of bond portfolio management and the various types of portfolio strategies, active and structured, the latter designed to achieve the performance of some predetermined benchmark. These strategies include indexing, the subject of Chapter 23, and liability funding strategies (immunization and cash flow matching), the subject of Chapter 24. Measuring and evaluating the investment performance of a fixed-income portfolio manager are explained Chapter 25.

In the last four chapters, the various instruments that can be used to control portfolio risk are explained. Chapter 26 covers interest-rate futures contracts; Chapter 27, interest-rate options; and Chapter 28, interest-rate swaps and interest-rate agreements (caps, floors, collars, and compound options). Coverage includes the pricing of these contracts and their role in bond portfolio management. Credit derivatives are the subject of Chapter 29.

Questions

1. Which sector of the U.S. bond market is referred to as the tax-exempt sector?
2. What is meant by a mortgage-backed security?
3. Who are the major types of issuers of bonds in the United States?
4. What is the cash flow of a 10-year bond that pays coupon interest semiannually, has a coupon rate of 7%, and has a par value of $100,000?
5. What is the cash flow of a seven-year bond that pays no coupon interest and has a par value of $10,000?
6. Give three reasons why the maturity of a bond is important.
7. Generally, in terms of years, how does one classify bonds as short term, intermediate term, and long term?
8. Explain whether or not an investor can determine today what the cash flow of a floating-rate bond will be.
9. Suppose that the coupon reset formula for a floating-rate bond is:

   1-month LIBOR + 220 basis points

   a. What is the reference rate?
   b. What is the quoted margin?
   c. Suppose that on a coupon reset date that 1-month LIBOR is 2.8%. What will the coupon rate be for the period?
10. What is an inverse-floating-rate bond?
11. What is a deferred coupon bond?

12. a. What is meant by an amortizing security?
    b. Why is the maturity of an amortizing security not a useful measure?
13. What is a bond with an embedded option?
14. What does the call provision for a bond entitle the issuer to do?
15. a. What is the advantage of a call provision for an issuer?
    b. What are the disadvantages of a call provision for the bondholder?
16. What does the put provision for a bond entitle the bondholder to do?
17. What are a convertible bond and an exchangeable bond?
18. How do market participants gauge the default risk of a bond issue?
19. Comment on the following statement: Credit risk is more than the risk that an issuer will default.
20. Does an investor who purchases a zero-coupon bond face reinvestment risk?
21. What risks does a U.S. investor who purchases a French corporation's bond whose cash flows are denominated in euros face?
22. What is meant by marking a position to market?
23. Why are liquidity risk and interest-rate risk important to institutional investors even if they plan to hold a bond to its maturity date?
24. What is risk risk?
25. Explain whether the secondary markets for common stocks and bonds are the same.
26. What is a price-risk transferring innovation?

CHAPTER

2 | PRICING OF BONDS

After reading this chapter you will understand:

- the time value of money

- how to calculate the price of a bond

- that to price a bond it is necessary to estimate the expected cash flows and determine the appropriate yield at which to discount the expected cash flows

- why the price of a bond changes in the direction opposite to the change in required yield

- that the relationship between price and yield of an option-free bond is convex

- the relationship between coupon rate, required yield, and price

- how the price of a bond changes as it approaches maturity

- the reasons why the price of a bond changes

- the complications of pricing bonds

- the pricing of floating-rate and inverse-floating-rate securities

- what accrued interest is and how bond prices are quoted

In this chapter we explain how the price of a bond is determined, and in the next we discuss how the yield on a bond is measured. Basic to understanding pricing models and yield measures is an understanding of the time value of money. Therefore, we begin this chapter with a review of this concept.

REVIEW OF TIME VALUE OF MONEY

The notion that money has a time value is one of the basic concepts in the analysis of any financial instrument. Money has time value because of the opportunity to invest it at some interest rate.

13

Future Value

To determine the future value of any sum of money invested today, equation (2.1) can be used:

$$P_n = P_0 (1 + r)^n \qquad\qquad (2.1)$$

where:

n = number of periods
P_n = future value n periods from now (in dollars)
P_0 = original principal (in dollars)
r = interest rate per period (in decimal form)

The expression $(1 + r)^n$ represents the future value of $1 invested today for n periods at a compounding rate of r.

For example, suppose that a pension fund manager invests $10 million in a financial instrument that promises to pay 9.2% per year for six years. The future value of the $10 million investment is $16,956,500; that is,

$$
\begin{aligned}
P_6 &= \$10,000,000(1.092)^6 \\
&= \$10,000,000(1.69565) \\
&= \$16,956,500
\end{aligned}
$$

This example demonstrates how to compute the future value when interest is paid once per year (i.e., the period is equal to the number of years). When interest is paid more than one time per year, both the interest rate and the number of periods used to compute the future value must be adjusted as follows:

$$r = \frac{\text{annual interest rate}}{\text{number of times interest is paid per year}}$$

$$n = \text{number of times interest is paid per year} \times \text{number of years}$$

For example, suppose that the portfolio manager in the first example invests $10 million in a financial instrument that promises to pay an annual interest rate of 9.2% for six years, but the interest is paid semiannually (i.e., twice per year). Then

$$r = \frac{0.092}{2} = 0.046$$
$$n = 2 \times 6 = 12$$

and

$$
\begin{aligned}
P_{12} &= \$10,000,000(1.046)^{12} \\
&= \$10,000,000(1.71546) \\
&= \$17,154,600
\end{aligned}
$$

Notice that the future value of $10 million when interest is paid semiannually ($17,154,600) is greater than when interest is paid annually ($16,956,500), even though the same annual rate is applied to both investments. The higher future value when interest is paid semiannually reflects the greater opportunity for reinvesting the interest paid.

Future Value of an Ordinary Annuity

When the same amount of money is invested periodically, it is referred to as an **annuity**. When the first investment occurs one period from now, it is referred to as an **ordinary annuity**. The future value of an ordinary annuity can be found by finding the future value of each investment at the end of the investment horizon and then adding these future values. However, it is easier to compute the future value of an ordinary annuity using the equation

$$P_n = A\left[\frac{(1+r)^n - 1}{r}\right] \tag{2.2}$$

where A is the amount of the annuity (in dollars). The term in brackets is the **future value of an ordinary annuity of \$1** at the end of n periods.

To see how this formula can be applied, suppose that a portfolio manager purchases \$20 million par value of a 15-year bond that promises to pay 10% interest per year. The issuer makes a payment once a year, with the first annual interest payment occurring one year from now. How much will the portfolio manager have if (1) the bond is held until it matures 15 years from now, and (2) annual payments are invested at an annual interest rate of 8%?

The amount that the portfolio manager will have at the end of 15 years will be equal to:

1. The \$20 million when the bond matures.
2. 15 annual interest payments of \$2,000,000 ($0.10 \times$ \$20 million).
3. The interest earned by investing the annual interest payments at 8% per year.

We can determine the sum of the second and third items by applying equation (2.2). In this illustration the annuity is \$2,000,000 per year. Therefore,

$$A = \$2,000,000$$
$$r = 0.08$$
$$n = 15$$

and

$$P_{15} = \$2,000,000\left[\frac{(1.08)^{15} - 1}{0.08}\right]$$
$$= \$2,000,000\left[\frac{3.17217 - 1}{0.08}\right]$$
$$= \$2,000,000\,[27.152125]$$
$$= \$54,304,250$$

The future value of the ordinary annuity of \$2,000,000 per year for 15 years invested at 8% is \$54,304,250. Because \$30,000,000 ($15 \times$ \$2,000,000) of this future value represents the total dollar amount of annual interest payments made by the issuer and invested by the portfolio manager, the balance of \$24,304,250 (\$54,304,250 − \$30,000,000) is the interest earned by reinvesting these annual interest payments. Thus, the total dollars that the portfolio manager will have at the end of 15 years by making the investment will be:

Par (maturity) value	$20,000,000
Interest payments	30,000,000
Interest on reinvestment of interest payments	24,304,250
Total future dollars	$74,304,250

As you shall see in Chapter 3, it is necessary to calculate these total future dollars at the end of a portfolio manager's investment horizon in order to assess the relative value of a bond.

Let's rework the analysis for this bond assuming that the interest is paid every six months (based on an annual rate), with the first six-month payment to be received and immediately invested six months from now. We shall assume that the semiannual interest payments can be reinvested at an annual interest rate of 8%.

Interest payments received every six months are $1,000,000. The future value of the 30 semiannual interest payments of $1,000,000 to be received plus the interest earned by investing the interest payments is found as follows:

$$A = \$1,000,000$$
$$r = \frac{0.08}{2} = 0.04$$
$$n = 15 \times 2 = 30$$
$$P_{30} = \$1,000,000 \left[\frac{(1.04)^{30} - 1}{0.04} \right]$$
$$= \$1,000,000 \left[\frac{3.2434 - 1}{0.04} \right]$$
$$= \$1,000,000[56.085]$$
$$= \$56,085,000$$

Because the interest payments are equal to $30,000,000, the interest earned on the interest payments reinvested is $26,085,000. The opportunity for more frequent reinvestment of interest payments received makes the interest earned of $26,085,000 from reinvesting the interest payments greater than the $24,304,250 interest earned when interest is paid only one time per year.

The total future dollars that the portfolio manager will have at the end of 15 years by making the investment are as follows:

Par (maturity) value	$20,000,000
Interest payments	30,000,000
Interest on reinvestment of interest payments	26,085,000
Total future dollars	$76,085,000

Present Value

We have explained how to compute the future value of an investment. Now we illustrate how to work the process in reverse; that is, we show how to determine the amount of money that must be invested today in order to realize a specific future value. This amount is called the **present value**. Because, as we explain later in this chapter, the price of any financial instrument is the present value of its expected cash flows, it is necessary to understand present value to be able to price fixed-income instruments.

What we are interested in is how to determine the amount of money that must be invested today at an interest rate of r per period for n periods to produce a specific future value. This can be done by solving the formula for the future value given by equation (2.1) for the original principal (P_0):

$$P_0 = P_n \left[\frac{1}{(1+r)^n} \right]$$

Instead of using P_0, however, we denote the present value by PV. Therefore, the present value formula can be rewritten as

$$PV = P_n \left[\frac{1}{(1+r)^n} \right] \tag{2.3}$$

The term in brackets is the present value of $1; that is, it indicates how much must be set aside today, earning an interest rate of r per period, in order to have $1 n periods from now.

The process of computing the present value is also referred to as **discounting**. Therefore, the present value is sometimes referred to as the **discounted value**, and the interest rate is referred to as the **discount rate**.

To illustrate how to apply equation (2.3), suppose that a portfolio manager has the opportunity to purchase a financial instrument that promises to pay $5 million seven years from now with no interim cash flows. Assuming that the portfolio manager wants to earn an annual interest rate of 10% on this investment, the present value of this investment is computed as follows:

$$r = 0.10$$
$$n = 7$$
$$P_7 = \$5,000,000$$
$$PV = \$5,000,000 \left[\frac{1}{(1.10)^7} \right]$$
$$= \$5,000,000 \left[\frac{1}{1.948717} \right]$$
$$= \$5,000,000 \left[0.513158 \right]$$
$$= \$2,565,791$$

The equation shows that if $2,565,791 is invested today at 10% annual interest, the investment will grow to $5 million at the end of seven years. Suppose that this financial instrument is actually selling for more than $2,565,791. Then the portfolio manager would be earning less than 10% by investing in this financial instrument at a purchase price greater than $2,565,791. The reverse is true if the financial instrument is selling for less than $2,565,791. Then the portfolio manager would be earning more than 10%.

There are two properties of present value that you should recognize. First, for a given future value at a specified time in the future, the higher the interest rate (or discount rate), the lower the present value. The reason the present value decreases as the interest rate increases should be easy to understand: The higher the interest rate that can be earned on any sum invested today, the less has to be invested today to realize a specified future value.

The second property of present value is that for a given interest rate (discount rate), the further into the future the future value will be received, the lower its present value. The reason is that the further into the future a given future value is to be received, the more opportunity there is for interest to accumulate. Thus, fewer dollars have to be invested.

Present Value of a Series of Future Values

In most applications in portfolio management a financial instrument will offer a series of future values. To determine the present value of a series of future values, the present value of each future value must first be computed. Then these present values are added together to obtain the present value of the entire series of future values.

Mathematically, this can be expressed as follows:

$$PV = \sum_{t=1}^{n} \frac{P_t}{(1+r)^t} \tag{2.4}$$

For example, suppose that a portfolio manager is considering the purchase of a financial instrument that promises to make these payments:

Years from Now	Promised Payment by Issuer
1	$ 100
2	100
3	100
4	100
5	1,100

Assume that the portfolio manager wants a 6.25% annual interest rate on this investment. The present value of such an investment can be computed as follows:

Years from Now	Future Value of Payment	Present Value of $1 at 6.25%	Present Value of Payment
1	$ 100	0.9412	$ 94.12
2	100	0.8858	88.58
3	100	0.8337	83.37
4	100	0.7847	78.47
5	1,100	0.7385	812.35
		Present value =	$1,156.89

Present Value of an Ordinary Annuity

When the same dollar amount of money is received each period or paid each year, the series is referred to as an **annuity**. When the first payment is received one period from now, the annuity is called an **ordinary annuity**. When the first payment is immediate, the annuity is called an **annuity due**. In all the applications discussed in this book, we shall deal with ordinary annuities. To compute the present value of an ordinary annuity, the present value of each future value can be computed and then summed. Alternatively, a formula for the present value of an ordinary annuity can be used:

$$PV = A \left[\frac{1 - \dfrac{1}{(1+r)^n}}{r} \right] \tag{2.5}$$

where A is the amount of the annuity (in dollars). The term in brackets is the **present value of an ordinary annuity of \$1 for n periods**.

Suppose that an investor expects to receive \$100 at the end of each year for the next eight years from an investment and that the appropriate discount rate to be used for discounting is 9%. The present value of this ordinary annuity is

$$A = \$100$$
$$r = 0.09$$
$$n = 8$$

$$PV = \$100 \left[\frac{1 - \dfrac{1}{(1.09)^8}}{0.09} \right]$$

$$= \$100 \left[\frac{1 - \dfrac{1}{1.99256}}{0.09} \right]$$

$$= \$100 \left[\frac{1 - 0.501867}{0.09} \right]$$

$$= \$100 \left[5.534811 \right]$$

$$= \$553.48$$

Present Value When Payments Occur More Than Once per Year

In our computations of the present value we have assumed that the future value to be received or paid occurs each year. In practice, the future value to be received may occur more than once per year. When that is the case, the formulas we have developed for determining the present value must be modified in two ways. First, the annual interest rate is divided by the frequency per year.[1] For example, if the future values are received

---

[1]Technically, this is not the proper way for adjusting the annual interest rate. The technically proper method of adjustment is discussed in Chapter 3.

semiannually, the annual interest rate is divided by 2; if they are paid or received quarterly, the annual interest rate is divided by 4. Second, the number of periods when the future value will be received must be adjusted by multiplying the number of years by the frequency per year.

PRICING A BOND

The price of any financial instrument is equal to the present value of the expected cash flows from the financial instrument. Therefore, determining the price requires

1. An estimate of the expected cash flows
2. An estimate of the appropriate required yield

The expected cash flows for some financial instruments are simple to compute; for others, the task is more difficult. The required yield reflects the yield for financial instruments with **comparable risk**, or **alternative (or substitute) investments**.

The first step in determining the price of a bond is to determine its cash flows. The cash flows for a bond that the issuer cannot retire prior to its stated maturity date (i.e., a noncallable bond[2]) consist of

1. Periodic coupon interest payments to the maturity date
2. The par (or maturity) value at maturity

Our illustrations of bond pricing use three assumptions to simplify the analysis:

1. The coupon payments are made every six months. (For most domestic bond issues, coupon interest is, in fact, paid semiannually.)
2. The next coupon payment for the bond is received exactly six months from now.
3. The coupon interest is fixed for the term of the bond.

Consequently, the cash flow for a noncallable bond consists of an annuity of a fixed coupon interest payment paid semiannually and the par or maturity value. For example, a 20-year bond with a 10% coupon rate and a par or maturity value of $1,000 has the following cash flows from coupon interest:

$$\text{annual coupon interest} = \$1,000 \times 0.10$$
$$= \$100$$
$$\text{semiannual coupon interest} = \$100/2$$
$$= \$50$$

Therefore, there are 40 semiannual cash flows of $50, and a $1,000 cash flow 40 six-month periods from now. Notice the treatment of the par value. It is *not* treated as if it

---

[2]In Chapter 17 we discuss the pricing of callable bonds.

is received 20 years from now. Instead, it is treated on a basis consistent with the coupon payments, which are semiannual.

The required yield is determined by investigating the yields offered on comparable bonds in the market. By comparable, we mean noncallable bonds of the same credit quality and the same maturity.[3] The required yield typically is expressed as an annual interest rate. When the cash flows occur semiannually, the market convention is to use one-half the annual interest rate as the periodic interest rate with which to discount the cash flows.

Given the cash flows of a bond and the required yield, we have all the analytical tools to price a bond. As the price of a bond is the present value of the cash flows, it is determined by adding these two present values:

1. The present value of the semiannual coupon payments
2. The present value of the par or maturity value at the maturity date

In general, the price of a bond can be computed using the following formula:

$$P = \frac{C}{1+r} + \frac{C}{(1+r)^2} + \frac{C}{(1+r)^3} + \ldots + \frac{C}{(1+r)^n} + \frac{M}{(1+r)^n}$$

or

$$P = \sum_{t=1}^{n} \frac{C}{(1+r)^t} + \frac{M}{(1+r)^n} \qquad (2.6)$$

where:
P = price (in dollars)
n = number of periods (number of years times 2)
C = semiannual coupon payment (in dollars)
r = periodic interest rate (required annual yield divided by 2)
M = maturity value
t = time period when the payment is to be received

Because the semiannual coupon payments are equivalent to an ordinary annuity, applying equation (2.5) for the present value of an ordinary annuity gives the present value of the coupon payments:

$$C \left[\frac{1 - \frac{1}{(1+r)^n}}{r} \right] \qquad (2.7)$$

---

[3]In Chapter 4 we introduce a measure of interest-rate risk known as duration. There, instead of talking in terms of bonds with the same maturity as being comparable, we recast the analysis in terms of duration.

To illustrate how to compute the price of a bond, consider a 20-year 10% coupon bond with a par value of $1,000. Let's suppose that the required yield on this bond is 11%. The cash flows for this bond are as follows:

1. 40 semiannual coupon payments of $50
2. $1,000 to be received 40 six-month periods from now

The semiannual or periodic interest rate (or periodic required yield) is 5.5% (11% divided by 2).

The present value of the 40 semiannual coupon payments of $50 discounted at 5.5% is $802.31, calculated as

$$C = \$50$$
$$n = 40$$
$$r = 0.055$$

$$= \$50 \left[\frac{1 - \dfrac{1}{(1.055)^{40}}}{0.055} \right]$$

$$= \$50 \left[\frac{1 - \dfrac{1}{8.51332}}{0.055} \right]$$

$$= \$50 \left[\frac{1 - 0.117463}{0.055} \right]$$

$$= \$50 [16.04613]$$
$$= \$802.31$$

The present value of the par or maturity value of $1,000 received 40 six-month periods from now, discounted at 5.5%, is $117.46, as follows:

$$\frac{\$1,000}{(1.055)^{40}} = \frac{\$1,000}{8.51332} = \$117.46$$

The price of the bond is then equal to the sum of the two present values:

Present value of coupon payments	$802.31
+ Present value of par (maturity value)	117.46
Price	$919.77

Suppose that, instead of an 11% required yield, the required yield is 6.8%. The price of the bond would then be $1,347.04, demonstrated as follows.

The present value of the coupon payments using a periodic interest rate of 3.4% (6.8%/2) is

$$\$50\left[\frac{1-\frac{1}{(1.034)^{40}}}{0.034}\right]=\$50[21.69029]$$

$$=\$1,084.51$$

The present value of the par or maturity value of $1,000 received *40 six-month periods from now* discounted at 3.4% is

$$\frac{\$1,000}{(1.034)^{40}}=\$262.53$$

The price of the bond is then as follows:

Present value of coupon payments	$1,084.51
+ Present value of par (maturity value)	262.53
Price	$1,347.04

If the required yield is equal to the coupon rate of 10%, the price of the bond would be its par value, $1,000, as the following calculations demonstrate.

Using a periodic interest rate of 5.0% (10%/2), the present value of the coupon payments is

$$\$50\left[\frac{1-\frac{1}{(1.050)^{40}}}{0.050}\right]=\$50[17.15909]$$

$$=\$857.95$$

The present value of the par or maturity value of $1,000 received *40 six-month periods from now* discounted at 5% is

$$\frac{\$1,000}{(1.050)^{40}}=\$142.05$$

The price of the bond is then as follows:

Present value of coupon payments	$ 857.95
+ Present value of par (maturity value)	142.05
Price	$1,000.00

Pricing Zero-Coupon Bonds

Some bonds do not make any periodic coupon payments. Instead, the investor realizes interest as the difference between the maturity value and the purchase price. These bonds are called **zero-coupon bonds**. The price of a zero-coupon bond is calculated by substituting zero for C in equation (2.6):

$$P = \frac{M}{(1+r)^n} \qquad (2.8)$$

Equation (2.8) states that the price of a zero-coupon bond is simply the present value of the maturity value. In the present value computation, however, the number of periods used for discounting is not the number of years to maturity of the bond, but rather double the number of years. The discount rate is one-half the required annual yield. For example, the price of a zero-coupon bond that matures 15 years from now, if the maturity value is $1,000 and the required yield is 9.4%, is $252.12, as shown:

$$M = \$1,000$$

$$r = 0.047 \left(= \frac{0.094}{2} \right)$$

$$n = 30 (= 2 \times 15)$$

$$P = \frac{\$1,000}{(1.047)^{30}}$$

$$= \frac{\$1,000}{3.96644}$$

$$= \$252.12$$

Price-Yield Relationship

A fundamental property of a bond is that its price changes in the opposite direction from the change in the required yield. The reason is that the price of the bond is the present value of the cash flows. As the required yield increases, the present value of the cash flow decreases; hence the price decreases. The opposite is true when the required yield decreases: The present value of the cash flows increases, and therefore the price of the bond increases. This can be seen by examining the price for the 20-year 10% bond when the required yield is 11%, 10%, and 6.8%. Exhibit 2-1 shows the price of the 20-year 10% coupon bond for various required yields.

If we graph the price-yield relationship for any noncallable bond, we will find that it has the "bowed" shape shown in Exhibit 2-2. This shape is referred to as convex. The convexity of the price-yield relationship has important implications for the investment properties of a bond, as we explain in Chapter 4.

Relationship Between Coupon Rate, Required Yield, and Price

As yields in the marketplace change, the only variable that can change to compensate an investor for the new required yield in the market is the price of the bond. When the coupon rate is equal to the required yield, the price of the bond will be equal to its par value, as we demonstrated for the 20-year 10% coupon bond.

Yield	Price	Yield	Price
0.045	$1,720.32	0.110	$919.77
0.050	1,627.57	0.115	883.50
0.055	1,541.76	0.120	849.54
0.060	1,462.30	0.125	817.70
0.065	1,388.65	0.130	787.82
0.070	1,320.33	0.135	759.75
0.075	1,256.89	0.140	733.37
0.080	1,197.93	0.145	708.53
0.085	1,143.08	0.150	685.14
0.090	1,092.01	0.155	663.08
0.095	1,044.41	0.160	642.26
0.100	1,000.00	0.165	622.59
0.105	958.53		

EXHIBIT 2-1   Price-Yield Relationship for a 20-Year 10% Coupon Bond

When yields in the marketplace rise above the coupon rate at *a given point in time*, the price of the bond adjusts so that an investor contemplating the purchase of the bond can realize some additional interest. If it did not, investors would not buy the issue because it offers a below market yield; the resulting lack of demand would cause the price to fall and thus the yield on the bond to increase. This is how a bond's price falls below its par value.

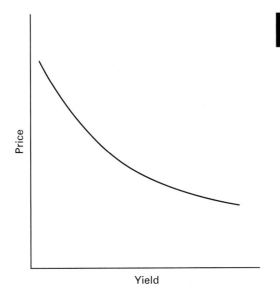

EXHIBIT 2-2   Shape of Price-Yield Relationship

The capital appreciation realized by holding the bond to maturity represents a form of interest to a new investor to compensate for a coupon rate that is lower than the required yield. When a bond sells below its par value, it is said to be selling at a **discount**. In our earlier calculation of bond price we saw that when the required yield is greater than the coupon rate, the price of the bond is always lower than the par value ($1,000).

When the required yield in the market is below the coupon rate, the bond must sell above its par value. This is because investors who have the opportunity to purchase the bond at par would be getting a coupon rate in excess of what the market requires. As a result, investors would bid up the price of the bond because its yield is so attractive. The price would eventually be bid up to a level where the bond offers the required yield in the market. A bond whose price is above its par value is said to be selling at a **premium**. The relationship between coupon rate, required yield, and price can be summarized as follows:

coupon rate < required yield ↔ price < par (discount bond)

coupon rate = required yield ↔ price = par

coupon rate > required yield ↔ price > par (premium bond)

Relationship Between Bond Price and Time If Interest Rates Are Unchanged

If the required yield does not change between the time the bond is purchased and the maturity date, what will happen to the price of the bond? For a bond selling at par value, the coupon rate is equal to the required yield. As the bond moves closer to maturity, the bond will continue to sell at par value. Its price will remain constant as the bond moves toward the maturity date.

The price of a bond will *not* remain constant for a bond selling at a premium or a discount. Exhibit 2-3 shows the time path of a 20-year 10% coupon bond selling at a discount and the same bond selling at a premium as it approaches maturity. Notice that the discount bond increases in price as it approaches maturity, assuming that the required yield does not change. For a premium bond, the opposite occurs. For both bonds, the price will equal par value at the maturity date.

Reasons for the Change in the Price of a Bond

The price of a bond will change for one or more of the following three reasons:

1. There is a change in the required yield owing to changes in the credit quality of the issuer.
2. There is a change in the price of the bond selling at a premium or a discount, without any change in the required yield, simply because the bond is moving toward maturity.
3. There is a change in the required yield owing to a change in the yield on comparable bonds (i.e., a change in the yield required by the market).

Reasons 2 and 3 for a change in price are discussed in this chapter. Predicting a change in an issue's credit quality (reason 1) before that change is recognized by the market is one of the challenges of investment management.

EXHIBIT 2-3   Time Path for the Price of a 20-Year 10% Bond Selling at a Discount and Premium as It Approaches Maturity

Year	Price of Discount Bond Selling to Yield 12%	Price of Premium Bond Selling to Yield 7.8%
20.0	$ 849.54	$ 1,221.00
19.5	850.51	1,218.62
19.0	851.54	1,216.14
18.5	852.63	1,213.57
18.0	853.79	1,210.90
17.5	855.02	1,208.13
17.0	856.32	1,205.24
16.5	857.70	1,202.25
16.0	859.16	1,199.14
15.5	860.71	1,195.90
15.0	862.35	1,192.54
14.5	864.09	1,189.05
14.0	865.94	1,185.43
13.5	867.89	1,181.66
13.0	869.97	1,177.74
12.5	872.17	1,173.67
12.0	874.50	1,169.45
11.5	876.97	1,165.06
11.0	879.58	1,160.49
10.5	882.36	1,155.75
10.0	885.30	1,150.83
9.5	888.42	1,145.71
9.0	891.72	1,140.39
8.5	895.23	1,134.87
8.0	898.94	1,129.13
7.5	902.88	1,123.16
7.0	907.05	1,116.97
6.5	911.47	1,110.53
6.0	916.16	1,103.84
5.5	921.13	1,096.89
5.0	926.40	1,089.67
4.5	931.98	1,082.16
4.0	937.90	1,074.37
3.5	944.18	1,066.27
3.0	950.83	1,057.85
2.5	957.88	1,049.11
2.0	965.35	1,040.02
1.5	973.27	1,030.58
1.0	981.67	1,020.78
0.5	990.57	1,010.59
0.0	1,000.00	1,000.00

COMPLICATIONS

The framework for pricing a bond discussed in this chapter assumes that:

1. The next coupon payment is exactly six months away.
2. The cash flows are known.
3. The appropriate required yield can be determined.
4. One rate is used to discount all cash flows.

Let's look at the implications of each assumption for the pricing of a bond.

Next Coupon Payment Due in Less than Six Months

When an investor purchases a bond whose next coupon payment is due in less than six months, the accepted method for computing the price of the bond is as follows:

$$P = \sum_{t=1}^{n} \frac{C}{(1+r)^v (1+r)^{t-1}} + \frac{M}{(1+r)^v (1+r)^{n-1}} \qquad (2.9)$$

where:

$$v = \frac{\text{days between settlement and next coupon}}{\text{days in six-month period}}$$

Note that when v is 1 (i.e., when the next coupon payment is six months away) equation (2.9) reduces to equation (2.6).

Cash Flows May Not Be Known

For noncallable bonds, assuming that the issuer does not default, the cash flows are known. For most bonds, however, the cash flows are not known with certainty. This is because an issuer may call a bond before the stated maturity date. With callable bonds, the cash flow will, in fact, depend on the level of current interest rates relative to the coupon rate. For example, the issuer will typically call a bond when interest rates drop far enough below the coupon rate so that it is economical to retire the bond issue prior to maturity and issue new bonds at a lower coupon rate.[4] Consequently, the cash flows of bonds that may be called prior to maturity are dependent on current interest rates in the marketplace.

Determining the Appropriate Required Yield

All required yields are benchmarked off yields offered by Treasury securities, the subject of Chapter 5. The analytical framework that we develop in this book is one of decomposing the required yield for a bond into its component parts, as we discuss in later chapters.

---

[4]Mortgage-backed securities, discussed in Chapters 11 and 12, are another example; the individual borrowers have the right to prepay all or part of the mortgage obligation prior to the scheduled due date.

One Discount Rate Applicable to All Cash Flows

Our pricing analysis has assumed that it is appropriate to discount each cash flow using the same discount rate. As explained in Chapter 5, a bond can be viewed as a package of zero-coupon bonds, in which case a unique discount rate should be used to determine the present value of each cash flow.

PRICING FLOATING-RATE AND INVERSE-FLOATING-RATE SECURITIES

The cash flow is not known for either a floating-rate or an inverse-floating-rate security; it will depend on the reference rate in the future.

Price of a Floater

The coupon rate of a floating-rate security (or **floater**) is equal to a reference rate plus some spread or margin. For example, the coupon rate of a floater can reset at the rate on a three-month Treasury bill (the reference rate) plus 50 basis points (the spread). The price of a floater depends on two factors: (1) the spread over the reference rate and (2) any restrictions that may be imposed on the resetting of the coupon rate. For example, a floater may have a maximum coupon rate called a **cap** or a minimum coupon rate called a **floor**. The price of a floater will trade close to its par value as long as (1) the spread above the reference rate that the market requires is unchanged and (2) neither the cap nor the floor is reached.[5]

If the market requires a larger (smaller) spread, the price of a floater will trade below (above) par. If the coupon rate is restricted from changing to the reference rate plus the spread because of the cap, then the price of a floater will trade below par.

Price of an Inverse Floater

In general, an inverse floater is created from a fixed-rate security.[6] The security from which the inverse floater is created is called the **collateral**. From the collateral two bonds are created: a floater and an inverse floater. This is depicted in Exhibit 2-4.

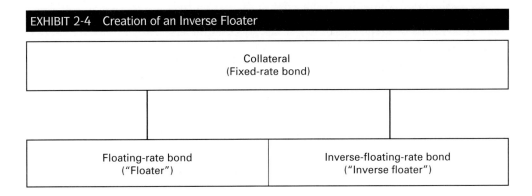

EXHIBIT 2-4   Creation of an Inverse Floater

Collateral
(Fixed-rate bond)

Floating-rate bond
("Floater")

Inverse-floating-rate bond
("Inverse floater")

---

[5] In between coupon reset dates, the floater can trade above or below par.
[6] Inverse floaters are also created using interest-rate swaps without the need to create a floater.

The two bonds are created such that (1) the total coupon interest paid to the two bonds in each period is less than or equal to the collateral's coupon interest in each period and (2) the total par value of the two bonds is less than or equal to the collateral's total par value. Equivalently, the floater and inverse floater are structured so that the cash flow from the collateral will be sufficient to satisfy the obligation of the two bonds.

For example, consider a 10-year 7.5% coupon semiannual-pay bond. Suppose that $100 million of the bond is used as collateral to create a floater with a par value of $50 million and an inverse floater with a par value of $50 million. Suppose that the coupon rate is reset every six months based on the following formula:

Floater coupon: reference rate + 1%
Inverse floater coupon: 14% − reference rate

Notice that the total par value of the floater and inverse floater equals the par value of the collateral, $100 million. The weighted average of the coupon rate of the combination of the two bonds is

$$0.5(\text{reference rate} + 1\%) + 0.5(14\% - \text{reference rate}) = 7.5\%$$

Thus, regardless of the level of the reference rate, the combined coupon rate for the two bonds is equal to the coupon rate of the collateral, 7.5%.

There is one problem with the coupon formulas given here. Suppose that the reference rate exceeds 14%. Then the formula for the coupon rate for the inverse floater will be negative. To prevent this from happening, a floor is placed on the coupon rate for the inverse floater. Typically, the floor is set at zero. Because of the floor, the coupon rate on the floater must be restricted so that the coupon interest paid to the two bonds does not exceed the collateral's coupon interest. In our hypothetical structure, the maximum coupon rate that must be imposed on the floater is 15%. Thus, when a floater and an inverse floater are created from the collateral, a floor is imposed on the inverse and a cap is imposed on the floater.

The valuation of the cap and the floor is beyond our discussion at this point. Here it is sufficient to point out that the price of an inverse floater is found by determining the price of the collateral and the price of the floater. This can be seen as follows:

collateral's price = floater's price + inverse's price

Therefore,

inverse's price = collateral's price − floater's price

Notice that the factors that affect the price of an inverse floater are affected by the reference rate only to the extent that it affects the restrictions on the floater's rate. This is quite an important result. Some investors mistakenly believe that because the coupon rate rises, the price of an inverse floater should increase if the reference rate decreases. This is not true. The key in pricing an inverse floater is how changes in interest rates affect the price of the collateral. The reference rate is important only to the extent that it restricts the coupon rate of the floater.

PRICE QUOTES AND ACCRUED INTEREST

Price Quotes

Throughout this chapter we have assumed that the maturity or par value of a bond is $1,000. A bond may have a maturity or par value greater or less than $1,000. Consequently, when quoting bond prices, traders quote the price as a percentage of par value.

A bond selling at par is quoted as 100, meaning 100% of its par value. A bond selling at a discount will be selling for less than 100; a bond selling at a premium will be selling for more than 100. The examples in Exhibit 2-5 illustrate how a price quote is converted into a dollar price.

In later chapters we will describe the convention for quoting specific security types.

Accrued Interest

When an investor purchases a bond between coupon payments, the investor must compensate the seller of the bond for the coupon interest earned from the time of the last coupon payment to the settlement date of the bond.[7] This amount is called **accrued interest**. The computation of accrued interest depends on the type of bond. For a Treasury coupon security (discussed in Chapter 6), accrued interest is based on the actual number of days the bond is held by the seller. For corporate and municipal bonds, accrued interest is based on a 360-day year, with each month having 30 days.

The amount that the buyer pays the seller is the agreed-upon price plus accrued interest. This is often referred to as the **full price** or **dirty price**. The price of a bond without accrued interest is called the **clean price**.

EXHIBIT 2-5   Price Quotes Converted into a Dollar Price

(1) Price Quote	(2) Converted to a Decimal [= (1)/100]	(3) Par Value	(4) Dollar Price [= (2) × (3)]
97	0.9700000	$ 10,000	$ 9,700.00
$85\frac{1}{2}$	0.8550000	100,000	85,500.00
$90\frac{1}{4}$	0.9025000	5,000	4,512.50
$80\frac{1}{8}$	0.8012500	10,000	8,012.50
$76\frac{5}{32}$	0.7615625	1,000,000	761,562.50
$86\frac{11}{64}$	0.8617188	100,000	86,171.88
100	1.0000000	50,000	50,000.00
109	1.0900000	1,000	1,090.00
$103\frac{3}{4}$	1.0375000	100,000	103,750.00
$105\frac{3}{8}$	1.0537500	25,000	26,343.75
$103\frac{19}{32}$	1.0359375	1,000,000	1,035,937.50

---

[7]The exceptions are bonds that are in default. Such bonds are said to be quoted **flat**; that is, without accrued interest.

SUMMARY

In this chapter we have shown how to determine the price of a noncallable bond. The price is simply the present value of the bond's expected cash flows, the discount rate being equal to the yield offered on comparable bonds. For a noncallable bond, the cash flows are the coupon payments and the par value or maturity value. For a zero-coupon bond, there are no coupon payments. The price is equal to the present value of the maturity value, where the number of periods used to compute the present value is double the number of years and the discount rate is a semiannual yield.

The higher (lower) the required yield, the lower (higher) the price of a bond. Therefore, a bond's price changes in the opposite direction from the change in the required yield. When the coupon rate is equal to the required yield, the bond will sell at its par value. When the coupon rate is less (greater) than the required yield, the bond will sell for less (more) than its par value and is said to be selling at a discount (premium).

Over time, the price of a premium or discount bond will change even if the required yield does not change. Assuming that the credit quality of the issuer is unchanged, the price change on any bond can be decomposed into a portion attributable to a change in the required yield and a portion attributable to the time path of the bond. The price of a floating-rate bond will trade close to par value if the spread required by the market does not change and there are no restrictions on the coupon rate. The price of an inverse floater depends on the price of the collateral from which it is created and the price of the floater.

Questions

1. A pension fund manager invests $10 million in a debt obligation that promises to pay 7.3% per year for four years. What is the future value of the $10 million?

2. Suppose that a life insurance company has guaranteed a payment of $14 million to a pension fund 4.5 years from now. If the life insurance company receives a premium of $10.4 million from the pension fund and can invest the entire premium for 4.5 years at an annual interest rate of 6.25%, will it have sufficient funds from this investment to meet the $14 million obligation?

3. a. The portfolio manager of a tax-exempt fund is considering investing $500,000 in a debt instrument that pays an annual interest rate of 5.7% for four years. At the end of four years, the portfolio manager plans to reinvest the proceeds for three more years and expects that for the three-year period, an annual interest rate of 7.2% can be earned. What is the future value of this investment?

   b. Suppose that the portfolio manager in Question 3, part a, has the opportunity to invest the $500,000 for seven years in a debt obligation that promises to pay an annual interest rate of 6.1% compounded semiannually. Is this investment alternative more attractive than the one in Question 3, part a?

4. Suppose that a portfolio manager purchases $10 million of par value of an eight-year bond that has a coupon rate of 7% and pays interest once per year. The first annual coupon payment will be made one year from now. How much will the portfolio manager have if she (1) holds the bond until it matures eight years from now, and (2) can reinvest all the annual interest payments at an annual interest rate of 6.2%?

5. a. If the discount rate that is used to calculate the present value of a debt obligation's cash flow is increased, what happens to the price of that debt obligation?

   b. Suppose that the discount rate used to calculate the present value of a debt obligation's cash flow is x%. Suppose also that the only cash flow for this debt obligation is $200,000 four years from now and

$200,000 five years from now. For which of these cash flows will the present value be greater?

6. The pension fund obligation of a corporation is calculated as the present value of the actuarially projected benefits that will have to be paid to beneficiaries. Why is the interest rate used to discount the projected benefits important?

7. A pension fund manager knows that the following liabilities must be satisfied:

Years from Now	Liability (in millions)
1	$2.0
2	3.0
3	5.4
4	5.8

Suppose that the pension fund manager wants to invest a sum of money that will satisfy this liability stream. Assuming that any amount that can be invested today can earn an annual interest rate of 7.6%, how much must be invested today to satisfy this liability stream?

8. Calculate for each of the following bonds the price per $1,000 of par value assuming semiannual coupon payments.

Bond	Coupon Rate (%)	Years to Maturity	Required Yield (%)
A	8	9	7
B	9	20	9
C	6	15	10
D	0	14	8

9. Consider a bond selling at par ($100) with a coupon rate of 6% and 10 years to maturity.
   a. What is the price of this bond if the required yield is 15%?
   b. What is the price of this bond if the required yield increases from 15% to 16%, and by what percentage did the price of this bond change?

   c. What is the price of this bond if the required yield is 5%?
   d. What is the price of this bond if the required yield increases from 5% to 6%, and by what percentage did the price of this bond change?
   e. From your answers to Question 9, parts b and d, what can you say about the relative price volatility of a bond in high- compared with low-interest-rate environments?

10. Suppose that you purchased a debt obligation three years ago at its par value of $100,000 and nine years remaining to maturity. The market price of this debt obligation today is $90,000. What are some reasons why the price of this debt obligation could have declined since you purchased it three years ago?

11. Suppose that you are reviewing a price sheet for bonds and see the following prices (per $100 par value) reported. You observe what seem to be several errors. Without calculating the price of each bond, indicate which bonds seem to be reported incorrectly and explain why.

Bond	Price	Coupon Rate (%)	Required Yield (%)
U	90	6	9
V	96	9	8
W	110	8	6
X	105	0	5
Y	107	7	9
Z	100	6	6

12. What is the maximum price of a bond?
13. What is the "dirty" price of a bond?
14. Explain why you agree or disagree with the following statement: "The price of a floater will always trade at its par value."
15. Explain why you agree or disagree with the following statement: "The price of an inverse floater will increase when the reference rate decreases."

CHAPTER

3 | MEASURING YIELD

After reading this chapter you will understand:

- how to calculate the yield on any investment

- how to calculate the current yield, yield to maturity, yield to call, yield to put, and cash flow yield

- how to calculate the yield for a portfolio

- how to calculate the discount margin for a floating-rate security

- the three potential sources of a bond's return

- what reinvestment risk is

- the limitations of conventional yield measures

- how to calculate the total return for a bond

- why the total return is superior to conventional yield measures

- how to use horizon analysis to assess the potential return performance of a bond

- the ways that a change in yield can be measured

In Chapter 2 we showed how to determine the price of a bond, and we described the relationship between price and yield. In this chapter we discuss various yield measures and their meaning for evaluating the relative attractiveness of a bond. We will also explain the ways in which a change in yield is calculated. We begin with an explanation of how to compute the yield on any investment.

COMPUTING THE YIELD OR INTERNAL RATE OF RETURN ON ANY INVESTMENT

The yield on any investment is the interest rate that will make the present value of the cash flows from the investment equal to the price (or cost) of the investment. Mathematically, the yield on any investment, y, is the interest rate that satisfies the equation

$$P = \frac{CF_1}{1+y} + \frac{CF_2}{(1+y)^2} + \frac{CF_3}{(1+y)^3} + \cdots + \frac{CF_N}{(1+y)^N}$$

This expression can be rewritten in shorthand notation as

$$P = \sum_{t=1}^{N} \frac{CF_t}{(1+y)^t} \qquad (3.1)$$

where:

CF_t = cash flow in year t
P = price of the investment
N = number of years

The yield calculated from this relationship is also called the **internal rate of return**.
    Solving for the yield (y) requires a trial-and-error (iterative) procedure. The objective is to find the interest rate that will make the present value of the cash flows equal to the price. An example demonstrates how this is done.
    Suppose that a financial instrument selling for $903.10 promises to make the following annual payments:

Years from Now	Promised Annual Payments (Cash Flow to Investor)
1	$ 100
2	100
3	100
4	1,000

To compute yield, different interest rates must be tried until the present value of the cash flows is equal to $903.10 (the price of the financial instrument). Trying an annual interest rate of 10% gives the following present value:

Years from Now	Promised Annual Payments (Cash Flow to Investor)	Present Value of Cash Flow at 10%
1	$ 100	$ 90.91
2	100	82.64
3	100	75.13
4	1,000	683.01
		Present value = $931.69

Because the present value computed using a 10% interest rate exceeds the price of $903.10, a higher interest rate must be used, to reduce the present value. If a 12% interest rate is used, the present value is $875.71, computed as follows:

Years from Now	Promised Annual Payments (Cash Flow to Investor)	Present Value of Cash Flow at 12%
1	$ 100	$ 89.29
2	100	79.72
3	100	71.18
4	1,000	635.52
		Present value = $875.71

Using 12%, the present value of the cash flow is less than the price of the financial instrument. Therefore, a lower interest rate must be tried, to increase the present value. Using an 11% interest rate:

Years from Now	Promised Annual Payments (Cash Flow to Investor)	Present Value of Cash Flow at 11%
1	$ 100	$ 90.09
2	100	81.16
3	100	73.12
4	1,000	658.73
		Present value = $903.10

Using 11%, the present value of the cash flow is equal to the price of the financial instrument. Therefore, the yield is 11%.

Although the formula for the yield is based on annual cash flows, it can be generalized to any number of periodic payments in a year. The generalized formula for determining the yield is

$$P = \sum_{t=1}^{N} \frac{CF_t}{(1+y)^t} \qquad (3.2)$$

where:

CF_t = cash flow in period t
 n = number of periods

Keep in mind that the yield computed is now the yield for the period. That is, if the cash flows are semiannual, the yield is a semiannual yield. If the cash flows are monthly, the yield is a monthly yield. To compute the *simple* annual interest rate, the yield for the period is multiplied by the number of periods in the year.

Special Case: Investment with Only One Future Cash Flow

In one special case it is not necessary to go through the time-consuming trial-and-error procedure to determine the yield. This is where there is only one future cash flow from the investment. When an investment has only one future cash flow at period $n(CF_n)$, equation (3.2) reduces to

$$P = \frac{CF_n}{(1+y)^n}$$

Solving for yield, y, we obtain

$$y = \left[\frac{CF_n}{P}\right]^{1/n} - 1 \tag{3.3}$$

To illustrate how to use equation (3.3), suppose that a financial instrument currently selling for \$62,321.30 promises to pay \$100,000 six years from now. The yield for this investment is 8.20%, as follows:

$$
\begin{aligned}
y &= \left[\frac{100,000.00}{62,321.30}\right]^{1/6} - 1 \\
&= (1.60459)^{1/6} - 1 \\
&= 1.082 - 1 \\
&= 0.082 \text{ or } 8.2\%
\end{aligned}
$$

Note in equation (3.3) that the ratio of the future cash flow in period n to the price of the financial instrument (i.e., CF_n/P) is equal to the future value per \$1 invested.

Annualizing Yields

In Chapter 2 we annualized interest rates by multiplying by the number of periods in a year, and we called the resulting value the **simple annual interest rate**. For example, a semiannual yield is annualized by multiplying by 2. Alternatively, an annual interest rate is converted to a semiannual interest rate by dividing by 2.

This simplified procedure for computing the annual interest rate given a periodic (weekly, monthly, quarterly, semiannually, and so on) interest rate is not accurate. To obtain an effective annual yield associated with a periodic interest rate, the following formula is used:

$$\text{effective annual yield} = (1 + \text{periodic interest rate})^m - 1$$

where m is the frequency of payments per year. For example, suppose that the periodic interest rate is 4% and the frequency of payments is twice per year. Then

$$
\begin{aligned}
\text{effective annual yield} &= (1.04)^2 - 1 = 1.0816 - 1 \\
&= 0.0816 \text{ or } 8.16\%
\end{aligned}
$$

If interest is paid quarterly, the periodic interest rate is 2% (8%/4), and the effective annual yield is 8.24%, as follows:

$$\text{effective annual yield} = (1.02)^4 - 1 = 1.0824 - 1$$
$$= 0.0824 \text{ or } 8.24\%$$

We can also determine the periodic interest rate that will produce a given annual interest rate by solving the effective annual yield equation for the periodic interest rate. Solving, we find that

$$\text{periodic interest rate} = (1 + \text{effective annual yield})^{1/m} - 1$$

For example, the periodic quarterly interest rate that would produce an effective annual yield of 12% is

$$\text{periodic interest rate} = (1.12)^{1/4} - 1 = 1.0287 - 1$$
$$= 0.0287 \text{ or } 2.87\%$$

CONVENTIONAL YIELD MEASURES

There are several bond yield measures commonly quoted by dealers and used by portfolio managers. In this section we discuss each yield measure and show how it is computed. In the next section we critically evaluate yield measures in terms of their usefulness in identifying the relative value of a bond.

Current Yield

Current yield relates the annual coupon interest to the market price. The formula for the current yield is

$$\text{current yield} = \frac{\text{annual dollar coupon interest}}{\text{price}}$$

For example, the current yield for a 15-year 7% coupon bond with a par value of $1,000 selling for $769.40 is 9.10%:

$$\text{current yield} = \frac{\$70}{\$769.40} = 0.0910 \text{ or } 9.10\%$$

The current yield calculation takes into account only the coupon interest and no other source of return that will affect an investor's yield. No consideration is given to the capital gain that the investor will realize when a bond is purchased at a discount and held to maturity; nor is there any recognition of the capital loss that the investor will realize if a bond purchased at a premium is held to maturity. The time value of money is also ignored.

Yield to Maturity

In the first section of this chapter we explained how to compute the yield or internal rate of return on any investment. The yield is the interest rate that will make the present value of the cash flows equal to the price (or initial investment). The **yield to maturity** is computed in the same way as the yield (internal rate of return); the cash flows are those that the investor would realize by holding the bond to maturity. For a semiannual pay bond, the yield to maturity is found by first computing the periodic interest rate, y, that satisfies the relationship

$$P = \frac{C}{1+y} + \frac{C}{(1+y)^2} + \frac{C}{(1+y)^3} + \cdots + \frac{C}{(1+y)^n} + \frac{M}{(1+y)^n}$$

$$P = \sum_{t=1}^{n} \frac{C}{(1+y)^t} + \frac{M}{(1+y)^n} \qquad \text{(3.4)}$$

where:

P = price of the bond
C = *semiannual* coupon interest (in dollars)
M = maturity value (in dollars)
n = number of periods (number of years $\times$ 2)

For a semiannual pay bond, doubling the periodic interest rate or discount rate (y) gives the yield to maturity. However, recall from our discussion of annualizing yields that doubling the periodic interest rate understates the effective annual yield. Despite this, the market convention is to compute the yield to maturity by doubling the periodic interest rate, y, that satisfies equation (3.4). The yield to maturity computed on the basis of this market convention is called the **bond-equivalent yield.**

The computation of the yield to maturity requires a trial-and-error procedure. To illustrate the computation, consider the bond that we used to compute the current yield. The cash flow for this bond is (1) 30 coupon payments of $35 every six months and (2) $1,000 to be paid 30 six-month periods from now.

To get y in equation (3.4), different interest rates must be tried until the present value of the cash flows is equal to the price of $769.42. The present value of the cash flows of the bond for several periodic interest rates is as follows:

Annual Interest Rate (%)	Semiannual Rate y (%)	Present Value of 30 Payments of $35[a]	Present Value of $1,000 30 Periods from Now[b]	Present Value of Cash Flows
9.00	4.50	$570.11	$267.00	$837.11
9.50	4.75	553.71	248.53	802.24
10.00	5.00	538.04	231.38	769.42
10.50	5.25	532.04	215.45	738.49
11.00	5.50	508.68	200.64	709.32

[a]The present value of the coupon payments is found using the formula

$$\$35 \left[\frac{1 - \frac{1}{(1+y)^{30}}}{y} \right]$$

[b]The present value of the maturity value is found using the formula

$$\$1,000 \left[\frac{1}{(1+y)^{30}} \right]$$

When a 5% semiannual interest rate is used, the present value of the cash flows is $769.42. Therefore, y is 5%, and the yield to maturity on a bond-equivalent basis is 10%. It is much easier to compute the yield to maturity for a zero-coupon bond because equation (3.3) can be used. As the cash flow in period n is the maturity value M, equation (3.3) can be rewritten as[1]

$$y = \left[\frac{M}{P} \right]^{1/n} - 1 \tag{3.5}$$

For example, for a 10-year zero-coupon bond with a maturity value of $1,000, selling for $439.18, y is 4.2%:

$$y = \left[\frac{\$1,000}{\$439.18} \right]^{1/20} - 1 = (2.27697)^{0.05} - 1$$
$$= 1.042 - 1$$
$$= 0.042$$

Note that the number of periods is equal to 20 semiannual periods, which is double the number of years. The number of years is not used because we want a yield value that may be compared with alternative coupon bonds. To get the bond-equivalent annual yield, we must double y, which gives us 8.4%.

The yield-to-maturity calculation takes into account not only the current coupon income but also any capital gain or loss that the investor will realize by *holding the bond to maturity*. In addition, the yield to maturity considers the timing of the cash flows. The relationship among the coupon rate, current yield, and yield to maturity looks like this:

Bond Selling at:	Relationship
Par	Coupon rate = current yield = yield to maturity
Discount	Coupon rate < current yield < yield to maturity
Premium	Coupon rate > current yield > yield to maturity

Yield to Call

As explained in Chapter 1, the issuer may be entitled to call a bond prior to the stated maturity date. When the bond may be called and at what price are specified at the time the bond is issued. The price at which the bond may be called is referred to as the **call price**. For some issues, the call price is the same regardless of when the issue is called. For other callable issues, the call price depends on when the issue is called. That is, there is a **call schedule** that specifies a call price for each call date.

---

[1]That is, M is substituted for CF_n.

For callable issues, the practice has been to calculate a **yield to call** as well as a yield to maturity. The yield to call assumes that the issuer will call the bond at some assumed call date and the call price is then the call price specified in the call schedule. Typically, investors calculate a **yield to first call** or **yield to next call**, a **yield to first par call**, and **yield to refunding**. The yield to first call is computed for an issue that is not currently callable, while the yield to next call is computed for an issue that is currently callable. The yield to refunding is computed assuming the issue will be called on the first date the issue is refundable. (In Chapter 7 we see that an issue may be callable but there may be a period when the issue may not be called using a lower cost of funds than the issue itself (i.e., the issue is nonrefundable).

The procedure for calculating the yield to any assumed call date is the same as for any yield calculation: Determine the interest rate that will make the present value of the expected cash flows equal to the bond's price. In the case of yield to first call, the expected cash flows are the coupon payments to the first call date and the call price as specified in the call schedule. For the yield to first par call, the expected cash flows are the coupon payments to the first date at which the issuer may call the bond at par value plus the last cash flow of par value.

Mathematically, the yield to call can be expressed as follows:

$$P = \frac{C}{1+y} + \frac{C}{(1+y)^2} + \frac{C}{(1+y)^3} + \cdots + \frac{C}{(1+y)^{n^*}} + \frac{M^*}{(1+y)^{n^*}}$$

$$P = \sum_{t=1}^{n^*} \frac{C}{(1+y)^t} + \frac{M^*}{(1+y)^n} \tag{3.6}$$

where:

M^* = call price (in dollars)
n^* = number of periods until the assumed call date (number of years $\times 2$)

For a semiannual pay bond, doubling the periodic interest rate (y) gives the yield to call on a bond-equivalent basis.

To illustrate the computation, consider an 18-year 11% coupon bond with a maturity value of $1,000 selling for $1,169. Suppose that the first call date is 8 years from now and that the call price is $1,055. The cash flows for this bond if it is called in 13 years are (1) 26 coupon payments of $55 every six months, and (2) $1,055 due in 16 six-month periods from now.

The value for y in equation (3.6) is the one that will make the present value of the cash flows to the first call date equal to the bond's price of $1,169. The process of finding the yield to first call is the same as that for finding the yield to maturity. The present value at several periodic interest rates is as follows:

Annual Interest Rate (%)	Semiannual Rate y (%)	Present Value of 16 Payments of $55[a]	Present Value of $1,055 16 Periods from Now[b]	Present Value of Cash Flows
8.000	4.0000	$640.88	$563.27	$1,204.15
8.250	4.1250	635.01	552.55	1,187.56
8.500	4.2500	629.22	542.05	1,171.26
8.535	4.2675	628.41	540.59	1,169.00
8.600	4.3000	626.92	537.90	1,164.83

[a]The present value of the coupon payments is found using the formula

$$\$55\left[\frac{1-\dfrac{1}{(1+y)^{16}}}{y}\right]$$

[b]The present value of the call price is found using the formula

$$\$1,055\left[\frac{1}{(1+y)^{16}}\right]$$

Because a periodic interest rate of 4.2675% makes the present value of the cash flows equal to the price, 4.2675% is y, the yield to first call. Therefore, the yield to first call on a bond-equivalent basis is 8.535%.

Suppose that the first par call date for this bond is 13 years from now. Then the yield to first par call is the interest rate that will make the present value of $55 every six months for the next 26 six-month periods plus the par value of $1,000 26 six-month periods from now equal to the price of $1,169. It is left as an exercise for the reader to show that the semiannual interest rate that equates the present value of the cash flows to the price is 4.3965%. Therefore, 8.793% is the yield to first par call.

Yield to Put

As explained in Chapter 1, an issue can be putable. This means that the bondholder can force the issuer to buy the issue at a specified price. As with a callable issue, a putable issue can have a put schedule. The schedule specifies when the issue can be put and the price, called the put price.

When an issue is putable, a **yield to put** is calculated. The yield to put is the interest rate that makes the present value of the cash flows to the assumed put date plus the put price on that date as set forth in the put schedule equal to the bond's price. The formula is the same as equation (3.6), but M^* is now defined as the put price and n^* as the number of periods until the assumed put date. The procedure is the same as calculating yield to maturity and yield to call.

For example, consider again the 11% coupon 18-year issue selling for $1,169. Assume that the issue is putable at par ($1,000) in five years. The yield to put is the interest rate that makes the present value of $55 per period for 10 six-month periods plus the put price of $1,000 equal to the $1,169. It is left to the reader to demonstrate that a discount rate of 3.471% will result in this equality. Doubling this rate gives 6.942% and is the yield to put.

Yield to Worst

A practice in the industry is for an investor to calculate the yield to maturity, the yield to every possible call date, and the yield to every possible put date. The minimum of all of these yields is called the **yield to worst**.

Cash Flow Yield

In later chapters we will cover fixed income securities whose cash flows include scheduled principal repayments prior to maturity. That is, the cash flow in each period includes interest plus principal repayment. Such securities are called **amortizing securities**. Mortgage-backed securities and asset-backed securities are examples. In addition, the amount that the borrower can repay in principal may exceed the scheduled amount. This excess amount of principal repayment over the amount scheduled is called a **prepayment**. Thus, for amortizing securities, the cash flow each period consists of three components: (1) coupon interest, (2) scheduled principal repayment, and (3) prepayments.

For amortizing securities, market participants calculate a **cash flow yield**. It is the interest rate that will make the present value of the projected cash flows equal to the market price. The difficulty is projecting what the prepayment will be in each period. We will illustrate this calculation in Chapter 11.

Yield (Internal Rate of Return) for a Portfolio

The yield for a portfolio of bonds is not simply the average or weighted average of the yield to maturity of the individual bond issues in the portfolio. It is computed by determining the cash flows for the portfolio and determining the interest rate that will make the present value of the cash flows equal to the market value of the portfolio.[2] Consider a three-bond portfolio as follows:

Bond	Coupon Rate (%)	Maturity (years)	Par Value	Price	Yield to Maturity (%)
A	7.0	5	$10,000,000	$9,209,000	9.0
B	10.5	7	20,000,000	20,000,000	10.5
C	6.0	3	30,000,000	28,050,000	8.5

To simplify the illustration, it is assumed that the coupon payment date is the same for each bond. The portfolio's total market value is $57,259,000. The cash flow for each bond in the portfolio and for the entire portfolio follows:

---

[2]In Chapter 4 we discuss the concept of duration. A good approximation to the yield for a portfolio can be obtained by using duration to weight the yield to maturity of the individual bonds in the portfolio.

Period Cash Flow Received	Bond A	Bond B	Bond C	Portfolio
1	$ 350,000	$ 1,050,000	$ 900,000	$ 2,300,000
2	350,000	1,050,000	900,000	2,300,000
3	350,000	1,050,000	900,000	2,300,000
4	350,000	1,050,000	900,000	2,300,000
5	350,000	1,050,000	900,000	2,300,000
6	350,000	1,050,000	30,900,000	32,300,000
7	350,000	1,050,000	—	1,400,000
8	350,000	1,050,000	—	1,400,000
9	350,000	1,050,000	—	1,400,000
10	10,350,000	1,050,000	—	11,400,000
11	—	1,050,000	—	1,050,000
12	—	1,050,000	—	1,050,000
13	—	1,050,000	—	1,050,000
14	—	21,050,000	—	21,050,000

To determine the yield (internal rate of return) for this three-bond portfolio, the interest rate must be found that makes the present value of the cash flows shown in the last column of the preceding table equal to $57,259,000 (the total market value of the portfolio). If an interest rate of 4.77% is used, the present value of the cash flows will equal $57,259,000. Doubling 4.77% gives 9.54%, which is the yield on the portfolio on a bond-equivalent basis.

Yield Spread Measures for Floating-Rate Securities

The coupon rate for a floating-rate security changes periodically based on the coupon reset formula which has as its components the reference rate and the quoted margin. Since the future value for the reference rate is unknown, it is not possible to determine the cash flows. This means that a yield to maturity cannot be calculated. Instead, there are several conventional measures used as margin or spread measures cited by market participants for floaters. These include spread for life (or simple margin), adjusted simple margin, adjusted total margin, and discount margin.[3]

The most popular of these measures is discount margin, so we will discuss this measure and its limitations below. This measure estimates the average margin over the reference rate that the investor can expect to earn over the life of the security. The procedure for calculating the discount margin is as follows:

Step 1: Determine the cash flows assuming that the reference rate does not change over the life of the security.

Step 2: Select a margin (spread).

Step 3: Discount the cash flows found in step 1 by the current value of the reference rate plus the margin selected in step 2.

Step 4: Compare the present value of the cash flows as calculated in step 3 with the price. If the present value is equal to the security's price, the discount

---

[3]For a discussion of these alternative measures, see Chapter 3 in Frank J. Fabozzi and Steven V. Mann, *Floating Rate Securities* (New York: John Wiley & Sons, 2000).

margin is the margin assumed in step 2. If the present value is not equal to the security's price, go back to step 2 and try a different margin.

For a security selling at par, the discount margin is simply the spread over the reference rate.

To illustrate the calculation, suppose that a six-year floating-rate security selling for 99.3098 pays a rate based on some reference rate plus 80 basis points. The coupon rate is reset every six months. Assume that the current value of the reference rate is 10%. Exhibit 3-1 shows the calculation of the discount margin for this security. The first column shows the current value of the reference rate. The second column sets forth the cash flows for the security. The cash flow for the first 11 periods is equal to one-half the current value of the reference rate (5%) plus the semiannual spread of 40 basis points multiplied by 100. In the twelfth six-month period, the cash flow is 5.4 plus the maturity value of 100. The top row of the last five columns shows the assumed margin. The rows below the assumed margin show the present value of each cash flow. The last row gives the total present value of the cash flows.

For the five assumed yield spreads, the present value is equal to the price of the floating-rate security (99.3098) when the assumed margin is 96 basis points. Therefore, the discount margin on a semiannual basis is 48 basis points and 96 basis points on an annual basis. (Notice that the discount margin is 80 basis points, the same as the spread over the reference rate when the security is selling at par.)

EXHIBIT 3-1   Calculation of the Discount Margin for a Floating-Rate Security

Floating-rate security:
    Maturity: six years
    Coupon rate: reference rate + 80 basis points
    Reset every six months

			Present Value of Cash Flow at Assumed Annual Margin (basis points)				
Period	Reference Rate	Cash Flow[a]	80	84	88	96	100
1	10%	5.4	5.1233	5.1224	5.1214	5.1195	5.1185
2	10	5.4	4.8609	4.8590	4.8572	4.8535	4.8516
3	10	5.4	4.6118	4.6092	4.6066	4.6013	4.5987
4	10	5.4	4.3755	4.3722	4.3689	4.3623	4.3590
5	10	5.4	4.1514	4.1474	4.1435	4.1356	4.1317
6	10	5.4	3.9387	3.9342	3.9297	3.9208	3.9163
7	10	5.4	3.7369	3.7319	3.7270	3.7171	3.7122
8	10	5.4	3.5454	3.5401	3.5347	3.5240	3.5186
9	10	5.4	3.3638	3.3580	3.3523	3.3409	3.3352
10	10	5.4	3.1914	3.1854	3.1794	3.1673	3.1613
11	10	5.4	3.0279	3.0216	3.0153	3.0028	2.9965
12	10	105.4	56.0729	55.9454	55.8182	55.5647	55.4385
		Present value =	100.0000	99.8269	99.6541	99.3098	99.1381

[a]For periods 1–11: cash flow = 100 (reference rate + assumed margin)(0.5); for period 12: cash flow = 100 (reference rate + assumed margin)(0.5) + 100.

A drawback of the discount margin as a measure of the potential return from investing in a floating-rate security is that the discount margin approach assumes that the reference rate will not change over the life of the security. Second, if the floating-rate security has a cap or floor, this is not taken into consideration.

POTENTIAL SOURCES OF A BOND'S DOLLAR RETURN

An investor who purchases a bond can expect to receive a dollar return from one or more of these sources:

1. The periodic coupon interest payments made by the issuer
2. Any capital gain (or capital loss—negative dollar return) when the bond matures, is called, or is sold
3. Interest income generated from reinvestment of the periodic cash flows

The last component of the potential dollar return is referred to as **reinvestment income**. For a standard bond that makes only coupon payments and no periodic principal payments prior to the maturity date, the interim cash flows are simply the coupon payments. Consequently, for such bonds the reinvestment income is simply interest earned from reinvesting the coupon interest payments. For these bonds, the third component of the potential source of dollar return is referred to as the **interest-on-interest component**. For amortizing securities, the reinvestment income is the interest income from reinvesting both the coupon interest payments and periodic principal repayments prior to the maturity date. In our subsequent discussion, we will look at the sources of return for nonamortizing securities (that is, bonds in which no periodic principal is repaid prior to the maturity date).

Any measure of a bond's potential yield should take into consideration each of these three potential sources of return. The current yield considers only the coupon interest payments. No consideration is given to any capital gain (or loss) or interest on interest. The yield to maturity takes into account coupon interest and any capital gain (or loss). It also considers the interest-on-interest component. However, as will be demonstrated later, implicit in the yield-to-maturity computation is the assumption that the coupon payments can be reinvested at the computed yield to maturity. The yield to maturity, therefore, is a *promised* yield—that is, it will be realized only if (1) the bond is held to maturity, and (2) the coupon interest payments are reinvested at the yield to maturity. If neither (1) nor (2) occurs, the actual yield realized by an investor can be greater than or less than the yield to maturity.

The yield to call also takes into account all three potential sources of return. In this case, the assumption is that the coupon payments can be reinvested at the yield to call. Therefore, the yield-to-call measure suffers from the same drawback as the yield to maturity in that it assumes coupon interest payments are reinvested at the computed yield to call. Also, it assumes that the bond will be called by the issuer on the assumed call date.

The cash flow yield, which will be more fully discussed in Chapter 11, also takes into consideration all three sources as is the case with yield to maturity, but it makes two additional assumptions. First, it assumes that the periodic principal repayments are reinvested at the computed cash flow yield. Second, it assumes that the prepayments projected to obtain the cash flows are actually realized.

Determining the Interest-on-Interest Dollar Return

Let's focus on nonamortizing securities. The interest-on-interest component can represent a substantial portion of a bond's potential return. The potential total dollar return from coupon interest and interest on interest can be computed by applying the future value of an annuity formula given in Chapter 2. Letting r denote the semiannual re-investment rate, the interest on interest plus the total coupon payments can be found from the equation

$$\begin{matrix} \text{coupon interest} \\ + \\ \text{interest on interest} \end{matrix} = C\left[\frac{(1+r)^n - 1}{r}\right] \qquad (3.7)$$

The total dollar amount of coupon interest is found by multiplying the semiannual coupon interest by the number of periods:

$$\text{total coupon interest} = nC$$

The interest-on-interest component is then the difference between the coupon interest plus interest on interest and the total dollar coupon interest, as expressed by the formula

$$\text{interest on interest} = C\left[\frac{(1+r)^n - 1}{r}\right] - nC \qquad (3.8)$$

The yield-to-maturity measure assumes that the reinvestment rate is the yield to maturity.

For example, let's consider the 15-year 7% bond that we have used to illustrate how to compute current yield and yield to maturity. If the price of this bond per $1,000 of par value is $769.40, the yield to maturity for this bond is 10%. Assuming an annual reinvestment rate of 10% or a semiannual reinvestment rate of 5%, the interest on interest plus total coupon payments using equation (3.7) is

$$\begin{matrix} \text{coupon interest} \\ + \\ \text{interest on interest} \end{matrix} = \$35\left[\frac{(1.05)^{30} - 1}{0.05}\right]$$

Using equation (3.8), the interest-on-interest component is

$$\text{interest on interest} = \$2{,}325.36 - 30(\$35)$$
$$= \$1{,}275.36$$

Yield to Maturity and Reinvestment Risk

Let's look at the potential total dollar return from holding this bond to maturity. As mentioned earlier, the total dollar return comes from three sources:

1. Total coupon interest of $1,050 (coupon interest of $35 every six months for 15 years)
2. Interest on interest of $1,275.36 earned from reinvesting the semiannual coupon interest payments at 5% every six months
3. A capital gain of $230.60 ($1,000 minus $769.40)

The potential total dollar return if the coupons can be reinvested at the yield to maturity of 10% is then $2,555.96.

Notice that if an investor places the money that would have been used to purchase this bond, $769.40, in a savings account earning 5% semiannually for 15 years, the future value of the savings account would be

$$\$769.40(1.05)^{30} = \$3,325.30$$

For the initial investment of $769.40, the total dollar return is $2,555.90.

So, an investor who invests $769.40 for 15 years at 10% per year (5% semiannually) expects to receive at the end of 15 years the initial investment of $769.40 plus $2,555.90. Ignoring rounding errors, this is what we found by breaking down the dollar return on the bond assuming a reinvestment rate equal to the yield to maturity of 10%. Thus, it can be seen that for the bond to yield 10%, the investor must generate $1,275.36 by reinvesting the coupon payments. This means that to generate a yield to maturity of 10%, approximately half ($1,275.36/$2,555.96) of this bond's total dollar return must come from the reinvestment of the coupon payments.

The investor will realize the yield to maturity at the time of purchase only if the bond is held to maturity and the coupon payments can be reinvested at the computed yield to maturity. The risk that the investor faces is that future reinvestment rates will be less than the yield to maturity at the time the bond is purchased. This risk is referred to as **reinvestment risk**.

There are two characteristics of a bond that determine the importance of the interest-on-interest component and therefore the degree of reinvestment risk: maturity and coupon. For a given yield to maturity and a given coupon rate, the longer the maturity, the more dependent the bond's total dollar return is on the interest-on-interest component in order to realize the yield to maturity at the time of purchase. In other words, the longer the maturity, the greater the reinvestment risk. The implication is that the yield-to-maturity measure for long-term coupon bonds tells little about the potential yield that an investor may realize if the bond is held to maturity. For long-term bonds, the interest-on-interest component may be as high as 80% of the bond's potential total dollar return.

Turning to the coupon rate, for a given maturity and a given yield to maturity, the higher the coupon rate, the more dependent the bond's total dollar return will be on the reinvestment of the coupon payments in order to produce the yield to maturity anticipated at the time of purchase. This means that when maturity and yield to maturity are held constant, premium bonds are more dependent on the interest-on-interest component than are bonds selling at par. Discount bonds are less dependent on the interest-on-interest component than are bonds selling at par. For zero-coupon bonds, none of the bond's total dollar return is dependent on the interest-on-interest component, so a zero-coupon bond has zero reinvestment risk if held to maturity. Thus, the yield earned on a zero-coupon bond held to maturity is equal to the promised yield to maturity.

Cash Flow Yield and Reinvestment Risk

For amortizing securities, reinvestment risk is even greater than for nonamortizing securities. The reason is that the investor must now reinvest the periodic principal repayments in addition to the periodic coupon interest payments. Moreover, as explained later in this book when we cover the two major types of amortizing securities—mortgage-backed securities and asset-backed securities—the cash flows are monthly, not semiannually as with nonamortizing securities. Consequently, the investor must not only reinvest periodic coupon interest payments and principal, but must do it more often. This increases reinvestment risk.

There is one more aspect of nonamortizing securities that adds to their reinvestment risk. Typically, for nonamortizing securities the borrower can accelerate the periodic principal repayment. That is, the borrower can prepay. But a borrower will typically prepay when interest rates decline. Consequently, if a borrower prepays when interest rates decline, the investor faces greater reinvestment risk because he or she must reinvest the prepaid principal at a lower interest rate.

TOTAL RETURN

In the preceding section we explain that the yield to maturity is a **promised** yield. At the time of purchase an investor is promised a yield, as measured by the yield to maturity, if both of the following conditions are satisfied:

1. The bond is held to maturity.
2. All coupon interest payments are reinvested at the yield to maturity.

We focused on the second assumption, and we showed that the interest-on-interest component for a bond may constitute a substantial portion of the bond's total dollar return. Therefore, reinvesting the coupon interest payments at a rate of interest less than the yield to maturity will produce a lower yield than the yield to maturity.

Rather than assuming that the coupon interest payments are reinvested at the yield to maturity, an investor can make an explicit assumption about the reinvestment rate based on personal expectations. The **total return** is a measure of yield that incorporates an explicit assumption about the reinvestment rate.

Let's take a careful look at the first assumption—that a bond will be held to maturity. Suppose, for example, that an investor who has a five-year investment horizon is considering the following four bonds:

Bond	Coupon (%)	Maturity (years)	Yield to Maturity (%)
A	5	3	9.0
B	6	20	8.6
C	11	15	9.2
D	8	5	8.0

Assuming that all four bonds are of the same credit quality, which is most attractive to this investor? An investor who selects bond C because it offers the highest yield to maturity is failing to recognize that the investment horizon calls for selling the bond after five years, at a price that depends on the yield required in the market for 10-year

11% coupon bonds at the time. Hence there could be a capital gain or capital loss that will make the return higher or lower than the yield to maturity promised now. Moreover, the higher coupon on bond C relative to the other three bonds means that more of this bond's return will be dependent on the reinvestment of coupon interest payments.

Bond A offers the second highest yield to maturity. On the surface, it seems to be particularly attractive because it eliminates the problem of realizing a possible capital loss when the bond must be sold prior to the maturity date. Moreover, the reinvestment risk seems to be less than for the other three bonds because the coupon rate is the lowest. However, the investor would not be eliminating the reinvestment risk because after three years the proceeds received at maturity must be reinvested for two more years. The yield that the investor will realize depends on interest rates three years from now on two-year bonds when the proceeds must be rolled over.

The yield to maturity does not seem to be helping us to identify the best bond. How, then, do we find out which is the best bond? The answer depends on the investor's expectations. Specifically, it depends on the investor's planned investment horizon. Also, for bonds with a maturity longer than the investment horizon, it depends on the investor's expectations about required yields in the market at the end of the planned investment horizon. Consequently, any of these bonds can be the best alternative, depending on some reinvestment rate and some future required yield at the end of the planned investment horizon. The total return measure takes these expectations into account and will determine the best investment for the investor, depending on personal expectations.

The yield-to-call measure is subject to the same problems as the yield to maturity. First, it assumes that the bond will be held until the first call date. Second, it assumes that the coupon interest payments will be reinvested at the yield to call. If an investor's planned investment horizon is shorter than the time to the first call date, the bond may have to be sold for less than its acquisition cost. If, on the other hand, the investment horizon is longer than the time to the first call date, there is the problem of reinvesting the proceeds from the time the bond is called until the end of the planned investment horizon. Consequently, the yield to call does not tell us very much. The total return, however, can accommodate the analysis of callable bonds.

Computing the Total Return for a Bond

The idea underlying total return is simple. The objective is first to compute the total future dollars that will result from investing in a bond assuming a particular reinvestment rate. The total return is then computed as the interest rate that will make the initial investment in the bond grow to the computed total future dollars.

The procedure for computing the total return for a bond held over some investment horizon can be summarized as follows. For an assumed reinvestment rate, the dollar return that will be available at the end of the investment horizon can be computed for both the coupon interest payments and the interest-on-interest component. In addition, at the end of the planned investment horizon the investor will receive either the par value or some other value (based on the market yield on the bond when it is sold). The total return is then the interest rate that will make the amount invested in the bond (i.e., the current market price plus accrued interest) grow to the future dollars available at the end of the planned investment horizon.

More formally, the steps for computing the total return for a bond held over some investment horizon are as follows:

Step 1: Compute the total coupon payments plus the interest on interest based on the assumed reinvestment rate. The coupon payments plus the interest on interest can be computed using equation (3.7). The reinvestment rate in this case is one-half the annual interest rate that the investor assumes can be earned on the reinvestment of coupon interest payments.

Step 2: Determine the projected sale price at the end of the planned investment horizon. The projected sale price will depend on the projected required yield at the end of the planned investment horizon. The projected sale price will be equal to the present value of the remaining cash flows of the bond discounted at the projected required yield.

Step 3: Sum the values computed in steps 1 and 2. The sum is the total future dollars that will be received from the investment, given the assumed reinvestment rate and the projected required yield at the end of the investment horizon.[4]

Step 4: To obtain the semiannual total return, use the formula

$$\left[\frac{\text{total future dollars}}{\text{purchase price of bond}} \right]^{1/h} - 1 \tag{3.9}$$

where h is the number of six-month periods in the investment horizon. Notice that this formula is simply an application of equation (3.3), the yield for an investment with just one future cash flow.

Step 5: As interest is assumed to be paid semiannually, double the interest rate found in step 4. The resulting interest rate is the total return.

To illustrate computation of the total return, suppose that an investor with a three-year investment horizon is considering purchasing a 20-year 8% coupon bond for $828.40. The yield to maturity for this bond is 10%. The investor expects to be able to reinvest the coupon interest payments at an annual interest rate of 6% and that at the end of the planned investment horizon the then-17-year bond will be selling to offer a yield to maturity of 7%. The total return for this bond is found as follows:

Step 1: Compute the total coupon payments plus the interest on interest, assuming an annual reinvestment rate of 6%, or 3% every six months. The coupon payments are $40 every six months for three years or six periods

---

[4]The total future dollars computed here differ from the total dollar return that we used in showing the importance of the interest-on-interest component in the preceding section. The total dollar return there includes only the capital gain (or capital loss if there was one), not the purchase price, which is included in calculating the total future dollars; that is,

total dollar return = total future dollars − purchase price of bond

(the planned investment horizon). Applying equation (3.7), the total cou-pon interest plus interest on interest is

$$\begin{array}{c} \text{coupon interest} \\ + \\ \text{interest on interest} \end{array} = \$40\left[\frac{(1.03)^6 - 1}{0.03}\right] = \$40\left[\frac{1.194052 - 1}{0.03}\right]$$

$$= \$40[6.4684]$$
$$= \$258.74$$

Step 2: Determining the projected sale price at the end of three years, assuming that the required yield to maturity for 17-year bonds is 7%, is accom-plished by calculating the present value of 34 coupon payments of $40 plus the present value of the maturity value of $1,000, discounted at 3.5%. The projected sale price is $1,098.51.[5]

Step 3: Adding the amounts in steps 1 and 2 gives total future dollars of $1,357.25.

Step 4: To obtain the semiannual total return, compute the following:

$$\left[\frac{\$1,375.25}{\$828.40}\right]^{1/6} - 1 = (1.63840)^{0.16667} - 1 = 1.0858 - 1$$
$$= 0.0858 \text{ or } 8.58\%$$

Step 5: Double 8.58%, for a total return of 17.16%.

There is no need in this case to assume that the reinvestment rate will be constant for the entire investment horizon. An example will show how the total return measure can accommodate multiple reinvestment rates.

Suppose that an investor has a six-year investment horizon. The investor is consider-ing a 13-year 9% coupon bond selling at par. The investor's expectations are as follows:

1. The first four semiannual coupon payments can be reinvested from the time of receipt to the end of the investment horizon at a simple annual interest rate of 8%.

---

[5]The present value of the 34 coupon payments discounted at 3.5% is

$$\$40\left[\frac{1 - \dfrac{1}{(1.035)^{34}}}{0.035}\right] = \$788.03$$

The present value of the maturity value discounted at 3.5% is

$$\frac{\$1,000}{(1.035)^{34}} = \$310.48$$

The projected sale price is $788.03 plus $310.48, or $1,098.51.

2. The last eight semiannual coupon payments can be reinvested from the time of receipt to the end of the investment horizon at a 10% simple annual interest rate.
3. The required yield to maturity on seven-year bonds at the end of the investment horizon will be 10.6%.

Using these three assumptions, the total return is computed as follows:

Step 1: Coupon payments of $45 every six months for six years (the investment horizon) will be received. The coupon interest plus interest on interest for the first four coupon payments, assuming a semiannual reinvestment rate of 4%, is

$$
\begin{array}{c}
\text{coupon interest} \\
+ \\
\text{interest on interest}
\end{array}
= \$45\left[\frac{(1.04)^4 - 1}{0.04}\right]
$$

$$= \$191.09$$

This gives the coupon plus interest on interest as of the end of the second year (four periods). Reinvested at 4% until the end of the planned investment horizon, four years or eight periods later, $191.09 will grow to

$$\$191.09(1.04)^8 = \$261.52$$

The coupon interest plus interest on interest for the last eight coupon payments, assuming a semiannual reinvestment rate of 5%, is

$$
\begin{array}{c}
\text{coupon interest} \\
+ \\
\text{interest on interest}
\end{array}
= \$45\left[\frac{(1.05)^8 - 1}{0.05}\right]
$$

$$= \$429.71$$

The coupon interest plus interest on interest from all 12 coupon interest payments is $691.23 ($261.52 + $429.71).

Step 2: The projected sale price of the bond, assuming that the required yield is 10.6%, is $922.31.[6]

---

[6]The present value of the coupon payments discounted at 5.3% is

$$\$45\left[\frac{1 - \dfrac{1}{\left(1.053\right)^{14}}}{0.053}\right] = \$437.02$$

The present value of the maturity value discounted at 5.3% is

$$\frac{\$1,000}{(1.053)^{14}} = \$485.29$$

The projected sale price is $437.02 plus $485.29, or $922.31.

Step 3: The total future dollars are $1,613.54 ($691.23 + $922.31).

Step 4: Compute the following:

$$\left[\frac{\$1,613.54}{\$1,000.00}\right]^{1/12} - 1 = (1.61354)^{0.08333} - 1$$
$$= 1.0407 - 1$$
$$= 0.0407 \text{ or } 4.07\%$$

Step 5: Doubling 4.07% gives a total return of 8.14%.

APPLICATIONS OF THE TOTAL RETURN (HORIZON ANALYSIS)

The total return measure allows a portfolio manager to project the performance of a bond on the basis of the planned investment horizon and expectations concerning re-investment rates and future market yields. This permits the portfolio manager to evaluate which of several potential bonds considered for acquisition will perform best over the planned investment horizon. As we have emphasized, this cannot be done using the yield to maturity as a measure of relative value.

Using total return to assess performance over some investment horizon is called **horizon analysis**. When a total return is calculated over an investment horizon, it is referred to as a **horizon return**. In this book we use the terms *horizon return* and *total return* interchangeably.

Horizon analysis is also used to evaluate bond swaps. In a bond swap the portfolio manager considers exchanging a bond held in the portfolio for another bond. When the objective of the bond swap is to enhance the return of the portfolio over the planned investment horizon, the total return for the bond being considered for purchase can be computed and compared with the total return for the bond held in the portfolio to determine if the bond being held should be replaced. We discuss several bond swap strategies in Chapter 25.

An often-cited objection to the total return measure is that it requires the portfolio manager to formulate assumptions about reinvestment rates and future yields as well as to think in terms of an investment horizon. Unfortunately, some portfolio managers find comfort in measures such as the yield to maturity and yield to call simply because they do not require incorporating any particular expectations. The horizon analysis framework, however, enables the portfolio manager to analyze the performance of a bond under different interest-rate scenarios for reinvestment rates and future market yields. Only by investigating multiple scenarios can the portfolio manager see how sensitive the bond's performance will be to each scenario. Chapter 20 explains a framework for incorporating the market's expectation of future interest rates.

CALCULATING YIELD CHANGES

When interest rates or yields change between two time periods, there are two ways that in practice the change is calculated: the absolute yield change and the percentage yield change.

The **absolute yield change** (also called the **absolute rate change**) is measured in basis points and is simply the absolute value of the difference between the two yields. That is,

absolute yield change (in basis points) = |initial yield − new yield| × 100

For example, consider the following three yields over three months:

Month 1	4.45%
Month 2	5.11%
Month 3	4.82%

Then the absolute yield changes are computed as shown below:

absolute yield change from month 1 to month 2 = |4.45% − 5.11%| × 100 = 66 basis points
absolute yield change from month 2 to month 3 = |5.11% − 4.82%| × 100 = 29 basis points

The **percentage yield change** is computed as the natural logarithm of the ratio of the change in yield as shown below:

percentage yield change = 100 × ln (new yield/initial yield)

where ln is the natural logarithm.

Using the three monthly yields earlier, the percentage yield changes are:

absolute yield change from month 1 to month 2 = ln(5.11%/4.45%) = 13.83%
absolute yield change from month 2 to month 3 = ln(4.82%/5.11%) = −5.84%

SUMMARY

In this chapter we have explained the conventional yield measures commonly used by bond market participants: current yield, yield to maturity, yield to call, yield to put, yield to worst, and cash flow yield. We then reviewed the three potential sources of dollar return from investing in a bond—coupon interest, reinvestment income, and capital gain (or loss)—and showed that none of the conventional yield measures deals satisfactorily with all of these sources. The current yield measure fails to consider both reinvestment income and capital gain (or loss). The yield to maturity considers all three sources but is deficient in assuming that all coupon interest can be reinvested at the yield to maturity. The risk that the coupon payments will be reinvested at a rate less than the yield to maturity is called reinvestment risk. The yield to call has the same shortcoming; it assumes that the coupon interest can be reinvested at the yield to call. The cash flow yield makes the same assumptions as the yield to maturity, plus it assumes that periodic principal payments can be reinvested at the computed cash flow yield and that the prepayments are actually realized. We then presented a yield measure, the total return, that is a more meaningful measure for assessing the relative attractiveness of a bond given the investor's or the portfolio manager's expectations and planned investment horizon. The change in yield between two periods can be calculated in terms of the absolute yield change or the percentage yield change.

Questions

1. A debt obligation offers the following payments:

Years from Now	Cash Flow to Investor
1	$2,000
2	2,000
3	2,500
4	4,000

    Suppose that the price of this debt obligation is $7,704. What is the yield or internal rate of return offered by this debt obligation?

2. What is the effective annual yield if the semiannual periodic interest rate is 4.3%?

3. What is the yield to maturity of a bond?

4. What is the yield to maturity calculated on a bond-equivalent basis?

5. a. Show the cash flows for the following four bonds, each of which has a par value of $1,000 and pays interest semiannually:

Bond	Coupon Rate (%)	Number of Years to Maturity	Price
W	7	5	$884.20
X	8	7	948.90
Y	9	4	967.70
Z	0	10	456.39

    b. Calculate the yield to maturity for the four bonds.

6. A portfolio manager is considering buying two bonds. Bond A matures in three years and has a coupon rate of 10% payable semi-annually. Bond B, of the same credit quality, matures in 10 years and has a coupon rate of 12% payable semiannually. Both bonds are priced at par.

    a. Suppose that the portfolio manager plans to hold the bond that is purchased for three years. Which would be the best bond for the portfolio manager to purchase?

    b. Suppose that the portfolio manager plans to hold the bond that is purchased for six years instead of three years. In this case, which would be the best bond for the portfolio manager to purchase?

    c. Suppose that the portfolio manager is managing the assets of a life insurance company that has issued a five-year guaranteed investment contract (GIC). The interest rate that the life insurance company has agreed to pay is 9% on a semiannual basis. Which of the two bonds should the portfolio manager purchase to ensure that the GIC payments will be satisfied and that a profit will be generated by the life insurance company?

7. Consider the following bond:
    Coupon rate = 11%
    Maturity = 18 years
    Par value = $1,000
    First par call in 13 years
    Only put date in five years and putable at par value

    Suppose that the market price for this bond is $1,169.

    a. Show that the yield to maturity for this bond is 9.077%.

    b. Show that the yield to first par call is 8.793%.

    c. Show that the yield to put is 6.942%.

    d. Suppose that the call schedule for this bond is as follows:
    Can be called in eight years at $1,055
    Can be called in 13 years at $1,000
    And suppose this bond can only be put in five years and assume that the yield to first par call is 8.535%. What is the yield to worst for this bond?

8. a. What is meant by an amortizing security?

    b. What are the three components of the cash flow for an amortizing security?

    c. What is meant by a cash flow yield?

9. How is the internal rate of return of a portfolio calculated?

10. What is the limitation of using the internal rate of return of a portfolio as a measure of the portfolio's yield?

11. Suppose that the coupon rate of a floating-rate security resets every six months at a spread of 70 basis points over the reference rate. If the bond is trading at below par value, explain whether the discount margin is greater than or less than 70 basis points.

12. An investor is considering the purchase of a 20-year 7% coupon bond selling for $816 and a par value of $1,000. The yield to maturity for this bond is 9%.
    a. What would be the total future dollars if this investor invested $816 for 20 years earning 9% compounded semiannually?
    b. What are the total coupon payments over the life of this bond?
    c. What would be the total future dollars from the coupon payments and the repayment of principal at the end of 20 years?
    d. For the bond to produce the same total future dollars as in part a, how much must the interest on interest be?
    e. Calculate the interest on interest from the bond assuming that the semiannual coupon payments can be reinvested at 4.5% every six months and demonstrate that the resulting amount is the same as in part d.

13. What is the total return for a 20-year zero-coupon bond that is offering a yield to maturity of 8% if the bond is held to maturity?

14. Explain why the total return from holding a bond to maturity will be between the yield to maturity and the reinvestment rate.

15. For a long-term high-yield coupon bond, do you think that the total return from holding a bond to maturity will be closer to the yield to maturity or the reinvestment rate?

16. Suppose that an investor with a five-year investment horizon is considering purchasing a seven-year 9% coupon bond selling at par. The investor expects that he can reinvest the coupon payments at an annual interest rate of 9.4% and that at the end of the investment horizon two-year bonds will be selling to offer a yield to maturity of 11.2%. What is the total return for this bond?

17. Two portfolio managers are discussing the investment characteristics of amortizing securities. Manager A believes that the advantage of these securities relative to nonamortizing securities is that because the periodic cash flows include principal repayments as well as coupon payments, the manager can generate greater re-investment income. In addition, the payments are typically monthly so even greater reinvestment income can be generated. Manager B believes that the need to re-invest monthly and the need to invest larger amounts than just coupon interest payments make amortizing securities less attractive. Whom do you agree with and why?

18. Assuming the following yields:

    Week 1: 3.84%
    Week 2: 3.51%
    Week 3: 3.95%

    a. Compute the absolute yield change and percentage yield change from week 1 to week 2.
    b. Compute the absolute yield change and percentage yield change from week 2 to week 3.

CHAPTER

4

BOND PRICE VOLATILITY

After reading this chapter you will understand:

- the price–yield relationship of an option-free bond

- the factors that affect the price volatility of a bond when yields change

- the price-volatility properties of an option-free bond

- how to calculate the price value of a basis point

- how to calculate and interpret the Macaulay duration, modified duration, and dollar duration of a bond

- why duration is a measure of a bond's price sensitivity to yield changes

- the spread duration measure for fixed-rate and floating rate bonds

- how to compute the duration of a portfolio and contribution to portfolio duration

- limitations of using duration as a measure of price volatility

- how price change estimated by duration can be adjusted for a bond's convexity

- how to approximate the duration and convexity of a bond

- the duration of an inverse floater

- how to measure a portfolio's sensitivity to a nonparallel shift in interest rates (key rate duration and yield curve reshaping duration)

To employ effective bond portfolio strategies, it is necessary to understand the price volatility of bonds resulting from changes in interest rates. The purpose of this chapter is to explain the price volatility characteristics of a bond and to present several measures to quantify price volatility.

REVIEW OF THE PRICE–YIELD RELATIONSHIP FOR OPTION-FREE BONDS

As we explain in Chapter 2, a fundamental principle of an option-free bond (i.e., a bond that does not have an embedded option) is that the price of the bond changes in the direction opposite to that of a change in the required yield for the bond. This principle follows from the fact that the price of a bond is equal to the present value of its expected cash flows. An increase (decrease) in the required yield decreases (increases) the present value of its expected cash flows and therefore decreases (increases) the bond's price. Exhibit 4-1 illustrates this property for the following six hypothetical bonds, where the bond prices are shown assuming a par value of $100 and interest paid semiannually:

1. A 9% coupon bond with 5 years to maturity
2. A 9% coupon bond with 25 years to maturity
3. A 6% coupon bond with 5 years to maturity
4. A 6% coupon bond with 25 years to maturity
5. A zero-coupon bond with 5 years to maturity
6. A zero-coupon bond with 25 years to maturity

When the price–yield relationship for any option-free bond is graphed, it exhibits the shape shown in Exhibit 4-2. Notice that as the required yield rises, the price of the option-free bond declines. This relationship is not linear, however (i.e., it is not a straight line). The shape of the price–yield relationship for any option-free bond is referred to as **convex**.

EXHIBT 4-1 Price–Yield Relationship for Six Hypothetical Bonds

Required Yield (%)	Price at Required Yield (coupon/maturity in years)					
	9%/5	9%/25	6%/5	6%/25	0%/5	0%/25
6.00	112.7953	138.5946	100.0000	100.0000	74.4094	22.8107
7.00	108.3166	123.4556	95.8417	88.2722	70.8919	17.9053
8.00	104.0554	110.7410	91.8891	78.5178	67.5564	14.0713
8.50	102.0027	105.1482	89.9864	74.2587	65.9537	12.4795
8.90	100.3966	100.9961	88.4983	71.1105	64.7017	11.3391
8.99	100.0395	100.0988	88.1676	70.4318	64.4236	11.0975
9.00	100.0000	100.0000	88.1309	70.3570	64.3928	11.0710
9.01	99.9604	99.9013	88.0943	70.2824	64.3620	11.0445
9.10	99.6053	99.0199	87.7654	69.6164	64.0855	10.8093
9.50	98.0459	95.2539	86.3214	66.7773	62.8723	9.8242
10.00	96.1391	90.8720	84.5565	63.4881	61.3913	8.7204
11.00	92.4624	83.0685	81.1559	57.6712	58.5431	6.8767
12.00	88.9599	76.3572	77.9197	52.7144	55.8395	5.4288

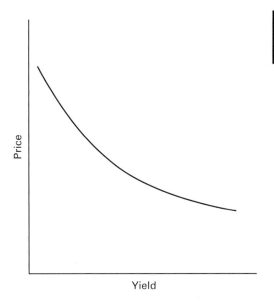

EXHIBIT 4-2   Shape of Price–Yield
Relationship for an
Option-Free Bond

The price–yield relationship that we have discussed refers to an instantaneous change in the required yield. As we explain in Chapter 2, the price of a bond will change over time as a result of (1) a change in the perceived credit risk of the issuer, (2) a discount or premium bond approaching the maturity date, and (3) a change in market interest rates.

PRICE VOLATILITY CHARACTERISTICS OF OPTION-FREE BONDS

Exhibit 4-3 shows for the six hypothetical bonds in Exhibit 4-1 the percentage change in the bond's price for various changes in the required yield, assuming that the initial yield for all six bonds is 9%. An examination of Exhibit 4-3 reveals several properties concerning the price volatility of an option-free bond.

Property 1: Although the prices of all option-free bonds move in the opposite direction from the change in yield required, the percentage price change is not the same for all bonds.

Property 2: For very small changes in the yield required, the percentage price change for a given bond is roughly the same, whether the yield required increases or decreases.

Property 3: For large changes in the required yield, the percentage price change is not the same for an increase in the required yield as it is for a decrease in the required yield.

Property 4: For a given large change in basis points, the percentage price increase is greater than the percentage price decrease.

The implication of property 4 is that if an investor owns a bond (i.e., is "long" a bond), the price appreciation that will be realized if the required yield decreases is greater than the capital loss that will be realized if the required yield rises by the same

EXHIBIT 4-3   Instantaneous Percentage Price Change for Six Hypothetical Bonds

Six hypothetical bonds, priced initially to yield 9%:
9% coupon, 5 years to maturity, price = $100.0000
9% coupon, 25 years to maturity, price = 100.0000
6% coupon, 5 years to maturity, price = 88.1309
6% coupon, 25 years to maturity, price = 70.3570
0% coupon, 5 years to maturity, price = 64.3928
0% coupon, 25 years to maturity, price = 11.0710

Yield (%) Changes to:	Change in Basis Points	Percentage Price Change (coupon/maturity in years)					
		9%/5	9%/25	6%/5	6%/25	0%/5	0%/25
6.00	−300	12.80	38.59	13.47	42.13	15.56	106.04
7.00	−200	8.32	23.46	8.75	25.46	10.09	61.73
8.00	−100	4.06	10.74	4.26	11.60	4.91	27.10
8.50	−50	2.00	5.15	2.11	5.55	2.42	12.72
8.90	−10	0.40	1.00	0.42	1.07	0.48	2.42
8.99	−1	0.04	0.10	0.04	0.11	0.05	0.24
9.01	1	−0.04	−0.10	−0.04	−0.11	−0.05	−0.24
9.10	10	−0.39	−0.98	−0.41	−1.05	−0.48	−2.36
9.50	50	−1.95	−4.75	−2.05	−5.09	−2.36	−11.26
10.00	100	−3.86	−9.13	−4.06	−9.76	−4.66	−21.23
11.00	200	−7.54	−16.93	−7.91	−18.03	−9.08	−37.89
12.00	300	−11.04	−23.64	−11.59	−25.08	−13.28	−50.96

number of basis points. For an investor who is "short" a bond, the reverse is true: The potential capital loss is greater than the potential capital gain if the required yield changes by a given number of basis points.

An explanation for these four properties of bond price volatility lies in the convex shape of the price–yield relationship. We will investigate this in more detail later in the chapter.

Characteristics of a Bond That Affect Its Price Volatility

There are two characteristics of an option-free bond that determine its price volatility: coupon and term to maturity.

Characteristic 1: For a given term to maturity and initial yield, the price volatility of a bond is greater, the lower the coupon rate. This characteristic can be seen by comparing the 9%, 6%, and zero-coupon bonds with the same maturity.

Characteristic 2: For a given coupon rate and initial yield, the longer the term to maturity, the greater the price volatility. This can be seen in Exhibit 4-3 by comparing the five-year bonds with the 25-year bonds with the same coupon.

An implication of the second characteristic is that investors who want to increase a portfolio's price volatility because they expect interest rates to fall, all other factors being constant, should hold bonds with long maturities in the portfolio. To reduce a portfolio's price volatility in anticipation of a rise in interest rates, bonds with shorter-term maturities should be held in the portfolio.

Effects of Yield to Maturity

We cannot ignore the fact that credit considerations cause different bonds to trade at different yields, even if they have the same coupon and maturity. How, then, holding other factors constant, does the yield to maturity affect a bond's price volatility? As it turns out, the higher the yield to maturity at which a bond trades, the lower the price volatility.

To see this, compare the 9% 25-year bond trading at various yield levels in Exhibit 4-4. The first column shows the yield level the bond is trading at, and the second column gives the initial price. The third column indicates the bond's price if yields change by 100 basis points. The fourth and fifth columns show the dollar price change and the percentage price change. Note in these last two columns that the higher the initial yield, the lower the price volatility. An implication of this is that for a given change in yields, price volatility is greater when yield levels in the market are low, and price volatility is lower when yield levels are high.

EXHIBIT 4-4   Price Change for a 100-Basis-Point Change in Yield for a 9% 25-Year Bond Trading at Different Yield Levels

Yield Level (%)	Initial Price	New Price[a]	Price Decline	Percent Decline
7	$123.46	$110.74	$12.72	10.30
8	110.74	100.00	10.74	9.70
9	100.00	90.87	9.13	9.13
10	90.87	83.07	7.80	8.58
11	83.07	76.36	6.71	8.08
12	76.36	70.55	5.81	7.61
13	70.55	65.50	5.05	7.16
14	65.50	61.08	4.42	6.75

[a]As a result of a 100-basis-point increase in yield.

MEASURES OF BOND PRICE VOLATILITY

Money managers, arbitrageurs, and traders need to have a way to measure a bond's price volatility to implement hedging and trading strategies. Three measures that are commonly employed are (1) price value of a basis point, (2) yield value of a price change, and (3) duration.

Price Value of a Basis Point

The **price value of a basis point**, also referred to as the **dollar value of an 01**, is the change in the price of the bond if the required yield changes by 1 basis point. Note that this measure of price volatility indicates **dollar price volatility** as opposed to percentage price volatility (price change as a percent of the initial price). Typically, the price value of a basis point is expressed as the absolute value of the change in price. Owing to property 2 of the price–yield relationship, price volatility is the same for an increase or a decrease of 1 basis point in required yield.

We can illustrate how to calculate the price value of a basis point by using the six bonds in Exhibit 4-1. For each bond, the initial price, the price after increasing the required yield by 1 basis point (from 9% to 9.01%), and the price value of a basis point (the difference between the two prices) are as follows:

Bond	Initial Price (9% yield)	Price at 9.01%	Price Value of a Basis Point[a]
5-year 9% coupon	100.0000	99.9604	0.0396
25-year 9% coupon	100.0000	99.9013	0.0987
5-year 6% coupon	88.1309	88.0945	0.0364
25-year 6% coupon	70.3570	70.2824	0.0746
5-year zero-coupon	64.3928	64.3620	0.0308
25-year zero-coupon	11.0710	11.0445	0.0265

[a]Absolute value per $100 of par value.

Because this measure of price volatility is in terms of dollar price change, dividing the price value of a basis point by the initial price gives the percentage price change for a 1-basis-point change in yield.

Yield Value of a Price Change

Another measure of the price volatility of a bond used by investors is the change in the yield for a specified price change. This is estimated by first calculating the bond's yield to maturity if the bond's price is decreased by, say, X dollars. Then the difference between the initial yield and the new yield is the yield value of an X dollar price change. The smaller this value, the greater the dollar price volatility, because it would take a smaller change in yield to produce a price change of X dollars.

Duration

In Chapter 2 we explained that the price of an option-free bond can be expressed mathematically as follows:[1]

$$P = \frac{C}{1+y} + \frac{C}{(1+y)^2} + \cdots + \frac{C}{(1+y)^n} + \frac{M}{(1+y)^n} \tag{4.1}$$

where:

P = price of the bond
C = semiannual coupon interest (in dollars)

---

[1]Equation (4.1) assumes that the next coupon payment is exactly six months from now and that there is no accrued interest. As we explain at the end of Chapter 2, it is not difficult to extend the model to account for the first coupon payment occurring less than six months from the valuation date and to adjust the price to include accrued interest.

y = one-half the yield to maturity or required yield
n = number of semiannual periods (number of years $\times$ 2)
M = maturity value (in dollars)

To determine the approximate change in price for a small change in yield, the first derivative of equation (4.1) with respect to the required yield can be computed as

$$\frac{dP}{dy} = \frac{(-1)C}{(1+y)^2} + \frac{(-2)C}{(1+y)^3} + \cdots + \frac{(-n)C}{(1+y)^{n+1}} + \frac{(-n)M}{(1+y)^{n+1}} \qquad (4.2)$$

Rearranging equation (4.2), we obtain

$$\frac{dP}{dy} = -\frac{1}{1+y}\left[\frac{1C}{1+y} + \frac{2C}{(1+y)^2} + \cdots + \frac{nC}{(1+y)^n} + \frac{nM}{(1+y)^n}\right] \qquad (4.3)$$

The term in brackets is the weighted average term to maturity of the cash flows from the bond, where the weights are the present value of the cash flow.

Equation (4.3) indicates the approximate dollar price change for a small change in the required yield. Dividing both sides of equation (4.3) by P gives the approximate percentage price change:

$$\frac{dP}{dy}\frac{1}{P} = -\frac{1}{1+y}\left[\frac{1C}{1+y} + \frac{2C}{(1+y)^2} + \cdots + \frac{nC}{(1+y)^n} + \frac{nM}{(1+y)^n}\right]\frac{1}{P} \qquad (4.4)$$

The expression in brackets divided by the price (or here multiplied by the reciprocal of the price) is commonly referred to as **Macaulay duration**;[2] that is,

$$\text{Macaulay duration} = \frac{\dfrac{1C}{1+y} + \dfrac{2C}{(1+y)^2} + \cdots + \dfrac{nC}{(1+y)^n} + \dfrac{nM}{(1+y)^n}}{P}$$

---

[2]In a 1938 National Bureau of Economic Research study on bond yields, Frederick Macaulay coined this term and used this measure rather than maturity as a proxy for the average length of time that a bond investment is outstanding. [See Frederick Macaulay, *Some Theoretical Problems Suggested by the Movement of Interest Rates, Bond Yields, and Stock Prices in the U.S. Since 1856* (New York: National Bureau of Economic Research, 1938).] In examining the interest rate sensitivity of financial institutions, Redington and Samuelson independently developed the duration concept. (See F. M. Redington, "Review of the Principle of Life Office Valuation," *Journal of the Institute of Actuaries*, 1952, pp. 286–340; and Paul A. Samuelson, "The Effect of Interest Rate Increases on the Banking System," *American Economic Review*, March 1945, pp. 16–27.)

which can be rewritten as

$$\text{Macaulay duration} = \frac{\displaystyle\sum_{t=1}^{n} \frac{tC}{(1+y)^t} + \frac{nM}{(1+y)^n}}{P} \tag{4.5}$$

Substituting Macaulay duration into equation (4.4) for the approximate percentage price change gives

$$\frac{dP}{dy}\frac{1}{P} = -\frac{1}{1+y} \times \text{Macaulay duration} \tag{4.6}$$

Investors commonly refer to the ratio of Macaulay duration to $1 + y$ as **modified duration**; that is,

$$\text{modified duration} = \frac{\text{Macaulay duration}}{1+y} \tag{4.7}$$

Substituting equation (4.7) into equation (4.6) gives

$$\frac{dP}{dy}\frac{1}{P} = -\text{modified duration} \tag{4.8}$$

Equation (4.8) states that modified duration is related to the approximate percentage change in price for a given change in yield. Because for all option-free bonds modified duration is positive, equation (4.8) states that there is an inverse relationship between modified duration and the approximate percentage change in price for a given yield change. This is to be expected from the fundamental principle that bond prices move in the opposite direction of the change in interest rates.

Exhibits 4-5 and 4-6 show the computation of the Macaulay duration and modified duration of two five-year coupon bonds. The durations computed in these exhibits are in terms of duration per period. Consequently, the durations are in half-years because the cash flows of the bonds occur every six months. To adjust the durations to an annual figure, the durations must be divided by 2, as shown at the bottom of Exhibits 4–5 and 4–6. In general, if the cash flows occur m times per year, the durations are adjusted by dividing by m; that is,

$$\text{duration in years} = \frac{\text{duration in } m \text{ periods per year}}{m}$$

EXHIBIT 4-5   Calculation of Macaulay Duration and Modified Duration for 5-Year 9% Bond Selling to Yield 9%

Coupon rate: 9.00%
Term (years): 5
Initial yield: 9.00%

Period, t	Cash Flow[a]	PV of $1 at 4.5%	PV of CF	$t \times PVCF$[b]
1	$ 4.50	0.956937	4.306220	4.30622
2	4.50	0.915729	4.120785	8.24156
3	4.50	0.876296	3.943335	11.83000
4	4.50	0.838561	3.773526	15.09410
5	4.50	0.802451	3.611030	18.05514
6	4.50	0.767895	3.455531	20.73318
7	4.50	0.734828	3.306728	23.14709
8	4.50	0.703185	3.164333	25.31466
9	4.50	0.672904	3.028070	27.25262
10	104.50	0.643927	67.290443	672.90442
			100.0	826.87899

[a]Cash flow per $100 of par value.

$$\text{Macaulay duration (in half years)} = \frac{826.87899}{100.000000} = 8.27$$

$$\text{Macaulay duration (in years)} = \frac{8.27}{2} = 4.13$$

$$\text{Macaulay duration} = \frac{4.13}{1.0450} = 3.96$$

[b]Values are rounded.

Macaulay duration in years and modified duration for the six hypothetical bonds are as follows:

Bond	Macaulay Duration (years)	Modified Duration
9%/5-year	4.13	3.96
9%/25-year	10.33	9.88
6%/5-year	4.35	4.16
6%/25-year	11.10	10.62
0%/5-year	5.00	4.78
0%/25-year	25.00	23.92

Rather than use equation (4.5) to calculate Macaulay duration and then equation (4.7) to obtain modified duration, we can derive an alternative formula that does not require the extensive calculations required by equation (4.5). This is done by rewriting the price of a bond in terms of its two components: (1) the present value of an annuity, where the annuity is the sum of the coupon payments, and (2) the present

EXHIBIT 4-6 Calculation of Macaulay Duration and Modified Duration for 5-Year 6% Bond Selling to Yield 9%

Coupon rate: 6.00%
Term (years): 5
Initial yield: 9.00%

Period, t	Cash Flow[a]	PV of $1 at 4.5%	PV of CF	$t \times$ PVCF[b]
1	$ 3.00	0.956937	2.870813	2.87081
2	3.00	0.915729	2.747190	5.49437
3	3.00	0.876296	2.628890	7.88666
4	3.00	0.838561	2.515684	10.06273
5	3.00	0.802451	2.407353	12.03676
6	3.00	0.767895	2.303687	13.82212
7	3.00	0.734828	2.204485	15.43139
8	3.00	0.703185	2.109555	16.87644
9	3.00	0.672904	2.018713	18.16841
10	103.00	0.643927	66.324551	663.24551
Total			88.130923	765.89520

[a]Cash flow per $100 of par value.

$$\text{Macaulay duration (in half years)} = \frac{765.89520}{88.130923} = 8.69$$

$$\text{Macaulay duration (in years)} = \frac{8.69}{2} = 4.35$$

$$\text{Macaulay duration} = \frac{4.35}{1.0450} = 4.16$$

[b]Values are rounded.

value of the par value. That is, the price of a bond per $100 of par value can be written as follows:[3]

$$P = C \left[\frac{1 - \frac{1}{(1+y)^n}}{y} \right] + \frac{100}{(1+y)^n} \tag{4.9}$$

By taking the first derivative of equation (4.9) and dividing by P, we obtain another formula for modified duration:

$$\text{modified duration} = \frac{\frac{C}{y^2}\left[1 - \frac{1}{(1+y)^n}\right] + \frac{n(100 - C/y)}{(1+y)^{n+1}}}{P} \tag{4.10}$$

[3]The first term in equation (4.9) is the present value of the coupon payments from equation (2.7) discounting at y.

where the price is expressed as a percentage of par value. Macaulay duration can be expressed by multiplying equation (4.10) by $(1 + y)$. To illustrate how to apply equation (4.10), consider the 25-year 6% bond selling at 70.357 to yield 9%. Then

$$
\begin{aligned}
C &= 3(0.06 \times 100 \times 1/2) \\
y &= 0.045 \ (0.09 \times 1/2) \\
n &= 50 \\
p &= 70.357
\end{aligned}
$$

Substituting into equation (4.10) yields

$$
\begin{aligned}
\text{modified duration} &= \frac{\dfrac{3}{(0.045)^2}\left[1 - \dfrac{1}{(1.045)^{50}}\right] + \dfrac{50(100 - 3/0.045)}{(1.045)^{51}}}{70.357} \\
&= \frac{1,481.481(0.88929) + 176.5704}{70.357} \\
&= 21.23508
\end{aligned}
$$

Converting to an annual number by dividing by 2 gives a modified duration of 10.62. Multiplying by 1.045 gives 11.10, which is Macaulay duration.

Properties of Duration

As can be seen from the various durations computed for the six hypothetical bonds, the modified duration and Macaulay duration of a coupon bond are less than the maturity. It should be obvious from the formula that the Macaulay duration of a zero-coupon bond is equal to its maturity; a zero-coupon bond's modified duration, however, is less than its maturity. Also, the lower the coupon, generally the greater the modified and Macaulay duration of the bond.[4]

There is a consistency between the properties of bond price volatility we discussed earlier and the properties of modified duration. We showed earlier that when all other factors are constant, the longer the maturity, the greater the price volatility. A property of modified duration is that when all other factors are constant, the longer the maturity, the greater the modified duration. We also showed that the lower the coupon rate, all other factors being constant, the greater the bond price volatility. As we have just seen, generally the lower the coupon rate, the greater the modified duration. Thus, the greater the modified duration, the greater the price volatility.

Finally, as we noted earlier, another factor that will influence the price volatility is the yield to maturity. All other factors constant, the higher the yield level, the lower the price volatility. The same property holds for modified duration, as can be seen in the following table, which shows the modified duration of a 25-year 9% coupon bond at various yield levels:

---

[4]This property does not hold for long-maturity deep-discount bonds.

Yield (%)	Modified Duration
7	11.21
8	10.53
9	9.88
10	9.27
11	8.70
12	8.16
13	7.66
14	7.21

Approximating the Percentage Price Change

If we multiply both sides of equation (4.8) by the change in the required yield (dy), we have the following relationship:

$$\frac{dP}{P} = -\text{modified duration} \times dy \qquad\qquad \textbf{(4.11)}$$

Equation (4.11) can be used to approximate the percentage price change for a given change in required yield.

To illustrate the relationship, consider the 25-year 6% bond selling at 70.3570 to yield 9%. The modified duration for this bond is 10.62. If yields increase instantaneously from 9% to 9.10%, a yield change of +0.0010 (10 basis points), the *approximate* percentage change in price using equation (4.11) is

$$-10.62\,(+0.0010) = -0.0106 \text{ or } -1.06\%$$

Notice from Exhibit 4-3 that the actual percentage change in price is −1.05%. Similarly, if yields decrease instantaneously from 9% to 8.90% (a 10-basis-point decrease), the approximate percentage change in price using equation (4.11) would be +1.06%. According to Exhibit 4-3, the actual percentage price change would be +1.07%. This example illustrates that for small changes in the required yield, modified duration gives a good approximation of the percentage change in price.

Instead of a small change in required yield, let's assume that yields increase by 200 basis points, from 9% to 11% (a yield change of +0.02). The approximate percentage change in price using equation (4.11) is

$$210.62(+0.02) = -0.2124 = -21.24\%$$

How good is this approximation? As can be seen from Exhibit 4-3, the actual percentage change in price is only −18.03%. Moreover, if the required yield decreased by 200 basis points, from 9% to 7%, the approximate percentage change in price based on duration would be +21.24%, compared with an actual percentage change in price of +25.46%. Modified duration provides not only a flawed approximation but also a symmetric percentage price change, which, as we point out earlier in this chapter, is not a property of the price–yield relationship for bonds when there are large changes in yield.

We can use equation (4.11) to provide an interpretation of modified duration. Suppose that the yield on any bond changes by 100 basis points. Then, substituting 100 basis points (0.01) into equation (4.11), the following is obtained:

$$\frac{dP}{P} = -\text{modified duration } (0.01) = -\text{modified duration } (\%)$$

Thus, *modified duration can be interpreted as the approximate percentage change in price for a 100-basis-point change in yield.*

Approximating the Dollar Price Change

Modified duration is a proxy for the percentage change in price. Investors also like to know the dollar price volatility of a bond. Of course, equation (4.2) can be used to compute the dollar price volatility. Alternatively, multiplying both sides of equation (4.8) by P gives

$$\frac{dP}{dy} = (-\text{modified duration})P \qquad\qquad \textbf{(4.12)}$$

The expression on the right-hand side is called **dollar duration**:

$$\text{dollar duration} = -(\text{modified duration})P \qquad\qquad \textbf{(4.13)}$$

When we know the percentage price change and the initial price, the estimated dollar price change using modified duration can be determined. Alternatively, the estimated dollar price change can be obtained by multiplying both sides of equation (4.11) by P, giving

$$dP = -(\text{modified duration})P(dy)$$

From equation (4.13) we can substitute dollar duration for the product of modified duration and P. Thus

$$dP = -(\text{dollar duration})(dy) \qquad\qquad \textbf{(4.14)}$$

For small changes in the required yield, equation (4.14) does a good job in estimating the change in price. For example, consider the 6% 25-year bond selling at 70.3570 to yield 9%. The dollar duration is 747.2009. For a 1-basis-point (0.0001) increase in the required yield, the estimated price change per $100 of face value is

$$dP = -(\$747.2009)(0.0001)$$
$$= -\$0.0747$$

From Exhibit 4-1 we see that the actual price is 70.2824. The actual price change would therefore be 0.0746 (70.2824 − 70.3570). Notice that the dollar duration for a 1-basis-point change is the same as the price value of a basis point.

Now let's see what happens when there is a large change in the required yield for the same bond. If the required yield increases from 9% to 11% (or 200 basis points), the approximate dollar price change per $100 par value is

$$dP = -(\$747.2009)(0.02)$$
$$= -\$14.94$$

From Exhibit 4-1 we see that the actual price for this bond if the required yield is 11% is 57.6712. Thus, the actual price decline is 12.6858 (57.6712 − 70.3570). The estimated dollar price change is more than the actual price change. The reverse is true for a decrease in the required yield. This result is consistent with what we illustrated earlier. When there are large movements in the required yield, dollar duration or modified duration is not adequate to approximate the price reaction. Duration will overestimate the price change when the required yield rises, thereby underestimating the new price. When the required yield falls, duration will underestimate the price change and thereby underestimate the new price.

Spread Duration

Market participants compute a measure called *spread duration*. However, this measure is used in two ways. One use is for fixed-rate bonds and the other for floating-rate bonds.

Consider first fixed-rate bonds. As we have explained, duration is a measure of the change in the value of a bond when rates change. The interest rate that is assumed to shift is the Treasury rate. However, as explained in the next chapter, for non-Treasury bonds the yield for such securities is equal to the Treasury yield plus a spread to the Treasury yield cure. The spread represents compensation for credit risk. The price of a non-Treasury bond is exposed to a change in the spread, and we referred to this in Chapter 1 as credit spread risk. The credit spread can change even though Treasury yields are unchanged because the spread required by the market changes. A measure of how a non-Treasury bond's price will change if the spread sought by the market changes is referred to as **spread duration**. For a Treasury security, the spread duration is zero.

Spread duration is used in different ways even when dealing with fixed-rate bonds. As we will see in future chapters, there are different spread measures.[5] Consequently, in using this measure it is important to know what spread measure is being used. A spread duration for a fixed-rate security is interpreted as follows: It is the approximate change in the price of a fixed-rate bond for a 100-basis-point change in the spread.

As explained in Chapter 2, a floating-rate security's price sensitivity will depend on whether the spread that the market wants changes. Recall that the spread is reflected in the quoted margin in the coupon reset formula. The quoted margin is fixed over the life of a typical floater. Spread duration is a measure used to estimate the sensitivity of

---

[5]Specifically, for fixed-rate bonds there is the nominal spread, zero-volatility spread, and option-adjusted spread.

a floater's price sensitivity to a change in the spread. A spread duration of 1.4 for a floater would mean that if the spread the market requires changes by 100 basis points, the floater's price will change by about 1.4%.

Portfolio Duration

Thus far we have looked at the duration of an individual bond. The duration of a portfolio is simply the weighted average duration of the bonds in the portfolios. That is, the duration of each bond in the portfolio is weighted by its percentage within the portfolio. For example, consider the following four-bond portfolio with a total market value of $100 million:

Bond	Market Value	Portfolio Weight	Duration
A	$10 million	0.10	4
B	$40 million	0.40	7
C	$30 million	0.30	6
D	$20 million	0.20	2

The portfolio weight for a bond is simply the market value of the bond divided by the total market value of $100 million. The portfolio duration is then

$$0.1 \times 4 + 0.4 \times 7 + 0.3 \times 6 + 0.2 \times 2 = 5.4$$

The portfolio's duration is 5.4 and interpreted as follows: If all the yields affecting the four bonds in the portfolio change by 100 basis points, the portfolio's value will change by approximately 5.4%.

Portfolio managers look at their interest rate exposure to a particular issue in terms of its **contribution to portfolio duration**. This measure is found by multiplying the weight of the issue in the portfolio by the duration of the individual issue. That is,

contribution to portfolio duration = weight of issue in portfolio × duration of issue

For example, for the four-bond portfolio whose portfolio duration was computed previously the contribution to portfolio duration for each issue is shown in the last column of the following table:

Bond	Market Value	Weight in Portfolio	Duration	Contribution to Duration
A	$ 10,000,000	0.10	4	0.40
B	$ 40,000,000	0.40	7	2.80
C	$ 30,000,000	0.30	6	1.80
D	$ 20,000,000	0.20	2	0.40
Total	$100,000,000	1.00		5.40

Moreover, portfolio managers look at portfolio duration for sectors of the bond market. The procedure is the same for computing the contribution to portfolio duration of a sector as it is for computing the contribution to portfolio duration of an individual issue. For example, if A is the government bond sector, B is the federal agency bond sector, C is the corporate bond sector, and D is the mortgage sector, then the contribution to portfolio duration of each sector would be the value shown in the last column in the previous table.

The exposure can also be cast in terms of dollar exposure. To do this, the dollar duration of the issue or sector is used instead of the duration of the issue or sector.

A spread duration for a portfolio of fixed-rate bonds can also be computed. In this case, the portfolio duration is divided into two durations. The first is the duration of the portfolio with respect to changes in the level of Treasury rates. The second is the spread duration.

CONVEXITY

The three measures for price volatility that we describe in the preceding section are good measures for small changes in yield or price. We have explained how these measures are related. Exhibit 4-7 does this more formally.

Because all the duration measures are only approximations for small changes in yield, they do not capture the effect of the convexity of a bond on its price performance

---

EXHIBIT 4-7   Measures of Bond Price Volatility and Their Relationships to One Another

Notation:

D = Macaulay duration
D^* = modified duration
PVBP = price value of a basis point
y = yield to maturity in decimal form
Y = yield to maturity in percentage terms ($Y = 100 \times y$)
P = price of bond
m = number of coupons per year

Relationships:

$D^* = \dfrac{D}{1 + y/m}$ by definition

$\dfrac{\Delta P/P}{\Delta y} \approx D^*$ to a close approximation for a small Δy

$\Delta P/\Delta Y \approx$ slope of price–yield curve to a close approximation for a small ΔY

$PVBP \approx \dfrac{D^* \times P}{10,000}$ to a close approximation

For bonds at or near par:

$PVBP \approx D^*/100$ to a close approximation

$D^* \approx \Delta P/\Delta Y$ to a close approximation for a small ΔY

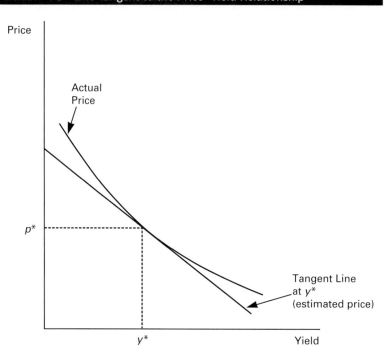

EXHIBIT 4-8 Line Tangent to the Price–Yield Relationship

when yields change by more than a small amount. The duration measure can be supplemented with an additional measure to capture the curvature or convexity of a bond. In this section we tie together the convex price–yield relationship for a bond and several of the properties of bond price volatility discussed earlier.

In Exhibit 4-8 a tangent line is drawn to the price–yield relationship at yield y^*. The tangent shows the rate of change of price with respect to a change in interest rates at that point (yield level). The slope of the tangent line is closely related to the price value of a basis point. Consequently, for a given starting price, the tangent (which tells the rate of absolute price changes) is closely related to the duration of the bond (which tells about the rate of percentage of price changes). The steeper the tangent line, the greater the duration; the flatter the tangent line, the lower the duration. Thus for a given starting price, the tangent line and the duration can be used interchangeably and can be thought of as one and the same method of estimating the rate of price changes.

Notice what happens to duration (steepness of the tangent line) as yield changes: As yield increases (decreases), duration decreases (increases). This property holds for all option-free bonds, as we noted earlier.

If we draw a vertical line from any yield (on the horizontal axis), as in Exhibit 4-9, the distance between the horizontal axis and the tangent line represents the price approximated by using duration starting with the initial yield y^*. The approximation will always understate the actual price. This agrees with what we demonstrated earlier about the relationship between duration (and the tangent line) and the approximate

EXIHIBIT 4-9   Price Approximation Using Duration

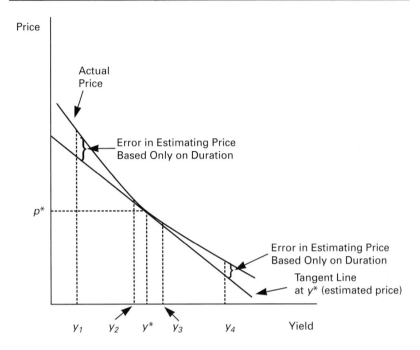

price change. When yields decrease, the estimated price change will be less than the actual price change, thereby underestimating the actual price. On the other hand, when yields increase, the estimated price change will be greater than the actual price change, resulting in an underestimate of the actual price.

For small changes in yield, the tangent line and duration do a good job in estimating the actual price. However, the farther away from the initial yield y^*, the worse the approximation. It should be apparent that the accuracy of the approximation depends on the convexity of the price–yield relationship for the bond.

Measuring Convexity

Duration (modified or dollar) attempts to estimate a convex relationship with a straight line (the tangent line). Is it possible to specify a mathematical relationship that provides a better approximation to the price change of the bond if the required yield changes?

We can use the first two terms of a Taylor series to approximate the price change as follows:[6]

$$dP = \frac{dP}{dy}dy + \frac{1}{2}\frac{d^2P}{dy^2}(dy)^2 + \text{error} \qquad \textbf{(4.15)}$$

---

[6]A Taylor series, discussed in calculus textbooks, can be used to approximate a mathematical function. Here, the mathematical function to be approximated is the price function.

Dividing both sides of equation (4.15) by P to get the percentage price change gives us

$$\frac{dP}{P} = \frac{dP}{dy}\frac{1}{P}dy + \frac{1}{2}\frac{d^2P}{dy^2}\frac{1}{P}(dy)^2 + \frac{\text{error}}{P} \qquad \textbf{(4.16)}$$

The first term on the right-hand side of equation (4.15) is equation (4.14); that is, it is the dollar price change based on dollar duration. Thus, the first term in equation (4.15) is our approximation of the price change based on duration. In equation (4.16), the first term on the right-hand side is the approximate percentage change in price based on modified duration.

The second term in equations (4.15) and (4.16) includes the second derivative of the price function [equation (4.1)]. It is the second derivative that is used as a proxy measure to correct for the convexity of the price–yield relationship. Market participants refer to the second derivative of price [equation (4.1)] as the **dollar convexity measure** of the bond; that is,

$$\text{dollar convexity measure} = \frac{d^2P}{dy^2} \qquad \textbf{(4.17)}$$

The product of the dollar convexity measure and the square of the change in the required yield indicates the estimated price change due to convexity. That is, the approximate change in price due to convexity is

$$dP = (\text{dollar convexity measure})(dy)^2 \qquad \textbf{(4.18)}$$

The second derivative divided by price is a measure of the percentage change in the price of the bond due to convexity and is referred to simply as the **convexity measure**; that is,

$$\text{convexity measure} = \frac{d^2P}{dy^2}\frac{1}{P} \qquad \textbf{(4.19)}$$

and the percentage price change due to convexity is

$$\frac{dP}{P} = \frac{1}{2}(\text{convexity measure})(dy)^2 \qquad \textbf{(4.20)}$$

The second derivative of the price equation (4.1) is

$$\frac{d^2P}{dy^2} = \sum_{t=1}^{n}\frac{t(t+1)C}{(1+y)^{t+2}} + \frac{n(n+1)M}{(1+y)^{n+2}} \qquad \textbf{(4.21)}$$

EXIHIBIT 4-10   Calculation of Convexity Measure and Dollar Convexity Measure for Five-Year 9% Bond Selling to Yield 9%

Coupon rate: 9.00%
Term (years): 5
Initial yield: 9.00%
Price: 100

Period, t	Cash Flow[a]	$\dfrac{1}{(1.045)^{t+2}}$	$t(t+1)CF$	$\dfrac{t(t+1)CF}{(1.045)^{t+2}}$
1	$4.50	0.876296	9	7.886
2	$4.50	0.838561	27	22.641
3	$4.50	0.802451	54	43.332
4	$4.50	0.767895	90	69.110
5	$4.50	0.734828	135	99.201
6	$4.50	0.703185	189	132.901
7	$4.50	0.672904	252	169.571
8	$4.50	0.643927	324	208.632
9	$4.50	0.616198	405	249.560
10	$104.50	0.589663	11,495	6,778.186
			12,980	7,781.020

[a]Cash flow per $100 of par value.

$$\text{Second derivative} = 7{,}781.02$$

$$\text{Convexity measure (half years)} = \frac{7{,}781.020}{100.0000} = 77.8102$$

$$\text{Convexity measure (years)} = \frac{77.8102}{4} = 19.4526$$

$$\text{Dollar convexity measure} = 100 \times 19.4526 = 1{,}945.26$$

Exhibits 4–10 and 4–11 demonstrate how to calculate the second derivative [equation (4.21)], annualized dollar convexity measure, and annualized convexity measure for the two five-year coupon bonds. The convexity measure is in terms of periods squared. To convert the convexity measures to an annual figure, equations (4.17) and (4.19) must be divided by 4 (which is 2 squared). In general, if the cash flows occur m times per year, convexity is adjusted to an annual figure as follows:

$$\text{convexity measure in years} = \frac{\text{convexity measure in } m \text{ periods per year}}{m^2}$$

Annualized convexity measure and annualized dollar convexity measure for our six hypothetical bonds can be summarized as follows:

EXHIBIT 4-11   Calculation of Convexity Measure and Dollar Convexity Measure for Five-Year 6% Bond Selling to Yield 9%

Coupon rate: 6.00%
Term (years): 5
Initial yield: 9.00%
Price: 88.1309

Period, t	Cash Flow[a]	$\dfrac{1}{(1.045)^{t+2}}$	$t(t+1)CF$	$\dfrac{t(t+1)CF}{(1.045)^{t+2}}$
1	$3.00	0.876296	6	5.257
2	$3.00	0.838561	18	15.094
3	$3.00	0.802451	36	28.888
4	$3.00	0.767895	60	46.073
5	$3.00	0.734828	90	66.134
6	$3.00	0.703185	126	88.601
7	$3.00	0.672904	168	113.047
8	$3.00	0.643927	216	139.088
9	$3.00	0.616198	270	166.373
10	$103.00	0.589663	11,330	6,680.891
			12,320	7,349.446

[a]Cash flow per $100 of par value.

$$\text{Second derivative} = 7{,}349.45$$

$$\text{Convexity measure (half years)} = \frac{7{,}349.45}{88.1309} = 83.3924$$

$$\text{Convexity measure (years)} = \frac{83.3924}{4} = 20.8481$$

$$\text{Dollar convexity measure} = 88.1309 \times 20.8481 = 1{,}837.36$$

Bond (per $100 par)	Second Derivative	Annualized Convexity Measure (per $100 par)	Annualized Dollar Convexity Measure
9%/5-year	7,781.02	19.45	$ 1,945.26
9%/25-year	64,288.42	160.72	16,072.00
6%/5-year	7,349.45	20.85	1,837.36
6%/25-year	51,476.26	182.92	12,869.70
0%/5-year	6,486.30	25.18	1,621.42
0%/25-year	25,851.93	583.78	6,463.02

Alternatively, the second derivative can be determined by taking the second derivative of equation (4.9). By doing so, we can simplify equation (4.21) as follows:

$$\frac{d^2 P}{dy^2} = \frac{2C}{y^3}\left[1 - \frac{1}{(1+y)^n}\right] - \frac{2Cn}{y^2(1+y)^{n+1}} + \frac{n(n+1)(100 - C/y)}{(1+y)^{n+2}} \tag{4.22}$$

To illustrate how to use equation (4.22), consider the 25-year 6% bond selling at 70.357 to yield 9%. The second derivative is

$$\frac{2(3)}{(0.045)^3}\left[1-\frac{1}{(1.045)^{50}}\right]-\frac{2(3)(50)}{(0.045)^2(1.045)^{51}}+\frac{50(51)(100-3/0.045)}{(1.045)^{52}}$$

$$= 65,843.62(0.88929) - 15,695.14 + 8,617.31$$
$$= 51,476.26$$

This agrees with the value reported earlier.

Approximating Percentage Price Change Using Duration and Convexity Measures

Equation (4.16) tells us that the percentage price change of a bond can be estimated using both duration and convexity measure. To illustrate how this is done, consider the 25-year 6% bond selling to yield 9%. The modified duration for this bond is 10.62, and the convexity measure is 182.92. If the required yield increases by 200 basis points, from 9% to 11%, the approximate percentage change in the price of the bond is

percentage change in price due to duration from equation (4.11)
$$= -(\text{modified duration})(dy)$$
$$= -(10.62)(0.02) = -0.2124 = -21.24\%$$

percentage change in price due to convexity from equation (4.20)
$$= \frac{1}{2}(\text{convexity measure})(dy)^2$$
$$= \frac{1}{2}(182.92)(0.02)^2 = 0.0366 = 3.66\%$$

The estimated percentage price change due to duration and convexity is

$$-21.24\% + 3.66\% = -17.58\%$$

From Exhibit 4-3 we see that the actual change is −18.03%. Using duration and convexity measures together gives a better approximation of the actual price change for a large movement in the required yield. Suppose, instead, that the required yield decreases by 200 basis points. Then the approximate percentage change in the price of the bond using modified duration and convexity is

percentage change in price due to duration from equation (4.11)
$$= -(\text{modified duration})(dy)$$
$$= -(10.62)(-0.02) = +0.2124 = +21.24\%$$

percentage change in price due to convexity from equation (4.20)

$$= \frac{1}{2}(\text{convexity measure})(dy)^2$$

$$= \frac{1}{2}(182.92)(-0.02)^2 = 0.0366 = 3.66\%$$

The estimated percentage price change due to duration and convexity is

$$+21.24\% + 3.66\% = 24.90\%$$

From Exhibit 4-3 we see that the actual change is +25.46%. Once again, using both duration and convexity measure provides a good approximation of the actual price change for a large movement in the required yield.

Some Notes on Convexity

There are three points that should be kept in mind regarding a bond's convexity and convexity measure. First, it is important to understand the distinction between the use of the term *convexity*, which refers to the general shape of the price–yield relationship, and the term *convexity measure*, which is related to the quantification of how the price of the bond will change when interest rates change.

The second point has to do with how to interpret the convexity measure. Recall that for duration, the interpretation of this measure is straightforward. A duration of 4, for example, is interpreted as the approximate percentage change in the price of the bond for a 100-basis-point change in interest rates. How do we interpret a convexity measure? It's not that simple because the approximate percentage change in price due to convexity is affected by the square of the change in rates, as shown in equation (4.20). In that equation, the approximate percentage change in price due to convexity is the product of three numbers: (1) $\frac{1}{2}$, (2) convexity measure, and (3) the square of the change in yield.

The final point is that in practice different vendors of analytical systems and different writers compute the convexity measure in different ways. To see why, look back at equation (4.16) and focus on the second term on the right-hand side of the equation. In equation (4.19), we used part of that equation to define the convexity measure. Specifically, the convexity measure is the product of the second derivative and the reciprocal of the price. Suppose instead that we defined the convexity measure from the second term of equation (4.16) to be

$$\text{convexity measure} = \frac{1}{2}\frac{d^2p}{dy^2}\frac{1}{P}$$

That is, the convexity measure shown is just one-half the convexity measure given by equation (4.19). Does it make a difference? Not at all. We must just make sure that we make the adjustment to the relationship between the approximate percentage price change due to convexity and the convexity measure accordingly. Specifically, in equation (4.20), the relationship would be changed as follows:

$$\frac{dP}{P} = (\text{convexity measure}) \times (dy)^2$$

The bottom line is that the approximate percentage price change due to convexity is the same regardless of whether the preceding equation or equation (4.20) is used. This relates to our second point. The interpretation of the convexity measure on a stand-alone basis is not meaningful because different vendors and writers may scale the measure in different ways. What is important is relating the convexity measure and the change in yield (squared).

Value of Convexity

Up to this point, we have focused on how taking convexity into account can improve the approximation of a bond's price change for a given yield change. The convexity of a bond, however, has another important investment implication, which is illustrated in Exhibit 4-12. The exhibit shows two bonds, A and B. The two bonds have the same duration and are offering the same yield; they have different convexities, however. Bond B is more convex (bowed) than bond A.

What is the implication of the greater convexity for B? Whether the market yield rises or falls, B will have a higher price. That is, if the required yield rises, the capital loss on bond B will be less than it will be on bond A. A fall in the required yield will generate greater price appreciation for B than for A.

Generally, the market will take the greater convexity of B compared with A into account in pricing the two bonds. That is, the market will price convexity. Consequently, although there may be times when a situation such as that depicted in Exhibit 4-12 will exist, generally the market will require investors to "pay up" (accept a lower yield) for the greater convexity offered by bond B.

The question is: How much should the market want investors to pay up for convexity? Look again at Exhibit 4-12. Notice that if investors expect that market yields will change by very little—that is, they expect low interest rate volatility—the advantage of owning bond B over bond A is insignificant because both bonds will offer

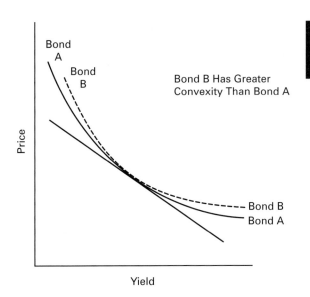

EXHIBIT 4-12   Comparison of Convexity of Two Bonds

Bond A

Bond B

Bond B Has Greater Convexity Than Bond A

Bond B
Bond A

Price

Yield

approximately the same price for small changes in yield. In this case, investors should not be willing to pay much for convexity. In fact, if the market is pricing convexity high, which means that A will be offering a higher yield than B, investors with expectations of low interest rate volatility would probably be willing to "sell convexity"—that is, to sell B if they own it and buy A. In contrast, if investors expect substantial interest rate volatility, bond B would probably sell at a much lower yield than A.

Properties of Convexity

All option-free bonds have the following convexity properties.

Property 1: As the required yield increases (decreases), the convexity of a bond decreases (increases). This property is referred to as **positive convexity**.

An implication of positive convexity is that the duration of an option-free bond moves in the right direction as market yields change. That is, if market yields rise, the price of a bond will fall. The price decline is slowed down by a decline in the duration of the bond as market yields rise. In contrast, should market yields fall, duration increases so that percentage price change accelerates. With an option-free bond, both these changes in duration occur.

This is portrayed graphically in Exhibit 4-13. The slope of the tangent line in the exhibit gets flatter as the required yield increases. A flatter tangent line means a smaller duration as the required yield rises. In contrast, the tangent line gets steeper as the required yield decreases, implying that the duration gets larger. This property will hold for all option-free bonds. Also, from this graphical presentation we can see that the convexity is actually measuring the rate of change of the dollar duration as market yields change.

Property 2: For a given yield and maturity, the lower the coupon, the greater the convexity of a bond.

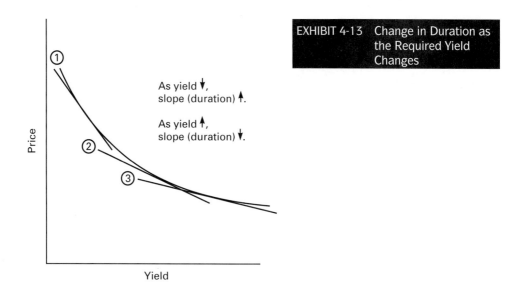

EXHIBIT 4-13 Change in Duration as the Required Yield Changes

As yield ↓, slope (duration) ↑.

As yield ↑, slope (duration) ↓.

Price

Yield

This can be seen from the computed convexity of our hypothetical bonds. Of the three five-year bonds, the zero-coupon bond has the highest convexity, and the 9% coupon bond has the lowest convexity. The same is true of the 25-year bonds.

Property 3: For a given yield and modified duration, the lower the coupon, the smaller the convexity.

The investment implication of property 3 is that zero-coupon bonds have the lowest convexity for a given modified duration.

ADDITIONAL CONCERNS WHEN USING DURATION

Our illustrations have demonstrated that relying on duration as the sole measure of the price volatility of a bond may mislead investors. There are two other concerns about using duration that we should point out.

First, in the derivation of the relationship between modified duration and bond price volatility, we started with the price equation (4.1). This price equation assumes that all cash flows for the bond are discounted at the same discount rate. The appropriateness of this assumption is examined in Chapter 5 where we analyze the yield curve. Essentially, the derivation of equation (4.3) assumes that the yield curve is flat and all shifts are parallel. In Chapter 22 we show the limitations of applying duration when this assumption does not hold, and the yield curve does not shift in a parallel fashion. This is extremely important when we try to use a portfolio's duration to quantify the responsiveness of a portfolio's value to a change in interest rates. If a portfolio has bonds with different maturities, the duration measure may not provide a good estimate for unequal changes in interest rates of different maturities. At the end of this chapter, we'll look at one approach to measuring the sensitivity of a portfolio when interest rates for all maturities do not change by the same number of basis points.

Our second concern is misapplication of duration to bonds with embedded options. The principles we have illustrated apply only to option-free bonds. When changes in yields result in a change in the expected cash flow for a bond, which is the case for bonds with embedded options, the duration and convexity measures are appropriate only in certain circumstances. We discuss the price volatility of bonds with embedded options in Chapters 17 and 18.

The duration measure introduced in those chapters that takes into account any embedded options is called **effective duration**.

DON'T THINK OF DURATION AS A MEASURE OF TIME

Unfortunately, market participants often confuse the main purpose of duration by constantly referring to it as some measure of the weighted average life of a bond. This is because of the original use of duration by Macaulay. If you rely on this interpretation of duration, it will be difficult for you to understand why a bond with a maturity of 20 years can have a duration greater than 20 years. For example, in Chapter 12 we discuss collateralized mortgage obligation (CMO) bond classes. Certain CMO bond classes have a greater duration than the underlying mortgage loans. That is, a CMO bond class can have a duration of 40 although the underlying mortgage loans from which the CMO is created can have a maturity of 30 years. Also, some CMO bond classes have a negative duration. How can this happen?

The answer to this puzzle is that duration is the approximate percentage change in price for a small change in interest rates. In fact, as explained earlier, a good way to remember duration is that it is the approximate percentage change in price for a 100-basis-point change in interest rates.

Certain CMO bond classes are leveraged instruments whose price sensitivity or duration, as a result, are a multiple of the underlying mortgage loans from which they were created. Thus, a CMO bond class with a duration of 40 does not mean that it has some type of weighted average life of 40 years. Instead, it means that for a 100-basis-point change in yield, that bond's price will change by roughly 40%.

Similarly, we interpret the duration of an option in the same way. A call option can have a duration of 20 when the time to expiration of the option is one year.[7] This is confusing to someone who interprets duration as some measure of the life of an option. What it means is that if yields change by 100 basis points for the bond underlying the option, the value of the option will change by approximately 20%.

APPROXIMATING A BOND'S DURATION AND CONVEXITY MEASURE

When we understand that duration is related to percentage price change, a simple formula can be used to calculate the approximate duration of a bond or any other more complex derivative securities or options described throughout this book. All we are interested in is the percentage price change of a bond when interest rates change by a small amount. This can be found quite easily by the following procedure:

Step 1:   Increase the yield on the bond by a small number of basis points and determine the new price at this higher yield level. We denote this new price by P_+.

Step 2:   Decrease the yield on the bond by the same number of basis points and calculate the new price. We will denote this new price by P_-.

Step 3:   Letting P_0 be the initial price, duration can be approximated using the following formula:

$$\text{approximate duration} = \frac{P_- - P_+}{2(P_0)(\Delta y)} \tag{4.23}$$

where Δy is the change in yield used to calculate the new prices (in decimal form). What the formula is measuring is the average percentage price change (relative to the initial price) per 1-basis-point change in yield.

---

[7]We see how to measure the duration of an option in Chapter 27.

To see how good this approximation is, let's apply it to the 25-year 6% coupon bond trading at 9%. All the necessary information is provided in Exhibit 4-2. The initial price (P_0) is 70.3570. The steps are as follows:

Step 1: Increase the yield on the bond by 10 basis points from 9% to 9.1%. Thus, Δy is 0.001. The new price (P_+) is 69.6164.

Step 2: Decrease the yield on the bond by 10 basis points from 9% to 8.9%. The new price (P_-) is 71.1105.

Step 3: Because the initial price, P_0, is 70.3570, the duration can be approximated as follows:

$$\text{approximate duration} = \frac{71.1105 - 69.6164}{2(70.3570)(0.001)} = 10.62$$

How good is the approximation? The modified duration as calculated by using equations (4.5) and (4.7) is 10.62.

If an investor is interested in the duration of any financial instrument, equation (4.23) can be used. However, to use the equation, it is necessary to have a good pricing model to get the new prices in steps 1 and 2. These models are discussed in later chapters. *It is important to emphasize here that duration is a by-product of a pricing model. If the pricing model is poor, the resulting duration estimate is poor.*

Similarly, the convexity measure of any bond can be approximated using the following formula:

$$\text{approximate convexity measure} = \frac{P_+ + P_- - 2P_0}{P_0(\Delta y)^2} \qquad \textbf{(4.24)}$$

Using our previous illustration, the approximate convexity measure is

$$\text{approximate convexity measure} = \frac{71.1105 + 69.6164 - 2(70.3570)}{70.3570(0.001)^2} = 183.3$$

As reported previously, the convexity measure calculated by formula is 182.92. Thus, equation (4.24) does a fine job.

As we noted earlier, the convexity measure can be measured in a different way. Equation (4.24) can be rewritten to include 2 in the denominator. All this means is that when the percentage change in price due to convexity is computed using equation (4.20), the $\frac{1}{2}$ should be eliminated.

Duration of an Inverse Floater

In Chapter 2 we discussed how an inverse floater is created and how it is priced. Here we will look at the duration of an inverse floater. The duration of the inverse floater is related to the duration of the collateral and the duration of the floater. Assuming that the duration of the floater is close to zero, it can be shown that the duration of an inverse floater is as follows:[8]

$$\text{duration of inverse floater} = (1 + L)(\text{duration of collateral}) \times \frac{\text{collateral price}}{\text{inverse price}}$$

where L is the ratio of the par value of the floater to the par value of the inverse floater. For example, if collateral with a par value of $100 million is used to create a floater with a par value of $80 million and an inverse floater with a par value of $20 million, L is 4 ($80 million/$20 million).

It is easy to see why an inverse's duration is a multiple of the collateral. Suppose that the par value of the collateral of $100 million is split as follows: $80 million for the floater and $20 million for the inverse floater. Suppose also that the collateral and inverse are trading at par so that the ratio of the prices is 1 and that the duration for the collateral is 8. For a 100-basis-point change in interest rates, the collateral's price will decline by 8% or $8 million (8% times $100 million). Assuming that the floater's price does not change when interest rates increase, the $8 million decline must come from the inverse floater. For the inverse floater to realize a decline in value of $8 million when its value is $20 million, the duration must be 40. That is, a duration of 40 will produce a 40% change in value or $8 million (40% times $20 million). Thus, the duration is five times the collateral's duration of 8. Or equivalently, because L is 4, it is $(1 + 4)$ times the collateral's duration.

Notice that even if the maturity of the collateral is 30 years, the duration of the inverse is greater than the maturity of the collateral. Investors who interpret duration as some time of weighted life of a security would be surprised by this result.

MEASURING A BOND PORTFOLIO'S RESPONSIVENESS TO NONPARALLEL CHANGES IN INTEREST RATES

We noted earlier in this chapter when we identified the shortcoming of duration that this measure may be inadequate in measuring how a security's price or a portfolio's value will change when interest rates do not change in a parallel manner. (We will discuss how yield curve shifts in Chapter 5.) This is particularly the case for a bond portfolio. As a result, it is necessary to be able to measure the exposure of a bond or bond portfolio to shifts in the yield curve. There have been several approaches that have been suggested for measuring this exposure. There have been several approaches to measuring yield curve risk. The two major ones are yield curve reshaping duration and key rate duration. We describe each below.[9]

---

[8]William R. Leach, "A Portfolio Manager's Perspective of Inverses and Inverse IOs," Chapter 9 in Frank J. Fabozzi (ed.), *Advances in the Valuation and Management of Mortgage-Backed Securities* (New Hope, PA: Frank J. Fabozzi Associates, 1998).

[9]The other measures are yield curve reshaping duration and yield curve specific duration. These measures are discussed in Chapter 7 of Frank J. Fabozzi, *Duration, Convexity, and Other Bond Risk Measures* (New Hope, PA: Frank J. Fabozzi Associates, 1999). The discussion in this section on key rate duration is adapted from that chapter.

Yield Curve Reshaping Duration

The first approach concentrates on the sensitivity of a portfolio to a change in the slope of the yield curve. The initial step in this approach is to define what is meant by the slope of the yield curve. Market participants have used different definitions. Some define yield curve slope as the difference in the Treasury yield curve at two maturity levels. For instance, the yield curve slope can be defined as the difference between the yield on a proxy for the long-term Treasury bond (30-year Treasury) and the 2-year on-the-run Treasury. Some have defined the short maturity point as the 6-month rate.

One of the first measures of this approach was introduced by three researchers at Salomon Brothers (now Salomon Smith Barney), Klaffky, Ma, and Nozari.[10] They called the measure that they suggest **yield curve reshaping duration**. They focus on three maturity points on the yield curve: 2-year, 10-year, and 30-year. Using these three points they then calculate the spread between the 10-year and 2-year yield and refer to this as the spread for the short end of the yield curve; the spread between the 30-year and the 10-year is computed and referred to as the spread for the long end of the yield curve. Klaffky, Ma, and Nozari refer to the sensitivity of a portfolio to changes in the short end of the yield curve as **short-end duration** (SEDUR) and to changes in the long-end of the yield curve as **long-end duration** (LEDUR). These concepts, however, are applicable to other points on the yield curve.

To calculate the SEDUR of the portfolio, first the change in each security's price is calculated for

1. a steepening of the yield curve at the short end by x basis points
2. a flattening of the yield curve at the short end by x basis points

The portfolio value for a steepening of the yield curve is then computed by adding up the value of every security in the portfolio after the steepening. We will denote this value as $V_{SE,S}$ where V stands for portfolio value, SE for short end of the yield curve, and S for steepening. Similarly, the portfolio value after the flattening is obtained by summing up the value of each security in the portfolio and the resulting value will be denoted by $V_{SE,F}$ where F denotes flattening. The SEDUR is then computed as follows:

$$\text{SEDUR} = \frac{V_{SE,S} - V_{SE,F}}{2\,(V_0)\,(\Delta y)}$$

where V_0 is the initial value of the portfolio (the value before any steepening or flattening) and Δy is the number of basis points used to compute the steepening and flattening of the yield curve (x).

Compare the above equation to equation (4.23) for approximating duration. Notice that it is the same formula where V is used instead of P and P_- and P_+ are replaced by $V_{SE,S}$ and $V_{SE,F}$, respectively.

[10]Thomas E. Klaffky, Y. Y. Ma, and Ardavan Nozari, "Managing Yield Curve Exposure: Introducing Reshaping Durations," *Journal of Fixed Income* (December 1992), pp. 5–15.

To compute the LEDUR of the portfolio, the change in each security's price is first calculated for

1. a flattening of the yield curve at the long end by x basis points
2. a steepening of the yield curve at the long end by x basis points

The value for the portfolio after each shift is computed and denoted by $V_{LE,F}$ and $V_{LE,S}$ where LE denotes the long-end of the yield curve. Then LEDUR is calculated from the following formula:

$$\text{LEDUR} = \frac{V_{LE,F} - V_{LE,S}}{2\,(V_0)\,(\Delta y)}$$

SEDUR and LEDUR are interpreted as follows. SEDUR is the approximate percentage change in the value of a portfolio for a 100-basis-point change in the slope of the short-end of the yield curve. LEDUR is the approximate percentage change in the value of a portfolio for a 100-basis-point change in the slope of the long-end of the yield curve.

Key Rate Duration

The most popular measure for estimating the sensitivity of a security or a portfolio to changes in the yield curve is key rate duration. The basic principle of key rate duration is to change the yield for a particular maturity of the yield curve and determine the sensitivity of a security or portfolio to that change holding all other yields constant. The sensitivity of the change in value to a particular change in yield is called **rate duration**. There is a rate duration for every point on the yield curve. Consequently, there is not one rate duration, but a vector of durations representing each maturity on the yield curve. The total change in value of a bond or a portfolio if all rates change by the same number of basis points is simply the duration of a security or portfolio we discussed earlier in this chapter.

The notion of using multiple durations was first suggested in 1988 by Donald Chambers and Willard Carleton; they called it **duration vectors**.[11] Robert Reitano suggested a similar approach in a series of papers and called the durations partial durations.[12] The most popular version of this approach is that developed by Thomas Ho in 1992, who called it rate duration.[13]

Ho's approach focuses on 11 key maturities of a Treasury curve, which we will describe in Chapter 5. The specific curve used in the analysis is called the Treasury spot

---

[11]Donald Chambers and Willard Carleton, "A Generalized Approach to Duration," *Research in Finance* 7(1988).

[12]See, for example, Robert R. Reitano, "Non-Parallel Yield Curve Shifts and Durational Leverage," *Journal of Portfolio Management*, Summer 1990, pp. 62–67, and "A Multivariate Approach to Duration Analysis," *ARCH* 2 (1989).

[13]Thomas S. Y. Ho, "Key Rate Durations: Measure of Interest Rate Risk," *Journal of Fixed Income*, September 1992, pp. 29–44.

rate curve; this important curve shows the relationship between maturity and yields on Treasury zero-coupon securities (see Chapter 5 for a detailed discussion). The rate durations are called **key rate durations**. The specific maturities on the spot rate curve for which a key rate duration is measured are 3 months, 1 year, 2 years, 3 years, 5 years, 7 years, 10 years, 15 years, 20 years, 25 years, and 30 years. Changes in rates between any two key rates are calculated using a linear approximation.

A key rate duration for a particular portfolio maturity should be interpreted as follows: Holding the yield for all other maturities constant, the key rate duration is the approximate percentage change in the value of a portfolio (or bond) for a 100-basis-point change in the yield for the maturity whose rate has been changed. Thus, a key rate duration is quantified by changing the yield of the maturity of interest and determining how the value or price changes. In fact, equation (4.23) is used. The prices denoted by P_- and P_+ in the equation are the prices in the case of a bond and the portfolio values in the case of a bond portfolio found by holding all other interest rates constant and changing the yield for the maturity whose key rate duration is sought.

Let's look at three actual portfolios to make the concept of key rate duration more concrete. Exhibit 4-14 shows three portfolios consisting of different maturity Treasury securities as of March 22, 2006. The duration for each portfolio is the same, 4.26.[14] The key rate durations differ for each portfolio. Look at the 30-year key rate duration for each portfolio. For the first portfolio in the exhibit, the 30-year duration is 0.675. This means that if the 30-year Treasury spot rate changes by 100 basis points and the spot rate for all other maturities does not change, the portfolio's value will change by approximately 0.675%. For the second portfolio, the 30-year key rate duration is close to zero; thus, for a 100-basis-point change in the 30-year Treasury spot rate and holding the spot rate for all other maturities the same, the second portfolio's value will not change. The third portfolio's 30-year key rate duration is 0.594, so its value will change by 0.594% for a 100-basis-point change assuming no change in the spot rate for other maturities.

From this illustration it can be seen that despite the same portfolio duration for all three portfolios (4.26), they will each be expected to react in a different way if the 30-year spot rate changes. Exhibit 4-14 indicates that each portfolio will have quite different reactions to changes in the interest rate for different maturities.

SUMMARY

The price–yield relationship for all option-free bonds is convex. There are three properties of the price volatility of an option-free bond: (1) for small changes in yield, the percentage price change is symmetric; (2) for large changes in yield, the percentage price change is asymmetric; and (3) for large changes in yield the price appreciation is greater than the price depreciation for a given change in yield.

The price volatility of an option-free bond is affected by two characteristics of a bond (maturity and coupon) and the yield level at which a bond trades. For a given maturity and yield, the lower the coupon rate, the greater the price volatility. For a given coupon rate and yield, the longer the maturity, the greater the price volatility. For a given coupon rate and maturity, the price volatility is greater the lower the yield.

---

[14]Note that the three portfolios are labeled "ladder portfolio," "barbell portfolio," and "bullet portfolio." We'll see why in Chapter 22.

EXHIBIT 4-14   Key Rate Durations For Three Treasury Portfolios (March 22, 2006)

Barbell Portfolio		Bullet Portfolio		Ladder Portfolio	
Treasury Issue	Weight (%)	Treasury Issue	Weight (%)	Treasury Issue	Weight (%)
2.625% 05/15/2008	3.71	3.875% 02/15/2013	0.50	14.000% 11/15/2011	36.47
4.000% 02/15/2015	14.95	3.875% 09/15/2010	69.73	10.375% 11/15/2012	13.92
4.250% 08/15/2015	9.12	4.250% 01/15/2011	29.41	12.000% 08/15/2013	7.81
4.500% 02/15/2036	6.90	4.500% 02/15/2036	0.35	12.500% 08/15/2014	8.57
4.625% 02/29/2008	65.31			6.000% 02/15/2026	6.06
				6.750% 08/15/2026	2.58
				5.375% 02/15/2031	2.89
				5.000% 08/15/2011	4.55
				4.000% 02/15/2015	7.74
				4.500% 02/15/2036	4.57
				4.500% 02/15/2016	4.85

Key Rate Durations

Vertices	Barbell	Bullet	Ladder
0.0833	0.0000	0.0000	0.0015
0.25	0.0017	0.0014	0.0045
0.50	0.0092	0.0087	0.1273
1	0.0662	0.0290	0.1768
2	1.2480	0.0744	0.2880
3	0.0513	0.1071	0.2430
4	0.0448	1.5132	0.1520
5	0.0790	2.4525	0.2280
7	0.5131	0.0287	0.3626
10	1.3210	0.0060	0.9770
20	0.2520	0.0120	1.1040
30	0.6750	0.0330	0.5940
Duration	4.2613	4.2660	4.2586

NOTE: This exhibit was prepared for the author by Dan Sinnreich and Oren Cheyette of MSCI Barra using Cosmos.

There are two measures of bond price volatility: price value of a basis point and duration. We focused on the various duration measures—Macaulay duration, modified duration, and dollar duration—showing the relationship between bond price volatility and each of these measures. Modified duration is the approximate percentage change in price for a 100-basis-point change in yield. The dollar duration is the approximate dollar price change.

Duration does a good job of estimating a bond's percentage price change for a small change in yield. However, it does not do as good a job for a large change in yield. The percentage price change due to convexity can be used to supplement the approximate price change using duration. Together, the duration and convexity measures provide an excellent approximation of the price change when yields change.

Duration is an approximation of price change assuming a parallel shift in the yield curve. Duration should not be interpreted as a measure of the weighted life of a bond. For certain bonds, the modified duration can be greater than the maturity of a bond. Duration and convexity can be approximated by looking at how the price of a bond changes when the yield is changed up and down by a small number of basis points. For a fixed-rate bond and a floating-rate bond, a spread measure can be calculated. The duration of an inverse floater is a multiple of the duration of the collateral from which it is created.

The duration of a portfolio is the weighted average duration of the bonds constituting the portfolio. When a manager attempts to gauge the sensitivity of a bond portfolio to changes in interest rates by computing a portfolio's duration, it is assumed that the interest rate for all maturities changes by the same number of basis points. To estimate the sensitivity of a bond portfolio to unequal changes in interest rates, two approaches have been used. The first is yield curve reshaping duration. Here two measures are computed: short-end duration and long-end duration. The former measures the exposure of a portfolio to changes in the short-end of the yield curve and the latter exposure to the long-end of the yield curve. The more popular approach is key rate duration. A rate duration is the approximate change in the value of a portfolio (or bond) to a change in the interest rate of a particular maturity assuming that the interest rate for all other maturities is held constant. Practitioners compute a key rate duration, which is simply the rate duration for key maturities.

Questions

1. The price value of a basis point will be the same regardless if the yield is increased or decreased by 1 basis point. However, the price value of 100 basis points (i.e., the change in price for a 100-basis-point change in interest rates) will not be the same if the yield is increased or decreased by 100 basis points. Why?

2. Calculate the requested measures for bonds A and B (assume that each bond pays interest semiannually):

	A	B
Coupon	8%	9%
Yield to maturity	8%	8%
Maturity (years)	2	5
Par	$100.00	$100.00
Price	$100.00	$104.055

   a. Price value of a basis point
   b. Macaulay duration
   c. Modified duration
   d. The approximate duration using the shortcut formula by changing yields by 20 basis points and compare your answer with the convexity measure calculated in part c.
   e. Convexity measure
   f. The approximate convexity measure using the shortcut formula by changing yields by 20 basis points and compare your answer to the convexity measure calculated in part e.

3. Can you tell from the following information which of the following three bonds will have the greatest price volatility, assuming that each is trading to offer the same yield to maturity?

Bond	Coupon Rate (%)	Maturity (years)
X	8	9
Y	10	11
Z	11	12

4. For bonds A and B in Question 2:
   a. Calculate the actual price of the bonds for a 100-basis-point increase in interest rates.

b. Using duration, estimate the price of the bonds for a 100-basis-point increase in interest rates.

c. Using both duration and convexity measure, estimate the price of the bonds for a 100-basis-point increase in interest rates.

d. Comment on the accuracy of your results in parts b and c, and state why one approximation is closer to the actual price than the other.

e. Without working through calculations, indicate whether the duration of the two bonds would be higher or lower if the yield to maturity is 10% rather than 8%.

5. State why you would agree or disagree with the following statement: As the duration of a zero-coupon bond is equal to its maturity, the price responsiveness of a zero-coupon bond to yield changes is the same regardless of the level of interest rates.

6. State why you would agree or disagree with the following statement: When interest rates are low, there will be little difference between the Macaulay duration and modified duration measures.

7. State why you would agree or disagree with the following statement: If two bonds have the same dollar duration, yield, and price, their dollar price sensitivity will be the same for a given change in interest rates.

8. State why you would agree or disagree with the following statement: For a 1-basis-point change in yield, the price value of a basis point is equal to the dollar duration.

9. The November 26, 1990, issue of *BondWeek* includes an article, "Van Kampen Merritt Shortens." The article begins as follows: "Peter Hegel, first v.p. at Van Kampen Merritt Investment Advisory, is shortening his $3 billion portfolio from 110% of his normal duration of 6 years to 103–105% because he thinks that in the short run the bond rally is near an end." Explain Hegel's strategy and the use of the duration measure in this context.

10. Consider the following two Treasury securities:

Bond	Price	Modified Duration
A	$100	6
B	80	7

Which bond will have the greater dollar price volatility for a 25-basis-point change in interest rates?

11. What are the limitations of using duration as a measure of a bond's price sensitivity to interest-rate changes?

12. The following excerpt is taken from an article titled "Denver Investment to Make $800 Million Treasury Move," which appeared in the December 9, 1991, issue of *BondWeek*, p. 1: "Denver Investment Advisors will swap $800 million of long zero-coupon Treasuries for intermediate Treasuries. . . . The move would shorten the duration of its $2.5 billion fixed-income portfolio. . . ."

Why would the swap described here shorten the duration of the portfolio?

13. You are a portfolio manager who has presented a report to a client. The report indicates the duration of each security in the portfolio. One of the securities has a maturity of 15 years but a duration of 25. The client believes that there is an error in the report because he believes that the duration cannot be greater than the security's maturity. What would be your response to this client?

14. a. Suppose that the spread duration for a fixed-rate bond is 2.5. What is the approximate change in the bond's price if the spread changes by 50 basis points?

b. What is the spread duration of a Treasury security?

15. What is meant by the spread duration for a floating-rate bond?

16. Explain why the duration of an inverse floater is a multiple of the duration of the collateral from which the inverse floater is created.

17. Consider the following portfolio:

Bond	Market Value	Duration
W	$13 million	2
X	$27 million	7
Y	$60 million	8
Z	$40 million	14

a. What is the portfolio's duration?

b. If interest rates for all maturities change by 50 basis points, what is the approximate percentage change in the value of the portfolio?

c. What is the contribution to portfolio duration for each bond?

18. "If two portfolios have the same duration, the change in their value when interest rates change will be the same." Explain why you agree or disagree with this statement.

19. In the fifth edition of *The Handbook of Fixed Income Securities* (Irwin Professional Publishing, 1997), page 104 gives the following formula for the approximate convexity measure:

$$\frac{P_+ + P_- - 2(P_0)}{2(P_0)(\Delta y)^2}$$

where the variables are defined as in equation (4.24) of this chapter. Compare this formula with the approximate convexity measure given by equation (4.24). Which formula is correct?

20. a. How is the short-end duration of a portfolio computed?

b. How is the long-end duration of a portfolio computed?

c. How is the short end and long end of a portfolio defined?

d. Suppose that the SEDUR of a portfolio is 3. What is the approximate change in the portfolio's value if the slope of the short end of the yield curve changed by 25 basis points?

21. a. Explain what a 10-year key rate duration of 0.35 means?

b. How is a key rate duration computed?

CHAPTER

5

FACTORS AFFECTING BOND YIELDS AND THE TERM STRUCTURE OF INTEREST RATES

After reading this chapter you will understand:

- ■ why the yield on a Treasury security is the base interest rate

- ■ the factors that affect the yield spread between two bonds

- ■ what a yield curve is

- ■ a spot rate and a spot rate curve

- ■ how theoretical spot rates are derived using arbitrage arguments from the Treasury yield curve

- ■ what the term structure of interest rates is

- ■ why the price of a Treasury bond should be based on theoretical spot rates

- ■ a forward rate and how a forward rate is derived

- ■ how long-term rates are related to the current short-term rate and short-term forward rates

- ■ why forward rates should be viewed as hedgeable rates

- ■ the various theories about the determinants of the shape of the term structure: pure expectations theory, the liquidity theory, the preferred habitat theory, and the market segmentation theory

- ■ the main economic influences on the shape of the Treasury yield curve

In all financial markets throughout the world, there is not one yield offered on all bonds. The yield offered on a particular bond depends on a myriad of factors having to do with the type of issuer, the characteristics of the bond issue, and the state of the economy. In this chapter we look at the factors that affect the yield offered in the bond market. We begin with the minimum interest rate that an investor wants from investing in a bond, the yield on U.S. Treasury securities. Then we describe why the yield on a non-U.S. Treasury security will differ from that of a U.S. Treasury security. Finally, we focus on one particular factor that affects the yield offered on a security: maturity. The pattern of interest rates on securities of the same issuer but with different maturities is called the term structure of interest rates. The importance of analyzing the term structure of interest rates for U.S. Treasury securities is explained.

BASE INTEREST RATE

The securities issued by the U.S. Department of the Treasury are backed by the full faith and credit of the U.S. government. Consequently, market participants throughout the world view them as having no credit risk. As such, interest rates on Treasury securities are the key interest rates in the U.S. economy as well as in international capital markets. The large size of any single issue has contributed to making the Treasury market the most active and hence the most liquid market in the world.

The minimum interest rate that investors want is referred to as the **base interest rate** or **benchmark interest rate** that investors will demand for investing in a non-Treasury security. This rate is the yield to maturity (hereafter referred to as simply **yield**) offered on a comparable maturity Treasury security that was most recently issued ("on the run"). So, for example, if an investor wanted to purchase a 10-year bond on October 7, 2005, the minimum yield the investor would seek is 4.36% (see Exhibit 5-1).

EXHIBIT 5-1   U.S. Treasury Security Yields on October 7, 2005

Maturity	Yield (%)
1-month	3.33
3-month	3.61
6-month	3.99
1-year	4.17
2-year	4.19
3-year	4.21
5-year	4.23
10-year	4.36
30-year	4.57

Lehman Brothers, *Global Relative Value,* October 11, 2005, p. 161.

RISK PREMIUM

Market participants talk of interest rates on non-Treasury securities as **trading at a spread** to a particular on-the-run Treasury security. This spread, called a **risk premium**, reflects the additional risks the investor faces by acquiring a security that is not issued by the U.S. government. Thus, we can express the interest rate offered on a non-Treasury security as

$$\text{base interest rate} + \text{spread}$$

or, equivalently,

$$\text{base interest rate} + \text{risk premium}$$

Yield spreads can be measured in terms of the difference between the yield on two bonds. The difference is measured in basis points. Unless otherwise stated, yield spreads are typically measured in this way. Yield spreads can also be measured on a relative basis by taking the ratio of the yield spread to the yield level. This is called a **relative yield spread**:

$$\text{relative yield spread} = \frac{\text{yield on bond A} - \text{yield on bond B}}{\text{yield on bond B}}$$

Sometimes bonds are compared in terms of a **yield ratio**, the quotient of two bond yields:

$$\text{yield ratio} = \frac{\text{yield on bond A}}{\text{yield on bond B}}$$

The factors that affect the yield spread include (1) the type of issuer, (2) the issuer's perceived credit worthiness, (3) the term or maturity of the instrument, (4) provisions that grant either the issuer or the investor the option to do something, (5) the taxability of the interest received by investors, and (6) the expected liquidity of the security.

Types of Issuers

The bond market is classified by the type of issuer, including the U.S. government, U.S. government agencies, municipal governments, credit (domestic and foreign corporations), and foreign governments. These classifications are referred to as **market sectors**. Different sectors are generally perceived to represent different risks and rewards. Some market sectors are further subdivided into categories intended to reflect common economic characteristics. For example, within the credit market sector, issuers are classified as follows: (1) industrial, (2) utility, (3) finance, and (4) noncorporate. Excluding the Treasury market sector, the other market sectors have a wide range of issuers, each with different abilities to satisfy their contractual obligations. Therefore, a key feature of a debt obligation is the nature of the issuer.

The spread between the interest rate offered in two sectors of the bond market with the same maturity is referred to as an **intermarket sector spread**. The most common intermarket sector spread calculated is the spread between Treasury securities and some sector of the non-Treasury market with the same maturity. Exhibit 5-2 shows the

EXHIBIT 5-2 Approximate Benchmark Bid Spreads of the 20 Largest Issuers in the High-Yield Index, October 6, 2005

| | Issuer's Largest Issue | | | | | | | Issuer | |
| | | | | Price | | Bid Spread (bp) | | | |
	Coupon	Maturity	Rating	Current	1-wk Chg.	Current	1-Wk Chg.	Amt. Out. ($ 000)	% of Index
CCH I LLC	11.000	10/1/2015	CAA3	93.75	-3.75	773	63	3,525.000	4.71
QWEST SERVICES CORP	13.500	12/15/2010	B2	114.25	-0.25	224	9	2,202.896	3.71
GENERAL MOTORS - GLOBAL	8.375	7/15/2033	BA2	77.75	-0.25	635	1	3,000.000	3.40
MCI INC	7.688	5/1/2009	B2	103.75	0.00	171	-7	1,982.537	3.02
SUNGARD DATA SYSTEMS INC	9.125	8/15/2013	B3	103.00	-0.63	423	9	1,600.000	2.38
AES CORP	8.750	5/15/2013	BA3	109.50	0.00	211	-3	1,200.000	1.93
NOVELIS INC	7.250	2/15/2015	B2	95.00	0.00	365	-4	1,400.000	1.91
EL PASO PRODUCTION HLDG	7.750	6/1/2003	B3	104.50	0.00	255	-4	1,200.000	1.83
NRG ENERGY INC	8.000	12/15/2013	B1	110.50	4.00	132	-119	1,113.892	1.79
WYNN LAS VEGAS LLC/CORP	6.625	12/1/2014	B2	94.50	-0.50	310	4	1,297.840	1.79
TRUMP ENTERTAINMENT RESORTS	8.500	6/1/2015	CAA1	96.75	0.00	464	-4	1,250.000	1.78
TEXAS GENCO LLC	6.875	12/15/2014	B2	107.50	6.00	135	-107	1,125.000	1.75
CROWN EURO HOLDINGS SA	9.500	3/1/2011	B1	108.75	-0.50	202	29	1,084.725	1.69
MIDWEST GENERATION LLC	8.750	5/1/2034	B2	111.00	0.50	216	-18	1,000.000	1.63
CASE NEW HOLLAND INC	9.250	8/1/2011	BA3	105.50	-0.50	336	12	1,049.210	1.60
TENET HEALTHCARE CORP	9.875	7/1/2014	B3	103.63	-0.87	489	10	1,000.000	1.51
MGM MIRAGE INC	6.000	10/1/2009	BA2	98.25	-0.75	231	22	1,049.035	1.47
DYNEGY INC	10.125	7/15/2013	B3	111.25	0.25	305	-12	900.000	1.45
L-3 COMMS CORP	6.375	10/15/2015	BA2	100.13	-0.63	199	6	1,000.000	1.44
DIRECTV HOLDINGS/FINANCE	6.375	6/15/2015	BA2	98.75	-0.25	219	0	1,000.000	1.43
Average				**102.40**	**0.09**	**315**	**-6**		

*Based on issuers qualifying for our VLI High Yield Index.

approximate benchmark spread between the largest issuers in the Lehman Brothers High-Yield Index and Treasury securities with approximately the same maturity. The spread between two issues within a market sector is called an **intramarket sector spread**.

Perceived Credit Worthiness of Issuer

Default risk refers to the risk that the issuer of a bond may be unable to make timely principal and/or interest payments. Most market participants rely primarily on commercial rating companies to assess the default risk of an issuer. We discuss these rating companies in Chapter 7.

The spread between Treasury securities and non-Treasury securities that are identical in all respects except for quality is referred to as a **credit spread**. It is important to keep in mind what is meant by "identical in all respects except for quality." As explained in Chapters 4 and 7 and discussed further subsequently, issues may have provisions that can be beneficial or detrimental to a bondholder. If these provisions are absent in a Treasury issue but present in a non-Treasury under examination, the credit spread would be distorted because it reflects the value of these other provisions.

Inclusion of Options

It is not uncommon for a bond issue to include a provision that gives either the bondholder or the issuer an option to take some action against the other party. Such embedded options are discussed throughout this book. The most common type of option in a bond issue is the call provision that grants the issuer the right to retire the debt, fully or partially, before the scheduled maturity date. The inclusion of a call feature benefits issuers by allowing them to replace an old bond issue with a lower-interest-cost issue should interest rates in the market decline. Effectively, a call provision allows the issuer to alter the maturity of a bond. A call provision is detrimental to the bondholder because the bondholder must reinvest the proceeds received at a lower interest rate.

The presence of an embedded option has an effect on the spread of an issue relative to a Treasury security and the spread relative to otherwise comparable issues that do not have an embedded option. In general, market participants will require a larger spread to a comparable Treasury security for an issue with an embedded option that is favorable to the issuer (e.g., a call option) than for an issue without such an option. In contrast, market participants will require a smaller spread to a comparable Treasury security for an issue with an embedded option that is favorable to the investor (e.g., put option or conversion option). In fact, for a bond with an option that is favorable to an investor, the interest rate on an issue may be less than that on a comparable Treasury security!

Taxability of Interest

Unless exempted under the federal income tax code, interest income is taxable at the federal level. In addition to federal income taxes, there may be state and local taxes on interest income.

The federal tax code specifically exempts the interest income from qualified municipal bond issues from taxation at the federal level. Because of the tax-exempt feature of municipal bonds, the yield on municipal bonds is less than that on Treasuries with the same maturity.

The yield on a taxable bond issue after federal income taxes are paid is called the **after-tax yield**:

$$\text{after-tax yield} = \text{pretax yield} \times (1 - \text{marginal tax rate})$$

Of course, the marginal tax rate varies among investors. For example, suppose that a taxable bond issue offers a yield of 5% and is acquired by an investor facing a marginal tax rate of 35%. The after-tax yield would then be

$$\text{after-tax yield} = 0.05 \times (1 - 0.35) = 3.25\%$$

Alternatively, we can determine the yield that must be offered on a taxable bond issue to give the same after-tax yield as a tax-exempt issue. This yield, called the **equivalent taxable yield**, is determined as follows:

$$\text{equivalent taxable yield} = \frac{\text{tax-exempt yield}}{1 - \text{marginal tax rate}}$$

For example, consider an investor facing a 35% marginal tax rate who purchases a tax-exempt issue with a yield of 3.4%. The equivalent taxable yield is then

$$\text{equivalent taxable yield} = \frac{0.034}{1 - 0.35} = 0.0523 = 5.23\%$$

Notice that the higher the marginal tax rate, the higher the equivalent taxable yield. For example, in our previous example, if the marginal tax rate is 45% rather than 35%, the equivalent taxable yield would be 6.18% rather than 5.23%:

$$\text{equivalent taxable yield} = \frac{0.034}{1 - 0.45} = 0.0618 = 6.18\%$$

The municipal bond market is divided into two major sectors: general obligations and revenue bonds. The revenue bond sector is further decomposed into the following sectors: (1) housing, (2) power, (3) hospitals, and (4) insured. For the tax-exempt bond market, the benchmark for calculating spreads is not Treasuries. Rather, it is a generic AAA general obligation bond with a specified maturity.

State and local governments may tax interest income on bond issues that are exempt from federal income taxes. Some municipalities exempt interest income from all municipal issues from taxation; others do not. Some states exempt interest income from bonds issued by municipalities within the state but tax the interest income from bonds issued by municipalities outside the state. The implication is that two municipal securities of the same quality rating and the same maturity may trade at some spread because of the relative demand for bonds of municipalities in different states. For example, in a high-income-tax state such as New York, the demand for bonds of municipalities will drive down their yield relative to municipalities in a low-income-tax state such as Florida. Municipalities are not permitted to tax the interest income from securities issued by the U.S. Treasury. Thus, part of the spread between Treasury securities and taxable non-Treasury securities of the same maturity reflects the value of the exemption from state and local taxes.

Expected Liquidity of an Issue

Bonds trade with different degrees of liquidity. The greater the expected liquidity, the lower the yield that investors would require. As noted earlier, Treasury securities are the most liquid securities in the world. The lower yield offered on Treasury securities relative to non-Treasury securities reflects the difference in liquidity. Even within the Treasury market, on-the-run issues have greater liquidity than off-the-run issues. One study finds that while default risk explains the majority of the risk premium between corporate bonds and Treasury securities, a significant factor that affects the risk premium is corporate bond illiquidity.[1]

Financeability of an Issue

A portfolio manager can use an issue as collateral for borrowing funds. By borrowing funds, a portfolio manager can create leverage. We will discuss this strategy in Chapter 22. The typical market used by portfolio managers to borrow funds using a security as collateral for a loan is the repurchase agreement market or "repo" market. We will discuss this market and the repo agreement in Chapter 22.

Basically, when a portfolio manager wants to borrow funds via a repo agreement, a dealer provides the funds. The interest rate the dealer charges is called the repo rate. There is not one repo rate but a structure of rates depending on the maturity of the loan and the specific issue being financed. With respect to the latter, there are times when dealers are in need of particular issues to cover a short position. When a dealer needs a particular issue, that dealer will be willing to offer to lend funds at a lower repo rate than the general repo rate in the market. The dealer is willing to offer attractive financing because it can use the collateral (i.e., the particular issue it needs) to cover a short position for the life of the repo agreement. Because such issues offer below-market financing opportunities, the price of such issues will be bid up, and therefore their yield is less than otherwise comparable issues. The spread between the yield on such issues and issues that do not offer a below-market repo rate reflects the financing advantage. This spread is commonly observed in the Treasury market between on-the-run and off-the-run issues. Consequently, the spread between on-the-run and off-the-run issues of approximately the same maturity reflects not only differences in liquidity but any financing advantage. This spread not only occurs between on-the-run and off-the-run issues. There are times in the market when particular off-the-run issues are needed by dealers for various activities that they perform.

Term to Maturity

As we explained in Chapter 2, the price of a bond will fluctuate over its life as yields in the market change. The time remaining on a bond's life is referred to as its **term to maturity** or simply **maturity**. As demonstrated in Chapter 4, the volatility of a bond's

---

[1]Francis A. Longstaff, Sanjay Mithal, and Eric Neis, "Coprorate Yield Spreads: Default Risk or Liquidity? New Evidence from the Credit Default Swap Market," *Journal of Finance* (October 2005), pp. 2213–2253.

price is dependent on its term to maturity. More specifically, with all other factors constant, the longer the term to maturity of a bond, the greater the price volatility resulting from a change in market yields. Generally, bonds are classified into three **maturity sectors**: Bonds with a term to maturity of between 1 to 5 years are considered **short term**; bonds with a term to maturity between 5 and 12 years are viewed as **intermediate term**; and **long-term** bonds are those with a term to maturity greater than 12 years. The spread between any two maturity sectors of the market is called a **maturity spread**. The relationship between the yields on otherwise comparable securities with different maturities is called the **term structure of interest rates**.

TERM STRUCTURE OF INTEREST RATES

The term structure of interest rates plays a key role in the valuation of bonds. For this reason, we devote a good deal of space to this important topic.

Yield Curve

The graphical depiction of the relationship between the yield on bonds of the same credit quality but different maturities is known as the **yield curve**. In the past, most investors have constructed yield curves from observations of prices and yields in the Treasury market. Two factors account for this tendency. First, Treasury securities are free of default risk, and differences in credit worthiness do not affect yields. Therefore, these instruments are directly comparable. Second, as the largest and most active bond market, the Treasury market offers the fewest problems of illiquidity or infrequent trading. The disadvantage, as noted previously, is that the yields may be biased downward because they reflect favorable financing opportunities.

Exhibit 5-3 shows three typical shapes that have been observed for the yield curve.

From a practical viewpoint, as we explained earlier in this chapter, a key function of the Treasury yield curve is to serve as a benchmark for pricing bonds and to set yields in all other sectors of the debt market: bank loans, mortgages, corporate debt, and international bonds. However, market participants are coming to realize that the traditionally constructed Treasury yield curve is an unsatisfactory measure of the relation between required yield and maturity. The key reason is that securities with the same maturity may actually carry different yields. As we explain in the next section, this phenomenon reflects the role and impact of differences in the bonds' coupon rates. Hence, it is necessary to develop more accurate and reliable estimates of the Treasury yield curve. In what follows we show the problems posed by traditional approaches to the Treasury yield curve and offer the correct approach to building a yield curve. This approach consists of identifying yields that apply to zero-coupon bonds and therefore eliminates the problem of coupon rate differences in the yield-maturity relationship.

Why the Yield Curve Should Not Be Used to Price a Bond

The price of a bond is the present value of its cash flow. However, in our illustrations and our discussion of the pricing of a bond in Chapter 2, we assume that one interest rate should be used to discount all the bond's cash flows. The appropriate interest rate is the yield on a Treasury security, with the same maturity as the bond, plus an appropriate risk premium.

EXHIBIT 5-3   Three Shapes That Have Been Observed for the Yield Curve

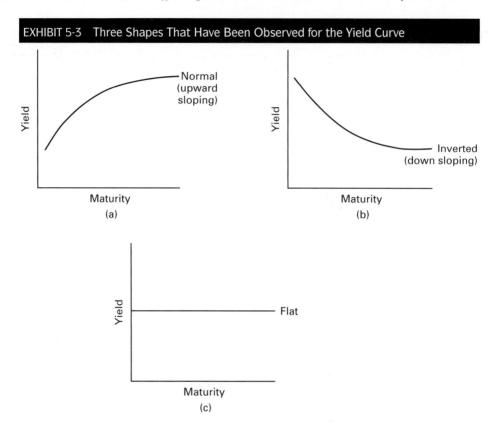

As noted previously, however, there is a problem with using the Treasury yield curve to determine the appropriate yield at which to discount the cash flow of a bond. To illustrate this problem, consider the following two hypothetical five-year Treasury bonds, A and B. The difference between these two Treasury bonds is the coupon rate, which is 12% for A and 3% for B. The cash flow for these two bonds per $100 of par value for the 10 six-month periods (five years) to maturity would be:

Period	Cash Flow for A	Cash Flow for B
1–9	$ 6.00	$ 1.50
10	106.00	101.50

Because of the different cash flow patterns, it is not appropriate to use the same interest rate to discount all cash flows. Instead, each cash flow should be discounted at a unique interest rate that is appropriate for the time period in which the cash flow will be received. But what should be the interest rate for each period?

The correct way to think about bonds A and B is not as bonds but as packages of cash flows. More specifically, they are packages of zero-coupon instruments. Thus, the interest earned is the difference between the maturity value and the price paid. For example, bond A can be viewed as 10 zero-coupon instruments: one with a maturity value of $6 maturing six months from now, a second with a maturity value of $6 maturing 1 year from now, a third with a maturity value of $6 maturing 1.5 years from now, and so on. The final zero-coupon instrument matures 10 six-month periods from now and has a maturity value of $106. Similarly, bond B can be viewed as 10 zero-coupon instruments with maturity values of $1.50 for the first nine six-month periods and $101.50 for the last six-month period. Obviously, in the case of each coupon bond (A or B), the value or price of the bond is equal to the total value of its component zero-coupon instruments.

In general, any bond can be viewed as a package of zero-coupon instruments. That is, each zero-coupon instrument in the package has a maturity equal to its coupon payment date or, in the case of the principal, the maturity date. The value of the bond should equal the value of all the component zero-coupon instruments. If this does not hold, it is possible for a market participant to generate riskless profits by stripping off the coupon payments and creating stripped securities (see Chapter 6).

To determine the value of each zero-coupon instrument, it is necessary to know the yield on a zero-coupon Treasury with that same maturity. This yield is called the **spot rate**, and the graphical depiction of the relationship between the spot rate and maturity is called the **spot rate curve**. Because there are no zero-coupon Treasury debt issues with a maturity greater than one year, it is not possible to construct such a curve solely from observations of market activity on Treasury securities. Rather, it is necessary to derive this curve from theoretical considerations as applied to the yields of the actually traded Treasury debt securities. Such a curve is called a **theoretical spot rate curve** and is the graphical depiction of the **term structure of interest rate**.

Constructing the Theoretical Spot Rate Curve for Treasuries[2]

A default-free theoretical spot rate curve can be constructed from the yield on Treasury securities. The Treasury issues that are candidates for inclusion are

1. on-the-run Treasury issues
2. on-the-run Treasury issues and selected off-the-run Treasury issues
3. all Treasury coupon securities and bills
4. Treasury coupon strips

Each type of Treasury is explained in the next chapter. After the securities that are to be included in the construction of the theoretical spot rate curve are selected, the methodology for constructing the curve must be determined. The methodology depends on the securities included. If Treasury coupon strips are used, the procedure is simple, because the observed yields are the spot rates. If the on-the-run Treasury issues with or without selected off-the-run Treasury issues are used, a methodology called **bootstrapping** is used. When all Treasury coupon securities and bills are used, then elaborate statistical techniques are used.

---

[2]This discussion draws from Chapter 5 in Frank J. Fabozzi, *Fixed Income Analysis for the Chartered Financial Analyst* (New Hope, PA: Frank J. Fabozzi Associates, 2000).

On-the-Run Treasury Issues

The **on-the-run Treasury issues** are the most recently auctioned issue of a given maturity. These issues include the 3-month and 6-month Treasury bills; the 2-year, 5-year, and 10-year Treasury notes; and the 30-year Treasury bond. Treasury bills are zero-coupon instruments; the notes and the bond are coupon securities.

There is an observed yield for each of the on-the-run issues. For the coupon issues, these yields are not the yields used in the analysis when the issue is not trading at par. Instead, for each on-the-run coupon issue, the estimated yield necessary to make the issue trade at par is used. The resulting on-the-run yield curve is called the **par coupon curve**.

The goal is to construct a theoretical spot rate curve with 60 semiannual spot rates: 6-month rate to 30-year rate. Excluding the three-month bill, there are only six maturity points available when only on-the-run issues are used. The 54 missing maturity points are interpolated from the surrounding maturity points on the par yield curve. The simplest interpolation method, and the one most commonly used, is linear extrapolation. Specifically, given the yield on the par coupon curve at two maturity points, the following is calculated:

$$\frac{\text{yield at higher maturity} - \text{yield at lower maturity}}{\text{number of semiannual periods between the two maturity points}}$$

Then, the yield for all intermediate semiannual maturity points is found by adding to the yield at the lower maturity the amount computed here.

For example, suppose that the yield from the par yield curve for the two-year and five-year on-the-run issues is 6% and 6.6%, respectively. There are six semiannual periods between these two maturity points. The extrapolated yield for the 2.0, 2.5, 3.0, 3.5, 4.0, and 4.5 maturity points is found as follows. Calculate

$$\frac{6.6\% - 6\%}{6} = 0.10\%$$

Then

$$
\begin{aligned}
\text{2.5-year yield} &= 6.00\% + 0.10\% = 6.10\% \\
\text{3.0-year yield} &= 6.10\% + 0.10\% = 6.20\% \\
\text{3.5-year yield} &= 6.20\% + 0.10\% = 6.30\% \\
\text{4.0-year yield} &= 6.30\% + 0.10\% = 6.40\% \\
\text{4.5-year yield} &= 6.40\% + 0.10\% = 6.50\%
\end{aligned}
$$

There are two problems with using just the on-the-run issues. First, there is a large gap between some of the maturities points, which may result in misleading yields for those maturity points when estimated using the linear interpolation method. Specifically, the concern is with the large gap between the 5-year and 10-year maturity points and the 10-year and 30-year maturity points. The second problem is that the yields for the on-the-run issues themselves may be misleading because most offer the favorable financing opportunity in the repo market mentioned earlier. This means that the true yield is greater than the quoted (observed) yield.

Now let's look at how the par yield curve is converted into the theoretical spot rate curve using bootstrapping. For simplicity, we will illustrate this methodology to calculate the theoretical spot rate curve for only 10 years. That is, 20 semiannual spot rates will be computed. Suppose that the par yield curve is the one shown in Exhibit 5-4.[3]

To explain the process of estimating the theoretical spot rate curve from observed yields on Treasury securities, we use the data for the price, annualized yield (yield to maturity), and maturity of the 20 hypothetical Treasury securities shown in Exhibit 5-4. Each security is assumed to have a market price equal to its par value, so that the yield to maturity and the coupon rate are equal.

Throughout the analysis and illustrations to come, it is important to remember that the basic principle is that the value of the Treasury coupon security should be equal to the value of the package of zero-coupon Treasury securities that duplicates the coupon bond's cash flow.

Consider the six-month Treasury bill in Exhibit 5-4. As explained in Chapter 6, a Treasury bill is a zero-coupon instrument; hence, its annualized yield of 5.25% is equal to the spot rate. Similarly, for the one-year Treasury, the cited yield of 5.5% is the one-year

FIGURE 5-4 Maturity and Yield to Maturity for 20 Hypothetical Treasury Securities[a]

Period	Years	Yield to Maturity/Coupon Rate (%)
1	0.5	5.25
2	1.0	5.50
3	1.5	5.75
4	2.0	6.00
5	2.5	6.25
6	3.0	6.50
7	3.5	6.75
8	4.0	6.80
9	4.5	7.00
10	5.0	7.10
11	5.5	7.15
12	6.0	7.20
13	6.5	7.30
14	7.0	7.35
15	7.5	7.40
16	8.0	7.50
17	8.5	7.60
18	9.0	7.60
19	9.5	7.70
20	10.0	7.80

[a]All bonds with the exception of the six-month and one-year issues are at par (100). For these issues the coupon rate is equal to the yield to maturity. The six-month and one-year issues are zero-coupon instruments and the price is less than par.

---

[3]Note that the intermediate maturity points in Exhibit 5-4 were not calculated using the linear interpolation procedure.

spot rate. Given these two spot rates, we can compute the spot rate for a theoretical 1.5-year zero-coupon Treasury. The price of a theoretical 1.5-year zero-coupon Treasury should equal the present value of three cash flows from an actual 1.5-year coupon Treasury, where the yield used for discounting is the spot rate corresponding to the cash flow. Exhibit 5-4 shows the coupon rate for a 1.5-year Treasury as 5.75%. Using $100 as par, the cash flow for this Treasury security is

$$
\begin{array}{lll}
\text{0.5 year:} & 0.0575 \times \$100 \times 0.5 = & \$\quad 2.875 \\
\text{1.0 year:} & 0.0575 \times \$100 \times 0.5 = & 2.875 \\
\text{1.5 years:} & 0.0575 \times \$100 \times 0.5 + \$100 = & 102.875
\end{array}
$$

The present value of the cash flow is then

$$
\frac{2.875}{1+z_1} + \frac{2.875}{(1+z_2)^2} + \frac{102.875}{(1+z_3)^3}
$$

where:

z_1 = one-half the annualized 6-month theoretical spot rate
z_2 = one-half the 1-year theoretical spot rate
z_3 = one-half the annual value of the 1.5-year theoretical spot rate

Because the six-month spot rate and one-year spot rate are 5.25% and 5.50%, respectively, we know these facts:

$$
z_1 = 0.02625 \text{ and } z_2 = 0.0275
$$

We can compute the present value of the 1.5-year coupon Treasury security as

$$
\frac{2.875}{1.02625} + \frac{2.875}{(1.0275)^2} + \frac{102.875}{(1+z_3)^3}
$$

Because the price of the 1.5-year coupon Treasury security is $100, the following relationship must hold:

$$
100 = \frac{2.875}{1.02625} + \frac{2.875}{(1.0275)^2} + \frac{102.875}{(1+z_3)^3}
$$

We can solve for the theoretical 1.5-year spot rate as follows:

$$
100 = 2.801461 + 2.723166 + \frac{102.875}{(1+z_3)^3}
$$

$$
94.47537 = \frac{102.875}{(1+z_3)^3}
$$

$$
(1+z_3)^3 = 1.028798
$$

$$
z_3 = 0.028798
$$

Doubling this yield, we obtain the bond-equivalent yield of 0.0576 or 5.76%, which is the theoretical 1.5-year spot rate. That rate is the rate that the market would apply to a 1.5-year zero-coupon Treasury security if, in fact, such a security existed.

Given the theoretical 1.5-year spot rate, we can obtain the theoretical 2-year spot rate. The cash flow for the two-year coupon Treasury in Exhibit 5-4 is

0.5 year:	$0.060 \times \$100 \times 0.5 = \$ \quad 3.00$
1.0 year:	$0.060 \times \$100 \times 0.5 = \quad 3.00$
1.5 years:	$0.060 \times \$100 \times 0.5 = \quad 3.00$
2.0 years:	$0.060 \times \$100 \times 0.5 + \$100 = \quad 103.00$

The present value of the cash flow is then

$$\frac{3.00}{1+z_1} + \frac{3.00}{(1+z_2)^2} + \frac{3.00}{(1+z_3)^3} + \frac{103.00}{(1+z_4)^4}$$

where z_4 is one-half the two-year theoretical spot rate. Because the 6-month spot rate, 1-year spot rate, and 1.5-year spot rate are 5.25%, 5.50%, and 5.76%, respectively, then

$$z_1 = 0.02625 \quad z_2 = 0.0275 \quad z_3 = 0.028798$$

Therefore, the present value of the two-year coupon Treasury security is

$$\frac{3.00}{1.002625} + \frac{3.00}{(1.0275)^2} + \frac{3.00}{(1.028798)^3} + \frac{103.00}{(1+z_4)^4}$$

Because the price of the two-year coupon Treasury security is $100, the following relationship must hold:

$$100 = \frac{3.00}{1.002625} + \frac{3.00}{(1.0275)^2} + \frac{3.00}{(1.028798)^3} + \frac{103.00}{(1+z_4)^4}$$

We can solve for the theoretical two-year spot rate as follows:

$$100 = 2.92326 + 2.84156 + 2.75506 + \frac{103.00}{(1+z_4)^4}$$

$$91.48011 = \frac{103.00}{(1+z_4)^4}$$

$$(1+z_4)^4 = 1.125927$$

$$z_4 = 0.030095$$

Doubling this yield, we obtain the theoretical two-year spot rate bond-equivalent yield of 6.02%.

One can follow this approach sequentially to derive the theoretical 2.5-year spot rate from the calculated values of z_1, z_2, z_3, z_4 (the 6-month, 1-year, 1.5-year, and 2-year rates), and the price and coupon of the bond with a maturity of 2.5 years. Further, one could derive theoretical spot rates for the remaining 15 half-yearly rates.

The spot rates using this process are shown in Exhibit 5-5. They represent the term structure of interest rates for maturities up to 10 years at the particular time to which the bond price quotations refer.

Exhibit 5-6 shows the theoretical spot rate curve estimated on August 13, 1996, by applying the bootstrapping methodology to on-the-run issues. Also shown in the exhibit are the rates based on the coupon strips. Note the significant divergence between the coupon strips and the rates generated from bootstrapping after the six-year maturity point.

On-the-Run Treasury Issues and Selected Off-the-Run Treasury Issues

As noted previously, one of the problems with using just the on-the-run issues is the large gaps between maturities, particularly after five years. To mitigate this problem, some dealers and vendors use selected off-the-run Treasury issues. Typically, the issues used are the 20-year issue and 25-year issue. Given the par coupon curve including any off-the-run selected issues, the linear extrapolation method is used to fill in the gaps for

EXHIBIT 5-5   Theoretical Spot Rates

Period	Years	Spot Rate (%)
1	0.5	5.25
2	1.0	5.50
3	1.5	5.76
4	2.0	6.02
5	2.5	6.28
6	3.0	6.55
7	3.5	6.82
8	4.0	6.87
9	4.5	7.09
10	5.0	7.20
11	5.5	7.26
12	6.0	7.31
13	6.5	7.43
14	7.0	7.48
15	7.5	7.54
16	8.0	7.67
17	8.5	7.80
18	9.0	7.79
19	9.5	7.93
20	10.0	8.07

EXHIBIT 5-6	Comparison of Theoretical Annual Spot Rates Using Bootstrapping Methodology, Merrill Lynch Exponential Spline Methodology, and Coupon Strips on August 13, 1996

	Bootstrapping Using On-the-Run Issues	Bootstrapping Using On-the-Run Issues + 20-Year and 25-Year Issues	Exponential Spline	Coupon Strip
1	5.62	5.62	5.69	5.60
2	5.98	5.98	6.00	5.98
3	6.17	6.17	6.18	6.17
4	6.27	6.27	6.29	6.27
5	6.36	6.36	6.37	6.35
6	6.42	6.42	6.44	6.42
7	6.47	6.47	6.51	6.51
8	6.53	6.53	6.58	6.60
9	6.59	6.59	6.65	6.68
10	6.66	6.66	6.71	6.74
11	6.66	6.68	6.77	6.79
12	6.67	6.72	6.83	6.84
13	6.68	6.75	6.89	6.90
14	6.69	6.78	6.94	6.94
15	6.71	6.82	6.98	6.98
16	6.72	6.86	7.02	7.03
17	6.73	6.89	7.06	7.06
18	6.75	6.94	7.09	7.07
19	6.77	6.98	7.12	7.10
20	6.78	7.02	7.14	7.11
21	6.80	7.04	7.16	7.13
22	6.82	7.04	7.16	7.14
23	6.84	7.05	7.16	7.14
24	6.86	7.05	7.15	7.13
25	6.88	7.06	7.12	7.10
26	6.90	7.01	7.08	7.06
27	6.92	6.96	7.02	6.98
28	6.95	6.91	6.95	6.95
29	6.98	6.86	6.85	6.88
30	7.00	6.81	6.74	6.85[a]

[a]29.5 yrs.

Source: The data points were provided by Philip H. Galdi, Analyst at Merrill Lynch, and Shenglin Lu, Analyst at Merrill Lynch. These data were used to construct the spot rate curves in Philip H. Galdi and Shenglin Lu, *Analyzing Risk and Relative Value of Corporate and Government Securities*, Merrill Lynch & Co., Global Securities Research & Economics Group, Fixed Income Analytics, 1997. Copyright © 1997 Merrill Lynch, Pierce, Fenner & Smith Incorporated.

the other maturities. The bootstrapping method is then used to construct the theoretical spot rate curve.

Exhibit 5-6 compares the theoretical annual spot rates on August 13, 1996, using the bootstrapping methodology applied to (1) the on-run-issues and (2) the on-the-run issues plus the 20-year and 25-year off-the-run issues. The table also includes the coupon strip rates. Notice how much closer the theoretical spot rate curve comes to the coupon strips curve when the on-the-run issues are supplemented with the 20-year and 25-year off-the-run issues.

All Treasury Coupon Securities and Bills

Using only on-the-run issues, even when extended to include a few off-the-run issues, fails to recognize the information embodied in Treasury prices that are not included in the analysis. Thus, it is argued that it is more appropriate to use all Treasury coupon securities and bills to construct the theoretical spot rate curve. Some practitioners do not use callable Treasury bonds.[4]

When all coupon securities and bills are used, statistical methodologies must be employed to construct the theoretical spot rate curve rather than bootstrapping because there may be more than one yield for each maturity. Several statistical methodologies have been proposed to estimate the spot rate curve. The most common methodology used is "exponential spline fitting."[5] An adjustment for the effect of taxes and for call features on U.S. Treasury bonds can be incorporated into the statistical model. A discussion of this statistical methodology is beyond the scope this book.[6]

Exhibit 5-6 provides a comparison of the theoretical spot rate constructed on August 13, 1996, using coupon strips with those of the exponential spline methodology as developed by Merrill Lynch and the bootstrapping methodology. Notice how close the spot rates based on the spline methodology are to the coupon strips, particularly after the six-year maturity point.

Treasury Coupon Strips

As explained in the next chapter, Treasury coupon strips are zero-coupon Treasury securities. It would seem logical that the observed yield on strips could be used to construct an actual spot rate curve rather than go through the procedure we describe here. There are three problems with using the observed rates on strips. First, the liquidity of the strips market is not as great as that of the Treasury coupon market. Thus, the observed rates on strips reflect a premium for liquidity.

---

[4]A common practice is to filter the Treasury securities universe to eliminate securities that offer advantageous financing in the repo market.
[5]Willard R. Carleton and Ian Cooper, "Estimation and Uses of the Term Structure of Interest Rates," *Journal of Finance,* September 1976, pp. 1067–1083; J. Huston McCulloch, "Measuring the Term Structure of Interest Rates," *Journal of Business,* January 1971, pp. 19–31; and McCulloch, "The Tax Adjusted Yield Curve," *Journal of Finance,* June 1975, pp. 811–830.
[6]See Oldrich A. Vasicek and H. Gifford Fong, "Term Structure Modeling Using Exponential Splines," *Journal of Finance,* May 1982, pp. 339–358. For an example of a dealer model, see Arnold Shapiro et al., *Merrill Lynch Exponential Spline Model,* Merrill Lynch & Co., Global Securities Research & Economics Group, Fixed Income Analytics, August 8, 1994.

Second, the tax treatment of strips is different from that of Treasury coupon securities. Specifically, the accrued interest on strips is taxed even though no cash is received by the investor. Thus, they are negative cash flow securities to taxable entities; as a result, their yield reflects this tax disadvantage.

Finally, there are maturity sectors in which non–U.S. investors find it advantageous to trade off yield for tax advantages associated with a strip. Specifically, certain foreign tax authorities allow their citizens to treat the difference between the maturity value and the purchase price as a capital gain and tax this gain at a favorable tax rate. Some will grant this favorable treatment only when the strip is created from the principal rather than the coupon. For this reason, those who use Treasury strips to represent theoretical spot rates restrict the issues included to coupon strips.

Using the Theoretical Spot Rate Curve

We can now apply the spot rates to price a bond. In Chapter 2 we showed how to price a bond assuming that each cash flow is discounted at one discount rate. Exhibit 5-7 shows how to value a Treasury bond properly using the theoretical spot rates. The

EXHIBIT 5-7   Determining the Theoretical Value of a 10% 10-Year Treasury Security Using the Theoretical Spot Rates

Period	Year	Cash Flow	Spot Rate (%)	PV of $1 at Spot Rate	PV of Cash Flow
1	0.5	5	5.25	0.974421	4.872107
2	1.0	5	5.50	0.947188	4.735942
3	1.5	5	5.76	0.918351	4.591756
4	2.0	5	6.02	0.888156	4.440782
5	2.5	5	6.28	0.856724	4.283619
6	3.0	5	6.55	0.824206	4.12103
7	3.5	5	6.82	0.790757	3.953783
8	4.0	5	6.87	0.763256	3.81628
9	4.5	5	7.09	0.730718	3.653589
10	5.0	5	7.20	0.701952	3.509758
11	5.5	5	7.26	0.675697	3.378483
12	6.0	5	7.31	0.650028	3.250138
13	6.5	5	7.43	0.622448	3.112238
14	7.0	5	7.48	0.597889	2.989446
15	7.5	5	7.54	0.573919	2.869594
16	8.0	5	7.67	0.547625	2.738125
17	8.5	5	7.80	0.521766	2.608831
18	9.0	5	7.79	0.502665	2.513325
19	9.5	5	7.93	0.477729	2.388643
20	10.0	105	8.07	0.453268	47.593170

Theoretical value = 115.4206

bond in the illustration is a hypothetical 10-year Treasury security with a coupon rate of 10%.

The third column of the exhibit shows the cash flow per $100 of par value for each of the 20 six-month periods. The fourth column shows the theoretical spot rate for each maturity given in Exhibit 5-5. The fifth column gives the present value of $1 when discounted at the theoretical spot rate shown in the fourth column. The last column gives the present value of the cash flow, found by multiplying the third column by the fifth column. The theoretical price of this bond is the sum of the present values in the last column, $115.4206.

Although we have stated that the price of a Treasury security should be equal to the present value of its cash flow where each cash flow is discounted at the theoretical spot rates, the question is: What forces a Treasury to be priced based on the spot rates? The answer is that arbitrage forces this. For example, the theoretical price of $115.4206 can be viewed as the value of a package of zero-coupon instruments. That is, if this 10% 10-year Treasury security is purchased and then stripped, it will generate proceeds of $115.4206. The stripped Treasury securities created are the securities we describe in Chapter 6.

Now suppose, instead, that the market priced the 10% 10-year Treasury security based on the yield to maturity of 10-year Treasury securities as indicated by the yield curve. As can be seen in Exhibit 5-4, the yield to maturity for 10-year Treasury securities is 7.8%. If the 10% 10-year Treasury security is priced using a discount rate of 7.8%, its price would be $115.0826, a price that is less than its theoretical value. A government securities dealer who had the opportunity to buy this Treasury security for $115.0826 would buy it, then strip it and sell the zero-coupon securities created. As we just noted, the total proceeds from this process would be $115.4206. Thus, the dealer would realize an arbitrage profit of $0.338 per $100 of par value purchased. The actions of dealers to capture this arbitrage profit would drive up the price of this Treasury security. Only when the price reaches $115.4206—the theoretical value when the cash flows are discounted at the theoretical spot rates—will the arbitrage disappear. It is this action that forces Treasury securities to be priced based on the theoretical spot rates.

Spot Rates and the Base Interest Rate

We can now modify our earlier statement about the base interest rate for a given maturity. It is not simply the yield on the on-the-run Treasury security for that maturity, but the theoretical Treasury spot rate for that maturity. It is to the theoretical Treasury spot rates that a risk premium must be added in order to value a non-Treasury security.

Forward Rates

Thus, we have seen that from the yield curve we can extrapolate the theoretical spot rates. In addition, we can extrapolate what some market participants refer to as the market's consensus of future interest rates. To see the importance of knowing the market's consensus for future interest rates, consider the following two investment alternatives for an investor who has a one-year investment horizon.

1. **Alternative 1:** Buy a one-year instrument.
2. **Alternative 2:** Buy a six-month instrument and when it matures in six months, buy another six-month instrument.

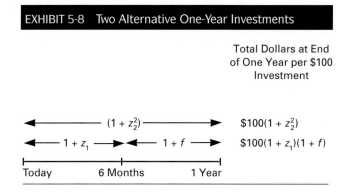

EXHIBIT 5-8   Two Alternative One-Year Investments

With alternative 1, the investor will realize the one-year spot rate and that rate is known with certainty. In contrast, with alternative 2, the investor will realize the six-month spot rate, but the six-month rate six months from now is unknown. Therefore, for alternative 2, the rate that will be earned over one year is not known with certainty. This is illustrated in Exhibit 5-8.

Suppose that this investor expected that six months from now the six-month rate will be higher than it is today. The investor might then feel that alternative 2 would be the better investment. However, this is not necessarily true. To understand why and to appreciate the need to understand why it is necessary to know what the market's consensus of future interest rates is, let's continue with our illustration.

The investor will be indifferent to the two alternatives if they produce the same total dollars over the one-year investment horizon. Given the one-year spot rate, there is some rate on a six-month instrument six months from now that will make the investor indifferent between the two alternatives. We denote that rate by f.

The value of f can be readily determined given the theoretical one-year spot rate and the six-month spot rate. If an investor placed $100 in a one-year instrument (alternative 1), the total dollars that will be generated at the end of one year is

$$\text{total dollars at end of year for alternative } 1 = \$100(1 + z_2)^2 \qquad \textbf{(5.1)}$$

where z_2 is the one-year spot rate. (Remember that we are working in six-month periods, so the subscript 2 represents two six-month periods, or one year.)

The proceeds from investing at the six-month spot rate will generate the following total dollars at the end of six months:

$$\text{total dollars at end of six months for alternative } 2 = \$100(1 + z_1) \qquad \textbf{(5.2)}$$

where z_1 is the six-month spot rate. If the amount in equation (5.2) is reinvested at the six-month rate six months from now, which we denoted f, the total dollars at the end of one year would be

$$\text{total dollars at end of year for alternative } 2 = \$100(1 + z_1)(1 + f) \qquad \textbf{(5.3)}$$

The investor will be indifferent between the two alternatives if the total dollars are the same. This will occur if equation (5.1) is equal to equation (5.3). Setting these two equations equal we get the following:

$$\$100(1 + z_2)^2 = \$100(1 + z_1)(1 + f)\qquad\qquad\textbf{(5.4)}$$

Solving equation (5.4) for f, we get

$$f = \frac{(1+z_2)^2}{1+z_1} - 1\qquad\qquad\textbf{(5.5)}$$

Doubling f gives the bond-equivalent yield for the six-month rate six months from now in which we are interested.

We can illustrate the use of equation (5.5) with the theoretical spot rates shown in Exhibit 5-5. From that exhibit we know that

$$\text{six-month spot rate} = 0.0525; \text{therefore}, z_1 = 0.2625$$
$$\text{one-year spot rate} = 0.0550; \text{therefore}, z_2 = 0.2750$$

Substituting into equation (5.5), we have

$$f = \frac{(1.02750)^2}{1.02625} - 1$$
$$= 0.028752$$

Therefore, the annual rate for f on a bond-equivalent basis is 5.75% (2.8752% $\times$ 2).

Here is how we use this rate of 5.75%. If the six-month rate six months from now is less than 5.75%, the total dollars at the end of one year would be higher by investing in the one-year instrument (alternative 1). If the six-month rate six months from now is greater than 5.75%, the total dollars at the end of one year would be higher by investing in the six-month instrument and reinvesting the proceeds six months from now at the six-month rate at the time (alternative 2). Of course, if the six-month rate six months from now is 5.75%, the two alternatives give the same total number of dollars at the end of one year.

Now that we have the rate for f that we are interested in and we know how that rate can be used, let's return to the question we posed at the outset. From Exhibit 5-5 the six-month spot rate is 5.25%. Suppose that the investor expects that six months from now, the six-month rate will be 5.60%. That is, the investor expects that the six-month rate will be higher than its current level. Should the investor select alternative 2 because the six-month rate six months from now is expected to be higher? The answer is no. As we explained earlier, if the rate is less than 5.75%, alternative 1 is the better alternative. Because this investor expects a rate of 5.60%, he should select alternative 1 despite the fact that he expects the six-month rate to be higher than it is today.

This is a somewhat surprising result for some investors, but the reason for this is that the market prices its expectations of future interest rates into the rates offered on investments with different maturities. This is why knowing the market's consensus of future interest rates is critical. The rate that we determined for f is the market's consensus for the six-month rate six months from now. A future interest rate calculated from either the spot rates or the yield curve is called a **forward rate**.

Relationship Between Six-Month Forward Rates and Spot Rates

In general, the relationship between a t-period spot rate, the current six-month spot rate, and the six-month forward rates is as follows:

$$z_t = [(1 + z_1)(1 + f_1)(1 + f_2)(1 + f_3) \ldots (1 + f_{t-1})]^{1/t} - 1 \qquad (5.6)$$

where f_t is the six-month forward rate beginning t six-month periods from now.

To illustrate how to use equation (5.6), let's look at how the five-year (10-period) spot rate is related to the six-month forward rates. Six-month forward rates were calculated for the spot rate given in Exhibit 5-5. The values for f_1 through f_9 are as follows:

$$f_1 = 0.02875 \quad f_2 = 0.03140 \quad f_3 = 0.03670 \quad f_4 = 0.03945$$
$$f_5 = 0.04320 \quad f_6 = 0.03605 \quad f_7 = 0.04455 \quad f_8 = 0.04100$$
$$f_9 = 0.03885$$

The six-month spot rate is 2.625% (5.25% on a bond-equivalent basis). Substituting these values into equation (5.6) we have

$$z_{10} = [(1.02875)(1.02625)(1.03140)(1.03670)(1.03945)(1.04320)(1.03605)(1.04455)$$
$$\cdot (1.04100)(1.03855)]^{1/10} - 1 = 0.036 = 3.6\%$$

Note that when doubled this value agrees with the five-year (10-period) spot rate shown in Exhibit 5-5.

Other Forward Rates

We can take this sort of analysis much further. It is not necessary to limit ourselves to six-month forward rates. The spot rates can be used to calculate the forward rate for any time in the future for any investment horizon. As examples, the following can be calculated:

- The two-year forward rate five years from now
- The six-year forward rate 10 years from now
- The seven-year forward rate three years from now

Forward Rate as a Hedgeable Rate

A natural question about forward rates is how well they do at predicting future interest rates. Studies have demonstrated that forward rates do not do a good job in predicting future interest rates.[7] Then why the big deal about understanding forward

---

[7] Eugene F. Fama, "Forward Rates as Predictors of Future Spot Rates," *Journal of Financial Economics*, Vol. 3, No. 4, 1976, pp. 361–377.

rates? As we demonstrated in our illustration of how to select between two alternative investments, the reason is that the forward rates indicate how an investor's expectations must differ from the market's consensus in order to make the correct decision.

In our illustration the six-month forward rate may not be realized. That is irrelevant. The fact is that the six-month forward rate indicated to the investor that if his expectation about the six-month rate six months from now is less than 5.75%, he would be better off with alternative 1.

For this reason, as well as others explained later, some market participants prefer not to talk about forward rates as being market consensus rates. Instead, they refer to forward rates as being **hedgeable rates**. For example, by buying the one-year security, the investor was able to hedge the six-month rate six months from now.

Determinants of the Shape of the Term Structure

If we plot the term structure—the yield to maturity, or the spot rate, at successive maturities against maturity—what is it likely to look like? Exhibit 5-3 shows three typical shapes that have been observed in the U.S. markets, as well as non-U.S. markets. Part (a) shows an upward-sloping yield curve; that is, yield rises steadily as maturity increases. This shape is commonly referred to as a **normal** or **positive yield curve**. Part (b) shows a downward-sloping or **inverted** yield curve, where yields decline as maturity increases. Finally, part (c) shows a **flat** yield curve.

Two major theories have evolved to account for these observed shapes of the yield curve: **expectations theories** and **market segmentation theory**.

There are several forms of the **expectations theory: pure expectations theory, liquidity theory**, and **preferred habitat theory**. Expectations theories share a hypothesis about the behavior of short-term forward rates and also assume that the forward rates in current long-term bonds are closely related to the market's expectations about future short-term rates. These three theories differ, however, as to whether other factors also affect forward rates, and how. The pure expectations theory postulates that no systematic factors other than expected future short-term rates affect forward rates; the liquidity theory and the preferred habitat theory assert that there are other factors. Accordingly, the last two forms of the expectations theory are sometimes referred to as **biased expectations theories**. Exhibit 5-9 depicts the relationships among these three theories.

Pure Expectations Theory

According to the pure expectations theory, the forward rates exclusively represent the expected future rates. Thus, the entire term structure at a given time reflects the market's current expectations of the family of future short-term rates. Under this view, a rising term structure, as in part (a) of Exhibit 5-3, must indicate that the market expects short-term rates to rise throughout the relevant future. Similarly, a flat term structure reflects an expectation that future short-term rates will be mostly constant, and a falling term structure must reflect an expectation that future short rates will decline steadily.

We can illustrate this theory by considering how the expectation of a rising short-term future rate would affect the behavior of various market participants so as to result in a rising yield curve. Assume an initially flat term structure, and suppose that subsequent economic news leads market participants to expect interest rates to rise.

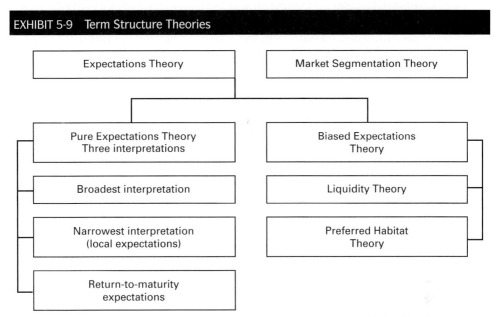

EXHIBIT 5-9   Term Structure Theories

Source: Frank J. Fabozzi, *Valuation of Fixed Income Securities and Derivatives,* Third Edition (New Hope, PA: Frank J. Fabozzi Associates, 1998), p. 53.

1. Those market participants interested in a long-term investment would not want to buy long-term bonds because they would expect the yield structure to rise sooner or later, resulting in a price decline for the bonds and a capital loss on the long-term bonds purchased. Instead, they would want to invest in short-term debt obligations until the rise in yield had occurred, permitting them to reinvest their funds at the higher yield.
2. Speculators expecting rising rates would anticipate a decline in the price of long-term bonds and therefore would want to sell any long-term bonds they own and possibly to "sell-short" some they do not now own. (Should interest rates rise as expected, the price of longer-term bonds will fall. Because the speculator sold these bonds short and can then purchase them at a lower price to cover the short sale, a profit will be earned.) Speculators will reinvest in short-term debt obligations.
3. Borrowers wishing to acquire long-term funds would be pulled toward borrowing now in the long end of the market by the expectation that borrowing at a later time would be more expensive.

All these responses would tend either to lower the net demand for, or to increase the supply of, long-maturity bonds, and all three responses would increase demand for short-term debt obligations. This would require a rise in long-term yields in relation to short-term yields; that is, these actions by investors, speculators, and borrowers would tilt the term structure upward until it is consistent with expectations of higher future interest rates. By analogous reasoning, an unexpected event leading to the expectation of lower future rates will result in the yield curve sloping down.

Unfortunately, the pure expectations theory suffers from one shortcoming, which, qualitatively, is quite serious. It neglects the risks inherent in investing in bonds and similar instruments. If forward rates were perfect predictors of future interest rates, the future prices of bonds would be known with certainty. The return over any investment period would be certain and independent of the maturity of the instrument initially acquired and of the time at which the investor needed to liquidate the instrument. However, with uncertainty about future interest rates and hence about future prices of bonds, these instruments become risky investments in the sense that the return over some investment horizon is unknown.

There are two risks that cause uncertainty about the return over some investment horizon: price risk and reinvestment risk. The first is the uncertainty about the price of the bond at the end of the investment horizon. For example, an investor who plans to invest for five years might consider the following three investment alternatives: (1) invest in a five-year bond and hold it for five years, (2) invest in a 12-year bond and sell it at the end of five years, and (3) invest in a 30-year bond and sell it at the end of five years. The return that will be realized for the second and third alternatives is not known because the price of each long-term bond at the end of five years is not known. In the case of the 12-year bond, the price will depend on the yield on seven-year debt securities five years from now; and the price of the 30-year bond will depend on the yield on 25-year bonds five years from now. Because forward rates implied in the current term structure for a future 12-year bond and a future 25-year bond are not perfect predictors of the actual future rates, there is uncertainty about the price for both bonds five years from now. Thus, there is price risk; that is, the risk that the price of the bond will be lower than currently expected at the end of the investment horizon. As explained in Chapter 4, an important feature of price risk is that it is greater the longer the maturity of the bond.

The second risk has to do with the uncertainty about the rate at which the proceeds from a bond can be reinvested until the expected maturity date; that is, reinvestment risk. For example, an investor who plans to invest for five years might consider the following three alternative investments: (1) invest in a five-year bond and hold it for five years; (2) invest in a six-month instrument and when it matures, reinvest the proceeds in six-month instruments over the entire five-year investment horizon; and (3) invest in a two-year bond and when it matures, reinvest the proceeds in a three-year bond. The risk in the second and third alternatives is that the return over the five-year investment horizon is unknown because rates at which the proceeds can be reinvested until maturity are unknown.

There are several interpretations of the pure expectations theory that have been put forth by economists. These interpretations are not exact equivalents nor are they consistent with each other, in large part because they offer different treatments of the two risks associated with realizing a return that we have just explained.[8]

The broadest interpretation of the pure expectations theory suggests that investors expect the return for any investment horizon to be the same, regardless of the maturity strategy selected.[9] For example, consider an investor who has a five-year investment

---

[8]These formulations are summarized by John Cox, Jonathan Ingersoll, Jr., and Stephen Ross, "A Reexamination of Traditional Hypotheses about the Term Structure of Interest Rates," *Journal of Finance*, September 1981, pp. 769–799.

[9]F. Lutz, "The Structure of Interest Rates," *Quarterly Journal of Economics*, 1940–41, pp. 36–63.

horizon. According to this theory, it makes no difference if a five-year, 12-year, or 30-year bond is purchased and held for five years because the investor expects the return from all three bonds to be the same over five years. A major criticism of this very broad interpretation of the theory is that, because of price risk associated with investing in bonds with a maturity greater than the investment horizon, the expected returns from these three very different bond investments should differ in significant ways.[10]

A second interpretation, referred to as the **local expectations theory**, a form of pure expectations theory, suggests that the returns on bonds of different maturities will be the same over a short-term investment horizon. For example, if an investor has a six-month investment horizon, buying a 5-year, 10-year, or 20-year bond will produce the same six-month return. It has been demonstrated that the local expectations formulation, which is narrow in scope, is the only one of the interpretations of the pure expectations theory that can be sustained in equilibrium.[11]

The third and final interpretation of the pure expectations theory suggests that the return that an investor will realize by rolling over short-term bonds to some investment horizon will be the same as holding a zero-coupon bond with a maturity that is the same as that investment horizon. (Because a zero-coupon bond has no reinvestment risk, future interest rates over the investment horizon do not affect the return.) This variant is called the **return-to-maturity expectations interpretation**. For example, let's assume that an investor has a five-year investment horizon. By buying a five-year zero-coupon bond and holding it to maturity, the investor's return is the difference between the maturity value and the price of the bond, all divided by the price of the bond. According to return-to-maturity expectations, the same return will be realized by buying a six-month instrument and rolling it over for five years. The validity of this interpretation is currently subject to considerable doubt.

Liquidity Theory

We have explained that the drawback of the pure expectations theory is that it does not consider the risks associated with investing in bonds. There is the risk in holding a long-term bond for one period, and that risk increases with the bond's maturity because maturity and price volatility are directly related.

Given this uncertainty and the reasonable consideration that investors typically do not like uncertainty, some economists and financial analysts have suggested a different theory. This theory states that investors will hold longer-term maturities if they are offered a long-term rate higher than the average of expected future rates by a risk premium that is positively related to the term to maturity.[12] Put differently, the forward rates should reflect both interest-rate expectations and a "liquidity" premium (really a risk premium), and the premium should be higher for longer maturities.

According to this theory, which is called the **liquidity theory of the term structure**, the implied forward rates will not be an unbiased estimate of the market's expectations of future interest rates because they embody a liquidity premium. Thus an upward-sloping yield curve may reflect expectations that future interest rates either (1) will

---

[10]Cox, Ingersoll, and Ross, "A Reexamination of Traditional Hypotheses about the Term Structure of Interest Rates," pp. 774–775.
[11]Ibid.
[12]John R. Hicks, *Value and Capital*, 2nd ed. (London: Oxford University Press, 1946), pp. 141–145.

rise, or (2) will be flat or even fall, but with a liquidity premium increasing fast enough with maturity so as to produce an upward-sloping yield curve.

Preferred Habitat Theory

Another theory, the preferred habitat theory, also adopts the view that the term structure reflects the expectation of the future path of interest rates as well as a risk premium. However, the preferred habitat theory rejects the assertion that the risk premium must rise uniformly with maturity.[13] Proponents of the preferred habitat theory say that the risk premium would rise uniformly with maturity only if all investors intend to liquidate their investment at the shortest possible date while all borrowers are anxious to borrow long. This assumption can be rejected since institutions have holding periods dictated by the nature of their liabilities.

The preferred habitat theory asserts that to the extent that the demand and supply of funds in a given maturity range do not match, some lenders and borrowers will be induced to shift to maturities showing the opposite imbalances. However, they will need to be compensated by an appropriate risk premium whose magnitude will reflect the extent of aversion to either price or reinvestment risk.

Thus, this theory proposes that the shape of the yield curve is determined by both expectations of future interest rates and a risk premium, positive or negative, to induce market participants to shift out of their preferred habitat. Clearly, according to this theory, yield curves sloping up, down, flat, or humped are all possible.

Market Segmentation Theory

The market segmentation theory also recognizes that investors have preferred habitats dictated by the nature of their liabilities. This theory also proposes that the major reason for the shape of the yield curve lies in asset–liability management constraints (either regulatory or self-imposed) and/or creditors (borrowers) restricting their lending (financing) to specific maturity sectors.[14] However, the market segmentation theory differs from the preferred habitat theory in that it assumes that neither investors nor borrowers are willing to shift from one maturity sector to another to take advantage of opportunities arising from differences between expectations and forward rates. Thus, for the segmentation theory, the shape of the yield curve is determined by the supply of and demand for securities within each maturity sector.

The Main Influences on the Shape of the Yield Curve

A body of work by Antti Ilmanen provides the most comprehensive research on the main influences of the shape of the Treasury yield curve.[15] He finds that the three main influences are

1. the market's expectations of future rate changes
2. bond risk premiums
3. convexity bias

---

[13]Franco Modigliani and Richard Sutch, "Innovations in Interest Rate Policy," *American Economic Review*, May 1966, pp. 178–197.
[14]This theory was suggested in J. M. Culbertson, "The Term Structure of Interest Rates," *Quarterly Journal of Economics*, November 1957, pp. 489–504.
[15]The research first appeared as a report published by Salomon Brothers. Different parts of the research report were then published. See Antti Ilmanen, "Market's Rate Expectations and Forward Rates," *Journal of*

In our discussion of the pure expectations theory of the term structure, we explained how market expectations of future rate changes influence the shape of the yield curve. Let's look at the last two influences.

Bond risk premiums are the expected return differentials across Treasury securities of different maturities. As explained in the previous section, there are theories of the term structure of interest rates that hypothesize why expected returns will vary by maturity. However, the theories disagree with respect to whether the risk premium is positive or negative. For example, the liquidity theory of the term structure would argue that the risk premium should increase with maturity; the market segmentation theory says that the bond risk premium can be positive or negative.

Ilmanen investigated the effect of the behavior of the bond risk premium using historical average *returns* on U.S. Treasury securities. Exhibit 5-10 shows the empirical average return curve as a function of average duration (not maturity) for the period 1972 to 2001. (Recall from Chapter 4 that duration is a measure of the price sensitivity of a bond to changes in interest rates.) Also shown in Exhibit 5-10 is the theoretical expected return curve based on expectations only (the first influence listed above). Notice that this curve is linear (i.e., it increases linearly with duration). In contrast, notice that the empirical evidence suggests that the bond risk premiums are not linear in duration. Instead, the empirical evidence suggests that at the front-end of the yield

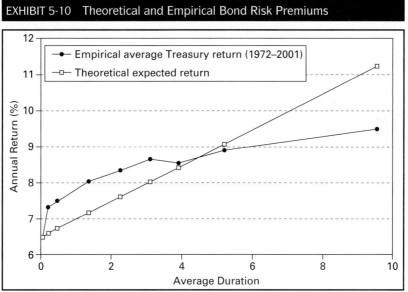

EXHIBIT 5-10   Theoretical and Empirical Bond Risk Premiums

Source: Exhibit 8-3 in Antti Ilmanen, "Overview of Forward Rate Analysis," Chapter 8 in Frank J. Fabozzi (ed.), *The Handbook of Fixed Income Securities* (New York: McGraw Hill, 2005).

Fixed Income (September 1996), pp. 8–22; Antti Ilmanen, "Does Duration Extension Enhance Long-Term Expected Returns?" *Journal of Fixed Income* (September 1996), pp. 23–36; Antti Ilmanen, Convexity Bias in the Yield Curve," Chapter 3 in Narasimgan Jegadeesh and Bruce Tuckman (eds.), *Advanced Fixed-Income Valuation Tools* (New York: Wiley, 2000); and Antti Ilmanen, "Overview of Forward Rate Analysis," Chapter 8 in Frank J. Fabozzi (ed.), *The Handbook of Fixed Income Securities* (New York, NY: McGraw Hill, 2005).

curve (i.e., up to a duration of 3), bond risk premiums increase steeply with duration. However, after a duration of 3 the bond risk premiums increase slowly. Ilmanen suggests that the shape shown in Exhibit 5-10 "may reflect the demand for long-term bonds from pension funds and other long-duration liability holders."[16]

Now let's look to the convexity bias influence, an influence that Ilmanen argues is the least well known of the three influences. Let's recall the concept of convexity described in Chapter 4. When interest rates change by a large number of basis points, a Treasury security's price change will not be the same for an increase and decrease in interest rates. More specifically, the price appreciation when interest rates fall will be greater than the price decline when interest rates rise by the same number of basis points. For example, if interest rates decline by 100 basis points, the price of a Treasury security might appreciate by 20%, but if interest rates increase by 100 basis points, the price of the same Treasury security might decline by only 15%. This attractive property of a bond is due to the shape of the relationship between price and yield described in Chapter 4 and is referred to as the bond's convexity. The longer the maturity, the more convexity the security has. That is, longer-term Treasury securities have a more attractive feature due to convexity than shorter-term Treasury securities. As a result, investors are willing to pay more for longer-term Treasury securities and therefore accept lower returns. This influence on the shape of the Treasury yield curve is what is referred to as the **convexity bias**.

SUMMARY

In all economies, there is not just one interest rate but a structure of interest rates. The difference between the yield on any two bonds is called the yield spread. The base interest rate is the yield on a Treasury security. The yield spread between a non-Treasury security and a comparable on-the-run Treasury security is called a risk premium. The factors that affect the spread include (1) the type of issuer (e.g., agency, corporate, municipality), (2) the issuer's perceived credit worthiness as measured by the rating system of commercial rating companies, (3) the term or maturity of the instrument, (4) the embedded options in a bond issue (e.g., call, put, or conversion provisions), (5) the taxability of interest income at the federal and municipal levels, (6) the expected liquidity of the issue, and (7) the financeability of an issue.

The relationship between yield and maturity is referred to as the term structure of interest rates. The graphical depiction of the relationship between the yield on bonds of the same credit quality but different maturities is known as the yield curve.

There is a problem with using the Treasury yield curve to determine the one yield at which to discount all the cash payments of any bond. Each cash flow should be discounted at a unique interest rate that is applicable to the time period when the cash flow is to be received. Because any bond can be viewed as a package of zero-coupon instruments, its value should equal the value of all the component zero-coupon instruments. The rate on a zero-coupon bond is called the spot rate. The relationship between the spot rate and maturity is called the term structure of interest rates.

A default-free theoretical spot rate curve can be constructed from the yield on Treasury securities using either (1) only on-the-run Treasury issues, (2) on-the-run Treasury issues and selected off-the-run Treasury issues, (3) all Treasury coupon securities

---

[16]Ilmanen, "Overview of Forward Rate Analysis," p. 167.

and bills, and (4) Treasury coupon strips. When the securities used are either (1) or (2) a method known as bootstrapping is used. More complex statistical techniques are used when all Treasury coupon securities and bills are used.

Under certain assumptions, the market's expectation of future interest rates can be extrapolated from the theoretical Treasury spot rate curve. The resulting forward rate is called the implied forward rate. The spot rate is related to the current six-month spot rate and the implied six-month forward rates.

Several theories have been proposed about the determination of the term structure: pure expectations theory, the biased expectations theory (the liquidity theory and preferred habitat theory), and the market segmentation theory. All the expectation theories hypothesize that the one-period forward rates represent the market's expectations of future actual rates. The pure expectations theory asserts that it is the only factor. The biased expectations theories assert that there are other factors.

Empirical evidence suggests that the three main influences on the shape of the Treasury yield curve are (1) the market's expectations of future rate changes, (2) bond risk premiums, and (3) convexity bias.

Questions

1. In the September 13, 1996, *Weekly Market Update* published by Goldman, Sachs & Co., the following information was reported in various exhibits for the Treasury market as of the close of business Thursday, September 12, 1996:

On-the-Run Treasuries

Maturity	Yield (%)
3 months	5.29
6 months	5.49
1 year	5.90
2 years	6.27
3 years	6.45
5 years	6.63
10 years	6.87
30 years	7.08

Key Off-the-Run Treasuries

Issue	Yield (%)
Old 5-year	6.65
Old 10-year	6.89
Old 30-year	7.12

a. What is the credit risk associated with a Treasury security?

b. Why is the Treasury yield considered the base interest rate?

c. What is meant by on-the-run Treasuries?

d. What is meant by off-the-run Treasuries?

e. What is the yield spread between (1) the off-the-run 10-year Treasury issue and the on-the-run 10-year Treasury issue, and (2) the off-the-run 30-year Treasury issue and the on-the-run 30-year Treasury issue?

f. What does the yield spread between the off-the-run Treasury issue and the on-the-run Treasury issue reflect?

2. In the May 29, 1992, *Weekly Market Update* published by Goldman, Sachs & Co., the following information was reported in various exhibits for certain corporate bonds as of the close of business Thursday, May 28, 1992:

Issuer	Rating	Yield (%)	Spread (basis points)	Treasury Benchmark (years)
General Electric Capital Co	Triple A	7.87	50	10
Mobil Corp	Double A	7.77	40	10
Southern Bell Tel & Teleg	Triple A	8.60	72	30
Bell Tel Co Pa	Double A	8.66	78	30
AMR Corp	Triple B	9.43	155	30

a. What does rating mean?

b. Which of the five bonds has the greatest credit risk?

c. What is meant by spread?

d. What is meant by Treasury benchmark?

e. Why do each of the spreads reported reflect a risk premium?

3. For the corporate bond issues reported in Question 2, answer the following questions:

a. What is the yield spread between the Southern Bell Telephone and Telegraph bond issue and the Bell Telephone Company (Pennsylvania) bond issue?

b. The Southern Bell Telephone and Telegraph bond issue is not callable, but the Bell Telephone Company (Pennsylvania) bond issue is callable. What does the yield spread in part a reflect?

c. AMR Corp. is the parent company of American Airlines and is therefore classified in the transportation industry. The issue is not callable. What is the yield spread between AMR Corp. and Southern Bell Telephone and Telegraph bond issue, and what does this spread reflect?

d. What is the spread between the General Electric Capital Co. issue and the Mobil Corp. issue?

e. The Mobil Corp. issue is not callable. However, the General Electric Capital Co. issue is callable. How does this information help you in understanding the spread between these two issues?

4. The yield spread between two corporate bond issues reflects more than just differences in their credit risk. What other factors would the spread reflect?

5. In the May 29, 1992, *Weekly Market Update* published by Goldman, Sachs & Co., the following information was reported in an exhibit for high-grade, tax-exempt securities as of the close of business Thursday, May 28, 1992:

Maturity (years)	Yield (%)	Yield (%) as a Percentage of Treasury Yield
1	3.20	76.5
3	4.65	80.4
5	5.10	76.4
10	5.80	78.7
30	6.50	82.5

a. What is meant by a tax-exempt security?

b. What is meant by high-grade issue?

c. Why is the yield on a tax-exempt security less than the yield on a Treasury security of the same maturity?

d. What is the equivalent taxable yield?

e. Also reported in the same issue of the Goldman, Sachs report is information on intramarket yield spreads. What are these?

6. a. What is an embedded option in a bond?

b. Give three examples of an embedded option that might be included in a bond issue.

c. Does an embedded option increase or decrease the risk premium relative to the base interest rate?

7. a. What is a yield curve?

b. Why is the Treasury yield curve the one that is most closely watched by market participants?

8. What is a spot rate?

9. Explain why it is inappropriate to use one yield to discount all the cash flows of a financial asset.

10. Explain why a financial asset can be viewed as a package of zero-coupon instruments.

11. How are spot rates related to forward rates?

12. You are a financial consultant. At various times you have heard comments on interest rates from one of your clients. How would you respond to each of the following comments?

a. "The yield curve is upward-sloping today. This suggests that the market consensus is that interest rates are expected to increase in the future."

b. "I can't make any sense out of today's term structure. For short-term yields (up to three years) the spot rates increase with maturity; for maturities greater than three years but less than eight years, the spot rates decline with maturity; and for maturities greater than eight years the spot rates are virtually the same for each maturity. There is simply no theory that explains a term structure with this shape."

c. "When I want to determine the market's consensus of future interest rates, I calculate the forward rates."

13. You observe the yields of the following Treasury securities (all yields are shown on a bond-equivalent basis):

Year	Yield to Maturity (%)	Spot Rate (%)	Year	Yield to Maturity (%)	Spot Rate (%)
0.5	5.25	5.25	5.5	7.75	7.97
1.0	5.50	5.50	6.0	8.00	8.27
1.5	5.75	5.76	6.5	8.25	8.59
2.0	6.00	?	7.0	8.50	8.92
2.5	6.25	?	7.5	8.75	9.25
3.0	6.50	?	8.0	9.00	9.61
3.5	6.75	?	8.5	9.25	9.97
4.0	7.00	?	9.0	9.50	10.36
4.5	7.25	?	9.5	9.75	10.77
5.0	7.50	?	10.0	10.00	11.20

All the securities maturing from 1.5 years on are selling at par. The 0.5- and 1.0-year securities are zero-coupon instruments.
a. Calculate the missing spot rates.
b. What should the price of a 6% six-year Treasury security be?
c. What is the six-month forward rate starting in the sixth year?

14. You observe the following Treasury yields (all yields are shown on a bond-equivalent basis):

Year	Yield to Maturity (%)	Spot Rate (%)
0.5	10.00	10.00
1.0	9.75	9.75
1.5	9.50	9.48
2.0	9.25	9.22
2.5	9.00	8.95
3.0	8.75	8.68
3.5	8.50	8.41
4.0	8.25	8.14
4.5	8.00	7.86
5.0	7.75	7.58
5.5	7.50	7.30
6.0	7.25	7.02
6.5	7.00	6.74
7.0	6.75	6.46
7.5	6.50	6.18
8.0	6.25	5.90
8.5	6.00	5.62
9.0	5.75	5.35
9.5	5.50	?
10.0	5.25	?

All the securities maturing from 1.5 years on are selling at par. The 0.5- and 1.0-year securities are zero-coupon instruments.
a. Calculate the missing spot rates.
b. What should the price of a 5% four-year Treasury security be?

15. What Treasury issues can be used to construct the theoretical spot rate curve?

16. What are the problems with using only on-the-run Treasury issues to construct the theoretical spot rate curve?

17. When all Treasury issues are used to construct the theoretical spot rate curve, what methodology is used to construct the curve?

18. a. What are the limitations of using Treasury strips to construct the theoretical spot rate curve?
   b. When Treasury strips are used to construct the curve, why are only coupon strips used?

19. What actions force a Treasury's bond price to be valued in the market at the present value of the cash flows discounted at the Treasury spot rates?

20. Explain the role that forward rates play in making investment decisions.

21. "Forward rates are poor predictors of the actual future rates that are realized. Consequently, they are of little value to an investor." Explain why you agree or disagree with this statement.

22. Bart Simpson is considering two alternative investments. The first alternative is to invest in an instrument that matures in two years. The second alternative is to invest in an

instrument that matures in one year and at the end of one year, reinvest the proceeds in a one-year instrument. He believes that one-year interest rates one year from now will be higher than they are today and therefore is leaning in favor of the second alternative. What would you recommend to Bart Simpson?

23. a. What is the common hypothesis about the behavior of short-term forward rates shared by the various forms of the expectations theory?

  b. What is price risk and reinvestment risk and how do these two risks affect the pure expectations theory?

  c. Give three interpretations of the pure expectations theory.

24. a. What are the two biased expectations theories about the term structure of interest rates?

  b. What are the underlying hypotheses of these two theories?

25. a. "Empirical evidence suggests that with respect to bond risk premiums that influence the shape of the Treasury yield curve, there is a linear relationship between Treasury average returns and duration." Explain whether you agree or disagree with this statement. If you disagree, explain the type of relationship that has been observed.

  b. What is meant by the "convexity bias" influence on the shape of the Treasury yield curve?

CHAPTER 6

TREASURY AND AGENCY SECURITIES MARKETS

After reading this chapter you will understand:

- the different types of securities issued by the Treasury

- the operation of the primary market for Treasury securities

- the role of government dealers and government brokers

- the secondary market for Treasury securities

- how Treasury securities are quoted in the secondary market

- the zero-coupon Treasury securities market

- the difference between government-sponsored enterprises and federally related institutions

The second largest sector of the bond market (after the mortgage market) is the market for U.S. Treasury securities; the smallest sector is the U.S. government agency securities market. We discuss them together in this chapter. We'll explain in more detail in Chapter 11, a majority of the securities backed by a pool of mortgages are guaranteed by a federally sponsored agency of the U.S. government. These securities are classified as part of the mortgage-backed securities market rather than as U.S. government agency securities.

TREASURY SECURITIES

Treasury securities are issued by the U.S. Department of the Treasury and are backed by the full faith and credit of the U.S. government. Consequently, market participants view them as having no credit risk. Interest rates on Treasury securities are the benchmark interest rates throughout the U.S. economy as well as in international capital markets. In Chapter 5 we described this important role played by Treasury securities.

Two factors account for the prominent role of U.S. Treasury securities: volume (in terms of dollars outstanding) and liquidity. The Department of the Treasury is the largest single issuer of debt in the world. The large volume of total debt and the large size of any single issue have contributed to making the Treasury market the most active and hence the most liquid market in the world. The dealer spread between bid and ask price is considerably narrower than in other sectors of the bond market.[1]

Treasury securities are available in book-entry form at the Federal Reserve Bank. This means that the investor receives only a receipt as evidence of ownership instead of an engraved certificate. An advantage of book entry is ease in transferring ownership of the security. Interest income from Treasury securities is subject to federal income taxes but is exempt from state and local income taxes.

Types of Treasury Securities

The Treasury issues marketable and nonmarketable securities. Our focus here is on marketable securities.[2] Marketable Treasury securities are categorized as **fixed-principal securities** or **inflation-indexed securities**. We describe each type below.

Fixed-Principal Treasury Securities

Fixed-income principal securities include Treasury bills, Treasury notes, and Treasury bonds.

Treasury bills are issued at a discount to par value, have no coupon rate, and mature at par value. The current practice of the Treasury is to issue all securities with a maturity of one year or less as discount securities. As discount securities, Treasury bills do not pay coupon interest. Instead, Treasury bills are issued at a discount from their maturity value; the return to the investor is the difference between the maturity value and the purchase price.

All securities with initial maturities of two years or more are issued as coupon securities. Coupon securities are issued at approximately par and, in the case of fixed-principal securities, mature at par value. Treasury coupon securities issued with original maturities of more than one year and no more than 10 years are called **Treasury notes**. Treasury coupon securities with original maturities greater than 10 years are called **Treasury bonds**.[3] While a few issues of the outstanding bonds are callable, the Treasury has not issued new callable Treasury securities since 1984.

Treasury Inflation Protection Securities

On January 29, 1997, the U.S. Department of the Treasury issued for the first time Treasury securities that adjust for inflation. These securities are popularly referred to as **Treasury inflation protection securities**, or TIPS. The first issue was a 10-year note.

---

[1]For a further discussion of the Treasury secondary market, see Frank J. Fabozzi and Michael J. Fleming, "U.S. Treasury Securities," Chapter 7 in Frank J. Fabozzi (ed.), *The Handbook of Financial Instruments* (Hoboken, NJ: John Wiley & Sons, 2002). Parts of this chapter draw from that work.

[2]Nonmarketable securities issued by the Treasury include savings bonds that are sold to individuals, and state and local government series (SLGS) securities that are sold to state and local government issuers of tax-exempt securities.

[3]On quote sheets, an "n" is used to denote a Treasury note. No notation typically follows an issue to identify it as a bond.

Subsequently, the Treasury issued a 5-year note in July 1997 and a 30-year bond in 1998.

TIPS work as follows. The coupon rate on an issue is set at a fixed rate. That rate is determined via the auction process described later in this section. The coupon rate is called the "real rate" since it is the rate that the investor ultimately earns above the inflation rate. The inflation index that the government has decided to use for the inflation adjustment is the non-seasonally adjusted U.S. City Average All Items Consumer Price Index for All Urban Consumers (CPI-U).

The adjustment for inflation is as follows. The principal that the Treasury Department will base both the dollar amount of the coupon payment and the maturity value on is adjusted semiannually. This is called the **inflation-adjusted principal**. For example, suppose that the coupon rate for a TIPS is 3.5% and the annual inflation rate is 3%. Suppose further that an investor purchases on January 1 $100,000 par value (principal) of this issue. The semiannual inflation rate is 1.5% (3% divided by 2). The inflation-adjusted principal at the end of the first six-month period is found by multiplying the original par value by one plus the semiannual inflation rate. In our example, the inflation-adjusted principal at the end of the first six-month period is $101,500. It is this inflation-adjusted principal that is the basis for computing the coupon interest for the first six-month period. The coupon payment is then 1.75% (one-half the real rate of 3.5%) multiplied by the inflation-adjusted principal at the coupon payment date ($101,500). The coupon payment is therefore $1,776.25.

Let's look at the next six months. The inflation-adjusted principal at the beginning of the period is $101,500. Suppose that the semiannual inflation rate for the second six-month period is 1%. Then the inflation-adjusted principal at the end of the second six-month period is the inflation-adjusted principal at the beginning of the six-month period ($101,500) increased by the semiannual inflation rate (1%). The adjustment to the principal is $1,015 (1% times $101,500). So, the inflation-adjusted principal at the end of the second six-month period (December 31 in our example) is $102,515 ($101,500 + $1,015). The coupon interest that will be paid to the investor at the second coupon payment date is found by multiplying the inflation-adjusted principal on the coupon payment date ($102,515) by one-half the real rate (i.e., one-half of 3.5%). That is, the coupon payment will be $1,794.01.

As can be seen, part of the adjustment for inflation comes in the coupon payment since it is based on the inflation-adjusted principal. However, the U.S. government has decided to tax the adjustment each year. This feature reduces the attractiveness of TIPS as investments in accounts of tax-paying entities.

Because of the possibility of disinflation (i.e., price declines), the inflation-adjusted principal at maturity may turn out to be less than the initial par value. However, the Treasury has structured TIPS so that they are redeemed at the greater of the inflation-adjusted principal and the initial par value.

An inflation-adjusted principal must be calculated for a settlement date. The inflation-adjusted principal is defined in terms of an index ratio, which is the ratio of the reference CPI for the settlement date to the reference CPI for the issue date. The reference CPI is calculated with a three-month lag. For example, the reference CPI for May 1 is the CPI-U reported in February. The U.S. Department of the Treasury publishes and makes available on its Web site (www.publicdebt.treas.gov) a daily index ratio for an issue. Exhibit 6-1 provides an example.

TREASURY INFLATION-PROTECTED SECURITIES (TIPS)
Ref CPI and Index Ratios for
October 2005

		3-3/8% 10-Year TIPS Series A-2007 9128272M3 January 15, 1997 February 6, 1997 April 15, 1997 January 15, 2007 158.43548	3-5/8% 10-Year TIPS Series A-2008 9128273T7 January 15, 1998 January 15, 1998 October 15, 1998 January 15, 2008 161.55484	3-5/8% 30-Year TIPS TIPS of April 2028 912810FD5 April 15, 1998 April 15, 1998 July 15, 1998 April 15, 2028 161.74000	3-7/8% 10-Year TIPS Series A-2009 9128274Y5 January 15, 1999 January 15, 1999 July 15, 1999 January 15, 2009 164.00000
Date	**Ref CPI**	**Index Ratio**	**Index Ratio**	**Index Ratio**	**Index Ratio**
Oct. 1 2005	195.40000	1.23331	1.20950	1.20811	1.19146
Oct. 2 2005	195.43226	1.23351	1.20970	1.20831	1.19166
Oct. 3 2005	195.46452	1.23372	1.20990	1.20851	1.19186
Oct. 4 2005	195.49677	1.23392	1.21010	1.20871	1.19205
Oct. 5 2005	195.52903	1.23412	1.21030	1.20891	1.19225
Oct. 6 2005	195.56129	1.23433	1.21049	1.20911	1.19245
Oct. 7 2005	195.59355	1.23453	1.21069	1.20931	1.19264
Oct. 8 2005	195.62581	1.23473	1.21089	1.20951	1.19284
Oct. 9 2005	195.65806	1.23494	1.21109	1.20971	1.19304
Oct. 10 2005	195.69032	1.23514	1.21129	1.20991	1.19323
Oct. 11 2005	195.72258	1.23535	1.21149	1.21011	1.19343
Oct. 12 2005	195.75484	1.23555	1.21169	1.21031	1.19363
Oct. 13 2005	195.78710	1.23575	1.21189	1.21051	1.19382
Oct. 14 2005	195.81935	1.23596	1.21209	1.21070	1.19402
Oct. 15 2005	195.85161	1.23616	1.21229	1.21090	1.19422
Oct. 16 2005	195.88387	1.23636	1.21249	1.21110	1.19441
Oct. 17 2005	195.91613	1.23657	1.21269	1.21130	1.19461
Oct. 18 2005	195.94839	1.23677	1.21289	1.21150	1.19481
Oct. 19 2005	195.98065	1.23697	1.21309	1.21170	1.19500
Oct. 20 2005	196.01290	1.23718	1.21329	1.21190	1.19520
Oct. 21 2005	196.04516	1.23738	1.21349	1.21210	1.19540
Oct. 22 2005	196.07742	1.23759	1.21369	1.21230	1.19559
Oct. 23 2005	196.10968	1.23779	1.21389	1.21250	1.19579
Oct. 24 2005	196.14194	1.23799	1.21409	1.21270	1.19599
Oct. 25 2005	196.17419	1.23820	1.21429	1.21290	1.19618
Oct. 26 2005	196.20645	1.23840	1.21449	1.21310	1.19638
Oct. 27 2005	196.23871	1.23860	1.21469	1.21330	1.19658
Oct. 28 2005	196.27097	1.23881	1.21489	1.21350	1.19677
Oct. 29 2005	196.30323	1.23901	1.21509	1.21370	1.19697
Oct. 30 2005	196.33548	1.23921	1.21529	1.21390	1.19717
Oct. 31 2005	196.36774	1.23942	1.21549	1.21410	1.19736
CPI-U (NSA) for :	June 2005 194.5	July 2005 195.4		July 2005 195.4	August 2005 196.4

Security:
Description:
CUSIP Number:
Dated Date:
Original Issue Date:
Additional Issue Date(s):
Maturity Date:
Ref CPI on Dated Date:

EXHIBIT 6-1 (continued)

TREASURY INFLATION-PROTECTED SECURITIES (TIPS)
Ref CPI and Index Ratios for
October 2005

		3-7/8% 30-Year TIPS	4-1/4% 10-Year TIPS	3-1/2% 10-Year TIPS	3-3/8% 30-1/2-Year TIPS
Security:					
Description:		TIPS of April 2029	Series A-2010	Series A-2011	TIPS of April 2032
CUSIP Number:		912810FH6	9128275W8	912827GR8	912810FQ6
Dated Date:		April 15, 1999	January 15, 2000	January 15, 2001	October 15, 2001
Original Issue Date:		April 15, 1999	January 18, 2000	January 16, 2001	October 15, 2001
Additional Issue Date(s):		October 15, 1999 / October 16, 2000	July 17, 2000	July 16, 2001	
Maturity Date:		April 15, 2029	January 15, 2010	January 15, 2011	April 15, 2032
Ref CPI on Dated Date:		164.39333	168.24516	174.04516	177.50000
Date	Ref CPI	Index Ratio	Index Ratio	Index Ratio	Index Ratio
Oct. 1 2005	195.40000	1.18861	1.16140	1.12270	1.10085
Oct. 2 2005	195.43226	1.18881	1.16159	1.12288	1.10103
Oct. 3 2005	195.46452	1.18901	1.16178	1.12307	1.10121
Oct. 4 2005	195.49677	1.18920	1.16198	1.12325	1.10139
Oct. 5 2005	195.52903	1.18940	1.16217	1.12344	1.10157
Oct. 6 2005	195.56129	1.18959	1.16236	1.12362	1.10175
Oct. 7 2005	195.59355	1.18979	1.16255	1.12381	1.10194
Oct. 8 2005	195.62581	1.18999	1.16274	1.12399	1.10212
Oct. 9 2005	195.65806	1.19018	1.16293	1.12418	1.10230
Oct. 10 2005	195.69032	1.19038	1.16313	1.12437	1.10248
Oct. 11 2005	195.72258	1.19057	1.16332	1.12455	1.10266
Oct. 12 2005	195.75484	1.19077	1.16351	1.12474	1.10284
Oct. 13 2005	195.78710	1.19097	1.16370	1.12492	1.10303
Oct. 14 2005	195.81935	1.19116	1.16389	1.12511	1.10321
Oct. 15 2005	195.85161	1.19136	1.16408	1.12529	1.10339
Oct. 16 2005	195.88387	1.19156	1.16428	1.12548	1.10357
Oct. 17 2005	195.91613	1.19175	1.16447	1.12566	1.10375
Oct. 18 2005	195.94839	1.19195	1.16466	1.12585	1.10393
Oct. 19 2005	195.98065	1.19214	1.16485	1.12603	1.10412
Oct. 20 2005	196.01290	1.19234	1.16504	1.12622	1.10430
Oct. 21 2005	196.04516	1.19254	1.16524	1.12640	1.10448
Oct. 22 2005	196.07742	1.19273	1.16543	1.12659	1.10466
Oct. 23 2005	196.10968	1.19293	1.16562	1.12677	1.10484
Oct. 24 2005	196.14194	1.19313	1.16581	1.12696	1.10503
Oct. 25 2005	196.17419	1.19332	1.16600	1.12715	1.10521
Oct. 26 2005	196.20645	1.19352	1.16619	1.12733	1.10539
Oct. 27 2005	196.23871	1.19371	1.16639	1.12752	1.10557
Oct. 28 2005	196.27097	1.19391	1.16658	1.12770	1.10575
Oct. 29 2005	196.30323	1.19411	1.16677	1.12789	1.10593
Oct. 30 2005	196.33548	1.19430	1.16696	1.12807	1.10612
Oct. 31 2005	196.36774	1.19450	1.16715	1.12826	1.10630
CPI-U (NSA) for :	June 2005	194.5	July 2005 195.4	August 2005 196.4	

EXHIBIT 6-1 (continued)

TREASURY INFLATION-PROTECTED SECURITIES (TIPS)
Ref CPI and Index Ratios for October 2005

		3-3/8% 10-Year TIPS Series A-2012 912827TJ5 January 15, 2002 January 15, 2002	3% 10-Year TIPS Series C-2012 912828AF7 July 15, 2002 July 15, 2002 October 15, 2002 January 15, 2003	1-7/8% 10-Year TIPS Series C-2013 912828BD1 July 15, 2003 July 15, 2003 October 15, 2003	2% 10-Year TIPS Series A-2014 912828BW9 January 15, 2004 January 15, 2004 January 15, 2004 April 15, 2004
Security / Description / CUSIP / Dated / Orig. / Addl. Issue:					
Maturity Date:		January 15, 2012	July 15, 2012	July 15, 2013	January 15, 2014
Ref CPI on Dated Date:		177.56452	179.80000	183.66452	184.77419
Date	Ref CPI	Index Ratio	Index Ratio	Index Ratio	Index Ratio
Oct. 1 2005	195.40000	1.10045	1.08676	1.06390	1.05751
Oct. 2 2005	195.43226	1.10063	1.08694	1.06407	1.05768
Oct. 3 2005	195.46452	1.10081	1.08712	1.06425	1.05786
Oct. 4 2005	195.49677	1.10099	1.08730	1.06442	1.05803
Oct. 5 2005	195.52903	1.10117	1.08748	1.06460	1.05821
Oct. 6 2005	195.56129	1.10135	1.08766	1.06477	1.05838
Oct. 7 2005	195.59355	1.10154	1.08784	1.06495	1.05855
Oct. 8 2005	195.62581	1.10172	1.08802	1.06513	1.05873
Oct. 9 2005	195.65806	1.10190	1.08820	1.06530	1.05890
Oct. 10 2005	195.69032	1.10208	1.08838	1.06548	1.05908
Oct. 11 2005	195.72258	1.10226	1.08856	1.06565	1.05925
Oct. 12 2005	195.75484	1.10244	1.08874	1.06583	1.05943
Oct. 13 2005	195.78710	1.10263	1.08892	1.06600	1.05960
Oct. 14 2005	195.81935	1.10281	1.08910	1.06618	1.05978
Oct. 15 2005	195.85161	1.10299	1.08927	1.06636	1.05995
Oct. 16 2005	195.88387	1.10317	1.08945	1.06653	1.06013
Oct. 17 2005	195.91613	1.10335	1.08963	1.06671	1.06030
Oct. 18 2005	195.94839	1.10353	1.08981	1.06688	1.06047
Oct. 19 2005	195.98065	1.10372	1.08999	1.06706	1.06065
Oct. 20 2005	196.01290	1.10390	1.09017	1.06723	1.06082
Oct. 21 2005	196.04516	1.10408	1.09035	1.06741	1.06100
Oct. 22 2005	196.07742	1.10426	1.09053	1.06758	1.06117
Oct. 23 2005	196.10968	1.10444	1.09071	1.06776	1.06135
Oct. 24 2005	196.14194	1.10462	1.09089	1.06794	1.06152
Oct. 25 2005	196.17419	1.10481	1.09107	1.06811	1.06170
Oct. 26 2005	196.20645	1.10499	1.09125	1.06829	1.06187
Oct. 27 2005	196.23871	1.10517	1.09143	1.06846	1.06205
Oct. 28 2005	196.27097	1.10535	1.09161	1.06864	1.06222
Oct. 29 2005	196.30323	1.10553	1.09179	1.06881	1.06240
Oct. 30 2005	196.33548	1.10571	1.09197	1.06899	1.06257
Oct. 31 2005	196.36774	1.10590	1.09215	1.06917	1.06274
CPI-U (NSA) for :	June 2005 194.5		July 2005 195.4		August 2005 196.4

132

EXHIBIT 6-1   (continued)

TREASURY INFLATION-PROTECTED SECURITIES (TIPS)
Ref CPI and Index Ratios for October 2005

	2% 10-Year TIPS	2-3/8% 20-1/2-Year TIPS	0-7/8% 5-1/2-Year TIPS	1-5/8% 10-Year TIPS
Security: Description:	Series D-2014	TIPS of January 2025	Series D-2010	Series A-2015
CUSIP Number:	912828CP3	912810FR4	912828CZ1	912828DH0
Dated Date:	July 15, 2004	July 15, 2004	October 15, 2004	January 15, 2005
Original Issue Date:	July 15, 2004	July 30, 2004	October 29, 2004	January 18, 2005
Additional Issue Date(s):	October 15, 2004	January 31, 2005 / July 29, 2005	April 29, 2005	April 15, 2005
Maturity Date:	July 15, 2014	January 15, 2025	April 15, 2010	January 15, 2015
Ref CPI on Dated Date:	188.49677	188.49677	189.44516	190.94516

Date		Ref CPI	Index Ratio	Index Ratio	Index Ratio	Index Ratio
Oct. 1	2005	195.40000	1.03662	1.03662	1.03143	1.02333
Oct. 2	2005	195.43226	1.03679	1.03679	1.03160	1.02350
Oct. 3	2005	195.46452	1.03696	1.03696	1.03177	1.02367
Oct. 4	2005	195.49677	1.03714	1.03714	1.03194	1.02384
Oct. 5	2005	195.52903	1.03731	1.03731	1.03211	1.02401
Oct. 6	2005	195.56129	1.03748	1.03748	1.03228	1.02418
Oct. 7	2005	195.59355	1.03765	1.03765	1.03245	1.02434
Oct. 8	2005	195.62581	1.03782	1.03782	1.03263	1.02451
Oct. 9	2005	195.65806	1.03799	1.03799	1.03280	1.02468
Oct. 10	2005	195.69032	1.03816	1.03816	1.03297	1.02485
Oct. 11	2005	195.72258	1.03833	1.03833	1.03314	1.02502
Oct. 12	2005	195.75484	1.03851	1.03851	1.03331	1.02519
Oct. 13	2005	195.78710	1.03868	1.03868	1.03348	1.02536
Oct. 14	2005	195.81935	1.03885	1.03885	1.03365	1.02553
Oct. 15	2005	195.85161	1.03902	1.03902	1.03382	1.02570
Oct. 16	2005	195.88387	1.03919	1.03919	1.03399	1.02586
Oct. 17	2005	195.91613	1.03936	1.03936	1.03416	1.02603
Oct. 18	2005	195.94839	1.03953	1.03953	1.03433	1.02620
Oct. 19	2005	195.98065	1.03970	1.03970	1.03450	1.02637
Oct. 20	2005	196.01290	1.03987	1.03987	1.03467	1.02654
Oct. 21	2005	196.04516	1.04005	1.04005	1.03484	1.02671
Oct. 22	2005	196.07742	1.04022	1.04022	1.03501	1.02688
Oct. 23	2005	196.10968	1.04039	1.04039	1.03518	1.02705
Oct. 24	2005	196.14194	1.04056	1.04056	1.03535	1.02722
Oct. 25	2005	196.17419	1.04073	1.04073	1.03552	1.02738
Oct. 26	2005	196.20645	1.04090	1.04090	1.03569	1.02755
Oct. 27	2005	196.23871	1.04107	1.04107	1.03586	1.02772
Oct. 28	2005	196.27097	1.04124	1.04124	1.03603	1.02789
Oct. 29	2005	196.30323	1.04141	1.04141	1.03620	1.02806
Oct. 30	2005	196.33548	1.04159	1.04159	1.03637	1.02823
Oct. 31	2005	196.36774	1.04176	1.04176	1.03654	1.02840
CPI-U (NSA) for :		June 2005 194.5	July 2005 194.5	July 2005 195.4	July 2005 195.4	August 2005 196.4

EXHIBIT 6-1 (continued)

TREASURY INFLATION-PROTECTED SECURITIES (TIPS)
Ref CPI and Index Ratios for October 2005

Security:	
Description:	1-7/8% 10-Year TIPS
CUSIP Number:	Series D-2015
	912828EA4
Dated Date:	July 15, 2005
Original Issue Date:	July 15, 2005
Additional Issue Date(s):	
Maturity Date:	July 15, 2015
Ref CPI on Dated Date:	194.50968

Date		Ref CPI	Index Ratio
Oct.	1	2005	195.40000	1.00458
Oct.	2	2005	195.43226	1.00474
Oct.	3	2005	195.46452	1.00491
Oct.	4	2005	195.49677	1.00507
Oct.	5	2005	195.52903	1.00524
Oct.	6	2005	195.56129	1.00541
Oct.	7	2005	195.59355	1.00557
Oct.	8	2005	195.62581	1.00574
Oct.	9	2005	195.65806	1.00590
Oct.	10	2005	195.69032	1.00607
Oct.	11	2005	195.72258	1.00624
Oct.	12	2005	195.75484	1.00640
Oct.	13	2005	195.78710	1.00657
Oct.	14	2005	195.81935	1.00673
Oct.	15	2005	195.85161	1.00690
Oct.	16	2005	195.88387	1.00706
Oct.	17	2005	195.91613	1.00723
Oct.	18	2005	195.94839	1.00740
Oct.	19	2005	195.98065	1.00756
Oct.	20	2005	196.01290	1.00773
Oct.	21	2005	196.04516	1.00789
Oct.	22	2005	196.07742	1.00806
Oct.	23	2005	196.10968	1.00823
Oct.	24	2005	196.14194	1.00839
Oct.	25	2005	196.17419	1.00856
Oct.	26	2005	196.20645	1.00872
Oct.	27	2005	196.23871	1.00889
Oct.	28	2005	196.27097	1.00906
Oct.	29	2005	196.30323	1.00922
Oct.	30	2005	196.33548	1.00939
Oct.	31	2005	196.36774	1.00955

CPI-U (NSA) for :	June 2005	194.5	July 2005	195.4	August 2005	196.4

The Treasury Auction Process

The Public Debt Act of 1942 grants the Department of the Treasury considerable discretion in deciding on the terms for a marketable security. An issue may be sold on an interest-bearing or discount basis and may be sold on a competitive or other basis, at whatever prices the Secretary of the Treasury may establish. However, Congress imposes a restriction on the total amount of bonds outstanding. Although Congress has granted an exemption to this restriction, there have been times when the failure of Congress to extend the exemption has resulted in the delay or cancellation of a Treasury bond offering.

Treasury securities are sold in the primary market through sealed-bid auctions. Each auction is announced several days in advance by means of a Treasury Department press release or press conference. The announcement provides details of the offering, including the offering amount and the term and type of security being offered, and describes some of the auction rules and procedures. Treasury auctions are open to all entities.

Auction Process

The U.S. Department of the Treasury makes the determination of the procedure for auctioning new Treasury securities, when to auction them, and what maturities to issue. There are periodic changes in the auction cycles and the maturity of the issues auctioned. The Treasury auctions on a regular cycle Treasury bills with maturities of 4 weeks, 13 weeks (3 months), and 26 weeks (6 months). At irregular intervals the Treasury issues **cash management bills** with maturities ranging from a few days to about six months. The Treasury auctions 2-, 3-, 5-, and 10-year Treasury notes. Exhibits 6-2 and 6-3 show the announcement of Treasury auctions. Exhibit 6-2 shows the announcement of the Treasury August quarterly financing on August 3, 2005. The auctions for three Treasury notes are shown: 3-year notes, 5-year notes, and 10-year notes. Exhibit 6-3 shows the announcement of a 10-year TIPS announced on July 11, 2005. The Treasury had issued 30-year Treasury bonds on a regular basis but suspended doing so in October 2001. However, in 2005 the Treasury announced it would resume the sale of 30-year bonds twice a year, beginning with a bond to mature in February 2036.

While the Treasury regularly offers new securities at auction, it often offers additional amounts of outstanding securities. This is referred to as a "reopening" of an issue. The Treasury has established a regular schedule of reopenings for the 5- and 10-year issues.

To maintain the sizes of its new issues and help manage the maturity of its debt, the Treasury launched a debt buyback program. Under the program, the Treasury redeems outstanding unmatured Treasury securities by purchasing them in the secondary market through reverse auctions.

Determination of the Results of an Auction

The auction for Treasury securities is conducted on a competitive bid basis. There are actually two types of bids that may be submitted by a bidder: noncompetitive bids and competitive bids. A **noncompetitive bid** is submitted by an entity that is willing to purchase the auctioned security at the yield that is determined by the auction process.

When a noncompetitive bid is submitted, the bidder only specifies the quantity sought. The quantity in a noncompetitive bid may not exceed $5 million. A **competitive bid** specifies both the quantity sought and the yield at which the bidder is willing to purchase the auctioned security.

The auction results are determined by first deducting the total noncompetitive tenders and nonpublic purchases (such as purchases by the Federal Reserve) from the total securities being auctioned. The remainder is the amount to be awarded to the competitive bidders. The competitive bids are then arranged from the lowest yield bid to the highest yield bid submitted. (This is equivalent to arranging the bids from the highest price to the lowest price that bidders are willing to pay.) Starting from the

---

EXHIBIT 6-2 Example of a U.S. Treasury Announcement of Fixed-Principal Notes

DEPARTMENT OF THE TREASURY

TREASURY NEWS

OFFICE OF PUBLIC AFFAIRS •1500 PENNSYLVENIA AVENUE, N.W.• WASHINGTON. D.C.• 20220• (202) 622-2960

EMBARGOED UNTIL 9:00 A.M.   CONTACT: Offiece of Financing
August 3, 2005   202/504-3550

                        TREASURY AUGUST QUARTERLY FINANCING

        The treasury will aution $18,000 million of 3-years notes, $13,000 million of
5 year notes, and $13,000 million of 10-year notes to refund #18,552 million of
publicly held securities maturing August 15, 2005, and to raise approximately $25,448
million of new cash.

        In addition to the public holdings, Federal Reserve Banks, for their own
accounts, hold $5,721 million of the maturing securities, which may be refunded by
issuing additional amounts of the new securities.

        Up to $1,000 million in noncompetitive bids from Foreign and International
Monetary Authority (FIMA) accounts bidding through the Federal Reserve Bank of New
York will be included within the offering amount of each acution. These
noncompetitive bids will have a limit of $100 million per account and will be accepted
in the order of smallest to largest, up to the aggregate award limit of $1,000
million.

        TreasuryDirect customers requested that we reinvest their maturing holdings of
approximately $19 million into the 3-year note, $7 million into the 5-year note, and
$7 million into the 10-year note.

        The auctions being announced today will be conducted in the single-price auction
format. All competitive and noncompetitive awards will be at the highest yeild of
accpeted competitive tenders. The allocation percentage applied to bids awarded at
the highest yeild will be rounded up to the next hundredth of a whole percentage
point, e.g., 17.13%

        The notes being offered today are eligible for the STRIPS program.

        This offering of Treasury securities is governed by the terms and conditions set
forth in the Uniform offering Circular for the Sale and Issue of Marketable Book-Entry
Treasury Bills, Notes, and Bonds (31 CFR Part 356, ad amended)

        Details about the notes are gives in the attached offering highlights.

                                        oOo

Attachment

EXHIBIT 6-2 (continued)

AUGUST 2005 QUARTERLY FINANCING

August 3, 2005

	3-year notes	5-year notes	10-year notes
Offering Amount................................	$18,000 million	$13,000 million	$13,000 million
Maximum Award (35% of Offering Amount).......	$ 6,300 million	$ 4,550 million	$ 4,550 million
Maximum Recognized Bid at a Single Yeild......	$ 6,300 million	$ 4,550 million	$ 4,550 million
NLP Reporting Threshold........................	$ 6,300 million	$ 4,550 million	$ 4,550 million

Description of Offering:

	3-year notes	5-year notes	10-year notes
Term and type of security......................	3-year notes	5-year notes	10-year notes
Series...	P-2008	M-2010	E-2015
CUSIP number...................................	912828 EC 0	912828 ED 8	912828 EE 6
Auction date...................................	August 8, 2005	August 10. 2005	August 11, 2005
Issue date.....................................	August 15, 2005	August 15, 2005	August 15, 2005
Dated date.....................................	August 15, 2005	August 15, 2005	August 15, 2005
Maturity date..................................	August 15, 2008	August 15, 2010	August 15, 2015
Interest rate..................................	Determined based on the highest accepted competitive bid	Determined based on the highest accepted competitive bid	Determined based on the highest accepted competitive bid
Amount currently outstanding...................	Not applicable	Not applicable	Not applicabel
Yeild..	Determined at auction	Determined at auction	Determined at auciton
Interest payment dates.........................	February 15 and August 15	February 15 and August 15	February 15 and August 15
Minimum bid amount and multiples...............	$1,000	$1,000	$1,000
Accrued interest payable by investor...........	None	None	None
Premium or discount............................	Determined at auction	Determined at auction	Determined at auction

STRIPS Information:

	3-year notes	5-year notes	10-year notes
Minimum amount requires........................	$1,000	$1,000	$1,000
Corpus CUSIP number............................	912820 LZ 8	912820 MA 2	912820 MB 0
Due date(s) and CUSIP number(s)................	Not applicable	Not applicable	Not applicable

The following rules apply to all securities mentioned above:

Submission of Bids:

Noncomoetitive bids: Accepted in full up to $5 million at the highest accepted yield.

Foreign and International Monetary Authority (FIMA) bids: Noncompetitive bids submitted through the Federal Reserve Banks as
agents for FIMA accounts. Accepted in order of size from smallest to largest with no more than $100 million awarded per account.
The total noncompetitive amount awarded to Federal Reserve Bank as agents for FIMA accounts will not exceed $1,000 million. A
single bid that would cause the limit to be exceeded will be partially accepted in the amount that brings the aggregate award total
to the $1,000 million limit. However, if there are two or more bids of equal amounts that would cause the limit to be exceeded,
each will be prorated to avoid exceeding the limit.

Competitive bids:

(1) Must be expressed as a yield with three decimals, e.g., 7.123%.

(2) Net long position (NLP) for each bidder must be reproted when the sum of the total bid amount, at all yields, and the
    net long position equals or exceeds the NLP reporting threshold stated above.

(3) Net long position must be determined as of one-half hour prior to the closing time for receipt of competitive tenders.

Receipt of Tenders:

Noncompetitive tenders......Prior to 12:00 noon eastern daylight saving time on auction day

Competitive tenders.........Prior to 1:00 p.m. eastern daylight saving time on auction day

Payment Terms...............By charge to a funds account at a Federal Reserve Bank on issue date, or payment of full par amount with tender.
    TreasuryDirect customers can use the Pay Direct feature which authorizes a charge to their account of record at
    their financial institution on issue date.

137

lowest yield bid, all competitive bids are accepted until the amount to be distributed to the competitive bidders is completely allocated. The highest yield accepted by the Treasury is referred to as the **stop-out yield** (or **high yield**). Bidders whose bid is higher than the stop-out yield are not distributed any of the new issue (i.e., they are unsuccessful bidders). Bidders whose bid was the stop-out yield (i.e., the highest yield accepted by the Treasury) are awarded a proportionate amount for which they bid. For example, suppose that $2 billion was tendered for at the stop-out yield but only $1 billion remains to be allocated after allocating to all bidders who bid lower than the stop-out yield. Then each bidder who bid the stop-out yield will receive 50% of the amount for which they tendered. So, if an entity tendered for $5 million, then that entity would be awarded only $2.5 million.

Within an hour following the 1:00 P.M. auction deadline, the Treasury announces the auction results. Announced results include the stop-out yield, the associated price, and the proportion of securities awarded to those investors who bid exactly the stop-out

---

EXHIBIT 6-3   Example of a U.S. Treasury Announcement of a TIPS Note

DEPARTMENT OF THE TREASURY

TREASURY N E W S

OFFICE OF PUBLIC AFFAIRS •1500 PENNSYLVENIA AVENUE, N.W.•WASHINGTON. D.C.• 20220•(202) 622-2960

EMBARGOED UNTIL, 11:00 A.M.   CONTACT: office of Financing
July 11, 2205   202/504-3550

    TREASURY OFFERS 10-YEAR TREASURY INFLATION-PROTECTED SECURITIES (TIPS)

    The Treasury will auction $9,000 million of 10-Year Treasury inflation-
protected securities to raise new cash

    Up to $1,000 million in noncompetitive bids from foreign and International
Monetary Authority (FIMA) accounts bidding through the Federal Reserve Bank of New
York will be included within the offering amount of the auction. These noncompetitive
bids will have a limit of $100 million per account and will be accepted in the order
of smallest to largest, up to the aggregate award limit of $1,000 million.

    The auction will be conducted in the single-price auction format. All
competitive and noncompetitive awards will be at the highest yield of accepted
competitive tenders. The allocation percentage applied to bids awarded at the
highest yield will be rounded up to the nest hundredth of a whole percentage
point, e.g., 17.13%

    The securities being offered today are eligible for the STRIPS program.

    This offering of Treasury secutities is governed by the terms and
conditions set forth in the Uniform Offering circular for the Sale and Issue of
Marketable Book-Entry Treasury Bills, Notea; and Bonds (31 CFR Parts 356, as
amended).

    Details about the security are given in the attached offering highlights.

Attachment

EXHIBIT 6-3   (continued)

```
                    Highlights of treasury offering to the public of
            10-year treasury inflation-protected securities to be issued july 15, 2005

                                                                     July 11, 2005
Offering Amount ................................. $9,000 million
Maximum Award (35% of Offering Amount) ............ $3,150 million
Maximum Recognized Bid at a Single Yield .......... $3,150 million
NLP Reporting Threshold ......................... $3,150 millon

Description of offering:
Term and type of security ....................... 10-year Treasury inflation-
                                                  Protected securities
Series .......................................... D-2015
CUSIP number .................................... 912828 EA 4
Auction data .................................... July 14, 2005
Issue data ...................................... July 15, 2005
Dated data ...................................... July 15, 2005
Maturity data ................................... July 15, 2015
Interest rate ................................... Determined based on the highest
                                                  accepted competitive bid
Real yield ...................................... Determined based on the highest
Interest payment dates .......................... Janyary 15 and July 15
Minimum bid amount and multiples ................. $1,000
Accrued interest ................................ None
Premium or discount ............................. Determined at auction

Strips information:
Minimum amount required ......................... $1,000
Corpus CUSIP number ............................. 912820 LX 3
Due date(s) and CUSIP number(s)
for additional TIIN(s) .......................... Not Applicable

Submission of Bids:
Noncompetitive bids:
Accepted in full up to $5 million at the highest accepted yield.
Foreign and International Monetary Authority (FIMA) bids: Noncompetitive bids submitted
     through the Federal Reserve Banks as agents for FIMA accounts. Accepted in order of
     size from smallest to largest with no more than $100 millon awared per account.
     The total noncompetitive amount awarded to Federal Reserve Banks as agents for FIMA
     accounts will not exceed $1,000 million. A single bid that would cause the limit to
     be exceeded will be partially accepted in the amount that brings the aggregate award
     total to the $1,000 million limit. However, if there are two or more bids of equal
     amounts that would cause the limit to be exceeded, each will be prorated to avoid
     exceeding the limit.
Competitive bids:
(1) Must be expressed as a real yield with three decimals, e.g., 3,123%
(2) Net long position for each bidder must be reported when the sum of the total bid
     amount, at all yields, and the net long position equals or exceeds the NLP reporting
     threshold stated above.
(3) Net long position must be determined as of one-half hour prior to the closing time for
     receipt of competitive tenders.

Receipt of Tenders:
Noncompetitive tenders: Prior to 12:00 noon eastern daylight saving time on auction day.
Competitive tenders: Prior to 1:00 p.m. eastern daylight saving time on auction day.
Payment Terms: By charge to a funds account at Federal Reserve Bank on issue date, or
payment of full per amount with tender. TreasuryDirect customers can use the Pay Direct
feature which authorizes a charge to their account of record at their financial
institution on issue date.
Indexing Information:       CPI Base Reference Period ... 1982-1984
                           Ref CPI 07/15/2005............ 194,50968
                           Index Ratio 07/15/2005........ 1,00000
```

yield. Also announced is the quantity of noncompetitive tenders, the median-yield bid, and the ratio of the total amount bid for by the public to the amount awarded to the public (called the **bid-to-cover ratio**). For notes and bonds, the announcement includes the coupon rate of the new security. The coupon rate is set to be that rate (in increments of $^1/_8$ of 1%) that produces the price closest to, but not above, par when evaluated at the yield awarded to successful bidders.

The results of the auctions for the 10-year Treasury notes announced in Exhibits 6-2 and 6-3 are shown in Exhibits 6-4 and 6-5. To determine the winning bidders, the bids are arranged from the lowest bid yield to the highest bid yield. The Treasury reported that the lowest bid yield was 5.290%. The high bid yield accepted for the fixed-principal 10-year Treasury note was 4.350%. All bidders that bid less than 4.350% were awarded the amount that they bid. The Treasury reported that "Tenders at the high yield were allotted 57.72%." This means that if an entity bid for $10 million at 4.350%, that entity was awarded $5.772 million.

Now we know how the winning bidders are determined and the amount that successful bidders will be allotted, the next question is the yield at which they are awarded

EXHIBIT 6-4 Example of the Results of a Treasury Auction for a 10-Year Fixed-Principal Note

PUBLIC DEBT NEWS

Department of the Treasury • Bureau of the Public Debt • Washington, DC 20239

```
              TREASURY SECURITY AUCTION RESULTS
              BUREAU OF THE PUBLIC DEBT - WASHINGTON DC

FOR IMMEDIATE RELEASE                  CONTACT:    Office of Financing
August 11, 2005                                    202-504-3550

          RESULTS OF TREASURY'S AUCTION OF 10-YEAR NOTES

Interest Rate:  4 1/4%            Issue Date:     August 15, 2005
Series:         E-2015            Dated Date:     August 15, 2005
CUSIP No:       912828EE6         Maturity Date:  August 15, 2015


          High Yield:  4.350%    Price: 99.196069

   All noncompetitive and successful competitive bidders were awarded
securities at the high yield.  Tenders at the high yield were
allotted  57.72%.  All tenders at lower yields were accepted in full.

          AMOUNTS TENDERED AND ACCEPTED (in thousands)

     Tender Type              Tendered             Accepted
     -----------         -----------------    -----------------
     Competitive         $    33,527,634      $    12,833,605
     Noncompetitive               66,421               66,421
     FIMA (noncompetitive)       100,000              100,000
                         -----------------    -----------------
        SUBTOTAL              33,694,055           13,000,026 1/

     Federal Reserve          1,472,161            1,472,161
                         -----------------    -----------------
     TOTAL              $    35,166,216      $    14,472,187

   Median yield   4.337%:  50% of the amount of accepted competitive tenders
was tendered at or below that rate.  Low yield   4.290%:   5% of the amount
of accepted competitive tenders was tendered at or below that rate.

Bid-to-Cover Ratio = 33,694,055 / 13,000,026 = 2.59

1/ Awards to TREASURY DIRECT = $36,205,000
```

EXHIBIT 6-5   Example of the Results of a Treasury Auction for a 10-Year TIPS Note

PUBLIC DEBT NEWS

Department of the Treasury • Bureau of the Public Debt • Washington, DC 20239

```
                       TREASURY SECURITY AUCTION RESULTS
                      BUREAU OF THE PUBLIC DEBT - WASHINGTON DC

FOR IMMEDIATE RELEASE                        CONTACT:     Office of Financing
July 14, 2005                                             202-504-3550

     RESULTS OF TREASURY'S AUCTION OF 10-YEAR INFLATION-INDEXED NOTES

Interest Rate:  1 7/8%                 Issue Date:      July 15, 2005
Series:         D-2015                 Dated Date:      July 15, 2005
CUSIP No:       912828EA4              Maturity Date:   July 15, 2015
TIIN Conversion Factor per $1,000 =    4.819811538 1/

               High Yield:   1.939%    Price:  99.420765

     All noncompetitive and successful competitive bidders were awarded
securities at the high yield.  Tenders at the high yield were
allotted   7.24%.  All tenders at lower yields were accepted in full.

              AMOUNTS TENDERED AND ACCEPTED (in thousands)

     Tender Type                   Tendered              Accepted
     -----------                 -----------           -----------
     Competitive            $     15,028,350      $      8,878,910
     Noncompetitive                   71,091                71,091
     FIMA (noncompetitive)           50,000                50,000
                                 -----------           -----------
          SUBTOTAL                15,149,441             9,000,001 2/

     Federal Reserve                       0                     0
                                 -----------           -----------
     TOTAL                  $     15,149,441      $      9,000,001

     Median yield   1.860%:  50% of the amount of accepted competitive tenders
was tendered at or below that rate.  Low yield   1.750%:   5% of the amount
of accepted competitive tenders was tendered at or below that rate.

Bid-to-Cover Ratio = 15,149,441 / 9,000,001 = 1.68

1/ This factor is used to calculate the Adjusted Values for any TIIN face
   amount and will be maintained to 2-decimals on Book-entry systems.
2/ Awards to TREASURY DIRECT = $24,068,000
```

the auctioned security. All U.S. Treasury auctions are **single-price auctions**. In a single-price auction, all bidders are awarded securities at the highest yield of accepted competitive tenders (i.e., the high yield).[4] In the case of the 10-year Treasury auction whose results are reported in Exhibit 6-4, all bidders (competitive and noncompetitive) were awarded securities at a yield of 4.350%.

The Treasury does not offer securities with a coupon rate of 4.35%. The practice of the Treasury is to adjust the coupon rate and the price so that the yield offered on the security is equal to the stop-out yield. In the case of the 10-year Treasury auction, the coupon rate was set at 4.25% (slightly below the high yield of 4.350%) and the price

---

[4]This type of auction is called a "Dutch auction."

that successful bidders paid for the issue was slightly below par value to reflect the lower coupon rate.

Secondary Market

The secondary market for Treasury securities is an over-the-counter market where a group of U.S. government securities dealers offers continuous bid and ask prices on outstanding Treasuries. There is virtual 24-hour trading of Treasury securities. The three primary trading locations are New York, London, and Tokyo. The normal settlement period for Treasury securities is the business day after the transaction day ("next day" settlement).

The most recently auctioned issue is referred to as the **on-the-run issue** or the **current issue**. Securities that are replaced by the on-the-run issue are called **off-the-run issues**. At a given point in time there may be more than one off-the-run issue with approximately the same remaining maturity as the on-the-run issue. Treasury securities are traded prior to the time they are issued by the Treasury. This component of the Treasury secondary market is called the **when-issued market**, or **wi market**. When-issued trading for both bills and coupon securities extends from the day the auction is announced until the issue day.

Government dealers trade with the investing public and with other dealer firms. When they trade with each other, it is through intermediaries known as **interdealer brokers**. Dealers leave firm bids and offers with interdealer brokers who display the highest bid and lowest offer in a computer network tied to each trading desk and displayed on a monitor. Dealers use interdealer brokers because of the speed and efficiency with which trades can be accomplished. Interdealer brokers keep the names of the dealers involved in trades confidential. The quotes provided on the government dealer screens represent prices in the "inside" or "interdealer" market.

Price Quotes for Treasury Bills

The convention for quoting bids and offers is different for Treasury bills and Treasury coupon securities. Bids and offers on Treasury bills are quoted in a special way. Unlike bonds that pay coupon interest, Treasury bill values are quoted on a **bank discount basis**, not on a price basis. The yield on a bank discount basis is computed as follows:

$$Y_d = \frac{D}{F} \times \frac{360}{t}$$

where

Y_d = annualized yield on a bank discount basis (expressed as a decimal)
D = dollar discount, which is equal to the difference between the face value and the price
F = face value
t = number of days remaining to maturity

As an example, a Treasury bill with 100 days to maturity, a face value of $100,000, and selling for $99,100 would be quoted at 3.24% on a bank discount basis:

$$D = \$100,000 - \$99,100$$
$$= \$900$$

Therefore,

$$Y_d = \frac{\$900}{\$100,000} \times \frac{360}{100} = 3.24\%$$

Given the yield on a bank discount basis, the price of a Treasury bill is found by first solving the formula for Y_d for the dollar discount (D), as follows:

$$D = Y_d \times F \times t/360$$

The price is then

$$\text{price} = F - D$$

For the 100-day Treasury bill with a face value of $100,000, if the yield on a bank discount basis is quoted as 3.24%, D is equal to

$$D = 0.0324 \times \$100,000 \times 100/360$$
$$= \$900$$

Therefore,

$$\text{price} = \$100,000 - \$900 = \$99,100$$

The quoted yield on a bank discount basis is not a meaningful measure of the return from holding a Treasury bill for two reasons. First, the measure is based on a face-value investment rather than on the actual dollar amount invested. Second, the yield is annualized according to a 360-day rather than a 365-day year, making it difficult to compare Treasury bill yields with Treasury notes and bonds, which pay interest on a 365-day basis. The use of 360 days for a year is a money market convention for some money market instruments, however. Despite its shortcomings as a measure of return, this is the method that dealers have adopted to quote Treasury bills. Many dealer quote sheets, and some reporting services, provide two other yield measures that attempt to make the quoted yield comparable to that for a coupon bond and other money market instruments.

The measure that seeks to make the Treasury bill quote comparable to Treasury notes and bonds is called the **bond equivalent yield**, which we explained in Chapter 3. The **CD equivalent yield** (also called the **money market equivalent yield**) makes the quoted yield on a Treasury bill more comparable to yield quotations on other money market instruments that pay interest on a 360-day basis. It does this by taking into consideration the price of the Treasury bill rather than its face value. The formula for the CD equivalent yield is

$$\text{CD equivalent yield} = \frac{360 Y_d}{360 - t(Y_d)}$$

As an illustration, consider once again the hypothetical 100-day Treasury bill with a face value of $100,000, selling for $99,100, and offering a yield on a bank discount basis of 3.24%.

$$\text{CD equivalent yield} = \frac{360(0.0324)}{360 - 100(0.0324)} = 0.327 = 3.27\%$$

Quotes on Treasury Coupon Securities

Treasury coupon securities are quoted in a different manner than Treasury bills—on a price basis in points where one point equals 1% of par.[5] The points are split into units of *32nds*, so that a price of 96-14, for example, refers to a price of 96 and 14 *32nds*, or 96.4375 per 100 of par value. The following are other examples of converting a quote to a price per $100 of par value:

Quote	No. of 32nds	Price per $100 par
91-19	19	91.59375
107-22	22	107.6875
109-06	6	109.1875

The 32nds are themselves often split by the addition of a plus sign or a number. A plus sign indicates that half a *32nd* (or a *64th*) is added to the price, and a number indicates how many eighths of *32nds* (or *256ths*) are added to the price. A price of 96-14+, therefore, refers to a price of 96 plus 14 *32nds* plus 1 64th, or 96.453125, and a price of 96-142 refers to a price of 96 plus 14 *32nds* plus 2 256ths, or 96.4453125. The following are other examples of converting a quote to a price per $100 of par value:

Quote	No. of 32nds	No. of 64ths	No. of 256ths	Price per $100 par
91-19+	19	1		91.609375
107-222	22		2	107.6953125
109-066	6		6	109.2109375

In addition to price, the yield to maturity is typically reported alongside the price.

When an investor purchases a bond between coupon payments, if the issuer is not in default, the buyer must compensate the seller of the bond for the coupon interest earned from the time of the last coupon payment to the settlement date of the bond. This amount is called **accrued interest**.

When calculating accrued interest, three pieces of information are needed: (1) the number of days in the accrued interest period, (2) the number of days in the coupon period, and (3) the dollar amount of the coupon payment. The number of days in the accrued interest period represents the number of days over which the investor has earned interest. Given these values, the accrued interest (AI) assuming semiannual payments is calculated as follows:

$$AI = \frac{\text{annual dollar coupon}}{2} \times \frac{\text{days in AI period}}{\text{days in coupon period}}$$

---

[5]Notes and bonds are quoted in yield terms in when-issued trading because coupon rates for new notes and bonds are not set until after these securities are auctioned.

For example, suppose that (1) there are 50 days in the accrued interest period, (2) there are 183 days in a coupon period, and (3) the annual dollar coupon per $100 of par value is $8. Then the accrued interest is

$$AI = \frac{\$8}{2} \times \frac{50}{183} = \$1.0929$$

The calculation of the number of days in the accrued interest period and the number of days in the coupon period begins with the determination of three key dates: the trade date, settlement date, and date of previous coupon payment. The **trade date** is the date on which the transaction is executed. The **settlement date** is the date a transaction is completed. For Treasury securities, settlement is the next business day after the trade date. Interest accrues on a Treasury coupon security from and including the date of the previous coupon payment up to but excluding the settlement date.

The number of days in the accrued interest period and the number of days in the coupon period may not be simply the actual number of calendar days between two dates. The reason is that there is a market convention for each type of security that specifies how to determine the number of days between two dates. These conventions are called day count conventions. There are different day count conventions for Treasury securities than for government agency securities, municipal bonds, and corporate bonds.

For Treasury coupon securities, the day count convention used is to determine the actual number of days between two dates. This is referred to as the **actual/actual day count convention**. For example, consider a Treasury coupon security whose previous coupon payment was May 15. The next coupon payment would be on November 15. Suppose this Treasury security is purchased with a settlement date of September 10. First, the number of days of accrued interest is calculated. The actual number of days between May 15 (the previous coupon date) and September 10 (the settlement date) is 118 days, as follows:

May 15 to May 31	17 days
June	30 days
July	31 days
August	31 days
September 1 to September 10	9 days
Actual number of days	118 days

The number of days in the coupon period is the actual number of days between May 15 and November 15, which is 184 days. The number of days between the settlement date (September 10) and the next coupon date (November 15) is therefore 66 days (184 days–118 days). Notice that in computing the number of days from May 15 to May 31, May 15 is counted in determining the number of days in the accrued interest period; however, the settlement date (September 10) is not included.

STRIPPED TREASURY SECURITIES

The Treasury does not issue zero-coupon notes or bonds. However, because of the demand for zero-coupon instruments with no credit risk, the private sector has created such securities. The profit potential for a government dealer who strips a Treasury security lies in arbitrage resulting from the mispricing of the security. We explained the reason for this in Chapter 5.

To illustrate the process, a process referred to as **coupon stripping**, suppose that $500 million of a 10-year fixed-principal Treasury note with a coupon rate of 5% is purchased by a dealer firm to create zero-coupon Treasury securities. The cash flow from this Treasury note is 20 semiannual payments of $12.5 million each ($500 million times 0.05 divided by 2) and the repayment of principal (also called the **corpus**) of $500 million 10 years from now. As there are 11 different payments to be made by the Treasury, a security representing a single payment claim on each payment is issued, which is effectively a zero-coupon Treasury security. The amount of the maturity value for a security backed by a particular payment, whether coupon or corpus, depends on the amount of the payment to be made by the Treasury on the underlying Treasury note. In our example, 20 zero-coupon Treasury securities each have a maturity value of $12.5 million, and one zero-coupon Treasury security, backed by the corpus, has a maturity value of $500 million. The maturity dates for the zero-coupon Treasury securities coincide with the corresponding payment dates by the Treasury.

Zero-coupon Treasury securities were first created in August 1982 by dealer firms. The problem with these securities were that they were identified with particular dealers and therefore reduced liquidity. Moreover, the process involved legal and insurance costs. In February 1985, the Treasury announced its **Separate Trading of Registered Interest and Principal of Securities (STRIPS)** program to facilitate the stripping of designated Treasury securities. Today, all Treasury notes and bonds (fixed-principal and inflation-indexed) are eligible for stripping. The zero-coupon Treasury securities created under the STRIPS program are direct obligations of the U.S. government. Moreover, the securities clear through the Federal Reserve's book-entry system.

There may be confusion when a market participant refers to a "stripped Treasury." Today, a stripped Treasury typically means a STRIPS product. However, because there are trademark products and other types of pre-STRIPS zero-coupon products still outstanding, an investor should clarify what product is the subject of the discussion. In the chapters that follow, we will refer to stripped Treasury securities as simply "strips."

On dealer quote sheets and vendor screens, STRIPS are identified by whether the cash flow is created from the coupon (denoted ci), principal from a Treasury bond (denoted bp), or principal from a Treasury note (denoted np). Strips created from the coupon are called **coupon strips** and strips created from the principal are called **principal strips**. The reason why a distinction is made between coupon strips and principal strips has to do with the tax treatment by non–U.S. entities, as discussed in the next section.

All fixed-principal notes and bonds that pay interest on the same dates are assigned the same CUSIP number. For example, fixed-principal notes and bonds that pay interest on April 15 and October 15 are stripped. The coupon strips that are payable on the same day have the same CUSIP number. The principal strips of each fixed-principal note and bond, in contrast, are assigned a unique CUSIP number, and principal strips with different CUSIP numbers that pay on the same day are not interchangeable.

Tax Treatment

A disadvantage of a taxable entity investing in stripped Treasury securities is that accrued interest is taxed each year even though interest is not paid. Thus, these instruments are negative cash flow instruments until the maturity date. They have negative cash flow because tax payments on interest earned but not received in cash must be made. One reason for distinguishing between coupon strips and principal strips is that some foreign buyers have a preference for principal strips. This preference is due to the tax treatment of the interest in their home country. The tax laws of some countries treat the interest from a principal strip as a capital gain, which receives a preferential tax treatment (i.e., lower tax rate) compared with ordinary interest income if the stripped security was created from a coupon strip.

Reconstituting a Bond

In our illustration of coupon stripping in Chapter 5, the price of the Treasury security is less than its theoretical price. Suppose, instead, that the Treasury security is greater than its theoretical price. In such cases, investors can purchase in the market a package of zero-coupon Treasury securities such that the cash flow of the package of securities replicates the cash flow of the mispriced coupon Treasury security. By doing so, the investor will realize a yield higher than the yield on the coupon Treasury security. This process is called **reconstitution**.

It is the process of coupon stripping and reconstituting that will prevent the actual spot rate curve observed on zero-coupon Treasuries from departing significantly from the theoretical spot rate curve. As more stripping and reconstituting occurs, forces of demand and supply will cause rates to return to their theoretical spot rate levels. This is, in fact, what has happened in the Treasury market and in other government bond markets throughout the world.

FEDERAL AGENCY SECURITIES

Federal agency securities can be classified by the type of issuer: those issued by federally related institutions and those issued by government-sponsored enterprises. Those federal agencies that provide credit for the housing market issue two types of securities: debentures and mortgage-backed securities. Our focus here is on the former securities. We discuss mortgage-backed securities in Chapters 12 and 13.

Federally Related Institutions

Federally related institutions are arms of the federal government and generally do not issue securities directly in the marketplace. Federally related institutions include the Export-Import Bank of the United States, Tennessee Valley Authority (TVA), Commodity Credit Corporation, Farmers Housing Administration, General Services Administration, Government National Mortgage Association, Maritime Administration, Private Export Funding Corporation, Rural Electrification Administration, Rural Telephone Bank, Small

Business Administration, and Washington Metropolitan Area Transit Authority. Interest income on securities issued by federally related institutions is exempt from state and local income taxes.

All federally related institutions are exempt from SEC registration. With the exception of securities of the TVA and the Private Export Funding Corporation, the securities are backed by the full faith and credit of the U.S. government. In recent years, the major issuer of these securities has been the TVA; most federally related institutions do not issue securities.

Tennessee Valley Authority

The TVA was established by Congress in 1933 primarily to provide flood control, navigation, and agricultural and industrial development. Created to promote the use of electric power in the Tennessee Valley region, the TVA is the largest public power system in the United States. The TVA primarily finances its capital requirements through internally generated funds and by issuing debt. The TVA issues a variety of debt securities in U.S. dollars and other currencies. The debt obligations issued by the TVA may be issued only to provide capital for its power program or to refund outstanding debt obligations.

TVA debt obligations are not guaranteed by the U.S. government. However, the securities are rated triple A by Moody's and Standard and Poor's. The rating is based on the TVA's status as a wholly owned corporate agency of the U.S. government and the view of the rating agencies of the TVA's financial strengths. These strengths include (1) the requirements that bondholders of power bonds are given a first pledge of payment from net power proceeds and (2) that electricity rates charged by the TVA are sufficient to ensure both the full payment of annual debt service and operating and capital costs.

There are issues targeted to individual investors (retail debt offerings) and institutional investors (nonretail offerings). For retail offerings, there are standard callable bonds (2000 Series A through Series E and 1998 Series A Estate Features), with one interesting investment feature. There is an "estate feature" that allows the bonds to be redeemed at par value plus accrued interest upon the death of the bondholder. The Putable Automatic Rate Reset Securities (PARRS) bonds (1999 Series A and 1998 Series D) are noncallable but have two interesting features. First, they have a fixed coupon rate for the first five years. Then there is an annual reset provision that provides for a reduction in the issue's coupon rate under certain conditions. Second, the bondholder has the right to put the bond at par value plus accrued interest if and when the coupon rate is reduced. More recently, the TVA has issued "electronotes." The retail bonds (as well as electronotes) just described are referred to as "power bonds." There are retail bonds that are "subordinated debt." That is, they are subordinated to the power bonds. The only outstanding issue is the 1996 Series A Quarterly Income Debt Securities (QIDS).

For institutional investors, the TVA has global bonds outstanding (e.g., 2001 Series A, 2001 Series C, 2000 Series G, 1999 Series B, 1998 Series G, 1998 Series C, 1995 Series E, and 1995 Series A) that are noncallable and issued in U.S. dollars. There are two global issues denominated in British pounds that are noncallable (1998 Series H and 2001 Series B) and a deal (1996 Series Global) initially issued in German marks, now denominated in euros. There are putable issues that may not be called (2000

Series F Put, 1997 Series C Exchange, and 1996 Series A Double Put). There is even one issue that is inflation indexed (1997 Series A Inflation-Indexed VIPS).

Government-Sponsored Enterprises[6]

Government-sponsored enterprises (GSEs) are privately owned, publicly chartered entities. They were created by Congress to reduce the cost of capital for certain borrowing sectors of the economy deemed to be important enough to warrant assistance. The entities in these sectors include farmers, homeowners, and students. The enabling legislation dealing with a GSE is reviewed periodically; GSEs issue securities directly in the marketplace. The market for these securities, while smaller than that of Treasury securities, has in recent years become an active and important sector of the bond market. GSEs are also issuers of foreign currency denominated and U.S. dollar global bonds.

Today there are five GSEs that currently issue debentures: Federal National Mortgage Association, Federal Home Loan Mortgage Corporation, Federal Agricultural Mortgage Corporation, Federal Farm Credit Bank System, and Federal Home Loan Bank System.[7] The Federal National Mortgage Association, Federal Home Loan Mortgage Corporation, and Federal Home Loan Bank are responsible for providing credit to the housing sectors. The Federal Agricultural Mortgage Corporation provides the same function for agricultural mortgage loans. The Federal Farm Credit Bank System is responsible for the credit market in the agricultural sector of the economy.

The interest earned on obligations of the Federal Home Loan Bank System and the Federal Farm Credit Bank System are exempt from state and local income taxes. In addition to the debt obligations issued by these five GSEs, there are issues outstanding by one-time GSE issuers that have been dismantled. These GSEs include the Financing Corporation, Resolution Trust Corporation, and Farm Credit Assistance Corporation.

The price quotation conventions for GSE securities will vary between types of debt. Short-term GSE **discount notes** are quoted on a yield basis, the same as that for Treasury bills explained earlier in this chapter. The most liquid GSE issues are generally quoted on two primary bases: (1) a price basis, like Treasury securities; that is, the bid and ask price quotations are expressed as a percentage of par plus fractional 32nds of a point; and (2) a spread basis, as an indicated yield spread in basis points, off a choice of proxy curves or issue. The Treasury market is the most popular bellwether proxy from which most GSE debt is quoted. The less liquid GSE securities types, such as callable debt, that contain some form of optionality, may be quoted on a yield spread basis off either Treasuries, U.S. dollar interest rate swaps curve (the interest rate swap market is described in detail in Chapter 28), or a yield curve referencing GSE debt or a particular GSE issue. Some GSE issues trade with almost the same liquidity as Treasury securities. Other issues that are supported only by a few dealers trade much like off-the-run corporate bonds.

---

[6]For a further discussion of GSEs, see Frank J. Fabozzi and George P. Kegler, "Federal Agency Securities," Frank J. Fabozzi (ed.) Chapter 9 in *The Handbook of Financial Instruments* (Hoboken, NJ: John Wiley & Sons, 2002).

[7]The Student Loan Marketing Association (nicknamed Sallie Mae) was until 2005 a GSE with the mandate to provide funds to support student loans for higher education.

In the following sections we briefly describe the five GSEs that currently issue securities and the three former GSEs that have outstanding issues.

Federal National Mortgage Association (Fannie Mae)

In the 1930s, Congress created a federally related institution, the Federal National Mortgage Association, popularly known as "Fannie Mae," which was charged with the responsibility to create a liquid secondary market for mortgages. Fannie Mae was to accomplish this objective by buying and selling mortgages. In 1968, Congress divided Fannie Mae into two entities: (1) the current Fannie Mae and (2) the Government National Mortgage Association (popularly known as "Ginnie Mae"). Ginnie Mae's function is to use the "full faith and credit of the U.S. government" to support the market for government-insured mortgages. (The mortgage-backed securities guaranteed by Ginnie Mae are discussed in Chapter 11.) While starting out as a federally related institution, today Fannie Mae is a GSE.

Fannie Mae issues **Benchmark Bills**, **Benchmark Notes**, **Benchmark Bonds**, **Callable Benchmark Notes**, **Subordinated Benchmark Notes**, **Investment Notes**, callable securities, and structured notes. Benchmark Notes and Benchmark Bonds are noncallable instruments. The minimum issue size is $4 billion for Benchmark Notes and $2 billion for Benchmark Bonds. Issued quarterly are 2-, 3-, 5-, 10-, and 30-year maturities.

In 2001 Fannie Mae began issuing subordinated securities (**Fannie Mae Subordinated Benchmark Notes**). These are unsecured subordinated obligations of Fannie Mae that rank junior in right of payment to all of Fannie Mae's existing and future obligations. The payment structure is as follows. Separately the affected corporation must defer payment of interest on all outstanding subordinated debt if certain conditions are realized. Deferral of interest is not permitted for more than five consecutive years nor beyond the maturity date. Accrual of interest is compounded at the issue's coupon rate. During any deferral period, the effected Fannie Mae may not declare or pay dividends on, redeem, purchase, or acquire its common stock or its preferred stock.

Federal Home Loan Mortgage Corporation (Freddie Mac)

In 1970 Congress created the Federal Home Loan Mortgage Corporation (Freddie Mac). The reason for the creation of Freddie Mac was to provide support for conventional mortgages. These mortgages are not guaranteed by the U.S. government.

Freddie Mac issues **Reference Bills**, discount notes, medium-term notes, **Reference Notes**, **Reference Bonds**, **Callable Reference Notes**, **Euro Reference Notes** (debt denominated in euros), and global bonds. Reference Bills and discount notes are issued with maturities of one year or less. Reference Notes and Bonds have maturities of 2 to 30 years and Callable Reference Notes have maturities of 2 to 10 years. Freddie Mac will issue and/or reopen Reference Bills, Reference Notes, 30-year Reference Bonds, and Euro Reference Notes according to a published issuance calendar and within minimum issue size guidelines. Freddie Mac Reference Notes and Reference Bonds are eligible for stripping.

Both Freddie Mac and Fannie Mae issue bullet and callable medium-term notes (MTNs) and structured notes, instruments described in Chapter 7. There are securities denominated in U.S. dollars as well as issues denominated in a wide range of foreign currencies.

In 2001, Freddie Mac also began issuing subordinated securities (called **Freddie Mac Subs**). These securities have the same feature as the Fannie Mae Subordinated Benchmark Notes.

The Federal Home Loan Bank System

The Federal Home Loan Bank System (FHLBanks) consists of the 12 district Federal Home Loan Banks and their member banks. The Federal Home Loan Bank Board was originally responsible for regulating all federally chartered savings and loan associations and savings banks, as well as state-chartered institutions insured by the Federal Savings and Loan Insurance Corporation. These responsibilities have been curtailed since 1989.

The major source of debt funding for the Federal Home Loan Banks is the issuance of **consolidated debt obligations**, which are joint and several obligations of the 12 Federal Home Loan Banks. Consolidated FHLBank discount notes with maturities from 1 to 360 days are issued daily. The FHLBanks have several programs to facilitate the issuance of certain bond types. The TAP Issue program was launched in 1999. This program aggregates FHLBank demand for six common (1.5-, 2-, 3-, 5-, 7-, and 10-year) bullet maturities, and then offers them daily through competitive auctions. These issues feature standardized terms and are re-opened via auction for three-month periods, enabling them to reach multi-billion dollar size. TAP Issues can also be reopened as they roll down the curve. Callable bonds are issued daily, primarily as customized issues for institutional investors.

The Federal Agricultural Mortgage Corporation

The Federal Agricultural Mortgage Corporation (Farmer Mac) provides a secondary market for first mortgage agricultural real estate loans. It was created by Congress in 1998 to improve the availability of mortgage credit to farmers and ranchers as well as rural homeowners, businesses, and communities. It does so by purchasing qualified loans from lenders in the same way as Freddie Mac and Fannie Mae. Farmer Mac raises funds by selling debentures and mortgage-backed securities backed by the loans purchased. The latter securities are called **agricultural mortgage-backed securities** (AMBS). The debentures that are issued include discount notes and medium-term notes.

Federal Farm Credit Bank System

The purpose of the Federal Farm Credit Bank System (FFCBS) is to facilitate adequate, dependable credit and related services to the agricultural sector of the economy. The Farm Credit Bank System consists of three entities: the Federal Land Banks, Federal Intermediate Credit Banks, and Banks for Cooperatives. Prior to 1979, each entity issued securities in its own name. Starting in 1979, they began to issue debt on a consolidated basis as "joint and several obligations" of the FFCBS. All financing for the FFCBS is arranged through the Federal Farm Credit Banks Funding Corporation (FFCBFC), which issues consolidated obligations.

The FFCBFC issues discount notes that are offered daily through posted rates. Calendar Bonds of three- and six-month maturities are offered monthly. Designated Bonds of typically two-year maturities can be offered twice monthly as either a new issue or re-opening. Unscheduled Bonds are issued throughout the month in varying sizes and structures either by competitive bidding or based on requests from institutional investors. Master Notes are issued as individually tailored daily investment agreements that are typically designed for a single investor.

Financing Corporation

The deposits of savings and loans were once insured by the Federal Savings and Loan Insurance Corporation (FSLIC), overseen by the Federal Home Loan Bank Board. When difficulties encountered in the savings and loan industry raised concerns about FSLIC's ability to meet its responsibility to insure deposits, Congress passed the Competitive Equality and Banking Act in 1987. This legislation included provisions to recapitalize FSLIC and establish a new government-sponsored agency, the Financing Corporation (FICO), to issue debt in order to provide funding for FICO. FICO issued its first bonds in September 1987 — a 30-year non-callable $500 million issue. The principal of these bonds is backed by zero-coupon Treasury securities. The legislation permitted FICO to issue up to $10.825 billion but not more than $3.75 billion in any one year. FICO was legislated to be dismantled in 2026, or after all securities have matured, whichever comes sooner.

Resolution Trust Corporation

The 1987 legislation that created FICO did not go far enough to resolve the problems facing the beleaguered savings and loan industry. In 1989, Congress passed more comprehensive legislation, the Financial Institutions Reform, Recovery and Enforcement Act (FIRREA). This legislation had three key elements. First, it transferred supervision of savings and loans to a newly created Office of Thrift Supervision. Second, it shifted the FSLIC insurance function to a Savings Association Insurance Fund, placed under the supervision of the Federal Deposit Insurance Corporation. Third, it established the Resolution Trust Corporation (RTC) as a GSE charged with the responsibility of liquidating or bailing out insolvent savings and loan institutions. The RTC obtained its funding from the Resolution Funding Corporation (REFCORP), which was authorized to issue up to $40 billion of long-term bonds. The principal of this debt is backed by zero-coupon Treasury bonds. REFCORP has issued both 30-year and 40-year bonds.

Farm Credit Financial Assistance Corporation

In the 1980s, the FFCBS faced financial difficulties because of defaults on loans made to farmers. The defaults were caused largely by high interest rates in the late 1970s and early 1980s and by depressed prices on agricultural products. To recapitalize the Federal Farm Credit Bank System, Congress created the Farm Credit Financial Assistance Corporation (FACO) in 1987. This federally sponsored agency was authorized to issue debt to assist the FFCBS. FACO bonds, unlike the debt of other GSEs, are backed by the Treasury.

GSE Credit Risk

With the exception of the securities issued by the Farm Credit Financial Assistance Corporation, GSE securities are not backed by the full faith and credit of the U.S. government, as is the case with Treasury securities. Consequently, investors purchasing

GSEs are exposed to credit risk. The yield spread between these securities and Treasury securities of comparable maturity reflects differences in perceived credit risk and liquidity. The spread attributable to credit risk reflects any financial difficulty faced by the issuing GSEs and the likelihood that the federal government will allow the GSE to default on its outstanding obligations.

SUMMARY

The U.S. Treasury market is closely watched by all participants in the financial markets because interest rates on Treasury securities are the benchmark interest rates throughout the world. The Treasury issues three types of securities: bills, notes, and bonds. Treasury bills have a maturity of one year or less, are sold at a discount from par, and do not make periodic interest payments. Treasury notes and bonds are coupon securities. The Treasury issues coupon securities with a fixed principal and an inflation-protected principal. The coupon payment for the latter is tied to the Consumer Price Index and the securities are popularly referred to as Treasury Inflation Protection Securities, or TIPS.

Treasury securities are issued on a competitive bid auction basis, according to a regular auction cycle. The auction process relies on the participation of the primary government securities dealers, with which the Federal Reserve deals directly. The secondary market for Treasury securities is an over-the-counter market, where dealers trade with the general investing public and with other dealers. In the secondary market, Treasury bills are quoted on a bank discount basis; Treasury coupon securities are quoted on a price basis.

Although the Treasury does not issue zero-coupon Treasury securities, government dealers have created these instruments synthetically by a process called coupon stripping. Zero-coupon Treasury securities include trademarks and STRIPS. Creation of trademark zero-coupon Treasury securities has ceased; STRIPS now dominate the market and are simply referred to as Treasury strips. The motivation for government dealers to create these securities is the arbitrage opportunities available.

Government-sponsored enterprises securities and federally related institution securities constitute the federal agency securities market. The former are privately owned, publicly chartered entities created to reduce the cost of borrowing for certain sectors of the economy. The two major GSEs that have issued debentures are Fannie Mae and Freddie Mac. Federally related institutions are arms of the federal government whose debt is generally guaranteed by the U.S. government. The only issuer of federally related institution securities is the Tennessee Valley Authority. The securities of this federal agency are not guaranteed by the U.S. government.

Questions

1. What are the differences among a Treasury bill, a Treasury note, and a Treasury bond?
2. The following questions are about Treasury Inflation Protected Securities (TIPS).
   a. What is meant by the "real rate"?
   b. What is meant by the "inflation-adjusted principal"?
   c. Suppose that the coupon rate for a TIPS is 3%. Suppose further that an investor purchases $10,000 of par value (initial principal) of this issue today

and that the semiannual inflation rate is 1%.

1. What is the dollar coupon interest that will be paid in cash at the end of the first six months?
2. What is the inflation-adjusted principal at the end of six months?

d. Suppose that an investor buys a five-year TIPS and there is deflation for the entire period. What is the principal that will be paid by the Department of the Treasury at the maturity date?

e. What is the purpose of the daily index ratio?

f. How is interest income on TIPS treated at the federal income tax level?

3. What is the when-issued market?

4. Why do government dealers use government brokers?

5. Suppose that the price of a Treasury bill with 90 days to maturity and a $1 million face value is $980,000. What is the yield on a bank discount basis?

6. The bid and ask yields for a Treasury bill were quoted by a dealer as 5.91% and 5.89%, respectively. Shouldn't the bid yield be less than the ask yield, because the bid yield indicates how much the dealer is willing to pay and the ask yield is what the dealer is willing to sell the Treasury bill for?

7. Assuming a $100,000 par value, calculate the dollar price for the following Treasury coupon securities given the quoted price:
   a. 84.14
   b. 84.14+
   c. 103.284
   d. 105.059

8. In a Treasury auction what is meant by:
   a. a noncompetitive bidder?
   b. the high yield?
   c. the bid-to-cover ratio?

9. In a Treasury auction, how is the price that a competitive bidder must pay determined in a single-price auction format?

10. In a Treasury auction, how is the price that a noncompetitive bidder must pay determined in a single-price auction format?

11. Suppose that a Treasury coupon security is purchased on April 8 and that the last coupon payment was on February 15. Assume that the year in which this security is purchased is not a leap year.
    a. How many days are in the accrued interest period?
    b. If the coupon rate for this Treasury security is 7% and the par value of the issue purchased is $1 million, what is the accrued interest?

12. a. What is meant by coupon stripping in the Treasury market?
    b. What is created as a result of coupon stripping in the Treasury market?

13. Why is a stripped Treasury security identified by whether it is created from the coupon or the principal?

14. What is the federal income tax treatment of accrued interest income on stripped Treasury securities?

15. What is the difference between a government-sponsored enterprise and a federally related institution?

16. Explain whether you agree or disagree with the following statement: "The securities issued by all federally related institutions are guaranteed by the full faith and credit of the U.S. government."

17. What are the major securities issued by Fannie Mae and Freddie Mac?

CHAPTER

7

CORPORATE DEBT INSTRUMENTS

After reading this chapter you will understand:

- the key provisions of a corporate bond issue

- provisions for paying off a bond issue prior to the stated maturity date

- corporate bond ratings and what investment-grade bonds and noninvestment-grade (or high-yield) bonds are

- event risk

- bond structures that have been used in the high-yield bond market

- empirical evidence concerning the historical risk and return pattern in the corporate bond market

- what a recovery rating is

- the secondary market for corporate bonds

- the private-placement market for corporate bonds

- a medium-term note

- the difference between the primary offering of a medium-term note and a corporate bond

- what a structured medium-term note is and the flexibility it affords issuers

- what commercial paper is and why it is issued

- the credit ratings of commercial paper

- the difference between directly placed and dealer-placed commercial paper

- the basic provisions in the Bankruptcy Reform Act of 1978 and its amendments

- the difference between a liquidation and a reorganization

- the principle of absolute priority in a bankruptcy and the different hypotheses as to why there is a violation of absolute priority

Corporate debt instruments are financial obligations of a corporation that have priority over its common stock and preferred stock in the case of bankruptcy. Corporate debt instruments can be classified as follows: (1) corporate bonds, (2) medium-term notes, (3) commercial paper, and (4) asset-backed securities. In this chapter we discuss these instruments. We postpone the discussion of convertible corporate bonds to Chapter 19 and asset-backed securities until Chapter 14.

CORPORATE BONDS

Corporate bonds are classified by the type of issuer. The four general classifications are (1) public utilities, (2) transportations, (3) banks/finance, and (4) industrials.[1] Finer breakdowns are often made to create more homogeneous groupings. For example, public utilities are subdivided into electric power companies, gas distribution companies, water companies, and communication companies. Transportations are divided further into airlines, railroads, and trucking companies. Banks/finance include both money center banks and regional banks, savings and loans, brokerage firms, insurance companies, and finance companies. Industrials are the catchall class and the most heterogeneous of the groupings with respect to investment characteristics. Industrials include manufacturers, mining companies, merchandising, retailers, energy companies, and service-related industries.

At one time, in the bond market indexes that will be discussed in Chapter 23, there was a corporate bond sector. Today, corporate bonds are included in the credit sector of the major bond indexes such as the Lehman Brothers U.S. Aggregate Bond Index. Within the credit sector, corporate bonds are categorized into industrial, utility, and finance subsectors.

Features of a Corporate Bond Issue

The essential features of a corporate bond are relatively simple. The corporate issuer promises to pay a specified percentage of par value on designated dates (the coupon payments) and to repay par or principal value of the bond at maturity. Failure to pay either the principal or interest when due constitutes legal default, and investors can go to court to enforce the contract. Bondholders, as creditors, have a prior legal claim over common and preferred stockholders as to both income and assets of the corporation for the principal and interest due them.

The promises of corporate bond issuers and the rights of investors who buy them are set forth in great detail in contracts called **bond indentures**. The covenants or restrictions on management are important in the analysis of the credit risk of a corporate issue. Covenants are described in Chapter 20. If bondholders were handed the complete indenture, they would have trouble understanding the language and even greater difficulty in determining from time to time whether the corporate issuer were keeping all the promises made. These problems are solved for the most part by

---

[1]Traditionally, the Yankee and Canadian bonds are considered part of the corporate bond market. These issues include dollar-denominated bonds issued in the United States by sovereign governments, local governments, and non-U.S. corporations.

bringing in a corporate trustee as a third party to the contract. The indenture is made out to the corporate trustee as a representative of the interests of bondholders; that is, a trustee acts in a fiduciary capacity for investors who own the bond issue. A corporate trustee is a bond or trust company with a corporate trust department whose officers are experts in performing the functions of a trustee.

Most corporate bonds are **term bonds**; that is, they run for a term of years, then become due and payable. Any amount of the liability that has not been paid off prior to maturity must be paid off at that time. The term may be long or short. Generally, obligations due in under 10 years from the date of issue are called **notes**. (However, the word *notes* has been used to describe particular types of securities that can have maturities considerably longer than 10 years.) Most corporate borrowings take the form of **bonds** due in 20 to 30 years. Term bonds may be retired by payment at final maturity or retired prior to maturity if provided for in the indenture. Some corporate bond issues are arranged so that specified principal amounts become due on specified dates. Such issues are called **serial bonds**. Equipment trust certificates (discussed later) are structured as serial bonds.

Security for Bonds

Either real property (using a mortgage) or personal property may be pledged to offer security beyond the issuer's general credit standing. A mortgage bond grants the bondholders a lien against the pledged assets; that is, a legal right to sell the mortgaged property to satisfy unpaid obligations to the bondholders. In practice, foreclosure and sale of mortgaged property is unusual. Usually in the case of default, a financial reorganization of the issuer provides for settlement of the debt to bondholders. The mortgage lien is important, though, because it gives the mortgage bondholders a strong bargaining position relative to other creditors in determining the terms of any reorganization.

Some companies do not own fixed assets or other real property and so have nothing on which they can give a mortgage lien to secure bondholders. Instead, they own securities of other companies; they are holding companies, and the other companies are subsidiaries. To satisfy the desire of bondholders for security, they will pledge stocks, notes, bonds or whatever other kind of obligations they own. These assets are termed **collateral** (or personal property); bonds secured by such assets are called **collateral trust bonds**.

Many years ago the railway companies developed a way of financing purchase of cars and locomotives (**rolling stock**) in a way that enabled them to borrow at just about the lowest rates in the corporate bond market. Railway rolling stock has for a long time been seen as excellent security for debt. The equipment is sufficiently standardized that it can be used by one railroad as well as another. It can be readily moved from the tracks of one railroad to another's, and there is generally a good market for lease or sale of cars and locomotives. The railroads have taken advantage of these characteristics of rolling stock by developing a legal arrangement for giving investors a legal claim on it that is different from, and generally superior to, a mortgage lien. The legal arrangement vests legal title to railway equipment in a trustee.

The procedure works like this. A railway company orders some cars and locomotives from a manufacturer. The manufacturer then transfers legal title to the equipment to a trustee, who in turn leases it to the railroad, and at the same time sells equipment trust certificates to obtain the funds to pay the manufacturer. The trustee collects lease payments from the railroad and uses the money to pay interest and principal on the certificates. The principal is therefore paid off on specified dates. Although the railway companies developed the equipment trust arrangement, it has been used since by companies engaged in providing other kinds of transportation. For example, trucking companies finance the purchase of huge fleets of trucks in the same manner; airlines use this kind of financing to purchase transport planes; and international oil companies use it to buy huge tankers.

Debenture bonds are debt securities not secured by a specific pledge of property, but that does not mean that they have no claim on property of issuers or on their earnings. Debenture bondholders have the claim of general creditors on all assets of the issuer not pledged specifically to secure other debt—and they have a claim on pledged assets even to the extent that these assets have more value than necessary to satisfy secured creditors. Subordinated debenture bonds rank after secured debt, after debenture bonds, and often after some general creditors in their claim on assets and earnings.

The type of security issued determines the cost to the corporation. For a given corporation, mortgage bonds will cost less than debenture bonds, and debenture bonds will cost less than subordinated debenture bonds.

Guaranteed bonds are obligations guaranteed by another entity. The safety of a guaranteed bond depends upon the guarantor's financial capability as well as the financial capability of the issuer. The terms of the guarantee may call for the guarantor to guarantee the payment of interest and/or repayment of the principal.

It is important to recognize that the superior legal status of any debt security will not prevent bondholders from suffering financial loss when the issuer's ability to generate cash flow adequate to pay its obligations is seriously eroded.

Provisions for Paying Off Bonds

Most corporate issues have a call provision allowing the issuer an option to buy back all or part of the issue prior to the stated maturity date. Some issues specify that the issuer must retire a predetermined amount of the issue periodically. Various types of corporate call provisions are discussed in the following sections.[2]

(1) Call and refund provisions   An important question in negotiating the terms of a new bond issue is whether the issuer shall have the right to redeem the entire amount of bonds outstanding on a date before maturity. Issuers generally want this right because they recognize that at some time in the future the general level of interest rates may fall sufficiently below the issue's coupon rate that redeeming the issue and replacing it with another issue with a lower coupon rate would be attractive. This right is a disadvantage to the bondholder.

A company wanting to retire a debt issue prior to maturity usually must pay a premium over the par value for the privilege. The initial call premium on long-term debt traditionally has been the interest coupon plus par or the initial reoffering price (in some cases it is the higher of the two). Thus, a 30-year bond initially priced at 100 with a 10% coupon may have a call price of 110% for the first year, scaled down in relatively equal amounts to par starting in year 21 to maturity.

---

[2]For a more detailed explanation of corporate call provisions, see Richard S. Wilson and Frank J. Fabozzi, *Corporate Bonds: Structures and Analysis* (Buckingham, PA: Frank J. Fabozzi Associates, 1995).

Instead of a specified fixed premium that must be paid by the issuer if the bond is called, a bond may have a **make-whole premium provision**, also called a **yield-maintenance premium provision**. The provision specifies a formula for determining the premium that the issuer must pay to call an issue and is such that the amount of the premium, when added to the principal amount and reinvested at the redemption date in U.S. Treasury securities having the same remaining life, would provide a yield equal to the original yield. The premium plus the principal at which the issue is called is referred to as the **make-whole redemption price**. The purpose of the make-whole premium is to protect the yield of those investors who purchased the issue at issuance.

Anheuser-Busch Companies, Inc., offered $200 million of 10% debentures in mid-1988 at 100% of par; the maturity is July 1, 2018. Exhibit 7-1 shows the redemption

---

EXHIBIT 7-1 Redemption Schedule for Anheuser-Busch Companies, Inc., 10% Sinking Fund Debentures Due July 1, 2018

The Debentures will be redeemable at the option of the Company at any time in whole or in part, upon not fewer than 30 nor more than 60 days' notice, at the following redemption prices (which are expressed in percentages of principal amount) in each case together with accrued interest to the date fixed for redemption:

If redeemed during the 12 months beginning July 1,

Redemption	
1988	110.0%
1989	109.5%
1990	109.0%
1991	108.5%
1992	108.0%
1993	107.5%
1994	107.0%
1995	106.5%
1996	106.0%
1997	105.5%
1998	105.0%
1999	104.5%
2000	104.0%
2001	103.5%
2002	103.0%
2003	102.5%
2004	102.0%
2005	101.5%
2006	101.0%
2007	100.5%
2008 and thereafter	100.0%

Provided, however, that prior to July 1, 1998, the Company may not redeem any of the Debentures pursuant to such option, directly or indirectly, from or in anticipation of the proceeds of the issuance of any indebtedness for money borrowed having an interest cost of less than 10% per annum.

Source: Prospectus dated June 23, 1988.

schedule for the bonds. Note that the initial call price is equal to the coupon plus the reoffering price. Subsequent redemption prices are in decrements of 50 basis points (0.5 of 1%) to par starting July 1, 2008. (Note that the entire issue was called at 106.50 effective May 2, 1996.) Some issues only show the call premium, such as 8.583%, 8.154%, or 7.725%, instead of the whole price.

The prices shown in Exhibit 7-1 are called the **regular** or **general redemption prices**. There are also **special redemption prices** for debt redeemed through the sinking fund (discussed next) and through other provisions, and the proceeds from the confiscation of property through the right of eminent domain. The special redemption price is usually par, but in the case of some utility issues it initially may be the public offering price, which is amortized down to par (if a premium) over the life of the bonds.

At the time of issuance, the Anheuser-Busch debentures were currently callable; that is, the company could redeem the bonds at any time at the general redemption prices cited previously subject only to the 10-year prohibition against lower-cost refunding. Other issues may not be called for any reason for a certain number of years.

If a debt does not have any protection against early call, it is said to be a currently callable issue, as is the Anheuser issue. But most new bond issues, even if currently callable, usually have some restrictions against certain types of early redemption. The most common restriction is that prohibiting the refunding of the bonds for a certain number of years. Bonds that are noncallable for the issue's life are more common than bonds that are nonrefundable for life but otherwise callable.

Many investors are confused by the terms **noncallable** and **nonrefundable**. Hess and Winn said: "The terms **noncallable** and **nonrefundable** are often used rather loosely as interchangeable entities, although from a technical standpoint they have different meanings."[3] Call protection is much more absolute than refunding protection. Although there may be certain exceptions to absolute or complete call protection in some cases (such as sinking funds and the redemption of debt under certain mandatory provisions), it still provides greater assurance against premature and unwanted redemption than does refunding protection. Refunding prohibition merely prevents redemption only from certain sources, namely the proceeds of other debt issues sold at a lower cost of money. The holder is protected only if interest rates decline, and the borrower can obtain lower-cost money to pay off the debt. The Anheuser bonds cannot be redeemed prior to July 2, 1998, if the company raises the funds from a new issue with an interest cost lower than 10%. There is nothing to prevent the company from calling the bonds within the 10-year refunding protected period from debt sold at a higher rate (although it normally wouldn't do so) or from funds obtained through other means.

Refunding means to replace an old bond issue with a new one, often at a lower interest cost. In the *Florida Power & Light* case the judge said:

> The terms *redemption* and *refunding* are not synonymous. A *redemption* is simply a call of bonds. A *refunding* occurs when the issuer sells bonds in order to use the proceeds to redeem an earlier series of bonds. The refunding bond issue being sold is closely linked to the one being redeemed by contractual language and proximity in time so that the proceeds will be available to pay

---

[3] Arleigh P. Hess, Jr., and Willis J. Winn, *The Value of the Call Privilege* (Philadelphia: University of Pennsylvania, 1962), p. 24.

for the redemption. Otherwise, the issuer would be taking an inordinate risk that market conditions would change between the redemption of the earlier issue and the sale of the later issue.[4]

Beginning in early 1986 a number of industrial companies issued long-term debt with extended call protection, not refunding protection. A number are noncallable for the issue's life. For such issues the prospectus expressly prohibits redemption prior to maturity. These noncallable-for-life issues are referred to as **bullet bonds**. Other issues carry 15 years of call protection, such as Eastman Kodak's 9.95% debentures due July 1, 2018, and not callable prior to July 1, 2003. However, this does not prevent the issuer from offering to repurchase the issue via a tender offer. In fact, out of the original $125 million of the Eastman Kodak issue, only about $3 million remained outstanding as of September 2005. The majority of the issue was retired via a fixed spread tender offer in October 1994.

Bonds can be called in whole (the entire issue) or in part (only a portion). When less than the entire issue is called, the specific bonds to be called are selected randomly or on a pro rata basis. When bonds are selected randomly, the serial number of the certificates is published in the *Wall Street Journal* and major metropolitan dailies.

(2) Sinking fund provision   Corporate bond indentures may require the issuer to retire a specified portion of an issue each year. This is referred to as a **sinking fund requirement**. This kind of provision for repayment of corporate debt may be designed to liquidate all of a bond issue by the maturity date, or it may be arranged to pay only a part of the total by the end of the term. If only a part is paid, the remainder is called a **balloon maturity**. The purpose of the sinking fund provision is to reduce credit risk.

Generally, the issuer may satisfy the sinking fund requirement by either (1) making a cash payment of the face amount of the bonds to be retired to the corporate trustee, who then calls the bonds for redemption using a lottery, or (2) delivering to the trustee bonds purchased in the open market that have a total face value equal to the amount that must be retired. If the bonds are retired using the first method, interest payments stop at the redemption date.

Usually, the periodic payments required for sinking fund purposes will be the same for each period. A few indentures might permit variable periodic payments, where payments change according to certain prescribed conditions set forth in the indenture. Many corporate bond indentures include a provision that grants the issuer the option to retire more than the amount stipulated for sinking fund retirement. This is referred to as an **accelerated sinking fund provision**.

Usually, the sinking fund call price is the par value if the bonds were originally sold at par. When issued at a price in excess of par, the call price generally starts at the issuance price and scales down to par as the issue approaches maturity.

Accrued Interest

As explained in Chapter 2, in addition to the agreed-upon price, the buyer must pay the seller accrued interest. Market convention for determining the number of days in a corporate bond coupon period and the number of days from the last coupon payment

[4]*Lucas et al. v. Florida Power & Light Company*, Final Judgment, paragraph 77.

to settlement date differs from that for a Treasury coupon security. Whereas a calendar year has 365 days (366 days in the case of a leap year), corporate bond interest is computed as if the year were 360 days. Each month in a corporate bond year is 30 days, whether it is February, April, or August. A 12% coupon corporate bond pays $120 per year per $1,000 par value, accruing interest at $10 per month or $0.33333 per day. The accrued interest on a 12% corporate bond for three months is $30; for three months and 25 days, $38.33, and so on. The corporate calendar is referred to as "30/360."

Corporate Bond Ratings

Professional money managers use various techniques to analyze information on companies and bond issues in order to estimate the ability of the issuer to live up to its future contractual obligations.[5] This activity is known as **credit analysis** and is the subject of Chapter 20.

Some large institutional investors and many investment banking firms have their own credit analysis departments. Few individual investors and institutional bond investors, though, do their own analysis. Instead, they rely primarily on nationally recognized rating companies that perform credit analysis and issue their conclusions in the form of ratings. The three commercial rating companies are (1) Moody's Investors Service, (2) Standard & Poor's Corporation, and (3) FitchRatings. The rating systems use similar symbols, as shown in Exhibit 7-2. The factors considered by rating agencies in assigning a credit rating are discussed in Chapter 20.

In all three systems, the term **high grade** means low credit risk, or conversely, high probability of future payments. The highest-grade bonds are designated by Moody's by the letters Aaa, and by the other two agencies by AAA. The next highest grade is Aa or AA; for the third grade all rating agencies use A. The next three grades are Baa or BBB, Ba or BB, and B, respectively. There are also C grades. Standard & Poor's and Fitch use plus or minus signs to provide a narrower credit quality breakdown within each class, and Moody's uses 1, 2, or 3 for the same purpose. Bonds rated triple A (AAA or Aaa) are said to be **prime**; double A (AA or Aa) are of **high quality**; single A issues are called **upper medium grade**, and triple B are **medium grade**. Lower-rated bonds are said to have speculative elements or to be distinctly speculative.

Bond issues that are assigned a rating in the top four categories are referred to as **investment-grade bonds**. Issues that carry a rating below the top four categories are referred to as **noninvestment-grade bonds**, or more popularly as **high-yield bonds** or **junk bonds**. Thus, the corporate bond market can be divided into two sectors: the investment-grade and noninvestment-grade markets.

Rating agencies monitor the bonds and issuers that they have rated. A rating agency may announce that it is reviewing a particular credit rating, and may go further and state that the outcome of the review may result in a downgrade (i.e., a lower credit rating being assigned) or upgrade (i.e., a higher credit rating being assigned). When this announcement is made by a rating agency, the issue or issuer is said to be under credit watch.

The rating agencies accumulate statistics on how ratings change over various periods of time. A table that specifies this information is called a **rating transition matrix**.

---

[5]For an in-depth discussion of credit analysis, see Jane Tripp Howe, "Credit Analysis for Corporate Bonds," Chapter 15 in Frank J. Fabozzi (ed.), *The Handbook of Corporate Debt Instruments* (New Hope, PA: Frank J. Fabozzi Associates, 1998).

| EXHIBIT 7-2 | Summary of Corporate Bond Ratings Systems and Symbols | | |

Moody's	S&P	Fitch	Brief Definition
Investment Grade: High Credit Worthiness			
Aaa	AAA	AAA	Gilt edge, prime, maximum safety
Aa1	AA+	AA+	
Aa2	AA	AA	Very high grade, high quality
Aa3	AA–	AA–	
A1	A+	A+	
A2	A	A	Upper medium grade
A3	A–	A–	
Baa1	BBB+	BBB+	
Baa2	BBB	BBB	Lower medium grade
Baa3	BBB2	BBB2	
Distinctly Speculative: Low Creditworthiness			
Ba1	BB+	BB+	
Ba2	BB	BB	Low grade, speculative
Ba3	BB–	BB–	
B1	B+	B+	
B2	B	B	Highly speculative
B3	B–	B–2	
Predominantly Speculative: Substantial Risk or in Default			
	CCC+		
Caa	CCC	CCC	Substantial risk, in poor standing
	CCC–		
Ca	CC	CC	May be in default, extremely speculative
C	C	C	Even more speculative than those above
	CI		CI = Income bonds; no interest is being paid
		DDD	Default
		DD	
	D	D	

Exhibit 7-3 shows a hypothetical one-year rating transition matrix. Here is how to interpret the table. The rows indicate the rating at the beginning of a year. The columns show the rating at the end of the year. For example, look at the second row. This row shows the transition for Aa-rated bonds at the beginning of a year. The number 91.40 in the second row means that on average 91.40% of Aa-rated bonds at the beginning of the year remained Aa rated at year end. The value 1.50 means that on average 1.50% of Aa-rated bonds at the beginning of the year were upgraded to Aaa. The value 0.50 means that on average 0.50% of Aa-rated bonds at the beginning of the year were downgraded to a Baa rating. From Exhibit 7-3 it can be seen that the probability of a

| EXHIBIT 7-3   Hypothetical One-Year Rating Transition Matrix | | | | | | | | |

Rating at Start of Year	Rating at End of Year							
	Aaa	Aa	A	Baa	Ba	B	C or D	Total
Aaa	91.00	8.30	0.70	0.00	0.00	0.00	0.00	100.00
Aa	1.50	91.40	6.60	0.50	0.20	0.00	0.00	100.00
A	0.10	3.00	91.20	5.10	0.40	0.20	0.00	100.00
Baa	0.00	0.20	5.80	88.00	5.00	0.90	0.10	100.00

downgrade is much higher than an upgrade for investment grade bonds. That attribute is actually observed in rating transition matrices reported by rating agencies.

Default Rates

Exhibit 7-4 provides information about defaults or restructuring under distressed conditions from 1978 through the first half of 2005 for high-yield bonds in the United States and Canada. The information shown in the first three columns is the par value outstanding for the year, the amount defaulted, and the default rate. (We will discuss the other columns later in this chapter.) The annual default rate reported in the exhibit is measured by the par value of the high-yield corporate bonds that have defaulted in a given calendar year divided by the total par value outstanding of high-yield corporate bonds during the year. The weighted average default rate for the period 1978–2004 was 4.86%.

Event Risk

In Chapter 5 we described various types of risk. Occasionally, the ability of an issuer to make interest and principal payments changes seriously and unexpectedly because of (1) a natural or industrial accident or some regulatory change, or (2) a takeover or corporate restructuring. These risks are referred to generically as **event risk**. Examples of the first type of event risk would be a change in the accounting treatment of loan losses for commercial banks or cancellation of nuclear plants by public utilities.

A good example of the second type of event risk is the 1988 takeover of RJR Nabisco for $25 billion through a financing technique known as a **leveraged buyout** (LBO). The new company took on a substantial amount of debt incurred to finance the acquisition of the firm.[6] In the case of RJR Nabisco, the debt and equity after the leveraged buyout were $29.9 and $1.2 billion, respectively. Because the corporation must service a larger amount of debt, its bond quality rating was reduced; RJR Nabisco's quality rating as assigned by Moody's dropped from A1 to B3. To see how much more investors demanded because of the company's new capital structure with a greater proportion of debt, look at panel a of Exhibit 7-5. The exhibit shows the impact of the initial LBO bid announcement on yield spreads for RJR Nabisco's debt. The yield spread to a benchmark Treasury increased from about 100 basis points to 350 basis points.

---

[6]For a discussion of event risk associated with takeovers, see N. R. Vijayarghavan and Randy Snook, "Takeover Event Risk and Corporate Bond Portfolio Management," in Frank J. Fabozzi (ed.), *Advances and Innovations in Bond and Mortgage Markets* (Chicago: Probus Publishing, 1989).

| EXHIBIT 7-4 | Default Rates and Losses,[a] 1978–First Half of 2005 | | | | | |

Year	Par Value Outstanding ($) Millions	Par Value of Default ($) Millions	Default Rate (%)	Weighted Price After Default	Weighted Coupon (%)	Default Loss (%)
2005(H1)	$ 939,300	3,551	0.38%	$ 49.7	10.38%	0.21%[b]
2004	933,100	11,657	1.25	57.7	10.30	0.59[b]
2003	825,000	38,451	4.66	45.5	9.55	2.76[b]
2002	757,000	96,858	12.79	25.3	9.37	10.15[b]
2001	649,000	63,609	9.80	25.5	9.18	7.76
2000	597,200	30,295	5.07	26.4	8.54	3.95
1999	567,400	23,532	4.15	27.9	10.55	3.21
1998	465,500	7,464	1.60	35.9	9.46	1.10
1997	335,400	4,200	1.25	54.2	11.87	0.65
1996	271,000	3,336	1.23	51.9	8.92	0.65
1995	240,000	4,551	1.90	40.6	11.83	1.24
1994	235,000	3,418	1.45	39.4	10.25	0.96
1993	206,907	2,287	1.11	56.6	12.98	0.56
1992	163,000	5,545	8.40	50.1	12.32	1.91
1991	183,600	18,862	10.27	36.0	11.59	7.16
1990	181,000	18,354	10.14	23.4	12.94	8.42
1989	189,258	8,110	4.29	38.3	13.40	2.93
1988	148,187	3,944	2.66	43.6	11.91	1.66
1987	129,657	7,486	5.78	75.9	12.07	1.74
1986	90,243	3,156	3.50	34.5	10.61	2.48
1985	58,088	992	1.71	45.9	13.69	1.04
1984	40,939	344	0.84	48.6	12.23	0.48
1983	27,492	301	1.09	55.7	10.11	0.54
1982	18,109	577	3.19	38.6	9.61	2.11
1981	17,115	27	0.16	72.0	15.75	0.15
1980	14,935	224	1.50	21.1	8.43	1.25
1979	10,356	20	0.19	31.0	10.63	0.14
1978	8,946	119	1.33	60.0	8.38	0.59
Arithmetic Average, 1978–2004			**3.57%**	**$43.02**	**10.98%**	**2.45%**
Weighted Average, 1978–2004			**4.86%**			**3.51%**

[a]Excludes defaulted issues.
[b]Default loss rate adjusted for fallen angels is 9.3% in 2002, 1.82% in 2003, 0.59% in 2004, and 0.21% in 1H 2005.

Source: Figure 7 in Edward I. Altman with Brent Pasternack and William Stonberg, "High Yield Bond and Distressed Debt Default and Returns: First-Half 2005 Update," New York University Salomon Center, Leonard N. Stern School of Business.

EXHIBIT 7-5   Illustration of Event Risk

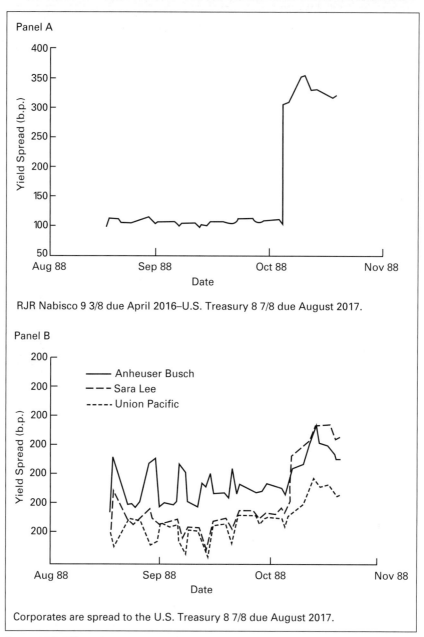

RJR Nabisco 9 3/8 due April 2016–U.S. Treasury 8 7/8 due August 2017.

Corporates are spread to the U.S. Treasury 8 7/8 due August 2017.

Source: N. R. Vijayarghavan and Randy Snook, "Takeover Event Risk and Corporate Bond Portfolio Management," in Frank J. Fabozzi (ed.), *Advances and Innovations in Bond and Mortgage Markets* (Chicago: Probus Publishing, 1989), p. 56.

Event risk can have spillover effects on other firms. A nuclear accident, for example, will affect all utilities producing nuclear power. And in the case of takeovers, consider once again the RJR Nabisco LBO. An LBO of $25 billion was considered impractical prior to the RJR Nabisco LBO, but the RJR transaction showed that size was not an obstacle, and other large firms previously thought to be unlikely candidates for an LBO became fair game. To see the spillover effect, look at panel b of Exhibit 7-5, which shows how event risk fears caused yield spreads to widen for three large firms.

High-Yield Corporate Bond Sector

As we have noted, high-yield bonds, commonly called junk bonds, are issues with quality ratings below triple B. Bond issues in this sector of the market may have been rated investment grade at the time of issuance and have been downgraded subsequently to noninvestment grade, or they may have been rated noninvestment grade at the time of issuance, called **original-issue high-yield bonds**. Bonds that have been downgraded fall into two groups: (1) issues that have been downgraded because the issuer voluntarily significantly increased their debt as a result of a leveraged buyout or a recapitalization, and (2) issues that have been downgraded for other reasons. The latter issues are commonly referred to as "fallen angels."

In the early years of the high-yield market, all the issues had a conventional structure; that is, the issues paid a fixed coupon rate and were term bonds. Today, however, there are more complex bond structures in the high-yield corporate bond sector, particularly for bonds issued for LBO financing and recapitalizations producing higher debt. The structures we describe next have features that are more attractive to issuers. In an LBO or a recapitalization, the heavy interest payment burden that the corporation assumes places severe cash flow constraints on the firm. To reduce this burden, firms involved in LBOs and recapitalizations have issued bonds with **deferred coupon structures** that permit the issuer to avoid using cash to make interest payments for a period of three to seven years. There are three types of deferred coupon structures: (1) deferred-interest bonds, (2) step-up bonds, and (3) payment-in-kind bonds.

Deferred-interest bonds are the most common type of deferred coupon structure. These bonds sell at a deep discount and do not pay interest for an initial period, typically from three to seven years. (Because no interest is paid for the initial period, these bonds are sometimes referred to as zero-coupon bonds.) **Step-up bonds** do pay coupon interest, but the coupon rate is low for an initial period and then increases ("steps up") to a higher coupon rate. Finally, **payment-in-kind (PIK) bonds** give the issuer an option to pay cash at a coupon payment date or give the bondholder a similar bond (i.e., a bond with the same coupon rate and a par value equal to the amount of the coupon payment that would have been paid). The period during which the issuer can make this choice varies from 5 to 10 years.

In late 1987, a junk bond came to market with a structure allowing the issuer to reset the coupon rate so that the bond will trade at a predetermined price.[7] The coupon rate may reset annually or even more frequently, or reset only one time over the life of the bond. Generally, the coupon rate at reset time will be the average of rates suggested by two investment banking firms. The new rate will then reflect (1) the level

---

[7]Most of the bonds have a coupon reset formula that requires the issuer to reset the coupon so that the bond will trade at a price of $101.

of interest rates at the reset date, and (2) the credit spread the market wants on the issue at the reset date. This structure is called an **extendable reset**.

Notice the difference between an extendable reset bond and a floating-rate issue as described earlier. In a floating-rate issue, the coupon rate resets according to a fixed spread over some benchmark, with the spread specified in the indenture. The amount of the spread reflects market conditions at the time the issue is offered. The coupon rate on an extendable reset bond by contrast is reset based on market conditions (as suggested by several investment banking firms) at the time of the reset date. Moreover, the new coupon rate reflects the new level of interest rates and the new spread that investors seek.

The advantage to issuers of extendable reset bonds is again that they can be assured of a long-term source of funds based on short-term rates. For investors, the advantage of these bonds is that the coupon rate will reset to the market rate—both the level of interest rates and the credit spread, in principle keeping the issue at par. In fact, experience with reset bonds has not been favorable during the recent period of difficulties in the high-yield bond market. The sudden substantial increase in default risk has meant that the rise in the rate needed to keep the issue at par was so large that it would have insured the bankruptcy of the firm. As a result, the rise in the coupon rate has been insufficient to keep the issue at the stipulated price.

Performance of High-Yield Bonds

There have been several studies of the risk and return in the high-yield bond market. Historically, the promised yields offered on high-yield bonds have been substantial. The last column in Exhibit 7-6 shows the promised yield spread of high-yield bonds over 10-year Treasury securities for the period 1978 to the first half of 2005. (As explained in Chapter 3, the yield to maturity is a measure of the promised yield because it assumes that the security is held to maturity, coupon payments can be reinvested at the computed yield to maturity, and the issue does not default. Thus, the difference between two promised yields is a promised yield spread.) As can be seen in the last column of the exhibit, the promised yield spread varied by year. It ranged from a low of 281 basis points in 1978 to a high of 1,050 basis points in 1990. The annual average promised yield spread for the 28-year period was 490 basis points. Are the promised yield spreads justified by the higher potential default rate for high-yield corporate bonds? This important question has been investigated extensively.

Most of the research on the high-yield-bond sector focuses on default rates. From an investment perspective, default rates by themselves are not of paramount significance: It is perfectly possible for a portfolio of high-yield bonds to suffer defaults and to outperform Treasuries at the same time, provided that the yield spread of the portfolio is sufficiently high to offset the losses from default. Furthermore, because holders of defaulted bonds typically recover a portion of the par amount of their investment, the default loss rate is lower than the default rate. Therefore, focusing exclusively on default rates merely highlights the worst possible outcome that a diversified portfolio of high-yield bonds would suffer, assuming that all defaulted bonds would be totally worthless. Assessing the potential rewards from investing in this market sector requires understanding not only default and default loss rates, but also total returns offered over various investment horizons.

EXHIBIT 7-6	Ten-Year Treasury and High Yield Bonds[a]—Annual Returns, Yields, and Spreads, 1978–First Half of 2005					
	Return (%)			Promised Yield (%)		
Year	HY	Treasury	Spread	HY	Treasury	Spread
2005(H1)	0.82	4.09	(3.27)	7.98	3.94	4.04
2004	10.79	4.87	5.92	7.35	4.21	3.14
2003	30.62	1.25	29.37	8.00	4.26	3.74
2002	(1.53)	14.66	(16.19)	12.38	3.82	8.56
2001	5.44	4.01	1.43	12.31	5.04	7.27
2000	(5.68)	14.45	(20.13)	14.56	5.12	9.44
1999	1.73	(8.41)	10.14	11.41	6.44	4.97
1998	4.04	12.77	(8.73)	10.04	4.65	5.39
1997	14.27	11.16	3.11	9.20	5.75	3.45
1996	11.24	0.04	11.20	9.58	6.42	3.16
1995	22.40	23.58	(1.18)	9.76	5.58	4.18
1994	(2.55)	(8.29)	5.74	11.50	7.83	3.67
1993	18.33	12.08	6.25	9.08	5.80	3.28
1992	18.29	6.50	11.79	10.44	6.69	3.75
1991	43.23	17.18	26.05	12.56	6.70	5.86
1990	(8.46)	6.88	(15.34)	18.57	8.07	10.50
1989	1.98	16.72	(14.74)	15.17	7.93	7.24
1988	15.25	6.34	8.91	13.70	9.15	4.55
1987	4.57	(2.67)	7.24	13.89	8.83	5.06
1986	16.50	24.08	(7.58)	12.67	7.21	5.46
1985	26.08	31.54	(5.46)	13.50	8.99	4.51
1984	8.50	14.82	(6.32)	14.97	11.87	3.10
1983	21.80	2.23	19.57	15.74	10.70	5.04
1982	32.45	42.08	(9.63)	17.84	13.86	3.98
1981	7.56	0.48	7.08	16.97	12.08	3.69
1980	(1.00)	(2.96)	1.96	13.46	10.23	3.23
1979	3.69	(0.86)	4.55	12.07	9.13	2.94
1978	7.57	(1.11)	8.68	10.92	8.11	2.81
Arithmetic Annual Average						
1978–2004	**11.37**	**9.02**	**2.36**	**12.47**	**7.57**	**4.90**
Std dev.	**12.45**	**11.92**	**12.34**	**2.85**	**2.61**	**2.06**
Compound Annual Average						
1978–2004	**11.16**	**8.76**			**2.41**	

[a]End of year yields. HY High yield.
From: Citigroup's High Yield Composite Index.

Source: Figure 9 in Edward I. Altman with Brent Pasternack and William Stonberg, "High Yield Bond and Distressed Debt Default and Returns: First-Half 2005 Update," New York University Salomon Center, Leonard N. Stern School of Business.

We discussed default rates earlier (see Exhibit 7-4).[8] Now let's look at the historical loss rate realized by investors in high-yield corporate bonds. This rate, referred to as a **default loss rate**, is reported in the last column of Exhibit 7-4. The methodology for computing the default loss rate, developed by Edward Altman, is as follows. First, the **default loss of principal** is computed by multiplying the default rate for the year by the average loss of principal. The average loss of principal is computed by first determining the recovery per $100 of par value. The recovery per $100 of par value uses the weighted average price of all issues after default. The difference between par value of $100 and the recovery of principal is the default loss of principal. Next the **default loss of coupon** is computed. This is found by multiplying the default rate by the weighted average coupon rate divided by 2 (because the coupon payments are semiannual). The default loss rate is then the sum of the default loss of principal and the default loss of coupon. The weighted average default loss rate for the entire period was 3.51%. This indicates that the weighted average recovery rate is 96.49%.

Now let's look at the total return of the high-yield corporate bond sector because, as we noted earlier, default rates do not tell us how a sector has performed. There have been several such total return studies published that cover different time periods.[9] These studies make different assumptions about factors such as default rate computations, recovery rates, reinvestment rates, and the treatment of default.

Despite the differences in time periods and methodologies, none of the studies seems to suggest that investing in high-yield corporate bonds offers exceptional value. Rather, the findings are consistent with what we stated at the outset of this section: In the long run, high-yield corporate bonds have outperformed both investment grade corporate bonds and Treasuries but have been outperformed by common stock. Therefore, any claim of superior or inferior performance by advocates and critics of this sector of the bond market must be taken with the greatest caution.

Exhibit 7-6 provides a summary of the return on high-yield corporate bonds versus 10-year Treasuries for the years 1978 to the first half of 2005. As expected, there are some years in which 10-year Treasuries have outperformed the high-yield corporate bond market. However, over the entire period, both the arithmetic annual return and the compounded annual return of high-yield corporate bonds exceeded that of 10-year Treasuries by more than 230 basis points.

Recovery Ratings

While credit ratings provide guidance for the likelihood of default and recovery given default, the market needed better recovery information for specific bond issues. In response to this need, two ratings agencies, Fitch and Standard & Poor's, developed

---

[8]The first studies were by Edward I. Altman, "Measuring Corporate Bond Mortality and Performance," *Journal of Finance*, September 1989, pp. 909–922; Edward I. Altman and Scott A. Nammacher, *Investing in Junk Bonds* (New York: Wiley, 1987); and Paul Asquith, David W. Mullins, Jr., and Eric D. Wolff, "Original Issue High Yield Bonds: Aging Analysis of Defaults Exchanges and Calls," *Journal of Finance*, September 1989, pp. 923–952.

[9]See, for example, Rayner Cheung, Joseph C. Bencivenga, and Frank J. Fabozzi, "Original Issue High-Yield Bonds: Historical Return and Default Experiences 1977–1989," *Journal of Fixed Income*, September 1992, pp. 58–76; Marshall E. Blume, Donald B. Keim, and Sandeep A. Patel, "Returns and Volatility of Low-Grade Bonds 1977–1989," *Journal of Finance*, March 1991, pp. 49–74; and Bradford Cornell and K. Green, "The Investment Performance of Low-Grade Bond Funds," *Journal of Finance*, March 1991, pp. 29–48.

recovery rating systems for corporate bonds. The recovery ratings were introduced by Standard & Poor's in December 2003. The recovery ratings were for secured debt. The S&P recovery ratings use an ordinal scale of 1+ through 5. Each recovery rating category, shown in Exhibit 7-7, corresponds to a specific range of recovery values.

In July 2005, Fitch introduced a recovery rating system for corporate bonds rated single B and below. The factors considered in assigning a recovery rating to an issue by Fitch are (1) the collateral, (2) the seniority relative to other obligations in the capital structure, and (3) the expected value of the issuer in distress. The recovery rating system does not attempt to precisely predict a given level of recovery. Rather, the ratings are in the form of an ordinal scale and referred to accordingly as a *Recovery Ratings Scale*. The Recovery Ratings Scale is given in Exhibit 7-8. Despite the recovery ratings being in relative terms, Fitch also provides recovery bands in terms of securities that have characteristics in line with securities historically recovering current principal and related interest. The recovery bands for each recovery rating are shown in the last column of Exhibit 7-8.

Secondary Market for Corporate Bonds

As with all bonds, the principal second market for corporate bonds is the over-the-counter market. The major concern is market transparency.

Trade Reporting and Compliance Engine

Efforts to increase price transparency in the U.S. corporate debt market resulted in the introduction in July 2002 by the National Association of Securities Dealers (NASD) in a mandatory reporting of over-the-counter secondary market transactions for corporate bonds that met specific criteria. The reporting system, the Trade Reporting and Compliance Engine (also known as "TRACE"), requires that all broker/dealers who are NASD member firms report transactions in corporate bonds to TRACE. When first introduced in July 2002, TRACE included only 500 U.S. investment-grade corporate bonds with an original issue size of $1 billion. Since then, the criteria for reporting transactions in TRACE resulted by October 2004 in 17,000 corporate bond issues

---

EXHIBIT 7-7   FitchRating Recovery Rating System

Recovery Rating	Recovery Prospect[a]	Recovery Band[b]
R1	Outstanding	91%–100%
R2	Superior	71%–90%
R3	Good	51%–70%
R4	Average	31%–50%
R5	Below average	11%–30%
R6	Poor recovery	0%–10%

[a]Recovery prospect given default.
[b]Recovery bands in terms of securities that have characteristics in line with securities historically recovering current principal and related interest.

This exhibit was prepared by the author based on the recovery rating system described in publications by FitchRatings.

EXHIBIT 7-8   S&P Recovery Ratings for Secured Debt

Recovery Rate	Ultimate Recovery of Principal	Indicative Recovery Expectation
1+	Highest expectation of full recovery of principal	100% of principal
1	High expectation of full recovery of principal	100% of principal
2	Substantial recovery of principal	80%–100% of principal
3	Meaningful recovery of principal	50%–80% of principal
4	Marginal recovery of principal	25%–50% of principal
5	Negligible recovery of principal	0%–25% of principal

being included, including most high-yield bonds. By February 2005, reporting criteria resulted in almost the entire corporate bond universe being included in TRACE (29,000 publicly traded issues).

At the end of each trading day, market aggregate statistics are published on corporate bond market activity. End of day recap information provided includes (1) the number of securities and total par amount traded, (2) advances, declines, and 52-week highs and lows, and (3) the 10 most active investment grade, high-yield, and convertible bonds for the day.

Electronic Bond Trading

Traditionally, corporate bond trading has been an OTC market conducted via telephone and based on broker-dealer trading desks, which take principal positions in corporate bonds in order to fulfill buy and sell orders of their customers. There has been a transition away from this traditional form of bond trading and toward electronic trading.[10] Electronic bond trading makes up about 30% of corporate bond trading. The major advantages of electronic trading over traditional corporate bond trading are (1) providing liquidity to the markets, (2) price discovery (particularly for less liquid markets), (3) use of new technologies, and (4) trading and portfolio management efficiencies.[11] As an example of the last advantage, a portfolio manager can load buy/sell orders in a web site, trade from these orders, and then clear these orders.

There are the following five types of electronic corporate bond trading systems:

- auction systems
- cross-matching systems
- interdealer systems
- multidealer systems
- single-dealer systems

[10]For an explanation for the reasons for the transitions to electronic bond trading and why the trend is expected to continue, see Frank J. Jones and Frank J. Fabozzi, "The Primary and Secondary Bond Markets," *The Handbook of Fixed Income Securities:* 7th ed. (New York: McGraw Hill, 2005).
[11]Jones and Fabozzi, "The Primary and Secondary Bond Markets," p. 47.

Auction systems allow market participants to conduct electronic auctions of securities offerings for both new issues in the primary markets and secondary market offerings. Auction systems are not typically used. **Cross-matching systems** bring dealers and institutional investors together in electronic trading networks that provide real-time or periodic cross-matching sessions. Buy and sell orders are executed automatically when matched. **Interdealer systems** allow dealers to execute transactions electronically with other dealers via the anonymous services of "brokers' brokers." The clients of dealers are not involved in interdealer systems. **Multidealer systems** allow customers with consolidated orders from two or more dealers that give the customers the ability to execute from among multiple quotes. Multidealer systems also called **client-to-dealer systems**, typically display to customers the best bid or offer price of those posted by all dealers. The participating dealer usually acts as the principal in the transaction. **Single-dealer systems** permit investors to execute transactions directly with the specific dealer desired; this dealer acts as a principal in the transaction with access to the dealer by the investor, which increasingly has been through the Internet. Single-dealer systems therefore simply replace telephone contact between a single dealer and a customer with Internet contact.

Private-Placement Market for Corporate Bonds

Securities privately placed are exempt from registration with the SEC because they are issued in transactions that do not involve a public offering. The private-placement market has undergone a major change since the adoption of SEC Rule 144A in 1990, which allows the trading of privately placed securities among qualified institutional buyers. Not all private placements are Rule 144A private placement. Consequently, the private-placement market can be divided into two sectors. First is the traditional private-placement market, which includes non-144A securities. Second is the market for 144A securities.

Rule 144A private placements are now underwritten by investment bankers on a firm commitment basis, just as with publicly issued bonds. The features in these issues are similar to those of publicly issued bonds. For example, the restrictions imposed on the borrower are less onerous than for traditional private-placement issues. For underwritten issues, the size of the offering is comparable to that of publicly offered bonds.

Unlike publicly issued bonds, the issuers of privately placed issues tend to be less well known. In this way, the private-placement market shares a common characteristic with the bank loan market that we will discuss later in this chapter. Borrowers in the publicly issued bond market are typically large corporations. Issuers of privately placed bonds tend to be medium-sized corporations. Those corporations that borrow from banks tend to be small corporations.

Although the liquidity of issues has increased since Rule 144A became effective, it is still not comparable to that of publicly offered issues. Yields on privately placed debt issues are still higher than those on publicly offered bonds. However, one market observer reports that the premium that must be paid by borrowers in the private placement market has decreased as investment banking firms have committed capital and trading personnel to making markets for securities issued under Rule 144A.

MEDIUM-TERM NOTES

A **medium-term note** (MTN) is a corporate debt instrument, with the unique characteristic that notes are offered continuously to investors by an agent of the issuer. Investors can select from several maturity ranges: 9 months to 1 year, more than 1 year to 18 months, more than 18 months to 2 years, and so on up to 30 years. Medium-term notes are registered with the SEC under Rule 415 (the shelf registration rule), which gives a corporation the maximum flexibility for issuing securities on a continuous basis.

The term *medium-term note* to describe this corporate debt instrument is misleading. Traditionally, the term *note* or *medium-term note* was used to refer to debt issues with a maturity greater than 1 year but less than 15 years. Certainly, this is not a characteristic of MTNs because they have been sold with maturities from 9 months to 30 years and even longer. For example, in July 1993, Walt Disney Corporation issued a security with a 100-year maturity off its MTN shelf registration.

General Motors Acceptance Corporation first used MTNs in 1972 to fund automobile loans with maturities of five years and less. The purpose of the MTN was to fill the funding gap between commercial paper and long-term bonds. It is for this reason that they are referred to as "medium term." The MTNs were issued directly to investors without the use of an agent. Only a few corporations issued MTNs in the 1970s. About $800 million of MTNs were outstanding by 1981. The market was hampered from developing for two reasons. First, because the issues must be registered with the SEC, registration costs made the issuance of MTNs expensive relative to other funding sources. This cost could be avoided by placing MTNs privately. However, as we explained earlier in this chapter, private placements carry a higher interest cost. Second, there was no secondary market for MTNs.

The modern-day MTN was pioneered by Merrill Lynch in 1981. The first MTN issuer was Ford Motor Credit company. By 1983, GMAC and Chrysler Financial used Merrill Lynch as an agent to issue MTNs. Merrill Lynch and other investment banking firms committed funds to make a secondary market for MTNs, thereby improving liquidity. In 1982, Rule 415 was adopted, making it easier for issuers to sell registered securities on a continuous basis.

Although we elected to discuss MTNs in our discussion of domestic corporate debt, they are also issued by foreign corporations, federal agencies, supranational institutions, and sovereign countries.

In 2004, there were 440 U.S. corporations that issued MTNs—198 financial corporations and 242 nonfinancial corporations.[12] Exhibit 7-9 shows the issuance in 2004 by credit rating.

Borrowers have flexibility in designing MTNs to satisfy their own needs. They can issue fixed- or floating-rate debt. The coupon payments can be denominated in U.S. dollars or in a foreign currency. Earlier in this chapter we described the various security structures; MTNs have been designed with the same features. For example, there are MTNs backed by equipment trust certificates issued by railways and subordinated notes issued by bank holding companies. In Chapter 14 we discuss asset-backed securities. There are asset-backed MTNs.

---

[12] 2004 Federal Reserve survey of medium-term note market, Table 2 (www.federalreserve.gov/releases/medterm).

EXHIBIT 7-9	Dollar Volume of Gross Issuance of Medium-Term Notes, by Rating Category of Issuer (millions of dollars)

Issuer	
All U.S. Corporations	$294,752
AAA	104,046
AA	80,128
A	98,482
BBB	2,551
BB	0
B	0
Other	9,554

Source: 2004 Federal Reserve survey of medium-term note market, Table 6 *(www.federalreserve.gov/releases/medterm).*

When the treasurer of a corporation is contemplating an offering of either an MTN or corporate bonds, there are two factors that affect the decision. The most obvious is the cost of the funds raised after consideration of registration and distribution costs. This cost is referred to as the **all-in-cost of funds**. The second is the flexibility afforded to the issuer in structuring the offering. The tremendous growth in the MTN market is evidence of the relative advantage of MTNs with respect to cost and flexibility for some offerings. However, the fact that there are corporations that raise funds by issuing both bonds and MTNs is evidence that there is no absolute advantage in all instances and market environments.

Primary Market

Medium-term notes differ from corporate bonds in the manner in which they are distributed to investors when they are initially sold. Although some investment-grade corporate bond issues are sold on a best-efforts basis, typically they are underwritten by investment bankers. Traditionally, MTNs have been distributed on a best-efforts basis by either an investment banking firm or other broker/dealers acting as agents. Another difference between corporate bonds and MTNs when they are offered is that MTNs are usually sold in relatively small amounts on a continuous or an intermittent basis, whereas corporate bonds are sold in large, discrete offerings.

A corporation that wants an MTN program will file a shell registration with the SEC for the offering of securities. Although the SEC registration for MTN offerings is between $100 and $1 billion, after the total is sold, the issuer can file another shelf registration. The registration will include a list of the investment banking firms, usually two to four, that the corporation has arranged to act as agents to distribute the MTNs. The large New York–based investment banking firms dominate the distribution market for MTNs.

The issuer then posts rates over a range of maturities: for example, 9 months to 1 year, 1 year to 18 months, 18 months to 2 years, and annually thereafter. Exhibit 7-10 provides an example of an offering rate schedule for an MTN program. Usually, an issuer will post rates as a spread over a Treasury security of comparable maturity. For

EXHIBIT 7-10   Offering Rate Schedule for a Medium-Term Note Program

Medium-Term Notes			Treasury Securities	
Maturity Range	Yield (%)	Yield Spread of MTN over Treasury Securities	Maturity	Yield (%)
9 months to 12 months	a	a	9 months	3.35
12 months to 18 months	a	a	12 months	3.50
18 months to 2 years	a	a	18 months	3.80
2 years to 3 years	4.35	35	2 years	4.00
3 years to 4 years	5.05	55	3 years	4.50
4 years to 5 years	5.60	60	4 years	5.00
5 years to 6 years	6.05	60	5 years	5.45
6 years to 7 years	6.10	40	6 years	5.70
7 years to 8 years	6.30	40	7 years	5.90
8 years to 9 years	6.45	40	8 years	6.05
9 years to 10 years	6.60	40	9 years	6.20
10 years	6.70	40	10 years	6.30

ªNo rate posted.

Source: Leland E. Crabbe, "Anatomy of the Medium-Term Note Market," *Federal Reserve Bulletin,* August 1993, pp. 751–768.

example, in the two-to three-year maturity range, the offering rate is 35 basis points over the two-year Treasury. Because the two-year Treasury is shown in the table at 4%, the offering rate is 4.35%. Rates will not be posted for maturity ranges that the issuer does not desire to sell. For example, in Exhibit 7-10 the issuer does not wish to sell MTNs with a maturity of less than two years.

The agents will then make the offering rate schedule available to their investor base interested in MTNs. An investor who is interested in the offering will contact the agent. In turn, the agent contacts the issuer to confirm the terms of the transaction. Because the maturity range in the offering rate schedule does not specify a specific maturity date, the investor can choose the final maturity subject to approval by the issuer. The minimum size that an investor can purchase of an MTN offering typically ranges from $1 million to $25 million.

The rate offering schedule can be changed at any time by the issuer either in response to changing market conditions or because the issuer has raised the desired amount of funds at a given maturity. In the latter case, the issuer can either not post a rate for that maturity range or lower the rate.

Structured MTNs

At one time the typical MTN was a fixed-rate debenture that was noncallable. It is common today for issuers of MTNs to couple their offerings with transactions in the derivative markets (options, futures/forwards, swaps, caps, and floors) so as to create debt obligations with more interesting risk–return features than are available in the corporate bond market. Specifically, an issue can be floating-rate over all or part of the life of the security, and the coupon reset formula can be based on a benchmark interest rate, equity index or individual stock price, a foreign exchange rate, or a commodity index. Inverse floaters are created in the structured MTN market. MTNs can have various embedded options included.

MTNs created when the issuer simultaneously transacts in the derivative markets are called **structured notes**. The most common derivative instrument used in creating structured notes is a swap. The development of the MTN market has been fostered by commercial banks involved in the swap market. By using the derivative markets in combination with an offering, borrowers are able to create investment vehicles that are more customized for institutional investors to satisfy their investment objectives, even though they are forbidden from using swaps for hedging. Moreover, it allows institutional investors who are restricted to investing in investment-grade debt issues the opportunity to participate in other asset classes to make a market play. For example, an investor who buys an MTN whose coupon rate is tied to the performance of the S&P 500 is participating in the equity market without owning common stock. If the coupon rate is tied to a foreign stock index, the investor is participating in the equity market of a foreign country without owning foreign common stock. In exchange for creating a structured note product, borrowers can reduce their funding costs.

How do borrowers or their agents find investors who are willing to buy structured notes? In a typical offering of a corporate bond, the sales force of the underwriting firm will solicit interest in the offering from its customer base. That is, the sales force will make an inquiry. In the structured note market, the process is often quite different. Because of the small size of an offering and the flexibility to customize the offering in the swap market, investors can approach an issuer through its agent about designing a security for their needs. This process of customers inquiring of issuers or their agents to design a security is called a **reverse inquiry**. Transactions that originate from reverse inquiries account for a significant share of MTN transactions.[13]

COMMERCIAL PAPER

Commercial paper is a short-term unsecured promissory note that is issued in the open market and that represents the obligation of the issuing corporation. The primary purpose of commercial paper was to provide short-term funds for seasonal and working capital needs. Corporations use commercial paper for other purposes. For example, it has been used for **bridge financing**. For example, suppose that a corporation needs long-term funds to build a plant or acquire equipment. Rather than raising long-term funds immediately, the corporation may elect to postpone the offering until more favorable capital market conditions prevail. The funds raised by issuing commercial paper are used until longer-term securities are sold. Commercial paper is sometimes used as bridge financing to finance corporate takeovers. Moreover, the interest-rate-swaps market encouraged the use of the commercial paper market. In an interest-rate

---

[13]Leonard E. Crabbe, "Medium-Term Notes and Structured Notes," Chapter 3 in *The Handbook of Corporate Debt Instruments*.

swap, one party exchanges a fixed rate for a floating rate. Corporate issuers would issue commercial paper and use the interest-rate swap to convert the floating interest rate on commercial paper into a fixed interest rate.

The minimum round-lot transaction is $100,000, although some issuers will sell commercial paper in denominations of $25,000. There is very little secondary trading of commercial paper. Typically, an investor in commercial paper is an entity that plans to hold it until maturity. This is understandable because an investor can purchase commercial paper in a direct transaction with the issuer that will issue paper with the specific maturity the investor desires.

Characteristics of Commercial Paper

In the United States, commercial paper ranges in maturity from 1 day to 270 days. The reason that the maturity of commercial paper does not exceed 270 days is as follows. The Securities Act of 1933 requires that securities be registered with the SEC. Special provisions in the 1933 act exempt commercial paper from registration as long as the maturity does not exceed 270 days. Hence, to avoid the costs associated with registering issues with the SEC, firms rarely issue commercial paper with maturities exceeding 270 days. Another consideration in determining the maturity is whether the commercial paper would be eligible collateral for a bank that wanted to borrow from the Federal Reserve Bank's discount window. To be eligible, the maturity of the paper may not exceed 90 days. Because eligible paper trades at lower cost than paper that is not eligible, issuers prefer to issue paper whose maturity does not exceed 90 days. According to the Federal Reserve Bank of New York, commercial paper does not exceed 30 days.[14] To pay off holders of maturing paper, issuers generally use the proceeds obtained by selling new commercial paper. This process is often described as **rolling over** short-term paper. The risk that the investor in commercial paper faces is that the issuer will be unable to issue new paper at maturity. As a safeguard against this **rollover risk**, commercial paper is typically backed by unused bank credit lines. Because there is a commitment fee charged by a bank for providing a credit line, this safeguard increases the effective cost of issuing commercial paper.

Issuers of Commercial Paper

There are more than 1,700 issuers of commercial paper in the United States. Corporate issuers of commercial paper can be divided into financial companies and nonfinancial companies. There has been significantly greater use of commercial paper by financial companies.

There are three types of financial companies: captive finance companies, bank-related finance companies, and independent finance companies. Captive finance companies are subsidiaries of equipment manufacturing companies. Their primary purpose is to secure financing for the customers of the parent company. For example, the three major U.S. automobile manufacturers have captive finance companies: General Motors Acceptance Corporation (GMAC), Ford Credit, and Chrysler Financial. GMAC is by the far the largest issuer of commercial paper in the United States. Furthermore, a bank

---

[14]Fedpoint 29: Commercial Paper (www.ny.frb.org/pihome/fedpoint/fed29.html).

holding company may have a subsidiary that is a finance company, which provides loans to enable individuals and businesses to acquire a wide range of products. Independent finance companies are those that are not subsidiaries of equipment manufacturing firms or bank holding companies.

Although the issuers of commercial paper typically have high credit ratings, smaller and less well-known companies with lower credit ratings have been able to issue paper. They have been able to do so by means of credit support from a firm with a high credit rating (such paper is called **credit-supported commercial paper**) or by collateralizing the issue with high-quality assets (such paper is called **asset-backed commercial paper**). An example of credit-supported commercial paper is one supported by a letter of credit. The terms of a letter of credit specify that the bank issuing the letter guarantees that the bank will pay off the paper when it comes due, if the issuer fails to do so. The bank will charge a fee for the letter of credit. From the issuer's perspective, the fee enables it to enter the commercial paper market and thereby obtain funding at a lower cost than that of bank borrowing. Commercial paper issued with this credit enhancement is referred to as **LOC paper**. The credit enhancement may also take the form of a surety bond from an insurance company.[15]

Default Risk and Credit Ratings

With one exception, between 1971 and mid-1989 there were no defaults on commercial paper.[16] With the weakening economy in the late 1980s, three defaults occurred in 1989 and four in 1990. This and two other factors caused corporate medium- and lower-quality-rated issuers to get out of commercial paper. The first factor was that banks became reluctant to provide backup facilities for these issuers. The introduction of the risk-based capital requirements for commercial banks made these commitments less attractive. Second, the demand for medium-grade commercial paper by money market mutual funds, the major buyer of commercial paper, was reduced by several SEC rulings in 1991. Specifically, at one time there was no restriction on medium-grade commercial paper that money market mutual funds could hold. Now there are.

The three companies that rate corporate bonds and medium-term notes also rate commercial paper. The ratings assigned by these three rating companies are shown in Exhibit 7-11. As with the ratings on other securities, commercial paper ratings are categorized as either **investment grade** or **noninvestment grade**. As with corporate bond ratings, rating agencies publish rating transition matrices for commercial paper ratings.

Directly Placed versus Dealer-Placed Paper

Commercial paper is classified as either direct paper or dealer-placed paper. **Directly placed paper** is sold by the issuing firm directly to investors without the help of an agent or an intermediary. (An issuer may set up its own dealer firm to handle sales.)

---

[15]A surety bond is a policy written by an insurance company to protect another party against loss or violation of a contract.

[16]Mitchell A. Post, "The Evolution of the U.S. Commercial Paper Market Since 1980," *Federal Reserve Bulletin*, December 1992, p. 888. The one exception was Manville Corporation in August 1982, which defaulted after filing in bankruptcy court for protection against potential liability from lawsuits related to injuries and deaths from asbestos.

EXHIBIT 7-11   Commercial Paper Ratings[a]

	Commercial Rating Company		
Category	Fitch	Moody's	S&P
Investment grade	F-1+		A-1+
	F-1	P-1	A-1
	F-2	P-2	A-2
	F-3	P-3	A-3
Noninvestment grade	F-S	NP (not prime)	B
			C
In default	D		D

[a]The definition of ratings varies by rating agency.

Source: Mitchell A. Post, "The Evolution of the U.S. Commercial Paper Market Since 1980," *Federal Reserve Bulletin*, December 1992, p. 882.

A large majority of the issuers of direct paper are financial companies. These entities require continuous funds in order to provide loans to customers. As a result, they find it cost-effective to establish a sales force to sell their commercial paper directly to investors. An institutional investor can find information about the rates posted by issuers on Bloomberg Financial Markets, Telerate/Bridge, Reuters, and the Internet (at cpmarket.com).[17]

General Electric Capital Corporation (GE Capital) is an example of a direct issuer, having issued commercial paper for more than 50 years. GE Capital is the principal financial services arm of General Electric Company and is now the largest and most active direct issuer in the United States, with commercial paper outstanding of about $73 billion. The Corporate Treasury unit of GE Capital manages the commercial paper programs of General Electric Company, GE Capital Services, GE Capital, and other GE-related programs. These programs include the following as of July 30, 2004:

		Ratings	
Issuer	Program Size (Billions)	S&P	Moody's
General Electric Capital Corporation	$ 60.0	Al+	Pl
General Electric Capital Services, Inc.	7.0	Al+	Pl
General Electric Company	6.0	Al+	Pl

The paper is marketed directly to institutional investors on a continuous basis by Corporate Treasury or through GECC Capital Markets Group, Inc. (an NASD registered broker-dealer).

---

[17]*cpmarket.com* is the first Internet browser-based portal for commercial paper transactions.

Dealer-placed commercial paper requires the services of an agent to sell an issuer's paper. The agent distributes the paper on a best efforts underwriting basis by commercial banks and securities houses.

Tier 1 and Tier 2 Paper

A major investor in commercial paper is money market mutual funds. However, there are restrictions imposed on money market mutual funds by the SEC. Specifically, Rule 2a-7 of the Investment Company Act of 1940 limits the credit risk exposure of money market mutual funds by restricting their investments to "eligible" paper. Eligibility is defined in terms of the credit ratings shown in Exhibit 7-11. To be eligible paper, the issue must carry one of the two highest ratings ("1" or "2") from at least two of the nationally recognized statistical ratings agencies. Tier-1 paper is defined as eligible paper that is rated "1" by at least two of the rating agencies; tier-2 paper security is defined as eligible paper that is not a tier-1 security.

Money market funds may hold no more than 5% of their assets in tier-1 paper of any individual issuer and no more than 1% of their assets in the tier-2 paper of any individual issuer. Furthermore, the holding of tier-2 paper may not represent more than 5% of the fund's assets.

Secondary Market

Despite the fact that the commercial paper market is larger than markets for other money market instruments, secondary trading activity is much smaller. The typical investor in commercial paper is an entity that plans to hold it until maturity, given that an investor can purchase commercial paper with the specific maturity desired. Should an investor's economic circumstances change so that there is a need to sell the paper, it can be sold back to the dealer or, in the case of directly placed paper, the issuer will repurchase it.

Yields on Commercial Paper

Like Treasury bills, commercial paper is a discount instrument. That is, it is sold at a price that is less than its maturity value. The difference between the maturity value and the price paid is the interest earned by the investor, although there is some commercial paper that is issued as an interest-bearing instrument. For commercial paper, a year is treated as having 360 days.

The yield offered on commercial paper tracks that of other money market instruments. The commercial paper rate is higher than that on Treasury bills for the same maturity. There are three reasons for this. First, the investor in commercial paper is exposed to credit risk. Second, interest earned from investing in Treasury bills is exempt from state and local income taxes. As a result, commercial paper has to offer a higher yield to offset this tax advantage. Finally, commercial paper is less liquid than Treasury bills. The liquidity premium demanded is probably small, however, because investors typically follow a buy-and-hold strategy with commercial paper and so are less concerned with liquidity.

The yield on commercial paper is higher by a few basis points than the yield on certificates of deposit for the same maturity. The higher yield available on commercial paper is attributable to the poorer liquidity relative to certificates of deposit.

BANKRUPTCY AND CREDITOR RIGHTS

The holder of a corporate debt instrument has priority over the equity owners in the case of bankruptcy of a corporation, and as we have explained, there are creditors who have priority over other creditors. In this section we provide an overview of the bankruptcy process and then look at what actually happens to creditors in bankruptcies.

Bankruptcy Process

The law governing bankruptcy in the United States is the Bankruptcy Reform Act of 1978.[18] One purpose of the act is to set forth the rules for a corporation to be either liquidated or reorganized. The **liquidation** of a corporation means that all the assets will be distributed to the holders of claims of the corporation and no corporate entity will survive. In a **reorganization**, a new corporate entity will result. Some holders of the claim of the bankrupt corporation will receive cash in exchange for their claims; others may receive new securities in the corporation that results from the reorganization; and still others may receive a combination of both cash and new securities in the resulting corporation.

Another purpose of the bankruptcy act is to give a corporation time to decide whether to reorganize or liquidate and then have the necessary time to formulate a plan to accomplish either a reorganization or liquidation. This is achieved because when a corporation files for bankruptcy, the act grants the corporation protection from creditors who seek to collect their claims.[19] A company that files for protection under the bankruptcy act generally becomes a **debtor in possession**, and continues to operate its business under the supervision of the court.

The bankruptcy act is composed of 15 chapters, each chapter covering a particular type of bankruptcy. Of particular interest to us are two of the chapters, Chapter 7 and Chapter 11. Chapter 7 deals with the liquidation of a company; Chapter 11 deals with the reorganization of a company.

Absolute Priority: Theory and Practice

When a company is liquidated, creditors receive distributions based on the **absolute priority rule** to the extent that assets are available. The absolute priority rule is the principle that senior creditors are paid in full before junior creditors are paid anything. For secured creditors and unsecured creditors, the absolute priority rule guarantees their seniority to equity holders.

In liquidations, the absolute priority rule generally holds. In contrast, there is a good body of literature that argues that strict absolute priority has not been upheld by

---

[18]For a discussion of the Bankruptcy Reform Act of 1978 and a nontechnical description of its principal features, see Jane Tripp Howe, "Investing in Chapter 11 and Other Distressed Companies," Chapter 20 in Fabozzi and Fabozzi (eds.), *The Handbook of Fixed Income Securities*, 4th ed.
[19]The petition for bankruptcy can be filed either by the company itself, in which case it is called a **voluntary bankruptcy**, or be filed by its creditors, in which case it is called an **involuntary bankruptcy**.

the courts or the SEC.[20] Studies of actual reorganizations under Chapter 11 have found that the violation of absolute priority is the rule rather the exception.[21]

There are several hypotheses that have been suggested as to why in a reorganization the distribution made to claimholders will diverge from that required by the absolute priority principle. The **incentive hypothesis** argues that the longer the negotiation process among the parties, the greater the bankruptcy costs and the smaller the amount to be distributed to all parties. This is because in a reorganization, a committee representing the various claimholders is appointed with the purpose of formulating a plan of reorganization. To be accepted, a plan of reorganization must be approved by at least two-thirds of the amount and a majority of the number of claims voting and at least two-thirds of the outstanding shares of each class of interests. Consequently, a long-lasting bargaining process is expected. The longer the negotiation process among the parties, the more likely that the company will be operated in a manner that is not in the best interest of the creditors and, as a result, the smaller the amount to be distributed to all parties. Because all impaired classes, including equity holders, generally must approve the plan of reorganization, creditors often convince equity holders to accept the plan by offering to distribute some value to them.

The **recontracting process hypothesis** argues that the violation of absolute priority reflects a recontracting process between stockholders and senior creditors that gives recognition to the ability of management to preserve value on behalf of stockholders.[22] According to the **stockholders' influence on the reorganization plan hypothesis**, creditors are less informed about the true economic operating conditions of the firm than management. As the distribution to creditors in the plan of reorganization is based on the valuation by the firm, creditors without perfect information easily suffer the loss.[23] According to Wruck, managers generally have a better understanding than creditors or stockholders about a firm's internal operations while creditors and stockholders can have better information about industry trends. Management may therefore use its superior knowledge to present the data in a manner that reinforces its position.[24]

The essence of the **strategic bargaining process hypothesis** is that the increasing complexity of firms that declare bankruptcy will accentuate the negotiating process

---

[20]See, for example, William H. Meckling, "Financial Markets, Default, and Bankruptcy," *Law and Contemporary Problems*, Vol. 41, 1977, pp. 124–177; Merton H. Miller, "The Wealth Transfers of Bankruptcy: Some Illustrative Examples," *Law and Contemporary Problems*, Vol. 41, 1977, pp. 39–46; Jerome B. Warner, "Bankruptcy, Absolute Priority, and the Pricing of Risky Debt Claims," *Journal of Financial Economics*, Vol. 4, 1977, pp. 239–276; and Thomas H. Jackson, "Of Liquidation, Continuation, and Delay: An Analysis of Bankruptcy Policy and Nonbankruptcy Rules," *American Bankruptcy Law Journal*, Vol. 60, 1986, pp. 399–428.

[21]See Julian R. Franks and Walter N. Torous, "An Empirical Investigation of U.S. Firms in Reorganization," *Journal of Finance*, July 1989, pp. 747–769; Lawrence A. Weiss, "Bankruptcy Resolution: Direct Costs and Violation of Priority of Claims," *Journal of Financial Economics*, 1990, pp. 285–314; and Frank J. Fabozzi, Jane Tripp Howe, Takashi Makabe, and Toshihide Sudo, "Recent Evidence on the Distribution Patterns in Chapter 11 Reorganizations," *Journal of Fixed Income*, Spring 1993, pp. 6–23.

[22]Douglas G. Baird and Thomas H. Jackson, "Bargaining After the Fall and the Contours of the Absolute Priority Rule," *University of Chicago Law Review*, Vol. 55, 1988, pp. 738–789.

[23]L. A. Bebchuk, "A New Approach to Corporate Reorganizations," *Harvard Law Review*, Vol. 101, 1988, pp. 775–804.

[24]Karen Hooper Wruck, "Financial Distress, Reorganization, and Organizational Efficiency," *Journal of Financial Economics*, Vol. 27, 1990, pp. 419–444.

and result in an even higher incidence of violation of the absolute priority rule. The probable outcome is further supported by the increased number of official committees in the reorganization process, as well as the increased number of financial and legal advisors.

There are some who argue that creditors will receive a higher value in reorganization than they would in liquidation, in part because of the costs associated with liquidation.[25] Finally, the lack of symmetry in the tax system (negative taxes are not permitted, although loss deductions may be carried forward) results in situations in which the only way to use all current loss deductions is to merge.[26] The tax system may encourage continuance or merger and discourage bankruptcy.

Consequently, although investors in the debt of a corporation may feel that they have priority over the equity owners and priority over other classes of debtors, the actual outcome of a bankruptcy may be far different from what the terms of the debt agreement state.

One study examined the extent of violation of the absolute priority rule among three broad groups: secured creditors, unsecured creditors, and equity holders, and also among various types of debt and equity securities.[27] They also provided evidence on which asset class bears the cost of violations of absolute priority and an initial estimate of total distributed value relative to liquidation value. Their findings suggest that unsecured creditors bear a disproportionate cost of reorganization and that more senior unsecured creditors may bear a disproportionate cost relative to the junior unsecured creditors, whereas equity holders often benefit from violations of absolute priority.

SUMMARY

Corporate bonds are debts obligating a corporation to pay periodic interest with full repayment at maturity. The promises of the corporate bond issuer and the rights of the investors are set forth in the bond indenture. Provisions to be specified include call and sinking fund provisions, as well as limitations on further debt and on management powers.

Security for bonds may be real or personal property. A mortgage bond grants the bondholders a lien against the pledged assets. Collateral trust bonds are secured by securities owned by the issuer. Debenture bonds are not secured by a specific pledge of property; bondholders have the claim of general creditors on all assets of the issuer not pledged specifically to secure other debt. Subordinated debenture bonds are issues that rank after secured debt, after debenture bonds, and often after some general creditors in their claim on assets and earnings.

The credit risk of a corporate borrower can be gauged by the quality rating assigned by the three nationally recognized rating companies. Issues rated in the top ratings of both raters are referred to as investment-grade bonds; those below the top four ratings are called noninvestment-grade bonds, high-yield bonds, or junk bonds.

---

[25]Michael C. Jensen, "Eclipse of the Public Corporation," *Harvard Business Review*, Vol. 89, 1989, pp. 61–62, and Wruck, "Financial Distress, Reorganization, and Organizational Efficiency."

[26]J. I. Bulow and J. B. Shoven, "The Bankruptcy Decision," *Bell Journal of Economics*, 1978. For a further discussion of the importance of NOLs and the current tax law, see Fabozzi et al., "Recent Evidence on the Distribution Patterns in Chapter 11 Reorganizations."

[27]Fabozzi et al., "Recent Evidence on the Distribution Patterns in Chapter 11 Reorganizations."

Event risk refers to the possibility of an event that leads investors to doubt the ability of an issuer to make interest and principal payments. Event risk can occur because of a natural or industrial accident, or a takeover or corporate restructuring.

The high-yield sector of the corporate bond market is the market for noninvestment-grade corporate bonds. Several complex bond structures are issued in the high-yield sector of the corporate bond market. These include deferred-coupon bonds (deferred-interest bonds, step-up bonds, and payment-in-kind bonds) and extendable reset bonds.

Studies of high-yield corporate bonds have found that they outperformed both investment-grade corporate bonds and Treasuries but have been outperformed by common stock.

Medium-term notes are corporate debt obligations offered on a continuous basis. They are registered with the SEC under the shelf registration rule and are offered through agents. The rates posted are for various maturity ranges, with maturities as short as 9 months to as long as 30 years. Medium-term notes have been issued simultaneously with transactions in the derivatives market, particularly the swap market, to create structured MTNs. These products allow issuers greater flexibility in creating MTNs that are attractive to investors who seek to hedge or undertake a market play that they might otherwise be prohibited from doing.

Commercial paper is a short-term unsecured promissory note issued in the open market that represents the obligation of the issuing entity. It is sold on a discount basis. To avoid SEC registration, the maturity of commercial paper is less than 270 days. Generally, commercial paper maturity is less than 30 days. Financial and nonfinancial corporations issue commercial paper, with the majority issued by the former. The commercial paper market was limited to entities with strong credit ratings, but lower-rated issuers have used credit enhancements to enter the market. Direct paper is sold by the issuing firm directly to investors without using a securities dealer as an intermediary; with dealer-placed commercial paper, the issuer uses the services of a securities firm to sell its paper. There is little liquidity in the commercial paper market.

The Bankruptcy Reform Act of 1978 as amended governs the bankruptcy process in the United States. Chapter 7 of the bankruptcy act deals with the liquidation of a company. Chapter 11 deals with the reorganization of a company. Creditors receive distributions based on the absolute priority rule to the extent assets are available. This means that senior creditors are paid in full before junior creditors are paid anything. Generally, this rule holds in the case of liquidations. In contrast, the absolute priority rule is typically violated in a reorganization.

Questions

1. a. What are the corporate bond classifications used by bond information services?
   b. How are corporate bonds treated in the Lehman Brothers U.S. Aggregate Bond Index?
2. a. What is meant by a make-whole premium provision?
   b. What is the purpose of this provision?

3. a. What is the difference between refunding protection and call protection?
   b. Which protection provides the investor with greater protection that the bonds will be acquired by the issuer prior to the stated maturity date?
4. a. What is a bullet bond?
   b. Can a bullet bond be redeemed prior to the stated maturity date?

5. a. What is a sinking fund requirement in a bond issue?
    b. "A sinking fund provision in a bond issue benefits the investor." Do you agree with this statement?
6. Who are the companies that assign ratings to debt obligations?
7. What is the difference between a fallen angel and an original-issue high-yield bond?
8. a. What is event risk?
    b. Give two examples of event risk.
9. "A floating-rate note and an extendable reset bond both have coupon rates readjusted periodically. Therefore, they are basically the same instrument." Do you agree with this statement?
10. a. What is a payment-in-kind bond?
    b. An investor who purchases a payment-in-kind bond will find that increased interest rate volatility will have an adverse economic impact. If interest rates rise substantially, there will be an adverse consequence. So too will a substantial decline in interest rates have adverse consequences. Why?
11. What is a rating transition matrix?
12. Indicate why you agree or disagree with the following statements pertaining to the private-placement corporate debt market:
    a. "Since Rule 144A became effective, all privately placed issues can be bought and sold in the market."
    b. "Traditionally privately placed issues are now similar to publicly offered securities."
13. Indicate why you agree or disagree with the following statement: "Investing in the junk bond market offers the opportunity to realize superior investment returns compared with other debt instruments and common stock."
14. What is meant by a default loss rate and how is it computed?
15. What is the significance of a secured position if the absolute priority rule is typically not followed in a reorganization?
16. What is meant by an issue or issuer being placed on a credit watch?
17. Explain the various ways in which default rates are quoted.
18. What is the difference between a credit rating and recovery rating?
19. What are the major advantages cited for electronic bond trading relative to transacting in the traditional secondary bond market?
20. a. In what ways does an MTN differ from a corporate bond?
    b. What derivative instrument is commonly used in creating a structured MTN?
21. Indicate why you agree or disagree with the following statements:
    a. "Most MTN issues are rated noninvestment grade at the time of offering."
    b. "Typically, a corporate issuer with an MTN program will post rates for every maturity range."
    c. "An offering rate schedule for an MTN program is fixed for two years after the securities are registered."
22. What is reverse inquiry?
23. Why is commercial paper an alternative to short-term bank borrowing for a corporation?
24. What is the difference between directly placed paper and dealer-placed paper?
25. What does the yield spread between commercial paper and Treasury bills of the same maturity reflect?
26. Why does commercial paper have a maturity of less than 270 days?
27. What is meant by tier-1 and tier-2 commercial paper?
28. a. What is the difference between a liquidation and a reorganization?
    b. What is the difference between a Chapter 7 and Chapter 11 bankruptcy filing?
29. What is a debtor in possession?
30. What is the principle of absolute priority?
31. Comment on the following statement: "An investor who purchases the mortgage bonds of a corporation knows that should the corporation become bankrupt, mortgage bondholders will be paid in full before the common stockholders receive any proceeds."
32. Give three reasons to explain why absolute priority might be violated in a reorganization.

CHAPTER

8 | MUNICIPAL SECURITIES

After reading this chapter you will understand:

- the two basic security structures: general obligation bonds and revenue bonds

- the flow of funds structure for revenue bonds

- municipal bonds with hybrid structures and special bond security structures such as refunded bonds and insured municipal bonds

- the different types of tax-exempt short-term municipal securities

- what municipal derivative securities are

- how municipal inverse floaters are created

- the tax risk that investors face when investing in municipal securities

- yield spreads within the municipal market

- the shape of the municipal yield curve

- the primary and secondary markets for municipal securities

- the taxable municipal bond market

Municipal securities are issued by state and local governments and by governmental entities such as "authorities" or special districts. There are both tax-exempt and taxable municipal bonds. "Tax-exempt" means that interest on municipal bonds is exempt from federal income taxation, and it may or may not be taxable at the state and local levels. Most municipal bonds outstanding are tax-exempt. Municipal securities come in a variety of types, with different redemption features, credit risks, and liquidity.

Municipal securities are issued for various purposes. Short-term notes typically are sold in anticipation of the receipt of funds from taxes or receipt of proceeds from the sale of a bond issue, for example. Proceeds from the sale of short-term notes permit the issuing municipality to cover seasonal and temporary imbalances between outlays for expenditures and inflows from taxes.

Municipalities issue long-term bonds as the principal means for financing both

1. long-term capital projects such as schools, bridges, roads, and airports; and
2. long-term budget deficits that arise from current operations.

TYPES AND FEATURES OF MUNICIPAL SECURITIES

There are basically two different types of municipal bond security structures: tax-backed bonds and revenue bonds. There are also securities that share characteristics of both tax-backed and revenue bonds.

Tax-Backed Debt

Tax-backed debt obligations are instruments issued by states, counties, special districts, cities, towns, and school districts that are secured by some form of tax revenue. Tax-backed debt includes general obligation debt, appropriation-backed obligations, and debt obligations supported by public credit enhancement programs. We discuss each here.

General Obligation Debt

The broadest type of tax-backed debt is **general obligation debt**. There are two types of general obligation pledges: unlimited and limited. An **unlimited tax general obligation debt** is the stronger form of general obligation pledge because it is secured by the issuer's unlimited taxing power. The tax revenue sources include corporate and individual income taxes, sales taxes, and property taxes. Unlimited tax general obligation debt is said to be secured by the full faith and credit of the issuer. A **limited tax general obligation debt** is a limited tax pledge because for such debt there is a statutory limit on tax rates that the issuer may levy to service the debt.

Certain general obligation bonds are secured not only by the issuer's general taxing powers to create revenues accumulated in a general fund, but also by certain identified fees, grants, and special charges, which provide additional revenues from outside the general fund. Such bonds are known as **double-barreled** in security because of the dual nature of the revenue sources. For example, the debt obligations issued by special-purpose service systems may be secured by a pledge of property taxes, a pledge of special fees/operating revenue from the service provided, or a pledge of both property taxes and special fees/operating revenues. In the last case, they are double-barreled.

Appropriation-Backed Obligations

Agencies or authorities of several states have issued bonds that carry a potential state liability for making up shortfalls in the issuing entity's obligation. The appropriation of funds from the state's general tax revenue must be approved by the state legislature. However, the state's pledge is not binding. Debt obligations with this nonbinding pledge of tax revenue are called **moral obligation bonds**. Because a moral obligation bond requires legislative approval to appropriate the funds, it is classified as an appropriation-backed obligation. The purpose of the moral obligation pledge is to enhance the credit worthiness of the issuing entity. However, the investor must rely on the best efforts of the state to approve the appropriation. Another type of appropriation-backed obligation is lease-backed debt.

Debt Obligations Supported by Public Credit Enhancement Programs

While a moral obligation is a form of credit enhancement provided by a state, it is not a legally enforceable or legally binding obligation of the state. There are entities that have issued debt that carries some form of public credit enhancement that is legally enforceable. This occurs when there is a guarantee by the state or a federal agency or when there is an obligation to automatically withhold and deploy state aid to pay any defaulted debt service by the issuing entity. Typically, the latter form of public credit enhancement is used for debt obligations of a state's school systems.

Some examples of state credit enhancement programs include Virginia's bond guarantee program that authorizes the governor to withhold state aid payments to a municipality and divert those funds to pay principal and interest to a municipality's general obligation holders in the event of a default. South Carolina's constitution requires mandatory withholding of state aid by the state treasurer if a school district is not capable of meeting its general obligation debt. Texas created the Permanent School Fund to guarantee the timely payment of principal and interest of the debt obligations of qualified school districts. The fund's income is obtained from land and mineral rights owned by the state of Texas.

Revenue Bonds

The second basic type of security structure is found in a revenue bond. Such bonds are issued for either project or enterprise financings in which the bond issuers pledge to the bondholders the revenues generated by the operating projects financed. A feasibility study is performed before the endeavor is undertaken to determine whether it can be self-supporting.

For a revenue bond, the revenue of the enterprise is pledged to service the debt of the issue. The details of how revenue received by the enterprise will be disbursed are set forth in the trust indenture. Typically, the flow of funds for a revenue bond is as follows. First, all revenues from the enterprise are put into a revenue fund. It is from the revenue fund that disbursements for expenses are made to the following funds: **operation and maintenance fund**, **sinking fund**, **debt service reserve fund**, **renewal and replacement fund**, **reserve maintenance fund**, and **surplus fund**.[1]

Operations of the enterprise have priority over the servicing of the issue's debt, and cash needed to operate the enterprise is deposited from the revenue fund into the operation and maintenance fund. The pledge of revenue to the bondholders is a net revenue pledge, net meaning after operation expenses, so cash required to service the debt is deposited next in the sinking fund. Disbursements are then made to bondholders as specified in the trust indenture. Any remaining cash is then distributed to the reserve funds. The purpose of the debt service reserve fund is to accumulate cash to cover any shortfall of future revenue to service the issue's debt. The specific amount that must be

---

[1]There are structures in which it is legally permissible for others to tap the revenues of the enterprise prior to the disbursement set forth in the flow of funds structure described next. For example, it is possible that the revenue bond could be structured such that the revenue is first applied to the general obligation of the municipality that has issued the bond.

deposited is stated in the trust indenture. The function of the renewal and replacement fund is to accumulate cash for regularly scheduled major repairs and equipment replacement. The function of the reserve maintenance fund is to accumulate cash for extraordinary maintenance or replacement costs that might arise. Finally, if any cash remains after disbursement for operations, debt servicing, and reserves, it is deposited in the surplus fund. The issuer can use the cash in this fund in any way it deems appropriate.

There are various restrictive covenants included in the trust indenture for a revenue bond to protect the bondholders. A rate, or user charge, covenant dictates how charges will be set on the product or service sold by the enterprise. The covenant could specify that the minimum charges be set so as to satisfy both expenses and debt servicing, or to yield a higher rate to provide for a certain amount of reserves. An additional bond's covenant indicates whether additional bonds with the same lien may be issued. If additional bonds with the same lien may be issued, conditions that must first be satisfied are specified. Other covenants specify that the facility may not be sold, the amount of insurance to be maintained, requirements for recordkeeping and for the auditing of the enterprise's financial statements by an independent accounting firm, and requirements for maintaining the facilities in good order.

Following are examples of revenue bonds.[2]

Airport Revenue Bonds

The revenues securing these bonds usually come from either traffic-generated sources—such as landing fees, concession fees, and airline fueling fees—or lease revenues from one or more airlines for the use of a specific facility such as a terminal or hangar.

College and University Revenue Bonds

The revenues securing these bonds usually include dormitory room rental fees, tuition payments, and sometimes the general assets of the college or university as well.

Hospital Revenue Bonds

The security for hospital revenue bonds usually depends on federal and state reimbursement programs (such as Medicaid and Medicare), third-party commercial payers (such as Blue Cross, health maintenance organizations, and private insurance), and individual patient payments.

Single-Family Mortgage Revenue Bonds

These bonds are usually secured by the mortgages and loan repayments on single-family homes. Security features vary but can include Federal Housing Administration (FHA), Veterans Administration (VA), or private mortgage insurance.[3]

Multifamily Revenue Bonds

These revenue bonds are usually issued for multifamily housing projects for senior citizens and low-income families. Some housing revenue bonds are secured by mortgages that are federally insured; others receive federal government operating subsidies or interest-cost subsidies; still others receive only local property tax reductions as subsidies.

---

[2]The descriptions are adapted from various writings coauthored with Sylvan G. Feldstein of The Guardian Life.
[3]Mortgage insurance is discussed in Chapter 10.

Public Power Revenue Bonds

These bonds are secured by revenues to be produced from electrical operating plants. Some bonds are for a single issuer, who constructs and operates power plants and then sells the electricity. Other public power revenue bonds are issued by groups of public and private investor-owned utilities for the joint financing of the construction of one or more power plants.

Resource Recovery Revenue Bonds

A resource recovery facility converts refuse (solid waste) into commercially salable energy, recoverable products, and a residue to be landfilled. The major revenues securing these bonds usually are (1) fees paid by those who deliver the waste to the facility for disposal; (2) revenues from steam, electricity, or refuse-derived fuel sold to either an electric power company or another energy user; and (3) revenues from the sale of recoverable materials such as aluminum and steel scrap.

Seaport Revenue Bonds

The security for these bonds can include specific lease agreements with the benefiting companies, or pledged marine terminal and cargo tonnage fees.

Student Loan Revenue Bonds

Student loan repayments under student loan revenue bond programs are sometimes 100% guaranteed either directly by the federal government or by a state guaranty agency.

Toll Road and Gas Tax Revenue Bonds

There are generally two types of highway revenue bonds. Bond proceeds of the first type are used to build such specific revenue-producing facilities as toll roads, bridges, and tunnels. For these pure enterprise-type revenue bonds, the revenues pledged usually are the monies collected through tolls. The second type of highway revenue bond is one in which bondholders are paid by earmarked revenues outside of toll collections, such as gasoline taxes, automobile registration payments, and driver's license fees.

Water Revenue Bonds

Water revenue bonds are issued to finance the construction of water treatment plants, pumping stations, collection facilities, and distribution systems. Revenues usually come from connection fees and charges paid by users of the water systems.

Hybrid and Special Bond Securities

Some municipal bonds that have the basic characteristics of general obligation bonds and revenue bonds have more issue-specific structures as well. Some examples are insured bonds, bank-backed municipal bonds, refunded bonds, structured/asset-backed securities, and "troubled city" bailout bonds.

Insured Bonds

Insured bonds, in addition to being secured by the issuer's revenue, are also backed by insurance policies written by commercial insurance companies. Insurance on a municipal bond is an agreement by an insurance company to pay the bondholder any bond principal and/or coupon interest that is due on a stated maturity date but that has not been paid by the bond issuer. When issued, this municipal bond insurance usually extends for the term of the bond issue, and it cannot be canceled by the insurance company.

Because municipal bond insurance reduces credit risk for the investor, the marketability of certain municipal bonds can be greatly expanded. Municipal bonds that benefit most from the insurance would include lower-quality bonds; bonds issued by smaller governmental units not widely known in the financial community; bonds that have a sound, though complex and difficult-to-understand, security structure; and bonds issued by infrequent local-government borrowers who do not have a general market following among investors.

Of course, a major factor for an issuer to obtain bond insurance is that its credit worthiness without the insurance is substantially lower than what it would be with the insurance. That is, the interest cost savings are only of sufficient magnitude to offset the cost of the insurance premium when the underlying credit worthiness of the issuer is lower. In general, although insured municipal bonds sell at yields lower than they would without the insurance, they tend to have yields higher than other AAA-rated bonds.

There are two major groups of municipal bond insurers. The first includes the monoline companies that are primarily in the business of insuring municipal bonds. Almost all of the companies that are now insuring municipal bonds can be characterized as monoline in structure. The second group of municipal bond insurers includes the multiline property and casualty companies that usually have a wide base of business, including insurance for fires, collisions, hurricanes, and health problems. Most new issues in the municipal bond market today are insured by the following monoline insurers: AMBAC Indemnity Corporation (AMBAC); Financial Guaranty Insurance Company (FGIC); Financial Security Assurance, Inc. (FSA); and Municipal Bond Investors Assurance Corporation (MBIA Corp.).

Bank-Backed Municipal Bonds

Since the 1980s, municipal obligations have been increasingly supported by various types of credit facilities provided by commercial banks. The support is in addition to the issuer's cash flow revenues.

There are three basic types of bank support: letter of credit, irrevocable line of credit, and revolving line of credit. A **letter-of-credit agreement** is the strongest type of support available from a commercial bank. Under this arrangement, the bank is required to advance funds to the trustee if a default has occurred. An **irrevocable line of credit** is not a guarantee of the bond issue, although it does provide a level of security. A **revolving line of credit** is a liquidity-type credit facility that provides a source of liquidity for payment of maturing debt in the event that no other funds of the issuer are currently available. Because a bank can cancel a revolving line of credit without notice if the issuer fails to meet certain covenants, bond security depends entirely on the credit worthiness of the municipal issuer.

Refunded Bonds

Although originally issued as either revenue or general obligation bonds, municipals are sometimes refunded. A refunding usually occurs when the original bonds are escrowed or collateralized by direct obligations guaranteed by the U.S. government.

By this it is meant that a portfolio of securities guaranteed by the U.S. government is placed in trust. The portfolio of securities is assembled such that the cash flow from all the securities matches the obligations that the issuer must pay. For example, suppose that a municipality has a 7% $100 million issue with 12 years remaining to maturity. The municipality's obligation is to make payments of $3.5 million every 6 months for the next 12 years and $100 million 12 years from now. If the issuer wants to refund this issue, a portfolio of U.S. government obligations can be purchased that has a cash flow of $3.5 million every 6 months for the next 12 years and $100 million 12 years from now.

When this portfolio of securities whose cash flow matches that of the municipality's obligation is in place, the refunded bonds are no longer secured as either general obligation or revenue bonds. The bonds are now supported by the portfolio of securities held in an escrow fund. Such bonds, if escrowed with securities guaranteed by the U.S. government, have little if any credit risk. They are the safest municipal bond investments available.

The escrow fund for a refunded municipal bond can be structured so that the refunded bonds are to be called at the first possible call date or a subsequent call date established in the original bond indenture. Such bonds are known as **prerefunded municipal bonds**. Although refunded bonds are usually retired at their first or subsequent call date, some are structured to match the debt obligation to the retirement date. Such bonds are known as **escrowed-to-maturity** bonds.

There are three reasons why a municipal issuer may refund an issue by creating an escrow fund. First, many refunded issues were originally issued as revenue bonds. Included in revenue issues are restrictive-bond covenants. The municipality may wish to eliminate these restrictions. The creation of an escrow fund to pay the bondholders legally eliminates any restrictive-bond covenants. This is the motivation for the escrowed-to-maturity bonds. Second, some issues are refunded in order to alter the maturity schedule of the obligation. Finally, when interest rates have declined after a municipal security has been issued, there is a tax arbitrage opportunity available to the issuer by paying existing bondholders a lower interest rate and using the proceeds to create a portfolio of U.S. government securities paying a higher interest rate.[4] This is the motivation for the prerefunded bonds.

Structured/Asset-Backed Bonds

In recent years, state and local governments began issuing bonds where the debt service is to be paid from so-called dedicated revenues such as sales taxes, tobacco settlement payments, fees, and penalty payments. These structures mimic the asset-backed bonds that are discussed in Chapter 14. Asset-backed bonds are also referred to as **dedicated revenue bonds and structured bonds**.

---

[4]Because the interest rate that a municipality must pay on borrowed funds is less than the interest rate paid by the U.S. government, in the absence of any restrictions in the tax code, a municipal issuer can realize a tax arbitrage. This can be done by issuing a bond and immediately investing the proceeds in a U.S. government security. There are tax rules that prevent such arbitrage. Should a municipal issuer violate the tax-arbitrage rules, the Internal Revenue Service will rule the issue to be taxable. However, if subsequent to the issuance of a bond interest rates decline so that the issuer will find it advantageous to call the bond, the establishment of the escrow fund will not violate the tax-arbitrage rules.

These bonds have unique risks compared to other types of revenue bonds. Consider, for example, bonds backed by tobacco settlement payments. In 1998, the four largest tobacco companies (Philip Morris; R. J. Reynolds; Brown & Williamson; and Lorillard) reached a settlement with 46 state attorneys general to pay over the following 25 years a total of $206 billion. States and municipalities began to sell bonds backed by the future payments of the tobacco companies. New York City was the first to do so in November 1999 with a bond offering of $709 million. The credit risk associated with these bonds is that they depend on the ability of the tobacco companies to make the payments.

Troubled City Bailout Bonds

Troubled city bailout bonds are structured to appear as pure revenue bonds, but in essence they are not. Revenues come from general-purpose taxes and revenues that otherwise would have gone to the state's or the city's general fund. These bond structures were created to bail out underlying general obligation bond issuers from severe budget deficits. Examples are the New York State Municipal Assistance Corporation of the City of New York Bonds (MAC) and the State of Illinois Chicago School Finance Authority Bonds.

Redemption Features

Municipal bonds are issued with one of two debt retirement structures, or a combination. Either a bond has a serial maturity structure or it has a term maturity structure. A **serial maturity structure** requires a portion of the debt obligation to be retired each year. A **term maturity structure** provides for the debt obligation to be repaid on a final date.

Usually, term bonds have maturities ranging from 20 to 40 years and retirement schedules (sinking fund provisions) that begin 5 to 10 years before the final term maturity. Municipal bonds may be called prior to the stated maturity date, either according to a mandatory sinking fund or at the option of the issuer. In revenue bonds there is a catastrophe call provision that requires the issuer to call the entire issue if the facility is destroyed.

Special Investment Features

There are zero-coupon bonds, floating-rate bonds, and putable bonds in the municipal bond market.

In the municipal bond market there are two types of zero-coupon bonds. One type is issued at a very deep discount and matures at par. The difference between the par value and the purchase price represents a predetermined compound yield. These zero-coupon bonds are similar to those issued in the taxable bond market for Treasuries and corporates. The second type is called a **municipal multiplier**, or **compound interest bond**. This is a bond issued at par that has interest payments. The interest payments are not distributed to the holder of the bond until maturity, but the issuer agrees to reinvest the undistributed interest payments at the bond's yield to maturity when it was issued. For example, suppose that a 10% 10-year coupon bond with a par value of $5,000 is sold at par to yield 10%. Every six months the maturity value of this bond is increased by 5% of the maturity value of the previous six months. At the end of

10 years, the maturity value of the bond will be equal to $13,266.[5] In the case of a 10 year zero-coupon bond priced to yield 10%, the bond would have a maturity value of $5,000 but sell for $1,884 when issued.[6]

MUNICIPAL MONEY MARKET PRODUCTS

Tax-exempt money market products include notes, commercial paper, variable-rate demand obligations, and a hybrid of the last two products.

Municipal Notes

Municipal notes include tax anticipation notes (TANs), revenue anticipation notes (RANs), grant anticipation notes (GANs), and bond anticipation notes (BANs). These are temporary borrowings by states, local governments, and special jurisdictions. Usually, notes are issued for a period of 12 months, although it is not uncommon for notes to be issued for periods as short as three months and for as long as three years. TANs and RANs (also known as TRANs) are issued in anticipation of the collection of taxes or other expected revenues. These are borrowings to even out irregular flows into the treasuries of the issuing entity. BANs are issued in anticipation of the sale of long-term bonds.

Tax-Exempt Commercial Paper

As with commercial paper issued by corporations, tax-exempt commercial paper is used by municipalities to raise funds on a short-term basis ranging from 1 to 270 days. The dealer sets interest rates for various maturity dates and the investor then selects the desired date. Provisions in the 1986 tax act have restricted the issuance of tax-exempt commercial paper. Specifically, the act limits the new issuance of municipal obligations that is tax exempt, and as a result, every maturity of a tax-exempt municipal issuance is considered a new debt issuance. Consequently, very limited issuance of tax-exempt commercial paper exists. Instead, issuers use one of the next two products to raise short-term funds.

Variable-Rate Demand Obligations

Variable-rate demand obligations (VRDOs) are floating-rate obligations that have a nominal long-term maturity but have a coupon rate that is reset either daily or every seven days. The investor has an option to put the issue back to the trustee at any time with seven days' notice. The put price is par plus accrued interest.

---

[5]This is found by computing the future value of $5,000 twenty periods from now using a 5% interest rate. That is,

$$\$5,000 \times (1.05)^{20} = \$13,266$$

[6]This is found by computing the present value of $5,000 twenty periods from now by using a 5% interest rate. That is,

$$\$5,000 \times \frac{1}{(1.05)^{20}} = \$1,884$$

Commercial Paper/VRDO Hybrid

The commercial paper/VRDO hybrid is customized to meet the cash flow needs of an investor. As with tax-exempt commercial paper, there is flexibility in structuring the maturity, because the remarketing agent establishes interest rates for a range of maturities. Although the instrument may have a long nominal maturity, there is a put provision, as with a VRDO. Put periods can range from 1 day to more than 360 days. On the put date, the investor can put back the bonds, receiving principal and interest, or the investor can elect to extend the maturity at the new interest rate and put date posted by the remarketing agent at that time. Thus, the investor has two choices when initially purchasing this instrument: the interest rate and the put date. Interest is generally paid on the put date if the date is within 180 days. If the put date is more than 180 days forward, interest is paid semiannually.

Commercial paper dealers market these products under a proprietary name. For example, the Merrill Lynch product is called unit priced demand adjustable tax-exempt securities, or UPDATES. Lehman Brothers markets these simply as money market municipals. Goldman Sachs refers to these securities as flexible rate notes and Smith Barney Shearson markets them as BITS (bond interest term series).

MUNICIPAL DERIVATIVE SECURITIES

In recent years, a number of municipal products have been created from the basic fixed-rate municipal bond. This has been done by splitting up cash flows of newly issued bonds as well as bonds existing in the secondary markets. These products have been created by dividing the coupon interest payments and principal payments into two or more bond classes, or **tranches**. The resulting bond classes may have far different yield and price volatility characteristics than the underlying fixed-rate municipal bond from which they were created. By expanding the risk/return profile available in the municipal marketplace, institutional investors have more flexibility in structuring municipal bond portfolios either to satisfy a specific asset–liability objective or to make an interest rate or yield curve bet. In exchange for such benefits, municipal issuers benefit by being able to issue securities at a lower interest cost.

The name *derivative securities* has been attributed to these bond classes because they derive their value from the underlying fixed-rate municipal bond. Much of the development in this market has paralleled that of the taxable (specifically, the mortgage-backed securities) market discussed in Chapter 11. The ability of investment bankers to create these securities has been enhanced by the development of the municipal swap market. Next we give two examples of municipal derivative securities.

Floaters/Inverse Floaters

A common type of derivative security is one in which two classes of securities, a **floating-rate security** and an **inverse-floating-rate bond**, are created from a fixed-rate bond. The coupon rate on the floating-rate security is reset based on the results of a Dutch auction. The auction can take place anywhere between 7 and 35 days. The coupon rate on the floating-rate security changes in the same direction as market rates. The inverse-floating-rate bond receives the residual interest; that is, the coupon interest paid on this bond is the difference between the fixed rate on the underlying bond and the rate on the floating-rate security. Thus, the coupon rate on the inverse-floating-rate bond changes in the opposite direction of interest rates.

The sum of the interest paid on the floater and inverse floater (plus fees associated with the auction) must always equal the sum of the fixed-rate bond from which they were created. A floor (a minimum interest rate) is established on the inverse floater. Typically, the floor is zero. As a result, a cap (maximum interest rate) will be imposed on the floater such that the combined floor of zero on the inverse floater and the cap on the floater is equal to the total interest rate on the fixed-rate bond from which they were created.

Inverse floaters can be created in one of three ways. First, a municipal dealer can buy in the secondary market a fixed-rate municipal bond and place it in a trust. The trust then issues a floater and an inverse floater. The second method is similar to the first except that the municipal dealer uses a newly issued municipal bond to create a floater and an inverse floater as illustrated in Exhibit 8-1. The third method is to create an inverse floater without the need to create a floater. This is done using the municipal swaps market and is discussed in Chapter 28.

The dealer determines the ratio of floaters to inverse floaters. For example, an investment banking firm may purchase $100 million of the underlying bond in the secondary market and issue $50 million of floaters and $50 million of inverse floaters. The dealer may opt for a 60/40 or any other split. The split of floaters/inverse floaters determines the leverage of the inverse floaters and thus affects its price volatility when interest rates change. In Chapter 4, we explained that the duration of an inverse floater is a multiple of the underlying fixed-rate issue from which it was created. The multiple is determined by the leverage. To date, the most popular split of floaters and inverse floaters has been 50/50. In such instances, the inverse floater will have double the duration of the fixed-rate bond from which it is created. Determination of the leverage will be set based on the desires of investors at the time of the transaction.

The investor in the inverse floater can purchase the corresponding floater at auction and combine her two positions to effectively own the underlying fixed-rate bond. This can be done if interest rates are rising and the investor wishes to close out her inverse floater position. Because the market for inverse floaters is not highly liquid at this time, this represents an easy way to convert her position into a synthetic fixed-rate bond. In the future, the investor may opt to split the issue again, retaining the inverse floater. This is a valuable option for investors. As a result, the yield on this bond will generally be less than the yield on a comparable fixed-rate bond that does not have this option.

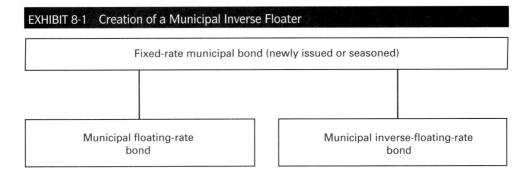

EXHIBIT 8-1   Creation of a Municipal Inverse Floater

Several investment banking firms active in the municipal bond market have developed proprietary products. Merrill Lynch's institutional floaters are called FLOATS and its inverse floaters are called RITES (residual interest tax-exempt securities). Goldman Sachs' proprietary products are called PARS (periodic auction reset securities), which are floaters, and INFLOS, which are inverse floaters. Lehman Brothers' proprietary products are called RIBs (residual interest bonds) and SAVRS (select auction variable-rate securities).

Strips and Partial Strips

Municipal strip obligations are created when a municipal bond's cash flows are used to back zero-coupon instruments. The maturity value of each zero-coupon bond represents a cash flow on the underlying security. These are similar to the strips that are created in the Treasury market that we described in Chapter 6. One example of this in the municipal bond market is Merrill Lynch's M-TIGRS.

Partial strips have also been created from cash bonds, which are zero-coupon instruments to a particular date, such as a call date, and then are converted into coupon-paying instruments. These are called **convertibles** or **step-up bonds**. Merrill Lynch markets these as LIMOS. Goldman Sachs uses the name GAINS for these instruments.

Other products can be created by allocating the interest payments and principal of a fixed-coupon-rate municipal bond to more than two bond classes. For example, consider a noncallable/nonputable $100 million par value issue with a coupon rate of 6%. From this fixed-rate issue, it would be possible to create three bond classes: (1) $60 million par value of a 4% fixed-rate coupon bond, (2) a floating-rate bond with a par value of $20 million and a coupon rate that floats based on the J. J. Kenny index plus 200 basis points, and (3) an inverse floating rate with a par value of $20 million, which receives the residual interest from the difference between the underlying issue and the coupon on the floating-rate class. Notice that the total par value of the collateral is distributed among the three bond classes, as is the fixed coupon interest on the underlying issue. In addition to creating a floater and an inverse floater, a synthetic fixed-rate municipal bond selling at a discount has also been created. This is because in this illustration the required coupon rate on the underlying municipal bond would be 6% for it to sell at par, but the fixed-rate bond class created has the same maturity and only a 4% coupon rate. Thus, it will sell at a discount. An investor who prefers a discount security (which has higher volatility than a similar bond selling at par, as explained in Chapter 4) because of an anticipated decline in interest rates but finds it difficult to obtain such bonds in the marketplace will be attracted to this synthetic bond.

These types of structures were introduced by Lehman Brothers in February 1993 as part of a $95.6 million offering of the Pennsylvania Housing Agency and again a month later in a $740 million offering of the Puerto Rico Telephone Agency.[7] These are collectively called **pieces and strips**.

---

[7]Aaron Pressman, "Lehman's 'Strips and Pieces' Allow Investors Multitude of Options in Structuring Portfolios," *The Bond Buyer*, March 26, 1993.

CREDIT RISK

Although municipal bonds at one time were considered second in safety only to U.S. Treasury securities, today there are new concerns about the credit risks of municipal securities.[8] The first concern came out of the New York City billion-dollar financial crisis in 1975. On February 25, 1975, the State of New York's Urban Development Corporation defaulted on a $100 million note issue that was the obligation of New York City; many market participants had been convinced that the State of New York would not allow the issue to default. Although New York City was later able to obtain a $140 million revolving credit from banks to cure the default, lenders became concerned that the city would face difficulties in repaying its accumulated debt, which stood at $14 billion on March 31, 1975. This financial crisis sent a loud and clear warning to market participants in general—regardless of supposedly ironclad protection for the bondholder, when issuers such as large cities have severe financial difficulties, the financial stakes of public employee unions, vendors, and community groups may be dominant forces in balancing budgets. This reality was reinforced by the federal bankruptcy law that took effect in October 1979, which made it easier for the issuer of a municipal security to go into bankruptcy.

The second reason for concern about municipal securities credit risk is the proliferation in this market of innovative financing techniques to secure new bond issues. In addition to the established general obligation bonds and revenue bonds, there are now more non–voter-approved, innovative, and legally untested security mechanisms. These innovative financing mechanisms include "moral obligation" bonds and commercial bank-backed letters of credit bonds, to name a few. What distinguishes these newer bonds from the more traditional general obligation and revenue bonds is that there is no history of court decisions or other case law that firmly establishes the rights of the bondholders and the obligations of the issuers. It is not possible to determine in advance the probable legal outcome if the newer financing mechanisms were to be challenged in court. This is illustrated most dramatically by the bonds of the Washington Public Power Supply System (WPPSS), where bondholder rights to certain revenues were not upheld by the highest court in the state of Washington.

As with corporate bonds, some institutional investors in the municipal bond market rely on their own in-house municipal credit analysts for determining the credit worthiness of a municipal issue; other investors rely on the nationally recognized rating companies. The two leading rating companies are Moody's and Standard & Poor's, and the assigned rating system is essentially the same as that used for corporate bonds.

In evaluating general obligation bonds, the commercial rating companies assess information in four basic categories.[9] The first category includes information on the issuer's debt structure to determine the overall debt burden. The second category relates to the issuer's ability and political discipline to maintain sound budgetary policy. The focus of attention here usually is on the issuer's general operating funds and

---

[8]For a history of defaults of municipal bonds, see Chapter 2 in Sylvan G. Feldstein and Frank J. Fabozzi, *The Dow Jones–Irwin Guide to Municipal Bonds* (Homewood, IL: Dow Jones–Irwin, 1987).

[9]Although there are many similarities in how Moody's and Standard & Poor's approach the credit rating of general obligation bonds, there are differences in their approaches as well. For a discussion of these differences, see Feldstein and Fabozzi, *The Dow Jones–Irwin Guide to Municipal Bonds.*

whether it has maintained at least balanced budgets over three to five years. The third category involves determining the specific local taxes and intergovernmental revenues available to the issuer as well as obtaining historical information both on tax collection rates, which are important when looking at property tax levies, and on the dependence of local budgets on specific revenue sources. The fourth and last category of information necessary to the credit analysis is an assessment of the issuer's overall socioeconomic environment. The determinations that have to be made here include trends of local employment distribution and composition, population growth, real estate property valuation, and personal income, among other economic factors.

Although there are numerous security structures for revenue bonds, the underlying principle in rating is whether the project being financed will generate sufficient cash flow to satisfy the obligations due bondholders.[10] A natural question to ask is: How good are the ratings? Of the municipal securities that were rated by a commercial rating company in 1929 and plunged into default in 1932, 78% had been rated AA or better, and 48% had been rated AAA. Since then the ability of rating agencies to assess the credit worthiness of municipal securities has evolved to a level of general industry acceptance and respectability. In most instances, ratings adequately describe the financial condition of the issuers and identify the credit risk factors. A small but significant number of recent instances still have caused market participants to reexamine their reliance on the opinions of the rating companies. One example is the bonds of the WPPSS mentioned previously. The two major commercial rating companies gave their highest ratings to these bonds in the early 1980s. While these high-quality ratings were in effect, WPPSS sold more than $8 billion in long-term bonds. By 1986 more than $2 billion of these bonds were in default.

RISKS ASSOCIATED WITH INVESTING IN MUNICIPAL SECURITIES

The investor in municipal securities is exposed to the same risks affecting corporate bonds plus an additional one that may be labeled **tax risk**. There are two types of tax risk to which tax-exempt municipal securities buyers are exposed. The first is the risk that the federal income tax rate will be reduced. The higher the marginal tax rate, the greater the value of the tax exemption feature. As the marginal tax rate declines, the price of a tax-exempt municipal security will decline. When in 1995 there were Congressional proposals regarding the introduction of a flat tax with a low tax rate, tax-exempt municipal bonds began trading at lower prices.

The second type of tax risk is that a municipal bond issued as a tax-exempt issue may eventually be declared to be taxable by the Internal Revenue Service. This may occur because many municipal revenue bonds have elaborate security structures that could be subject to future adverse congressional action and IRS interpretation. A loss of the tax exemption feature will cause the municipal bond to decline in value in order to provide a yield comparable to similar taxable bonds. As an example, in June 1980,

---

[10]A comprehensive discussion of the analysis of various revenue bond structures is found in Sylvan G. Feldstein, Frank J. Fabozzi, and Irving M. Pollack (eds.), *The Municipal Bond Handbook*, Vol. II (Homewood, IL: Dow Jones-Irwin, 1983); and Feldstein and Fabozzi, *The Dow Jones–Irwin Guide to Municipal Bonds*.

the Battery Park City Authority sold $97.315 million in notes, which at the time of issuance legal counsel advised were exempt from federal income taxation. In November 1980, however, the IRS held that interest on these notes was not exempt. The issue was not settled until September 1981, when the Authority and the IRS signed a formal agreement resolving the matter so as to make the interest on the notes tax-exempt.

YIELDS ON MUNICIPAL BONDS

As explained in Chapter 5, a common yield measure used to compare the yield on a tax-exempt municipal bond with a comparable taxable bond is the equivalent taxable yield. The equivalent taxable yield is computed as follows:

$$\text{equivalent taxable yield} = \frac{\text{tax-exempt yield}}{1 - \text{marginal tax rate}}$$

For example, suppose that an investor in the 40% marginal tax bracket is considering the acquisition of a tax-exempt municipal bond that offers a yield of 6.5%. The equivalent taxable yield is 10.83%, as follows:

$$\text{equivalent taxable yield} = \frac{0.065}{1 - 0.40} = 0.1083$$

When computing the equivalent taxable yield, the traditionally computed yield to maturity is not the tax-exempt yield if the issue is selling at a discount because only the coupon interest is exempt from federal income taxes. Instead, the yield to maturity after an assumed tax rate on the capital gain is computed and used in the numerator of the formula shown here. The yield to maturity after an assumed tax on the capital gain is calculated in the same manner as the traditional yield to maturity as explained in Chapter 3.

Yield Spreads

Because of the tax-exempt feature of municipal bonds, the yield on municipal bonds is less than that on Treasuries with the same maturity. The yield on municipal bonds is compared to the yield on Treasury bonds with the same maturity by computing the following ratio:

$$\text{yield ratio} = \frac{\text{yield on municipal bond}}{\text{yield on same maturity Treasury bond}}$$

The yield ratio has changed over time. The higher the tax rate, the more attractive the tax-exempt feature and the lower the yield ratio. The ratio of municipal yields to Treasury yields varies over time. For example, the yield ratio for 10-year AAA general obligation bonds and 10-year Treasury securities varied in the 1990s from a low of 0.72 on September 30, 1994, to a high of 0.94 on September 30, 1998.

The ratio of municipal yields to Treasury yields varies over time. Yield spreads within the municipal bond market are attributable to differences between credit ratings (i.e., credit spreads), sectors within markets (intramarket spreads), and differences between maturities (maturity spreads).

Our statement in Chapter 5 about credit spreads between credit ratings for corporate bonds over the interest-rate cycle is true for municipal bonds: Credit spreads widen during recessionary periods but narrow during periods of economic prosperity. Another factor that can cause changes in the credit spread is a temporary oversupply of issues within a market sector. For example, a substantial new-issue volume of high-grade state general obligation bonds may tend to decrease the spread between high-grade and lower-grade revenue bonds. In a weak market environment, it is easier for high-grade municipal bonds to come to market than weaker ones. Therefore, it is not uncommon for high grades to flood weak markets at the same time there is a relative scarcity of medium- and lower-grade municipal bond issues.

In the municipal bond market, several benchmark curves exist. In general, a benchmark yield curve is constructed for AAA-quality-rated state general obligation bonds. In the Treasury and corporate bond markets, it is not unusual to find at different times all three shapes for the yield curve described in Chapter 5. In general, the municipal yield curve is positively sloped.

Bonds of municipal issuers located in certain states yield considerably less than issues of identical credit quality that come from other states that trade in the general market. One reason for this is that states often exempt interest from in-state issues from state and local personal income taxes, whereas interest from out-of-state issues is generally not exempt. Consequently, in states with high income taxes, such as New York and California, strong investor demand for in-state issues will reduce their yields relative to bonds of issuers located in states where state and local income taxes are not important considerations (e.g., Florida).

MUNICIPAL BOND MARKET

Primary Market

A substantial number of municipal obligations are brought to market each week. A state or local government can market its new issue by offering bonds publicly to the investing community or by placing them privately with a small group of investors. When a public offering is selected, the issue usually is underwritten by investment bankers and/or municipal bond departments of commercial banks. Public offerings may be marketed by either competitive bidding or direct negotiations with underwriters. When an issue is marketed via competitive bidding, the issue is awarded to the bidder submitting the best bid.

Usually, state and local governments require a competitive sale to be announced in a recognized financial publication, such as the *Bond Buyer*, which is a trade publication for the municipal bond industry. The *Bond Buyer* also provides information on upcoming competitive sales and most negotiated sales, as well as the results of previous weeks.

Most states mandate that general obligation issues be marketed through competitive bidding, but generally this is not required for revenue bonds. Recent scandals involving financial contributions of underwriters to elected officials have made some municipalities concerned with whether they are receiving the lowest-cost funding possible. Consequently, more municipalities are requiring competitive bidding for both general obligation and revenue issues.

An **official statement** describing the issue and the issuer is prepared for new offerings. Municipal bonds have legal opinions that are summarized in the official statement. The relationship of the legal opinion to the safety of the bond is twofold. First, bond counsel determines if the issuer is indeed legally able to issue the bonds. Second, bond counsel verifies that the issuer has prepared for the bond sale properly by having enacted various required ordinances, resolutions, and trust indentures and without violating any other laws and regulations.

Secondary Market

Municipal bonds are traded in the over-the-counter market supported by municipal bond dealers across the country. Markets are maintained on smaller issuers (referred to as **local general credits**) by regional brokerage firms, local banks, and by some of the larger Wall Street firms. Larger issuers (referred to as **general names**) are supported by the larger brokerage firms and banks, many of whom have investment banking relationships with these issuers. There are brokers who serve as intermediaries in the sale of large blocks of municipal bonds among dealers and large institutional investors. Since 2000, bonds in the secondary market as well as some new competitive and negotiated issues began to be auctioned and sold over the Internet by large and small broker-dealers to institutional and individual investors.

In the municipal bond markets, an odd lot of bonds is $25,000 or less in par value for retail investors. For institutions, anything below $100,000 in par value is considered an odd lot. Dealer spreads depend on several factors: For the retail investor, the spread can range from as low as one-fourth of one point ($12.50 per $5,000 par value) on large blocks of actively traded bonds to four points ($200 per $5,000 of par value) for odd-lot sales of an inactive issue. For institutional investors, the dealer spread rarely exceeds one-half of one point ($25 per $5,000 of par value).

The convention for both corporate and Treasury bonds is to quote prices as a percentage of par value with 100 equal to par. Municipal bonds, however, generally are traded and quoted in terms of yield (yield to maturity or yield to call). The price of the bond in this case is called a **basis price**. The exception is certain long-maturity revenue bonds. A bond traded and quoted in dollar prices (actually, as a percentage of par value) is called a **dollar bond**.

Actual price and trade information for specific municipal bonds is available on a daily basis at no charge via the Internet at www.investinginbonds.com. It is the home page of the Bond Market Association. The trade information provided is from the Municipal Securities Rulemaking Board and Standard & Poor's J. J. Kenny. The original source of the trades reported are transactions between two dealers and a dealer with an institutional or retail customer (individual investor).

THE TAXABLE MUNICIPAL BOND MARKET

Taxable municipal bonds are bonds whose interest is taxed at the federal income tax level. Because there is no tax advantage, an issuer must offer a higher yield than for another tax-exempt municipal bond. The yield must be higher than the yield on U.S. government bonds because an investor faces credit risk by investing in a taxable municipal bond. The investors in taxable municipal bonds are investors who view them as alternatives to corporate bonds.

Why would a municipality want to issue a taxable municipal bond and thereby have to pay a higher yield than if it issued a tax-exempt municipal bond? There are three reasons for this. First, prior to 1986, there were many more activities that municipalities could finance by issuing tax-exempt municipal bonds. U.S. Congress felt that some of these activities should not be financed with tax-exempt municipal bonds because such activities do not benefit the public at large. As a result, Congress passed the Tax Reform Act of 1986, which imposed restrictions on what types of projects could be financed using tax-exempt municipal bonds. For example, within a particular project there is a maximum amount imposed on the issuance of tax-exempt municipal bonds for private activity bonds—the maximum amount is the greater of $150 million or $50 per state resident per year. As a result, municipalities had to finance these restricted activities in the taxable bond market.

The second reason is that the U.S. income tax code imposes restrictions on arbitrage opportunities that a municipality can realize from its financing activities. The third reason is that municipalities do not view their potential investor base as solely U.S. investors. Some issuers, for example, have been active issuers of bonds outside of the United States. When bonds are issued outside of the United States, the investor does not benefit from the tax-exempt feature. These last two reasons have to do with the flexibility afforded a municipality by using the taxable bond market rather than the tax-exempt bond market.

The most common types of activities for taxable municipal bonds used for financing are (1) local sports facilities, (2) investor-led housing projects, (3) advanced refunding of issues that are not permitted to be refunded because the tax law prohibits such activity, and (4) underfunded pension plan obligations of the municipality.

SUMMARY

Municipal securities are issued by state and local governments and their authorities, with the coupon interest on most issues being exempt from federal income taxes. The two basic security structures are tax-backed debt and revenue bonds. The former is secured by the issuer's general taxing power. Revenue bonds are used to finance specific projects and are dependent on revenues from those projects to satisfy the obligations. There are also hybrid securities that have certain characteristics of both general obligation and revenue bonds, and some securities that have unique structures. Municipal money market products include notes, commercial paper, variable-rate demand notes, and a hybrid of commercial paper and variable-rate demand notes. Derivative securities have been created from the basic fixed-rate municipal bond, the most popular being inverse floaters.

Municipal bonds may be retired with a serial maturity structure, a term maturity structure, or a combination. As in the case of corporate bonds, there are zero-coupon bonds and floating-rate bonds. Investing in municipal securities exposes investors to the same qualitative risks as investing in corporate bonds, with the additional risk that a change in the tax law may affect the price of municipal securities adversely.

Because of the tax-exempt feature, yields on municipal securities are lower than those on comparably rated taxable securities. Within the municipal bond market, there are credit spreads and maturity spreads. Typically, the municipal yield curve is upward sloping. Moreover, there are yield spreads related to differences between in-state issues and general market issues.

While the municipal bond market is dominated by tax-exempt municipal bonds, there are taxable municipal bonds. These bonds are issued by state and local governments due to restrictions on what financing activities a municipality may provide tax-exempt financing for and the flexibility they offer in terms of not having to comply with U.S. income tax laws in making financing decisions and issuing bonds outside of the United States.

Questions

1. Explain why you agree or disagree with the following statements:
   a. "All municipal bonds are exempt from federal income taxes."
   b. "All municipal bonds are exempt from state and local taxes."
2. If Congress changes the tax law so as to increase marginal tax rates, what will happen to the price of municipal bonds?
3. What is the difference between a general obligation bond and a revenue bond?
4. Which type of municipal bond would an investor analyze using an approach similar to that for analyzing a corporate bond?
5. In a revenue bond, which fund has priority when funds are disbursed from the reserve fund, the operation and maintenance fund, or the debt service reserve fund?
6. In a revenue bond, what is a catastrophe call provision?
7. What is the tax risk associated with investing in a municipal bond?
8. "An insured municipal bond is safer than an uninsured municipal bond." Indicate whether you agree or disagree with this statement.
9. In your view, would the typical AAA- or AA-rated municipal bond be insured?
10. Explain the different types of refunded bonds.
11. Give two reasons why an issuing municipality would want to refund an outstanding bond issue.
12. a. What are the three basic types of bank support for a bank-backed municipal security?

   b. Which is the strongest type of support available from a commercial bank?
13. What are TAN, RAN, GAN, and BAN?
14. Why has there been a decline in the issuance of tax-exempt commercial paper?
15. a. Explain how an inverse-floating-rate municipal bond can be created.
   b. Who determines the leverage of an inverse floater?
   c. What is the duration of an inverse floater?
16. For years, observers and analysts of the debt market believed that municipal securities were free of any risk of default. Why do most people now believe that municipal debt can carry a substantial amount of credit or default risk?
17. a. What is the equivalent taxable yield for an investor facing a 40% marginal tax rate, and who can purchase a tax-exempt municipal bond with a yield of 7.2?
   b. What are the limitations of using the equivalent taxable yield as a measure of relative value of a tax-exempt bond versus a taxable bond?
18. a. What is typically the benchmark yield curve in the municipal bond market?
   b. What can you say about the typical relationship between the yield on short- and long-term municipal bonds?
19. How does the steepness of the Treasury yield curve compare with that of the municipal yield curve?
20. Explain why the market for taxable municipal bonds competes for investors with the corporate bond market.

CHAPTER

9

NON–U.S. BONDS

After reading this chapter you will understand:

- the reasons for the globalization of financial markets

- the classification of global financial markets

- what the foreign bond market is

- what a global bond is

- the foreign exchange risk exposure of an investor who invests in nondollar-denominated bonds

- what a Eurobond is and the different types of Eurobond structures

- the classification of the global bond market in terms of trading blocs

- the euro government bond market

- the methods of distribution of new government bonds

- the issuance of linkers by sovereign issuers

- the motivation for investing in nondollar bonds

- factors considered in the rating of sovereign bonds

- how to compare yields on U.S. bonds and Eurobonds

- the Pfandbriefe market

- emerging market bonds

U.S. investors have become increasingly aware of non–U.S. interest-rate movements and their relationship to U.S. interest rates. In addition, foreign countries have liberalized their bond markets, making them more liquid and more accessible to international investors. In many cases, withholding taxes have been eliminated or reduced. Futures and options markets have been developed on government bonds in several major countries, permitting more effective implementation of hedging and arbitrage strategies. And in general, there is an increased awareness of the non–U.S. bond markets as potential sources of return enhancement and/or risk reduction. As a result, U.S. bond managers — mainly money managers who manage pension funds or other institutional monies, and mutual fund managers or others who manage retail monies — have increasingly adopted a global approach and invested in bonds from several countries.

Many global investors participate only in the foreign government bond markets rather than the nongovernment bond markets, because of the low credit risk, the liquidity, and the simplicity of the government markets. While nongovernment markets ("semigovernment," local government, corporate, and mortgage bond markets) provide higher yields, they also have greater credit risks, and foreign investors may not be ready to accept alien credit risks and less liquidity. In this chapter we look at the Eurobond market and several non–U.S. government bond markets.

CLASSIFICATION OF GLOBAL BOND MARKETS

There is no uniform system for classifying the sectors of the global bond market, although one possible classification is as follows. From the perspective of a given country, the global bond market can be classified into two markets: an internal bond market and an external bond market. The **internal bond market** is also called the **national bond market**. It can be decomposed into two parts: the domestic bond market and the foreign bond market. The **domestic bond market** is where issuers domiciled in the country issue bonds and where those bonds are subsequently traded. Exhibit 9-1 provides a schematic presentation of this classification system.

The **foreign bond market** of a country is where bonds of issuers not domiciled in the country are issued and traded. For example, in the United States the foreign bond market is the market where bonds are issued by non–U.S. entities and then subsequently traded. Bonds traded in the U.S. foreign bond market are nicknamed **Yankee bonds**. In Japan, a yen-denominated bond issued by a British corporation and subsequently traded in Japan's bond market is part of the Japanese foreign bond market. Yen-denominated bonds issued by non-Japanese entities are nicknamed **Samurai bonds**. Foreign bonds in the United Kingdom are referred to as **bulldog bonds**, in the Netherlands as **Rembrandt bonds**, and in Spain as **matador bonds**.

EXHIBIT 9-1   Classification of Global Financial Markets

Regulatory authorities in the country where the bond is issued impose certain rules governing the issuance of foreign bonds. These may include (1) restrictions on the bond structures that may be issued (e.g., unsecured debt, zero-coupon bonds, convertible bonds, and so on), (2) restrictions on the minimum or maximum size of an issue and/or the frequency with which an issuer may come to market, (3) a waiting period before an issuer can bring the issue to market (imposed to avoid an oversupply of issues), (4) a minimum quality standard (credit rating) for the issue or issuer, (5) disclosure and periodic reporting requirements, and (6) restrictions on the types of financial institutions permitted to underwrite issues. The 1980s have been characterized by general government relaxation or abolition of these restrictions so as to open up their bond market to issuers.

The **external bond market**, also called the **international bond market**, includes bonds with the following distinguishing features: (1) they are underwritten by an international syndicate; (2) at issuance they are offered simultaneously to investors in a number of countries; (3) they are issued outside the jurisdiction of any single country; and (4) they are in unregistered form. The external bond market is commonly referred to as the **offshore bond market**, or, more popularly, the **Eurobond market**. The classification used here is by no means universally accepted. Some market observers refer to the external bond market as consisting of the foreign bond market and the Eurobond market.

A **global bond** is one that is issued simultaneously in several bond markets throughout the world. Here are four examples of global bonds issued in 2005:

- On July 2005, the Asian Development Bank (ADB) issued a U.S. $1 billion five-year global bond. The issue was distributed as follows: 65% in Asia, 15% in the United States, and 20% in Europe.
- In September 2005, the Inter-American Development Bank issued a $1 billion global bond issue with a 10-year maturity. Investors in Asia acquired 63% of the issue; investors in the Americas 21%, and investors in Europe, the Middle East, and Africa purchased the balance.
- In February 2005, the World Bank issued a U.S. $750 million 30-year global bond. The bonds were placed 50% with North American investors, 35% with European investors, and 15% with Asian investors.
- In June 2005, Republic of Italy issued U.S. $3 billion of a 3-year global bond. The distribution breakdown on a regional basis was 56% in Asia, 17% in the United Kingdom, 12% in North America, 8% in the rest of Europe, and 7% in the Middle East.

Another way to classify the world's bond market is in terms of trading blocs. The trading blocs used by practitioners for this classification are[1]

1. dollar bloc
2. European bloc
3. Japan
4. emerging markets

---

[1] See Christopher B. Steward, J. Hank Lynch, and Frank J. Fabozzi, "International Bond Portfolio Management," forthcoming in Frank J. Fabozzi (ed.), *Fixed Income Readings for the Chartered Financial Analysts Program* (New Hope, PA: Frank J. Fabozzi Associates, 2004).

The **dollar bloc** includes the United States, Canada, Australia, and New Zealand. The **European bloc** is subdivided into two groups: (1) the **euro zone market bloc**, which has a common currency (Germany, France, Holland, Belgium, Luxembourg, Austria, Italy, Spain, Finland, Portugal, and Greece), the euro, and (2) the **non-euro zone market bloc** (Norway, Denmark, and Sweden). The United Kingdom often trades more on its own, influenced by both the euro zone and the United States, as well as its own economic fundamentals.

The trading bloc construct is useful because each bloc has a benchmark market that greatly influences price movements in the other markets. Investors are often focused more on the spread level of, say, Denmark to Germany, than the absolute level of yields in Denmark.

FOREIGN EXCHANGE RISK AND BOND RETURNS

The return to U.S. investors from investments in non–U.S. bonds that are denominated in a foreign currency consists of two components: (1) the return on the security measured in the currency in which the bond is denominated (called **local currency return**), which results from coupon payments, reinvestment income, and capital gains/losses; and (2) changes in the foreign exchange rate.

An **exchange rate** is the amount of one currency that can be exchanged for another currency or the price of one currency in terms of another currency. Since the early 1970s, exchange rates between currencies have been free to float, with market forces determining the relative value of a currency.[2] Thus, each day a currency's value may stay the same, increase, or decrease relative to that of another currency. When a currency declines in value relative to another currency, it is said to have **depreciated** relative to the other currency. Alternatively, this is the same as saying that the other currency has **appreciated**.

From the perspective of a U.S. investor, the cash flows of assets denominated in a foreign currency expose the investor to uncertainty as to the cash flow in U.S. dollars. The actual U.S. dollars that the investor gets depend on the exchange rate between the U.S. dollar and the foreign currency at the time the nondollar cash flow is received and exchanged for U.S. dollars. If the foreign currency depreciates (declines in value) relative to the U.S. dollar, the dollar value of the cash flows will be proportionately less. This risk is referred to as **foreign exchange risk**. This risk can be hedged with foreign exchange spot, forwards, futures, or options instruments (although there is a cost of hedging).

Several reasons have been offered for why U.S. investors should allocate a portion of their fixed income portfolio to nondollar bonds. The party line is that diversifying bond investments across countries—particularly with the currency hedged—may provide diversification resulting in a reduction in risk. This is generally demonstrated using modern portfolio theory by showing that investors can realize a higher expected return for a given level of risk (as measured by the standard deviation of return) by adding nondollar bonds in a portfolio containing U.S. bonds. Although there was ample

---

[2]In practice, national monetary authorities can intervene in the foreign exchange market for their currency for a variety of economic reasons, so the current foreign exchange system is sometimes referred to as a *managed* floating rate system.

evidence in the 1980s and early 1990s that this might have been true, recent evidence suggests that the reduction in risk may not be that great.[3]

One study suggests that while the diversification benefits may not be that great, a powerful reason for a U.S. investor to invest in nondollar bonds is "the increased opportunities to find value that multiple markets provide" but it is hard to quantify such a benefit because it depends on the investor's talents.[4] That is, nondollar bond investments—with the currency hedged—permits investment strategies based on interest rate changes in various countries, thereby providing additional dimensions to the actual investment decision or a broader range of investment choices. Another reason given for nondollar bond investing is that the decision not to hedge the currency component can then be regarded as an active currency play.

EUROBOND MARKET

The Eurobond market is divided into sectors depending on the currency in which the issue is denominated. For example, when Eurobonds are denominated in U.S. dollars, they are referred to as **Eurodollar bonds**. Eurobonds denominated in Japanese yen are referred to as **Euroyen bonds**.

In recent years it has become increasingly difficult to classify a bond issue as a foreign bond or a Eurobond based on the distinguishing characteristics that we cited earlier. We noted that the most important characteristic of a Eurobond offering is the composition of the underwriting syndicate. Yet "bought deals"—when there is only one underwriter—are becoming increasingly common. A bond offering in which there is only one underwriter and in which the issue is placed primarily outside the national market of both the issuer and underwriter would not traditionally be classified as a Eurobond offering. Another characteristic of a Eurobond is that it is not regulated by the single country whose currency is used to pay bondholders. In practice, however, only the United States and Canada do not place restrictions on U.S. dollar– or Canadian dollar–denominated issues sold outside their two countries. Regulators of other countries whose currencies are used in Eurobond issues have closely supervised such offerings. Their power to regulate Eurobond offerings comes from their ability to impose foreign exchange and/or capital restrictions.

Although Eurobonds are typically registered on a national stock exchange, the most common being the Luxembourg, London, or Zurich exchanges, the bulk of all trading is in the over-the-counter market. Listing is purely to circumvent restrictions imposed on some institutional investors who are prohibited from purchasing securities that are not listed on an exchange. Some of the stronger issuers privately place issues with international institutional investors.

Issuers of foreign bonds include national governments and their subdivisions, corporations (financial and nonfinancial), and supranationals. A **supranational** is an entity

---

[3]See Robert Litterman, "Nondollar Bond Markets: Opportunities for U.S. Portfolio Managers." *Fixed Income Research* (New York: Goldman, Sachs & Co., April 1992); and Michael R. Rosenberg, "International Fixed Income Investing: Theory and Practice," Chapter 49 in Frank J. Fabozzi (ed.), *The Handbook of Fixed Income Securities* (New York: McGraw-Hill, 2001).
[4]Litterman, "Nondollar Bond Markets," pp. 2–3.

that is formed by two or more central governments through international treaties. The purpose for creating a supranational is to promote economic development for the member countries. Two examples of supranational institutions are the International Bank for Reconstruction and Development, popularly referred to as the World Bank, and the Inter-American Development Bank. The general objective of the former is to improve the efficiency of the international financial and trading markets. The objective of the latter supranational is to promote economic growth in the developing countries of the Americas.

In the Eurobond market, indications for trades are initially expressed on a spread basis. In the U.S. market, the spread is relative to the U.S. Treasury yield curve. In the Eurobond market, the spread is expressed either relative to the interest rate swap curve (see Chapter 28) or over a specified government benchmark. Trades of less than $5 million are typically considered odd lots; because they are less efficient for dealers to handle, this impacts the price. It is rare that a trade will exceed $50 million.[5]

Corporate Bonds and Covenants

In Chapter 20, covenants for U.S. corporate bonds will be discussed. In the Eurobond market, there is a debate regarding the relatively weak protection afforded by covenants. The chief reason for this is that investors in corporate Eurobonds are geographically diverse. As a result, it makes it difficult for potential bond investors to agree on what form of covenants offer true protection.

For investment-grade corporate issues in the Eurobond market, documentation is somewhat standardized. According to David Munves, the key terms and conditions in Eurobond documentation are:

- *Governing law.* Most transactions are governed by U.K. law, although New York state law is an occasional alternative.
- *Security.* As a rule, issues are not secured by the company's assets.
- *Negative pledges.* Negative pledges are common. They prohibit an issuer from creating security interests on its assets, unless all bondholders receive the same level of security.
- *Subordination.* Except for bank or insurance capital issues, most bonds are sold on a senior basis.
- *Cross-default clauses.* Cross-default clauses state that if an issuer defaults on other borrowings, then the bonds will become due and payable. The definition of which borrowings are covered can vary. The cross-default clause usually carves out defaults in borrowings up to a certain threshold (e.g., $10,000) to prevent a minor trade dispute or overlooked invoice from allowing the bondholders to put the bonds back to the issuer.
- *Prohibition on the sale of material assets.* In order to protect bondholders, most documentation prohibits the sale or transfer of material assets or subsidiaries. As with cross-default clauses, the definition of material can vary considerably.[6]

---

[5]David Munves, "The Eurobond Market," Chapter 6 in Frank J. Fabozzi and Moorad Choudhry (eds.), *The Handbook of European Fixed Income Securities* (Hoboken, NJ: John Wiley & Sons, 2003).
[6]Munves, "The Eurobond Market," p. 193.

Securities Issued in the Eurobond Market

The Eurobond market has been characterized by new and innovative bond structures to accommodate particular needs of issuers and investors. There are, of course, the "plain vanilla," fixed-rate coupon bonds, referred to as **Euro straights**. Because these are issued on an unsecured basis, they are usually issued by high-quality entities.

Coupon payments are made annually, rather than semiannually, because of the higher cost of distributing interest to geographically dispersed bondholders. There are also zero-coupon bond issues and deferred-coupon issues, both of which were described in earlier chapters.

Floating-Rate Notes

There are a wide variety of floating-rate Eurobond notes. The coupon rate on a floating-rate note is some stated margin over the London interbank offered rate (LIBOR), the bid on LIBOR (referred to as LIBID), or the arithmetic average of LIBOR and LIBID (referred to as LIMEAN). The size of the spread reflects the perceived credit risk of the issuer, margins available in the syndicated loan market, and the liquidity of the issue. Typical reset periods for the coupon rate are either every six months or every quarter, with the rate tied to six-month or three-month LIBOR, respectively; that is, the length of the reset period and the maturity of the index used to establish the rate for the period are matched.

Many issues have either a minimum coupon rate (or floor) that the coupon rate cannot fall below and a maximum coupon rate (or cap) that the coupon rate cannot rise above. An issue that has both a floor and a cap is said to be **collared**. There are some issues that grant the borrower the right to convert the floating coupon rate into a fixed coupon rate at some time. There are some issues referred to as **drop-lock bonds**, which automatically change the floating coupon rate into a fixed coupon rate under certain circumstances.

A floating-rate note issue will either have a stated maturity date or it may be a **perpetual (also called undated) issue** (i.e., with no stated maturity date). The perpetual issue was introduced into the Eurobond market in 1984. For floating-rate notes that do mature, the term is usually greater than 5 years, with the typical maturity being between 7 and 12 years. There are callable and putable floating-rate notes; some issues are both callable and putable.

Dual-Currency Bonds

There are issues that pay coupon interest in one currency but pay the principal in a different currency. Such issues are called **dual-currency issues**. For the first type of dual-currency bond, the exchange rate that is used to convert the principal and coupon payments into a specific currency is specified at the time the bond is issued. The second type differs from the first in that the applicable exchange rate is the rate that prevails at the time a cash flow is made (i.e., at the spot exchange rate at the time a payment is made). The third type is one that offers to either the investor or the issuer the choice of currency. These bonds are commonly referred to as **option currency bonds**.

Convertible Bonds and Bonds with Warrants

A convertible Eurobond is one that can be converted into another asset. Bonds with attached warrants represent a large part of the Eurobond market. A warrant grants the owner of the warrant the right to enter into another financial transaction with the issuer if the owner will benefit as a result of exercising. Most warrants are detachable from the host bond; that is, the bondholder may detach the warrant from the bond and sell it.

There are a wide array of bonds with warrants: equity warrants, debt warrants, and currency warrants. An **equity warrant** permits the warrant owner to buy the common stock of the issuer at a specified price. A **debt warrant** entitles the warrant owner to buy additional bonds from the issuer at the same price and yield as the host bond. The debt warrant owner will benefit if interest rates decline because a bond with a higher coupon can be purchased from the same issuer. A **currency warrant** permits the warrant owner to exchange one currency for another at a set price (i.e., a fixed exchange rate). This feature protects the bondholder against a depreciation of the foreign currency in which the bond's cash flows are denominated.

Coupon Step-Up and Step-Down Bonds

In Chapter 1 we described how the coupon rate can step up over time due to either the passage of time or a change in the reference interest rate. A unique structure in the Eurobond market, particularly for large issues of telecom bonds, has been coupon step-up and step-down provisions where the change in the coupon is triggered by a change in the issuer's credit rating. A rating upgrade would result in a lower coupon rate while a rating downgrade would result in a higher coupon rate.

Comparing Yields on U.S. Bonds and Eurodollar Bonds

Because Eurodollar bonds pay annually rather than semiannually, an adjustment is required to make a direct comparison between the yield to maturity on a U.S. fixed-rate bond and that on a Eurodollar fixed-rate bond. Given the yield to maturity on a Eurodollar fixed-rate bond, its bond-equivalent yield is computed as follows:

bond-equivalent yield of Eurodollar bond

$$= 2[(1 + \text{yield to maturity on Eurodollar bond})^{1/2} - 1]$$

For example, suppose that the yield to maturity on a Eurodollar bond is 6%. Then the bond-equivalent yield is

$$2[(1.06)^{1/2} - 1] = 0.0591 = 5.91\%$$

Notice that the bond-equivalent yield will always be less than the Eurodollar bond's yield to maturity.

To convert the bond-equivalent yield of a U.S. bond issue to an annual-pay basis so that it can be compared to the yield to maturity of a Eurodollar bond, the following formula can be used:

yield to maturity on annual-pay basis

$$= \left(1 + \frac{\text{yield to maturity on bond-equivalent basis}}{2}\right)^2 - 1$$

For example, suppose that the yield to maturity of a U.S. bond issue quoted on a bond-equivalent yield basis is 5.5%. The yield to maturity on an annual-pay basis would be

$$[(1.0275)^2 - 1] = 0.0558 = 5.58\%$$

The yield to maturity on an annual basis is always greater than the yield to maturity on a bond-equivalent basis.

NON–U.S. GOVERNMENT BOND MARKETS

The institutional settings for government bond markets throughout the world vary considerably, and these variations may affect liquidity and the ways in which strategies are implemented, or, more precisely, affect the tactics of investment strategies. For example, in the government bond market different primary market issuance practices may affect the liquidity and the price behavior of specific government bonds in a country. The nature of the secondary market affects the ease and cost of trading. The importance of the benchmark effect in various countries may influence which bonds to trade and hold. In addition, yields are calculated according to different methods in various countries, and these differences will affect the interpretation of yield spreads. Withholding and transfer tax practices also affect global investment strategies.

The two largest non–U.S. government bond markets are those in Japan and Germany. Japanese government securities, referred to as JGBs, include medium-term bonds and long-dated bonds. There are two types of medium-term bonds: bonds with coupons and zero-coupon bonds. Bonds with coupons have maturities of two, three, and four years. The other type of medium-term bond is the five-year zero-coupon bond. Long-dated bonds are interest bearing. The German government issues bonds (called *Bunds*) with maturities from 8–30 years and notes, *Bundesobligationen* (Bobls), which have a maturity of five years.

It was not until the early 1990s that a liquid government bond market in Continental Europe developed. The market grew throughout the decade. However, the Euro government bond market (excludes the bonds issued by the U.K. government, gilts) was characterized as a fragmented market and, as a result, could not develop the type of liquidity that characterized the U.S. Treasury market. The difference in the currency used by each country hindered that integrated market and liquidity.[7]

In January 1999, the structure of the market changed with the start of the European Monetary Union (EMU). The EMU, combined with the decline in the U.S. Treasury issuance of securities, has resulted in the Euro government bond market becoming the largest government bond market in the world in terms of size and number of issues. As of June 2005, the euro zone government market was almost twice the size of the U.S. government bond market (€5.4 trillion versus €2.8 trillion). The average size of euro zone government bonds is €12 billion.[8]

---

[7]Antonio Villarroya, "The Euro Government Bond Market," Chapter 5 in *The Handbook of European Fixed Income Securities*.

[8]Emanuele Ravano, "10 Surprising Facts About the Euro Zone Bond Market 6½ Years Later," July 2005, available at http://Europe.pimco.com/LeftNav/Latest+Pbulications/2005/Eurosone+Bond+Market+July+2005.htm.

EXHIBIT 9-2	Euro Country Government Bond Market: Relative Size and Credit Ratings as of October 2005			

Country	Market Share (%)	Moody's	S&P	Fitch
Austria	4	Aaa	AAA	AAA
Belgium	7	Aa1	AA+	AA
Finland	1	Aaa	AAA	AAA
France	21	Aaa	AAA	AAA
Germany	24	Aaa	AAA	AAA
Greece	5	A1	A	A
Ireland	1	Aaa	AAA	AAA
Italy	22	Aa	2AA-	AA
Netherlands	6	Aaa	AAA	AAA
Portugal	2	Aa	2AA-	AA
Spain	8	Aaa	AAA	AAA

Source: Data provided by Antonio Villarroya of Merrill Lynch.

The relative size of the government bond markets in the 11 countries in the euro zone as of October 2005 is reported in Exhibit 9-2. The three largest government bond markets — German (24%), Italian (22%), and French (21%) — represent about two-thirds of the market. The Italian government issues (1) bonds, *Buoni del Tresoro Poliennali* (BTPs), with a fixed-rate that are issued with original maturities of 5, 10, and 30 years, (2) floating-rate notes, *Certificati di Credito del Tresoro* (CCTs), typically with a 7-year maturity and referenced to the Italian Treasury bill rate, and (3) 2-year zero-coupon notes, *Certificati di Tresoro a Zero Coupon* (CTZs). The French Treasury issues long-dated bonds, *Obligation Assimilable du Tresor* (OATS), with maturities up to 30 years and notes, *Tresor a Taux Fixe et a Interet Annuel* (BTANs), with a maturity between 2 and 5 years.

Within the Euro bond market, the government bond sector represents half of the market of Euro-denominated bonds, followed by the German Pfandbfriefe market.

Exhibit 9-2 shows the rating for each Euro government issuer. Factors considered by the rating agencies in assigning a rating to sovereign issuers are discussed later.

As explained in Chapter 6, a security can be stripped — that is, each interest and the one principal payment can be separated and sold as a separate security. While many Euro government bonds can be stripped, the stripped securities are not as liquid as that of U.S. Treasury strips.

Methods of Distribution of New Government Securities

We described the primary market for distribution of U.S. Treasury securities in Chapter 6. There are four methods that have been used in distributing new securities of central governments: the regular calendar auction/Dutch style system, the regular calendar auction/minimum-price offering, the ad hoc auction system, and the tap system.

In the **regular calendar auction/Dutch style auction system**, there is a regular calendar auction and winning bidders are allocated securities at the yield (price) they bid. In the **regular calendar auction/minimum-price offering system**, there is a regular calendar of offering. The price (yield) at which winning bidders are awarded the securities is different from the Dutch style auction. Rather than awarding a winning bidder at the yield (price) they bid, all winning bidders are awarded securities at the highest yield accepted by the government (i.e., the stop-out yield). For example, if the highest yield or stop-out yield for a government issue at auction is 5.14% and someone bids 5.12%, that bidder would be awarded the securities at 5.12%. In contrast, with the minimum-price offering method, that bidder would be awarded securities at 5.14%, which means a lower price than at the bid price of 5.12%. In Chapter 6, we referred to this auction method as a single-price auction and is the auction method used in the U.S. government market. The regular calendar auction/minimum-price offering method is used in Germany and France.

In the **ad hoc auction system**, governments announce auctions when prevailing market conditions appear favorable. It is only at the time of the auction that the amount to be auctioned and the maturity of the security to be offered are announced. This is one of the methods used by the Bank of England in distributing British government bonds. From the issuing government's perspective, there are two advantages of an ad hoc auction system over a regular calendar auction. First, a regular calendar auction introduces greater market volatility than an ad hoc auction does because yields tend to rise as the announced auction date approaches and then fall afterward. Second, there is reduced flexibility in raising funds with a regular calendar auction.

In a **tap system**, additional bonds of a previously outstanding bond issue are auctioned. The government announces periodically that it is adding this new supply.

Inflation-Indexed Bonds

In the United States, the U.S. Treasury issues fixed-rate bonds and bonds whose coupon rate is indexed to the rate of inflation. As explained in Chapter 6, these issues are referred to as Treasury Inflation Protection Securities, or TIPS. Outside the United States, bond coupon rates are linked to the rate of inflation and are referred to as **linkers**.[9]

Exhibit 9-3 shows the size of the inflation-linked government market by the major issuers in terms of local face value and market value as of September 30, 2005. The market value is U.S. $809.9 billion. The number of issues for each country is also shown. As can be seen, the United States is by far the largest issuer of inflation-linked government securities, followed by the United Kingdom and then France.

The indexes are typically linked to a consumer price index (CPI); however, within a country the index may differ. For example, in France about 56% of the inflation-linked bonds were indexed to the French CPI (excluding tobacco) and 44% to the Eurozone's Harmonised Index of Consumer Prices (HICP) (excluding tobacco).

---

[9]For comprehensive coverage of the use and analysis of linkers in the European bond market, see "European Inflation-Linked Bonds," Chapter 8 in *The Handbook of European Fixed Income Securities*.

EXHIBIT 9-3	Government Inflation-Linked Market as of 9/30/05				

Country	Face Value (local, millions)	Market Value (local, millions)	No. of Issues	Foreign Market Value (USD, millions)	Market Share (%)
Australia	6,020	8,978	3	6,856	0.85
Canada	19,725	34,292	4	29,547	3.65
Sweden	179,393	251,132	6	32,490	4.01
France	81,454	100,271	9	120,891	14.93
United Kingdom	46,889	105,047	9	185,839	22.95
United States	278,370	338,509	17	338,509	41.80
South Africa	39,116	61,442	4	9,664	1.19
Greece	5,200	6,788	1	8,184	1.01
Japan	1,971,400	1,958,621	5	17,281	2.13
Italy	45,549	50,273	4	60,612	7.48
Total			62	809,872	100.00

Source: Exhibit prepared from data supplied by Robert Tzucker of Barclays Capital.

Sovereign Bond Ratings

Sovereign debt is the obligation of a country's central government. Whereas U.S. government debt is not rated by any nationally recognized statistical rating organization, the debt of other national governments is rated. For the reasons discussed subsequently, there are two sovereign debt ratings assigned by rating agencies: a local currency debt rating and a foreign currency debt rating.

Standard & Poor's, Moody's, and Fitch all assign ratings to sovereign bonds. In this section, we will discuss the factors considered by Standard & Poor's in deriving their ratings. The categorization of these factors is summarized in Exhibit 9-4. The two general categories are economic risk and political risk. The former category is an assessment of the ability of a government to satisfy its obligations. Both quantitative and qualitative analyses are used in assessing economic risk. Political risk is an assessment of the willingness of a government to satisfy its obligations. A government may have the ability to pay but may be unwilling to pay. Political risk is assessed based on qualitative analysis of the economic and political factors that influence a government's economic policies.

The reason for distinguishing between local debt ratings and foreign currency debt ratings is that historically, the default frequency differs by the currency denomination of the debt. Specifically, defaults have been greater on foreign currency-denominated debt. The reason for the difference in default rates for local currency debt and foreign currency debt is that if a government is willing to raise taxes and control its domestic financial system, it can generate sufficient local currency to meet its local currency debt obligation. This is not the case with foreign currency-denominated debt. A national government must purchase foreign currency to meet a debt obligation in that foreign currency and therefore has less control with respect to its exchange rate. Thus,

EXHIBIT 9-4   Sovereign Ratings Methodology Profile

Political risk

- Stability and legitimacy of political institutions
- Popular participation in political processes
- Orderliness of leadership succession
- Transparency in economic policy decisions and objectives
- Public security
- Geopolitical risk

Income and economic structure

- Prosperity, diversity, and degree to which economy is market oriented
- Income disparities
- Effectiveness of financial sector in intermediating funds; availability of credit
- Competitiveness and profitability of nonfinancial private sector
- Efficiency of public sector
- Protectionism and other nonmarket influences
- Labor flexibility

Economic growth prospects

- Size and composition of savings and investment
- Rate and pattern of economic growth

Fiscal flexibility

- General government revenue, expenditure, and surplus/deficit trends
- Revenue-raising flexibility and efficiency
- Expenditure effectiveness and pressures
- Timeliness, coverage, and transparency in reporting
- Pension obligations

General government debt burden

- General government gross and net (of assets) debt as a percent of GDP
- Share of revenue devoted to interest
- Currency composition and maturity profile
- Depth and breadth of local capital markets

Off-budget and contingent liabilities

- Size and health of NFPEs
- Robustness of financial sector

Monetary flexibility

- Price behavior in economic cycles
- Money and credit expansion
- Compatibility of exchange-rate regime and monetary goals
- Institutional factors, such as central bank independence
- Range and efficiency of monetary policy tools

EXHIBIT 9-4 (continued)

External liquidity
- Impact of fiscal and monetary policies on external accounts
- Structure of the current account
- Composition of capital flows
- Reserve adequacy

Public sector external debt burden
- Gross and net public sector debt, including structured debt, as a percent of CAR
- Maturity profile, currency composition, and sensitivity to interest rate changes
- Access to concessional funding
- Debt service burden

Private sector external debt burden
- Gross and net financial sector external debt, including deposits and structured debt, as a percent of CAR
- Gross and net nonfinancial private sector external debt, including structured debt, as a percent of CAR
- Maturity profile, currency composition, and sensitivity to interest rate changes
- Access to concessional funding
- Debt service burden

CAR—Current account receipts, NFPEs—Nonfinancial public sector enterprises.

Source: In David T. Beers and Marie Cavanaugh, "Sovereign Credit Ratings: A Primer," Standard & Poor's, September 27, 2005. The material is reproduced with permission of Standard & Poor's, a division of the McGraw-Hill Companies, Inc.

a significant depreciation of the local currency relative to a foreign currency in which a debt obligation is denominated will impair a national government's ability to satisfy such obligation.

The implication of this is that the factors S&P analyzes in assessing the credit worthiness of a national government's local currency debt and foreign currency debt will differ to some extent. In assessing the credit quality of local currency debt, for example, S&P emphasizes domestic government policies that foster or impede timely debt service. For foreign currency debt, credit analysis by S&P focuses on the interaction of domestic and foreign government policies. S&P analyzes a country's balance of payments and the structure of its external balance sheet. The areas of analysis with respect to its external balance sheet are the net public debt, total net external debt, and net external liabilities.

It should be emphasized that sovereign ratings are relatively new and that ratings agencies continue to refine their methodology for assigning credit ratings. For example, consider the experience in the 1997–1998 Asian financial crisis (also referred to as the Asian currency crisis). The crisis started in July 1997 in Thailand.

The two countries most affected in addition to Thailand were South Korea and Indonesia. Exhibit 9-5 shows the ratings of these three countries from June 25, 1997 (just before the crisis) and the rating changes over the crisis period. Notice that Thailand and South Korea were rated investment grade about a month before the crisis. The ratings were not changed even after the crisis. In fact, it was not until September–October 1997 that these countries were downgraded. It was not until the end of 1997/early 1998 that there was the downgrading of these countries by the largest number of rating notches.

EXHIBIT 9-5   Ratings for Indonesia, Thailand, and South Korea During the Asian Financial Crisis

Indonesia

	Moody's			Standard & Poor's	
Date	Rating	Change[a]	Date	Rating	Change[a]
25/6/97	Baa3	—	25/6/97	BBB	—
27/12/97	Ba1	−1	10/10/97	BBB−	−1
9/1/98	B2	−5	31/12/97	BB+	−2
			9/1/98	BB	−3
			27/1/98	B	−6

Republic of Korea

	Moody's			Fitch	
Date	Rating	Change[a]	Date	Rating	Change[a]
25/6/97	A1	—	25/6/97	AA−	—
27/11/97	A3	−2	11/11/97	A+	−1
10/12/97	Baa2	−4	26/11/97	A	−2
21/12/97	Ba1	−6	11/12/97	BBB−	−6

Thailand

	Moody's			Standard & Poor's	
Date	Rating	Change[a]	Date	Rating	Change[a]
25/6/97	A3	—	25/6/97	A	—
1/10/97	Baa1	−1	3/9/97	A−	−1
27/11/97	Baa3	−3	24/10/97	BBB	−3
21/12/97	Ba1	−4	8/1/98	BBB−	−4

[a]Change is measured by the number of rating steps between the former and the new rating. A negative sign shows a downgrading

Source: Frank Packer, "Credit Ratings and the East Asian Financial Crisis," Presentation at the Workshop on Economic Monitoring of Financial Systems in East and South-East Asia, organized by the ADB Institute and PECC Manila, June 25–26, 1998. This report was prepared when Frank Packer was employed at the Federal Reserve Bank of New York.

THE PFANDBRIEFE MARKET

While our focus in this chapter is on a macro view of the non–U.S. bond market, there is one non-government bond market that is quite important—the German mortgage-bond market. This market, called the **Pfandbriefe market**, is the largest asset in the European bond market and the sixth largest in the world.[10] The bonds in this market, *Pfandbriefe*, are issued by mortgage banks in Germany. This bond sector is highly regulated. Because the bonds are backed by mortgage pools, they are referred to as **covered bonds** and, as a result, are viewed as highly secure bonds. This is because in the case of insolvency of the issuing mortgage bank, the bondholders of the covered bonds have a priority with respect to the underlying loan pool. In fact, there has not been a single case of insolvency in this market since its inception more than a century ago.

There are two types of Pfandbriefe that differ based on the borrowing entity for the loan. *Ofentliche Pfandbriefe* are bonds fully collateralized by loans to public-sector entities. These bonds are called **Public Pfandbriefe**. When the bonds are fully collateralized by residential and commercial mortgages, they are called **Hypotheken Pfandbriefe** or **Mortgage Pfandbriefe**.

The Pfandbriefe market is further divided into **Traditional Pfandbriefe** and **Jumbo Pfandbriefe**. The former represents the market for issues of smaller size. Historically, it has been an illiquid and fragmented market and, as a result, has not attracted much interest from non-German investors. The tap method was used for issuing Traditional Pfandbriefe.

The sector of the Pfandbriefe market that has received the greatest interest from global institutional bond investors is the Jumbo Pfandbriefe sector. This sector, started in the mid-1990s, is referred to as *Jumbo* because the minimum size of an issue is €500 million. Because of its size, it attracted non-German institutional money managers. The liquidity of the Jumbo Pfandbriefe market is further enhanced by the obligations of the dealers participating in an issuance. There are at least three dealers that are in the syndicate and all the dealers agree to quote for the life of the issue bid and offer prices for lots up to €15 million during the usual trading hours. The popularity of the Jumbo Pfandbriefe can be seen by the rise of its role in the European market in less than a decade. By early 2003 the size of the Jumbo Pfandbriefe exceeded €400 billion, making it Europe's fourth largest bond market behind the government bond markets of Italy, Germany, and France.

EMERGING MARKET BONDS

The financial markets of Latin America, Asia (with the exception of Japan), and Eastern Europe are viewed as emerging markets. Investing in the government bonds of emerging market countries entails considerably more credit risk than investing in the government bonds of major industrialized countries. Standard & Poor's and Moody's rate emerging market sovereign debt. Although there are exceptions, the securities issued by governments of emerging market countries are denominated in U.S. dollars.

Governments of emerging market countries issue either Brady bonds, Eurobonds, or global bonds. We have discussed Eurobonds and global bonds earlier in this chapter.

---

[10]For a further discussion of this market, see Graham H. Cross, "The German Pfandbriefe Market and Covered Bonds Market," Chapter 7 in *The Handbook of European Fixed Income Markets*.

Brady bonds are basically bonds that represent a restructuring of nonperforming bank loans of governments into marketable securities. An agreement for the restructuring of nonperforming bank loans was first worked out between Mexico and the United States by the then-Secretary of the Treasury Nicholas Brady—hence, nicknamed "Brady bonds." The agreement called for U.S. government and multilateral support to provide relief for principal and interest payments owed to banks outside Mexico, if Mexico successfully implemented certain structural reforms. This U.S. government program was then extended to the government debt of other emerging markets.

From 1989–1997, 17 countries, referred to as "Brady countries," took advantage of this program issuing about US$170 billion over that period.[11] There are two types of Brady bonds. The first type covers the interest due on these loans ("past-due interest bonds"). The second type covers the principal amount owed on the bank loans ("principal bonds"). Principal bonds have maturities at issuance from 25 to 30 years and are bullet bonds. They are more frequently traded than the past-due interest bonds, and therefore, have better liquidity. The principal bonds fall into two categories: par and discount bonds. Par principal bonds have a fixed rate; discount principal bonds have a floating rate.

The face value of emerging market government bonds outstanding of the domestic market was about US$440 billion as of year-end 2003. The majority of these issues were in global bonds or Eurobonds. The amount of Brady bonds is about only 10% of the amount issued by emerging market governments. The decline in the share of Brady bonds from the US$170 billion issued is due to the retirement of these bonds by their issuers and the fact that many countries have been able to improve their financial condition so as to raise more funds by issuing global bonds and Eurobonds.

SUMMARY

In this chapter the Eurobond market and the non–U.S. government bond markets are discussed. The global bond market can be classified into two markets: the internal or national bond market, which consists of a domestic bond market and a foreign bond market, and the external or international bond market (or Eurobond market).

The Eurobond market is divided into sectors based on the currency in which the issue is denominated. Many innovative bond structures have been introduced in the Eurobond market.

When a U.S. investor purchases non–U.S. bonds that are denominated in a foreign currency, the return to be realized will consist of two components. The first component is the local currency return, which results from coupon payments, reinvestment income, and capital gains/losses. The second component is any foreign exchange gain or loss resulting from converting the nondollar cash flows to U.S. dollars. Foreign exchange risk is the risk that the foreign currency depreciates (declines in value) relative to the U.S. dollar, resulting in the U.S. dollar value of the cash flows being lower.

Although it is often stated that the primary motivation to investing in non–U.S. bonds is that it provides diversification benefits, such benefits may not be significant.

---

[11]The majority of Brady bonds were issued by countries in Latin America. About three quarters of all Brady bonds were issued by four countries: Brazil, Mexico, Argentina, and Venezuela. See Jane Sachar Brauer, "Emerging Markets Debt," Chapter 26 in Frank J. Fabozzi (ed.), *The Handbook of Fixed Income Securities* 7th Ed. (New York: McGraw-Hill, 2005).

Rather, investing in non–U.S. bonds gives a money manager the opportunity to capitalize on factors that affect bond prices in non–U.S. markets and permits a currency play. Sovereign debt is the obligation of a country's central government. Ratings are assigned separately for local currency denominated debt and foreign currency denominated debt. The two general categories analyzed by rating companies in assigning ratings are economic risk and political risk.

Investors in the debt of governments of emerging countries are exposed to credit risk. Governments of emerging market countries issue either Brady bonds, Eurobonds, or global bonds. While at one time Brady bonds were a major part of the emerging bond market, they are less important today. Euroclear and Cedel are two clearing systems that handle Eurobond transactions as well as provide dealer financing and a securities borrowing service.

Questions

1. What risk is faced by a U.S. life insurance company that buys British government bonds?
2. Why do U.S. investors who invest in non–U.S. bonds prefer foreign government bonds?
3. What institutional factors of a foreign government bond market affect the tactics of investment strategies?
4. "The strongest argument for investing in nondollar bonds is that there are diversification benefits." Explain why you agree or disagree with this statement.
5. What arguments are offered for investing in nondollar bonds?
6. What is the difference between LIBID and LIMEAN?
7. What is the foreign bond market of a country?
8. What is a global bond?
9. Describe the trading blocs that are used in classifying the world's bond markets.
10. What is a Eurobond?
11. What are the different types of warrants that have been included in Eurobond offerings?
12. This excerpt, which discusses dual currency bonds, is taken from the *International Capital Market*, published in 1989 by the European Investment Bank:

The generic name of dual-currency bonds hides many different variations which are difficult to characterize in detail. These variations on the same basic concept have given birth to specific names like Index Currency Option Notes (ICON), foreign interest payment bonds (FIPS), forex-linked bonds, heaven and hell bonds, to name but a few. Despite this diversity it is, however, possible to attempt a broad-brush classification of the various types of dual-currency bonds.

The first category covers bond issues denominated in one currency but for which coupon and repayment of the principal are made in another designated currency at an exchange rate fixed at the time of issue. A second category comprises dual-currency bonds in which coupon payments and redemption proceeds are made in a currency different from the currency of denomination at the spot exchange rate that will prevail at the time of payment.

Within this category, one finds the forex-linked bonds, foreign currency bonds and heaven and hell bonds. A final category includes bonds which offer to issuers or the holder the choice of the currency in which payments and/or redemptions are to be made at the future spot exchange rate. ICONs fall into this latter category because there is an implicit option due to the exchange rate revision formula. Usually, these bonds are referred to as option currency bonds.

Irrespective of the above-mentioned categories, all dual-currency bonds expose the issuers and the holders to some form of foreign exchange risk. . . . Pricing dual-currency bonds is therefore an application of option pricing, as the bonds can be looked at as a combination of a straight bond and a currency option. The value of the straight bond component is obtained according to traditional fixed-rate bond valuation models. The pricing of the option component is, ex post, equal to the difference between the dual currency bond price and its straight bond component. . . .

a. Why do all currency bonds "expose the issuers and the holders to some form of foreign exchange risk" regardless of the category of bond?

b. Do you agree that the pricing of all dual-currency bonds is an application of option pricing?

c. Why should the price of the option component be "equal to the difference between the dual currency bond price and its bond component"?

13. a. Why do rating agencies assign a different rating to the debt of a sovereign entity based on whether the debt is denominated in a local currency or a foreign currency?

b. What are the two general categories of risk analyzed by Standard & Poor's in assigning a sovereign rating?

14. a. What are the four types of securities issued by the Japanese government?

b. How is the benchmark government issue determined in the Japanese bond market?

15. What is a gilt?

16. Suppose that the yield to maturity on a Eurodollar bond is 7.8%. What is the bond-equivalent yield?

17. What are the different methods for the issuance of government securities?

18. What is the debate regarding covenants in corporate bonds in the Eurobond market?

19. Explain the step-up and step-down structure used in the Eurobond market.

20. a. What is the Pfandbriefe market?

b. What is a Jumbo Pfandbriefe, and why has it attracted non-German bond investors?

21. What risk associated with the government bonds of emerging countries is not viewed as being present in industrialized countries?

22. a. What are Brady bonds?

b. What are the two types of Brady bonds?

c. Explain whether you agree or disagree with the following statement: "Brady bonds are the dominant form of emerging market government bonds."

CHAPTER

10 RESIDENTIAL MORTGAGE LOANS

After reading this chapter you will understand:

■ what a mortgage is

■ who the major originators of residential mortgages are and what they do with mortgage loans after origination

■ the factors that mortgage originators consider when granting a mortgage loan

■ what mortgage servicing involves

■ the various types of mortgage insurance

■ the fixed-rate, level-payment, fully amortized mortgage instrument and its cash flow characteristics

■ the characteristics of the following mortgage designs: adjustable-rate mortgages, hybrid adjustable-rate mortgages, prepayment penalty mortgages, balloon mortgages, and interest-only mortgages

■ the difference between a prime and subprime mortgage loan

■ the cash flow components of all mortgage loans

■ what prepayments are and their impact on the cash flow

■ the risks associated with investing in mortgages

■ the factors that affect the credit risk on mortgage loans

A lthough the American dream may be to own a home, the major portion of the funds to purchase one must be borrowed. The market where these funds are borrowed is called the mortgage market. This chapter and the two that follow describe residential mortgage loans and the various securities created by using mortgage loans as collateral. In this chapter we focus on individual mortgage loans: the characteristics of mortgage loans, the participants (mortgage originators and investors) in this market, the more popular mortgage loan designs, and the market for mortgage loans. In Chapter 13 we cover commercial loans and securities backed by commercial loans.

WHAT IS A MORTGAGE?

A **mortgage** is a loan secured by the collateral of specified real estate property, which obliges the borrower to make a predetermined series of payments. The mortgage gives the lender (the mortgagee) the right of foreclosure on the loan if the borrower (the mortgagor) defaults. That is, if the borrower fails to make the contracted payments, the lender can seize the property to ensure that the debt is paid off.

When the lender makes the loan based on the credit of the borrower and on the collateral for the mortgage, the mortgage is said to be a **conventional mortgage**. The lender also may take out mortgage insurance to provide a guarantee for the fulfillment of the borrower's obligations. There are three forms of mortgage insurance that are guaranteed by the U.S. government if the borrower can qualify: Federal Housing Administration (FHA), Veterans Administration (VA), and Federal Farmers Administration (FmHA) insurance. There are also private mortgage insurers. The cost of mortgage insurance is paid to the guarantor by the mortgage originator but passed along to the borrower in the form of higher mortgage payments.

The types of real estate properties that can be mortgaged are divided into two broad categories: *residential* and *nonresidential* properties. The former category includes houses, condominiums, cooperatives, and apartments. Residential real estate can be subdivided into single-family (one-to-four-family) structures and multifamily structures (apartment buildings in which more than four families reside). Nonresidential property includes commercial and farm properties. Our focus in this chapter and the next two is on residential mortgage loans.

PARTICIPANTS IN THE MORTGAGE MARKET

In addition to the ultimate lenders of funds and the government agencies described in the next chapter, there are three groups involved in the market: mortgage originators, mortgage servicers, and mortgage insurers.

Mortgage Originators

The original lender is called the **mortgage originator**. Mortgage originators include thrifts, commercial banks, mortgage bankers, life insurance companies, and pension funds. The three largest originators for all types of residential mortgages are thrifts, commercial banks, and mortgage bankers. Originators may generate income for themselves in one or more ways. First, they typically charge an origination fee. This fee is expressed in terms of points, where each point represents 1% of the borrowed funds. For example, an origination fee of two points on a $100,000 mortgage represents $2,000. Originators also charge application fees and certain processing fees.

The second source of revenue is the profit that might be generated from selling a mortgage at a higher price than it originally cost. This profit is called **secondary marketing profit**. Of course, if mortgage rates rise, an originator will realize a loss when the mortgages are sold in the secondary market. Finally, the mortgage originator may hold the mortgage in its investment portfolio.

A potential homeowner who wants to borrow funds to purchase a home will apply for a loan from a mortgage originator. Upon completion of the application form, which provides financial information about the applicant and payment of an application fee, the mortgage originator will perform a credit evaluation of the applicant. The two primary factors in determining whether the funds will be lent are the **payment-to-income** (PTI) ratio and the **loan-to-value** (LTV) ratio. The PTI, the ratio of monthly payments (both mortgage and real estate tax payments) to monthly income, is a measure of the ability of the applicant to make monthly payments. The lower this ratio, the greater the likelihood that the applicant will be able to meet the required payments. The difference between the purchase price of the property and the amount borrowed is the borrower's down payment. The LTV is the ratio of the amount of the loan to the market (or appraised) value of the property. The lower this ratio, the more protection the lender has if the applicant defaults and the property must be repossessed and sold.

Mortgage originators can either (1) hold the mortgage in their portfolio, (2) sell the mortgage to an investor who wishes to hold the mortgage or who will place the mortgage in a pool of mortgages to be used as collateral for the issuance of a security, or (3) use the mortgage themselves as collateral for the issuance of a security. When a mortgage is used as collateral for the issuance of a security, the mortgage is said to be **securitized**. In Chapter 11 we discuss the process of securitizing mortgages.

When a mortgage originator intends to sell the mortgage, it will obtain a commitment from the potential investor (buyer). Two federally sponsored credit agencies and several private companies buy mortgages. As these agencies and private companies pool these mortgages and sell them to investors, they are called **conduits**.

The two agencies, the Federal Home Loan Mortgage Corporation and the Federal National Mortgage Association (discussed further), purchase only conforming mortgages. A **conforming mortgage** is one that meets the underwriting standards established by these agencies for being in a pool of mortgages underlying a security that they guarantee. We will discuss these underwriting standards later in this chapter. If an applicant does not satisfy the underwriting standards, the mortgage is called a **nonconforming mortgage**.[1] Mortgages acquired by the agency may be held as investments in their portfolio or securitized. The securities offered are discussed in Chapter 11.

Mortgage Servicers

Every mortgage loan must be serviced. Servicing of a mortgage loan involves collecting monthly payments and forwarding proceeds to owners of the loan, sending payment notices to mortgagors, reminding mortgagors when payments are overdue, maintaining records of principal balances, administering an escrow balance for real estate taxes and

---

[1] Loans that exceed the maximum loan amount and thus do not qualify as conforming mortgages are called **jumbo loans**.

insurance purposes, initiating foreclosure proceedings if necessary, and furnishing tax information to mortgagors when applicable.

Mortgage servicers include bank-related entities, thrift-related entities, and mortgage bankers. There are five sources of revenue from mortgage servicing. The primary source is the **servicing fee**. This fee is a fixed percentage of the outstanding mortgage balance. Consequently, the revenue from servicing declines over time as the mortgage balance amortizes. The second source of servicing income arises from the interest that can be earned by the servicer from the escrow balance that the borrower often maintains with the servicer. The third source of revenue is the float earned on the monthly mortgage payment. This opportunity arises because of the delay permitted between the time the servicer receives the payment and the time that the payment must be sent to the investor. Fourth, there are several sources of ancillary income. First, a late fee is charged by the servicer if the payment is not made on time. Second, many servicers receive commissions from cross-selling their borrowers' credit life and other insurance products. Third, fees can also be generated from selling mailing lists.

Finally, there are other benefits of servicing rights for servicers who are also lenders. Their portfolio of borrowers is a potential source for other loans, such as second mortgages, automobile loans, and credit cards.

Mortgage Insurers

There are two types of mortgage-related insurance. The first type, originated by the lender to insure against default by the borrower, is called **mortgage insurance** or **private mortgage insurance**. It is usually required by lenders on loans with LTV ratios greater than 80%. The amount insured will be some percentage of the loan and may decline as the LTV ratio declines. Although the insurance is required by the lender, its cost is borne by the borrower, usually through a higher contract rate. Mortgage insurance can be obtained from a private mortgage insurance company or, if the borrower qualifies, from the FHA, VA, or FmHA.

The second type of mortgage-related insurance is acquired by the borrower, usually with a life insurance company, and is typically called **credit life**. Unlike mortgage insurance, this type of insurance is not required by the lender. The policy provides for a continuation of mortgage payments after the death of the insured person, which allows the survivors to continue living in the house. Because the insurance coverage decreases as the mortgage balance declines, this type of mortgage insurance is simply a term policy.

Although both types of insurance have a beneficial effect on the credit worthiness of the borrower, the first type is more important from the lender's perspective. Mortgage insurance is sought by the lender when the borrower is viewed as being capable of meeting the monthly mortgage payments but does not have enough funds for a large down payment. For example, suppose that a borrower seeks financing of $100,000 to purchase a single-family residence for $110,000, thus making a down payment of $10,000. The LTV ratio is 90.9%, exceeding the uninsured maximum LTV of 80%. Even if the lender's credit analysis indicates that the borrower's PTI ratio is acceptable, the mortgage loan cannot be extended. However, if a private mortgage insurance company insures a portion of the loan, the lender is afforded protection. Mortgage insurance companies will write policies to insure a maximum of 20% of loans with an LTV ranging from 80% to 90%, and a maximum of 25% of loans with an

LTV ranging from 90% to 95%. The lender is still exposed to default by the borrower on the noninsured portion of the mortgage loan, and in the case of private mortgage insurers, exposed as well to the risk that the insurer will default.

ALTERNATIVE MORTGAGE INSTRUMENTS

There are many types of mortgage loans from which a borrower can select. We review several of the more popular mortgage designs here.

The interest rate on a mortgage loan is called the **note rate** and is greater than the risk-free interest rate, in particular the yield on a Treasury security of comparable maturity. The spread reflects the higher costs of collection, the costs associated with default which are not eliminated despite the collateral, poorer liquidity, and uncertainty concerning the timing of the cash flow (which we explain later). The frequency of payment is typically monthly, and the prevailing term of the mortgage is 20 to 30 years, although in recent years an increasing number of 15-year mortgages have been originated.

Level-Payment Fixed-Rate Mortgage

The basic idea behind the design of the level-payment fixed-rate mortgage, or simply level-payment mortgage, is that the borrower pays interest and repays principal in equal installments over an agreed-upon period of time, called the maturity or term of the mortgage. Thus, at the end of the term the loan has been fully amortized.

Each monthly mortgage payment for a level-payment mortgage is due on the first of each month and consists of

1. Interest of one-twelfth of the fixed annual interest rate times the amount of the outstanding mortgage balance at the beginning of the previous month.
2. A repayment of a portion of the outstanding mortgage balance (principal).

The difference between the monthly mortgage payment and the portion of the payment that represents interest equals the amount that is applied to reduce the outstanding mortgage balance. The monthly mortgage payment is designed so that after the last scheduled monthly payment of the loan is made, the amount of the outstanding mortgage balance is zero (i.e., the mortgage is fully repaid).

To illustrate a level-payment fixed-rate mortgage, consider a 30-year (360-month) $100,000 mortgage with an 8.125% note rate. The monthly mortgage payment would be $742.50. (The formula for calculating the monthly mortgage payment is given later.)

Exhibit 10-1 shows for selected months how each monthly mortgage payment is divided between interest and repayment of principal. At the beginning of month 1, the mortgage balance is $100,000, the amount of the original loan. The mortgage payment for month 1 includes interest on the $100,000 borrowed for the month. Because the interest rate is 8.125%, the monthly interest rate is 0.0067708 (0.08125 divided by 12). Interest for month 1 is therefore $677.08 ($100,000 times 0.0067708). The $65.41 difference between the monthly mortgage payment of $742.50 and the interest of $677.08 is the portion of the monthly mortgage payment that represents repayment of principal. This $65.41 in month 1 reduces the mortgage balance.

| EXHIBIT 10-1 | Amortization Schedule of a Level Payment Fixed-Rate Mortgage | | | | |

Mortgage loan: $100,000
Note rate: 8.125%
Monthly payment: $742.50
Term of loan: 30 years (360 months)

Month	Beginning Mortgage Balance	Monthly Payment	Monthly Interest	Sch. Princ. Repay.	Ending Mortgage Balance
1	100,000.00	742.50	677.08	65.41	99,934.59
2	99,934.59	742.50	676.64	65.86	99,868.73
3	99,868.73	742.50	676.19	66.30	99,802.43
4	99,802.43	742.50	675.75	66.75	99,735.68
25	98,301.53	742.50	665.58	76.91	98,224.62
26	98,224.62	742.50	665.06	77.43	98,147.19
27	98,147.19	742.50	664.54	77.96	98,069.23
74	93,849.98	742.50	635.44	107.05	93,742.93
75	93,742.93	742.50	634.72	107.78	93,635.15
76	93,635.15	742.50	633.99	108.51	93,526.64
141	84,811.77	742.50	574.25	168.25	84,643.52
142	84,643.52	742.50	573.11	169.39	84,474.13
143	84,474.13	742.50	571.96	170.54	84,303.59
184	76,446.29	742.50	517.61	224.89	76,221.40
185	76,221.40	742.50	516.08	226.41	75,994.99
186	75,994.99	742.50	514.55	227.95	75,767.04
233	63,430.19	742.50	429.48	313.02	63,117.17
234	63,117.17	742.50	427.36	315.14	62,802.03
235	62,802.03	742.50	425.22	317.28	62,484.75
289	42,200.92	742.50	285.74	456.76	41,744.15
290	41,744.15	742.50	282.64	459.85	41,284.30
291	41,284.30	742.50	279.53	462.97	40,821.33
321	25,941.42	742.50	175.65	566.85	25,374.57
322	25,374.57	742.50	171.81	570.69	24,803.88
323	24,803.88	742.50	167.94	574.55	24,229.32
358	2,197.66	742.50	14.88	727.62	1,470.05
359	1,470.05	742.50	9.95	732.54	737.50
360	737.50	742.50	4.99	737.50	0.00

The mortgage balance at the end of month 1 (beginning of month 2) is then $99,934.59 ($100,000 minus $65.41). The interest for the second monthly mortgage payment is $676.64, the monthly interest rate (0.0066708) times the mortgage balance at the beginning of month 2 ($99,934.59). The difference between the $742.50 monthly mortgage payment and the $676.64 interest is $65.86, representing the amount of the mortgage balance paid off with that monthly mortgage payment. Notice that the last mortgage payment in month 360 is sufficient to pay off the remaining mortgage balance. When a loan repayment schedule is structured in this way, so that the payments made by the borrower will completely pay off the interest and principal, the loan is said to be **fully amortizing**. Exhibit 10-1 is then referred to as an **amortization schedule**.

As Exhibit 10-1 clearly shows, *the portion of the monthly mortgage payment applied to interest declines each month and the portion applied to reducing the mortgage balance increases.* The reason for this is that as the mortgage balance is reduced with each monthly mortgage payment, the interest on the mortgage balance declines. Because the monthly mortgage payment is fixed, an increasingly larger portion of the monthly payment is applied to reduce the principal in each subsequent month.

Servicing Fee

What was ignored in the amortization is the portion of the cash flow that must be paid to the servicer of the mortgage. The servicing fee is a specified portion of the note rate. The monthly cash flow from a mortgage loan, regardless of the mortgage design, can therefore be decomposed into three parts: (1) the servicing fee, (2) the interest payment net of the servicing fee, and (3) the scheduled principal repayment.

Determining the Monthly Mortgage Payment

To compute the monthly mortgage payment for a level-payment mortgage requires the application of the formula for the present value of an ordinary annuity formula presented in Chapter 2. The formula is

$$PV = A\left[\frac{1-(1+i)^{-n}}{i}\right]$$

where:

A = amount of the annuity ($)
n = number of periods
PV = present value of an annuity ($)
i = periodic interest rate

We can redefine the terms in the foregoing formula for a level-payment mortgage as follows:

$$MB_0 = MP\left[\frac{1-(1+i)^{-n}}{i}\right]$$

where:

MP = monthly mortgage payment ($)
n = number of months
MB_0 = original mortgage balance ($)
i = simple monthly note rate (annual note rate/12)

Solving for the monthly mortgage payment (MP) gives

$$MP = \frac{MB_0}{\frac{1-(1+i)^{-n}}{i}}$$

Alternatively, this can be expressed in a simplified form as follows:

$$MP = MB_0 \left[\frac{i(1+i)^n}{(1+i)^n - 1} \right]$$

The term in brackets is called the **payment factor** or **annuity factor**. It is the monthly payment for a $1 mortgage loan with a note rate of i and a term of n months.

To illustrate how the formula is applied, we'll use the $100,000 30-year, 8.125% mortgage that we discussed previously. Thus, $n = 360$, $MB_0 = \$100,000$, and $i = 0.0067708$ (20.08125/12). The monthly mortgage payment is then

$$MP = \$100,000 \left[\frac{0.0067708(1.0067708)^{360}}{(1.0067708)^{360} - 1} \right]$$

$$= \$100,000 \left[\frac{0.0067708(11.35063)}{11.35063 - 1} \right]$$

$$= \$100,000[0.007425]$$

$$= \$742.50$$

This agrees with the monthly mortgage payment we used in Exhibit 10-1. The payment factor or annuity factor is 0.007425.

Adjustable-Rate Mortgage

An **adjustable-rate mortgage** (ARM) is a loan in which the contract rate is reset periodically in accordance with some appropriately chosen reference rate, typically one based on a short-term interest rate. Outstanding ARMs call for resetting the contract rate either every month, six months, year, two years, three years, or five years. The contract rate at the reset date is equal to a reference rate plus a spread. The amount of the spread reflects market conditions, the features of the ARM, and the increased cost of servicing an ARM compared with a fixed-rate mortgage.

Reference Rates

Two categories of reference rates have been used in ARMs: (1) market-determined rates, and (2) calculated rates based on the cost of funds for thrifts. Market-determined rates have been limited to Treasury-based rates. The reference rate will have an important impact on the performance of an ARM and how it is priced.

Cost of funds for thrifts indexes are calculated based on the monthly weighted-average interest cost for liabilities of thrifts. The two most popular are the Eleventh Federal Home Loan Bank Board District Cost of Funds Index (COFI) and the National Cost of Funds Index, the former being the most popular.

The Eleventh District includes the states of California, Arizona, and Nevada. The cost of funds is calculated by first computing the monthly interest expenses for all thrifts included in the Eleventh District. The interest expenses are summed and then divided by the average of the beginning and ending monthly balance. The index value is reported with a one-month lag. For example, June's Eleventh District COFI is reported in July. The contract rate for a mortgage based on the Eleventh District COFI is usually reset based on the previous month's reported index rate. For example, if the reset date is August, the index rate reported in July will be used to set the contract rate. Consequently, there is a two-month lag by the time the average cost of funds is reflected in the contract rate. This obviously is an advantage to the borrower when interest rates are rising and a disadvantage to the investor. The opposite is true when interest rates are falling.

The National Cost of Funds Index is calculated based on all federally insured S&Ls. A median cost of funds is calculated rather than an average. This index is reported with about a 1.5-month delay. The contract rate is typically reset based on the most recently reported index value.

Features of Adjustable-Rate Mortgages

To encourage borrowers to accept ARMs rather than fixed-rate mortgages, mortgage originators generally offer an initial contract rate that is less than the prevailing market mortgage rate. This below-market initial contract rate, set by the mortgage originator based on competitive market conditions, is commonly referred to as a **teaser rate**. At the reset date, the reference rate plus the spread determines the new contract rate. For example, suppose that one-year ARMs are typically offering a 175-basis-point spread over the reference rate. Suppose also that the reference rate is 5.0%, so that the initial contract rate should be 6.75%. The mortgage originator might set an initial contract rate of 6.05%, a rate 70 basis points below the current value of the reference rate plus the spread.

A pure ARM is one that resets periodically and has no other terms that affect the monthly mortgage payment. However, the monthly mortgage payment, and hence the investor's cash flow, are affected by other terms. These are due to (1) periodic caps, and (2) lifetime rate caps and floors. Rate caps limit the amount that the contract rate may increase or decrease at the reset date. A lifetime cap sets the maximum contract rate over the term of the loan.

An ARM mortgage design that has become extremely popular is the **hybrid ARM**. In this mortgage design, the mortgage rate is fixed for a period of time and floats thereafter. For example, for a 30-year mortgage, a hybrid mortgage can have a fixed rate for three years and then become an ARM after year 3. While the frequency of resetting after year 3 can be any length of time, typically it is one year. These mortgages are typically referred to as 3/1, 5/1, 7/1, and 10/1 ARMs, where the first term refers to the period in years during which the mortgage rate is fixed and the second term refers to the frequency of reset during the adjustable-rate period.

A variation of the hybrid ARM is the **interest-only hybrid ARM**.[2] The purpose of this mortgage design is to reduce the homeowner's *initial* monthly payments. With an interest-only hybrid ARM, the homeowner's mortgage payment consists of only the interest associated with the loan until the reset date. At the end of the fixed period, the principal is amortized at a floating rate over the remaining life of the loan.

Balloon Mortgages

In a **balloon mortgage**, the borrower is given long-term financing by the lender, but at specified future dates the contract rate is renegotiated. Thus, the lender is providing long-term funds for what is effectively short-term borrowing, how short depending on

---

[2]While origination of interest-only mortgage loans is also available with fixed-rate mortgages, most of the interest-only loans have been for hybrid ARMs.

the frequency of the renegotiation period. Effectively, it is a short-term balloon loan in which the lender agrees to provide financing for the remainder of the term of the mortgage. The balloon payment is the original amount borrowed less the amount amortized. Thus, in a balloon mortgage, the actual maturity is shorter than the stated maturity.

This mortgage design, though much discussed in the late 1970s and throughout the 1980s, did not catch on until 1990. Two government-sponsored enterprises, discussed in Chapter 11, the Federal National Mortgage Association (Fannie Mae) and the Federal Home Loan Mortgage Corporation (Freddie Mac) have programs for the purchase of these mortgages. Freddie Mac's 30-year balloon, for example, can have either a renegotiation period of five years ("30-due-in-5") or seven years ("30-due-in-7"). If certain conditions are met, Freddie Mac guarantees the extension of the loan.

Prepayment Penalty Mortgages[3]

Most mortgages outstanding do not penalize the borrower for prepaying any part or all of the outstanding mortgage balance. However, there are **prepayment penalty mortgages** (PPMs) that are available to borrowers. The laws and regulations governing the imposition of prepayment penalties are established at the federal and state levels. Usually, the applicable laws for fixed-rate mortgages are specified at the state level. Some states do not permit prepayment penalties on fixed-rate mortgages with a first lien. Other states do permit prepayment penalties but restrict the type of penalty. For some mortgage designs, such as adjustable-rate and balloon mortgages, federal laws override state laws.[4]

The basic structure of a PPM includes a specified time period during which prepayments are not permitted except for the sale of the mortgaged property. This time period is called the **lockout period**. Typically, this period is either three or five years. Depending on the structure, a certain amount of prepayments can be made during the lockout period without the imposition of a prepayment penalty. The common prepayment penalty structure is one that allows partial prepayments up to 20% of the original loan amount in any consecutive 12-month period without a prepayment penalty. When a prepayment penalty is imposed, it typically takes the following form:[5]

- For a three-year lockout period, the prepayment penalty is the lesser of 2% of any prepayment amount within three years that is greater than 20% of the original mortgage, or six months of interest on the portion of the prepayment amount that exceeds 20% of the original principal balance.
- For a five-year lockout period, the prepayment penalty is six months' interest on any prepayment amount in the first five years that is greater than 20% of the original principal balance.

[3]Portions of the discussion on mortgage design and those that follow draw from Anand K. Bhattacharya, Frank J. Fabozzi, and S. Esther Chang, "Overview of the Mortgage Market," in Frank J. Fabozzi (ed.), *The Handbook of Mortgage-Backed Securities*, 5th ed. (New York: McGraw-Hill, 2001), Chapter 1.
[4]For a discussion of these laws and regulations, see Anand K. Bhattacharya and Paul C. Wang, "Prepayment Penalty MBS," in *The Handbook of Mortgage-Backed Securities*. The information in this section draws from that chapter.
[5]The prepayment penalty structures are explained in Bhattacharya and Wang, "Prepayment Penalty MBS," op. cit.

For example, suppose that a borrower with a PPM with a note rate of 8.5%, original principal balance of $150,000, and a lockout period of five years refinances within the first five years and prepays the entire balance. The prepayment penalty will be six months of interest on the amount prepaid in excess of 20% of the original principal balance. Since 80% of the original principal balance of $150,000 is $120,000 and interest for one year at 8.5% is $10,200 (8.5% times $120,000), the prepayment penalty is six-months' interest: $5,100.

The motivation for the PPM is that it reduces prepayment risk (discussed later in this chapter) for the lender during the lockout period. It does so by effectively making it more costly for the borrower to prepay. In exchange for this reduction in prepayment risk, the lender will offer a note rate that is lower than an otherwise comparable mortgage loan without a prepayment penalty.

Reverse Mortgages

Reverse mortgages are designed for senior home owners who want to convert their home equity into cash. Fannie Mae, for instance, offers two types of reverse mortgages for senior borrowers. The Home Keeper Mortgage is an adjustable-rate conventional reverse mortgage for borrowers who are at least 62 years of age and who either own the home outright or have a low amount of unpaid principal balance. The maximum amount that can be borrowed is based upon the homeowner's age, the property's value, and the interest rate. The borrower does not have to repay the loan until he or she no longer occupies the home as a principal residence and cannot be forced to sell or vacate the home to pay off the loan as long as the property is maintained. The other type of reverse mortgage, Home Keeper for Home Purchase, enables senior borrowers to buy a new home with a combination of personal funds and a calculated amount of reverse mortgage that is based upon the borrower's age, number of borrowers, the adjusted property value, and the equity share option chosen.

NONCONFORMING MORTGAGES

There are alternative mortgage designs that have been introduced by mortgage originators for those homeowners who could not qualify for or do not want a conforming mortgage. Basically, mortgages are available for those loans that do not satisfy one or more of the underwriting standards of Fannie Mae, Freddie Mac, and Ginnie Mae, and these mortgages, as explained earlier are called nonconforming mortgages. The underwriting standards deal with the amount of the loan, the credit worthiness of the borrower, documentation for the loan, and the purpose of the loan.[6] A **conventional, nonconforming loan** is a nonconforming loan that does not have any credit guarantee (i.e., no government or private mortgage insurance).

The maximum loan sizes for one- to four-family homes (referred to as the "conforming balance limit") is determined every year. For Fannie Mae and Freddie Mac, the conforming balance limits for one- to four-family homes were as follows for 2005:

---

[6]For a more detailed discussion, see Anand K. Bhattacharya, Frank J. Fabozzi, and William Berliner, "An Overview of Mortgages and the Mortgage Market," Chapter 1 in Frank J. Fabozzi (ed.), *The Handbook of Mortgage-Backed Securities*, 6th ed. (New York: McGraw Hill, 2006).

one-family: $359,650; two-family: $460,400; three-family: $556,500; and four-family: $691,600.[7] Loans larger than the conforming limit are classified as **jumbo loans**.

Mortgage lenders make funds available to credit borrowers who fail to qualify for a mortgage due to the underwriting standards relating to credit worthiness. **Subprime** refers to borrowers whose credit has been impaired but generally have sufficient equity in their homes to mitigate the credit exposure, allowing the lender to place less weight on the credit profile in making the lending decision.

An **alt-A loan** refers to loans made to borrowers who generally have high credit scores but who have variable incomes, are unable or unwilling to document a stable income history, or are buying second homes or investment properties. In such respects, alt-A loans allow reduced or alternate forms of documentation to qualify the loan. An alt-A loan borrower, however, should not be confused with borrowers with blemished credits. The typical alt-A borrower has an excellent credit rating referred to as an A rating, and hence the loan is referred to as an alt-A loan, which is especially important to the originator because the credit quality of the borrower must compensate for the lack of other necessary documentation. What is appealing to borrowers about the alt-A program is the flexibility that the program offers in terms of documentation. A fast-growing product area consists of loans to borrowers with both modestly impaired credit and less rigorous documentation, categorized under the general umbrella of **alt-B loans**.

Traditionally for a conventional, conforming loan, borrowers were required to make a down payment of 20% when qualifying for a mortgage. However, today a borrower with good credit has the option of making a lesser or no down payment, resulting in loans with higher LTVs. Hence, these mortgage loans are called **high-LTV loans**. For borrowers interested in conventional, nonconforming loans, programs available for 103% LTV require no down payment because 100% of the home's price, as well as an additional 3% for closing costs, can be financed into the mortgage.

RISKS ASSOCIATED WITH INVESTING IN MORTGAGES

Investors are exposed to four main risks by investing in mortgage loans: (1) credit risk, (2) liquidity risk, (3) interest rate risk, and (4) prepayment risk.

Credit Risk

Credit risk is the risk that the homeowner/borrower will default. An investor who purchases securities backed by a pool of mortgage loans may or may not be concerned with the credit risk associated with the borrowers whose loans are backing the security. For example, in the next chapter we will discuss securities guaranteed by the Government National Mortgage Association (Ginnie Mae). These securities are backed by the full faith and credit of the U.S. government. So, the credit risk of the underlying borrowers is not a concern to investors. There are securities backed by mortgage loans that are guaranteed by the Federal National Mortgage Association (Fannie Mae) and the Federal

---

[7]The conforming balance limits for Ginnie Mae loans are somewhat more complex than those for the GSEs.

Home Loan Mortgage Corporation (Freddie Mac). The investor is not concerned with the risk of individual borrowers.

When we discuss mortgage-backed securities in the next two chapters, it will be seen that the concern is with the credit risk of a pool (or collection) of mortgage loans where the issuer is neither Ginnie Mae, Fannie Mae, nor Freddie Mac. The securities not backed by any of these entities are referred to as nonagency mortgage-backed securities. Credit analysis of pools of mortgage loans that back nonagency mortgage-backed securities relies upon an unusual combination of large-scale statistical aggregate analysis and micro loan-by-loan analysis. This combination arises from knowing that out of a pool of 1,000 newly originated mortgages, it is virtually certain that at least 10 will be defaulted upon and go into foreclosure, but there is no way of knowing which 10.

The expectation that 10 or more homeowners will default is based on studies of millions of mortgages conducted by private mortgage insurers, federal agencies, and the three credit rating agencies. But not all of these studies are relevant to the default experience of mortgages collateralizing nonagency mortgage-backed securities. For example, studies by private mortgage companies focus only on mortgage defaults on loans with high LTV ratios, as would those done on FHA/VA mortgages. And by definition, studies of mortgages that meet Fannie Mae and Freddie Mac standards are not relevant. That leaves studies by the three rating agencies—Standard & Poor's, Moody's, and Fitch.

Rating agencies need to evaluate the magnitude of a potential loss of a pool of loans in order to assign a credit rating to a security backed by a pool of mortgage loans. As we will see when we discuss nonagency mortgage-backed securities, a rating agency will require an issuer to provide credit support in order to obtain a specific credit rating. Thus, rating agencies do an extensive analysis of defaults on mortgage loans.

While there is a wide range of mortgage designs, rating agencies in their credit analysis establish a benchmark to assess the credit risk of mortgage pools. Specifically, rating agencies compare a mortgage pool to a pool of what is called **prime loans**. A prime loan is a 30-year fixed-rate mortgage with a 75% to 80% loan-to-value ratio (discussed shortly) that is fully documented for the purchase of an owner-occupied single-family detached house. These characteristics describe the most common mortgage type generally associated with the lowest default rates. Except where noted later, loans with almost any other characteristic generally are assumed to have a greater frequency of default.

Loan-to-Value Ratio and Seasoning

A mortgage's **loan-to-value (LTV) ratio** has been found in numerous studies to be the single most important determinant of its likelihood of default, and therefore the amount of required credit enhancement. The rationale is straightforward: Homeowners with large amounts of equity in their properties are unlikely to default. They will either try to protect this equity by remaining current or, if they fail, sell the house or refinance it to unlock the equity. In any case, the lender is protected by the buyer's self-interest. On the other hand, if the borrower has little or no equity in the property, the value of the default option is much greater.

At one time, rating agencies and other participants in the mortgage market considered the LTV only at the time of origination (called the **original LTV**) in their analysis of credit risk. Because of periods in which there has been a decline in housing prices, the **current LTV** has become the focus of attention. The current LTV is the

LTV based on the current unpaid mortgage balance and the estimated current market value of the property. Specifically, the concern is that a decline in housing prices can result in a current LTV that is considerably greater than the original LTV. This would result in greater credit risk for such mortgage loans than at the time of origination. As a result, seasoning now is as likely to be a negative for a mortgage pool as it is to be a positive. It is little comfort to own a pool of original 80% LTV mortgages from California originated in 1995 because many of the borrowers may owe more than their houses are worth due to a decline in housing prices in some regions of that state; their LTVs will exceed 100%. Moreover, the prepayment option has been taken away for these borrowers.

One study found that delinquency/default rates for mortgages with LTVs of 105% and 110% are 7.5% and 10%, respectively, compared with 5% for 100% LTVs.[8] This study also shows that delinquency rates are higher for first mortgages whose borrowers have taken out second mortgages or home equity lines of credit even if their combined equity positions are identical. That is, if homeowner A has an 80% first mortgage and homeowner B has a 65% first mortgage with the same note rate as A and a 15% second mortgage, homeowner B is a poorer credit risk. This heightened risk probably is a result of homeowner B's higher monthly payment.

As a special case of homeowners with second mortgages, consider borrowers who take out secondary financing as part of a purchase transaction. For example, the seller of the house—an individual if the house is a resale, the developer/builder if the house is new—may lend the buyer all or part of the down payment to facilitate the transaction. One study found that the foreclosure rate for such transactions is nearly triple the rate of all transactions.[9]

Mortgage Term

Amortization increases the equity a homeowner has in a property, which reduces the likelihood of default. Because amortization schedules for terms less than 30 years accumulate equity faster, credit risk is greater the longer the mortgage term, all other factors equal. Thus, the credit risk for a 15-year mortgage loan is less than that of a 30-year mortgage loan, all other factors equal.

Mortgage Type

Fixed-rate mortgages are considered prime because both the borrower and the lender know the monthly payment and amortization schedule with certainty. Presumably, the loan was underwritten considering this payment stream and the borrower's current income.

Both lender and borrower are uncertain about the future payment schedule for ARMs. Because most ARMs have lower initial (teaser) rates, underwriting usually is done to ensure that the borrower will be able to meet the monthly payment assuming the rate adjusts up to the fully indexed rate at the first reset date. Beyond that first date, however, there is uncertainty both about the future stream of payments and the borrower's

---

[8]Douglas L. Bendt, Chuck Ramsey, and Frank J. Fabozzi, "The Rating Agencies' Approach," Chapter 13 in Frank J. Fabozzi, Chuck Ramsey, and Michael Marz (eds.), *The Handbook of Nonagency Mortgage-Backed Securities*, 2nd ed. (New Hope, PA: Frank J. Fabozzi Associates, 2000).
[9]Bendt, Ramsey, and Fabozzi, "The Rating Agencies' Approach."

ability to meet higher payments. Future payment schedules for other mortgage types such as balloons are known, but uncertainty about the borrower's income still exists.

Transaction Type

Mortgages taken out for cash-out refinancings are considered riskier than mortgages taken out for purchases, chiefly because the homeowner is reducing the equity in the home. In addition, the fact that the homeowner is taking out cash may be an indication of need, which could indicate shakier finances, and the homeowner's monthly payment will increase. On the other hand, a no-cash refinancing—in which the rate is reduced—lowers the monthly payment and speeds the rate of amortization, so there are no penalties.

Documentation

Borrowers must supply documents to lenders in order to obtain a loan. These documents cover where the borrower obtained the down payment and income verification. Full documentation generally means that the borrower has supplied income, employment, and asset verification sufficient to meet the underwriting standards of Fannie Mae and Freddie Mac. A borrower can obtain a mortgage loan without supplying full documentation. Mortgage loans based on low, alternative, or reduced documentation mean that at least one form of documentation was not supplied, perhaps, for example, because the borrower is self-employed. In this case, because the income stream is likely to be more volatile, the borrower is more likely to default.

No documentation loans generally are made as hard money loans (i.e., the value of the collateral is the most important criterion in the lending decision). Typically, lenders require larger down payments for these types of loans.

Occupancy Status

Property owners obviously have a greater vested interest in not defaulting on a mortgage on a house in which they live. Thus, mortgages for second homes or rental property are viewed as having greater credit risk.

Property Type

Generally, single-family detached houses are the most desirable properties because they are larger, more private, and include more land. Moreover, the supply of condominiums or townhouses is more likely to become overbuilt in a local area with the addition of a single large project, potentially increasing the volatility of prices and the length of time needed to sell a property. Thus, all other factors constant, mortgage loans backed by properties other than single-family detached houses are viewed as having greater credit risk.

Mortgage Size/House Price

Most mortgages are sold into nonagency mortgage-backed securities because the dollar amounts exceed the agency conforming limits. The rating agencies make the strong presumption that higher-valued properties with larger mortgages have greater credit risk.

Credit Worthiness of the Borrower

Although loan originators place a great deal of emphasis on borrowers' credit histories, these data are not available to the rating agencies. The Fair Credit Reporting Act restricts access to such information to parties involved in a credit extension decision. As a result, the agencies use credit proxies such as the debt-to-income ratio, the note rate, past delinquencies or seasoned loans, or either originators' credit scores (e.g., A, B, C, or D) or credit scores by vendors.

There are several firms that collect data on the payment histories of individuals from lending institutions and statistical models to evaluate and quantify individual credit worthiness in terms of a credit score. Basically, a credit score is a numerical grade of the credit history of the borrower. The three most popular credit reporting companies that compute credit scores are Experian, Transunion, and Equifax. While the credit scores have different underlying methodologies, the scores generically are referred to as "FICO scores."[10] Typically, a lender will obtain more than one score in order to minimize the impact of variations in credit scores across providers.[11] FICO scores range from 350 to 850. The higher the FICO score, the lower the credit risk. The general rule of thumb is that a borrower needs a credit score of 660 or higher to qualify as "prime" credit. Borrowers with a credit score below this level can obtain loans either through government programs (mainly the FHA) or through subprime lending programs.

Liquidity Risk

Although there is an active secondary market for mortgage loans, the fact is that bid–ask spreads are large compared with other debt instruments (i.e., mortgage loans tend to be rather illiquid because they are large and indivisible).

The bid–ask spread on mortgage loans varies. Typical spreads are around ten 32nds, with aggressive bidding reducing spreads to eight 32nds when collateral is needed to create mortgage-backed securities. For mortgage loans with unusual collateral, spreads are much wider — the odder the collateral, the higher the spread.

Interest-Rate Risk

Because a mortgage loan is a debt instrument, and long-term on the average — indeed, one of the longest — its price will move in the direction opposite to market interest rates. Moreover, because the borrower can repay the loan at any time, the investor faces the same problem of negative convexity when rates decline as that of the holder of any callable bond. This is discussed further in Chapter 17.

Prepayment Risk

In our illustration of the cash flow from a level-payment fixed-rate mortgage, we assumed that the homeowner would not pay any portion of the mortgage balance off prior to the scheduled due date. However, homeowners do pay off all or part of their mortgage balance prior to the maturity date. Payments made in excess of the scheduled principal repayments are called **prepayments**.

Prepayments occur for one of several reasons. First, homeowners prepay the entire mortgage when they sell their home. The sale of a home may be due to (1) a change of employment that necessitates moving, (2) the purchase of a more expensive home ("trading up"), or (3) a divorce in which the settlement requires sale of the marital residence. Second, as we explained earlier in this chapter, the borrower has the right to pay off all or part of the mortgage balance at any time. Effectively, someone who invests

---

[10]This is because credit scoring companies generally use a model developed by Fair, Isaacs & Company. The model uses 45 criteria to rank the credit worthiness of an individual.

[11]In such cases, if the lender obtains all three scores, generally the middle score is used, whereas the convention is to use the lower score in the case of the availability of only two scores.

in a mortgage has granted the borrower an option to prepay the mortgage and the debtor will have an incentive to do so as market rates fall below the contract rate. Third, in the case of homeowners who cannot meet their mortgage obligations, the property is repossessed and sold. The proceeds from the sale are used to pay off the mortgage in the case of a conventional mortgage. For an insured mortgage, the insurer will pay off the mortgage balance. Finally, if property is destroyed by fire or another insured catastrophe occurs, the insurance proceeds are used to pay off the mortgage. The effect of prepayments is that the cash flow from a mortgage is not known with certainty. This is true for all mortgage loans, not just level-payment fixed-rate mortgages.

In the next chapter, securities backed by a pool of mortgage loans that overcome many of the drawbacks of investing directly in mortgage loans are described.

SUMMARY

A mortgage is a loan secured by the collateral of some specified real estate property, which obliges the borrower to make a predetermined series of payments. Because of the nature of mortgage loans, there are three groups involved in the market: mortgage originators, mortgage servicers, and mortgage insurers. The original lender is called the mortgage originator.

The interest rate on a mortgage loan is generally above the risk-free interest rate, in particular the yield on a Treasury security of comparable maturity, with the spread reflecting the costs of servicing the loan, the costs associated with default which are not eliminated despite the collateral, poorer liquidity, and the uncertainty concerning the timing of the cash flow.

There is a wide range of mortgage designs. These include the level-payment fixed rate mortgage, the adjustable-rate mortgage (including variations such as the hybrid ARM and interest-only hybrid ARM), the balloon mortgage, the prepayment penalty mortgage, and the reverse mortgage. For borrowers who fail to satisfy the underwriting standards of the GSEs, there are subprime loans, alt-A and alt-B loans, and high LTV loans.

The monthly cash flow from a mortgage loan, regardless of the mortgage design, can be decomposed into three parts: (1) the servicing fee, (2) the interest payment, and (3) the scheduled principal repayment. There is uncertainty associated with investing in a mortgage because of prepayments; that is, the cash flow is not known with certainty. This uncertainty is called prepayment risk. Those investing in mortgages also face liquidity risk and price risk and may be exposed to credit risk.

Questions

1. a. What are the sources of revenue arising from mortgage origination?
   b. What are the risks associated with the mortgage origination process?
2. What are the two primary factors in determining whether funds will be lent to an applicant for a mortgage loan?
3. What is a conventional mortgage?
4. What can mortgage originators do with a loan after originating it?
5. What are a conforming mortgage and a nonconforming mortgage?
6. What are the sources of revenue from mortgage servicing?
7. Why is the note rate on a mortgage loan not the same as the interest rate that the investor of the mortgage loan receives?
8. a. What are the two types of mortgage insurance?

b. Which is the more important type of insurance from the lender's perspective?

9. a. What are the components of the cash flow of a mortgage loan?

   b. Why is the cash flow of a mortgage unknown?

10. What is a prepayment?

11. In what sense has the investor in a mortgage granted the borrower (homeowner) a call option?

12. a. What are the two categories of reference rates used in adjustable-rate mortgages?

    b. Which category of reference rate would you expect to increase faster when interest rates are rising? Why?

13. What types of features are included in an adjustable-rate mortgage to restrict how the note rate may change at the reset date?

14. a. What is a hybrid mortgage?

    b. What is an interest-only hybrid mortgage?

    c. Why would you expect that an interest-only hybrid mortgage would have greater credit risk than an adjustable-rate mortgage?

15. a. Does a prepayment penalty mortgage prohibit prepayments?

    b. What are the benefits of a prepayment penalty mortgage from the perspective of the borrower?

    c. How does the borrower benefit from a prepayment penalty mortgage?

16. What is the motivation for the creation of a reverse mortgage?

17. Explain why you agree or disagree with each of the following statements:

    a. Only borrowers with highly impaired credit can obtain a high LTV loan.

    b. An alt-A loan is a conventional, conforming loan.

    c. An alt-B loan is a subprime loan.

18. Why is an alt-A loan obtained?

19. a. What is a balloon mortgage?

    b. What is the actual final maturity of a balloon mortgage?

20. Explain why in a fixed-rate level-payment mortgage the amount of the mortgage payment applied to interest declines over time while the amount applied to the repayment of principal increases.

21. Consider the following fixed-rate level-payment mortgage:

$$\text{maturity} = 360 \text{ months}$$
$$\text{amount borrowed} = \$150,000$$
$$\text{note rate} = 8\%$$

What is the monthly mortgage payment?

22. For the following fixed-rate level-payment mortgage, construct an amortization schedule for the first 10 months:

$$\text{maturity} = 360 \text{ months}$$
$$\text{amount borrowed} = \$100,000$$
$$\text{note rate} = 10\%$$
$$\text{monthly mortgage payment} = \$877.57$$

23. What is the most important factor that has been found to gauge the risk that a borrower will default?

24. a. What is the original LTV of a mortgage loan?

    b. What is the current LTV of a mortgage loan?

    c. What is the problem with using the original LTV to assess the likelihood that a seasoned mortgage will default?

25. In assessing the credit risk of a pool of mortgage loans, the rating agency compares a pool to a pool of prime loans. What is meant by a prime loan?

26. a. What is meant by a FICO score?

    b. What is the relationship between FICO scores and credit risk?

CHAPTER

11

MORTGAGE PASS-THROUGH SECURITIES

After reading this chapter you will understand:

- what a mortgage pass-through security is

- the cash flow characteristics of mortgage pass-through securities

- the importance of prepayments projections in estimating the cash flow of a mortgage pass-through security

- the WAC and WAM of a pass-through security

- the different types of agency pass-through securities

- what nonagency pass-through securities are and the different ways in which they can be credit enhanced

- what the PSA prepayment benchmark is and how it is used for determining the cash flow of a pass-through security

- the factors that affect prepayments

- what the PSA standard default assumption curve is

- what a nonagency mortgage security is

- the different types of credit enhancement for a nonagency mortgage-backed security

- what the cash flow yield is and its limitations

- how the average life of a mortgage pass-through security is calculated

- why prepayment risk can be divided into contraction risk and extension risk

- the market trading conventions of mortgage pass-through securities

A mortgage pass-through security, or simply a pass-through, is created when one or more mortgage holders form a collection (pool) of mortgages and sell shares or participation certificates in the pool. From the pass-through, two further derivative mortgage-backed securities are created: collateralized mortgage obligations and stripped mortgage-backed securities, which we discuss in Chapter 12. The pass-through is the subject of this chapter.

CASH FLOW CHARACTERISTICS

The cash flow of a mortgage pass-through security depends on the cash flow of the underlying mortgages. As we explained in Chapter 10, the cash flow consists of monthly mortgage payments representing interest, the scheduled repayment of principal, and any prepayments. The creation of a pass-through and its cash flow are diagrammed in Exhibit 11-1.

Payments are made to security holders each month. Neither the amount nor the timing, however, of the cash flow from the pool of mortgages is identical to that of the cash flow passed through to investors. The monthly cash flow for a pass-through is less than the monthly cash flow of the underlying mortgages by an amount equal to servicing and other fees. The other fees are those charged by the issuer or guarantor of the pass-through for guaranteeing the issue. The coupon rate on a pass-through, called the **pass-through coupon rate**, is less than the mortgage rate on the underlying pool of mortgage loans by an amount equal to the servicing and guaranteeing fees.

The timing of the cash flow is also different. The monthly mortgage payment is due from each mortgagor on the first day of each month, but there is a delay in passing through the corresponding monthly cash flow to the security holders. The length of the delay varies by the type of pass-through security.

Because of prepayments, the cash flow of a pass-through is also not known with certainty. The various conventions for estimating the cash flow are discussed later in the chapter.

WAC AND WAM

Not all of the mortgages that are included in a pool of mortgages that are securitized have the same mortgage rate and the same maturity. Consequently, when describing a pass-through security, a weighted-average coupon rate and a weighted-average maturity are determined.

A **weighted-average coupon rate (WAC)** is found by weighting the mortgage rate of each mortgage loan in the pool by the amount of the mortgage outstanding. A **weighted-average maturity (WAM)** is found by weighting the remaining number of months to maturity for each mortgage loan in the pool by the amount of the mortgage outstanding.

EXHIBIT 11-1   Creation of a Pass-Through and Its Cash Flow

Each loan is for $100,000

Total loans: $1 million

AGENCY PASS-THROUGHS

There are three major types of pass-throughs, guaranteed by three organizations: Government National Mortgage Association (Ginnie Mae), Federal Home Loan Mortgage Corporation (Freddie Mac), and Federal National Mortgage Association (Fannie Mae). These are called **agency pass-throughs**.

An agency can provide one of two types of guarantees. One type of guarantee is the timely payment of both interest and principal, meaning that interest and principal will be paid when due, even if some of the mortgagors fail to make their monthly mortgage payments. Pass-throughs with this type of guarantee are referred to as **fully**

modified pass-throughs. The second type also guarantees both interest and principal payments, but it guarantees only the timely payment of interest. The scheduled principal is passed through as it is collected, with a guarantee that the scheduled payment will be made no later than a specified date. Pass-throughs with this type of guarantee are called **modified pass-throughs**.

Ginnie Mae pass-throughs are guaranteed by the full faith and credit of the U.S. government. For this reason, Ginnie Mae pass-throughs are viewed as risk-free in terms of default risk, just like Treasury securities. The security guaranteed by Ginnie Mae is called a **mortgage-backed security (MBS)**. All Ginnie Mae MBSs are fully modified pass-throughs. Only mortgage loans insured or guaranteed by either the Rural Housing Service, the Veterans Administration, or the Farmers Home Administration can be included in a mortgage pool guaranteed by Ginnie Mae.

Freddie Mac issues a pass-through called a **participation certificate (PC)**. Although a guarantee of Freddie Mac is not a guarantee by the U.S. government, most market participants view Freddie Mac PCs as similar, although not identical, in credit worthiness to Ginnie Mae pass-throughs. In 1990, Freddie Mac introduced its **Gold PC**, which has stronger guarantees than other PCs it issues and will be the only type of PC issued in the future. Specifically, non-Gold PCs that have been issued are modified pass-throughs. All Gold PCs issued are fully modified pass-throughs. For modified PCs issued by Freddie Mac, the scheduled principal is passed through as it is collected, with Freddie Mac guaranteeing only that the scheduled payment will be made no later than one year after it is due.

The pass-throughs issued by Fannie Mae are called mortgage-backed securities (MBSs). Like a Freddie Mac PC, a Fannie Mae MBS is not an obligation of the federal government. All Fannie Mae MBSs are fully modified pass-throughs.

As explained in Chapter 6, Fannie Mae and Freddie Mac are government-sponsored enterprises (GSEs). In the marketplace, the mortgage pass-through securities issued by these two GSEs are referred to as **conventional pass-through securities**. However, we will refer to them as agency pass-through securities in this book.

NONAGENCY PASS-THROUGHS

Nonagency pass-through securities are issued by commercial banks, thrifts, and private conduits. Private conduits purchase nonconforming mortgages, pool them, and then sell pass-throughs in which the collateral is the underlying pool of nonconforming mortgages. The private conduits that issue pass-throughs are doing what the government created the agency conduits to do, without any guarantees (implicit or explicit) from the U.S. government. Nonagency mortgage pass-throughs must be registered with the Securities and Exchange Commission. They are rated by the same four nationally recognized companies that rate debt obligations. The development of credit enhancement has been the key to the success of this market.

Credit Enhancement
The primary factors considered by the nationally recognized rating companies in assigning a rating are the type of property (single-family residences, condominiums), the type of loan (fixed-rate level payment, adjustable rate, balloon), the term of the

loans, the geographical dispersion of the loans, the loan size (conforming loans, jumbo loans), the amount of seasoning of the loans, and the purpose of the loans (purchase or refinancing). Typically, a double A or triple A rating is sought. The amount of credit enhancement necessary depends on what the rating agency requires to bring the attributes of a particular pool of mortgages to the credit rating sought.

We will provide a brief review of the different types of credit enhancement mechanisms in Chapter 14 where we discuss asset-backed securities.

External Credit Enhancements

External credit enhancements come in the form of third-party guarantees that provide for first-loss protection against losses up to a specified level, for example, 10%. The most common forms of external enhancements are bond insurance and pool insurance. Bond insurance provides the same function as in municipal bond structures. The insurance is provided by a monoline insurance company.

Pool insurance policies cover losses resulting from defaults and foreclosures. Policies are typically written for a dollar amount of coverage that continues in force throughout the life of the pool. However, some policies are written so that the dollar amount of coverage declines as the pool seasons as long as two conditions are met: (1) the credit performance is better than expected, and (2) the rating agencies that rated the issue approve. Because only defaults and foreclosures are covered, additional insurance must be obtained to cover losses resulting from bankruptcy (i.e., court-mandated modification of mortgage debt), fraud arising in the origination process, and special hazards (i.e., losses resulting from events not covered by a standard homeowner's insurance policy).

The rating of the third-party guarantor must be at least as high as the rating sought. Thus, if the third-party guarantor has an A rating, a AAA rating for the asset-backed security cannot be obtained by using only this guarantee.[1] The disadvantage of a third-party guarantee is that if the rating of the third-party guarantor is downgraded, the security's rating may be downgraded depending on the historical performance of the collateral. Therefore, it is imperative that an investor perform credit analysis on both the collateral (the loans) and the third-party guarantor.

Internal Credit Enhancements

Internal credit enhancements come in more complicated forms than external credit enhancements and may alter the cash flow characteristics of the loans even in the absence of default. The most common forms of internal credit enhancement are reserve funds, overcollateralization, and senior/subordinate structures.

Reserve funds   **Reserve funds** come in two forms, cash reserve funds and excess spread accounts. **Cash reserve funds** are straight deposits of cash generated from issuance proceeds. In this case, part of the underwriting profits from the deal are deposited into a hypothecated fund that typically invests in money market instruments. Cash reserve funds are typically used in conjunction with other forms of credit enhancement.

---

[1] It is for this reason that letter of credits from banks are rare as a credit enhancement. There are few international banks with a triple A rating.

Excess spread accounts involve the allocation of excess spread or cash into a separate reserve account after paying out the net coupon, servicing fee, and all other expenses on a monthly basis. For example, suppose that the gross WAC is 7.75%, the servicing and other fees are 0.25%, and the net WAC is 7.25%. This means that there is excess spread of 0.25%. The amount in the reserve account will gradually increase and can be used to pay for possible future losses.

Overcollateralization   **Overcollateralization** involves establishing a pool of assets with a greater principal amount than the principal amount of the pool of mortgage loans. For example, the principal amount of an issue may be $300 million, but the principal amount of the pool of mortgages is $305 million.

Senior/subordinate structure   The most widely used internal credit support structure by far is the senior/subordinate structure. The subordinate bond class is the first to absorb all losses on the underlying collateral, thus protecting the senior bond class. For example, a $100 million deal can be divided into two bond classes: a $92.25 million senior bond class and a $7.75 million subordinate bond class. The subordination level in this hypothetical structure is 7.75%. The subordinate bond class will absorb all losses up to $7.75 million and the senior bond class will start to experience losses thereafter. So if there is $5 million of losses, the subordinate bond class will realize this loss. Thus it would realize a 64.5% loss ($5/$7.75). If, instead, there is $10 million of losses, the subordinate bond class will experience $7.75 million of losses or a 100% loss and the senior bond class will experience a loss of $2.25 million ($10 million minus $7.75 million), or a 2.4% loss ($2.25/$92.25).

The subordinate bond class holder obviously would require a yield premium to take on the greater default risk exposure relative to the senior bond class. This setup is another form of self-insurance in which the senior bond class holder is giving up yield spread to the subordinate bond class holder. This form of credit enhancement still does not affect cash flow characteristics of the senior bond class except in the form of prepayment. To the extent that losses are within the subordination level, the senior bond class holder will receive principal as if a prepayment has occurred.

Almost all existing senior/subordinate structures also incorporate a **shifting interest structure**. A shifting interest structure redirects prepayments disproportionally from the subordinate bond class to the senior bond class according to a specified schedule. The rationale for the shifting interest structure is to have enough insurance outstanding to cover future losses. We will illustrate the shifting interest mechanism in Chapter 14.

PREPAYMENT CONVENTIONS AND CASH FLOW[2]

To value a pass-through security, it is necessary to project its cash flow. The difficulty is that the cash flow is unknown because of prepayments. The only way to project a cash flow is to make some assumption about the prepayment rate over the life of the

[2]This section and the one to follow are adapted from Chapter 3 of Fabozzi and Ramsey, *Collateralized Mortgage Obligations: Structures and Analysis.*

underlying mortgage pool. The prepayment rate assumed is called the **prepayment speed** or, simply, **speed**. The yield calculated based on the projected cash flow is called a **cash flow yield**.

Estimating the cash flow from a pass-through requires making an assumption about future prepayments. Several conventions have been used as a benchmark for prepayment rates: (1) Federal Housing Administration (FHA) experience, (2) the conditional prepayment rate, and (3) the Public Securities Association (PSA) prepayment benchmark. Although the first convention is no longer used, we discuss it because of its historical significance.

In the early stages of the development of the pass-through market, cash flows were calculated assuming no prepayments for the first 12 years, at which time all the mortgages in the pool were assumed to prepay. This naive approach was replaced by the **FHA prepayment experience** approach, which also is no longer in use. This prepayment assumption, based on the prepayment experience for 30-year mortgages derived from an FHA table on mortgage survival factors, was once the most commonly used benchmark for prepayment rates. It calls for the projection of the cash flow for a mortgage pool on the assumption that the prepayment rate will be the same as the FHA experience with 30-year mortgage loans.

Despite the method's past popularity, prepayments based on FHA experience are not necessarily indicative of the prepayment rate for a particular pool, mainly because FHA prepayments are for mortgages originated over all sorts of interest-rate periods. Prepayment rates are tied to interest-rate cycles, however, so an average prepayment rate over various cycles is not very useful in estimating prepayments. Moreover, new FHA tables are published periodically, causing confusion about the FHA table on which prepayments should be based. Finally, because FHA mortgages are assumable, unlike FNMA, FHLMC, and most nonconforming mortgages that have due-on-sale provisions, FHA statistics underestimate prepayments for non-FHA mortgages. Because estimated prepayments using FHA experience may be misleading, the resulting cash flow is not meaningful for valuing pass-throughs.

Conditional Prepayment Rate

Another benchmark for projecting prepayments and the cash flow of a pass-through requires assuming that some fraction of the remaining principal in the pool is prepaid each month for the remaining term of the mortgage. The prepayment rate assumed for a pool, called the **conditional prepayment rate (CPR)**, is based on the characteristics of the pool (including its historical prepayment experience) and the current and expected future economic environment. It is referred to as a conditional rate because it is conditional on the remaining mortgage balance.

Single-Monthly Mortality Rate

The CPR is an annual prepayment rate. To estimate monthly prepayments, the CPR must be converted into a monthly prepayment rate, commonly referred to as the **single-monthly mortality rate (SMM)**. A formula can be used to determine the SMM for a given CPR:

$$SMM = 1 - (1 - CPR)^{1/12} \qquad \textbf{(11.1)}$$

Suppose that the CPR used to estimate prepayments is 6%. The corresponding SMM is

$$SMM = 1 - (1 - 0.06)^{1/12}$$
$$= 1 - (0.94)^{0.08333} = 0.005143$$

SMM Rate and Monthly Prepayment

An SMM of $w\%$ means that approximately $w\%$ of the remaining mortgage balance at the beginning of the month, less the scheduled principal payment, will prepay that month. That is,

prepayment for month t

$$= SMM \times (\text{beginning mortgage balance for month } t$$
$$- \text{scheduled principal payment for month } t) \qquad \textbf{(11.2)}$$

For example, suppose that an investor owns a pass-through in which the remaining mortgage balance at the beginning of some month is $290 million. Assuming that the SMM is 0.5143% and the scheduled principal payment is $3 million, the estimated prepayment for the month is

$$0.005143(\$290,000,000 - \$3,000,000) = \$1,476,041$$

PSA Prepayment Benchmark

The Public Securities Association (PSA) prepayment benchmark is expressed as a monthly series of annual prepayment rates.[3] The PSA benchmark assumes that prepayment rates are low for newly originated mortgages and then will speed up as the mortgages become seasoned.

The PSA benchmark assumes the following CPRs for 30-year mortgages: (1) a CPR of 0.2% for the first month, increased by 0.2% per year per month for the next 30 months when it reaches 6% per year, and (2) a 6% CPR for the remaining years. This benchmark, referred to as "100% PSA" or simply "100 PSA," is depicted graphically in Exhibit 11-2. Mathematically, 100 PSA can be expressed as follows:

$$\text{If } t \le 30: \quad CPR = 6\% \ (t/30)$$
$$\text{If } t > 30: \quad CPR = 6\%$$

where t is the number of months since the mortgage originated.

Slower or faster speeds are then referred to as some percentage of PSA. For example, 50 PSA means one-half the CPR of the PSA benchmark prepayment rate; 150 PSA means 1.5 times the CPR of the PSA benchmark prepayment rate; 300 PSA means 3 times the CPR of the benchmark prepayment rate. A prepayment rate of 0 PSA means that no prepayments are assumed.

---

[3]This benchmark is commonly referred to as a *prepayment model*, suggesting that it can be used to estimate prepayments. Characterization of this benchmark as a prepayment model is inappropriate. It is simply a market convention of prepayment behavior.

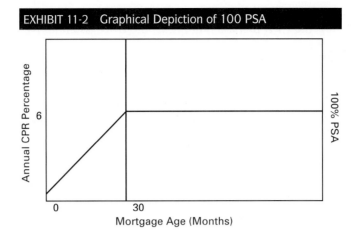

EXHIBIT 11-2   Graphical Depiction of 100 PSA

The CPR is converted to an SMM using equation (11.1). For example, the SMMs for month 5, month 20, and months 31 through 360 assuming 100 PSA are calculated as follows:

For month 5:
$$CPR = 6\%(5/30) = 1\% = 0.01$$
$$SMM = 1 - (1 - 0.01)^{1/12}$$
$$= 1 - (0.99)^{0.083333} = 0.000837$$

For month 20:
$$CPR = 6\%(20/30) = 4\% = 0.04$$
$$SMM = 1 - (1 - 0.04)^{1/12}$$
$$= 1 - (0.96)^{0.083333} = 0.003396$$

For months 31–360:
$$CPR = 6\%$$
$$SMM = 1 - (1 - 0.06)^{1/12}$$
$$= 1 - (0.94)^{0.083333} = 0.005143$$

The SMMs for month 5, month 20, and months 31 through 360 assuming 165 PSA are computed as follows:

For month 5:
$$CPR = 6\%(5/30) = 1\% = 0.01$$
$$165\ PSA = 1.65(0.01) = 0.0165$$
$$SMM = 1 - (1 - 0.0165)^{1/12}$$
$$= 1 - (0.9835)^{0.083333} = 0.001386$$

For month 20:
$$CPR = 6\%(20/30) = 4\% = 0.04$$
$$165\ PSA = 1.65(.04) = 0.066$$
$$SMM = 1 - (1 - 0.066)^{1/12}$$
$$= 1 - (0.934)^{0.083333} = 0.005674$$

For months 31–360:
$$CPR = 6\%$$
$$165\ PSA = 1.65(0.06) = 0.099$$
$$SMM = 1 - (1 - 0.099)^{1/12}$$
$$= 1 - (0.901)^{0.083333} = 0.007828$$

Notice that the SMM assuming 165 PSA is not just 1.65 times the SMM assuming 100 PSA. It is the CPR that is a multiple of the CPR assuming 100 PSA.

Monthly Cash Flow Construction

We now show how to construct a monthly cash flow for a hypothetical pass-through given a PSA assumption. For the purpose of this illustration, the underlying mortgages for this hypothetical pass-through are assumed to be fixed-rate level-payment mortgages with a WAC rate of 8.125%. It will be assumed that the pass-through rate is 7.5%, with a WAM of 357 months.

Exhibit 11-3 shows the cash flow for selected months assuming 100 PSA. The cash flow is broken down into three components: (1) interest (based on the pass-through rate), (2) the regularly scheduled principal repayment, and (3) prepayments based on 100 PSA.

Let's walk through Exhibit 11-3 column by column.

Column 1   This is the month.

Column 2   This column gives the outstanding mortgage balance at the beginning of the month. It is equal to the outstanding balance at the beginning of the preceding month reduced by the total principal payment in the preceding month.

Column 3   This column shows the SMM for 100 PSA. Two things should be noted in this column. First, for month 1, the SMM is for a pass-through that has been seasoned three months. That is, the CPR is 0.8%. This is because the WAM is 357. Second, from month 27 on, the SMM is 0.00514, which corresponds to a CPR of 6%.

EXHIBIT 11-3   Monthly Cash Flow for a $400 Million 7.5% Pass-Through Rate with a WAC of 8.125% and a WAM of 357 Months Assuming 100 PSA

(1)	(2) Outstanding	(3)	(4) Mortgage	(5)	(6) Scheduled	(7)	(8) Total	(9)
Month	Balance	SMM	Payment	Interest	Principal	Prepayment	Principal	Cash Flow
1	400,000,000	0.00067	2,975,868	2,500,000	267,535	267,470	535,005	3,035,005
2	399,464,995	0.00084	2,973,877	2,496,656	269,166	334,198	603,364	3,100,020
3	398,861,631	0.00101	2,971,387	2,492,885	270,762	400,800	671,562	3,164,447
4	398,190,069	0.00117	2,968,399	2,488,688	272,321	467,243	739,564	3,228,252
5	397,450,505	0.00134	2,964,914	2,484,066	273,843	533,493	807,335	3,291,401
6	396,643,170	0.00151	2,960,931	2,479,020	275,327	599,514	874,841	3,353,860
7	395,768,329	0.00168	2,956,453	2,473,552	276,772	665,273	942,045	3,415,597
8	394,826,284	0.00185	2,951,480	2,467,664	278,177	730,736	1,008,913	3,476,577
9	393,817,371	0.00202	2,946,013	2,461,359	279,542	795,869	1,075,410	3,536,769
10	392,741,961	0.00219	2,940,056	2,454,637	280,865	860,637	1,141,502	3,596,140
11	391,600,459	0.00236	2,933,608	2,447,503	282,147	925,008	1,207,155	3,654,658
12	390,393,304	0.00254	2,926,674	2,439,958	283,386	988,948	1,272,333	3,712,291
13	389,120,971	0.00271	2,919,254	2,432,006	284,581	1,052,423	1,337,004	3,769,010
14	387,783,966	0.00288	2,911,353	2,423,650	285,733	1,115,402	1,401,134	3,824,784
15	386,382,832	0.00305	2,902,973	2,414,893	286,839	1,177,851	1,464,690	3,879,583
16	384,918,142	0.00322	2,894,117	2,405,738	287,900	1,239,739	1,527,639	3,933,378
17	383,390,502	0.00340	2,884,789	2,396,191	288,915	1,301,033	1,589,949	3,986,139

EXHIBIT 11-3   (continued)

(1) Month	(2) Outstanding Balance	(3) SMM	(4) Mortgage Payment	(5) Interest	(6) Scheduled Principal	(7) Prepayment	(8) Total Principal	(9) Cash Flow
18	381,800,553	0.00357	2,874,992	2,386,253	289,884	1,361,703	1,651,587	4,037,840
19	380,148,966	0.00374	2,864,730	2,375,931	290,805	1,421,717	1,712,522	4,088,453
20	378,436,444	0.00392	2,854,008	2,365,228	291,678	1,481,046	1,772,724	4,137,952
21	376,663,720	0.00409	2,842,830	2,354,148	292,503	1,539,658	1,832,161	4,186,309
22	374,831,559	0.00427	2,831,201	2,342,697	293,279	1,597,525	1,890,804	4,233,501
23	372,940,755	0.00444	2,819,125	2,330,880	294,005	1,654,618	1,948,623	4,279,503
24	370,992,132	0.00462	2,806,607	2,318,701	294,681	1,710,908	2,005,589	4,324,290
25	368,986,543	0.00479	2,793,654	2,306,166	295,307	1,766,368	2,061,675	4,367,841
26	366,924,868	0.00497	2,780,270	2,293,280	295,883	1,820,970	2,116,852	4,410,133
27	364,808,016	0.00514	2,766,461	2,280,050	296,406	1,874,688	2,171,092	4,451,144
28	362,636,921	0.00514	2,752,233	2,266,481	296,879	1,863,519	2,160,398	4,426,879
29	360,476,523	0.00514	2,738,078	2,252,978	297,351	1,852,406	2,149,758	4,402,736
30	358,326,766	0.00514	2,723,996	2,239,542	297,825	1,841,347	2,139,173	4,378,715
⋮								
100	231,249,776	0.00514	1,898,682	1,445,311	332,928	1,187,608	1,520,537	2,965,848
101	229,729,239	0.00514	1,888,917	1,435,808	333,459	1,179,785	1,513,244	2,949,052
102	228,215,995	0.00514	1,879,202	1,426,350	333,990	1,172,000	1,505,990	2,932,340
103	226,710,004	0.00514	1,869,538	1,416,938	334,522	1,164,252	1,498,774	2,915,712
104	225,211,230	0.00514	1,859,923	1,407,570	335,055	1,156,541	1,491,596	2,899,166
105	223,719,634	0.00514	1,850,357	1,398,248	335,589	1,148,867	1,484,456	2,882,703
⋮								
200	109,791,339	0.00514	1,133,751	686,196	390,372	562,651	953,023	1,639,219
201	108,838,316	0.00514	1,127,920	680,239	390,994	557,746	948,740	1,628,980
202	107,889,576	0.00514	1,122,119	674,310	391,617	552,863	944,480	1,618,790
203	106,945,096	0.00514	1,116,348	668,407	392,241	548,003	940,243	1,608,650
204	106,004,852	0.00514	1,110,607	662,530	392,866	543,164	936,029	1,598,560
205	105,068,823	0.00514	1,104,895	656,680	393,491	538,347	931,838	1,588,518
⋮								
300	32,383,611	0.00514	676,991	202,398	457,727	164,195	621,923	824,320
301	31,761,689	0.00514	673,510	198,511	458,457	160,993	619,449	817,960
302	31,142,239	0.00514	670,046	194,639	459,187	157,803	616,990	811,629
303	30,525,249	0.00514	666,600	190,783	459,918	154,626	614,545	805,328
304	29,910,704	0.00514	663,171	186,942	460,651	151,462	612,113	799,055
305	29,298,591	0.00514	659,761	183,116	461,385	148,310	609,695	792,811
⋮								
350	4060,411	0.00514	523,138	25,378	495,645	18,334	513,979	539,356
351	3,546,432	0.00514	520,447	22,165	496,435	15,686	512,121	534,286
352	3,034,311	0.00514	517,770	18,964	497,226	13,048	510,274	529,238
353	2,524,037	0.00514	515,107	15,775	498,018	10,420	508,437	524,213
354	2,015,600	0.00514	512,458	12,597	498,811	7,801	506,612	519,209
355	1,508,988	0.00514	509,823	9,431	499,606	5,191	504,797	514,228
356	1,004,191	0.00514	507,201	6,276	500,401	2,591	502,992	509,269
357	501,199	0.00514	504,592	3,132	501,199	0	501,199	504,331

Column 4   The total monthly mortgage payment is shown in this column. Notice that the total monthly mortgage payment declines over time as prepayments reduce the mortgage balance outstanding. There is a formula to determine what the monthly mortgage balance will be for each month given prepayments.[4]

Column 5   The monthly interest paid to the pass-through investor is found in this column. This value is determined by multiplying the outstanding mortgage balance at the beginning of the month by the pass-through rate of 7.5% and dividing by 12.

Column 6   This column gives the regularly scheduled principal repayment. This is the difference between the total monthly mortgage payment (the amount shown in column 4) and the gross coupon interest for the month. The gross coupon interest is 8.125% multiplied by the outstanding mortgage balance at the beginning of the month, then divided by 12.

Column 7   The prepayment for the month is reported in this column. The prepayment is found by using equation (11.2). So, for example, in month 100, the beginning mortgage balance is $231,249,776, the scheduled principal payment is $332,298, and the SMM at 100 PSA is 0.00514301 (only 0.00514 is shown in the table, to save space), so the prepayment is

$$0.00514301(\$231,249,776 - \$332,928) = \$1,187,608$$

Column 8   The total principal payment, which is the sum of columns 6 and 7, is shown in this column.

Column 9   The projected monthly cash flow for this pass-through is shown in this last column. The monthly cash flow is the sum of the interest paid to the pass-through investor (column 5) and the total principal payments for the month (column 8).

Exhibit 11-4 shows selected monthly cash flows for the same pass-through assuming 165 PSA.

Beware of Conventions

The PSA prepayment benchmark is simply a market convention. It is the product of a study by the PSA based on FHA prepayment experience. Data that the PSA committee examined seemed to suggest that mortgages became seasoned (i.e., prepayment rates tended to level off) after 30 months and the CPR tended to be 6%. How, though, did the PSA come up with the CPRs used for months 1 through 29? In fact, these numbers are not based on empirical evidence but on a linear increase from month 1 to month 30 so that at month 30 the CPR is 6%. Moreover, the same benchmark or seasoning process is used in quoting pass-throughs regardless of the collateral: 30- and 15-year loans, fixed- or adjustable-rate loans, and conventional or VA/FHA-insured loans.

Astute money managers recognize that the CPR is a convenient shorthand enabling market participants to quote yield and/or price, but that as a convention in determining value it has many limitations.

---

[4]The formula is presented in Chapter 20 of Frank J. Fabozzi, *Fixed Income Mathematics: Analytical and Statistical Techniques* (Chicago: Probus Publishing, 1993).

EXHIBIT 11-4 Monthly Cash Flow for a $400 Million 7.5% Pass-Through Rate with a WAC of 8.125% and a WAM of 357 Months Assuming 165 PSA

(1) Month	(2) Outstanding Balance	(3) SMM	(4) Mortgage Payment	(5) Interest	(6) Scheduled Principal	(7) Prepayment	(8) Total Principal	(9) Total Cash Flow
1	400,000,000	0.00111	2,975,868	2,500,000	267,535	442,389	709,923	3,209,923
2	399,290,077	0.00139	2,972,575	2,495,563	269,048	552,847	821,896	3,317,459
3	398,468,181	0.00167	2,968,456	2,490,426	270,495	663,065	933,560	3,423,986
4	397,534,621	0.00195	2,963,513	2,484,591	271,873	772,949	1,044,822	3,529,413
5	396,489,799	0.00223	2,957,747	2,478,061	273,181	882,405	1,155,586	3,633,647
6	395,334,213	0.00251	2,951,160	2,470,839	274,418	991,341	1,265,759	3,736,598
7	394,068,454	0.00279	2,943,755	2,462,928	275,583	1,099,664	1,375,246	3,838,174
8	392,693,208	0.00308	2,935,534	2,454,333	276,674	1,207,280	1,483,954	3,938,287
9	391,209,254	0.00336	2,926,503	2,445,058	277,690	1,314,099	1,591,789	4,036,847
10	389,617,464	0.00365	2,916,666	2,435,109	278,631	1,420,029	1,698,659	4,133,769
11	387,918,805	0.00393	2,906,028	2,424,493	279,494	1,524,979	1,804,473	4,228,965
12	386,114,332	0.00422	2,894,595	2,413,215	280,280	1,628,859	1,909,139	4,322,353
13	384,205,194	0.00451	2,882,375	2,401,282	280,986	1,731,581	2,012,567	4,413,850
14	382,192,626	0.00480	2,869,375	2,388,704	281,613	1,833,058	2,114,670	4,503,374
15	380,077,956	0.00509	2,855,603	2,375,487	282,159	1,933,203	2,215,361	4,590,848
16	377,862,595	0.00538	2,841,068	2,361,641	282,623	2,031,931	2,314,554	4,676,195
17	375,548,041	0.00567	2,825,779	2,347,175	283,006	2,129,159	2,412,164	4,759,339
18	373,135,877	0.00597	2,809,746	2,332,099	283,305	2,224,805	2,508,110	4,840,210
19	370,627,766	0.00626	2,792,980	2,316,424	283,521	2,318,790	2,602,312	4,918,735
20	368,025,455	0.00656	2,775,493	2,300,159	283,654	2,411,036	2,694,690	4,994,849
21	365,330,765	0.00685	2,757,296	2,283,317	283,702	2,501,466	2,785,169	5,068,486
22	362,545,596	0.00715	2,738,402	2,265,910	283,666	2,590,008	2,873,674	5,139,584
23	359,671,922	0.00745	2,718,823	2,247,950	283,545	2,676,588	2,960,133	5,208,083
24	356,711,789	0.00775	2,698,575	2,229,449	283,338	2,761,139	3,044,477	5,273,926
25	353,667,312	0.00805	2,677,670	2,210,421	283,047	2,843,593	3,126,640	5,337,061
26	350,540,672	0.00835	2,656,123	2,190,879	282,671	2,923,885	3,206,556	5,397,435
27	347,334,116	0.00865	2,633,950	2,170,838	282,209	3,001,955	3,284,164	5,455,002
28	344,049,952	0.00865	2,611,167	2,150,312	281,662	2,973,553	3,255,215	5,405,527
29	340,794,737	0.00865	2,588,581	2,129,967	281,116	2,945,400	3,226,516	5,356,483
30	337,568,221	0.00865	2,566,190	2,109,801	280,572	2,917,496	3,198,067	5,307,869
⋮								
100	170,142,350	0.00865	1,396,958	1,063,390	244,953	1,469,591	1,714,544	2,777,933
101	168,427,806	0.00865	1,384,875	1,052,674	244,478	1,454,765	1,699,243	2,751,916
102	166,728,563	0.00865	1,372,896	1,042,054	244,004	1,440,071	1,684,075	2,726,128
103	165,044,489	0.00865	1,361,020	1,031,528	243,531	1,425,508	1,669,039	2,700,567
104	163,375,450	0.00865	1,349,248	1,021,097	243,060	1,411,075	1,654,134	2,675,231
105	161,721,315	0.00865	1,337,577	1,010,758	242,589	1,396,771	1,639,359	2,650,118
⋮								
200	56,746,664	0.00865	585,990	354,667	201,767	489,106	690,874	1,045,540
201	56,055,790	0.00865	580,921	350,349	201,377	483,134	684,510	1,034,859
202	55,371,280	0.00865	575,896	346,070	200,986	477,216	678,202	1,024,273
203	54,693,077	0.00865	570,915	341,832	200,597	471,353	671,950	1,013,782

(continued)

EXHIBIT 11-4   (continued)

(1) Month	(2) Outstanding Balance	(3) SMM	(4) Mortgage Payment	(5) Interest	(6) Scheduled Principal	(7) Prepayment	(8) Total Principal	(9) Total Cash Flow
204	54,021,127	0.00865	565,976	337,632	200,208	465,544	665,752	1,003,384
205	53,355,375	0.00865	561,081	333,471	199,820	459,789	659,609	993,080
⋮								
300	11,758,141	0.00865	245,808	73,488	166,196	100,269	266,465	339,953
301	11,491,677	0.00865	243,682	71,823	165,874	97,967	263,841	335,664
302	11,227,836	0.00865	241,574	70,174	165,552	95,687	261,240	331,414
303	10,966,596	0.00865	239,485	68,541	165,232	93,430	258,662	327,203
304	10,707,934	0.00865	237,413	66,925	164,912	91,196	256,107	323,032
305	10,451,827	0.00865	235,360	65,324	164,592	88,983	253,575	318,899
⋮								
350	1,235,674	0.00865	159,202	7,723	150,836	9,384	160,220	167,943
351	1,075,454	0.00865	157,825	6,722	150,544	8,000	158,544	165,266
352	916,910	0.00865	156,460	5,731	150,252	6,631	156,883	162,614
353	760,027	0.00865	155,107	4,750	149,961	5,277	155,238	159,988
354	604,789	0.00865	153,765	3,780	149,670	3,937	153,607	157,387
355	451,182	0.00865	152,435	2,820	149,380	2,611	151,991	154,811
356	299,191	0.00865	151,117	1,870	149,091	1,298	150,389	152,259
357	148,802	0.00865	149,809	930	148,802	0	148,802	149,732

FACTORS AFFECTING PREPAYMENTS AND PREPAYMENT MODELING

A prepayment model is a statistical model that is used to forecast prepayments. It begins by modeling the statistical relationships among the factors that are expected to affect prepayments. Wall Street firms that sell mortgage-backed securities and independent research firms have developed prepayment models.

At one time, because of the data limitations about the individual loans in the pool backing a mortgage-backed security, prepayment models viewed borrowers as generic with the only significant difference in borrowers being due to (1) how borrowers respond, on average, to refinancing opportunities based on their mortgage rate relative to the market rate, the loan age (i.e., the length of time their mortgage has been outstanding) and (2) the type of loan (i.e., fixed-rate fully amortizing, balloon loans, ARMs). Today, much more data are available, particularly for nonagency MBS, regarding borrower and loan attributes. The attributes that modelers have found to be important in the nonagency MBS market have been applied to the agency MBS market using proxy measures where data for individual loans are not available. As a result, more variables are now used to compute prepayments that are attributable to refinancing and housing turnover.

Modelers have developed different prepayment models for agency and nonagency mortgage-backed securities. We describe the model for each next. In our discussion we will use the prepayment models developed by Bear Stearns, a major dealer in the mortgage market.

Agency Prepayment Models

There is much less borrower and loan data provided for agency MBS than for non-agency MBS. As a result, prepayment modeling has been done at the pool level rather than the loan level.

The Bear Stearns agency prepayment model consists of three components:

- housing turnover
- cash-out refinancing
- rate/term refinancing

Housing turnover means existing home sales. The two factors that impact existing home sales include:

- family relocation due to changes in employment and family status (e.g., change in family size, divorce)
- trade-up and trade-down activity attributable to changes in interest rates, income, and home prices.

In general, housing turnover is insensitive to the level of mortgage rates.

Cash-out refinancing means refinancing by a borrower in order to monetize the price appreciation of the property. Obviously, prepayments due to cash-out refinancing will depend on the increase in housing prices in the economy or region where the property is located. Adding to the incentive for borrowers to monetize price appreciation is the favorable tax law regarding the taxation of capital gains. The federal income tax rules exempt gains up to $500,000. Thus, cash-out refinancing may be economic despite a rising mortgage rate and considering transaction costs. Basically, cash-out refinancing is more like housing turnover refinancing because of its tie to housing prices and its insensitivity to mortgage rates.

Rate/term refinancing means that the borrower has obtained a new mortgage on the existing property to save either on interest cost or shortening the life of the mortgage with no increase in the monthly payment. The homeowner's incentive to refinance is based on the projected present value of the dollar interest savings from the lower mortgage rate after deducting the estimated transaction costs to refinance.

In prepayment modeling, what measure is used to proxy for the savings incentive for a rate/term refinancing? One simple proxy would be to use the difference between the prevailing mortgage rate and the note rate on the homeowner's loan. However, this is not a good proxy. The reason is that a difference of 100 basis points between the homeowner's note rate and the prevailing mortgage rate has a greater impact on the borrower's savings if the borrower's note rate is 11% rather than 6%. Practitioners who have developed prepayment models have found that a better, although not perfect, proxy for capturing the incentive to refinance is the ratio of the borrower's note rate to the current mortgage rate. This ratio is called the **refinancing ratio**. For agency data, the WAC is the numerator. A refinancing ratio less than 1 means that the borrower's mortgage rate is less than the prevailing mortgage rate, and, therefore, there is no incentive for rate/term refinancing; a refinancing ratio of 1 means that the borrower has no incentive to refinance because his rate is the same as the market rate. When the refinancing ratio exceeds unity, there is an incentive to refinance.

For agency MBS, there are two other minor reasons for prepayments: curtailments and defaults. A **curtailment** is a prepayment of part of the outstanding loan balance. The motivation is the desire of the borrower to reduce the outstanding loan balance but not pay it off completely. A default of the borrower results in the foreclosure of the property and payment of the principal outstanding to the security holders. One study finds that these two reasons for prepayments for agency MBS since 2000 has been less than 1% CPR.[5]

Now let's look at these factors for agency MBS more closely.

Housing Turnover Component

Studies have found factors that have produced a relatively stable, long-term level of housing turnover rates that vary within a reasonable range. We already discussed the PSA benchmark. This is the baseline that was used in the agency MBS market from 1987 through the early 1990s based on conforming mortgages—the mortgages backing agency MBS was the one developed by the Public Securities Association. The baseline for seasoned mortgage pools (i.e., seasoned 30 months or longer) was 6%.

How good is this baseline? Not bad for the period 1988 through the end of 1997 according to a study by Westhoff and Srinivasan.[6] For this period, they found that aggregate housing turnover rates averaged 5.9% with a standard deviation of only $\frac{1}{2}$ of 1%. However, when they examined the period 1998 through 2001, annual housing turnover rates averaged 7.3%. The increase from 5.9% to 7.3% was due to the 8% annual price appreciation in housing prices over that period. Thus, the 6% benchmark for housing turnover when one used the PSA benchmark may no longer be appropriate.

The factors in the Bear Stearns model to forecast prepayments due to housing turnover are

- seasoning effect
- housing price appreciation effect
- seasonality effect

Because of transactions costs and moving costs, one might not expect that a newly acquired home will be sold shortly after it is purchased. The 30-month ramp in the baseline PSA model is a reflection of this view. However, due to periods of substantial refinancing (i.e., refinancing waves), there is evidence that a 30-month aging period is no longer an appropriate description of the seasoning process because the home-owner's tenure in the home (which does not necessarily correspond to the age of the loan due to refinancing) must be recognized. For example, a homeowner who resided in a home for 10 years but refinanced six months ago would view the decision to sell his home differently than someone who just move moved into a home six months ago. Consequently, this must be accounted for. In the Bear Stearns model, for example,

---

[5]Dale Westhoff and V. S. Srinivasan, "Agency Prepayment Model: Modeling the Dynamics of Borrower Attributes." Chapter 25 in Frank J. Fabozzi (ed.), *The Handbook of Mortgage-Backed Securities* (New York: McGraw-Hill, 2006).
[6]Westhoff and Srinivasan, "Agency Prepayment Model: Modeling the Dynamics of Borrower Attributes."

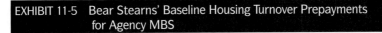

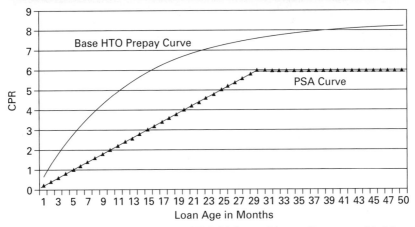

EXHIBIT 11-5   Bear Stearns' Baseline Housing Turnover Prepayments for Agency MBS

Source: Exhibit 25-2 in Dale Westhoff and V. S. Srinivasan, "Agency Prepayment Model: Modeling the Dynamics of Borrower Attributes," Chapter 25 in Frank J. Fabozzi (ed.), *The Handbook of Mortgage-Backed Securities* (New York: McGraw Hill, 2006).

the *baseline* housing turnover prepayment curve for agency 30-year current coupon purchase mortgages, future home price appreciation of 3.5%, and no seasonality is shown in Exhibit 11-5. For comparative purposes, the PSA benchmark is also shown in the exhibit. According to the Bear Stearns model, aging occurs faster than the PSA benchmark, with prepayment rates reaching 6% CPR in about 15 months (rather than 30 months) and prepayments peaking after 40 months at around 8% CPR and then leveling off at just below 7.5% CPR.

With respect to housing appreciation, over time the LTV of a loan changes. This is due to (1) the amortization of the loan and (2) the change in the value of the home. As explained earlier, there is an incentive for cash-out refinancing if the value of a home appreciates. Thus, in prepayment modeling to estimate prepayments attributable to housing appreciation, a proxy is needed to capture the change in the value of the LTV for a pool. In the Bear Stearns agency prepayment model, this is captured by constructing a composite *home appreciation index* (HPI).[7] For the Bear Stearns agency model, Exhibit 11-6 shows housing turnover prepayments against the composite HPI. For the five relative coupons shown in the exhibit, we see the effects on housing turnover prepayment forecasts of relative coupon and various levels of home price appreciation. For example, the prepayment model suggests that if the property values for a pool have increased 20% since origination, depending on whether the pool's WAC

---

[7]Almost 920,000 pools in the Bear Stearns' fixed-rate agency database are used to construct the HPI. The agencies do not release LTV information. However, originator panel data suggest that when the vast majority of Fannie Mae and Freddie Mac pools are originated, the LTV is between 75% and 80%. For Ginnie Mae pools, LTV exceeds 95% at origination.

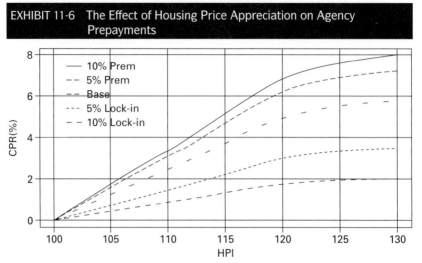

EXHIBIT 11-6 The Effect of Housing Price Appreciation on Agency Prepayments

Source: Exhibit 25-4 in Dale Westhoff and V. S. Srinivasan, "Agency Prepayment Model: Modeling the Dynamics of Borrower Attributes," Chapter 25 in Frank J. Fabozzi (ed.), *The Handbook of Mortgage-Backed Securities* (New York: McGraw Hill, 2006).

is a 10% discount, current coupon, or a 10% premium, the pool's housing turnover prepayments will increase by approximately 2%, 5%, or 7% CPR, respectively.

There is a well-documented seasonal pattern in prepayments. This pattern, referred to as the **seasonality effect**,[8] is related to activity in the primary housing market, with home buying increasing in the spring and gradually reaching a peak in late summer. Home buying declines in the fall and winter. Mirroring this activity are the prepayments that result from the turnover of housing as home buyers sell their existing homes and purchase new ones. Prepayments are low in the winter months and begin to rise in the spring, reaching a peak in the summer months. However, probably because of delays in passing through prepayments, the peak may not be observed until early fall.

Cash-Out Refinancing Component

As noted earlier, cash-out refinancing is driven by price appreciation since origination of the loans in the pool. A proxy measure for price appreciation must be used. For the Bear Stearns agency prepayment model, the pool's HPI is used and Exhibit 11-7 illustrates the cash-out refinancing incentives for four assumed rates of appreciation of the HPI. The horizontal axis in the exhibit is the ratio of the pool's WAC to the prevailing market rate. A ratio greater than 1 means that there is an incentive to refinance while a ratio below 1 means that the borrower will incur a higher interest rate to refinance. According to the Bear Stearns agency model, projected prepayments attributable to cash-out refinancing (1) exist for all ratios greater than 0.6, (2) prepayments increase

---

[8]Don't get seasonality and seasoning confused. Seasonality is the time of the year; seasoning is the aging of a loan.

EXHIBIT 11-7   The Effect of Housing Price Appreciation on Cash-Out
Refinancing on Agency Prepayments

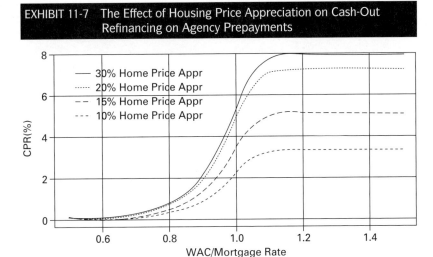

Source: Exhibit 25-9 in Dale Westhoff and V. S. Srinivasan, "Agency Prepayment Model:
Modeling the Dynamics of Borrower Attributes," Chapter 25 in Frank J. Fabozzi (ed.),
The Handbook of Mortgage-Backed Securities (New York: McGraw Hill, 2006).

as the ratio increases, and (3) the greater the price appreciation for a given ratio, the
greater the projected prepayments.

Rate/Term Refinancing Component

The refinancing decision is not based solely on the mortgage rate relative to the
prevailing market rate but a host of other borrower circumstances. This is reflected in
the **S-curve for prepayments**, which is graphically illustrated in Exhibit 11-7. The reason
for the observed S-curve for prepayments is that as the rate ratio increases, the CPR
(i.e., prepayment rate) increases. There is some level of the rate ratio, however, at which
the prepayment rate tends to level off. The reason for this leveling of the prepayment
rate is because the only borrowers remaining in the pool are those that cannot obtain
refinancing or those who have other reasons why refinancing does not make sense.

The S-curve is not sufficient for modeling the refinancing rate/term refinancing.
This is because the S-curve fails to adequately account for two dynamics of borrower
attributes that impact refinancing decisions: (1) the burnout effect and the threshold
media effect. The **burnout effect** occurs because the composition of borrowers in a
mortgage pool changes over time due to seasoning and refinancing patterns. More
specifically, as mortgage rates decline, those borrowers in the pool who are the most
interest-rate sensitive prepay. The balance of the borrowers in the pool are less rate
sensitive but as mortgage rates continue to decline, these borrowers prepay. As mortgage rates continue down, there is less additional prepayment activity and at some
point, the incentive to refinance is "burned out."

Modelers have used different approaches for accounting for the burnout effect in
agency prepayments models. The Bear Stearns agency model, for example, uses the following pool-level variables as proxies for the attributes of the borrowers in the pool:
original term, loan purpose, weighted average contract rate (WAC), weighted average

EXHIBIT 11-8   Baseline Refinancing Function (S-Curve) for the Bear Stearns' Agency Prepayment Model for an "Ordinary" Pool of Agency Borrowers

Source: Exhibit 25-13 in Dale Westhoff and V. S. Srinivasan, "Agency Prepayment Model: Modeling the Dynamics of Borrower Attributes," Chapter 25 in Frank J. Fabozzi (ed.), *The Handbook of Mortgage-Backed Securities* (New York: McGraw Hill, 2006).

loan age (WALA), loan size, rate premium over the benchmark conforming rate, changes in the pool level HPI, and a yield curve slope term. Exhibit 11-8 shows the *baseline* refinancing function (S-curve) for the Bear Stearns agency prepayment model for an "ordinary" pool of agency borrowers with the following attributes: original loan balance of $125,000; loan age of 12 months; no rate premium at origination; no prior opportunities to refinance; and 3.5% annual home price appreciation. When the attributes change, the S-curve changes. For example, Exhibit 11-9 illustrates the model's baseline S-curves for $25,000 loan size increments ranging between $75,000 and $200,000. From the exhibit we see that relative to loans with balances less than $100,000, loan balances that exceed $150,000 generally show from 1.5 to 2.5 times more refinancing sensitivity.

The **threshold-media effect** is so-named because borrowers are more aware of the refinancing opportunities available due to heavy media reporting and mortgage banking advertisements when mortgage rates drop to historic low levels.

Nonagency Prepayment Models

The components of nonagency prepayment models are the same components used in agency prepayment models.[9] However, because the issuer of nonagency MBS provides more detailed loan-level information, a prepayment model is estimated for each type

---

[9]For a discussion of the Bear Stearns nonagency prepayment model, see Dale Westhoff and V. S. Srinivasan, "Prepayment Models to Value Nonagency MBS," Chapter 28, *The Handbook of Mortgage-Backed Securities*. For a discussion of the prepayment factors found for one issuer, Option One, see Glenn Schultz, Christopher Flanagan, and Christopher Muth, "Modeling Non-Prime Mortgage Prepayment, Delinquency, and Default," Chapter 30 in *The Handbook of Mortgage-Backed Securities*.

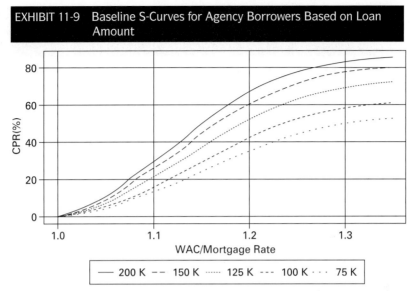

EXHIBIT 11-9   Baseline S-Curves for Agency Borrowers Based on Loan Amount

Source: Exhibit 25-18 in Dale Westhoff and V. S. Srinivasan, "Agency Prepayment Model: Modeling the Dynamics of Borrower Attributes," Chapter 25 in Frank J. Fabozzi (ed.), *The Handbook of Mortgage-Backed Securities* (New York: McGraw Hill, 2006).

of loan. For each type of *representative* loan, a baseline for the components is constructed, and then the baseline is modified for different permutations of loan-level characteristics.

Consider first the baseline nonagency refinancing profile for the Bear Stearns' nonagency MBS model. Exhibit 11-10 shows the baseline projected prepayment rate across a wide range of refinancing incentives for each of the three representative loan types (jumbo, alt-A, and alt-A conforming) used as collateral in nonagency deals.[10] For comparison purposes, the projected prepayment rate for agency (conforming) loans is also shown in the same exhibit. For each type of loan, the Bear Stearns nonagency prepayment model provides projected prepayment rates attributable to factors such as size of the loan, rate premium, documentation, occupancy status, and current LTV.

CASH FLOW FOR NONAGENCY PASS-THROUGHS

In agency pass-through securities, the cash flow is not affected by defaults and delinquencies. For nonagency pass-throughs, the effect of defaults and delinquencies must be considered. With the increase in the issuance of nonagency pass-through securities (as

---

[10]In the analysis, a representative jumbo is defined as having the following characteristics: new, full documentation, purchase loan; single-family detached home, owner-occupied property, with a $300,000 loan balance, 75% LTV, and no rate premium (i.e., no spread above the prevailing mortgage jumbo rate). A representative alt-A is defined by modification of the representative jumbo loan. Specifically, it has a $150,000 loan balance, limited documentation, and 90-basis-point-rate premium.

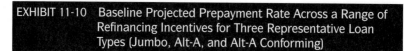

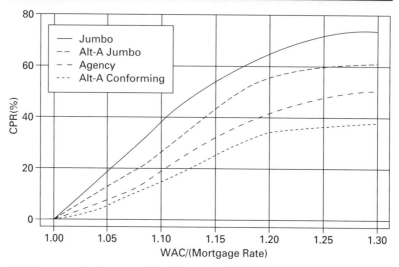

Source: Exhibit 28-4 in Dale Westhoff and V. S. Srinivasan, "Prepayment Models to Value Nonagency MBS," Chapter 28 in Frank J. Fabozzi (ed.), *The Handbook of Mortgage-Backed Securities* (New York: McGraw Hill, 2006).

well as nonagency CMOs, described in Chapter 12), a standardized benchmark for default rates has been introduced by the Public Securities Association (PSA). The PSA standard default assumption (SDA) benchmark gives the annual default rate for a mortgage pool as a function of the seasoning of the mortgages. The PSA SDA benchmark, or 100 SDA, specifies the following:

1. The default rate in month 1 is 0.02% and increases by 0.02% up to month 30, so that in month 30, the default rate is 0.60%.
2. From month 30 to month 60, the default rate remains at 0.60%.
3. From month 61 to month 120, the default rate declines from 0.60% to 0.03%.
4. From month 120 on, the default rate remains constant at 0.03%.

This pattern is illustrated in Exhibit 11-11.

As with the PSA prepayment benchmark, multiples of the benchmark are found by multiplying the default rate by the assumed multiple. For example, 200 SDA means the following pattern:

1. The default rate in month 1 is 0.04% and increases by 0.04% up to month 30, so that in month 30, the default rate is 1.20%.
2. From month 30 to month 60, the default rate remains at 1.20%.
3. From month 61 to month 120, the default rate declines from 1.20% to 0.06%.
4. From month 120 on, the default rate remains constant at 0.06%.

A 0 SDA means that no defaults are assumed.

EXHIBIT 11-11   PSA Standard Default Assumption Benchmark (100 SDA)

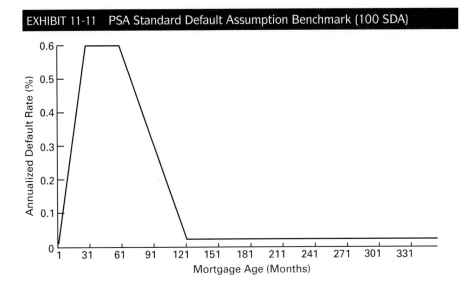

CASH FLOW YIELD

Given the projected cash flow and the price of a pass-through, its yield can be calculated. The yield is the interest rate that will make the present value of the expected cash flow equal to the price. A yield computed in this manner is known as a **cash flow yield**.

Bond-Equivalent Yield

For a pass-through, the yield that makes the present value of the cash flow equal to the price is a monthly interest rate. The next step is to annualize the monthly yield. According to market convention, to compare the yield for a pass-through to that of a Treasury or corporate bond, the monthly yield should not be annualized just by multiplying the monthly yield by 12. The reason is that a Treasury bond and a corporate bond pay interest semiannually, whereas a pass-through has a monthly cash flow. By reinvesting monthly cash flows, the pass-through holder has the opportunity to generate greater interest than can be earned by a bond holder who has only semiannual coupon payments to reinvest. Therefore, the yield on a pass-through must be calculated so as to make it comparable to the yield to maturity for a bond.

This is accomplished by computing the **bond-equivalent yield**. As explained in Chapter 3, this is simply a market convention for annualizing any fixed-income instrument that pays interest more than once a year. The bond-equivalent yield is found by doubling a semiannual yield. For a pass-through security, the semiannual yield is

$$\text{semiannual cash flow yield} = (1 + y_M)^6 - 1$$

where y_M is the monthly interest rate that will equate the present value of the projected monthly cash flow to the price of the pass-through. The bond-equivalent yield is found by doubling the semiannual cash flow yield; that is,

$$\text{bond-equivalent yield} = 2[(1 + y_M)^6 - 1]$$

Limitations of Cash Flow Yield Measure

The yield corresponding to a price must be qualified by an assumption concerning prepayments. Although yields are frequently quoted, remember that the yield is based on some underlying prepayment assumption. Consequently, a yield of 9% based on 150% PSA means that it is assumed that the underlying mortgages will prepay at a rate equal to 150% PSA. A yield number without qualification as to the prepayment assumption is meaningless.

In fact, even with specification of the prepayment assumption, the yield number is meaningless in terms of the relative value of a pass-through. For an investor to realize the yield based on some PSA assumption, a number of conditions must be met: (1) the investor must reinvest all the cash flows at the calculated yield, (2) the investor must hold the pass-through security until all the mortgages have been paid off, and (3) the assumed prepayment rate must actually occur over the life of the pass-through. Moreover, in the case of private-label pass-throughs, the assumed default and delinquencies must actually occur. Now, if all this is likely, we can trust the yield numbers. Otherwise, investors must be cautious in using yield numbers to evaluate pass-through securities.

Yield Spread to Treasuries

Although we have explained that it is not possible to calculate a yield with certainty, it has been stated that pass-through securities offer a higher yield than Treasury securities. Typically, the comparison is between Ginnie Mae pass-through securities and Treasuries, for both are free of default risk. Presumably, the difference between the two yields primarily represents prepayment risk. The question should be whether the premium the investor receives in terms of higher yield for bearing prepayment risk is adequate. This is where option-pricing models applied to pass-through securities have been used. Option-pricing models let us determine if the pass-through security is offering the proper compensation for accepting prepayment risk.

The yield spread between private-label pass-through securities and agency pass-through securities reflects both credit risk and prepayment risk. The reason for the difference in prepayment risk lies in the nature of the underlying mortgages. For example, in the case of Ginnie Mae pass-through securities, the underlying mortgages are FHA or VA-insured mortgages. Borrowers who obtain such government guarantees have different prepayment characteristics than those of holders of non–government-insured mortgages. Specifically, when interest rates decline, prepayments on FHA/VA-insured mortgages do not increase as fast as those for non–FHA/VA-insured mortgages. This reflects the fact that borrowers who obtain government-guaranteed mortgages typically do not have the ability to take on refinancing costs as rates decline. There are similar differences between the prepayment patterns of Ginnie Mae pass-through securities and the two other agency pass-through securities.

EXHIBIT 11-12   Average Life of a Pass-Through Based on Different PSA Prepayment Assumptions

PSA speed	50	100	165	200	300	400	500	600	700
Average life	15.11	11.66	8.76	7.68	5.63	4.44	3.68	3.16	2.78

When we speak of comparing the yield of a mortgage pass-through security to a comparable Treasury, what does "comparable" mean? The stated maturity of a mortgage pass-through security is an inappropriate measure because of prepayments. Instead, market participants have used two measures: Macaulay duration and average life. As we explained in Chapter 4, Macaulay duration is a weighted-average term to maturity where the weights are the present value of the cash flows. The more commonly used measure is the average life.

Average Life

The **average life** of a mortgage-backed security is the average time to receipt of principal payments (scheduled principal payments and projected prepayments), weighted by the amount of principal expected. Mathematically, the average life is expressed as follows:

$$\text{average life} = \sum_{t=1}^{T} \frac{t \times \text{principal received at time } t}{12(\text{total principal})}$$

where T is the number of months. The average life of a pass-through depends on the PSA prepayment assumption. To see this, the average life is shown in Exhibit 11-12 for different prepayment speeds for the pass-through we used to illustrate the cash flow for 100 PSA and 165 PSA in Exhibits 11-3 and 11-4.

PREPAYMENT RISK AND ASSET/LIABILITY MANAGEMENT

An investor who owns pass-through securities does not know what the cash flow will be because that depends on prepayments. The risk associated with prepayments is called **prepayment risk**. To understand prepayment risk, suppose that an investor buys a 10% coupon Ginnie Mae at a time when mortgage rates are 10%. Let's consider what will happen to prepayments if mortgage rates decline to, say, 6%. There will be two adverse consequences. First, we know from the basic property of fixed-income securities that the price of an option-free bond will rise. But in the case of a pass-through security, the rise in price will not be as large as that of an option-free bond because a fall in interest rates increases the borrower's incentive to prepay the loan and refinance the debt at a lower rate. This results in the same adverse consequence faced by holders of callable corporate and municipal bonds. As in the case of those instruments, the upside price potential of a pass-through security is truncated because of prepayments. This characteristic, as we explain in Chapter 17, is referred to as **negative convexity**.

This should not be surprising, because a mortgage loan effectively grants the borrower the right to call the loan at par value. The second adverse consequence is that the cash flow must be reinvested at a lower rate. These two adverse consequences when mortgage rates decline are referred to as **contraction risk**.

Now let's look at what happens if mortgage rates rise to 15%. The price of the pass-through, like the price of any bond, will decline. But again it will decline more because the higher rates will tend to slow down the rate of prepayment, in effect increasing the amount invested at the coupon rate, which is lower than the market rate. Prepayments will slow down because homeowners will not refinance or partially prepay their mortgages when mortgage rates are higher than the contract rate of 10%. Of course, this is just the time when investors want prepayments to speed up so that they can reinvest the prepayments at the higher market interest rate. This adverse consequence of rising mortgage rates is called **extension risk**.

Therefore, prepayment risk encompasses contraction risk and extension risk. Prepayment risk makes pass-through securities unattractive for certain financial institutions to hold from an asset–liability perspective. Let's look at why particular institutional investors may find pass-throughs unattractive:

1. Thrifts and commercial banks want to lock in a spread over their cost of funds. Their funds are raised on a short-term basis. If they invest in fixed-rate pass-through securities, they will be mismatched because a pass-through is a longer-term security. In particular, depository institutions are exposed to extension risk when they invest in pass-through securities.

2. To satisfy certain obligations of insurance companies, pass-through securities may be unattractive. More specifically, consider a life insurance company that has issued a four-year GIC. The uncertainty about the cash flow from a pass-through security and the likelihood that slow prepayments will result in the instrument being long term make it an unappealing investment vehicle for such accounts. In such instances, a pass-through security exposes the insurance company to extension risk.

3. Consider a pension fund that wants to satisfy long-term liabilities by locking in prevailing interest rates. Buying a pass-through security exposes the pension fund to the risk that prepayments will speed up and the maturity of the investment will shorten considerably. Prepayments will speed up when interest rates decline, thereby forcing reinvestment of prepayments at a lower interest rate. In this case the pension fund is exposed to contraction risk.

We can see that some institutional investors are concerned with extension risk and others with contraction risk when they purchase a pass-through security. Is it possible to alter the cash flow of a pass-through so as to reduce the contraction risk and extension risk for institutional investors? This can be done, as we shall see later in Chapter 12.

It should be understood that prepayments are not necessarily an adverse event for an investor. The effect on investment performance will depend upon whether the pass-through is purchased at a discount or at a premium. Prepayments enhance the return from holding a pass-through if it is purchased at a discount, for two reasons. First, the investor realizes a capital gain equal to the difference between the par value and the price paid. Second, a pass-through will trade at a discount because the pass-through's coupon rate is lower than the current coupon rate for newly issued pass-throughs.

Consequently, prepayments allow the investor to reinvest the proceeds at a higher coupon rate. For a pass-through purchased at a premium to par, prepayments reduce investment returns for two reasons: (1) the investor realizes a capital loss equal to the difference between the price paid and par, and (2) the proceeds must be reinvested at a lower coupon rate.

SECONDARY MARKET TRADING

Pass-throughs are quoted in the same manner as U.S. Treasury coupon securities. A quote of 94-05 means 94 and 5/32nds of par value, or 94.15625% of par value. As we explain in our discussion of prepayments, the yield corresponding to a price must be qualified by an assumption concerning prepayments.

Pass-throughs are identified by a pool prefix and pool number provided by the agency. The prefix indicates the type of pass-through. For example, a pool prefix of 20 for a Freddie Mac PC means that the underlying pool consists of conventional mortgages with an original maturity of 15 years. A pool prefix of AR for a Ginnie Mae MBS means that the underlying pool consists of adjustable-rate mortgages. The pool number indicates the specific mortgages underlying the pass-through and the issuer of the pass-through.

Many trades occur while a pool is still unspecified, and therefore no pool information is known at the time of the trade. This kind of trade is known as a "TBA" (to be announced) trade. When an investor purchases, say, $1 million GNMA 8s on a TBA basis, the investor can receive up to three pools, with pool numbers being announced shortly before the settlement date. Three pools can be delivered because the PSA has established guidelines for standards of delivery and settlement of mortgage-backed securities,[11] under which our hypothetical TBA trade permits three possible pools to be delivered. The option of what pools to deliver is left to the seller, as long as selection and delivery satisfy the PSA guidelines. In contrast to TBA trades, a pool number may be specified. In this case the transaction will involve delivery of the pool specifically designated.

There are many seasoned issues of the same agency with the same coupon rate outstanding at a given point in time. For example, there are more than 30,000 pools of 30-year Ginnie Mae MBSs outstanding with a coupon rate of 9%. One pass-through may be backed by a pool of mortgage loans in which all the properties are located in California, whereas another may be backed by a pool of mortgage loans in which all the properties are in Minnesota. Yet another may be backed by a pool of mortgage loans in which the properties are from several regions in the country. So which pool are dealers referring to when they talk about Ginnie Mae 9s? They do not refer to any specific pool but instead to a generic security, although the prepayment characteristics of pass-throughs with underlying pools from different parts of the country are different.

---

[11]Public Securities Association, *Uniform Practices for the Clearance and Settlement of Mortgage-Backed Securities*. More specifically, the requirement for good delivery permits a maximum of three pools per $1 million traded, or a maximum of four pools per $1 million for coupons of 12% or more.

Thus, the projected prepayment rates for pass-throughs reported by dealer firms are for generic pass-throughs. A particular pool purchased may have a materially different prepayment speed from the generic. Moreover, when an investor purchases a pass-through without specifying a pool number, the seller can deliver the worst-paying pools as long as the pools delivered satisfy good delivery requirements.

Prior to March 1999, the PSA delivery standards allowed the seller in a TBA trade to under- or over-deliver by 1% per $1 million traded. So, if $1 million of par value is sold at par, the seller could deliver as little as $990,000 or as much as $1,010,000. The seller would select the amount to deliver based on prevailing prices. This was a valuable option to sellers in a TBA trade and a disadvantage to buyers. In March 1999, the PSA changed its delivery standards so that the seller in a TBA trade may only under- or over-deliver by 0.1%. Consequently, the value of this delivery option to the seller is now minimal.

SUMMARY

A mortgage pass-through security is created when one or more mortgage holders form a collection (pool) of mortgages and sell shares or participation certificates in the pool. The monthly cash flow of a pass-through depends on the cash flow of the underlying mortgages and therefore consists of monthly mortgage payments representing interest, the scheduled repayment of principal, and any prepayments. The cash flow is less than that of the underlying mortgages by an amount equal to servicing and any guarantor fees. As with individual mortgage loans, because of prepayments the cash flow of a pass-through is not known with certainty.

The major types of pass-throughs are agency pass-throughs issued by Ginnie Mae, Freddie Mac, and Fannie Mae. There are two types of guarantees that may be provided by an agency: (1) timely payment of both interest and principal, and (2) timely payment of interest and eventual payment of the scheduled principal when it is collected but no later than a specified date. Ginnie Mae pass-throughs are guaranteed by the full faith and credit of the U.S. government and consequently are viewed as risk-free in terms of default risk. Freddie Mac and Fannie Mae are government-sponsored enterprises, and therefore their guarantee does not carry the full faith and credit of the U.S. government.

Nonagency pass-throughs are issued by entities such as commercial banks, thrifts, and private conduits. Unlike agency pass-throughs, these pass-throughs are rated by the nationally recognized rating companies and require some form of credit enhancement to obtain a high credit rating. Credit enhancement may be internal or external, or a combination of both.

Estimating the cash flow from a pass-through requires forecasting prepayments. The current convention is to use the PSA prepayment benchmark, which is a series of conditional prepayment rates, to obtain the cash flow.

A prepayment model begins by modeling the statistical relationships among the factors that are expected to affect prepayments. At one time, because of data limitations on borrower and loan attributes, prepayment modelers viewed borrowers as generic with the only significant difference in borrowers being due to refinancing opportunities, loan age, and loan type. Today, prepayment models incorporate more factors regarding borrower and loan attributes in their models. The key components of prepayment models are housing turnover, cash-out refinancing, and rate/term refinancing.

For nonagency pass-throughs, the effect of defaults and delinquencies on the cash flow must be considered. A standardized benchmark for default rates has been introduced by the PSA. The PSA SDA benchmark gives the annual default rate for a mortgage pool as a function of the seasoning of the mortgages.

Given the projected cash flow and the market price of a pass-through, a cash flow yield can be calculated. Investors must recognize that the PSA prepayment benchmark is a convention enabling market participants to quote yield and/or price but that it has many limitations for determining the value of a pass-through. The yield spread is quoted as the difference between the cash flow yield and the yield to maturity of a comparable Treasury. A measure commonly used to estimate the life of a pass-through is its average life.

The prepayment risk associated with investing in mortgage pass-through securities can be decomposed into contraction risk and extension risk. Prepayment risk makes pass-through securities unattractive for certain financial institutions to hold from an asset–liability perspective.

Pass-throughs are quoted in the same manner as U.S. Treasury coupon securities. They are identified by a pool prefix and pool number. A TBA trade occurs while a pool is still unspecified, and therefore no pool information is known at the time of the trade. The seller has the right in this case to deliver pass-throughs backed by pools that satisfy the PSA requirements for good delivery.

Questions

1. What is a mortgage pass-through security?
2. Describe the cash flow of a mortgage pass-through security.
3. What are the WAC and WAM of a pass-through security?
4. What are the different types of agency pass-through securities?
5. Which type of agency pass-through carries the full faith and credit of the U.S. government?
6. If the borrower whose mortgage is included in an agency pass-through fails to make a mortgage payment, what is the impact on the cash flow to the investor?
7. What is a nonagency pass-through security?
8. What is the disadvantage of a nonagency pass-through that is credit enhanced with a third-party guarantee?
9. What is a senior-subordinate structure?
10. Why is overcollateralization a form of credit enhancement for a nonagency pass-through security?

11. Why is an assumed prepayment speed necessary to project the cash flow of a pass-through?
12. What does a conditional prepayment rate of 8% mean?
13. Indicate whether you agree or disagree with the following statement: "The PSA prepayment benchmark is a model for forecasting prepayments for a pass-through security."
14. a. Complete the following table:

| | CPR Assuming: | | |
Month	100% PSA	70% PSA	320% PSA
1			
4			
9			
27			
40			
120			
340			

b. Complete the following table:

SMM Assuming:

Month	100% PSA	70% PSA	320% PSA
1			
4			
9			
27			
40			
120			
340			

15. Complete the following table (in thousands of dollars) assuming a prepayment rate of 165 PSA:
    Original balance: $100,000,000
    Pass-through rate: 9.0%
    WAM: 360 months

Month	Out. Bal.	SMM	Mortg. Pay.	Interest	Sch. Prin.	Pre-pay.	Tot. Prin.	Cash Flow	Total CF
1	100,000		841						
2	99,934		841						

16. What is meant by prepayments due to
    a. housing turnover
    b. cash-out refinancing
    c. rate/term refinancing
17. a. What factor can be used as a proxy for cash-out refinancing incentives?
    b. Why are prepayments attributable to cash-out refinancing likely to be insensitive to changes in mortgage rates?

18. What is the S-curve for prepayments and explain the reason for the shape?
19. a. What is the burnout effect?
    b. What is the threshold media effect?
20. Why was the PSA Standard Default curve introduced?
21. a. What is the cash flow yield of a mortgage pass-through security?
    b. What are the limitations of cash flow yield measures for a mortgage pass-through security?
    c. What is the bond-equivalent yield if the monthly cash flow yield is 0.7%?
22. What is the average life of a pass-through, and what does it depend on?
23. a. What are contraction risk and extension risk?
    b. Why would a pass-through with a WAM of 350 months be an unattractive investment for a savings and loan association?
24. a. Distinguish between a TBA and specified pool trade.
    b. What delivery options are granted to the seller in a TBA trade?

CHAPTER

12

COLLATERALIZED MORTGAGE OBLIGATIONS AND STRIPPED MORTGAGE-BACKED SECURITIES

After reading this chapter you will understand:

- why and how a collateralized mortgage obligation is created

- what a sequential-pay CMO is

- how the average life of a sequential-pay CMO compares to that of the collateral from which it is created

- what an accrual tranche is and its effect on the average life of sequential-pay tranches in the CMO structure

- how a floater and an inverse floater are created from a CMO tranche

- what a planned amortization class tranche is and how it is created

- how the prepayment protection for a planned amortization class changes over time

- what a support tranche is and the substantial prepayment risk to which it exposes investors

- what a support bond with a schedule is

- what a notional IO is and how it is created

- what a REMIC is

- the difference between an agency CMO, a private-label CMO, and a whole loan CMO

- how stripped mortgage-backed securities are created
- the various types of stripped mortgage-backed securities
- the investment characteristics of stripped mortgage-backed securities

Ⅰn this chapter we discuss collateralized mortgage obligations and stripped mortgage-backed securities. Because these securities derive their cash flow from underlying mortgage collateral such as pass-throughs or a pool of whole loans, they are referred to as derivative mortgage-backed securities products.

COLLATERALIZED MORTGAGE OBLIGATIONS[1]

At the close of Chapter 11, we discussed the prepayment risks associated with investing in pass-throughs: contraction risk and extension risk. We note there that some institutional investors are concerned with extension risk when they invest in a pass-through, whereas others are more concerned with contraction risk. Fortunately, redirecting cash flows from a pass-through to various bond classes makes it possible to redistribute prepayment risk for investors who want to reduce their exposure to prepayment risk. Because the total prepayment risk of a pass-through will not be changed by altering the cash flows, other investors must be found who are willing to accept the unwanted prepayment risk.

Collateralized mortgage obligations (CMOs) are bond classes created by redirecting the cash flows of mortgage-related products so as to mitigate prepayment risk. The mere creation of a CMO cannot eliminate prepayment risk; it can only transfer the various forms of this risk among different classes of bondholders. The technique of redistributing the coupon interest and principal from the underlying mortgage-related products to different classes, so that a CMO class has a different coupon rate from that for the underlying collateral, results in instruments that have varying risk-return characteristics that may be more suitable to the needs and expectations of investors, thereby broadening the appeal of mortgage-backed products to various traditional fixed-income investors.

CMO Structure

A CMO is a security backed by a pool of pass-throughs, whole loans, or stripped mortgage-backed securities (explained later in the chapter). CMOs are structured so that there are several classes of bondholders with varying stated maturities. When there is more than one class of bondholders with the same level of credit priority, the structure is called a **pay-through structure**, as opposed to a **pass-through structure** in which there is only one class of bondholders at a given level of credit priority.

---

[1]This section is adapted from Chapters 1 to 7 of Frank J. Fabozzi and Charles Ramsey, *Collateralized Mortgage Obligations: Structures and Analysis*, 3rd ed. (New Hope, PA: Frank J. Fabozzi Associates, 1999).

The bond classes created are commonly referred to as **tranches**. The principal payments from the underlying collateral are used to retire the tranches on a priority basis according to terms specified in the prospectus. In the following sections we describe the various types of CMO tranches.

Sequential-Pay Tranches

The first CMO was created in 1983 and was structured so that each class of bond would be retired sequentially. Such structures are referred to as **sequential-pay CMOs**. To illustrate a sequential-pay CMO, we discuss FJF-01,[2] a hypothetical deal made up to illustrate the basic features of the structure. The collateral for this hypothetical CMO is a hypothetical pass-through with a total par value of $400 million and the following characteristics: (1) the pass-through coupon rate is 7.5%, (2) the weighted-average coupon (WAC) is 8.125%, and (3) the weighted-average maturity (WAM) is 357 months. This is the same pass-through that we used in Chapter 11 to describe the cash flow of a pass-through based on some PSA assumption.

From this $400 million of collateral, four bond classes or tranches are created. Their characteristics are summarized in Exhibit 12-1. The total par value of the four tranches is equal to the par value of the collateral (i.e., the pass-through security). In this simple structure, the coupon rate is the same for each tranche and also the same as the coupon rate on the collateral. There is no reason why this must be so, and in fact, typically the coupon rate varies by tranche.

Now remember that a CMO is created by redistributing the cash flow—interest and principal—to the different tranches based on a set of payment rules. The payment

---

EXHIBIT 12-1   FJF-01: Hypothetical Four-Tranche Sequential-Pay Structure[a]

Tranche	Par Amount	Coupon Rate (%)
A	$194,500,000	7.5
B	36,000,000	7.5
C	96,500,000	7.5
D	73,000,000	7.5
	$400,000,000	

[a]*Payment rules*:

1. *For payment of periodic coupon interest:* Disburse periodic coupon interest to each tranche on the basis of the amount of principal outstanding at the beginning of the period.
2. *For disbursement of principal payments:* Disburse principal payments to tranche A until it is paid off completely. After tranche A is paid off completely, disburse principal payments to tranche B until it is paid off completely. After tranche B is paid off completely, disburse principal payments to tranche C until it is paid off completely. After tranche C is paid off completely, disburse principal payments to tranche D until it is paid off completely.

---

[2]All CMO structures are given a name. In our illustration we use FJF, the initials of the author of this book.

rules at the bottom of Exhibit 12-1 describe how the cash flow from the pass-through (i.e., collateral) is to be distributed to the four tranches. There are separate rules for the payment of the coupon interest and the payment of principal, the principal being the total of the regularly scheduled principal payment and any prepayments.

In FJF-01, each tranche receives periodic coupon interest payments based on the amount of the outstanding balance at the beginning of the month. The disbursement of the principal, however, is made in a special way. A tranche is not entitled to receive principal until the entire principal of the preceding tranche has been paid off. More specifically, tranche A receives all the principal payments until the entire principal amount owed to that bond class, $194,500,000, is paid off; then tranche B begins to receive principal and continues to do so until it is paid the entire $36,000,000. Tranche C then receives principal, and when it is paid off, tranche D starts receiving principal payments.

Although the priority rules for the disbursement of the principal payments are known, the precise amount of the principal in each period is not. This will depend on the cash flow, and therefore principal payments, of the collateral, which depends on the actual prepayment rate of the collateral. An assumed PSA speed allows the cash flow to be projected. Exhibit 11-5 shows the cash flow (interest, regularly scheduled principal repayment, and prepayments) assuming 165 PSA. Assuming that the collateral does prepay at 165 PSA, the cash flow available to all four tranches of FJF-01 will be precisely the cash flow shown in Exhibit 12-2.

To demonstrate how the priority rules for FJF-01 work, Exhibit 12-2 shows the cash flow for selected months assuming that the collateral prepays at 165 PSA. For each tranche, the exhibit shows (1) the balance at the end of the month, (2) the principal paid down (regularly scheduled principal repayment plus prepayments), and (3) interest. In month 1, the cash flow for the collateral consists of a principal payment of $709,923 and interest of $2.5 million (0.075 times $400 million divided by 12). The interest payment is distributed to the four tranches based on the amount of the par value outstanding. So, for example, tranche A receives $1,215,625 (0.075 times $194,500,000 divided by 12) of the $2.5 million. The principal, however, is all distributed to tranche A. Therefore, the cash flow for tranche A in month 1 is $1,925,548. The principal balance at the end of month 1 for tranche A is $193,790,076 (the original principal balance of $194,500,000 less the principal payment of $709,923). No principal payment is distributed to the three other tranches because there is still a principal balance outstanding for tranche A. This will be true for months 2 through 80.

After month 81, the principal balance will be zero for tranche A. For the collateral, the cash flow in month 81 is $3,318,521, consisting of a principal payment of $2,032,196 and interest of $1,286,325. At the beginning of month 81 (end of month 80), the principal balance for tranche A is $311,926. Therefore, $311,926 of the $2,032,196 of the principal payment from the collateral will be disbursed to tranche A. After this payment is made, no additional principal payments are made to this tranche as the principal balance is zero. The remaining principal payment from the collateral, $1,720,271, is disbursed to tranche B. According to the assumed prepayment speed of 165 PSA, tranche B then begins receiving principal payments in month 81.

Exhibit 12-2 shows that tranche B is fully paid off by month 100, when tranche C now begins to receive principal payments. Tranche C is not fully paid off until month 178, at which time bond class D begins receiving the remaining principal payments. The maturity (i.e., the time until the principal is fully paid off) for these four tranches

EXHIBIT 12-2 Monthly Cash Flow for Selected Months for FJF-01 Assuming 165 PSA

	Tranche A			Tranche B		
Mo.	Balance	Principal	Interest	Balance	Principal	Interest
1	194,500,000	709,923	1,215,625	36,000,000	0	225,000
2	193,790,077	821,896	1,211,188	36,000,000	0	225,000
3	192,968,181	933,560	1,206,051	36,000,000	0	225,000
4	192,034,621	1,044,822	1,200,216	36,000,000	0	225,000
5	190,989,799	1,155,586	1,193,686	36,000,000	0	225,000
6	189,834,213	1,265,759	1,186,464	36,000,000	0	225,000
7	188,568,454	1,375,246	1,178,553	36,000,000	0	225,000
8	187,193,208	1,483,954	1,169,958	36,000,000	0	225,000
9	185,709,254	1,591,789	1,160,683	36,000,000	0	225,000
10	184,117,464	1,698,659	1,150,734	36,000,000	0	225,000
11	182,418,805	1,804,473	1,140,118	36,000,000	0	225,000
12	180,614,332	1,909,139	1,128,840	36,000,000	0	225,000
75	12,893,479	2,143,974	80,584	36,000,000	0	225,000
76	10,749,504	2,124,935	67,184	36,000,000	0	225,000
77	8,624,569	2,106,062	53,904	36,000,000	0	225,000
78	6,518,507	2,087,353	40,741	36,000,000	0	225,000
79	4,431,154	2,068,807	27,695	36,000,000	0	225,000
80	2,362,347	2,050,422	14,765	36,000,000	0	225,000
81	311,926	311,926	1,950	36,000,000	1,720,271	225,000
82	0	0	0	34,279,729	2,014,130	214,248
83	0	0	0	32,265,599	1,996,221	201,660
84	0	0	0	30,269,378	1,978,468	189,184
85	0	0	0	28,290,911	1,960,869	176,818
95	0	0	0	9,449,331	1,793,089	59,058
96	0	0	0	7,656,242	1,777,104	47,852
97	0	0	0	5,879,138	1,761,258	36,745
98	0	0	0	4,117,880	1,745,550	25,737
99	0	0	0	2,372,329	1,729,979	14,827
100	0	0	0	642,350	642,350	4,015
101	0	0	0	0	0	0
102	0	0	0	0	0	0
103	0	0	0	0	0	0
104	0	0	0	0	0	0
105	0	0	0	0	0	0
1	96,500,000	0	603,125	73,000,000	0	456,250
2	96,500,000	0	603,125	73,000,000	0	456,250
3	96,500,000	0	603,125	73,000,000	0	456,250
4	96,500,000	0	603,125	73,000,000	0	456,250

(continued)

EXHIBIT 12-2   (continued)

Mo.	Tranche A			Tranche B		
	Balance	Principal	Interest	Balance	Principal	Interest
5	96,500,000	0	603,125	73,000,000	0	456,250
6	96,500,000	0	603,125	73,000,000	0	456,250
7	96,500,000	0	603,125	73,000,000	0	456,250
8	96,500,000	0	603,125	73,000,000	0	456,250
9	96,500,000	0	603,125	73,000,000	0	456,250
10	96,500,000	0	603,125	73,000,000	0	456,250
11	96,500,000	0	603,125	73,000,000	0	456,250
12	96,500,000	0	603,125	73,000,000	0	456,250
95	96,500,000	0	603,125	73,000,000	0	456,250
96	96,500,000	0	603,125	73,000,000	0	456,250
97	96,500,000	0	603,125	73,000,000	0	456,250
98	96,500,000	0	603,125	73,000,000	0	456,250
99	96,500,000	0	603,125	73,000,000	0	456,250
100	96,500,000	1,072,194	603,125	73,000,000	0	456,250
101	95,427,806	1,699,243	596,424	73,000,000	0	456,250
102	93,728,563	1,684,075	585,804	73,000,000	0	456,250
103	92,044,489	1,669,039	575,278	73,000,000	0	456,250
104	90,375,450	1,654,134	564,847	73,000,000	0	456,250
105	88,721,315	1,639,359	554,508	73,000,000	0	456,250
175	3,260,287	869,602	20,377	73,000,000	0	456,250
176	2,390,685	861,673	14,942	73,000,000	0	456,250
177	1,529,013	853,813	9,556	73,000,000	0	456,250
178	675,199	675,199	4,220	73,000,000	170,824	456,250
179	0	0	0	72,829,176	838,300	455,182
180	0	0	0	71,990,876	830,646	449,943
181	0	0	0	71,160,230	823,058	444,751
182	0	0	0	70,337,173	815,536	439,607
183	0	0	0	69,521,637	808,081	434,510
184	0	0	0	68,713,556	800,690	429,460
185	0	0	0	67,912,866	793,365	424,455
350	0	0	0	1,235,674	160,220	7,723
351	0	0	0	1,075,454	158,544	6,722
352	0	0	0	916,910	156,883	5,731
353	0	0	0	760,027	155,238	4,750
354	0	0	0	604,789	153,607	3,780
355	0	0	0	451,182	151,991	2,820
356	0	0	0	299,191	150,389	1,870
357	0	0	0	148,802	148,802	930

| EXHIBIT 12-3   Average Life for the Collateral and the Four Tranches of FJF-01 |

Prepayment Speed (PSA)	Average Life for				
	Collateral	Tranche A	Tranche B	Tranche C	Tranche D
50	15.11	7.48	15.98	21.02	27.24
100	11.66	4.90	10.86	15.78	24.58
165	8.76	3.48	7.49	11.19	20.27
200	7.68	3.05	6.42	9.60	18.11
300	5.63	2.32	4.64	6.81	13.36
400	4.44	1.94	3.70	5.31	10.34
500	3.68	1.69	3.12	4.38	8.35
600	3.16	1.51	2.74	3.75	6.96
700	2.78	1.38	2.47	3.30	5.95

assuming 165 PSA would be 81 months for tranche A, 100 months for tranche B, 178 months for tranche C, and 357 months for tranche D.

The **principal pay-down window** for a tranche is the time period between the beginning and the ending of the principal payments to that tranche. So, for example, for tranche A, the principal pay-down window would be month 1 to month 81 assuming 165 PSA. For tranche B it is from month 82 to month 100. The window is also specified in terms of the length of the time from the beginning of the principal pay-down window to the end of the principal pay-down window. For tranche A, the window would be stated as 80 months, for tranche B, 19 months.

Let's look at what has been accomplished by creating the CMO. First, in Chapter 11 we indicated that the average life of the pass-through is 8.76 years, assuming a prepayment speed of 165 PSA. Exhibit 12-3 reports the average life of the collateral and the four tranches assuming different prepayment speeds. Notice that the four tranches have average lives that are both shorter and longer than the collateral, thereby attracting investors who have a preference for an average life different from that of the collateral.

There is still a major problem: There is considerable variability of the average life for the tranches. We'll see later how this can be tackled. However, there is some protection provided for each tranche against prepayment risk. This is because prioritizing the distribution of principal (i.e., establishing the payment rules for principal) effectively protects the shorter-term tranche A in this structure against extension risk. This protection must come from somewhere, so it comes from the three other tranches. Similarly, tranches C and D provide protection against extension risk for tranches A and B. At the same time, tranches C and D benefit because they are provided protection against contraction risk, the protection coming from tranches A and B.

Accrual Bonds

In FJF-01, the payment rules for interest provide for all tranches to be paid interest each month. In many sequential-pay CMO structures, at least one tranche does not receive current interest. Instead, the interest for that tranche would accrue and be added to the principal balance. Such a bond class is commonly referred to as an **accrual**

EXHIBIT 12-4   FJF-02: Hypothetical Four-Tranche Sequential-Pay Structure with an Accrual Bond Class[a]

Tranche	Par Amount	Coupon Rate (%)
A	$194,500,000	7.5
B	36,000,000	7.5
C	96,500,000	7.5
Z (accrual)	73,000,000	7.5
	$400,000,000	

[a]*Payment rules:*

1. *For payment of periodic coupon interest:* Disburse periodic coupon interest to tranches A, B, and C on the basis of the amount of principal outstanding at the beginning of the period. For tranche Z, accrue the interest based on the principal plus accrued interest in the preceding period. The interest for tranche Z is to be paid to the earlier tranches as a principal pay down.
2. *For disbursement of principal payments:* Disburse principal payments to tranche A until it is completely paid off. After tranche A is paid off completely, disburse principal payments to tranche B until it is paid off completely. After tranche B is paid off completely, disburse principal payments to tranche C until it is paid off completely. After tranche C is paid off completely, disburse principal payments to tranche Z, until the original principal balance plus accrued interest is paid off completely.

tranche, or a **Z bond** (because the bond is similar to a zero-coupon bond). The interest that would have been paid to the accrual bond class is then used to speed up the pay down of the principal balance of earlier bond classes.

To see this, consider FJF-02, a hypothetical CMO structure with the same collateral as FJF-01 and with four tranches, each with a coupon rate of 7.5%. The difference is in the last tranche, Z, which is an accrual. The structure for FJF-02 is shown in Exhibit 12-4.

Exhibit 12-5 shows cash flows for selected months for tranches A and B. Let's look at month 1 and compare it with month 1 in Exhibit 12-2. Both cash flows are based on 165 PSA. The principal payment from the collateral is $709,923. In FJF-01, this is the principal pay down for tranche A. In FJF-02, the interest for tranche Z, $456,250, is not paid to that tranche but instead is used to pay down the principal of tranche A. So the principal payment to tranche A in Exhibit 12-5 is $1,166,173, the collateral's principal payment of $709,923 plus the interest of $456,250 that was diverted from tranche Z.

The expected final maturity for tranches A, B, and C has shortened as a result of the inclusion of tranche Z. The final payout for tranche A is 64 months rather than 81 months; for tranche B it is 77 months rather than 100 months; and for tranche C it is 112 rather than 178 months.

The average lives for tranches A, B, and C are shorter in FJF-02 than in FJF-01 because of the inclusion of the accrual bond. For example, at 165 PSA, the average lives are as follows:

Structure	Tranche A	Tranche B	Tranche C
FJF-02	2.90	5.86	7.87
FJF-01	3.48	7.49	11.19

EXHIBIT 12-5	Monthly Cash Flow for Selected Month for Tranches A and B of FJF-02 Assuming 165 PSA

| | | Tranche A | | | Tranche B | |
Mo.	Balance	Principal	Interest	Balance	Principal	Interest
1	194,500,000	1,166,173	1,215,625	36,000,000	0	225,000
2	193,333,827	1,280,997	1,208,336	36,000,000	0	225,000
3	192,052,829	1,395,531	1,200,330	36,000,000	0	225,000
4	190,657,298	1,509,680	1,191,608	36,000,000	0	225,000
5	189,147,619	1,623,350	1,182,173	36,000,000	0	225,000
6	187,524,269	1,736,446	1,172,027	36,000,000	0	225,000
7	185,787,823	1,848,875	1,161,174	36,000,000	0	225,000
8	183,938,947	1,960,543	1,149,618	36,000,000	0	225,000
9	181,978,404	2,071,357	1,137,365	36,000,000	0	225,000
10	179,907,047	2,181,225	1,124,419	36,000,000	0	225,000
11	177,725,822	2,290,054	1,110,786	36,000,000	0	225,000
12	175,435,768	2,397,755	1,096,474	36,000,000	0	225,000
60	15,023,406	3,109,398	93,896	36,000,000	0	225,000
61	11,914,007	3,091,812	74,463	36,000,000	0	225,000
62	8,822,195	3,074,441	55,139	36,000,000	0	225,000
63	5,747,754	3,057,282	35,923	36,000,000	0	225,000
64	2,690,472	2,690,472	16,815	36,000,000	349,863	225,000
65	0	0	0	35,650,137	3,023,598	222,813
66	0	0	0	32,626,540	3,007,069	203,916
67	0	0	0	29,619,470	2,990,748	185,122
68	0	0	0	26,628,722	2,974,633	166,430
69	0	0	0	23,654,089	2,958,722	147,838
70	0	0	0	20,695,367	2,943,014	129,346
71	0	0	0	17,752,353	2,927,508	110,952
72	0	0	0	14,824,845	2,912,203	92,655
73	0	0	0	11,912,642	2,897,096	74,454
74	0	0	0	9,015,546	2,882,187	56,347
75	0	0	0	6,133,358	2,867,475	38,333
76	0	0	0	3,265,883	2,852,958	20,412
77	0	0	0	412,925	412,925	2,581
78	0	0	0	0	0	0

The reason for the shortening of the nonaccrual tranches is that the interest that would be paid to the accrual bond is being allocated to the other tranches. Tranche Z in FJF-02 will have a longer average life than that of tranche D in FJF-01.

Thus, shorter-term tranches and a longer-term tranche are created by including an accrual bond. The accrual bond has appeal to investors who are concerned with reinvestment risk. Because there are no coupon payments to reinvest, reinvestment risk is eliminated until all the other tranches are paid off.

Floating-Rate Tranches

The CMO structures discussed previously offer a fixed coupon rate on all tranches. If CMO classes could be created only with fixed-rate coupons, the market for CMOs would be limited. Many financial institutions prefer floating-rate assets, which provide a better match for their liabilities.

Floating-rate tranches can be created from fixed-rate tranches by creating a floater and an inverse floater. We illustrate the creation of a floating-rate and an inverse-floating-rate bond class using the hypothetical CMO structure FJF-02, which is a four-tranche sequential-pay structure with an accrual bond. We can select any of the tranches from which to create a floating-rate and an inverse-floating-rate tranche. In fact, we can create these two securities for more than one of the four tranches or for only a portion of one tranche.

In this case, we create a floater and an inverse floater from tranche C. The par value for this tranche is $96.5 million, and we create two tranches that have a combined par value of $96.5 million. We refer to this CMO structure with a floater and an inverse floater as FJF-03. It has five tranches, designated A, B, FL, IFL, and Z, where FL is the floating-rate tranche and IFL is the inverse-floating-rate tranche. Exhibit 12-6 describes FJF-03. Any reference rate can be used to create a floater and the corresponding inverse floater. The reference rate for setting the coupon-rate for FL and IFL in FJF-03 is taken as one-month LIBOR.

EXHIBIT 12-6   FJF-03: Hypothetical Five-Tranche Sequential-Pay Structure with Floater, Inverse Floater, and Accrual Bond Classes[a]

Tranche	Par Amount	Coupon Rate (%)
A	$194,500,000	7.50
B	36,000,000	7.50
FL	72,375,000	1-month LIBOR + 0.50
IFL	24,125,000	28.50 – 3 × (1-month LIBOR)
Z (accrual)	73,000,000	7.50
	$400,000,000	

---

[a]*Payment rules:*

1. *For payment of periodic coupon interest:* Disburse periodic coupon interest to tranches A, B, FL, and IFL on the basis of the amount of principal outstanding at the beginning of the period. For tranche Z, accrue the interest based on the principal plus accrued interest in the preceding period. The interest for tranche Z is to be paid to the earlier tranches as a principal pay down. The maximum coupon rate for FL is 10%; the minimum coupon rate for IFL is 0%.

2. *For disbursement of principal payments:* Disburse principal payments to tranche A until it is paid off completely. After tranche A is paid off completely, disburse principal payments to tranche B until it is paid off completely. After tranche B is paid off completely, disburse principal payments to tranches FL and IFL until they are paid off completely. The principal payments between tranches FL and IFL should be made in the following way: 75% to tranche FL and 25% to tranche IFL. After tranches FL and IFL are paid off completely, disburse principal payments to tranche Z until the original principal balance plus accrued interest is paid off completely.

The amount of the par value of the floating-rate tranche will be some portion of the $96.5 million. There is an infinite number of ways to cut up the $96.5 million between the floater and inverse floater, and final partitioning will be driven by the demands of investors. In the FJF-03 structure, we made the floater from $72,375,000 or 75% of the $96.5 million. The coupon rate on the floater is set at one-month LIBOR plus 50 basis points. So, for example, if LIBOR is 3.75% at the reset date, the coupon rate on the floater is 3.75% + 0.5%, or 4.25%. There is a cap on the coupon rate for the floater (discussed later).

Unlike a floating-rate note in the corporate bond market, whose principal is unchanged over the life of the instrument, the floater's principal balance declines over time as principal payments are made. The principal payments to the floater are determined by the principal payments from the tranche from which the floater is created. In our CMO structure, this is tranche C.

Because the floater's par value is $72,375,000 of the $96.5 million, the balance is the inverse floater. Assuming that one-month LIBOR is the reference rate, the coupon rate on the inverse floater takes the following form:

$$K - L \times (\text{one-month LIBOR})$$

In FJF-03, K is set at 28.50% and L at 3. Thus, if one-month LIBOR is 3.75%, the coupon rate for the month is

$$28.50\% - 3(3.75\%) = 17.25\%$$

K is the cap or maximum coupon rate for the inverse floater. In FJF-03, the cap for the inverse floater is 28.50%.

The L or multiple in the formula to determine the coupon rate for the inverse floater is called the **coupon leverage**. The higher the coupon leverage, the more the inverse floater's coupon rate changes for a given change in one-month LIBOR. For example, a coupon leverage of 3.0 means that a 100-basis-point change in one-month LIBOR will change the coupon rate on the inverse floater by 300 basis points; a coupon leverage of 0.7 means that the coupon rate will change by 70 basis points for a 100-basis-point change in one-month LIBOR. Inverse floaters with a wide variety of coupon leverages are available in the market. Participants refer to low-leverage inverse floaters as those with a coupon leverage between 0.5 and 2.1; medium-leverage as those with a coupon leverage higher than 2.1 but not exceeding 4.5; and high-leverage as those with a coupon leverage higher than 4.5. At the time of issuance, the issuer determines the coupon leverage according to investor desire. In FJF-03 the coupon leverage is set at 3.

Let's see how the total interest paid on the floater and inverse floater can be supported by the bond class with a coupon rate of 7.5% from which they are created. The coupon rate for the floating-rate class is

$$\text{one-month LIBOR} + 0.50$$

For the inverse floater the coupon rate is

$$28.50 - 3 \times (\text{one-month LIBOR})$$

Because the floater is 75% of the $96.5 million and the inverse floater is 25%, the weighted-average coupon rate is

$$0.75 \text{ (floater coupon rate)} + 0.25 \text{ (inverse floater coupon rate)}$$

The weighted average coupon rate is 7.5%, regardless of the level of LIBOR. For example, if one-month LIBOR is 9%, then

$$\text{floater coupon rate} = 9.0\% + 0.5\% = 9.5\%$$
$$\text{inverse floater coupon rate} = 28.5 - 3(9.0\%) = 1.5\%$$

The weighted-average coupon rate is

$$0.75(9.5\%) + 0.25(1.5\%) = 7.5\%$$

Consequently, the 7.5% coupon rate on the bond class from which these two classes were created can support the aggregate interest payments that must be made to them. As in the case of the floater, the principal pay down of an inverse floater will be a proportionate amount of the principal pay down of bond class C.

Because one-month LIBOR is always positive, the coupon rate paid to the floating-rate bond class cannot be negative. If there are no restrictions placed on the coupon rate for the inverse floater, however, it is possible for the coupon rate for that bond class to be negative. To prevent this, a floor, or minimum, can be placed on the coupon rate. In many structures, the floor is set at zero. Once a floor is set for the inverse floater, a cap or ceiling is imposed on the floater. In FJF-03, a floor of zero is set for the inverse floater. The floor results in a cap or maximum coupon rate for the floater of 10%. This is found by substituting zero for the coupon rate of the inverse floater in the formula for the weighted-average coupon rate, and then setting the formula equal to 7.5%.

The cap for the floater and the inverse floater, the floor for the inverse floater, the coupon leverage, and the margin spread are not determined independently. Given four of these variables, the fifth will be determined.

Planned Amortization Class Tranches

The CMO innovations discussed previously attracted many institutional investors who had previously either avoided investing in mortgage-backed securities or allocated only a nominal portion of their portfolio to this sector of the fixed-income market. Although some traditional corporate bond buyers shifted their allocation to CMOs, a majority of institutional investors remained on the sidelines, concerned about investing in an instrument that they continued to perceive as posing significant prepayment risk because of the substantial average life variability, despite the innovations designed to reduce prepayment risk.

Potential demand for a CMO product with less uncertainty about the cash flow increased in the mid-1980s because of two trends in the corporate bond market. First was the increased event risk faced by investors, highlighted by the RJR Nabisco leveraged buyout in 1988. The second trend was a decline in the number of AAA-rated corporate issues. Traditional corporate bond buyers sought a structure with both the characteristics of a corporate bond (either a bullet maturity or a sinking fund type of schedule of principal repayment) and high credit quality. Although CMOs satisfied the second condition, they did not satisfy the first.

In March 1987, the M.D.C. Mortgage Funding Corporation CMO Series O included a class of bonds referred to as **stabilized mortgage reduction term (SMRT) bonds**;

another class in its CMO Series P was referred to as **planned amortization class (PAC) bonds**. The Oxford Acceptance Corporation III Series C CMOs included a class of bonds referred to as a **planned redemption obligation (PRO) bonds**. The characteristic common to these three bonds is that if the prepayments are within a specified range, the cash flow pattern is known.

The greater predictability of the cash flow for these classes of bonds, now referred to exclusively as PAC bonds, occurs because there is a principal repayment schedule that must be satisfied. PAC bondholders have priority over all other classes in the CMO issue in receiving principal payments from the underlying collateral. The greater certainty of the cash flow for the PAC bonds comes at the expense of the non-PAC classes, called **support** or **companion bonds**. It is these bonds that absorb the prepayment risk. Because PAC bonds have protection against both extension risk and contraction risk, they are said to provide **two-sided prepayment protection**.

To illustrate how to create a PAC bond, we will use as collateral the $400 million pass-through with a coupon rate of 7.5%, an 8.125% WAC, and a WAM of 357 months. The second column of Exhibit 12-7 shows the principal payment (regularly scheduled

EXHIBIT 12-7	Monthly Principal Payment for $400 Million 7.5% Coupon Pass-Through with an 8.125% WAC and a 357 WAM Assuming Prepayment Rates of 90 PSA and 300 PSA		
Month	At 90% PSA	At 300% PSA	Minimum Principal Payment—the PAC Schedule
1	508,169.52	1,075,931.20	508,169.52
2	569,843.43	1,279,412.11	569,843.43
3	631,377.11	1,482,194.45	631,377.11
4	692,741.89	1,683,966.17	692,741.89
5	753,909.12	1,884,414.62	753,909.12
6	814,850.22	2,083,227.31	814,850.22
7	875,536.68	2,280,092.68	875,536.68
8	935,940.10	2,474,700.92	935,940.10
9	996,032.19	2,666,744.77	996,032.19
10	1,055,784.82	2,855,920.32	1,055,784.82
11	1,115,170.01	3,041,927.81	1,115,170.01
12	1,174,160.00	3,224,472.44	1,174,160.00
13	1,232,727.22	3,403,265.17	1,232,727.22
14	1,290,844.32	3,578,023.49	1,290,844.32
15	1,348,484.24	3,748,472.23	1,348,484.24
16	1,405,620.17	3,914,344.26	1,405,620.17
17	1,462,225.60	4,075,381.29	1,462,225.60
18	1,518,274.36	4,231,334.57	1,518,274.36
101	1,458,719.34	1,510,072.17	1,458,719.34
102	1,452,725.55	1,484,126.59	1,452,725.55
103	1,446,761.00	1,458,618.04	1,446,761.00
			(continued)

EXHIBIT 12-7   (continued)

104	1,440,825.55	1,433,539.23	1,433,539.23
105	1,434,919.07	1,408,883.01	1,408,883.01
211	949,482.58	213,309.00	213,309.00
212	946,033.34	209,409.09	209,409.09
213	942,601.99	205,577.05	205,577.05
346	618,684.59	13,269.17	13,269.17
347	617,071.58	12,944.51	12,944.51
348	615,468.65	12,626.21	12,626.21
349	613,875.77	12,314.16	3,432.32
350	612,292.88	12,008.25	0
351	610,719.96	11,708.38	0
352	609,156.96	11,414.42	0
353	607,603.84	11,126.28	0
354	606,060.57	10,843.85	0
355	604,527.09	10,567.02	0
356	603,003.38	10,295.70	0
357	601,489.39	10,029.78	0

principal repayment plus prepayments) for selected months assuming a prepayment speed of 90 PSA, and the next column shows the principal payments for selected months assuming that the pass-through prepays at 300 PSA.

The last column of Exhibit 12-7 gives the *minimum* principal payment if the collateral speed is 90 PSA or 300 PSA for months 1 to 349. (After month 346, the outstanding principal balance will be paid off if the prepayment speed is between 90 PSA and 300 PSA.) For example, in the first month, the principal payment would be $508,169.52 if the collateral prepays at 90 PSA and $1,075,931.20 if the collateral prepays at 300 PSA. Thus, the minimum principal payment is $508,169.52, as reported in the last column of Exhibit 12-7. In month 103, the minimum principal payment is also the amount if the prepayment speed is 90 PSA, $1,446,761, compared with $1,458,618.04 for 300 PSA. In month 104, however, a prepayment speed of 300 PSA would produce a principal payment of $1,433,539.23, which is less than the principal payment of $1,440,825.55 assuming 90 PSA. So $1,433,539.23 is reported in the last column of Exhibit 12-7. In fact, from month 104 on, the minimum principal payment is the one that would result assuming a prepayment speed of 300 PSA.

In fact, if the collateral prepays at *any* speed between 90 PSA and 300 PSA, the minimum principal payment would be the amount reported in the last column of Exhibit 12-7. For example, if we had included principal payment figures assuming a prepayment speed of 200 PSA, the minimum principal payment would not change; from month 11 through month 103, the minimum principal payment is that generated from 90 PSA, but from month 104 on, the minimum principal payment is that generated from 300 PSA.

EXHIBIT 12-8 FJF-04: CMO Structure with One PAC Bond and One Support Bond[a]

Tranche	Par Amount	Coupon Rate (%)
P (PAC)	$243,800,000	7.5
S (Support)	156,200,000	7.5
	$400,000,000	

[a]*Payment rules:*

1. *For payment of periodic coupon interest:* Disburse periodic coupon interest to each tranche on the basis of the amount of principal outstanding at the beginning of the period.
2. *For disbursement of principal payments:* Disburse principal payments to tranche P based on its schedule of principal repayments. Tranche P has priority with respect to current and future principal payments to satisfy the schedule. Any excess principal payments in a month over the amount necessary to satisfy the schedule for tranche P are paid to tranche S. When tranche S is paid off completely, all principal payments are to be made to tranche P regardless of the schedule.

This characteristic of the collateral allows for the creation of a PAC bond, assuming that the collateral prepays over its life at a speed between 90 PSA to 300 PSA. A schedule of principal repayments that the PAC bondholders are entitled to receive before any other bond class in the CMO is specified. The monthly schedule of principal repayments is as specified in the last column of Exhibit 12-7, which shows the minimum principal payment. Although there is no assurance that the collateral will prepay between these two speeds, a PAC bond can be structured to assume that it will.

Exhibit 12-8 shows a CMO structure, FJF-04, created from the $400 million, 7.5% coupon pass-through with a WAC of 8.125% and a WAM of 357 months. There are just two bond classes in this structure: a 7.5% coupon PAC bond created assuming 90 to 300 PSA with a par value of $243.8 million, and a support bond with a par value of $156.2 million. The two speeds used to create a PAC bond are called the **initial PAC collars** (or **initial PAC bands**); in our case 90 PSA is the lower collar and 300 PSA the upper collar.

Exhibit 12-9 reports the average life for the PAC bond and the support bond in FJF-04 assuming various *actual* prepayment speeds. Notice that between 90 PSA and 300 PSA, the average life for the PAC bond is stable at 7.26 years. However, at slower or faster PSA speeds, the schedule is broken, and the average life changes, lengthening when the prepayment speed is less than 90 PSA and shortening when it is greater than 300 PSA. Even so, there is much greater variability for the average life of the support bond.

Creating a Series of PAC Bonds

Most CMO PAC structures have more than one class of PAC bonds. We created six PAC bonds from FJF-04, which we call FJF-05. Information about this CMO structure is reported in Exhibit 12-10. The total par value of the six PAC bonds is equal to $243.8 million, which is the amount of the single PAC bond in FJF-04.

EXHIBIT 12-9 Average Life for Pac Bond and Support Bond in FJF-04 Assuming Various Prepayment Speeds

Prepayment Rate (PSA)	PAC Bond (P)	Support Bond (S)
0	15.97	27.26
50	9.44	24.00
90	7.26	18.56
100	7.26	18.56
150	7.26	12.57
165	7.26	11.16
200	7.26	8.38
250	7.26	5.37
300	7.26	3.13
350	6.56	2.51
400	5.92	2.17
450	5.38	1.94
500	4.93	1.77
700	3.70	1.37

EXHIBIT 12-10 FJF-05: CMO Structure with Six PAC Bonds and One Support Bond[a]

Tranche	Par Amount	Coupon Rate (%)
P-A	$85,000,000	7.5
P-B	8,000,000	7.5
P-C	35,000,000	7.5
P-D	45,000,000	7.5
P-E	40,000,000	7.5
P-F	30,800,000	7.5
S	156,200,000	7.5
	$400,000,000	

[a]*Payment rules:*

1. *For payment of periodic coupon interest:* Disburse periodic coupon interest to each tranche on the basis of the amount of principal outstanding at the beginning of the period.
2. *For disbursement of principal payments:* Disburse principal payments to tranches P-A to P-F based on their respective schedules of principal repayments. Tranche P-A has priority with respect to current and future principal payments to satisfy the schedule. Any excess principal payments in a month over the amount necessary to satisfy the schedule for tranche P-A are paid to tranche S. When tranche P-A is paid off completely, tranche P-B has priority, then tranche P-C, and so on. When tranche S is paid off completely, all principal payments are to be made to the remaining PAC tranches in order of priority regardless of the schedule.

EXHIBIT 12-11   Average Life for the Six PAC Bonds in FJF-05 Assuming Various Prepayment Speeds

Prepayment Rate (PSA)	PAC Bonds					
	P-A	P-B	P-C	P-D	P-E	P-F
0	8.46	14.61	16.49	19.41	21.91	23.76
50	3.58	6.82	8.36	11.30	14.50	18.20
90	2.58	4.72	5.78	7.89	10.83	16.92
100	2.58	4.72	5.78	7.89	10.83	16.92
150	2.58	4.72	5.78	7.89	10.83	16.92
165	2.58	4.72	5.78	7.89	10.83	16.92
200	2.58	4.72	5.78	7.89	10.83	16.92
250	2.58	4.72	5.78	7.89	10.83	16.92
300	2.58	4.72	5.78	7.89	10.83	16.92
350	2.58	4.72	5.49	6.95	9.24	14.91
400	2.57	4.37	4.91	6.17	8.33	13.21
450	2.50	3.97	4.44	5.56	7.45	11.81
500	2.40	3.65	4.07	5.06	6.74	10.65
700	2.06	2.82	3.10	3.75	4.88	7.51

Exhibit 12-11 shows the average life for the six PAC bonds and the support bond in FJF-05 at various prepayment speeds. From a PAC bond in FJF-04 with an average life of 7.26, we have created six bonds with an average life as short as 2.58 years (P-A) and as long as 16.92 years (P-F) if prepayments stay within 90 PSA and 300 PSA.

As expected, the average lives are stable if the prepayment speed is between 90 PSA and 300 PSA. Notice that even outside this range the average life is stable for several of the PAC bonds. For example, the PAC P-A bond is stable even if prepayment speeds are as high as 400 PSA. For the PAC P-B, the average life does not vary when prepayments are in the initial collar until prepayments are greater than 350 PSA. Why is it that the shorter the PAC, the more protection it has against faster prepayments?

To understand why this is so, remember that there are $156.2 million in support bonds that are protecting the $85 million of PAC P-A. Thus, even if prepayments are faster than the initial upper collar, there may be sufficient support bonds to assure the satisfaction of the schedule. In fact, as can be seen from Exhibit 12-11, even if prepayments are at 400 PSA over the life of the collateral, the average life is unchanged.

Now consider PAC P-B. The support bonds are providing protection for both the $85 million of PAC P-A and $93 million of PAC P-B. As can be seen from Exhibit 12-11, prepayments could be 350 PSA and the average life is still unchanged. From Exhibit 12-11 it can be seen that the degree of protection against extension risk increases the shorter the PAC. Thus, whereas the initial collar may be 90 to 300 PSA, the **effective collar** is wider for the shorter PAC tranches. Exhibit 12-12 shows the effective collar for the six PAC tranches in FJF-04.

EXHIBIT 12-12	Effective Collars for Each Pac Tranche in FJF-04

Amount of Support Bonds: $156.2 Million	
Tranche	Effective Collar
P-A	90–450 PSA
P-B	90–350 PSA
P-C	90–300 PSA
P-D	90–300 PSA
P-E	90–300 PSA
P-F	90–300 PSA

PAC Window

As we explained earlier, the length of time over which scheduled principal repayments are made is referred to as the window. A PAC window can be wide or narrow. The narrower a PAC window, the more it resembles a corporate bond with a bullet payment. PAC buyers appear to prefer tight windows, although institutional investors facing a liability schedule are generally better off with a window that more closely matches the liabilities. Investor demand dictates the PAC windows that issuers will create. Investor demand in turn is governed by the nature of investor liabilities.

Effective Collars and Actual Prepayments

As we have emphasized several times, the creation of a mortgage-backed security cannot make prepayment risk disappear. This is true for both a pass-through and a CMO. Thus, the reduction in prepayment risk (both extension risk and contraction risk) that a PAC offers must come from somewhere.

Where does the prepayment protection come from? It comes from the support bonds. It is the support bonds that forego principal payments if the collateral prepayments are slow; support bonds do not receive any principal until the PAC bonds receive the scheduled principal repayment. This reduces the risk that the PAC bonds will extend. Similarly, it is the support bonds that absorb any principal payments in excess of the scheduled principal payments that are made. This reduces the contraction risk of the PAC bonds. *Thus, the key to the prepayment protection offered by a PAC bond is the amount of support bonds outstanding. If the support bonds are paid off quickly because of faster-than-expected prepayments, there is no longer any protection for the PAC bonds.* In fact, in FJF-05, if the support bond is paid off, the structure is effectively reduced to a sequential-pay CMO.

The support bonds can be thought of as bodyguards for the PAC bondholders. When the bullets fly (i.e., prepayments occur) it is the bodyguards that get killed off first. The bodyguards are there to absorb the bullets. When all the bodyguards are killed off (i.e., the support bonds paid off with faster-than-expected prepayments), the PAC bonds must fend for themselves; they are exposed to all the bullets.

The top panel of Exhibit 12-13 shows what happens to the average life for all PAC tranches of FJF-05 one year from now if prepayments for the first 12 months are the speed shown and the future speed is the same as the first 12 months. For example, if the

EXHIBIT 12-13   Average Life for PAC Tranches of FJF-05 One Year from Now Assuming Various Prepayment Speeds for the First 12 Months

Speed for First 12 Months	Thereafter	PAC					
		P-A	P-B	P-C	P-D	P-E	P-F
90 PSA	90 PSA	1.81	3.72	4.77	6.89	9.82	15.91
100 PSA	100 PSA	1.81	3.72	4.77	6.89	9.82	15.91
165 PSA	165 PSA	1.81	3.72	4.77	6.89	9.82	15.91
200 PSA	200 PSA	1.81	3.72	4.77	6.89	9.82	15.91
300 PSA	300 PSA	1.81	3.72	4.77	6.89	9.82	15.91
400 PSA	400 PSA	1.80	3.37	3.90	5.17	7.32	12.21
600 PSA	600 PSA	1.41	2.16	2.50	3.29	4.65	7.83
800 PSA	800 PSA	1.09	1.56	1.79	2.34	3.28	5.48
Speed for First 12 Months	Thereafter	PAC					
		P-A	P-B	P-C	P-D	P-E	P-F
42 CPR	90 PSA	2.73	6.17	8.26	12.78	18.86	25.42
42 CPR	100 PSA	2.52	5.69	7.63	11.92	17.93	24.92
42 CPR	165 PSA	1.70	3.77	5.06	8.08	12.91	21.07
42 CPR	200 PSA	1.46	3.19	4.28	6.83	11.03	18.94
42 CPR	300 PSA	1.05	2.24	2.96	4.69	7.61	13.97
42 CPR	400 PSA	0.84	1.74	2.28	3.55	5.72	10.67
42 CPR	600 PSA	0.60	1.23	1.57	2.37	3.73	6.92
42 CPR	800 PSA	0.47	0.97	1.22	1.77	2.71	4.92

collateral prepays at 165 PSA for the first 12 months and then prepays at the same speed thereafter, the average life one year from now will be 1.81 years. Notice that for all the PAC tranches the average life is still stable for the initial collar. In contrast, the second panel shows what will happen to the average life one year from now if the collateral pays at 42 CPR for the first 12 months and prepays at the indicated speed thereafter. We selected 42 CPR so that the support bonds will be paid off by the end of the first year. The structure is now effectively a sequential-pay structure and, as indicated by the average lives reported in the exhibit, there is substantial average life variability for the original PAC tranches. A comparison of the lower and upper panel clearly demonstrates the role of the support bonds.

With the bodyguard metaphor for the support bonds in mind, let's consider two questions asked by CMO buyers:

1. Will the schedule of principal repayments be satisfied if prepayments are faster than the initial upper collar?
2. Will the schedule of principal repayments be satisfied as long as prepayments stay within the initial collar?

Let's address the first question. The initial upper collar for FJF-05 is 300 PSA. Suppose that actual prepayments are 500 PSA for seven consecutive months; will this disrupt the schedule of principal repayments? The answer is: It depends!

To answer this question we need two pieces of information. First, when does the 500 PSA occur? Second, what has been the actual prepayment experience up to the time that prepayments are 500 PSA? For example, suppose that six years from now is when the prepayments reach 500 PSA and also suppose that for the past six years the actual prepayment speed has been 90 PSA every month. This means that there are more bodyguards (i.e., support bonds) around than was expected when the PAC was structured at the initial collar. In establishing the schedule of principal repayments, it was assumed that the bodyguards would be killed off at 300 PSA, but the actual prepayment experience results in them being killed off at only 90 PSA. Thus, six years from now when the 500 PSA is assumed to occur, there are more bodyguards than expected. Thus, a 500 PSA for seven consecutive months may have no effect on the ability of the schedule of principal repayments to be met.

In contrast, suppose that the actual prepayment experience for the first six years is 300 PSA (the upper collar of the initial PAC collar). In this case, there are no extra bodyguards around. As a result, any prepayment speeds faster than 300 PSA, such as 500 PSA in our example, jeopardize satisfaction of the principal repayment schedule and increase extension risk. This does not mean that the schedule will be **busted**—the term used in the CMO market when a PAC schedule is broken. It does mean that the prepayment protection is reduced.

It should be clear from these observations that the initial collars are not particularly useful in assessing the prepayment protection for a seasoned PAC bond. This is most important to understand, as it is common for CMO buyers to compare prepayment protection of PACs in different CMO structures, and conclude that the greater protection is offered by the one with the wider collar. This approach is inadequate because it is actual prepayment experience that determines the degree of prepayment protection as well as the expected future prepayment behavior of the collateral.

The way to determine this protection is to calculate the effective collar for a seasoned PAC bond. An effective collar for a seasoned PAC is the lower and the upper PSA that can occur in the future and still allow maintenance of the schedule of principal repayments.

The effective collar changes every month. An extended period over which actual prepayments are below the upper range of the initial PAC collar will result in an increase in the upper range of the effective collar. This is because there will be more bodyguards around than anticipated. An extended period of prepayments slower than the lower range of the initial PAC collar will raise the lower range of the effective collar. This is because it will take faster prepayments to make up the shortfall of the scheduled principal payments not made plus the scheduled future principal payments.

The PAC schedule may not be satisfied even if the actual prepayments never fall outside the initial collar. This may seem surprising because our previous analysis indicated that the average life would not change if prepayments are at either extreme of the initial collar. However, recall that all of our previous analysis has been based on a single PSA speed for the life of the structure.

Let's use vector analysis to see what happens to the effective collar if the prepayments are at the initial upper collar for a certain number of months. Exhibit 12-14 shows the average life two years from now for the PAC bond in FJF-04 assuming that prepayments are 300 PSA for the first 24 months. Notice that the average life is stable at six years if the prepayments for the following months are between 115 PSA and

EXHIBIT 12-14   Average Life Two Years from Now for
               PAC Bond of FJF-04 Assuming
               Prepayments of 300 PSA for First
               24 Months

PSA from Year 2 on	Average Life (years)
95	6.43
105	6.11
115	6.01
120	6.00
125	6.00
300	6.00
305	5.62

300 PSA. That is, the effective PAC collar is no longer the initial collar. Instead, the lower collar has shifted upward. This means that the protection from year 2 on is for 115 to 300 PSA, a narrower band than initially even though the earlier prepayments did not exceed the initial upper collar.

Providing Greater Prepayment Protection for PACs

There are two ways to provide greater protection for PAC bonds: lockouts and reverse PAC structures. One obvious way to provide greater protection for PAC bonds is to issue fewer PAC bonds relative to support bonds. In FJF-05, for example, rather than creating the six PAC bonds with a total par value of $243.8 million, we could use only $158.8 million of the $400 million of collateral to create these bonds, by reducing the amount of each of the six PAC bonds. An alternative is not to issue one of the PAC bonds, typically the shorter-term one. For example, suppose that we create only the last five of the six PAC bonds in FJF-05. The $85 million for PAC P-A is then used to create more support bonds. Such a CMO structure with no principal payments to a PAC bond class in the earlier years is referred to as a **lockout structure**.

A lockout structure provides greater prepayment protection to all PAC bonds in the CMO structure. One way to provide greater prepayment protection to only some PAC bonds is to alter the principal payment rules for distributing principal when all the support bonds have been paid off. In FJF-05, for example, when the support bond in this structure is paid off, the structure effectively becomes a sequential-pay structure. For PAC P-A this means that although there is protection against extension risk, as this tranche receives principal payments before the other five PAC bonds, there is no protection against contraction.

To provide greater protection to PAC P-A, the payment rules after all support bonds have been paid off can be specified so that any principal payments in excess of the scheduled amount will be paid to the last PAC bond, P-F. Thus, PAC P-F is exposed to greater contraction risk, which provides the other five PAC bonds with more protection against contraction risk. The principal payment rules would also specify that when the support bond and PAC P-F bond are paid off, all principal payments in excess of the scheduled amounts to earlier tranches are to be paid to the next-to-last PAC bond, PAC P-E in our example.

A CMO structure requiring any excess principal payments to be made to the longer PAC bonds after all support bonds are paid off is called a **reverse PAC structure**.

Other PAC Tranches

Earlier we described how the collateral can be used to create a CMO with accrual bonds, floaters, and inverse floaters bonds. In addition, interest-only and principal-only tranches (described later) can be created. These same types of bond classes can be created from a PAC bond. The difference between the bond classes described and those created from a PAC bond is simply the prepayment protection offered by the PAC structure.

Targeted Amortization Class Bonds

A **targeted amortization class (TAC) bond** resembles a PAC bond in that both have a schedule of principal repayment. The difference between a PAC bond and a TAC bond is that the former has a wide PSA range over which the schedule of principal repayment is protected against contraction risk and extension risk. A TAC bond, in contrast, has a single PSA rate from which the schedule of principal repayment is protected. As a result, the prepayment protection afforded the TAC bond is less than that for a PAC bond.

The creation of a bond with a schedule of principal repayments based on a single prepayment rate results in protection against contraction risk but not extension risk. Thus, whereas PAC bonds are said to have two-sided prepayment protection, TAC bonds have one-sided prepayment protection. Such a bond is acceptable to institutional investors who are not overly concerned with some extension risk but greatly concerned with contraction risk.

Some institutional investors are interested in protection against extension risk but are willing to accept contraction risk. This is the opposite protection from that sought by the buyers of TAC bonds. The structures created to provide such protection are referred to as **reverse TAC bonds**.

Very Accurately Determined Maturity Bonds

Accrual or Z bonds have been used in CMO structures as support for bonds called **very accurately determined maturity (VADM)** or **guaranteed final maturity bonds**. In this case the interest accruing (i.e., not being paid out) on a Z bond is used to pay the interest and principal on a VADM bond. This effectively provides protection against extension risk even if prepayments slow down, because the interest accruing on the Z bond will be sufficient to pay off the scheduled principal and interest on the VADM bond. Thus, the maximum final maturity can be determined with a high degree of certainty. If prepayments are high, resulting in the supporting Z bond being paid off faster, however, a VADM bond can shorten.

A VADM is similar in character to a reverse TAC. For structures with similar collateral, however, a VADM bond offers greater protection against extension risk. Moreover, most VADMs will not shorten significantly if prepayments speed up. Thus, they offer greater protection against contraction risk compared with a reverse TAC with the same underlying collateral. Compared with PACs, VADM bonds have greater absolute protection against extension risk, and though VADM bonds do not have as much protection against contraction risk, as noted previously, the structures that have included these bonds are such that contraction risk is generally not significant.

Interest-Only and Principal-Only Tranches

As we explain later in this chapter, stripped mortgage-backed securities are created by paying all the principal to one bond class and all the interest to another bond class. These two classes are referred to as the **principal-only (PO) bond class** and the **interest-only (IO) bond class**. We discuss the investment characteristics of these securities later.

CMO structures can be created so that a tranche can receive only the principal or only the interest. For example, consider FJF-01. Tranche B in this structure can be divided into two tranches, a principal-only tranche and an interest-only tranche.

Notional IOS

In our previous illustrations, we used a CMO structure in which all the tranches have the same coupon rate (7.5%) and that coupon rate is the same as the collateral. In practice, the same coupon rate would not be given to each tranche. Instead, the coupon rate would depend on the term structure of interest rates and the average life of the tranche, among other things.

In the earlier CMO deals, all of the excess interest between the coupon rate on the tranches and the coupon interest on the collateral was paid to an equity class referred to as the **CMO residual**. This is no longer the practice today. Instead, a tranche is created that receives the excess coupon interest. This tranche is called a **notional interest-only (IO) class** and also referred to as a **structured IO**.

To see how a notional IO is created, consider the CMO structure shown in Exhibit 12-15, FJF-06. This is the same structure as FJF-02 except that the coupon rate varies by tranche and there is a class denoted IO, which is the class of interest to us.

Notice that for this structure the par amount for the IO class is shown as $52,566,667 and the coupon rate is 7.5%. This is an IO class, so there is no par amount. The amount shown is the amount on which the interest payments will be determined, not the amount that will be paid to the holder of this bond. Therefore, it is called a **notional amount**.

Let's look at how the notional amount is determined. Consider first tranche A. The par value is $194.5 million and the coupon rate is 6%. Because the collateral's coupon rate is 7.5%, the excess interest is 150 basis points (1.5%). Therefore, an IO with a 1.5% coupon rate and a notional amount of $194.5 million can be created from tranche A. However, this is equivalent to an IO with a notional amount of $38.9 million and a coupon rate of 7.5%. Mathematically, this notional amount is found as follows:

$$\text{notional amount for 7.5\% IO} = \frac{\text{tranche's par value} \times \text{excess interest}}{0.075}$$

where:

excess interest = collateral coupon rate – tranche coupon rate

For example, for tranche A,

EXHIBIT 12-15 FJF-06: Hypothetical Five Tranche Sequential Pay with an Accrual Tranche and an Interest-Only Tranche[a]

Tranche	Par Amount	Notional Amount	Coupon Rate (%)
A	$194,500,000		6.00
B	36,000,000		6.50
C	96,500,000		7.00
Z	73,000,000		7.25
IO		52,566,667	7.50
	$400,000,000		

[a]*Payment rules:*

1. *For payment of periodic coupon interest*: Disburse periodic coupon interest to tranches A, B, and C on the basis of the amount of principal outstanding at the beginning of the period. For tranche Z, accrue the interest based on the principal plus accrued interest in the preceding period. The interest for tranche Z is to be paid to the earlier tranches as a principal pay down. Disburse periodic interest to the IO tranche based on the notional amount at the beginning of the period.
2. *For disbursement of principal payments*: Disburse principal payments to tranche A until it is paid off completely. After tranche A is paid off completely, disburse principal payments to tranche B until it is paid off completely. After tranche B is paid off completely, disburse principal payments to tranche C until it is paid off completely. After tranche C is paid off completely, disburse principal payments to tranche Z until the original principal balance plus accrued interest is paid off completely.

$$\text{excess interest} = 0.075 - 0.060 = 0.015$$
$$\text{tranche's par value} = \$194,500,000$$
$$\text{notional amount for 7.5\% IO} = \frac{\$194,500,000 \times 0.015}{0.075}$$
$$= \$38,900,000$$

Similarly, from tranche B with a par value of $36 million, the excess interest is 100 basis points (1%), and therefore an IO with a coupon rate of 1% and a notional amount of $36 million can be created. But this is equivalent to creating an IO with a notional amount of $4.8 million and a coupon rate of 7.5%. This procedure is shown in the following table for all four tranches.

Tranche	Par Amount	Excess Interest	Notional Amount for a 7.5% Coupon Rate IO
A	$194,500,000	1.50	$38,900,000
B	36,000,000	1.00	4,800,000
C	96,500,000	0.50	6,433,333
Z	73,000,000	0.25	2,433,333
	Notional amount for 7.5% IO		$52,566,666

Support Bonds

The support bonds—or bodyguards—are the bonds that provide prepayment protection for the PAC tranches. Consequently, they are exposed to the greatest level of prepayment risk. Because of this, investors must be particularly careful in assessing the cash flow characteristics of support bonds to reduce the likelihood of adverse portfolio consequences due to prepayments.

The support bond typically is divided into different bond classes. All the bond classes we have discussed earlier in this section are available, including sequential-pay support bond classes, floater and inverse floater support bond classes, and accrual support bond classes.

The support bond can even be partitioned so as to create support bond classes with a schedule of principal repayments. That is, support bond classes that are PAC bonds can be created. In a structure with a PAC bond and a support bond with a PAC schedule of principal repayments, the former is called a PAC I bond or level I PAC bond or PAC1 and the latter a PAC II bond or level II PAC bond. Although PAC II bonds have greater prepayment protection than the support bond classes without a schedule of principal repayments, the prepayment protection is less than that provided PAC I bonds.

Credit Risk

A CMO can be viewed as a business entity. The assets of this business are the collateral; that is, the pass-through securities or pool of mortgage loans backing the deal. The collateral for a CMO is held in trust for the exclusive benefit of all the bondholders. The liabilities are the payments due to the CMO bond classes. The liability obligation consists of the par value and periodic interest payment that is owed to each class of bond. The CMO or, equivalently, the business, is structured so that even under the worst possible consequences concerning prepayments, all the liabilities will be satisfied.

Credit risk exposure depends on who has issued the CMO. An issuer is either (1) Freddie Mac, Fannie Mae, or Ginnie Mae, or (2) a private entity. Those CMOs issued by the former are referred to as **agency CMOs**. Those issued by a private entity are called **nonagency CMOs** and can be divided into two types. A private entity that issues a CMO but whose underlying collateral is a pool of pass-throughs guaranteed by an agency is called a **private-label CMO**. If the collateral for a CMO is a pool of unsecuritized mortgage loans, the structure is referred to as a **whole loan CMO**. Today, the most common type of nonagency CMO is a whole loan CMO. Consequently, market participants use the terms **nonagency CMO** and **whole loan CMO** interchangeably.

As we noted in Chapter 11, the guarantee of a government-sponsored enterprise depends on the financial capacity of the agency. CMOs issued by private entities are rated by commercial rating agencies. There are various ways that such issues can be credit enhanced, as described in Chapter 14 when we discuss asset-backed securities.

Tax Considerations

The issuer of a CMO wants to be sure that the trust created to pass through the interest and principal payments is not treated as a taxable entity. A provision of the Tax Reform Act of 1986, called the Real Estate Mortgage Investment Conduit (REMIC), specifies the requirements that an issuer must fulfill so that the legal entity created to issue a CMO is not taxable. Most CMOs today are created as REMICs. Although it is common to hear market participants refer to a CMO as a REMIC, not all CMOs are REMICs.

STRIPPED MORTGAGE-BACKED SECURITIES

Stripped mortgage-backed securities (MBSs), introduced by Fannie Mae in 1986, are another example of derivative mortgage products. A pass-through divides the cash flow from the underlying pool of mortgages on a pro rata basis across the security holders. A stripped MBS is created by altering the distribution of principal and interest from a pro rata distribution to an unequal distribution. Some of the securities thus created will have a price/yield relationship that is different from the price/yield relationship of the underlying mortgage pool. There are three types of stripped MBS: (1) synthetic-coupon pass-throughs, (2) interest-only/principal-only securities, and (3) CMO strips.

Synthetic-Coupon Pass-Throughs

The first generation of stripped mortgage-backed securities is called synthetic-coupon pass-throughs. This is because the unequal distribution of coupon and principal results in a synthetic coupon rate that is different from that of the underlying collateral.

Interest-Only/Principal-Only Securities

In early 1987, stripped MBS began to be issued where all the interest is allocated to one class (the IO class) and all the principal to the other class (the PO class). The IO class receives no principal payments. IOs and POs are referred to as **mortgage strips**.

The PO security is purchased at a substantial discount from par value. The yield an investor will realize depends on the speed at which prepayments are made. The faster the prepayments, the higher the yield the investor will realize. For example, suppose that there is a pass-through backed by 30-year mortgages with $400 million in par value and that investors can purchase POs backed by this pass-through for $175 million. The dollar return on this investment will be $225 million. How quickly that dollar return is recovered by PO investors determines the yield that will be realized. In the extreme case, if all the homeowners in the underlying mortgage pool decide to prepay their mortgage loans immediately, PO investors will realize the $225 million immediately. At the other extreme, if all homeowners decide to keep their houses for 30 years and make no prepayments, the $225 million will be spread out over 30 years, which will result in a lower yield for PO investors.

Let's look at how the price of the PO can be expected to change as mortgage rates in the market change. When mortgage rates decline below the coupon rate, prepayments are expected to speed up, accelerating payments to the PO holder. Thus, the cash flow of a PO improves (in the sense that principal repayments are received earlier). The cash flow will be discounted at a lower interest rate because the mortgage rate in the market has declined. The result is that the price of a PO will increase when mortgage rates decline. When mortgage rates rise above the coupon rate, prepayments are expected to slow down. The cash flow deteriorates (in the sense of it taking longer to recover principal repayments). Coupled with a higher discount rate, the price of a PO will fall when mortgage rates rise.

When an IO is purchased there is no par value. In contrast to the PO investor, the IO investor wants prepayments to be slow. The reason is that the IO investor receives only interest on the amount of the principal outstanding. As prepayments are made, the outstanding principal declines, and less dollar interest is received. In fact, if prepayments are too fast, the IO investor may not recover the amount paid for the IO.

Let's look at the expected price response of an IO to changes in mortgage rates. If mortgage rates decline below the coupon rate, prepayments are expected to accelerate. This results in a deterioration of the expected cash flow for an IO. Although the cash flow will be discounted at a lower rate, the net effect is typically a decline in the price of an IO. If mortgage rates rise above the coupon rate, the expected cash flow improves but the cash flow is discounted at a higher interest rate. The net effect may be either a rise or a fall for the IO. Thus, we see an interesting characteristic of an IO: Its price tends to move in the same direction as the change in mortgage rates. This effect occurs (1) when mortgage rates fall below the coupon rate, and (2) for some range of mortgage rates above the coupon rate.

An example of this effect can be seen in Exhibit 12-16, which shows for various mortgage rates the price of (1) a 9% pass-through, (2) a PO created from this pass-through, and (3) an IO created from this pass-through. Notice that as mortgage rates decline below 9%, the price of the pass-through does not respond much. This is the negative convexity (or price compression) property of pass-throughs. For the PO security, the price falls monotonically as mortgage rates rise. For the IO security, at mortgage rates above approximately 11%, the price declines as mortgage rates rise; as mortgage rates fall below about 11%, the price of an IO falls as mortgage rates decline. Both POs and IOs exhibit substantial price volatility when mortgage rates change. The

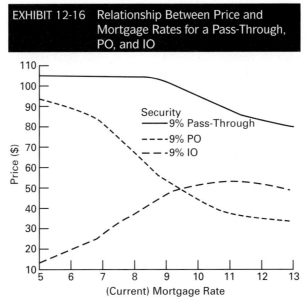

EXHIBIT 12-16 Relationship Between Price and Mortgage Rates for a Pass-Through, PO, and IO

Source: Adapted from Steven J. Carlson and Timothy D. Sears, "Stripped Mortgage Pass-Throughs: New Tools for Investors," in Frank J. Fabozzi, ed., *The Handbook of Mortgage-Backed Securities*, rev. ed. (Chicago: Probus Publishing, 1988), p. 564.

greater price volatility of the IO and PO compared with the pass-through from which they were created can be seen by the steepness of a tangent line to the curves at any given mortgage rate.

CMOs that are backed by POs are referred to as **PO-collateralized CMOs**.

CMO Strips

One of the classes in a CMO structure can be a principal-only or an interest-only class. These are called CMO strips or structured IOs. Earlier we discussed how CMO strip tranches can be created.

SUMMARY

Collateralized mortgage obligations are bond classes created by redirecting the cash flows of mortgage-related products (pass-throughs and whole loans). The creation of a CMO cannot eliminate prepayment risk; it can only redistribute the various forms of this risk among different classes of bonds called tranches.

In a CMO there are rules for the distribution of interest and principal from the collateral. The first CMOs were structured so that each class of bond would be retired sequentially, and hence such structures are referred to as sequential-pay CMOs. The average life of the tranches differs from that of the collateral. An accrual tranche allows the creation of even shorter-term and longer-term average life tranches than in a sequential-pay CMO without the inclusion of an accrual tranche. From any of the fixed-rate tranches, a floater and an inverse can be created. Also, an interest-only and a principal-only tranche can be created from a tranche. A notional IO is a tranche created from the difference between the collateral's coupon interest and the total coupon interest paid to the tranches.

Despite the redistribution of prepayment risk with sequential-pay and accrual CMOs, there is still considerable prepayment risk. That is, there is still considerable average life variability for a given tranche. This problem has been mitigated by the creation of a planned amortization class tranche. This type of CMO tranche reduces average life variability. The bonds included in a CMO structure that provide the better protection for PAC tranches are the support or companion tranches. There are various ways in which greater prepayment protection can be provided for some or all of the PAC bonds within a CMO structure. These include a lockout and a reverse PAC structure.

Targeted amortization class bonds are created so as to provide protection against contraction risk but not against extension risk. A reverse TAC also provides one-sided protection: protection against extension risk but not against contraction risk. A very accurately determined maturity bond also provides protection against extension risk.

Support bonds are the riskiest tranche within a CMO structure. From support bonds other types of bonds can be created. For example, a part of the support bonds can be carved up to create support bonds with a principal repayment schedule. Such bonds are referred to as PAC II or level II PAC bonds.

The credit risk exposure depends on whether the issuer is an agency (i.e., the issuer is Ginnie Mae, Fannie Mae, or Freddie Mac) or a nonagency CMO. Agency CMOs are perceived to have no credit risk. Nonagency CMOs can be divided into private-label

CMOs in which the underlying collateral is a pool of agency pass-throughs, and whole loan CMOs, in which the underlying collateral is a pool of whole loans. Nonagency CMOs expose investors to credit risk.

A stripped MBS is created by assigning distribution of principal and interest of the underlying pass-through security in unequal portions to two classes of bonds. The result is that the two bonds will have a different price/yield relationship from that of the underlying pass-through. There are three types of stripped MBS: (1) synthetic-coupon pass-throughs, (2) interest-only/principal-only securities, and (3) CMO strips.

Questions

1. How does a CMO alter the cash flow from mortgages so as to shift the prepayment risk across various classes of bondholders?
2. Why is a CMO called a pay-through structure?
3. a."By creating a CMO, an issuer eliminates the prepayment risk associated with the underlying mortgages." Do you agree with this statement?
   b. Wall Street often refers to CMOs as "customized securities." Explain why.
4. In a discussion of the CMO market, the popular press sometimes refers to this sector of the mortgage-backed securities market as the riskiest sector and the pass-through sector as the safest sector. Comment.
5. Explain the effect on the average lives of sequential-pay structures of including an accrual tranche in a CMO structure.
6. What types of investors would be attracted to an accrual bond?
7. Suppose that a tranche from which an inverse floater is created has an average life of five years. What will the average life of the inverse floater be?
8. This quotation is taken from a 1991 issue of *BondWeek*:

   First Interstate Bank of Texas will look into buying several different types of collateralized mortgage obligation tranches when it starts up its buy program sometime after the second quarter of 1991, according to Jules Pollard, v.p. Pollard said he will consider replacing maturing adjustable-rate mortgage pass-throughs with short companion

   tranches and planned amortization classes because the ARMS have become rich . . . . Pollard did not provide a dollar figure on the planned investments, which will be made to match fund the bank's liabilities. When he does invest he said he prefers government-guaranteed securities or those with implied guarantees.

   a. Explain the types of securities that Pollard is buying and selling.
   b. Given the preference stated in the last sentence of the quotation, what issuers is he likely to prefer? What issuers would he reject?

9. Describe how the schedule for a PAC tranche is created.
10. Explain the role of a support bond in a CMO structure.
11. What was the motivation for the creation of PAC bonds?
12. Suppose that a savings and loan association has decided to invest in mortgage-backed securities and is considering the following two securities: (i) a Freddie Mac pass-through security with a WAM of 340 months or (ii) a PAC tranche of a Freddie Mac CMO issue with an average life of two years. Which mortgage-backed security would probably be better from an asset/liability perspective?
13. Suppose that a PAC bond is created assuming prepayments speeds of 80 PSA and 350 PSA. If the collateral pays at 100 PSA over its life, what will this PAC tranche's average life be?
14. Suppose that $1 billion of pass-throughs is used to create a CMO structure with a PAC

bond with a par value of $700 million and a support bond with a par value of $300 million.

a. Which of the following will have the greatest average life variability: (i) the collateral, (ii) the PAC bond, or (iii) the support bond? Why?

b. Which of the following will have the least average life variability: (i) the collateral, (ii) the PAC bond, or (iii) the support bond? Why?

15. Suppose that the $1 billion of collateral in Question 14 was divided into a PAC bond with a par value of $800 million and a support bond with a par value of $200 million. Will the PAC bond in this CMO structure have more or less protection than the PAC bond in Question 14?

16. Suppose that $1 billion of pass-throughs is used to create a CMO structure with a PAC bond with a par value of $700 million (PAC I), a support bond with a schedule (PAC II) with a par value of $100 million, and a support bond without a schedule with a par value of $200 million.

a. Will the PAC I or PAC II have the smaller average life variability? Why?

b. Will the support bond without a schedule or the PAC II have the greater average life variability? Why?

17. In a CMO structure with several PAC bonds, explain why, when the support bonds are paid off, the structure will be just like a sequential-pay CMO.

18. Suppose that for the first four years of a CMO, prepayments are well within the initial PAC collar. What will happen to the effective upper collar?

19. Consider the following CMO structure backed by 8% collateral:

Tranche	Par Amount (in millions)	Coupon Rate (%)
A	$300	6.50
B	250	6.75
C	200	7.25
D	250	7.75

Suppose that a client wants a notional IO with a coupon rate of 8%. Calculate the notional amount for this notional IO.

20. An issuer is considering the following two CMO structures:

Structure I

Tranche	Par Amount (in millions)	Coupon Rate (%)
A	$150	6.50
B	100	6.75
C	200	7.25
D	150	7.75
E	100	8.00
F	500	8.50

Tranches A to E are a sequence of PAC Is and F is the support bond.

Structure II

Tranche	Par Amount (in millions)	Coupon Rate (%)
A	$150	6.50
B	100	6.75
C	200	7.25
D	150	7.75
E	100	8.00
F	200	8.25
G	300	?

Tranches A to E are a sequence of PAC Is, F is a PAC II, and G is a support bond without a PAC schedule.

a. In structure II, tranche G is created from tranche F in structure I. What is the coupon rate for tranche G assuming that the combined coupon rate for tranches F and G in structure II should be 8.5%?

b. What is the effect on the value and average life of tranches A to E by including the PAC II in structure II?

c. What is the difference in the average life variability of tranche G in structure II and tranche F in structure II?

21.a. What is the role of a lockout in a CMO structure?

b. Explain why in a reverse PAC bond structure the longest average life bond can turn out to be effectively a support bond if all the support bonds in the structure are paid off.

22. What type of prepayment protection is afforded each of the following: (a) a TAC bond, (b) a reverse TAC bond, (c) a VADM?

23. What types of CMO issues require a credit rating?

24. What is a whole loan CMO?

25. What is a REMIC?

26. Indicate why you agree or disagree with the following statement: "All CMOs are REMICs."

27. a. What is a principal-only security? What is an interest-only security?

    b. How is the price of an interest-only security expected to change when interest rates change?

28. Suppose that 8% coupon pass-throughs are stripped into two classes. Class X-1 receives 75% of the principal and 10% of the interest. Class X-2 receives 25% of the principal and 90% of the interest.

    a. What type of stripped MBS would this be?

    b. What is the effective coupon rate on Class X-1?

    c. What is the effective coupon rate on Class X-2?

13

COMMERCIAL MORTGAGE-BACKED SECURITIES

After reading this chapter you will understand:

- ◼ how commercial mortgage loans differ from residential mortgage loans

- ◼ the different property types for which commercial mortgage loans are obtained

- ◼ the two indicators of performance used for evaluating commercial mortgage loans—debt-to-service coverage ratio and loan-to-value ratio

- ◼ the different types of call protection provided for in commercial mortgage loans and in a commercial mortgage-backed security

- ◼ what balloon risk is for a commercial mortgage loan and a commercial mortgage-backed security

- ◼ differences in structuring a commercial mortgage-backed and residential mortgage-backed securities transaction

- ◼ the structural features of a commercial mortgage-backed security deal

- ◼ how prepayment premiums may be distributed among bondholders in a commercial mortgage-backed security

- ◼ the difference between a single borrower/multi-property deal and a conduit deal

- ◼ the different types of servicers in a commercial mortgage-backed securities deal

- ◼ factors to consider in the analysis of the collateral of a commercial mortgage-backed security

- ◼ why it is important to stress test a deal's structure

The mortgage market consists of residential mortgages and commercial mortgages. Residential mortgage loans are for properties with one to four single-family units. Residential mortgage-backed securities are the securities we discussed in the previous two chapters that are backed by residential mortgage loans. In this chapter, we look at commercial mortgages and securities backed by commercial mortgages—**commercial mortgage-backed securities** (CMBS).

COMMERCIAL MORTGAGE LOANS

Commercial mortgage loans are for income-producing properties. These properties include:

- multifamily properties (i.e., apartment buildings)
- office buildings
- industrial properties (including warehouses)
- shopping centers
- hotels
- health care facilities (e.g., senior housing care facilities)

A commercial mortgage loan is originated either to finance a commercial purchase or to refinance a prior mortgage obligation. Unlike residential mortgage loans where the lender relies on the ability of the borrower to repay and has recourse to the borrower if the payment terms are not satisfied, commercial mortgage loans are **non-recourse loans**. This means that the lender can only look to the income-producing property backing the loan for interest and principal repayment.

Indicators of Potential Performance

Because commercial mortgage loans are non-recourse loans, the lender looks only to the property to generate sufficient cash flow to repay principal and to pay interest. If there is a default, the lender looks to the proceeds from the sale of the property for repayment and has no recourse to the borrower for any unpaid balance. There are different risks associated with investing in each property type. Later in this chapter an excerpt from an actual CMBS transaction that describes these risks by property type will be presented.

Regardless of the property type, the two measures that have been found to be key indicators of the potential credit performance are the debt-to-service coverage ratio and the loan-to-value ratio.

The **debt-to-service coverage ratio** (DSC ratio) is the ratio of a property's **net operating income** (NOI) divided by the debt service. The NOI is defined as the rental income reduced by cash operating expenses (adjusted for a replacement reserve). A ratio greater than 1 means that the cash flow from the property is sufficient to cover debt servicing. The higher the ratio, the more likely it is that the borrower will be able to meet debt servicing from the property's cash flow.

As explained in Chapter 10, studies of residential mortgage loans have found that the key predictor of default is the **loan-to-value ratio**. For residential mortgage loans, "value" is either market value or appraised value. For income-producing properties, the value of the property is based on the fundamental principles of valuation: the value of an asset is the present value of the expected cash flow. Valuation requires projecting an asset's cash flow and discounting at an appropriate interest rate(s). In valuing commercial property, the cash flow is the future NOI. A discount rate (a single rate), referred to as the "capitalization rate," reflecting the risks associated with the cash flow is then used to compute the present value of the future NOI. Consequently, there can be considerable variation in the estimates of NOI and the appropriate capitalization rate in estimating a property's market value. Thus, analysts are skeptical about estimates of market value and the resulting LTVs reported for properties.

Call Protection

For residential mortgage loans, only prepayment penalty mortgages provide protection against prepayments. For commercial mortgage loans, call protection can take the following forms:

- prepayment lockout
- defeasance
- prepayment penalty points
- yield maintenance charges

Prepayment Lockout

A **prepayment lockout** is a contractual agreement that prohibits any prepayments during a specified period of time, called the **lockout period**. The lockout period can be from 2 to 10 years. After the lockout period, call protection usually comes in the form of either prepayment penalty points or yield maintenance charges. Prepayment lockout and defeasance (discussed next) are the strongest forms of prepayment protection.

Defeasance

With **defeasance**, the borrower provides sufficient funds for the servicer to invest in a portfolio of Treasury securities that replicates the cash flows that would exist in the absence of prepayments.[1] For the reason explained later when we describe CMBS, this form of prepayment protection has become the most popular.

Prepayment Penalty Points

Prepayment penalty points are predetermined penalties that must be paid by the borrower if the borrower wishes to refinance. For example, 5-4-3-2-1 is a common prepayment penalty point structure. That is, if the borrower wishes to prepay during the first year, he must pay a 5% penalty for a total of $105 rather than $100; in the second year, a 4% penalty would apply, and so on.

It has been argued that the prepayment penalty points are not an effective means for discouraging refinancing. However, prepayment penalty points may be superior to yield maintenance charges in a rising rate environment. This is because prepayments do occur when rates rise. With yield maintenance, the penalty will be zero (unless there is a "yield maintenance floor" that imposes a minimum penalty). In contrast, with prepayment penalty points, there will be a penalty even in a rising rate environment.

Yield Maintenance Charge

Yield maintenance charge, in its simplest terms, is designed to make the lender indifferent as to the timing of prepayments. The yield maintenance charge, also called the make whole charge, makes it uneconomical to refinance solely to get a lower mortgage rate. The simplest and most restrictive form of yield maintenance charge ("Treasury flat yield maintenance") penalizes the borrower based on the difference between the mortgage coupon and the prevailing Treasury rate.

---

[1]Defeasance is a method used by municipal bond issuers for prerefunding a bond issue.

There are several methods that have been used in practice to compute the yield maintenance charge. These methods include the simple model, the bullet model, the single discount factor model, the multiple discount factor model, the interest difference model, and the truncated interest difference model.[2] To provide further protection to lenders, there are often yield maintenance floors that impose a minimum charge.

Balloon Maturity Provisions

Commercial mortgage loans are typically balloon loans requiring substantial principal payment at the end of the balloon term. If the borrower fails to make the balloon payment, the borrower is in default. The lender may extend the loan and in so doing will typically modify the original loan terms. During the work-out period for the loan, a higher interest rate will be charged, the **default interest rate**.

The risk that a borrower will not be able to make the balloon payment because either the borrower cannot arrange for refinancing at the balloon payment date or cannot sell the property to generate sufficient funds to pay off the balloon balance is called **balloon risk**. Since the term of the loan will be extended by the lender during the work-out period, balloon risk is also referred to as **extension risk**.

COMMERCIAL MORTGAGE-BACKED SECURITIES

Many types of commercial loans can be sold by the originator as a commercial whole loan or structured into a commercial mortgage-backed security (CMBS) transaction. A **commercial mortgage-backed security** is a security backed by one or more commercial mortgage loans. The whole loan market, which is largely dominated by insurance companies and banks, is focused on loans between $10 and $50 million issued on traditional property types (multifamily, retail, office, and industrial). CMBS transactions, on the other hand, can involve loans of virtually any size (from as small as $1 million to single property transactions as large as $200 million) and/or property type.

As with residential mortgage-backed securities (RMBS), CMBS can be issued by an agency (Ginnie Mae, Fannie Mae, or Freddie Mac) or nonagency. Nonagency CMBS represent the major part of the CMBS market. Our focus in this chapter is on nonagency CMBS.

Differences Between CMBS and Nonagency RMBS Structuring

The structure of a transaction is the same as in a nonagency RMBS in that most structures have multiple bond classes (tranches) with different ratings, and there are rules for the distribution of interest and principal to the bond classes. However, there are three major differences due to the features of the underlying loans.[3]

First, as explained earlier, prepayment terms for commercial mortgages differ significantly from residential mortgages. The former impose prepayment penalties or

---

[2]For a description of these methods, see Da Cheng, Adrian Cooper, and Jason Huang, "Understanding Prepayments in CMBS Deals," Chapter 8 in Frank J. Fabozzi and David Jacob, *The Handbook of Commercial Mortgage-Backed Securities* (Hoboken, NJ: John Wiley & Sons, 1999).

[3]David P. Jacob, James M. Manzi, and Frank J. Fabozzi, "The Impact of Structuring on CMBS Bond Class Performance." Chapter 51 in Frank J. Fabozzi (ed.), *The Handbook of Mortgage-Backed Securities*, 6th ed. (New York: McGraw-Hill, 2006).

restrictions on prepayments. While there are residential mortgages with prepayment penalties, they are a small fraction of the market.[4] In structuring a CMBS, there are rules for the allocation of any prepayment penalties among the bondholders. In addition, if there is a defeasance, the credit risk of a CMBS virtually disappears because it is then backed by U.S. Treasury securities. In fact, it is because investors like the defeasance feature for commercial mortgages used as collateral for a CMBS that defeasance has become the most popular type of prepayment protection.

The second difference in structuring is due to the significant difference between commercial and residential mortgages with respect to the role of the servicer when there is a default. In commercial mortgages, the loan can be transferred by the servicer to the *special* servicer when the borrower is in default, imminent default, or in violation of covenants. The key here is that it is transferred when there is an imminent default. The special servicer has the responsibility of modifying the loan terms in the case of an imminent default to reduce the likelihood of default. There is no equivalent feature for a residential mortgage in the case of an imminent default. The particular choice of action that may be taken by the special servicer in a commercial mortgage will generally have different effects on the various bond classes on a CMBS structure. Moreover, there can be a default due to failure to make the balloon payment at the end of the loan term. There can be differences in loans as to how to deal with defaults due to a failure to meet the balloon payment. Thus, balloon risk must be taken into account in structuring a CMBS transaction, which because of the significant size of the payment, can have a considerable impact on the cash flow of the structure. Balloon risk is not something that has to be dealt with in structuring an RMBS.

The third difference in structuring between CMBS and RMBS has to do with the role of the buyers when the structure is being created. More specifically, typically potential buyers of the junior bond classes are first sought by the issuer before the deal is structured. The potential buyers first review the proposed pool of mortgage loans and in the review process may, depending on market demand for CMBS product, request the removal of some loans from the pool. This phase in the structuring process, which one does not find in RMBS transactions, provides an additional layer of security for the senior buyers, particularly because some of the buyers of the junior classes have tended to be knowledgeable real estate investors.

Structural Features of a CMBS Transaction

To understand the features of a CMBS transaction, let's look at an actual deal. Exhibit 13-1 shows the Banc of America Commercial Mortgage, Series 2001-1. The deal was issued in June 2001. There are 18 tranches in this deal that were offered to the public.[5] For each tranche, the following are reported in Exhibit 13-1: ratings (original and current as of 11/15/02), the balance of the tranche at the cutoff date ("cutoff balance"), the balance as of 11/15/02 (the "current balance"), the coupon rate, and a description of each tranche.

---

[4]In RMBS with prepayment penalty mortgages, traditionally the penalties paid have been held by the servicer independent of the securitization. A more recent trend is to create a tranche that passes the penalty through to the investor (which may be either a private investor or the servicer). Investors in interest-only securities like them as a hedge.

[5]There were the residual certificates consisting of Class R-I, Class R-II, Class R-III, class R-IIIU, and Class R-IV Certificates.

EXHIBIT 13-1 Banc of America Commercial Mortgage, Series 2001-1 Transaction

	Lead Underwriter: Banc of America	Currency: USD	Deal Type: Fusion	Master Servicer: GMAC	Trustee: Wells Fargo
	Cutoff Balance: $948,131,109	Cutoff Loan Count: 185	Cutoff Date: 6/28/2001		Special Servicer: LENNAR PARTNERS
Loans: 185	**Current:** 98.31%	**30 Days:** 0.22%	**Special:** 1.47%	**DSCR Cutoff:** 1.35	**LTV:** 71.37%
Balance: $936,128,023	**60 Days:** 0.00%	**90+ Days:** 1.47%	**Foreclosed:** 0.00% **Bankruptcy:** 0.00% **REO:** 0.00%	**Current DSCR:** 1.52	**LTV:** 71.37%
Factor: 0.98					

Bond	CUSIP	Original Fitch/S&P/MDY	Current Fitch/S&P/MDY	Cutoff Balance	Current Balance	Factor	Original Credit Support	Current Credit Support	Coupon	Desc.
A-1	05947UBL1	AAA/NA/Aaa	AAA/NA/Aaa	$161,603,149	$149,600,063	0.93	22.01	22.3	6.09	SEN_FIX
A-2	05947UBM9	NA/NA/NA	AAA/NA/Aaa	$527,811,659	$527,811,659	1	22.01	22.3	6.5	SEN_FIX
A-2F	05947UCC0	NA/NA/NA	AAA/NA/Aaa	$50,000,000	$50,000,000	1	22.01	22.3	2.16	SEN_FLT
B	05947UBP2	AA/NA/Aa2	AA/NA/Aa2	$35,576,642	$35,576,642	1	18.26	18.5	6.67	MEZ_FIX
C	05947UBQ0	A+/NA/A1	A+/NA/A1	$21,345,985	$21,345,985	1	16.01	16.22	6.77	MEZ_FIX_CAP
D	05947UBR8	A/NA/A2	A/NA/A2	$18,974,209	$18,974,209	1	14.01	14.19	6.85	MEZ_FIX_CAP
E	05947UBS6	A-/NA/A3	A-/NA/A3	$9,487,105	$9,487,105	1	13.01	13.17	6.97	MEZ_FIX_CAP
F	05947UBT4	BBB+/NA/Baa1	BBB+/NA/Baa1	$18,974,209	$18,974,209	1	12.01	12.16	7.22	MEZ_FIX_CAP
G	05947UBU1	BBB/NA/Baa2	BBB/NA/Baa2	$18,974,209	$18,974,209	1	10.01	10.13	7.32	MEZ FIX CAP
H	05947UBV9	BBB-/NA/Baa3	BBB-/NA/Baa3	$14,230,657	$14,230,657	1	8.51	8.61	7.51	MEZ_FIX_CAP
J	05947UCD8	NA/NA/NA	BB+/NA/Ba1	$13,281,946	$13,281,946	1	7.1	7.2	6.13	JUN_FIX
K	05947UBW7	NA/NA/NA	BB/NA/Ba2	$23,480,584	$23,480,584	1	4.63	4.69	6.13	JUN_FIX
L	05947UBX5	NA/NA/NA	BB-/NA/Ba3	$2,134,598	$2,134,598	1	4.4	4.46	6.13	JUN_FIX
M	05947UBY3	NA/NA/NA	B+/NA/B1	$5,538,842	$5,538,842	1	3.82	3.87	6.13	JUN_FIX
N	05947UBZ0	NA/NA/NA	B/NA/B2	$6,788,329	$6,788,329	1	3.1	3.14	6.13	JUN_FIX
O	05947UCA4	NA/NA/NA	B-/NA/B3	$5,883,218	$5,883,218	1	2.48	2.51	6.13	JUN_FIX
P	05947UCB2	NA/NA/NA	NA/NA/NA	$23,532,872	$23,532,872	1	0	0	6.13	JUN_FIX
X	05947UBN7	AAA/NA/Aaa	AAA/NA/Aaa	$948,131,109	$936,128,024	0.99	0	0	1.09	SEN_FLT_IO

Information as of: 11/15/2002

Source: RealPoint.

The tranches were rated by all three rating agencies. By looking at the original and current ratings, it can be seen that no tranche was downgraded by any of the rating agencies subsequent to issuance.

The tranches are classified as senior (SEN), mezzanine (MEZ), and junior (JUN). The senior certificates include Class A-1, Class A-2, Class A-2F, and Class X. All but one senior tranche and the interest-only tranche have a fixed coupon rate. For the one tranche that has a floating rate, Class A-2F, the coupon reset formula is LIBOR plus 36 basis points. Since all of the commercial mortgage loans backing this deal have a fixed rate, this means that there is a mismatch between the interest obligation for Class A-2F and the interest obligation from the collateral. This is dealt with in this deal by using an interest rate swap, a derivative instrument that we will discuss in Chapter 28.[6]

As of 11/15/02 only Class A-1 has paid down. The factor of 0.93 means that 93% of the original principal was paid down. Look also at Class X, which is the interest-only tranche. More specifically, it is a structured IO as described in Chapter 12. The notional amount for this senior tranche is based on all of the senior bonds outstanding. Since Class A-1 has paid down a part of the principal, the effect on Class X was to reduce the notional amount to 99% of the original notional amount. Hence, 0.99 is shown as the factor.

The principal and interest payments are distributed in descending order as follows:

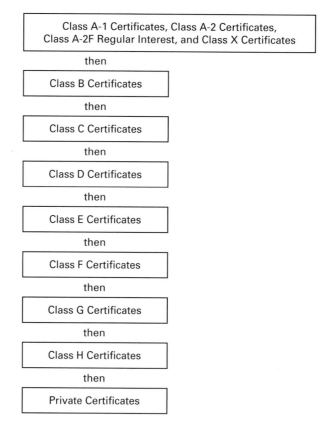

---

[6]In Chapter 15, when we discuss collateralized debt obligations, we will see how an interest-rate swap is used in a structured product.

Exhibit 13-2 provides more specific information about the distributions of interest and principal from the supplementary prospectus.

When there are mortgage loan losses, they are allocated in ascending order to the bond classes. Because Class X is an interest-only security, no principal payments or loan losses are allocated to that class. However, the notional amount for Class X is reduced by principal payments or loan losses.

EXHIBIT 13-2   Order of Priority for Distributions of Interest and Principal for Banc of America Commercial Mortgages, Series 2001-1 from Prospectus

On each Distribution Date, the Trustee will apply the Available Distribution Amount for such date for the following purposes and in the following order of priority:

A. Amount and Order of Distributions

First, Class A-1, Class A-2, Class A-2F Regular Interest and Class X: To interest on Class A-1, Class A-2, Class A-2F Regular Interest and Class X, pro rata, in accordance with their interest entitlements.

Second, Class A-1, Class A-2 and Class A-2F Regular Interest: To the extent of funds available for principal, sequentially on Class A-1, then pro rata to Class A-2 and Class A-2F Regular Interest, until each class is reduced to zero.

Third, Class A-1, Class A-2 and Class A-2F Regular Interest: To reimburse Class A-1, Class A-2, and Class A-2F Regular Interest pro rata, for any previously unreimbursed losses on the mortgage loans allocable to principal that were previously borne by those classes.

Fourth, Class B: To Class B as follows: (a) to interest on Class B in the amount of its interest entitlement; (b) to the extent of funds available for principal, to principal on Class B until reduced to zero; and (c) to reimburse Class B for any previously unreimbursed losses on the mortgage loans allocable to principal that were previously borne by that class.

Fifth, Class C: To Class C in a manner analogous to the Class B allocations of the fourth step.

Sixth, Class D: To Class D in a manner analogous to the Class B allocations of the fourth step.

Seventh, Class E: To Class E in a manner analogous to the Class B allocations of the fourth step.

Eighth: Class F: To Class F in a manner analogous to the Class B allocations of the fourth step.

Ninth: Class G: To Class G in a manner analogous to the Class B allocations of the fourth step.

Tenth: Class H: To Class H in a manner analogous to the Class B allocations of the fourth step.

Finally, Private Certificates: In the amounts and order of priority provided for in the Pooling Agreement.

The distributions referred to in priority Second above, will be made pro rata among the Class A-1 Certificates, Class A-2 Certificates and Class A-2F Regular Interest when the Certificate Balances of the Subordinate Certificates have been reduced to zero and in any event on the final Distribution Date as described.

Source: Supplementary Prospectus, p. S-16.

The credit enhancements that were described for nonagency RMBS in the previous chapter can be used in CMBS structures. Typically, the primary form of credit support is the senior-subordinated structure such as in the Banc of America Commercial Mortgage, Series 2001-1 deal. The credit support provided at the time of issuance and as of 11/15/02 is shown in the exhibit.

Prepayment Protection and Distributions of Prepayment Premiums

In a CMBS structure, there are two levels of prepayment protection. The first is at the loan level. As described earlier, there are various forms of prepayment protection provided (lockouts, prepayment penalty points, yield maintenance, and defeasance). The second is at the structure level. For example, the senior tranches can be structured to pay off sequentially as described in Chapter 12 in a CMO structure.

For the Banc of America Commercial Mortgage, Series 2001-1 deal, the prepayment protection was described in the prospectus supplement as follows:

- approximately 80.2% of the initial loan pool balance generally permits defeasance only, and prohibits any voluntary principal prepayment until two to seven months prior to the maturity date of the mortgage loans
- one mortgage loan equal to 0.8% of the initial pool balance permits defeasance after the expiration of an initial lockout period, then permits voluntary principal prepayment
- for approximately 19.0% of the initial loan balance, voluntary principal prepayments are permitted during certain periods. Any such prepayments are subject to a prepayment penalty

Exhibit 13-3 provides information on prepayments in tabular form as set forth in the prospectus supplement.

When a defeasance takes place, there is no distribution made to the bondholders. Since there are no penalties or charges, there is no issue as to how any penalties paid by the borrower are to be distributed among the bondholders in a CMBS structure. When there are prepayment penalty points, there are rules for distributing the penalty among the CMBS bondholders. In the case of loans with a yield maintenance provision, several methods are used in practice for distributing the yield maintenance charge and, depending on the method specified in a deal, not all bondholders in a CMBS may be made whole. These methods include the principal allocation method, base interest method, bond yield maintenance method, and present value yield loss method.[7] Prepayment penalties and yield maintenance charges are referred to as **prepayment premiums**. Exhibit 13-4 provides an excerpt from the supplementary prospectus for the Banc of America Commercial Mortgage, Series 2001-1 deal explaining the rules for distributions of prepayment premiums. The interest base method is used.

It is because of the substantial prepayment protection at the loan and structure level that a CMBS is not viewed in the market in the same way as a nonagency RMBS. Rather, CMBS trades in the market like a corporate bond rather than a nonagency RMBS.

---

[7]For a description of these methods, see Cheng, Cooper, and Huang, "Understanding Prepayments in CMBS Deals."

EXHIBIT 13-3   Payment Lockout/Prepayment Analysis Based on Outstanding Principal Balance All Mortgage Loans: Banc of America Commercial Mortgage, Series 2001–1 Transaction

	June 2001	June 2002	June 2003	June 2004	June 2005	June 2006	June 2007
Locked Out	99.79%	99.80%	98.21%	95.08%	84.29%	81.12%	81.10%
Yield Maintenance	0.00%	0.00%	1.61%	4.70%	14.11%	17.44%	17.25%
5%	0.00%	0.00%	0.00%	0.00%	1.39%	0.00%	0.00%
4%	0.00%	0.00%	0.00%	0.00%	0.00%	1.39%	0.00%
3%	0.00%	0.00%	0.00%	0.00%	0.00%	0.00%	1.39%
2%	0.00%	0.00%	0.00%	0.00%	0.00%	0.00%	0.00%
1%	0.21%	0.20%	0.19%	0.22%	0.20%	0.04%	0.04%
No Penalty	0.00%	0.00%	0.00%	0.00%	0.00%	0.00%	0.21%
Total	100.00%	100.00%	100.00%	100.00%	100.00%	100.00%	100.00%
Total Beginning Balance (in millions)	$948.13	$939.70	$930.50	$919.92	$907.96	$894.81	$879.47
Percent of Initial Balance 100.00%	99.11%	98.14%	97.02%	95.76%	94.38%	92.76%	

	June 2008	June 2009	June 2010	June 2011	June 2012	June 2013	June 2014
Locked Out	81.12%	79.28%	74.00%	38.37%	62.30%	57.40%	48.92%
Yield Maintenance	17.45%	17.94%	13.69%	20.22%	37.70%	42.60%	51.08%
5%	0.00%	0.00%	0.00%	0.00%	0.00%	0.00%	0.00%
4%	0.00%	0.00%	0.00%	0.00%	0.00%	0.00%	0.00%
3%	0.00%	0.00%	0.00%	0.00%	0.00%	0.00%	0.00%
2%	1.39%	0.00%	0.00%	0.00%	0.00%	0.00%	0.00%
1%	0.04%	1.46%	0.00%	0.00%	0.00%	0.00%	0.00%
No Penalty	0.00%	1.33%	12.32%	41.41%	0.00%	0.00%	0.00%
Total	100.00%	100.00%	100.00%	100.00%	100.00%	100.00%	100.00%
Total Beginning Balance (in millions)	$859.75	$800.98	$706.15	$3.86	$1.94	$1.59	$1.21
Percent of Initial Balance	90.68%	84.48%	74.48%	0.41%	0.20%	0.17%	0.13%

	June 2015
Locked Out	30.64%
Yield Maintenance	69.36%
5%	0.00%
4%	0.00%
3%	0.00%
2%	0.00%
1%	0.00%
No Penalty	0.00%
Total	100.00%
Total Beginning Balance (in millions)	$0.79
Percent of Initial Balance	0.08%

Source: Supplementary Prospectus.

EXHIBIT 13-4 Distributions of Prepayment Premiums for Banc of America Commercial Mortgage, Series 2001-1 from Supplementary Prospectus

On any Distribution Date, Prepayment Premiums collected during the related Collection Period are required to be distributed to the holders of the Classes of Offered Certificates (other than the Class A-2F Certificates) and the Class A-2F Regular Interest as described below.

On each Distribution Date, Prepayment Premiums collected on the Mortgage Loans during the related Prepayment Period will be distributed by the Trustee to the following Classes: to the Class A-1, Class A-2, Class B, Class C, Class D, Class E, Class F, Class G and Class H Certificates and the Class A-2F Regular.

Interest, in an amount equal to the product of (a) a fraction, not greater than 1, whose numerator is the amount distributed as principal to such Class on such Distribution Date, and whose denominator is the total amount distributed as principal to the Class A-1, Class A-2, Class B, Class C, Class D, Class E, Class F, Class G, Class H, Class J, Class K, Class L, Class M, Class N, Class O and Class P Certificates and the Class A-2F Regular Interest on such Distribution Date, (b) the Base Interest Fraction for the related principal payment on such Class of Certificates, and (c) the aggregate amount of Prepayment Premiums collected on such principal prepayments during the related Prepayment Period. In connection with the Class A-2F Regular Interest, so long as the Swap Contract is in effect, any Prepayment Premium distributable in respect of the Class A-2F Regular Interest will be payable to the Swap Counterparty pursuant to the terms of the Swap Contract. If the Swap Contract is no longer in effect, any Prepayment Premium paid to the Class A-2F Regular Interest will be paid to the holders of the Class A-2F Certificates. Any Prepayment Premiums collected during the related Prepayment Period remaining after such distributions will be distributed to the holders of the Class X Certificates.

The "Base Interest Fraction" with respect to any principal prepayment on any Mortgage Loan and with respect to any class of Offered Certificates (other than the Class A-2F Certificates) and the Class A-2F Regular Interest is a fraction (a) whose numerator is the amount, if any, by which (i) the Pass-Through Rate on such Class of Certificates exceeds (ii) the discount rate used in accordance with the related Mortgage Loan documents in calculating the Prepayment Premium with respect to such Principal Prepayment and (b) whose denominator is the amount, if any, by which (i) the Mortgage Rate on such Mortgage Loan exceeds (ii) the discount rate used in accordance with the related Mortgage Loan documents in calculating the yield maintenance charge with respect to such principal prepayment. However, under no circumstances shall the Base Interest Fraction be greater than one. If such discount rate is greater than or equal to the lesser of (x) the Mortgage Rate on such Mortgage Loan and (y) the Pass-Through Rate described in the preceding sentence, then the Base Interest Fraction will equal zero.

Source: Supplementary Prospectus, pp. S-82–S-83.

Balloon Risk in CMBS Deals

As explained earlier, commercial mortgage loans have a balloon maturity provision. Balloon risk, or extension risk, is the risk that the borrower will fail to refinance to meet the balloon payment. Therefore, CMBS with senior-subordinated structures face the risk that all loans must be refinanced to pay off the most senior bondholders. Therefore, the balloon risk of the most senior tranche may be equivalent to that of the most junior bond class in the deal.

There are two types of structural provisions that can be present in CMBS transactions to mitigate balloon risk: internal tail and external tail. The **internal tail** requires the borrower to document efforts to refinance the loan within one year of the balloon maturity date. Within six months prior to the balloon maturity date, the borrower must obtain a refinancing commitment. With an **external tail**, the maturity date for the CMBS issue is set to be longer than the balloon payment for the pool of commercial mortgage loans. Since this gives the borrower the time to arrange refinancing while avoiding default on the bond obligations, it is the method preferred by rating agencies.

For the Banc of America Commercial Mortgage, Series 2001-1, 187 of the commercial mortgage loans (93.5% of the initial pool balance) have balloon payments due at their maturity (assuming that they are not prepaid). At the time of issuance, 183 of the loans (86.6% of the initial pool balance) had balloon payments that were due during the period from April 2010 through April 2011.

Types of Deals

The two major classifications for CMBS deals are single borrower/multi-property deals and multi-property conduit deals.

Single Borrower/Multi-Property Deals

As the name suggests, in a single borrower/ multi-property deal there is one borrower and multiple properties. Three key structural features in such deals are the cross-collateralization feature, cross-default feature, and property release provisions.

The **cross-collateralization feature** is a mechanism whereby the properties that collateralize the individual loans in the mortgage pool are pledged against each loan. The **cross-default feature** permits the lender to call each loan within the mortgage pool when any one property defaults. By including these two features, the principal and interest payments of all the properties are available to meet the obligations of all the loans. As a result, a shortfall on an individual loan would not make it delinquent if the principal and interest payments from other loans in the mortgage pool are not less than the amount of the shortfall.[8]

Because there is a single borrower, there is concern that the borrower can benefit by removing the best properties from the mortgage pool by prepaying the balance and selling those properties. This action would result in a deterioration of the structural protection afforded the bondholders. The objective of **property release provisions** is to protect the investor against such an action by the borrower. Two examples of a property release provision are (1) a requirement that if any property is sold, the borrower must retire more than the initial mortgage balance in the pool (say, 125%) and (2) a sale may not take place if the DSC ratios after a proposed sale are less than prior to the sale.

---

[8]For an illustration of the importance of these two features, see Frank J. Fabozzi and John N. Dunlevy, *Real Estate-Backed Securities* (Hoboken, NJ: John Wiley & Sons, 2001), pp. 139–140.

Multi-Borrower Deals

The second type of deal is one that involves loans by conduits. Conduits are commercial-lending entities that are established for the sole purpose of generating collateral to securitize, and the CMBS transactions that result are called **conduit deals**. The rating agencies refer to conduit transactions as **multi-borrower deals**. The Banc of America Commercial Mortgage, Series 2001-1 deal is a conduit or multi-borrower deal. When a conduit deal contains one large property for more than $50 million and then smaller loans, it is referred to as a **fusion conduit deal**. The deal that we have been discussing is a fusion conduit deal because the first property listed in the exhibit has a loan balance greater than $50 million.

In a conduit there can be more than one originator. In the deal we have been discussing, 110 of the 185 loans were originated by either Banc of America (or its conduit participants) or were acquired by Banc of America from various third-party originators (generally comprised of commercial banks or affiliates of commercial banks). The mortgage loans originated by Banc of America constituted about 74.5% of the initial mortgage pool.

Services

As with a nonagency RMBS, a servicer is required and plays an important role. The responsibilities of the servicer include collecting monthly loan payments, keeping records relating to payments, maintaining property escrow for taxes and insurance, monitoring the condition of underlying properties, preparing reports for the trustee, and transferring collected funds to the trustee for payment to bondholders.

Depending on the transaction, there are several types of servicers. The three most common in CMBS transactions are the sub-servicer, the master servicer, and the special servicer. The **sub-servicer** collects all payments and gathers property information, which is then sent to the master servicer. The **master servicer** is responsible for (1) overseeing the deal, (2) verifying that all servicing agreements are being maintained, and (3) facilitating the timely payment of interest and principal. This last function is critical for a CMBS transaction. If a loan is in default, it is the master servicer that must provide for servicing advances. To fulfill this role, the master servicer must have the financial capacity to provide advances. The master servicer in the Banc of America Commercial Mortgage, Series 2001-1 deal is GMAC Commercial Mortgage Corporation.

The duties of a **special servicer** arise only when a loan becomes more than 60 days past due. Typically, the special servicer has the authority to (1) extend the loan, (2) make loan modifications, (3) restructure the loan, or (4) foreclose on the loan and sell the property. Lennar Partners, Inc., is the special servicer for the Banc of America Commercial Mortgage, Series 2001-1 deal.

Analysis of the Collateral

Because of the non-recourse nature of commercial mortgage loans, CMBS investors must view each property as a stand-alone business and evaluate each property using the measures discussed earlier (DSC and LTV ratios). While there are fundamental principles of assessing credit risk that apply to all property types, traditional approaches to assessing the credit risk of the collateral differ for CMBS than for nonagency RMBS. For nonagency RMBS, the loans typically are lumped into buckets based on certain loan characteristics, and assumptions regarding default rates and

Property Name	Prop. Type	City	State	Zip Code	Cutoff Balance	Current Balance	% of Deal	Maturity Date	Coupon	Loan Status
315 Park Avenue	OF	New York	NY	10010	$87,200,000	$87,200,000	9.31	4/1/2011	6.70%	C
701 Gateway Office Building	OF	South San Francisco	CA	94080	$33,952,359	$33,519,899	3.58	4/1/2011	7.14%	C
One Lake Park Office Building	OF	Richardson	TX	75080	$25,523,893	$25,223,645	2.69	2/1/2011	7.55%	C
PCS Holdings Corp Office Building	OF	Scottsdale	AZ	85260	$24,573,859	$24,138,495	2.57	1/1/2011	8.00%	C
RCA—Royal St. Moritz Apartments	MF	Grapevine	TX	76051	$20,800,000	$20,800,000	2.22	4/1/2011	7.06%	C
Talley Plaza	OF	Phoenix	AZ	85008	$17,945,954	$17,732,303	1.89	2/1/2011	7.50%	C
Historic Mission Inn	HT	Riverside	CA	92501	$17,912,607	$17,611,823	1.88	1/1/2011	8.29%	C
Northwest—Hidden Valley	OF	Bellevue	WA	98004	$16,490,787	$16,293,071	1.74	5/1/2011	7.36%	C
Keswick Village Apartments	MF	Conyers	GA	30013	$15,900,000	$15,900,000	1.69	4/1/2011	6.88%	C
Calverton Office Building #5	OF	Beltsville	MD	20705	$15,972,832	$15,796,224	1.68	3/1/2011	7.75%	C
Waretech Industrial Park	IN	Grand Blanc	MI	48439	$15,642,813	$15,476,135	1.65	12/1/2010	8.00%	C
Freeport Office Center IV	OF	Irving	TX	75063	$14,854,242	$14,567,244	1.55	5/1/2010	7.42%	C
Ballantyne Commons East	RT	Charlotte	NC	28277	$14,552,572	$14,326,955	1.53	2/1/2010	6.69%	C
Macrott Courtyard—Embassy Row	HT	Washington	DC	20036	$13,324,256	$13,117,968	1.4	1/1/2010	9.20%	C
Eagle One Distribution Warehouse	IN	Atlanta	GA	30336	$12,891,152	$12,651,603	1.35	4/1/2011	7.60%	C
Porest Park Apartments	MF	Forest Park	OH	45240	$12,461,491	$12,308,477	1.31	2/1/2011	7.37%	C
RCA—Regency Arms	MF	Houston	TX	77057	$11,080,000	$11,080,000	1.18	4/1/2011	7.06%	C
Colonial Pines Apartments	MF	Lindenwold	NJ	8021	$11,059,635	$11,059,635	1.18	10/1/2010	8.33%	C
Eagle Two Distribution Warehouse	IN	Atlanta	GA	30336	$11,202,104	$10,993,942	1.17	4/1/2011	7.60%	C
Columbia Apartment Portfolio (Roll-Up)	MF	Columbia	MO		$11,061,025	$10,930,156	1.16	1/1/2011	7.55%	C
Lake Jasmine Apartments	MF	Orlando	FL	32839	$10,959,222	$10,821,627	1.15	1/1/2011	7.30%	C
Stealth II	OF	Cecil Township	PA	15317	$10,817,504	$10,630,338	1.13	10/1/2010	8.25%	C
Willows Corporate Center	OF	Redmond	WA	98052	$10,484,382	$10,381,007	1.1	3/1/2011	8.20%	C
Marlboro Village Center	RT	Upper Marlboro	MD	20772	$10,385,641	$10,255,211	1.09	4/1/2011	7.20%	C

prepayment rates are then made regarding each bucket. In contrast, for commercial mortgage loans, the unique economic characteristics of each income-producing property in a pool backing a CMBS deal require that credit analysis be performed on a loan-by-loan basis not only at the time of issuance, but also be monitored on an on-going basis. The starting point in the analysis is an investigation of the underwriting standards of the originators of the loans in the mortgage pool.

Exhibit 13-5 shows 24 of the 185 properties that comprise the collateral for the Banc of America Commercial Mortgage, Series 2001-1 deal. For each property, the following information is shown: property, property type, location (city, state, and zip code), mortgage loan balance (as of cutoff date and as of 11/15/02), percentage of the deal, maturity date, coupon rate (i.e., loan interest rate), and loan status. As of 11/15/02, all but three loans were current, representing 98.3% of the then-mortgage balance for the pool. One of the three loans (0.22% of the mortgage balance for the pool) was 30 days delinquent and two loans (1.47% of the mortgage balance for the pool) were delinquent 90+ days.

Performance Indicators for Properties

For all properties backing a CMBS deal, a weighted-average DSC ratio and a weighted-average LTV is computed. An analysis of the credit quality of a CMBS structure will also look at the dispersion of the DSC and LTV ratios for the underlying loans. For example, one might look at the percentage of a deal with a DSC ratio below a certain value. As can be seen from Exhibit 13-1, the weighted-average DSC ratio was 1.35× at the time of issuance and improved by 11/15/02 to 1.52×. The weighted-average LTV was 71.37% at the time of issuance and was the same on 11/15/02.

Property Types

In analyzing the collateral, the types of income-producing properties are examined. In general, investors prefer deals that are not concentrated in one property type. For the Banc of America Commercial Mortgage, Series 2001-1, the distribution of property type for the initial pool balance is shown in Exhibit 13-6. The risks associated with each property type are identified in the supplementary prospectus. Exhibit 13-7 is an excerpt from the prospectus that describes these risks for each property type in Banc of America Commercial Mortgage, Series 2001-1 deal.

Geographical Distribution of Properties

Investors are also interested in the geographical dispersion of the properties. The concern is that if the properties are concentrated in one geographical region, investors would be exposed to economic downturns that may be unique to that geographical region. Exhibit 13-5 lists the geographical location of each property for the Banc of America Commercial Mortgage, Series 2001-1 deal. A summary of the geographical locations included in the supplementary prospectus is provided in Exhibit 13-8.

Stress Testing Structures

As noted earlier in this chapter, an analysis of the credit quality of the tranches in a CMBS involves looking at the commercial loans on a loan-by-loan basis. Rating agencies and analysts will then stress test the structure with respect to a combination of default and prepayment assumptions.

EXHIBIT 13-6 Distribution of Property Type for Banc of America
Commercial Mortgage, Series 2001-1

Property Type	Initial Pool Balance (%)
Multifamily	30.2
Retail	9.9*
Industrial	13.0
Office	36.3
Self-storage	3.1
Hotel	4.2
Mobile Home	3.4

*Breakdown for Retail: Unanchored, 3.1%; Shadow Anchored, 0.5%;
and Anchored, 6.3%

Source: Supplementary Prospectus, p. S-6.

EXHIBIT 13-7 Description of Risks by Property Type in the Prospectus for Banc of
America Commercial Mortgage, Series 2001-1

Risks Particular to Multifamily Properties

Multifamily properties secure 64 of the Mortgage Loans, representing 30.2% of the
Initial Pool Balance.

Several factors may adversely affect the value and successful operation of a multifamily
property, including:

- the physical attributes of the apartment building (e.g., its age, appearance and
  construction quality);
- the location of the property (e.g., a change in the neighborhood over time);
- the ability and willingness of management to provide adequate maintenance and
  insurance;
- the types of services or amenities the property provides;
- the property's reputation;
- the level of mortgage interest rates (which may encourage tenants to purchase
  rather than lease housing);
- the tenant mix, such as the tenant population being predominantly students or
  being heavily dependent on workers from a particular business or personnel from
  a local military base;
- the presence of competing properties;
- adverse local or national economic conditions which may limit the amount of rent
  that may be charged and may result in a reduction of timely rent payments or a
  reduction in occupancy levels; and
- state and local regulations which may affect the building owner's ability to increase
  rent to market rent for an equivalent apartment.

(continued)

EXHIBIT 13-7   (continued)

Risks Particular to Mobile Home Properties

Mobile home properties secure 15 of the Mortgage Loans representing 3.4% of the Initial Pool Balance. Significant factors determining the value of such properties are generally similar to the factors affecting the value of multifamily residential properties. In addition, these properties are special purpose properties that could not be readily converted to general residential, retail or office use. In fact, certain states also regulate changes in mobile home park use and require that the landlord give written notice to its tenants a substantial period of time prior to the projected change. Consequently, if the operation of any of such properties becomes unprofitable such that the borrower becomes unable to meet its obligation on the related Mortgage Loan, the liquidation value of the related property may be substantially less, relative to the amount owing on the Mortgage Loan, than would be the case if such properties were readily adaptable to other uses.

Risks Particular to Retail Properties

Retail properties secure 30 of the Mortgage Loans, representing 9.9% of the Initial Pool Balance.

Several factors may adversely affect the value and successful operation of a retail property, including:

- changes in consumer spending patterns, local competitive conditions (such as the supply of retail space or the existence or construction of new competitive shopping centers or shopping malls);
- alternative forms of retailing (such as direct mail, video shopping networks and internet web sites which reduce the need for retail space by retail companies);
- the quality and philosophy of management;
- the safety, convenience and attractiveness of the property to tenants and their customers or clients;
- the public perception of the safety of customers at shopping malls and shopping centers;
- the need to make major repairs or improvements to satisfy the needs of major tenants; and
- traffic patterns and access to major thoroughfares.

The general strength of retail sales also directly affects retail properties. The retailing industry is currently undergoing consolidation due to many factors, including growth in discount and alternative forms of retailing. If the sales by tenants in the Mortgaged Properties that contain retail space were to decline, the rents that are based on a percentage of revenues may also decline, and tenants may be unable to pay the fixed portion of their rents or other occupancy costs. The cessation of business by a significant tenant can adversely affect a retail property, not only because of rent and other factors specific to such tenant, but also because significant tenants at a retail property play an important part in generating customer traffic and making a retail property a desirable location for other tenants at such property. In addition, certain tenants at retail properties may be entitled to terminate their leases if an anchor tenant fails to renew or terminates its lease, becomes the subject of a bankruptcy proceeding or ceases operations at such property.

EXHIBIT 13-7   (continued)

Risks Particular to Office Properties

Office properties secure 36 of the Mortgage Loans, representing approximately 36.3% of the Initial Pool Balance.

A large number of factors may adversely affect the value of office properties, including:

- the number and quality of an office building's tenants;
- the physical attributes of the building in relation to competing buildings (e.g., age, condition, design, access to transportation and ability to offer certain amenities, such as sophisticated building systems);
- the desirability of the area as a business location; and
- the strength and nature of the local economy (including labor costs and quality, tax environment and quality of life for employees).

In addition, there may be significant costs associated with tenant improvements, leasing commissions and concessions in connection with reletting office space. Moreover, the cost of refitting office space for a new tenant is often higher than the cost of refitting other types of property.

Risks Particular to Industrial Properties

Industrial Properties secure 27 of the Mortgage Loans representing 13.0% of the Initial Pool Balance.

Significant factors determining the value of industrial properties include:

- the quality of tenants;
- building design and adaptability (e.g., clear heights, column spacing, zoning restrictions, number of bays and bay depths, divisibility and truck turning radius); and
- the location of the property (e.g., proximity to supply sources and customers, availability of labor and accessibility to distribution channels).

In addition, industrial properties may be adversely affected by reduced demand for industrial space occasioned by a decline in a particular industrial space occasioned by a decline in a particular industry segment, and a particular industrial property may be difficult to release to another tenant or may become functionally obsolete relative to newer properties.

Risks Particular to Hotels

Properties operated as hotels secure 3 of the Mortgage Loans, representing approximately 4.2% of the Initial Pool Balance.

Various factors may adversely affect the economic performance of a hotel, including:

- adverse economic and social conditions, either local, regional or national (which may limit the amount that can be charged for a room and reduce occupancy levels);
- the construction of competing hotels or resorts;
- continuing expenditures for modernizing, refurbishing, and maintaining existing facilities prior to the expiration of their anticipated useful lives;
- a deterioration in the financial strength or managerial capabilities of the owner and operator of a hotel; and
- changes in travel patterns caused by changes in access, energy prices, strikes, relocation of highways, the construction of additional highways or other factors.

(continued)

EXHIBIT 13-7 (continued)

Because hotel rooms generally are rented for short periods of time, the financial performance of hotels tends to be affected by adverse economic conditions and competition more quickly than other commercial properties. Moreover, the hotel and lodging industry is generally seasonal in nature and different seasons affect different hotels depending on type and location. This seasonality can be expected to cause periodic fluctuations in a hotel property's room and restaurant revenues, occupancy levels, room rates and operating expenses. In addition, the franchise license may be owned by an entity operating the hotel and not the borrower or, if the franchise license is owned by the borrower, the transferability of the related franchise license agreement may be restricted and, in the event of a foreclosure on a hotel property, the mortgagee may not have the right to use the franchise license without the franchisor's consent. Furthermore, the ability of a hotel to attract customers, and some of such hotel's revenues, may depend in large part on its having a liquor license. Such a license may not be transferable, and there can be no assurance that a new license could be obtained promptly or at all.

Risks Particular to Self-Storage Properties

Self-storage properties secure 11 of the mortgage loans, representing approximately 3.1% of the aggregate principal balance of the pool of mortgage loans as of the Cut-off Date. Self-storage properties are considered vulnerable to competition, because both acquisition costs and break-even occupancy are relatively low. The conversion of self-storage facilities to alternative uses would generally require substantial capital expenditures. Thus, if the operation of any of the self-storage mortgaged properties becomes unprofitable due to

- decreased demand;
- competition;
- age of improvements; or
- other factors so that the borrower becomes unable to meet its obligations on the related mortgage loan, the liquidation value of that self-storage mortgaged property may be substantially less, relative to the amount owing on the mortgage loan, than if the self-storage mortgaged property were readily adaptable to other uses.

Tenant privacy, anonymity and efficient access may heighten environmental risks. No environmental assessment of a mortgaged property included an inspection of the contents of the self-storage units included in the self-storage mortgaged properties and there is no assurance that all of the units included in the self-storage mortgaged properties are free from hazardous substances or other pollutants or contaminants or will remain so in the future.

Source: Supplementary Prospectus, pp. S-27–S-30.

In stress testing default risk, the following three key assumptions are made. The first is the annual rate of defaults as measured by the conditional default rate (CDR). The benchmark CDRs typically used by rating agencies and analysts are those based on the default experience of commercial loans in the 1970s and 1980s. For example, it is

EXHIBIT 13-8	Geographical Dispersion of the Properties in Banc of America Commercial Mortgage, Series 2001-1

Property Location	No. of Mortgaged Properties	Aggregate Balance	% of Initial Pool Balance
CA	41	$166,661,508	17.6%
TX	16	110,975,773	11.7
NY	7	104,003,232	11.0
WA	10	62,029,810	6.5
GA	8	56,493,903	6.0
MD	6	56,072,939	5.9
AZ	7	51,603,989	5.4
FL	16	40,674,151	4.3
OH	10	34,491,197	3.6
NJ	4	30,736,272	3.2
SC	5	8,977,385	0.9
OR	5	24,043,667	2.5
PA	7	23,168,537	2.4
MI	3	18,215,181	1.9
MO	4	16,591,537	1.7
MS	2	14,982,232	1.6
NC	1	14,552,572	1.5
DC	1	13,324,256	1.4
NV	4	13,268,807	1.4
LA	2	12,029,769	1.3
IL	4	12,499,947	1.3
IN	6	9,980,475	1.1
DE	1	7,366,340	0.8
HI	1	5,977,522	0.6
OK	1	5,579,602	0.6
AL	2	5,005,363	0.5
TN	3	5,137,918	0.5
UT	2	4,334,133	0.5
VA	1	2,387,786	0.3
MA	1	4,183,415	0.4
CO	4	2,593,061	0.3
IA	1	2,577,382	0.3
ID	3	2,509,507	0.3
WV	2	3,315,253	0.3
KS	1	1,786,686	0.2

Source: Supplementary Prospectus, p. 2.

not uncommon for analysts to assume a CDR of 2% to stress test strong deals and 3% to test weaker deals.[9] However, Patrick Corcoran and Joshua Phillips have argued that, for a variety of reasons, the default experience of the 1970s and 1980s is inappropriate for stress testing default risk in today's CMBS market. They believe that "the modern CMBS market has benefited primarily from the tougher oversight and discipline provided by the public markets, and highlighted by rating agency leadership."[10] Specifically, there is much stronger cash coverage in deals today and reduced property cash flows.

A second important assumption is the timing of the defaults. A default can occur sometime early in the term of the loan or at the balloon date (when refinancing is required). The earlier defaults occur, the more adverse the impact will be on the performance of the deal. A third important assumption is the percentage of the loan balance that will be lost when a default occurs. This measure is called the loss severity.

To illustrate the importance of the assumptions on stress testing, Corcoran and Phillips used three stress test scenarios for a representative conduit deal to assess the impact on each bond class. Exhibit 13-9 shows the bond classes in the structure. The loans are 10-year balloon loans with a 30-year amortization. For each scenario, the loss severity assumed was 33% and no voluntary prepayments were assumed (i.e, a CPR of zero is assumed).

EXHIBIT 13-9 Scenario Bond Spreads			
	Base Case: Default Scenarios		
Bond Classes	0 CDR 0 CPR	2 CDR 0 CPR	Model Defaults 0 CPR	Balloon Default Scenario 0 CPR
AAA-5 yr	98	93	97	98
AAA-10 yr	123	123	123	123
AA	137	137	137	137
A	160	160	160	160
BBB	195	195	195	195
BBB-	275	275	275	271
BB	575	575	575	556
B/B-	725	22	443	420
B-	950	−1585	−406	−220
UR	1706	−2921	−16	689
X	450	127	369	475

Source: Table 2 in Patrick Corcoran and Joshua Phillips, "Stress and Defaults in CMBS Deals: Theory and Evidence," *JP Morgan Credit Research* (June 18, 1999), p. 5.

---

[9]See Patrick Corcoran and Joshua Phillips, "Stress and Defaults in CMBS Deals: Theory and Evidence," *JP Morgan Credit Research* (June 18, 1999), p. 1.

[10]Corcoran and Phillips, "Stress and Defaults in CMBS Deals: Theory and Evidence," p. 1.

The three stress test scenarios that they analyzed are:

Scenario 1 (2% CDR Scenario): A 2% CDR per year. (For the 10-year loan pool with a 30-year amortization schedule, this means cumulative defaults over the 10-year loan of 16.7%.)

Scenario 2 (Model Default Scenario): Annual default rates over 10 years based on a model developed by Corcoran and Kao.[11] The default model produces a cumulative default rate for 10 years of 14%. However, the pattern of defaults is such that there is a delay or backloading of defaults. This scenario does not allow for the stronger DSC ratios that exist in today's CMBS market compared to those of the 1970s and 1980s.

Scenario 3 (Balloon Default Scenario): Default rates from the Corcoran–Kao model are used as in Scenario 1, producing a cumulative default rate for 10 years of 14%. However, the defaults are assumed to occur at the 10-year balloon date. Effectively, this scenario does allow for the stronger DSC ratios in today's CMBS market compared to the 1970s and 1980s.

Exhibit 13-9 shows the results of the analysis on the spread. The spread reported is a "credit-adjusted spread." This is a spread measure based on cash flows adjusted for the assumed defaults for the scenario. The second column shows the base case results—a CDR of zero. The next three columns show the results of the 2% CDR scenario, model default scenario, and balloon default scenario. As can be seen, for the B-rated tranche, the credit-adjusted spread is small in the 2% CDR scenario but roughly the same in the other two scenarios. However, even though positive in those scenarios, the spread is less than for the BB tranche. For the BBB and higher rated tranches, the credit-adjusted spreads are equal; for the BB tranche the balloon default scenario shows a slightly lower credit-adjusted spread compared to the other two scenarios.

While the scenarios used in the Corcoran–Phillips illustration test solely for defaults, a more complete analysis recognizes that prepayments must be considered and that there is an interaction between default rates and prepayment rates linked by changes in interest rates. In stress testing, it is important to take both defaults and prepayments not due to default into account. For example, Michael Ervolini, Harold Haig, and Michael Megliola have demonstrated how credit-driven prepayment and default analysis can be used for stress testing.[12]

The model that they present specifies conditions for prepayments and for defaults. Prepayments occur when permitted and when it will result in net proceeds to the borrower (after adjusting for any prepayment penalties). So, assessing prepayments requires modeling how the yield curve will change over the investment horizon. The conditions for default occur when NOI is insufficient to meet debt service. This is modeled to assess the default possibility for each loan rather than an assumed constant CDR. Assumptions regarding when the defaults will occur and the severity of loss must be made. In addition, the refinanceability of each property is modeled.

---

[11]Patrick Corcoran and Duen-Li Kao, "Assessing Credit Risk of CMBS," Chapter 13 in Fabozzi and Jacob, *The Handbook of Commercial Mortgage-Backed Securities*.
[12]See Michael A. Ervolini, Harold J. A. Haig, and Michael Megliola, "Credit-Driven Prepayment and Default Analysis," Chapter 14 in Fabozzi and Jacob, *The Handbook of Commercial Mortgage-Backed Securities*.

SUMMARY

Commercial mortgage loans are for income-producing properties. Unlike residential mortgage loans where the lender relies on the ability of the borrower to repay and has recourse to the borrower if the payment terms are not satisfied, commercial mortgage loans are non-recourse loans. Consequently, the lender looks only to the property to generate sufficient cash flow to repay principal and to pay interest and, if there is a default, the lender looks to the proceeds from the sale of the property for repayment.

Two measures that have been found to be important measures of potential credit performance for a commercial mortgage loan are the debt-to-service coverage ratio and the loan-to-value ratio. For commercial mortgage loans, call protection can take the following forms: prepayment lockout, defeasance, prepayment penalty points, or yield maintenance charges. Commercial mortgage loans are typically balloon loans requiring substantial principal payment at the end of the balloon term. If the borrower fails to make the balloon payment, the borrower is in default. Balloon risk, also called extension risk, is the risk that a borrower will not be able to make the balloon payment because either the borrower cannot arrange for refinancing at the balloon payment date or cannot sell the property to generate sufficient funds to pay off the balloon balance.

CMBS are issued by federal agencies (Ginnie Mae, Fannie Mae, or Freddie Mac) and nonagencies. The structure of a transaction is the same as in a nonagency residential mortgage-backed security, with the typical structure having multiple bond classes with different ratings. There are rules for the distribution of interest and principal to the bond classes and the distribution of losses. However, there are differences in structuring transactions due to prepayment features, the role of the special servicer in the case of imminent default, and the role of potential investors when the deal is being structured.

In a CMBS structure, there is call protection at the loan level and the structure level. When there are prepayment premiums (i.e., prepayment penalty points or yield maintenance charges), there are rules for distributing the prepayment premiums among the CMBS bondholders. In a CMBS deal there are two types of structural provisions that can be present in CMBS transactions to mitigate balloon risk: internal tail and external tail. A CMBS trades in the market like a corporate bond rather than a nonagency RMBS because of its substantial prepayment protection at the loan and structure level.

There are two major classifications for CMBS deals. One type is the single borrower/multi-property deal. Three key structural features in these deals are the cross-collateralization feature, cross-default feature, and property release provisions. The second type of CMBS deal is the multi-borrower deal, also called a conduit deal. A conduit is a commercial-lending entity that is established for the sole purpose of generating collateral to securitize.

Depending on the transactions, there are several types of servicers. The three most common in CMBS transactions are the sub-servicer, the master servicer, and the special servicer.

Because of the non-recourse nature of commercial mortgage loans, investors must view each property as a stand-alone business. The unique economic characteristics of each income-producing property in a pool backing a CMBS deal require that credit analysis be performed on a loan-by-loan basis not only at the time of issuance, but also monitored on an ongoing basis. The starting point is investigating the underwriting standards of the originators of the loans in the mortgage pool. An analysis of the credit quality of a CMBS structure will also look at the dispersion of the DSC ratios and LTV ratios for the underlying loans, the types of income-producing properties, and the geographical dispersion of the properties.

Rating agencies and analysts will then stress test the structure with respect to a combination of default and prepayment assumptions. In stress testing default risk, alternative assumptions are made regarding the conditional default rate, the timing of the defaults, and the percentage of the loss severity.

Questions

1. How does a commercial mortgage loan differ from a residential mortgage loan?
2. How is the net operating income (NOI) of a commercial property determined?
3. Why might an investor be skeptical about the loan-to-value ratio for a commercial mortgage loan?
4. Explain the underlying principle for a yield maintenance charge.
5. What types of prepayment protection provisions result in a prepayment premium being paid if a borrower prepays?
6. Why is balloon risk referred to as extension risk?
7. What are the major differences in structuring CMBS and RMBS transactions?
8. In a commercial mortgage-backed security, what is the concern that the bondholders have when there is a prepayment premium paid by a borrower?
9. In a defeasance, why is an investor not concerned with prepayment premiums?
10. Explain why commercial mortgage-backed securities do not trade like residential mortgage-backed securities in the market.
11. With respect to the mitigation of balloon risk, what is meant by
    a. an internal tail?
    b. an external tail?
12. Explain each of the following features and their significance in a single borrower/multi-property CMBS transaction:
    a. cross-collateralization feature
    b. cross-default feature
    c. property release provision
13. a. How does a single borrower/multi-property deal differ from a conduit deal?
    b. What is meant by a fusion conduit deal?
14. What are the typical duties of a special servicer?
15. How does the analysis of a commercial mortgage-backed security differ from that of a residential mortgage-backed security?
16. Why is it not adequate to look at the weighted-average debt-to-service coverage ratio and weighted-average loan-to-value ratio for the pool of commercial mortgage loans in assessing the potential performance of a CMBS transaction?
17. Why is it important to look at the dispersion of property types and geographical location of properties in analyzing a CMBS transaction?

CHAPTER

14 | ASSET-BACKED SECURITIES

After reading this chapter you will understand:

- how asset-backed securities are created

- the basic structure of a securitization

- the parties to a securitization

- the primary motivation for raising funds via a securitization

- the role of the special purpose vehicle

- the different types of structures: self liquidating and revolving

- the various forms of credit enhancement

- shifting interest mechanism and step down provisions

- the different types of optional call provisions

- the cash flow characteristics of the major types of asset-backed securities

- the credit risks associated with asset-backed securities and how they are analyzed.

In Chapters 11, 12, and 13 we discussed securities backed by a pool of mortgage loans, residential and commercial. A security created by pooling loans other than mortgage loans is referred to as an **asset-backed security** (ABS). Although in some countries the term "asset-backed securities" refers to all types of loans securitized (including mortgage loans), in the United States the convention is to distinguish between mortgage-backed securities (i.e., securities backed by mortgage loans) and asset-backed securities (i.e., securities backed by assets other than mortgage loans). To add another layer of confusion, there are certain types of mortgage loans that in the United States are classified as part of the asset-backed securities market: home equity loans and manufactured housing loans.

The types of assets that have been securitized fall into the following two general categories: (1) consumer asset-backed securities and residential mortgage-backed securities (MBS) and (2) commercial asset-backed securities. Consumer ABS and residential MBS securitizations include:

- mortgage-backed and home equity securities
- auto loans and leases
- credit card receivables
- manufactured housing loans
- student loans
- other consumer loans such as home improvement loans

Commercial ABS securitizations include:

- trade receivables (e.g., health care receivables)
- equipment leasing
- operating assets (e.g., aircraft, marine cargo containers)
- entertainment assets (e.g., film rights, music publishing royalties)
- franchise loans
- small business loans
- commercial mortgage loans

The broad-based bond market indexes include an ABS sector. The five largest subsectors within this sector are: (1) credit card receivable ABS, (2) auto ABS, (3) home equity ABS, (4) rate reduction bonds (also called stranded cost ABS), and (5) manufactured housing ABS. Commercial mortgage-backed securities (CMBS), the subject of Chapter 13, is treated as a separate sector in the broad-based bond market indexes.

In this chapter, we will discuss the basic features of asset-backed securities and provide an overview of the five major asset-backed security types described above.

CREATION OF AN ABS

To explain how an ABS is created and the parties to a securitization, we will use an illustration. Suppose that Exception Dental Equipment, Inc., manufactures high-quality dental equipment. While the company has cash sales, a bulk of its sales are from installment sales contracts. An installment sale contract is a loan to the buyer of the dental equipment (i.e., a dental practice) wherein the buyer agrees to repay Exceptional Dental Equipment, Inc., over a specified period of time for the amount borrowed plus interest. The dental equipment purchased is the collateral for the loan. We will assume that the loans are all for five years.

The credit department of Exceptional Dental Equipment, Inc., makes the decision as to whether or not to extend credit to a customer. That is, the credit department will receive a credit application from a potential customer and, based on criteria established by the company, will decide on whether to make a loan. The criteria for granting a loan are referred to as **underwriting standards**. Because Exceptional Dental Equipment, Inc., is granting the loan, the company is referred to as the **originator** of the loan.

Moreover, Exceptional Dental Equipment, Inc., may have a department that is responsible for servicing the loan. As explained in previous chapters, servicing involves collecting payments from borrowers, notifying borrowers who may be delinquent, and, when necessary, recovering and disposing of the collateral (i.e., the dental equipment in our illustration) if the borrower fails to make the contractual loan payments. While the servicer of the loans need not be the originator of the loans, in our illustration we are assuming that Exceptional Dental Equipment, Inc., is the servicer.

Now let's get to how these loans are used in a securitization transaction. We will assume that Exceptional Dental Equipment, Inc., has more than $300 million of install-ment sales contracts. We will further assume that Exceptional Dental Equipment, Inc., wants to raise $300 million. Rather than issuing corporate bonds for $300 million, the treasurer of the corporation decides to raise the funds via a securitization. To do so, Exceptional Dental Equipment, Inc., will set up a legal entity referred to as a **special purpose vehicle** (SPV). At this point, we will not explain the purpose of this legal entity, but it will be made clearer later that the SPV is critical in a securitization trans-action. In our illustration, the SPV that is set up is called DE Asset Trust (DEAT). Exceptional Dental Equipment, Inc., will then sell to DEAT $300 million of the loans. Exceptional Dental Equipment, Inc., will receive from DEAT $300 million in cash, the amount of funds it wanted to raise. DEAT obtains the $300 million by selling securities that are backed by the $300 million of loans. The securities are the asset-backed securi-ties we referred to earlier.

The Parties to a Securitization

Let's make sure we understand the parties to a securitization. In our hypothetical secu-ritization, Exceptional Dental Equipment, Inc., is not the issuer of the ABS (although it is sometimes referred to as the issuer because it is the entity that ultimately raises the funds). Rather, it originated the loans. Hence, in this transaction, Exceptional Dental Equipment, Inc., is called the "seller." The reason it is referred to as the "seller" is because it sold the receivables to DEAT. Exceptional Dental Equipment, Inc., is also called the "originator" because it originated the loans. The SPV in a securitization is referred to as the "issuer" or "trust" in the prospectus.

While in our simple transaction Exceptional Dental Equipment, Inc., manufactured the dental equipment and originated the loans, there is another type of securitization transaction involving another company, called a **conduit**, that buys the loans and securi-tizes them. For example, consider a hypothetical company Dental Equipment Financing Corporation whose business is to provide financing to dental equipment manufactures who want to sell their equipment on an installment basis. Dental Equip-ment Financing Corporation would then develop a relationship with manufacturers of dental equip-ment (such as Exceptional Dental Equipment, Inc.) to purchase their installment con-tracts. Dental Equipment Financing Corporation would then warehouse the installment contracts purchased until it had a sufficient amount to sell to an SPV, which would then issue the ABS.

There will be a trustee for the securities issued. The responsibilities of the trustee are to represent the interests of the bond classes by monitoring compliance with covenants and in the event of default enforce remedies as specified in the governing documents.[1]

Transaction Structure

In creating the various bond classes (or tranches) in a securitization, there will be rules for distribution of principal and interest. As explained in Chapters 11 and 12, the creation of the different bond classes results in securities with different risk-return characteristics. The structure is designed to create bond classes with investment characteristics that are more attractive to institutional investors. By doing so, the entity seeking to raise funds can obtain the best price for the securities it sells (referred to as "best execution").

As explained in Chapter 11, nonagency MBS are credit enhanced. The two general forms of credit enhancement are internal and external credit enhancement. All asset-backed securities are credit enhanced. Credit enhancement levels are determined relative to a specific rating desired by the seller/servicer for a security by each rating agency. Typically in a securitization, there are at least two classes of bond holders: senior bond classes and subordinate bond classes. This structure is called a senior-subordinate structure, and we described it in Chapter 11.

Role of the SPV

To understand the role of the SPV, we need to understand why a corporation would want to raise funds via securitization rather than simply issue corporate bonds. There are four principal reasons why a corporation may elect to raise funds via a securitization rather than a corporate bond. They are:

1. The potential for reducing funding costs
2. To diversify funding sources
3. To accelerate earnings for financial reporting purposes
4. For regulated entities, potential relief from capital requirements

We will only focus on the first of these reasons in order to see the critical role of the SPV in a securitization.[2]

Let's suppose that Exceptional Dental Equipment, Inc., has a double B credit rating (i.e., a below investment-grade credit rating). If it wants to raise funds equal to $300 million by issuing a corporate bond, its funding cost would be whatever the benchmark Treasury yield is plus a credit spread for double B issuers. Suppose, instead, that Exceptional Dental Equipment, Inc., uses $300 million of its installment sales contracts (i.e., the loans it has made to customers) as collateral for a bond issue. What will be its funding cost? It probably will be the same as if it issued a corporate bond. The reason is that if Exceptional Dental Equipment, Inc., defaults on any of its outstanding debt, the creditors will go after all of its assets, including the loans to its customers.

---

[1]For a further discussion of the role of the trustee in a securitization, see Karen Cook and F. Jim Della Sala, "The Role of the Trustee in Asset-Backed Securities," Chapter 7 in Frank J. Fabozzi (ed.) *Handbook of Structured Financial Products* (Hoboken, NJ: John Wiley & Sons, 1998).
[2]For a discussion of the other reasons, see W. Alexander Roever and Frank J. Fabozzi, "Primer on Securitization," *Journal of Structured and Project Finance,* Summer 2003, pp. 5–19.

Suppose that Exceptional Dental Equipment, Inc., can create a legal entity and sell the loans to that entity. That entity is the special purpose vehicle. In our illustration, the SPV is DEAT. If the sale of the loans by Exceptional Dental Equipment, Inc., to DEAT is done properly,[3] DEAT then legally owns the receivables, not Exceptional Dental Equipment, Inc. As a result, if Exceptional Dental Equipment, Inc., is ever forced into bankruptcy while the loans sold to DEAT are still outstanding, the creditors of Exceptional Dental Equipment, Inc., cannot recover the loans because they are legally owned by DEAT.

The legal implication is that when DEAT issues the ABS that are backed by the loans, investors contemplating the purchase of any bond class will evaluate the credit risk associated with collecting the payments due on the loans independent of the credit rating of Exceptional Dental Equipment, Inc. The credit rating will be assigned to the different bond classes created in the securitization and will depend on how the rating agencies will evaluate the credit risk based on the collateral (i.e., the loans). In turn, this will depend on the credit enhancement for each bond class. So, due to the SPV, quality of the collateral, and credit enhancement, a corporation can raise funds via a securitization where some of the bond classes have a credit rating better than the corporation seeking to raise funds and that in the aggregate the funding cost is less than issuing corporate bonds.

Credit Enhancements

In Chapter 11, we briefly reviewed the different forms of credit enhancement for nonagency MBS. They include external credit enhancement and internal credit enhancement. The credit enhancement forms are used both individually and in combination, depending on the loan types that are backing the securities.

External credit enhancement involves a guarantee from a third party. The risk faced by an investor is the potential for the third party to be downgraded, and, as a result, the bond classes guaranteed by the third party may be downgraded. The most common form of external credit enhancement is **bond insurance** and is referred to as a **surety bond** or a **wrap**. Bond insurance is a financial guarantee from a monoline insurance company requiring that the insurer guarantee the timely payments of principal and interest if these payments cannot be satisfied from the cash flow from the underlying loan pool. The principal payments will be made without acceleration, except if the insurer elects to do so. Ambac Assurance Corporation (Ambac), Financial Guaranty Insurance Corporation (FGIC), Financial Security Assurance (FSA), Municipal Bond Insurance Corporation (MBIA), and BIAXLCA/XLFA are the primary insurers as of the end of 2005.

Internal credit enhancements come in more complicated forms than external credit enhancements and may alter the cash flow characteristics of the loans even in the absence of default. Credit enhancement levels (i.e., the amount of subordination for each form of enhancement utilized within a deal) are determined by the rating agencies from which the issuer seeks a rating for the bond classes. This is referred to as "sizing" the transaction and is based on the rating agencies' expectations for the performance of the loans collateralizing the deal in question.

---

[3]More specifically, it has to be a sale of the loans at a fair market value.

Most securitization transactions that employ internal credit enhancements follow a predetermined schedule that prioritizes the manner in which principal and interest generated by the underlying collateral must be used. This schedule, which is explained in the deal's prospectus, is known as the **cash flow waterfall**, or simply the **waterfall**. At the top of the waterfall would be cash flows due to senior bondholders (interest and principal, depending upon the principal repayment schedule) as well as some standard fees and expenses (e.g., administration and servicing fee). After the cash flow obligations at the top of the waterfall are met, cash flows down to lower priority classes (those rated AA, A, BBB bond classes and so on). The cash flows that remain after all of the scheduled periodic payment obligations are met is the **excess spread**. The excess spread is the first line of defense against collateral losses, since deals that are structured to have a large amount of excess spread can absorb relatively large levels of collateral losses. If the excess spread is fully eaten away by losses, the next lowest-rated class will begin to be negatively affected by credit losses.

The most common forms of internal credit enhancement are senior/subordinate structures, overcollateralization, and reserve funds. In Chapter 11 we described each of these forms of internal credit enhancement. However, we mentioned in that chapter that an important credit enhancement mechanism for securitizations backed by residential mortgage loans is the shifting interest mechanism. We describe this next, as well as other provisions in a senior/subordinate structure that are important: step down provisions.

Shifting Interest Mechanism in a Senior/Subordinate Structure

Almost all existing senior/subordinate structures backed by residential mortgage loans also incorporate a shifting interest mechanism. This mechanism redirects prepayments disproportionately from the subordinate bond class to the senior bond class according to a specified schedule. As mentioned in Chapter 11, the rationale for the shifting interest structure is to have enough subordinate bond classes outstanding to cover future credit losses.

The basic credit concern that investors in the senior bond class have is that while the subordinate bond classes provide a certain level of credit protection for the senior bond class at the closing of the deal, the level of protection may deteriorate over time due to prepayments and certain liquidation proceeds. The objective is to distribute these payments of principal such that the credit protection for the senior bond class does not deteriorate over time.

The percentage of the mortgage balance of the subordinate bond class to that of the mortgage balance for the entire deal is called the **level of subordination** or the **subordinate interest**. The higher the percentage, the greater the level of protection for the senior bond class. The subordinate interest changes after the deal is closed due to prepayments. That is, the subordinate interest shifts (hence the term "shifting interest"). The purpose of a shifting interest mechanism is to allocate prepayments so that the subordinate interest is maintained at an acceptable level to protect the senior bond class.

The prospectus will specify how different scheduled principal payments and prepayments will be allocated between the senior bond class and the subordinate bond class. The scheduled principal payments are allocated based on the senior percentage. The **senior percentage**, also called the **senior interest**, is defined as the ratio of the balance of the senior bond class to the balance of the entire deal and is equal to 100% minus the subordinate interest. So, if in some month the senior percentage is 82% and the scheduled principal payment is $1 million, the senior bond class will get $820,000 ($0.082 \times \$1,000,000$) and the subordinate bond class $180,000 ($1,000,000 − $820,000).

Allocation of the prepayments is based on the **senior prepayment percentage** (in some deals called the **accelerated distribution percentage**.) This is defined as follows:

$$\text{Senior percentage} + \text{Shifting interest percentage} \times \text{Subordinate interest}$$

The "shifting interest percentage" in the formula above is specified in the prospectus. To illustrate the formula, suppose that in some month the senior interest is 82%, the subordinate interest is 18%, and the shifting interest percentage is 70%. The senior prepayment percentage for that month is:

$$82\% + 0.70 \times 18\% = 94.6\%$$

Thus, if prepayments for the month are $1,000,000, then $946,000 is allocated to the senior bond class and $54,000 to the subordinate bond class.

The prospectus will provide the shifting interest percentage schedule for calculating the senior prepayment percentage. A commonly used shifting interest percentage schedule is as follows:

Year after issuance	Shifting interest percentage
1–5	100
6	70
7	60
8	40
9	20
after year 9	0

The shifting interest percentage schedule given in the prospectus is the "base" schedule. The schedule can change over time depending on the performance of the collateral. If the performance is such that the credit protection is deteriorating or may deteriorate, the base shifting interest percentages are overridden and a higher allocation of prepayments is made to the senior bond class. Performance analysis of the collateral is undertaken by the trustee for determining whether to override the base schedule. The performance analysis is in terms of tests and if the collateral or structure fails any of the tests, this will trigger an override of the base schedule. The tests are described next.

While the shifting interest structure is beneficial to the senior bond class holder from a credit standpoint, it does alter the cash flow characteristics of the senior bond class even in the absence of defaults. The size of the subordination also matters. A larger subordinate class redirects a higher proportion of prepayments to the senior bond class, thereby shortening the average life even further.

Deal Step-Down Provisions

An important feature in analyzing senior/subordinate bond classes or deals backed by residential mortgages is the deal's **step-down provisions**. These provisions allow for the reduction in credit support over time. As noted previously, a concern that investors in the senior bond class have is that if the collateral performance is deteriorating, step down provisions should be altered. The provisions that prevent the credit support from stepping down are called "triggers." Principal payments from the subordinate bond classes are diverted to the senior bond class if a trigger is reached. The diversion of principal varies from issuer to issuer. The most conservative approach is to stop all principal payments from being distributed to the subordinate bond classes. Alternatively, some issuers allow the subordinate bond classes to receive regularly scheduled principal (amortization) on a pro rata basis but divert all prepayments to the senior bond class.

There are two triggers based on the level of credit performance required to be passed before the credit support can be reduced: a delinquency trigger and loss trigger. The triggers are expressed in the form of a test that is applied in each period. The **delinquency test**, in its most common form, prevents any step-down from taking place as long as the current over 60-day delinquency rate exceeds a specified percentage of the then-current pool balance. The **principal loss test** prevents a step-down from occurring if cumulative losses exceed a certain limit (which changes over time) of the original balance.

In addition to triggers based on the performance of the collateral, there is a **balance test**. This test involves comparing the change in the senior interest from the closing of the deal to the current month. If the senior interest has increased, the balance test is failed, triggering a revision of the base schedule for the allocation of principal payments from the subordinate bond classes to the senior bond class. Unlike a trigger that will increase the allocation to the senior bond class, there are balance tests that will increase the allocation to the subordinate bond class. This can occur where the subordinate interest improves by a significant amount. That amount is set forth in the prospectus. For example, the prospectus may set forth that if the subordinate interest doubles, the base schedule is overridden such that more is allocated to the subordinate bond class.

Optional Clean-Up Call Provisions

For ABS there is an optional clean-up call provision granted to the trustee. There are several types of clean-up call provisions: percent of collateral call, percent of collateral call, percent of tranche clean-up call, call on or after specified date, latter of percent or date call, auction call, and insurer call.

In a **percent of collateral call**, the outstanding bonds can be called at par value if the outstanding collateral's balance falls below a predetermined percent of the original collateral's balance. This is the most common type of clean-up call provision for amortizing assets, and the predetermined level is typically 10%.

A **percent of bonds clean-up call** provision is similar to a percent of collateral call except that the percent that triggers the call is the percent of the amount of the bonds outstanding relative to the original amount of bonds issued. A **percent of tranche clean-up call** bases the right to call on the percent of the tranche's par value outstanding relative to the tranche's original par value.

A **call on or after specified date** operates just like a standard bond call provision. In a **latter of percent or date call**, the outstanding bond classes can be called if either (1) the collateral outstanding reaches a predetermined level before the specified call date or (2) the call date has been reached even if the collateral outstanding is above the predetermined level. In an **auction call**, at a certain date a call will be exercised if an auction results in the outstanding collateral being sold at a price greater than its par value. The premium over par value received from the auctioned collateral is retained by the trustee and eventually paid to the seller through the residual.

In addition to the above clean-up call provisions, which permit the trustee to call the bonds, there may be an **insurer call**. Such a call permits the insurer to call the bonds if the collateral's cumulative loss history reaches a predetermined level.

Example of an Actual Securitization

Let's look at an actual securitization—Caterpillar Financial Asset Trust 1997-A. For this securitization, Caterpillar Financial Asset Trust 1997-A is the SPV and the issuer and the trust. The collateral (i.e., financial assets) for the transaction is a pool of retail installment sales contracts that are secured by new and used machinery manufactured primarily by Caterpillar, Inc. The retail installment sales contracts carry a fixed interest rate and were originated by the Caterpillar Financial Funding Corporation, a wholly-owned subsidiary of Caterpillar Financial Services Corporation. Caterpillar Financial Services Corporation is a wholly-owned subsidiary of Caterpillar, Inc., and because it sold the retail installment sales contracts to Caterpillar Financial Asset Trust 1997-A, Caterpillar Financial Funding Corporation is referred to in the prospectus as the "Seller."

The prospectus states that:

> THE NOTES REPRESENT OBLIGATIONS OF THE ISSUER ONLY AND DO NOT REPRESENT OBLIGATIONS OF OR INTERESTS IN CATERPILLAR FINANCIAL FUNDING CORPORATION, CATERPIL-LAR FINANCIAL SERVICES CORPORATION, CATERPILLAR, INC. OR ANY OF THEIR RESPECTIVE AFFILIATES.

As noted above, this is the key feature in a securitization transaction—the separation of the collateral from the creditors of Caterpillar, Inc. The servicer of the retail installment sales contracts is Caterpillar Financial Services Corporation, a wholly-owned finance subsidiary of Caterpillar, Inc. and is referred to as the "Servicer" in the prospectus. For servicing the collateral, Caterpillar Financial Services Corporation receives a servicing fee of 100 basis points of the outstanding loan balance.

The securities were issued on May 19, 1997, and had a par value of $337,970,000. In the prospectus the securities were referred to as "asset-backed notes." The structure was as follows. There were four rated bond classes:

Bond Class	Par Value
Class A-1	$ 88,000,000
Class A-2	$128,000,000
Class A-3	$108,100,000
Class B	$ 13,870,000

This is a senior-subordinate structure. The senior bond classes in this transaction are Class A-1, Class A-2, and Class A-3. The subordinate class is Class B. The cash flow waterfall is as follows. The senior classes are paid off in sequence—first Class A-1 is paid principal until it is paid off its entire balance, then Class A-2 starts receiving principal payments until it is paid off entirely, and then finally Class A-3 is paid off. Class B begins receiving principal payments after Class A-3 is paid off. Any losses on the collateral are realized by Class B. If the losses exceed $13,870,000 (the par value of Class B) less the losses that can be absorbed by the reserve account, the senior classes absorb the loss on a pro rata basis.

COLLATERAL TYPE AND SECURITIZATION STRUCTURE

Structuring a securitization will depend on the characteristics of the underlying assets. Here we will discuss how two characteristics affect the structure: amortization and interest rate. Specifically, the structure depends on whether (1) the assets are amortizing or nonamortizing and (2) the interest rate on the collateral is fixed or floating.

Amortizing Versus Nonamortizing Assets

The collateral in a securitization can be classified as either amortizing or nonamortizing assets. **Amortizing assets** are loans in which the borrower's periodic payment consists of scheduled principal and interest payments over the life of the loan. The schedule for the repayment of the principal is called an **amortization schedule**. The standard residential mortgage loan falls into this category. Auto loans and certain types of home equity loans (specifically, closed-end home equity loans discussed later in this chapter) are amortizing assets.

The amortization schedule for the collateral can be created on a pool level or a loan level. In pool-level analysis it is assumed that all loans comprising the collateral are identical. For an amortizing asset, the amortization schedule is based on the gross weighted average coupon (GWAC) and weighted average maturity (WAM) for that single loan. Pool-level analysis is appropriate where the underlying loans are homogeneous. Loan-level analysis involves amortizing each loan (or group of homogeneous loans).

As explained in Chapter 11, a prepayment is any excess payment over the scheduled principal payment. For an amortizing asset, projection of the cash flows requires projecting prepayments. In contrast to amortizing assets, **nonamortizing assets** do not have a schedule for the periodic payments that the individual borrower must make. Instead, a nonamortizing asset is one in which the borrower must make a minimum periodic payment. If that payment is less than the interest on the outstanding loan balance, the shortfall is added to the outstanding loan balance. If the periodic payment is greater than the interest on the outstanding loan balance, then the difference is applied to the reduction of the outstanding loan balance. Because there is no schedule of principal payments (i.e., no amortization schedule) for a nonamortizing asset, the concept of a prepayment does not apply. Credit card receivables are examples of nonamortizing assets.

Typically when amortizing assets are securitized, the collateral is fixed over the life of the structure. That is, no new assets are acquired. The collateral composition stays the same except for prepayments and defaults. Consequently, all principal received by the trust is paid out to the bond classes. The structure in this case is referred to as a **self-liquidating structure**. In the case of nonamortizing assets, for a period of time, referred to as the **lockout period** or **revolving period**, all principal received is used to purchase new collateral. Hence, new assets are being added to the collateral, and this structure is referred to as a **revolving structure**. After the lockout period, called the **amortization period**, principal received is distributed to the bond classes.

Fixed-Rate Versus Floating-Rate Assets

The assets that are securitized can have a fixed rate or a floating rate. This impacts the structure in terms of the coupon rate for the bonds issued. For example, a structure with all floating-rate bond classes backed by collateral consisting of only fixed-rate contracts exposes bondholders to interest rate risk. If the reference rate for the floating-rate bond classes increases sufficiently, there could be a shortfall between the interest received from the collateral and the aggregate interest payment that must be made to the bond classes. If the collateral consists of only floating-rate contracts and the bond classes all have a fixed coupon rate, the exposure in this case is that the reference rate for the contracts will decline sufficiently so that the interest paid by the borrowers will be less than the total interest due to the bondholders.

To deal with situations where there may be a mismatch between the cash flow characteristics of the asset and the liabilities, interest rate derivative instruments are used in a securitization. The two common interest rate derivatives used are interest rate swaps and interest rate caps, both described in Chapter 28.[4]

CREDIT RISKS ASSOCIATED WITH INVESTING IN ABS

Investors in ABS are exposed to credit risk and rely on rating agencies to evaluate that risk for the bond classes in a securitization. While the three agencies have different approaches in assigning credit ratings, they do focus on the same areas of analysis. Moody's, for example, investigates: (1) asset risks, (2) structural risks, and (3) third parties to the structure.[5] We discuss each next. In addition, rating agencies analyze the legal structure (i.e., the SPV). We also discuss the legal issue regarding securitizations in general.

Asset Risks

Evaluating asset risks involves the analysis of the credit quality of the collateral. The rating agencies will look at the underlying borrower's ability to pay and the borrower's equity in the asset. The reason for looking at the latter is because it is a key determinant as to whether the underlying borrower will default or sell the asset and pay off a loan. The rating agencies will look at the experience of the originators of the underlying loans and will assess whether the loans underlying a specific transaction have the same characteristics as the experience reported by the seller.

The concentration of loans is examined. The underlying principle of asset securitization is that a large number of borrowers in a pool will reduce the credit risk via diversification. If there are a few borrowers in the pool that are significant in size relative to the entire pool balance, this diversification benefit can be lost, resulting in a higher level of credit risk referred to as **concentration risk**. To reduce concentration risk, concentration limits on the amount or percentage of receivables from any one borrower, region of the

---

[4]For an explanation of how interest rate derivatives are used in securitizations, see Frank J. Fabozzi, Raymond Morel, and Brian D. Grow, "Use of Interest Rate Derivatives in Securitization Transactions," *Journal of Structured Finance,* Summer 2005, pp. 22–27.

[5]Andrew A. Silver, "Rating Structured Securities," Chapter 5 in Frank J. Fabozzi (ed.), *Issuer Perspectives on Securities* (Hoboken, NJ: John Wiley & Sons, 1998).

country, or industry (in the case of commercial assets) will be established by rating agencies. If at issuance the concentration limit is exceeded, some or all of the bond classes will receive a lower credit rating than if the concentration limit was within the established range. Subsequent to issuance, bond classes may be downgraded if the concentration limit is exceeded.

Employing statistical analysis, the rating agencies assess the most likely loss to a bond class that would result from the performance of the collateral. This is done by analyzing various scenarios that the rating agencies specify. Based on the result of the analysis, the rating agencies compute both a weighted average loss and variability of loss for each bond class. To appreciate why the variability of loss is important, suppose that a bond class has protection against a 7% loss in the value of the collateral due to defaults. To simplify the illustration, suppose that a rating agency evaluates two equally likely scenarios and that in the first scenario the loss is 6% and in the second scenario 4%. The weighted average loss is 5%. This is less than the 7% loss that a bond class has protection against and therefore the rating agency would expect that it is unlikely that the bond class will realize a loss. Let's change the two outcomes now. Suppose that the outcome of the two scenarios is that the loss is 8% in the first scenario and 2% in the second scenario. While the expected value for the loss is still 5%, the variability of the loss is much greater than before. In fact, if in the second scenario an 8% loss occurs, the bond class would realize a loss of 1% (8% loss in the scenario minus the 7% protection).

Structural Risks

The decision on the structure is up to the seller. Once selected, the rating agencies examine the extent to which the cash flow from the collateral can satisfy all of the obligations of the bond classes in the securitization. The cash flow of the underlying collateral is interest and principal repayment. The cash flow payments that must be made are interest and principal to investors, servicing fees, and any other expenses for which the issuer is liable. This is described by the structure's cash flow waterfall. The rating agencies analyze the structure to test whether the collateral's cash flows match the payments that must be made to satisfy the issuer's obligations. This requires that the rating agency make assumptions about losses and delinquencies and consider various interest rate scenarios after taking into consideration credit enhancements.

In considering the structure, the rating agencies will consider (1) the loss allocation (how losses will be allocated among the bond classes in the structure), (2) the cash flow allocation (i.e., the cash flow waterfall), (3) the interest rate spread between the interest earned on the collateral and the interest paid to the bond classes plus the servicing fee, (4) the potential for a trigger event to occur that will cause the early amortization of a deal (discussed later), and (5) how credit enhancement may change over time.

Third-Party Providers

In a securitization, several third parties are involved. These include third-party credit guarantors (most commonly bond insurers), the servicer, a trustee, issuer's counsel, a guaranteed investment contract provider (this entity insures the reinvestment rate on investable funds), and accountants. The rating agency will investigate all third-party providers. For the third-party guarantors, the rating agencies will perform a credit analysis of their ability to pay.

All loans must be serviced. Servicing involves collecting payments from borrowers, notifying borrowers who may be delinquent, and, when necessary, recovering and disposing of the collateral if the borrower does not make loan repayments by a specified time. The servicer is responsible for these activities. Moreover, while still viewed as a "third party" in many securitizations, the servicer is likely to be the originator of the loans used as the collateral.

In addition to the administration of the loan portfolio as just described, the servicer is responsible for distributing the proceeds collected from the borrowers to the different bond classes in the structure according to the cash flow waterfall. Where there are floating-rate securities in the transaction, the servicer will determine the interest rate for the period. The servicer may also be responsible for advancing payments when there are delinquencies in payments (that are likely to be collected in the future), resulting in a temporary shortfall in the payments that must be made to the bondholders.

The role of the servicer is critical in a securitization. Therefore, rating agencies look at the ability of a servicer to perform all the activities that a servicer will be responsible for before they assign a rating to the bonds in a transaction. For example, the following factors are reviewed when evaluating servicers: servicing history, experience, underwriting standard for loan originations, servicing capabilities, human resources, financial condition, and growth/competition/business environment. Transactions where there is a concern about the ability of a servicer to perform are either not rated or the rating agency may require a backup servicer.

Recent cases have made rating agencies pay even closer attention to the importance of the underlying business of the seller/originator, the strength of the servicer, and the economics that will produce the cash flows for the collateral. Primarily, this was as a result of the alleged fraud of National Century Financial Enterprises (NCFE), purchaser of health care receivables that were then securitized and serviced, and DVI, a securitizer of medical equipment leases. In addition, NCFE and DVI highlighted the need for a trustee to be more proactive if the performance of the servicer deteriorates. That is, the trustee's role should be expanded beyond the traditional function of merely performing the ongoing tests on the collateral that are set forth in the deal documents. This is, in fact, happening in recent deals where the trustee under certain circumstances can take on an expanded role. This is referred to as a **trustee event trigger**.

Potential Legal Challenges

The long-standing view is that investors in ABS are protected from the creditors of the seller of the collateral. That is, when the seller of the collateral transfers it to the trust (the SPV), the transfer represents a "true sale" and therefore in the case of the seller's bankruptcy, the bankruptcy court cannot penetrate the trust to recover the collateral or cash flow from the collateral. However, this issue has never been fully tested. The closest challenge was the bankruptcy of LTV Steel Company. In the bankruptcy, LTV argued that its securitizations were not true sales and therefore it should be entitled to the cash flows that it transferred to the trust. Although the case was settled and the settlement included a summary finding that the LTV's securitizations were a true sale, the court's decision to permit LTV to use the cash flows prior to the settlement is a major concern to investors.

There are also concerns regarding the outcome of a bankruptcy involving Conseco Finance. The firm filed for bankruptcy in December 2002. Conseco Finance had been the largest originator of manufactured housing loans, as well as originator of other types of asset types. At the time of filing, Conseco was the servicer for its prior securitizations, charging a servicing fee of 50 basis points. The bankruptcy court took the position that a 50 basis points servicing fee was not adequate compensation, ordering it to be increased (to 115 basis points). That increase in the servicing fee was obtained by reducing the excess spread in the securitization transactions that Conseco was servicing. As a result of a reduction in the excess spread, the credit enhancement levels for the transactions being serviced were reduced and several of the subordinate tranches in those transactions were downgraded.[6]

REVIEW OF SEVERAL MAJOR TYPES OF ABS

The five largest sectors within the ABS market are: (1) credit card receivable-backed securities, (2) auto loan-backed securities, (3) home equity loan-backed securities, (4) rate reduction bonds, and (5) manufactured housing loan-backed securities. Next we provide a summary of these securities.

Credit Card Receivable-Backed Securities

Credit cards are issued by banks (e.g., Visa and MasterCard), retailers (e.g., JC Penney and Sears), and travel and entertainment companies (e.g., American Express). The cash flow for a pool of credit card receivables consists of finance charges collected, fees, and principal. Finance charges collected represent the periodic interest the credit card borrower is charged based on the unpaid balance after the grace period. Fees include late payment fees and any annual membership fees. Interest to the bond classes is paid periodically (e.g., monthly, quarterly, or semiannually). The interest rate may be fixed or floating.

Structure of the Transaction

A credit card receivable is a nonamortizing asset and therefore has a revolving structure. During the lockout period the principal payments made by credit card borrowers comprising the pool are retained by the trustee and reinvested in additional receivables to maintain the size of the pool. The lockout period can vary from 18 months to 10 years. So, during the lockout period, the cash flow that is paid out to the bond classes is based on finance charges collected and fees. The lockout period is followed by the principal amortization period where the principal is no longer reinvested but paid to bond holders.

There are provisions in credit card receivable-backed securities that require early amortization of the principal if certain events occur. Such a provision, which is referred to as either an **early amortization provision** or a **rapid amortization provision**, is included to safeguard the credit quality of the structure. The only way that the principal cash flows can be altered is by triggering the early amortization provision. Typically, early

---

[6]For a further discussion of the implications of the Conseco Finance bankruptcy, see Frank J. Fabozzi, "The Structured Finance Market: An Investor's Perspective," *Financial Analysts Journal*, May–June 2005, pp. 27–40.

amortization allows for the rapid return of principal in the event that the three-month average excess spread earned on the receivables falls to zero or less. When early amortization occurs, the bond classes are retired sequentially (i.e., first the AAA bond then the AA rated bond, etc.). This is accomplished by distributing the principal payments to the specified bond class instead of using those payments to acquire more receivables. The length of time until the return of principal is largely a function of the monthly payment rate that we describe next.

Performance of the Portfolio of Receivables

The following concepts must be understood in order to assess the performance of the portfolio of receivables and the ability of the collateral to satisfy the interest obligation and repay principal as scheduled: gross portfolio yield, charge-offs, net portfolio yield, delinquencies, and monthly payment rate.

The **gross portfolio yield** includes finance charges collected and fees. **Charge-offs** represent the accounts charged off as uncollectible. **Net portfolio yield** is equal to gross portfolio yield minus charge-offs. The net portfolio yield is important because it is from this yield that the bondholders will receive interest payments. So, for example, if the weighted average coupon that must be paid to the various bond classes in the structure is 6% and the net portfolio yield for the month is 5%, there is the risk that the bondholder obligations will not be satisfied.

Delinquencies are the percentages of receivables that are past due for a specified number of months, usually 30, 60, and 90 days. They are considered an indicator of potential future charge-offs.

The **monthly payment rate** (MPR) expresses the monthly payment (which includes finance charges, fees, and any principal repayment) of a credit card receivable portfolio as a percentage of credit card debt outstanding in the previous month. For example, suppose a $600 million credit card receivable portfolio in February realized $60 million of payments in March. The MPR for March would then be 10% ($60 million divided by $600 million). The MPR is important for two reasons. First, if the MPR reaches an extremely low level, there is a chance that there will be extension risk with respect to the principal payments to the bond classes. Second, if the MPR is very low, then there is a chance that there will not be sufficient cash flows to pay off principal. This is one of the events that could trigger the early amortization provision.

Auto Loan-Backed Securities

Auto loan-backed securities are issued by the financial subsidiaries of auto manufacturers (domestic and foreign), commercial banks, and independent finance companies and small financial institutions specializing in auto loans. The cash flow for auto loan-backed securities consists of regularly scheduled monthly loan payments (interest and scheduled principal repayments) and any prepayments. For securities backed by auto loans, prepayments result from (1) sales and trade-ins requiring full payoff of the loan, (2) repossession and subsequent resale of the automobile, (3) loss or destruction of the vehicle, (4) payoff of the loan with cash to save on the interest cost, and (5) financing of the loan at a lower interest cost. While refinancings may be a major reason for prepayments of residential mortgage loans, they are of minor importance for automobile loans.

Prepayments for auto loan-backed securities are measured in terms of the **absolute prepayment speed** (ABS).[7] The ABS measure is the monthly prepayment expressed as a percentage of the original collateral amount. As explained in Chapter 11, the single-monthy mortality rate (SMM) is the monthly conditional prepayment rate (CPR) based on the prior month's balance. There is a mathematical relationship between the ABS and SMM. Given the SMM (expressed as a decimal), the ABS (expressed as a decimal) is obtained as follows:

$$ABS = \frac{SMM}{1 + SMM \times (M - 1)}$$

where M is the number of months after origination (i.e., loan age).

For example, suppose that the SMM is 2.1%, or 0.021, in month 32. Then the ABS is

$$ABS = \frac{0.021}{1 + 0.021 \times (32 - 1)} = 0.0127 = 1.27\%$$

Given the ABS, the SMM is obtained as follows:

$$SMM = \frac{ABS}{1 - ABS \times (M - 1)}$$

The SMM can then be converted to a CPR using the formula given in Chapter 11.

To illustrate the formula, suppose that the ABS is 1.5%, or 0.015, in month 26. Then the SMM is

$$SMM = \frac{0.015}{1 - 0.015 \times (26 - 1)} = 0.024 = 24\%$$

Home Equity Loan-Backed Securities

A **home equity loan** (HEL) is a loan backed by residential property. Typically the borrower has either an impaired credit history and/or the payment-to-income ratio is too high for the loan to qualify as a conforming loan for securitization by Ginnie Mae, Fannie Mae, or Freddie Mac. While home equity loans can be either closed end or open end, most home equity loan securitizations are backed by closed-end HELs. A closed-end HEL is designed the same way as a fully amortizing residential mortgage loan. That is, it has a fixed maturity, and the payments are structured to fully amortize the loan by the maturity date. An open-end HEL is a line of credit.

There are both fixed-rate and variable-rate closed-end HELs. Typically, variable-rate loans have a reference rate that is LIBOR and have periodic caps and lifetime caps. The cash flow of a pool of closed-end HELs is comprised of interest, regularly scheduled principal repayments, and prepayments, just as with mortgage-backed securities described in Chapter 11. Thus, it is necessary to have a prepayment model and

---

[7]The abbreviation *ABS* was probably used because it was the first prepayment measure used for asset-backed securities.

a default model to forecast cash flows. The prepayment speed is measured in terms of CPR.

Borrower characteristics and the seasoning process must be kept in mind when trying to assess prepayments for a particular deal. In the prospectus of an offering, a base-case prepayment assumption is made—the initial speed and the amount of time until the collateral is expected to be seasoned. Thus, the prepayment benchmark is issuer specific. The benchmark speed in the prospectus is called the **prospectus prepayment curve** or PPC. Slower or faster prepayments speeds are a multiple of the PPC. For example, in the prospectus for the Contimortgage Home Equity Loan Trust 1996-1, the base case prepayment assumption for the fixed-rate mortgages in the pool is as follows (p. 3–37):

> . . . a 100% Prepayment Assumption assumes conditional prepayment rates of 4% per annum of the then outstanding principal balance of the Home Equity Loans in the Fixed Rate Group in the first month of the life of the mortgage loans and an additional 1.455% (precisely 16/11%) per annum in each month thereafter until the twelfth month. Beginning in the twelfth month and in each month thereafter during the life of the mortgage loans, 100% Prepayment Assumption assumes a conditional prepayment rate of 20% per annum each month.

Therefore, if an investor analyzed the deal based on 200% PPC, this means doubling the CPRs cited in the excerpt and using 12 months for seasoning.

In the Champion Home Equity Loan Trust 1996-1, the base case prepayment assumption is specified in the prospectus as follows (p. S-28):

> The model used with respect to the Fixed Rate Certificates (the "Prepayment Ramp") assumes that the Home Equity Loans in Loan Group One prepay at a rate of 4% CPR in the first month after origination, and an additional 1.5% each month thereafter until the 14th month. Beginning in the 15th month and each month thereafter, the Prepayment Ramp assumes a prepayment rate of 25% CPR.

Thus, 100% PPC is based on the preceding CPRs assuming seasoning after 14 months.

The securities backed by the adjustable-rate (or variable-rate) HELs are called **HEL floaters**. To increase the attractiveness of home equity loan-backed securities to institutional investors, the securities typically have been created using a reference rate of 1-month LIBOR. Because of (1) the mismatch between the reference rate on the underlying loans (typically 6-month LIBOR) and that of the HEL floater (1-month LIBOR) and (2) the periodic and life caps of the underlying loans, there is a cap on the coupon rate for the HEL floater. Unlike a typical floater, which has a cap that is fixed throughout the security's life, the effective cap of an HEL floater is variable. The effective cap, referred to as the **available funds cap**, will depend on the amount of funds generated by the net coupon on the principal, less any fees.

Rate Reduction Bonds

Rate reduction bonds are backed by a special charge (tariff) included in the utility bills of utility customers in. The charge, called the **competitive transition charge** (or CTC), is effectively a legislated asset. It is the result of the movement to make the electric utility industry more competitive by deregulating the industry. Prior to deregulation, electric utilities were entitled to set utility rates so as to earn a competitive return on the assets on their balance sheet. After deregulation, the setting of utility rates to recover a competitive return was no long permissible. As a result, many electric utilities had a substantial amount of assets that they acquired prior to deregulation that would likely become uneconomic and utilities would no longer be assured that they could charge a high enough rate to recover the costs of these assets. These assets are referred to as "stranded assets" and the associated costs referred to as "stranded costs." For this reason, rate reduction bonds are also known as **stranded cost bonds** or **stranded asset bonds**. Some market participants refer to this sector of the ABS market as the "utilities" sector.

The CTC is collected by the utility over a specific period of time. Because the state legislature designates the CTC to be a statutory property right, it can be sold by a utility to an SPV and securitized. It is the legislative designation of the CTC as an asset that makes rate reduction bonds different from the typical asset securitized.

The CTC is initially calculated based on projections of utility usage and the ability to collect revenues. However, actual collection experience may differ from initial projections. Because of this, there is a "true-up" mechanism in these securitizations. This mechanism permits the utility to recompute the CTC on a periodic basis over the term of the securitization based on actual collection experience. The advantage of the true-up mechanism to the bond classes is that it provides cash flow stability as well as a form of credit enhancement.

Manufactured Housing-Backed Securities

Manufactured housing-backed securities are backed by loans for manufactured homes. In contrast to site-built homes, manufactured homes are built at a factory and then transported to a manufactured home community or private land. The typical loan for a manufactured home is 15 to 20 years and may be either a mortgage loan (for both the land and the home) or a consumer retail installment loan.

The loan repayment is structured to fully amortize the amount borrowed. Therefore, as with residential mortgage loans and HELs, the cash flow consists of net interest, regularly scheduled principal, and prepayments. It has been observed that prepayments tend to be more stable for manufactured housing-backed securities because they are not as sensitive to refinancing. There are several reasons for this. First, the loan balances for many loans are typically small so that there is no significant dollar savings from refinancing. Second, the rate of depreciation of some manufactured homes (such as mobile homes) may be such that in the earlier years depreciation is greater than the amount of the loan paid off. This makes it difficult to refinance the loan. Finally, borrowers are typically of lower credit quality and therefore find it difficult to obtain funds to refinance.

As with residential mortgage loans and HELs, prepayments on manufactured housing-backed securities are measured in terms of CPR. The payment structure is the same as with home equity loan-backed securities.

SUMMARY

Asset-backed securities are created by pooling loans and receivables through a process known as securitization. The main parties to a securitization are the seller/originator (party seeking to raise funds), special purpose vehicle, and servicer. The motivation for issuing asset-backed securities rather than issuing a corporate bond is the potential reduction in funding cost. The key to this savings is the role of the special purpose vehicle.

ABS are credit enhanced to provide greater protection to bond classes against defaults. There are two general types of credit enhancement structures: external and internal. External credit enhancements come in the form of third-party guarantees, the most common being bond insurance. Internal credit enhancements include reserve funds (cash reserves and excess spread), overcollateralization, and senior/subordinate structures. An important provision in a senior/subordinate structure for securitizations backed by residential mortgage loans to protect the senior bond classes is the shifting interest mechanism. Another important provision is the step down provision.

In analyzing credit risk, the rating agencies will examine asset risks, structural risks, and third parties to the structure. Based on this analysis, a rating agency will determine the amount of credit enhancement needed for a bond class to receive a specific credit rating.

The five largest sectors of the ABS market are securities backed by credit card receivables, closed-end home equity loans, auto loans, a tariff charged by electric utilities, and manufactured housing loans.

Questions

1. Why is the entity seeking to raise funds through a securitization referred to as the "seller" or the "originator"?

2. In achieving the benefits associated with a securitization, why is the special purpose vehicle important to the transaction?

3. In a securitization, what is the difference between a servicer and a special purpose vehicle?

4. What is meant by a cash flow waterfall?

5. Explain the difference in the treatment of principal received for a self-liquidating trust and a revolving trust.

6. In a securitization, what is (a) a lockout period and (b) an early amortization provision?

7. a. Why is credit enhancement required in a securitization?
   b. What entity determines the amount of securities needed in a securitization?

8. Why is the MPR for credit card receivable-backed securities important?

9. What is the limitation of a third-party guarantee as a form of credit enhancement?

10. An asset-backed security has been credit enhanced with a letter of credit from a bank with a single A credit rating. If this is the only form of credit enhancement, explain whether this issue can be assigned a triple A credit rating at the time of issuance.

11. A corporation is considering a securitization and is considering two possible credit enhancement structures backed by a pool of automobile loans. Total principal value underlying the asset-backed security is $300 million.

Principal Value for:	Structure I	Structure II
Pool of automobile loans	$304 million	$301 million
Senior class	250	270
Subordinate class	50	30

   a. Which structure would receive a higher credit rating and why?
   b. What form of credit enhancement is being used in both structures?

12. a. Why is a shifting interest mechanism included in a securitization where the collateral is residential mortgage loans?
   b. Why would a shifting interest mechanism *not* be included in a securitization where the assets being securitized do not have prepayments?

13. Suppose that for a securitization with a shifting interest mechanism you are given the following information for some month:

$$\text{subordinate interest} = 25\%$$
$$\text{shifting interest percentage} = 85\%$$
$$\text{regularly scheduled principal payment} = \$3,000,000$$
$$\text{prepayments} = \$1,200,000$$

   a. What is the senior prepayment percentage for the month?

   b. How much of the $3,000,000 regularly scheduled principal payment is distributed to the senior class?

   c. How much of the $1,200,000 is distributed to the senior class?

14. What is the purpose of the step down provisions in a securitization?

15. a. What is meant by concentration risk?

   b. How do rating agencies seek to limit the exposure of a pool of loans to concentration risk?

16. What is the difference between pool-level and loan-level analysis?

17. How do optional call provisions in a securitization differ from that of a call provision in a standard corporate bond?

18. What factors do the rating agencies consider in analyzing the structural risk in a securitization?

19. Why would an interest rate derivative be using in a securitization structure?

20. The following questions relate to auto loan-backed securities:

   a. What is the cash flow for an auto loan-backed security?

   b. Why are prepayments of minor importance for automobile loan-backed securities?

   c. How are prepayments on pools of auto loans measured?

21. The following questions relate to credit card receivable-backed securities:

   a. What happens to the principal repaid by borrowers in a credit card receivable-backed security during the lockout period?

   b. What is the role of the early amortization provision in a credit card receivable-backed security structure?

   c. How can the cash flow of a credit card receivable-backed security be altered prior to the principal-amortization period?

   d. Why is the monthly payment rate an important measure to examine when considering investing in a credit card receivable-backed security?

22. The following questions relate to home equity loan-backed securities:

   a. What is the cash flow of a closed-end home equity loan-backed security?

   b. How are prepayments on these securities measured?

   c. What is meant by the prospectus prepayment curve?

23. In a home equity loan-backed transaction, what is meant by an available funds cap and how does this cap differ from a typical cap in a floating-rate security?

24. The following questions relate to rate reduction bonds:

   a. What asset is the collateral?

   b. What is a true up provision in a securitization creating rate reduction bonds?

25. The following questions relate to manufactured housing-backed securities:

   a. What is the cash flow of a manufactured housing-backed security?

   b. How are prepayments measured for manufactured housing-backed securities?

   c. Why are prepayments on manufactured housing-backed securities less insensitive to prepayments due to refinancing compared to securities backed by other types of residential mortgage loans?

CHAPTER

15 COLLATERALIZED DEBT OBLIGATIONS

After reading this chapter you will understand:

■ what is meant by a collateralized debt obligation, collateralized bond obligation, and collateralized loan obligation

■ the structure of a collateralized debt obligation and the role of the collateral manager

■ the difference between an arbitrage and balance sheet transaction

■ the economics underlying an arbitrage transaction

■ the motivation for a balance sheet transaction

■ the difference between a cash flow transaction and a market value transaction

■ the types of restrictions imposed on management in a collateralized debt obligation

■ the difference between a cash and synthetic transaction

■ the need for an interest-rate swap in a cash transaction

■ the role of a credit default swap in a synthetic transaction

A collateralized debt obligation (CDO) is a security backed by a diversified pool of one or more of the following types of debt obligations:

- U.S. domestic investment-grade and high-yield corporate bonds
- U.S. domestic bank loans
- emerging market bonds
- special situation loans and distressed debt
- foreign bank loans
- asset-backed securities
- residential and commercial mortgage-backed securities

When the underlying pool of debt obligations consists of bond-type instruments (corporate and emerging market bonds), a CDO is referred to as a **collateralized bond obligation** (CBO).[1] When the underlying pool of debt obligations is bank loans, a CDO is referred to as a **collateralized loan obligation** (CLO).

It is common in the fixed-income market to refer to CDOs as a type of asset-backed security. However, the structure and investment characteristics of a CDO warrant a classification of its own. In this chapter we explain the basic CDO structure, the types of CDOs, and the risks associated with investing in CDOs.[2] The creation of these structures requires the use of derivative instruments, specifically interest-rate swaps (covered in Chapter 28) or credit default swaps (covered in Chapter 29). However, we will be able to describe the essential elements of CDOs without knowledge of these derivative instruments.

STRUCTURE OF A CDO

In a CDO structure, there is a **collateral manager** responsible for managing the portfolio of debt obligations. The portfolio of debt obligations in which the collateral manager invests is referred to as the **collateral**. The individual issues held that comprise the collateral are referred to as the **collateral assets**.

The funds to purchase the collateral assets are obtained from the issuance of debt obligations. These debt obligations are referred to as **tranches**. The tranches include:

- senior tranches
- mezzanine tranches
- subordinate/equity tranche

A CDO may or may not have a mezzanine tranche.

There will be a rating sought for all but the subordinate/equity tranche. For the senior tranches, at least an A rating is typically sought. For the mezzanine tranches, a rating of BBB but no less than B is sought. The subordinate/equity tranche receives the residual cash flow; hence, no rating is sought for this tranche. There are restrictions imposed as to what the collateral manager may do and certain tests that must be satisfied for the CDO to maintain the credit rating assigned at the time of issuance. We'll discuss some of these requirements later.

The ability of the collateral manager to make the interest payments to the tranches and pay off the tranches as they mature depends on the performance of the collateral. The proceeds to meet the obligations to the CDO tranches (interest and principal repayment) can come from

- coupon interest payments from the collateral assets
- maturing of collateral assets
- sale of collateral assets

---

[1] A CDO that includes primarily asset-backed securities and residential and commercial mortgage-backed securities is called a "structured CDO" by some dealer firms.

[2] For a more detailed discussion of CDOs, see Douglas J. Lucas, Laurie S. Goodman, and Frank J. Fabozzi, *Collateralized Debt Obligations: Structures and Analysis*, 2nd Edition (Hoboken, NJ: John Wiley & Sons, 2006).

In a typical structure, one or more of the tranches has a floating rate. With the exception of deals backed by bank loans that pay a floating rate, the collateral manager invests in fixed-rate bonds. Now that presents a problem—paying tranche investors a floating rate and investing in assets with a fixed rate. To deal with this problem, the collateral manager uses derivative instruments to be able to convert a portion of the fixed-rate payments from the assets into floating-rate cash flow to pay floating-rate tranches. In particular, interest-rate swaps are used. This instrument allows a market participant to swap fixed-rate payments for floating-rate payments or vice versa. Because of the mismatch between the nature of the cash flows of the debt obligations in which the collateral manager invests and the floating-rate liability of any of the tranches, the collateral manager must use an interest-rate swap. A rating agency will require the use of swaps to eliminate this mismatch.

Arbitrage Versus Balance Sheet Transactions

CDOs are categorized based on the motivation of the sponsor of the transaction. If the motivation of the sponsor is to earn the spread between the yield offered on the collateral and the payments made to the various tranches in the structure, then the transaction is referred to as an **arbitrage transaction**. If the motivation of the sponsor is to remove debt instruments (primarily loans) from its balance sheet, then the transaction is referred to as a **balance sheet transaction**. Sponsors of balance sheet transactions are typically financial institutions such as banks seeking to reduce their capital requirements specified by bank regulators by removing loans from their balance sheet. Our focus in this chapter is on arbitrage transactions.

Cash Versus Synthetic Structures

CDOs are also classified in terms of **cash CDO structures** and **synthetic CDO structures**. The latter involve the use of credit derivatives. At the outset of this chapter, we will focus on cash CDO structures. The last section of this chapter will cover synthetic CDO structures.

ARBITRAGE TRANSACTIONS

The key as to whether it is economically feasible to create an arbitrage CDO is whether a structure can offer a competitive return for the subordinate/equity tranche.

To understand how the subordinate/equity tranche generates cash flows, consider the following basic $100 million CDO structure with the coupon rate to be offered at the time of issuance as follows:

Tranche	Par Value	Coupon Type	Coupon Rate
Senior	$80,000,000	Floating	LIBOR + 70 basis points
Mezzanine	10,000,000	Fixed	Treasury rate + 200 basis points
Subordinate/Equity	10,000,000	—	—

We will make the following assumptions:

- the collateral consists of bonds that all mature in 10 years
- the coupon rate for every bond is a fixed rate
- the fixed rate at the time of purchase of each bond is the 10-year Treasury rate plus 400 basis points

Suppose the collateral manager enters into an interest-rate swap agreement with another party with a notional principal of $80 million in which it agrees to do the following:

- pay a fixed rate each year equal to the 10-year Treasury rate plus 100 basis points
- receive LIBOR

The interest-rate agreement is simply an agreement to periodically exchange interest payments. The payments are benchmarked off a notional amount. This amount is not exchanged between the two parties; it is used simply to determine the dollar interest payment of each party. This is all we need to know about an interest-rate swap in order to understand the economics of an arbitrage CDO transaction.[3] Keep in mind, the goal is to show how the subordinate/equity tranche can be expected to generate a return.

Let's assume that the 10-year Treasury rate at the time the CDO is issued is 7%. Now we can walk through the cash flows for each year. Look first at the collateral. The collateral will pay interest each year (assuming no defaults) equal to the 10-year Treasury rate of 7% plus 400 basis points. So the interest will be:

Interest from collateral: $11\% \times \$100,000,000 = \$11,000,000$

Now let's determine the interest that must be paid to the senior and mezzanine tranches. For the senior tranche, the interest payment will be:

Interest to senior tranche: $\$80,000,000 \times (\text{LIBOR} + 70 \text{ bp})$

The coupon rate for the mezzanine tranche is 7% plus 200 basis points. So, the coupon rate is 9% and the interest is:

Interest to mezzanine tranche: $9\% \times \$10,000,000 = \$900,000$

Finally, let's look at the interest-rate swap. In this agreement, the collateral manager is agreeing to pay some third party (called the swap counterparty) 7% each year (the 10-year Treasury rate) plus 100 basis points, or 8%. But 8% of what? As explained above, in an interest-rate swap payments are based on a notional amount. In our illustration, the notional amount is $80 million. The collateral manager selected the $80 million because this is the amount of principal for the senior tranche. So, the collateral manager pays to the swap counterparty:

Interest to swap counterparty: $8\% \times \$80,000,000 = \$6,400,000$

---

[3]Interest-rate swaps are covered in Chapter 28.

The interest payment received from the swap counterparty is LIBOR based on a notional amount of $80 million. That is,

$$\text{Interest from swap counterparty: } \$80,000,000 \times \text{LIBOR}$$

Now we can put this all together. Let's look at the interest coming into the CDO:

Interest from collateral	$= \$11,000,000$
Interest from swap counterparty	$= \$80,000,000 \times \text{LIBOR}$
Total interest received	$= \$11,000,000 + \$80,000,000 \times \text{LIBOR}$

The interest to be paid out to the senior and mezzanine tranches and to the swap counterparty include:

Interest to senior tranche	$= \$80,000,000 \times (\text{LIBOR} + 70 \text{ bp})$
Interest to mezzanine tranche	$= \$900,000$
Interest to swap counterparty	$= \$6,400,000$
Total interest paid	$= \$7,300,000 + \$80,000,000 \times (\text{LIBOR} + 70 \text{ bp})$

Netting the interest payments coming in and going out we have:

Total interest received	$= \$11,000,000 + \$80,000,000 \times \text{LIBOR}$
Total interest paid	$= \$7,300,000 + \$80,000,000 \times (\text{LIBOR} + 70 \text{ bp})$
Net interest	$= \$3,700,000 - \$80,000,000 \times (70 \text{ bp})$

Since 70 bp times $80 million is $560,000, the net interest remaining is $3,140,000 ($3,700,000 – $560,000). From this amount any fees (including the asset management fee) must be paid. The balance is then the amount available to pay the subordinate/equity tranche. Suppose that these fees are $634,000. Then the cash flow available to the subordinate/equity tranche is $2.5 million. Since the tranche has a par value of $10 million and is assumed to be sold at par, this means that the potential return is 25%.

In our illustration, some simplifying assumptions were made. For example, it is assumed that there are no defaults. It is assumed that all of the issues purchased by the collateral manager are noncallable (or not prepayable), and, therefore, the coupon rate would not decline because issues are called. Moreover, as explained later, after some period, the collateral manager must begin repaying principal to the senior and mezzanine tranches. Consequently, the interest-rate swap must be structured to take this into account since the entire amount of the senior tranche is not outstanding for the life of the collateral.

Despite the simplifying assumptions, the illustration does demonstrate the basic economics of arbitrage CDO structures, the need for the use of an interest-rate swap, and how the subordinate/equity tranche will realize a return. In determining whether or not to

CHAPTER 15 Collateralized Debt Obligations 353

create a CDO, dealers will look to see if there is a potential return available to the equity tranche of a minimum amount. The threshold return is based on market conditions.

Early Termination

A deal can be terminated early if certain events or default occur. These events basically relate to conditions that are established that would materially adversely impact the performance of the collateral. Such events include

- failure to comply with certain covenants
- failure to meet payments (interest and/or principal) to the senior tranches
- bankruptcy of the issuing entity of the CDO
- departure of the collateral management team if an acceptable replacement is not found

Types of Arbitrage Transactions

Arbitrage transactions can be divided into two types depending on the primary source of the proceeds from the collateral to satisfy the obligation to the tranches. If the primary source is the interest and maturing principal from the collateral, then the transaction is referred to as a **cash flow transaction**. If instead the proceeds to meet the obligations depend heavily on the total return generated from the collateral (i.e., interest income, capital gain, and maturing principal), then the transaction is referred to as a **market value transaction**.

CASH FLOW TRANSACTIONS

In a cash flow transaction, the objective of the collateral manager is to generate cash flow for the senior and mezzanine tranches without the need to actively trade bonds. Because the cash flows from the structure are designed to accomplish the objective for each tranche, restrictions are imposed on the collateral manager. The collateral manager is not free to buy and sell bonds. The conditions for disposing of issues held are specified and are usually driven by credit risk considerations. Also, in assembling the portfolio, the collateral manager must meet certain requirements set forth by the rating agency or agencies that rate the transaction.

There are three relevant periods. The first is the **ramp-up period**. This is the period that follows the closing date of the transaction where the collateral manager begins investing the proceeds from the sale of the debt obligations issued. This period usually lasts from one to two years. The **reinvestment period** or **revolving period** is where principal proceeds are reinvested and is usually for five or more years. In the final period, the collateral is sold and the debtholders are paid off.

Distribution of Income

Income is derived from interest income from the collateral assets and capital appreciation. The income is then used as follows. Payments are first made to the trustee and administrators and then to the senior collateral manager. Once these fees are paid, then the senior tranches are paid their interest. At this point, before any other payments are made, certain tests must be passed. These tests are called **coverage tests** and are discussed later. If the coverage tests are passed, then interest is paid to the mezzanine tranches. Once the mezzanine tranches are paid, interest is paid to the subordinate/equity tranche.

In contrast, if the coverage tests are not passed, then payments are made to protect the senior tranches. The remaining income after paying the fees and senior tranche interest is used to redeem the senior tranches (i.e., pay off principal) until the coverage tests are brought into compliance. If the senior tranches are paid off fully because the coverage tests are not brought into compliance, then any remaining income is used to redeem the mezzanine tranches. Any remaining income is then used to redeem the subordinate/equity tranche.

Distribution of Principal Cash Flow
The principal cash flow is distributed as follows after the payment of the fees to the trustees, administrators, and senior managers. If there is a shortfall in interest paid to the senior tranches, principal proceeds are used to make up the shortfall. Assuming that the coverage tests are satisfied, during the reinvestment period the principal is reinvested. After the reinvestment period or if the coverage tests are failed, the principal cash flow is used to pay down the senior tranches until the coverage tests are satisfied. If all the senior tranches are paid down, then the mezzanine tranches are paid off, followed by the subordinate/equity tranche.

After all the debt obligations are satisfied in full, if permissible, the equity investors are paid. Typically, there are also incentive fees paid to management based on performance. Usually a target return for the equity investors is established at the inception of the transaction. Management is then permitted to share on some pro-rated basis once the target return is achieved.

The collateral manager must monitor the collateral to ensure that certain tests are being met. There are two types of tests imposed by rating agencies: quality tests and coverage tests.

Restrictions on Management: Quality Tests
In rating a transaction, the rating agencies are concerned with the diversity of the assets. Consequently, there are tests that relate to the diversity of the assets. These tests are called **quality tests**. A collateral manager may not undertake a trade that will result in the violation of any of the quality tests. Quality tests include

- a minimum asset diversity score
- a minimum weighted-average rating
- maturity restrictions
- restrictions imposed on the concentration of bonds in certain countries or geographical regions for collateral consisting of emerging market bonds

Diversity Score
A **diversity score** is a measure that is constructed to gauge the diversity of the collateral's assets. Moody's has developed such a measure. The greater the score value, the lower the likelihood of default. The measure uses the binomial probability distribution

to estimate the number of collateral assets that will default over the life of the CDO. It is beyond the scope of this chapter to discuss this measure and the theory underlying its construction. Rather, what is important to understand is that every time the composition of the collateral changes, a diversity score is computed. There is a minimum diversity score needed to achieve a particular rating.

Weighted-Average Rating

A measure is also needed to gauge the credit quality of the collateral. Certainly one can describe the distribution of the credit ratings of the collateral in terms of the percentage of the collateral's asset in each credit rating. However, such a measure would be of limited use in establishing tests for a minimum credit rating for the collateral. There is a need to have one figure that summarizes the rating distribution test. Moody's and Fitch have developed a measure to summarize the rating distribution. This is commonly referred to as the **weighted-average rating factor** (WARF) for the collateral. This involves assigning a numerical value to each rating. These numerical values are referred to as "rating factors." For example, Moody's assigns a rating factor of 1 for Aaa-rated issues, scaling up to 10,000 for Ca-rated issues. For each collateral asset, the current face value of the issue is multiplied by its corresponding rating factor. The values are then summed to give the WARF, and a WARF value would then correspond to a rating for the collateral. The collateral manager must maintain a minimum average rating score.

Unlike Moody's and Fitch, S&P uses a different system. S&P specifies **required rating percentages** that the collateral must maintain. Specifically, S&P requires strict percentage limits for lower rated assets in the collateral.

Restrictions on Management: Coverage Tests

There are tests to ensure that the performance of the collateral is sufficient to make payments to the various tranches. These tests are called **coverage tests**. There are two types of coverage tests:

- par value tests
- interest coverage ratio tests

Recall that if the coverage tests are violated, then income from the collateral is diverted to pay down the senior tranches.

A separate par value test is used for each rated bond issued in the transaction. A **par value test** specifies that the par value of the collateral be at least a specified percentage above the liability to the bondholders. For example, suppose that the par value of the senior notes in a CDO deal is $80 million. The par value test might specify that the collateral's par value (i.e., the aggregate par value for all the collateral assets) must be 120% of the par value of the senior notes. That is, the par value of the collateral must be at least $96 million ($80 million times 120%). Basically, this is an **overcollateralization test** for a rated bond issued since it is a measure of the cushion provided by the collateral's assets over the obligation to the bondholders *in terms of par value.*

The percentage in the par value test is called the **trigger**, and as indicated, the trigger is different for each rated bond. Specifically, the trigger declines as the rating declines. For example, if the trigger for the senior notes is 120%, then the trigger will be less than 120% for the mezzanine tranches. This simply means that the overcollateralization in terms of par value declines as the rating of a bond issued in the transaction declines.

While par value tests focus on the market value of the collateral relative to the par value of the bonds issued, **interest coverage tests** look at the ability to meet interest payments when due.

MARKET VALUE TRANSACTIONS

In a market value transaction, the cash flow generated to pay the bondholders depends upon the ability of the collateral manager to maintain and improve the market value of the collateral. Funds to be used for liability principal payments are obtained from liquidating the collateral. Liability interest payments can be made from collateral interest receipts, as well as collateral liquidation proceeds. Ratings are based on price volatility, liquidity, and market value of the collateral assets. The collateral manager focuses on maximizing total return while minimizing volatility.

Market value transactions represent a small portion of CDO transactions. They are used for certain types of collateral where the cash flows are not predictable with a reasonable degree of certainty. Creating a cash flow transaction structure is very difficult when the collateral has unpredictable cash flows. They are also used by collateral managers who want the greater flexibility for trading permitted by a market value structure and other buyers of the subordinate/equity tranches that feel the greater expected return warrants the use of this structure.

As with cash value transactions, market value transactions do have tests with respect to overcollateralization, diversity, and concentration. We will take a closer look at the difference between the overcollateralization tests for market value transactions later. Moreover, there are other constraints but these constraints are less than those in cash flow transactions.

The order of priority of the principal payments in the capital structure is as follows. Fees are paid first for trustees, administrators, and managers. After these fees are paid, the senior facility and the senior notes are paid. The two classes in the capital structure are treated equally in their rights to their claim on cash proceeds from the collateral. That is, their payments are prorated if there is a shortfall. If the senior facility or senior notes are amortizing, they would have the next priority on the cash proceeds from the collateral with respect to the payment of the principal due. The senior-subordinated notes would be paid, followed by the subordinated notes. All of this assumes that the overcollateralization tests are satisfied. If not, the senior notes are then paid down until the overcollateralization tests are brought into compliance.

When rating a cash flow transaction, the rating agencies look at the ability of the collateral to generate sufficient current cash flow to pay interest and principal on rated notes issued by the CDO. The ratings are based on the effect of collateral defaults and recoveries on the receipt of timely interest and principal payments from the collateral. It is the job of the collateral manager to concentrate efforts on controlling defaults and recoveries. If the overcollateralization tests are not met, then cash flow is diverted from the mezzanine and subordinated classes to pay down senior notes, or cash flow is trapped in a reserve account. Failing the overcollateralization tests does not force sale of the collateral.

Overcollateralization Tests

Overcollateralization tests in market value transactions are based on the market value of the collateral, not the par value. Market value overcollateralization tests require that the market value of the collateral be adjusted as explained later to obtain an adjusted market value for the collateral. Using this adjusted market value for the collateral, if the overcollateralization tests are failed, sale of some of the collateral assets and redemption of some of the liabilities may be required to bring the overcollateralization ratios back into compliance.[4]

The advance rates are the key in the overcollateralization tests and critical in market value transactions. Advance rates are determined by the rating agencies based on a combination of three factors: (1) price volatility, (2) correlation among securities, and (3) liquidity. The rating agencies begin by classifying asset types. For example, Moody's asset types are:[5]

Performing Bank Loans Valued $0.90 and above
Distressed Bank Loans Valued $0.85 and above
Performing High-Yield Bonds Rated Baa
Performing High-Yield Bonds Rated B
Distressed Bank Loans Valued Below $0.85
Performing High-Yield Valued Below Caa
Distressed Bonds
Reorganized Equities

There is then an advance rate assigned to each asset type based on (1) the structure of the transaction and (2) the composition of the collateral. For example, suppose that a structure has only one rated tranche. This means that there is only a senior tranche and no mezzanine tranche. Consequently, all of the protection for the senior tranche must come from the collateral. The following table shows the advance rates for performing high-yield bonds rated B assigned by Moody's to obtain a target rating of Aaa, Aa3, A3, or Baa3 if the collateral contains one asset type:[6]

	Target Rating			
	Aaa	Aa3	A3	Baa3
20 Issuers and 5 Industries	0.72	0.77	0.80	0.85
40 Issuers and 10 Industries	0.74	0.80	0.83	0.76

---

[4]There are other alternatives to bring the collateral into compliance: Higher credit-rated assets that have higher advance rates can be substituted for lower credit-rated assets with lower advance rates.
[5]Yvonne Fu Falcone and Jeremy Gluck, "Moody's Approach to Market-Value CDOs," Special Report, *Structured Finance*, April 8, 1998.
[6]The advance rates were obtained from tables reported in Falcone and Gluck, "Moody's Approach to Market-Value CDOs."

As will be seen when we illustrate how to use advance rates, the higher the advance rate, the greater the adjusted market value for a collateral asset. Notice that the lower the credit rating sought for a single tranche, the higher the advance rate. That is, it will be easier to pass an overcollateralization test the lower the credit rating sought. Also notice that the more issuers in a structure and the more industries, the higher the advance rate for a given target rating.

Our illustration is only for deals with a single tranche and one asset type. When there is more than one tranche and more than one asset type, the advance rates are different. The way that they change is systematic. For example, if there is a mezzanine tranche, then part of the protection afforded the senior tranche comes from the mezzanine tranche. Thus, the advance rates reported in the preceding table would be higher for the senior tranche. Moreover, when there is more than one asset type, the advance rate depends on the correlation between the asset types in the collateral.

Now that we have a general understanding of advance rates, let's see how they are used. Suppose that the collateral consists of three asset types with the assumed advance ratings for the particular rating sought for a tranche:

Asset Type	Market Value	Advance Rate
Performing High-Yield Bonds Rated Baa	$50 million	0.80
Performing High-Yield Bonds Rated B	$30 million	0.75
Performing High-Yield Valued Below Caa	$20 million	0.70

The market value of the collateral is $100 million. The adjusted market value that must be used in the overcollateralization tests for this tranche would then be found by multiplying the market value of an asset type by the advance rate and then summing over all asset types. So, for our hypothetical collateral, the adjusted market value is found as follows:

$$\$50,000,000 \times 0.80 + \$30,000,000 \times 0.75 + \$20,000,000 \times 0.70 = \$76,500,000$$

SYNTHETIC CDOS

The CDO structures discussed thus far are called **cash CDO structures**. They are so named because the collateral assets are owned. In recent years, the fastest growing sector of the CDO market is the **synthetic CDO structure**. The name follows from the fact that the collateral assets are not actually owned. Instead, in a synthetic CDO the collateral absorbs the economic risks associated with specified assets but does not have legal ownership of those assets. There are both synthetic balance sheet and synthetic arbitrage CDO structures.[7]

---

[7]For a further discussion of synthetic balance sheet CDO structures and synthetic arbitrage CDO structures, see Chapters 12 and 13 in Lucas, Goodman, and Fabozzi, *Collateralized Debt Obligations: Structures and Analysis*.

The creation of a synthetic CDO structure requires the use of a credit derivative.[8] More specifically, the type of credit derivative used is a **credit default swap**. A credit default swap allows market participants that own an asset to transfer the credit risk associated with that asset to another party without transferring the legal ownership of that asset. For example, a bank may own a portfolio of bank loans and is therefore exposed to the credit risk of the bank loans in the portfolio. A credit default swap can be used to transfer the credit risk of all or a portion of the bank loans to another party without transferring the bank loans to that party.

Let's take a brief look at a credit default swap. This derivative instrument is conceptually similar to an insurance policy. There is a credit protection buyer and a credit protection seller. The credit protection buyer pays a fee (premium) to the credit protection seller. If a "credit event" occurs, then the credit protection seller must make a payment to the credit protection buyer. Credit events on a debt instrument may include bankruptcy, failure to pay when due, downgrading of an issue, debt repudiation, and debt restructuring. The defining of a credit event is obviously critical in credit derivatives and we will discuss credit events further in Chapter 29 when we cover credit derivatives.

With this basic information about credit default swaps, let's look at the basic structure of a synthetic CDO. As with a cash CDO structure, liabilities are issued. The proceeds received from the tranches will be invested by the collateral manager in assets with low risk. In addition, the collateral manager will enter into a credit default swap with another entity in which it will provide credit protection. Because it is selling credit protection, the collateral manager will receive the credit default swap fee.

On the other side of the credit default swap will be a credit protection buyer who will be paying the fee. This entity will be a financial institution seeking to shed the credit risk of some of its assets. For example, it could be a bank that is using the credit default swap for some specifically defined loans in the bank's portfolio. These loans are referred to as the **reference assets** in the credit default swap.

If a credit event does not occur, the return realized by the collateral manager that will be available to meet the structure's obligations will be the return on the collateral consisting of low risk assets plus the fee received from the credit default swap. If there is a default on any of the referenced assets, the collateral manager must make a payment to the counterparty. This reduces the return available to meet the structure's obligations.

SUMMARY

A collateralized debt obligation is a security backed by a diversified pool of one or more debt obligations. A CDO in which the collateral assets are bond-type instruments is called a collateralized bond obligation. A collateralized loan obligation is a CDO where the collateral assets are bank loans.

A collateral manager is responsible for managing the collateral subject to restrictions imposed regarding the composition of the collateral. The funds to purchase the

---

[8]Credit derivatives are discussed in Chapter 29.

collateral assets come from the issuance of debt obligations. These debt obligations include senior tranches, mezzanine tranches, and a subordinate/equity tranche. The ability of the collateral manager to make the interest payments to the tranches and pay off the tranches as they mature depends on the performance of the collateral.

CDOs are categorized as either arbitrage transactions or balance sheet transactions. The categorization depends on the motivation of the sponsor of the transaction. In an arbitrage transaction, the sponsor seeks to earn the spread between the yield offered on the collateral assets and the payments made to the various tranches in the structure. In a balance sheet transaction, the sponsor's motivation is to remove debt instruments from its balance sheet. Interest-rate swaps are often used in CDO structures due to the mismatch between the characteristics of the collateral cash flow and some of the liabilities.

Arbitrage transactions are further classified as cash flow transactions and market value transactions. The classification depends on the source of funds from the collateral to satisfy the obligation to the tranches. In a cash flow transaction, the primary source is the interest and maturing principal from the collateral assets. In a market value transaction, the proceeds to meet the obligations depend heavily on the total return generated from the portfolio (i.e., interest income, capital gain, and maturing principal).

The collateral manager must monitor the collateral to ensure that certain tests are being met. There are two types of tests imposed by rating agencies: quality tests and coverage tests. Quality tests involve diversity measures, weighted-average ratings, maturity restrictions, and concentration limits. Coverage tests include par value tests and interest coverage ratio tests. Par value tests are also called overcollateralization tests. In a cash flow structure, overcollateralization tests use the par value of the collateral assets. In a market value transaction, the market value of the collateral, adjusted for the advance rate of the collateral assets, is used in the overcollateralization tests. Advance rates are determined by the rating agencies based on a combination of three factors: price volatility, correlation among securities, and liquidity. The higher the advance rate, the greater the adjusted market value for a collateral asset.

CDOs are also classified in terms of cash CDO structures and synthetic CDO structures. In the latter structure, a credit default swap is used.

Questions

1. What is the motivation of a sponsor for an arbitrage CDO?
2. What is the motivation of a sponsor for a balance sheet CDO?
3. Why is the subordinate/equity tranche of a CDO not rated?
4. a. What are the sources of funds that are used in a CDO to pay bondholders?
   b. How does the source of funds affect the classification of a CDO as a cash flow CDO and a market value CDO?
5. a. If there is a shortfall in interest paid to the senior tranches of a CDO, how is the shortfall made up?

   b. If coverage tests are failed for a CDO, how is the principal received from the collateral used?
6. What events can result in the early termination of a CDO structure?
7. How do overcollateralization tests for cash flow transactions differ from those of market value transactions?
8. a. What is the role of advance rates in overcollateralization tests?
   b. What factors affect the advance rates?
9. What is the purpose of a diversity score?
10. How is the credit quality of the collateral measured in a CDO structure?

11. Suppose that the collateral of a market value CDO consists of the following three asset types:

Asset Type	Market Value	Advance Rate
Performing High-Yield Bonds Rated Baa	$90 million	0.85
Performing High-Yield Bonds Rated B	$40 million	0.78
Performing High-Yield Valued Below Caa	$30 million	0.71

In an overcollateralization test, what market value is used?

12. Explain why you agree or disagree with the following statement: "The collateral manager for a CDO is free to actively manage the portfolio without any constraints."

13. Consider the following basic $150 million CDO structure with the coupon rate to be offered at the time of issuance as shown:

Tranche	Par Value	Coupon Rate
Senior	$100,000,000	LIBOR + 50 basis points
Mezzanine	$ 30,000,000	Treasury rate + 200 basis points
Subordinated/ Equity	$ 20,000,000	

Assume the following:

- The collateral consists of bonds that all mature in 10 years.
- The coupon rate for every bond is the 10-year Treasury rate plus 300 basis points.
- The collateral manager enters into an interest-rate swap agreement with another party with a notional amount of $100 million.
- In the interest-rate swap the collateral manager agrees to pay a fixed rate each year equal to the 10-year Treasury rate plus 100 basis points and receive LIBOR.

a. Why is an interest-rate swap needed?
b. What is the potential return for the subordinate/equity tranche assuming no defaults?
c. Why will the actual return be less than the return computed?

14. a. In a synthetic CDO, what is the source of funds for making payments to bondholders?
b. How do defaults on the reference assets impact the ability to pay bondholders?

15. In a synthetic CDO, what is the role of a credit default swap?

16 INTEREST-RATE MODELS

After reading this chapter you will understand:

- what an interest-rate model is

- how an interest-rate model is represented mathematically

- the characteristics of an interest-rate model: drift, volatility, and mean reversion

- what a one-factor interest-rate model is

- the difference between an arbitrage-free model and an equilibrium model

- the different types of arbitrage-free models and why they are used in practice

- the difference between a normal model and a lognormal model

- the empirical evidence on interest rate changes

- considerations in selecting an interest rate model

- how to calculate historical volatility

In implementing bond portfolio strategies there are two important activities that a manager will undertake. One will be the determination of whether the bonds that are purchase and sale candidates are fairly priced. The same applies to any interest-rate derivatives that the manager may want to employ to control interest-rate risk or potentially enhance returns. Second, a manager will want to assess the performance of a portfolio over realistic future interest-rate scenarios. For both of these activities, the manager will have to rely on an interest-rate model.

Future interest rates are, of course, unknown. The description of the uncertainty about future interest rates is mathematically described by an interest-rate model. More specifically, an **interest-rate model** is a probabilistic description of how interest rates can change over time. In this chapter we provide an overview of interest-rate models. Our focus will be on *nominal* interest rates rather than *real* interest rates (i.e., the nominal interest rate reduced by the inflation rate). At the end of this chapter, we will see how interest-rate volatility is computed using historical data.

MATHEMATICAL DESCRIPTION OF ONE-FACTOR INTEREST-RATE MODELS

Interest-rate models must incorporate statistical properties of interest-rate movements. These properties are (1) drift, (2) volatility, and (3) mean reversion. We will describe each property next. The commonly used mathematical tool for describing the movement of interest rates that can incorporate these properties is **stochastic differential equations** (SDEs). A rigorous treatment of interest-rate modeling requires an understanding of this specialized topic in mathematics. Because SDEs are typically not covered in finance courses (except in financial engineering programs), we provide only the basic elements of the subject here. It is also worth noting that SDEs are used in the pricing of options, the most well-known model being the Black-Scholes model that we will describe in Chapter 27.

The most common interest-rate model used to describe the behavior of interest rates assumes that short-term interest rates follow some statistical process and that other interest rates in the term structure are related to short-term rates. The short-term interest rate (i.e., short rate) is the only one that is assumed to drive the rates of all other maturities. Hence, these models are referred to as **one-factor models**. The other rates are not randomly determined once the short rate is specified. Using arbitrage arguments, the rate for all other maturities is determined.

There are also multi-factor models that have been proposed in the literature. The most common multi-factor model is a two-factor model where a long-term rate is the second factor. In practice, however, one-factor models are used because of the difficulty of applying even a two-factor model. The high correlation between rate changes for different maturities provides some support for the use of a one-factor model as well as empirical evidence that supports the position that a level shift in interest rates accounts for the major portion of the change in the yield curve.[1] Consequently, our focus is on one-factor models.

While the value of the short rate at some future time is uncertain, the pattern by which it changes over time can be assumed. In statistical terminology, this pattern or behavior is called a **stochastic process**. Thus, describing the dynamics of the short rate means specifying the stochastic process that describes the movement of the short rate. It is assumed that the short rate is a continuous random variable and therefore the stochastic process used is a **continuous-time stochastic process**.

There are different types of continuous-time stochastic processes, and we describe those used in interest-rate modeling next. In all of these models because time is a

---

[1] Note that a one-factor model should not be used in valuing financial instruments where the payoff depends on the shape of the spot rate curve rather than simply the level of interest rates. Examples would be dual index floaters and yield curve options.

continuous variable, the letter *d* is used to denote the "change in" some variable. Specifically, in the models below we will let

> *r* = the short rate and therefore *dr* denotes the change in the short rate
> *t* = time and therefore *dt* denotes the change in time or equivalently the length of the time interval (*dt* is a very small interval of time)
> *z* = a random term and *dz* denotes a random process

A Basic Continuous-Time Stochastic Process

Let's start with a basic continuous-time stochastic process for describing the dynamics of the short rate given by:

$$dr = bdt + \sigma dz \tag{16.1}$$

where

dr, dt, and *dz* were defined above and
σ = standard deviation of the changes in the short rate
b = expected direction of rate change

The expected direction of the change in the short rate (*b*) is called the **drift term** and σ is called the **volatility term**.[2]

In words, equation (16.1) says that the change in the short rate (*dr*) over the time interval (*dt*) depends on:

1. the expected direction of the change in the short rate (*b*) and
2. a random process (*dz*) that is affected by volatility

The random nature of the change in the short rate comes from the random process *dz*. The assumptions are that

1. the random term *z* follows a normal distribution with a mean of zero and a standard deviation of one (i.e., is a standardized normal distribution).
2. the change in the short rate is proportional to the value of the random term, which depends on the standard deviation of the change in the short rate.
3. the change in the short rate for any two different short intervals of time are independent.

Based on the assumptions above, important properties can be shown for equation (16.1). The expected value of the change in the short rate is equal to *b*, the drift term. Notice that in the special case where the drift term is equal to zero, equation (16.1) tells us that expected value of the change in the short rate is zero. This means that the expected value for the short rate is its current value. Note that in the special case where the drift term is zero and the variance is one, it can be shown that the variance of the change in the short rate over some interval of length *T* is equal to *T* and therefore the standard deviation is the square root of *T*.

---

[2]A special case of the SDE described by equation (16.1) when *b* is equal to zero and σ is equal to one is called a standard Wiener process and is the building block for constructing models in continuous time.

Itô Process

Notice that in equation (16.1) neither the drift term nor the standard deviation of the change in the short rate depend on either the level of the short rate and time. So, for example, suppose the current short rate is 3%, then the SDE given by equation (16.1) assumes that b is the same if the current short rate is 12%. There are economic reasons that might suggest that the expected direction of the rate change will depend on the level of the current short rate. The same is true for σ.

We can change the dynamics of the drift term and the dynamics of the volatility term by allowing these two parameters to depend on the level of the short rate and/or time. We can denote that the drift term depends on both the level of the short rate and time by $b(r,t)$. Similarly, we can denote the volatility term by $\sigma(r,t)$. We can then write

$$dr = b(r,t)\, dt + \sigma\,(r,t)\, dz \tag{16.2}$$

The continuous-time stochastic model given by equation (16.2) is called an **Itô process**.

Specifying the Dynamics of the Drift Term

In specifying the dynamics of the drift term, one can specify that the drift term depends on the level of the short rate by assuming it follows a **mean-reversion process**. By mean reversion it is meant that some long-run stable mean value for the short rate is assumed. We will denote this value by $\bar{r}$. So, if r is greater than $\bar{r}$, the direction of change in the short rate will move down in the direction of the long-run stable value and vice versa. However, in specifying the mean-reversion process, it is necessary to indicate the speed at which the short rate will move or converge to the long-run stable mean value. This parameter is called the **speed of adjustment** and we will denote it by α. Thus, the mean-reversion process that specifies the dynamics of the drift term is:

$$b(r,t) = -\alpha(r - \bar{r}) \tag{16.3}$$

Specifying the Dynamics of the Volatility Term

There have been several formulations of the dynamics of the volatility term. If volatility is not assumed to depend on time, then $\sigma(r,t) = \sigma(r)$. In general, the dynamics of the volatility term can be specified as follows:

$$\sigma\, r^{\gamma}\, dz \tag{16.4}$$

where γ is equal to the **constant elasticity of variance**. Equation (16.4) is called the **constant elasticity of variance model** (CEV model). The CEV model allows us to distinguish between the different specifications of the dynamics of the volatility term for the various interest-rate models suggested by researchers.

Let's look at three cases for γ: 0, 1, and ½. Substituting these values for γ into equation (16.4) we get the following models identified by the researchers who first proposed them:

$\gamma = 0$:	$\sigma(r,t) = \sigma$;	Vasicek specification[3]
$\gamma = 1$:	$\sigma(r,t) = \sigma\, r$	Dothan specification[4]
$\gamma = $ ½:	$\sigma(r,t) = \sigma\sqrt{r}$	Cox-Ingersoll-Ross specification[5]

In the Vasicek specification, volatility is independent of the level of the short rate as in equation (16.1) and is referred to as the **normal model**. In the normal model, it is possible for negative interest rates to be generated. In the Dothan specification, volatility is proportional to the short rate. This model is referred to as the **proportional volatility model**. The Cox-Ingersoll-Ross (CIR) specification, referred to for obvious reasons as the **square-root model**, makes the volatility proportional to the square rate of the short rate. Negative interest rates are not possible in the square-root model.

One can combine the dynamics of the drift term and volatility term to create the following commonly used interest rate model:

$$dr = -\alpha(r - \bar{r})\,dt + \alpha\sqrt{r}\,dz$$

(16.5)

Notice that this model specifies a mean-reversion process for the drift term and the square root model for volatility. The model given by equation (16.5) is referred to as the **mean-reverting square-root model**.

ARBITRAGE-FREE VERSUS EQUILIBRIUM MODELS

Interest-rate models fall into two general categories: arbitrage models and equilibrium models. We describe both in this section.

Arbitrage-Free Models

In **arbitrage-free models**, also referred to as **no-arbitrage models**, the analysis begins with the observed market price of a set of financial instruments. The financial instruments can include cash market instruments and interest-rate derivatives, and they are referred to as the **benchmark instruments** or **reference set**. The underlying assumption is that the benchmark instruments are fairly priced. A random process for the generation of the term structure is assumed. The random process assumes a drift term for interest rates and volatility of interest rates. Based on the random process and the assumed value for the parameter that represents the drift term, a computational

---

[3]Oldrich A. Vasicek, "An Equilibrium Characterization of the Term Structure," *Journal of Financial Economics*, 1977, pp. 177–188.
[4]L. Uri Dothan, "On the Term Structure of Interest Rates," *Journal of Financial Economics*, 1978, pp. 59–69.
[5]John C. Cox, Jonathan E. Ingersoll, Jr, and Stephen A. Ross. "A Theory of the Term Structure of Interest Rates," *Econometrica*, 1985, pp. 385–407.

procedure is used to calculate the term structure of interest rates (i.e., the spot rate curve) such that the valuation process generates the observed market prices for the benchmark instruments. The model is referred to as arbitrage-free because it matches the observed prices of the benchmark instruments. In other words, one cannot realize an arbitrage profit by pursuing a strategy based on the value of the securities generated by the model and the observed market price. Non-benchmark instruments are then valued using the term structure of interest rates estimated and the volatility assumed.

We'll describe how this is done in the next chapter where we will start with the price of benchmark bonds, generate a spot rate curve that matches the market prices of the benchmark bonds, and then use the model to generate the theoretical price of non-benchmark bonds. The arbitrage-free model is also used to value certain derivatives (options, caps, floors, and swaptions) using a consistent framework for valuing cash market instruments. In Chapters 27 and 28, we'll see how the arbitrage-free model is used to value option-type derivatives.

The most popular arbitrage-free interest-rate models used for valuation are[6]

- the Ho-Lee model
- the Hull-White model
- the Kalotay-Williams-Fabozzi model
- the Black-Karasinki model
- the Black-Derman-Toy model
- the Heath-Jarrow-Morton model

The first arbitrage-free interest-rate model was introduced by Ho and Lee in 1986.[7] In the Ho-Lee model, there is no mean reversion and volatility is independent of the level of the short rate. That is, it is a normal model [i.e, $\gamma = 0$ in equation (16.4)]. The Hull-White model is also a normal model.[8] Unlike the Ho-Lee model, however, it allows for mean reversion. Thus, the Hull-White model is the first arbitrage-free, mean-reverting normal model.

The last three models listed above are lognormal models. In the Kalotay-Williams-Fabozzi (KWF) model,[9] changes in the short-rate are modeled by modeling the natural logarithm of r; no allowance for mean reversion is considered in the model. It is this model that will be used in the next chapter to value bonds with embedded options. The Black-Karasinski model[10] is a generalization of the KWF model by allowing for mean reversion. That is, the Black-Karasinski model is the logarithmic extension of the KWF model in the same way that the Hull-White model is the normal model extension of the

---

[6]For a more detailed discussion including a discussion of the solution to these models, see Gerald W. Buetow, Frank J. Fabozzi, and James Sochacki, "A Review of No Arbitrage Interest Rate Models," Chapter 3 in Frank J. Fabozzi (ed.), *Interest Rate, Term Structure, and Valuation Modeling* (Hoboken, NJ: John Wiley & Sons, 2002).
[7]Thomas Ho and Sang Lee, "Term Structure Movements and Pricing Interest Rate Contingent Claims," *Journal of Finance*, 1986, pp. 1011–1029.
[8]John Hull and Alan White, "Pricing Interest Rate Derivative Securities," *Review of Financial Studies*, 1990, pp. 573–592.
[9]Andrew Kalotay, George Williams, and Frank J. Fabozzi, "A Model for the Valuation of Bonds and Embedded Options," *Financial Analyst Journal*, May–June 1993, pp. 35–46.
[10]Fisher Black and Piotr Karasinski, "Bond and Option Pricing When Short Rates are Lognormal," *Financial Analyst Journal*, July–August 1991, pp. 52–59.

Ho-Lee model. The Black-Derman-Toy (BDT) model[11] allows for mean reversion. However, unlike the Black-Karasinski model, mean reversion is endogenous to the model. The mean reversion in the BDT model is determined by market conditions.

The Heath-Jarrow-Morton (HJM) model is a general continuous time, multi-factor model.[12] The HJM model has received considerable attention in the industry as well as in the finance literature. Many other no-arbitrage models are shown to be special cases of the HJM model. The HJM model does not require assumptions about investor preferences but instead only requires a description of the volatility structure of forward interest rates. A special case of the one-factor HJM model is derived by Jeffrey.[13]

Equilibrium Models

A fair characterization of arbitrage-free models is that they allow one to interpolate the term structure of interest rates from a set of observed market prices at one point in time assuming that one can rely on the market prices used. **Equilibrium models**, however, are models that seek to describe the dynamics of the term structure using fundamental economic variables that are assumed to affect the interest-rate process. In the modeling process, restrictions are imposed allowing for the derivation of closed-form solutions for equilibrium prices of bonds and interest rate derivatives. In these models (1) a functional form of the interest-rate volatility is assumed and (2) how the drift moves up and down over time is assumed.

In characterizing the difference between arbitrage-free and equilibrium models, one can think of the distinction being whether the model is designed to be consistent with any initial term structure, or whether the parameterization implies a particular family of term structure of interest rates. Arbitrage-free models have the deficiency that the initial term structure is an input rather than being explained by the model. Basically, equilibrium models and arbitrage models are seeking to do different things.

While there have been many developments in equilibrium models, the best known models are the Vasicek and CIR models discussed previously and the Brennan and Schwartz,[14] and Longstaff and Schwartz models.[15] To implement these models, estimates of the parameters of the assumed interest-rate process are needed, including the parameters of the volatility function for interest rates. These estimated parameters are typically obtained using econometric techniques using historical yield curves without regard to how the final model matches any market prices.

---

[11]Fischer Black, Emanuel Derman, and William Toy, "A One Factor Model of Interest Rates and Its Application to the Treasury Bond Options," *Financial Analyst Journal*, January–February 1990, pp. 33–39.
[12]David Heath, Robert A. Jarrow, and Andrew J. Morton, "Bond Pricing and the Term Structure of Interest Rates: A New Methodology for Contingent Claims Valuation," *Econometrica*, 60, 1992, pp. 77–105. The Brace-Gatarek-Musiela model is a particular implementation of the HJM model, which corresponds to a specific choice of the volatility term: Alan Brace, Dariusz Gatarek, and Marcek Musiela, "The Market Model of Interest Rate Dynamics," *Mathematical Finance*, 7, 1997, pp. 127–155.
[13]Andrew Jeffrey, "Single Factor Heath-Jarrow-Morton Term Structure Models Based on Spot Interest Rate Dynamics," *Journal of Financial and Quantitative Analysis*, 30, 1995, pp. 619–642.
[14]Michael Brennan and Eduardo Schwartz, "A Continuous Time Approach to the Pricing of Bonds," *Journal of Banking and Finance*, 1979, pp. 133–155; "An Equilibrium Model of Bond Pricing and a Test of Market Efficiency," *Journal of Financial and Quantitative Analysis*, 1982, pp. 301–329.
[15]Francis Longstaff and Eduardo Schwartz, "Interest Rate Volatility and the Term Structure: A Two-Factor General Equilibrium Model," *Journal of Finance*, 1992, pp. 1259–1282.

In practice, there are two concerns with implementing and using equilibrium models. First, many economic theories start with an assumption about the class of utility functions to describe how investors make choices. Equilibrium models are no exception: the model builder must specify the assumed class of utility functions. Second, as noted previously, these models are not calibrated to the market so that the prices obtained from the model can lead to arbitrage opportunities in the current term structure.[16] These models are such that volatility is an input into the model rather than output that can be extracted from observed prices for financial instruments.

EMPIRICAL EVIDENCE ON INTEREST-RATE CHANGES

Now that we are familiar with the different types of interest-rate models, let's look at empirical evidence regarding the historical movement of interest rates. Our motivation for doing so is to help in assessing the various arbitrage-free interest-rate models. Specifically, in our review of interest-rate models, we encountered the following issues:

1. The choice between normal models (i.e., volatility is independent of the level of interest rates) and logarithm models.
2. If interest rates are highly unlikely to be negative, then interest-rate models that allow for negative rates may be less suitable as a description of the interest-rate process.

Accordingly, we present evidence regarding:

- the relationship between interest-rate volatility and the level of interest rates
- negative interest rates

Recall from Chapter 3 that the change in interest rates can be measured by either the absolute rate change (absolute value of the change in spread in basis points between two time periods) or percentage rate change (computed as the natural logarithm of the ratio of the yield for two time periods).

Volatility of Rates and the Level of Interest Rates

We will first look at the historical movement to examine the issue as to whether interest-rate volatility is affected by the level of interest rates or independent of the level of interest rates. In the former case, the higher the level of interest rates, the greater the interest-rate volatility. That is, there is a positive correlation between the level of interest rates and interest-rate volatility. If the two are independent, a low correlation would exist.

The dependence of volatility on the level of interest rates has been examined by several researchers. The earlier research focused on short-term rates and employed a statistical time series model called generalized autoregressive conditional

---

[16]To deal with this, Dybvig has suggested an approach that has been used by some commercial vendors of analytical systems. See Philip Dybvig, "Bond and Bond Option Pricing Based on the Current Term Structure," in Michael A.H. Dempster and Stanley Pliska (eds.), *Mathematics of Derivatives Securities* (Cambridge, U.K.: Cambridge University Press, 1997).

heteroscedasticity (GARCH).[17] With respect to short-term rates, the findings were inconclusive.

Rather than focusing on the short-term rate, Oren Cheyette of MSCI Barra examined all the spot rates for the Treasury yield curve for the period 1977 to early 1996, a period covering a wide range of interest rates and different Federal Reserve policies.[18] He finds that for different periods there are different degrees of dependence of volatility on the level of interest rates. (Interest-rate changes are measured as absolute rate changes in Cheyette's study.) Specifically, in the high interest-rate environment of the late 1970s and early 1980s where interest rates exceeded 10%, there was a positive correlation between interest-rate volatility and the level of interest rates. However, when interest rates were below 10%, the relationship was weak. Hence, the findings suggest that since the 1980s, interest-rate volatility has been independent of the level of interest rates. These conclusions were supported in a study by Levin of the Treasury 10-year rate from 1980 to 2003 and the 10-year swap rate from 1989 to 2003.[19]

The implication is that in modeling interest rates, one can assume that interest-rate volatility is independent of the level of interest rates in an environment where rates are less than double digit. That is, in modeling the dynamics of the volatility term the normal model can be used.

Negative Interest Rates

Our focus is on nominal interest rates. While we know that real interest rates (rates adjusted for inflation) in an economy have been negative, it is generally thought that it is impossible for the nominal interest rate to be negative. The reason is that if the nominal rate is negative, investors will simply hold cash. However, there have been time periods in countries where interest rates have been negative for a brief time period, refuting the notion that investors would not be willing to lend at negative interest rates.

For example, during the Great Depression in the United States, financial historians have identified periods where Treasury securities traded at a negative yield. Japan provides another example. In early November 1998, Western banks charged Japanese banks interest of 3 to 6 basis points to hold 2- or 3-month yen deposits that Japanese banks were unwilling to deposit with local institutions because of the perceived instability of Japan's financial system. The yield on 3-month Japanese Treasury bills during one trading day in November 1998 fell to −5 basis points, although the closing yield was positive.

---

[17]See, for example, K. C. Chan, G. A. Karolyi, Francis A. Longstaff, and Anthony B. Sanders, "An Empirical Comparison of Alternative Models of the Short Rate," *Journal of Finance* 47:3, 1992, pp.1209–1227; Robin J. Brenner, Richard H. Harjes, and Kenneth F. Kroner, "Another Look at Alternative Models of the Short-Term Interest Rate," *Journal of Financial and Quantitative Analysis*, 31, 1996, pp. 85–107; and, Yacine Aït-Sahalia, "Testing Continuous Time Models of the Spot Interest Rate," *Review of Financial Studies*, 9:2, 1996, pp. 385–426.

[18]Oren Cheyette, "Interest Rate Models," Chapter 1 in *Interest Rate, Term Structure, and Valuation Modeling*.

[19]Alexander Levin, "Interest Rate Model Selection," *Journal of Portfolio Management*, Winter 2004, pp. 74–86.

It is fair to say that while negative interest rates are not impossible, they are unlikely. The significance of this is that one might argue that an interest-rate model should not permit negative interest rates (or negative rates greater than a few basis points). Yet, this may occur in a model where volatility is measured in terms of basis points—as in the normal model. In contrast, if interest-rate volatility is measured in terms of the percentage yield change (i.e., logarithm of the yield ratio), interest rates cannot be negative. Hence, a stated advantage of using an interest-rate model whose volatility is dependent on the level of interest rates is that negative returns are not possible. How critical is this assumption in deciding whether to use a lognormal model rather than a normal model? We address this in the next section.

SELECTING AN INTEREST-RATE MODEL

Cheyette provides guidance in the selection of an interest rate model. He writes:

> It may seem that one's major concern in choosing an interest-rate model should be the accuracy with which it represents the empirical volatility of the term structure of rates, and its ability to fit market prices of vanilla derivatives such as at-the-money caps and swaptions. These are clearly important criteria, but they are not decisive. The first criterion is hard to pin down, depending strongly on what historical period one chooses to examine. The second criterion is easy to satisfy for most commonly used models, by the simple (though unappealing) expedient of permitting predicted future volatility to be time dependent. So, while important, this concern doesn't really do much to narrow the choices.[20]

Moreover, as Cheyette notes, the ease of application is a critical issue in selecting an interest-rate model. While our focus in this chapter has been on describing interest-rate models, there is the implementation issue. For consistency in valuation, a portfolio manager would want a model that can be used to value all financial instruments that are included in a portfolio. In practice, writing efficient algorithms to value all financial instruments that may be included in a portfolio for some interest-rate models that have been proposed in the literature is "difficult or impossible."[21]

Based on the empirical evidence, Cheyette and Levin have concluded that the normal model is a suitable model. Cheyette argues that for typical initial spot rate curves and volatility parameters, the probability that negative rates would be generated by the model is quite small.[22] What is important from a practical perspective is not just whether the normal model admits the possibility of negative interest rates but whether negative interest rates may have a significant impact on the pricing of financial instruments. Cheyette tests this by pricing a call option on a zero-coupon bond and concluded that: "The oft raised bogeyman of negative interest rates proves to have little

---

[20]Cheyette, "Interest Rate Models," p. 4.
[21]Cheyette, "Interest Rate Models," p. 4.
[22]Cheyette, "Interest Rate Models," p. 10.

consequence for option pricing, since negative rates occur with very low probability for reasonable values of the model parameters and initial term structure."[23]

Levin who empirically investigated the issue for valuing mortgage-backed securities also concluded that the normal model, in particular the Hull-White model, is appropriate. He states: "It will not lead to sizable mispricing even in the worst mortgage-irrelevant case."[24] But, as he notes, "This conclusion, however, certainly merits periodic review."[25]

ESTIMATING INTEREST-RATE VOLATILITY USING HISTORICAL DATA

As we have seen, one of the inputs into an interest-rate model is interest-rate volatility. Where does a practitioner obtain this value in order to implement an interest-rate model? Market participants estimate yield volatility in one of two ways. The first way is by estimating historical interest volatility. This method uses historical interest rates to calculate the standard deviation of interest-rate changes and for obvious reasons is referred to as **historical volatility**. The second method is more complicated to explain at this juncture of the book. It involves using models for valuing option-type derivative instruments to obtain an estimate of what the market expects interest-rate volatility is. Basically, in any option pricing model, the only input that is not observed in the model is interest-rate volatility. What is done in practice is to assume that the observed price for an option-type derivative is priced according to some option pricing model. The calculation then involves determining what interest-rate volatility will make the market price of the option-type derivative equal to the value generated by the option pricing model. Since the expected interest-rate volatility obtained is being "backed out" of the model, it is referred to as **implied volatility**.

We use the data in Exhibit 16-1 to explain how to calculate the historical volatility as measured by the standard deviation based on the absolute rate change and the percentage change in rates. The historical interest rates shown in Exhibit 16-1 are the weekly returns for one-month LIBOR from 7/30/2004 to 7/29/2005. The observations are based on bid rates for Eurodollar deposits collected around 9:30 A.M. Eastern time.[26] The calculation can be performed on an electronic spreadsheet. The *weekly* standard deviation is reported in the exhibit. For the absolute rate change, it is 2.32 basis points; for the percentage rate change, it is 1.33%.

The weekly measures must be annualized. The formula for annualizing a weekly standard deviation is[27]

$$\text{Weekly standard deviation} \times \sqrt{52}$$

---

[23]Cheyette, "Interest Rate Models," p. 25.
[24]Levin, "Interest Rate Model Selection," p. 85.
[25]Levin, "Interest Rate Model Selection," p. 85.
[26]The data were obtained from the Federal Reserve Statistical Release H.15.
[27]In the annualizing formula, there is an assumption made when the square root of the number of time periods in a year is used. The assumption is that the correlation between the interest rate changes over time is not significant. The term *serial correlation* is used to describe this correlation.

EXHIBIT 16-1	Data for Calculating Historical Volatility: One-Month from 7/30/2004 to 7/29/2005		
Date	1-Month LIBOR (%)	Absolute Rate Change (bps)	Percentage Rate Change (%)
7/30/2004	1.43		
8/6/2004	1.49	6	4.110
8/13/2004	1.51	2	1.333
8/20/2004	1.52	1	0.660
8/27/2004	1.54	2	1.307
9/3/2004	1.59	5	3.195
9/10/2004	1.67	8	4.909
9/17/2004	1.73	6	3.530
9/24/2004	1.77	4	2.286
10/1/2004	1.77	0	0.000
10/8/2004	1.78	1	0.563
10/15/2004	1.81	3	1.671
10/22/2004	1.86	5	2.725
10/29/2004	1.9	4	2.128
11/5/2004	1.98	8	4.124
11/12/2004	2.03	5	2.494
11/19/2004	2.06	3	1.467
11/26/2004	2.11	5	2.398
12/3/2004	2.24	13	5.979
12/10/2004	2.3	6	2.643
12/17/2004	2.35	5	2.151
12/24/2004	2.34	1	−0.426
12/31/2004	2.34	0	0.000
1/7/2005	2.34	0	0.000
1/14/2005	2.39	5	2.114
1/21/2005	2.44	5	2.070
1/28/2005	2.5	6	2.429
2/4/2005	2.53	3	1.193
2/11/2005	2.53	0	0.000
2/18/2005	2.53	0	0.000
2/25/2005	2.59	6	2.344
3/4/2005	2.66	7	2.667
3/11/2005	2.71	5	1.862
3/18/2005	2.77	6	2.190
3/25/2005	2.79	2	0.719
4/1/2005	2.81	2	0.714
4/8/2005	2.85	4	1.413
4/15/2005	2.89	4	1.394
4/22/2005	2.95	6	2.055
4/29/2005	3.01	6	2.013
			(continued)

EXHIBIT 16-1   (continued)

Date	1-Month LIBOR (%)	Absolute Rate Change (bps)	Percentage Rate Change (%)
5/6/2005	3.04	3	0.992
5/13/2005	3.03	1	−0.329
5/20/2005	3.02	1	−0.331
5/27/2005	3.03	1	0.331
6/3/2005	3.08	5	1.637
6/10/2005	3.12	4	1.290
6/17/2005	3.19	7	2.219
6/24/2005	3.25	6	1.863
7/1/2005	3.28	3	0.919
7/8/2005	3.29	1	0.304
7/15/2005	3.32	3	0.908
7/22/2005	3.38	6	1.791
7/29/2005	3.44	6	1.760
Average		3.98	1.69
Weekly Variance		6.84	1.78
Weekly Std Dev.		2.62	1.33
Annualized Std. Dev.		18.86	9.62

Annualizing the two weekly volatility measures:

$$Absolute\ rate\ change: 2.32 \times \sqrt{52} = 18.86\ basis\ points$$
$$Logarithm\ percentage\ change: 1.33 \times \sqrt{52} = 9.62\%$$

If we use daily or monthly data to compute the standard deviation, the following formula would be used to annualize:

$$Monthly\ standard\ deviation \times \sqrt{12}$$
$$Daily\ standard\ deviation \times \sqrt{Number\ of\ trading\ days\ in\ a\ year}$$

Note that annualizing of the daily volatility requires that the number of days in a year be determined. Market practice varies with respect to the number of trading days in the year that should be used in the annualizing formula above. Typically, either 250 days or 260 days are used. For many traders who use daily rates, the difference in the calculated historical annual volatility could be significant depending on the number of trading days assumed in a year. Specifically, the difference in the factor that the daily standard deviation will be multiplied by depending on the number of days assumed in the year is:

Days Assumed	Square Root of Days Assumed
250	15.81
260	16.12

SUMMARY

An interest-rate model is a probabilistic description of how interest rates can change over time. A stochastic differential equation is the most commonly used mathematical tool for describing interest-rate movements that incorporate statistical properties of interest-rate movements (drift, volatility, and mean reversion).

In practice, one-factor models are used to describe the behavior of interest rates; they assume that short-term interest rates follow some statistical process and that other interest rates in the term structure are related to short-term rates. In a one-factor model, the SDE expresses the interest rate movement in terms of the change in the short rate over the time interval based on two components: (1) the expected direction of the change in the short rate (the drift term) and (2) a random process (the volatility term).

Interest-rate models fall into two general categories: arbitrage-free models and equilibrium models. For the former models, the analysis begins with the observed market price of benchmark instruments that are assumed to be fairly priced, and using those prices one derives a term structure that is consistent with observed market prices for the benchmark instruments. The model is referred to as arbitrage-free because it matches the observed prices of the benchmark instruments. Equilibrium models attempt to describe the dynamics of the term structure using fundamental economic variables that are assumed to affect the interest-rate process. In practice, because of the difficulties of implementing equilibrium models, arbitrage-free models are used.

The classification of a model as normal or lognormal is based on the assumed dynamics of the random component of the SDE. Normal models assume that interest-rate volatility is independent of the level of rates and therefore admits the possibility of negative interest rates. The lognormal models assume that interest-rate volatility is proportional to the level of rates, and therefore negative interest rates are not possible.

Empirical evidence reviewed in this chapter regarding the relationship between interest-rate volatility and the level of rates suggests that the relationship is weak at interest rate levels below 10%. However, for rates exceeding 10%, there tends to be a positive relationship. This evidence suggests that in rate environments below 10%, a normal model would be more descriptive of the behavior of interest rates than the lognormal model. Moreover, empirical tests suggest that the impact of negative interest rates on pricing is minimal, and therefore one should not be overly concerned that a normal model admits the possibility of negative interest rates.

Interest-rate volatility can be estimated using historical volatility or implied volatility. Historical volatility is calculated from observed rates over some period of time. When calculating historical volatility using daily observations, differences in annualized volatility occur for a given set of observations because of the different assumptions that can be made about the number of trading days in a year. Implied volatility is obtained using an option pricing model and observed prices for option-type derivative instruments.

Questions

1. What is meant by an interest-rate model?
2. Explain the following three properties of an interest-rate model:
   a. drift
   b. volatility
   c. mean reversion
3. What is the commonly used mathematical tool for describing the movement of interest rates that can incorporate the properties of an interest-rate model?
4. a. Why is the most common interest-rate model used to describe the behavior of interest rates a one-factor model?
   b. What is the one-factor in a one-factor interest-rate model?
5. What is meant by
   a. a normal model of interest rates?
   b. a lognormal model of interest rates?
6. Explain the treatment of the dynamics of the volatility term for the following interest-rate models:
   a. Vasicek model
   b. Dothan model
   c. Cox-Ingersoll-Ross model
7. What is an arbitrage-free interest-rate model?
8. a. What are the general characteristics of the Ho-Lee arbitrage-free interest-rate model?

   b. How does the Ho-Lee arbitrage-free interest-rate model differ from the Hull-White arbitrage-free interest-rate model?
9. What is an equilibrium interest-rate model?
10. Explain why in practice arbitrage-free models are typically used rather than equilibrium models.
11. a. What is the empirical evidence on the relationship between volatility and the level of interest rates?
    b. Explain whether the historical evidence supports the use of a normal model or a lognormal model.
12. Comment on the following statement: "If an interest-rate model allows the possibility of negative interest rates, then it is not useful in practice."
13. a. What is meant by historical volatility?
    b. What is meant by implied volatility?
14. Suppose that the following weekly interest-rate volatility estimates are computed:
    absolute rate change = 3.85 basis points
    percentage rate change = 2.14%
    a. What is the annualized volatility for the absolute rate change?
    b. What is the annualized volatility for the percentage rate change?

CHAPTER

17

ANALYSIS OF BONDS WITH EMBEDDED OPTIONS

After reading this chapter you will understand:

- the drawbacks of the traditional yield spread analysis

- what static spread is and under what conditions it would differ from the traditional yield spread

- the disadvantages of a callable bond from the investor's perspective

- the yield to worst and the pitfalls of the traditional approach to valuing callable bonds

- the price–yield relationship for a callable bond

- negative convexity and when a callable bond may exhibit it

- how the value of a bond with an embedded option can be decomposed

- the lattice method and how it is used to value a bond with an embedded option

- how a binomial interest-rate tree is constructed to be consistent with the prices for the on-the-run issues of an issuer and a given volatility assumption

- what an option-adjusted spread is and how it is calculated using the binomial method

- the limitations of using modified duration and standard convexity as a measure of the price sensitivity of a bond with an embedded option

- the difference between effective duration and modified duration

- how effective duration and effective convexity are calculated using the binomial method

In earlier chapters we discussed pricing, yield measures, and price volatility for bonds without options. In Chapter 2 we saw that the price of a bond was based on the present value of its cash flow. A bond with an embedded option is one in which either the issuer or the bondholder has the option to alter a bond's cash flows. In this chapter we look at how to analyze bonds with embedded options. Because the most common type of option embedded in a bond is a call option, our primary focus is on callable bonds. We begin by looking at the limitations of traditional yield spread analysis. Although corporate bonds are used in our examples, the analysis presented in this chapter is equally applicable to agency securities and municipal securities. In the next chapter we focus on the analysis of mortgage-backed securities.

DRAWBACKS OF TRADITIONAL YIELD SPREAD ANALYSIS

Traditional analysis of the yield premium for a non-Treasury bond involves calculating the difference between the yield to maturity (or yield to call) of the bond in question and the yield to maturity of a comparable-maturity Treasury. The latter is obtained from the Treasury yield curve. For example, consider two 8.8% coupon 25-year bonds:

Issue	Price	Yield to Maturity (%)
Treasury	$96.6133	9.15
Corporate	87.0798	10.24

The yield spread for these two bonds as traditionally computed is 109 basis points (10.24% minus 9.15%). The drawbacks of this convention, however, are (1) the yield for both bonds fails to take into consideration the term structure of interest rates, and (2) in the case of callable and/or putable bonds, expected interest rate volatility may alter the cash flow of a bond. For now, let's focus only on the first problem: failure to incorporate the term structure of interest rates.

STATIC SPREAD: AN ALTERNATIVE TO YIELD SPREAD

In traditional yield spread analysis, an investor compares the yield to maturity of a bond with the yield to maturity of a similar maturity on-the-run Treasury security. This means that the yield to maturity of a 25-year zero-coupon corporate bond and an 8.8% coupon 25-year corporate coupon bond would both be compared to a benchmark 25-year Treasury security. Such a comparison makes little sense, because the cash flow characteristics of the two corporate bonds will not be the same as that of the benchmark Treasury.

The proper way to compare non-Treasury bonds of the same maturity but with different coupon rates is to compare them with a portfolio of Treasury securities that have the same cash flow. For example, consider the 8.8% 25-year corporate bond selling for $87.0798. The cash flow per $100 par value for this corporate bond, assuming that interest rates do not change (i.e., assuming static interest rates), is 49 six-month payments of $4.40 and a payment in 25 years (50 six-month periods) of $104.40. A portfolio that will replicate this cash flow would include 50 zero-coupon Treasury securities with maturities coinciding with the amount and timing of the cash flows of the corporate bond. The corporate bond's value is equal to the present value of all the cash flows.

The corporate bond's value, assuming that the cash flows are riskless, will equal the present value of the replicating portfolio of Treasury securities. In turn, these cash flows are valued at the Treasury spot rates. Exhibit 17-1 shows how to calculate the price of a risk-free 8.8% 25-year bond assuming the Treasury spot rate curve shown in the exhibit. The price would be $96.6133. The corporate bond's price is $87.0798, less than the package of zero-coupon Treasury securities, because investors in fact require a yield premium for the risk associated with holding a corporate bond rather than a riskless package of Treasury securities.

The **static spread**, also referred to as the **zero-volatility spread**, is a measure of the spread that the investor would realize over the entire Treasury spot rate curve if the bond

EXHIBIT 17-1   Calculation of Price of a 25-Year 8.8% Coupon Bond Using Treasury Spot Rates

Period	Cash Flow	Treasury Spot Rate (%)	Present Value
1	4.4	7.00000	4.2512
2	4.4	7.04999	4.1055
3	4.4	7.09998	3.9628
4	4.4	7.12498	3.8251
5	4.4	7.13998	3.6922
6	4.4	7.16665	3.5622
7	4.4	7.19997	3.4351
8	4.4	7.26240	3.3077
9	4.4	7.33315	3.1820
10	4.4	7.38977	3.0611
11	4.4	7.44517	2.9434
12	4.4	7.49135	2.8302
13	4.4	7.53810	2.7200
14	4.4	7.57819	2.6141
15	4.4	7.61959	2.5112
16	4.4	7.66205	2.4111
17	4.4	7.70538	2.3139
18	4.4	7.74391	2.2207
19	4.4	7.78888	2.1291
20	4.4	7.83434	2.0404
21	4.4	8.22300	1.8879
22	4.4	8.33333	1.7923
23	4.4	8.40000	1.7080
24	4.4	8.50000	1.6204
25	4.4	8.54230	1.5465
26	4.4	8.72345	1.4500
27	4.4	8.90000	1.3581
28	4.4	9.00000	1.2829

(*continued*)

EXHIBIT 17-1   (continued)

Period	Cash Flow	Treasury Spot Rate (%)	Present Value
29	4.4	9.01450	1.2252
30	4.4	9.23000	1.1367
31	4.4	9.39000	1.0611
32	4.4	9.44840	1.0045
33	4.4	9.50000	0.9514
34	4.4	9.50000	0.9083
35	4.4	9.50000	0.8671
36	4.4	9.50000	0.8278
37	4.4	9.55000	0.7833
38	4.4	9.56000	0.7462
39	4.4	9.58000	0.7095
40	4.4	9.58000	0.6771
41	4.4	9.60000	0.6436
42	4.4	9.70000	0.6020
43	4.4	9.80000	0.5625
44	4.4	9.90000	0.5251
45	4.4	10.00000	0.4897
46	4.4	10.10000	0.4563
47	4.4	10.30000	0.4154
48	4.4	10.50000	0.3774
49	4.4	10.60000	0.3503
50	104.4	10.80000	7.5278
Theoretical price			96.6134

is held to maturity. It is not a spread off one point on the Treasury yield curve, as is the traditional yield spread. The static spread is calculated as the spread that will make the present value of the cash flows from the corporate bond, when discounted at the Treasury spot rate plus the spread, equal to the corporate bond's price. A trial-and-error procedure is required to determine the static spread.

To illustrate how this is done, let's use the corporate bond in the first illustration. Select a spread, say, 100 basis points. To each Treasury spot rate shown in the third column in Exhibit 17-2, 100 basis points is added. So, for example, the 14-year (period 28) spot rate is 10% (9% plus 1%). The spot rate plus 100 basis points is then used to calculate the present value of $88.5474. Because the present value is not equal to the corporate bond's price ($87.0796), the static spread is not 100 basis points. If a spread of 110 basis points is tried, it can be seen from the next-to-last column of Exhibit 17-2 that the present value is $87.8029; again, because this is not equal to the corporate bond's price, 110 basis points is not the static spread. The last column of Exhibit 17-2 shows the present value when a 120-basis-point spread is tried. The present value is equal to the corporate bond price. Therefore, 120 basis points is the static spread, compared to the traditional yield spread of 109 basis points.

Exhibit 17-3 shows the static spread and the traditional yield spread for bonds with various maturities and prices, assuming the Treasury spot rates shown in Exhibit 17-1.

EXHIBIT 17-2   Calculation of the Static Spread for a 25-Year 8.8% Coupon Corporate Bond

Period	Cash Flow	Treasury Spot Rate (%)	Present Value if Spread Used Is: 100 BP	110 BP	120 BP
1	4.4	7.00000	4.2308	4.2287	4.2267
2	4.4	7.04999	4.0661	4.0622	4.0583
3	4.4	7.09998	3.9059	3.9003	3.8947
4	4.4	7.12498	3.7521	3.7449	3.7377
5	4.4	7.13998	3.6043	3.5957	3.5871
6	4.4	7.16665	3.4607	3.4508	3.4408
7	4.4	7.19997	3.3212	3.3101	3.2990
8	4.4	7.26240	3.1828	3.1706	3.1584
9	4.4	7.33315	3.0472	3.0340	3.0210
10	4.4	7.38977	2.9174	2.9034	2.8895
11	4.4	7.44517	2.7917	2.7770	2.7624
12	4.4	7.49135	2.6715	2.6562	2.6409
13	4.4	7.53810	2.5552	2.5394	2.5236
14	4.4	7.57819	2.4440	2.4277	2.4115
15	4.4	7.61959	2.3366	2.3198	2.3032
16	4.4	7.66205	2.2327	2.2157	2.1988
17	4.4	7.70538	2.1325	2.1152	2.0981
18	4.4	7.74391	2.0368	2.0193	2.0020
19	4.4	7.78888	1.9435	1.9259	1.9085
20	4.4	7.83434	1.8536	1.8359	1.8184
21	4.4	8.22300	1.7072	1.6902	1.6733
22	4.4	8.33333	1.6131	1.5963	1.5796
23	4.4	8.40000	1.5300	1.5132	1.4967
24	4.4	8.50000	1.4446	1.4282	1.4119
25	4.4	8.54230	1.3722	1.3559	1.3398
26	4.4	8.72345	1.2806	1.2648	1.2492
27	4.4	8.90000	1.1938	1.1785	1.1635
28	4.4	9.00000	1.1224	1.1075	1.0929
29	4.4	9.01450	1.0668	1.0522	1.0378
30	4.4	9.23000	0.9852	0.9712	0.9575
31	4.4	9.39000	0.9154	0.9020	0.8888
32	4.4	9.44840	0.8625	0.8495	0.8367
33	4.4	9.50000	0.8131	0.8004	0.7880
34	4.4	9.50000	0.7725	0.7601	0.7480
35	4.4	9.50000	0.7340	0.7219	0.7100
36	4.4	9.50000	0.6974	0.6855	0.6739
37	4.4	9.55000	0.6568	0.6453	0.6341
38	4.4	9.56000	0.6227	0.6116	0.6007
39	4.4	9.58000	0.5893	0.5785	0.5679
40	4.4	9.58000	0.5597	0.5492	0.5389

(*continued*)

EXHIBIT 17-2   (continued)

			Present Value if Spread Used Is:		
Period	Cash Flow	Treasury Spot Rate (%)	100 BP	110 BP	120 BP
41	4.4	9.60000	0.5295	0.5193	0.5093
42	4.4	9.70000	0.4929	0.4832	0.4737
43	4.4	9.80000	0.4585	0.4492	0.4401
44	4.4	9.90000	0.4260	0.4172	0.4086
45	4.4	10.00000	0.3955	0.3871	0.3789
46	4.4	10.10000	0.3668	0.3588	0.3511
47	4.4	10.30000	0.3323	0.3250	0.3179
48	4.4	10.50000	0.3006	0.2939	0.2873
49	4.4	10.60000	0.2778	0.2714	0.2652
50	104.4	10.80000	5.9416	5.8030	5.6677
Total present value			88.5474	87.8029	87.0796

EXHIBIT 17-3   Comparison of Traditional Yield Spread and Static Spread for Various Bonds[a]

			Spread (basis points)		
Bond	Price	Yield to Maturity (%)	Traditional	Static	Difference
25-year 8.8% Coupon Bond					
Treasury	96.6133	9.15	—	—	—
A	88.5473	10.06	91	100	9
B	87.8031	10.15	100	110	10
C	87.0798	10.24	109	120	11
15-year 8.8% Coupon Bond					
Treasury	101.9603	8.57	—	—	—
D	94.1928	9.54	97	100	3
E	93.4639	9.63	106	110	4
F	92.7433	9.73	116	120	4
10-year 8.8% Coupon Bond					
Treasury	107.4906	7.71	—	—	—
G	100.6137	8.71	100	100	0
H	99.9585	8.81	110	110	0
I	99.3088	8.91	120	120	0
5-year 8.8% Coupon Bond					
Treasury	105.9555	7.36	—	—	—
J	101.7919	8.35	99	100	1
K	101.3867	8.45	109	110	1
L	100.9836	8.55	119	120	1

[a]Assumes Treasury spot rate curve given in Exhibit 17-1.

Notice that the shorter the maturity of the bond, the less the static spread will differ from the traditional yield spread. The magnitude of the difference between the traditional yield spread and the static spread also depends on the shape of the yield curve. The steeper the yield curve, the more the difference for a given coupon and maturity.

Another reason for the small differences in Exhibit 17-3 is that the corporate bond makes a bullet payment at maturity. The difference between the traditional yield spread and the static spread will be considerably greater for sinking fund bonds and mortgage-backed securities in a steep yield curve environment.

CALLABLE BONDS AND THEIR INVESTMENT CHARACTERISTICS

Now that we know the problems with the traditional yield spread analysis, let's introduce another complexity: the callability of an issue. We begin by examining the characteristics of a callable bond. The holder of a callable bond has given the issuer the right to call the issue prior to the expiration date. The presence of a call option results in two disadvantages to the bondholder.

First, callable bonds expose bondholders to reinvestment risk, because an issuer will call a bond when the yield on bonds in the market is lower than the issue's coupon rate. For example, if the coupon rate on a callable corporate bond is 13% and prevailing market yields are 7%, the issuer will find it economical to call the 13% issue and refund it with a 7% issue. From the investor's perspective, the proceeds received will have to be reinvested at a lower interest rate.

Second, as we explain later in this chapter, the price appreciation potential for a callable bond in a declining interest-rate environment is limited. This is because the market will increasingly expect the bond to be redeemed at the call price as interest rates fall. This phenomenon for a callable bond is referred to as **price compression**.

Because of the disadvantages associated with callable bonds, these instruments often feature a period of call protection, an initial period when bonds may not be called. Still, given both price compression and reinvestment risk, why would any investor want to own a callable bond? If the investor receives sufficient potential compensation in the form of a higher potential yield, an investor would be willing to accept call risk.

Traditional Valuation Methodology for Callable Bonds

When a bond is callable, the practice has been to calculate a **yield to worst**. As explained in Chapter 3, the yield to worst is the smallest of the yield to maturity and the yield to call for all possible call dates. The yield to worst is the yield that the traditional approach has investors believing should be used in relative value analysis of callable bonds.

We explained in Chapter 3 the limitations of the **yield to call** as a measure of the potential return of a security. The yield to call does consider all three sources of potential return from owning a bond. However, as in the case of the yield to maturity, it assumes that all cash flows can be reinvested at the computed yield—in this case the yield to call—until the assumed call date. Moreover, the yield to call assumes that (1) the investor will hold the bond to the assumed call date, and (2) the issuer will call the bond on that date.

Often, these underlying assumptions about the yield to call are unrealistic because they do not take into account how an investor will reinvest the proceeds if the issue is called. For example, consider two bonds, M and N. Suppose that the yield to maturity for bond M, a five-year noncallable bond, is 10%, and the yield to call for bond N is 10.5% assuming that the bond will be called in three years. Which bond is better for an investor with a five-year investment horizon? It is not possible to tell for the yields cited. If the investor intends to hold the bond for five years and the issuer calls the bond after three years, the total dollars that will be available at the end of five years will depend on the interest rate that can be earned from investing funds from the call date to the end of the investment horizon.

Price–Yield Relationship for a Callable Bond

As explained in Chapter 4, the price–yield relationship for an option-free bond is convex. Exhibit 17-4 shows the price–yield relationship for both a noncallable bond and the same bond if it is callable. The convex curve *a–a'* is the price–yield relationship for the non-callable (option-free) bond. The unusual shaped curve denoted by *a–b* is the price–yield relationship for the callable bond.

   The reason for the shape of the price–yield relationship for the callable bond is as follows. When the prevailing market yield for comparable bonds is higher than the coupon interest on the bond, it is unlikely that the issuer will call the bond. For example, if the coupon rate on a bond is 8% and the prevailing yield on comparable bonds is 16%, it is highly improbable that the issuer will call an 8% coupon bond so that it can issue a 16% coupon bond. The bond is unlikely to be called, so the callable bond will have the same convex price–yield relationship as a noncallable bond when yields are greater than y^*. However, even when the coupon rate is just below the market yield,

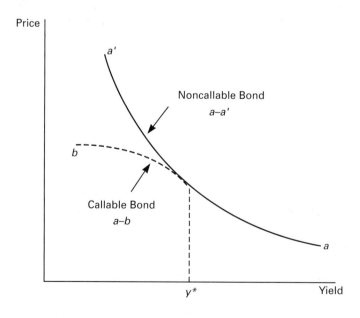

EXHIBIT 17-4   Price–Yield Relationship for a Noncallable and a Callable Bond

investors may not pay the same price for the callable bond had it been noncallable because there is still the chance the market yield may drop further, making it beneficial for the issuer to call the bond.

As yields in the market decline, the likelihood that yields will decline further so that the issuer will benefit from calling the bond increases. The exact yield level at which investors begin to view the issue likely to be called may not be known, but we do know that there is some level. In Exhibit 17-4, at yield levels below y^*, the price–yield relationship for the callable bond departs from the price–yield relationship for the noncallable bond. Consider a bond that is callable at 104. If market yield would price a comparable noncallable bond at 109, rational investors would not pay 109 for the callable bond. If they did and the bond was called, investors would receive 104 (the call price) for a bond they purchased for 109.

Notice that for a range of yields below y^*, there is price compression—that is, there is limited price appreciation as yields decline. The portion of the callable bond price–yield relationship below y^* is said to be negatively convex.

Negative convexity means that the price appreciation will be less than the price depreciation for a large change in yield of a given number of basis points. For a bond that is option-free and exhibits positive convexity, the price appreciation will be greater than the price depreciation for a large change in yield. The price changes resulting from bonds exhibiting positive convexity and negative convexity are shown in Exhibit 17-5.

It is important to understand that a bond can still trade above its call price even if it is highly likely to be called. For example, consider a callable bond with a 10-year 13% coupon rate that is callable in one year at a call price of 104. Suppose that the yield on 10-year bonds is 6% and that the yield on one-year bonds is 5%. In a 6% interest rate environment for 10-year bonds, investors will expect that the issue will be called in one year. Thus, investors will treat this issue as if it is a one-year bond and price it accordingly. The price must reflect the fact that the investor will receive a 13% coupon rate for one year. The price of this bond would be the present value of the two cash flows, which are (1) $6.50 (per $100 of par value) of coupon interest six months from now, and (2) $6.50 coupon interest plus the call price of $104 one year from now. Discounting the two cash flows at the 5% prevailing market yield (2.5% every six months) for one-year bonds, the price is

$$\frac{\$6.5}{1.025} + \frac{\$110.5}{(1.025)^2} = \$111.52$$

The price is greater than the call price. Consequently, an investor will be willing to pay a higher price than the call price to purchase this bond.

EXHIBIT 17-5 Price Volatility Implications of Positive and Negative Convexity

	Absolute Value of Percentage Price Change	
Change in Interest Rates	Positive Convexity	Negative Convexity
−100 basis points	X%	Less than Y%
+100 basis points	Less than X%	Y%

COMPONENTS OF A BOND WITH AN EMBEDDED OPTION

To develop a framework for analyzing a bond with an embedded option, it is necessary to decompose a bond into its component parts. A **callable bond** is a bond in which the bondholder has sold the issuer an option (more specifically, a call option) that allows the issuer to repurchase the contractual cash flows of the bond from the time the bond is first callable until the maturity date.

Consider the following two bonds: (1) a callable bond with an 8% coupon, 20 years to maturity, and callable in five years at 104, and (2) a 10-year 9% coupon bond callable immediately at par. For the first bond, the bondholder owns a five-year noncallable bond and has sold a call option granting the issuer the right to call away from the bondholder 15 years of cash flows five years from now for a price of 104. The investor who owns the second bond has a 10-year noncallable bond and has sold a call option granting the issuer the right to call immediately the entire 10-year contractual cash flows, or any cash flows remaining at the time the issue is called, for 100.

Effectively, the owner of a callable bond is entering into two separate transactions. First, she buys a noncallable bond from the issuer for which she pays some price. Then, she sells the issuer a call option for which she receives the option price.

In terms of price, a callable bond is therefore equal to the price of the two components parts; that is,

$$\text{callable bond price} = \text{noncallable bond price} - \text{call option price}$$

The reason the call option price is subtracted from the price of the noncallable bond is that when the bondholder sells a call option, she receives the option price. Graphically, this can be seen in Exhibit 17-6. The difference between the price of the noncallable bond and the callable bond at any given yield is the price of the embedded call option.[1]

The same logic applies to **putable bonds**. In the case of a putable bond, the bondholder has the right to sell the bond to the issuer at a designated price and time. A putable bond can be broken into two separate transactions. First, the investor buys a noncallable bond. Second, the investor buys an option from the issuer that allows the investor to sell the bond to the issuer. The price of a putable bond is then

$$\text{putable bond price} = \text{nonputable bond price} + \text{put option price}$$

---

[1]Actually, the position is more complicated than we have described. The issuer may be entitled to call the bond at the first call date and anytime thereafter, or at the first call date and any subsequent coupon anniversary. Thus, the investor has effectively sold an American-type call option to the issuer, but the call price may vary with the date the call option is exercised. This is because the call schedule for a bond may have a different call price depending on the call date. Moreover, the underlying bond for the call option is the remaining coupon payments that would have been made by the issuer had the bond not been called. For exposition purposes, it is easier to understand the principles associated with the investment characteristics of callable corporate bonds by describing the investor's position as long a noncallable bond and short a call option.

EXHIBIT 17-6   Decomposition of Price of a Callable Bond

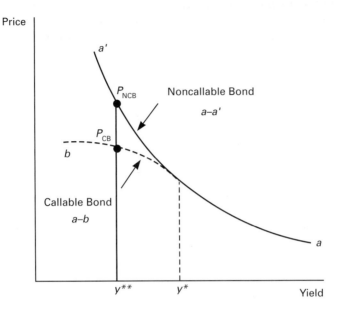

Note: At y^{**} yield level:
$$P_{NCB} = \text{noncallable bond price}$$
$$P_{CB} = \text{callable bond price}$$
$$P_{NCB} - P_{CB} = \text{call option price}$$

VALUATION MODEL[2]

Thus far, we described a way to think conceptually about bonds with embedded options. More specifically, the value of a callable bond is equal to the value of a comparable noncallable bond minus the value of the call option. In this section a model for valuing bonds with embedded options is presented.

The valuation principles that we have discussed so far in this book are used here. Specifically, we saw two important things in Chapter 5. First, it is inappropriate to use a single rate to discount all the cash flows of a bond. Second, the correct rate to use to discount each cash flow is the theoretical spot rate. This is equivalent to discounting at a series of forward rates.

What we have to add to the valuation process is how interest-rate volatility affects the value of a bond through its effects on the embedded options. There are three models depending on the structure of the security to be analyzed. The first is a model for a

[2]The valuation model described in this section was first introduced in Andrew J. Kalotay, George O. Williams, and Frank J. Fabozzi, "A Model for the Valuation of Bonds and Embedded Options," *Financial Analysts Journal*, May–June 1993, pp. 35–46.

bond that is not a mortgage-backed security or asset-backed security that can be exercised at more than one time over its life. An example is a 10-year corporate bond that is callable beginning three years from now on every coupon anniversary date. It is the valuation model for such a bond that is discussed in this section. The second case is a bond with an embedded option where the option can be exercised only once. An example is a callable bond that can be exercised only on a specific date. Bonds with this characteristic are issued by the government-sponsored enterprises Fannie Mae and Freddie Mac. We will discuss the approach to valuing such bonds later in this chapter. The third model is for a mortgage-backed security or certain types of asset-backed securities. The model used, Monte Carlo simulation, is explained and illustrated in the next chapter.

We begin with a review of the valuation of bonds without embedded options.

Valuation of Option-Free Bonds

In Chapter 5 we said that the price of an option-free bond is the present value of the cash flows discounted at the spot rates. To illustrate this, let's use the following hypothetical yield curve:

Maturity (years)	Yield to Maturity (%)	Market Value
1	3.50	100
2	4.00	100
3	4.50	100

We will be simplifying the illustration by assuming annual-pay bonds. Using the bootstrapping methodology described in Chapter 5, the spot rates and the one-year forward rates can be obtained.

Year	Spot Rate (%)	One-Year Forward Rate (%)
1	3.500	3.500
2	4.010	4.523
3	4.541	5.580

Now consider an option-free bond with three years remaining to maturity and a coupon rate of 5.25%. The price of this bond can be calculated in one of two ways, both producing the same result. First, the coupon payments can be discounted at the zero-coupon rates:

$$\frac{\$5.25}{(1.035)} + \frac{\$5.25}{(1.0401)^2} + \frac{\$100 + \$5.25}{(1.04541)^3} = \$102.075$$

The second way is to discount by the one-year forward rates:

$$\frac{\$5.25}{(1.035)} + \frac{\$5.25}{(1.035)(1.04523)} + \frac{\$100 + \$5.25}{(1.035)(1.04523)(1.05580)} = \$102.075$$

Introducing Interest-Rate Volatility

When we allow for embedded options, consideration must be given to interest-rate volatility. This can be done by introducing an **interest-rate tree**, also referred to as an **interest-rate lattice**. This tree is nothing more than a graphical depiction of the one-period forward rates over time based on some assumed interest-rate model and interest-rate volatility.

Interest-Rate Model

As explained in the previous chapter, an **interest-rate model** is a probabilistic description of how interest rates can change over the life of a financial instrument being evaluated. An interest-rate model does this by making an assumption about the relationship between (1) the level of short-term interest rates and (2) interest-rate volatility. Standard deviation of interest rates is used as the measure of interest-rate volatility.

The interest-rate models commonly used are arbitrage-free models based on how short-term interest rates can evolve (i.e., change) over time. As explained in Chapter 16, models based solely on movements in the short-term interest rate are referred to as one-factor models

Interest-Rate Lattice

Exhibit 17-7 shows an example of the most basic type of interest-rate lattice or tree, a **binomial interest-rate tree**. The corresponding model is referred to as the **binomial model**. In this model, it is assumed that interest rates can realize one of two possible rates in the next period. In the valuation model we present in this chapter we will use the binomial model. Valuation models that assume that interest rates can take on three possible rates in the next period are called **trinomial models**. More complex models exist that assume that more than three possible rates in the next period can be realized.

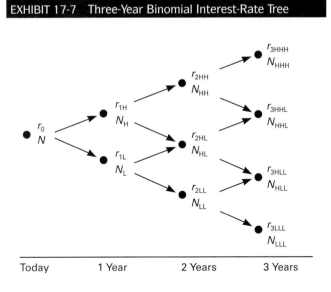

EXHIBIT 17-7   Three-Year Binomial Interest-Rate Tree

Returning to the binomial interest-rate tree in Exhibit 17-7, each node (bold circle) represents a time period that is equal to one year from the node to its left. Each node is labeled with an N, representing **node**, and a subscript that indicates the path that one-year forward rates took to get to that node. H represents the *higher* of the two forward rates and L the *lower* of the two forward rates from the preceding year. For example, node N_{HH} means that to get to that node the following path for one-year rates occurred: The one-year rate realized is the higher of the two rates in the first year and then the higher of the one-year rates in the second year.[3]

Look first at the point denoted N in Exhibit 17-7. This is the root of the tree and is nothing more than the current one-year rate, or equivalently, the one-year forward rate, which we denote by r_0. In the model, a one-factor interest-rate model is assumed. More specifically, it is assumed that the one-year forward rate can evolve over time based on a random process called a **lognormal random walk** with a certain volatility.

We will use the following notation to describe the tree in the first year. Let

σ = assumed volatility of the one-year forward rate
$r_{1,L}$ = the lower one-year rate one year from now
$r_{1,H}$ = the higher one-year rate one year from now

The relationship between $r_{1,L}$ and $r_{1,H}$ is as follows:

$$r_{1,H} = r_{1,L}(e^2\sigma)$$

where e is the base of the natural logarithm 2.71828. For example, suppose that $r_{1,L}$ is 4.074% and σ is 10% per year; then

$$r_{1,H} = 4.074\%(e^{2\times0.10}) = 4.976\%$$

In the second year, there are three possible values for the one-year rate, which we will denote as follows:

$r_{2,LL}$ = one-year rate in second year assuming the lower rate in the first year and the lower rate in the second year
$r_{2,HH}$ = one-year rate in second year assuming the higher rate in the first year and the higher rate in the second year
$r_{2,HL}$ = one-year rate in second year assuming the higher rate in the first year and the lower rate in the second year or equivalently the lower rate in the first year and the higher rate in the second year

The relationship between $r_{2,LL}$ and the other two one-year rates is as follows:

$$r_{2,HH} = r_{2,LL}(e^4\sigma)$$

and

$$r_{2,HL} = r_{2,LL}(e^2\sigma)$$

---

[3]Note that N_{HL} is equivalent to N_{LH}: in the second year, and that in the third year N_{HHL} is equivalent to N_{HLH} and N_{LHH} and that N_{HLL} is equivalent to N_{LLH}. We have simply selected one label for a node rather than clutter up the figure with unnecessary information.

So, for example, if $r_{2,LL}$ is 4.53%, then assuming once again that σ is 10%,

$$r_{2,HH} = 4.53\%(e^{4\times0.10}) = 6.757\%$$

and

$$r_{2,HL} = 4.53\%(e^{2\times0.10}) = 5.532\%$$

Exhibit 17-7 shows the notation for the binomial interest-rate tree in the third year. We can simplify the notation by letting r_t be the lower one-year forward rate t years from now because all the other forward rates t years from now depend on that rate. Exhibit 17-8 shows the interest-rate tree using this simplified notation.

Before we go on to show how to use this binomial interest-rate tree to value bonds, let's focus on two issues here. First, what does the volatility parameter σ in the expression $e^{2}\sigma$ represent? Second, how do we find the value of the bond at each node?

Volatility and the Standard Deviation

It can be shown that the standard deviation of the one-year forward rate is equal to $r_0 \sigma$.[4] The standard deviation is a statistical measure of volatility. For now it is important to see that the process that we assumed generates the binomial interest-rate tree (or

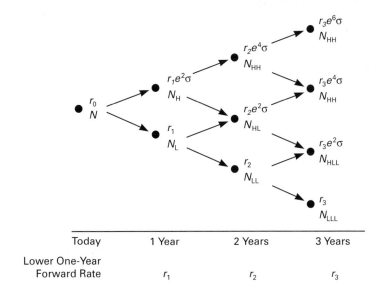

EXHIBIT 17-8 Three-Year Binomial Interest-Rate Tree with One-Year Forward Rates

---

[4]This can be seen by noting that $e^{2\sigma} \approx 1 + 2\sigma$. Then the standard deviation of one-period forward rates is

$$\frac{re^{2\sigma} - r}{2} \approx \frac{r + 2\sigma r - r}{2} \approx \sigma r$$

equivalently, the forward rates) implies that volatility is measured relative to the current level of rates. For example, if σ is 10% and the one-year rate (r_0) is 4%, the standard deviation of the one-year forward rate is 4% × 10% = 0.4% or 40 basis points. However, if the current one-year rate is 12%, the standard deviation of the one-year forward rate would be 12% × 10% or 120 basis points.

Determining the Value at a Node

The answer to the second question about how we find the value of the bond at a node is as follows. First calculate the bond's value at the two nodes to the right of the node where we want to obtain the bond's value. For example, in Exhibit 17-8, suppose that we want to determine the bond's value at node N_H. The bond's value at node N_{HH} and N_{HL} must be determined. Hold aside for now how we get these two values because as we will see, the process involves starting from the last year in the tree and working backward to get the final solution we want, so these two values will be known.

Effectively what we are saying is that if we are at some node, the value at that node will depend on the future cash flows. In turn, the future cash flows depend on (1) the bond's value one year from now, and (2) the coupon payment one year from now. The latter is known. The former depends on whether the one-year rate is the higher or lower rate. The bond's value depending on whether the rate is the higher or lower rate is reported at the two nodes to the right of the node that is the focus of our attention. So the cash flow at a node will be either (1) the bond's value if the short rate is the higher rate plus the coupon payment, or (2) the bond's value if the short rate is the lower rate plus the coupon payment. For example, suppose that we are interested in the bond's value at N_H. The cash flow will be either the bond's value at N_{HH} plus the coupon payment or the bond's value at N_{HL} plus the coupon payment.

To get the bond's value at a node we follow the fundamental rule for valuation: The value is the present value of the expected cash flows. The appropriate discount rate to use is the one-year forward rate at the node. Now there are two present values in this case: the present value if the one-year rate is the higher rate and the value if it is the lower rate. Because it is assumed that the probability of both outcomes is equal, an average of the two present values is computed. This is illustrated in Exhibit 17-9 for any node assuming that the one-year forward rate is r_* at the node where the valuation is sought and letting

$$V_H = \text{the bond's value for the higher one-year rate}$$
$$V_L = \text{the bond's value for the lower one-year rate}$$
$$C = \text{coupon payment}$$

Using our notation, the cash flow at a node is either:

$$V_H + C \text{ for the higher one-year rate, or}$$
$$V_L + C \text{ for the lower one-year rate}$$

EXHIBIT 17-9   Calculating a Value at a Node

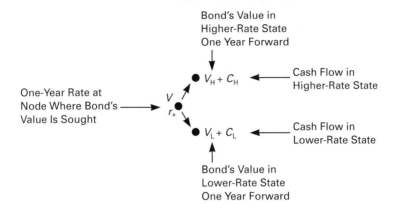

The present value of these two cash flows using the one-year rate at the node, r_*, is

$$\frac{V_H + C}{1 + r_*} \quad \text{present value for the higher one-year rate}$$

$$\frac{V_L + C}{1 + r_*} \quad \text{present value for the lower one-year rate}$$

Then the value of the bond at the node is found as follows:

$$\text{value at a node} = \frac{1}{2}\left[\frac{V_H + C}{1 + r_*} + \frac{V_L + C}{1 + r_*}\right]$$

Constructing the Binomial Interest-Rate Tree

To see how to construct the binomial interest-rate tree, let's use the assumed current on-the-run yields that we used earlier. We will assume that volatility, σ, is 10% and construct a two-year model using the two-year bond with a coupon rate of 4%.

Exhibit 17-10 shows a more detailed binomial interest-rate tree because at each node the cash flow is shown. We'll see how all the values reported in the exhibit are obtained. The root rate for the tree, r_0, is simply the current one-year rate, 3.5%.

In the first year there are two possible one-year rates, the higher rate and the lower rate. What we want to find is the two forward rates that will be consistent with the volatility assumption, the process that is assumed to generate the forward rates, and the observed market value of the bond. There is no simple formula for this. It must be found by an iterative process (i.e., trial and error). The steps are described and illustrated next.

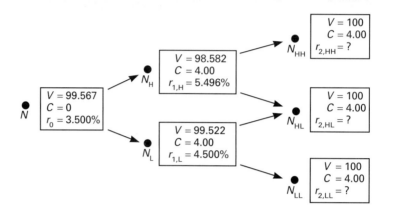

EXHIBIT 17-10   Finding the One-Year Forward Rates for Year 1 Using the Two-Year 4% On-the-Run: First Trial

Step 1: Select a value for r_1. Recall that r_1 is the lower one-year forward rate one year from now. In this first trial we *arbitrarily* selected a value of 4.5%.

Step 2: Determine the corresponding value for the higher one-year forward rate. As explained earlier, this rate is related to the lower one-year forward rate as follows: $r_1 e^{2\sigma}$. Because r_1 is 4.5%, the higher one-year forward rate is 5.496% ($= 4.5\%\ e^{2\times 0.10}$). This value is reported in Exhibit 17-10 at node N_H.

Step 3: Compute the bond's value one year from now. This value is determined as follows:

3a. The bond's value two years from now must be determined. In our example this is simple. We are using a two-year bond, so the bond's value is its maturity value ($100) plus its final coupon payment ($4). Thus, it is $104.

3b. Calculate the present value of the bond's value found in 3a using the higher rate. In our example the appropriate discount rate is the one-year higher forward rate, 5.496%. The present value is $98.582 (= $104/1.05496). This is the value of V_H that we referred to earlier.

3c. Calculate the present value of the bond's value found in 3a using the lower rate. The discount rate used is then the lower one-year forward rate, 4.5%. The value is $99.522 (= $104/1.045) and is the value of V_L.

3d. Add the coupon to V_H and V_L to get the cash flow at N_H and N_L, respectively. In our example we have $102.582 for the higher rate and $103.522 for the lower rate.

3e. Calculate the present value of the two values using the one-year forward rate using r_*. At this point in the valuation, r_* is the root rate, 3.50%. Therefore,

$$\frac{V_H + C}{1 + r_*} = \frac{\$102.582}{1.035} = \$99.113$$

and

$$\frac{V_L + C}{1 + r_*} = \frac{\$103.522}{1.035} = \$100.021$$

Step 4:   Calculate the average present value of the two cash flows in step 3. This is the value we referred to earlier as

$$\text{value at a node} = \frac{1}{2}\left[\frac{V_H + C}{1 + r_*} + \frac{V_L + C}{1 + r_*}\right].$$

In our example, we have

$$\text{value at a node} = \frac{1}{2}(\$99.113 + \$100.021) = \$99.567$$

Step 5:   Compare the value in step 4 with the bond's market value. If the two values are the same, the r_1 used in this trial is the one we seek. This is the one-year forward rate that would then be used in the binomial interest-rate tree for the lower rate, and the corresponding rate would be for the higher rate. If, instead, the value found in step 4 is not equal to the market value of the bond, this means that the value r_1 in this trial is not the one-period forward rate that is consistent with (1) the volatility assumption of 10%, (2) the process assumed to generate the one-year forward rate, and (3) the observed market value of the bond. In this case the five steps are repeated with a different value for r_1.

In this example, when r_1 is 4.5% we get a value of $99.567 in step 4, which is less than the observed market value of $100. Therefore, 4.5% is too large and the five steps must be repeated, trying a lower value for r_1.

Let's jump right to the correct value for r_1 in this example and rework steps 1 through 5. This occurs when r_1 is 4.074%. The corresponding binomial interest-rate tree is shown in Exhibit 17-11.

Step 1:   In this trial we select a value of 4.074% for r_1.
Step 2:   The corresponding value for the higher one-year forward rate is 4.976% (4.074% $e^{2\times0.10}$).
Step 3:   The bond's value one year from now is determined as follows:

    3a. The bond's value two years from now is $104, just as in the first trial.

    3b. The present value of the bond's value found in 3a for the higher rate, V_H, is $99.070 (= $104/1.04976).

    3c. The present value of the bond's value found in 3a for the lower rate, V_L, is $99.929 (= $104/1.04074).

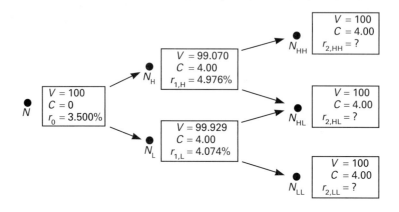

EXHIBIT 17-11 One-Year Forward Rates for Year 1 Using the Two-Year 4% On-the-Run Issue

3d. Adding the coupon to V_H and V_L, we get $103.071 as the cash flow for the higher rate and $103.929 as the cash flow for the lower rate.

3e. The present value of the two cash flows using the one-year forward rate at the node to the left, 3.5%, gives

$$\frac{V_H + C}{1 + r_*} = \frac{\$103.071}{1.035} = \$99.586$$

and

$$\frac{V_L + C}{1 + r_*} = \frac{\$103.929}{1.035} = \$100.414$$

Step 4: The average present value is $100, which is the value at the node.

Step 5: Because the average present value is equal to the observed market value of $100, r_1 is 4.074%.

We're not done. Suppose that we want to "grow" this tree for one more year—that is, we want to determine r_2. Now we will use the three-year on-the-run issue, the 4.5% coupon bond, to get r_2. The same five steps are used in an iterative process to find the one-year forward rate two years from now. But now our objective is as follows: Find the value for r_2 that will produce an average present value at node N_H equal to the bond value at that node ($98.074) and will also produce an average present value at node N_L equal to the bond value at that node ($99.926). When this value is found, we know that given the forward rate we found for r_1, the bond's value at the root—the value of ultimate interest to us—will be $100, the observed market price.

It can be demonstrated that the value of r_2 that will produce that desired outcome is 4.530%. Exhibit 17-12 shows the completed binomial interest-rate tree. It is this tree that we can use to value any option-free bond or bond with embedded options.

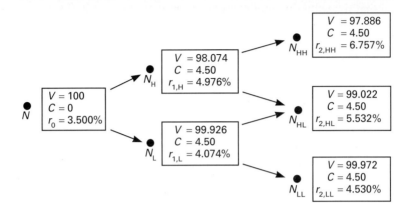

EXHIBIT 17-12 One-Year Forward Rates for Year 2 Using the Three-Year 4.5% On-the-Run Issue

The binomial interest-rate tree constructed is said to be an **arbitrage-free tree**. It is so named because it fairly prices the on-the-run issues.

Application to Valuing an Option-Free Bond

To illustrate how to use the binomial interest-rate tree, consider a 5.25% corporate bond that has two years remaining to maturity and is option-free. Also assume that the issuer's on-the-run yield curve is the one given earlier, and hence the appropriate binomial interest-rate tree is the one in Exhibit 17-12. Exhibit 17-13 shows the various values in the discounting process and produces a bond value of $102.075.

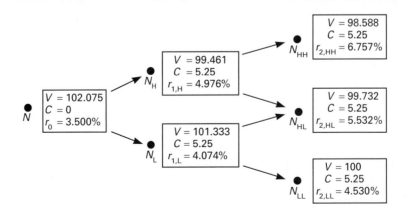

EXHIBIT 17-13 Valuing an Option-Free Corporate Bond with Three Years to Maturity and a Coupon Rate of 5.25%

It is important to note that this value is identical to the bond value found earlier when we discounted at either the zero-coupon rates or the one-year forward rates. We should expect to find this result because our bond is option free. This clearly demonstrates that the valuation model is consistent with the standard valuation model for an option-free bond.

Valuing a Callable Corporate Bond

Now we demonstrate how the binomial interest-rate tree can be applied to value a callable corporate bond. The valuation process proceeds in the same fashion as in the case of an option-free bond but with one exception: When the call option may be exercised by the issuer, the bond value at a node must be changed to reflect the lesser of its value if it is not called (i.e., the value obtained by applying the recursive valuation formula described previously) and the call price.

For example, consider a 5.25% corporate bond with three years remaining to maturity that is callable in one year at $100. Exhibit 17-14 shows the values at each node of the binomial interest-rate tree. The discounting process is identical to that shown in Exhibit 17-13 except that at two nodes, N_L and N_{LL}, the values from the recursive valuation formula ($101.001 at N_L and $100.689 at N_{LL}) exceed the call price ($100) and therefore have been struck out and replaced with $100. Each time a value derived from the recursive valuation formula has been replaced, the process for finding the values at that node is reworked starting with the period to the right. The value for this callable bond is $101.432.

The question that we have not addressed in our illustration but which is nonetheless important is the circumstances under which the issuer will call the bond. A discussion of the call rule is beyond the scope of this chapter. Basically, it involves determining when it is economical on an after-tax basis for the issuer to call the bond.

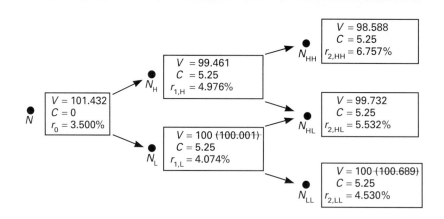

EXHIBIT 17-14   Valuing a Callable Corporate Bond with Three Years to Maturity, a Coupon Rate of 5.25%, and Callable in One Year at 100

Determining the Call Option Value (or Option Cost)

As explained in Chapter 14, the value of a callable bond is expressed as the difference between the value of a noncallable bond and the value of the call option. This relationship can also be expressed as follows:

value of a call option = value of a noncallable bond − value of a callable bond

But we have just seen how the value of a noncallable bond and the value of a callable bond can be determined. The difference between the two values is therefore the value of the call option. In our illustration, the value of the noncallable bond is $102.075 and the value of the callable bond is $101.432, so the value of the call option is $0.643.

Extension to Other Embedded Options

The bond valuation framework presented here can be used to analyze other embedded options, such as put options, caps and floors on floating-rate notes, and the optional accelerated redemption granted to an issuer in fulfilling its sinking fund requirement.[5] For example, let's consider a putable bond. Suppose that a 5.25% corporate bond with three years remaining to maturity is putable in one year at par ($100). Also assume that the appropriate binomial interest-rate tree for this issuer is the one in Exhibit 17-12. Exhibit 17-15 shows the binomial interest-rate tree with the bond values altered at two nodes (N_{HH} and N_{LH}) because the bond values at these two nodes exceed $100, the value at which the bond can be put. The value of this putable bond is $102.523.

Because the value of a nonputable bond can be expressed as the value of a putable bond minus the value of a put option on that bond, this means that

value of a put option = value of a nonputable bond − value of a putable bond

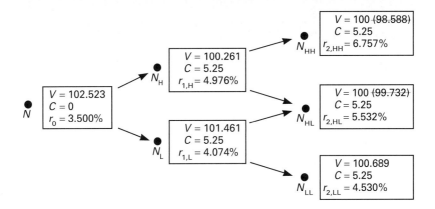

EXHIBIT 17-15 Valuing a Putable Corporate Bond with Three Years to Maturity, a Coupon Rate of 5.25%, and Putable in One Year at 100

---

[5]Andrew Kalotay and George O. Williams, "The Valuation and Management of Bonds with Sinking Fund Provisions," *Financial Analysis Journal*, March–April 1992, pp. 59–67.

In our example, because the value of the putable bond is $102.523 and the value of the corresponding nonputable bond is $102.075, the value of the put option is –$0.448. The negative sign indicates that the issuer has sold the option, or equivalently, the investor has purchased the option.

The framework can also be used to value a bond with multiple or interrelated embedded options. The bond values at each node are altered based on whether one of the options is exercised.

Incorporating Default Risk

Recently, John Finnerty has extended the basic binomial model just explained to incorporate default risk.[6] The extension involves adjusting the expected cash flows for the probability of a payment default and the expected amount of cash that will be recovered when a default occurs. This extension then requires the manager to estimate (1) the historical default experience of bonds with a similar rating and (2) the expected amount that will be recovered. Empirical data collected by the commercial rating agencies and several well-known studies by Edward Altman allow a manager to do a good job of estimating this required data.

An explanation of specifically how the adjustments are made to the model is beyond the scope of this chapter. The article by Finnerty provides not only a detailed discussion of the valuation process but also illustrates how the model was applied to value a pay-in-kind debenture bond of Bucyrus-Erie Company, an issue that was rated non-investment grade at the time of the analysis and had multiple embedded options.

Modeling Risk

The user of any valuation model is exposed to **modeling risk**. This is the risk that the output of the model is incorrect because the assumptions upon which it is based are incorrect. Consequently, it is imperative that the results of a valuation model be stress-tested for modeling risk by altering the assumptions.

A critical assumption in the valuation model is the volatility assumption. For a callable bond, a higher (lower) volatility assumption lowers (raises) its value. For a putable bond, a higher (lower) volatility assumption raises (lowers) its value.

OPTION-ADJUSTED SPREAD

What an investor seeks to do is to buy securities whose value is greater than their market price. A valuation model such as the one just described allows an investor to estimate the value of a security, which at this point would be sufficient to determine the fairness of the price of the security. That is, the investor can say that this bond is one point cheap or two points cheap and so on.

A valuation model need not stop here, however. Instead, it can convert the divergence between the price observed in the market for the security and the value derived

---

[6]John D. Finnerty, "Adjusting the Binomial Model for Default Risk," *Journal of Portfolio Management,* Winter 1999, pp. 93–104.

from the model into a yield spread measure. This step is necessary because most market participants find it more convenient to think about yield spread than about price differences.

The **option-adjusted spread (OAS)** was developed as a measure of the yield spread (in basis points) that can be used to convert dollar differences between value and price. Thus, basically, the OAS is used to reconcile value with market price. But what is it a "spread" over? The OAS is a spread over the spot rate curve or benchmark used in the valuation. The reason that the resulting spread is referred to as *option-adjusted* is because the cash flows of the security whose value we seek are adjusted to reflect the embedded option.

In the case of the binomial method, the OAS is a spread over the binomial interest-rate tree. Some market participants construct the binomial interest-rate tree using the Treasury spot rates. In this case, the OAS reflects the richness or cheapness of the security, if any, plus a credit spread. Other market participants construct the binomial interest-rate tree from the issuer's spot rate curve. In this case, the credit risk is already incorporated into the analysis, and the OAS therefore reflects the richness or cheapness of a security. Therefore, it is critical to know the on-the-run issues that the modeler used to construct the binomial interest-rate tree.

Translating OAS to Theoretical Value

Although the product of a valuation model is the OAS, the process can be worked in reverse. For a specified OAS, the valuation model can determine the theoretical value of the security that is consistent with that OAS. As with the theoretical value, the OAS is affected by the assumed interest rate volatility. The higher (lower) the expected interest rate volatility, the lower (higher) the OAS.

Determining the Option Value in Spread Terms

Earlier we described how the dollar value of the option is calculated. The option value in spread terms is determined as follows:

$$\text{option value (in basis points)} = \text{static spread} - \text{OAS}$$

EFFECTIVE DURATION AND CONVEXITY

As explained in Chapter 4, money managers also want to know the price sensitivity of a bond when interest rates change. Modified duration is a measure of the sensitivity of a bond's price to interest-rate changes, *assuming that the expected cash flow does not change with interest rates*. Consequently, modified duration may not be an appropriate measure for bonds with embedded options because the expected cash flows change as interest rates change. For example, when interest rates fall, the expected cash flow for a callable bond may change. In the case of a putable bond, a rise in interest rates may change the expected cash flow.

Although modified duration may be inappropriate as a measure of a bond's price sensitivity to interest rate changes, there is a duration measure that is more appropriate for bonds with embedded options. Because duration measures price responsiveness to

changes in interest rates, the duration for a bond with an embedded option can be estimated by letting interest rates change by a small number of basis points above and
below the prevailing yield, and seeing how the prices change. As explained in Chapter 4,
in general, the duration for *any* bond can be *approximated* as follows:

$$\text{duration} = \frac{P_- - P_+}{2(P_0)(\Delta y)}$$

where:

P_- = price if yield is decreased by x basis points
P_+ = price if yield is increased by x basis points
P_0 = initial price (per \$100 of par value)
Δy = change in rate used to calculate price (x basis points in decimal form)

In Chapter 4 we showed how the application of this formula to an option-free bond
gives the modified duration because the cash flows do not change when yields change.
    When the approximate duration formula is applied to a bond with an embedded
option, the new prices at the higher and lower yield levels should reflect the value from
the valuation model. Duration calculated in this way is called **effective duration** or
option-adjusted duration.
    In general, the relationships among duration, modified duration, and effective
duration are as follows. Duration is a generic concept that indicates the responsiveness
of a bond to a change in interest rates. Modified duration is a duration measure in
which the cash flow is not assumed to change when interest rates change. In contrast,
effective duration measures the responsiveness of a bond's price taking into account
that the expected cash flow will change as interest rates change due to the embedded
option. The difference between modified duration and effective duration for a bond
with an embedded option can be quite dramatic. For example, a callable bond could
have a modified duration of 5 and an effective duration of 3. For certain highly leveraged mortgage-backed securities, the bond could have a modified duration of 7 and an
effective duration of 50! The differences between modified duration and effective
duration are summarized in Exhibit 17-16.
    Similarly, the standard convexity measure may be inappropriate for a bond with
embedded options because it does not consider the effect of a change in interest rates
on the bond's cash flow. As explained in Chapter 4, the convexity of any bond can be
approximated using the following formula:

$$\frac{P_+ + P_- - 2(P_0)}{(P_0)(\Delta y)^2}$$

When the prices used in this formula assume that the cash flows do not change when
yields change, the resulting convexity is a good approximation of the standard convexity for an option-free bond. When the prices used in the formula are derived by
changing the cash flows when yields change, the resulting convexity is called **effective
convexity**.

EXHIBIT 17-16   Modified Duration Versus Effective Duration

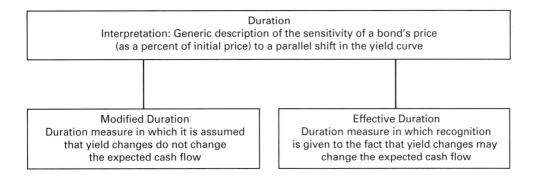

Using the binomial method, the procedure for calculating the value of P_+ that should be used to calculate effective duration and effective convexity is as follows:

Step 1:   Calculate the OAS for the issue.
Step 2:   Shift the on-the-run yield curve up by a small number of basis points.
Step 3:   Construct a binomial interest-rate tree based on the new yield curve in step 2.
Step 4:   To each of the short rates in the binomial interest-rate tree, add the OAS to obtain an adjusted tree.
Step 5:   Use the adjusted tree found in step 4 to determine the value of the security, which is P_+.

To determine the value of P_-, the same five steps are followed except that in step 2 the on-the-run yield curve is shifted down by a small number of basis points.

SUMMARY

The traditional yield spread approach fails to take three factors into account: (1) the term structure of interest rates, (2) the options embedded in the bond, and (3) the expected volatility of interest rates. The static spread measures the spread over the Treasury spot rate curve assuming that interest rates will not change in the future.

The potential investor in a callable bond must be compensated for the risk that the issuer will call the bond prior to the stated maturity date. The two risks faced by a potential investor are reinvestment risk and truncated price appreciation when yields decline (i.e., negative convexity).

The traditional methodology for valuing bonds with embedded options relies on the yield to worst. The limitations of yield numbers are now well recognized. Moreover, the traditional methodology does not consider how future interest-rate volatility will affect the value of the embedded option.

To value a bond with an embedded option, it is necessary to understand that the bond can be decomposed into an option-free component and an option component.

CHAPTER 17 *Analysis of Bonds with Embedded Options*

The binomial method can be used to value a bond with an embedded option. It involves generating a binomial interest-rate tree based on (1) an issuer's yield curve, (2) an interest-rate model, and (3) an assumed interest-rate volatility. The binomial interest-rate tree provides the appropriate volatility-dependent one-period forward rates that should be used to discount the expected cash flows of a bond. Critical to the valuation process is an assumption about expected interest-rate volatility.

The option-adjusted spread (OAS) converts the cheapness or richness of a bond into a spread over the future possible spot rate curves. The spread is option adjusted because it allows for future interest-rate volatility to affect the cash flows.

Modified duration and standard convexity, used to measure the interest-rate sensitivity of an option-free bond, may be inappropriate for a bond with an embedded option because these measures assume that cash flows do not change as interest rates change. The duration and convexity can be approximated for any bond, whether it is option-free or a bond with an embedded option. The approximation involves determining how the price of the bond changes if interest rates go up or down by a small number of basis points. If interest rates are changed it is assumed that the cash flows do not change, the resulting measures are modified duration and standard convexity. However, when the cash flows are allowed to change when interest rates change, the resulting measures are called effective duration and effective convexity.

Questions

1. What are the two drawbacks of the traditional approach to the valuation of bonds with embedded options?
2. Is the static spread for a three-year 9% coupon corporate bond selling at 105.58, given the following theoretical Treasury spot rate values equal to 50, 100, or 120 basis points?

Month	Spot Rate (%)
1	4.0
2	4.2
3	4.9
4	5.4
5	5.7
6	6.0

3. Under what conditions would the traditional yield spread be close to the static spread?
4. Why is the investor of a callable bond exposed to reinvestment risk?
5. What is negative convexity?
6. Does a callable bond exhibit negative or positive convexity?

7. Suppose that you are given the following information about two callable bonds that can be called immediately:

	Estimated Percentage Change in Price if Interest Rates Change by:	
	−100 basis points	+100 basis points
Bond ABC	+5	−8
Bond XYZ	+22	−16

You are told that both of these bonds have the same maturity and that the coupon rate of one bond is 7% and of the other is 13%. Suppose that the yield curve for both issuers is flat at 8%. Based on this information, which bond is the lower coupon bond and which is the higher coupon bond? Explain why.

8. The theoretical value of a noncallable bond is $103; the theoretical value of a callable bond is $101. Determine the theoretical value of the call option.

9. Explain why you agree or disagree with the following statement: "The value of a putable

bond is never greater than the value of an otherwise comparable option-free bond."

10. Explain why you agree or disagree with the following statement: "An investor should be unwilling to pay more than the call price for a bond that is likely to be called."

11. In Robert Litterman, Jose Scheinkman, and Laurence Weiss, "Volatility and the Yield Curve," *Journal of Fixed Income*, Premier Issue, 1991, p. 49, the following statement was made: "Many fixed income securities (e.g., callable bonds) contain embedded options whose prices are sensitive to the level of volatility. Modeling the additional impact of volatility on the value of the coupons allows for a better understanding of the price behavior of these securities." Explain why.

12. If an on-the-run issue for an issuer is evaluated properly using a binomial model, how would the theoretical value compare to the actual market price?

13. The current on-the-run yields for the Ramsey Corporation are as follows:

Maturity (years)	Yield to Maturity (%)	Market Price
1	7.5	100
2	7.6	100
3	7.7	100

Assume that each bond is an annual-pay bond. Each bond is trading at par, so its coupon rate is equal to its yield to maturity.

a. Using the bootstrapping methodology, complete the following table:

Year	Spot Rate (%)	One-Year Forward Rate (%)
1		
2		
3		

b. Using the spot rates, what would be the value of an 8.5% option-free bond of this issuer?

c. Using the one-year forward rates, what would be the value of an 8.5% coupon option-free bond of this issuer?

d. Using the binomial model (which assumes that one-year rates undergo a

lognormal random walk with volatility σ), show that if σ is assumed to be 10%, the lower one-year forward rate one year from now *cannot* be 7%.

e. Demonstrate that if σ is assumed to be 10%, the lower one-year forward rate one year from now is 6.944%.

f. Demonstrate that if σ is assumed to be 10%, the lower one-year forward rate two years from now is approximately 6.437%.

g. Show the binomial interest-rate tree that should be used to value any bond of this issuer.

h. Determine the value of an 8.5% coupon option-free bond for this issuer using the binomial interest-rate tree given in part g.

i. Determine the value of an 8.5% coupon bond that is callable at par (100) assuming that the issue will be called if the price exceeds par.

14. Explain how an increase in expected interest-rate volatility can decrease the value of a callable bond.

15. a. What is meant by the option-adjusted spread?
    b. What is the spread relative to?

16. "The option-adjusted spread measures the yield spread over the Treasury on-the-run yield curve." Explain why you agree or disagree with this statement.

17. What is the effect of greater expected interest-rate volatility on the option-adjusted spread of a security?

18. The following excerpt is taken from an article titled "Call Provisions Drop Off" that appeared in the January 27, 1992, issue of *BondWeek*, p. 2:

Issuance of callable long-term bonds dropped off further last year as interest rates fell, removing the incentive for many issuers to pay extra for the provision, said Street capital market officials. . . .

The shift toward noncallable issues, which began in the late 1980s, reflects the secular trend of investors unwilling to bear prepayment risk and possibly the cyclical trend that corporations believe that interest rates have hit all time lows. . . .

a. What "incentive" is this article referring to in the first sentence of the excerpt?
b. Why would issuers not be willing to pay for this incentive if they feel that interest rates will continue to decline?

19. The following excerpt is taken from an article titled "Eagle Eyes High-Coupon Callable Corporates" that appeared in the January 20, 1992, issue of *BondWeek*, p. 7:

If the bond market rallies further, Eagle Asset Management may take profits, trading $8 million of seven- to 10-year Treasuries for high-coupon single-A industrials that are callable in two to four years according to Joseph Blanton, senior V.P. He thinks a further rally is unlikely, however. . . .

The corporates have a 95% chance of being called in two to four years and are treated as two- to four-year paper in calculating the duration of the portfolio, Blanton said. . . .

a. Why is modified duration an inappropriate measure for a high-coupon callable bond?
b. What would be a better measure than modified duration?
c. Why would the replacement of 10-year Treasuries with high-coupon callable bonds reduce the portfolio's duration?

ANALYSIS OF RESIDENTIAL MORTGAGE-BACKED SECURITIES *

After reading this chapter you will understand:

■ the cash flow yield methodology for analyzing residential mortgage-backed securities

■ the limitations of the cash flow yield methodology

■ how the effective duration and convexity are calculated for the cash flow yield methodology

■ one measure for estimating prepayment sensitivity

■ why the Monte Carlo simulation methodology is used to value residential mortgage-backed securities

■ how interest-rate paths are simulated in a Monte Carlo simulation methodology

■ how the Monte Carlo simulation methodology can be used to determine the theoretical value of a residential mortgage-backed security

■ how the option-adjusted spread, effective duration, and effective convexity are computed using the Monte Carlo simulation methodology

■ the complexities of modeling collateralized mortgage obligations

■ the limitations of option-adjusted spread

■ modeling risk and how it can be stress tested

---

*This chapter is adapted from Chapters 9 and 10 of Frank J. Fabozzi, Chuck Ramsey, and Frank Ramirez, *Collateralized Mortgage Obligations: Structures and Analysis* (Buckingham, PA: Frank J. Fabozzi Associates, 1994).

■ how the total return is calculated for a residential mortgage-backed security

■ the difficulties of applying the total return framework to residential mortgage-backed securities

There are two approaches to the analysis of residential mortgage-backed securities (including pass-throughs, collateralized mortgage obligations, and stripped mortgage-backed securities): (1) the static cash flow yield methodology, and (2) the Monte Carlo simulation methodology. The Monte Carlo simulation methodology provides the theoretical value of a residential mortgage-backed security. That is, it is a valuation model. A product of this valuation model, as with all valuation models, is the option-adjusted spread (OAS). In this chapter we review the static cash flow yield methodology and its limitations and then focus on the Monte Carlo simulation methodology. The framework provided in this chapter applies to agency and nonagency residential mortgage-backed securities including home equity loan–backed securities and manufactured housing–backed securities.

STATIC CASH FLOW YIELD METHODOLOGY

The static cash flow yield methodology is the simplest to use, although we shall see that it offers little insight into the relative value of a residential mortgage-backed security (RMBS). It begins with the computation of the cash flow yield measure that we described for pass-throughs in Chapter 11. The cash flow yield is based on some prepayment assumption.

To illustrate the cash flow yield, we'll use one of the CMO structures we developed in Chapter 12, FJF-06. This structure is summarized in Exhibit 12–15. Exhibit 18-1 summarizes cash flow yields according to various PSA prepayment assumptions for the four tranches assuming different purchase prices. Notice that the greater the discount assumed to be paid for the tranche, the more a tranche will benefit from faster prepayments. The converse is true for a tranche for which a premium is paid. The faster the prepayments, the lower the cash flow yield.

Vector Analysis

One practice that market participants use to overcome the drawback of the PSA benchmark is to assume that the PSA speed can change over time. This technique is referred to as **vector analysis**. A **vector** is simply a set of numbers. In the case of prepayments, it is a vector of prepayment speeds. Vector analysis is particularly useful for CMO tranches that are dramatically affected by the initial slowing down of prepayments, and then speeding up of prepayments, or vice versa.

Exhibit 18-2 reports the cash flow yield using vector analysis for the four tranches and collateral of FJF-06. The top panel shows the cash flow yield assuming 165 PSA. Nine vectors are then shown assuming that the PSA is constant from months 1 to 36,

EXHIBIT 18-1 Price Cash Flow Yield Table for the Four Tranches in FJF-06

Tranche A: Orig. par: $194,500,000; type: sequential; coupon: 6.00% (fixed)

If Price Paid Is:	50.00 PSA	100.00 PSA	165.00 PSA	250.00 PSA	400.00 PSA	500.00 PSA	700.00 PSA	1000.00 PSA
90–24	08.37	09.01	09.76	10.61	11.87	12.59	13.88	15.63
91–24	8.09	8.66	9.32	10.07	11.17	11.81	12.94	14.47
92–24	7.82	8.31	8.88	9.53	10.49	11.03	12.01	13.33
93–24	7.56	7.97	8.45	9.00	9.81	10.27	11.10	12.22
94–24	7.29	7.63	8.03	8.48	9.14	9.52	10.20	11.12
95–24	7.03	7.30	7.61	7.97	8.49	8.79	9.32	10.04
96–24	6.78	6.97	7.20	7.46	7.85	8.06	8.45	8.98
97–24	6.53	6.65	6.80	6.97	7.21	7.35	7.60	7.94
98–24	6.28	6.34	6.40	6.48	6.59	6.65	6.76	6.91
99–24	6.04	6.02	6.01	6.00	5.97	5.96	5.94	5.91
100–24	5.79	5.72	5.62	5.52	5.37	5.28	5.13	4.92
101–24	5.56	5.41	5.24	5.05	4.77	4.61	4.33	3.95
102–24	5.33	5.12	4.87	4.59	4.18	3.95	3.54	2.99
103–24	5.10	4.82	4.50	4.14	3.61	3.30	2.77	2.05
104–24	4.87	4.53	4.14	3.69	3.04	2.66	2.01	1.12
105–24	4.65	4.25	3.78	3.25	2.47	2.03	1.26	0.21
106–24	4.42	3.96	3.42	2.81	1.92	1.41	0.52	−0.68
107–24	4.21	3.69	3.07	2.38	1.37	0.80	−0.21	−1.57
108–24	3.99	3.41	2.73	1.96	0.83	0.20	−0.93	−2.44
109–24	3.78	3.14	2.39	1.54	0.30	−0.40	−1.64	−3.29
Average life:	5.09	3.80	2.93	2.33	1.79	1.58	1.31	1.07
Mod. duration:	4.12	3.22	2.57	2.09	1.64	1.46	1.22	1.00
Exp. maturity:	9.40	7.15	5.40	4.15	3.07	2.65	2.24	1.82

(*continued*)

and then changes for months 37 through 138, and again changes for months 139 through 357.

Limitations of the Cash Flow Yield

As we have noted several times already, the yield to maturity has two shortcomings as a measure of a bond's potential return: (1) It is assumed that the coupon payments can be reinvested at a rate equal to the yield to maturity, and (2) it is assumed that the bond is held to maturity. These shortcomings are equally present in application of the cash flow yield measure: (1) the projected cash flows are assumed to be reinvested at the cash flow yield, and (2) the RMBS is assumed to be held until the final payout based on some prepayment assumption. The importance of reinvestment risk, the risk that the cash flow will be reinvested at a rate less than the cash flow yield, is particularly important for many RMBS because payments come as frequently as every month. The cash flow yield, moreover, is dependent on realization

EXHIBIT 18-1:   (continued)

Tranche B: Orig. par: $36,000,000; type: sequential; coupon: 6.50% (fixed)

If Price Paid Is:	50.00 PSA	100.00 PSA	165.00 PSA	250.00 PSA	400.00 PSA	500.00 PSA	700.00 PSA	1000.00 PSA
90–31	7.85	8.12	8.49	8.95	9.69	10.13	10.89	11.83
91–31	7.69	7.93	8.25	8.66	9.31	9.70	10.36	11.18
92–31	7.54	7.75	8.02	8.37	8.94	9.27	9.84	10.55
93–31	7.39	7.57	7.80	8.09	8.57	8.85	9.33	9.92
94–31	7.24	7.39	7.58	7.82	8.20	8.43	8.82	9.31
95–31	7.10	7.21	7.35	7.54	7.84	8.02	8.32	8.70
96–31	6.95	7.03	7.14	7.27	7.49	7.61	7.83	8.10
97–31	6.81	6.86	6.92	7.00	7.13	7.21	7.34	7.51
98–31	6.67	6.69	6.71	6.74	6.79	6.82	6.86	6.92
99–31	6.53	6.52	6.50	6.48	6.45	6.42	6.39	6.35
100–31	6.39	6.35	6.29	6.22	6.11	6.04	5.92	5.78
101–31	6.26	6.19	6.09	5.97	5.77	5.66	5.46	5.22
102–31	6.13	6.02	5.89	5.72	5.44	5.28	5.00	4.66
103–31	5.99	5.86	5.69	5.47	5.12	4.91	4.55	4.12
104–31	5.86	5.70	5.49	5.22	4.79	4.54	4.11	3.58
105–31	5.74	5.55	5.30	4.98	4.48	4.18	3.67	3.04
106–31	5.61	5.39	5.10	4.74	4.16	3.82	3.23	2.51
107–31	5.48	5.24	4.91	4.50	3.85	3.46	2.80	1.99
108–31	5.36	5.08	4.72	4.27	3.54	3.11	2.38	1.48
109–31	5.24	4.93	4.54	4.04	3.24	2.76	1.96	0.97
Average life:	10.17	7.76	5.93	4.58	3.35	2.89	2.35	1.90
Mod. duration:	7.23	5.92	4.78	3.84	2.92	2.56	2.11	1.74
Exp. maturity:	10.90	8.40	6.49	4.99	3.65	3.15	2.49	1.99

of the projected cash flow according to some prepayment rate. If actual pre-payments vary from the prepayment rate assumed, the cash flow yield will not be realized.

Yield Spread to Treasuries

It should be clear that at the time of purchase it is not possible to determine an exact yield for a RMBS; the yield will depend on the actual prepayment experience of the mortgages in the pool. Nevertheless, the convention in all fixed-income markets is to measure the yield on a non-Treasury security to that of a "comparable" Treasury security.

The repayment of principal over time makes it inappropriate to compare the yield of a RMBS to a Treasury of a stated maturity. Instead, market participants have used two measures: Macaulay duration (as explained in Chapter 4) and average life (as explained in Chapter 11).

EXHIBIT 18-1   (continued)

Tranche C: Orig. par: $96,500,000; type: sequential; coupon: 7.00% (fixed)

If Price Paid Is:	50.00 PSA	100.00 PSA	165.00 PSA	250.00 PSA	400.00 PSA	500.00 PSA	700.00 PSA	1000.00 PSA
90–03	8.34	8.53	8.80	9.15	9.77	10.16	10.89	11.85
91–03	8.20	8.37	8.61	8.92	9.47	9.81	10.46	11.31
92–03	8.06	8.21	8.42	8.70	9.17	9.48	10.05	10.79
93–03	7.92	8.06	8.24	8.47	8.88	9.14	9.63	10.27
94–03	7.79	7.90	8.05	8.25	8.60	8.81	9.22	9.76
95–03	7.66	7.75	7.87	8.03	8.31	8.49	8.82	9.25
96–03	7.53	7.60	7.69	7.82	8.03	8.17	8.42	8.76
97–03	7.40	7.45	7.52	7.61	7.76	7.85	8.03	8.26
98–03	7.28	7.31	7.35	7.40	7.48	7.54	7.64	7.78
99–03	7.15	7.16	7.17	7.19	7.21	7.23	7.26	7.30
100–03	7.03	7.02	7.01	6.98	6.95	6.93	6.88	6.83
101–03	6.91	6.88	6.84	6.78	6.69	6.63	6.51	6.36
102–03	6.79	6.74	6.67	6.58	6.43	6.33	6.14	5.90
103–03	6.67	6.61	6.51	6.39	6.17	6.03	5.78	5.45
104–03	6.56	6.47	6.35	6.19	5.92	5.74	5.42	5.00
105–03	6.44	6.34	6.19	6.00	5.67	5.46	5.07	4.56
106–03	6.33	6.21	6.03	5.81	5.42	5.17	4.72	4.12
107–03	6.22	6.08	5.88	5.62	5.18	4.89	4.37	3.69
108–03	6.11	5.95	5.73	5.43	4.94	4.62	4.03	3.26
109–03	6.00	5.82	5.57	5.25	4.70	4.34	3.69	2.84
Average life:	12.77	10.16	7.98	6.24	4.54	3.87	3.04	2.37
Mod. duration:	8.18	7.04	5.92	4.89	3.76	3.28	2.65	2.12
Exp. maturity:	14.57	11.90	9.57	7.65	5.57	4.74	3.65	2.82

(*continued*)

Static Spread

As explained in Chapter 17, the practice of spreading the yield to the average life on the interpolated Treasury yield curve is improper for an amortizing bond even in the absence of interest-rate volatility. What should be done instead is to calculate what is called the **static spread**. This is the yield spread in a static scenario (i.e., no volatility of interest rates) of the bond over the entire theoretical Treasury spot rate curve, not a single point on the Treasury yield curve.

As explained in Chapter 17, the magnitude of the difference between the traditional yield spread and the static yield spread depends on the steepness of the yield curve: The steeper the curve, the greater the difference between the two values. In a relatively flat interest-rate environment, the difference between the traditional yield spread and the static spread will be small.

There are two ways to compute the static spread for RMBS. One way is to use today's yield curve to discount future cash flows and keep the mortgage refinancing rate fixed at today's mortgage rate. Because the mortgage refinancing rate is fixed,

EXHIBIT 18-1 (continued)

Tranche Z: Orig. par: $73,000,000; type: sequential; coupon: 7.35% (fixed)

If Price Paid Is:	50.00 PSA	100.00 PSA	165.00 PSA	250.00 PSA	400.00 PSA	500.00 PSA	700.00 PSA	1000.00 PSA
90–01	7.87	7.96	8.09	8.27	8.61	8.84	9.33	10.10
91–01	7.82	7.89	8.00	8.16	8.47	8.68	9.11	9.79
92–01	7.76	7.83	7.93	8.07	8.33	8.51	8.89	9.49
93–01	7.71	7.76	7.85	7.97	8.20	8.35	8.68	9.20
94–01	7.65	7.70	7.77	7.87	8.06	8.19	8.47	8.90
95–01	7.60	7.63	7.69	7.77	7.93	8.04	8.26	8.61
96–01	7.54	7.57	7.62	7.68	7.80	7.88	8.05	8.33
97–01	7.49	7.51	7.54	7.59	7.67	7.73	7.85	8.04
98–01	7.44	7.45	7.47	7.49	7.54	7.58	7.65	7.76
99–01	7.38	7.39	7.39	7.40	7.42	7.43	7.45	7.49
100–01	7.33	7.33	7.32	7.31	7.29	7.28	7.26	7.21
101–01	7.28	7.27	7.25	7.22	7.17	7.14	7.06	6.95
102–01	7.23	7.21	7.18	7.13	7.05	6.99	6.87	6.68
103–01	7.18	7.15	7.11	7.05	6.93	6.85	6.68	6.42
104–01	7.13	7.09	7.04	6.96	6.81	6.71	6.49	6.16
105–01	7.08	7.04	6.97	6.88	6.69	6.57	6.31	5.90
106–01	7.04	6.98	6.90	6.79	6.58	6.43	6.13	5.65
107–01	6.99	6.93	6.84	6.71	6.46	6.29	5.94	5.39
108–01	6.94	6.87	6.77	6.62	6.35	6.16	5.77	5.15
109–01	6.89	6.82	6.70	6.54	6.24	6.03	5.59	4.90
Average life:	22.39	19.57	16.21	12.78	9.01	7.46	5.49	3.88
Mod. duration:	19.42	16.68	13.81	11.08	8.06	6.78	5.11	3.67
Exp. maturity:	29.74	29.74	29.74	29.74	29.74	29.74	29.74	24.24

Note: Calculated using SFW Software, copyright © 1989 by Wall Street Analytics, Inc.

the investor can usually specify a reasonable prepayment rate for the life of the security. Using this prepayment rate, the bond's future cash flow can be estimated. Use of this approach to calculate the static spread recognizes different prices today of dollars to be delivered at future dates. This results in the proper discounting of cash flows while keeping the mortgage rate fixed. Effectively, today's prices indicate what the future discount rates will be, but the best estimates of future rates are today's rates.

The second way to calculate the static spread allows the mortgage rate to go up the curve as implied by the forward interest rates. This procedure is sometimes called the **zero-volatility OAS**. In this case a prepayment model is needed to determine the vector of future prepayment rates implied by the vector of future refinancing rates. A money manager using static spread should determine which approach is used in the calculation.

EXHIBIT 18-2 Vector Analysis of Cash Flow Yield for Four Tranches of FJF-06 and Collateral Assumptions

	Coupon (%)	Price	Cash flow yield at 165 PSA (%)
Tranche A	6.00	99–24	6.00
Tranche B	6.50	99–31	6.50
Tranche C	7.00	100–03	7.00
Tranche Z	7.25	100–01	7.25
Collateral	7.50	100–00	?

		PSA Vector Scenario								
	Months	(1)	(2)	(3)	(4)	(5)	(6)	(7)	(8)	(9)
	1–36	165	165	165	165	165	165	165	165	165
Tranchel	37–138	50	50	300	400	400	400	400	500	600
Parameter	139–357	250	400	400	200	700	500	165	200	1000
Tranche A										
Cash flow yield		6.02	6.02	6.01	6.00	6.00	6.00	6.00	6.00	6.00
Average life		3.51	3.51	2.71	2.63	2.63	2.63	2.63	2.58	2.54
Modified duration		2.97	2.97	2.40	2.34	2.34	2.34	2.34	2.30	2.27
Tranche B										
Cash flow yield		6.52	6.52	6.48	6.48	6.48	6.48	6.48	6.47	6.46
Average life		8.51	8.51	4.82	4.39	4.39	4.39	4.39	4.11	3.91
Modified duration		6.35	6.35	4.02	3.71	3.71	3.71	3.71	3.50	3.36
Tranche C										
Cash flow yield		7.03	7.03	6.98	6.97	6.97	6.97	6.97	6.96	6.95
Average life		11.15	11.07	6.24	5.52	5.52	5.52	5.52	5.04	4.68
Modified duration		7.50	7.47	4.89	4.43	4.43	4.43	4.43	4.11	3.87
Tranche D										
Cash flow yield		7.26	7.25	7.21	7.19	7.19	7.20	7.20	7.17	7.14
Average life		17.08	15.29	11.47	10.49	9.55	11.42	10.65	8.92	7.49
Modified duration		15.44	14.19	10.28	9.19	8.76	9.56	9.26	8.01	6.98
Collateral										
Cash flow yield		7.54	7.53	7.50	7.49	7.49	7.49	7.49	7.48	7.47
Average life		10.90	10.05	6.31	5.68	5.40	5.95	5.72	5.02	4.48
Modified duration		6.47	6.25	4.50	4.14	4.07	4.21	4.16	3.82	3.55

Note: Calculated using SFW Software, copyright © 1989 by Wall Street Analytics, Inc.

Effective Duration

Modified duration is a measure of the sensitivity of a bond's price to interest-rate changes, assuming that the expected cash flow does not change with interest rates. Modified duration is consequently not an appropriate measure for mortgage-backed securities, because prepayments do cause the projected cash flow to change as interest rates change. When interest rates fall (rise), prepayments are expected to rise (fall). As a result, when interest rates fall (rise), duration may decrease (increase) rather than increase (decrease). As we explained in Chapter 17, this property is referred to as **negative convexity**.

Negative convexity has the same impact on the price performance of a RMBS as it does on the performance of a callable bond (discussed in Chapter 17). When interest rates decline, a bond with an embedded call option, which is what a RMBS is, will not perform as well as an option-free bond. Although modified duration is an inappropriate measure of interest-rate sensitivity, there is a way to allow for changing prepayment rates on cash flow as interest rates change. This is achieved by calculating the **effective duration**, which allows for changing cash flow when interest rates change.

To illustrate calculation of effective duration for CMO classes, consider FJF-06 once again. The structure is summarized in the top panel of Exhibit 18-3. The second panel provides all the data necessary to calculate modified duration and effective duration of the four tranches and the collateral. This panel shows the assumed cash flow yield and the corresponding initial price for the tranches assuming a prepayment speed

---

EXHIBIT 18-3 Calculation of Effective Duration and Convexity for FJF-06

Structure of FRR-06

Class	Par Amount	Coupon Rate (%)
A	$194,500,000	6.00
B	36,000,000	6.50
C	96,500,000	7.00
Z (accrual)	73,000,000	7.25
R	0	0
Collateral	$400,000,000	7.50

			NEW PRICE 165% PSA		NEW PRICE CFY	
	Cash Flow	Initial	CFY Change (bp)		Change (bp)/New PSA	
Class	Yield (%)	Price	+25 bp	−25bp	+25/150	−25/200
A	6.00	99.7813	99.0625	100.5313	99.0313	100.4375
B	6.50	100.0313	98.6250	101.5000	98.5625	101.2813
C	7.00	100.2813	98.4063	102.1875	98.3438	101.9063
Z	7.25	100.6250	98.0625	103.2500	98.0313	103.0313
Coll.	7.50	100.1250	98.7500	101.5000	98.7188	101.3438

Modified Duration/Convexity and Effective Duration/Convexity

Class	Modified Duration	Effective Duration	Standard Convexity	Effective Convexity
A	2.94	2.82	25.055	−75.164
B	5.75	5.44	49.984	−174.945
C	7.54	7.11	24.930	−249.299
Z	10.31	9.94	49.689	−149.068
Coll.	5.49	5.24	0	−149.813

of 165 PSA. The two columns following the initial prices give the new prices if the cash flow yield is changed by 25 basis points and assuming no change in the prepayment speed. The last two columns show new prices if the cash flow yield changes by 25 basis points and the prepayment speed is assumed to change; it decreases to 150 PSA if the cash flow yield increases by 25 basis points, and it increases to 200 PSA if the cash flow yield decreases by 25 basis points.

Exhibit 18-3 reports the modified duration and effective duration. To illustrate the calculation, consider tranche C. The data for calculating modified duration using the approximation formula is

$$P_- = 102.1875 \quad P_+ = 98.4063 \quad P_0 = 100.2813 \quad \Delta y = 0.0025$$

Substituting into the duration formula yields

$$\text{modified duration} = \frac{102.1875 - 98.4063}{2(100.2813)(0.0025)} = 7.54$$

The effective duration for the same bond class is calculated as follows:

$$P_- = 101.9063 \text{ (at 200 PSA)} \quad P_+ = 98.3438 \text{ (at 150 PSA)} \quad P_0 = 100.2813 \quad \Delta y = 0.0025$$

Substituting into the formula gives

$$\text{effective duration} = \frac{101.9063 - 98.3438}{2(100.2813)(0.0025)} = 7.11$$

Notice that for all four tranches and the collateral, the effective duration is less than the modified duration.

The divergence between modified duration and effective duration is much more dramatic for bond classes trading at a substantial discount from par or at a substantial premium over par. To demonstrate this, we can create another hypothetical CMO structure, which differs from FJF-06 by including a PO class and an IO class made up from tranche C. Let's look at the duration for the PO class. Assuming that the cash flow yield for the PO class is 7%, based on 165 PSA, the following prices are obtained:

	New Price		New Price	
Initial Price	165 PSA 7.25% CFY	165 PSA 6.75% CFY	150 PSA 7.25% CFY	200 PSA 6.75% CFY
60.3125	59.2500	61.3750	57.6563	64.5938

The modified duration for this PO is 7.05. The effective duration of 23.01 is dramatically different.

Effective Convexity

Exhibit 18-3 reports the standard convexity and the effective convexity for the four tranches in FJF-06 and the collateral. To illustrate the convexity formula, consider once again tranche C in FJF-06. The standard convexity is approximated as follows:

$$\frac{98.4063 - 102.1875 - 2(100.2813)}{(100.2813)(0.0025)^2} = 24.930$$

The effective convexity is

$$\frac{98.3438 + 101.9063 - 2(100.2813)}{(100.2813)(0.0025)^2} = -249.299$$

Note the significant difference in the two convexity measures here and in Exhibit 18-3. The standard convexity indicates that the four tranches have positive convexity, whereas the effective convexity indicates they have negative convexity. The difference is even more dramatic for bonds not trading near par. For a PO created from tranche C, the standard convexity is close to zero whereas the effective convexity is 2,155! This means that if yields change by 100 basis points, the percentage change in price due to convexity would be

$$2,155(0.01)^2(100) = 21.6\%$$

Prepayment Sensitivity Measure

The value of a RMBS will depend on prepayments. To assess prepayment sensitivity, market participants have used the following measure: the basis point change in the price of an RMBS for a 1% increase in prepayments. Specifically, prepayment sensitivity is defined as

P_0 = initial price (per $100 par value) at assumed prepayment speed
P_s = price (per $100 par value) assuming a 1% increase in prepayment speed

$$\text{prepayment sensitivity} = (P_s - P_0) \times 100$$

For example, suppose that for some RMBS at 300 PSA the price is 106.10. A 1% increase in the PSA prepayment rate means that PSA increases from 300 PSA to 303 PSA. Suppose that at 303 PSA the price is recomputed using a valuation model to be 106.01. Therefore,

$$P_0 = 106.10$$
$$P_s = 106.08$$

$$\text{prepayment sensitivity} = (106.01 - 106.10) \times 100 = -9$$

Notice that a security that is adversely affected by an increase in prepayment speeds will have a negative prepayment sensitivity while a security that benefits from an increase in prepayment speed will have a positive prepayment sensitivity.

MONTE CARLO SIMULATION METHODOLOGY[1]

For some fixed-income securities and derivative instruments, the periodic cash flows are **path dependent**. This means that the cash flows received in one period are determined not only by the current and future interest-rate levels but also by the path that interest rates took to get to the current level.

In the case of mortgage pass-through securities, prepayments are path dependent because this month's prepayment rate depends on whether there have been prior opportunities to refinance since the underlying mortgages were originated. Unlike mortgage loans, the decision as to whether a corporate issuer will elect to refund an issue when the current rate is below the issue's coupon rate is not dependent on how rates evolved over time to the current level.

Moreover, in the case of adjustable-rate pass-throughs (ARMs), prepayments are not only path dependent but the periodic coupon rate depends on the history of the reference rate upon which the coupon rate is determined. This is because ARMs have periodic caps and floors as well as a lifetime cap and floor. For example, an ARM whose coupon rate resets annually could have the following restriction on the coupon rate: (1) The rate cannot change by more than 200 basis points each year, and (2) the rate cannot be more than 500 basis points from the initial coupon rate.

Pools of pass-throughs are used as collateral for the creation of collateralized mortgage obligations (CMOs). Consequently, for CMOs there are typically two sources of path dependency in a CMO tranche's cash flows. First, the collateral prepayments are path dependent, as discussed previously. Second, the cash flow to be received in the current month by a CMO tranche depends on the outstanding balances of the other tranches in the deal. Thus, we need the history of prepayments to calculate these balances.

Because of the path dependency of a RMBS's cash flow, the Monte Carlo simulation method is used for these securities rather than the static method described in Chapter 17.

Conceptually, the valuation of pass-throughs using the Monte Carlo method is simple. In practice, however, it is very complex. The simulation involves generating a set of cash flows based on simulated future mortgage refinancing rates, which in turn imply simulated prepayment rates.

Valuation modeling for CMOs is similar to valuation modeling for pass-throughs, although the difficulties are amplified because, as we explained in Chapter 12, the issuer has sliced and diced both the prepayment risk and the interest-rate risk into smaller pieces called tranches. The sensitivity of the pass-throughs composing the collateral to these two risks is not transmitted equally to every tranche. Some of the tranches wind up more sensitive to prepayment risk and interest-rate risk than the collateral, whereas some of them are much less sensitive.

---

[1]Portions of the material in this section and the one to follow are adapted from Frank J. Fabozzi and Scott F. Richard, "Valuation of CMOs," in Frank J. Fabozzi (ed.), *CMO Portfolio Management* (Summit, NJ: Frank J. Fabozzi Associates, 1994). In the finance literature several recursive valuation models (i.e., models described in the previous chapter for valuing bonds with embedded options) have been proposed. However, in practice these models have not been used.

The objective of the money manager is to figure out how the value of the collateral gets transmitted to the CMO tranches. More specifically, the objective is to find out where the value goes and where the risk goes so that the money manager can identify the tranches with low risk and high value: the ones we want to buy. The good news is that this combination usually exists in every deal. The bad news is that in every deal there are usually tranches with low value and high risk.

Using Simulation to Generate Interest-Rate Paths and Cash Flows

The typical model that Wall Street firms and commercial vendors use to generate random interest-rate paths takes as input today's term structure of interest rates and a volatility assumption. The term structure of interest rates is the theoretical spot rate (or zero-coupon) curve implied by today's Treasury securities. The volatility assumption determines the dispersion of future interest rates in the simulation. The simulations should be normalized so that the average simulated price of a zero-coupon Treasury bond equals today's actual price.

Each model has its own model of the evolution of future interest rates and its own volatility assumptions. Typically, there are no significant differences in the interest-rate models of dealer firms and vendors, although their volatility assumptions can be significantly different.

The random paths of interest rates should be generated from an arbitrage-free model of the future term structure of interest rates. By *arbitrage-free* it is meant that the model replicates today's term structure of interest rates, an input of the model, and that for all future dates there is no possible arbitrage within the model.

The simulation works by generating many scenarios of future interest-rate paths. In each month of the scenario, a monthly interest rate and a mortgage refinancing rate are generated. The monthly interest rates are used to discount the projected cash flows in the scenario. The mortgage refinancing rate is needed to determine the cash flow because it represents the opportunity cost the mortgagor is facing at that time.

If the refinancing rates are high relative to the mortgagor's contract rate, the mortgagor will have less incentive to refinance, or even a positive disincentive (i.e., the homeowner will avoid moving, to avoid refinancing). If the refinancing rate is low relative to the mortgagor's contract rate, the mortgagor has an incentive to refinance.

Prepayments are projected by feeding the refinancing rate and loan characteristics, such as age, into a prepayment model. In the case of a nonagency deal, the prepayments can be involuntary. By involuntary it is meant that prepayments can arise because of a default by homeowners. Thus, in the modeling of prepayments, defaults must be projected. Modeling prepayments due to defaults involve projecting the severity of defaults (i.e., determining what the recovery rates are) and the timing of defaults. Given the projected prepayments (voluntary and involuntary), the cash flow along an interest-rate path can be determined.

To make this more concrete, consider a newly issued mortgage pass-through security with a maturity of 360 months. Exhibit 18-4 shows N simulated interest-rate path scenarios. Each scenario consists of a path of 360 simulated one-month future interest rates. Just how many paths should be generated is explained later. Exhibit 18-5 shows the paths of simulated mortgage refinancing rates corresponding to the scenarios

---

EXHIBIT 18-4 Simulated Paths of One-Month Future Interest Rates

Month	Interest-Rate Path Number[a]					
	1	2	3	...	n	... N
1	$f_1(1)$	$f_1(2)$	$f_1(3)$		$f_1(n)$	$f_1(N)$
2	$f_2(1)$	$f_2(2)$	$f_2(3)$		$f_2(n)$	$f_2(N)$
3	$f_3(1)$	$f_3(2)$	$f_3(3)$		$f_3(n)$	$f_3(N)$
4	$f_4(1)$	$f_4(2)$	$f_4(3)$		$f_4(n)$	$f_4(N)$
⋮						
t	$f_t(1)$	$f_t(2)$	$f_t(3)$		$f_t(n)$	$f_t(N)$
⋮						
358	$f_{358}(1)$	$f_{358}(2)$	$f_{358}(3)$		$f_{358}(n)$	$f_{358}(N)$
359	$f_{359}(1)$	$f_{359}(2)$	$f_{359}(3)$		$f_{359}(n)$	$f_{359}(N)$
360	$f_{360}(1)$	$f_{360}(2)$	$f_{360}(3)$		$f_{360}(n)$	$f_{360}(N)$

[a]Notation: $f_t(n)$, one-month future interest rate for month t on path n; N, total number of interest-rate paths.

EXHIBIT 18-5 Simulated Paths of Mortgage Refinancing Rates

Month	Interest-Rate Path Number[a]					
	1	2	3	...	n	... N
1	$r_1(1)$	$r_1(2)$	$r_1(3)$		$r_1(n)$	$r_1(N)$
2	$r_2(1)$	$r_2(2)$	$r_2(3)$		$r_2(n)$	$r_2(N)$
3	$r_3(1)$	$r_3(2)$	$r_3(3)$		$r_3(n)$	$r_3(N)$
4	$r_4(1)$	$r_4(2)$	$r_4(3)$		$r_4(n)$	$r_4(N)$
⋮						
t	$r_t(1)$	$r_t(2)$	$r_t(3)$		$r_t(n)$	$r_t(N)$
⋮						
358	$r_{358}(1)$	$r_{358}(2)$	$r_{358}(3)$		$r_{358}(n)$	$r_{358}(N)$
359	$r_{359}(1)$	$r_{359}(2)$	$r_{359}(3)$		$r_{359}(n)$	$r_{359}(N)$
360	$r_{360}(1)$	$r_{360}(2)$	$r_{360}(3)$		$r_{360}(n)$	$r_{360}(N)$

[a]Notation: $r_t(n)$, mortgage refinancing rate for month t on path n; N, total number of interest-rate paths.

---

shown in Exhibit 18-4. Assuming these mortgage refinancing rates, the cash flow for each scenario path is shown in Exhibit 18-6.

Calculating the Present Value for a Scenario Interest-Rate Path

Given the cash flow on an interest-rate path, its present value can be calculated. The discount rate for determining the present value is the simulated spot rate for each month on the interest-rate path plus an appropriate spread. The spot rate on a path can

EXHIBIT 18-6	Simulated Cash Flow on Each of the Interest-Rate Paths						

	Interest-Rate Path Number[a]						
Month	1	2	3	...	n	...	N
1	$C_1(1)$	$C_1(2)$	$C_1(3)$		$C_1(n)$		$C_1(N)$
2	$C_2(1)$	$C_2(2)$	$C_2(3)$		$C_2(n)$		$C_2(N)$
3	$C_3(1)$	$C_3(2)$	$C_3(3)$		$C_3(n)$		$C_3(N)$
4	$C_4(1)$	$C_4(2)$	$C_4(3)$		$C_4(n)$		$C_4(N)$
$\vdots$							
t	$C_t(1)$	$C_t(2)$	$C_t(3)$		$C_t(n)$		$C_t(N)$
$\vdots$							
358	$C_{358}(1)$	$C_{358}(2)$	$C_{358}(3)$		$C_{358}(n)$		$C_{358}(N)$
359	$C_{359}(1)$	$C_{359}(2)$	$C_{359}(3)$		$C_{359}(n)$		$C_{359}(N)$
360	$C_{360}(1)$	$C_{360}(2)$	$C_{360}(3)$		$C_{360}(n)$		$C_{360}(N)$

[a]Notation: $C_t(n)$, cash flow for month t on path n; N, total number of interest-rate paths.

be determined from the simulated future monthly rates. The relationship that holds between the simulated spot rate for month T on path n and the simulated future one-month rates is

$$z_T(n) = \{[1 + f_1(n)][1 + f_2(n)] \ldots [1 + f_T(n)]\}^{1/T} - 1$$

where:

$z_T(n)$ = simulated spot rate for month T on path n
$f_j(n)$ = simulated future one-month rate for month j on path n

Consequently, the interest-rate path for the simulated future one-month rates can be converted to the interest-rate path for the simulated monthly spot rates as shown in Exhibit 18-7.

Therefore, the present value of the cash flow for month T on interest-rate path n discounted at the simulated spot rate for month T plus some spread is

$$PV[C_T(n)] = \frac{C_T(n)}{[1 + z_T(n) + K]^{1/T}}$$

where:

$PV[C_T(n)]$ = present value of cash flow for month T on path n
$C_T(n)$ = cash flow for month T on path n
$z_T(n)$ = spot rate for month T on path n
K = appropriate risk-adjusted spread

EXHIBIT 18-7   Simulated Paths of Monthly Spot Rates

Month	Interest-Rate Path Number[a]					
	1	2	3	...	n ...	N
1	$z_1(1)$	$z_1(2)$	$z_1(3)$		$z_1(n)$	$z_1(N)$
2	$z_2(1)$	$z_2(2)$	$z_2(3)$		$z_2(n)$	$z_2(N)$
3	$z_3(1)$	$z_3(2)$	$z_3(3)$		$z_3(n)$	$z_3(N)$
4	$z_4(1)$	$z_4(2)$	$z_4(3)$		$z_4(n)$	$z_4(N)$
⋮						
t	$z_t(1)$	$z_t(2)$	$z_t(3)$		$z_t(n)$	$z_t(N)$
⋮						
358	$z_{358}(1)$	$z_{358}(2)$	$z_{358}(3)$		$z_{358}(n)$	$z_{358}(N)$
359	$z_{359}(1)$	$z_{359}(2)$	$z_{359}(3)$		$z_{359}(n)$	$z_{359}(N)$
360	$z_{360}(1)$	$z_{360}(2)$	$z_{360}(3)$		$z_{360}(n)$	$z_{360}(N)$

[a]Notation: $z_t(n)$, spot rate for month t on path n; N, total number of interest-rate paths.

The present value for path n is the sum of the present value of the cash flow for each month on path n. That is,

$$PV[\text{path}(n)] = (1/360)\ \{PV[C_1(n)] + PV[C_2(n)] + \ldots + PV[C_{360}(n)]\}$$

where $PV[\text{path}(n)]$ is the present value of interest-rate path n.

Determining the Theoretical Value

The present value of a given interest-rate path can be thought of as the theoretical value of a pass-through if that path was actually realized. The theoretical value of the pass-through can be determined by calculating the average of the theoretical value of all the interest-rate paths. That is, the theoretical value is equal to

$$\text{theoretical value} = (1/N)\{PV[\text{path}(1)] + PV[\text{path}(2)] + \cdots + PV[\text{path}(N)]\}$$

This procedure for valuing a pass-through is also followed for a CMO tranche. The cash flow for each month on each interest-rate path is found according to the principal repayment and interest distribution rules of the deal. To do this, a CMO structuring model is needed. In any analysis of CMOs, one of the major stumbling blocks is getting a good CMO structuring model.

Looking at the Distribution of the Path Values

The theoretical value generated by the Monte Carlo simulation method is the average of the path values. There is valuable information in the distribution of the path values. For example, consider a well-protected PAC bond. If the theoretical value generated from the Monte Carlo simulation method is 88 and the standard deviation of the path values is 1 point, there is not a great deal of dispersion in the path values. In contrast, suppose that the model indicates that the theoretical value for a support bond is 77 and the standard deviation of the path values is 10 points. Clearly, there is substantial dispersion of the path values and, as a result, the investor is warned about the potential variability of the model's value.[2]

Simulated Average Life

In Chapter 11 the average-life measure for a mortgage-backed security was introduced. The average life reported in a Monte Carlo analysis is the average of the average lives along the interest-rate paths. That is, for each interest-rate path, there is an average life. The average of these average lives is the average life reported. As with the theoretical value, additional information is conveyed by the distribution of the average life. The greater the range and standard deviation of the average life, the more uncertainty there is about the security's average life.

Option-Adjusted Spread

As explained in Chapter 17, the option-adjusted spread is a measure of the yield spread that can be used to convert dollar differences between value and price. It represents a spread over the issuer's spot rate curve or benchmark.

In the Monte Carlo model, the OAS is the spread K that when added to all the spot rates on all interest-rate paths will make the average present value of the paths equal to the observed market price (plus accrued interest). Mathematically, OAS is the spread that will satisfy the following condition:

$$\text{market price} = (1/N)\{\text{PV}[\text{path}(1)] + \text{PV}[\text{path}(2)] + \cdots + \text{PV}[\text{path}(N)]\}$$

where N is the number of interest-rate paths.

Option Cost

The implied cost of the option embedded in any RMBS can be obtained by calculating the difference between the OAS at the assumed volatility of interest rates and the static spread. That is,

$$\text{option cost} = \text{static spread} - \text{option-adjusted spread}$$

The reason that the option cost is measured in this way is as follows. In an environment of no interest-rate changes, the investor would earn the static spread. When future interest rates are uncertain, the spread is less, however, because of the homeowner's option to prepay; the OAS reflects the spread after adjusting for this option. Therefore, the option cost is the difference between the spread that would be earned in a static interest-rate environment (the static spread) and the spread after adjusting for the homeowner's option.

---

[2]For illustrations, see Robert W. Kopprasch, "A Further Look at Option-Adjusted Spread Analysis," Chapter 30 in Frank J. Fabozzi (ed.), *The Handbook of Mortgage-Backed Securities* (Burr Ridge, IL: Irwin Professional Publishing, 1995).

In general, a tranche's option cost is more stable than its OAS in the face of market movements. This interesting feature is useful in reducing the computational costs of calculating the OAS as the market moves. For small market moves, the OAS of a tranche may be approximated by recalculating the static spread (which is relatively cheap and easy to calculate) and subtracting its option cost.

Effective Duration and Convexity

In Chapter 17 we explained how to determine the effective duration and effective convexity for any security. These measures can be calculated using the Monte Carlo method as follows. First, the bond's OAS is found using the current term structure of interest rates. Next, the bond is repriced holding OAS constant but shifting the term structure. Two shifts are used to get the prices needed to apply the effective duration and effective convexity formulas: In one, yields are increased, in the second, they are decreased.

Selecting the Number of Interest-Rate Paths

Let's now address the question of the number of scenario paths or repetitions, N, needed to value a RMBS. A typical OAS run will be done for 512 to 1,024 interest-rate paths. The scenarios generated using the simulation method look very realistic and, furthermore, reproduce today's Treasury curve. By employing this technique, the money manager is effectively saying that Treasuries are fairly priced today and that the objective is to determine whether a specific RMBS is rich or cheap relative to Treasuries.

The number of interest-rate paths determines how "good" the estimate is, not relative to the truth but relative to the model. The more paths, the more average spread tends to settle down. It is a statistical sampling problem.

Most Monte Carlo simulation models employ some from of **variance reduction** to cut down on the number of sample paths necessary to get a good statistical sample. Variance reduction techniques allow us to obtain price estimates within a tick. By this we mean that if the model is used to generate more scenarios, price estimates from the model will not change by more than a tick. For example, if 1,024 paths are used to obtain the estimated price for a tranche, there is little more information to be had from the model by generating more than that number of paths. (For some very sensitive CMO tranches, more paths may be needed to estimate prices within one tick.)

Limitations of the OAS Measure

Although the OAS measure is much more useful than the static cash flow yield measure, it still suffers from major pitfalls.[3] These limitations apply not only to the OAS for RMBS but also the OAS produced from a binomial model. First, as noted earlier, the OAS is a product of the valuation model. The valuation model may be poorly constructed because it fails to capture the true factors that affect the value of particular securities. Second, in Monte Carlo simulation the interest-rate paths must be adjusted so that on-the-run Treasuries are valued properly. That is, the value of an on-the-run

---

[3]These pitfalls have been described and documented in David F. Babbel and Stavros A. Zenios, "Pitfalls in the Analysis of Option-Adjusted Spreads," *Financial Analysts Journal,* July–August 1992, pp. 65–69.

Treasury is equal to its market price or, equivalently, its OAS is zero. The process of adjusting the interest-rate paths to achieve that result is ad hoc.

A third problem with the OAS is that it assumes a constant OAS for each interest-rate path and over time for a given interest-rate path. If there is a term structure to the OAS, this is not captured by having a single OAS number. Finally, the OAS is dependent on the volatility assumption, the prepayment assumption in the case of RMBS, and the rules for refunding in the case of corporate bonds.

In addition, there is a problem with calculating an OAS for a portfolio by taking a weighted average of the OAS of the individual portfolio holdings.[4] Instead, if an OAS for a portfolio is sought, it is necessary to obtain the portfolio's cash flow along each interest-rate path. The OAS is then the spread that will make the average portfolio value equal to the portfolio's market value.

Illustration[5]

In this section we use a plain vanilla deal to show how CMOs can be analyzed using the Monte Carlo simulation method. The plain vanilla sequential-pay CMO bond structure in our illustration is FNMA 89-97. A diagram of the principal allocation structure is given in Exhibit 18-8. The structure includes five tranches, A, B, C, D, and Z, and a residual class. Tranche Z is an accrual bond, and tranche D class is an IOette.[6] The focus of our analysis is on tranches A, B, C, and Z.

The top panel of Exhibit 18-9 shows the OAS and the option cost for the collateral and the four tranches in the CMO structure. The OAS for the collateral is 70 basis points. Because the option cost is 45 basis points, the static spread is 115 basis points

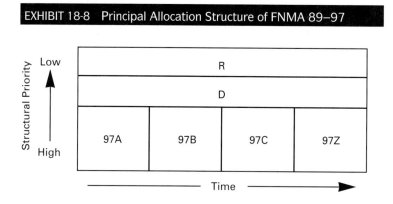

EXHIBIT 18-8   Principal Allocation Structure of FNMA 89–97

[4]Kopprasch, "A Further Look at Option-Adjusted Spread Analysis."
[5]For additional illustrations, see Frank J. Fabozzi, Scott F. Richard, and David S. Horovitz, "Valuation of Mortgage-Backed Securities," Chapter 25 in Frank J. Fabozzi (ed.), *The Handbook of Mortgage-Backed Securities*, 5th ed. (New York: McGraw-Hill, 2001).
[6]This is a form of an interest-only tranche that has a nominal par value. Until 1992, all tranches in a CMO structure had to have some par value. As explained in Chapter 12, today, notional IOs are created.

EXHIBIT 18-9 Analysis of FNMA 89-97 Classes A, B, C, and Z (as of 4/27/90)

	Base Case (Assumes 12% Interest-Rate Volatility)	
	Option-Adjusted Spread (basis points)	Option Cost (basis points)
Collateral	70	45
Tranches		
A	23	29
B	46	41
C	59	36
Z	74	50

	Prepayments at 80% and 120% of Prepayment Model (Assumes 12% Interest-Rate Volatility)			
	New Option-Adjusted Spread (basis points)		Change in Price per $100 par (holding OAS constant)	
	80%	120%	80%	120%
Collateral	70	71	$0.00	$0.04
Tranches				
A	8	40	–0.43	0.48
B	31	65	–0.86	1.10
C	53	73	–0.41	0.95
Z	72	93	–0.28	2.70

	Interest-Rate Volatility of 8% and 16%			
	New Option-Adjusted Spread (basis points)		Change in Price per $100 par (holding OAS constant)	
	8%	16%	8%	16%
Collateral	92	46	$1.03	–$1.01
Tranches				
A	38	5	0.42	–0.51
B	67	21	1.22	–1.45
C	77	39	1.22	–1.36
Z	99	50	3.55	–3.41

(70 basis points plus 45 basis points). The weighted-average OAS of all the tranches (including the residual) is equal to the OAS of the collateral.

At the time this analysis was performed, April 27, 1990, the Treasury yield curve was not steep. As we noted earlier, in such a yield curve environment the static spread will not differ significantly from the traditionally computed yield spread. Thus, for the four tranches shown in Exhibit 18-9, the static spread is 52 for A, 87 for B, 95 for C, and 124 for D.

Notice that the tranches did not share the OAS equally. The same is true for the option cost. The value tended to go toward the longer tranches, something that occurs in the typical deal. Both the static spread and the option cost increase as the maturity increases. The only tranches where there appears to be a bit of a bargain are B and C. A money manager contemplating the purchase of one of these middle tranches can see that C offers a higher OAS than B and appears to bear less of the risk, as measured by the option cost. The problem a money manager may encounter is that he might not be permitted to extend out as long as the C tranche because of duration, maturity, or average-life constraints.

Now let's look at modeling risk. Examination of the sensitivity of the tranches to changes in prepayments and interest-rate volatility will help us to understand the interaction of the tranches in the structure and who is bearing the risk.

We begin with prepayments. Specifically, we keep the same interest-rate paths as those used to get the OAS in the base case (the top panel of Exhibit 18-9) but reduce the prepayment rate on each interest-rate path to 80% of the projected rate.

As can be seen in the second panel of Exhibit 18-9, slowing down prepayments does not change the OAS for the collateral and its price at all. This is because the collateral is trading close to par. Tranches created by this collateral do not behave the same way, however. The exhibit reports two results of the sensitivity analysis. First, it indicates the change in the OAS. Second, it indicates the change in the price, holding the OAS constant at the base case.

To see how a money manager can use the information in the second panel, consider tranche A. At 80% of the prepayment speed, the OAS for this class declines from 23 basis points to 8 basis points. If the OAS is held constant, the panel indicates that the buyer of tranche A would lose $0.43 per $100 par value.

Notice that for all the tranches reported in Exhibit 18-9 there is a loss. How could all four tranches lose if prepayments are slowed down and the collateral does not lose value? This is because tranche D and the residual (R), which are not reported in the exhibit, got all the benefit of that slowdown. Notice that tranche Z is actually fairly well protected, so it does not lose much value as a result of the slowdown of prepayments. Tranche B by contrast is severely affected.

Also shown in the second panel of the exhibit is the second part of our experiment that tests the sensitivity of prepayments: The prepayment rate is assumed to be 120% of the base case. Once again, as the collateral is trading at close to par, its price does not move very much, about four cents per $100 of par value. In fact, because the collateral is trading slightly below par, the speeding up of prepayments will make the collateral look better while the OAS increases by only one basis point.

Now look at the four tranches. They all benefited. The results reported in the exhibit indicate that a money manager who is willing to go out to the long end of the curve, such as tranche Z, would realize most of the benefits of that speedup of prepayments. Because the four tranches benefited and the benefit to the collateral was minor, tranche D, the IOette, and the residual were affected adversely. In general, IO types of tranches will be affected adversely by a speedup.

Now let's look at the sensitivity to the interest-rate volatility assumption, 12% in the base case. Two experiments are performed: reducing the volatility assumption to 8% and increasing it to 16%. These results are reported in the third panel of Exhibit 18-9.

Reducing the volatility to 8% increases the dollar price of the collateral by $1 and increases the OAS from 70 in the base case to 92. This $1 increase in the price of the collateral is not equally distributed, however, among the four tranches. Most of the increase in value is realized by the longer tranches. The OAS gain for each of the tranches follows more or less the OAS durations of those tranches. This makes sense, because the longer the duration, the greater the risk, and when volatility declines, the reward is greater for the risk accepted.

At the higher level of assumed interest-rate volatility of 16%, the collateral is affected severely. The collateral's loss is distributed among the tranches in the expected manner: The longer the duration, the greater the loss. In this case tranche D and the residual are the least affected.

Using the OAS from the Monte Carlo simulation methodology, a fair conclusion can be made about this simple plain vanilla structure: What you see is what you get. The only surprise in this structure seems to be tranches B and C. In general, however, a money manager willing to extend duration gets paid for that risk.

TOTAL RETURN ANALYSIS

Neither the static cash flow methodology nor the Monte Carlo simulation methodology will tell a money manager whether investment objectives can be satisfied. The performance evaluation of an individual RMBS requires specification of an investment horizon, whose length for most financial institutions is dictated by the nature of its liabilities.

The measure that should be used to assess the performance of a security or a portfolio over some investment horizon is the total return that we discussed in Chapter 3. The total dollars received from investing in a RMBS consist of

1. The projected cash flow from the projected interest payments and the projected principal repayment (scheduled plus prepayments).
2. The interest earned on reinvestment of the projected interest payments and the projected principal prepayments.
3. The projected price of the RMBS at the end of the investment horizon.

To obtain the cash flow, a prepayment rate over the investment horizon must be assumed. The second step requires assumption of a reinvestment rate. Finally, either of the methodologies described in this chapter—cash flow yield or Monte Carlo simulation—can be used to calculate the price at the end of the investment horizon under a particular set of assumptions. Either approach requires assumption of the prepayment rate and the Treasury rates (i.e., the yield curve) at the end of the investment horizon. The cash flow yield methodology uses an assumed spread to a comparable Treasury to determine the required cash flow yield, which is then used to compute the projected price. The Monte Carlo simulation methodology requires an assumed OAS at the investment horizon. From this assumption, the OAS methodology can produce the horizon price.

To test the sensitivity of total return to various alternative assumptions scenario analysis is helpful. Its limitation is that only a small number of potential scenarios can be considered, and it fails to take into consideration the dynamics of changes in the yield curve and the dynamics of the deal structure.

Horizon Price for CMO Tranches

The most difficult part of estimating total return is projecting the price at the horizon date. In the case of a CMO tranche the price depends on the characteristics of the tranche and the spread to Treasuries *at the termination date.* The key determinants are the "quality" of the tranche, its average life (or duration), and its convexity.

Quality refers to the type of CMO tranche. Consider, for example, that an investor can purchase a CMO tranche that is a PAC bond but as a result of projected prepayments could become a sequential-pay tranche. As another example, suppose that a PAC bond is the longest-average-life tranche in a reverse PAC structure. Projected prepayments in this case might occur in an amount to change the class from a long-average-life PAC tranche to a support tranche. The converse is that the quality of a tranche may improve as well as deteriorate. For example, the effective collar for a PAC tranche could widen at the horizon date when prepayment circumstances increase the par amount of support tranches outstanding as a proportion of the deal.

OAS Total Return

The total return and OAS frameworks can be combined to determine the projected price at the horizon date. At the end of the investment horizon, it is necessary to specify how the OAS is expected to change. The horizon price can be "backed out" of the Monte Carlo simulation model.

Assumptions about the OAS value at the investment horizon reflect the expectations of the money manager. It is common to assume that the OAS at the horizon date will be the same as the OAS at the time of purchase. A total return calculated using this assumption is sometimes referred to as a **constant-OAS total return**. Alternatively, active total return managers will make bets on how the OAS will change—either widening or tightening. The total return framework can be used to assess how sensitive the performance of a RMBS is to changes in the OAS.

SUMMARY

There are two methodologies commonly used to analyze all RMBS (agency, nonagency, home equity loan–backed and manufactured housing–backed deals): cash flow yield methodology and Monte Carlo simulation methodology. The cash flow yield is the interest rate that will make the present value of the projected cash flow from a RMBS equal to its market price. The cash flow yield assumes that (1) all the cash flows can be reinvested at a rate equal to the cash flow yield, (2) the RMBS is held to the maturity date, and (3) the prepayment speed used to project the cash flow will be realized. In addition, the cash flow yield methodology fails to recognize that future interest-rate changes will affect the cash flow.

Modified duration is not a good measure of price volatility for RMBS because it assumes that the cash flow does not change as yield changes. Effective duration does take into consideration how yield changes will affect prepayments and therefore cash flow.

A RMBS is a security whose cash flow is path dependent. This means that cash flow received in one period is determined not only by the current and future interest-rate levels, but also by the path that interest rates took to get to the current level.

A methodology used to analyze path-dependent cash flow securities is the Monte Carlo simulation. This methodology involves randomly generating many scenarios of future interest-rate paths, where the interest-rate paths are generated based on some volatility assumption for interest rates.

The random paths of interest rates should be generated from an arbitrage-free model of the future term structure of interest rates. The Monte Carlo simulation methodology applied to RMBS involves randomly generating a set of cash flows based on simulated future mortgage refinancing rates. The theoretical value of a security on any interest-rate path is the present value of the cash flow on that path, where the spot rates are those on the corresponding interest-rate path. The theoretical value of a security is the average of the theoretical values over all the interest-rate paths. Information about the distribution of the path values is useful in understanding the variability around the theoretical value. The average life reported is the average of the average lives from all the interest-rate paths and information about the distribution of the average life is useful.

In the Monte Carlo simulation methodology, the option-adjusted spread is the spread that when added to all the spot rates on all interest-rate paths will make the average present value of the paths equal to the observed market price (plus accrued interest). The effective duration and effective convexity are calculated using the Monte Carlo simulation methodology by holding the OAS constant and shifting the term structure up and down.

Total return is the correct measure for assessing the potential performance of CMO tranches over a specified investment horizon. The static cash flow yield or Monte Carlo simulation methodology can be incorporated into a total return framework to calculate the mortgage-backed security's price at the horizon date. Scenario analysis is one way to evaluate the risk associated with investing in a RMBS.

Questions

1. Suppose you are told that the cash flow yield of a pass-through security is 9% and that you are seeking to invest in a security with a yield greater than 8.8%.
   a. What additional information would you need to know before you might invest in this pass-through security?
   b. What are the limitations of the cash flow yield for assessing the potential return from investing in a RMBS?

2. Using the cash flow yield methodology, a spread is calculated over a comparable Treasury security. How is a comparable Treasury determined?

3. What is vector analysis?

4. In the calculation of effective duration and effective convexity, why is a prepayment model needed?

5. The following excerpt is taken from an article titled "Fidelity Eyes $250 Million Move into Premium PACs and I-Os" that appeared in the January 27, 1992, issue of *BondWeek*, pp. 1 and 21:

   Three Fidelity investment mortgage funds are considering investing this quarter a total of $250 million in premium planned amortization classes of collateralized mortgage obligations and some interest-only strips, said Jim Wolfson, portfolio manager . . . .
   Wolfson . . . will look mainly at PACs backed by 9–10% Federal Home Loan Mortgage Corp. and Federal National Mortgage Association pass-throughs. These have higher option-adjusted

spreads than regular agency pass-throughs, or similar premium Government National Mortgage Association-backed, PACs, he said. He expects I-Os will start to perform better as prepayments start to slow later in this quarter.

The higher yields on I-Os and premium PACs compensate for their higher prepayment risk, said Wolfson. "You get paid in yield to take on negative convexity," he said. He does not feel prepayments will accelerate. . . .

a. Why would premium PACs and interest-only strips offer higher yields if the market expects that prepayments will accelerate or are highly uncertain?

b. What does Wolfson mean when he says: "You get paid in yield to take on negative convexity"?

c. What measure is Wolfson using to assess the risks associated with prepayments?

6. In an article titled "CUNA Mutual Looks for Noncallable Corporates" that appeared in the November 4, 1991, issue of *BondWeek*, p. 6, Joe Goglia, a portfolio manager for CUNA Mutual Insurance Group, stated that he invests in "planned amortization class tranches, which have less exposure to prepayment risk and are more positively convex than other mortgage-backeds." Is this true?

7. What is a path-dependent cash flow security?

8. Why is a pass-through security a path-dependent cash flow security?

9. Give two reasons why a CMO tranche is a path-dependent cash flow security.

10. Explain how, given the cash flow on the simulated interest-rate paths, the theoretical value of a RMBS is determined.

11. Explain how, given the cash flow on the simulated interest-rate paths, the average life of a RMBS is determined.

12. Suppose that a support bond is being analyzed using the Monte Carlo simulation methodology. The theoretical value using 1,500 interest-rate paths is 88. The range

for the path present values is a low of 50 and a high of 115. The standard deviation is 15 points. How much confidence would you place on the theoretical value of 88?

13. In a well-protected PAC structure, what would you expect the distribution of the path present values and average lives to be compared to a support bond from the same CMO structure?

14. Suppose that the following values for a RMBS are correct for each prepayment assumption:

PSA Assumption	Value of Security
192	112.10
194	111.80
200	111.20
202	111.05
210	110.70

Assume that the value of the security in the market is 111.20 based on 200 PSA. What is the prepayment sensitivity of this security?

15. An analysis of a CMO structure using the Monte Carlo method indicated the following, assuming 12% volatility:

	OAS (basis points)	Static Spread (basis points)
Collateral	80	120
Tranche		
PAC I A	40	60
PAC I B	55	80
PAC I C	65	95
PAC II	95	125
Support	75	250

a. Calculate the option cost for each tranche.

b. Which tranche is clearly too rich?

c. What would happen to the static spread for each tranche if a 15% volatility is assumed?

d. What would happen to the OAS for each tranche if a 15% volatility is assumed?

16. Why would the option-adjusted spread vary across dealer firms?

17. Explain how the number of interest-rate paths used in the Monte Carlo simulation methodology is determined.

18. Explain why you agree or disagree with the following statement: "When the Monte Carlo simulation methodology is used to value a RMBS, a PSA assumption is employed for all interest-rate paths."

19. What assumption is made about the OAS in calculating the effective duration and effective convexity of a RMBS?

20. What are the limitations of the option-adjusted spread measure?

21. What assumptions are required to assess the potential total return of a RMBS?

22. What are the complications of assessing the potential total return of a CMO tranched using the total return framework?

CHAPTER

19

ANALYSIS OF CONVERTIBLE BONDS

After reading this chapter you will understand:

- what a convertible bond is

- what an exchangeable bond is

- the basic features of a convertible security

- conversion value, market conversion price, conversion premium per share, conversion premium ratio, and premium over straight value of a convertible bond

- the investment features of a convertible security

- what the minimum value of a convertible bond is

- the premium payback period

- the downside risk associated with a convertible bond

- the pros and cons of investing in a convertible bond

- types of investors in convertible bonds

- the options approach to valuing a convertible bond

- why an option pricing approach is needed to value convertible securities properly

In Chapter 7 we described convertible bonds. In this chapter we explain methodologies for analyzing them, beginning with a review of the basic provisions of convertible bonds.

CONVERTIBLE BOND PROVISIONS

The conversion provision in a corporate bond issue grants the bondholder the right to convert the bond into a predetermined number of shares of common stock of the issuer. A **convertible bond**, colloquially referred to as a "convert," is therefore a corporate

432

bond with a call option to buy the common stock of the issuer. **Exchangeable bonds** grant the bondholder the right to exchange the bonds for the common stock of a firm *other* than the issuer of the bond.

The number of shares of common stock that the bondholder will receive from exercising the call option of a convertible bond or an exchangeable bond is called the **conversion ratio**. The conversion privilege may extend for all or only some portion of the bond's life, and the stated conversion ratio may fall over time. It is always adjusted proportionately for stock splits and stock dividends. There are some convertible bonds that may have an initial nonconversion period. That period can be from 6 to 12 months.

Upon conversion, the bondholder typically receives from the issuer the underlying shares. This is referred to as a **physical settle**. There are issues where the issuer may have the choice of paying the bondholder the cash value of the underlying shares. This is referred to as a **cash settle**.

At the time of issuance of a convertible bond, the issuer has effectively granted the bondholder the right to purchase the common stock at a price equal to

$$\frac{\text{par value of convertible bond}}{\text{conversion ratio}}$$

Along with the conversion privilege granted to the bondholder, most convertible bonds are callable at the option of the issuer as of a certain date. This standard type of call option in a convertible bond is called an **unprotected call**. There is another type of call feature that is included in some convertible bond issues: The bond may only be called if the price of the underlying stock (or the average stock price over some number of days) exceeds a specified trigger price. This type of call is known as a **protected call**. Some convertible bonds are putable. Put options can be classified as hard puts and soft puts. A **hard put** is one in which the convertible security must be redeemed by the issuer only for cash. In the case of a **soft put**, the issuer has the option to redeem the convertible security for cash, common stock, subordinated notes, or a combination of the three. Most converts include another type of put should there be a change in control of the corporation. Typically, an investor can put the bond at par or slightly above par if a specified percent of the shares (typically 51) is acquired by another entity. The put price is payable in cash (i.e., a hard put).

A new type of convertible bond has been issued in recent years that has been motivated by Generally Accepted Accounting Principles.[1] This type of convertible bond grants the bondholder the right to convert only when the price of the underlying stock exceeds a specified threshold price for a specified number of trading days. Until that time, the bondholder is not entitled to convert.[2] This type of convertible bond that grants contingent conversion is called a **contingent convertible bond** and nicknamed a "CoCo" bond. While introduced in late 1999, by 2003, CoCo bonds accounted for more than 70% of new convertible bond issuance.[3]

---

[1]For an explanation, see Mihir Bhattacharya, "Convertible Securities and Their Valuation," Chapter 60 in Frank J. Fabozzi (ed.). *Handbook of Fixed Income Securities*, 7th ed. (New York: McGraw-Hill, 2005).
[2]For those familiar with options, this type of option is referred to as a "knock-in option."
[3]Bhattacharya, "Convertible Securities and Their Valuation," p. 1404.

At one time, most convertible bonds were issued with maturities of 25 years or more. In recent years, the trend has been to issue convertible bonds with 5- to 10-year maturities.

Illustration

To illustrate how to analyze a convertible bond, we will use the same hypothetical bond throughout the chapter, an XYZ bond:

$$\text{maturity} = 10 \text{ years}$$
$$\text{coupon rate} = 10\%$$
$$\text{conversion ratio} = 50$$
$$\text{par value} = \$1,000$$
$$\text{current market price of XYZ bond} = \$950$$
$$\text{current market price of XYZ common stock} = \$17$$
$$\text{dividends per share} = \$1$$

We will assume that this convertible bond is neither callable nor putable.

The conversion price for the XYZ bond is

$$\text{conversion price} = \frac{\$1,000}{50} = \$20$$

MINIMUM VALUE OF A CONVERTIBLE BOND

The **conversion value** of a convertible bond is the value of the bond if it is converted immediately.[4] That is,

$$\text{conversion value} = \text{market price of common stock} \times \text{conversion ratio}$$

The minimum price of a convertible bond is the greater of[5]

1. Its conversion value, or
2. Its value as a corporate bond without the conversion option—that is, based on the convertible bond's cash flows if not converted (i.e., a plain vanilla bond). This value is called its **straight value**.

To estimate the straight value, we must determine the required yield on a nonconvertible bond with the same quality rating and similar investment characteristics. Given this estimated required yield, the straight value is then the present value of the bond's cash flows using this yield to discount the cash flows.

If the convertible bond does not sell for the greater of these two values, arbitrage profits could be realized. For example, suppose that the conversion value is greater than the straight value, and the bond trades at its straight value. An investor can buy the convertible bond at the straight value and convert it. By doing so, the investor realizes a

---

[4]Technically, the standard textbook definition of conversion value given here is theoretically incorrect because as bondholders convert, the price of the stock will decline. The theoretically correct definition for the conversion value is that it is the product of the conversion ratio and the stock price *after* conversion.
[5]If the conversion value is the greater of the two values, it is possible for the convertible bond to trade below the conversion value. This can occur for the following reasons: (1) There are restrictions that prevent the investor from converting, (2) the underlying stock is illiquid, and (3) an anticipated forced conversion will result in loss of accrued interest of a high coupon issue. See Mihir Bhattacharya, "Convertible Securities and Their Valuation," p. 1395.

gain equal to the difference between the conversion value and the straight value. Suppose, instead, that the straight value is greater than the conversion value, and the bond trades at its conversion value. By buying the convertible at the conversion value, the investor will realize a higher yield than a comparable straight bond.

Illustration

For the XYZ convertible bond, the conversion value is equal to

$$\text{conversion value} = \$17 \times 50 = \$850$$

To determine the straight value, it is necessary to determine what comparable bonds are trading for in the market. Suppose that comparable bonds are trading to yield 14%. The straight value is then the price of a 10% 10-year bond selling to yield 14%. The price for such a bond would be $788.[6]

Given a conversion value of $850 and a straight value of $788, the minimum price for the XYZ bond is $850. To see this, note that if the bond is selling at its straight value rather than its conversion value, an investor could buy the bond for $788 and simultaneously sell 50 shares of XYZ stock at $17 per share. When the short sale of the stock is covered when the bond is converted, the transaction would produce an arbitrage profit of $62 per XYZ bond purchased. The only way to eliminate this arbitrage profit is for the XYZ bond to sell for $850, its conversion value.

Suppose, instead, that comparable nonconvertible bonds are trading to yield 11.8%. Then the straight value of XYZ bond would be $896. The minimum price for the XYZ bond must be its straight value in this case because that is a value higher than the conversion value of $850. To see this, suppose that the market price of the XYZ bond is $850. At this price, the yield would be about 12.7%, 90 basis points greater than comparable nonconvertible bonds. Investors would find the bond attractive. As investors buy the bond, they will bid up its price to where the new yield is 11.8%.

MARKET CONVERSION PRICE

The price that an investor effectively pays for the common stock if the convertible bond is purchased and then converted into the common stock is called the **market conversion price**.[7] It is found as follows:

$$\text{market conversion price} = \frac{\text{market price of convertible bond}}{\text{conversion ratio}}$$

The market conversion price is a useful benchmark because when the actual market price of the stock rises above the market conversion price, any further stock price increase is certain to increase the value of the convertible bond by at least the same percentage. Therefore, the market conversion price can be viewed as a break-even point.

An investor who purchases a convertible bond rather than the underlying stock typically pays a premium over the current market price of the stock. This premium per

---

[6]Actually, it is $788.10, but $788 will be used in our illustrations.
[7]The market conversion price is also called the **conversion parity price**.

share is equal to the difference between the market conversion price and the current market price of the common stock. That is,

market conversion premium per share

$$= \text{market conversion price} - \text{current market price}$$

The market conversion premium per share is usually expressed as a percentage of the current market price as follows:

$$\text{market conversion premium ratio} = \frac{\text{conversion premium per share}}{\text{market price of common stock}}$$

Why would someone be willing to pay a premium to buy this stock? Recall that the minimum price of a convertible bond is the greater of its conversion value or its straight value. Thus, as the stock price declines, the price of the convertible bond will not fall below its straight value. The straight value therefore acts as a floor for the convertible bond price.

Viewed in this context, the market conversion premium per share can be seen as the price of a call option. As explained in Chapter 27, the buyer of a call option limits the downside risk to the option price. In the case of a convertible bond, for a premium, the bondholder limits the downside risk to the straight value of the bond. The difference between the buyer of a call option and the buyer of a convertible bond is that the former knows precisely the dollar amount of the downside risk, whereas the latter knows only that the most that can be lost is the difference between the convertible bond price and the straight value. The straight value at some future date, however, is not known; the value will change as the interest rate changes.

Illustration

At a market price of $950, a stock price of $17, and a conversion ratio of 50, the market conversion price, market conversion premium per share, and market conversion premium ratio of the XYZ convertible bond are calculated as follows:

$$\text{market conversion price} = \frac{\$950}{50} = \$19$$

$$\text{market conversion premium per share} = \$19 - \$17 = \$2$$

$$\text{market conversion premium ratio} = \frac{\$2}{\$17} = 0.118 \text{ or } 11.8\%$$

CURRENT INCOME OF CONVERTIBLE BOND VERSUS STOCK

As an offset to the market conversion premium per share, investing in the convertible bond rather than buying the stock directly generally means that the investor realizes higher current income from the coupon interest paid on the convertible bond than would be received as dividends paid on the number of shares equal to the conversion ratio. Analysts evaluating a convertible bond typically compute the time it takes to recover the premium per share by computing the **premium payback period** (which is also known as the **break-even time**). This is computed as follows:

$$\frac{\text{market conversion premium per share}}{\text{favorable income differential per share}}$$

where the favorable income differential per share is equal to[8]

$$\frac{\text{coupon interest from bond } - \text{ (conversion ratio} \times \text{dividend per share)}}{\text{conversion ratio}}$$

Notice that the premium payback period does *not* take into account the time value of money.

Illustration

For the XYZ convertible bond, the market conversion premium per share is $2. The favorable income differential per share is found as follows:

$$\text{coupon interest from bond} = 0.10 \times \$1{,}000 = \$100$$
$$\text{conversion ratio} \times \text{dividend per share} = 50 \times \$1 = \$50$$

Therefore,

$$\text{favorable income differential per share} = \frac{\$100 - \$50}{50} = \$1$$

and

$$\text{premium payback period} = \frac{\$2}{\$1} = 2 \text{ years}$$

Without considering the time value of money, the investor would recover the market conversion premium per share in two years.

DOWNSIDE RISK WITH A CONVERTIBLE BOND

Investors usually use the straight value of the bond as a measure of the downside risk of a convertible bond because the price of the convertible bond cannot fall below this value. Thus, the straight value acts as the *current* floor for the price of the convertible bond. The downside risk is measured as a percentage of the straight value and computed as follows:

$$\text{premium over straight value} = \frac{\text{market price of the convertible bond}}{\text{straight value}} - 1$$

---

[8]A more precise methodology for calculating the favorable income from holding the convertible is recommended in Luke Knecht and Mike McCowin, "Valuing Convertible Securities," in Frank J. Fabozzi (ed.), *Advances and Innovations in Bond and Mortgage Markets* (Chicago: Probus Publishing, 1989). In most cases the conventional formula presented in the text is sufficient.

The higher the premium over straight value, all other factors constant, the less attractive the convertible bond.

Despite its use in practice, this measure of downside risk is flawed because the straight value (the floor) changes as interest rates change. If interest rates rise (fall), the straight value falls (rises) making the floor fall (rise). Therefore, the downside risk changes as interest rates change.

Illustration

Earlier we said that if comparable nonconvertible bonds are trading to yield 14%, the straight value of the XYZ bond would be $788. The premium over straight value is then

$$\text{premium over straight value} = \frac{\$950}{\$788} - 1 = 0.21 \text{ or } 21\%$$

If the yield on a comparable nonconvertible bond is 11.8% instead of 14%, the straight value would be $896 and the premium over straight value would be

$$\text{premium over straight value} = \frac{\$950}{\$896} - 1 = 0.06 \text{ or } 6\%$$

INVESTMENT CHARACTERISTICS OF A CONVERTIBLE BOND

The investment characteristics of a convertible bond depend on the stock price. If the price of the stock is low, so that the straight value is considerably higher than the conversion value, the bond will trade much like a straight bond. The convertible bond in such instances is referred to as a **bond equivalent** or a **busted convertible**.

When the price of the stock is such that the conversion value is considerably higher than the straight value, the convertible bond will trade as if it were an equity instrument; in this case it is said to be an **equity equivalent**. In such cases the market conversion premium per share will be small.

Between these two cases, bond equivalent and equity equivalent, the convertible bond trades as a **hybrid security**, having the characteristics of both a bond and an equity instrument.

PROS AND CONS OF INVESTING IN A CONVERTIBLE BOND

So far we have presented several measures that can be used to analyze convertible bonds. Let's use the XYZ convertible bond to drive home the pros and cons of investing in a convertible bond.

Suppose that an investor is considering purchase of a stock or a convertible bond. The stock can be purchased in the market for $17. By buying the convertible bond, the investor is effectively purchasing the stock for $19 (the market conversion price per share).

Look at the outcome one month from now, assuming that XYZ stock rises to $34. An investor buying the stock would realize a gain of $17 ($34 − $17) on a $17 investment, or a 100% return. In contrast, the conversion value for the bond would be $1,700 ($34 × 50). Because the price of XYZ bond is $950, the investor would realize a return of about 79%. The return would in fact probably be slightly higher because the convertible bond would trade at a slight premium to its conversion value. The reason for the lower return by buying the convertible bond rather than the stock directly is that the investor has effectively paid $2 per share more for the stock. Thus, the investor realizes a gain based on a stock price of $19 rather than $17.

So far, we've illustrated the advantage of owning the stock rather than the bond when the price of the stock rises. Let's look at the situation where the stock declines in value to $7. The investor who buys the stock now realizes a loss of $10 per share for a return of −59%. The conversion value of the XYZ bond likewise drops, to $350 ($7 × 50). Its price, however, will not fall to that level. Recall from our earlier discussion that the minimum price of a convertible bond will be the greater of its conversion value or its straight value. Assuming that the straight value is $788, and it does not change over the one-month period, the value of XYZ bond will fall to only $788. This means that the investor realizes a loss of only 17%. The loss would be even less in fact because the convertible bond would trade at a premium to its straight value.

The critical assumption in this analysis is that the straight value does not change, although it can change for any of the reasons cited in Chapter 2. More specifically, if interest rates rise in the economy, the straight value will decline. Even if interest rates do not rise, the perceived credit worthiness of the issuer may deteriorate, causing investors to demand a higher yield. In fact, the stock price and the yield required by investors are not independent. When the price of the stock drops precipitously, as in our $17 to $7 illustration, the perceived credit worthiness of the issuer may decline, causing a decline in the straight value. In any event, although the straight value may decline, it still is a floor (albeit a moving floor) for the convertible bond price. In our illustration, the straight value would have to fall about $390 (59% loss on $950) to equal the loss on the stock purchase.

The illustration clearly demonstrates that there are benefits and drawbacks of investing in convertible bonds. The disadvantage is the upside potential given up because a premium per share must be paid. An advantage is the reduction in downside risk (as determined by the straight value), with the opportunity to recoup the premium per share through the higher current income from owning the convertible bond.

A portfolio manager is interested in the total return from holding a convertible bond. The benchmark to compare the total return is the performance of the underlying common stock. The manager must therefore examine the total return using scenario analysis.

Call Risk

Convertible issues are callable by the issuer. This is a valuable feature for issuers, who deem the current market price of their stock undervalued enough so that selling stock directly would dilute the equity of current stockholders. The firm would prefer to raise equity funds over incurring debt, so it issues a convertible, setting the conversion ratio on the basis of a stock price it regards as acceptable. When the market price reaches the conversion point, the firm will want to see the conversion happen in view of the risk that the price may drop in the future. This gives the firm an interest in forcing conversion, even though this is not in the interest of the owners of the security whose price is likely to be adversely affected by the call.

Takeover Risk

Corporate takeovers represent another risk to investing in convertible bonds. If an issuer is acquired by another company or by its own management (as in the case of a management-led leveraged buyout), the stock price may not appreciate sufficiently for the holders of the convertible bond to benefit from the conversion feature. As the stock of the acquired company may no longer trade after a takeover, the investor can be left with a bond that pays a lower coupon rate than comparable-risk corporate bonds.

TYPES OF INVESTORS IN CONVERTIBLE BONDS

The types of convertible investors typically found in the market are classified as: defensive equity managers, equity managers seeking income, bond portfolio managers, convertible specialists, arbitrageurs, and insurance companies.[9]

As explained previously, convertible bonds offer the possibility of downside protection but still allow the potential for participation in the underlying stock's price appreciation. Defensive equity portfolio managers participate in the convertible bond market for that reason. Also explained previously, there is typically an income advantage by holding a convertible bond rather than the common stock, but the convertible bond still provides the opportunity to participate in the price appreciation of the common stock. However, the tradeoff is that some price appreciation potential for the common stock's price is sacrificed because of the higher price that must be paid for the convertible bond rather than buying the common stock directly. Equity managers seeking income are willing to accept this trade.

While convertible securities typically offer an income advantage compared to buying the common stock, they have an income disadvantage compared to a straight bond. There are bond portfolio managers who are willing to accept a lower income in exchange for the opportunity to benefit from the appreciation in the common stock price.

There are investment managers who specialize in solely convertible securities. Convertible bond arbitrageurs follow a strategy of purchasing what they believe to be undervalued (i.e., cheap) convertible bonds and selling short the underlying stock. The assessment of the undervaluation of a convertible bond is typically based on proprietary technical models. Leverage is used by the arbitrageur who seeks to capture profits from changes in valuation and volatility. There are a limited number of asset managers who follow this strategy because of the relative illiquidity of convertibles and the limited number of convertible issues in the marketplace.

Insurance company regulations require that companies in this industry maintain capital reserves. The amount of the capital reserves are based on the risk of the insurance company's portfolio. Because stocks are riskier than bonds, regulators require more capital be held for stocks than bonds. For this reason, insurance companies are important participants in the market, investing in convertible bonds in order to obtain equity exposure but reduce capital requirements.

---

[9]Chris P. Dialynas and John C. Ritchie, Jr., "Convertible Securities and Their Investment Characteristics," Chapter 59 in *Handbook of Fixed Income Securities*, 7th ed.

OPTIONS APPROACH

In our discussion of convertible bonds, we did not address the following questions:

1. What is a fa\ir value for the conversion premium per share?
2. How do we handle convertible bonds with call and/or put options?
3. How does a change in interest rates affect the stock price?

The option pricing approach to valuation described in Chapter 17 can help us answer these questions. Consider first a noncallable/nonputable convertible bond. The investor who purchases this bond would be entering into two separate transactions: (1) buying a noncallable/nonputable straight bond, and (2) buying a call option (or warrant) on the stock, where the number of shares that can be purchased with the call option is equal to the conversion ratio.

The question is: What is the fair value for the call option? The fair value depends on the factors (discussed in Chapter 27) that affect the price of a call option. One key factor is the expected price volatility of the stock: the more the expected price volatility, the greater the value of the call option. The theoretical value of a call option can be valued using the Black–Scholes option pricing model[10] or the binomial option pricing model.[11] As a first approximation to the value of a convertible bond, the formula would be

convertible bond value = straight value + price of the call option on the stock

The price of the call option is added to the straight value because the investor has purchased a call option on the stock.

Now let's add in a common feature of a convertible bond: the issuer's right to call the bond. The issuer can force conversion by calling the bond. For example, suppose that the call price is $1,030 per $1,000 par and the conversion value is $1,700. If the issuer calls the bonds, the optimal strategy for the investor is to convert the bond and receive shares worth $1,700.[12] The investor, however, loses any premium over the conversion value that is reflected in the market price. Therefore, the analysis of convertible bonds must take into account the value of the issuer's right to call the bond. This depends, in turn, on (1) future interest rate volatility, and (2) economic factors that determine whether it is optimal for the issuer to call the bond.

The Black–Scholes option pricing model cannot handle this situation. Instead, the binomial option pricing model can be used simultaneously to value the bondholder's call option on the stock and the issuer's right to call the bonds. The bondholder's put option can also be accommodated. To link interest rates and stock prices together (the third question we raised previously), statistical analysis of historical movements of these two variables must be estimated and incorporated into the model.

---

[10]Fischer Black and Myron Scholes, "The Pricing of Corporate Liabilities," *Journal of Political Economy*, May–June 1973, pp. 637–659.

[11]John C. Cox, Stephen A. Ross, and Mark Rubinstein, "Option Pricing: A Simplified Approach," *Journal of Financial Economics*, September 1979, pp. 229–263; Richard J. Rendleman and Brit J. Bartter, "Two-State Option Pricing," *Journal of Finance*, December 1979, pp. 1093–1110; and William F. Sharpe, *Investments* (Upper Saddle River, NJ: Prentice Hall, 1981), Chapter 16.

[12]Actually, the conversion value would be less than $1,700 because the per-share value after conversion would decline.

The option pricing approach offers a great deal of promise and models have been proposed as far back as 1977.[13] In the experience of the author, the most complicated model employed by practitioners uses the Black–Scholes model and tests the sensitivity of the factors that affect any other embedded options.[14]

SUMMARY

In this chapter we have discussed the basic provisions of convertible bonds and explored a framework for evaluating these bonds. Analysis of a convertible bond requires calculation of the conversion value, straight value, market conversion price, market conversion premium ratio, and premium payback period.

The downside risk of a convertible bond usually is estimated by calculating the premium over straight value. The limitation of this measure is that the straight value (the floor) changes as interest rates change. Convertible bond investors are also subject to call risk and takeover risk.

The option pricing approach can be used to determine the fair value of the embedded call option. The value of the call option following this approach is estimated using some equity option pricing model such as the Black–Scholes model.

Questions

1. In the October 26, 1992, prospectus summary of the Staples 5% convertible subordinated debentures due 1999, the offering stated: "Convertible into Common Stock at a conversion price of $45 per share. . . ." If the par value is $1,000, what is the conversion ratio?
2. What is the difference between a soft put and a hard put?
3. This excerpt is taken from an article titled "Caywood Looks for Convertibles," which appeared in the January 13, 1992, issue of *BondWeek*, p. 7:

   Caywood Christian Capital Management will invest new money in its $400 million high-yield portfolio in "busted convertibles," double- and triple-B rated convertible bonds of companies . . . , said James Caywood, CEO. Caywood likes these convertibles as they trade at discounts and are unlikely to be called, he said.

   a. What is a busted convertible?
   b. What is the premium over straight value at which these bonds would trade?
   c. Why does Mr. Caywood seek convertibles with higher investment-grade ratings?
   d. Why is Mr. Caywood interested in call protection?
4. Explain the limitation of using premium over straight value as a measure of the downside risk of a convertible bond.
5. This excerpt comes from an article titled "Bartlett Likes Convertibles" in the October 7, 1991, issue of *BondWeek*, p. 7:

[13]See, for example, Michael Brennan and Eduardo Schwartz, "Convertible Bonds: Valuation and Optimal Strategies for Call and Conversion," *Journal of Finance*, December 1977, pp. 1699–1715; Jonathan Ingersoll, "A Contingent-Claims Valuation of Convertible Securities," *Journal of Financial Economics*, May 1977, pp. 289–322; Michael Brennan and Eduardo Schwartz, "Analyzing Convertible Bonds," *Journal of Financial and Quantitative Analysis*, November 1980, pp. 907–929; and George Constantinides, "Warrant Exercise and Bond Conversion in Competitive Markets," *Journal of Financial Economics*, September 1984, pp. 371–398.
[14]See, for example, Mihir Bhattacharya and Yu Zhu, "Valuation and Analysis of Convertible Securities," Chapter 36 in Frank J. Fabozzi and T. Dessa Fabozzi (eds.), *The Handbook of Fixed Income Securities* (Burr Ridge, IL: Irwin Professional Publishing, 1995); and Frank J. Fabozzi, *Valuation of Fixed Income Securities and Derivatives* (New Hope, PA: Frank J. Fabozzi Associates, 1995), Chapter 9.

Bartlett & Co. is selectively looking for opportunities in convertible bonds that are trading cheaply because the equity of the issuer has dropped in value, according to Dale Rabiner, director of fixed income at the $800 million Cincinnati-based fund. Rabiner said he looks for five-year convertibles trading at yields comparable to straight bonds of companies he believes will rebound.

Discuss this strategy for investing in convertible bonds.

6. Consider a convertible bond as follows:

par value = $1,000
coupon rate = 9.5%
market price of convertible bond = $1,000
conversion ratio = 37.383
estimated straight value of bond = $510
yield to maturity of straight bond = 18.7%

Assume that the price of the common stock is $23 and that the dividend per share is $0.75 per year.

a. Calculate each of the following:
   1. Conversion value
   2. Market conversion price
   3. Conversion premium per share
   4. Conversion premium ratio
   5. Premium over straight value
   6. Favorable income differential per share
   7. Premium payback period
b. Suppose that the price of the common stock increases from $23 to $46.
   1. What will be the approximate return realized from investing in the convertible bond?
   2. What would be the return realized if $23 had been invested in the common stock?
   3. Why would the return on investing in the common stock directly be higher than investing in the convertible bond?
c. Suppose that the price of the common stock declines from $23 to $8.
   1. What will be the approximate return realized from investing in the convertible bond?
   2. What would be the return realized if $23 had been invested in the common stock?

3. Why would the return on investing in the convertible bond be higher than investing in the common stock directly?
7. A Merrill Lynch note structure called a *liquid yield option note* (LYON) is a zero-coupon instrument that is convertible into the common stock of the issuer. The conversion ratio is fixed for the entire life of the note. If investors wish to convert to the shares of the issuer, they must exchange the LYON for the stock. As a result, the conversion price increases over time. Why?
8. What is a contingent convertible bond?
9. Why are insurance companies participants in the convertible bond market?
10. The following quotes are from Mihir Bhattacharya, "Convertible Securities and Their Valuation," Chapter 51 in Frank J. Fabozzi (ed.), *The Handbook of Fixed Income Securities*, 6th ed. (New York: McGraw-Hill, 2001).
   a. "Increased debt market volatility has driven home the point of *duration risk* inherent in any security with a fixed income component, including converts. The increased volatility of the spreads (over Treasury or other interest rate benchmarks) has heightened investor sensitivity to the reliability of the *fixed income floor* or *bond value* of the convert." What message is the author trying to convey to investors?
   b. "Convertibles have equity and interest rate options, and occasionally, currency options, embedded in them. Issuers and investors are becoming even more aware that option valuation is driven by, among other factors: (a) equity volatility; (b) interest rate volatility; and (c) spread volatility. In some situations the embedded options may easily be separated and valued. However, in the vast majority of cases, they interact with each other and so prove difficult, if not impossible, to separate. Investors should be aware of the inherent danger of attempting to value the embedded options as if they were separable options." Explain why the factors mentioned in the quote affect the value of a convertible bond and why the factors interact.

20

CORPORATE BOND
CREDIT ANALYSIS

After reading this chapter you will understand:

- the major areas of bond credit analysis: covenants, collateral, and ability to pay

- the reason why covenants must be analyzed

- what factors are considered in evaluating the ability of an issuer to satisfy its obligations

- what factors are considered in assessing a company's business risk

- why an analysis of a company must be looked at relative to the industry in which it operates

- the reasons corporate governance risk is important and how it can be mitigated

- key financial ratios

- the relationship between corporate bond credit analysis and common stock analysis

A s explained in Chapter 1, credit risk encompasses three types of risk: default risk, credit spread risk, and credit downgrade risk. Since the credit rating companies (Moody's Investors Service, Standard & Poor's, and Fitch Ratings) have well-developed methodologies for analyzing the default risk of a corporate bond, we will describe factors that they consider in this chapter. The framework for analysis that we describe in this chapter is referred as "traditional credit analysis." In the next chapter we will explain credit risk models for assessing credit risk and look at the potential advantage of the output of such models relative to credit ratings.

There are two appendices to this chapter. Appendix A is a report by two high-yield credit analysts, Eric Selle and Stephanie Renegar, at Wachovia Securities on the Lear Corporation. This comprehensive report illustrates all of the key elements discussed in this chapter (and more), and we make continuous reference to the relevant portions. Appendix B shows a recommendation of one credit analyst, Martin Fridson, that ties together credit issues and analytical measures discussed earlier in this book.

OVERVIEW OF CORPORATE BOND CREDIT ANALYSIS

In the analysis of the default risk of a corporate bond issuer and specific bond issues, there are three areas that are analyzed by bond credit analysts:

1. the protections afforded to bondholders that are provided by covenants limiting management's discretion
2. the collateral available for the bondholder should the issuer fail to make the required payments
3. the ability of an issuer to make the contractual payments to bondholders

In this section, we briefly describe these three areas of analysis.

Analysis of Covenants

An analysis of the indenture is part of a credit review of a corporation's bond issue. The indenture provisions establish rules for several important areas of operation for corporate management. These provisions are safeguards for the bondholder. Indenture provisions should be analyzed carefully. A general description of the indenture is found in a company's prospectus for its bond offering. However, it is often stated that the indenture provisions are only summarized. Often, the covenants are ambiguous. The analyst must pay careful attention to the definitions in indentures because they vary from indenture to indenture. For examples of a summary of a bank and bond covenant, see pages 28 to 30 in the Lear Corp. report in Appendix A.

The importance of understanding covenants was summarized by one high-yield portfolio manager, Robert Levine, as follows:

> Covenants provide insight into a company's strategy. As part of the credit process, one must read covenants within the context of the corporate strategy. It is not sufficient to hire a lawyer to review the covenants because a lawyer might miss the critical factors necessary to make the appropriate decision. Also, loopholes in covenants often provide clues about the intentions of management teams.[1]

There are two general types of covenants. **Affirmative covenants** call upon the corporation to make promises to do certain things. **Negative covenants**, also called **restrictive covenants**, require that the borrower not take certain actions. There are an infinite variety of restrictions that can be placed on borrowers in the form of negative covenants.

---

[1] Robert Levine, "Unique Factors in Managing High-Yield Bond Portfolios," in Frank K. Reilly (ed.), *High-Yield Bonds: Analysis and Risk Assessment* (Charlottesville, VA: Association for Investment Management and Research, 1990), p. 35.

Some of the more common restrictive covenants include various limitations on the company's ability to incur debt since unrestricted borrowing can be highly detrimental to the bondholders. Consequently, bondholders may want to include limits on the absolute dollar amount of debt that may be outstanding or may require some type of fixed charge coverage ratio test. We will discuss these types of ratios later in the chapter. The two most common tests are the maintenance test and the debt incurrence test. The **maintenance test** requires the borrower's ratio of earnings available for interest or fixed charges to be at least a certain minimum figure on each required reporting date (such as quarterly or annually) for a certain preceding period. The **debt incurrence test** only comes into play when the company wishes to do additional borrowing. In order to take on additional debt, the required interest or fixed charge coverage figure adjusted for the new debt must be at a certain minimum level for the required period prior to the financing. Debt incurrence tests are generally considered less stringent than maintenance provisions. There could also be **cash flow tests** (or **cash flow requirements**) and **working capital maintenance provisions**.

Some indentures may prohibit subsidiaries from borrowing from all other companies except the parent. Indentures often classify subsidiaries as restricted or unrestricted. Restricted subsidiaries are those considered to be consolidated for financial test purposes; unrestricted subsidiaries (often foreign and certain special-purpose companies) are those excluded from the covenants governing the parent. Often, subsidiaries are classified as unrestricted in order to allow them to finance themselves through outside sources of funds.

Analysis of Collateral

A corporate debt obligation can be secured or unsecured. In the case of the liquidation of a corporation, proceeds from a bankruptcy are distributed to creditors based on the absolute priority rule. In contrast, as explained in Chapter 7, seldom does the absolute priority rules hold in a reorganization. What is typically observed in such cases is that the corporation's unsecured creditors may receive distributions for the entire amount of their claim and common stockholders may receive some distribution, while secured creditors may receive only a portion of their claim. Secured creditors are willing to allow distribution to unsecured creditors and common stockholders in order to obtain approval for the plan of reorganization, a plan that requires approval of all parties.

The question is then, what does a "secured position" mean in the case of a reorganization if the absolute priority rule is not followed in a reorganization? The claim position of a secured creditor is important in terms of the negotiation process. However, because absolute priority is not followed and the final distribution in a reorganization depends on the bargaining ability of the parties, some analysts place less emphasis on collateral compared to covenants and business risk. To see an example of the importance of security holders' priority of claims in a bankruptcy valuation, see page 6 of the Lear Corp. report in Appendix A.

Assessing an Issuer's Ability to Pay

In assessing the ability of an issuer to service its debt (i.e., make timely payment of interest and principal), one immediately thinks about the crunching of numbers based on the financial statements of the issuing corporation. While that is extremely important, the ability of an issuer to generate cash flow goes considerably beyond the calculation and

analysis of a myriad of financial ratios and cash flow measures that can be used as a basic assessment of a company's financial risk. Analysts also look at qualitative factors such as the issuer's business risk and corporate governance risk to assess the issuer's ability to pay.

Thus, an evaluation of an issuer's ability to pay involves analysis of

1. business risk
2. corporate governance risk
3. financial risk

We describe the analysis of each of these in the following sections.

ANALYSIS OF BUSINESS RISK

Business risk is defined as the risk associated with operating cash flows. Operating cash flows are not certain because the revenues and the expenditures comprising the cash flows are uncertain. Revenues depend on conditions in the economy as a whole and the industry in which the company operates, as well as the actions of management and its competitors. Expenditures for operations are comprised of variable costs and fixed costs, and these costs depend on a myriad of factors. In the Lear Corp. report in Appendix A, the analysts who authored the report derive their model assumptions off of their estimates of the breakdown of variable and fixed costs (see page 22).

In assessing business risk, the three rating agencies look at the same general areas. Standard & Poor's (S&P) states that in analyzing business risk it considers country risk, industry characteristics, company position, product portfolio/marketing, technology, cost efficiency, strategic and operational management competence, and profitability/peer group comparisons.[2] Moody's investigates industry trends, national political and regulatory environment, management quality and attitude towards risk-taking, and basic operating and competitive position.[3] Fitch reviews industry trends, operating environment, market position, and management.[4]

An analysis of industry trends is important because it is only within the context of an industry that company analysis is valid. For example, suppose that the growth rate for a company over the past three years was 20% per year. In isolation, that may appear to be an attractive growth rate. However, suppose that over the same time period, the industry in which the company operates has been growing at 45% over the same period. While there could be many factors to explain the discrepancy in the relative performance, one might conclude that the company is competitively weak. Industry consideration should be considered in a global context. For example, consider the automobile industry. It is not sufficient to consider the competitive position of companies in this industry without taking into account their global competitive position. The need for many companies to become globally competitive increases as the barriers to international trade are broken down. For an example of the use of industry analysis

---

[2]Standard & Poor's Corporation, *Corporate Rating Criteria*, 2005, p. 20.
[3]Moody's Investors Service, *Industrial Company Rating Methodology*, July 1998, p. 3.
[4]FitchRatings, *Corporate Rating Methodology*, undated, pp. 1–2.

to help analyze a specific credit, see pages 22 to 23 in the Lear Corp. report in Appendix A.

Regarding industry analysis, S&P notes:

> While any particular profile category can be the overriding rating considera-tion, the industry risk assessment can be a key factor in determining the rating to which any participant in the industry can aspire. It would be hard to imagine assigning "AA" and "AAA" debt ratings to companies with extensive participa-tion in industries of above-average risk, regardless of how conservative their financial posture. Examples of these industries are integrated steel makers, tire and rubber companies, home-builders, and most of the mining sector. [5]

Furthermore, S&P notes:

> . . . the industry risk assessment sets the stage for analyzing specific company risk factors and establishing the priority of these factors in the overall evalua-tion. For example, if technology is a critical competitive factor, R&D prowess is stressed. If the industry produces a commodity, cost of production assumes major importance.[6]

Regarding industry analysis, Moody's states:

> This first facet of our analysis focuses on industry trends that provide impor-tant indications of future profitability, asset values, upcoming financing needs, and potential liabilities. For companies that operate in several industries, it is critical that each major business segment is analyzed separately, looking at each industry from a global perspective. The same is true for companies with significant operations or markets in many countries.[7]

Fitch writes that:

> Major industry developments are considered in relation to their likely effect on future performance. The inherent riskiness and/or cyclicality of an industry may result in an absolute ceiling for ratings within that industry. Therefore, an issuer in such an industry is unlikely to receive the highest rating possible ("AAA") despite having a conservative financial profile, while not all issuers in low-risk industries can expect high ratings. Instead, many credit issues are weighed in conjunction with the risk characteristics of the industry to arrive at an accurate evaluation of credit quality. [8]

---

[5]Standard & Poor's Corporation, *Corporate Rating Criteria*, p. 20.
[6]Standard & Poor's Corporation, *Corporate Rating Criteria*, p. 21.
[7]Moody's Investors Service, *Industrial Company Rating Methodology*, p. 4.
[8]Fitch Ratings, *Corporate Rating Methodology*, p. 1.

It has been suggested that the following areas will provide a credit analyst with a sufficient framework to properly interpret a company's economic prospects: economic cylicality, growth prospects, research and development expenses, competition, sources of supply, degree of regulation, and labor.[9] These general areas encompass most of the areas that the rating agencies have identified for assessing business risk. We will briefly describe each of these areas.

One of the first areas of analysis is investigating how closely the industry follows gross domestic product (GDP) growth. This is done in order to understand the industry's economic cylicality. Note, however, that economic growth as measured by the growth in GDP may not always be the most suitable benchmark for the potential growth of an industry. There are some industries that are sensitive to many economic variables, and often various industry sub-sectors move countercyclically or at least with different lags in relation to the general economy. For some industries, growth may be somewhat dependent on general economic growth but be more sensitive to demographic changes. Related to the analysis of economic cyclicality is the growth prospects of the industry. This requires an analysis as to whether the industry's growth is projected to increase and thereafter be maintained at a high level or is it expected to decline. The analyst develops growth scenarios to assess the implications of industry growth for the company.

To assess the growth prospects, a credit analyst will have to investigate the dependence on research and development (R&D) expenditures for maintaining or expanding the company's market position. While the company under analysis may be currently well positioned with the industry in which it operates, the lack of financial capacity to continue a technological lead or at least expend a sufficient amount of money to keep technologically current will likely result in a deterioration of its relative position in the long run (see page 8 of the Lear Corp. report in Appendix A).

Competition is based on a variety of factors and depends on the nature of the industry. As Moody's notes,

> Competition can be based on price, quality of product, distribution capabilities, image, product differentiation, service, or some other factor. Competition may be on a national basis, as is the case with major appliances. In other industries, such as chemicals, competition is global, and in still others, such as cement, competition is strictly regional. The basis for competition determines which factors are analyzed for a given company.[10]

With respect to pricing, the credit analyst will look at the market structure of an industry (e.g., unregulated monopoly, oligopoly, etc.) because of its implications on pricing flexibility. Moreover, market structure is important if it bears on one of the other industry factors identified previously: sources of supply. A company that is not self-sufficient in its factors of production but is sufficiently powerful in its industry to pass along increased costs is in a stronger position than a company that is in an industry where none or only a modest portion of increased costs can be passed on to cus-

---

[9]Frank J. Fabozzi, "Credit Analysis for Corporate Bonds," chapter 32 in Frank J. Fabozzi (ed.), *The Handbook of Fixed Income Securities* (New York, NY: McGraw-Hill, 2005), p. 735.
[10]Moody's Investors Service, *Industrial Company Rating Methodology*, p. 21.

tomers. In the Lear Corp. report, the authors of the report describe how Lear's inability to pass on higher raw material costs has negatively affected the credit (see pages 11 and 13).

With respect to regulation, the concern should not be with its existence or absence in an industry per se. Rather, the focus with respect to regulation should be on the direction of regulation and its potential impact on the current and prospective profitability of the company. Regulation also encompasses government intervention in non-U.S. operations of a company. With respect to its analysis of a company's global risk, S&P states:

> Is there a particular risk to the company that the government may change the rules through import/export restrictions; direct intervention in service quality or levels; redefining boundaries of competition (such as service areas); altering existing barriers to entry; changing subsidies; changing antitrust legislation; changing the maximum percentage level of foreign ownership participation; or changing terms to concession contracts for utilities? For extractive industries, is there a risk of government contract renegotiation?[11]

A key component in the cost structure of an industry is labor. (For analysis of a company's labor situation, see "Labor-Intensive Production" and the "Restructuring Plans" sections (page 9) in the Lear Corp. report in Appendix A.) In analyzing the labor situation, the credit analyst will examine if the industry is heavily unionized and, if so, will study: (1) whether management has the flexibility to reduce the labor force, (2) when does the prevailing labor contract come up for renewal, and (3) the historical occurrence of strikes. In nonunionized companies, the credit analyst will look at the prospect of potential unionization. Also in analyzing an industry, the requirements for particular specialists are examined.

CORPORATE GOVERNANCE RISK

Corporate governance issues involve (1) the ownership structure of the corporation, (2) the practices followed by management, and (3) policies for financial disclosure. The eagerness of corporate management to present favorable results to shareholders and the market has been a major factor in several of the corporate scandals in recent years. Chief executive officers (CEOs), chief financial officers, and the board of directors are being held directly accountable for disclosures in financial statements and other corporate decisions.

The underlying economic theory regarding many of the corporate governance issues is the principal-agency relationship between the senior managers and the shareholders of corporations.[12] The agent, a corporation's senior management, is charged with the responsibility of acting on behalf of the principal, the shareholders

---

[11]Standard & Poor's Corporation, *Corporate Rating Criteria*, p. 39.
[12]The seminal paper on the agency-principal relationship in corporate finance is Michael Jensen and William Meckling, "Theory and the Firm: Managerial Behavior, Agency Costs and Ownership Structure," *Journal of Financial Economics* (October 1976), pp. 305–360.

of the corporation. In a principal-agency relationship, there is the potential for the agent not to pursue the best interest of the principal, but instead pursue a policy in its own self-interest.

There are mechanisms that can mitigate the likelihood that management will act in its own self-interest. The mechanisms fall into two general categories. The first is to more strongly align the interests of management with those of shareholders. This can be accomplished by granting management an economically meaningful equity interest in the company. Also, manager compensation can be linked to the performance of the company's common stock.

The second category of mechanism is by means of the company's internal corporate control systems, which can provide a way for effectively monitoring the performance and decision-making behavior of management. For example, it would allow the timely removal of the CEO by the board of directors who believe that a CEO's performance is not in the best interest of the shareholders. In general, there are several critical features of an internal corporate control system that are necessary for the effective monitoring of management. What has been clear in corporate scandals is that there was a breakdown of the internal corporate control systems that lead to corporate difficulties and the destruction of shareholder wealth.

Because of the important role played by the board of directors, the structure and composition of the board are critical for effective corporate governance. The key is to remove the influence of the CEO and senior management on board members. This can be done in several ways. First, while there is no optimal board size, the more members there are, the less likely the influence of the CEO. With more board members, a larger number of committees can be formed to deal with important corporate matters.[13] Second, the composition of the committee should have a majority of independent directors, and the committees should include only independent directors.[14] Finally, there are corporate governance specialists who believe that the CEO should not be the chairman of the board of directors because such a practice allows the CEO to exert too much influence over board members and other important corporate actions.[15]

There are standards and codes of best practice for effective corporate governance.[16] The standards and codes of best practice go beyond applicable securities law. The expectation is that the adoption of best practice for corporate governance is a signal to investors about the character of management. There is empirical evidence

---

[13]At a minimum, there should be an auditing committee, a nominating committee (for board members), and a compensation committee.

[14]There are two classes of members of the board of directors. Directors who are employees or management or have some economic interest as set forth by the SEC (for example, a former employee with a pension fund, the relative of senior management, or an employee of an investment banking firm that has underwritten the company's securities) are referred to as "inside directors." Board members who do not fall into the category of inside directors are referred to as "outside directors" or "independent directors."

[15]This is a position that has been taken by the Securities and Exchange Commission.

[16]The standards of best practice that have become widely accepted as a benchmark are those set forth by the Organisation of Economic Cooperation and Development (OECD) in 1999. Other entities that have established standards and codes for corporate governance are the Commonwealth Association for Corporate Governance, the International Corporate Governance Network, and the Business Roundtable. Countries have established their own code and standards using the OECD principles.

supporting the relationship between corporate governance and bond ratings (and hence bond yields).[17]

Several organizations have developed services that assess corporate governance and express their view in the form of a rating. Generally, these ratings are made public at the option of the company requesting an evaluation. One such service is offered by S&P, which produces a Corporate Governance Score based on a review of both publicly available information, interviews with senior management and directors, and confidential information that S&P may have available from its credit rating of the corporation's debt. The score is based on four key elements evaluated by S&P:[18]

1. Ownership structure and external influences
   - Transparency of ownership structure
   - Concentration and influence of ownership and external stakeholders

2. Shareholder rights and stakeholder relations
   - Shareholder meeting and voting procedures
   - Ownership rights and takeover defenses
   - Stakeholder relations

3. Transparency, disclosure, and audit
   - Content of public disclosure
   - Timing of and access to public disclosure
   - Audit process

4. Board structure and effectiveness
   - Board structure and independence
   - Role and effectiveness of the board
   - Director and senior executive compensation

Based on S&P's analysis of the four key elements listed previously, its assessment of the company's corporate governance practices and policies and how its policies serve shareholders and other stakeholders is reflected in the Corporate Governance Score. The score ranges from 10 (the highest score) to 1 (the lowest score).

In addition to corporate governance, credit analysts look at the quality of management in assessing a corporation's ability to pay. Moody's notes the following regarding the quality of management:

> Although difficult to quantify, management quality is one of the most important factors supporting an issuer's credit strength. When the unexpected occurs, it is a management's ability to react appropriately that will sustain the company's performance. Assessment of management's plans in comparison with those of their industry peers can also provide important insights into the company's ability to compete, how likely it is to use debt capacity, its

[17]See Sanjeev Bhojraj and Partha Sengupta, "Effect of Corporate Governance on Bond Ratings and Yields: The Role of Institutional Investors and Outside Directors," *Journal of Business*, 76, 2003, pp. 455–476.
[18]Standard & Poor's, *Corporate Governance Evaluations & Scores*, undated, p. 2.

treatment of its subsidiaries, its relationship with regulators, and its position vis-à-vis all fundamentals affecting the company's long-term credit strength.[19]

In assessing management quality, Moody's tries to understand the business strategies and policies formulated by management. The factors Moody's considers are: (1) strategic direction, (2) financial philosophy, (3) conservatism, (4) track record, (5) succession planning, and (6) control systems.

FINANCIAL RISK

Having achieved an understanding of a corporation's business risk and corporate governance risk, the analyst is ready to move on to assessing financial risk. This involves traditional ratio analysis and other factors affecting the firm's financing. Next we provide a brief summary of some of the more important financial ratios: interest coverage, leverage, cash flow, net assets, and working capital. Once these ratios are calculated, it is necessary to analyze their absolute levels relative to those of the industry.

Before performing an analysis of the financial statement, the analyst must determine if the industry in which the company operates has any special accounting practices, such as those in the insurance industry. If so, an analyst should become familiar with industry practices. Moreover, the analyst must review the accounting policies to determine whether management is employing liberal or conservative policies in applying generally accepted accounting principles (GAAP). An analyst should be aware of changes in GAAP policies by the company and the reason for any changes. Since historical data are analyzed, the analyst should recognize that companies adjust prior years' results to accommodate discontinued operations and changes in accounting that can hide unfavorable trends. This can be done by assessing the trends for the company's unadjusted and adjusted results.

Interest Coverage

An **interest coverage ratio** measures the number of times interest charges are covered on a pretax basis. Typically, interest coverage ratios that are used and published are pretax as opposed to after-tax because interest payments are a pretax expense. **Pretax interest coverage ratio** is calculated by dividing pretax income plus interest charges by total interest charges. The higher this ratio, the lower the credit risk, all other factors the same. If a company has a pretax interest ratio that is less than 1×, it must borrow or use cash flow or proceeds from the sale of assets to meet its interest payments. For the Lear Corp., the authors of the report define interest coverage as the ratio of EBITDA, or operating earnings (excluding noncash restructuring charges and depreciation and amortization) over consolidated interest expense.

A calculation of simple pretax interest coverage would be misleading if there are fixed obligations other than interest that are significant. In this case, a more appropriate

---

[19]Moody's Investors Service, *Industrial Company Rating Methodology*, p. 6.

coverage ratio would include these other fixed obligations, and the resulting ratio is called a **fixed charge coverage ratio**. An example of other significant fixed obligations is lease payments. An analyst must also be aware of any contingent liabilities, such as a company's guaranteeing another company's debt.

Rather than use pretax income, cash flow can be used, and the computed ratio is called a **cash flow ratio**. We will discuss the various cash flow ratios later.

Leverage

A second important ratio is a **leverage ratio**. While there is no one definition for leverage, the most common one is the ratio of long-term debt to total capitalization. The higher the level of debt, the higher the percentage of operating income that must be used to satisfy fixed obligations. In calculating leverage, it is common to use the company's capitalization structure as stated in the most recent balance sheet. To supplement this measure, the analyst should calculate capitalization using a market approximation for the value of the common stock. For Lear Corp., the authors of the report define the leverage ratio as the ratio of total debt to EBITDA for a trailing 12-month period.

In analyzing a highly leveraged company (i.e., a company with a high leverage ratio), the margin of safety must be analyzed. The **margin of safety** is defined as the percentage by which operating income could decline and still be sufficient to allow the company to meet its fixed obligations. (Page 6 of the Lear Corp. report in Appendix A shows the margin or safety analysis.) The degree of leverage and margin of safety varies dramatically among industries.

Recognition must be given to the company's operating leases. Such leases represent an alternative to financing assets with borrowed funds. The existence of material operating leases can therefore understate a company's leverage. Operating leases should be capitalized to give a true measure of leverage.

Two other factors should be considered: the maturity structure of the debt and bank lines of credit. With respect to the first, the analyst would want to know the percentage of debt that is coming due within the next five years and how that debt will be refinanced. For the latter, a company's bank lines of credit often constitute a significant portion of its total debt. These lines of credit should be closely analyzed in order to determine the flexibility afforded to the company. The lines of credit should be evaluated in terms of undrawn capacity as well as security interests granted. (See Exhibit 21 on page 21 of the Lear Corp. report in Appendix A for an analysis of the amount of the credit's borrowing capacity that is driven by bank covenants.) The analysis also involves a determination as to whether the line contains a "material adverse change" clause under which the bank may withdraw a line of credit.

Cash Flow

The need to look at cash flow is emphasized by S&P:

Cash flow analysis is the single most critical aspect of all credit rating decisions. It takes on added importance for speculative-grade issuers. While companies with investment-grade ratings generally have ready access to external cash to cover temporary shortfalls, junk-bond issuers lack this degree of flexibility and have fewer alternatives to internally generated cash for servicing debt.[20]

How is cash flow defined? S&P notes that: "Discussions about cash flow often suffer from lack of uniform definition of terms."[21] S&P discussed four cash flow concepts: operating cash flow, free operating cash flow, discretionary cash flow, and prefinancing cash flow. Given a cash flow measure, cash flow ratios are calculated. These ratios are simply variants of the coverage ratio described earlier.

The statement of cash flows is required to be published in financial statements along with the income statement and balance sheet. The statement of cash flows is a summary over a period of time of a company's cash flows broken out by operating, investing, and financing activities. Analysts then reformat this information, combining it with information from the income statement to obtain what they view as a better description of the company's activities. S&P, for example, first calculates what it refers to as **funds from operations** (defined as net income adjusted for depreciation and other noncash debits and credits). **Operating cash flow** is funds from operations reduced by changes in the investment in working capital (current assets less current liabilities). Subtracting capital expenditures gives what S&P defines as **free operating cash flow**. It is from this cash flow that dividends and acquisitions can be made. Deducting cash dividends from free operating cash flow gives **discretionary cash flow**. Adjusting discretionary cash flow for managerial discretionary decisions for acquisition of other companies, the disposal of assets (e.g., lines of business or subsidiaries), and other sources or uses of cash gives prefinancing cash flow. As stated by S&P, **prefinancing cash flow** "represents the extent to which company cash flow from all internal sources have been sufficient to cover all internal needs."[22] In the Lear Corp. report in Appendix A, the analysts who authored the report define free cash flow as EBITDA less total interest expense, income tax expense, cash used or gained from management of working capital, capital expenditures, dividends, cash restructuring and asset sales or purchases (see page 6).

Cash flow measures can then be used to calculate various cash flow ratios. The ratio used often depends on the type of company being analyzed. According to S&P:

> Where long-term viability is more assured (i.e., higher in the rating spectrum) there can be greater emphasis on the level of funds from operations and its relation to total debt burden. These measures clearly differentiate between levels of protection over time. Focusing on debt service coverage and free cash flow becomes more critical in the analysis of a weaker company. Speculative-grade issuers typically face near-term vulnerabilities, which are better measured by free cash flow ratios.[23]

Net Assets

A fourth important ratio is net assets to total debt. In the analysis of this ratio, consideration should be given to the liquidation value of the assets. Liquidation value will

---

[20]Standard & Poor's Corporation, *Corporate Rating Criteria*, p. 26.
[21]Standard & Poor's Corporation, *Corporate Rating Criteria*, p. 27.
[22]Standard & Poor's Corporation, *Corporate Rating Criteria*, p. 27.
[23]Standard & Poor's Corporation, *Corporate Rating Criteria*, p. 27.

often differ dramatically from the value stated on the balance sheet. In addition to the assets' market value, some consideration should be given to the liquidity of the assets. A company with a high percentage of its assets in cash and marketable securities is in a much stronger asset position than a company whose primary assets are illiquid real estate. Finally, consideration should be given to several other financial variables including intangible assets, pension liabilities, and the age and condition of the plant.

Working Capital

Working capital is defined as current assets less current liabilities. Working capital is considered a primary measure of a company's financial flexibility. Other such measures include the *current ratio* (current assets divided by current liabilities) and the *acid test* (cash, marketable securities, and receivables divided by current liabilities). The stronger the company's liquidity measures, the better it can weather a downturn in business and reduction in cash flow.

In assessing this variable, the normal working capital requirements of a company and industry should be considered. The components of working capital should also be analyzed. Although accounts receivable are considered to be liquid, an increase in the average days receivables are outstanding may be an indication that a higher level of working capital is needed for the efficient running of the operation. In addition, companies frequently have account receivable financing, some with recourse provisions. In this scenario, comparisons among companies in the same industry may be distorted. For an example of the analysis of working capital, see page 8 of the Lear Corp. report in Appendix A.

CORPORATE BOND CREDIT ANALYSIS AND EQUITY ANALYSIS

The analysis of business risk, corporate governance risk, and financial risk described previously involves the same type of analysis that a common stock analyst would undertake. Many fixed income portfolio managers strongly believe that corporate bond analysis, particularly high-yield bond analysis, should be viewed from an equity analyst's perspective. As Stephen Esser notes:

> Using an equity approach, or at least considering the hybrid nature of high-yield debt, can either validate or contradict the results of traditional credit analysis, causing the analyst to dig further.[24]

He further states:

> For those who work with investing in high-yield bonds, whether issued by public or private companies, dynamic, equity-oriented analysis is invaluable. If analysts think about whether they would want to buy a particular high-yield company's stock and what will happen to the future equity value of that

---

[24]Stephen F. Esser, "High-Yield Bond Analysis: The Equity Perspective," in Ashwinpaul C. Sondhi (ed.), *Credit Analysis of Nontraditional Debt Securities* (Charlottesville, VA: Association for Investment Management and Research, 1995), p. 47.

company, they have a useful approach because, as equity values go up, so does the equity cushion beneath the company's debt. All else being equal, the bonds then become better credits and should go up in value relative to competing bond investments.[25]

SUMMARY

Corporate bond credit analysis involves an assessment of bondholder protections set forth in the bond indenture, the collateral available for the bondholder should the issuer fail to make the required payments, and the capacity of an issuer to fulfill its payment obligations. Covenants contained in the bond indenture set forth limitations on management and, as a result, provide safeguard provisions for bondholders. While collateral analysis is important, there is a question of what a secured position means in the case of a reorganization if the absolute priority rule is not followed in a reorganization. In assessing the ability of an issuer to service its debt, analysts look at a myriad of financial ratios as well as qualitative factors such as the issuer's business risk and corporate government risk.

In assessing the ability of an issuer to service its debt, analysts assess the issuer's business risk, corporate governance risk, and financial risk. Business risk is the risk associated with operating cash flows. In assessing business risk, some of the main factors considered are industry characteristics and trends, the company's market and competitive positions, management characteristics, and national political and regulatory environment. Corporate governance risk involves assessing (1) the ownership structure of the corporation, (2) the practices followed by management, and (3) policies for financial disclosure. Assessing financial risk involves traditional ratio analysis and other factors affecting the firm's financing. The more important financial ratios analyzed are interest coverage, leverage, cash flow, net assets, and working capital.

Some fixed income portfolio managers strongly believe that corporate bond analysis should be viewed from an equity analyst's perspective. This is particularly the case in analyzing high-yield bonds.

Questions

1. a. What is the difference between a positive and negative covenant?
    b. What is the purpose of the analysis of covenants in assessing the credit risk of an issuer?
2. a. What is a maintenance test?
    b. What is a debt incurrence test and when does it come into play?
3. Some credit analysts place less emphasis on collateral compared to covenants and business risk. Explain why.

4. Why do credit analysts begin with an analysis of the industry in assessing the business risk of a corporate issuer?
5. What is the purpose of a credit analyst investigating the market structure of an industry (e.g., unregulated monopoly, oligopoly, etc.)?
6. What should be the focus of an analyst with respect to the regulation of an industry?
7. In analyzing the labor situation in an industry in which a corporate issue operates, what should the credit analyst examine?

---

[25]Esser, "High-Yield Bond Analysis: The Equity Perspective," p. 54.

8. The underlying economic theory regarding many corporate governance issues is the principal-agency relationship between the senior managers and the shareholders of corporations. Explain this relationship.

9. With respect to corporate governance, what are the mechanisms that can mitigate the likelihood that management will act in its own self-interest?

10. a. What are corporate governance ratings?
    b. Are corporate governance ratings reported to the investing public?
    c. What factors are considered by services that assign corporate governance ratings?

11. Explain what a credit analyst should do in preparation for an analysis of the financial statements.

12. a. What is the purpose of an interest coverage ratio?
    b. What does an interest coverage ratio of 1.8 × mean?
    c. Why are interest coverage ratios typically computed on a pretax basis?

d. Why would a fixed-charge coverage ratio be materially different from an interest coverage ratio?

13. a. What is the purpose of a leverage ratio?
    b. What measures are used in a leverage ratio for total capitalization?
    c. What is the margin of safety measure?

14. Why do analysts investigate the bank lines of credit that a corporation has?

15. Explain each of the following:
    a. funds from operation
    b. operating cash flow
    c. free operating cash flow
    d. discretionary cash flow
    e. prefinancing cash flow.

16. In the analysis of net assets, what factors should be considered?

17. a. What is meant by working capital?
    b. Why is an analysis of working capital important?

18. Why do analysts of high-yield corporate bonds feel that the analysis should be viewed from an equity analyst's perspective?

WACHOVIA SECURITIES

High Yield Research

November 10, 2005

Eric J. Selle, CFA
eric.selle@wachovia.com
704-383-4086
Stephanie Renegar
stephanie.renegar@wachovia.com
704-715-7038

Lear Corp. (LEA)

Initiating With an Outperform Recommendation on the 8.11% Senior Notes due 2009 and an Underperform Recommendation on the 5.75% Senior Notes due 2014

Coupon	Issue	Maturity	Moody's/ S&P	Amt. Out. ($mm)	Next Call	Call Price	Recent Price*	Current Yield	YTW	Spread	CDS Levels
8.11%	Notes	5/15/2009	Ba2/BB+	800.0	NC	NC	92.75	8.74%	10.65%	614	685/700
5.75%	Notes	8/1/2014	Ba2/BB+	399.2	NC	NC	79.00	7.28%	9.32%	473	

* Represents the offer price for the 8.11% notes and the bid price for the 5.75% notes

We are basing our recommendation on the following factors:

Our concerns over short-term volatility in cash flow and balance sheet metrics:

- **Deteriorating Credit Profile.** We foresee that Lear's credit profile will be under pressure until mid-2006 as unfavorable mix hits revenues and higher raw material price increases COGS and working capital needs.
- **Customer and Mix Issues.** For FY2004, the Big 3 accounted for over 67% of Lear's sales. Due to market share losses, from 1999- LTM Q3 2005 the CAGR for NA production for the Big 3 has fallen by 3.8%, while all other OEM production has increased by 6.8%. Furthermore, Lear derived nearly half of its FY2004 sales from light trucks and SUVs.

Our longer-term outlook on the credit:

- **Adequate Liquidity.** We believe Lear's liquidity position ($135.4 million in cash on its balance sheet at 10/1, and we calculate the company had $544.2 million in covenant-constrained availability) provides the company with sufficient funds for its expected cash needs over the next 15 months.
- **Clean Capital Structure.** We estimate given Lear's current debt levels, the company's EBITDA would have to drop below $512 million, (or 30.2% from

Contents

Recommendation
Merits
Concerns
Company Facts
Financials
Model
    Assumptions
Industry
    Outlook
Relative Value
Bank Covenants
Bond Covenants

LTM 10/1/2005 EBITDA of $733.5 million) in order for the unsecured bondholders to not be made whole (see Exhibit 4 on page 6).

- **Strong Market Position.** Lear commands #1 global market share in its largest operating segment (seating) and #2 global market share in both door panels and flooring and acoustics.
- **Large Backlog.** Lear's high quality products have helped the company build a solid backlog of future business. We expect these net new sales to translate into $270 million in additional EBITDA in FY2006 (see Exhibit 22 on page 22), or incremental EBITDA growth of 36.8% over Lear's LTM 10/1/05 EBITDA of $733.5 million.

Recommendation

In our opinion, Lear is one of the more solvent auto suppliers in our coverage universe due to its clean capital structure, considerable liquidity and solid working capital management. Its seating systems are world-class in quality (#1 U.S. and global market share) and we feel that these attributes have allowed the company to build a considerable backlog to OEMs across the globe.

Despite these positive attributes, we have reservations about the credit. First, the company's revenue mix is weighted towards Ford and GM (55% of Lear's 2004 sales) with considerable concentration on these OEMs' light duty truck platforms (28% and 21% of Lear's 2004 sales were generated by production of SUVs and light trucks, respectively). Not only do these two OEMs continue to lose market share in the U.S. (over 200 bps over the past 3 years), but high gas prices, changing consumer preferences, competitive Asian offerings and the end of the accelerated tax depreciation law have caused SUV sales to plummet (total SUV sales in the U.S. have fallen almost 13% YTD). Furthermore, Lear is a heavy user of steel and resin-based plastics and we expect its profits to continue to be hurt by soaring prices and limited supplies of these inputs. Finally, the considerable decline in free cash flow (Lear burned over $360 million in Q3) concerns us, as we expect Lear's FY2005 leverage ratio to rise over a turn to 3.6x (versus 2.3x at FYE2004). Although cash restructuring ($21 million in Q3) should generate future cost savings, asset write-downs (a $670 million charge to goodwill and $74 million in fixed asset impairments taken in Q3) were necessary and the increase in working capital ($271 million in Q3) can be partially explained by the elimination in fast-pay programs and raw material inflation, we believe that overhang from these recent operating challenges will hinder Lear's ability to lower debt until Q3 2006.

We believe these challenges worsen the relative value argument, particularly for holders of Lear's 5.75% senior notes. For example, Metaldyne, Corp. and Dura Automotive Systems, Inc.' senior notes have similar current senior leverage metrics (see Exhibit 13 on page 14) and offer over 300 bps of spread versus Lear's 5.75% senior notes. In addition, the offer side of Lear's 8.11% notes represents 133 bps of YTW versus the bid side of its 5.75% notes, despite the maturity being over five years earlier. Due to the uncertainty surrounding the sector and the low relative YTW offered we are initiating coverage of Lear's 5.75% senior notes with an under perform recommendation.

In turn, we expect the benefits of Lear's restructuring, the recovery in its customers' production rates and Lear's incremental sales to materialize over the next year. Due to our longer-term view of the credit's stability, the bonds' short duration (3 and a half years) and relative value offered (represents over 200 bps of YTW versus the BB index), we are initiating coverage on Lear's 8.11% notes with an outperform recommendation. Our higher rating of these bonds with a higher dollar price is bullish, as we believe most of the negative news is already baked into the bonds' prices and expect the yield curve to normalize within the next two quarters. Over the next several months, we view GM's increased production, the sale of GMAC and the absence of a strike at Delphi as events that could stabilize Lear's fundamental picture.

Exhibit 1: Lear Corp. Financial Summary

($million)	FY 12/31/1998	FY 12/31/1999	FY 12/31/2000	FY 12/31/2001	FY 12/31/2002	FY 12/31/2003	FY 12/31/2004	FY 12/31/05E	FY 12/31/06E
Revenue	9,059.4	12,428.8	14,072.8	13,624.7	14,424.6	15,746.7	16,960.0	17,106.6	18,133.0
EBITDA	744.1	1,130.8	1,317.5	915.9	1,044.1	1,094.6	1,123.5	673.0	950.0
EBITDA Margin	8.2%	9.1%	9.4%	6.7%	7.2%	7.0%	6.6%	3.9%	5.2%
Interest Coverage	6.7x	4.8x	4.2x	3.6x	5.0x	5.9x	6.8x	3.6x	4.9x
(EBITDA-Capex)/Total Interest Expense	3.6x	3.1x	3.1x	2.5x	3.7x	3.9x	4.2x	0.6x	2.2x
Total Debt/ EBITDA	2.1x	3.1x	2.3x	2.7x	2.1x	1.9x	2.3x	3.6x	2.8x
Net Debt/ EBITDA	2.1x	3.0x	2.3x	2.6x	2.0x	1.7x	1.7x	3.4x	2.7x

Source: Company reports and Wachovia Securities' estimates.

Investment Merits

- **Liquidity**

The principal reason certain automotive suppliers have filed for bankruptcy over the past year is due to cash crunches, as the impact of the elimination of fast-pay programs, rising raw material prices and production cuts have sapped liquidity.

However, we do not foresee a liquidity issue for Lear. The company had $135.4 million in cash on its balance sheet at 10/1, and we calculate the company had $544.2 million in covenant-constrained availability under its $1.7 billion revolver.

Exhibit 2: Calculation of Lear Corp. Covenant-Constrained Liquidity (10/1/05)

For LTM 10/1/05 ($ millions)	
EBITDA	733.5
Leverage Covenant	3.75x
Maximum Net Debt Allowed Under Covenant Constraints	**2750.6**
less: Net Debt Outstanding at 10/1/05	2206.4
Covenant-Constrained Availability	**544.2**

Source: Company Reports and Wachovia Securities

We believe Lear's liquidity position provides the company with sufficient funds for the following expected cash needs over the next 15 months:
- About $99.0 million in cash restructuring charges in FY2005 ($24.0 million incurred YTD and we expect $75 million more Q4 2005). In FY2006, we expect $134.4 million in cash restructuring charges.
- We expect capital expenditures for FY2005 to increase to $564.3 million (compared to $429.0 in FY2004), due to Lear's significant backlog, as well as its

focus on expanding its global footprint. After ramping up for new business, the company expects its 2006 capital expenditures to fall to more normalized levels (we expect FY2006 capex to total approximately $520.0 million).

- We expect cash interest of $180.5 million in FY2005 and $179.0 million in FY2006.
- On Aug. 16, Lear filed an 8-K stating it was interested in pursuing a joint venture with Collins & Aikman. We expect this action to follow the divestiture of a large portion of its interiors businesses. Lear's actions are not expected to require capital, as the company intends to find a private equity backer to finance a portion of the transaction, with Lear contributing assets. In fact, as Lear desires to retain less than 50% ownership, the company may receive some cash proceeds for its asset contribution. However, we estimate the absence of the majority of the EBITDA generated by Lear's interiors segment will boost leverage by 0.6x (see Exhibit 12 on page 13).
- Lear could acquire assets in order to diversify its revenue base away from North America and the Big 2 in particular.
- Taking into account the cash restructuring, capex swings and our expectation of EBITDA growth in FY2006, we expect Lear to end 2006 with $617.1 million in covenant-constrained liquidity under its revolver.

Exhibit 3: Lear Corp. Free Cash Flow Analysis

 WACHOVIA SECURITIES

($ millions)	Q1 2005A	Q2 2005A	Q3 2005A	Q4 2005E	FY 2005E	Q1 2006E	Q2 2006E	Q3 2006E	Q4 2006E	FY 2006E
EBITDA	143.3	147.3	129.0	253.4	673.0	215.7	271.7	202.8	259.7	950.0
OPEB Expense	6.8	7.9	7.5	0.2	22.4	7.4	8.6	8.2	0.2	24.4
Bank-Defined EBITDA	150.1	155.2	136.5	253.6	695.4	223.1	280.3	211.0	260.0	974.4
Cash Restructuring	0.0	2.9	21.1	75.0	99.0	33.6	33.6	33.6	33.6	134.4
Cash Pension	14.5	14.5	14.5	14.5	58.0	15.0	15.0	15.0	15.0	60.0
Cash OPEB	0.0	0.0	0.0	0.0	0.0	0.0	0.0	0.0	0.0	0.0
Cash Taxes	63.5	29.7	0.0	12.0	105.2	5.0	26.8	0.0	22.5	54.3
Cash Interest	28.9	68.0	36.0	47.6	180.5	39.8	50.2	40.5	48.5	179.0
Capex	129.4	149.7	135.2	150.0	564.3	130.0	130.0	130.0	130.0	520.0
Dividends	16.8	15.0	16.8	16.8	65.4	16.8	16.8	16.8	16.8	67.2
Stock Repurchase	25.4	0.0	0.0	0.0	25.4	0.0	0.0	0.0	0.0	0.0
Working Capital	13.6	-311.8	271.1	50.0	22.9	200.0	150.0	-125.0	-75.0	150.0
(Debt Issuance)/Bond Maturity	0.0	600.0	-400.0	0.0	200.0	0.0	0.0	0.0	0.0	0.0
Asset (Sales)/ Purchases	0.0	0.0	0.0	0.0	0.0	0.0	0.0	0.0	0.0	0.0
(Sources) / Uses of Cash[1]	292.1	568.0	94.7	365.8	1,320.6	440.2	422.4	110.9	191.4	1,164.9
Free Cash Flow	-148.8	-420.7	34.3	-112.5	-647.7	-224.5	-150.7	92.0	68.3	-214.9
Cash	525.6	132.9	135.4	135.4	135.4	135.4	135.4	135.4	135.4	135.4
Availability under Revolving Credit Facility	1,356.1	1,150.1	544.2	279.5	279.5	141.6	204.3	530.3	617.1	617.1
Liquidity	1,881.7	1,283.0	679.6	414.9	414.9	277.0	339.7	665.7	752.5	752.5
Revolver Borrowings	0.0	0.0	100.0	210.5	210.5	435.0	585.7	493.7	425.4	425.4
Term Loan	0.0	0.0	400.0	400.0	400.0	400.0	400.0	400.0	400.0	400.0
Bonds	2,412.1	1,793.8	1,793.8	1,793.8	1,793.8	1,793.8	1,793.8	1,793.8	1,793.8	1,793.8
Other	110.4	99.2	48.0	50.0	50.0	50.0	50.0	50.0	50.0	50.0
Total Debt	2,522.5	1,893.0	2,341.8	2,454.3	2,454.3	2,678.8	2,829.5	2,737.5	2,669.2	2,669.2
Accounts Receivable Securitization	0.0	129.9	129.9	129.9	129.9	129.9	129.9	129.9	129.9	129.9
Total Debt and Securitizations	2,522.5	2,022.9	2,471.7	2,584.2	2,584.2	2,808.7	2,959.4	2,867.4	2,799.1	2,799.1
Net Lev as defined by Bank Covenants	1.90x	1.90x	3.07x	3.52x	3.52x	3.48x	3.16x	2.82x	2.73x	2.73x
Bank Covenant	3.25x	3.25x	3.75x	3.75x	3.75x	3.50x	3.25x	3.25x	3.25x	3.25x

1. Certain drivers of cash flow (pension, OPEB, interest and taxes) are Wachovia's calculations.
Source: Company Reports and Wachovia Securities' estimates

Lear Corp. (LEA)
November 10, 2005

HIGH YIELD RESEARCH

- **Clean Capital Structure**

At 10/1/05, Lear's secured leverage was 0.7x, versus a 1.0x average for similarly-rated automotive supplier credits. In Exhibit 4, we estimate given Lear's current debt levels, the company's EBITDA would have to drop below $512 million, (or 30.2% from LTM 10/1/2005 EBITDA of $733.5) in order for the unsecured bondholders to not be made whole. EBITDA of $512 million is also significantly below our FY2005 EBITDA estimate of $673.0 million and FY2006 EBITDA estimate of $950.0 million. Although we expect Lear's FY2005 total leverage be 3.6x, leverage based on current bond prices is only 2.8x. Therefore, we believe these bonds have a considerable cushion should fundamentals deteriorate.

Lear's strong balance sheet also prepares the company during difficult automotive environments, as OEMs are more inclined to award new business to stronger companies. In addition, Lear has dry powder to potentially make a low-multiple acquisition to diversify its footprint and customer base or to pay for far-reaching restructurings to right-size and focus its operating base.

Exhibit 4: Lear Corp. Distressed Valuation

($ millions)	Current Wachovia Estimates	EBITDA Drop needed to hit Senior Debtholders
2005 Estimated EBITDA [1]	**673.0**	**512.0**
Pension Expense	58.0	58.0
Core Pre-Legacy EBITDA	731.0	570.0
TEV Multiple	5.0x	5.0x
Total Enterprise Value	3,655.0	2,850.0
plus Cash	135.4	135.4
less Working Capital Adjustment [2]	129.9	129.9
Total Enterprise Value available to Debt	**3,660.5**	**2,855.5**
Secured Debt [3]	660.5	821.5
Secured Leverage	**1.0X**	**1.6X**
Remaining Proceeds for Senior and Subordinated Debt	3,000.0	2,034.0
Senior Debt	1,793.8	1,793.8
Unfunded Pension Obligations	236.3	236.3
% Recovery	**100%**	**100%**
Remaining Proceeds for Subordinated Debt	969.9	3.9

1) Wachovia Securities estimates
2) Includes off balance sheet accounts receivables securitizations and factoring as well as normalizing
   accounts payable to 60 days
3) Using Wachovia Securities estimate for 2005 year end debt levels.
Source: Company Reports and Wachovia Securities

- **Strong Market Position.**
Lear commands #1 global market share in its largest operating segment (seating) and #2 global market share in door panels and flooring and acoustics. Lear's significant market share is a competitive advantage that boosts both sales and profitability, as Lear can offer its global customers "one stop shopping" by combining its seating and interior products with electronic content.

The company's scale and integrated interior product offering also serve as a barrier to entry. For example, on Sept. 29, Ford Motor Co. announced it was entering into new long-term agreements with select suppliers to better align its businesses and increase future collaboration. Lear was one of seven companies named in Ford's initial round of key suppliers. As a result of this initiative, Ford announced it would be lowering the amount of suppliers it uses by 50%.

Exhibit 5: Lear Corp. Global Market Position (FY2003)

	North America	Europe	Global
Seating Systems	#1	#1	#1
Door Panels	#1	#3	#2
Flooring & Acoustics	#2	#8	#2
Headliners	#2	#3	#3
Electrical Distribution	#3	#3	#3
Instrument Panels	#5	#4	#7

Source: Company Reports

- **Large Backlog**

Lear's high quality products have helped the company build a solid backlog of future business. According to management, Lear has a very active new product schedule, particularly over the next three years[1]. At 10/26, over $3.8 billion in incremental sales are expected to be executed in the period 2005-2007. We expect a portion of these net new sales to translate into $270 million in additional EBITDA in FY2006 (see Exhibit 22 on page 22). This represents incremental EBITDA growth of 36.8% over Lear's LTM 10/1/05 EBITDA of $733.5 million.

Exhibit 6: Lear Corp.-Reported Backlog at Q2 2005*

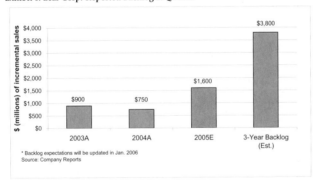

* Backlog expectations will be updated in Jan. 2006
Source: Company Reports

- **Geographic Diversity**

Lear continues to focus on driving new business in Asia and Europe. For example, from 1999 to 2004, Lear's U.S. sales have dropped from 49.0% of total revenues to 36.6%. We think this growth away from the Big 3 will be will be positive for both revenue growth and cash flow, given the production trends in North America over

---

[1] Lear's incremental backlog reflects formally awarded new programs, targeted programs for which Lear believes there is a substantial likelihood of award, phased-out and canceled programs, estimates regarding customer-mandated changes in selling prices and estimates of expected changes in vehicle content.

the past 5 years. For example, from 1999-YTD 2005, the CAGR for NA production for the Big 3 has fallen by 3.8%, while all other production has increased by 6.8%.

Exhibit 7: Lear Corp. Geographic Revenue Split (FY2004)

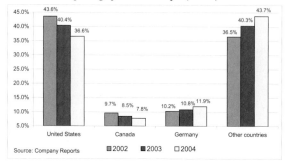

Source: Company Reports   ▤ 2002   ▪ 2003   ☐ 2004

- **Technology**

Lear owns intellectual property, including patents, copyrights, proprietary tools and technologies and trade secrets. For example, the company held 2,700 patents and patent applications pending worldwide at 12/31/04. Lear's focus on technology has allowed the company to be one of the world leaders in seating systems, flooring and acoustic components, and door panels. One recent new product that has stemmed from these efforts is Lear's tire pressuring monitor system, the "Intellitire," which can monitor pressure and temperatures from inside the vehicle wheel.

To enhance its technological edge, Lear maintains six advanced technology centers and several customer-focused product engineering centers, and spent $198 million on research and development (R&D) in fiscal 2004, or about 1.3% of the company's operating costs. These up-front costs are essential to gain new business and stay cost-competitive. For example, in June 2005 Lear bought injection molding machinery (called the Quadloc-Tandem Index, or QTI system) that allows the company to manufacture large interior and exterior plastic panels with multiple materials in one machine, which reduces production space and improves part quality.

- **Working Capital Management**

We believe Lear's working capital management is the best among its peers. This tight management of capital is primarily due to extremely thin inventories. The company only holds about 2 weeks in inventory, the bulk of which is raw materials (only about 31% of Lear's inventory at 7/2/05 was work-in-process or finished goods).

Lear Corp. (LEA)
November 10, 2005

WACHOVIA SECURITIES
HIGH YIELD RESEARCH

Exhibit 8: Lear Corp. Cash Cycle Analysis (LTM Q3 2005)[1]

	ArvinMeritor, Inc. (ARM)	Dana Corp. (DCN)	Lear Corp. (LEA)	Tenneco Automotive, Inc. (TEN)	TRW Automotive, Inc. (TRW)	Average (excl. LEA)
A/R Days	62	67	58	55	56	60
Inventory Days	26	39	16	40	22	32
Payable Days	65	57	70	72	57	63
Cash Cycle	**23**	**49**	**4**	**23**	**21**	**29**
% Inventory that is WIP, Finished Goods	58.7%	60.9%	30.7%	73.3%	53.7%	55.5%

A/R: Accounts receivable., WIP: Work-in-process
1. ARM and DCN numbers are as of 6/30/05. All inventory % numbers are as of 6/30/05.
Source: Company reports and Wachovia Securities

Investment Concerns

- **Deteriorating Credit Profile**

We foresee that Lear's credit profile will be under pressure until mid-2006. In Q4 2005, we expect vehicle production rates to improve, which should increase Lear's capital expenditures and working capital requirements. Furthermore, higher steel and resin prices could increase COGS and working capital needs. We estimate that this cash burn will keep Lear's respective leverage and net leverage at about 2.8x and 2.7x for FYE 2006. While these leverage points are lower than the bulk of Lear's comps, total leverage had fallen to below 2.0x when the company was upgraded to high grade in July 2003 (S&P) and Dec. 2003 (Moody's). Due to an increase in leverage from 1.9x at FYE2003 to 2.7x at LTM 7/2/05 (pro forma for the $400 million term loan), the company's bonds were downgraded from high grade to high yield (unsecured ratings were lowered to Ba2/BB+ on 7/25/05 by Moody's and 8/2/05 by S&P). We have seen leverage continue to increase since then to 3.2x (3.0x net leverage) for LTM 10/2/05. In addition, we believe Lear would be willing to take on more leverage via restructuring, acquisitions, or capital requirements to fund new business. We expect Lear's total leverage to peak at 3.6x for FYE2005.

We are also concerned about the longer-term trend in Lear's EBITDA margins. From FY1999-LTM 10/2/2005, high raw material costs, Lear's platform weighting and OEM price-downs have caused the company's EBITDA to drop by a CAGR of 7.3% versus the company's sales CAGR of positive 5.6%. We do not feel that Lear will be able to substantially improve its margins without a significant shift in customer/platform weighting, as well as product shifts to Lear's higher-margin electronic and electrical segment (15.8% of FY2004 revenues, 26.4% of FY2004 EBITDA). We are not as concerned about growth in Lear's capital expenditures, as they typically fall to more normalized levels after the company ramps up for new product launches. In fact, Lear has historically posted strong free cash flow and has brought down debt in years following large outflows for capital expenditures and tooling. For example, in FY1999, Lear spent $391.4 million for capital expenditures to ramp-up for new business. In FY2000, Lear posted year-over-year sales growth of

13.2%, a 26 bp improvement in EBITDA margin and spent $69.1 million less in capex. Similarly, over the past year much of Lear's cash has been spent to launch new business in FY2006-2007. However, we may not see quite as dramatic a drop in capital expenditures year over year, as the company intends to invest in low-cost, non-US production areas in order grab part of the growing book of the Big 3's Asian and Eastern European business.

- **Customer Concentration**

For FY2004, the Big 3 accounted for over 67% of Lear's sales. Due to market share losses, from 1999- LTM Q3 2005 the CAGR for NA production for the Big 3 has fallen by 3.8%, while all other OEM production has increased by 6.8%. In 2005, Lear expects total industry production to fall by 2% versus 2004 and production for its top 15 platforms in North America (most of which are light truck platforms with the Big 3, see Exhibits 10 and 11 on page 11) to decline by 8%. This persistent slowdown in production is occurring alongside price concessions demanded from the OEMs. Longer term, we believe these price and volume declines are unsustainable for Big 3 suppliers.

Exhibit 9: Lear Corp. Customer Split as a Percentage of Revenue

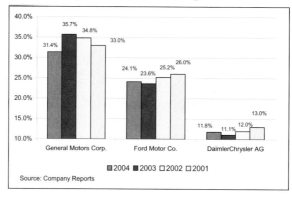

Source: Company Reports

- **Current Platform Weighting**

Lear's product segment weighting of 28% SUVs and 21% light trucks concerns us. In 2005, unfavorable mix and lower production volumes have already had a negative impact on Lear's revenues of $1.4 billion in Q1-Q3 2005, and a negative impact on gross margin of $239 million and $237 million in Q2 2005 and Q1 2005, respectively. Longer term, we are concerned about changes in customer preferences due to increasing gasoline prices. Furthermore, we do not foresee the GMT900 (launching in early 2006) providing much of a boost to GM's longer-term future production schedules due to competitive offerings from foreign competitors, high gas prices, the elimination of the accelerated tax depreciation bill in December 2004 and a mix shift to crossover utility vehicles.

Lear Corp. (LEA)
November 10, 2005

Exhibit 10: Lear Corp. Vehicle Categories (FY2004)

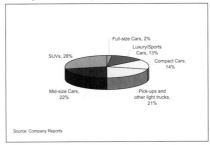

Source: Company Reports

Exhibit 11: Lear Corp. Principal Platform Production Volumes[1]

	H1 Production	Q3 Production
Ford Explorer/Mountaineer	(41%)	(39%)
DCX Durango	(35%)	9%
DCX Ram	(26%)	(20%)
GM Yukon/Tahoe/Escalade	(24%)	(18%)
GM Grand Prix/LaCrosse/Impala/Regal	(20%)	4%
Ford Crown Victoria/Grand Marquis	(17%)	(23%)
GM Silverado/Sierra/Avalanche	(7%)	(2%)
DCX Jeep Liberty	(3%)	4%
Ford F-Series	(2%)	9%
BMW X5	(.1%)	8%
Subaru Legacy/Outback	10%	(24%)
Ford Escape/Tribute/Mariner	15%	(.2%)
Ford Five Hundred/Freestyle/Taurus/Sable	28%	10%
DCX Grand Cherokee	33%	115%
Ford Mustang[2]	51%	731%

1. From Ward's Autodata
2. Changeover in H2 2004
Company Reports and Ward's Autodata

- **Commodity Prices**

Raw materials represent about 67% of Lear's sales (approximately 73% of COGS, or $11.4 billion). Lear's major raw material inputs are steel (hot and cold-rolled), resins (including polypropylene and ABS) chemicals, energy and leather. While steel prices face easier year-over-year comparisons and leather prices tend to follow the beef market, resin prices have continued to rise over the past year. Although the company does not split out the size of these purchases, we expect that petroleum-based foams, plastics and resins represent 15% of COGS (slightly less than the 20% of COGS we estimate is used to purchase steel). The recent 20% price surges by

several plastics producers could lower Lear's Q4 profits. In addition, on Sept. 28, BP Plc., Sunoco, Inc. and Basell NV announced they will not be able to meet customer orders for polypropylene plastic as 42% of the North American polypropylene production capacity was down due to damage caused by hurricane Rita. Alleviating these concerns is the London Exchange's new plastics derivative contract, which should give automotive suppliers an opportunity to hedge their exposure to plastic resins beginning in late 2005/early 2006. Meanwhile, we estimate resin prices will grow 8% in FY2006 (versus our estimate of 35% year-over-year growth in Q4 2005) and steel prices will fall by 12% in FY2006 (versus our estimate of a 22.5% decline in Q4 2005).

- **Restructuring Plans**

Lear has announced a major restructuring plan that will affect over 20 manufacturing facilities and result in a 5%-7% headcount reduction worldwide (between 5,500-7,700 workers). We expect these actions will cost $250 million ($60 million in pre-tax restructuring charges have been incurred YTD), about $200 million, or 80%, of which Lear believes will be in cash. While we expect the restructuring to take approximately 3-6 months, Lear expects payback in about 2-3 years. We see these restructuring activities as positive in the long term, as Lear streamlines its current production base and expands into low-cost areas. For example, Lear's production capacity in low-cost countries is about 15% currently, but the company expects to increase its capacity to over 25%. Lear has targeted certain areas for this move, including China, India, the Phillippines, Eastern Europe, South Africa, and Mexico.

- **Potentially Acquisitive**

Lear has stated it would not sacrifice balance sheet strength to make an acquisition. However, the company's need to diversify its customer base away from the Big 3's NA production base may result in a leveraging acquisition in the short-term in order to benefit from cash flow growth and diversity in the longer-term.

- **Re-Sourcing of Business by GM**

Lear's GM platforms have had no timing or quality issues; however, GM is starting to bring certain aspects of interior sourcing back in-house (these actions do not affect Lear's GM backlog). While Lear believes that it can perform these services more efficiently (total interior sourcing includes the design, sourcing and engineering of the product), GM's focus is on cutting costs. As a result, we may see some more margin pressure as OEMs continue to rationalize costs.

- **Labor-Intensive Production**

Lear's seat production, such as its cut and sew operations, requires a considerable amount of labor per part. Furthermore, only about 15% of its manufacturing capacity is in low-cost areas. As a result, our calculations for certain labor-related efficiency metrics, such as sales/employee and EBITDA/employee, show Lear being 31% and 38% lower than the averages for our automotive supplier universe of $223,598 and $16,572, respectively. However, the company believes its latest restructuring (expected to take 3-6 months) will increase its capacity in low-cost areas to over 25%.

- **Interior Operations and Lear's Growth Story**

Interiors are Lear's lowest margin business, due to overcapacity in the marketplace, rising commodity prices, price concessions forced by the OEMs and irrational pricing by some of its competitors. As a result, Lear recently announced its intentions to divest some of its underperforming interior components operations.

On Aug. 16, Lear filed an 8-K stating it was interested in pursuing a joint venture with Collins & Aikman. We expect that Lear will end up divesting a large portion of its interiors businesses. As a result of Lear's intentions, during Q3, Lear wrote down $670 million of goodwill in relation to its interior business. We do not expect Lear's divestiture will require capital, as the company intends to find a private equity backer to finance a portion of the transaction, with Lear contributing assets. In fact, as Lear desires to retain less than 50% ownership, the company may receive some cash proceeds for its asset contribution. However, we estimate the absence of the majority of the EBITDA generated by Lear's interiors segment will boost leverage by 0.6x. Despite the possible increase in leverage, we are encouraged by the announcement, as interiors are a lower margin, more commodity-type business. In fact, for LTM 10/1/05 Lear's interiors business represented 17.4% of revenues, but only 12.1% of EBITDA.

Exhibit 12: Lear Corp. Possible Interiors Divestiture ($ millions)

LTM 10/1/2005	Lear Financials, Pre-Divestiture[1]	Less: Interiors Segment	Lear Financials, Post-Divestiture
Revenues	16978.0	2938.4	14039.6
EBITDA	733.5	122.6	610.9
EBITDA Margin	4.3%	4.2%	4.4%
Total Debt Leverage	3.2x		3.8x

1. Includes "other" revenues of $88.8 million and the corporate segment's and other charges to LTM EBITDA of $278.7 million.
Source: Company Reports and Wachovia Securities

- **Relative Value**

We believe that Dura's senior notes and Metaldyne's senior notes offer relative value versus Lear's 5.75% senior notes. While Metaldyne and Dura are lower rated, high-beta names, we believe there is significant upside in these bonds due to credit profile improvement (Metaldyne) and significant liquidity (Dura). We also believe their senior and maximum allowable leverage compare favorably to Lear. As a result, we recommend investors pick up 330 bps by going long Dura senior notes and Metaldyne senior notes while shorting Lear's 5.75% senior notes. Outside of these swap ideas, we currently have a buy rating on Metaldyne's 10% senior notes and an outperform rating on Dura's 8.625% senior notes.

Exhibit 13: Lear Relative Value Versus Metaldyne and Dura Senior Notes

	Lear 5.75% Senior Notes due 2014	Metaldyne 10% Senior Notes due 2012	Dura 8.625% Senior Notes due 2012
2005 EBITDA estimate ($ millions)	673.0	216.1	167.9
Estimated Total Debt through Senior Notes at 12/31/05	2440.2	587.4	543.6
Estimated Total Senior Leverage	**3.6x**	**2.7x**	**3.2x**
Estimated Bank Availabilty at 12/31/2005	153.8	88.4	155.0
Maximum Secured Leverage	**3.9x**	**3.1x**	**4.2x**
Senior Notes YTW	9.32%	12.62%	12.62%
Senior Notes STT	473	803	804
VERSUS LEAR 5.75% NOTES		**3.30%**	**3.30%**

1. Adds back our 12/31/05 cash estimate of $135.4 million for LEA's net leverage bank covenant.
Source: Company Reports and Wachovia Securities

Company Description

Lear is one of the leading global automotive interior systems suppliers, with capabilities in all five principal segments of the automotive interior market: seat systems, instrument panels and cockpit systems, overhead systems, door panels, and flooring and acoustic systems. The company is also one of the leading global suppliers of automotive electrical distribution systems. Lear supplies its products and services to every major automotive manufacturer in the world, including General Motors, Ford, DaimlerChrysler, BMW, PSA, Fiat, Volkswagen, Renault-Nissan, Mazda, Toyota, Subaru and Hyundai.

Headquartered in Southfield, MI, at FYE2004 the company conducted its operations through 271 facilities, including 165 production/manufacturing facilities, 52 administrative/technical support facilities, 45 assembly sites, six advanced technology centers and three distribution centers in 34 countries. Of Lear's 271 total facilities, which include facilities owned or leased by its consolidated subsidiaries, 126 are owned and 145 are leased. At Dec. 31, 2004, Lear employed 110,000 people worldwide.

Lear Corp. (LEA)
November 10, 2005

WACHOVIA SECURITIES

HIGH YIELD RESEARCH

Exhibit 14: Lear Corp. Customer Split (FY2004)

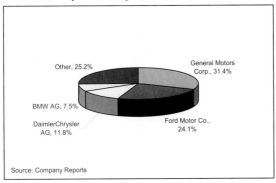

Source: Company Reports

Reporting Segments

Exhibit 15: Lear Corp. Segment Split (FY2004)

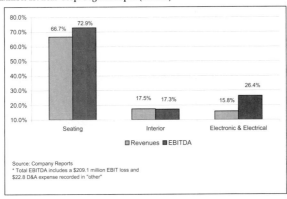

Source: Company Reports
* Total EBITDA includes a $209.1 million EBIT loss and
$22.8 D&A expense recorded in "other"

- Lear's seating segment (66.7% of FY2004 revenues, 72.9% of FY2004 EBITDA)
  includes seat systems and components.

- Lear's interior segment (17.5% of FY2004 revenues, 17.3% of FY2004 EBITDA) includes instrument panels and cockpit systems, overhead systems, door panels, flooring and acoustic systems and other interior products.

- Lear's electronic and electrical segment (15.8% of FY2004 revenues, 26.4% of FY2004 EBITDA) includes electronic products and electrical distribution systems, primarily wire harnesses and junction boxes; interior control and entertainment systems; and wireless systems.

Exhibit 16: Lear Corp. Product and Service Offerings

Product or Service	Description
People-Vehicle-Interface Methodology	Part of total interior integration: Lear will conduct consumer research of a target segment, apply industrial design, conduct technical analysis, engineer, conduct manufacturing process development to save time and lower costs, and certify products in the "validation" stage
Seating Systems	Lear produces seating systems for cars and light trucks that are fully assembled and prepared for installation. Lear's seats include manual and power features including lumbar supports, cushion and back bolsters and leg and thigh supports
Flooring and Acoustic Systems	Lear's Sonotec products include processes, technologies and products that provide solutions for automotive noise, vibration and harshness (NVH). Lear's applications range from engine side treatments, dash and wheelhouse insulators to floor and truck systems.
Door Panels and Trim	Specific components in this product segment include vinyl or cloth-covered appliques, arm rests, radio speaker grilles, map pocket compartments, carpet and sound-reducing insulation
Instrument Panels and Cockpit Systems	Instrument panels consist of complex coverings and foam, plastic and metal parts designed to house various components and act as a safety device. Cockpit systems include the instrument panel trim & pad, structural subsystem, electrical distribution system, climate control, driver control pedals, steering controls and passenger safety systems.
Overhead Systems	Headliners, lighting, visors, consoles, wiring and electronics that are located in the interior of the vehicle roof.
Electronic and electrical products	Wiring, electronics and switch/control products to integrate the overall electrical architecture of the vehicle.

Source: Company Reports

Corporate Structure

Exhibit 17: Lear Corp. Corporate Structure at 7/2/05 [1]

1. Lear Corp's Non-Guarantors generated 66.2% of its sales and 95.3% of its EBIT for LTM 7/2/2005. Excluding the $313.9 million EBIT loss for the Parent, Non-Guarantors generated 56.4% of EBIT.
2. Pro forma for $400 million term loan completed in August 2005
3. Tangible Assets include Equity Investments and Receivables in Affiliates
Source: Company Reports and Wachovia Securities' Estimates

Company History

Lear was founded in 1917 as American Metal Products, a Detroit manufacturer of tubular, welded and stamped assemblies for the automotive and aircraft industries. The modern company is the successor to the seat frame manufacturing business that, from its inception, served as a supplier to GM and Ford. In 1988, the company, formerly known as Lear Seating Corp., was taken private in a leveraged buyout transaction.

On Nov. 1, 1993, Lear significantly expanded its operations by acquiring certain segments of Ford Motor Co.'s NA seat cover and seat systems business for approximately $173 million in cash and $11 million in notes payable (approximately a 3.4x EBITDA multiple). This business consisted of an integrated U.S. and Mexican operation that produced seat covers for approximately 80% of Ford's NA production in 1993. As a result of this acquisition, Lear entered into a five-year supply agreement with Ford, becoming Ford's leading seat systems supplier.

On April 6, 1994, Lear Seating Corp. completed an initial public offering of 9.4 million shares at a price of $15.5/share. The proceeds were used to repay a portion of the company's credit facilities that were tapped to fund the acquisition of Ford's seat cover and seat systems business.

From 1994 to 2004, Lear made significant acquisitions that grew the company's revenues from $3.1 billion to $17.0 billion. These acquisitions are outlined in Exhibit 18. As a result of the expansion of the company's business from automotive seat systems to products for a vehicle's complete interior, the company changed its name to "Lear Corporation" from "Lear Seating Corporation" on May 9, 1996.

On Aug. 16, Lear filed an 8-K stating it was interested in pursuing a joint venture with Collins & Aikman. We expect this action to follow the divestiture of a large portion of its interiors businesses. Currently, interiors are Lear's lowest margin business, and the company had previously announced its intentions to divest some of its underperforming interior components operations. The new joint venture would require the two companies to contribute some or all of their respective interiors businesses into the newly formed entity. Lear believes the joint venture will help create an interior supplier large enough to command pricing power, especially for products like carpet and door panels. With a less integrated supplier base, the OEs are able to force price concessions, despite higher input prices for resin and steel.

We do not expect Lear's actions will require capital, as the company intends to find a private equity backer to finance a portion of the transaction, with Lear contributing assets. In fact, as Lear desires to retain less than 50% ownership, the company may receive some cash proceeds for its asset contribution. However, we estimate the absence of the majority of the EBITDA generated by Lear's interiors segment will boost leverage by 0.6x (see Exhibit 12 on page 13).

Exhibit 18: Lear Corp. Corporate Timeline

Date	Company Action	Business	Purchase/Sale Price	Sales Multiple[1]	Commentary
Jul-04	Acquired GHW Grote & Hartmann GmbH	Electronic Parts Distribution	$160.2 million, including assumed debt of $86.3 million	0.8x	75% of company's sales are in Europe, 15% in North America; Employed about 1,900 and had production facilities in 6 countries; main customers were VW, BMW, Ford, Opel, DCX, Renault, MAN and PSA
Jun-00	Sold Sealants & Rubber Business to GSC Industries, Inc.	Sealants and foam rubber	$92.5 million in cash	0.9x	Sold the business to focus on the company's main products; segment had 600 employees
Sep-99	Acquires 100% of Lear-Donnelly Overhead Systems (JV between Lear and Donnelly Corp.)	Headliners, sun visors, lighting & overhead consoles	NA	NA	The 50/50 JV was formed in 1997
Jun-99	Divests electric motor systems segment to Johnson Electric Holdings Ltd.	Industrial and automotive electric motors and starter motors for small gasoline engines	$310 million	0.9x	Used proceeds from sale to pay down debt under credit facilities; segment had 3,300 employees and locations in 10 countries
May-99	Acquires UT Automotive, Inc. from United Technologies Corp.	Electronics, wiring, interior systems	$2.3 billion in cash	0.8x	UT Automotive had 46,000 employees and 145 locations
Apr-99	Acquired Peregrine Windsor, Inc.	Seat Assemblies & Door Panels	NA	NA	Facility produced seat assemblies and door panels for General Motors; sales of $420 million
Feb-99	Sold acoustical insulation manufacturing and molding operation to Jason, Inc.	Acoustical Insulation	NA	NA	Based in Colne, England
Feb-99	Acquired Polovat & Ovatex	Flooring & Acoustic Products	NA	NA	The acquired operations had three plants in Poland, two plants in Italy and employed over 600 people. Annual sales of $45 million; supplier to Fiat and Daewoo.
Jan-99	Acquired a seating business from Hyundai Motor Co.	Seating	$87 million	0.4x	Seating business was about 3% of Hyundai's sales; had 605 employees
Sep-98	Delphi's Seat Business	Seat Production	$247 million ($.5 million of debt assumed)	NA	Seating business had 16 facilities in 10 countries
May-98	Acquired the A.W. Chapman Ltd. and A.W. Chapman Belgium nv subsidiaries of the Rodd Group Ltd.	Seat Mechanisms	NA	NA	The Chapman companies employed 600 and produced seat tracks, mechanisms & seat height adjustors, primarily for Ford Europe; companies had $70 million in revenues
May-98	Gruppo Pianfei S.r.L & Strapazzini Resine S.r.L.	Door panels, headliners, plastic interior components	NA	NA	NA
Aug-97	ITT Automotive Seat Sub-Systems Unit	Integrators of seat-back technology with seat adjuster systems	NA	NA	ITT had 1996 sales of $115 million
Jul-97	Keiper Car Seating GmbH & Co. KG	Seat Systems	$235 million	0.4x	Company had over 2,000 employees; significant customers included Mercedes, Audi, and VW; 1996 sales of $615 million
Jun-97	Acquired Dunlop Cox Ltd. From BTR Plc	Manual and electrically-powered seating mechanisms	$56.8 million in cash	1.4x	Dunlop had 400 employees and 1996 sales of $39.2 million; 4th largest seat mechanisms producer in Europe
1997	Empetek Autodily S.R.O.	Overhead systems	NA	NA	NA
Dec-96	Borealis Industrier AB	Instrument panels, door panels, climate systems, exterior trim & various components for the European auto & truck industry	$91.1 million	NA	Increased Lear's presence in the Western European market and strengthened its relationships with Volvo, Saab & Scania
Jul-96	Masland Corp.	Floor systems, acoustical products & luggage compartment trim	$473.8 million	NA	As a result of this acquisition, Lear held a 40% share of the floor and acoustic systems market in the US
May-96	Company changed its name to Lear Corp. from Lear Seating Corp.	NA	NA	NA	Name change was a result of the expansion from auto seats to products for vehicle's complete interior
Aug-95	Automotive Industries- AI	High-quality interior systems & under-hood components	NA	NA	As a result of this acquisition, Lear became one of the largest independent Tier I suppliers of automotive interior systems
Apr-94	Lear goes public	NA	NA	NA	Offered 9.4 million shares at $15.50

1. Wachovia Securities' Calculations
Source: Company Reports, Bloomberg L.P., and Wachovia Securities

Management

Robert E. Rossiter.   Mr. Rossiter has been Lear's Chairman and Chief Executive Officer since January 2003 and has served as our Chief Executive Officer since October 2000. Prior to his post as CEO, Mr. Rossiter served as President of Lear from 1984-Dec. 2002, as the company's COO from 1998-April 1997, and as the COO of Lear's International Operations from April 1997-Nov. 1998.

David C. Wajsgras. Mr. Wajsgras has served as Lear's Senior Vice President and Chief Financial Officer since January 2002. Prior to serving as CFO, Mr. Wajsgras was Lear's Vice President and Corporate Controller from Sept. 1999-Jan. 2002. Prior to joining Lear, Mr. Wajsgras served as Corporate Controller of Engelhard Corporation from Sept. 1997-Aug. 1999. He also was employed in various senior financial positions at AlliedSignal Inc. (now Honeywell International Inc.), including Chief Financial Officer of the Global Shared Services organization, from Mar. 1992-Sept. 1997.

Recent Results

Exhibit 19: Lear Corp. Recent Results

($ millions)	Q3 2004	Q3 2005	% Change	LTM 10/1/05
Sales	3,897.8	3,986.6	2.3%	16,978.0
EBITDA	**247.4**	**129.0**	**-47.9%**	**733.5**
EBITDA Margin	6.3%	3.2%	-310 bps	4.3%
Interest Coverage	**5.7x**	**2.9x**		**4.0x**
Leverage	**2.5x**	**4.5x**		**3.2x**
Net Leverage	2.0x	4.3x		3.0x

Source: Company reports.

For its fiscal Q3 ended Oct. 1, Lear Corp.'s total sales increased 2.3% year-over-year to $4.0 billion, as negative platform mix (a negative impact of $331 million) was offset by the addition of new business ($387 million) and favorable foreign exchange ($33 million). The gross margin fell 366 bps to 6.8%, due to unfavorable mix, commodity inflation (particularly for resins and chemicals which spiked even more after the recent hurricanes in the Gulf region) and restructuring actions (totaling $105 million). SG&A expenses as a percentage of sales fell 55 bps to 3.6%. Due to the decline in gross margin, Q3 EBITDA dropped 47.9% year-over-year to $129.0 million. LTM EBITDA of $733.5 million resulted in coverage and leverage of 4.0x and 3.2x, respectively.

Financial Condition

At Oct. 1, 2005, Lear had cash and marketable securities of $135.4 million, an increase of $2.5 million sequentially, as cash used in operations sapped up cash generated from Lear's $400 million term loan completed in August. We calculate that covenant-constrained liquidity under Lear's $1.7 billion revolver was $544.2 million at quarter-end. The company had $2.3 billion in debt, a sequential increase of $448.8 million, primarily due to the issuance of the term loan.

Exhibit 20: Lear Corp. Financial Summary

($ millions)	FYE 12/31/98	FYE 12/31/99	FYE 12/31/00	FYE 12/31/01	FYE 12/31/02	FYE 12/31/03	FYE 12/31/04	Q3 10/02/04	Q3 10/01/05	% Chg.	LTM 10/01/05	FYE 12/31/05E	FYE 12/31/06E
Revenue	9,059.4	12,428.8	14,072.8	13,624.7	14,424.6	15,746.7	16,960.0	3,897.8	3,986.6	2.3%	16,978.0	17,106.6	18,133.0
EBITDA	744.1	1,130.8	1,317.5	915.9	1,044.1	1,094.6	1,123.5	247.4	129.0	-47.9%	733.5	673.0	950.0
Interest Expense	110.5	235.1	316.2	254.7	210.5	186.6	165.5	43.3	45.1		182.0	186.1	195.0
Income Taxes	93.9	174.0	197.3	68.7	157.0	153.7	128.0	14.1	0.0		129.7	105.2	54.2
Capital Expenditures	351.4	391.4	322.3	267.0	272.6	375.6	429.0	91.1	135.2		559.6	564.3	520.0
Dividends	0.0	0.0	0.0	0.0	0.0	0.0	68.0	13.5	16.8		62.0	65.4	67.2
Net Acquisitions/Cash Restructuring	332.2	2,168.6	(105.1)	(50.6)	(7.3)	(20.0)	46.7	23.6	21.1		(26.8)	99.0	134.4
Changes in Working Capital	21.7	(42.6)	(141.5)	(296.5)	122.9	229.1	166.3	(45.6)	271.1		(50.6)	22.9	150.0
Free Cash Flow	(165.6)	(1,795.7)	728.3	672.6	288.4	169.6	120.0	107.4	(360.3)		(122.4)	(369.0)	(170.8)
EBITDA Margin	8.2%	9.1%	9.4%	6.7%	7.2%	7.0%	6.6%	6.3%	3.2%	-311 bps	4.3%	3.9%	5.2%
EBITDA/(Interest Expense)	6.7x	4.8x	4.2x	3.6x	5.0x	5.9x	6.8x	5.7x	2.9x		4.0x	3.6x	4.9x
EBITDA-Capex/(Interest)	3.6	3.1	3.1	2.5	3.7	3.9	4.2	3.6	(0.1)		1.0	0.6	2.2
Cash & Equivalents	30.0	106.9	98.8	87.6	91.7	169.3	584.9	501.6	135.4		135.4	135.4	135.4
Borrowing Capacity	1,070.0	1,548.0	1,843.9	1,447.0	2,033.0	1,946.0	1,648.0	1,655.0	544.2		544.2	279.5	617.1
Short-term Liquidity	1,100.0	1,654.9	1,942.7	1,534.6	2,124.7	2,115.3	2,232.9	2,156.6	679.6		679.6	414.9	752.5
Total Debt	1,562.6	3,492.0	3,080.1	2,486.6	2,174.0	2,074.3	2,535.1	2,490.8	2,341.8		2,341.8	2,454.3	2,669.2
Shareholders Equity	1,300.0	1,465.3	1,600.8	1,559.1	1,662.3	2,257.5	2,730.1	2,512.6	1,758.7		1,758.7	1,779.1	1,863.9
Net Debt/EBITDA	2.1	3.0	2.3	2.6	2.0	1.7	1.7	2.0	4.3		3.0	3.4	2.7
Total Debt/EBITDA	2.1x	3.1x	2.3x	2.7x	2.1x	1.9x	2.3x	2.5x	4.5x		3.2x	3.6x	2.8x
Shares Outstanding	68.0	67.7	65.8	65.3	71.3	73.3	74.7				67.2	67.1	67.1
Share Price	$38.50	$32.00	$24.81	$38.14	$33.28	$61.33	$61.01				$28.80	$28.80	$28.80
Equity Market Capital	2,618.9	2,167.8	1,633.7	2,490.7	2,372.5	4,498.3	4,559.1				1,935.4	1,932.5	1,932.5
Net Debt	1,532.6	3,385.1	2,981.3	2,399.0	2,082.3	1,905.0	1,950.2				2,206.4	2,318.9	2,533.8
Total Enterprise Value (TEV)	$4,151.5	$5,552.9	$4,615.0	$4,889.7	$4,454.8	$6,403.3	$6,509.3				$4,141.8	$4,251.4	$4,466.3
TEV/EBITDA	5.6x	4.9x	3.5x	5.3x	4.3x	5.8x	5.8x				5.6x	6.3x	4.7x

Capital Structure ($ in millions) as of 10/1//2005[1]

Cash	135.4
Availability	544.2
Revolver	$100.0
Term Loan due 2007	$400.0
5.75% Senior Notes, due 2014	$399.2
0-Coupon Convertible Senior Notes, due 2022	$293.2
8.125% Senior Notes, due 2008 (Eurodollar)	$301.4
8.11% Senior Notes, due 2009	$800.0
Other/ Current Debt/ Capital Lease	48.0
Total Debt	2341.8
Common Equity	1,758.7
Total Capital	4100.5

Debt Maturities ($ in millions) as of Dec. 31, 2004[3]

	Long-term Debt	Operating Leases
FYE 2005	668.2	88.4
2006	6.8	97.5
2007	9.2	59.2
2008	342.3	51.6
2009	805.4	39.9
Thereafter	703.2	113.0
	2,535.1	449.6

Bank Facility

Admin. Agent	BAS, JPM	BAS, JPM
Type	Revolver	Term Loan
Security	Secured by Capital Stock of Subs	Secured by Capital Stock of Subs
Amount	$1.7 billion	$400 million
Maturity	3/23/10	2/11/07
Rate	LIBOR + 150 bps	LIBOR + 150 bps
Ratings	NA/NA	
Covenants: Interest Coverage Ratio >= 3.5x		
Leverage Ratio[4] <= 3.25:1 for Q2 2005; 3.75:1 for Q3 2005-Q4 2005; 3.5:1 for Q1 2006; and 3.25:1 for Q2 2006 and thereafter		

Equity Ownership

AXA Financial, Inc.	15.1%
Wellington Management Co., LLP	6.4%
All Directors and executive officers as a group	1.0%

1. The 0% Convertible Notes are convertible into 7.5204 shares at a price/share of $52, convertible until 2/20/2022. The notes are callable and putable starting on 2/20/07.
2. The Leverage Ratio is defined as Net Debt (debt includes Receivables Financing Transactions over $500 million) to EBITDA (excludes OPEB expenses).
3. $600 million of notes matured in Q2 2005.
Source: Company Reports and Wachovia Securities' Estimates

Exhibit 21: Lear Corp. Quarterly Financial Summary

WACHOVIA SECURITIES

($millions)	Q4 12/31/04	Q1 4/02/05	Q2 7/02/05	Q3 10/01/05	LTM 10/01/05	Q3 12/31/05E	Q4 3/31/06E	Q1 6/30/06E	Q2 9/30/06E	LTM 9/30/06E
Revenue	4,286.1	4,286.0	4,419.3	3,986.6	16,978.0	4,414.7	4,543.2	4,684.5	4,225.8	17,868.1
EBITDA	313.9	143.3	147.3	129.0	733.5	253.4	215.7	271.7	202.8	943.6
Total Interest Expense	43.9	44.8	48.2	45.1	182.0	48.0	49.0	49.0	49.0	195.0
Taxes	36.5	63.5	29.7	0.0	129.7	12.0	5.0	26.8	0.0	43.7
Working Capital Use/(Source)	(23.5)	13.6	(311.8)	271.1	(50.6)	50.0	200.0	150.0	(125.0)	275.0
Capital Expenditures	145.3	129.4	149.7	135.2	559.6	150.0	130.0	130.0	130.0	540.0
Dividends	13.4	16.8	15.0	16.8	62.0	16.8	16.8	16.8	16.8	67.2
Net Acquisitions/Cash Restructuring	-50.8	0	2.9	21.1	(26.8)	75.0	33.6	33.6	33.6	175.8
Free Cash Flow	**149.1**	**(124.8)**	**213.6**	**(360.3)**	**(122.4)**	**(98.4)**	**(218.6)**	**(134.5)**	**98.4**	**(353.1)**
EBITDA Margin	7.3%	3.3%	3.3%	3.2%	44.0%	5.7%	4.7%	5.8%	4.8%	5.3%
EBITDA/Total Interest	**7.2x**	**3.2x**	**3.1x**	**2.9x**	**4.0x**	**5.3x**	**4.4x**	**5.5x**	**4.1x**	**4.8x**
EBITDA – Capex/Total Interest	7.7x	2.9x	9.5x	-3.2x	4.3x	4.2x	0.3x	2.5x	6.7x	3.4x
Cash and Equivalents	584.9	525.6	132.9	135.4	135.4	135.4	135.4	135.4	135.4	135.4
Borrowing Capacity	1,648.0	1,356.1	1,150.1	544.2	544.2	279.5	141.6	204.3	530.3	530.3
Short-Term Liquidity	2,232.9	1,881.7	1,283.0	679.6	679.6	414.9	277.0	339.7	665.7	665.7
Total Debt	2,535.1	2,522.5	1,893.0	2,341.8	2,341.8	2,454.3	2,678.8	2,829.5	2,737.5	2,737.5
Shareholders' Equity	2,730.1	2,651.9	2,520.6	1,758.7	1,758.7	1,779.1	1,786.8	1,828.7	1,828.6	1,828.6
Total Capitalization	5,265.2	5,174.4	4,413.6	4,100.5	4,100.5	4,233.4	4,465.6	4,658.2	4,566.1	4,566.1
Net Debt/EBITDA	1.6x	3.5x	3.0x	4.3x	3.0x	2.3x	2.9x	2.5x	3.2x	2.8x
Total Debt/EBITDA	**2.0x**	**4.4x**	**3.2x**	**4.5x**	**3.2x**	**2.4x**	**3.1x**	**2.6x**	**3.4x**	**2.9x**
Total Debt/Capital	48.1%	48.7%	42.9%	57.1%	57.1%	58.0%	60.0%	60.7%	60.0%	60.0%

Source: Company Reports and Wachovia Securities.

479

Model Assumptions

Exhibit 22: Model Assumptions for Lear Corp.

($million)	Impact on EBITDA	Assumption
Q4 2004 EBITDA	313.9	
New Business Wins and Acquisition Revenues	60.0	Expect $0.3 billion in incremental new sales and acquisition revenue in Q4 2005. Estimate a 20% contribution margin
Lower Production Volumes, Unfavorable Mix & Price Concessions	(37.2)	Estimate Q4 production for GM up 2%, Ford down 4% and other up 1%. Estimate 3% price concession and 30% contribution margin
Commodity price increases (steel, resin)	(3.8)	Estimate resin prices (assume 10% of COGS) increase by 35% and steel prices (assume 15% of COGS) decline 22.5% and 80% pass through to customers
Cash Restructuring	(75.0)	80% of total restructuring is cash
Higher healthcare and R&D expenses	(4.5)	Ramp up for new business
Q4 2005 EBITDA	253.4	
Q1-Q3 2005 EBITDA[1]	419.6	
2005 Estimated EBITDA[1]	673.0	
New Business Wins	270.0	Expect $1.35 billion in incremental new sales and acquisition revenue in FY2006. Estimate 20% contribution margin
Higher Production Volumes offset by Price Concessions and Unfavorable Mix	(158.4)	Estimate FY 2006 production for GM down 3%, Ford down 2% and other up 3%. Estimate 3% price concessions and a 30% contribution margin
Commodity price increases (steel, resin)	126.4	Estimate resin prices (assume 10% of COGS) increase by 8% and steel prices (assume 15% of COGS) decline 12%. Assume 80% pass through to customers
Cost Savings From Restructuring and other Cost Cuts	154.0	Assume company benefits for half year from cutting 7,700 employees at $40,000/year (wages and benefits). Company expects payback from restructuring in 2-3 years.
Litigation Expenses	30.0	Non-recurring charge from FY2005
Cash Restructuring	(134.4)	80% of total restructuring is cash
Higher healthcare and R&D expenses	(10.5)	Ramp up for new business
2006 Estimated EBITDA[1]	950.0	

1. EBITDA as adjusted for non-cash restructuring and impairment charges. Does not include certain add-backs for calculation of bank-defined EBITDA.
Source: Company reports, AutoNews, Bloomberg L.P. and Wachovia Securities' estimates.

Industry Recommendation: Maintaining Market Weight

Our current sector recommendation on the auto suppliers is market weight. We continue to see more selected opportunities in the space as our high-yield supplier index trades 672 bps wide to the high-yield market versus 25 bps wide at the beginning of January 2005 and 29 bps tight at the end of June 2004.

On a fundamental front, we believe that beginning in Q4, auto suppliers' cash flows will improve versus the previous year's results due to waning metal prices, better raw material recoveries, net new business and firming production schedules. We expect production rates to improve due to extremely lean inventory levels, important 2006 product launches and easy year over year comparisons. Although we are becoming more positive towards the sector, we are cautiously optimistic as we believe there are high expectations toward a 2006 recovery. Until we feel the market is entering into a solid fundamental position, we favor suppliers with revenue streams that are not principally tied to North American domestic vehicle production (i.e., non–North American production or exposure to commercial vehicles, heavy trucks and the aftermarket segment).

Still, we view the current Delphi labor talks as the biggest concern facing the industry. Although we expect strike rhetoric to intensify over the next three months, we continue to estimate the probability of a prolonged strike or major supply disruption at 40%, or less likely than a smooth transition. Through many conversations with the rank-and-file, we have become more convinced that the workers ultimately have to help preserve the value of the entities (GM and DPH) providing their post-retirement pension and other benefits. Our belief that these workers will act on behalf of their benefits leads us to conclude that an agreement involving dramatic paycuts and plant closures is achievable.

In summary, we believe the auto sector represents relative value versus the market. In our opinion, the sector's downgrade and bankruptcy cycle has peaked and most suppliers' liquidity profiles are sufficient. Furthermore, we expect the upcoming resolution to the union negotiations and selected restructurings (Ford, GM, DPH, VC, ARM, DCN and LEA) to be viewed as positive by investors. We would advise investors to take exposure in bonds that have yet to fully recover to prior levels and still trade around distressed values. However, we reiterate our market weight recommendation due to strike risk and weakened U.S. consumers' disposable income due to higher fuel, heating bills and installment debt expenses.

Competition

Delphi Corp. (DPH) Delphi is the second largest automotive supplier (based on FY2004 sales), designs and manufactures vehicle electronics, transportation components, integrated systems and modules and other electronic technology. The company currently has an expansive network of manufacturing sites, technical centers, sales offices and joint ventures in every major region of the world. For LTM 6/30/05, Delphi reported net sales of $27.6 billion and EBITDA of $260.0 million, which resulted in LTM leverage and net leverage of 15.1x and 11.3x, respectively.

Johnson Controls, Inc. (JCI) Johnson Controls supplies seating; instrument panels; overhead; floor consoles and door systems, including electronics; and batteries for more than 35 million vehicles annually. It also conducts business through its Control Group, which is a market leader in providing installed building control systems and technical and facility management services, including comfort, energy and security management for the nonresidential buildings market. For LTM June 30, Johnson Controls reported net sales of $28.4 billion and EBITDA of $1.8 billion, which resulted in LTM leverage and net leverage of 1.1x and 0.9x, respectively.

Robert Bosch GmbH. With headquarters in Germany, Bosch supplies antilock braking, fuel-injection systems, automotive electronics, starters and alternators for OEMs around the world. The company also produces industrial machinery and hand tools and owns 50% of Bosch-Siemens Hausgerate, a European appliance maker. Bosch, in its Blaupunkt unit, is a major manufacturer of vehicle audio equipment, and the Rexroth subsidiary makes electric, hydraulic and pneumatic machinery for applications ranging from automotive to mining. About 92% of the company is owned by Robert Bosch Stiftung, a charitable organization, and the Bosch family owns 7%.

Valeo SA. Valeo manufactures components, integrated systems and modules for cars and trucks. The company employed 72,100 workers at July 21, 2005 and had 130 production sites, 68 R&D centers, and 9 distribution platforms in 28 countries. Valeo's FY2004 revenue of 9.4 billion euros was split among electrical and electronic systems (50%), thermal systems (27%), aftermarket (18%) and transmissions (5%).

Visteon Corp. (VC) Visteon is a global supplier of automotive systems, modules and components to global vehicle manufacturers and the automotive aftermarket. Visteon and its joint ventures have a network of 136 manufacturing sites and 71 technical centers/sales offices in 25 countries worldwide. Visteon primarily operates in two business segments: Automotive Operations (97% of sales in fiscal 2004) and Glass Operations (3% of sales). Visteon's Automotive Operations supply automotive systems, modules and components in the following product areas: climate control, interior, exterior, powertrain, chassis and electronics. Visteon's LTM 9/30/05 sales of $18.8 billion and EBITDA of $287.0 million resulted in leverage and net leverage of 6.8x and 3.7x, respectively.

TRW Automotive, Inc. TRW supplies automotive systems, modules and components to global OEMs. TRW has leading market positions in its primary business lines, which encompass the design, manufacture and sale of active and passive safety-related products. Active safety-related products primarily refer to vehicle dynamic controls (such as braking and steering), and passive safety-related products principally referred to as occupant restraints (e.g., airbags and seat belts). About 85% of TRW's net sales are made directly to OEMs, and 7% of its products are sold in the aftermarket. For LTM 9/30/05, TRW reported net sales of $12.7 billion and EBITDA of $1.1 billion, which resulted in LTM leverage and net leverage of 2.6x and 2.4x, respectively.

WACHOVIA SECURITIES

Financial Summary ($millions)

($millions)	ArvinMeritor, Inc. (ARM)	Collins & Aikman Corp. (CKC)	Cooper Standard Automotive, Inc. (COOPER)	Dana, Corp. (DCN)[2]	Delphi, Corp. (DPH)[3]	Dura Operating Corp (DRRA)[5]	Lear Corp. (LEA)	Metaldyne, Corp. (METALD)	Remy Int'l Inc. (RMY)	Tenneco Automotive, Inc. (TEN)	Tower Automotive, Inc. (TWR)	TRW Automotive, Inc. (TRW)	Visteon Corp. (VC)	Average
Sales	8791.0	3960.4	1840.9	9534.0	27560.0	2362.5	16978.0	2169.1	1104.0	4448.0	3453.0	12693.0	18806.0	8744.1
EBITDA	406.0	338.3	170.6	508.0	260.0	170.9	733.5	217.6	83.5	412.0	262.2	1071.0	287.0	376.3
EBITDA Margin	4.6%	8.5%	9.3%	5.3%	0.9%	7.2%	4.3%	10.0%	7.6%	9.3%	7.6%	8.4%	1.5%	4.3%
Operating Profit	256.0	95.9	77.6	20.0	-1272.0	86.8	262.4	49.7	57.2	192.0	82.0	463.0	-357.0	-20.2
Operating Profit Margin	2.9%	2.4%	4.2%	0.2%	-4.6%	3.7%	1.5%	2.3%	5.2%	4.3%	2.4%	3.6%	-1.9%	-0.2%
Interest Expense	119.0	167.4	96.6	163.0	250.3	97.2	182.0	86.8	53.0	172.0	140.4	240.0	143.0	149.3
Capital Expenditures	146.0	201.8	57.2	317.0	1,092.0	67.9	559.6	145.5	35.4	143.0	131.4	526.0	676.0	329.4
Free Cash Flow	141.0	-30.9	16.8	28.0	-1082.3	5.8	-8.1	-14.7	-4.9	97.0	-8.6	305.0	-532.0	-102.4
EBITDA/Total Interest Expense	3.4x	2.0x	1.8x	3.1x	1.0x	1.8x	4.0x	2.5x	1.6x	2.4x	1.9x	4.5x	2.0x	2.4x
(EBITDA-Capex)/Interest Expense	2.2x	0.8x	1.2x	1.2x	-3.3x	1.1x	1.0x	0.8x	0.8x	1.6x	0.9x	2.3x	0.9x	0.5x
Total Debt/EBITDA	3.7x	4.7x	5.3x	4.3x	22.2x	6.9x	3.2x	4.6x	8.5x	3.5x	3.0x	2.6x	6.8x	5.0x
Bank Defined Leverage	NA	4.6x	4.5x	NA	NA	NA	NA	NA	NA	NA	NA	NA	NA	4.5x
Secured Leverage Ratio	0.3x	1.5x	2.1x	0.4x	10.6x	0.9x	0.7x	1.9x	2.5x	NA	3.0x	1.3x	1.9x	2.4x
(Total Obligations)/EBITDAR	5.0x	5.0x	5.5x	5.1x	24.8x	7.0x	3.9x	5.9x	8.7x	4.1x	8.0x	3.1x	8.4x	6.4x
TEV / EBITDA	6.4x	NA	NA	7.4x	28.4x	6.8x	6.1x	NA	NA	5.2x	5.0x	5.0x	6.6x	9.4x
Market Capitalization	1249.3	NA	NA	2257.2	2610.0	75.2	2362.8	NA	NA	798.5	NA	2678.6	775.9	1668.4
Cash	180.0	3.5	66.8	651.0	988.0	93.7	135.4	0.0	21.6	89.0	51.6	317.0	823.0	270.1
Availability	135.3	179.0	112.4	194.0	247.0	157.0	544.2	107.1	66.0	351.0	0.0	837.0	204.0	249.9
Liquidity	315.3	182.5	179.2	845.0	1,235.0	250.7	679.6	107.1	87.6	440.0	51.6	1,154.0	1,027.0	519.9

Capital Structure

	ARM	CKC	COOPER	DCN	DPH	DRRA	LEA	METALD	RMY	TEN	TWR	TRW	VC	Average
Revolver	0.0	59.4	0.0	0.0	1500.0	0.0	0.0	50.0	71.8	55.0	533.3	0.0	300.0	214.1
Term Loan	0.0	400.0	346.2	0.0	1000.0	147.8	400.0	350.6	0.0	832.0	0.0	1293.0	250.0	418.3
Capital Leases and other	118.0	35.3	8.6	211.0	263.0	0.0	99.3	20.1	16.0	42.0	259.8	87.0	0.0	86.8
Senior Notes	1355.0	500.0	200.0	1597.0	2000.0	401.4	1792.8	150.0	270.0	500.0	0.0	972.0	1177.0	622.0
Subordinated Notes	0.0	400.3	350.0	0.0	412.0	575.4	0.0	277.3	313.9	0.0	0.0	479.0	0.0	407.9
Convertible Notes	0.0	193.3	0.0	0.0	0.0	0.0	0.0	0.0	0.0	0.0	0.0	0.0	0.0	0.0
Preferred Equity	0.0	0.0	0.0	0.0	0.0	55.3	0.0	160.2	0.0	0.0	0.0	0.0	0.0	34.1
Other	39.0	0.0	0.0	370.0	588.0	0.0	48.7	0.0	36.1	0.0	0.0	0.0	228.0	110.3
Total Debt	1512.0	1588.3	904.8	2178.0	5763.0	1179.9	2341.8	1008.3	707.7	1429.0	793.1	2831.0	1955.0	1890.0
Accounts Receivables Securitization	156.0	160.7	0.0	110.0	250.0	0.0	279.0	101.9	40.0	97.0	0.0	0.0	62.0	93.4
Operating Leases	71.0	357.9	48.0	402.0	507.0	92.7	449.6	357.0	57.0	45.0	45.0	212.0	232.0	250.9
Total Unfunded Pension Obligations[4]	469.0	106.9	67.7	354.0	4346.0	64.8	236.3	101.9	245.0	245.0	108.1	599.0	870.0	593.2
Liabilities Subject to Compromise	0.0	NA	0.0	0.0	NA	0.0	0.0	0.0	0.0	0.0	1192.9	0.0	0.0	0.0
Total Obligations	2208.0	2213.8	1020.5	3044.0	10866.0	1337.4	3306.7	1569.1	823.2	1816.0	2094.0	3642.0	3139.0	2827.5

Customer Mix (FY2004)

	ARM	CKC	COOPER	DCN	DPH	DRRA	LEA	METALD	RMY	TEN	TWR	TRW	VC	Average
Big 3 Exposure	42%	75%	70%	36%	61%	39%	67%	67%	28%	42%	64%	43%	70%	55%
International Sales (Non NA)	48%	27%	35%	43%	31%	41%	56%	21%	20%	54%	29%	63%	33%	38%
Aftermarket Sales	NA	NA	NA	NA	5%	NA	NA	NA	54%	24%	NA	7%	6%	19%

Customer detail:
- ARM: DCX 19%, GM 13%, Ford 10%, VW 10%
- CKC: DCX 28%, Ford 25%, GM 22%
- COOPER: Ford 35%, GM 21%, DCX 14%
- DCN: F 25%, GM 11%
- DPH: GM 54%, Ford 4%, Renault Nissan 3%, VW 3%, DCX 3%
- DRRA: Ford 19%, GM 12%, Lear 11%, VW 9%, DCX 8%, RV 15%
- LEA: GM 31%, Ford 24%, DCX 12%
- METALD: DCX 33%, Ford 22%, GM 12%
- RMY: GM 28%, Int'l Truck 10%
- TEN: GM 18%, Ford 12%, VW 11%, DCX 8%
- TWR: Ford 35%, DCX 19%, GM 10%, Hyundai/Kia 9%, VW 5%, Fiat 4%, Toyota 3%
- TRW: Ford 17%, DCX 15%, VW 14%, GM 11%
- VC: Ford 70%

Product Mix (FY2004)

- ARM: Emissions 33%, Aperture Sys 18%, Undercarriage Sys 9%, Undercarriage and Drivetrain 9%, Systems for Commercial 34%, Specialty Sys 6%
- CKC: US & Mex. Plastics 34%, Int'l Plastics 32%, Global Soft Trim 34%
- COOPER: Sealing 47%, Fluid 34%, Noise, Vibration & Harshness 19%
- DCN: Axle 43%, Driveshaft 14%, Fluid Systems 9%, Structural 12%, Bearings & Sealing 10%, Other Engine 12%
- DPH: Electronics, Electrical, Safety & Interior 47%; Dynamics, Propulsion, & Thermal 46%; Auto Holdings Group 7%
- DRRA: Driver Control Sys 34%, Glass Control Sys 16%, Seating Control Sys 14%, Structural Door Models 9%, Exterior Trim Systems 7%, Engineered Assemblies 6%, Mobile Products 15%
- LEA: Seating 67%, Interior 17%, Electrical 16%
- METALD: Driveline 39%, Engine 32%, Chassis 29%
- RMY: Electrical Systems 67%, Power Drivetrain 7%, Core Services 6%
- TEN: Emission Control Sys 63%, Ride Control Sys 37%
- TWR: Body Struct/Assembly 43%, Lower Veh Structures 34%, Suspension & Powertrain Modules 12%, Suspension Components 8%
- TRW: Steering gears & sys 16.5%, Airbags 13.9%, Foundation brakes 13.3%, ABS & other brake Sys 8.9%, Seat belts 8.2%, Chassis Modules 5.3%, Linkage & Suspension 5.2%, Other 28.7%
- VC: Chassis Pdts & Sys 25%, Interior Pdts & Sys 21%, Climate Control Pdts & Sys 22%, Powertrain Pdts & Sys 18%, Electronic Pdts & Sys 12%, Exterior Pdts & Sys 5%, Glass Products 3%

1. CKC results are as of 9/30/04. ARM, COOPER, DCN, DPH, METALD, RMY, TWR results are as of 6/30/05.
2. Accounts for DCN on an equity basis other than data for TEV multiples, accounts receivable securitization, OPEB/pension liabilities, and operating leases.
3. Pro forma for DPH $1 billion term loan and $1.5 billion drawdown of $1,825 billion revolver.
4. Pensions are accounted for as of Sept. 30, 2004.

Source: Company reports and Wachovia Securities

Wachovia Securities Automotive Relative Value Analysis as of 11/04/05

Coupon	Issue	Maturity	Ratings	Amt. ($mm)	Bid Price ($)	Current Yield	YTW	YTW Spread	YTW Date	Next Call Date	Next Call Price ($)	CDS Bid/Offer	EBITDA ($mn)	EBITDA Margin	EBITDA/Int. Exp.	EBITDA – Capex/Int. Exp.	Total Debt/EBITDA	Net Debt/EBITDA	TEV/EBITDA
AUTO DEALERS', AUTO PARTS RETAILERS & WHOLESALE PARTS DISTRIBUTORS																			
American Tire Distributors, Inc. (ATD)													Pro Forma LTM 7/2/05						Private Equity: Investcorp S.A.
10.750%	Sr. Notes	4/01/13	Caa2/CCC+	150	95.00	11.32%	11.78%	717	4/01/13	4/01/09	105.38		65.1	4.6%	1.1x	1.0x	7.7x	7.7x	
Notes: The 10.75% Senior Notes were issued on 3/23/2005 at par to yield 10.75% and 622 bps stt.																			
Asbury Automotive Group, Inc. (ABG)													LTM 9/30/05						
9.000%	Sr. Notes	6/15/12	B3/B	250	98.63	9.13%	9.28%	467	6/15/12	6/15/07	104.50		184.1	3.3%	2.6x	1.6x	5.4x	5.3x	8.3x
8.000%	Sr. Sub Notes	3/15/14	B3/B	200	92.38	8.66%	9.33%	470	3/15/14	3/15/09	104.00		r55.9		3.9x		3.2x		6.6x
Notes: The 9% Senior Sub Notes were issued on 5/31/02 at par to yield 9.00% and 397 bps stt. The 8% Senior Sub Notes were issued on 12/18/03 at par to yield 8% and 384 stt. We maintain an outperform recommendation on these bonds.																			
AutoNation, Inc. (AN)													LTM 9/30/05						
9.000%	Sr. Notes	8/01/08	Ba2/BBB-	343	107.50	8.37%	5.99%	147	8/01/08	NC	NC		905.5	4.6%	4.9x	4.1x	2.9x	2.6x	8.4x
Notes: The 9% Senior Notes were issued on 8/1/01 at $98.73 to yield 9.25% and 418 bps stt. We maintain a market recommendation on these bonds.													873.3		9.7x		0.8x		7.1x
CSK Auto Corp. (CAO)													LTM 7/C/105						
7.000%	Sr. Notes	1/15/14	B2/B-	225	93.25	7.51%	8.15%	351	1/15/14	1/15/09	103.50		r50.5	9.5%	2.9x	2.6x	2.9x	2.7x	7.4x
Group 1 Automotive, Inc. (GPI)													LTM 9/30/05						
8.250%	Sr. Sub Notes	8/15/13	B1/B+	150	95.50	8.64%	9.07%	443	8/15/13	8/15/08	104.13		183.9	3.1%	3.3x	2.3x	4.5x	4.3x	7.9x
Notes: The 8.25% Senior Sub. Notes were issued on 8/8/03 at $98.34 to yield 8.5% and 430 bps stt. We maintain an outperform recommendation on these bonds.													148.2		7.5x		1.2x		5.6x
Pep Boys Manny Moe & Jack (PBY)													LTM 7/30/05						
7.500%	Sr. Sub Notes	12/15/14	B3/B-	200	93.00	8.06%	8.63%	397	12/15/14	12/15/09	103.75		37.0	3.9%	2.4x	-1.3x	5.5x	5.0x	13.7x
Notes: The 7.5% Senior Sub. Notes were issued on 12/14/2004 at $100.00 to yield 7.5% and 333 bps stt.																			
Sonic Automotive, Inc. (SAH)													LTM 9/30/05						
8.625%	Sr. Sub Notes	8/15/13	B2/B	275	95.75	9.01%	9.41%	477	8/15/13	8/15/08	104.31		256.5	3.3%	3.1x	1.9x	5.8x	5.8x	9.7x
Notes: The 8.625% Senior Sub. Notes were issued on 8/7/03 at $98.36 to yield 8.875% and 466 bps stt.													2*9.7		4.8x		3.1x		7.7x
A $75 million add-on to the 8.625% Senior Sub. Notes was priced on 11/21/03 at $105.00 to yield 7.9% and 335 bps stt. We maintain a market perform recommendation on these bonds.																			
United Auto Group, Inc. (UAG)													LTM 9/30/05						
9.625%	Sr. Sub Notes	3/15/12	B3/B	300	103.75	9.28%	8.57%	403	3/15/12	3/15/07	104.81		327.1	3.1%	3.2x	1.0x	5.0x	5.0x	9.9x
Notes: The 9.625% Senior Sub. Notes were issued on 3/15/02 at par to yield 9.625% and 432 bps stt. We maintain an outperform recommendation on these bonds.													273.0		5.7x		2.3x		8.1x
Subsector Average					97.19	8.89%	8.91%	430					257.3	4.4%	3.1x	1.7x	4.8x	4.8x	9.0x
HIGH YIELD AUTO SUPPLIERS																			
Accuride Corp. (ACW)													Pro Forma LTM 6/30/05						
8.500%	Sr. Sub Notes	2/01/15	Caa3/B-	275	96.75	8.79%	9.03%	437	2/01/15	2/01/10	104.25		185.7	16.0%	3.4x	2.9x	4.0x	3.8x	6.0x
Collins & Aikman Corp. (CKCR)													LTM 9/3/004						Private Equity: Heartland Industrial Partners, L.P.
10.750%	Sr. Notes	12/31/11	NA	500	48.00	22.40%	29.59%	2,499	12/31/11	12/31/06	105.38		328.3	8.5%	2.0x	0.8x	4.7x	4.7x	
12.875%	Sr. Sub Notes	8/24/12	NA	415	0.00	NA	NA	NA	NA	NC	NC								
Notes: The 12.875% Senior Sub. Notes were issued on 8/12/04 at $96.416 to yield 13.625% and 953 bps stt.																			
Cooper Standard Automotive, Inc. (COOPER)													LTM 6/34/2005						Private Equity: Cypress Group, L.L.C.
7.000%	Sr. Notes	12/15/12	B2/B	200	87.00	8.05%	9.56%	495	12/15/12	12/15/08	103.50		162.9	9.9%	4.7x	3.2x	4.9x	4.6x	
8.375%	Sr. Sub Notes	12/15/14	B3/B	350	76.50	10.95%	12.82%	816	12/15/14	12/15/09	104.19								
Delphi Corp. (DPH)													LTM 6/30/2005						NA
6.550%	Notes	6/15/06	Ca/D	500	66.50	9.85%	90.09%	8,585	6/15/06	NC	NC		260.0	0.9%	1.0x	-3.5x	15.1x	11.3x	
6.500%	Notes	5/01/09	Ca/D	500	64.50	10.08%	21.50%	1,698	5/01/09	NC	NC								
6.500%	Sr. Notes	8/15/13	Ca/D	500	65.80	9.88%	13.81%	918	8/15/13	NC	NC								
7.125%	Debentures	5/01/29	Ca/D	500	64.00	11.13%	11.63%	697	5/01/29	NC	NC								
Notes: We maintain a market perform recommendation on these bonds.																			
Dura Operating Corp. (DRRA)													LTM 10/c/2005						6.7x
9.000%	Sr. Notes	5/01/09	Caa2/CCC+	589	61.00	14.75%	26.96%	2,244	5/01/09	5/01/06	101.50	780/830	170.9	7.2%	1.8x	1.1x	6.9x	6.4x	
8.625%	Sr. Notes	4/15/12	Caa1/B-	400	84.25	10.24%	12.23%	764	4/15/12	4/15/07	104.31								
Notes: We maintain an outperform recommendation on these bonds.																			
Hayes Lemmerz International, Inc.													LTM 7/3/V05						5.0x
10.500%	Sr. Notes	6/15/10	Caa3/B-	163	82.50	12.73%	16.02%	1,145	6/15/10	6/15/07	105.25		165.1	7.0%	2.8x	0.1x	4.4x	4.2x	
Metaldyne, Corp. (METALD)													LTM 6/30/05						Private Equity: Heartland Industrial Partners, L.P.
10.000%	Sr. Notes	11/01/13	Caa1/CCC+	150	89.50	11.17%	12.09%	745	11/01/13	11/01/08	105.00		217.6	10.0%	2.5x	0.8x	4.4x	4.4x	
11.000%	Sr. Sub Notes	6/15/12	Caa2/CCC+	250	74.00	14.86%	17.86%	1,324	6/15/12	6/15/07	105.50								
Remy International, Inc. (RMY)													LTM 6/30/05						Private Equity: Citicorp Venture Capital Ltd.
8.625%	Sr. Notes	12/15/07	B3/CCC	145	85.00	10.15%	17.45%	1,321	12/15/07	12/15/05	100.00		83.0	8.1%	1.7x	1.0x	8.0x	7.7x	
	FRN Sr. Secured Notes	4/15/09	B2/CCC+	125	96.00	NA	8.98%	446	4/15/09	4/15/06	101.00								
11.000%	Sr. Sub Notes	5/01/09	Caa1/CCC	165	46.00	23.91%	41.77%	3,725	5/01/09	5/01/06	103.67								
9.375%	Sr. Sub Notes	4/15/12	Caa1/CCC	150	43.00	21.80%	29.74%	2,515	4/15/12	4/15/07	104.69								
Notes: On 4/8/04, the 9.375% Sr. Sub. Notes were issued at par to yield 9.375% and 548 bps stt and the floating Sr. notes were issued at par to yield 5.121% and 130 stt. We maintain an underperform recommendation on these four bonds.																			
Tower Automotive, Inc. (TWR)													LTM 6/30 05						NA
12.000%	Sr. Notes	6/01/13	NA	258	86.25	13.91%	15.11%	1,048	6/01/13	6/01/08	106.00		263.2	7.6%	1.9x	0.9x	7.5x	7.3x	
Notes: We maintain an underperform recommendation on these bonds.																			
Visteon, Corp. (VC)													LTM 6/30/05						5.9x
8.250%	Sr. Notes	8/01/10	B3/B-	700	93.00	8.87%	10.15%	558	8/01/10	NC	NC	510/535	372.0	2.0%	2.9x	-3.0x	5.2x	3.0x	
7.000%	Sr. Notes	3/10/14	B3/B-	450	84.50	8.28%	9.76%	512	3/10/14	NC	NC								
Notes: The 7% Notes were issued at $99.957 to yield 7% and 295 stt. We maintain an outperform recommendation on these bonds.																			
Subsector Average					73.47	13.14%	22.11%	1,755					22=5	7.7%	2.5x	0.4x	6.5x	5.7x	5.9x

Wachovia Securities Automotive Relative Value Analysis as of 11/04/05

Eric J. Selle, CFA (704) 383-4086/(800) 528 4580 — Automotive High Yield Research
Stephanie Renegar—High Yield Research

	Issue Data					Current Market Data								Summary Credit Data						
Coupon	Issue / Maturity	Ratings	Amt. ($mm)	Bid Price ($)	Current Yield	YTW	YTW Spread	YTW Date	Next Call Date	Price ($)	CDS Bid/Offer	EBITDA ($mm)	EBITDA Margin	EBITDA/Int. Exp.	EBITDA – Capex/Int. Exp.	Total Debt/EBITDA	Net Debt/EBITDA	TEV/EBITDA
HIGH GRADE/CROSSOVER SUPPLIERS & OEMs																		
American Axle & Manufacturing, Inc. (AXL)																		
5.250%	Sr. Notes / 2/11/14	Baa3/BBB-	250	82.46	6.37%	8.21%	358	2/11/14	NC	NC	480/500	LTM 9/30/05 332.7	9.8%	13.2x	0.3x	1.7x	1.7x	4.9x
ArvinMeritor, Inc. (ARM)																		
6.800%	Notes / 2/15/09	Ba2/BB	305	92.75	7.33%	9.42%	491	2/15/09	NC	NC	510/525	LTM 6/30/05 406.0	4.6%	3.4x	2.2x	3.7x	3.3x	6.0x
8.750%	Sr. Notes / 3/01/12	Ba2/BB	400	95.19	9.19%	9.79%	520	3/01/12	NC	NC								
Cooper Tire & Rubber Co. (CTBUS)																		
7.750%	Sr. Notes / 12/15/09	Ba2/BB+	266	99.50	7.79%	7.89%	335	12/15/09	NC	NC		LTM 6/30/05 159.6	7.7%	3.8x	-0.7x	4.3x	1.5x	6.8x
8.000%	Sr. Notes / 12/15/19	Ba2/BB+	225	92.50	8.65%	8.95%	429	12/15/19	NC	NC								
DaimlerChrysler AG (DCX)[2]																		
6.500%	Notes / 11/15/13	A3/BBB	2,000	102.86	6.32%	6.04%	141	11/15/13	NC	NC	71	FYE 12/31/04 20,279.0	10.5%	13.9x	7.5x	5.1x	4.6x	7.1x
Dana Corp. (DCN)																		
6.500%	Notes / 3/01/09	Baa2/BB	350	85.00	7.65%	12.13%	761	3/01/09	NC	NC	750/775	LTM 9/30/05 508.0	5.3%	3.1x	1.2x	4.3x	3.0x	5.2x
5.850%	Notes / 1/15/15	Baa2/BB	450	74.00	7.91%	10.29%	563	1/15/15	NC	NC								
7.000%	Notes / 3/01/29	Baa2/BB	400	78.50	8.92%	9.27%	461	3/01/29	NC	NC								
Notes: The 5.85% Senior Sub. Notes were issued at on 12/10/04 at $99.9530 to yield 162.5 bps stt.																		
Ford Motor, Co. (F)																		
8.875%	Notes / 4/01/06	Ba1/BB+	95	100.00	8.88%	8.88%	422	4/01/06	NC	NC	720/750	LTM 9/30/05 3,443.0	2.3%	3.2x	-1.4x	5.3x	0.2x	5.5x Consolidated
8.375%	Sr. Notes / 8/01/18	Ba1/BB+	500	69.00	9.42%	11.10%	645	8/01/18	NC	NC								
Ford Motor Credit, Co. (F)																		
7.000%	Notes / 10/01/13	Baa3/BB+	3,000	91.25	7.67%	8.55%	391	10/01/13	NC	NC	420/430	LTM 9/30/05 18,360.0	77.5%	1.7x	1.7x	6.8x	5.7x	
General Motors Corp. (GM)																		
7.125%	Sr. Notes / 7/15/13	B1/BB-	1,000	79.00	9.02%	11.28%	665	7/15/13	NC	NC	905/925	LTM 9/30/05 2,967.0	1.9%	1.1x	-2.0x	10.8x	4.3x	9.3x Consolidated
8.375%	Sr. Notes / 7/15/33	B1/BB-	3,000	73.75	11.36%	11.55%	689	7/15/33	NC	NC								
General Motors Acceptance Corp. (GM)																		
6.750%	Notes / 12/01/14	Ba1/BB	1,750	97.00	6.96%	7.21%	255	12/01/14	NC	NC	245/250	LTM 10/1/05 21,429.0	63.2%	1.8x	1.8x	11.8x	9.9x	9.3x
Lear Corp. (LEA)																		
8.110%	Sr. Notes / 5/15/09	Ba2/BB+	800	93.50	8.67%	10.36%	582	5/15/09	NC	NC	610/635	LTM 10/1/05 733.5	4.3%	4.0x	1.0x	3.2x	3.0x	5.8x
5.750%	Sr. Sub. Notes / 8/01/14	Ba2/BB+	400	81.25	7.08%	8.88%	422	8/01/14	NC	NC								
Notes: The 5.85% Senior Sub. Notes were issued at on 12/10/04 at $99.9530 to yield 162.5 bps stt. We currently have an underperform on the 5.75% notes and an outperform on the 8.11% notes																		
Navistar International Corp.																		
6.250%	Sr. Notes / 3/01/12	Ba3/BB-	400	89.75	6.96%	8.37%	378	3/01/12	3/01/09	103.13	320/375	LTM 7/31/05 842.0	7.3%	5.4x	4.9x	4.6x	3.1x	5.4x
Tenneco Automotive, Inc. (TEN)																		
10.250%	Sr. Notes / 7/15/13	B2/B-	475	109.00	9.40%	8.19%	364	7/15/13	7/15/08	105.13	350/400	LTM 6/30/05 412.0	9.3%	2.4x	1.6x	3.5x	3.3x	5.0x
8.625%	Sr. Sub. Notes / 11/15/14	B3/B-	500	95.75	9.01%	9.33%	467	11/15/14	11/15/09	104.31								
Notes: On 11/9/04 the 8.625% notes were issued at par to yield 443 bps stt.																		
TRW Automotive Holdings Corp. (TRW)																		
9.375%	Sr. Notes / 2/15/13	Ba3/BB-	825	108.00	8.68%	7.42%	294	2/15/13	2/15/08	104.69	210/235	LTM 9/30/05 1,071.0	8.4%	4.5x	2.3x	2.6x	2.3x	4.8x
11.000%	Sr. Sub. Notes / 2/15/13	B1/BB-	195	112.25	9.80%	7.32%	285	2/15/13	2/15/08	105.50								
Subsector Average				89.91	8.00%	8.81%	420					6,059.8	18.4%	4.8x	1.5x	5.3x	3.9x	5.7x
MOTORSPORTS COMPANIES																		
International Speedway Corp. (ISCA)																		
4.200%	Notes / 4/15/09	Baa2/BBB-	150	97.48	4.31%	5.01%	85	4/15/09	NC	NC		LTM 8/31/05 316.5	43.1%	22.6x	3.5x	1.2x	0.7x	9.7x
5.400%	Notes / 4/15/14	Baa2/BBB-	150	99.37	5.43%	5.49%	90	4/15/14	NC	NC								
Notes: The 4.2% notes were issued at $99.788 at a stt of 85 bps. The 5.4% notes were issued at $99.925 at a 105.0 stt. Recommendation suspended.																		
Speedway Motorsports, Inc. (TRK)																		
6.750%	Sr. Sub. Notes / 6/01/13	Ba2/B+	330	101.50	6.65%	6.43%	183	6/01/13	6/01/08	103.38		LTM 9/30/05 200.1	41.8%	8.7x	5.0x	2.2x	0.9x	8.6x
Notes: The company issued the 6.75% Sr Sub Nts at par (254 bps stt) on 6/29/2006 (upsized from $210 million). Recommendation suspended.																		
Subsector Average				99.45	5.46%	5.64%	119					258.3	42.4%	15.6x	4.3x	1.7x	0.8x	9.2x
Consolidated High Yield Weighted Average				87.22	9.48%	14.03%	948					313.9	5.2%	2.5x	0.9x	3.9x	3.3x	6.3x
Weighted Average- 10/28/2005				87.37	9.44%	13.78%	936					313.5	5.2%	2.5x	1.0x	3.9x	3.2x	6.2x

BBB Average 5.94%
HY Composite 8.18%
BB Average 7.26%
B Average 7.84%
CCC and lower 12.06%

1) Italicized statistics in the auto dealers section have floorplan interest and debt removed.
2) Credit statistics are for DaimlerChrysler AG on a consolidated basis.
Source: Company Reports and Wachovia Securities

Key Bank Covenants

Exhibit 24: Lear Corp. Key Bank Covenants

	Q2 2005	Q3 2005-Q4 2005	Q1 2006	Q2 2006 and thereafter
Maximum Leverage Ratio	3.25x	3.75x	3.5x	3.25x
Minimum Coverage Ratio	Q2 2005- Thereafter			
	3.5x			

Source: Company reports.

Lear's credit facility includes a $1.7 billion revolver, maturing March 23, 2010 and a $400 million term loan maturing February 11, 2007. The facility is secured by the capital stock of certain material subsidiaries. Here we outline the facility's principal financial covenants:

- **Maximum Leverage Ratio.** Lear must maintain a Leverage Ratio at or under 3.25x at July 2, 2005, 3.75x at October 1, 2005 and December 31, 2005, 3.50x at April 1, 2006 and 3.25x at each quarter-end thereafter. The Leverage Ratio is defined as the ratio of Consolidated Indebtedness to LTM Consolidated Operating Profit.

  Consolidated Indebtedness is defined as all Indebtedness (excluding trade and accounts payable, deferred compensation obligations for employees, and debt associated with Receivable Financing Transactions under $500 million), less any cash and cash equivalents. Consolidated Operating Profit is defined as Consolidated Net Income plus depreciation and amortization, expenses for taxes, Consolidated Interest Expense and minority interest expense. The definition of Consolidated Net Income excludes charges related to OPEB, extraordinary gains/losses, charges associated with the discharge of debt, write-offs of goodwill, restructuring charges related to the company's June 27th restructuring announcement not exceeding $250 million and any charges incurred due to the Seton Company lawsuit (not to exceed $22 million) and a lawsuit by one of Lear's European suppliers (not to exceed $8 million).

- **Minimum Interest Coverage Ratio.** Lear must maintain a minimum Interest Coverage Ratio at or over 3.5x, measured at the end of each quarter. The Interest Coverage Ratio is defined as the ratio of LTM Consolidated Interest Expense to LTM Consolidated Operating Profit (as defined above). Consolidated Interest Expense is defined as GAAP interest expense, excluding any amortization or write-off of deferred financing fees and any interest income.

- **Limitation on Subsidiary and Secured Indebtedness.** Lear cannot incur Subsidiary and Secured Indebtedness that exceeds 15% of Consolidated Assets (in the aggregate). In addition, Lear cannot incur Subsidiary and Secured Indebtedness that is secured by liens on any property, assets or receivables, in an amount exceeding 5% of Consolidated Assets. This calculation does not take into account any Subsidiary or Secured Indebtedness already outstanding.

Key Bond Covenants

Lear's 5.75% and 8.11% notes are unsecured obligations, ranking pari passu with all other unsecured and unsubordinated debt.

5.75% Senior Notes

- **Limitation on Liens**

Lear and its Restricted Subsidiaries cannot incur any Liens on any of their respective properties or assets unless the company equally and ratably secures the senior notes. However, this provision does not apply to Permitted Liens, liens securing obligations under the company's credit facilities, liens on receivables associated with Receivable Financing Transactions, liens associated with IRBs or other tax-favored or government-sponsored transactions, and other liens in an aggregate principal amount not exceeding 10% of Consolidated Assets.

- **Limitation on Sale and Lease-Back Transactions**

Lear and its Restricted Subsidiaries cannot enter into any sale and lease-back transaction, unless: the transaction is an inter-company transaction, the lease period is less than three years or within 120 days after the date of acquisition of the asset, Lear or its Restricted Subsidiaries would be allowed to create a lien on the assets to be leased (in an amount equal to the Attributable Value), or the proceeds of the sale are at least equal to their fair market value and the proceeds are used to acquire assets or to repay long-term debt.

8.11% Senior Notes

- **Limitation on Liens**

Lear and its Restricted Subsidiaries cannot incur any Liens on any of their respective properties or assets unless the company equally and ratably secures the senior notes. However, this provision does not apply to Permitted Liens, liens on shares of capital stock of Lear's subsidiaries securing obligations under the company's credit facilities, liens on receivables associated with Receivable Financing Transactions, liens associated with IRBs or other tax-favored or government-sponsored transactions, and other liens in an aggregate principal amount not exceeding 5% of Consolidated Assets.

- **Limitation on Sale and Lease-Back Transactions**

Lear and its Restricted Subsidiaries cannot enter into any sale and lease-back transaction, unless: the transaction is an inter-company transaction, the lease period is less than three years or within 120 days after the date of acquisition of the asset, Lear or its Restricted Subsidiaries would be allowed to create a lien on the assets to be leased (in an amount equal to the Attributable Value), or the proceeds of the sale are at least equal to their fair market value and the proceeds are used to acquire assets or to repay long-term debt.

DISCLOSURE APPENDIX

Additional information is available on request

Definition of Ratings

Buy: The security is trading cheap to its peer group and/or the market and has significant total return potential.
Outperform: On a relative basis, the security is expected to outperform its peer group and/or the market.
Market Perform: The security is expected to perform in line with its peer group and/or the market.
Underperform: On a relative basis, the security is expected to underperform its peer group and/or the market.
Sell: The security is trading rich to its peer group and/or the market and has the potential to significantly underperform based on fundamental reasons.

About Wachovia Securities

Wachovia Securities is the trade name for the corporate, investment banking, capital markets and securities research businesses of Wachovia Corporation and its subsidiaries, including Wachovia Capital Markets, LLC (WCM) and Wachovia Securities International Limited. Wachovia Securities is also the trade name for the retail brokerage businesses of WCM's affiliates, Wachovia Securities, LLC, Wachovia Securities Financial Networks, LLC, Wexford Clearing, LLC, and First Clearing LLC.

Wachovia Capital Markets, LLC, is a U.S. broker-dealer registered with the U.S. Securities and Exchange Commission and a member of the New York Stock Exchange, the National Association of Securities Dealers, Inc., and the Securities Investor Protection Corp. Wachovia Securities International Limited is a U.K. incorporated investment firm authorized and regulated by the Financial Services Authority.

Important Information for Non-U.S. Recipients

The securities and related financial instruments described herein may not be eligible for sale in all jurisdictions or to certain categories of investors. For certain non-U.S. institutional readers (including readers in the EEA), this report is distributed by Wachovia Securities International Limited. For the purposes of Section 21 of the U.K. Financial Services and Markets Act 2000, this report has been approved by Wachovia Securities International Limited. This research is not intended for, and should not be relied on by, private customers. Please consult your Financial Advisor or the Wachovia Securities office in your area for additional information. U.S. residents are directed to wachovia.com for investment and related services.

Important Disclosures Relating to Conflicts of Interest and Potential Conflicts of Interest

WCM, or any of its affiliates, has beneficial ownership of 1% or more of any class of common stock of ArvinMeritor, Inc., Dura Automotive Systems, Inc., Group 1 Automotive, Inc., and Sonic Automotive, Inc.

WCM, or any of its affiliates, intends to seek or expects to receive compensation for investment banking services from Asbury Automotive, Inc., AutoNation, Inc., Dana Corp., Dura Automotive Systems, Inc., Ford Motor Co., Lear Corp., Metaldyne Corp., PSA Inc., Remy International, Inc., and Toyota Motor Corp., in the next three months.

WCM, or its affiliates, managed or co-managed a public offering for, or was an initial purchaser in an unregistered offering of securities pursuant to Rule 144A of, Dana Corp., Ford Motor Co., General Motors Corp., Hyundai Motor Co., Toyota Motor Corp. and Volkswagen AG in the past 12 months.

WCM may sell or buy the subject securities to/from customers on a principal basis.

WCM does not compensate its research analysts based on specific investment banking transactions. WCM's research analysts receive compensation that is based on and affected by the overall profitability of their respective department and the firm, which includes, but is not limited to, investment banking revenue.

WCM Fixed Income Research analysts interact with the firm's trading and sales personnel in the ordinary course of business. The firm trades or may trade as a principal in the securities or related derivatives mentioned herein. The firm's interests may conflict with the interests of investors in those instruments.

Analyst's Certification

The research analyst(s) principally responsible for the report certifies to the following: all views expressed in this research report accurately reflect the analysts' personal views about any and all of the subject securities or issuers discussed; and no part of the research analysts' compensation was, is, or will be, directly or indirectly, related to the specific recommendations or views expressed by the research analyst(s) in this research report.

This report, IDs, and passwords are available at wachoviaresearch.com

APPENDIX B

Rich / Cheap

THE PRESENT 79-BASIS-POINT DIFFERENCE IN SPREADS BETWEEN THE **DOLLAR GENERAL** 8-5/8% OF 2010 AND THE **AUTONATION** 9% OF 2008 REPRESENTS THE MOST ATTRACTIVE SWAP POSSIBILITY AMONG NONDISTRESSED, HIGH YIELD, RETAILERS, BASED ON OUR FINANCIAL VALUATION MODEL. DOLLAR GENERAL HAS POSTED SOLID OPERATING RESULTS AND HAS MAINTAINED ITS AGGRESSIVE EXPANSION STRATEGY. MEANWHILE, AUTONATION IS FACING INTENSE COMPETITION IN A SOFTENING CAR MARKET.

Retailers: Dollar General and AutoNation

Our Rich/Cheap methodology identifies on a weekly basis an industry pair that offers potential as a long-short relative value trade.[†] (Note that the analysis does not preclude executing only one side of the proposed swap.) This week's analysis concentrates on the Retailers industry. **Exhibit 1** presents two potentially misvalued bonds with their Focus Issues model estimates and actual spreads. If we were to judge solely by the model-generated numbers, the **Dollar General** (NYSE: DG) 8-5/8% senior unsecured notes due June 15, 2010 would be 155 basis points too wide versus the **AutoNation** (NYSE: AN) 9% senior unsecured notes due August 1, 2008.

Exhibit 1: Focus Issues Model Estimates and Actual Spreads*
(Basis Points)

	Issues	Ratings	Price	Effective Duration**	Effective Convexity[‡]	Estimated	Actual	Potential Relative Value Pickup
BUY	Dollar General 8.625% 6/15/10	Ba2/BB+	110.625	4.090	0.629	231	302	
SELL	AutoNation 9% 8/1/08	Ba2/BBB-	112.625	3.354	0.137	307	223	
	Difference					-76	79	155

* Spreads as of August 11, 2004.
** Effective duration measures price sensitivity to changes in yields, taking into account embedded options such as early redemption provisions.
[‡] Effective convexity measures curvature of price sensitivity to a change in yields, taking into account embedded options such as early redemption provisions. A negative figure indicates that a bond's price increases less than duration predicts when rates fall, and decreases at least as much as duration predicts when rates rise.

Sources: Advantage Data, FridsonVision LLC.

As of August 11, 2004, the spread of the DG notes was 79 basis points wider than the AN issue's. Based on differences in coupon, coverage ratio, and EBIT (neither issue is rated below B-), a yield *giveup* of 76 would be predicted. **Exhibit 2** graphs the relationship between the spreads of this industry pair since January 2004. Note that from March to May, the two issues traded at a much tighter spread than currently. Moreover, the difference in spreads was reversed as recently as May 18, when it stood at a 1-basis-point yield pickup into the AN 9s.

[†] See "Rich/Cheap," *Leverage World* (August 1, 2003), pp. 1-5.

Source: Leverage World, August 3, 2004 Vol 2, No 33, pp. 6–9. *Leverage World* is published by FridsonVision LLC.

SECURITY SELECTION...

Exhibit 2: Spread for DG and AN notes

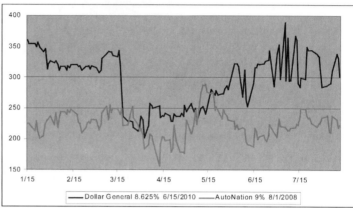

Source: Advantage Data.

Fundamental Factors

The two issues considered in this report were previously matched as a Rich/Cheap industry pair in our January 16, 2004 report.[2] In the first three months after that recommendation, the DG 8-5/8s, which were relatively cheap according to our analysis, delivered a total return of 4.27%, while AN 9s posted only a 1.06% return. Over the same period, the total return of the Lehman Brothers High Yield Retailers came to 1.05%. As the result of recent widening, DG notes are again significantly undervalued according to our model. Furthermore, the company has posted solid results in the latest quarter and has made significant progress on a number of meaningful cost-cutting initiatives. Meanwhile, the spread on AN's bond has failed to widen significantly following the July release of weak financial results for the second quarter of 2004. There is also a continuing lack of positive fundamental developments in automotive retailing.

We can identify two major fundamental factors that suggest that the divergence in spreads will disappear or decrease significantly:

- AutoNation is continuing to face intense price competition, which has led to decreasing profit margins on new vehicles, declining prices on used vehicles, and higher inventory-to-sales ratios. The used car market is especially challenging with generous incentives driving customers toward purchasing new cars. Furthermore, rising interest rates and oil prices make owning a car more expensive. It is therefore difficult for AN increase its revenues. Meanwhile, weak revenues in the latest quarter have already led to a 75-day inventory level, which the company's management deems to be too high. Getting rid of this extra supply would probably depress margins in the upcoming quarters.

---

[2] See "Rich/Cheap," *Leverage World* (January 16, 2004), pp. 4-7.

- Dollar General has continued pursuing its aggressive expansion strategy in 2004, despite a difficult retailing environment. Expanded shelf space, combined with a decent same-store sales increase, has allowed the company to post solid revenue growth in the latest quarter. Meanwhile, DG has invested in upgrading its supply chain with the introduction of automatic replenishment and perpetual inventory programs. These improvements should lower costs and produce better margins for the company. Finally, DG is still far from having nationwide penetration, providing the company ample room for expansion.

Dollar General

Description

DG, headquartered in Goodlettsville, Tennessee, is one of the largest discount retail chain operators in the United States. Originally started as a dry goods wholesaling operation, the company expanded into retail nearly 60 years ago. For the full year ending in January 2004, DG recorded sales of $6.9 billion, while posting net income of $301 million. Currently, the company has a single high yield issue with $200 million outstanding. Dollar General last tapped the high yield debt market in August 2000.

Overview

One of the fastest growing retailers, Dollar General has tripled the number of stores that it owns to about 7,000 during the latest eight years. Moreover, the expansion is unabating with the company well on its way to completing 695 store openings planned for 2004. DG has found a niche by serving small towns in the Southeast and Midwest, and has augmented its coverage with a recent entry into the Northeast. With approximately 70% of the company's stores located in small towns that could not provide enough demand for a competing store, Dollar General has been able to establish numerous local monopolies. This allowed the company to stop advertising in 1998, instead letting location and prices tell the story. Furthermore, this strategy has allowed DG to steer clear of heads-on competition with Wal-Mart, a killer of many small, regional chains over the years.

Recent Developments

On May 27, 2004, Dollar General reported solid financial results for the fiscal first quarter of 2004, with earnings per share of $0.20 coming in line with the First Call average estimate. Revenues rose by 11.4% to $1.75 billion from the preceding-year period, driven by a large number of new store openings. However, sales were also firm on a same-store basis with a 3% increase. In addition, the company was able to push its gross profit margin to 29.3% from 28.8% in the fiscal first quarter of 2003 by marking up prices on certain items. On the negative side, the company did report a slight uptick in its selling, general, and administrative expenses, partially due to increases in the cost of workers' compensation. On August 5, 2004, Dollar General reported a 3.6% increase in July same-store sales, which was in line with expectations.

AutoNation

AutoNation

Description

AN, headquartered in Fort Lauderdale, Florida, is the largest car dealer in the United States. Only eight years ago, the company was a midsized solid-waste firm, but has been transformed through numerous restructurings into a pure play auto dealer. For the full year 2003, AN recorded sales of $19.4 billion, while posting net income of $479 million. Currently, the company has a single high yield issue with $450 million outstanding. AutoNation last accessed the high yield debt market in November 2001.

Overview

The company was started in 1980 to conduct oil exploration and production, and to broker petroleum leases. After several metamorphoses, in 1995 the company found itself under the control of Wayne Huizenga, who was readying it for another remake. Huizenga used the solid-waste operations to secure public financing, then turned to consolidating a highly fragmented U.S. auto dealership market. The roll-up business strategy created regional clusters that shared inventory and enjoyed reduced marketing costs. The company has been successful in the new car market in the recent years, helped by low interest rates and manufacturers' promotions. However, the fact that demand began to soften late last year, combined with increases in interest rates and oil prices, could prove perilous for AN.

Recent Developments

On July 20, 2004, AutoNation reported weak financial results for the second quarter of 2004. Earnings per share of $0.35 were in line with the First Call average estimate, but Street estimates were revised downward just two weeks prior to the release, in response to the company's profit warning. Total revenues stayed flat at $5 billion compared to the preceding-year period, reflecting difficulties in the sector. AN was hurt by declining sales of Ford and GM vehicles, which are the two largest makes in which the company deals. Furthermore, retail sales declined by 1.1% in June, the largest such drop in sixteen months. Nevertheless, the company confirmed its full-year earnings estimate of $1.35 to $1.40 per share.

Retailers Industry Trends

According to index data provided by Lehman Brothers, the high yield Retailers index has returned 2.89% year to date. That is materially less than the total return of the broad Consumer Cyclical sector, at 4.49%. (The sector also includes the Automotive and Gaming industries.) At the same time, the 2.89% figure is slightly less than the overall U.S. Corporate High Yield Index's 3.31% year-to-date return. The underperformance was driven by uncertainty over economic conditions, which negatively affected revenues of large, discount department store chains. Furthermore, the fact that the Retailers index started 2004 priced at 107.34, compared to 102.84 for the overall high yield index, limited its potential for price appreciation.

LW

CHAPTER
21
CREDIT RISK MODELING

After reading this chapter you will understand:

- the difficulties of measuring credit risk exposure compared to interest rate risk exposure

- there are two basic types of credit risk models: structural models and reduced form models

- what a structural model is and the link to option theory

- the basic structural model (Black-Scholes-Merton model) and its extensions (Geske model and first-passage time model)

- what is meant by default correlations and the reason for using copulas in measuring portfolio credit risk

- the basic feature of reduced-form models

- the role of the Poisson process in reduced-form models

- the differences in the two major reduced-form models: Jarrow-Turnbull model and Duffie-Singleton model

- what an incomplete information model is

Credit risk models are used in finance to measure, monitor, and control a portfolio's credit risk. In fixed-income analysis they are also used in the pricing of credit risky debt instruments. Credit risk models are classified as either structural models or reduced-form models. There is considerable debate as to which type of model is the best to employ. This is not just a debate amongst academic theorists. Oftentimes, the parties to the debate are vendors that sell these models to asset management firms and financial institutions needing a credit risk management system.

We will provide the main elements of structural and reduced-form models in this chapter. In addition, there are structural/reduced-form hybrid models, and we will discuss one such model called the incomplete information model. A discussion of how the parameters of credit risk models are estimated is beyond the scope of this chapter.

DIFFICULTIES IN CREDIT RISK MODELING

In Chapter 4 we described how to quantify the interest rate risk of a bond and a bond portfolio. While there are complex securities where modeling the interest rate risk exposes the portfolio manager to modeling risk, quantifying interest risk exposure is less complicated than modeling credit risk exposure. Following are three reasons that this is so:

1. Credit default risk is a rare event and, as a result, the historical data needed to compute the inputs into a credit risk model (e.g., default rates and recovery rates) arc considerably less in comparison to the data available for the modeling of interest rate risk where, for example, historical U.S. Treasury prices are available on a daily basis for many decades.
2. Even with the default data that are available, it is much more difficult to draw any meaningful and possibly predictive conclusions about the probability of default because of the diversity of the corporations involved (in terms of industry sector, size, and leverage) and the lack of complete information regarding corporate practices.
3. There are various causes of default by a corporate borrower—ranging from microeconomic factors (such as poor management) to macroeconomic factors (such as high interest rates and recession)—that make default hard to predict.

Moreover, while our focus in this chapter will be on credit risk modeling for U.S. corporations, applying these models to non-U.S. entities is complicated by the fact that default is not a universal concept. Every country has its own bankruptcy code to deal with defaults. Furthermore, there is no assurance that the administrators of the bankruptcy law (e.g., bankruptcy judges in the United States) will apply the law in a manner that is consistent with the bankruptcy code. For example, as explained in Chapter 7, the U.S. bankruptcy code sets forth that when a corporation is liquidated, creditors receive distributions based on the "absolute priority rule" to the extent assets are available. The absolute priority rule is the principle that senior creditors are paid in full before junior creditors are paid anything. For secured creditors and unsecured creditors, the absolute priority rule guarantees their seniority to stockholders. In liquidations, the absolute priority rule generally holds. In contrast, there is a preponderance of evidence that shows that strict absolute priority has not been upheld by the courts in corporate reorganizations.

From what we have said so far, it seems unlikely that credit risk modeling will yield fruitful and meaningful information. Yet, credit risk models have long been employed in the finance and insurance industries. The focus of the early models was on generating forecasts of default rates, credit ratings, and credit spreads (measured relative to

U.S. Treasury securities).[1] From a portfolio perspective, the assumption was that credit default risk for corporate bonds is idiosyncratic and, therefore, can be diversified away in large portfolios containing corporate bonds. In credit risk modeling for individual corporate bonds, some risk-return measure (such as the Sharpe ratio) was used to evaluate the observed credit spreads.[2]

Since the mid-1990s, more sophisticated approaches to credit risk modeling have been proposed and made commercially available to portfolio managers. For one of these approaches that is commercially available, the theoretical foundation underlying the model dates back to the early 1970s.

OVERVIEW OF CREDIT RISK MODELING[3]

Credit risk modeling is used to:

- estimate the default probability
- price individual corporate bonds
- measure a portfolio's credit risk

The **default probability** (or **probability of default**) is the likelihood that a borrower will default sometime over the life of the debt obligation. By default it is meant that the borrow fails to honor the terms of the agreement, such as the failure to make a principal or coupon payment required under the agreement, or the violation of a covenant. It is common in practice to look at the default over the next one year. The default probability is sometimes referred to as an **expected default frequency**. To estimate the default probability for one year, a credit risk model requires the following: (1) a definition of what constitutes a default event, (2) a model of investor uncertainty (i.e., what information are we uncertain about?), and (3) how that information will evolve over time.[4]

---

[1]One of the approaches was a credit scoring model using multiple discriminant analysis developed by Edward Altman in 1968: Edward I. Altman, "Financial Bankruptcies, Discriminant Analysis and the Prediction of Corporate Bankruptcy," *Journal of Finance* (September 1968), pp. 589–609. There were subsequent updates of the model. See: Edward I. Altman, Robert G. Haldeman, and Paul Narayann, "Zeta Analysis: A New Model to Identify Bankruptcy Risk of Corporations," *Journal of Banking and Finance* (June 1977), pp. 29–54 and Chapters 8 and 9 in Edward I. Altman, *Corporate Financial Distress and Bankruptcy: A Complete Guide to Predicting and Avoiding Distress and Profiting from Bankruptcy* (New York, NY: John Wiley & Sons, 1993).

[2]See H. Gifford Fong and Frank J. Fabozzi, *Fixed Income Portfolio Management* (Homewood, IL: Dow Jones-Irwin, 1985). One of the problems with using the Sharpe measure for corporate bond returns is the assumed symmetric return distribution. However, corporate bond returns offer an asymmetric risk-reward property. As a result, traditional risk-reward measures such as the Sharpe ratio based on variance do not cope well with credit especially for bonds that may be crossover candidates—bonds that are candidates for shifting from high-yield to investment grade.

[3]A detailed discussion of the objectives of the credit risk modeling process is provided in Donald R. van Deventer and Kenji Imai, *Credit Risk Models and the Basel Accords* (Hoboken, NJ: John Wiley & Sons, 2003).

[4]Tim Backshall, Kay Giesecke, and Lisa Goldberg, "Credit Risk Modeling," Chapter 33 in Frank J. Fabozzi (ed.), *The Handbook of Fixed Income Securities* (New York, NY: McGraw-Hill, 2004), p. 779.

Given a credit risk model and observed market prices for corporate bonds and/or credit derivatives, a fair value for the credit spread for an illiquid or unpriced corporate bond with a given credit rating or other credit-based characteristic can be estimated. This credit spread is referred to as the **fair market credit spread**. The fair market credit spread is then used to price other credit risky assets with similar characteristics. To estimate the fair market credit spread, a credit risk model requires (1) a model that estimates recovery if a default occurs, (2) a model that shows the credit spread that investors want in order to accept systematic credit risk and idiosyncratic risk—as the spread is largely driven by uncertainty of the timing of default for this one company, and (3) a model of the risk-free rate.[5]

Measuring a portfolio's credit risk requires a model for linking the defaults of corporate bonds. One might think that this link can be estimated by looking at the correlations of defaults for corporate bond issuers in different sectors of the bond market. However, as will be explained later in this chapter, a different statistical tool is used.

CREDIT RATINGS VERSUS CREDIT RISK MODELS

Recall that a long-term credit rating is a prediction of the likelihood that an issuer or issue will default and the severity of the loss. Why not simply rely on credit ratings as a forecaster of default? Van Deventer of Kamakura Corporation, a vendor of credit risk models, provides the following reasons.[6] First, ratings are discrete with a limited number of rating grades, which were described in Chapter 20. In contrast, default probabilities are continuous and range from 0% to 100%. Second, while ratings are updated very infrequently, default probabilities can be estimated on a real-time basis. Van Deventer provides an example of the downgrade of Merck (from AAA to AA-) in 2004. The downgrade came three weeks after the withdrawal of a major drug that significantly impacted Merck's stock price. Finally, there is no clear maturity for a credit rating. While there is a separate short- and long-term credit rating, credit risk models provide a default probability by maturity (i.e., a term structure of default probabilities). This provides insight into the default probabilities for different phases of the business cycle.

STRUCTURAL MODELS

In 1973, Fischer Black and Myron Scholes developed a model for the pricing of options on common stock.[7] At the end of the article, the authors discussed an application of their option pricing model to corporate bond pricing by explaining how the stockholders

---

[5]Backshall, Giesecke, and Goldberg, "Credit Risk Modeling," pp. 779–780.
[6]Donald R. van Deventer "An Introduction to Credit Risk Models," Chapter 14 in Frank J. Fabozzi, Lionel Martellini, and Philippe Priaulet (eds), *Advanced Bond Portfolio Management: Best Practices in Modeling and Strategies* (forthcoming John Wiley & Sons, 2006).
[7]Fischer Black and Myron Scholes, "The Pricing of Options and Corporate Liabilities," *Journal of Political Economy*, 81 (1973), pp. 637–654.

can be viewed as having a call option on the value of the assets with the right being granted by the bondholders. A year after the publication of this seminal article, Robert Merton extended the framework provided by Black and Scholes to analyze how it can be used to value credit risky securities such as corporate bonds.[8] We'll provide the basics of what is now referred to as the Black-Scholes-Merton (BSM) model. As we review the model, we will see that there are many simplifying assumptions. There have been extensions of the BSM model to make the model more realistic and we will briefly describe them also.

The BSM model and its extensions are referred to as **structural models**. The fundamental feature that is common to all structural models is that default can be viewed as some type of option by the equity owners on the assets of the firm, and that the option is triggered (i.e., the corporation defaults) when the value of the corporation's assets declines below a certain default point.[9] The application of option pricing theory avoids the use of a risk premium and tries to use other marketable securities to price the option. The use of option pricing theory provides a significant improvement over traditional methods for valuing corporate bonds. The outputs of structural models show how the credit risk of a corporate bond is a function of the issuer's leverage and the volatility of the issuer's assets. The output of these models also provides information about how to hedge the default risk, which was not obtainable from traditional methods.

Structural models have been used by banks in making credit decisions and by bond portfolio managers. According to Wesley Phoa of Capital Groups Companies, structural models have been used by bond portfolio managers in one or more of the following ways:[10]

1. to estimate a corporate bond's default risk
2. to predict rating changes (upgrades and downgrades with particular interest in downgrades)
3. for a given corporate issuer with several issues in its capital structure, to identify relative value opportunities
4. to forecast changes in corporate bond credit spreads
5. from within the corporate bond market, to identify relative value opportunities
6. to evaluate the sensitivity of corporate bond credit spreads to equity prices

In assessing the merits of structural models, these potential uses must be kept in mind. Structural models may perform well in one area of application in bond portfolio management but turn out to be useless for other applications. When considering the potential use of structural models, it is important to be aware of the underlying assumptions of the model because it is these assumptions that may limit the usefulness of a model to one or more of the six areas mentioned previously.

---

[8]Robert Merton, "On the Pricing of Corporate Debt: The Risk Structure of Interest Rates," *Journal of Finance*, 29 (1974), pp. 449–470.
[9]Because of this feature, structural models are also known as "firm-value models."
[10]Wesley Phoa, "Implications of Merton Models for Corporate Bond Investors," Chapter 16 in Frank J. Fabozzi, Lionel Martellini, and Philippe Priaulet (eds), *Advanced Bond Portfolio Management: Best Practices in Modeling and Strategies* (Hoboken, NJ: John Wiley & Sons, 2006).

Fundamentals of the Black-Scholes-Merton Model[11]

In the BSM model, the following assumptions are made:

Assumption 1: A corporation has only one type of bond outstanding in its debt structure.

Assumption 2: The bond outstanding is a zero-coupon bond that matures in T years.

Assumption 3: There is a constant risk-free interest rate over the life of the bond.

Assumption 4: The payment to bondholders in the case of default of the corporation is made in accordance with the principle of absolute priority.

Assumption 5: Volatility is assumed to be constant.

Assumption 1 is obviously unrealistic, and extensions of the BSM model discussed later allow for multiple types of bond issues. Assumption 2 is important because it precludes a corporation from defaulting prior to the maturity date of the zero-coupon bond. The reason is that there are no payments that must be made and, therefore, no default based on missed payments if the outstanding debt is a zero-coupon bond. So, regardless of what happens to the value of the zero-coupon bond issued by the corporation between the time of issuance and its maturity date, there is nothing having to do with this bond that would result in a default event. Again, this assumption is unrealistic and there are models that allow for default prior to the maturity date.

To describe the model, we will let

$E(t)$ = the value of the corporation's equity at time t

$\quad A(t)$ = the value of the corporation's asset at time t

$\quad K$ = the maturity value of the zero-coupon bond issued by the corporation

At the maturity date of the zero-coupon bond, T, the value of the corporation's equity is $E(T)$ and the value of the corporation's assets is $A(T)$.

Now let's look at what can happen at the maturity date of the zero-coupon bond. There are only three possible scenarios at T:

Scenario 1: Total assets exceed the maturity value of the zero-coupon bond. That is, $A(T) > K$.

Scenario 2: Total assets are less than the maturity value of the zero-coupon bond. That is, $A(T) < K$.

Scenario 3: Total assets are equal to the maturity value of the zero-coupon bond. That is, $A(T) = K$.

The value of the equity at time T, $E(T)$, is the difference between the value of the assets, $A(T)$, and the maturity value of the zero-coupon bond, K. That is,

$$E(T) = A(T) - K$$

---

[11]For numerical illustrations of the BSM model, see Chapter 8 in Mark J. P. Anson, Frank J. Fabozzi, Moorad Choudhry, and Ren-Raw Chen, *Credit Derivatives: Instruments, Pricing, and Applications* (John Wiley & Sons, 2004).

In Scenario 1 (total assets exceed the maturity value of the zero-coupon bond), then

$$E(T) = A(T) - K > 0$$

That is, there is positive equity value, and the stockholders would be sure to pay off the bondholders in full in order to retain the corporation.

In Scenario 2 (total assets are less than the maturity value of the zero-coupon bond), then

$$E(T) = A(T) - K < 0$$

In this scenario, the stockholders would default and the bondholders would receive less than the maturity value of the bond. Effectively, the bondholders would own the corporation.

In Scenario 3 (total assets are equal to the maturity value of the zero-coupon bond), the value of the equity is zero. In this case, the stockholders would pay off the bondholders in full and own a corporation with zero value.

If we let $B(T)$ denote the value of the corporation's zero-coupon bond, then its value at the maturity date can be expressed as:

$$B(T) = A(T) - \max\left[A(T) - K, 0\right] \qquad \textbf{(21.1)}$$

The notation $\max\left[A(T) - K, 0\right]$ means the maximum of $A(T) - K$ and zero. In Scenario 1, $A(T) - K$ is positive so the maximum value is $A(T) - K$ and the value of the bond is K,

$$B(T) = A(T) - \left[A(T) - K\right] = K$$

In Scenario 2, $A(T) - K$ is negative and therefore $\max\left[A(T) - K, 0\right]$ is zero. Hence, the value of the bond is

$$B(T) = A(T) - 0 = A(T)$$

In Scenario 3, the value of the bond is simply K.

If we look closely at equation (21.1) we can see why Black and Scholes viewed the value of a corporate bond in terms of the value of an option. The term $\max\left[A(T) - K, 0\right]$ in equation (21.1) is the payoff of a call option with a strike price of K that expires at T, and the underlying is the corporation's assets. Since the term enters into the equation with a negative sign, this means a short position in a call option (i.e., the sale of a call option). So the position given by equation (21.1) is that the bondholder has a long position in the corporation's assets and has sold a call option to the common stockholders on the corporation's assets. The value of a corporate bond is valued accordingly: It is the value of the total assets reduced by the value of the call option. The call option can be valued by using an option pricing model such as the Black-Scholes model.

If we rewrite equation (21.1), we have another interpretation that is useful. The equation can be rewritten as

$$B(T) = K - \max\left[K - A(T), 0\right] \tag{21.2}$$

The results for each of the three scenarios will, of course, be the same as with equation (21.1). Again, the notation max $[K - A(T), 0]$ means the maximum of $K - A(T)$ and zero. In Scenario 1, $K - A(T)$ is negative so the maximum value is zero, and the value of the bond is K. In Scenario 2, $K - A(T)$ is positive and, therefore, max $[K - A(T), 0]$ is $K - A(T)$. Hence, the value of the bond is

$$B(T) = K - [K - A(T)] = A(T)$$

In Scenario 3, the value of the bond is simply K.

The term $[K - A(T)]$ is the payoff of a put option at time T written on the corporation's assets with a strike price K. Since this term enters into equation (21.2) with a negative sign, it is the payoff of a short put position. One can interpret the position given by equation (21.2) as a position in a risk-free bond reduced by the value of the put position that the stockholders sold to the bondholders on the corporation's assets.

To value the option using this approach to corporate bond valuation using an option pricing model, the following inputs are required:

1. the corporation's capital structure
2. the corporation's market value (typically derived from its stock price)
3. The volatility of the market value of the corporation (typically derived from the volatility of the stock's price)

Extensions of the BSM Model

Researchers have developed extensions of the BSM model by relaxing the assumptions. The mathematics in deriving the model becomes more complicated. Moreover, the type of option that is granted by the bondholders to the common stockholders is no longer a basic call option but rather a complex or exotic option. We do not cover such options in this book. Therefore, here we will only describe the extensions and their motivation, providing references for those who desire to study the topic further.

First, consider Assumption 1 (the corporation has only one type of bond outstanding). If the company has a series of zero-coupon bonds outstanding with different maturities, then it is quite easy for the BSM model to characterize default at different times. Geske demonstrated how this is done by using a "compound option" model.[12] A compound option is an option on another option. The main point of the Geske model is that defaults can be described as a series of contingent events and that later defaults are

---

[12]See Robert Geske, "The Valuation of Corporate Liabilities as Compound Options," *Journal of Financial and Quantitative Analysis*, 12 (1977), pp. 541–552. Also see Robert Geske and Herbert Johnson, "The Valuation of Corporate Liabilities as Compound Options: A Correction," *Journal of Financial and Quantitative Analysis*, 19 (1984), pp. 231–232. For a numerical illustration of the Geske model, see Chapter 8 in Anson, Fabozzi, Choudhry, and Chen, *Credit Derivatives: Instruments, Pricing, and Applications*.

contingent upon whether there was no prior default. Based on this notion, layers of contingent defaults build up a series of sequential compound options, one linking to the other.

Another series of models have been proposed to extend the BSM model to the case where default can occur not only at maturity but at any time prior to maturity. The underlying legal principle here is that there are typically covenants in a typical bond indenture granting the bondholders the right to restructure the corporation should the value of the corporate assets fall below a given amount, referred to as a **default barrier**. These models are referred to as **first-passage time models** with the first such model being proposed by Black and Cox.[13] In all of these models, a threshold is defined (default barrier) and default occurs when a corporation's asset value crosses that threshold. Default is viewed as a form of barrier option.[14] A barrier option is a path dependent option. For such options, both the payoff of the option and the survival of the option to the stated expiration date depends on whether the price of the underlying asset reaches a specified level over the life of the option.[15]

With respect to Assumption 3, a constant risk-free rate, Shimko, Tejima, and van Deventer extend the BSM model to allow for stochastic interest rates.[16]

Moody's KMV Model

A number of software/consulting companies have developed credit risk models based on structural models. The two most popular appear to be Moody's KMV Corporation and RiskMetric Group's CreditGrades. Both systems use the BSM model to model defaults using large databases of historical data. Here, we will describe the Moody's KMV model. This is not an endorsement of this company's products but merely to see the output of a commercial product based on the BMS model.

In the Moody's KMV methodology, information contained in equity prices and the balance sheet of corporate bond issuers is used to extract the probability of default, which it refers to as the **expected default frequency** (EDF) and is the probability of defaulting within a specified time period. So, a corporation with an EDF for a one-year time period of 3% has a 3% probability of defaulting within the next 12 months. The EDF is specific to a corporation, as any default of any security is legally applicable to all securities of the issuer (i.e., the corporation cannot "cherry-pick" which liabilities to default upon).

---

[13]Fischer Black and John Cox, "Valuing Corporate Securities: Some Effects of Bond Indenture Provisions," *Journal of Finance*, 31 (1976), pp. 351–367.

[14]Other extensions viewing default as a barrier option include: Francis Longstaff and Eduardo Schwartz, "A Simple Approach to Valuing Risky Fixed and Floating Rate Debt," *Journal of Finance*, 50 (1995), pp. 789–819; Eric Briys and Francois de Varenne, "Valuing Risky Fixed Rate Debt: An Extension," *Journal of Financial and Quantitative Analysis*, 32, (1997), pp. 239–248; Chunsheng Zhou, "An Analysis of Default Correlations and Multiple Defaults," *Review of Financial Studies* (2001), pp. 555–576; and Ming Huang and Jay Huang, "How Much of the Corporate-Treasury Yield Spread Is Due to Credit Risk?" working paper, Stanford University, 2002.

[15]This form of barrier option is also called a "down-and-out barrier" option. There are two types of barrier options: knock-out options and knock-in options. The former is an option that is terminated once a specified value is realized by the underlying asset. A knock-in option is an option that is activated once a specified value is realized by the underlying asset. For a further explanation of barrier options, see John Hull, *Options, Futures, and Other Derivatives* (New York: Prentice Hall, 2002).

[16]David C. Shimko, Naohiko Tejima, and Donald R. van Deventer, "The Pricing of Risky Debt When Interest Rates Are Stochastic," *Journal of Fixed Income* (September 1993), pp. 58–66.

Moreover, each EDF can be associated with a credit spread curve and a credit rating. The credit rating assigned by the model based on market prices is called a **market implied rating**. Instead of being aggregated into rating classes, corporations are categorized in the Moody's KMV methodology using a "distance-to-default index" measure.

There are three steps involved in computing a firm's EDF in the Moody's KMV methodology. First, the market value and volatility of a firm's assets need to be estimated. Second, using option pricing theory applied to the valuation of corporate bonds, the distance-to-default index measure is computed. Finally, the distance-to-default index measure is combined with a large dataset of actual default rates to compute the probability of default. This last step is the major advantage of the model and what also sets it most apart from the BSM approach.

Advantages and Disadvantages of Structural Models

From a theoretical perspective, structural models analyze default based on a reasonable assumption that it is a result of the value of the corporate issuer's assets falling below the value of its debt. In addition to providing default probabilities, these models allow a bond portfolio manager to see how the credit risk of corporate debt is a function of the leverage and the asset volatility of the issuer. Accordingly, the impact of a new stock or bond offering that will change the capital structure of a corporation can be assessed.

While superior to what was previously available, there are two concerns that have been expressed about structural models: difficult to calibrate and computationally burdensome. We first discussed the calibration of models to market data when we discussed interest rate models in Chapter 16. Calibration is a necessary first step in fixed-income trading because it allows traders to clearly see *relative prices* and hence be able to construct arbitrage trading strategies. To calibrate a structural model to price a corporate bond requires calibration to asset volatility, asset value, face value of the corporate issuer's debt, the default barrier (in the case of first-passage time models), and the risk-free rate.[17] While some of these values required for calibration can be estimated from market data (e.g., using Treasuries to estimate the risk-free rate), many are not observable or easy to obtain. The value of a corporation is estimated from stock prices for publicly traded corporations. Determining the face value of the corporation's debt may seem simple; however, in complex capital structures involving multiple bond issues, bank debt, guarantees on debt issues by others, pension liabilities, leasing obligations, and any interest rate derivatives that the issuer may be exposed to, it is not simple. For first-passage time models, a suitable default barrier must be estimated. Because of this difficulty, it is argued that structural models are not suitable for the frequent marking to market of credit contingent securities.

What we have just described is the problem with calibration for a single corporate bond issue. When assessing the credit risk of a portfolio of corporate bonds there is a further complication when implementing structural models. One must estimate the correlation between the issuers in the portfolio. The statistical tool for doing this is described next.

---

[17]To truly price the bond (in the real world) we actually need the risk premium also—as the standard BSM model will produce risk-neutral spreads.

From a computational perspective, the pricing of a corporate zero-coupon bond, for example, is just like pricing an option on a bond, a topic we cover in Chapter 27. However, for coupon-bearing corporate bonds the problem becomes one of pricing a compound option, a more difficult problem. To price a subordinated bond, it is necessary to simultaneously value all of the more senior debt (bonds and loans). Consequently, there is reluctance by some market participants to use structural models where there is a need for rapid and accurate pricing of corporate bonds.

The main application of structural models in practice appears to be in the area of credit risk analysis. Market participants have argued that structural models are more likely to be able to predict the credit quality of a corporate security than the reduced-form models that will be discussed later and are certainly more timely than rating agency actions or fundamental analysis described in the previous chapter. As a result, banks have found it a useful model for establishing credit lines with corporations and a useful tool in the risk analysis of portfolios of corporate bonds.

Estimating Portfolio Credit Risk: Default Correlation and Copulas

Thus far, we have discussed how structural models can be used in assessing the credit risk of an individual corporation. For a portfolio of corporate bonds, there is the risk that some event that triggers the default of one of the corporate bonds in the portfolio will adversely impact another corporate bond in the portfolio, thereby increasing the probability of the default of that second corporation. A commonly used statistical concept to gauge the dependence between two variables is correlation. In credit risk management, this type of risk is referred to as default correlation. One would expect that for corporate issuers in the same industry sector, **default correlation** is high.

Developers of credit risk models need an estimate of the default correlations in order to assess the credit risk of a portfolio and credit derivatives. The technique used to estimate the default correlation varies. For example, Moody's uses Monte Carlo simulation of historical data on rating transitions and defaults in its analysis. Another rating agency, Fitch Ratings, uses correlations based on equity price changes.

While we just noted that correlation quantifies the dependence between two variables, it should be noted that correlation is often incorrectly used to mean any notion of dependence between two variables. However, correlation is only one of several measures in statistics used to quantify a dependence structure, and there are reasons this measure is not a suitable one in the case of credit risk modeling. One reason is that the independence of two random variables implies a correlation that is equal to zero. However, conversely, a correlation of zero does not imply independence.

To see the relevance for credit risk management, suppose that there are numerous potential suppliers of a particular part to the automotive industry. Assume that ABC Company is one such supplying firm. From the perspective of the ABC Company, defaults of firms in the automotive industry are likely to have severe adverse economic consequence, potentially leading to its bankruptcy. Hence, from the perspective of an investor in ABC Company's bond, there is high default risk between ABC Company and the automotive industry. However, from the holder of the corporate bonds of companies in the automotive industry, the default of ABC Company is highly unlikely to have any impact on these companies. Thus, from the perspective of the automotive industry, the impact on default risk is likely to be zero.

Because of this asymmetrical dependence and other drawbacks of correlation as a measure of risk, many developers of credit risk models use different measures of dependence to understand the multivariate relationship between all of the bonds in a portfolio. The combination of individual default probabilities (or default distributions) and their dependence is known mathematically as a "copula." The background needed to understand copulas cannot be discussed here. What is important to understand is that by using copulas rather than simple correlations to gauge the nature of the dependency between two variables, a modeler can better handle the modeling of extreme events.

REDUCED-FORM MODELS

Reduced-form models were introduced in the mid 1990s. The two most notable reduced-form models are the Jarrow-Turnbull model[18] and the Duffie-Singleton model.[19]

The major difference between reduced-form models and structural models is how default is treated. As with all economic models, structural and reduced-form models are merely an abstract simplified mathematical representation of relationships between economic variables. The variables in an economic model contain endogenous variables and exogenous variables. An endogenous variable is a variable whose value is determined within the economic model; it is referred to as a "dependent" variable because its value is dependent on the other variables in the economic model. An exogenous variable is a variable whose value is determined outside the economic model and is referred to as an "independent" variable because its value is determined independent of the other variables in the economic model. In structural models, default is endogenous; in reduced-form models it is exogenous. As it turns out, specifying defaults exogenously, as is done in reduced-form models, greatly simplifies credit risk modeling because it ignores the constraint of defining what causes default and simply looks at the default event itself. Pricing of corporate bonds with different maturities can be seen as independent, unlike structural models where defaults of longer-maturity corporate bonds of an issuer are contingent on defaults of shorter-maturity corporate bonds of that same issuer.

The key elements in reduced-form models are: (1) the default-time, (2) recovery rate process, and (3) risk-free interest rate. The modeling of when a default occurs and the recovery process, if the issuer defaults, is how the reduced-form models that have been proposed differ. Accurately modeling the bankruptcy recovery process is not simple.[20]

---

[18]Robert Jarrow and Stuart Turnbull, "Pricing Derivatives on Financial Securities Subject to Default Risk," *Journal of Finance*, 50 (1995), pp. 53–86.
[19]Darrell Duffie and Kenneth Singleton, "Modeling the Term Structure of Defaultable Bonds," *Review of Financial Studies*, 12 (1999), pp. 687–720. The name "reduced form" was given by Darrell Duffie to distinguish it from structural models.
[20]Three models have been proposed to model the recovery process: (1) recovery of market value, (2) recovery of face value and accrued interest, and (3) recovery of Treasury value.

Recognition must be given to the trade-off between analytic tractability and practical applicability. Based on restrictive assumptions about the dynamics of the default and recovery processes, a closed-form solution to reduced-form models has been derived by their proposers.

The theoretical framework for reduced-form models is the Poisson process. We will provide a brief explanation of this simple stochastic process.

Poisson Process

In Chapter 16 in our description of interest rate modeling, we explained what a stochastic process is. A Poisson process is one of the most important classes of stochastic processes. To understand the Poisson process, we begin with a sequence or counter, which counts (i.e., $1, 2, \ldots$) the number of some defined event occurring from an initial point in time. We denote the value of this counter at time t as N_t. That is

$$N_t = \text{number of occurrences in the interval 0 to } t$$

Thus, N_t will increase by 1 for every occurrence of an event, and these increases are referred to as "increments."

The probability of an event occurring from one integer to the next over a small time interval dt is given by[21]

$$\text{Probability } [N_{t+dt} + N_{t-1} = 1] = \lambda dt$$

where the parameter λ is called the *intensity parameter* of the Poisson process. Similarly, the probability of no event occurring in the same time interval is simply given by

$$\text{Probability } [N_{t+dt} + N_{t-1} = 0] = 1 - \lambda dt$$

In reduced-form models, the event in a Poisson process is defined as a default. The intensity parameter in reduced-form models is called the **default intensity** and is a key parameter in the model. In fact, reduced-form models are also referred to as **intensity-based models** and **stochastic default rate models**. In the context of a reduced-form model, the default intensity at time t can be thought of in terms of a probability. More specifically, it is the *conditional* probability of default per unit time given that the corporation has not previously defaulted.[22] Consequently, the Poisson process basically describes the near-term default risk of a corporation.

---

[21]Recall in Chapter 16, where we mentioned stochastic differential equations, what dt represents: dt denotes the change in time or equivalently the length of the time interval and is a very small interval of time.
[22]Because it depends on the corporation not having previously defaulted, that is why it is a conditional probability.

The intensity parameter in the Poisson process can be specified in one of three ways. The first is simply as a deterministic or constant value that is independent of time *t*. In the previous formula that is how it is specified. The second way is to specify the intensity parameter as a deterministic function of time *t*. Finally, the intensity function can be specified as a random variable that depends on some exogenously specified state variables. For example, the default process can be correlated with the risk-free interest rate processes.[23] Most reduced-form models used in practice employ a stochastic intensity parameter to model the default process.

If we assume that the intensity parameter is a constant, then it can be demonstrated that the time it takes until the first default event occurs, called the **default time**, obeys an exponential distribution given by

$$\text{Probability } (T > t) = e^{-\lambda(T - t)}$$

The Jarrow-Turnbull Model

The Jarrow-Turnbull model is a simple model of default and recovery. It assumes that no matter when default occurs, the recovery payment is paid at the maturity date. By making the assumption that the recovery payment is made at maturity, Jarrow and Turnbull assume away any dependency between the bond price and the conditional default probability.

The basic Jarrow-Turnbull model has been extended by Jarrow, Lando, and Turnbull[24] to incorporate different credit ratings rather than of just two states (default and survival). That is, instead of a single state for default (and survival), there can be a number of probabilities, each for the probability of moving from one credit rating to another credit rating. This is done by providing the probabilities for these rating movements. Recall from our discussion in Chapter 20 that these probabilities can be obtained from the rating transition tables published periodically by the rating agencies. Thus, these extended reduced-form models deal with migration risk of credit ratings rather than default risk.

The Duffie-Singleton Model

The assumption that the recovery payment can occur only at maturity rather than when default actually occurs (or soon after) in the Jarrow-Turnbull model so that a closed-form solution can be derived is not realistic. This is one of two major drawbacks of that model. The second drawback is that the recovery amount can fluctuate randomly over time. The recovery amount fluctuates because it depends on the corporation's liquidation value at the time of default. As a result, it is possible to have scenarios for the Jarrow-Turnbull model wherein the recovery payment may exceed the price of the bond

---

[23]In such cases, a special type of Poisson process known as a Cox process (or doubly stochastic Poisson process) is used. For a discussion of the Cox process, see Chapter 10 in Svetlozar T. Rachev, Christian Menn, and Frank J. Fabozzi, *Fat-Tailed and Skewed Asset Return Distributions: Implications for Risk Management, Portfolio Selection, and Option Pricing* (Hoboken, NJ: John Wiley & Sons, 2005).
[24]Robert Jarrow, David Lando, and Stuart Turnbull, "A Markov Model for the Term Structure of Credit Spreads," *Review of Financial Studies*, 10 (1997), pp. 481–532.

at the time of default because the recovery rate is an exogenously specified percentage of the risk-free bonds.

In contrast, the model proposed by Duffie and Singleton (1) allows the recovery payment to occur at any time and (2) restricts the amount of recovery to be a fixed fraction of the non-default bond price at the time of default. Because of this second assumption, the Duffie-Singleton model is referred to as a **fractional recovery model** or **fractional recovery of predefault market value model**. The rationale for this assumption is as a corporate bond's credit quality deteriorates, its price falls. At the time of default, the recovery price will be some fraction of the final price that prevailed prior to default, and, as a result, one does not encounter the shortcoming of the Jarrow-Turnbull model that price can be greater than the price prior to default.

Advantages and Disadvantages of Reduced-Form Models

Because the default probabilities and recovery rates are exogenously specified in the model, one can use a series of risky zero-coupon bonds to calibrate out a default probability curve and hence a credit spread curve. The ability to quickly calibrate to the market so that traders can assess relative prices and construct arbitrage trading strategies is the major reason why reduced-form models are strongly favored by practitioners involved in the credit derivatives market.[25]

A criticism of reduced-form models is precisely the advantage cited by its proponents: It does not explain the economic reasoning behind default because it treats default as an exogenous event. Future refinements of reduced-form models will likely incorporate factors driving defaults into the modeling of the intensity rate and loss rate. One example is the linking of the intensity parameter to the value of the firm.[26] Moreover, reduced-form models suffer from the constraint that default is always treated as a surprise. This is rarely the case. Studies by the rating agencies indicate that there are very few corporate bonds that move from investment-grade quality right into default without a series of downgrades in between. Hence, default for such corporate bonds can be anticipated.

INCOMPLETE INFORMATION MODELS

In both structural and reduced-form models, no consideration is given to the fact that the information that investors use may be imperfect. In structural models, for example, firm value is based on the market evaluating correctly the value of the corporation. This could be due to off-balance sheet derivatives, lease financing, pension obligations, etc., all being based on generally accepted accounting principles but not reflecting a

---

[25]We will discuss credit derivatives in Chapter 29. For an illustration of the calibration process for the Jarrow-Turnbull model, see Chapter 9 in Anson, Fabozzi, Choudhry, and R. Chen, *Credit Derivatives: Instruments, Applications, and Pricing.*

[26]Sanjiv Das and Peter Tufano, "Pricing Credit—Sensitive Debt When Interest Rates, Credit Ratings, and Credit Spreads Are Stochastic," *Journal of Financial Engineering*, 5 (1996), pp. 161–198.

true economic state. Moreover, corporate scandals such as that of Enron, Tyco, WorldCom, and Parmalat are constant reminders that the financial information provided by corporations may be far from reflecting their true economic condition. For example, in first-passage time models, as explained earlier, a default barrier is required. Using the information by Enron, Tyco, and WorldCom would have resulted in misleading default barriers.

Incomplete information models take into account imperfect information reported in financial statements. While incomplete information models were proffered by several researchers,[27] Giesecke and Goldberg propose a structural/reduced form hybrid model based on incomplete information.[28] Their model, which is used by MSCI Barra, is a first-passage time model wherein it is assumed that investors do not know the default barrier. The approach allows a portfolio manager or credit analyst to include their view on the financial well-being of a company in calibrating the model to market data.

SUMMARY

In the first half of the 1970s, Black, Scholes, and Merton provided the underlying theory for all structural models. The basic idea is that a company defaults on its debt if the value of its assets falls below a certain default point and that the value of a corporate bond can be modeled as an option on these assets. With this insight, researchers were able to apply the same principles used for option pricing to the valuation of corporate bonds using the issuer's stock price and balance sheet data. The BSM model is based on some simplifying assumptions. There have been several modifications and extensions of the BSM model.

Reduced-form models do not look into the microeconomic factors of a company. Rather, they model directly the default probability or transition risk. The theoretical framework for reduced-form models is the Poisson process. The two most notable reduced-form models are the Jarrow-Turnbull and Duffie-Singleton models.

Both structural models and reduced-form models assume that the information reported by the issuing corporations is accurate. However, corporate bankruptcies in recent years that have been attributable to fraud and opaque/inaccurate financial accounting data have made practitioners aware that when modeling credit risk, there must be consideration of the possibility that information is imperfect. This has led to the development of incomplete information models. One such model that combines the structural and reduced-form models but incorporates incomplete information has been proposed by Giesecke and Goldberg.

---

[27]Darrell Duffie and David Lando, "Term Structures of Credit Spreads with Incomplete Accounting Information," *Econometrica*, 69 (2001), pp. 633–664; Umut Cetin, Robert A. Jarrow, Philip Protter, and Yildiray Yildirim, "Modeling Credit Risk with Partial Information," *Annals of Applied Probability*, 14 (2004), pp. 1167–1178; and Kay Giesecke, "Correlated Default with Incomplete Information," *Journal of Banking and Finance* 28 (2004), pp. 1521–1545.

[28]Kay Giesecke and Lisa Goldberg, "Forecasting Default in the Face of Uncertainty," *Journal of Derivatives* 12 (2004), pp. 14–25. For a further description of this model, see Backshall, Giesecke, and Goldberg, "Credit Risk Modeling," pp. 794–797.

Questions

1. Why is credit risk modeling more difficult than interest rate modeling?
2. A corporate bond portfolio manager was overhead asking: "Why do I need a credit risk model. I can get information about the probability of default from credit ratings?" How would you respond to this portfolio manager?
3. What is a common feature of all structural models?
4. Give two interpretations of the value of a bond from an option's perspective.
5. Explain how the Black-Scholes-Merton model has been extended to allow for multiple bond issues in a corporation's debt structure.
6. Explain how the Black-Scholes-Merton model has been extended to overcome the assumption that default can only occur at maturity.
7. How can structural models be used by bond portfolio managers?
8. Explain each of the following:
   a. expected default frequency
   b. market implied rating
   c. distance-to-default index measure
9. How does the treatment of default in structural models and reduced-form models differ?
10. How do the Jarrow-Turnbull and Duffie-Singleton reduced-form models differ?
11. How does the Jarrow-Turnbull-Lando model differ from the basic Jarrow-Turnbull model?
12. a. How is an event defined in the Poisson process?
    b. What is meant by the intensity parameter in the Poisson process?
13. a. What is the meaning of the default intensity parameter in a reduced-form model?
    b. What are the various ways that the default intensity parameter can be modeled in a reduced-form model?
14. What is meant by default correlation?
15. What is the drawback of the default correlation measure and what alternative measure is used in measuring portfolio credit risk?
16. What is the motivation for the development of incomplete information credit risk models.
17. Why is the calibration of a credit risk model to the market important in fixed income trading?

22

ACTIVE BOND PORTFOLIO MANAGEMENT STRATEGIES

After reading this chapter you will understand:

- the five basic steps involved in the investment management process

- the difference between active and passive strategies

- what tracking error is and how it is computed

- the difference between forward-looking and backward-looking tracking error

- the link between tracking error and active portfolio management

- the risk factors that affect a benchmark index

- the importance of knowing the market consensus before implementing an active strategy

- the different types of active bond portfolio strategies: interest-rate expectations strategies, yield curve strategies, yield spread strategies, option-adjusted spread-based strategies, and individual security selection strategies

- bullet, barbell, and ladder yield curve strategies

- the limitations of using duration and convexity to assess the potential performance of bond portfolio strategies

- why it is necessary to use the dollar duration when implementing a yield spread strategy

- how to assess the allocation of funds within the corporate bond sector

- why leveraging is used by managers and traders and the risks and rewards associated with leveraging

- how to leverage using the repo market

This chapter and the two that follow discuss bond portfolio management strategies. We begin with an overview of the investment management process and the factors to consider in the selection of a portfolio strategy, distinguishing between active portfolio strategies and structured portfolio strategies. Active strategies are discussed in this chapter, and structured portfolio strategies are the subject of the next two chapters.

OVERVIEW OF THE INVESTMENT MANAGEMENT PROCESS

Regardless of the type of financial institution, the investment management process involves the following five steps:

1. Setting investment objectives
2. Establishing investment policy
3. Selecting a portfolio strategy
4. Selecting assets
5. Measuring and evaluating performance

Setting Investment Objectives

The first step in the investment management process is setting investment objectives. The investment objective will vary by type of financial institution. For institutions such as pension funds, the investment objective is to generate sufficient cash flow from investments to satisfy pension obligations. For life insurance companies, the basic objective is to satisfy obligations stipulated in insurance policies and generate a profit. Most insurance products guarantee a dollar payment or a stream of dollar payments at some time in the future. The premium that the life insurance company charges a policyholder for one of its products will depend on the interest rate that the company can earn on its investments. To realize a profit, the life insurance company must earn a higher return on the premium it invests than the implicit (or explicit) interest rate it has guaranteed policyholders.

For institutions such as banks and thrifts, funds are obtained from the issuance of certificates of deposit, short-term money market instruments, or floating-rate notes. These funds are then invested in loans and marketable securities. The objective in this case is to earn a return on invested funds that is higher than the cost of acquiring those funds. For these sorts of institutions, investment objectives are dictated essentially by the nature of their liabilities—obligations to pension recipients, policyholders, and depositors. For investment companies (mutual funds), the investment objectives will be as set forth in a prospectus. With the exception of mutual funds that have a specified termination date (called **target term trusts**), there are no specific liabilities that must be met. Typically, the fund establishes a target dividend payout. Because of the importance of the nature of the liabilities in determining investment objectives, in Chapter 24 we examine this topic more closely.

Establishing Investment Policy

The second step in investment management is establishing policy guidelines for meeting the investment objectives. Setting policy begins with the asset allocation decision; that is, there must be a decision as to how the funds of the institution should be distributed among the major classes of investments (cash equivalents, equities, fixed-income securities, real estate, and foreign securities).

Client and regulatory constraints are considerations in establishing an investment policy. Examples of constraints that the sponsor of a pension fund might impose are the following: No funds may be invested in a bond of an issuer whose credit rating is below a specified level; no more than a predetermined percentage of the fund's assets may be invested in a particular industry; and options and futures may be used only to protect asset values, not for speculative purposes. Regulators of state-regulated institutions such as insurance companies (both life and property and casualty companies) may restrict the amount of funds allocated to certain major asset classes. Even the amount allocated within a major asset class may be restricted, depending on the characteristics of the particular asset. In the case of investment companies, restrictions on asset allocation are set forth in the prospectus when the fund is launched and may be changed only with approval of the fund's board of directors.

Tax and financial reporting implications must also be considered in adopting investment policies. For example, life insurance companies enjoy certain tax advantages that make investing in tax-exempt municipal securities generally unappealing. Because pension funds too are exempt from taxes, they also are not particularly interested in tax-exempt municipal securities.

Institutional investors must prepare periodic financial statements. These financial statements must be prepared in accordance with "generally accepted accounting principles" (GAAPs). Thus, the assets and liabilities reported are based on GAAP accounting. The accounting treatment for assets is governed by a relatively new accounting requirement, Statement of Financial Accounting Standards No. 115, more popularly referred to as FASB 115. Financial Accounting Standards Board Statements Nos. 87 and 88 and the Omnibus Budget Reconciliation Act of 1987 affect the ways in which pension funds establish investment policies.

It is unfortunate but true that financial reporting considerations can cause institutions to establish investment policies that may not be in the best interest of the institution in the long run. Basically, financial reporting considerations prior to the adoption of FASB 115 were due to the use of accounting for assets at cost rather than market value (i.e., marking assets to market). FASB 115 limited the use of reporting assets at cost.

Selecting a Portfolio Strategy

Selecting a portfolio strategy that is consistent with the objectives and policy guidelines of the client or institution is the third step in the investment management process. Portfolio strategies can be classified as either **active strategies** or **passive strategies**. Essential to all active strategies is specification of expectations about the factors that influence the performance of an asset class. In the case of active equity strategies, this may include forecasts of future earnings, dividends, or price/earnings ratios. In the case of active bond management, this may involve forecasts of future interest rates, future interest-rate volatility, or future yield spreads. Active portfolio strategies involving foreign securities will require forecasts of future exchange rates.

Passive strategies involve minimal expectational input. One popular type of passive strategy is indexing, whose objective is to replicate the performance of a predetermined index. Although indexing has been employed extensively in the management of equity portfolios, the use of indexing for managing bond portfolios is a relatively new practice.

Between the extremes of active and passive strategies have sprung up strategies that have elements of both. For example, the core of a portfolio may be indexed, with the balance managed actively or a portfolio may be primarily indexed but employ low-risk strategies to enhance the indexed portfolio's return. This strategy is commonly referred to as **enhanced indexing** or **indexing plus**.

In the bond area, several strategies classified as **structured portfolio strategies** have commonly been used. A structured portfolio strategy calls for design of a portfolio to achieve the performance of a predetermined benchmark. Such strategies are frequently followed when funding liabilities. When the predetermined benchmark is the generation of sufficient funds to satisfy a single liability, regardless of the course of future interest rates, a strategy known as **immunization** is often used. When the predetermined benchmark requires funding multiple future liabilities regardless of how interest rates change, strategies such as immunization, **cash flow matching** (or **dedication**), or **horizon matching** can be employed.

As part of the immunization and cash flow matching strategies, low-risk active management strategies can be employed. For example, contingent immunization strategy allows the portfolio manager to manage a portfolio actively until certain parameters are violated. If and when those parameters are violated, the portfolio is then immunized.

Indexing can also be considered a structured portfolio strategy, because the benchmark is to achieve the performance of a predetermined index.[1] In Chapter 23 and 24 we describe structured portfolio strategies: Chapter 23 focuses on indexing, and Chapter 24 on immunization and cash flow matching/dedication.

Given the choice among active, structured, or passive management, which should be selected? The answer depends on (1) the client or money manager's view of the pricing efficiency of the market, and (2) the nature of the liabilities to be satisfied. First let's consider the pricing efficiency of a market.

Pricing efficiency is taken to describe a market where prices at all times fully reflect all available information that is relevant to the valuation of securities. When a market is price-efficient, active strategies will not consistently produce superior returns after adjusting for (1) risk and (2) transactions costs.

What strategy should be pursued by an investor who believes that the market is sufficiently efficient that superior risk-adjusted returns cannot be realized consistently after accounting for transactions costs? Capital market theory argues that indexing is the strategy of choice.

But pricing efficiency is not the sole determinant of the type of investment strategy that should be employed. The nature of the liabilities is also of paramount importance. Although indexing may be a reasonable strategy for an institution that does not have a future liability stream to be satisfied, consider the circumstances in which pension funds operate. If a pension fund indexes its portfolio, the fund's return will be roughly the same as the index return. Yet the index may not provide a return that is sufficient to satisfy the fund's obligations. Consequently, for some institutions, such as pension funds and life insurance companies, structured portfolio strategies such as immunization

---

[1]Portfolio insurance strategies—strategies commonly used in the equity area to reproduce the payoff of a put option—where the objective is to ensure that the value of the portfolio does not fall below a predetermined level, are also viewed as structured portfolio strategies. However, portfolio insurance strategies are rarely used in the fixed-income area.

or dedication may be more appropriate to achieve investment objectives. Within the context of these strategies, an active or enhanced return strategy may be followed.

Selecting Assets

After a portfolio strategy is specified, the next step is to select the specific assets to be included in the portfolio, which requires an evaluation of individual securities. In an active strategy, this means identifying mispriced securities. In the case of bonds, the characteristics of a bond (i.e., coupon, maturity, credit quality, and options granted to either the issuer or bondholder) must be examined carefully to determine how these characteristics will influence the performance of the bond over some investment horizon.

It is in this phase that the investment manager attempts to construct an efficient portfolio. An efficient portfolio is one that provides the greatest expected return for a given level of risk, or, equivalently, the lowest risk for a given expected return.

Measuring and Evaluating Performance

The measurement and evaluation of investment performance is the last step in the investment management process. (Actually, it is technically not the "last" step because investment management is an ongoing process.) This step involves measuring the performance of the portfolio, then evaluating that performance relative to some benchmark. The benchmark selected for evaluating performance is called a **benchmark** or **normal portfolio**.

The benchmark portfolio may be a popular index such as the S&P 500 for equity portfolios or one of the bond indexes discussed in Chapter 23. Pension sponsors have worked with money managers and pension consultants to establish customized benchmark portfolios. Evaluating the performance of a money manager is not simple. Clients typically rely on the services of a firm that specializes in evaluating money managers.

Although the performance of a money manager according to some benchmark portfolio may seem superior, this does not necessarily mean that the portfolio satisfies its investment objective. For example, suppose that a life insurance company establishes as its objective the maximization of portfolio return and allocates 75% of the fund to stocks and the balance to bonds. Suppose further that the money manager responsible for the equity portfolio of this pension fund earns a return over a one-year horizon that is 200 basis points higher than the benchmark portfolio, which had a return of 2%. Assuming that the risk of the portfolio is similar to that of the benchmark portfolio, it would appear that the money manager outperformed the benchmark portfolio. Despite this performance, however, suppose that the life insurance company cannot meet its liabilities because the rate it must pay to policyholders is 7%. Then the failure is in establishing the investment objectives and setting policy, not in the money manager's performance.

TRACKING ERROR AND BOND PORTFOLIO STRATEGIES

Before discussing bond portfolio strategies, it is important to understand an important analytical concept. When a portfolio manager's benchmark is a bond market index, risk is not measured in terms of the standard deviation of the portfolio's return. Instead, risk is measured by the standard deviation of the return of the portfolio relative to the return of the benchmark index. This risk measure is called **tracking error**. Tracking error is also called **active risk**.

Calculation of Tracking Error

Tracking error is computed as follows:

Step 1: Compute the total return for a portfolio for each period.

Step 2: Obtain the total return for the benchmark index for each period.

Step 3: Obtain the difference between the values found in Step 1 and Step 2. The difference is referred to as the **active return**.

Step 4: Compute the standard deviation of the active returns. The resulting value is the tracking error.

Exhibit 22-1 shows the calculation of the tracking error for two hypothetical portfolios assuming that the benchmark is the Lehman Brothers Aggregate Bond Index. The observations are monthly for 2004. Portfolio A's monthly tracking error is 7.94 basis points. Notice that the monthly returns of the portfolio closely track the return of the benchmark index—that is, the active returns are small. In contrast, for Portfolio B,

---

EXHIBIT 22-1 Calculation of Tracking Error for Two Hypothetical Portfolios: Benchmark Is the Lehman Aggregate Bound Index

Observation period = January 2004–December 2004

| | Portfolio A | | |
Month in 2004	Portfolio Return (%)	Benchmark Index Return (%)	Active Return(%)
Jan	0.76	0.80	−0.04
Feb	1.00	1.08	−0.08
March	0.78	0.75	0.03
April	−2.51	−2.60	0.09
May	−0.47	−0.40	−0.07
June	0.61	0.57	0.05
July	1.08	0.99	0.09
Aug	1.81	1.91	−0.10
Sept	0.35	0.27	0.08
Oct	0.95	0.84	0.11
Nov	−0.89	−0.80	−0.09
Dec	0.95	0.92	0.03
Sum			0.095
Mean			0.0079
Variance			0.0063
Standard Deviation = Tracking error			0.0794
Tracking error (in basis points) =			7.94
			(continued)

EXHIBIT 22-1 (continued)

	Portfolio B		
Month in 2004	Portfolio Return (%)	Benchmark Index Return (%)	Active Return (%)
Jan	1.20	0.80	0.40
Feb	1.23	1.08	0.15
March	0.41	0.75	−0.34
April	−2.90	−2.60	−0.30
May	−0.20	−0.40	0.20
June	1.20	0.57	0.64
July	0.58	0.99	−0.41
Aug	1.06	1.91	−0.85
Sept	0.42	0.27	0.15
Oct	1.16	0.84	0.32
Nov	−1.80	−0.80	−1.00
Dec	1.12	0.92	0.20
Sum			−0.845
Mean			−0.0704
Variance			0.2562
Standard Deviation = Tracking error			0.5062
Tracking error (in basis points) =			50.62

Notes: active return = port folio return − benchmark index return
variance = sum of the squares of the deviations from the mean/11 (division by 11, which is number of observations minus 1)
standard deviation = tracking error = square root of variance.

the active returns are large and therefore the monthly tracking error is large—50.62 basis points.

The tracking error is also unique to the benchmark used. Exhibit 22-2 shows the tracking error for both portfolios using the Salomon Smith Barney BIG Index. The monthly tracking error for Portfolio A is 8.03 basis points compared to 7.94 basis points when the benchmark is the Lehman index; for Portfolio B it is 50.36 basis points versus 50.62 basis points.

The tracking error measurement is in terms of the observation period. If monthly returns are used, the tracking error is a monthly tracking error. If weekly returns are used, the tracking error is a weekly tracking error. Tracking error is annualized as follows:

When observations are monthly:
annual tracking error = monthly tracking error $\times \sqrt{12}$

When observations are weekly:
annual tracking error = monthly tracking error $\times \sqrt{52}$

Observation period = January 2004-December 2004

Portfolio A

Month in 2004	Portfolio Return (%)	Benchmark Index Return (%)	Active Return (%)
Jan	0.76	0.83	−0.06
Feb	1.00	1.07	−0.07
March	0.78	0.76	0.02
April	−2.51	−2.60	0.09
May	−0.47	−0.43	−0.04
June	0.61	0.59	0.02
July	1.08	0.99	0.09
Aug	1.81	1.98	−0.17
Sept	0.35	0.26	0.09
Oct	0.95	0.88	0.07
Nov	−0.89	−0.84	−0.06
Dec	0.95	0.96	−0.01
Sum			−0.041
Mean			−0.0034
Variance			0.0065
Standard Deviation = Tracking error			0.0803
Tracking error (in basis points) =			8.03

Portfolio B

Month in 2004	Portfolio Return (%)	Benchmark Index Return (%)	Active Return (%)
Jan	1.20	0.83	0.38
Feb	1.23	1.07	0.16
March	0.41	0.76	−0.35
April	−2.90	−2.60	−0.30
May	−0.20	−0.43	0.23
June	1.20	0.59	0.61
July	0.58	0.99	−0.41
Aug	1.06	1.98	−0.92
Sept	0.42	0.26	0.16
Oct	1.16	0.88	0.28
Nov	−1.80	−0.84	−0.97
Dec	1.12	0.96	0.16
Sum			−0.981
Mean			−0.0818
Variance			0.2536
Standard Deviation = Tracking error			0.5036
Tracking error (in basis points) =			50.36

Notes: active return = portfolio return − benchmark index return
variance = sum of the squares of the deviations from the mean/11 (division by 11, which is number of observations minus 1)
standard deviation = tracking error = square root of variance.

For example, when the Lehman index is used, the annual tracking error for Portfolio A and Portfolio B is

Annual tracking error for Portfolio A = 7.94 basis points $\times \sqrt{12}$ = 27.50 basis points
Annual tracking error for Portfolio B = 50.62 basis points $\times \sqrt{12}$ = 175.35 basis points

Two Faces of Tracking Error

We have just described how to calculate tracking error based on the actual active returns observed for a portfolio. Calculations computed for a portfolio based on a portfolio's actual active returns reflect the portfolio manager's decisions during the observation period with respect to the factors that we describe later in this chapter that affect tracking error. We call tracking error calculated from observed active returns for a portfolio **backward-looking tracking error**. It is also called the **ex-post tracking error** and the **actual tracking error**.

A problem with using backward-looking tracking error in bond portfolio management is that it does not reflect the effect of current decisions by the portfolio manager on the future active returns and hence the future tracking error that may be realized. If, for example, the manager significantly changes the portfolio's duration or allocation to the mortgage market sector today, then the backward-looking tracking error which is calculated using data from prior periods would not accurately reflect the current portfolio risks going forward. That is, the backward-looking tracking error will have little predictive value and can be misleading regarding portfolio risks going forward.

The portfolio manager needs a forward-looking estimate of tracking error to reflect the portfolio risk going forward. The way this is done in practice is by using the services of a commercial vendor or dealer firm that has modeled the factors that affect the tracking error associated with the bond market index that is the portfolio manager's benchmark. These models are called **multi-factor risk models**. Given a manager's current portfolio holdings, the portfolio's current exposure to the various risk factors can be calculated and compared to the benchmark's exposures to the factors. Using the differential factor exposures and the risks of the factors, a **forward-looking tracking error** for the portfolio can be computed. This tracking error is also referred to as **predicted tracking error** and **ex ante tracking error**.

Given a forward-looking tracking error, a range for the future possible portfolio active return can be calculated assuming that the active returns are normally distributed. For example, assume the following:

benchmark = Lehman Aggregate Bond Index
expected return for Lehman Aggregate Bond Index = 10%
forward-looking tracking error relative to Lehman Aggregate Bond Index =
    100 basis points

From the properties of a normal distribution we know the following:

Number of Standard Deviations	Range for Portfolio Active Return	Corresponding Range for Portfolio Return	Probability
1	−1%	9%–11%	67%
2	−2%	8%–12%	95%
3	−3%	7%–13%	99%

It should be noted that there is no guarantee that the forward-looking tracking error at the start of, say, a year would exactly match the backward-looking tracking error calculated at the end of the year. There are two reasons for this. The first is that as the year progresses and changes are made to the portfolio, the forward-looking tracking error estimate would change to reflect the new exposures. The second is that the accuracy of the forward-looking tracking error at the beginning of the year depends on the extent of the stability of the variances and correlations that commercial vendors use in their statistical models to estimate forward-looking tracking error. These problems notwithstanding, the average of forward-looking tracking error estimates obtained at different times during the year will be reasonably close to the backward-looking tracking error estimate obtained at the end of the year.

The forward-looking tracking error is useful in risk control and portfolio construction. The manager can immediately see the likely effect on tracking error of any intended change in the portfolio. Thus, scenario analysis can be performed by a portfolio manager to assess proposed portfolio strategies and eliminate those that would result in tracking error beyond a specified tolerance for risk.[2]

Tracking Error and Active Versus Passive Strategies

Now that we know what tracking error is, we can think of active versus passive bond portfolio strategies in terms of forward-looking tracking error. In constructing a portfolio, a manager can estimate its forward-looking tracking error. When a portfolio is constructed to have a forward-looking tracking error of zero, the manager has effectively designed the portfolio to replicate the performance of the benchmark. If the forward-looking tracking error is maintained for the entire investment period, the active return should be close to zero. Such a strategy—one with a forward-looking tracking error of zero or very small—indicates that the manager is pursing a passive strategy relative to the benchmark index. When the forward-looking tracking error is large, the manager is pursuing an active strategy.

Risk Factors and Portfolio Management Strategies

Forward-looking tracking error indicates the degree of active portfolio management being pursued by a manager. Therefore, it is necessary to understand what factors (referred to as **risk factors**) affect the performance of a manager's benchmark index. The degree to which the manager constructs a portfolio that has exposure to the risk factors that is different from the risk factors that affect the benchmark determines the forward-looking tracking error.

The risk factors affecting the Lehman Brothers Aggregate Bond Index have been investigated by Lev Dynkin, Jay Hyman, and Wei Wu.[3] A summary of the risk factors is provided in Exhibit 22-3. Dynkin, Hyman, and Wu first classify the risk factors into two types: systematic risk factors and non-systematic risk factors. **Systematic risk factors** are forces that affect all securities in a certain category in the benchmark index. **Non-systematic factor** risk is the risk that is not attributable to the systematic risk factors.

---

[2]For a parallel discussion regarding the role of tracking error for managing a common stock portfolio, see Raman Vardharaj, Frank J. Jones, and Frank J. Fabozzi, "Tracking Error and Common Stock Portfolio Management," Chapter 7 in Frank J. Fabozzi and Harry M. Markowitz (eds.), *The Theory and Practice of Investment Management* (New York: John Wiley & Sons, 2002).

[3]Lev Dynkin, Jay Hyman, and Wei Wu, "Multi-Factor Risk Factors and Their Applications," in Frank J. Fabozzi (ed.), *Professional Perspectives on Fixed Income Portfolio Management*, Volume 2 (New Hope, PA: Frank J. Fabozzi Associates, 2001).

EXHIBIT 22-3   Summary of Risk Factors for a Benchmark

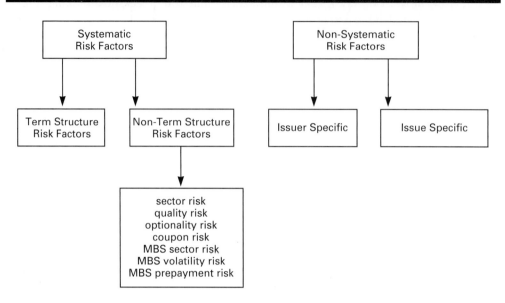

Systematic risk factors, in turn, are divided into two categories: term structure risk factors and non-term structure risk factors. **Term structure risk factors** are associated with changes in the shape of the term structure (level and shape changes). **Non-term structure risk factors** include the following:

- sector risk
- quality risk
- optionality risk
- coupon risk
- MBS sector risk
- MBS volatility risk
- MBS prepayment risk

Sector risk is the risk associated with exposure to the sectors of the benchmark index. For example, consider the Lehman Brother Aggregate Bond Index. At the macro level, these sectors include Treasury, agencies, corporates, residential mortgages, commercial mortgages, and asset-backed. Each of these sectors is divided further. For example, the corporate sector (called the credit sector) is divided into financial institutions, industrials, transportations, and utilities. In turn, each of these subsectors is further divided. The financial institutions subsector, for example, is broken down into the following: banking, brokerage, financial companies, insurance, and other. For the residential mortgage market (which includes agency pass-through securities), the breakdown is as follows: Ginnie Mae 30-year MBS, 15-year MBS, conventional MBS (Fannie Mae and Freddie Mac MBS), and balloon MBS. There is an even further breakdown by the coupon of the MBS (e.g., coupon rate less than 6%, between 6% and 7%, between 7% and 8%, between 8% and 9%, between 9% and 10%, and greater than 10%).

Quality risk is the risk associated with exposure to the credit rating of the securities in the benchmark index. The breakdown for the Lehman Brothers Aggregate Bond Index, which includes only investment-grade credits, is Aaa+, Aaa, Aa, A, Baa, and MBS. MBS includes credit exposure to the agency pass-through sector.

Optionality risk is the risk associated with an adverse impact on the embedded options of the securities in the benchmark index. This includes embedded options in callable and putable corporate bonds, MBS, and ABS. **Coupon risk** is the exposure of the securities in the benchmark index to different coupon rates.

The last three risks are associated with investing in residential mortgage pass-through securities. The first is **MBS sector risk**, which is the exposure to the sectors of the MBS market included in the benchmark: Ginnie Mae 30-year MBS, 15-year MBS, conventional MBS, and balloon MBS by coupon rate (less than 6%, between 6% and 7%, between 7% and 8%, between 8% and 9%, between 9% and 10%, and greater than 10%). As explained in Chapter 18, the value of an MBS depends on the expected interest rate volatility and prepayments. **MBS volatility risk** is the exposure of a benchmark index to changes in expected interest-rate volatility. **MBS prepayment risk** is the exposure of a benchmark index to changes in prepayments.

Non-systematic factor risks are classified as non-systematic risks associated with a particular issuer, **issuer-specific risk**, and those associated with a particular issue, **issue-specific risk**.

Determinants of Tracking Error

Once we know what the risk factors that are associated with a benchmark index, forward-looking tracking error can be estimated for a portfolio. The tracking error occurs because the portfolio constructed deviates from the risk factor exposures for the benchmark index. Here are two simple examples.

First, suppose that the duration for the Lehman Brothers Aggregate Bond Index is 4.3 and a portfolio manager constructs a portfolio with a duration of 4.9. Then there is different exposure to changes in the level of interest rates. This is one element of systematic term structure factor risk. What can be determined from the difference in durations is what the (forward-looking) tracking error due to the term structure risk factor will be.

As a second example, suppose that the manager has more exposure to the Baa-rated sector and less exposure to the Aa-rated sector than the Lehman Brothers Aggregate Bond Index. For this difference in exposure, the (forward-looking) tracking error due to the quality factor risk can be estimated.

In sum, the tracking error for a portfolio relative to a benchmark index can be decomposed as follows:

I. Tracking error due to systematic risk factors
   a. Tracking error due to term structure risk factor
   b. Tracking error due to non-term structure risk factors
      1. Tracking error due to sector
      2. Tracking error due to quality
      3. Tracking error due to optionality
      4. Tracking error due to coupon
      5. Tracking error due to MBS sector

6. Tracking error due to MBS volatility
7. Tracking error due to MBS prepayment

II. Tracking error due to non-systematic risk factors
  a. Tracking error due to issuer-specific risk
  b. Tracking error due to issue-specific risk

A manager provided with information about (forwarding-looking) tracking error for the current portfolio can quickly assess (1) if the risk exposure for the portfolio is one that is acceptable and (2) if the particular exposures are those desired. A client can in fact use forward-looking tracking error to communicate the degree of active portfolio management that it wants the portfolio manager to pursue.

Where are the forward-looking tracking errors obtained? Using historical returns, vendors of multi-factor risk models have constructed databases using statistical techniques that provide forward-looking tracking error.

ACTIVE PORTFOLIO STRATEGIES

Armed with an understanding of the risk factors for a benchmark index and how to gauge the risk exposure of a portfolio relative to a benchmark index using forward-looking tracking error, we now discuss various active portfolio strategies that are typically employed by managers.

Manager Expectations Versus the Market Consensus

A money manager who pursues an active strategy will position a portfolio to capitalize on expectations about future interest rates, but the potential outcome (as measured by total return) must be assessed before an active strategy is implemented. The primary reason for this is that the market (collectively) has certain expectations for future interest rates and these expectations are embodied into the market price of bonds. One lesson we learned in Chapter 5 when we discussed forward rates is that the outcome of a strategy will depend on how a manager's expectation differs from that of the market. Moreover, it does not make a difference if the market's expectation is correct. What is relevant is that the price of a bond embodies those expectations. The same is true for the strategies we discuss in this chapter.

Consequently, though some managers might refer to an "optimal strategy" that should be pursued given certain expectations, that is insufficient information in making an investment decision. If the market's expectations are the same as the manager's, bond prices reflect these expectations. For this reason we emphasize the use of the total return framework for evaluating active strategies rather than the blind pursuit of a strategy based merely on general statements such as "if you expect . . . , you should pursue . . . strategy."

Interest-Rate Expectations Strategies

A money manager who believes that he or she can accurately forecast the future level of interest rates will alter the portfolio's sensitivity to interest-rate changes. As duration is a measure of interest-rate sensitivity, this involves increasing a portfolio's duration if interest rates are expected to fall and reducing duration if interest rates are expected to rise. For those managers whose benchmark is a bond index, this means increasing the portfolio duration relative to the benchmark index if interest rates are expected to fall and reducing it if interest rates are expected to rise. The degree to which the duration of the managed portfolio is permitted to diverge from that of the benchmark index may be limited by the client.

A portfolio's duration may be altered by swapping (or exchanging) bonds in the portfolio for new bonds that will achieve the target portfolio duration. Such swaps are commonly referred to as **rate anticipation swaps**. Alternatively, a more efficient means for altering the duration of a bond portfolio is to use interest-rate futures contracts. As we explain in Chapter 26, buying futures increases a portfolio's duration, whereas selling futures decreases it.

The key to this active strategy is, of course, an ability to forecast the direction of future interest rates. The academic literature, however, does not support the view that interest rates can be forecasted so that risk-adjusted excess returns can be realized consistently. It is doubtful whether betting on future interest rates will provide a consistently superior return.

Although a manager may not pursue an active strategy based strictly on future interest-rate movements, there can be a tendency to make an interest-rate bet to cover inferior performance relative to a benchmark index. For example, suppose that a manager holds himself or herself out to a client as pursuing one of the active strategies discussed later in this chapter. Suppose further that the manager is evaluated over a one-year investment horizon and that three months before the end of the investment horizon the manager is performing below the client-specified benchmark index. If the manager believes the account will be lost because of underperformance, there is an incentive to bet on interest-rate movements. If the manager is correct, the account will be saved, although an incorrect bet will result in underperforming the benchmark index by a greater amount. A client can prevent this type of gaming by a manager by imposing constraints on the degree that the portfolio's duration can vary from that of the benchmark index. Also, in the performance-evaluation stage of the investment management process described in Chapter 25, decomposing the portfolio's return into the factors that generated the return will highlight the extent to which a portfolio's return is attributable to changes in the level of interest rates.

There are other active strategies that rely on forecasts of future interest-rate levels. Future interest rates, for instance, affect the value of options embedded in callable bonds and the value of prepayment options embedded in mortgage-backed securities. Callable corporate and municipal bonds with coupon rates above the expected future interest rate will underperform relative to noncallable bonds or low-coupon bonds. This is because of the negative convexity feature of callable bonds. For the wide range of mortgage-backed securities described in Chapters 11 and 12, the effect of interest rates on prepayments cause some to benefit from higher future interest rates and others to benefit from lower future interest rates.

Yield Curve Strategies

As we explained in Chapter 5, the yield curve for U.S. Treasury securities shows the relationship between their maturities and yields. The shape of this yield curve changes over time. **Yield curve strategies** involve positioning a portfolio to capitalize on expected changes in the shape of the Treasury yield curve. In this section we describe various ways in which the Treasury yield curve has shifted, the different types of yield curve strategies, the usefulness of duration as a measure of the price sensitivity of a bond or portfolio when the yield curve shifts, and how to assess the potential outcome of yield curve strategies.

Types of Shifts in the Yield Curve and Impact on Historical Returns

A shift in the yield curve refers to the relative change in the yield for each Treasury maturity. A **parallel shift in the yield curve** is a shift in which the change in the yield on all maturities is the same. A **nonparallel shift in the yield curve** indicates that the yield for maturities does not change by the same number of basis points.

Historically, two types of nonparallel yield curve shifts have been observed: a twist in the slope of the yield curve and a change in the humpedness of the yield curve. All of these shifts are portrayed graphically in Exhibit 22-4. A twist in the slope of the yield

EXHIBIT 22-4   Types of Yield Curve Shifts

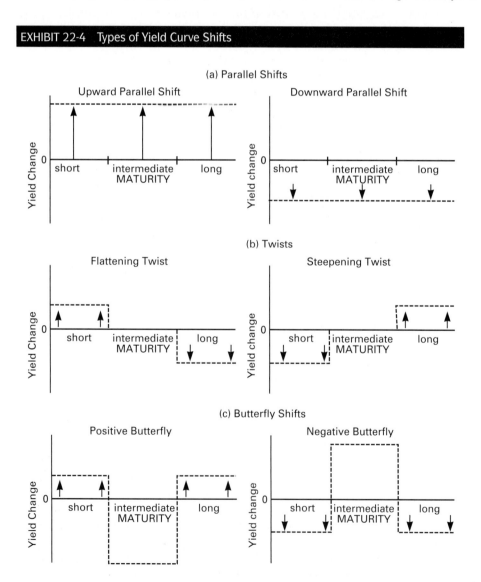

curve refers to a flattening or steepening of the yield curve. In practice, the slope of the yield curve is measured by the spread between some long-term Treasury yield and some short-term Treasury yield. For example, some practitioners refer to the slope as the difference between the 30-year Treasury yield and the one-year Treasury yield. Others refer to it as the spread between the 20-year Treasury yield and the two-year Treasury yield. Regardless of how it is defined, a **flattening of the yield curve** indicates that the yield spread between the yield on a long-term and a short-term Treasury has decreased; a **steepening of the yield curve** indicates that the yield spread between a long-term and a short-term Treasury has increased. The other type of nonparallel shift, a change in the humpedness of the yield curve, is referred to as a **butterfly shift**.

Frank Jones analyzed the types of yield curve shifts that occurred between 1979 and 1990.[4] He found that the three types of yield curve shifts are not independent, with the two most common types of yield curve shifts being (1) a downward shift in the yield curve combined with a steepening of the yield curve, and (2) an upward shift in the yield curve combined with a flattening of the yield curve. These two types of shifts in the yield curve are depicted in Exhibit 22-5. For example, his statistical analysis indicated that an upward parallel shift in the Treasury yield curve and a flattening of the yield curve have a correlation of 0.41. This suggests that an upward shift of the yield curve by 10 basis points is consistent with a 2.5-basis-point flattening of the yield curve. Moreover, he finds that an upward shift and flattening of the yield curve is correlated with a positive butterfly (less humpedness), whereas a downward shift and steepening of the yield curve is correlated with a negative butterfly (more humpedness).

Jones also provides empirical evidence of the importance of changes in the yield curve in determining returns of Treasury securities for various maturity sectors from 1979 to 1990. He finds that parallel shifts and twists in the yield curve are responsible for 91.6% of Treasury returns, 3.4% of the return is attributable to butterfly shifts and the balance, 5%, to unexplained factor shifts.[5] This discussion indicates that yield curve strategies require a forecast of the direction of the shift and a forecast of the type of twist.

Yield Curve Strategies

In portfolio strategies that seek to capitalize on expectations based on short-term movements in yields, the dominant source of return is the impact on the price of the securities in the portfolio. This means that the maturity of the securities in the portfolio will have an important impact on the portfolio's return. For example, a total return over a one-year investment horizon for a portfolio consisting of securities all maturing in one year will not be sensitive to changes in how the yield curve shifts one year from now. In contrast, the total return over a one-year investment horizon for a portfolio consisting of securities all maturing in 30 years will be sensitive to how the yield curve shifts because one year from now the value of the portfolio will depend on the yield offered on 29-year securities. As we know from Chapter 3, long maturity bonds have substantial price volatility when yields change.

---

[4]Frank J. Jones, "Yield Curve Strategies," *Journal of Fixed Income*, September 1991, pp. 43–48.
[5]These findings are consistent with those reported in Robert Litterman and Jose Scheinkman, "Common Factors Affecting Bond Returns," *Journal of Fixed Income*, June 1991, pp. 54–61.

EXHIBIT 22-5   Combinations of Yield Curve Shifts

Upward Shift/Flattening/Positive Butterfly

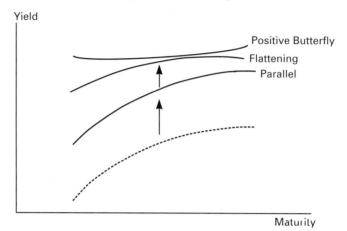

Downward Shift/Steepening/Negative Butterfly

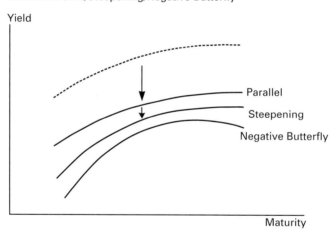

When the yield curve shifts, a portfolio consisting of equal proportions of securities maturing in one year and securities maturing in 30 years will have quite a different total return over a one-year investment horizon than the two portfolios we described previously. The price of the one-year securities in the portfolio will not be sensitive to how the one-year yield has changed, but the price of the 30-year securities will be highly sensitive to how long-term yields have changed.

The key point is that for short-term investment horizons, the spacing of the maturity of bonds in the portfolio will have a significant impact on the total return. Consequently, yield curve strategies involve positioning a portfolio with respect to the maturities of the securities across the maturity spectrum included in the portfolio. There are three yield curve strategies: (1) bullet strategies, (2) barbell strategies, and (3) ladder strategies. Each of these strategies is depicted in Exhibit 22-6.

EXHIBIT 22-6   Yield Curve Strategies: Bullet, Barbell, and Ladder

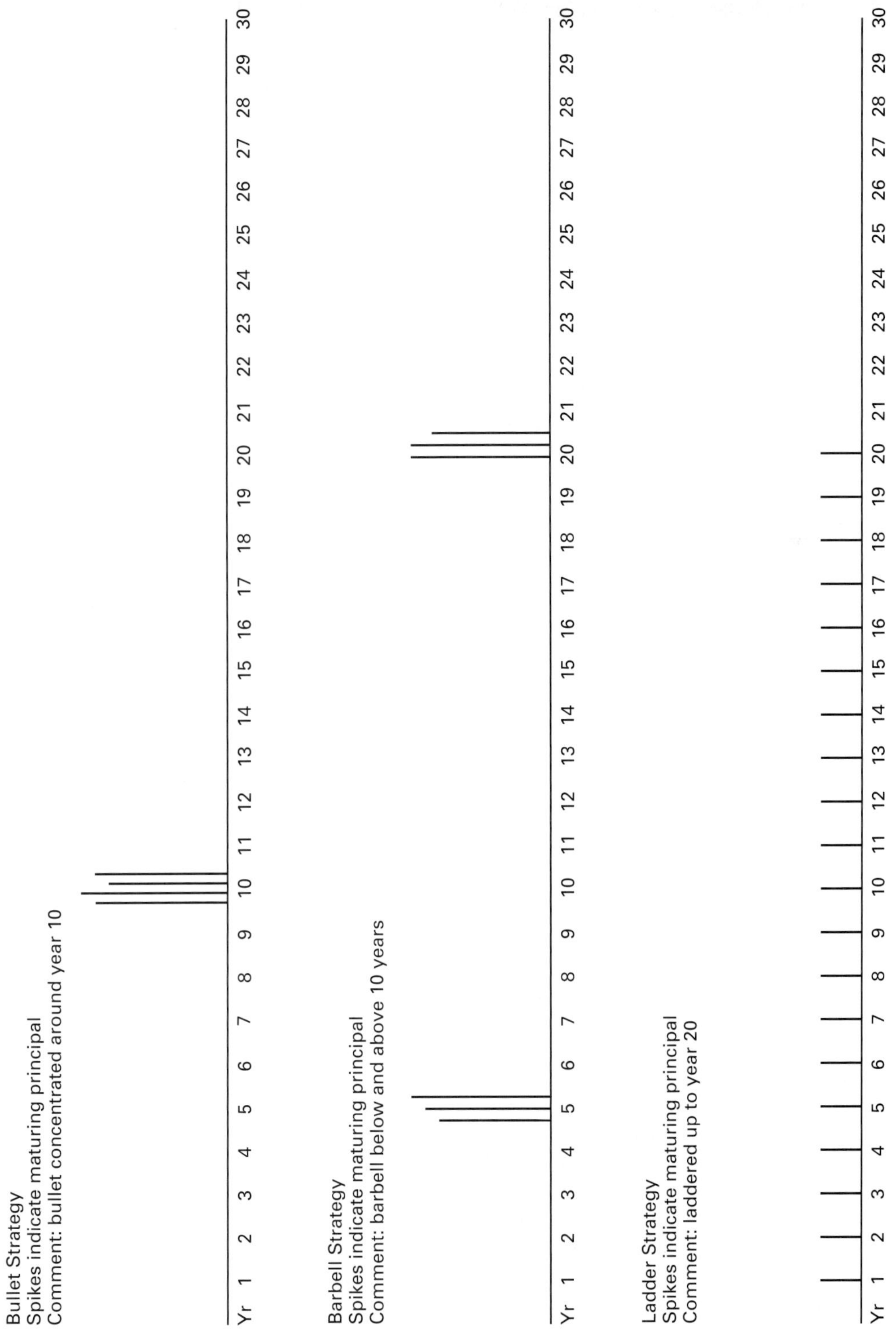

Bullet Strategy
Spikes indicate maturing principal
Comment: bullet concentrated around year 10

Yr 1 2 3 4 5 6 7 8 9 10 11 12 13 14 15 16 17 18 19 20 21 22 23 24 25 26 27 28 29 30

Barbell Strategy
Spikes indicate maturing principal
Comment: barbell below and above 10 years

Yr 1 2 3 4 5 6 7 8 9 10 11 12 13 14 15 16 17 18 19 20 21 22 23 24 25 26 27 28 29 30

Ladder Strategy
Spikes indicate maturing principal
Comment: laddered up to year 20

Yr 1 2 3 4 5 6 7 8 9 10 11 12 13 14 15 16 17 18 19 20 21 22 23 24 25 26 27 28 29 30

527

In a **bullet strategy**, the portfolio is constructed so that the maturity of the securities in the portfolio are highly concentrated at one point on the yield curve. In a **barbell strategy**, the maturity of the securities included in the portfolio are concentrated at two extreme maturities. Actually, in practice when managers refer to a barbell strategy it is relative to a bullet strategy. For example, a bullet strategy might be to create a portfolio with maturities concentrated around 10 years, whereas a corresponding barbell strategy might be a portfolio with 5- and 20-year maturities. In a **ladder strategy** the portfolio is constructed to have approximately equal amounts of each maturity. So, for example, a portfolio might have equal amounts of securities with one year to maturity, two years to maturity, and so on.

Each of these strategies will result in a different performance when the yield curve shifts. The actual performance will depend on both the type of shift and the magnitude of the shift. Thus, no general statements can be made about the optimal yield curve strategy. The framework for analyzing a yield curve strategy will be discussed later.

Duration and Yield Curve Shifts

Before discussing how to analyze yield curve strategies, let's reconsider the concept of duration and its role in approximating the price volatility of a bond portfolio when the yield curve shifts. In Chapter 4 we explained how duration is a measure of the sensitivity of the price of a bond or the value of a bond portfolio to changes in market yields. Thus, a portfolio with a duration of 4 means that if market yields change by 100 basis points, the portfolio will change by approximately 4%.

In explaining the limitations of duration, we indicated that there is an assumption made about how market yields change. Specifically, if a portfolio of bonds consists of 5-, 10-, and 20-year bonds, and the portfolio's duration is 4, what market yield is assumed to change when we say that this portfolio will change in value by 4% if yields change by 100 basis points? Is it the 5-year yield, the 10-year yield, or the 20-year yield? In fact, the assumption made when using duration as a measure of how the value of a portfolio will change if market yields change is that the yield on *all* maturities will change by the same number of basis points. Thus, if our three-bond portfolio has a duration of 4, the statement that the portfolio's value will change by 4% for a 100 basis-point change in yields actually should be stated as follows: The portfolio's value will change by 4% if the yield on 5-, 10-, and 20-year bonds all change by 100 basis points. That is, it is assumed that there is a parallel yield curve shift.

An illustration of what happens to a bond portfolio when the yield curve shift is not parallel is demonstrated in the next section. The key point of the illustration is that two portfolios with the same duration may perform quite differently when the yield curve shifts.

Analyzing Expected Yield Curve Strategies

The proper way to analyze any portfolio strategy is to look at its potential total return. We indicated this at the outset of this chapter. If a manager wants to assess the outcome of a portfolio for any assumed shift in the Treasury yield curve, this should be done by calculating the potential total return if that shift actually occurs.

We illustrate this by looking at the performance of two hypothetical portfolios of Treasury securities assuming different shifts in the Treasury yield curve. The three hypothetical Treasury securities shown in Exhibit 22-7 are considered for inclusion in

EXHIBIT 22-7	Three Hypothetical Treasury Securities					
Bond	Coupon (%)	Maturity (years)	Price Plus Accrued	Yield to Maturity (%)	Dollar Duration	Dollar Convexity
A	8.50	5	100	8.50	4.005	19.8164
B	9.50	20	100	9.50	8.882	124.1702
C	9.25	10	100	9.25	6.434	55.4506

our two portfolios.[6] Thus, for our illustration, the Treasury yield curve consists of these three Treasury securities: a short-term security (A, the 5-year security), an intermediate-term security (C, the 10-year security), and a long-term security (B, the 20-year security).

Consider the following two yield curve strategies: a bullet strategy and a barbell strategy. We will label the portfolios created based on these two strategies as the "bullet portfolio" and the "barbell portfolio" and they comprise the following:

- *Bullet portfolio:* 100% bond C
- *Barbell portfolio:* 50.2% bond A and 49.8% bond B

The bullet portfolio consists of only bond C, the 10-year bond. In our hypothetical portfolio, all the principal is received when bond C matures in 10 years. The barbell portfolio consists of almost an equal amount of the short- and long-term securities. It is the result of a barbell strategy because principal will be received at two ends of the maturity spectrum. Specifically, relative to the bullet portfolio, which in our illustration has all its principal being returned in 10 years, for the barbell portfolio the principal is being returned at shorter (5 years) and longer (20 years) dates.

As we explained in Chapter 4, dollar duration is a measure of the dollar price sensitivity of a bond or a portfolio. As indicated in Exhibit 22-7, the dollar duration for the bullet portfolio per 100-basis-point change in yield is 6.434. For the barbell portfolio, the dollar duration is just the weighted average of the dollar duration of the two bonds. Therefore,

dollar duration of barbell portfolio = 0.502(4.005) + 0.498(8.882) = 6.434

The dollar duration of the barbell portfolio is the same as that of the bullet portfolio. (In fact, the barbell portfolio was designed to produce this result.)

As we explained in Chapter 4, duration is just a first approximation of the change in price resulting from a change in interest rates. Convexity provides a second approximation. Although we did not discuss **dollar convexity**, it has a meaning similar to *convexity*, in that it provides a second approximation to the dollar price change. For two portfolios with the same dollar duration, the greater the convexity, the better the performance of a bond or a portfolio when yields change. What is necessary to understand for this illustration is that the larger the dollar convexity, the greater the dollar price

---

[6]This illustration is adapted from Ravi E. Dattatreya and Frank J. Fabozzi, *Active Total Return Management of Fixed Income Portfolios* (Chicago: Probus Publishing, 1989).

change due to a portfolio's convexity. As shown in Exhibit 22-7, the dollar convexity of the bullet portfolio is 55.4506. The dollar convexity for the barbell portfolio is a weighted average of the dollar convexity of the two bonds. That is,

dollar convexity of barbell portfolio = 0.502(19.8164) + 0.498(124.1702) = 71.7846

Therefore, the dollar convexity of the barbell portfolio is greater than that of the barbell portfolio.

Similarly, the yield for the two portfolios is not the same. The yield for the bullet portfolio is simply the yield to maturity of bond C, 9.25%. The traditional yield calculation for the barbell portfolio, which is found by taking a weighted average of the yield to maturity of the two bonds included in the portfolio, is 8.998%:

portfolio yield for barbell portfolio = 0.502(8.50%) + 0.498(9.50%) = 8.998%

This approach suggests that the yield of the bullet portfolio is 25.2 basis points greater than that of the barbell portfolio (9.25% − 8.998%). Although both portfolios have the same dollar duration, the yield of the bullet portfolio is greater than the yield of the barbell portfolio. However, the dollar convexity of the barbell portfolio is greater than that of the bullet portfolio. The difference in the two yields is sometimes referred to as the **cost of convexity** (i.e., giving up yield to get better convexity).

Now suppose that a portfolio manager with a six-month investment horizon has a choice of investing in the bullet portfolio or the barbell portfolio. Which one should he choose? The manager knows that (1) the two portfolios have the same dollar duration, (2) the yield for the bullet portfolio is greater than that of the barbell portfolio, and (3) the dollar convexity of the barbell portfolio is greater than that of the bullet portfolio. Actually, this information is not adequate in making the decision. What is necessary is to assess the potential total return when the yield curve shifts.

Exhibit 22-8 provides an analysis of the six-month total return of the two portfolios when the yield curve shifts.[7] The numbers reported in the exhibit are the difference in the total return for the two portfolios. Specifically, the following is shown:

difference in dollar return = bullet portfolio's total return
− barbell portfolio's total return

Thus, a positive value means that the bullet portfolio outperformed the barbell portfolio, and a negative sign means that the barbell portfolio outperformed the bullet portfolio.

Let's focus on the second column of Exhibit 22-8, which is labeled "parallel shift." This is the relative total return of the two portfolios over the six-month investment horizon assuming that the yield curve shifts in a parallel fashion. In this case parallel movement of the yield curve means that the yields for the short-term bond (A), the intermediate-term bond (C), and the long-term bond (B) change by the same number of basis points, shown in the "yield change" column of the table.

---

[7]Note that no assumption is needed for the reinvestment rate because the three bonds shown in Exhibit 22-7 are assumed to be trading right after a coupon payment has been made, and therefore there is no accrued interest.

EXHIBIT 22-8   Relative Performance of Bullet Portfolio and Barbell Portfolio over a Six-Month Investment Horizon[a]

Yield Change	Parallel Shift	Nonparallel Shift[b]	Nonparallel Shift[c] (%)
−5.000	−7.19	−10.69	−3.89
−4.750	−6.28	−9.61	−3.12
−4.500	−5.44	−8.62	−2.44
−4.250	−4.68	−7.71	−1.82
−4.000	−4.00	−6.88	−1.27
−3.750	−3.38	−6.13	−0.78
−3.500	−2.82	−5.44	−0.35
−3.250	−2.32	−4.82	0.03
−3.000	−1.88	−4.26	0.36
−2.750	−1.49	−3.75	0.65
−2.500	−1.15	−3.30	0.89
−2.250	−0.85	−2.90	1.09
−2.000	−0.59	−2.55	1.25
−1.750	−0.38	−2.24	1.37
−1.500	−0.20	−1.97	1.47
−1.250	−0.05	−1.74	1.53
−1.000	0.06	−1.54	1.57
−0.750	0.15	−1.38	1.58
−0.500	0.21	−1.24	1.57
−0.250	0.24	−1.14	1.53
0.000	0.25	−1.06	1.48
0.250	0.24	−1.01	1.41
0.500	0.21	−0.98	1.32
0.750	0.16	−0.97	1.21
1.000	0.09	−0.98	1.09
1.250	0.01	−1.00	0.96
1.500	−0.08	−1.05	0.81
1.750	−0.19	−1.10	0.66
2.000	−0.31	−1.18	0.49
2.250	−0.44	−1.26	0.32

[a]Performance is based on the difference in total return over a six-month investment horizon. Specifically,

$$\text{bullet portfolio's total return} - \text{barbell portfolio's total return}$$

Therefore, a negative value means that the barbell portfolio outperformed the bullet portfolio.
[b]Change in yield for bond C. Nonparallel shift as follows (flattening of yield curve):

$$\text{yield change bond A} = \text{yield change bond C} + 25 \text{ basis points}$$

$$\text{yield change bond B} = \text{yield change bond C} - 25 \text{ basis points}$$

[c]Change in yield for bond C. Nonparallel shift as follows (steepening of yield curve):

$$\text{yield change bond A} = \text{yield change bond C} - 25 \text{ basis points}$$

$$\text{yield change bond B} = \text{yield change bond C} + 25 \text{ basis points}$$

(continued)

EXHIBIT 22-8 (continued)

Yield Change	Parallel Shift	Nonparallel Shift[b]	Nonparallel Shift[c] (%)
2.500	−0.58	−1.36	0.14
2.750	−0.73	−1.46	−0.05
3.000	−0.88	−1.58	−0.24
3.250	−1.05	−1.70	−0.44
3.500	−1.21	−1.84	−0.64
3.750	−1.39	−1.98	−0.85
4.000	−1.57	−2.12	−1.06
4.250	−1.75	−2.27	−1.27
4.500	−1.93	−2.43	−1.48
4.750	−2.12	−2.58	−1.70
5.000	−2.31	−2.75	−1.92

Which portfolio is the better investment alternative if the yield curve shifts in a parallel fashion and the investment horizon is six months? The answer depends on the amount by which yields change. Notice that when yields change by less than 100 basis points, the bullet portfolio outperforms the barbell portfolio. The reverse is true if yields change by more than 100 basis points.

This illustration makes two key points. First, even if the yield curve shifts in a parallel fashion, two portfolios with the same dollar duration will not give the same performance. The reason is that the two portfolios do not have the same dollar convexity. The second point is that although with all other things equal it is better to have more convexity than less, the market charges for convexity in the form of a higher price or a lower yield. But the benefit of the greater convexity depends on how much yields change. As can be seen from the second column of Exhibit 22-8, if market yields change by less than 100 basis points (up or down), the bullet portfolio, which has less convexity, will provide a better total return.

Now let's look at what happens if the yield curve does not shift in a parallel fashion. The last two columns of Exhibit 22-8 show the relative performance of the two portfolios for a nonparallel shift of the yield curve. Specifically, the first nonparallel shift column assumes that if the yield on bond C (the intermediate-term bond) changes by the amount shown in the first column, bond A (the short-term bond) will change by the same amount plus 25 basis points, whereas bond B (the long-term bond) will change by the same amount shown in the first column less 25 basis points. Measuring the steepness of the yield curve as the spread between the long-term yield (yield on bond B) and the short-term yield (yield on Bond A), the spread has decreased by 50 basis points. As we noted earlier, such a nonparallel shift means a flattening of the yield curve. As can be seen in Exhibit 22-8, for this assumed yield curve shift, the barbell outperforms the bullet.

In the last column, the nonparallel shift assumes that for a change in bond C's yield, the yield on bond A will change by the same amount less 25 basis points, whereas that on bond B will change by the same amount plus 25 points: Thus, the spread between the long-term yield and the short-term yield has increased by 50 basis points, and the yield curve has steepened. In this case the bullet portfolio outperforms the barbell portfolio as long as the yield on bond C does not rise by more than 250 basis points or fall by more than 325 basis points.

The key point here is that looking at measures such as yield (yield to maturity or some type of portfolio yield measure), duration, or convexity tells us little about performance over some investment horizon, because performance depends on the magnitude of the change in yields and how the yield curve shifts. Therefore, when a manager wants to position a portfolio based on expectations as to how he might expect the yield curve to shift, it is imperative to perform total return analysis. For example, in a steepening yield curve environment, it is often stated that a bullet portfolio would be better than a barbell portfolio. As can be seen from Exhibit 22-8, it is not the case that a bullet portfolio would outperform a barbell portfolio. Whether the bullet portfolio outperforms the barbell depends on how much the yield curve steepens. An analysis similar to that in Exhibit 22-8 based on total return for different degrees of steepening of the yield curve clearly demonstrates to a manager whether a particular yield curve strategy will be superior to another. The same analysis can be performed to assess the potential outcome of a ladder strategy.

Complex Strategies

Thus far we have described the basics of yield curve strategies. A study by Fabozzi, Martinelli, and Priaulet finds evidence of the predictability in the time-varying shape of the U.S. term structure of interest rates using a more advanced econometric model.[8] Variables such as default spread, equity volatility, and short-term and forward rates are used to predict changes in the slope of the yield curve and (to a lesser extent) changes in its curvature. Systematic trading strategies based on butterfly swaps reveal that the evidence of predictability in the shape of the yield curve is both statistically and economically significant.

Yield Spread Strategies

As discussed in Chapter 5, the bond market is classified into sectors in several ways: by type of issuer (Treasury, agencies, corporates, and mortgage-backeds), quality or credit (risk-free Treasuries, AAA, AA, and so on), coupon (high-coupon/premium bonds, current-coupon/par bonds, and low-coupon/discount bonds), and maturity (short, intermediate, or long term). Yield spreads between maturity sectors involve changes in the yield curve as discussed in the preceding section.

Yield spread strategies involve positioning a portfolio to capitalize on expected changes in yield spreads between sectors of the bond market. Swapping (or exchanging) one bond for another when the manager believes that the prevailing yield spread between the two bonds in the market is out of line with their historical yield spread, and that the yield spread will realign by the end of the investment horizon, are called **intermarket spread swaps**.

Credit Spreads

Credit or quality spreads change because of expected changes in economic prospects. Credit spreads between Treasury and non-Treasury issues widen in a declining or contracting economy and narrow during economic expansion. The economic rationale is

---

[8]Frank J. Fabozzi, Lionel Martellini, and Philippe Priaulet, "Exploiting Predictability in the Time-Varying Shape of the Term Structure of Interest Rates," *Journal of Fixed Income*, June 2005, pp. 40–53. Specifically, they use a robust recursive modeling approach based on a Bayesian mixture of multifactor models.

that in a declining or contracting economy, corporations experience a decline in revenue and reduced cash flow, making it difficult for corporate issuers to service their contractual debt obligations. To induce investors to hold non-Treasury securities of lower-quality issuers, the yield spread relative to Treasury securities must widen. The converse is that during economic expansion and brisk economic activity, revenue and cash flow pick up, increasing the likelihood that corporate issuers will have the capacity to service their contractual debt obligations. Yield spreads between Treasury and federal agency securities will vary depending on investor expectations about the prospects that an implicit government guarantee will be honored.

Spreads Between Callable and Noncallable Securities

Spreads attributable to differences in callable and noncallable bonds and differences in coupons of callable bonds will change as a result of expected changes in (1) the direction of the change in interest rates, and (2) interest-rate volatility. An expected drop in the level of interest rates will widen the yield spread between callable bonds and noncallable bonds as the prospects that the issuer will exercise the call option increase. The reverse is true: The yield spread narrows if interest rates are expected to rise. As we explained in Chapter 17, an increase in interest-rate volatility increases the value of the embedded call option and thereby increases the yield spread between callable bonds and noncallable bonds. Expectations about the direction of the change in interest rates and interest-rate volatility will affect the yield spread between Treasury and mortgage pass-through securities and the yield spread between low-coupon and high-coupon pass-throughs in the same way as it affects the yield spreads for corporates.

Importance of Dollar Duration Weighting of Yield Spread Strategies

What is critical in assessing yield spread strategies is to compare positions that have the same dollar duration. To understand why, consider two bonds, X and Y. Suppose that the price of bond X is 80 with a modified duration of 5, and bond Y has a price of 90 with a modified duration of 4. Because modified duration is the approximate percentage change per 100-basis-point change in yield, a 100-basis-point change in yield for bond X would change its price by about 5%. Based on a price of 80, its price will change by about $4 per $80 of market value. Thus, its dollar duration for a 100-basis-point change in yield is $4 per $80 of market value. Similarly, for bond Y, its dollar duration for a 100-basis-point change in yield per $90 of market value can be determined. In this case it is $3.60. So if bonds X and Y are being considered as alternative investments in a strategy other than one based on anticipating interest-rate movements, the amount of each bond in the strategy should be such that they will both have the same dollar duration.

To illustrate this, suppose that a portfolio manager owns $10 million of par value of bond X, which has a market value of $8 million. The dollar duration of bond X per 100-basis-point change in yield for the $8 million market value is $400,000. Suppose further that this portfolio manager is considering exchanging bond X that it owns in its portfolio for bond Y. If the portfolio manager wants to have the same interest-rate exposure (i.e., dollar duration) for bond Y that she currently has for bond X, she will buy a market value amount of bond Y with the same dollar duration. If the portfolio manager purchased $10 million of *par value* of bond Y and therefore $9 million of *market value* of bond Y, the dollar price change per 100-basis-point change in yield would be only

$360,000. If, instead, the portfolio manager purchased $10 million of *market value* of bond Y, the dollar duration per 100-basis-point change in yield would be $400,000. Because bond Y is trading at 90, $11.11 million of par value of bond Y must be purchased to keep the dollar duration of the position from bond Y the same as for bond X.

Mathematically, this problem can be expressed as follows:

Let

$\$D_X$ = dollar duration per 100-basis-point change in yield for bond X
 for the market value of bond X held
MD_Y = modified duration for bond Y
MV_Y = market value of bond Y needed to obtain the same dollar duration as
 bond X

Then the following equation sets the dollar duration for bond X equal to the dollar duration for bond Y:

$$\$D_X = \frac{MD_Y}{100} MV_Y$$

Solving for MV_Y yields

$$MV_Y = \frac{\$D_X}{\dfrac{MD_Y}{100}}$$

Dividing by the price per $1 of par value of bond Y gives the par value of Y that has an approximately equivalent dollar duration as bond X.

In our illustration, $\$D_X$ is $400,000 and MD_Y is 4; then

$$MV_Y = \frac{\$400,000}{\dfrac{4}{100}} = \$10,000,000$$

The market value of bond Y is 90 per $100 of par value, so the price per $1 of par value is 0.9. Dividing $10 million by 0.9 indicates that the par value of bond Y that should be purchased is $11.11 million.

Failure to adjust a portfolio repositioning based on some expected change in yield spread so as to hold the dollar duration the same means that the outcome of the portfolio will be affected not only by the expected change in the yield spread but also by a change in the yield level. Thus, a manager would be making a conscious yield spread bet and possibly an undesired bet on the level of interest rates.

Individual Security Selection Strategies

There are several active strategies that money managers pursue to identify mispriced securities. The most common strategy identifies an issue as undervalued because either (1) its yield is higher than that of comparably rated issues, or (2) its yield is expected to decline (and price therefore rise) because credit analysis indicates that its rating will improve.

A swap in which a money manager exchanges one bond for another bond that is similar in terms of coupon, maturity, and credit quality, but offers a higher yield, is called a **substitution swap**. This swap depends on a capital market imperfection. Such situations sometimes exist in the bond market owing to temporary market imbalances and the fragmented nature of the non-Treasury bond market. The risk the money manager faces in making a substitution swap is that the bond purchased may not be truly identical to the bond for which it is exchanged. Moreover, typically, bonds will have similar but not identical maturities and coupons. This could lead to differences in the convexity of the two bonds, and any yield spread may reflect the cost of convexity.

An active strategy used in the mortgage-backed securities market is to identify individual issues of pass-throughs, CMO classes, or stripped MBS that are mispriced, given the assumed prepayment speed to price the security. Another active strategy commonly used in the mortgage-backed securities market is to create a package of securities that will have a better return profile for a wide range of interest-rate and yield curve scenarios than similar duration securities available in the market. Because of the fragmented nature of the mortgage-backed securities market and the complexity of the structures, such opportunities are not unusual.

Strategies for Asset Allocation Within Bond Sectors

The ability to outperform a benchmark index will depend on how the manager allocates funds within a bond sector relative to the composition of the benchmark index. As explained in the next chapter, the three major sectors of the broad-based bond market indexes are government/agencies, corporates, and mortgage-backed securities. Within the corporate sector, for example, the manager must decide how to allocate funds among the different credit ratings. (Only investment grade ratings are included in the broad-based bond market indexes.) In the case of mortgage-backed securities where only pass-through securities are included with different coupon rates, there is the decision of how to allocate funds among the different coupon issues. This is important because prepayment rates and the performance of pass-throughs will depend on the coupon issues selected by the manager.

We already discussed strategies that will affect the allocation decision among the bond sectors. Expected changes in the level of interest rates will affect the allocation of funds within the corporate and mortgage-backed securities sectors because the more attractive the call feature of a security, the worse it may perform in a declining interest rate environment due to negative convexity. Yield curve strategies would affect the maturity selection within sectors. While our previous focus was on strategies involving anticipated changes in credit spreads or OAS between sectors in the bond market, the same strategies are used in making intersector asset allocation decisions. Next we look at a framework for guiding and assessing the allocation of funds among the credit sectors within the corporate bond sector. This strategy was first suggest by Leland Crabbe.[9]

---

[9]Leland E. Crabbe, "A Framework for Corporate Bond Strategy," *Journal of Fixed Income*, June 1995, pp. 15–25.

The framework relies on the historical experience of credit quality changes. This information is captured in a table referred to as a *rating transition matrix* and shows on a percentage basis how ratings on issues change over time. Exhibit 22-9 shows a one-year rating transition matrix (table) based on a Moody's study for the period 1970–1993. Here is how to interpret the table. The rows indicate the rating at the beginning of a year. The columns show the rating at the end of the year. For example, look at the second row. This row shows the transition for Aa-rated bonds at the beginning of a year. The number 91.26 in the second row means that on average 91.26% of Aa-rated bonds at the beginning of the year remained Aa rated at year end. The value of 1.13 means that on average 1.13% of Aa-rated bonds at the beginning of the year were upgraded to Aaa. The value of 0.31 means that on average 0.31% of Aa-rated bonds at the beginning of the year were downgraded to a Baa rating.

From Exhibit 22-9 it should be clear that the probability of a downgrade is much higher than for an upgrade for investment grade bonds. While the historical rating transition matrix is a useful starting point since it represents an average over the study period (the 1970–1993 period in the exhibit), a manager must modify the matrix based on expectations of upgrades and downgrades given current and anticipated economic conditions.

Given the rating transition matrix that the manager expects, an *expected incremental return* can be calculated for each credit quality sector. This involves four steps. First, estimate what the spread over Treasuries will be for all ratings at the end of the investment horizon. Second, estimate the price change for upgraded and downgraded bonds based on the new spreads. Third, compute the return for upgraded and downgraded bonds based on the price change calculated in the first step and the coupon interest. Finally, calculate the expected incremental return for the credit quality sector by weighting the returns by the probabilities as given in the manager's rating transition matrix.

To illustrate this, suppose that the manager's rating transition matrix is the one shown in Exhibit 22-9. Second, suppose that the manager expects that the spreads will not change over the one year investment horizon. Consider the Aa-rated sector. Exhibit 22-10 shows the expected incremental return estimates for a portfolio consisting of only three-year Aa-rated bonds. The first column shows the initial spread. The second column is the rating at the end of the investment horizon. The horizon spread is the spread over Treasuries at the end of the investment horizon for each of the credit

EXHIBIT 22-9 One-Year Rating Transition Probabilities (%)							
	Aaa	Aa	A	Baa	Ba	Bb	C or D	Total
Aaa	91.90	7.38	0.72	0.00	0.00	0.00	0.00	100.00
Aa	1.13	91.26	7.09	0.31	0.21	0.00	0.00	100.00
A	0.10	2.56	91.20	5.33	0.61	0.20	0.00	100.00
Baa	0.00	0.21	5.36	87.94	5.46	0.82	0.21	100.00

Source: From Leland E. Crabbe, "A Framework for Corporate Bond Strategy," *Journal of Fixed Income,* June 1995, p. 16. Reprinted by permission of *Institutional Investor.*

EXHIBIT 22-10　Expected Incremental Return Estimates for Three-Year Aa-Rated Bonds over a One-Year Horizon

Initial Spread	Horizon Rating	Horizon Spread	Return over Treasuries (bp) ×	Transition Probability (%) =	Contribution to Incremental Return (bp)
30	Aaa	25	38	1.13	0.43
30	Aa	30	30	91.26	27.38
30	A	35	21	7.09	1.49
30	Baa	60	−24	0.31	−0.07
30	Ba	130	−147	0.21	−0.31
Portfolio Incremental Return over Treasuries = 28.90					

Source: From Leland E. Crabbe, "A Framework for Corporate Bond Strategy," *Journal of Fixed Income*, June 1995, p. 17. Reprinted by permission of *Institutional Investor*.

quality sectors for the three-year maturity sector shown in the second column. For example, if there is no change in the rating, the horizon spread is the same as the initial spread of 30 basis points. An upgrade reduces the spread, a downgrade increases it. The assumption in our illustration is that the horizon spread is the same as currently observed. The fourth column shows the horizon return over Treasuries based on price change and coupon interest. The next to the last column gives the probabilities from the rating transition matrix (i.e., the second row of Exhibit 22-9). The sum of the product of the fourth and fifth columns gives the expected incremental return over Treasuries of 28.9 basis points.

There are two reasons why the expected incremental return over Treasuries of 28.9 basis points is less than the initial spread of 30 basis points. First, the probability of an upgrade is significantly less than for a downgrade. Second, the steepness of the credit spread curve at the end of the investment horizon penalizes downgrades.

From this illustration it can be seen that the incremental return over Treasuries depends on the initial spread, the change in the spread, and the probability of a rating change.

The framework can be extended to any maturity sector. Exhibit 22-11 shows expected incremental returns over Treasuries assuming the rating transition matrix given in Exhibit 22-9 and assuming that the horizon spreads are the same as the initial spreads. For example, the second column in Exhibit 22-11 shows that the expected incremental return in the three-year maturity sector of the corporate bond market is 28.9 basis points for Aa-rated bonds and 46.3 basis points for Baa-rated bonds.

The exhibit provides a guide for assessing relative value within each maturity sector. Notice that for all rating sectors and maturity sectors, expected incremental returns are less than the initial spread. For the 3-year and 5-year maturity sectors, the ranking by expected incremental return is the same as for the ranking by initial spread. However, this is not true for the 10-year and 30-year maturity sectors. This is because of the significant influence of the duration of the bonds in these sectors and the steepness of the credit quality spread. Exhibit 22-11 can also be used to assess relative value among maturity sectors for a given rating sector.

	Initial Spread	Incremental Return	Initial Spread	Incremental Return	Initial Spread	Incremental Return	Initial Spread	Incremental Return
Aaa	25	24.2	30	28.4	35	31.7	45	34.6
Aa	30	28.9	35	31.4	40	30.3	55	34.8
A	35	31.1	45	37.3	55	37.9	75	42.7
Baa	60	46.3	70	39.9	85	21.9	115	27.4

EXHIBIT 22-11   Expected Incremental Returns over Treasuries When Rating Transitions Match Historical Experience (One-Year Horizon, bp)

Source: From Leland E. Crabbe, "A Framework for Corporate Bond Strategy," *Journal of Fixed Income*, June 1995, p. 18. Reprinted by permission of *Institutional Investor*.

While the illustrations assumed the rating transmission matrix in Exhibit 22-9 and that the spread over Treasuries at the end of the investment horizon would be unchanged from the initial spread, this will not be the case in practice. The manager will modify both assumptions based on prevailing and expected market conditions.

THE USE OF LEVERAGE

If permitted by investment guidelines, a manager may use leverage in an attempt to enhance portfolio returns. A portfolio manager can create leverage by borrowing funds in order to acquire a position in the market that is greater than if only cash were invested. For example, a manager may have cash to invest in the bond market of $50 million but wants an exposure of $200 million.

The funds available to invest without borrowing are referred to as the "equity." In our example, the equity is $50. A portfolio that does not contain any leverage is called an **unlevered portfolio**. A **levered portfolio** is a portfolio in which a manager has created leverage. The levered portfolio in this example is $200 million.

In this section we'll take a look at leverage. First, we'll look at why a manager uses leverage and the measurement of the duration of a portfolio that uses leverage. Then we will look at how a manager can create leverage using the repo market.

Motivation for Leverage

The basic principle in using leverage is that a manager wants to earn a return on the borrowed funds that is greater than the cost of the borrowed funds. The return from borrowing funds is produced from a higher income and/or greater price appreciation relative to a scenario in which no funds are borrowed.

Let's first look at the higher income that may be generated from a levered portfolio relative to an unlevered portfolio. If a manager can invest $50 million earning 5% for a year but borrow funds at a cost of 4.5% for a year, then the manager can generate for the year 50 basis points in income over its funding cost. By borrowing greater amounts, the manager can magnify the 50 basis points. This is a benefit of leveraging.

The risk of leveraging is that the return generated from the borrowed funds will be less than the funding cost. In our example, the risk is that if the return from investing the amount borrowed is less than 4.5%, then there will be negative return on the funds borrowed.

The return from investing the funds comes from two sources. The first is the interest income and the second is the change in the value of the security (or securities) at the end of the borrowing period. For example, suppose our manager invests all the funds borrowed in a security that matures in one year, is selling at par, and has a coupon rate of 5%. At the end of one year (the time period we assumed in our example that the manager borrowed the funds), the return is 5% if the issuer of the security pays off the bond at par. Suppose instead that the bond is a 10-year bond that can be purchased at par and has a coupon rate of 5%. Then the return over the one-year period for which the funds are borrowed will be 5% in interest income adjusted for how the price of the bond changes at the end of one year. At the end of one year, the 10-year bond is a 9-year bond and its price will be greater than or less than par depending on market rates at the end of one year. The risk, of course, is that the change in the value of the security will decline such that the return will be negative.

There are some managers who use leverage in the hopes of benefiting primarily from price changes. Small price changes will be magnified by using leveraging. For example, if a manager expects interest rates to fall, the manager can borrow funds to increase price exposure to the market. Effectively, the manager is increasing the duration of the portfolio, a point that we will return to later.

Thus, the risk associated with borrowing funds is that the security (or securities) in which the borrowed funds are invested may earn less than the cost of the borrowed funds due to failure to generate interest income plus capital appreciation as expected when the funds were borrowed.

Leveraging is a necessity for depository institutions (such as banks and savings and loan associations) because the spread over the cost of borrowed funds is typically small. The magnitude of the borrowing (i.e., the degree of leverage) is what produces an acceptable return for the institution. For traders, individual trades typically produce small spreads over funding costs. It is the leveraging of those trades that will generate a return needed to make them attractive to traders.

Duration of a Leveraged Portfolio

Now let's look at how to calculate the duration of a fund that has borrowed money. This can be done by using an example to understand the general principle.

Suppose that a portfolio has a market value of $100 million and the manager invests the proceeds in a bond with a duration of 3. This means that the manager would expect that for a 100-basis-point change in interest rates, the portfolio's value would change by approximately $3 million. For this unlevered fund, the duration of the portfolio is 3.

Suppose now that the manager of this portfolio can borrow an additional $300 million. This means that the levered fund will have $400 million to invest, consisting of $100 million that the manager has available before borrowing (i.e., the equity) and $300 million borrowed. All of the funds are invested in a bond with a duration of 3. Now let's look at what happens if interest rates change by 100 basis points. The levered portfolio's value will change by $12 million (3% times $400 million). This means that on an investment of $100 million, the portfolio's value changes by $12 million. The proper way to measure the portfolio's duration is relative to the unlevered amount or equity because the manager is concerned with the risk exposure relative to equity. Thus, the duration for the portfolio is 12 because a duration of 12 will change the portfolio's equity value of $100 million by 12% or $12 million for a 100-basis-point change in rates.

In general, the procedure for calculating the duration of a portfolio that uses leverage is as follows:

Step 1: Calculate the duration of the levered portfolio.
Step 2: Determine the dollar duration of the portfolio of the levered portfolio for a change in interest rates.
Step 3: Compute the ratio of the dollar duration of the levered portfolio to the value of the initial unlevered portfolio (i.e., initial equity).
Step 4: The duration of the unlevered portfolio is then found as follows:

$$\text{ratio computed in Step 3} \times \frac{100}{\text{rate change used in Step 2 in bps}} \times 100$$

To illustrate the procedure, suppose that the initial value of the unlevered portfolio is $100 million and the leveraged portfolio is $400 million ($100 million equity plus $300 million borrowed).

Step 1: Assume that calculation of the duration of the levered portfolio finds that the duration is 3.
Step 2: Let's use a 50-basis-point change in interest rates to compute the dollar duration. If the duration of the levered portfolio is 3, then the dollar duration for a 50-basis-point change in interest rates is $6 million (1.5% change for a 50-basis-point move times $400 million).
Step 3: The ratio of the dollar duration for a 50-basis-point change in interest rates to the $100 million initial market value of the unlevered portfolio is 0.06 ($6 million divided by $100 million).
Step 4: The duration of the unlevered portfolio is:

$$0.06 \times \frac{100}{50} \times 100 = 12$$

How to Create Leverage via the Repo Market

A manager can create leverage in one of two ways. One way is through the use of derivative instruments. As is explained in Chapters 26–28, interest-rate derivatives instruments can produce the same effect as leverage. The second way is to borrow funds via a collateralized loan arrangement. The two most common ways a money manager can borrow via a collateralized loan arrangement is through a reverse repurchase agreement or margin buying. The former is the most common transaction used by institutional money managers, so we discuss it next.

Repurchase Agreement

A **repurchase agreement** is the sale of a security with a commitment by the seller to buy the same security back from the purchaser at a specified price at a designated future date. The price at which the seller must subsequently repurchase the security for is called the **repurchase price**, and the date that the security must be repurchased is called the **repurchase date**. Basically, a repurchase agreement is a collateralized loan, where the collateral is the security sold and subsequently repurchased. The agreement is best explained with an illustration.

Suppose a government securities dealer has purchased $10 million of a particular Treasury security. The dealer uses the repurchase agreement or "repo" market to obtain financing. In the repo market the dealer can use the $10 million of the Treasury security as collateral for a loan. The term of the loan and the interest rate that the dealer agrees to pay are specified. The interest rate is called the **repo rate**. When the term of the loan is one day, it is called an **overnight repo**; a loan for more than one day is called a **term repo**. The transaction is referred to as a repurchase agreement because it calls for the sale of the security and its repurchase at a future date. Both the sale price and the purchase price are specified in the agreement. The difference between the purchase (repurchase) price and the sale price is the dollar interest cost of the loan.

Back to the dealer who needs to finance $10 million of a Treasury security that it purchased and plans to hold overnight. Suppose that a customer of the dealer has excess funds of $10 million. (The customer might be a municipality with tax receipts that it has just collected and no immediate need to disburse the funds.) The dealer would agree to deliver ("sell") $10 million of the Treasury security to the customer for an amount determined by the repo rate and buy ("repurchase") the same Treasury security from the customer for $10 million the next day. Suppose that the overnight repo rate is 6.5%. Then, as is explained subsequently, the dealer would agree to deliver the Treasury securities for $9,998,195 and repurchase the same securities for $10 million the next day. The $1,805 difference between the "sale" price of $9,998,195 and the repurchase price of $10 million is the dollar interest on the financing.

The following formula is used to calculate the dollar interest on a repo transaction:

$$\text{dollar interest} = (\text{dollar amount borrowed}) \times (\text{repo rate}) \times \text{repo term}/360$$

Notice that the interest is computed on a 360-day basis.

In our example, at a repo rate of 6.5% and a repo term of one day (overnight), the dollar interest is $1,805 as shown here:

$$\$9,998,195 \times 0.065 \times 1/360 = \$1,805$$

The advantage to the dealer of using the repo market for borrowing on a short-term basis is that the rate is lower than the cost of bank financing. (The reason for this is explained later.) From the customer's perspective, the repo market offers an attractive yield on a short-term secured transaction that is highly liquid.

Although the example illustrates financing a dealer's long position in the repo market, dealers can also use the market to cover a short position. For example, suppose a government dealer sold $10 million of Treasury securities two weeks ago and must now cover the position—that is, deliver the securities. The dealer can do a **reverse repo** (agree to buy the securities and sell them back). Of course, the dealer eventually would have to buy the Treasury security in the market in order to cover its short position. In this case, the dealer is actually making a collateralized loan to its customer; that is, in a reverse repo a party is lending funds. The customer may be using the funds obtained from the collateralized loan to create leverage.

There is a good deal of Wall Street jargon describing repo transactions. To understand it, remember that one party is lending money and accepting a security as collateral for the loan; the other party is borrowing money and providing collateral to borrow the money. When someone lends securities in order to receive cash (i.e., borrow money), that party is said to be "reversing out" securities. A party that lends money with the security as collateral is said to be "reversing in" securities. The expressions "to repo securities" and "to do repo" are also used. The former means that someone is going to finance securities using the security as collateral; the latter means that the party is going to invest in a repo. Finally, the expressions "selling collateral" and "buying collateral" are used to describe a party financing a security with a repo on the one hand and lending on the basis of collateral on the other.

Rather than using industry jargon, investment guidelines should be clear as to what a manager is permitted to do. For example, a client may have no objections to its money manager using a repo as a short-term investment; that is, the money manager may lend funds on a short-term basis. The investment guidelines will set forth how the loan arrangement should be structured to protect against credit risk. We'll discuss this next. However, if a client does not want a money manager to use the repo agreement as a vehicle for borrowing funds in order to create leverage, it should state so.

Although in our illustration we used Treasury securities as the collateral, the collateral in a repo is not limited to government securities. Money market instruments, federal agency securities, and mortgage-backed securities[10] are also used. In some specialized markets, whole loans are used as collateral

Credit Risks

Despite the fact that there may be high-quality collateral underlying a repo transaction, both parties to the transaction are exposed to credit risk. Why does credit risk occur in a repo transaction? Consider our initial example in which the dealer uses $10 million of government securities as collateral to borrow. If the dealer cannot repurchase the government securities, the customer may keep the collateral; if interest rates on government securities increase subsequent to the repo transaction, however, the market value of the government securities will decline, and the customer will own securities with a market value less than the amount it lent to the dealer. If the market value of the security rises instead, the dealer will be concerned with the return of the collateral, which then has a market value higher than the loan.

Repos should be carefully structured to reduce credit risk exposure. The amount lent should be less than the market value of the security used as collateral, thereby providing the lender with some cushion should the market value of the security decline. The amount by which the market value of the security used as collateral exceeds the value of the loan is called **repo margin** or simply **margin**. Margin is also referred to as the "haircut." Repo margin is generally between 1% and 3%. For borrowers of lower

---

[10]A special repo called a "dollar roll" is available when the security used as collateral is a mortgage pass-through security.

credit worthiness and/or when less liquid securities are used as collateral, the repo margin can be 10% or more.

Another practice to limit credit risk is to mark the collateral to market on a regular basis. (Marking a position to market means recording the value of a position at its market value.) When market value changes by a certain percentage, the repo position is adjusted accordingly.

One concern in structuring a repo is delivery of the collateral to the lender. The most obvious procedure is for the borrower to deliver the collateral to the lender or to the lender's clearing agent. In such instances, the collateral is said to be "delivered out." At the end of the repo term, the lender returns the collateral to the borrower in exchange for the principal and interest payment. This procedure may be too expensive, though, particularly for short-term repos, because of costs associated with delivering the collateral. The cost of delivery would be factored into the transaction by a lower repo rate than the borrower would be willing to pay. The risk of the lender not taking possession of the collateral is that the borrower may sell the security or use the same security as collateral for a repo with another party.

As an alternative to delivering out the collateral, the lender may agree to allow the borrower to hold the security in a segregated customer account. Of course, the lender still faces the risk that the borrower may use the collateral fraudulently by offering it as collateral for another repo transaction. If the borrower of the cash does not deliver out the collateral, but instead holds it, then the transaction is called a **hold-in-custody repo (HIC repo)**. Despite the credit risk associated with a HIC repo, it is used in some transactions when the collateral is difficult to deliver (such as in whole loans) or the transaction amount is small and the lender of funds is comfortable with the reputation of the borrower of the cash.

Another method is for the borrower to deliver the collateral to the lender's custodial account at the borrower's clearing bank. The custodian then has possession of the collateral that it holds on behalf of the lender. This practice reduces the cost of delivery because it is merely a transfer within the borrower's clearing bank. If, for example, a dealer enters into an overnight repo with Customer A, the next day the collateral is transferred back to the dealer. The dealer can then enter into a repo with Customer B for, say, five days without having to redeliver the collateral. The clearing bank simply establishes a custodian account for Customer B and holds the collateral in that account. This specialized type of repo arrangement is called a **tri-party repo**.

Determinants of the Repo Rate

There is not one repo rate. The rate varies from transaction to transaction depending on a variety of factors: quality of collateral, term of the repo, delivery requirement, availability of collateral, and the prevailing federal funds rate.

The higher the credit quality and liquidity of the collateral, the lower the repo rate. The effect of the term of the repo on the rate depends on the shape of the yield curve. As noted earlier, if delivery of the collateral to the lender is required, the repo rate will be lower. If the collateral can be deposited with the bank of the borrower, a higher repo rate is paid.

The more difficult it is to obtain the collateral, the lower the repo rate. To understand why this is so, remember that the borrower (or equivalently the seller of the collateral) has a security that lenders of cash want, for whatever reason. Such collateral is referred to as **hot** or **special collateral**. (Collateral that does not have this characteristic is referred to as **general collateral**.) The party that needs the hot collateral will be willing to lend funds at a lower repo rate in order to obtain the collateral.

Whereas these factors determine the repo rate on a particular transaction, the federal funds rate determines the general level of repo rates. The repo rate generally will be a rate lower than the federal funds rate, because a repo involves collateralized borrowing, whereas a federal funds transaction is unsecured borrowing.

SUMMARY

There are five basic steps in investment management. The first and principal step in the investment management process is setting investment objectives. The second step is establishing policy guidelines to satisfy the investment objectives; it begins with the asset allocation decision. The third step is selecting a portfolio strategy that is consistent with the objectives and policy guidelines of the client or institution. The fourth step is selecting the specific assets to be included in the portfolio. The measurement and evaluation of investment performance is the final step in the ongoing investment management process.

Tracking error, or active risk, is the standard deviation of a portfolio's return relative to the benchmark index. There are two types of tracking error—backward-looking tracking error and forward-looking tracking error. Backward-looking tracking error is calculated based on the actual performance of a portfolio relative to a benchmark index. Forward-looking tracking error is an estimate of how a portfolio will perform relative to a benchmark index in the future. Forward-looking tracking error is used in risk control and portfolio construction. The higher the forward-looking tracking error, the more the manager is pursuing a strategy in which the portfolio has a different risk profile than the benchmark index and there is, therefore, greater active management.

The risk factors affecting a portfolio are divided into systematic risk factors and non-systematic risk factors. In turn, each of these risk factors are further decomposed. For example, systematic risk factors are divided into term structure risk factors and non-term structure risk factors. In the case of the Lehman Brothers Aggregate Bond Index, the non-term structure risk factors are sector risk, quality risk, optionality risk, coupon risk, MBS sector risk, MBS volatility risk, and MBS prepayment risk. Non-systematic factor risks are classified as issuer-specific risk and issue-specific risk.

Active bond portfolio strategies seek to capitalize on expectations about changes in factors that will affect the price and therefore the performance of an issue over some investment horizon. The factors that affect a portfolio's return are (1) changes in the level of interest rates, (2) changes in the shape of the yield curve, (3) changes in yield spreads among bond sectors, (4) changes in the option-adjusted spread, and (5) changes in the yield spread for a particular bond. The total return framework should be used to assess how changes in these factors will affect the performance of a strategy over some investment horizon.

The performance of an actively managed portfolio will also be affected by how the manager allocates funds among the various sectors within a bond sector. In the case of the corporate bond sector, a framework that estimates the expected incremental return over Treasuries using a rating transition matrix can be used.

Leveraging involves creating an exposure to a market in excess of the exposure that can be obtained without borrowing funds. The objective is to earn a return in excess of the cost of the borrowed funds. The risk is that the manager will earn a return less than the cost of the borrowed funds. The return on the borrowed funds is realized from the interest earned plus the change in the value of the securities acquired. The duration of a portfolio is magnified by leveraging a portfolio.

The most common way in which a manager can borrow funds is via a repurchase agreement. This is a collateralized loan arrangement in which a party borrows funds. It is called a reverse repo agreement when a party lends funds. There is credit risk in a repo agreement, and there are mechanisms for mitigating this risk.

Questions

1. Why might the investment objective of a portfolio manager of a life insurance company be different from that of a mutual fund manager?

2. Explain how it can be possible for a portfolio manager to outperform a benchmark but still fail to meet the investment objective of a client.

3. What is the essential ingredient in all active portfolio strategies?

4. What is tracking error?

5. Explain why backward-looking tracking error has limitations for estimating a portfolio's future tracking error.

6. Why might one expect that for a manager pursuing an active management strategy that the backward-looking tracking error at the beginning of the year will deviate from the forward-looking tracking error at the beginning of the year?

7. a. Compute the tracking error from the following information:

Month 2001	Portfolio A's Return (%)	Lehman Aggregate Bond Index Return (%)
Jan	2.15	1.65
Feb	0.89	−0.10
March	1.15	0.52
April	−0.47	−0.60
May	1.71	0.65
June	0.10	0.33
July	1.04	2.31
Aug	2.70	1.10
Sept	0.66	1.23
Oct	2.15	2.02
Nov	−1.38	−0.61
Dec	−0.59	−1.20

b. Is the tracking error computed in part a a backward-looking or forward-looking tracking error?

c. Compare the tracking error found in part a to the tracking error found for Portfolios A and B in Exhibit 22-1. What can you say about the investment management strategy pursued by this portfolio manager?

8. Assume the following:

benchmark index = Salomon Smith Barney BIG Bond Index

expected return for benchmark index = 7%

forward-looking tracking error relative to Lehman Aggregate Bond Index = 200 basis points

Assuming that returns are normally distributed, complete the following table:

Number of Standard Deviations	Range for Portfolio Active Return	Corresponding Range for Portfolio Return	Probability
1			
2			
3			

9. At a meeting between a portfolio manager and a prospective client, the portfolio manager stated that her firm's bond investment strategy is a conservative one. The portfolio manager told the prospective client that she constructs a portfolio with a forward-looking tracking error that is typically between 250 and 300 basis points of a

client-specified bond index. Explain why you agree or disagree with the portfolio manager's statement that the portfolio strategy is a conservative one.

10. a. What is meant by systematic risk factors?
    b. What is the difference between term structure and non-term structure risk factors?
    c. What are the systematic risk factors associated with investing in the residential mortgage-backed sector of a benchmark index?

11. What is meant by tracking error due to systematic risk factors?

12. Suppose that the benchmark index for a portfolio manager is the Lehman Brothers Aggregate Bond Index. That bond market index includes only investment grade. Suppose that the portfolio manager decides to allocate a portion of the portfolio's fund to high-yield bonds. What would you expect would happen to the forward-looking tracking error due to quality risk?

13. a. What is an active portfolio strategy?
    b. What will determine whether an active or a passive portfolio strategy will be pursued?

14. What are the limitations of using duration and convexity measures in active portfolio strategies?

15. Next are two portfolios with a market value of $500 million. The bonds in both portfolios are trading at par value. The dollar duration of the two portfolios is the same.

Bonds Included in Portfolio I

Issue	Years to Maturity	Par Value (in millions)
A	2.0	$120
B	2.5	130
C	20.0	150
D	20.5	100

Bonds Included in Portfolio II

Issue	Years to Maturity	Par Value (in millions)
E	9.7	$200
F	10.0	230
G	10.2	70

a. Which portfolio can be characterized as a bullet portfolio?
b. Which portfolio can be characterized as a barbell portfolio?

c. The two portfolios have the same dollar duration; explain whether their performance will be the same if interest rates change.
d. If they will not perform the same, how would you go about determining which would perform best assuming that you have a six-month investment horizon?

16. Explain why you agree or disagree with the following statements:
    a. "It is always better to have a portfolio with more convexity than one with less convexity."
    b. "A bullet portfolio will always outperform a barbell portfolio with the same dollar duration if the yield curve steepens."

17. What is a laddered portfolio?

18. A portfolio manager owns $5 million par value of bond ABC. The bond is trading at 70 and has a modified duration of 6. The portfolio manager is considering swapping out of bond ABC and into bond XYZ. The price of this bond is 85 and it has a modified duration of 3.5.
    a. What is the dollar duration of bond ABC per 100-basis-point change in yield?
    b. What is the dollar duration for the $5 million position of bond ABC?
    c. How much in market value of bond XYZ should be purchased so that the dollar duration of bond XYZ will be approximately the same as that for bond ABC?
    d. How much in par value of bond XYZ should be purchased so that the dollar duration of bond XYZ will be approximately the same as that for bond ABC?

19. Explain why in implementing a yield spread strategy it is necessary to keep the dollar duration constant.

20. The excerpt that follows is taken from an article titled "Smith Plans to Shorten," which appeared in the January 27, 1992, issue of *BondWeek*, p. 6:

When the economy begins to rebound and interest rates start to move up, Smith Affiliated Capital will swap 30-year Treasuries for 10-year Treasuries and those with average remaining lives of nine years, according to Bob Smith, executive V.P. The New York firm doesn't expect this to occur until the end of this year or early next, however, and sees the yield on the 30-year Treasury first falling below 7%. Any new cash that comes in now will be put into 30-year Treasuries, Smith added.

What type of portfolio strategy is Smith Affiliated Capital pursuing?

21. The following excerpt is taken from an article titled "MERUS to Boost Corporates," which appeared in the January 27, 1992, issue of *BondWeek*, p. 6:

MERUS Capital Management will increase the allocation to corporates in its $790 million long investment-grade fixed-income portfolio by $39.5 million over the next six months to a year, according to George Wood, managing director. MERUS will add corporates rated single A or higher in the expectation that spreads will tighten as the economy recovers and that some credits may be upgraded.

What types of active portfolio strategies is MERUS Capital Management pursuing?

22. This excerpt comes from an article titled "Eagle Eyes High-Coupon Callable Corporates" in the January 20, 1992, issue of *BondWeek*, p. 7:

If the bond market rallies further, Eagle Asset Management may take profits, trading $8 million of seven- to 10-year Treasuries for high-coupon single-A industrials that are callable in two to four years according to Joseph Blanton, senior V.P. He thinks a further rally is unlikely, however.

Eagle has already sold seven- to 10-year Treasuries to buy $25 million of high-coupon, single-A nonbank financial credits. It made the move to cut the duration of its $160 million fixed income portfolio from 3.7 to 2.5 years, substantially lower than the 3.3-year duration of its bogey ... because it thinks the bond rally has run its course. ...

Blanton said he likes single-A industrials and financials with 9–10% coupons because these are selling at wide spreads of about 100–150 basis points off Treasuries.

What types of active portfolio strategies are being pursued by Eagle Asset Management?

23. The following excerpt is taken from an article titled "W.R. Lazard Buys Triple Bs," which appeared in the November 18, 1991, issue of *BondWeek*, p. 7:

W.R. Lazard & Co. is buying some corporate bonds rated triple B that it believes will be upgraded and some single As that the market perceives as risky but Lazard does not, according to William Schultz, V.P. The firm, which generally buys corporates rated single A or higher, is making the move to pick up yield, Schultz said.

What types of active portfolio strategies are being followed by W.R. Lazard & Co.?

24. In an article titled "Signet to Add Pass-Throughs," which appeared in the October 14, 1991, issue of *BondWeek*, p. 5, it was reported that Christian Goetz, assistant vice president of Signet Asset Management, "expects current coupons to outperform premium pass-throughs as the Fed lowers rates because mortgage holders will refinance premium mortgages." If Goetz pursues a strategy based on this, what type of active strategy is it?

25. The following excerpt comes from an article titled "Securities Counselors Eyes Cutting Duration" in the February 17, 1992, issue of *BondWeek*, p. 5:

Securities Counselors of Iowa will shorten the 5.3 year duration on its $250 million fixed-income portfolio once it is convinced interest rates are moving up and the economy is improving. ... It will shorten by holding in cash equivalents the proceeds from the sale of an undetermined amount of 10-year Treasuries and adding a small amount of high-grade electric utility bonds that have short-maturities if their spreads widen out at least 100 basis points. . . .

The portfolio is currently allocated 85% to Treasuries and 15% to agencies. It has not held corporate bonds since 1985, when it perceived as risky the barrage of hostile corporate tak eovers. . . .

a. Why would Securities Counselors want to shorten duration if it believes that interest rates will rise?

b. How does the purchase of cash equivalents and short-maturity high-grade utilities accomplish the goal of shortening the duration?

c. What risk is Securities Counselors indicating in the last sentence of the excerpt that it is seeking to avoid by not buying corporate bonds?

26. The next excerpt is taken from an article titled "Wood Struthers to Add High-Grade Corporates," which appeared in the February 17, 1992, issue of *BondWeek*, p. 5:

Wood Struthers & Winthrop is poised to add a wide range of high-grade corporates to its $600 million fixed-income portfolio. . . . It will increase its 25% corporate allocation to about 30% after the economy shows signs of improving. . . . It will sell Treasuries and agencies of undetermined maturities to make the purchase. . . .

Its duration is 4 1/2–5 years and is not expected to change significantly. . . .

Comment on this portfolio strategy.

27. Explain how a rating transition matrix can be used as a starting point in assessing how a manager may want to allocate funds to the different credit sectors of the corporate bond market.

28. What is the risk associated with the use of leverage?

29. Suppose that the initial value of an unlevered portfolio of Treasury securities is $200 million and the duration is 7. Suppose further that the manager can borrow $800 million and invest it in the identical Treasury securities so that the levered portfolio has a

value of $1 billion. What is the duration of this levered portfolio?

30. Suppose a manager wants to borrow $50 million of a Treasury security that it plans to purchase and hold for 20 days. The manager can enter into a repo agreement with a dealer firm that would provide financing at a 4.2% repo rate and a 2% margin requirement. What is the dollar interest cost that the manager will have to pay for the borrowed funds?

31. Two trustees of a pension fund are discussing repurchase agreements. Trustee A told Trustee B that she feels it is a safe short-term investment for the fund. Trustee B told Trustee A that repurchase agreements are highly speculative vehicles because they are leveraged instruments. You've been called in by the trustees to clarify the investment characteristics of repurchase agreements. What would you say to the trustees?

32. Suppose that a manager buys an adjustable-rate pass-through security backed by Freddie Mac or Fannie Mae, two government-sponsored enterprises. Suppose that the coupon rate is reset monthly based on the following coupon formula:

one-month LIBOR + 80 basis points

with a cap of 9% (i.e., maximum coupon rate of 9%).

Suppose that the manager can use these securities in a repo transaction in which (1) a repo margin of 5% is required, (2) the term of the repo is one month, and (3) the repo rate is one-month LIBOR plus 10 basis points. Also assume that the manager wishes to invest $1 million of his client's funds in these securities. The manager can purchase $20 million in par value of these securities because only $1 million is required. The amount borrowed would be $19 million. Thus, the manager realizes a spread of 70 basis points on the $19 million borrowed because LIBOR plus 80 basis points is earned in interest each month (coupon rate) and LIBOR plus 10 basis point is paid each month (repo rate).

What are the risks associated with this strategy?

33. Why is there credit risk in a repo transaction?

CHAPTER
23 | INDEXING

After reading this chapter you will understand:

- the objectives and motivation for bond indexing

- the advantages and disadvantages of bond indexing

- the three major broad-based bond market indexes

- the sectors of the broad-based indexes

- the three methodologies used for constructing an indexed portfolio

- the difficulties associated with implementing a bond indexing strategy

- the objectives and motivation for enhanced bond indexing

- the strategies used in enhanced indexing

In this chapter and the next we describe several structured portfolio strategies. Structured strategies generally do not rely on expectations of interest-rate movements or changes in yield spread relationships. Their objective, instead, is to design a portfolio that will achieve the performance of some predetermined benchmark. The target to achieve may be (1) the return on a specific benchmark index, (2) sufficient dollars to satisfy a future single liability, or (3) sufficient dollars to satisfy each liability of a future liability stream. The structured bond portfolio strategy used when the target to be achieved is replication of a predetermined benchmark index is called an indexing strategy. When the target objective is, instead, to generate sufficient funds to pay off predetermined future liabilities, the strategy is called a liability funding strategy. Indexing is discussed in this chapter; liability funding is discussed in Chapter 24.

OBJECTIVE OF AND MOTIVATION FOR BOND INDEXING

Bond indexing means designing a portfolio so that its performance will match the performance of some bond index. In indexing, performance is measured in terms of total rate of return achieved (or simply, total return) over some investment horizon. Total return over some investment horizon incorporates all three sources of return from holding a portfolio of bonds.

Several factors explain the popularity of bond indexing.[1] First, the empirical evidence suggests that historically the overall performance of active bond managers has been poor. Second is the reduced advisory management fees charged for an indexed portfolio compared to active management advisory fees. Advisory fees charged by active managers typically range from 15 to 50 basis points. The range for indexed portfolios, in contrast, is 1 to 20 basis points, with the upper range representing the fees for enhanced and customized benchmark funds, discussed later in this chapter. Some pension funds have decided to do away with advisory fees and to manage some or all of their funds in-house following an indexing strategy.

Lower nonadvisory fees, such as custodial fees, is the third explanation for the popularity of indexing. Finally, sponsors have greater control over external managers when an indexing strategy is selected. For example, in an actively managed portfolio, a sponsor who specifies a restriction on the portfolio's duration still gives the manager ample leeway to pursue strategies that may significantly underperform the index selected as a benchmark. In contrast, requiring an investment advisor to match an index gives little leeway to the manager and, as a result, should result in performance that does not significantly diverge from a benchmark.

Critics of indexing point out that although an indexing strategy matches the performance of some index, the performance of that index does not necessarily represent optimal performance. Moreover, matching an index does not mean that the manager will satisfy a client's return requirement objective. For example, if the objective of a life insurance company or a pension fund is to have sufficient funds to satisfy a predetermined liability, indexing only reduces the likelihood that performance will not be materially worse than the index. The index's return is not necessarily related to the sponsor's liability. Finally, matching an index means that a money manager is restricted to the sectors of the bond market that are in the index, even though there may be attractive opportunities in market sectors excluded from the index. While the broad-based bond market indexes typically include agency pass-through securities, other mortgage-backed securities such as nonagency mortgage-backed securities and collateralized mortgage obligations are generally not included. Yet it is in these newer markets that attractive returns to enhance performance may be available.

At the theoretical level, there are the well-known benefits of diversification as set forth in the Markowitz mean-variance portfolio theory.[2] Capital market theory tells us a market portfolio offers the highest level of return per unit of risk in an efficient

[1]Sharmin Mossavar-Rahmani, *Bond Index Funds* (Chicago: Probus Publishing, 1991), p. 212.
[2]Harry M. Markowitz, "Portfolio Selection," *Journal of Finance*, March 1952, pp. 71–91, and *Portfolio Selection: Efficient Diversification of Investment* (New York: Wiley, 1959).

market.[3] An efficient market is one in which market participants cannot consistently earn abnormal risk-adjusted returns after considering transactions costs. A combination of securities in a portfolio with characteristics similar to the market is able to capture the efficiency of the market. The theoretical market portfolio consists of all risky assets. The weight of each risky asset in the market portfolio is equal to the ratio of its market value to the aggregate market value of all risky assets. That is, the market portfolio is a capitalization-weighted (value-weighted) portfolio of all risky assets. Consequently, because a broad-based market index has more than 6,000 securities and represents most of the bond universe, if a portfolio manager can effectively replicate the performance of the index, a client will realize the benefits of diversification. In contrast, as noted by Kenneth Volpert of The Vanguard Group, while an extra large bond index fund would have 500 or more issues in its portfolio, most actively managed portfolios have far fewer issues and, as a result, will have greater exposure to non-systematic factor risks.[4] Consider, for example, the adverse outcome of poorly diversified active fund managers that held bonds issued by Enron.

Exhibit 23-1 summarizes the advantages and disadvantages of bond indexing.

EXHIBIT 23-1 Advantages and Disadvantages of Bond Indexing	
Advantages	**Disadvantages**
No dependence on expectations and little risk of underperforming the index	Bond indexes do not reflect optimal performance
Reduced advisory and non-advisory fees	Bond index may not match the sponsor's liabilities
Greater sponsor control	Restrictions on fund; management ignores opportunities

FACTORS TO CONSIDER IN SELECTING AN INDEX

A money manager who wishes to pursue an indexing strategy must determine which bond index to replicate. There are a number of bond indexes from which to select, and several factors influence the decision. The first is the investor's risk tolerance. Selection of an index that includes corporate bonds will expose the investor to credit risk. If this risk is unacceptable, an investor should avoid an index that includes this sector.

---

[3]William F. Sharpe, "Capital Asset Prices: A Theory of Market Equilibrium Under Conditions of Risk," *Journal of Finance*, September 1964, pp. 425–442.
[4]Kenneth E. Volpert, "Managing Indexed and Enhanced Indexed Bond Portfolios," Chapter 4 in Frank J. Fabozzi (ed.), *Fixed Income Readings for the Financial Analysts Program* (New Hope, PA: Frank J. Fabozzi Associates, 2000), p. 88.

The second factor influencing the selection of an index is the investor's objective. For example, although the total return of the various indexes tends to be highly positively correlated, the variability of total returns has been quite different. Therefore, an investor whose objective may be to minimize the variability of total returns will be biased toward one that has had, and expects to continue to have, low variability (i.e., a shorter duration relative to other indexes). Moreover, variability of total return may not be symmetric in rising and falling markets. Investors who have expectations about the future direction of interest rates will favor the index that is expected to perform better given their expectations.

BOND INDEXES

The wide range of bond market indexes available can be classified as broad-based market indexes and specialized market indexes. Why have broker/dealer firms developed and aggressively marketed their bond indexes? Enhancing the firm's image is only a minor reason. The key motivation lies in the potential profit that the firm will make by executing trades to set up an indexed portfolio and rebalance it. Typically, a broker/dealer charges a money manager who wants to set up or rebalance an index a nominal amount for providing the necessary data but expects that the bulk of the trades will be executed through its trading desks. Also, by keeping the makeup of the index proprietary, those firms attempt to lock in customers to using their index.

The two broad-based U.S. bond market indexes most commonly used by institutional investors are the Lehman Brothers U.S. Aggregate Bond Index and the Salomon Smith Barney (SSB) Broad Investment-Grade Bond Index (BIG). Another broad-based index is the Merrill Lynch Domestic Market Index. The correlation of the returns for each index exceeds 0.90.

There are more than 5,500 issues in all three broad-based bond indexes. They include only investment-grade securities. Each index is a market-value weighted index. That is, for each issue, the ratio of the market value of an issue relative to the market value of all issues in the index is used as the weight of the issue in all calculations.

The index is computed daily. The pricing of the securities in each index is as follows. The securities in the SSB BIG index are all trader priced. For the two other indexes, the securities are either trader priced or model priced.

To be able to match the performance of an index and to understand why there may be a slippage, a manager must understand the different ways in which an index provider handles the reinvestment of intra-month cash flows. For the SSB BIG index, these cash flows are assumed to be reinvested at the one-month Treasury bill rate. For the Merrill Lynch index, intra-month cash flows are assumed to be reinvested in the specific issue that generated the cash flow. There is no reinvestment of intra-month cash flows for the Lehman index.

Each index is broken into sectors. Exhibit 23-2 shows the sector breakdown for the Lehman Brothers U.S. Aggregate Bond Index and the percentage of each sector.

For the Lehman Brothers U.S. Aggregate Bond Index, the agency sector includes agency debentures, not mortgage-backed or asset-backed securities issued by federal agencies. The mortgage pass-through sector includes agency pass-through securities. What is not included in the index is agency collateralized mortgage obligations and

EXHIBIT 23-2   Sector Breakdown of the Lehman Brothers U.S.
Aggregate Bond Index (as of October 7, 2005)

Sector	Percentage of Index
Treasury	25.50
Agency	11.18
Mortgage pass-throughs	34.53
Commercial mortgage-backed	3.57
Asset-backed securities	1.23
Credit	23.97
Option-adjusted duration = 4.36	

agency stripped mortgage-backed securities. These mortgage derivatives products are not included because it would be double counting since they are created from agency pass-throughs. In constructing the index for the mortgage sector for the Lehman index, for example, Lehman groups more than 800,000 individual mortgage pools with a fixed-rate coupon into generic aggregates. These generic aggregates are defined in terms of agency (i.e., Ginnie Mae, Fannie Mae, and Freddie Mac), program type (i.e., 30-year, 15-year, balloon mortgages, etc.), coupon rate for the pass-through, and the year the pass-through was originated (i.e., vintage). For an issue to be included, it must have a minimum amount outstanding of $100 million and a minimum weighted-average maturity of one year. Agency pass-throughs backed by pools of adjustable-rate mortgages are not included in the mortgage index. The credit sector in the Lehman index includes corporate issues.

INDEXING METHODOLOGIES

After a money manager has decided to pursue an indexing strategy and has selected an index (broad-based bond market index, specialized market index, or customized benchmark), the next step is to construct a portfolio that will track the index. Any discrepancy between the performance of the indexed portfolio and the index (whether positive or negative) is referred to as **tracking error**. Tracking error has three sources: (1) transaction costs in constructing the indexed portfolio, (2) differences in the composition of the indexed portfolio and the index itself, and (3) discrepancies between prices used by the organization constructing the index and transaction prices paid by the indexer.

One approach in constructing the indexed portfolio is for the money manager to purchase all the issues in the index according to their weight in the benchmark index. However, substantial tracking error will result from the transaction costs (and other fees) associated with purchasing all the issues and reinvesting cash flow (maturing principal and coupon interest). A broad-based market index could include more than 5,000 issues, so large transaction costs may make this approach impractical. In addition, some issues in the index may not be available at the prices used in constructing the index.

Instead of purchasing all issues in the index, the money manager may purchase just a sample of issues. Although this approach reduces tracking error resulting from high transaction costs, it increases tracking error resulting from the mismatch of the indexed portfolio and the index.

Generally speaking, the fewer the number of issues used to replicate the index, the smaller the tracking error due to transaction costs but the greater the tracking error risk due to the mismatch of the characteristics of the indexed portfolio and the index. In contrast, the more issues purchased to replicate the index, the greater the tracking error due to transaction costs and the smaller the tracking error risk due to the mismatch of the indexed portfolio and the index. Obviously, then, there is a trade-off between tracking error and the number of issues used to construct the indexed portfolio.

There are three methodologies for designing a portfolio to replicate an index: (1) the stratified sampling or cell approach, (2) the optimization approach, and (3) the variance minimization approach. For each of these approaches, the initial question that the indexer must ask is: What factors affect a bond index's performance? Each approach assumes that the performance of an individual bond depends on a number of systematic factors that affect the performance of all bonds and on a factor unique to the individual issue. This last risk is diversifiable risk. The objective of the three approaches is to construct an indexed portfolio that eliminates this diversifiable risk.

Stratified Sampling or Cell Approach

Under the **stratified sampling approach to indexing**, the index is divided into cells, each cell representing a different characteristic of the index. The most common characteristics used to break down an index are (1) duration, (2) coupon, (3) maturity, (4) market sectors (Treasury, corporate, mortgage-backed), (5) credit rating, (6) call factors, and (7) sinking fund features. The last two factors are particularly important because the call and sinking fund features of an issue will affect its performance.

For example, suppose that a manager selects the following characteristics to partite in a Treasury/agency/corporate bond index:

Characteristic 1: effective duration range: (1) less than or equal to five years, and (2) greater than five years;

Characteristic 2: maturity range: (1) less than five years, (2) between five and 15 years, and (3) greater than or equal to 15 years;

Characteristic 3: market sectors: (1) Treasury, (2) agencies, and (3) corporates;

Characteristic 4: credit rating: (1) AAA, (2) AA, (3) A, and (4) BBB.

The total number of cells would be equal to 72 ($= 2 \times 3 \times 3 \times 4$).

The objective, then, is to select from all the issues in the index one or more issues in each cell that can be used to represent the entire cell. The total dollar amount purchased of the issues from each cell will be based on the percentage of the index's total market value that the cell represents. For example, if 40% of the market value of all the issues in the index is made up of corporate bonds, 40% of the market value of the indexed portfolio should be composed of corporate bond issues.

The number of cells that the indexer uses will depend on the dollar amount of the portfolio to be indexed. In indexing a portfolio of less than $50 million, for example, using a large number of cells would require purchasing odd lots of issues. This increases the cost of buying the issues to represent a cell and thus would increase the tracking error. Reducing the number of cells to overcome this problem increases tracking error risk of index mismatch because the characteristics of the indexed portfolio may differ materially from those of the index.

Optimization Approach

In the **optimization approach to indexing**, the money manager seeks to design an indexed portfolio that will match the cell breakdown as just described, and satisfy other constraints, but also optimize some objective. An objective might be to maximize the portfolio yield, to maximize convexity, or to maximize expected total returns.[5] Constraints other than matching the cell breakdown might include not purchasing more than a specified amount of one issuer or group of issuers, or overweighing certain sectors for enhanced indexing (discussed later).

The computational technique used to derive the optimal solution to the indexing problem in this approach is mathematical programming. When the objective function that the indexer seeks to optimize is a linear function, linear programming (a specific form of mathematical programming) is used. If the objective function is quadratic, the particular mathematical programming technique used is quadratic programming.

Tracking Error Minimization Using Multi-Factor Risk Models

In the previous chapter, forward-looking tracking error was explained. A portfolio can be constructed such that its forward-looking tracking error is minimized. Vendors of multi-factor risk models provide software that permits the construction of a portfolio that will accomplish tracking error minimization. The forward-looking tracking error for each security included in the index is obtained from a statistical analysis of historical returns.

LOGISTICAL PROBLEMS IN IMPLEMENTING AN INDEXING STRATEGY[6]

An indexer faces several logistical problems in constructing an indexed portfolio. First, the prices for each issue used by the organization that publishes the index may not be execution prices available to the indexer. In fact, they may be materially different from the prices offered by some dealers. In addition, the prices used by organizations reporting

---

[5]For a mathematical presentation of this approach as well as the variance minimization approach, see Christina Seix and Ravi Akoury, "Bond Indexation: The Optimal Quantitative Approach," *Journal of Portfolio Management*, Spring 1986, pp. 50–53. For an illustration, see Philip Galdi, "Indexing Fixed Income Portfolios," in Fabozzi and Garlicki (eds.), *Advances in Bond Analysis and Portfolio Strategies*.
[6]For a more detailed discussion, see Mossavar-Rahmani, *Bond Indexing Funds*.

the value of indexes are based on bid prices. Dealer ask prices, however, are the ones that the money manager would have to transact at when constructing or rebalancing the indexed portfolio. Thus, there will be a bias between the performance of the index and the indexed portfolio that is equal to the bid-ask spread.

Furthermore, there are logistical problems unique to certain sectors in the bond market. Consider first the corporate bond market. There are typically about 3,500 issues in the corporate bond sector of a broad-based index. Because of the illiquidity of this sector of the bond market, not only may the prices used by the organization that publishes the index be unreliable, but many of the issues may not even be available. Next, consider the mortgage-backed securities market. There are more than 800,000 agency pass-through issues. The organizations that publish indexes lump all these issues into a few hundred generic issues. The indexer is then faced with the difficult task of finding pass-through securities with the same risk–return profiles of these hypothetical issues.

Finally, recall that the total return depends on the reinvestment rate available on coupon interest. If the organization publishing the index regularly overestimates the reinvestment rate, the indexed portfolio could underperform the index by 10 to 15 basis points a year.[7]

ENHANCED INDEXING

So far we have discussed straight or "plain vanilla" indexing. The objective of an **enhanced indexing strategy** is to replicate the total return performance of some predetermined index. In enhanced indexing (also called "indexing plus"), the objective is consistently to exceed the total return performance of the index by an amount sufficient to justify a higher management advisory fee and a higher level of risk of underperforming the index. The total return on the index becomes the minimum total return objective rather than the target total return. Thus, enhanced indexing brings active strategies back into the portfolio management process, although they are assumed to employ only low-risk strategies.

Basically, any departure of a portfolio's composition from that of the benchmark represents the risk exposure of a portfolio. In plain vanilla indexing, the portfolio manager attempts to replicate the benchmark index as best as possible subject to the limitations discussed earlier regarding implementation. In enhanced indexing, there is a controlled departure of the portfolio's composition from that of the benchmark index. As the departure from the benchmark index becomes greater, the portfolio manager crosses over into the area of active management. Just where that crossover occurs differs from manager to manager.

Another way to define enhanced indexing is in terms of tracking error. While there is no industry standard, Kenneth Volpert, principal and senior portfolio manager at The Vanguard Group, feels that under normal conditions a tracking error of 1 to 15 basis

---

[7]Fran Hawthorne, "The Battle of the Bond Indexes," *Institutional Investor*, April 1986, p. 122.

points per year is reasonable.[8] However, sampling risk has increased in recent years as corporate issuer "blow-ups" have occured with greater frequency and with greater downside, which has resulted in actual tracking error being greater than model predicted tracking error. Many multi-factor risk models are being recalibrated to capture this greater idiosyncratic credit risk. For enhanced bond indexing, tracking error ranges from 15 to 50 basis points under normal conditions. The range in the tracking error is due to the wide range of enhanced indexing portfolio strategies that can be pursued.

What are some of the strategies employed in enhanced indexing? We discussed most of them in Chapter 22. Any of the strategies employed would involve only those issues in the index. Another strategy for enhancing total return is to use securities not included in the index. For example, the broad-based indexes do not include derivative mortgage-backed securities, such as collateralized mortgage obligations. If money managers pursuing enhanced index strategies believe that derivative mortgage-backed securities will outperform the agency pass-through securities in the index, they can substitute the former securities for the latter. Or the money manager may be able to create synthetic agency pass-through securities by using stripped mortgage-backed securities (interest-only and principal-only securities) that would exhibit better performance in certain interest-rate environments.

SUMMARY

Indexing a portfolio means designing a portfolio so that its total return will match the performance of some predetermined index. The indexing approach has been motivated by the poor historical performance of money managers and the lower management fees.

The three broad-based market indexes most commonly used by institutional investors are the Lehman Brothers Aggregate Index, the Salomon Smith Barney Broad Investment-Grade Bond Index, and the Merrill Lynch Domestic Market Index. The performance of these broad-based indexes is highly correlated.

Indexing requires selecting a bond index to be replicated and constructing a portfolio so as to minimize tracking error. The methodologies used to construct an indexed portfolio include the stratified sampling or cell approach, the optimization approach, and the tracking error minimization approach using multi-factor risk models. In an enhanced indexing strategy, the performance of the index becomes the minimum return objective that the portfolio manager attempts to achieve.

Questions

1. What factors support the use of bond indexing?
2. Is there any problem with a commercial bank using an indexing strategy to invest one-year funds on
which the bank has agreed to pay a fixed rate?
3. What are the three most commonly used broad-based bond market indexes used by institutional investors?

---

[8]Mr. Volpert provided this information via e-mail correspondence on February 7, 2003.

4. What are the major sectors covered by the broad-based market indexes?
5. What types of mortgage-backed securities are included in a broad-based market index?
6. Why is a reinvestment rate assumption needed in order to calculate the monthly total return of an index?
7. Why does tracking error occur in a bond indexing strategy?
8. What is the stratified sampling or cell approach to indexing?
9. What are the various types of enhanced bond indexing strategies?
10. How can a multi-factor risk model be used to design an indexed portfolio?
11. a. Explain how enhanced indexing differs from indexing.
    b. Explain how enhanced indexing differs from active management.

LIABILITY FUNDING STRATEGIES

After reading this chapter you will understand:

- the types of liabilities that an institution may face

- the two important dimensions of a liability: the amount and timing of the payment

- why the same factors that affect the risk of financial assets also affect liabilities

- the goals of asset/liability management

- the difference between an institution's accounting surplus, regulatory surplus, and economic surplus

- how assets are handled for accounting purposes

- how to use the duration of assets and liabilities to calculate the sensitivity of the economic surplus of an institution when interest rates change

- what a liability funding strategy is

- the risks associated with mismatching portfolio assets and liabilities

- what immunizing a portfolio is

- the basic principles of an immunization strategy and the role of duration in an immunization strategy

- the risks associated with immunizing a portfolio

- what a contingent immunization strategy is and the key factors in implementing such a strategy

- the two liability funding strategies when there are multiple liabilities: multiperiod liability immunization and cash flow matching

- the advantages and disadvantages of a multiple liability immunization strategy versus a cash flow matching strategy

■ how liability funding strategies can be extended to cases in which the liabilities are not known with certainty

■ what an active/immunization combination strategy is

In our discussion of the investment management process in Chapter 22, we explained that an investor must set objectives. For institutional investors, objectives are influenced by the nature of the institution's liabilities. Although investors are exposed to the same types of risks when they invest in financial assets, the nature of liabilities varies from institution to institution and is therefore the key factor in a portfolio manager's selection of the asset classes to include in a portfolio.

In this chapter we begin with the basic principles underlying the management of assets relative to liabilities, popularly referred to as **asset/liability management**. We then describe several structured portfolio strategies, strategies that seek to match the performance of a predetermined benchmark. Bond portfolio indexing, discussed in Chapter 23, is an example of such a strategy. There the benchmark is based on a bond index but may not actually satisfy the needs of the sponsoring institution. In this chapter we discuss **liability funding strategies** that select assets so that cash flows will equal or exceed the client's obligations. The client's liabilities, then, serve as the benchmark for portfolio performance. Specifically, when the liability is a single liability, an immunization strategy is employed. When there are multiple liabilities, there are two strategies to choose from: multiperiod immunization and cash flow matching.

GENERAL PRINCIPLES OF ASSET/LIABILITY MANAGEMENT

The nature of an institutional investor's liabilities will dictate the investment strategy it will request its money manager to pursue. Depository institutions, for example, seek to generate income by the spread between the return that they earn on their assets and the cost of their funds. Consequently, banking is referred to as **spread banking**. Life insurance companies are in the spread business. Pension funds are not in the spread business, in that they themselves do not raise funds in the market. Sponsors of defined benefit pension plans seek to cover the cost of pension obligations at a minimum cost that is borne by the sponsor of the pension plan. Most investment companies face no explicit costs for the funds they acquire and must satisfy no specific liability obligations.

Classification of Liabilities
A **liability** is a cash outlay that must be made at a specific time to satisfy the contractual terms of an issued obligation. An institutional investor is concerned with both the amount and timing of liabilities because its assets must produce the cash to meet any payments it has promised to make in a timely way. In fact, liabilities are classified according to the degree of certainty of their amount and timing, as shown in Exhibit 24-1. The classification assumes that the holder of the obligation will not cancel it prior to an actual or projected payout date.

EXHIBIT 24-1	Classification of Liabilities of Institutional Investors	

Liability Type	Amount of Cash Outlay	Timing of Cash Outlay
I	Known	Known
II	Known	Uncertain
III	Uncertain	Known
IV	Uncertain	Uncertain

The descriptions of cash outlays as either known or uncertain are undoubtedly broad. When we refer to a cash outlay as being uncertain, we do not mean that it cannot be predicted. There are some liabilities for which the "law of large numbers" makes it easier to predict the timing and/or amount of cash outlays. This work is typically done by actuaries, but even actuaries have difficulty predicting natural catastrophes, such as floods and earthquakes.

Next, we illustrate each type of risk category. The important thing to note is that just like assets, there are risks associated with liabilities. Some of these risks are affected by the same factors that affect asset risks.

Type I Liabilities

A type I liability is one for which both the amount and timing of the liabilities are known with certainty. An example is a liability in which an institution knows that it must pay $50,000 six months from now. Banks and thrifts know the amount that they are committed to pay (principal plus interest) on the maturity date of a fixed-rate deposit, assuming that the depositor does not withdraw funds prior to the maturity date.

Type I liabilities, however, are not limited to depository institutions. A major product sold by life insurance companies is a **guaranteed investment contract**, popularly referred to as a **GIC**. The obligation of the life insurance company under this contract is that for a sum of money (called a **premium**), it will guarantee an interest rate up to some specified maturity date. For example, suppose that a life insurance company, for a premium of $10 million, issues a five-year GIC agreeing to pay 10% compounded annually. The life insurance company knows that it must pay $16.11 million to the GIC policyholder in five years.[1]

Type II Liabilities

A type II liability is one for which the amount of cash outlay is known but the timing of the cash outlay is uncertain. The most obvious example of a type II liability is a life insurance policy. There are many types of life insurance policies, but the most basic type provides that for an annual premium, a life insurance company agrees to make a specified dollar payment to policy beneficiaries upon the death of the insured. Naturally, the timing of the insured's death is uncertain.

Type III Liabilities

A type III liability is one for which the timing of the cash outlay is known but the amount is uncertain. A two-year floating-rate CD in which the interest rate resets quarterly based

---

[1]This amount is determined as follows: $10,000,000 \times (1.10)^5$.

on a market interest rate is an example. Not surprisingly, there are also floating-rate GICs; these also fall into the type III liabilities category.

Type IV Liabilities

A type IV liability is one in which there is uncertainty as to both the amount and timing of the cash outlay. There are numerous insurance products and pension obligations in this category. Probably the most obvious examples are automobile and home insurance policies issued by property and casualty insurance companies. When, and if, a payment will have to be made to the policyholder is uncertain. Whenever damage is done to an insured asset, the amount of the payment that must be made is uncertain.

The liabilities of pension plans can also be type IV liabilities. In defined benefit plans, retirement benefits depend on the participant's income for a specified number of years before retirement and the total number of years the participant worked. This will affect the amount of the cash outlay. The timing of the cash outlay depends on when the employee elects to retire and whether the employee remains with the sponsoring plan until retirement. Moreover, both the amount and the timing will depend on how the employee elects to have payments made—over only the employee's life or those of the employee and spouse.

Liquidity Concerns

Because of uncertainty about the timing and/or the amount of the cash outlays, an institution must be prepared to have sufficient cash to satisfy its obligations. Also keep in mind that the entity that holds the obligation against the institution may have the right to change the nature of the obligation, perhaps incurring a penalty. For example, in the case of a CD, the depositor may request the withdrawal of funds prior to the maturity date. Typically, the deposit-accepting institution will grant this request but assess an early withdrawal penalty. In the case of certain types of investment companies, shareholders have the right to redeem their shares at any time. These rights add to the uncertainty of the liability from the point of view of the financial institution.

Similarly, some life insurance products have a cash surrender value. This means that at specified dates, the policyholder can exchange the policy for a lump-sum payment. Typically, the lump-sum payment will penalize the policyholder for turning in the policy. Some life insurance products have a loan value, which means that the policyholder has the right to borrow against the cash value of the policy. Both factors increase the uncertainty of the insurance company's liabilities.

In addition to uncertainty about the timing and amount of the cash outlays and the potential for the depositor or policyholder to withdraw cash early or borrow against a policy, an institution has to be concerned with possible reduction in cash inflows. In the case of a depository institution, this means the inability to obtain deposits. For insurance companies, it means reduced premiums because of the cancellation of policies. For certain types of investment companies, it means not being able to find new buyers for shares.

Surplus Management

The two goals of a financial institution are (1) to earn an adequate return on funds invested, and (2) to maintain a comfortable surplus of assets beyond liabilities. The task of managing funds of a financial institution to accomplish these goals is referred to as **asset/liability management** or **surplus management**. This task involves a trade-off between controlling the risk of a decline in the surplus and taking on acceptable risks in order to earn an adequate return on the funds invested. With respect to the risks, the manager must consider the risks of both the assets and the liabilities.

Institutions may calculate three types of surpluses: economic, accounting, and regulatory. The method of valuing assets and liabilities greatly affects the apparent health of a financial institution. Unrealistic valuation, although allowable under accounting procedures and regulations, is not sound investment practice.

Economic Surplus

The **economic surplus** of any entity is the difference between the market value of all its assets and the market value of its liabilities; that is,

economic surplus = market value of assets − market value of liabilities

Although the concept of a market value of assets may not seem unusual, one might ask: What is the market value of liabilities? This value is simply the present value of the liabilities, in which the liabilities are discounted at an appropriate interest rate. A rise in interest rates will therefore decrease the present value or market value of the liabilities; a decrease in interest rates will increase the present value or market value of liabilities. Thus, the economic surplus can be expressed as

economic surplus = market value of assets − present value of liabilities

For example, consider an institution that has a portfolio consisting only of bonds and liabilities. Let's look at what happens to the economic surplus if interest rates rise. This will cause the bonds to decline in value, but it will also cause the liabilities to decline in value. Both the assets and liabilities decline so the economic surplus can either increase, decrease, or not change. The net effect depends on the relative interest-rate sensitivity of the assets compared to the liabilities. Because duration is a measure of the responsiveness of cash flows to changes in interest rates, a duration can be calculated for liabilities in the same way in which it is calculated for assets. Thus, the duration of liabilities measures their responsiveness to a change in interest rates.

If the duration of the assets is greater than the duration of the liabilities, the economic surplus will increase if interest rates fall. For example, suppose that the current market value of a portfolio of assets is equal to $100 million, and the present value of liabilities is $90 million. Then the economic surplus is $10 million. Suppose that the duration of the assets is 5 and the duration of the liabilities is 3. Consider the following two scenarios:

Scenario 1: *Interest rates decline by 100 basis points.* Because the duration of the assets is 5, the market value of the assets will increase by approximately 5% or $5 million (5% × $100 million) to $105 million. The liabilities will also increase. If the duration of the liabilities is assumed to be 3, the present value of the liabilities will increase by $2.7 million (3% × $90 million) to $92.7 million. Thus, the surplus increased from $10 million to $12.3 million.

Scenario 2: *Interest rates rise by 100 basis points.* Because the duration of the assets is 5, the market value of the assets will decrease by approximately 5%, to $95 million. The liabilities will also decrease. If the duration of the liabilities is 3, the present value of the liabilities will decrease by $2.7 million to $87.3 million. The surplus is then reduced to $7.7 million from $10 million.

The net effect on the surplus depends on the duration or interest-rate sensitivity of the assets and liabilities so it is imperative that portfolio managers be able to measure this sensitivity for all assets and liabilities accurately.

Accounting Surplus

Institutional investors must prepare periodic financial statements. These financial statements must be prepared in accordance with **generally accepted accounting principles** (GAAP). Thus, the assets and liabilities reported are based on GAAP accounting. The accounting treatment for assets is governed by a relatively new accounting requirement, Statement of Financial Accounting Standards No. 115, more popularly referred to as FASB 115.[2] However, it does not deal with the accounting treatment for liabilities.

With respect to the financial reporting of assets, there are three possible methods for reporting: (1) amortized cost or historical cost, (2) market value, or (3) the lower of cost or market value. Despite the fact that the real cash flow is the same regardless of the accounting treatment, there can be substantial differences in the financial statements using these three methods.

In the **amortized cost method**, the value reported in the balance sheet reflects an adjustment to the acquisition cost for debt securities purchased at a discount or premium from their maturity value. This method is sometimes referred to as **book value accounting**. In the **market value accounting method**, the balance sheet reported value of an asset is its market value. When an asset is reported in the financial statements of an institution at its market value, it is said to be "marked to market." Finally, the **lower of cost** or **market method** requires comparison of market value to the amortized cost, with the lower of these two values reported in the balance sheet. The value reported cannot exceed the amortized cost.

FASB 115 specifies which of these three methods must be followed for assets. Specifically, the accounting treatment required for a security depends on how the security is classified. There are three classifications of investment accounts: (1) held to maturity, (2) available for sale, and (3) trading. The definition of each account is set forth in FASB 115, and we summarize each next.

The **held-to-maturity account** includes assets that the institution plans to hold until they mature. Obviously, the assets classified in this account cannot be common stock because they have no maturity. For all assets in the held-to-maturity account, the amortized cost method must be used.

An asset is classified as in the **available-for-sale account** if the institution does not have the ability to hold the asset to maturity or intends to sell it. An asset that is acquired for the purpose of earning a short-term trading profit from market movements is classified in the **trading account**. For all assets in the available-for-sale and trading accounts, market value accounting is used. Thus, these two accounts more accurately reflect the economic condition of the assets held by the institution. Exhibit 24-2 summarizes the accounting treatment of assets as set forth by FASB 115.

When financial statements are prepared, the change in the value of assets must be accounted for. An unrealized gain or loss occurs when the asset's value has changed

---

[2]FASB 115 was issued in May 1993 and became effective with fiscal years beginning after December 15, 1993.

EXHIBIT 24-2	Summary of Key Provisions of FASB 115		
Account Classification	Accounting Method for Assets	Will Affect Surplus	Will Affect Reported Earnings
Held to maturity	Amortized cost	No	No
Available for sale	Market value	Yes	No
Trading	Market value	Yes	Yes

but the gain or loss is not realized because the asset is not sold. For example, if an asset has a market value of $100 at the beginning of an accounting period and is held in the portfolio at the end of the accounting period with a market value of $110, the unrealized gain is $10.

Any unrealized gain or loss affects the accounting surplus. Specifically, an unrealized gain increases the surplus, and an unrealized loss reduces the accounting surplus. The unrealized gain or loss may or may not affect the reported earnings.

Under FASB 115, the accounting treatment for any unrealized gain or loss depends on the account in which the asset is classified. Specifically, any unrealized gain or loss is ignored for assets in the held-to-maturity account. Thus, for assets in this account there is no affect on reported earnings or the accounting surplus. For the other two accounts, any unrealized gain or loss affects the accounting surplus as described previously. However, there is a difference as to how reported earnings are affected. For assets classified in the available-for-sale account, unrealized gains or losses are not included in reported earnings; in contrast, for assets classified in the trading account, any gains or losses are included in reported earnings. These provisions are summarized in Exhibit 24-2.

Regulatory Surplus

Institutional investors that are regulated at the state or federal levels must provide financial reports to regulators based on regulatory accounting principles (RAP). RAP accounting for a regulated institution need not use the same rules as set forth by FASB 115 (i.e., GAAP accounting). Liabilities may or may not be reported at their present value, depending on the type of institution and the type of liability. The surplus as measured using RAP accounting, called **regulatory surplus**, may, as in the case of accounting surplus, differ materially from economic surplus.

IMMUNIZATION OF A PORTFOLIO TO SATISFY A SINGLE LIABILITY

In the balance of this chapter we focus on liability funding strategies. Tens of billions of dollars in pension monies went into these liability funding strategies in the early and mid-1980s when interest rates were high because of the strong incentive to reduce pension costs by locking in these rates. The insurance industry has also made widespread use of these strategies for their fixed-liability insurance products.

We begin with a strategy referred to as an **immunization strategy**. The person generally credited with pioneering this strategy, F. M. Reddington, defined immunization in 1952 as "the investment of the assets in such a way that the existing business is immune to a general change in the rate of interest."[3]

To comprehend the basic principles underlying the immunization of a portfolio against interest-rate changes so as to satisfy a single liability, consider the situation faced by a life insurance company that sells a guaranteed investment contract (GIC). Under this policy, for a lump-sum payment, a life insurance company guarantees that specified dollars will be paid to the policyholder at a specified future date. Or, equivalently, the life insurance company guarantees a specified rate of return on the payment. For example, suppose that a life insurance company sells a GIC that guarantees an interest rate of 6.25% every six months (12.5% on a bond-equivalent yield basis) for 5.5 years (11 six-month periods). Also suppose that the payment made by the policyholder is $8,820,262. Then, the value that the life insurance company has guaranteed the policyholder 5.5 years from now is

$$\$8,820,262(1.0625)^{11} = \$17,183,033$$

When investing the $8,820,262, the target accumulated value for the portfolio manager of the life insurance company is $17,183,033 after 5.5 years, which is the same as a target yield of 12.5% on a bond-equivalent basis.[4]

Suppose that the portfolio manager buys $8,820,262 par value of a bond selling at par with a 12.5% yield to maturity that matures in 5.5 years. Will the portfolio manager be assured of realizing the target yield of 12.5% or, equivalently, a target accumulated value of $17,183,033? As we explained in Chapter 3, the portfolio manager will realize a 12.5% yield only if the coupon interest payments can be reinvested at 6.25% every six months. That is, the accumulated value will depend on the reinvestment rate.

To demonstrate this, we will suppose that immediately after investing the $8,820,262 in the 12.5% coupon 5.5-year maturity bond, yields in the market change and stay at the new level for the remainder of the 5.5 years. Exhibit 24-3 illustrates what happens at the end of 5.5 years. The first column shows the new yield level. The second column shows the total coupon interest payments (which remains constant). The third column gives the interest on interest over the entire 5.5 years if the coupon interest payments are reinvested at the new yield level shown in the first column. The price of the bond at the end of 5.5 years shown in the fourth column is the par value. The fifth column is the accumulated value from all three sources: coupon interest, interest on interest, and bond price. The total return on a bond-equivalent yield basis is shown in the last column, according to the formula[5]

$$2\left[\left(\frac{\text{accumulated value}}{\$8,820,262}\right)^{1/11} - 1\right]$$

If yields do not change, so that the coupon payments can be reinvested at 12.5% (6.25% every six months), the portfolio manager will achieve the target accumulated

---

[3]The theory of immunization was first set forth in F. M. Reddington, "Review of the Principle of Life Office Valuation," *Journal of the Institute of Actuaries*, 1952, pp. 286–340.

[4]Actually, the life insurance company will not guarantee the interest rate that it expects to earn, but a lower rate. The spread between the interest rate earned and the interest rate it guarantees is the return for the risk of not achieving the target return.

[5]The procedure for calculating the total return is given in Chapter 3.

EXHIBIT 24-3   Accumulated Value and Total Return After 5.5 Years: 5.5-Year 12.5% Bond Selling to Yield 12.5%

Investment horizon (years): 5.5
Coupon rate: 0.125
Maturity (years): 5.5
Yield to maturity: 0.125
Price: 100
Par value purchased: $8,820,262
Purchase price: $8,820,262
Target accumulated value: $17,183,033

| | | After 5.5 Years | | | |
New Yield[a]	Coupon Interest	Interest on Interest	Price of Bond[b]	Accumulated Value	Total Return
0.160	$6,063,930	$3,112,167	$8,820,262	$17,996,360	0.1340
0.155	6,063,930	2,990,716	8,820,262	17,874,908	0.1326
0.145	6,063,930	2,753,177	8,820,262	17,637,369	0.1300
0.140	6,063,930	2,647,037	8,820,262	17,521,230	0.1288
0.135	6,063,930	2,522,618	8,820,262	17,406,810	0.1275
0.130	6,063,930	2,409,984	8,820,262	17,294,086	0.1262
0.125	6,063,930	2,298,840	8,820,262	17,183,033	0.1250
0.120	6,063,930	2,189,433	8,820,262	17,073,625	0.1238
0.115	6,063,930	2,081,648	8,820,262	16,965,840	0.1225
0.110	6,063,930	1,975,462	8,820,262	16,859,654	0.1213
0.105	6,063,930	1,870,852	8,820,262	16,755,044	0.1201
0.100	6,063,930	1,767,794	8,820,262	16,651,986	0.1189
0.095	6,063,930	1,666,266	8,820,262	16,550,458	0.1178
0.090	6,063,930	1,566,246	8,820,262	16,450,438	0.1166
0.085	6,063,930	1,467,712	8,820,262	16,351,904	0.1154
0.080	6,063,930	1,370,642	8,820,262	16,254,834	0.1143
0.075	6,063,930	1,275,014	8,820,262	16,159,206	0.1132
0.070	6,063,930	1,180,808	8,820,262	16,065,000	0.1120
0.065	6,063,930	1,088,003	8,820,262	15,972,195	0.1109
0.060	6,063,930	996,577	8,820,262	15,880,769	0.1098
0.055	6,063,930	906,511	8,820,262	15,790,703	0.1087
0.050	6,063,930	817,785	8,820,262	15,701,977	0.1077

[a]Immediate change in yield.
[b]Maturity value.

value. If market yields rise, an accumulated value (total return) higher than the target accumulated value (target yield) will be achieved. This is because the coupon interest payments can be reinvested at a higher rate than the initial yield to maturity. Contrast this with what happens when the yield declines. The accumulated value (total return) will be less than the target accumulated value (target yield). *Therefore, investing in a coupon bond with a yield to maturity equal to the target yield and a maturity equal to the investment horizon does not assure that the target accumulated value will be achieved.*

Suppose that instead of investing in a bond maturing in 5.5 years the portfolio manager invests in a 15-year bond with a coupon rate of 12.5% that is selling at par to yield 12.5%. Exhibit 24-4 presents the accumulated value and total return if the market yield changes immediately after the bond is purchased and remains at the new yield level. The fourth column of the table is the market price of a 12.5% coupon 9.5-year bond (because 5.5 years have passed), assuming the market yields shown in the first column. If the market yield increases, the portfolio will fail to achieve the target accumulated

EXHIBIT 24-4   Accumulated Value and Total Return After 5.5 Years: 15-Year 12.5% Bond Selling to Yield 12.5%

Investment horizon (years): 5.5
Coupon rate: 0.1250
Maturity (years): 15
Yield to maturity: 0.1250
Price: 100
Par value purchased: $8,820,262
Purchase price: $8,820,262
Target accumulated value: $17,183,033

| | | | After 5.5 Years | | |
New Yield[a]	Coupon Interest	Interest on Interest	Price of Bond	Accumulated Value	Total Return
0.160	$6,063,930	$3,112,167	$7,337,902	$16,513,999	0.1173
0.155	6,063,930	2,990,716	7,526,488	16,581,134	0.1181
0.145	6,063,930	2,753,177	7,925,481	16,742,588	0.1200
0.140	6,063,930	2,637,037	8,136,542	16,837,509	0.1211
0.135	6,063,930	2,522,618	8,355,777	16,942,325	0.1223
0.130	6,063,930	2,409,984	8,583,555	17,057,379	0.1236
0.125	6,063,930	2,298,840	8,820,262	17,183,032	0.1250
0.120	6,063,930	2,189,433	9,066,306	17,319,699	0.1265
0.115	6,063,930	2,081,648	9,322,113	17,467,691	0.1282
0.110	6,063,930	1,975,462	9,588,131	17,627,523	0.1299
0.105	6,063,930	1,870,852	9,864,831	17,799,613	0.1318
0.100	6,063,930	1,767,794	10,152,708	17,984,432	0.1338
0.095	6,063,930	1,666,266	10,452,281	18,182,477	0.1359
0.090	6,063,930	1,566,246	10,764,095	18,394,271	0.1382
0.085	6,063,930	1,467,712	11,088,723	18,620,365	0.1406
0.080	6,063,930	1,370,642	11,462,770	18,897,342	0.1431
0.075	6,063,930	1,275,014	11,778,867	19,117,811	0.1457
0.070	6,063,930	1,180,808	12,145,682	19,390,420	0.1485
0.065	6,063,930	1,088,003	12,527,914	19,679,847	0.1514
0.060	6,063,930	996,577	12,926,301	19,986,808	0.1544
0.055	6,063,930	906,511	13,341,617	20,312,058	0.1576
0.050	6,063,930	817,785	13,774,677	20,656,392	0.1609

[a]Immediate change in yield.

value; the opposite will be true if the market yield decreases: The accumulated value (total return) will exceed the target accumulated value (target yield).

The reason for this result can be seen Exhibit 24-5, which summarizes the change in interest on interest and the change in price resulting from a change in the market yield. For example, if the market yield rises instantaneously by 200 basis points, from 12.5% to 14.5%, interest on interest will be $454,336 greater; however, the market price of the bond will decrease by $894,781. The net effect is that the accumulated value will be $440,445 less than the target accumulated value. The reverse will be true if the market yield decreases. The change in the price of the bond will more than offset the decline in the interest on interest, resulting in an accumulated value that exceeds the target accumulated value.

Now we can see what is happening to the accumulated value. There is a trade-off between interest rate (or price) risk and reinvestment risk. For this 15-year bond, the target accumulated value will be realized only if the market yield does not increase.

Because neither a coupon bond with the same maturity nor a bond with a longer maturity ensures realization of the target accumulated value, perhaps a bond with a maturity shorter than 5.5 years will. Consider a 12.5% bond with six months remaining to

EXHIBIT 24-5	Change in Interest on Interest and Price Due to Interest Rate Change After 5.5 Years: 15-Year 12.5% Bond Selling to Yield 12.5%		
New Yield	Change in Interest on Interest	Change in Price	Total Change in Accumulated Value
0.160	$813,327	−$1,482,360	−$669,033
0.155	692,875	−1,293,774	−600,899
0.145	454,336	−894,781	−440,445
0.140	338,197	−683,720	−345,523
0.135	223,778	−464,485	−240,707
0.130	111,054	−236,707	−125,653
0.125	0	0	0
0.120	−109,407	246,044	136,637
0.115	−217,192	501,851	284,659
0.110	−323,378	767,869	444,491
0.105	−427,989	1,044,569	616,580
0.100	−531,046	1,332,446	801,400
0.095	−632,574	1,632,019	999,445
0.090	−732,594	1,943,833	1,211,239
0.085	−831,128	2,268,461	1,437,333
0.080	−928,198	2,606,508	1,678,310
0.075	−1,023,826	2,958,605	1,934,779
0.070	−1,118,032	3,325,420	2,207,388
0.065	−1,210,838	3,707,652	2,496,814
0.060	−1,302,263	4,106,039	2,803,776
0.055	−1,392,329	4,521,355	3,129,026
0.050	−1,481,055	4,954,415	3,473,360

maturity selling at par. Exhibit 24-6 shows the accumulated value and total return over the 5.5-year investment horizon. The second column shows the accumulated value after six months. The third column shows the value that is accumulated after 5.5 years by reinvesting the value accumulated after six months at the yield shown in the first column; that is,

$$\$9,371,528\left(1+\frac{\text{new yield}}{2}\right)^2$$

EXHIBIT 24-6 Accumulated Value and Total Return: Six-Month, 12.5% Bond Selling to Yield 12.5%

Investment horizon (years): 5.5
Coupon rate: 0.125
Maturity (years): 0.5
Yield to maturity: 0.125
Price: 100
Par value purchased: $8,820,262
Purchase price: $8,820,262
Target accumulated value: $17,183,033

| | | After 5.5 Years | |
New Yield[a]	After 6 Months	Accumulated Value	Total Return
0.160	$9,371,528	$20,232,427	0.1568
0.155	9,371,528	19,768,932	0.1523
0.145	9,371,528	18,870,501	0.1432
0.140	9,371,528	18,435,215	0.1386
0.135	9,371,528	18,008,986	0.1341
0.130	9,371,528	17,591,647	0.1295
0.125	9,371,528	17,183,033	0.1250
0.120	9,371,528	16,782,980	0.1205
0.115	9,371,528	16,391,330	0.1159
0.110	9,371,528	16,007,924	0.1114
0.105	9,371,528	15,632,609	0.1068
0.100	9,371,528	15,265,232	0.1023
0.095	9,371,528	14,905,644	0.0977
0.090	9,371,528	14,553,697	0.0932
0.085	9,371,528	14,209,247	0.0886
0.080	9,371,528	13,872,151	0.0841
0.075	9,371,528	13,542,270	0.0795
0.070	9,371,528	13,219,466	0.0749
0.065	9,371,528	12,903,604	0.0704
0.060	9,371,528	12,594,550	0.0658
0.055	9,371,528	12,292,175	0.0613
0.050	9,371,528	11,996,349	0.0567

[a]Immediate change in yield.

By investing in this six-month bond, the portfolio manager incurs no interest-rate risk, although there is reinvestment risk. The target accumulated value will be achieved only if the market yield remains at 12.5% or rises. Once again, the portfolio manager is not assured of achieving the target accumulated value.

If we assume there is a one-time instantaneous change in the market yield, is there a coupon bond that the portfolio manager can purchase to assure the target accumulated value whether the market yield rises or falls? The portfolio manager should look for a coupon bond so that however the market yield changes, the change in the interest on interest will be offset by the change in the price.

Consider, for example, an eight-year 10.125% coupon bond selling at 88.20262 to yield 12.5%. Suppose that $10,000,000 of par value of this bond is purchased for $8,820,262. Exhibit 24-7 provides the same information for this bond as Exhibits 24-3

EXHIBIT 24-7   Accumulated Value and Total Return: Eight-Year 10.125% Bond Selling to Yield 12.5%

Investment horizon (years): 5.5
Coupon rate: 0.10125
Maturity (years): 8
Yield to maturity: 0.125
Price: 88.20262
Par value purchased: $10,000,000
Purchase price: $8,820,262
Target accumulated value: $17,183,033

		After 5.5 Years			
New Yield[a]	Coupon Interest	Interest on Interest	Price of Bond	Accumulated Value	Total Return
0.160	$5,568,750	$2,858,028	$ 8,827,141	$17,253,919	0.1258
0.155	5,568,750	2,746,494	8,919,852	17,235,096	0.1256
0.145	5,568,750	2,528,352	9,109,054	17,206,156	0.1253
0.140	5,568,750	2,421,697	9,205,587	17,196,034	0.1251
0.135	5,568,750	2,316,621	9,303,435	17,188,806	0.1251
0.130	5,568,750	2,213,102	9,402,621	17,184,473	0.1250
0.125	5,568,750	2,111,117	9,503,166	17,183,033	0.1250
0.120	5,568,750	2,010,644	9,605,091	17,184,485	0.1250
0.115	5,568,750	1,911,661	9,708,420	17,188,831	0.1251
0.110	5,568,750	1,814,146	9,813,175	17,196,071	0.1251
0.105	5,568,750	1,718,078	9,919,380	17,206,208	0.1253
0.100	5,568,750	1,623,436	10,027,059	17,219,245	0.1254
0.095	5,568,750	1,530,199	10,136,236	17,235,185	0.1256
0.090	5,568,750	1,438,347	10,246,936	17,254,033	0.1258
0.085	5,568,750	1,347,859	10,359,184	17,275,793	0.1260
0.080	5,568,750	1,258,715	10,473,006	17,300,471	0.1263
0.075	5,568,750	1,170,897	10,588,428	17,328,075	0.1266

EXHIBIT 24-7   (continued)

New Yield[a]	Coupon Interest	Interest on Interest	Price of Bond	Accumulated Value	Total Return
			After 5.5 Years		
0.070	5,568,750	1,084,383	10,705,477	17,358,610	0.1270
0.065	5,568,750	999,156	10,824,180	17,392,086	0.1273
0.060	5,568,750	915,197	10,944,565	17,428,512	0.1277
0.055	5,568,750	832,486	11,066,660	17,467,896	0.1282
0.050	5,568,750	751,005	11,190,494	17,510,249	0.1268

[a]Immediate change in yield.

and 24–4 did for the previous bonds. Looking at the last two columns, we see that the accumulated value and the total return are never less than the target accumulated value and the target yield. Thus, the target accumulated value is assured regardless of what happens to the market yield. Exhibit 24-8 shows why. When the market yield rises, the

EXHIBIT 24-8   Change in Interest on Interest and Price Due to Interest Rate Change After 5.5 Years: Eight-Year 10.125% Bond Selling to Yield 12.5%

New Yield	Change in Interest on Interest	Change in Price	Total Change in Accumulated Value
0.160	$ 746,911	−$676,024	$70,887
0.155	635,377	−583,314	52,063
0.145	417,235	−394,112	23,123
0.140	310,580	−297,579	13,001
0.135	205,504	−199,730	5,774
0.130	101,985	−100,544	1,441
0.125	0	0	0
0.120	−100,473	101,925	1,452
0.115	−199,456	205,254	5,798
0.110	−296,971	310,010	13,039
0.105	−393,039	416,215	23,176
0.100	−487,681	523,894	36,213
0.095	−580,918	633,071	52,153
0.090	−672,770	743,771	71,001
0.085	763,258	856,019	92,761
0.080	−852,402	969,841	117,439
0.075	−940,221	1,085,263	145,042
0.070	−1,026,734	1,202,311	175,577
0.065	−1,111,961	1,321,014	209,053
0.060	−1,195,921	1,441,399	245,478
0.055	−1,278,632	1,563,494	284,862
0.050	−1,360,112	1,687,328	327,216

change in the interest on interest more than offsets the decline in price. When the market yield declines, the increase in price exceeds the decline in interest on interest.

Let's look at the characteristic of this bond that seems to assure that the target accumulated value will be realized regardless of how the market yield changes. The duration for each of the four bonds we have considered is shown in Exhibit 24-9. Recall from our earlier discussion of duration in this book that there is modified duration and effective duration. Because the bonds in our illustration are all assumed to be option-free bonds, modified duration is used. However, when portfolios include securities with embedded options, the effective duration is used. Throughout the remainder of the discussion in this chapter, when we refer to *duration* we mean the appropriate measure of duration given the types of securities in the portfolio. For most institutional portfolios, this will typically be effective duration.

Given the duration for each bond as shown in Exhibit 24-9, let's compare them to the duration of the liability. This is a simple liability because there is only one cash payment at the maturity date, and it is assumed that there is no embedded option in the liability. For an asset or a liability with only one cash flow, the duration is equal to the number of years to maturity divided by one plus one-half the yield. If the number of years to maturity is 5.5 years and the yield for a 5.5-year liability is 12.5%, then the duration is 5.5 divided by 1 plus 0.0625, or 5.18. We can see from Exhibit 24-9 that the duration of the eight-year 10.125% coupon issue has the same duration as the liability. This is the bond that assured immunization in our illustration.

This equality of the duration of the asset and the duration of the liability is the key to immunization. Generalizing this observation to bond portfolios from individual bonds, the key is: *To immunize a portfolio's target accumulated value (target yield), a portfolio manager must construct a bond portfolio such that (1) the duration of the portfolio is equal to the duration of the liability, and (2) the present value of the cash flow from the portfolio equals to the present value of the future liability.*

Often in discussions of immunization, the condition for immunization is cast in terms of Macaulay duration, a concept discussed in Chapter 4. The reason for the focus on Macaulay duration is that the bonds and liabilities are assumed to be option-free so that modified duration is appropriate and therefore from the relationship between modified duration and Macaulay duration, the analysis can be cast in terms of the latter.

Rebalancing an Immunized Portfolio

Our illustrations of the principles underlying immunization assume a one-time instantaneous change in the market yield. In practice, the market yield will fluctuate over the

EXHIBIT 24-9 Modified Durations of Selected Bonds	
Bond	Modified Duration
5.5-year 12.5% coupon, selling at par	3.90
15-year 12.5% coupon, selling at par	6.70
6-month 12.5% coupon, selling at par	0.48
8-year 10.125% coupon, selling for 88.20262	5.18

investment horizon. As a result, the duration of the portfolio will change as the market yield changes. In addition, the duration will change simply because of the passage of time.

Even in the face of changing market yields, a portfolio can be immunized if it is rebalanced so that its duration is equal to the duration of the liability's remaining time. For example, if the liability is initially 5.5 years, the initial portfolio should have a duration of 5.5 years. After six months, the liability will be five years, but the duration of the portfolio will probably be different from five years. This is because duration depends on the remaining time to maturity and the new level of yields, and there is no reason why the change in these two values should reduce the duration by exactly six months. Thus, the portfolio must be rebalanced so that its duration is five years. Six months later, the portfolio must be rebalanced again so that its duration will equal 4.5 years. And so on.

How often should the portfolio be rebalanced to adjust its duration? On the one hand, the more frequent rebalancing increases transactions costs, thereby reducing the likelihood of achieving the target yield. On the other hand, less frequent rebalancing will result in the duration wandering from the target duration, which will also reduce the likelihood of achieving the target yield. Thus, the portfolio manager faces a trade-off: Some transaction costs must be accepted to prevent the duration from wandering too far from its target, but some maladjustment in the duration must be accepted or transaction costs will become prohibitively high.

Immunization Risk

The sufficient condition for the immunization of a single liability is that the duration of the portfolio be equal to the duration of the liability. However, a portfolio will be immunized against interest-rate changes only if the yield curve is flat and any changes in the yield curve are parallel changes (i.e., interest rates move either up or down by the same number of basis points for all maturities). Recall from Chapter 4 that duration is a measure of price volatility for parallel shifts in the yield curve. If there is a change in interest rates that does not correspond to this shape-preserving shift, matching the portfolio's duration to the liability's duration will not assure immunization. That is, the target yield will no longer be the minimum total return for the portfolio.

As there are many duration-matched portfolios that can be constructed to immunize a liability, is it possible to construct one that has the lowest risk of not realizing the target yield? That is, in light of the uncertain way in which the yield curve may shift, is it possible to develop a criterion for minimizing the risk that a duration-matched portfolio will not be immunized? Fong and Vasicek[6] and Bierwag, Kaufman, and Toevs[7] explore this question. Exhibit 24-10 illustrates how to minimize immunization risk.

The spikes in the two panels of Exhibit 24-10 represent actual portfolio cash flows. The taller spikes depict the actual cash flows generated by securities that have matured, and the smaller spikes represent coupon payments. Portfolios A and B are both composed of two bonds with a portfolio's duration equal to the liability's duration. Portfolio A is, in effect, a barbell portfolio, one composed of short and long maturities and interim coupon

[6]H. Gifford Fong and Oldrich Vasicek, "A Risk Minimizing Strategy for Multiple Liability Immunization," *Journal of Finance*, December 1984, pp. 1541–1546.
[7]G. O. Bierwag, George K. Kaufman, and Alden Toevs, "Bond Immunization and Stochastic Process Risk," working paper, Center for Capital Market Research, University of Oregon, July 1981.

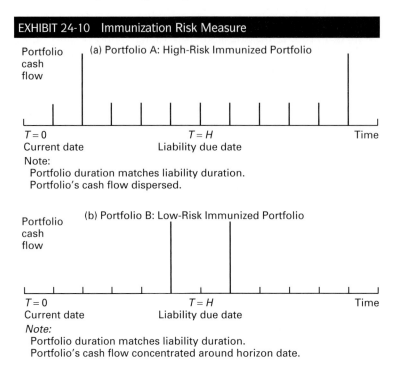

EXHIBIT 24-10   Immunization Risk Measure

(a) Portfolio A: High-Risk Immunized Portfolio

Portfolio cash flow

$T = 0$
Current date

$T = H$
Liability due date

Time

Note:
  Portfolio duration matches liability duration.
  Portfolio's cash flow dispersed.

(b) Portfolio B: Low-Risk Immunized Portfolio

Portfolio cash flow

$T = 0$
Current date

$T = H$
Liability due date

Time

Note:
  Portfolio duration matches liability duration.
  Portfolio's cash flow concentrated around horizon date.

payments. For portfolio B the two bonds mature very close to the date the liability is due, and the coupon payments are nominal over the investment horizon. Portfolio B is, in effect, a bullet portfolio.

We can now see why the barbell portfolio should be riskier than the bullet portfolio. Assume that both portfolios have durations equal to the liability's duration, so that each is immune to parallel changes in the yield curve. Suppose that the yield curve changes in a nonparallel way so that short-term interest rates decline while long-term interest rates increase. Both portfolios would then produce an accumulated value at the liability due date that is below the target accumulated value because they would experience a capital loss owing to the higher long-term interest rate and less interest on interest resulting from the lower reinvestment rate when the short-term interest rate declines.

The accumulated value for the barbell portfolio at the liability due date, however, would miss the target accumulated value by more than the bullet portfolio. There are two reasons for this. First, the lower reinvestment rates are experienced on the barbell portfolio for larger interim cash flows over a longer time period than on the bullet portfolio. Second, the portion of the barbell portfolio still outstanding at the end of the liability due date is much longer than the maturity of the bullet portfolio, resulting in a greater capital loss for the barbell than for the bullet. Thus, the bullet portfolio has less risk exposure than the barbell portfolio to any changes in the interest-rate structure that might occur.

What should be evident from this analysis is that immunization risk is the risk of reinvestment. The portfolio that has the least reinvestment risk will have the least immunization risk. When there is a high dispersion of cash flows around the liability due date, the portfolio is exposed to high reinvestment risk. When the cash flows are concentrated around the liability due date, as in the case of the bullet portfolio, the portfolio is subject to low reinvestment risk.

Fong and Vasicek have developed a measure of immunization risk. They have demonstrated that if the yield curve shifts in any arbitrary way, the relative change in the portfolio value will depend on the product of two terms. The first term depends solely on the characteristics of the investment portfolio. The second term is a function of interest-rate movement only. The second term characterizes the nature of the change in the shape of the yield curve. Because that change will be impossible to predict a priori, it is not possible to control for it. The first term, however, can be controlled for when constructing the immunized portfolio, because it depends solely on the composition of the portfolio. This first term, then, is a measure of risk for immunized portfolios and is equal to

$$\frac{CF_1(1-H)^2}{1+y} + \frac{CF_2(2-H)^2}{(1+y)^2} + \cdots + \frac{CF_n(n-H)^2}{(1+y)^n}$$

where:

CF_t = cash flow of the portfolio at time period t
H = length (in years) of the investment horizon or liability due date
y = yield for the portfolio
n = time to receipt of the last cash flow

The immunization risk measure agrees with our earlier graphic analysis of the relative risk associated with a barbell and a bullet portfolio. For the barbell portfolio (portfolio A in Exhibit 24-10), the portfolio's cash flow payments are widely dispersed in time and the immunization risk measure would be high. The portfolio cash flow payments for the bullet portfolio (portfolio B in Exhibit 24-10) are close to the liability due date so the immunization risk measure is low.

Notice that if all the cash flows are received at the liability due date, the immunization risk measure is zero. In such a case, the portfolio is equivalent to a pure discount security (zero-coupon security) that matures on the liability due date. If a portfolio can be constructed that replicates a pure discount security maturing on the liability due date, that portfolio will be the one with the lowest immunization risk. Typically, however, it is not possible to construct such an ideal portfolio.

The objective in constructing an immunized portfolio, then, is to match the portfolio's duration to the liability's duration and select the portfolio that minimizes the immunization risk. The immunization risk measure can be used to construct approximate confidence intervals for the target yield and the target accumulated value.

Zero-Coupon Bonds and Immunization

So far we have dealt with coupon bonds. An alternative approach to immunizing a portfolio against changes in the market yield is to invest in zero-coupon bonds with a maturity equal to the investment horizon. This is consistent with the basic principle of immunization because the duration of a zero-coupon bond is equal to the liability's duration. However, in practice, the yield on zero-coupon bonds is typically lower than the yield on coupon bonds. Thus, using zero-coupon bonds to fund a bullet liability requires more funds because a lower target yield (equal to the yield on the zero-coupon bond) is being locked in.

Suppose, for example, that a portfolio manager must invest funds to satisfy a known liability of $20 million five years from now. If a target yield of 10% on a bond-equivalent basis (5% every six months) can be locked in using zero-coupon Treasury bonds, the funds necessary to satisfy the $20 million liability will be $12,278,260, the present value of $20 million using a discount rate of 10% (5% semiannually).

Suppose, instead, that by using coupon Treasury securities, a target yield of 10.3% on a bond-equivalent basis (5.15% every six months) is possible. Then, the funds needed to satisfy the $20 million liability will be $12,104,240, the present value of $20 million discounted at 10.3% (5.15% semiannually). Thus, a target yield higher by 30 basis points would reduce the cost of funding the $20 million by $174,020 ($12,278,260 − $12,104,240). But the reduced cost comes at a price—the risk that the target yield will not be achieved.

Credit Risk and the Target Yield

The target yield may not be achieved if any of the bonds in the portfolio default or decrease in value because of credit quality deterioration. Restricting the universe of bonds that may be used in constructing an immunized portfolio to Treasury securities eliminates credit risk. The target yield that can be achieved, however, will be lower than that for bonds with credit risk so that the cost of funding a liability would be increased.

In most immunization applications, the client specifies an acceptable level of credit risk. Issues selected for the immunized portfolio are then restricted to those with that quality rating or higher. The more credit risk the client is willing to accept, the higher the achievable target yield, but the greater the risk that the immunized portfolio will fail to meet that target yield because of defaulted or downgraded issues. After the minimum credit risk is specified and the immunized portfolio is constructed, the portfolio manager must then monitor the individual issues for possible decreases in credit quality. Should an issue be downgraded below the minimum quality rating, that issue must be sold or the acceptable level of credit risk changed.

Call Risk

When the universe of acceptable issues includes corporate bonds, the target yield may be jeopardized if a callable issue is included that is subsequently called. Call risk can be avoided by restricting the universe of acceptable bonds to noncallable bonds and deep-discount callable bonds. This strategy does not come without a cost. Because noncallable and deep-discount bonds offer lower yields in a low-interest-rate environment, restricting the universe to these securities reduces the achievable target yield and therefore increases the cost of funding a liability. Also, it may be difficult to find acceptable noncallable bonds.

An immunized portfolio that includes callable bond issues must be carefully monitored so that issues likely to be called are sold and replaced with bond issues that have a lower probability of being called.

Constructing the Immunized Portfolio

When the universe of acceptable issues is established and any constraints are imposed, the portfolio manager has a large number of possible securities from which to construct an initial immunized portfolio and from which to select to rebalance an immunized portfolio. An objective function can be specified, and a portfolio that optimizes the objective function using mathematical programming tools can be determined. A common objective function, given the risk of immunization discussed earlier, is to minimize the immunization risk measure.[8]

Contingent Immunization

Contingent immunization is a strategy that consists of identifying both the available immunization target rate and a lower safety net level return with which the investor would be minimally satisfied.[9] The money manager pursues an active portfolio strategy until an adverse investment experience drives the then-available potential return—the combined active return from actual past experience and immunized return from expected future experience—down to the safety net level. When that point is reached, the money manager is obligated to immunize the portfolio completely and lock in the safety net level return. As long as the safety net is not violated, the money manager can continue to manage the portfolio actively. When the immunization mode is activated because the safety net is violated, the manager can no longer return to the active mode, unless, of course, the contingent immunization plan is abandoned.

To illustrate this strategy, suppose that a client investing $50 million is willing to accept a 10% rate of return over a four-year investment horizon at a time when a possible immunized rate of return is 12%. The 10% return is called the **safety net return**. The difference between the immunized return and the safety net return is called the **safety cushion**. In our example, the safety cushion is 200 basis points (12% minus 10%).

Because the initial portfolio value is $50 million, the minimum target value at the end of four years, based on semiannual compounding, is $73,872,772 [= $50,000,000(1.05)^8]. The rate of return at the time is 12% so the assets required at this time to achieve the minimum target value of $73,872,772 represent the present value of $73,872,772 discounted at 12% on a semiannual basis, which is $43,348,691 [= $73,872,772/(1.06)^8]. Therefore, the safety cushion of 200 basis points translates into an initial *dollar safety margin* of $6,651,309 ($50,000,000 − $43,348,691). Had the safety net of return been 11% instead of 10%, the safety cushion would have been 100 basis points and the initial dollar safety margin, $1,855,935. In other words, the smaller the safety cushion, the smaller the dollar safety margin. Exhibit 24-11 illustrates the contingency immunization strategy by showing the portfolio's initial value and for two scenarios six months later.

---

[8]For a discussion of alternative objective functions, see H. Gifford Fong and Frank J. Fabozzi, *Fixed Income Portfolio Management* (Homewood, IL: Dow Jones-Irwin, 1985), Chapter 6; Peter C. Christensen and Frank J. Fabozzi, "Bond Immunization: An Asset Liability Optimization Strategy," Chapter 31 in Frank J. Fabozzi and Irving M. Pollack (eds.), *The Handbook of Fixed Income Securities* (Homewood, IL: Dow Jones-Irwin, 1987); and Peter C. Christensen and Frank J. Fabozzi, "Dedicated Bond Portfolios," Chapter 32 in Frank J. Fabozzi (ed.), *The Handbook of Fixed Income Securities*, 3rd ed. (Homewood, IL: Business One-Irwin, 1991).
[9]Martin L. Leibowitz, "The Uses of Contingent Immunization," *Journal of Portfolio Management*, Fall 1981, pp. 51–55.

EXHIBIT 24-11   Contingency Immunization: Two Scenarios

Initial conditions:
$50 million investment
Achievable immunization rate: 12%
Safety net return: 10%
Planning horizon: 4 years

Initial investment:
20-year 12% coupon bond, selling at
par to yield 12%

| | Interest Rates | | |
| | Initial | Drops to 9% | Rises to 14.26% |
Scenario	Rate 12%	in 6 Months	in 6 Months
Minimum target value to horizon	$73,872,772	$73,872,772	$73,872,772
Current portfolio value	50,000,000	66,670,000	45,615,776
Present value of minimum target	43,348,691	54,283,888	45,614,893
Dollar safety margin (current value – present value of minimum target)	6,651,309	12,386,112	883
Management strategy	Active	Active	Immunize

Initially, the money manager pursues an active portfolio strategy within the contingent immunization strategy. Suppose that the money manager puts all the funds into a 20-year 12% coupon bond selling at par to yield 12%. Let's look at what happens if the market yield falls to 9% at the end of six months. The value of the portfolio at the end of six months would consist of (1) the value of the 19.5-year 12% coupon bond at a 9% market yield and (2) six months of coupon interest. The price of the bond would increase from 100 to 127.34 so that the price of $50 million of these bonds would rise to $63.67 million. Coupon interest is $3 million ($0.50 \times 0.12 \times \$50$ million). Thus, the portfolio value at the end of six months is $66.67 million.

How much would be necessary to achieve the minimum target return of $73,872,772 if a portfolio can be immunized at the current interest rate of 9%? The required dollar value is found by computing the present value of the minimum target return at 9% for 3.5 years. The required dollar amount is $54,283,888 [= \$73,872,772/(1.045)^7]$.

The portfolio value of $66.67 million is greater than the required portfolio value of $54,283,888. The money manager can therefore continue to manage the portfolio actively. The dollar safety margin is now $12,386,112 ($66,670,000 – $54,283,888). As long as the dollar safety margin is positive (i.e., the portfolio value is greater than the required portfolio value to achieve the minimum target value at the prevailing interest rate), the portfolio is actively managed.

Suppose that instead of declining to 9% in six months, interest rates rose to 14.26%. The market value of the bond would decline to $42,615,776. The portfolio value would then equal $45,615,776 (the market value of the bonds plus $3 million of coupon interest). The required dollar amount to achieve the minimum target value of $73,872,772 at the current interest rate (14.26%) would be $45,614,893 [= \$73,872,772/(1.0713)^7]$. The required dollar amount is approximately equal to the portfolio value (i.e., the dollar safety margin is almost zero). Thus, the money manager would be required to immunize the portfolio to achieve the minimum target value (safety net return) over the investment horizon.

The three key factors in implementing a contingent immunization strategy are (1) establishing accurate immunized initial and ongoing available target returns, (2) identifying a suitable and immunizable safety net return, and (3) designing an effective monitoring procedure to ensure that the safety net return is not violated.

STRUCTURING A PORTFOLIO TO SATISFY MULTIPLE LIABILITIES

Thus far we have discussed immunizing a single liability. For pension funds, there are multiple liabilities that must be satisfied—payments to the beneficiaries of the pension fund. A stream of liabilities must also be satisfied for a life insurance company that sells an insurance policy requiring multiple payments to policyholders, such as an annuity policy. There are two strategies that can be used to satisfy a liability stream: (1) multiperiod immunization, and (2) cash flow matching.

Multiperiod Immunization

Multiperiod immunization is a portfolio strategy in which a portfolio is created that will be capable of satisfying more than one predetermined future liability regardless if interest rates change. Even if there is a parallel shift in the yield curve, Bierwag, Kaufman, and Toevs demonstrate that matching the duration of the portfolio to the duration of the liabilities is not a sufficient condition to immunize a portfolio seeking to satisfy a liability stream.[10] Instead, it is necessary to decompose the portfolio payment stream in such a way that each liability is immunized by one of the component streams. The key to understanding this approach is recognizing that the payment stream on the portfolio, not the portfolio itself, must be decomposed in this manner. There may be no actual bonds that would give the component payment stream.

In the special case of a parallel shift of the yield curve, Fong and Vasicek demonstrate the necessary and sufficient conditions that must be satisfied to assure the immunization of multiple liabilities:[11]

1. The portfolio's duration must equal the duration of the liabilities.
2. The distribution of durations of individual portfolio assets must have a wider range than the distribution of the liabilities.[12]
3. The present value of the cash flows from the bond portfolio must equal the present value of the liability stream.

However, these conditions will immunize only in the case of a parallel shift in the yield curve. To cope with the problem of failure to immunize because of nonparallel shifts in the yield curve, Fong and Vasicek generalize the immunization risk measure

---

[10]G. O. Bierwag, George K. Kaufman, and Alden Toevs, "Immunization Strategies for Funding Multiple Liabilities," *Journal of Financial and Quantitative Analysis*, March 1983, pp. 113–124.

[11]Fong and Vasicek, "A Risk Minimizing Strategy for Multiple Liability Immunization."

[12]The reason for the second condition can be illustrated using an example. Suppose that a liability stream with 10 payments of $5 million each year is funded with a zero-coupon bond with a maturity (duration) equal to the duration of the liability stream. Suppose also that when the first $5 million payment is due, interest rates rise so that the value of the zero-coupon bond falls. Even though interest rates have increased, there is no offset to reinvestment income because the bond is a zero-coupon bond. Thus, there is no assurance that the portfolio will generate sufficient cash flow to satisfy the remaining liabilities. In the case of a single liability, the second condition is satisfied automatically.

for a single liability discussed earlier in this chapter to the multiple liability case. An optimal immunization strategy is to minimize this immunization risk measure subject to the three constraints mentioned previously (duration, dispersion of assets and liabilities, and equality of present value of asset cash flow and liability stream), as well as any other constraints that a client may impose.

In a series of articles, Reitano has explored the limitations of the parallel shift assumption.[13] He has also developed models that generalize the immunization of multiple liabilities to arbitrary yield curve shifts. His research makes it clear that classical multiple-period immunization can disguise the risks associated with nonparallel yield curve shifts and that a model that protects against one type of yield curve shift may allow a great deal of exposure and vulnerability to other types of shifts.

Cash Flow Matching

An alternative to multiperiod immunization is **cash flow matching**. This approach, also referred to as **dedicating a portfolio**, can be summarized as follows. A bond is selected with a maturity that matches the last liability stream. An amount of principal plus final coupon equal to the amount of the last liability stream is then invested in this bond. The remaining elements of the liability stream are then reduced by the coupon payments on this bond, and another bond is chosen for the new, reduced amount of the next-to-last liability. Going backward in time, this cash flow matching process is continued until all liabilities have been matched by the payment of the securities in the portfolio.

Exhibit 24-12 provides a simple illustration of this process for a five-year liability stream. Mathematical programming techniques can be employed to construct a least-cost cash flow matching portfolio from an acceptable universe of bonds.

The differences between the cash flow matching and multiperiod immunization strategies should be understood. First, unlike the immunization approach, the cash flow matching approach has no duration requirements. Second, with immunization, rebalancing is required even if interest rates do not change. In contrast, no rebalancing is necessary for cash flow matching except to delete and replace any issue whose quality rating has declined below an acceptable level. Third, there is no risk that the liabilities will not be satisfied (barring any defaults) with a cash flow–matched portfolio. For a portfolio constructed using multiperiod immunization, there is immunization risk due to reinvestment risk.

The differences just cited may seem to favor the use of cash flow matching. However, what we have ignored is the relative cost of the two strategies. Using the cost of the initial portfolio as an evaluation measure, Gifford Fong Associates has found that cash flow–matched portfolios, using a universe of corporate bonds rated at least AA, cost from 3% to 7% more in dollar terms than do multiperiod immunized portfolios. The reason cash flow matching is more expensive is that, typically, the matching of cash flows to liabilities is not perfect. This means that more funds than necessary must be set aside to match the liabilities. Optimization techniques used to design cash flow–matched

---

[13]Robert R. Reitano, "A Multivariate Approach to Immunization Theory," *Actuarial Research Clearing House*, Vol. 2, 1990; and "Multivariate Immunization Theory," *Transactions of the Society of Actuaries*, Vol. XLIII, 1991. For a detailed illustration of the relationship between the underlying yield curve shift and immunizations, see Robert R. Reitano, "Non-Parallel Yield Curve Shifts and Immunization," *Journal of Portfolio Management*, Spring 1992, pp. 36–43.

EXHIBIT 24-12   Cash Flow Matching Process

Assume: 5-year liability stream.
        Cash flow from bonds are annual.

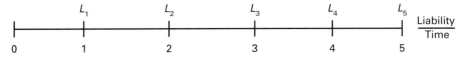

Step 1:
Cash flow from bond A selected to satisfy L_5
        Coupons $= A_s$; Principal $= A_p$ and $A_s + A_p = L_5$
Unfunded liabilities remaining:

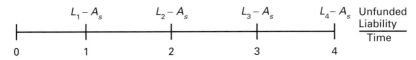

Step 2:
Cash flow from bond B selected to satisfy L_4
        Unfunded liability $= L_4 - A_s$
        Coupons $= B_s$; Principal $= B_p$ and $B_s + B_p = L_4 - A_s$
Unfunded liabilities remaining:

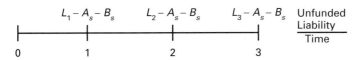

Step 3:
Cash flow from bond C selected to satisfy L_3
        Unfunded liability $= L_3 - A_s - B_s$
        Coupons $= C_s$; Principal $= C_p$ and $C_s + C_p = L_3 - A_s - B_s - C_s$
Unfunded liabilities remaining:

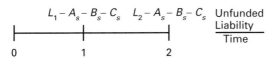

Step 4:
Cash flow from bond D selected to satisfy L_2
        Unfunded liability $= L_2 - A_s - B_s - C_s$
        Coupons $= D_s$; Principal $= D_p$ and $D_s + D_p = L_2 - A_s - B_s - C_s$
Unfunded liabilities remaining:

$L_1 - A_s - B_s - C_s - D_s$ Unfunded
                                 Liability
                                 ─────────
                                 Time

┣━━━━━━━━━━━━┫
0   1

Step 5:
Select bond E with a cash flow of $L_1 - A_s - B_s - C_s - D_s$

portfolios assume that excess funds are reinvested at a conservative reinvestment rate. With multiperiod immunization, all reinvestment returns are assumed to be locked in at a higher target rate of return. Therefore, money managers face a trade-off in deciding between the two strategies: avoidance of the risk of not satisfying the liability stream under cash flow matching versus the lower cost attainable with multiperiod immunization.

In the basic cash flow–matching technique, only asset cash flows occurring prior to a liability date can be used to satisfy the liability. The technique has been extended to handle situations in which cash flows occurring both before and after the liability date can be used to meet a liability.[14] This technique, called **symmetric cash matching**, allows for the short-term borrowing of funds to satisfy a liability prior to the liability due date. The opportunity to borrow short term so that symmetric cash matching can be employed results in a reduction in the cost of funding a liability.

A popular variation of multiperiod immunization and cash flow matching to fund liabilities is one that combines the two strategies. This strategy, referred to as **combination matching** or **horizon matching**, creates a portfolio that is duration matched with the added constraint that it be cash matched in the first few years, usually five years. The advantage of combination matching over multiperiod immunization is that liquidity needs are provided for in the initial cash flow–matched period. Cash flow matching the initial portion of the liability stream reduces the risk associated with nonparallel shifts of the yield curve. The disadvantage of combination matching over multiperiod immunization is that the cost is slightly greater.

Within the immunization and dedicated cash flow strategies, some portfolio managers are permitted to manage the portfolio actively by entering into bond swaps to enhance portfolio performance. Obviously, only small bets can be made, to minimize the likelihood that the liability payments will not be satisfied.

EXTENSIONS OF LIABILITY FUNDING STRATEGIES

As we explained at the outset of this chapter, liabilities may be uncertain with respect to both timing and amount of the payment. In the techniques we have discussed in this chapter, we have assumed that the timing and the amount of the cash payment of liabilities are known with certainty. That is, we assume that the liabilities are deterministic.

We assume, moreover, that the cash flows from the assets are known with certainty, although you have learned that most non-Treasury securities have embedded options that permit the borrower or the investor to alter the cash flows. Thus, the models presented in this chapter are referred to as **deterministic models** because they assume that the liability payments and the asset cash flows are known with certainty.

Since the mid-1980s, a good number of models have been developed to handle real-world situations in which liability payments and/or asset cash flows are uncertain. Such models are called **stochastic models**.[15] Such models require that the portfolio

[14]T. Dessa Fabozzi, Tom Tong, and Yu Zhu, "Extensions of Dedicated Bond Portfolio Techniques." Chapter 44 in Fabozzi (ed.), *The Handbook of Fixed Income Securities*, 3rd ed.
[15]For a review of such models, see Randall S. Hiller and Christian Schaack, "A Classification of Structured Bond Portfolio Modeling Techniques," *Journal of Portfolio Management*, Fall 1990, pp. 37–48.

manager incorporate an interest-rate model; that is, a model that describes the probability distribution for interest rates. Optimal portfolios then are solved for using a mathematical programming technique known as **stochastic programming**.

The complexity of stochastic models, however, has limited their application in practice. Nevertheless, they are gaining in popularity as more portfolio managers become comfortable with their sophistication. There is increasing awareness that stochastic models reduce the likelihood that the liability objective will not be satisfied and that transactions costs can be reduced through less frequent rebalancing of a portfolio derived from these models.

COMBINING ACTIVE AND IMMUNIZATION STRATEGIES

In our discussion of contingent immunization, the money manager is permitted to manage the portfolio actively until the safety net is violated. However, contingent immunization is not a combination or mixture strategy. The money manager is either in the immunization mode by choice or because the safety net is violated or in the active management mode. In contrast to an immunization strategy, an active/immunization combination strategy is a mixture of two strategies that are pursued by the money manager at the same point in time.

The immunization component of this strategy could be either a single-liability immunization or a multiple-liability immunization using the techniques discussed earlier in this chapter. In the single-liability immunization case, an assured return would be established so as to serve to stabilize the portfolio's total return. In the multiple-liability immunization case, the component to be immunized would be immunized now, with new requirements, as they become known, taken care of through reimmunization. This would be an adaptive strategy in that the immunization component would be based on an initial set of liabilities and modified over time to changes in future liabilities (e.g., for actuarial changes for the liabilities in the case of a pension fund). The active portion would continue to be free to maximize expected return, given some acceptable risk level.

The following formula suggested by Gifford Fong Associates can be used to determine the portion of the initial portfolio to be managed actively, with the balance immunized:[16]

$$\text{active component} = \frac{\text{immunization target rate} - \text{minimum return established by client}}{\text{immunization target rate} - \text{expected worst case active return}}$$

In the formula it is assumed that the immunization target return is greater than either the minimum return established by the client or the expected worst-case return from the actively managed portion of the portfolio.

As an illustration, assume that the available immunization target return is 7% per year, the minimum return acceptable to the client is 5%, and the expected worst-case

---

[16]*The Costs of Cash Flow Matching* (Santa Monica, CA: Gifford Fong Associates, 1981).

return for the actively managed portion of the portfolio is 2%. Then, the percentage in the active portion of the portfolio would be

$$\text{active component} = \frac{0.07 - 0.05}{0.07 - 0.02} = 0.40 \text{ or } 40\%$$

Notice from the formula for determining the active component that for any given immunization target return, the smaller the minimum acceptable return to the client and the larger the expected worst-case active return, the larger will be the percentage allocated to active management. Since the return values in the formula change over time, the money manager must monitor these values constantly, adjusting and rebalancing the allocation between the immunized and active components as appropriate. As long as the worst-case scenario is not violated—that is, as long as the actual return experienced does not drop below the expected worst-case active return—the minimum return for the portfolio established by the client will be achieved.

SUMMARY

The nature of their liabilities, as well as regulatory considerations, determines the investment strategy pursued by all institutional investors. By nature, liabilities vary with respect to the amount and timing of their payment. The liabilities will generally fall into one of the four types shown in Exhibit 24-1.

Surplus management is a more appropriate description of the activity of asset/liability management of an institution. The economic surplus of any entity is the difference between the market value of all its assets and the present value of its liabilities. Institutional investors will pursue a strategy either to maximize economic surplus or to hedge economic surplus against any adverse change in market conditions. In addition to economic surplus, there are accounting surplus and regulatory surplus. The former is based on GAAP accounting, specifically, FASB 115, and the latter on RAP accounting. To the extent that these two surplus measures may not reflect the true financial condition of an institution, future financial problems may arise.

Liability funding strategies involve designing a portfolio to produce sufficient funds to satisfy liabilities whether or not interest rates change. When there is only one future liability to be funded, an immunization strategy can be used. An immunization strategy is designed so that as interest rates change, interest-rate risk and reinvestment risk will offset each other in such a way that the minimum accumulated value (or minimum rate of return) becomes the target accumulated value (or target yield). An immunization strategy requires that a money manager create a bond portfolio with a duration equal to the duration of the liability. Because immunization theory is based on parallel shifts in the yield curve, the risk is that a portfolio will not be immunized even if the duration-matching condition is satisfied. Immunization risk can be quantified so that a portfolio that minimizes this risk can be constructed.

When there are multiple liabilities to be satisfied, either multiperiod immunization or cash flow matching can be used. Multiperiod immunization is a duration-matching strategy that exposes the portfolio to immunization risk. The cash flow–matching strategy does not impose any duration requirement. Although the only risk that the liabilities will not be satisfied is that issues will be called or will default, the dollar cost of a cash flow–matched portfolio may be higher than that of a portfolio constructed using a multiperiod immunization strategy.

Liability funding strategies in which the liability payments and the asset cash flows are known with certainty are deterministic models. In a stochastic model, either the liability payments or the asset cash flows, or both, are uncertain. Stochastic models require specification of a probability distribution for the process that generates interest rates.

A combination of active and immunization strategies can be pursued. Allocation of the portion of the portfolio to be actively managed is based on the immunization target rate, the minimum return acceptable to the client, and the expected worst-case return from the actively managed portfolio. In a contingent immunization strategy, a money manager is either actively managing the portfolio or immunizing it. Because both strategies are not pursued at the same time, contingent immunization is not a combination or mixture strategy.

Questions

1. What are the two dimensions of a liability?
2. Why is it not always simple to estimate the liability of an institution?
3. Why is asset/liability management best described as surplus management?
4. a. What is the economic surplus of an institution?
   b. What is the accounting surplus of an institution?
   c. What is the regulatory surplus of an institution?
   d. Which surplus best reflects the economic well-being of an institution?
   e. Under what circumstances are all three surplus measures the same?
5. Suppose that the present value of the liabilities of some financial institution is $600 million and the surplus $800 million. The duration of the liabilities is equal to 5. Suppose further that the portfolio of this financial institution includes only bonds and the duration for the portfolio is 6.
   a. What is the market value of the portfolio of bonds?
   b. What does a duration of 6 mean for the portfolio of assets?
   c. What does a duration of 5 mean for the liabilities?
   d. Suppose that interest rates increase by 50 basis points; what will be the approximate new value for the surplus?
   e. Suppose that interest rates decrease by 50 basis points; what will be the approximate new value for the surplus?
6. a. Why is the interest-rate sensitivity of an institution's assets and liabilities important?
   b. In 1986, Martin Leibowitz of Salomon Brothers, Inc., wrote a paper titled "Total Portfolio Duration: A New Perspective on Asset Allocation." What do you think a total portfolio duration means?
7. If an institution has liabilities that are interest-rate sensitive and invests in a portfolio of common stocks, can you determine what will happen to the institution's economic surplus if interest rates change?
8. The following quote is taken from Phillip D. Parker (Associate General Counsel of the SEC), "Market Value Accounting—An Idea Whose Time Has Come?" in Elliot P. Williams (ed.), *Managing Asset/Liability Portfolios* (Charlottesville, VA: Association for Investment Management and Research, 1991), published prior to the passage of FASB 115: "The use of market value accounting would eliminate any incentive to sell or retain investment securities for reasons of accounting treatment rather than business utility." Explain why this statement is correct. (Note that in historical accounting a loss is recognized only when a security is sold.)

9. Indicate why you agree or disagree with the following statements.
   a. "Under FASB 115 all assets must be marked to market."
   b. "The greater the price volatility of assets classified in the held-to-maturity account, the greater the volatility of the accounting surplus and reported earnings."

10. What is meant by immunizing a bond portfolio?

11. a. What is the basic underlying principle in an immunization strategy?
    b. Why may the matching of the maturity of a coupon bond to the remaining time to maturity of a liability fail to immunize a portfolio?

12. Why must an immunized portfolio be rebalanced periodically?

13. What are the risks associated with a bond immunization strategy?

14. "I can immunize a portfolio simply by investing in zero-coupon Treasury bonds." Comment on this statement.

15. Three portfolio managers are discussing a strategy for immunizing a portfolio so as to achieve a target yield. Manager A, whose portfolio consists of Treasury securities and option-free corporates, stated that the duration of the portfolio should be constructed so that the Macaulay duration of the portfolio is equal to the number of years until the liability must be paid. Manager B, with the same types of securities in his portfolio as Manager A, feels that Manager A is wrong because the portfolio should be constructed so that the modified duration of the portfolio is equal to the modified duration of the liabilities. Manager C believes Manager B is correct. However, unlike the portfolios of Managers A and B, Manager C invests in mortgage-backed securities and callable corporate bonds.

    Discuss the position taken by each manager and explain why they are correct.

16. Why is there greater risk in a multiperiod immunization strategy than a cash flow–matching strategy?

17. a. What is a contingent immunization strategy?
    b. What is the safety net cushion in a contingent immunization strategy?

c. Is it proper to classify a contingent immunization as a combination active/immunization strategy?

18. What is a combination matching strategy?

19. In a stochastic liability funding strategy, why is an interest-rate model needed?

20. Suppose that a client has granted a money manager permission to pursue an active/immunized combination strategy. Suppose further that the minimum return expected by the client is 9% and that the money manager believes that an achievable immunized target return is 4% and the worst possible return from the actively managed portion of the portfolio is 1%. Approximately how much should be allocated to the active component of the portfolio?

21. One of your clients, a newcomer to the life insurance business, questioned you about the following excerpt from Peter E. Christensen, Frank J. Fabozzi, and Anthony LoFaso, "Dedicated Bond Portfolios," Chapter 43 in Frank J. Fabozzi (ed.), *The Handbook of Fixed Income Securities* (Homewood, IL: Richard D. Irwin, 1991):

For financial intermediaries such as banks and insurance companies, there is a well-recognized need for a complete funding perspective. This need is best illustrated by the significant interest-rate risk assumed by many insurance carriers in the early years of their Guaranteed Investment Contract (GIC) products. A large volume of compound interest (zero coupon) and simple interest (annual pay) GICs were issued in three- through seven-year maturities in the positively sloped yield-curve environment of the mid-1970s. Proceeds from hundreds of the GIC issues were reinvested at higher rates in the longer 10- to 30-year private placement, commercial mortgage, and public bond instruments. At the time, industry expectations were that the GIC product would be very profitable because of the large positive spread between the higher "earned" rate on the longer assets and the lower "credited" rate on the GIC contracts.

By pricing GICs on a spread basis and investing the proceeds on a mismatched basis, companies gave little consideration to the rollover risk they were assuming in volatile markets. As rates rose dramatically in the late 1970s and early 1980s, carriers were exposed to disintermediation as GIC liabilities matured and the corresponding assets had 20 years remaining to maturity and were valued at only a fraction of their original cost.

Answer the following questions posed to you by your client.

a. "It is not clear to me what risk an issuer of a GIC is facing. A carrier can invest the proceeds in assets offering a higher yield than they are guaranteeing to GIC policyholders, so what's the problem? Isn't it just default risk that can be controlled by setting tight credit standards?"

b. "I understand that disintermediation means that when a policy matures, the funds are withdrawn from the insurance company by the policyholder. But why would a rise in interest rates cause GIC policyholders to withdraw their funds? The insurance company can simply guarantee a higher interest rate."

c. "What do the authors mean by 'pricing GICs on a spread basis and investing the proceeds on a mismatched basis,' and what is this 'rollover risk' they are referring to?"

22. Suppose that a life insurance company sells a five-year guaranteed investment contract that guarantees an interest rate of 7.5% per year on a bond-equivalent yield basis (or equivalently, 3.75% every six months for the next 10 six-month periods). Also suppose that the payment made by the policyholder is $9,642,899. Consider the following three investments that can be made by the portfolio manager:

Bond X: Buy $9,642,899 par value of an option-free bond selling at par with a 7.5% yield to maturity that matures in five years.

Bond Y: Buy $9,642,899 par value of an option-free bond selling at par with a 7.5% yield to maturity that matures in 12 years.

Bond Z: Buy $10,000,000 par value of a six-year 6.75% coupon option-free bond selling at 96.42899 to yield 7.5%.

a. Holding aside the spread that the insurance company seeks to make on the invested funds, demonstrate that the target accumulated value to meet the GIC obligation five years from now is $13,934,413.

b. Complete Table A assuming that the manager invests in bond X and immediately following the purchase, yields change and stay the same for the five-year investment horizon.

c. Based on Table A, under what circumstances will the investment in bond X fail to satisfy the target accumulated value?

d. Complete Table B, assuming that the manager invests in bond Y and immediately following the purchase, yields change and stay the same for the five-year investment horizon.

e. Based on Table B, under what circumstances will the investment in bond Y fail to satisfy the target accumulated value?

f. Complete Table C, assuming that the manager invests in bond Z and immediately following the purchase, yields change and stay the same for the five-year investment horizon.

g. Based on Table C, under what circumstances will the investment in bond Z fail to satisfy the target accumulated value?

h. What is the modified duration of the liability?

i. Complete the following table for the three bonds assuming that each bond is trading to yield 7.5%:

Bond	Modified Duration
5-year, 7.5% coupon, selling at par	
12-year, 7.5% coupon, selling at par	
6-year, 6.75% coupon selling for 96.42899	

j. For which bond is the modified duration equal to the duration of the liability?

k. Why in this example can one focus on modified duration rather than effective duration?

Table A
Accumulated Value and Total Return After Five Years: Five-Year 7.5% Bond
Selling to Yield 7.5%

Investment horizon (years): 5
Coupon rate: 7.50%
Maturity (years): 5
Yield to maturity: 7.50%
Price: 100.00000
Par value purchased: $9,642,899
Purchase price: $9,642,899
Target accumulated value: $13,934,413

New Yield (%)	Coupon	After Five Years			
		Interest on Interest	Price of Bond	Accumulated Value	Total Return (%)
11.00	$3,616,087	$1,039,753	$9,642,899	$14,298,739	8.04
10.00	3,616,087				
9.00	3,616,087				
8.00	3,616,087				
7.50	3,616,087				
7.00	3,616,087				
6.00	3,616,087				
5.00	3,616,087				
4.00	3,616,087	343,427	9,642,899	13,602,414	7.00

Table B
Accumulated Value and Total Return After Five Years: Twelve-Year 7.5% Bond
Selling to Yield 7.5%

Investment horizon (years): 5
Coupon rate: 7.5%
Maturity (years): 12
Yield to maturity: 7.5%
Price: 100.00000
Par value purchased: $9,642,899
Purchase price: $9,642,899
Target accumulated value: $13,934,413

New Yield (%)	Coupon	After Five Years			
		Interest on Interest	Price of Bond	Accumulated Value	Total Return (%)
11.00	$3,616,087	$1,039,753	$ 8,204,639	$12,680,479	5.55
10.00	3,616,087				
9.00	3,616,087				
8.00	3,616,087				
7.50	3,616,087				
7.00	3,616,087				
6.00	3,616,087				
5.00	3,616,087				
4.00	3,616,087	343,427	11,685,837	15,645,352	9.92

Table C

Accumulated Value and Total Return After Five Years: Six-Year 6.75% Bond
Selling to Yield 7.5%

Investment horizon (years): 5
Coupon rate: 6.75%
Maturity (years): 6
Yield to maturity: 7.5%
Price: 96.42899
Par value purchased: $10,000,000
Purchase price: $9,642,899
Target accumulated value: $13,934,413

New Yield (%)	Coupon	After Five Years			
		Interest on Interest	Price of Bond	Accumulated Value	Total Return (%)
11.00	$3,375,000	$970,432	$9,607,657	$13,953,089	7.53
10.00	3,375,000				
9.00	3,375,000				
8.00	3,375,000				
7.50	3,375,000				
7.00	3,375,000				
6.00	3,375,000				
5.00	3,375,000				
4.00	3,375,000	320,531	10,266,965	13,962,495	7.54

CHAPTER
25

BOND PERFORMANCE MEASUREMENT AND EVALUATION

After reading this chapter you will understand:

■ the difference between performance measurement and performance evaluation

■ the various methods for calculating the rate of return over some evaluation period: the arithmetic average rate of return, the time-weighted rate of return, and the dollar-weighted rate of return

■ the impact of client contributions and withdrawals on the calculated return

■ the method of calculating return that minimizes the effect of client contributions and withdrawals

■ why it is necessary to establish a benchmark

■ how normal portfolios are created and the difficulties of creating them

■ what a fixed-income performance attribution model is and why it is useful in assessing the performance of a money manager

In this chapter we will see how to measure and evaluate the investment performance of a fixed-income portfolio manager. *Performance measurement* involves the calculation of the return realized by a portfolio manager over some time interval, which we call the *evaluation period*. *Performance evaluation* is concerned with two issues. The first is to determine whether the manager added value by outperforming the established benchmark. The second is to determine how the manager achieved the calculated return. For example, as explained in Chapter 22, there are several active strategies that a fixed-income manager can employ. The decomposition of the performance results to explain the reasons why those results were achieved is called performance or return attribution analysis.

REQUIREMENTS FOR A BOND PERFORMANCE AND ATTRIBUTION ANALYSIS PROCESS

There are three desired requirements of a bond performance and attribution analysis process. The first is that the process be accurate. For example, as we will explain, there are several ways of measuring portfolio return. The return should recognize the time when each cash flow actually occurs, resulting in a much more accurate measure of the actual portfolio performance. The second requirement is that the process be informative. It should be capable of evaluating the managerial skills that go into fixed-income portfolio management. To be informative, the process must effectively address the key management skills and explain how these can be expressed in terms of realized performance. The final requirement is that the process be simple. Whatever the output of the process, it should be understood by the manager and client, or others who may be concerned with the performance of the portfolio. As we explain the process for analyzing bond performance in this chapter, these requirements should be kept in mind.

PERFORMANCE MEASUREMENT

The starting point for evaluating the performance of a manager is measuring return. As we will see, there are several important issues that must be addressed in developing a methodology for calculating a portfolio's return. Because different methodologies are available and these methodologies can lead to quite disparate results, it is difficult to compare the performances of managers. Consequently, there is a great deal of confusion concerning the meaning of the data provided by managers to their clients and their prospective clients. This has led to abuses by some managers in reporting performance results that are better than actual performance. To mitigate this problem the Committee for Performance Standards of the Association for Investment Management and Research (now the CFA Institute) has established standards for calculating performance results and how to present those results.

Alternative Return Measures

Let's begin with the basic concept. The dollar return realized on a portfolio for any evaluation period (i.e., a year, month, or week) is equal to the sum of (1) the difference between the market value of the portfolio at the end of the evaluation period and the market value at the beginning of the evaluation period, and (2) any distributions made from the portfolio. It is important that any capital or income distributions from the portfolio to a client or beneficiary of the portfolio be included.

The rate of return, or simply return, expresses the dollar return in terms of the amount of the market value at the beginning of the evaluation period. Thus, the return can be viewed as the amount (expressed as a fraction of the initial portfolio value) that can be withdrawn at the end of the evaluation period while maintaining the initial market value of the portfolio intact.

In equation form, the portfolio's return can be expressed as follows:

$$R_P = \frac{MV_1 - MV_0 + D}{MV_0} \qquad \textbf{(25.1)}$$

where:

R_p = return on the portfolio
MV_1 = portfolio market value at the end of the evaluation period
MV_0 = portfolio market value at the beginning of the evaluation period
D = cash distributions from the portfolio to the client during the evaluation period

To illustrate the calculation of a return, assume the following information for an external manager for a pension plan sponsor: The portfolio's market value at the beginning and end of the evaluation period is $25 million and $28 million, respectively, and during the evaluation period $1 million is distributed to the plan sponsor from investment income. Thus

$$MV_1 = \$28{,}000{,}000$$
$$MV_0 = \$25{,}000{,}000$$
$$D = \$1{,}000{,}000$$

Then

$$R_P = \frac{\$28{,}000{,}000 - \$25{,}000{,}000 + \$1{,}000{,}000}{\$25{,}000{,}000}$$

$$= 0.16 = 16\%$$

There are three assumptions in measuring return as given by equation (25.1). First, it assumes that cash inflows into the portfolio from interest income that occur during the evaluation period but are not distributed are reinvested in the portfolio. For example, suppose that during the evaluation period $2 million is received from interest income. This amount is reflected in the market value of the portfolio at the end of the period.

The second assumption is that if there are distributions from the portfolio, they occur at the end of the evaluation period or are held in the form of cash until the end of the evaluation period. In our example, $1 million is distributed to the plan sponsor. But when did that distribution actually occur? To understand why the timing of the distribution is important, consider two extreme cases: (1) the distribution is made at the end of the evaluation period, as assumed by equation (25.1), and (2) the distribution is made at the beginning of the evaluation period. In the first case, the manager had the use of the $1 million to invest for the entire evaluation period. By contrast, in the second case, the manager loses the opportunity to invest the funds until the end of the evaluation period. Consequently, the timing of the distribution will affect the return, but this is not considered in equation (25.1).

The third assumption is that there is no cash paid into the portfolio by the client. For example, suppose that sometime during the evaluation period, the plan sponsor gives an additional $1.5 million to the external manager to invest. Consequently, the market value of the portfolio at the end of the evaluation period, $28 million in our example, would reflect the contribution of $1.5 million. Equation (25.1) does not reflect that the ending market value of the portfolio is affected by the cash paid in by the sponsor. Moreover, the timing of this cash inflow will affect the calculated return.

Thus, while the return calculation for a portfolio using equation (25.1) can be determined for an evaluation period of any length of time, such as one day, one month, or five years, from a practical point of view the assumptions discussed previously limit its application. The longer the evaluation period, the more likely the assumptions will be violated. For example, it is highly likely that there may be more than one distribution to the client and more than one contribution from the client if the evaluation period is five years. Thus, a return calculation made over a long period of time, if longer than a few months, would not be very reliable because of the assumption underlying the calculations that all cash payments and inflows are made and received at the end of the period.

Not only does the violation of the assumptions make it difficult to compare the returns of two managers over some evaluation period, but it is also not useful for evaluating performance over different periods. For example, equation (25.1) will not give reliable information to compare the performance of a one-month evaluation period and a three-year evaluation period. To make such a comparison, the return must be expressed per unit of time, for example, per year.

The way to handle these practical issues is to calculate the return for a short unit of time such as a month or a quarter. We call the return so calculated the **subperiod return**. To get the return for the evaluation period, the subperiod returns are then averaged. So, for example, if the evaluation period is one year and 12 monthly returns are calculated, the monthly returns are the subperiod returns and they are averaged to get the one-year return. If a three-year return is sought and 12-quarterly returns can be calculated, quarterly returns are the subperiod returns and they are averaged to get the three-year return. The three-year return can then be converted into an annual return by the straightforward procedure described later.

There are three methodologies that have been used in practice to calculate the average of the subperiod returns: (1) the arithmetic average rate of return, (2) the time-weighted rate of return (also called the geometric rate of return), and (3) the dollar-weighted rate of return.

Arithmetic Average Rate of Return

The **arithmetic average rate of return** is an unweighted average of the subperiod returns. The general formula is

$$R_A = \frac{R_{P1} + R_{P2} + \cdots + R_{PN}}{N}$$

where:

R_A = arithmetic average rate of return
R_{Pk} = portfolio return for subperiod k as measured by equation (25.1), $k = 1, \ldots, N$
N = number of subperiods in the evaluation period

For example, if the portfolio returns [as measured by equation (25.1)] were −10%, 20%, and 5% in July, August, and September, respectively, the arithmetic average monthly return is 5%:

$$N = 3 \quad R_{P1} = -0.10 \quad R_{P2} = 0.20 \quad R_{P3} = 0.05$$

$$R_A = \frac{-0.10 + 0.20 + 0.05}{3} = 0.05 = 5\%$$

There is a major problem with using the arithmetic average rate of return. To see this problem, suppose that the initial market value of a portfolio is $28 million and the market values at the end of the next two months are $58 million and $28 million, and assume that there are no distributions or cash inflows from the client for either month. Then using equation (25.1) the subperiod return for the first month (R_{P1}) is 100% and the subperiod return for the second month (R_{P2}) is –50%. The arithmetic average rate of return is then 25%. Not a bad return! But think about this number. The portfolio's initial market value was $28 million. Its market value at the end of two months is $28 million. The return over this two-month evaluation period is zero. Yet the arithmetic average rate of return says that it is a whopping 25%.

Thus, it is improper to interpret the arithmetic average rate of return as a measure of the average return over an evaluation period. The proper interpretation is as follows: It is the average value of the withdrawals (expressed as a fraction of the initial portfolio market value) that can be made at the end of each subperiod while keeping the initial portfolio market value intact. In our first example in which the average monthly return is 5%, the investor must add 10% of the initial portfolio market value at the end of the first month, can withdraw 20% of the initial portfolio market value at the end of the second month, and can withdraw 5% of the initial portfolio market value at the end of the third month. In our second example, the average monthly return of 25% means that 100% of the initial portfolio market value ($28 million) can be withdrawn at the end of the first month and 50% must be added at the end of the second month.

Time-Weighted Rate of Return

The **time-weighted rate of return** measures the compounded rate of growth of the initial portfolio market value during the evaluation period, assuming that all cash distributions are reinvested in the portfolio. It is also commonly referred to as the **geometric rate of return** because it is computed by taking the geometric average of the portfolio sub-period returns computed from equation (25.1). The general formula is

$$R_T = [(1 + R_{P1})(1 + R_{P2}) \cdots (1 + R_{PN})]^{1/N} - 1$$

where R_T is the time-weighted rate of return and R_{Pk} and N are as defined earlier. For example, let us assume that the portfolio returns were –10%, 20%, and 5% in July, August, and September, as in the first example. The time-weighted rate of return is

$$R_T = \{[1 + (-0.10)](1 + 0.20)(1 + 0.05)\}^{1/3} - 1$$

$$= [(0.90)(1.20)(1.05)]^{1/3} - 1 = 0.043$$

If the time-weighted rate of return is 4.3% per month, one dollar invested in the portfolio at the beginning of July would have grown at a rate of 4.3% per month during the three-month evaluation period.

The time-weighted rate of return in the second example is 0%, as expected:

$$R_T = \{(1 + 1.00)[(1 + (-0.50)]\}^{1/2} - 1$$

$$= [(2.00)(0.50)]^{1/2} - 1 = 0\%$$

In general, the arithmetic and time-weighted average returns will give different values for the portfolio return over some evaluation period. This is because in computing the arithmetic average rate of return, the amount invested is assumed to be maintained (through additions or withdrawals) at its initial portfolio market value. The time-weighted return, on the other hand, is the return on a portfolio that varies in size because of the assumption that all proceeds are reinvested.

In general, the arithmetic average rate of return will exceed the time-weighted average rate of return. The exception is in the special situation where all the subperiod returns are the same, in which case the averages are identical. The magnitude of the difference between the two averages is smaller the less the variation in the subperiod returns over the evaluation period. For example, suppose that the evaluation period is four months and that the four monthly returns are as follows:

$$R_{P1} = 0.04 \qquad R_{P2} = 0.06 \qquad R_{P3} = 0.02 \qquad R_{P4} = -0.02$$

The average arithmetic rate of return is 2.5% and the time-weighted average rate of return is 2.46%. Not much of a difference. In our earlier example in which we calculated an average rate of return of 25% but a time-weighted average rate of return of 0%, the large discrepancy is due to the substantial variation in the two monthly returns.

Dollar-Weighted Rate of Return

The **dollar-weighted rate of return** is computed by finding the interest rate that will make the present value of the cash flows from all the subperiods in the evaluation period plus the terminal market value of the portfolio equal to the initial market value of the portfolio.

Cash flows are defined as follows:[1]

- A cash withdrawal is treated as a cash inflow. So, in the absence of any cash contribution made by a client for a given time period, a cash withdrawal (e.g., a distribution to a client) is a positive cash flow for that time period.
- A cash contribution is treated as a cash outflow. Consequently, in the absence of any cash withdrawal for a given time period, a cash contribution is treated as a negative cash flow for that period.
- If there are both cash contributions and cash withdrawals for a given time period, then the cash flow is as follows for that time period: If cash withdrawals exceed cash contributions, then there is a positive cash flow. If cash withdrawals are less than cash contributions, then there is a negative cash flow.

The dollar-weighted rate of return is simply an internal rate-of-return calculation and hence it is also called the **internal rate of return**. The general formula for the dollar-weighted return is

$$V_0 = \frac{C_1}{1 + R_D} + \frac{C_2}{(1 + R_D)^2} + \cdots + \frac{C_N + V_N}{(1 + R_D)^n}$$

---

[1]Here is a simple way of remembering how to handle cash withdrawals: Treat withdrawals the same way as you would ordinary bonds. To compute the yield for a bond, the cash flow for the coupon payments (i.e., a cash withdrawal from the investment) is positive. Since a cash withdrawal is a positive cash flow, a cash contribution is a negative cash flow.

where:

R_D = dollar-weighted rate of return
V_0 = initial market value of the portfolio
V_N = terminal market value of the portfolio
C_k = cash flow for the portfolio (cash inflows minus cash outflows) for subperiod
$k, k = 1, 2, \ldots, N$

Notice that it is not necessary to know the market value of the portfolio for each subperiod to determine the dollar-weighted rate of return. For example, consider a portfolio with a market value of $100,000 at the beginning of July, capital withdrawals of $5,000 at the end of months July, August, and September, no cash inflows from the client in any month, and a market value at the end of September of $110,000. Then V_0 = $100,000, $N = 3$, $C_1 = C_2 = C_3 = \$5,000$, $V_3 = \$110,000$, and R_D is the interest rate that satisfies the following equation:

$$\$100,000 = \frac{\$5,000}{1 + R_D} + \frac{\$5,000}{(1 + R_D)^2} + \frac{\$5,000 + \$110,000}{(1 + R_D)^3}$$

It can be verified that the interest rate that satisfies the expression above is 8.1%. This, then, is the dollar-weighted return.

The dollar-weighted rate of return and the time-weighted rate of return will produce the same result if no withdrawals or contributions occur over the evaluation period and all investment income is reinvested. The problem with the dollar-weighted rate of return is that it is affected by factors that are beyond the control of the manager. Specifically, any contributions made by the client or withdrawals that the client requires will affect the calculated return. This makes it difficult to compare the performance of two managers.

To see this, suppose that a pension plan sponsor engaged two managers, A and B, with $10 million given to A to manage and $200 million given to B. Suppose that

- both managers invest in identical portfolios (i.e., the two portfolios have the same securities and are held in the same proportion)
- for the following two months the rate of return on the two portfolios is 20% for month 1 and 50% for month 2
- the amount received in investment income is in cash
- the plan sponsor does not make an additional contribution to the portfolio of either manager

Under these assumptions, it is clear that the performance of both managers would be identical.

Suppose, instead, that the plan sponsor withdraws $4 million from A at the beginning of month 2. This means that A could not invest the entire amount at the end of month 1 and capture the 50% increase in the portfolio value. A's net cash flow would be as follows:

- For month 1: the cash flow is $6 million because $2 million (20% × $10 million) is realized in investment income and $4 million is withdrawn by the plan sponsor.
- For month 2: there is $8 million invested for the month—the $2 million of realized investment income in month 1 plus $6 million from the $10 million in month 1

minus the $4 million withdrawn. The realized income for month 2 is $4 million (50% × $8 million). The cash flow for month 2 is then $8 million plus $4 million or $2 million.

The dollar-weighted rate of return is then calculated as follows:

$$\$10 = \frac{\$6}{1+R_D} + \frac{\$12}{(1+R_D)^2} \rightarrow R_D = 28.4\%$$

For B, the cash inflow for month 1 is $40 million (20% × $200 million) and the portfolio value at the end of month 2 is $360 million (1.5 × $240 million). The dollar-weighted rate of return is

$$\$200 = \frac{\$40}{1+R_D} + \frac{\$330}{(1+R_D)^2} \rightarrow R_D = 38.8\%$$

These are quite different results for two managers who we agreed had identical performance. The withdrawal by the plan sponsor and the size of the withdrawal relative to the portfolio value had a significant impact on the calculated return. Notice also that even if the plan sponsor had withdrawn $4 million from B at the beginning of month 2, this would not have had as significant an impact. The problem would also have occurred if we assumed that the return in month 2 is –50% and that instead of A realizing a withdrawal of $4 million, the plan sponsor contributed $4 million.

Despite this limitation, the dollar-weighted rate of return does provide information. It indicates information about the growth of the fund that a client will find useful. This growth, however, is not attributable to the performance of the manager because of contributions and withdrawals.

Annualizing Returns

The evaluation period may be less than or greater than one year. Typically, return measures are reported as an average annual return. This requires the annualization of the subperiod returns. The subperiod returns are typically calculated for a period of less than one year for the reasons described earlier. The subperiod returns are then annualized using the following formula:

annual return = $(1 + \text{average period return})^{\text{number of periods in year}} - 1$

For example, suppose that the evaluation period is three years and a monthly period return is calculated. Suppose further that the average monthly return is 2%. Then the annual return would be

$$\text{annual return} = (1.02)^{12} - 1 = 26.8\%$$

Suppose instead that the period used to calculate returns is quarterly and the average quarterly return is 3%. Then the annual return is

$$\text{annual return} = (1.03)^4 - 1 = 12.6\%$$

PERFORMANCE ATTRIBUTION ANALYSIS

In the preceding section, we concentrated on performance measurement. Our focus in this section is on how to evaluate the performance of a manager to determine if the manager added value beyond what could have been achieved by a passive strategy in a benchmark portfolio and whether that performance was due to skill or luck.

Bond attribution models seek to identify the active management decisions that contributed to the performance of a portfolio and give a quantitative assessment of the contribution of these decisions. In Chapter 22 we explained active strategies in managing a fixed-income portfolio: interest-rate expectation strategies, yield curve expectations strategies, yield spread strategies, and individual security selection strategies. The performance of a portfolio can be decomposed in terms of these four strategies.

Benchmark Portfolios

To evaluate the performance of a manager, a client must specify a benchmark against which the manager will be measured. There are two types of benchmarks that have been used in evaluating fixed-income portfolio managers: (1) market indexes published by dealer firms and vendors, and (2) normal portfolios.

A **normal portfolio** is a customized benchmark that includes "a set of securities that contains all of the securities from which a manager normally chooses, weighted as the manager would weight them in a portfolio."[2] Thus, a normal portfolio is a specialized index. It is argued that normal portfolios are more appropriate benchmarks than market indexes because they control for investment management style, thereby representing a passive portfolio against which a manager can be evaluated.

The construction of a normal portfolio for a particular manager is no simple task.[3] The principle is to construct a portfolio that, given the historical portfolios held by the manager, will reflect that manager's style in terms of assets and the weighting of those assets. The construction of a normal portfolio for a manager requires (1) defining the universe of fixed-income securities to be included in the normal portfolio, and (2) determining how these securities should be weighted (i.e., equally weighted or capitalization weighted).

Defining the set of securities to be included in the normal portfolio begins with discussions between the client and the manager to determine the manager's investment style. Based on these discussions, the universe of all publicly traded securities is reduced to a subset that includes those securities that the manager considers eligible given his or her investment style.

Given these securities, the next question is how they should be weighted in the normal portfolio. The two choices are equal weighting or capitalization weighting of each security. Various methodologies can be used to determine the weights. These methodologies typically involve a statistical analysis of the historical holdings of a manager and the risk exposure contained in those holdings.

---

[2]Jon Christopherson, "Normal Portfolios: Construction of Customized Benchmarks," Chapter 6 in Frank J. Fabozzi (ed.), *Active Equity Portfolio Management* (New Hope, PA: Frank J. Fabozzi Associates, 1998), p. 92.
[3]See Mark Kritzman, "How to Build a Normal Portfolio in Three Easy Steps," *Journal of Portfolio Management*, Spring 1987, pp. 21–23.

Plan sponsors work with pension consultants to develop normal portfolios for a manager. The consultants use vendor systems that have been developed for performing the needed statistical analysis and the necessary optimization program to create a portfolio exhibiting similar factor positions to replicate the "normal" position of a manager. A plan sponsor must recognize that there is a cost to developing and updating the normal portfolio.

There are some who advocate the responsibility of developing normal portfolios should be left to the manager. However, many clients are reluctant to let their managers control the construction of normal portfolios because they believe that the managers will produce easily beaten, or "slow rabbit," benchmarks. Bailey and Tierney demonstrate that under reasonable conditions there is no long-term benefit for the manager to construct a "slow rabbit" benchmark and explain the disadvantage of a manager pursuing such a strategy.[4] In addition, they recommend that clients let managers control the benchmarks. Clients should, instead, focus their efforts on monitoring the quality of the benchmarks and the effectiveness of the managers' active management strategies.

Performance Attribution Analysis Model[5]

There are several vendors of performance attribution models. The performance attribution model described here is that of Gifford Fong Associates of Lafayette, California. The particular system that monitors and evaluates the performance of a fixed-income portfolio as well as the individual securities held in the portfolio is called BONDPAR. BONDPAR decomposes the return into those elements beyond the manager's control, such as the interest-rate environment and client-imposed-duration policy constraints, and those that the management process contributes to, such as interest-rate management, sector/quality allocations, and individual bond selection.

BONDPAR answers the following six questions: (1) How does each element of the manager's return compare with the same elements of return of the benchmark? (2) What is the cost of being in the bond market? (3) What effect do client policies have on portfolio returns? (4) Has the manager successfully anticipated interest-rate changes? (5) Has the manager been successful at selecting the issuing sector and quality groups that enhance the portfolio's performance? and (6) Has the manager improved returns by selecting individual bonds because of company fundamentals?

An explanation of the technology for decomposing the portfolio's return so that these questions can be answered is beyond the scope of this chapter.[6] Instead, we illustrate the product of the system with a hypothetical portfolio for the period February 28, 1990 to March 31, 1990 and how it answers the six questions. Exhibit 25-1 shows the holdings of the portfolio and the transactions during the period. Also shown for each security are the beginning and ending par amount, proceeds, accrued value, interest paid during the evaluation period, and capital gain or loss.

---

[4]Jeffery V. Bailey and David E. Tierney, "Gaming Manager Benchmarks," *Journal of Portfolio Management,* Summer 1993, pp. 37–40.
[5]This section is adapted from Chapter 12 in Frank J. Fabozzi and H. Gifford Fong, *Advanced Fixed Income Portfolio Management* (Chicago: Probus Publishing, 1994).
[6]An explanation of the technology is provided in Fabozzi and Fong, *Advanced Fixed Income Portfolio Management.*

EXHIBIT 25-1   Bond Performance Analysis Individual Security Listing and Transactions

Individual Security Listing[a]

Cusip	Bond Description	Initial/ Last Date	Beg/End Par ($000)	Beg/ End Prc (%)	Beg/ End Acc ($000)	Interest Paid ($000)	Capital Gain/ Loss ($000)
041033BM							
ARKANSAS POWER & LIGHT CO							
1 14.125%	11/1/14 E4	2/28/90	24500.000	98.689	1124.70		
		3/31/90	20000.000	98.765	1177.08	0.00	17.99
161610BA							
CHASE MANHATTAN CORP							
2 9.750%	9/15/99 F3	2/28/90	25000.000	99.969	1103.65		
		3/31/90	30000.000	100.080	130.00	1462.50	69.05
172921CT							
CITICORP MORTGAGES SECS INC							
3 9.500%	1/1/19 PS	2/28/90	76151.720	86.250	542.58		
		3/31/90	76151.720	85.031	602.87	602.87	−928.29
3024519X							
FHA INSURED PROJECT MORTGAGE							
4 7.400%	2/1/21 PS	2/28/90	73071.970	84.438	405.55		
		3/31/90	73071.970	83.875	450.61	450.61	−411.40
313400KK							
FEDERAL HOME LOAN MTG CORP							
5 12.250%	3/15/95 AG	2/28/90	30600.000	106.250	1718.93		
		3/31/90	30600.000	105.813	162.98	1874.25	−133.72
4581829H							
INTER-AMERICAN DEVELOPMENT							
6 11.000%	12/11/92 XI	2/28/90	5600.000	103.313	131.76		
		3/31/90	5600.000	102.813	188.22	0.00	−28.00
674599AW							
OCCIDENTAL PETROLEUM CORP							
7 11.750%	3/15/11 04	2/28/90	34000.000	102.875	1808.85		
		3/31/90	34000.000	102.500	177.56	1997.50	−127.50
912827TQ							
UNITED STATES TREASURY NOTES							
8 7.375%	5/15/96 TR	2/28/90	93500.000	94.156	2000.11		
		3/31/90	93500.000	93.594	2590.62	0.00	−525.47

[a]The Individual Security Listing is an optional report that is used to review the beginning and ending holdings, price, and accrued interest for all individual securities held during the evaluation period. This report also displays the amount of interest paid for individual securities during the evaluation period.

EXHIBIT 25-1   (continued)

Cusip	Bond Description	Initial/ Last Date	Beg/End Par ($000)	Beg/End Prc (%)	Beg/ End Acc ($000)	Interest Paid ($000)	Capital Gain/ Loss ($000)
912827WN							
UNITED STATES TREASURY NOTES							
9 9.250%	8/15/98 TR	3/13/90	92000.000	102.531	658.23		
		3/31/90	92000.000	102.969	1034.36	0.00	402.96
912827XM							
UNITED STATES TREASURY NOTES							
10 9.000%	5/15/92 TR	2/28/90	85900.000	101.031	2242.42		
		3/10/90	0.000	100.750	2498.69	0.00	−241.38

Transactions Report[b]

Cusip	Bond Description	Type of/ Transact	Trade Date	Settle Date	Par ($000)	Acc ($000)	Prc ($000)	Cost Proceeds ($000)
041033BM								
ARKANSAS POWER & LIGHT CO								
1 14.125%	11/1/14 E4	Sale	3/5/90	3/12/90	4500.000	231.30	98.751	4675.1
161610BA								
CHASE MANHATTAN CORP								
2 9.750%	9/15/99 F3	Purchase	3/6/90	3/13/90	5000.000	241.04	99.254	5203.7
912827XM								
UNITED STATES TREASURY NOTES								
10 9.000%	5/15/92 TR	Termsale	3/10/90	3/12/90	85900.000	2498.69	100.750	89042.9
912827WN								
UNITED STATES TREASURY NOTES								
9 9.250%	8/15/98 TR	Purchase	3/13/90	3/15/90	92000.000	658.23	102.531	94986.8

[b]The Transactions Report can be used to review the total cost and proceeds of all purchase and sale transactions during the evaluation period. This report displays the type of transaction, the trade and settlement date, the par amount in $000, the price of the transaction, and the accrued interest calculated by the BONDPAR system.

Exhibit 25-2 shows the results of the performance attribution analysis for the portfolio in Exhibit 25-1. Let's look first at the three columns in the exhibit. The "evaluation period return" column is the return and components of return for the portfolio over the evaluation period. The "bond equivalent annualized return" column is the annualized return and components of return for the portfolio over the evaluation period. The "Salomon B.I.G. Index" column shows the evaluation period return of a market index (benchmark). (After the merger of Salomon Brothers and Smith Barney, the name of this index was changed to the Salomon Smith Barney BIG Index. This broad-based bond market index was discussed in Chapter 23.)

EXHIBIT 25-2   Performance Attribution Analysis for a Portfolio with BONDPAR

	Eval. Period Return (%)	Bond Equiv. Annualized Return (%)	Salomen B.I.G. Index Eval. Period Return (%)
I. Interest-rate effect (SAL Treasury Index)			
1. Expected	0.66	7.93	0.66
2. Unexpected	−0.57	−6.87	−0.57
Subtotal	0.09	1.06	0.09
II. Policy effect			
3. Portfolio duration reqt. (4.60 years)	0.01	0.07	0.01
III. Interest rate management effect			
4. Duration	0.06	0.69	0.00
5. Convexity	−0.07	−0.84	−0.10
6. Yield curve shape change	−0.15	−1.78	0.10
Subtotal (options adjusted)	−0.16	−1.93	0.00
IV. Other management effects			
7. Sector/quality	0.18	2.15	0.10
8. Bond selectivity	0.32	3.79	0.00
9. Transactions cost	−0.03	−0.38	0.00
Subtotal	0.47	5.56	0.10
V. Total return	0.41	4.76	0.20
VI. Sources of return			
1. Capital gains	−0.44	−5.20	
2. Interest income	0.85	9.96	
Total return	0.41	4.76	

The decomposition of the evaluation period return is shown in the sections labeled I, II, III, and IV. Section I, interest-rate effect, is the return over the evaluation period of the full Treasury index. The values in this section are interpreted as follows. The subtotal 0.09 means that the actual monthly return on Treasuries was 9 basis points. The value of 0.66 indicates that the expected monthly return from investing in Treasury bonds over this period was 66 basis points. From where does this value come? Recall from Chapter 5 that we demonstrated that forward rates can be calculated from the Treasury yield curve. These rates are taken as the market's consensus of rates that can be earned. It is the forward rate that is the expected return that is reported in the row "expected." The unexpected return is the difference between the actual return of 9 basis points and the expected return of 66 basis points.

The results reported in the section "interest-rate effect" can be interpreted as the cost of being in the bond market. That is, if any investor wanted to invest in default-free bonds (i.e., Treasury securities) and simply bought a portfolio of Treasury securities, the return would have been 9 basis points. Therefore, this component of return is considered out of the manager's control because such a return would have been realized by anyone who decided to commit funds to the bond market.

Section II shows the **policy effect**. This information provides the necessary information to analyze the duration policy constraint specified by the manager's client. BOND-PAR calculates the portion of the total return due to the policy constraint and separates it from the interest-rate management effect. This effect, shown in section III, shows the option-adjusted default-free return for the portfolio. This component of return shows whether the manager has successfully anticipated interest-rate changes. The interest-rate management effect is broken into three subcomponents: (1) the duration effect, which is the effect on the return due to the magnitude of the yield curve shift;[7] (2) the convexity effect, which is the return component of managing the convexity of the portfolio; and (3) the yield curve shape change effect, which is the return due to the change in the shape of the yield curve (i.e., the residual return component not measured by duration and convexity).

Other management effects are shown in section IV. These are divided into three effects. The **sector/quality effect** is the return component that shows whether the manager successfully selected the sector and quality groups that performed better over the evaluation period. The **bond selectivity effect** is the return component due to the selection of individual bonds in the portfolio. **Transactions cost** refers to the hypothetical effect of transactions on the portfolio's return.

The last two sections, V and VI, provide summary information. **Total return** is the time-weighted total return for the evaluation period. This is the sum of the interest-rate effect, policy effect, interest-rate management effect, and other management effects. Section VI, sources of return, separates the return into capital gains (the change in price) and interest income.

Exhibit 25-2 shows the decomposition of return for the entire portfolio; the same analysis can be done for each security, as shown in Exhibit 25-3.

SUMMARY

Performance measurement involves calculation of the return realized by a money manager over some evaluation period. Performance evaluation is concerned with determining whether the money manager added value by outperforming the established benchmark and how the money manager achieved the calculated return.

The rate of return expresses the dollar return in terms of the amount of the initial investment (i.e., the initial market value of the portfolio). Three methodologies have been used in practice to calculate the average of the subperiod returns: (1) the arithmetic average rate of return, (2) the time-weighted (or geometric) rate of return, and (3) the dollar-weighted return. The arithmetic average rate of return is the average value of the withdrawals (expressed as a fraction of the initial portfolio market value) that can be made at the end of each period while keeping the initial portfolio market value intact. The time-weighted rate of return measures the compounded rate of growth of the initial portfolio over the evaluation period, assuming that all cash distributions are reinvested in the portfolio. The time-weighted return is the return on a portfolio that varies in size because of the assumption that all proceeds are reinvested. In general, the arithmetic average rate of return will exceed the time-weighted average

[7]Consistent with the concept of using the Treasury index to measure the unmanaged interest-rate effect, this component is measured relative to the duration of the Treasury index.

EXHIBIT 25-3 Performance Attribution Analysis for Each Security with BONDPAR[a]

Init. Face Value ($000) Bond Description	Initial Date	Last Date	Market Perf.		Portfolio Management				Total Return % =	Return Source	
			Market Expect +	Rate Change +	Init Rate +	Sector/ Qual. +	Selectivity +	Trans. Cost =		Capit. Gains +	Inter. Income
1 041033BM											
24500.0 ARKANSAS POWER & LIGHT CO 14.125% 11/1/14 E4 2 161610BA	2/28/90	3/31/90	0.66	−0.57	0.37	0.69	0.25	−.07	1.33	0.07	1.25
25000.0 CHASE MANHATTAN CORP 9.750% 9/15/99 F3 3 17292ICT	2/28/90	3/31/90	0.66	−0.57	−0.19	0.01	1.12	−.04	0.98	0.11	0.88
76151.7 CITICORP MORTGAGE SECS INC 9.500% 1/1/19 PS 4 3024519X	2/28/90	3/31/90	0.66	−0.57	−0.04	0.25	−0.70	00.00	−0.40	−1.31	0.91
73072.0 FHA INSURED PROJECT MORTGAG 7.400% 2/1/21 PS 5 313400KK	2/28/90	3/31/90	0.66	−0.57	−0.55	0.70	−0.10	00.00	0.14	−0.59	0.73
30600.0 FEDERAL HOME LOAN MTG CORP 12.250% 3/15/95 AG 6 4581829H	2/28/90	3/31/90	0.66	−0.57	−0.08	0.06	0.50	00.00	0.57	−0.39	0.96
5600.0 INTER-AMERICAN DEVELOPMENT 11.000% 12/11/92 XI 7 674599AW	2/28/90	3/31/90	0.66	−0.57	0.05	−0.03	0.37	00.00	0.48	−0.47	0.95
34000.0 OCCIDENTAL PETROLEUM CORP 11.750% 3/15/11 04 8 912827TQ	2/28/90	3/31/90	0.66	−0.57	−0.31	0.05	0.84	00.00	0.68	−0.35	1.02
93500.0 UNITED STATES TREASURY NOTE 7.375% 5/15/96 TR 9 912827WN	2/28/90	3/31/90	0.66	−0.57	−0.19	0.00	0.17	00.00	0.07	−0.58	0.66
92000.0 UNITED STATES TREASURY NOTE 9.250% 8/15/98 TR 10 912827XM	3/13/90	3/13/90	0.39	−0.33	−0.15	0.00	0.99	−0.06	0.82	0.42	0.40
85900.0 UNITED STATES TREASURY NOTE 9.000% 5/15/96 TR	2/28/90	3/10/90	0.21	−0.18	0.13	00.00	−0.08	−0.06	0.02	−0.27	0.29

[a]The *individual security performance* report lists the return components for all individual securities held during the evaluation period. *Initial face value* indicates in $000 the beginning holding position for the bond. *Bond description* displays the security's portfolio bond number, cusip number, coupon, maturity date, and sector/quality. *Initial date* and *Last date* display the evaluation period for the security being analyzed. The remaining columns break down the components of return for the individual security over the evaluation period.

rate of return. The magnitude of the difference between the two averages is smaller the less the variation in the subperiod returns over the evaluation period.

The dollar-weighted rate of return is computed by finding the interest rate that will make the present value of the cash flows from all the subperiods in the evaluation period plus the terminal market value of the portfolio equal to the initial market value of the portfolio. The dollar-weighted rate of return is an internal rate-of-return calculation and will produce the same result as the time-weighted rate of return if (1) no withdrawals or contributions occur over the evaluation period and (2) all dividends are reinvested. The problem with using the dollar-weighted rate of return to evaluate the performance of money managers is that it is affected by factors that are beyond the control of the money manager. Specifically, any contributions made by the client or withdrawals that the client requires will affect the calculated return, making it difficult to compare the performance of two money managers.

The role of performance evaluation is to determine if a money manager added value beyond what could have been achieved by a passive strategy in a benchmark portfolio.

The analysis requires the establishment of a benchmark. One such benchmark is a normal portfolio. This is a customized benchmark that includes a set of securities that contains the universe of securities that a manager normally selects from and weighted as the manager would weight them in a portfolio. Advocates claim that normal portfolios are more appropriate benchmarks than market indexes because they control for investment management style, thereby representing a passive portfolio against which a manager can be evaluated. It is neither an easy nor a costless process to construct normal portfolios.

In the fixed-income area, returns are attributed to those elements beyond the manager's control, such as the interest-rate environment and duration policy constraints imposed by a client, and those that the management process contributes to, such as interest-rate management, sector/quality allocations, and individual bond selection.

Questions

1. What is the difference between performance measurement and performance evaluation?
2. Suppose that the monthly return for two bond managers is as follows:

Month	Manager I	Manager II
1	9%	25%
2	13%	13%
3	22%	22%
4	−18%	−24%

What is the arithmetic average monthly rate of return for the two managers?
3. What is the time-weighted average monthly rate of return for the two managers in Question 2?
4. Why does the arithmetic average monthly rate of return diverge more from the time-weighted monthly rate of return for manager II than for manager I in Question 2?
5. Smith & Jones is a money management firm specializing in fixed-income securities. One of its clients gave the firm $100 million to manage. The market value for the portfolio for the four months after receiving the funds was as follows:

End of Month	Market Value (in millions)
1	$ 50
2	150
3	75
4	100

a. Calculate the rate of return for each month.

b. Smith & Jones reported to the client that over the four-month period the average monthly rate of return was 33.33%. How was that value obtained?

c. Is the average monthly rate of return of 33.33% indicative of the performance of Smith & Jones? If not, what would be a more appropriate measure?

6. The Mercury Company is a fixed-income management firm that manages the funds of pension plan sponsors. For one of its clients it manages $200 million. The cash flow for this particular client's portfolio for the past three months was $20 million, –$8 million, and $4 million. The market value of the portfolio at the end of three months was $208 million.

a. What is the dollar-weighted rate of return for this client's portfolio over the three-month period?

b. Suppose that the $8 million cash outflow in the second month was a result of withdrawals by the plan sponsor and that the cash flow after adjusting for this withdrawal is therefore zero. What would the dollar-weighted rate of return then be for this client's portfolio?

7. If the average monthly return for a portfolio is 1.23%, what is the annualized return?

8. If the average quarterly return for a portfolio is 1.78%, what is the annualized return?

9. What are the difficulties of constructing a normal portfolio?

CHAPTER

26

INTEREST-RATE FUTURES
CONTRACTS

After reading this chapter you will understand:

■ what a futures contract is

■ the differences between a futures and a forward contract

■ the basic features of various interest-rate futures contracts

■ the cheapest-to-deliver issue for a Treasury bond futures contract and how it is determined

■ how the theoretical price of a futures contract is determined

■ how the theoretical price of a Treasury bond futures contract is affected by the delivery options

■ how futures contracts can be used in bond portfolio management: speculation, changing duration, yield enhancement, and hedging

■ how to calculate the hedge ratio and the number of contracts to short when hedging with Treasury bond futures contracts

A futures contract is an agreement that requires a party to the agreement either to buy or sell something at a designated future date at a predetermined price. In this chapter we describe interest-rate futures contracts. Interest-rate options and options on futures are covered in Chapter 27. Interest-rate swaps and agreements are the subject of Chapter 28.

With the advent of interest-rate futures, options, swaps, caps, and floors, proactive portfolio risk management, in its broadest sense, assumes a new dimension. Money managers can achieve new degrees of freedom. It is now possible to alter the interest-rate sensitivity of a bond portfolio or an asset/liability position economically and quickly. These derivative contracts, so called because they derive their value from an underlying asset, offer money managers risk and return patterns that previously were either unavailable or too costly to create.

MECHANICS OF FUTURES TRADING

A **futures contract** is an agreement between a buyer (seller) and an established exchange or its clearinghouse in which the buyer (seller) agrees to take (make) delivery of something at a specified price at the end of a designated period of time. The price at which the parties agree to transact in the future is called the futures price. The designated date at which the parties must transact is called the **settlement** or **delivery date**.

To illustrate, suppose that there is a futures contract traded on an exchange where the something to be bought or sold is bond XYZ, and the settlement is three months from now. Assume further that Bob buys this futures contract, and Sally sells this futures contract, and the price at which they agree to transact in the future is $100. Then $100 is the **futures price**. At the settlement date, Sally will deliver bond XYZ to Bob. Bob will give Sally $100, the futures price.

Most financial futures contracts have settlement dates in the months of March, June, September, or December. This means that at a predetermined time in the contract settlement month the contract stops trading, and a price is determined by the exchange for settlement of the contract. The contract with the nearest settlement date is called the **nearby futures contract**. The next futures contract is the one that settles just after the nearby contract. The contract furthest away in time from settlement is called the **most distant futures contract**.

Opening Position

When an investor takes a position in the market by buying a futures contract, the investor is said to be in a **long position** or to be **long futures**. If, instead, the investor's opening position is the sale of a futures contract, the investor is said to be in a **short position** or **short futures**.

Liquidating a Position

A party to a futures contract has two choices on liquidation of the position. First, the position can be liquidated prior to the settlement date. For this purpose, the party must take an offsetting position in the same contract. For the buyer of a futures contract, this means selling the same number of identical futures contracts; for the seller of a futures contract, this means buying the same number of identical futures contracts.

The alternative is to wait until the settlement date. At that time, the party purchasing a futures contract accepts delivery of the underlying asset at the agreed-upon price; the party that sells a futures contract liquidates the position by delivering the underlying asset at the agreed-upon price. For some futures contracts that we describe in this chapter, settlement is made in cash only. Such contracts are referred to as **cash-settlement contracts**.

Role of the Clearinghouse

Associated with every futures exchange is a clearinghouse, which performs several functions. One of these functions is guaranteeing that the two parties to the transaction will perform. To see the importance of this function, consider potential problems in the futures transaction described earlier from the perspective of the two parties: Bob the buyer and Sally the seller. Each must be concerned with the other's ability to fulfill the obligation at the settlement date. Suppose that at the settlement date the price of bond XYZ in the cash market is $70. Sally can buy bond XYZ for $70 and deliver it to Bob, who, in turn, must pay her $100. If Bob does not have the capacity to pay $100 or refuses to pay, however, Sally has lost the opportunity to realize a profit of $30. Suppose, instead, that the price of bond XYZ in the cash market is $150 at the settlement date. In this case Bob is ready and willing to accept delivery of bond XYZ and pay the agreed-upon price of $100. If Sally does not have the ability or refuses to deliver bond XYZ, Bob has lost the opportunity to realize a profit of $50.

The clearinghouse exists to meet this problem. When an investor takes a position in the futures market, the clearinghouse takes the opposite position and agrees to satisfy the terms set forth in the contract. Because the clearinghouse exists, the investor need not worry about the financial strength and integrity of the party taking the opposite side of the contract. After initial execution of an order, the relationship between the two parties ends. The clearinghouse interposes itself as the buyer for every sale and the seller for every purchase. Thus, investors are free to liquidate their positions without involving the other party in the original contract and without worry that the other party may default. This is the reason why we define a futures contract as an agreement between a party and a clearinghouse associated with an exchange.

Besides its guarantee function, the clearinghouse makes it simple for parties to a futures contract to unwind their positions prior to the settlement date. Suppose that Bob wants to get out of his futures position. He will not have to seek out Sally and work out an agreement with her to terminate the original agreement. Instead, Bob can unwind his position by selling an identical futures contract. As far as the clearinghouse is concerned, its records will show that Bob has bought and sold an identical futures contract. At the settlement date, Sally will not deliver bond XYZ to Bob but will be instructed by the clearinghouse to deliver to someone who bought and still has an open futures position. In the same way, if Sally wants to unwind her position prior to the settlement date, she can buy an identical futures contract.

Margin Requirements

When a position is first taken in a futures contract, the investor must deposit a minimum dollar amount per contract as specified by the exchange. This amount, called the **initial margin**, is required as deposit for the contract.[1] The initial margin may be in the form of an interest-bearing security such as a Treasury bill. As the price of the futures contract fluctuates, the value of the investor's equity in the position changes. At the end of each trading day, the exchange determines the settlement price for the futures contract. This price is used to mark to market the investor's position so that any gain or loss from the position is reflected in the investor's equity account.

The **maintenance margin** is the minimum level (specified by the exchange) by which an investor's equity position may fall as a result of an unfavorable price movement before the investor is required to deposit additional margin. The additional margin deposited, called the **variation margin**, is the amount necessary to bring the equity in the account back to its initial margin level. Unlike initial margin, variation margin must be in cash, not in interest-bearing instruments. Any excess margin in the account may be withdrawn by the investor. If a party to a futures contract who is required to deposit variation margin fails to do so within 24 hours, the futures position is closed out.

---

[1]Individual brokerage firms are free to set margin requirements above the minimum established by the exchange.

Although there are initial and maintenance margin requirements for buying securities on margin, the concept of margin differs for securities and futures. When securities are acquired on margin, the difference between the price of the security and the initial margin is borrowed from the broker. The security purchased serves as collateral for the loan, and the investor pays interest. For futures contracts, the initial margin, in effect, serves as "good faith" money, an indication that the investor will satisfy the obligation of the contract. Normally, no money is borrowed by the investor.

Commissions

Commissions on futures contracts are fully negotiable. They are usually quoted on the basis of a **round turn**, a price that includes the opening and closing out of the futures contract. In most cases the commission is the same regardless of the maturity date or type of the underlying instrument. Commissions for institutional accounts vary enormously, ranging from a low of about $11 to a high of about $30 per contract.

FUTURES VERSUS FORWARD CONTRACTS

Just like a futures contract, a **forward contract** is an agreement for the future delivery of the underlying at a specified price at the end of a designated period of time. Futures contracts are standardized agreements as to the delivery date (or month) and quality of the deliverable and are traded on organized exchanges. A forward contract differs in that it is usually nonstandardized (i.e., the terms of each contract are negotiated individually between buyer and seller), there is no clearinghouse, and secondary markets are often nonexistent or extremely thin. Unlike a futures contract, which is an exchange-traded product, a forward contract is an over-the-counter instrument.

Because there is no clearinghouse that guarantees the performance of a counterparty in a forward contract, the parties to a forward contract are exposed to **counterparty risk**. Counterparty risk is the risk that the other party to the transaction will fail to perform. That is, a party to a forward contract is exposed to credit or default risk.

Although both futures and forward contracts set forth terms of delivery, futures contracts are not intended to be settled by delivery. In fact, generally less than 2% of outstanding contracts are settled by delivery. Forward contracts, in contrast, are intended for delivery.

A futures contract is marked to market at the end of each trading day, whereas a forward contract may or may not be marked to market. Just how much variation margin may be required by one or both parties of a forward contract depends on the terms negotiated. Therefore, although a futures contract is subject to interim cash flows as additional margin may be required in the case of adverse price movements, or as cash is withdrawn in the case of favorable price movements, variation margin may or may not result from a forward contract.

Finally, the parties in a forward contract are exposed to credit risk because either party may default on the obligation. Credit risk is minimal in the case of futures contracts because the clearinghouse associated with the exchange guarantees the other side of the transaction. Other than these differences, most of what we say about futures contracts applies to forward contracts.

RISK AND RETURN CHARACTERISTICS OF FUTURES CONTRACTS

The buyer of a futures contract will realize a profit if the futures price increases; the seller of a futures contract will realize a profit if the futures price decreases. For example, suppose that one month after Bob and Sally take their positions in the futures contract, the futures price of bond XYZ increases to $120. Bob, the buyer of the futures contract, could then sell the futures contract and realize a profit of $20. Effectively, at the settlement date he has agreed to buy bond XYZ for $100 and agreed to sell bond XYZ for $120. Sally, the seller of the futures contract, will realize a loss of $20.

If the futures price falls to $40 and Sally buys the contract, she realizes a profit of $60 because she agreed to sell bond XYZ for $100 and now can buy it for $40. Bob would realize a loss of $60. Thus, if the futures price decreases, the buyer of a futures contract realizes a loss while the seller of a futures contract realizes a profit.

Leveraging Aspect of Futures

When a position is taken in a futures contract, the party need not put up the entire amount of the investment. Instead, only initial margin must be put up. If Bob has $100 and wants to invest in bond XYZ because he believes its price will appreciate as a result of a decline in interest rates, he can buy one bond if bond XYZ is selling for $100. If the exchange where the futures contract for bond XYZ is traded requires an initial margin of $5, however, Bob can purchase 20 contracts with his $100 investment. (This example ignores the fact that Bob may need funds for variation margin.) His payoff will then depend on the price action of 20 XYZ bonds, not the one he could buy with $100. Thus, he can leverage the use of his funds. Although the degree of leverage available in the futures market varies from contract to contract, the leverage attainable is considerably greater than in the cash market.

At first, the leverage available in the futures market may suggest that the market benefits only those who want to speculate on price movements. This is not true. Futures markets can be used to reduce price risk. Without the leverage possible in futures transactions, the cost of reducing price risk using futures would be too high for many market participants.

CURRENTLY TRADED INTEREST-RATE FUTURES CONTRACTS

Several of the more important interest-rate futures contracts in the United States are described in the following sections. For the first three—Treasury bills futures contract, Eurodollar futures contract, and federal funds futures contract—the underlying interest rate is a short-term (money market) interest rate. For the other contracts—Treasury bond futures, Treasury notes futures, and municipal note index futures—the underlying interest rate is a longer term interest rate. Most major financial markets outside the United States have similar futures contracts in which the underlying security is a fixed-income security issued by the central government.

Treasury Bill Futures

Treasury bill futures, as well as the Eurodollar futures contracts described next, are futures contracts whose underlying instrument is a short-term debt obligation. The

Treasury bill futures contract, which is traded on the International Money Market (IMM), is based on a 13-week (three-month) Treasury bill with a face value of $1 million. More specifically, the seller of a Treasury bill futures contract agrees to deliver to the buyer at the settlement date a Treasury bill with 13 weeks remaining to maturity and a face value of $1 million. The Treasury bill delivered can be newly issued or seasoned. The futures price is the price at which the Treasury bill will be sold by the short and purchased by the long. For example, a Treasury bill futures contract that settles in nine months requires that nine months from now the short deliver to the long $1 million face value of a Treasury bill with 13 weeks remaining to maturity. The Treasury bill could be a newly issued 13-week Treasury bill or a Treasury bill that was issued one year prior to the settlement date and therefore at the settlement has only 13 weeks remaining to maturity.

As explained in Chapter 6, Treasury bills are quoted in the cash market in terms of the annualized yield on a bank discount basis

$$Y_d = \frac{D}{F} \times \frac{360}{t}$$

where:

Y_d = annualized yield on a bank discount basis (expressed as a decimal)
D = dollar discount, which is equal to the difference between the face value and the price of a bill maturing in t days
F = face value
t = number of days remaining to maturity.

The dollar discount (D) is found by

$$D = Y_d \times F \times \frac{t}{360}$$

In contrast, the Treasury bill futures contract is quoted not directly in terms of yield but instead on an index basis that is related to the yield on a bank discount basis as follows:

$$\text{index price} = 100 - (Y_d \times 100)$$

For example, if Y_d is 8%, the index price is

$$100 - (0.08 \times 100) = 92$$

Given the price of the futures contract, the yield on a bank discount basis for the futures contract is determined as follows:

$$Y_d = \frac{100 - \text{index price}}{100}$$

To see how this works, suppose that the index price for a Treasury bill futures contract is 92.52. The yield on a bank discount basis for this Treasury bill futures contract is

$$Y_d = \frac{100 - 92.52}{100} = 0.0748 \text{ or } 7.48\%$$

The invoice price that the buyer of $1 million face value of 13-week Treasury bills must pay at settlement is found by first computing the dollar discount, as follows:

$$D = Y_d \times \$1,000,000 \times \frac{t}{360}$$

where t is either 90 or 91 days.

Typically, the number of days to maturity of a 13-week Treasury bill is 91 days. The invoice price is then

$$\text{invoice price} = \$1,000,000 - D$$

For example, for the Treasury bill futures contract with an index price of 92.52 (and a yield on a bank discount basis of 7.48%), the dollar discount for the 13-week Treasury bill to be delivered with 91 days to maturity is

$$D = 0.0748 \times \$1,000,000 \times \frac{91}{360}$$
$$= \$18,907.78$$

The invoice price is

$$\text{invoice price} = \$1,000,000 - \$18,907.78 = \$981,092.22$$

The minimum index price fluctuation or "tick" for this futures contract is 0.01. A change of 0.01 for the minimum index price translates into a change in the yield on a bank discount basis of one basis point (0.0001). A change of one basis point will change the dollar discount, and therefore the invoice price, by

$$0.0001 \times \$1,000,000 \times \frac{t}{360}$$

For a 13-week Treasury bill with 91 days to maturity, the change in the dollar discount is

$$0.0001 \times \$1,000,000 \times \frac{91}{360} = \$25.28$$

For a 13-week Treasury bill with 90 days to maturity, the change in the dollar discount would be $25. Despite the fact that a 13-week Treasury bill typically has 91 days to maturity, market participants commonly refer to the value of a basis point for this futures contract as $25.

Eurodollar CD Futures

Eurodollar certificates of deposit (CDs) are denominated in dollars but represent the liabilities of banks outside the United States. The contracts are traded on both the International Monetary Market of the Chicago Mercantile Exchange and the London International Financial Futures Exchange. The rate paid on Eurodollar CDs is the London interbank offered rate (LIBOR).

The three-month Eurodollar CD is the underlying instrument for the Eurodollar CD futures contract. As with the Treasury bill futures contract, this contract is for $1 million of face value and is traded on an index price basis. The index price basis in which the contract is quoted is equal to 100 minus the annualized futures LIBOR. For example, a Eurodollar CD futures price of 94.00 means a futures three-month LIBOR of 6%.

The minimum price fluctuation (tick) for this contract is 0.01 (or 0.0001 in terms of LIBOR). This means that the price value of a basis point for this contract is $25, found as follows. The simple interest on $1 million for 90 days is equal to

$$\$1,000,000 \times (LIBOR \times 90/360)$$

If LIBOR changes by 1 basis point (0.0001), then

$$\$1,000,000 \times (0.0001 \times 90/360) = \$25$$

The Eurodollar CD futures contract is a cash settlement contract. That is, the parties settle in cash for the value of a Eurodollar CD based on LIBOR at the settlement date. The Eurodollar CD futures contract is one of the most heavily traded futures contracts in the world. It is frequently used to trade the short end of the yield curve, and many hedgers have found this contract to be the best hedging vehicle for a wide range of hedging situations.

Federal Funds Futures Contract

Depository institutions are required to maintain reserves at the Federal Reserve. At any given time, some banks have excess reserves while others have less than required. Banks that have excess reserves do not earn interest on those funds. However, they can lend those funds through the Federal Reserve to other banks that need reserves. The funds lent are called **federal funds**. The interest rate at which banks lend balances at the Federal Reserve to other banks on an overnight basis called the **federal funds rate** or simply **fed funds rate**.

Using its three tools of monetary policy—open market operations, reserve requirements, and discount rate—the Federal Reserve influences the demand for, and supply of, balances that banks hold at Federal Reserve Banks. By doing so, this alters the federal funds rate, which ultimately influences other short-term interest rates and long-term interest rates.

The 30-day federal funds futures contract, traded on the CBOT, is designed for financial institutions and businesses that want to control their exposure to movements in the federal funds rate. These contracts have a notional amount of $5 million and the contract can be written for the current month up to 24 months in the future. Underlying this contract is the simple average overnight federal funds rate (i.e., the effective rate) for the delivery month. As such, this contract is settled in cash on the last business day of the month. Just as the other short-term interest rate futures contracts discussed previously, prices are quoted on the basis of 100 minus the overnight federal funds rate for the delivery month. These contracts are marked to market using the effective daily federal funds rate as reported by the Federal Reserve Bank of New York.

Treasury Bond Futures

The Treasury bond futures contract is traded on the Chicago Board of Trade (CBOT). The underlying instrument for a Treasury bond futures contract is $100,000 par value of a hypothetical 20-year 6% coupon bond. The futures price is quoted in terms of par being 100. Quotes are in 32nds of 1%. Thus, a quote for a Treasury bond futures contract of 97-16 means 97 and 16/32nds, or 97.50. So if a buyer and seller agree on a futures price of 97-16, this means that the buyer agrees to accept delivery of the hypothetical underlying Treasury bond and pay 97.50% of par value, and the seller agrees to accept 97.50% of par value. Because the par value is $100,000, the futures price that the buyer and seller agree to transact for this hypothetical Treasury bond is $97,500.

The minimum price fluctuation for the Treasury bond futures contract is a 32nd of 1%. The dollar value of a 32nd for a $100,000 par value (the par value for the underlying Treasury bond) is $31.25. Thus, the minimum price fluctuation is $31.25 for this contract.

We have been referring to the underlying as a hypothetical Treasury bond. Does this mean that the contract is a cash settlement contract, as is the case with the Eurodollar CD futures contract? The answer is no. The seller of a Treasury bond futures who decides to make delivery rather than liquidate his position by buying back the contract prior to the settlement date must deliver some Treasury bond. But what Treasury bond? The CBOT allows the seller to deliver one of several Treasury bonds that the CBOT declares is acceptable for delivery. The specific bonds that the seller may deliver are published by the CBOT prior to the initial trading of a futures contract with a specific settlement date. Exhibit 26-1 shows the Treasury issues that the seller can select from to deliver to the buyer of six Treasury bond futures contract by settlement month. The CBOT makes its determination of the Treasury issues that are acceptable for delivery from all outstanding Treasury issues that meet the following criteria: An issue must have at least 15 years to maturity from the date of delivery if not callable; in the case of callable Treasury bonds, the issue must not be callable for at least 15 years from the first day of the delivery month. In addition to the eligible issues shown in the exhibit, newly issued Treasury bonds would qualify for delivery.

The delivery process for the Treasury bond futures contract makes the contract interesting. At the settlement date, the seller of a futures contract (the short) is required to deliver the buyer (the long) $100,000 par value of 96% 20-year Treasury bond. Because no such bond exists, the seller must choose from one of the acceptable deliverable Treasury bonds that the CBOT exchange has specified. Suppose that the seller is entitled to deliver $100,000 of a 5% 20-year Treasury bond to settle the futures contract. The value of this bond of course is less than the value of a 6% 20-year bond. If the seller delivers the 5% 20-year bond, this would be unfair to the buyer of the futures contract who contracted to receive $100,000 of a 6% 20-year Treasury bond. Alternatively, suppose that the seller delivers $100,000 of a 7% 20-year Treasury bond. The value of a 7% 20-year Treasury bond is greater than that of a 6% 20-year bond, so this would be a disadvantage to the seller.

How can this problem be resolved? To make delivery equitable to both parties, the CBOT has introduced **conversion factors** for determining the invoice price of each acceptable deliverable Treasury issue against the Treasury bond futures contract. The conversion factor is determined by the CBOT before a contract with a specific settlement date begins trading. Exhibit 26-1 shows for each of the acceptable Treasury issues for each contract the corresponding conversion factor.[2] The conversion factor is constant throughout the trading period of the futures contract for a given settlement month. The short must notify the long of the actual bond that will be delivered one day before the delivery date.

---

[2]The conversion factor is based on the price that a deliverable bond would sell for at the beginning of the delivery month if it were to yield 6%.

EXHIBIT 26-1   Treasury Bonds Acceptable for Delivery and Conversion Factors for Treasury Bond Futures by Settlement Month

		Settlement Month					
Coupon	Maturity Date	Sep. 2006	Dec. 2006	Mar. 2007	Jun. 2007	Sep. 2007	Dec. 2007
5 1/4	11/15/28	0.9090	0.9095	0.9101	0.9105	0.9111	0.9116
5 1/4	02/15/29	0.9084	0.9090	0.9095	0.9101	0.9105	0.9111
5 3/8	02/15/31	0.9206	0.9210	0.9213	0.9218	0.9221	0.9226
5 1/2	08/15/28	0.9396	0.9400	0.9403	0.9407	0.9410	0.9415
6	02/15/26	0.9999	1.0000	0.9999	1.0000	0.9999	1.0000
6 1/8	11/15/27	1.0148	1.0146	1.0146	1.0144	1.0144	1.0142
6 1/8	08/15/29	1.0153	1.0153	1.0151	1.0152	1.0150	1.0150
6 1/4	08/15/23	1.0261	1.0260	1.0256	1.0255	1.0251	1.0250
6 1/4	05/15/30	1.0313	1.0310	1.0310	1.0307	1.0306	1.0304
6 3/8	08/15/27	1.0441	1.0439	1.0435	1.0433	1.0429	1.0428
6 1/2	11/15/26	1.0578	1.0573	1.0570	1.0565	1.0562	1.0557
6 5/8	02/15/27	1.0726	1.0722	1.0716	1.0713	1.0707	1.0703
6 3/4	08/15/26	1.0860	1.0855	1.0848	1.0843	1.0836	1.0831
6 7/8	08/15/25	1.0976	1.0970	1.0961	1.0955	1.0946	1.0940
7 1/8	02/15/23	1.1156	1.1147	1.1135	1.1125	1.1113	1.1103
7 1/4	08/15/22	1.1261	1.1250	1.1236	1.1225	–	–
7 1/2	11/15/24	1.1637	1.1623	1.1612	1.1597	1.1585	1.1570
7 5/8	11/15/22	1.1657	1.1640	1.1625	1.1607	1.1593	–
7 5/8	02/15/25	1.1786	1.1774	1.1759	1.1746	1.1730	1.1717
7 7/8	02/15/21	–	–	–	–	–	–
8	11/15/21	1.1960	–	–	–	–	–
8 1/8	05/15/21	–	–	–	–	–	–
8 1/8	08/15/21	–	–	–	–	–	–
No. of eligible issues		20	19	19	19	18	17

The price that the buyer must pay the seller when a Treasury bond is delivered is called the **invoice price**. The invoice price is the settlement futures price plus accrued interest on the bonds delivered. However, as just noted, the seller can deliver one of several acceptable Treasury issues. To make delivery fair to both parties, the invoice price must be adjusted based on the actual Treasury issue delivered. It is the conversion factors that are used to adjust the invoice price. The invoice price is

invoice price = contract size × futures contract settlement price × conversion factor
+ accrued interest

Suppose that the Treasury bond futures contract settles at 94-08 and that the short elects to deliver a Treasury bond issue with a conversion factor of 1.20. The futures contract settlement price of 94-08 means 94.25% of par value. As the contract size is $100,000, the invoice price the buyer pays the seller is

$100,000 × 0.9425 × 1.20 + accrued interest = $113,100 + accrued interest

In selecting the issue to be delivered, the short will select from all the deliverable issues the one that is cheapest to deliver. This issue is referred to as the **cheapest-to-deliver issue**; it plays a key role in the pricing of this futures contract. The cheapest-to-deliver issue is determined by participants in the market as follows. For each of the acceptable Treasury issues from which the seller can select, the seller calculates the return that can be earned by buying that issue and delivering it at the settlement date. Note that the seller can calculate the return because she knows the price of the Treasury issue now and the futures price that she agrees to deliver the issue. The return so calculated is called the **implied repo rate**. The cheapest-to-deliver issue is then the one issue among all acceptable Treasury issues with the highest implied repo rate because it is the issue that would give the seller of the futures contract the highest return by buying and then delivering the issue. This is depicted in Exhibit 26-2.

In addition to the choice of which acceptable Treasury issue to deliver—sometimes referred to as the **quality option** or **swap option**—the short position has two more options granted under CBOT delivery guidelines. The short position is permitted to decide when in the delivery month delivery actually will take place. This is called the **timing option**. The other option is the right of the short position to give notice of intent to deliver up to 8:00 P.M. Chicago time after the closing of the exchange (3:15 P.M. Chicago time) on the date when the futures settlement price has been fixed. This option is referred to as the **wild card option**. The quality option, the timing option, and the wild card option (in sum referred to as the **delivery options**) mean that the long position can never be sure of which Treasury bond will be delivered or when it will be delivered. The delivery options are summarized in Exhibit 26-3.

EXHIBIT 26-2 Determination of Cheapest-to-Deliver Issue Based on the Implied Repo Rate

Implied repo rate: Rate of return by buying an acceptable Treasury issue, shorting the Treasury bond futures, and delivering the issue at the settlement date.

Buy this issue	Deliver this issue at futures price	Calculate return (implied repo rate)
Acceptable Treasury issue #1	Deliver issue #1	Implied repo rate #1
Acceptable Treasury issue #2	Deliver issue #2	Implied repo rate #2
Acceptable Treasury issue #3	Deliver issue #3	Implied repo rate #3
. . .	. . .	. . .
Acceptable Treasury issue #N	Deliver issue #N	Implied repo rate #N

The cheapest-to-deliver issue is that which produces the maximum implied repo rate.

EXHIBIT 26-3   Delivery Option Granted to the Short (Seller) of a CBOT Treasury Bond Futures Contract

Delivery Option	Description
Quality or swap option	Choice of which acceptable Treasury issue to deliver
Timing option	Choice of when in delivery month to deliver
Wild card option	Choice to deliver after the closing price of the futures contract is determined

Treasury Note Futures

There are three Treasury note futures contracts: 10-year, 5-year, and 2-year. All three contracts are modeled after the Treasury bond futures contract and are traded on the CBOT. The underlying instrument for the 10-year Treasury note futures contract is $100,000 par value of a hypothetical 10-year 6% Treasury note. There are several acceptable Treasury issues that may be delivered by the short. Exhibit 26-4 shows the issues that are acceptable for delivery to satisfy the several 10-year Treasury note futures contracts and the conversion factor for each issue. An issue is acceptable if the maturity is not less than 6.5 years and not greater than 10 years from the first day of the delivery month. The delivery options granted to the short position and the minimum price fluctuations are the same as for the Treasury bond futures contract.

For the five-year Treasury note futures contract, the underlying is $100,000 par value of a U.S. Treasury note that satisfies the following conditions: (1) an original maturity of not

EXHIBIT 26-4   Treasury Notes Acceptable for Delivery and Conversion Factors for 10-Treasury Notes Futures by Settlement Month

		Settlement Month					
Coupon	Maturity Date	Sep. 2006	Dec. 2006	Mar. 2007	Jun. 2007	Sep. 2007	Dec. 2007
3 5/8	05/15/13	0.8737	—	—	—	—	—
3 7/8	02/15/13	—	—	—	—	—	—
4	11/15/12	—	—	—	—	—	—
4	02/15/14	0.8837	0.8870	0.8902	0.8937	—	—
4	02/15/15	0.8713	0.8744	0.8774	0.8806	0.8837	0.8870
4 1/8	05/15/15	0.8766	0.8793	0.8822	0.8851	0.8881	0.8910
4 1/4	08/15/13	0.9040	0.9069	—	—	—	—
4 1/4	11/15/13	0.9012	0.9040	0.9069	—	—	—
4 1/4	08/15/14	0.8927	0.8955	0.8983	0.9012	0.9040	0.9069
4 1/4	11/15/14	0.8901	0.8927	0.8955	0.8983	0.9012	0.9040
4 1/4	08/15/15	0.8821	0.8848	0.8873	0.8901	0.8927	0.8955
4 3/8	08/15/12	—	—	—	—	—	—
4 3/4	05/15/14	0.9254	0.9273	0.9294	0.9314	0.9335	—
No. of eligible issues		10	9	8	7	6	5

more than five years and three months, (2) a remaining maturity no greater than five years and three months, and (3) a remaining maturity not less than four years and three months.

The underlying for the two-year Treasury note futures contract is $200,000 par value of a U.S. Treasury note with a remaining maturity of not more than two years and not less than one year and nine months. Moreover, the original maturity of the note delivered to satisfy the two-year futures cannot be more than five years and two months.

10-Year Municipal Note Index Futures Contract

A 10-year municipal note index futures contract is traded on the CBOT. The underlying for this contract is an index. The index includes between 100 and 250 high-grade tax-exempt securities. For an issue to be eligible for inclusion in the index, the issuer

- must have a credit rating assigned by both S&P and Moody's of AAA
- must have a principal size of at least $50 million
- must be a component (i.e., tranche) of a municipal issue with a total deal size of at least $200 million
- must have a remaining maturity of between 10 and 40 years from the first calendar day of the corresponding futures contract expiration
- must at issuance have a price of at least 90
- must pay semiannual interest at a fixed coupon rate that ranges from 3% to 9%

An issue can be callable or non-callable. However, if an issue is callable, it must have a first call date at least seven years from the first calendar day of the corresponding futures contract expiration. The issues comprising the index includes insured and uninsured bonds.

In constructing the index, there are three further restrictions: (1) no more than 5% of the bond in the index can be from any one issuer, (2) no more than 15% can be from any one state or U.S. territory, and (3) no more than 40% of the issues can be insured by any one issuer.

To assure that the index continues to accurately mirror the overall tax-exempt market, it is revised quarterly on the first business day of each February, May, August, and November. When the index is revised, issues that no longer meet the selection criteria explained previously will be eliminated from the index.

Every trading day the index is priced. Because the issues comprising the index do not typically trade each day, an independent pricing service, FT Interactive Data Corporation, provides prices for the individual issues and then calculates the closing value of the index. At the settlement date, the parties settle in cash. Settlement is based on the final settlement value based on the value of the index as determined by FT Interactive Data Corporation. The final settlement price is calculated as follows:

$$\text{final settlement value} = \$100,000 \,[5/r + (1 - 5/r)(\,1 + r/200)^{-20}]$$

where r is equal to the simple average yield-to-worst of the component bonds in the index for the last day of trading, expressed in percent terms and calculated to the nearest 1/10 of a basis point (e.g., 4.85%).

Swap Futures Contracts

Interest rate swaps are discussed in Chapter 28. The CBOT introduced a swap futures contract in 2001. The underlying instrument is the notional price of the fixed-rate side of a 10-year interest rate swap that has a notional principal equal to $100,000 and that exchanges semiannual interest payments at a fixed annual rate of 6% for floating interest rate payments based on 3-month LIBOR.

This swap futures contract is cash-settled with a settlement price determined by the International Swap and Derivatives Association (ISDA) benchmark 10-year swap rate on the last day of trading before the contract expires. This benchmark rate is published with a one-day lag in the Federal Reserve Board's statistical release H.15. Contracts have settlement months of March, June, September, and December just like the other CBOT interest rate futures contracts that we have discussed.

The London International Financial Futures Exchange (LIFFE) introduced the first swap futures contract called Swapnote®, which is referenced to the euro interest rate swap curve. Swapnotes are available in 2-, 5-, and 10-year maturities. The CME also lists a swap futures contract with maturities of 2, 5, and 10 years that is similar to the one listed on the CBOT.

PRICING AND ARBITRAGE IN THE INTEREST-RATE FUTURES MARKET

One of the primary concerns that most traders and investors have when taking a position in futures contracts is whether the futures price at which they transact will be a "fair" price. Buyers are concerned that the price may be too high and that they will be picked off by more experienced futures traders waiting to profit from the mistakes of the uninitiated. Sellers worry that the price is artificially low and that savvy traders may have manipulated the markets so that they can buy at bargain-basement prices. Furthermore, prospective participants frequently find no rational explanation for the sometimes violent ups and downs that occur in the futures markets. Theories about efficient markets give little comfort to anyone who knows of or has experienced the sudden losses that can occur in the highly leveraged futures markets.

Fortunately, the futures markets are not as irrational as they may at first seem; if they were, they would not have become so successful. The interest-rate futures markets are not perfectly efficient markets, but they probably come about as close as any market. Furthermore, there are both very clear reasons why futures prices are what they are and methods by which traders, investors, and borrowers can and will quickly eliminate any discrepancy between futures prices and their fair levels.

There are several different ways to price futures contracts. Fortunately, all lead to the same fair price for a given contract. Each approach relies on the "law of one price." This law states that a given financial asset (or liability) must have the same price regardless of the means by which it is created. We explain here one way in which futures contracts can be combined with cash market instruments to create cash flows that are identical to other cash securities.[3] The law of one price implies that the synthetically created cash securities must have the same price as the actual cash securities. Similarly, cash instruments can be combined to create cash flows that are identical to

---

[3]For the other ways to price futures contracts, see Chapter 5 in Mark Pitts and Frank J. Fabozzi, *Interest Rate Futures and Options* (Chicago: Probus Publishing, 1990).

futures contracts. By the law of one price, the futures contract must have the same price as the synthetic futures created from cash instruments.

Pricing of Futures Contracts

To understand how futures contracts should be priced, consider the following example. Suppose that a 20-year 100-par-value bond with a coupon rate of 12% is selling at par. Also suppose that this bond is the deliverable for a futures contract that settles in three months. If the current three-month interest rate at which funds can be loaned or borrowed is 8% per year, what should be the price of this futures contract?

Suppose that the price of the futures contract is 107. Consider the following strategy:

- Sell the futures contract at 107.
- Purchase the bond for 100.
- Borrow 100 for three months at 8% per year.

The borrowed funds are used to purchase the bond, resulting in no initial cash outlay for this strategy. Three months from now, the bond must be delivered to settle the futures contract, and the loan must be repaid. These trades will produce the following cash flows:

From Settlement of the Futures Contract:	
Flat price of bond	107
Accrued interest (12% for 3 months)	3
Total proceeds	110
From the Loan:	
Repayment of principal of loan	100
Interest on loan (8% for 3 months)	2
Total outlay	102
Profit	8

This strategy will guarantee a profit of 8. Moreover, the profit is generated with no initial outlay because the funds used to purchase the bond are borrowed. The profit will be realized *regardless of the futures price at the settlement date*. Obviously, in a well-functioning market, arbitrageurs would buy the bond and sell the futures, forcing the futures price down and bidding up the bond price so as to eliminate this profit. This strategy is called a **cash-and-carry trade**.

In contrast, suppose that the futures price is 92 instead of 107. Consider the following strategy:

- Buy the futures contract at 92.
- Sell (short) the bond for 100.
- Invest (lend) 100 for 3 months at 8% per year.

Once again, there is no initial cash outlay. Three months from now a bond will be purchased to settle the long position in the futures contract. That bond will then be used to cover the short position (i.e., to cover the short sale in the cash market). The outcome in three months would be as follows:

From Settlement of the Futures Contract:	
Flat price of bond	92
Accrued interest (12% for 3 months)	3
Total outlay	95
From the Loan:	
Principal received from maturing investment	100
Interest earned from the 3-month investment (8% for 3 months)	2
Total outlay	102
Profit	7

The profit of 7 is a pure arbitrage profit. It requires no initial cash outlay and will be realized *regardless of the futures price at the settlement date*. This strategy is called a **reverse cash-and-carry trade**.

There is a futures price that will eliminate the arbitrage profit, however. There will be no arbitrage if the futures price is 99. Let's look at what would happen if the two previous strategies are followed and the futures price is 99. First, consider the following cash-and-carry trade strategy:

- Sell the futures contract at 99.
- Purchase the bond for 100.
- Borrow 100 for three months at 8% per year.

In three months, the outcome would be as follows:

From Settlement of the Futures Contract:	
Flat price of bond	99
Accrued interest (12% for 3 months)	3
Total proceeds	102
From the Loan:	
Repayment of principal of loan	100
Interest on loan (8% for 3 months)	2
Total outlay	102
Profit	0

There is no arbitrage profit in this case.

Next, consider the following reverse cash-and-carry trade strategy:

- Buy the futures contract at 99.
- Sell (short) the bond for 100.
- Invest (lend) 100 for three months at 8% per year.

The outcome in three months would be as follows:

From Settlement of the Futures Contract:	
Flat price of bond	99
Accrued interest (12% for 3 months)	3
Total outlay	102
From the Loan:	
Principal received from maturing investment	100
Interest earned from the 3-month investment (8% for 3 months)	2
Total proceeds	102
Profit	0

Thus, neither strategy results in a profit. Hence the futures price of 99 is the theoretical futures price because any higher or lower futures price will permit arbitrage profits.

Theoretical Futures Price Based on Arbitrage Model

Considering the arbitrage arguments just presented, the theoretical futures price can be determined on the basis of the following information:

1. The price of the bond in the cash market.
2. The coupon rate on the bond. In our example, the coupon rate is 12% per year.
3. The interest rate for borrowing and lending until the settlement date. The borrowing and lending rate is referred to as the **financing rate**. In our example, the financing rate is 8% per year.

We will let

r = financing rate
c = current yield, or coupon rate divided by the cash market price
P = cash market price
F = futures price
t = time, in years, to the futures delivery date

and then consider the following cash-and-carry trade strategy that is initiated on a coupon date:

- Sell the futures contract at F.
- Purchase the bond for P.
- Borrow P until the settlement date at r.

The outcome at the settlement date is

From Settlement of the Futures Contract:	
Flat price of bond	F
Accrued interest	ctP
Total proceeds	$F + ctP$
From the Loan:	
Repayment of principal of loan	P
Interest on loan	rtP
Total outlay	$P + rtP$

The profit will be

$$\text{profit} = \text{total proceeds} - \text{total outlay}$$

$$= F + ctP - (P + rtP)$$

In equilibrium the theoretical futures price occurs where the profit from this trade is zero. Thus, to have equilibrium, the following must hold:

$$0 = F + ctP - (P + rtP)$$

Solving for the theoretical futures price, we have

$$F = P[1 + t(r - c)] \tag{26.1}$$

Alternatively, consider the following reverse cash-and-carry trade strategy:

- Buy the futures contract at *F*.
- Sell (short) the bond for *P*.
- Invest (lend) *P* at *r* until the settlement date.

The outcome at the settlement date would be

From Settlement of the Futures Contract:	
Flat price of bond	F
Accrued interest	ctP
Total outlay	$\overline{F + ctP}$
From the Loan:	
Proceeds received from maturing of investment	P
Interest earned	rtP
Total proceeds	$\overline{P + rtP}$

The profit will be

$$\text{profit} = \text{total proceeds} - \text{total outlay}$$

$$= P + rtP - (F + ctP)$$

Setting the profit equal to zero so that there will be no arbitrage profit and solving for the futures price, we obtain the same equation for the futures price as equation (26.1). Let's apply equation (26.1) to our preceding example, in which

$$r = 0.08$$
$$c = 0.12$$
$$P = 100$$
$$t = 0.25$$

Then the theoretical futures price is

$$F = 100[1 + 0.25(0.08 - 0.12)] = 99$$

This agrees with the theoretical futures price that we derived earlier.

The theoretical futures price may be at a premium to the cash market price (higher than the cash market price) or at a discount from the cash market price (lower than the cash market price), depending on $(r-c)$. The term $r-c$ is called the **net financing cost** because it adjusts the financing rate for the coupon interest earned. The net financing cost is more commonly called the **cost of carry**, or simply **carry**. **Positive carry** means that the current yield earned is greater than the financing cost; **negative carry** means that the financing cost exceeds the current yield. The relationships can be expressed as follows:

Carry	Futures Price
Positive $(c > r)$	Will sell at a discount to cash price $(F < P)$
Negative $(c > r)$	Will sell at a premium to cash price $(F > P)$
Zero $(c > r)$	Will be equal to cash price $(F = P)$

In the case of interest-rate futures, carry (the relationship between the short-term financing rate and the current yield on the bond) depends on the shape of the yield curve. When the yield curve is upward-sloping, the short-term financing rate will generally be less than the current yield on the bond, resulting in positive carry. The futures price will then sell at a discount to the cash price for the bond. The opposite will hold true when the yield curve is inverted.

Closer Look at the Theoretical Futures Price
To derive the theoretical futures price using the arbitrage argument, we made several assumptions, which have certain implications.

Interim Cash Flows
No interim cash flows due to variation margin or coupon interest payments were assumed in the model. However, we know that interim cash flows can occur for both of these reasons. Because we assumed no variation margin, the price derived is technically the theoretical price for a forward contract (which is not marked to market at the end of each trading day). If interest rates rise, the short position in futures will receive margin as the futures price decreases; the margin can then be re-invested at a higher interest rate. In contrast, if interest rates fall, there will be variation margin that must be financed by the short position; however, because interest rates have declined, financing will be possible at a lower cost. Thus, whichever way rates move, those who are short futures gain relative to those who are short forwards. Conversely, those who are long futures lose relative to those who are long forwards. These facts account for the difference between futures and forward prices.

Incorporating interim coupon payments into the pricing model is not difficult. However, the value of the coupon payments at the settlement date will depend on the interest rate at which they can be reinvested. The shorter the maturity of the futures contract and the lower the coupon rate, the less important the reinvestment income is in determining the futures price.

Short-Term Interest Rate (Financing Rate)

In deriving the theoretical futures price it is assumed that the borrowing and lending rates are equal. Typically, however, the borrowing rate is higher than the lending rate. We will let

$$r_B = \text{borrowing rate}$$
$$r_L = \text{lending rate}$$

Consider the following strategy:

- Sell the futures contract at F.
- Purchase the bond for P.
- Borrow P until the settlement date at r_B.

The futures price that would produce no arbitrage profit is

$$F = P[1 + t(r_B - c)] \qquad\qquad \textbf{(26.2)}$$

Now consider the following strategy:

- Buy the futures contract at F.
- Sell (short) the bond for P.
- Invest (lend) P at r_L until the settlement date.

The futures price that would produce no profit is

$$F = P[1 + t(r_L - c)] \qquad\qquad \textbf{(26.3)}$$

Equations (26.2) and (26.3) together provide boundaries for the theoretical futures price. Equation (26.2) provides the upper boundary and equation (26.3) the lower boundary. For example, assume that the borrowing rate is 8% per year and the lending rate is 6% per year. Then using equation (26.2) and the preceding example, the upper boundary is

$$F(\text{upper boundary}) = \$100[1 + 0.25\,(0.08 - 0.12)]$$
$$= \$99$$

The lower boundary using equation (23.3) is

$$F(\text{lower boundary}) = \$100[1 + 0.25\,(0.06 - 0.12)]$$
$$= \$98.50$$

In calculating these boundaries, we assume that no transaction costs are involved in taking the position. In actuality, the transaction costs of entering into and closing the cash position as well as the round-trip transaction costs for the futures contract must be considered and do affect the boundaries for the futures contract.

Deliverable Bond Is Not Known

The arbitrage arguments used to derive equation (26.1) assumed that only one instrument is deliverable. But the futures contracts on Treasury bonds and Treasury notes are designed to allow the short the choice of delivering one of a number of deliverable issues (the quality or swap option). Because there may be more than one deliverable, market participants track the price of each deliverable bond and determine which bond is the cheapest to deliver. The futures price will then trade in relation to the cheapest-to-deliver issue.

There is the risk that though an issue may be the cheapest to deliver at the time a position in the futures contract is taken, it may not be the cheapest to deliver after that time. A change in the cheapest-to-deliver issue can dramatically alter the futures price.

What are the implications of the quality (swap) option on the futures price? Because the swap option is an option granted by the long to the short, the long will want to pay less for the futures contract than indicated by equation (26.1). Therefore, as a result of the quality option, the theoretical futures price as given by equation (26.1) must be adjusted as follows:

$$F = P[1 + t(r - c)] - \text{value of quality option} \tag{26.4}$$

Market participants have employed theoretical models in attempting to estimate the fair value of the quality option. These models are beyond the scope of this chapter.[4]

Delivery Date Is Not Known

In the pricing model based on arbitrage arguments, a known delivery date is assumed. For Treasury bond and note futures contracts, the short has a timing and wild card option, so the long does not know when the securities will be delivered. The effect of the timing and wild card options on the theoretical futures price is the same as with the quality option. These delivery options should result in a theoretical futures price that is lower than the one suggested in equation (26.1), as shown here:

$$F = P[1 + t(r - c)] - \text{value of quality option} - \text{value of timing option} \\ - \text{value of wildcard option} \tag{26.5}$$

or alternatively,

$$F = P[1 + t(r - c)] - \text{delivery options} \tag{26.6}$$

Market participants attempt to value the delivery option in order to apply equation (26.6).

Deliverable Is Not a Basket of Securities

The municipal index futures contract is a cash settlement contract based on a basket of securities. The difficulty in arbitraging this futures contract is that it is too expensive to buy or sell every bond included in the index. Instead, a portfolio including a smaller number of bonds may be constructed to "track" the index. The arbitrage, however, is no longer risk-free because there is tracking error risk.

---

[4]Several studies have investigated the magnitude of the mispricing caused by the delivery option. See, for example, Gerald D. Gay and Steven Manaster, "The Quality Option Implicit in Futures Contracts," *Journal of Financial Economics*, September 1984, pp. 353–370; Gerald D. Gay and Steven Manaster, "Implicit Delivery Options and Optimal Delivery Strategies for Financial Futures Contracts," *Journal of Financial Economics*, May 1986, pp. 41–72; Alex Kane and Alan Marcus, "The Quality Option in the Treasury Bond Futures Market: An Empirical Assessment," *Journal of Futures Markets*, Summer 1986, pp. 231–248; Alex Kane and Alan Marcus, "Valuation and Optimal Exercise of the Wild Card Option in the Treasury Bond Futures Market," *Journal of Finance*, March 1986, pp. 195–207; and Michael J. Hemler, "The Quality Delivery Option in Treasury Bond Futures Contracts," doctoral dissertation, Graduate School of Business, University of Chicago, March 1988.

BOND PORTFOLIO MANAGEMENT APPLICATIONS

There are various ways in which a money manager can use interest-rate futures contracts.

Speculating on the Movement of Interest Rates

The price of a futures contract moves in the opposite direction from interest rates: When rates rise, the futures price will fall; when rates fall, the futures price will rise. A portfolio manager who wants to speculate that interest rates will rise (fall) can sell (buy) interest-rate futures. Before interest-rate futures were available, investors who wanted to speculate on interest rates did so with the long-term Treasury bond; they shorted the bond if they expected interest rates to rise, and they bought it if they expected interest rates to fall. Using interest-rate futures instead of the cash markets (instead of trading long-term Treasuries themselves) has three advantages. First, transactions costs for trading futures are lower than trading in the cash market. Second, margin requirements are lower for futures than for Treasury securities; using futures thus permits greater leverage. Finally, it is easier to sell short in the futures market than in the Treasury market. The leverage advantages in trading futures may encourage speculation on interest-rate movements; making speculation easier for investors is not the function of interest-rate futures contracts.

Controlling the Interest-Rate Risk of a Portfolio

Interest-rate futures can be used to alter the interest-rate sensitivity of a portfolio. Money managers with strong expectations about the direction of the future course of interest rates will adjust the durations of their portfolios so as to capitalize on their expectations. Specifically, if a manager expects rates to increase, the duration will be shortened; if interest rates are expected to decrease, the duration will be lengthened. Although money managers can alter the durations of their portfolios with cash market instruments, a quick and inexpensive means for doing so (on either a temporary or permanent basis) is to use futures contracts.

In addition to adjusting a portfolio based on anticipated interest-rate movements, futures contracts can be used in constructing a portfolio with a longer duration than is available with cash market securities. As an example of the latter, suppose that in a certain interest-rate environment a pension fund manager must structure a portfolio to have a duration of 15 years to accomplish a particular investment objective. Bonds with such a long duration may not be available. By buying the appropriate number and kind of interest-rate futures contracts, a pension fund manager can increase the portfolio's duration to the target level of 15.

A formula to approximate the number of futures contracts necessary to adjust the portfolio duration to a new level is

$$\text{approximate number of contracts} = \frac{(D_T - D_I)P_I}{D_F P_F}$$

where:

D_T = target effective duration for the portfolio
D_I = initial effective duration for the portfolio
P_I = initial market value of the portfolio

D_F = effective duration for the futures contact
P_F = market value of the futures contract

Notice that if the money manager wishes to increase the duration, D_T will be greater than D_I, and the equation will have a positive sign. This means that futures contracts will be purchased. The opposite is true if the objective is to shorten the portfolio duration.

Creating Synthetic Securities for Yield Enhancement

A cash market security can be created synthetically by taking a position in the futures contract together with the deliverable instrument. If the yield on the synthetic security is the same as the yield on the cash market security, there will be no arbitrage opportunity. Any difference between the two yields can be exploited so as to enhance the yield on the portfolio.

To see how, consider an investor who owns a 20-year Treasury bond and sells Treasury futures that call for the delivery of that particular bond three months from now. Although the maturity of the Treasury bond is 20 years, the investor has effectively shortened the maturity of the bond to three months.

Consequently, the long position in the 20-year bond and the short futures position are equivalent to a long position in a three-month riskless security. The position is riskless because the investor is locking in the price to be received three months from now—the futures price. By being long the bond and short the futures, the investor has synthetically created a three-month Treasury bill. The return the investor should expect to earn from this synthetic position should be the yield on a three-month Treasury bill. If the yield on the synthetic three-month Treasury bill is greater than the yield on the cash market Treasury bill, the investor can realize an enhanced yield by creating the synthetic short-term security. The fundamental relationship for creating synthetic securities is

$$RSP = CBP - FBP \qquad (26.7)$$

where:
RSP = riskless short-term security position
CBP = cash bond position
FBP = bond futures position

A negative sign before a position means a short position. In terms of our previous example, CBP is the long cash bond position, the negative sign before FBP refers to the short futures position, and RSP is the riskless synthetic three-month security or Treasury bill.

Equation (26.7) states that an investor who is long the cash market security and short the futures contract should expect to earn the rate of return on a risk-free security with the same maturity as the futures delivery date. Solving equation (26.7) for the long bond position, we have

$$CBP = RSP + FBP \qquad (26.8)$$

Equation (26.8) states that a cash bond position equals a short-term riskless security position plus a long bond futures position. Thus, a cash market bond can be created synthetically by buying a futures contract and investing in a Treasury bill. Solving equation (26.8) for the bond futures position, we have

$$FBP = CBP - RSP \qquad (26.9)$$

Equation (26.9) tells us that a long position in the futures contract can be created synthetically by taking a long position in the cash market bond and shorting the short-term riskless security. But shorting the short-term riskless security is equivalent to borrowing money. Notice that it was equation (26.9) that we used in deriving the theoretical futures price when the futures contract was underpriced. Recall that when the actual futures price is greater than the theoretical futures price, the strategy to obtain an arbitrage profit is to sell the futures contract and create a synthetic long futures position by buying the asset with borrowed funds. This is precisely what equation (26.9) states. In this case, instead of creating a synthetic cash market instrument as we did with equations (26.7) and (26.8), we have created a synthetic futures contract. The fact that the synthetic long futures position is cheaper than the actual long futures position provides an arbitrage opportunity. If we reverse the sign of both sides of equation (26.9), we can see how a short futures position can be created synthetically.

In an efficient market the opportunities for yield enhancement should not exist very long. But even in the absence of yield enhancement, money managers can use synthetic securities to hedge a portfolio position that they find difficult to hedge in the cash market either because of lack of liquidity or because of other constraints.

Hedging

Hedging with futures calls for taking a futures position as a temporary substitute for transactions to be made in the cash market at a later date. If cash and futures prices move together, any loss realized by the hedger from one position (whether cash or futures) will be offset by a profit on the other position. When the net profit or loss from the positions is exactly as anticipated, the hedge is referred to as a **perfect hedge**.

In practice, hedging is not that simple. The amount of net profit will not necessarily be as anticipated. The outcome of a hedge will depend on the relationship between the cash price and the futures price both when a hedge is placed and when it is lifted. The difference between the cash price and the futures price is the **basis**. The risk that the basis will change in an unpredictable way is called **basis risk**.

In bond portfolio management, typically, the bond to be hedged is not identical to the bond underlying the futures contract. This type of hedging is referred to as **cross hedging**. There may be substantial basis risk in cross hedging. An unhedged position is exposed to price risk, the risk that the cash market price will move adversely. A hedged position substitutes basis risk for price risk.

A **short (or sell) hedge** is used to protect against a decline in the cash price of a bond. To execute a short hedge, futures contracts are sold. By establishing a short hedge, the hedger has fixed the future cash price and transferred the price risk of ownership to the buyer of the futures contract. To understand why a short hedge might be executed, suppose that a pension fund manager knows that bonds must be liquidated in 40 days to make a $5 million payment to the beneficiaries of the pension fund. If interest rates rise during the 40-day period, more bonds will have to be liquidated to realize $5 million. To guard against this possibility, the manager can sell bonds in the futures market to lock in a selling price.

A **long (or buy) hedge** is undertaken to protect against an increase in the cash price of a bond. In a long hedge, the hedger buys a futures contract to lock in a purchase price. A pension fund manager might use a long hedge when substantial cash contributions are expected, and the manager is concerned that interest rates will fall. Also, a money manager who knows that bonds are maturing in the near future and expects that interest rates will fall can employ a long hedge to lock in a rate for the proceeds to be reinvested.

Conceptually, cross hedging is somewhat more complicated than hedging deliverable securities, because it involves two relationships. First, there is the relationship between the cheapest-to-deliver security and the futures contract. Second, there is the relationship between the security to be hedged and the cheapest-to-deliver security.

The Hedge Ratio
The key to minimizing risk in a cross hedge is to choose the right hedge ratio. The hedge ratio depends on volatility weighting, or weighting by relative changes in value. The purpose of a hedge is to use gains or losses from a futures position to offset any difference between the target sale price and the actual sale price of the asset. Accordingly, the hedge ratio is chosen with the intention of matching the volatility (i.e., the dollar change) of the futures contract to the volatility of the asset. Consequently, the hedge ratio is given by

$$\text{hedge ratio} = \frac{\text{volatility of bond to be hedged}}{\text{volatility of hedging instrument}} \qquad \textbf{(26.10)}$$

As equation (26.10) shows, if the bond to be hedged is more volatile than the hedging instrument, more of the hedging instrument will be needed.

Although it might be fairly clear why volatility is the key variable in determining the hedge ratio, *volatility* has many definitions. For hedging purposes we are concerned with volatility in absolute dollar terms. To calculate the dollar volatility of a bond, one must know the precise point in time that volatility is to be calculated (because volatility generally declines as a bond seasons) as well as the price or yield at which to calculate volatility (because higher yields generally reduce dollar volatility for a given yield change). The relevant point in the life of the bond for calculating volatility is the point at which the hedge will be lifted. Volatility at any other point is essentially irrelevant because the goal is to lock in a price or rate only on that particular day. Similarly, the relevant yield at which to calculate volatility initially is the target yield. Consequently, the "volatility of the bond to be hedged" referred to in equation (26.10) is the price value of a basis point for the bond on the date the hedge is expected to be delivered.[5]

An example shows why volatility weighting leads to the correct hedge ratio.[6] Suppose that on April 19, 1985, an investor owned the Southern Bell 11 3/4% bonds of 2023 and sold June 1985 Treasury bond futures to hedge a future sale of the bonds. This is an example of a cross hedge. Suppose that (1) the Treasury 7 5/8s of 2007 were

---

[5]The yield that is to be used on this date in order to determine the price value of a basis point is the forward rate. We discussed forward rates in Chapter 5.
[6]This example is adapted from Mark Pitts and Frank J. Fabozzi, *Interest Rate Futures and Options* (Chicago: Probus Publishing, 1989).

the cheapest-to-deliver issue on the contract and that they were trading at 11.50%, (2) the Southern Bell bonds were at 12.40%, and (3) the Treasury bond futures were at a price of 70. To simplify, assume also that the yield spread between the two bonds remains at 0.90% (i.e., 90 basis points) and that the anticipated sale date was the last business day in June 1985.

Because the conversion factor for the deliverable 7 5/8s for the June 1985 contract was 0.9660, the target price for hedging the 7 5/8s would be 67.62 (from 70×0.9660), and the target yield would be 11.789% (the yield at a price of 67.62). The yield on the telephone bonds is assumed to stay at 0.90% above the yield on the 7 5/8s, so the target yield for the Southern Bell bonds would be 12.689%, with a corresponding price of 92.628. At these target levels, the price value of a basis point (PVBP) for the 7 5/8s and telephone bonds are, respectively, 0.056332 and 0.072564. As indicated earlier, all these calculations are made using a settlement date equal to the anticipated sale date, in this case the end of June 1985. Thus, the relative price volatilities of the bonds to be hedged and the deliverable security are easily obtained from the assumed sale date and target prices.

However, to calculate the hedge ratio [equation (26.10)] we need the volatility not of the cheapest-to-deliver issue, but of the hedging instrument; that is, of the futures contract. Fortunately, knowing the volatility of the bond to be hedged relative to the cheapest-to-deliver issue and the volatility of the cheapest-to-deliver bond relative to the futures contract, we can easily obtain the relative volatilities that define the hedge ratio:

$$\text{hedge ratio} = \frac{\text{volatility of bond to be hedged}}{\text{volatility of CTD}}$$

$$\times \frac{\text{volatility of CTD}}{\text{volatility of hedging instrument}} \qquad \textbf{(26.11)}$$

where CTD is the cheapest-to-deliver issue. The second ratio can be shown to equal the conversion factor for the CTD. Assuming a fixed yield spread between the bond to be hedged and the cheapest-to-deliver issue, equation (26.11) can be rewritten as

$$\text{hedge ratio} = \frac{\text{PVBP of bond to be hedged}}{\text{PVBP of CTD}} \times \text{conversion factor for CTD} \qquad \textbf{(26.12)}$$

The hedge ratio at hand is therefore approximately 1.24 [from $(0.072564/0.056332) \times 0.9660$].

Given the hedge ratio, the number of contracts that must be short is determined as follows:

$$\text{number of contracts} = \text{hedge ratio} \times \frac{\text{par value to be hedged}}{\text{par value of contract}} \qquad \textbf{(26.13)}$$

Because the amount to be hedged is $10 million and each Treasury bond futures contract is for $100,000, this means that the number of futures contracts that must be sold is

EXHIBIT 26-5 Hedging a Nondeliverable Bond to a Delivery Date with Futures

Instrument to be hedged: Southern Bell 11 ¾ % of 4/19/23
Hedge ratio: 1.24
Price of futures contract when sold: 70
Target price for Southern Bell bonds: 92.628

Actual Sale Price of Telephone Bonds	Yield at Sale	Yield on Treas. 7⅝ [a]	Price of Treas. 7⅝	Futures Price[b]	Gain (Loss) on 124 Contracts ($10/0.01/Contract)	Effective Sale Price[c]
$ 7,600,000	15.468%	14.568%	54.590	56.511	$1,672,636	$9,272,636
7,800,000	15.072	14.172	56.167	58.144	1,470,144	9,270,144
8,000,000	14.696	13.769	57.741	59.773	1,268,148	9,268,148
8,200,000	14.338	13.438	59.313	61.401	1,066,276	9,266,276
8,400,000	13.996	13.096	60.887	63.030	864,280	9,264,280
8,600,000	13.671	12.771	62.451	64.649	663,524	9,263,524
8,800,000	13.359	12.459	64.018	66.271	462,396	9,262,396
9,000,000	13.061	12.161	65.580	67.888	261,888	9,261,888
9,200,000	12.776	11.876	67.134	69.497	62,372	9,262,372
9,400,000	12.503	11.603	68.683	71.100	(136,400)	9,263,600
9,600,000	12.240	11.340	70.233	72.705	(335,420)	9,264,580
9,800,000	11.988	11.088	71.773	74.299	(533,076)	9,266,924
10,000,000	11.745	10.845	73.312	75.892	(730,608)	9,269,392
10,200,000	11.512	10.612	74.839	77.473	(926,652)	9,273,348
10,400,000	11.287	10.387	76.364	79.052	(1,122,448)	9,277,552
10,600,000	11.070	10.170	77.884	80.625	(1,317,500)	9,282,500
10,800,000	10.861	9.961	79.394	82.188	(1,511,312)	9,288,688
11,000,000	10.659	9.759	80.889	83.746	(1,704,504)	9,295,496
11,200,000	10.463	9.563	82.403	85.303	(1,897,572)	9,302,428

[a]By assumption, the yield on the 7⅝ s of 2007 is 90 basis points lower than the yield on the Southern Bell bond.
[b]By convergence, the futures price equals the price of the 7⅝ s of 2007 divided by 0.9660 (the conversion factor).
[c]Transaction costs and the financing of margin flows are ignored.

$$\text{number of contracts} = \text{hedge ratio} \times \frac{\$10,000,000}{\$100,000}$$

$$= 1.24 \times 100 = 124 \text{ contracts} \qquad \textbf{(26.13A)}$$

Exhibit 26-5 shows that if the simplifying assumptions hold, a futures hedge using the recommended hedge ratio very nearly locks in the target price for $10 million face value of the telephone bonds.[7]

---

[7]In practice, most of the remaining error could be eliminated by frequent adjustments to the hedge ratio to account for the fact that the price value of a basis point changes as rates move up or down.

Another refinement in the hedging strategy is usually necessary for hedging non-deliverable securities. This refinement concerns the assumption about the relative yield spread between the cheapest-to-deliver bond and the bond to be hedged. In the prior discussion, we assumed that the yield spread was constant over time. Yield spreads, however, are not constant over time. They vary with the maturity of the instruments in question and the level of rates, as well as with many unpredictable and nonsystematic factors.

Regression analysis allows the hedger to capture the relationship between yield levels and yield spreads and use it to advantage. For hedging purposes, the variables are the yield on the bond to be hedged and the yield on the cheapest-to-deliver bond. The regression equation takes the form

$$\text{yield on bond to be hedged} = a + b \times \text{yield on CTD} + \text{error} \quad \textbf{(26.14)}$$

The regression procedure provides an estimate of b (the yield beta), which is the expected relative change in the two bonds. Our example that used constant spreads implicitly assumes that the yield beta, b in equation (26.14), equals 1.0 and that a equals 0.90 (because 0.90 is the assumed spread).

For the two issues in question, that is, the Southern Bell 11 3/4s and the Treasury 7 5/8s, the estimated yield beta was 1.05. Thus, yields on the corporate issue are expected to move 5% more than yields on the Treasury issue. To calculate the relative volatility of the two issues correctly, this fact must be taken into account; thus, the hedge ratio derived in our earlier example is multiplied by the factor 1.05. Consequently, instead of shorting 124 Treasury bond futures contracts to hedge $10 million of telephone bonds, the investor would short 130 contracts.

The formula for the hedge ratio, equation (26.12), is revised as follows to incorporate the impact of the yield beta:

$$\text{hedge ratio} = \frac{\text{PVBP of bond to be hedged}}{\text{PVBP of CTD}}$$
$$\times \text{ conversion factor for CTD} \times \text{yield beta} \quad \textbf{(26.15)}$$

where the yield beta is derived from the yield of the bond to be hedged regressed on the yield of the cheapest-to-deliver issue. As before, PVBP stands for the change in price for a one-basis-point change in yield.

The effect of a change in the cheapest-to-deliver issue and the yield spread can be assessed a priori. An exhibit similar to that of Exhibit 26-5 can be constructed under a wide range of assumptions. For example, at different yield levels at the date the hedge is to be lifted (the second column in Exhibit 26-5), a different yield spread may be appropriate and a different acceptable issue will be the CTD. The money manager can determine what this will do to the outcome of the hedge.

Allocating Funds Between Stocks and Bonds

A pension sponsor may wish to alter the composition of the pension's funds between stocks and bonds, that is, change its asset allocation. Suppose that a pension sponsor wants to shift a $1 billion fund from its current allocation of $500 million in stocks and $500 million in bonds to $300 million in stocks and $700 million in bonds. This can be done directly by selling $200 million of stocks and buying a similar amount of bonds. The costs associated with shifting funds in this manner are (1) the transactions costs with respect to commissions and bid-ask spreads, (2) the market impact costs, and (3) the disruption of the activities of the money managers employed by the pension sponsor.

An alternative course of action is to use interest-rate futures and stock index futures. Assume that the pension sponsor wants to shift $200 million from stocks to bonds. Buying an appropriate number of interest-rate futures and selling an appropriate number of stock index futures can achieve the desired exposure to stocks and bonds. Futures positions can be maintained or slowly liquidated as funds invested in the cash markets are actually shifted. The advantages of using financial futures contracts are as follows: (1) Transactions costs are lower, (2) market impact costs are avoided or reduced by allowing the sponsor time to buy and sell securities in the cash market, and (3) activities of the money managers employed by the pension sponsor are not disrupted.[8]

To determine the approximate number of interest-rate futures contracts needed to change the market value of the portfolio allocated to bonds, assuming that the duration of the portfolio is to remain constant, we can use the formula

$$\text{approximate number of contracts} = \frac{(P_T - P_I)D_I}{D_F P_F}$$

where P_T is the target market value allocated to bonds and the other terms are the same as in the formula given earlier to approximate the number of contracts to adjust a portfolio's duration. Notice that if the market value of the portfolio allocated to bonds is to be increased, the numerator of the equation will be positive. This means that futures contracts will be purchased. If funds are to be reallocated to stocks and withdrawn from bonds, the numerator of the equation will be negative, which means that interest-rate futures contracts will be sold.

SUMMARY

A futures contract is an agreement between a buyer (seller) and an established exchange or its clearinghouse in which the buyer (seller) agrees to take (make) delivery of something at a specified price (called the futures price) at the end of a designated period of time (called the settlement or delivery date). Associated with every futures exchange is a clearinghouse, which guarantees that the two parties to the transaction will perform and allows parties to unwind their position without the need to deal with the counterparty to the initial transaction. A party to a futures contract must comply with margin requirements (initial, maintenance, and variation margin). A forward contract differs from a futures contract in that it is usually nonstandardized (i.e., the terms of each contract are negotiated individually between buyer and seller), there is no clearinghouse, and secondary markets are often nonexistent or extremely thin.

---

[8]See Roger Clarke, "Asset Allocation Using Futures," Chapter 16 in Robert Arnott and Frank J. Fabozzi (eds.), *Asset Allocation* (Chicago: Probus Publishing, 1988); and Mark Zurak and Ravi Dattatreya, "Asset Allocation Using Futures Contracts," Chapter 20 in Frank J. Fabozzi and Gregory Kipnis (eds.), *The Handbook of Stock Index Futures and Options* (Homewood, IL: Probus Publishing, 1988).

Futures contracts traded on short-term interest rates are Treasury bill futures, Eurodollar CD futures, and Federal funds futures. Futures contracts traded on a longer-term interest rate are Treasury bond and note futures and the 10-year municipal note index futures.

The theoretical price of a futures contract is equal to the cash or spot price plus the cost of carry. The cost of carry is equal to the cost of financing the position less the cash yield on the underlying security. The shape of the yield curve will affect the cost of carry. There are several reasons why the actual futures price will depart from the theoretical futures price. In the case of the Treasury bond futures contracts, the delivery options granted to the seller reduce the actual futures price below the theoretical futures price suggested by the standard arbitrage model.

Interest-rate futures contracts can be used by money managers to speculate on the movement of interest rates, to control the interest-rate risk of a portfolio, to allocate funds between stocks and bonds, and to enhance returns when futures are mispriced.

Questions

1. Explain the differences between a futures contract and a forward contract.
2. a. What is counterparty risk?
   b. Why do both the buyer and seller of a forward contract face counterparty risk?
3. What does it mean if the cost of carry is positive for a Treasury bond futures contract?
4. If the Eurodollar CD futures contract is quoted at 91.75, what is the annualized futures three-month LIBOR?
5. How do you think the cost of carry will affect the decision of the short as to when in the delivery month the short will elect to deliver?
6. Explain the asymmetric effect on the variation margin and cash flow for the short and long in an interest-rate futures contract when interest rates change.
7. What are the delivery options granted to the seller of the Treasury bond futures contract?
8. How is the theoretical futures price of a Treasury bond futures contract affected by the delivery options granted to the short?
9. Explain how the shape of the yield curve influences the theoretical price of a Treasury bond futures contract.
10. Suppose that the conversion factor for a particular Treasury bond that is acceptable for delivery in a Treasury bond futures contract is 0.85 and that the futures price settles at 105. Assume also that the accrued interest

for this Treasury bond is 4. What is the invoice price if the seller delivers this Treasury bond at the settlement date?
11. Suppose that bond ABC is the underlying asset for a futures contract with settlement six months from now. You know the following about bond ABC and the futures contract: (1) In the cash market ABC is selling for $80 (par value is $100); (2) ABC pays $8 in coupon interest per year in two semiannual payments of $4, and the next semiannual payment is due exactly six months from now; and (3) the current six-month interest rate at which funds can be loaned or borrowed is 6%
    a. What is the theoretical futures price?
    b. What action would you take if the futures price is $83?
    c. What action would you take if the futures price is $76?
    d. Suppose that bond ABC pays interest quarterly instead of semiannually. If you know that you can reinvest any funds you receive three months from now at 1% for three months, what would the theoretical futures price for six-month settlement be?
    e. Suppose that the borrowing rate and lending rate are not equal. Instead, suppose that the current six-month borrowing rate is 8% and the six-month lending rate is 6%. What is the boundary for the theoretical futures price?

12. What is the implied repo rate?
13. Explain why the implied repo rate is important in determining the cheapest-to-deliver issue.
14. a. What is the underlying for the CBOT 10-year municipal note index futures contract?
    b. Why is the contract cash settled?
15. A manager wishes to hedge a bond with a par value of $20 million by selling Treasury bond futures. Suppose that (1) the conversion factor for the cheapest-to-deliver issue is 0.91, (2) the price value of a basis point of the cheapest-to-deliver issue at the settlement date is 0.06895, and (3) the price value of a basis point of the bond to be hedged is 0.05954.
    a. What is the hedge ratio?
    b. How many Treasury bond futures contracts should be sold to hedge the bond?
16. Suppose that a manager wants to reduce the duration of a portfolio. Explain how this can be done using Treasury bond futures contracts.
17. What risks are associated with hedging?
18. How could a money manager use a Treasury bond futures contract to hedge against increased interest rates over the next quarter?
19. Suppose that an institutional investor wants to hedge a portfolio of mortgage pass-through securities using Treasury bond futures contracts. What are the risks associated with such a hedge?
20. The following excerpt appeared in the article, "Duration," in the November 16, 1992, issue of *Derivatives Week*, p. 9: "TSA Capital Management in Los Angeles must determine duration of the futures contract it uses in order to match it with the dollar duration of the underlying, explains David Depew, principal and head of trading at the firm. Futures duration will be based on the duration of the underlying bond most likely to be delivered against the contract. . . ."
    a. Explain why it is necessary to know the dollar duration of the underlying in order to hedge.
    b. Why can the price value of basis point be used instead of the dollar duration?
21. You work for a conservative investment management firm. You recently asked one of the senior partners for permission to open up a futures account so that you could trade interest-rate futures as well as cash instruments. He replied, "Are you crazy? I might as well write you a check, wish you good luck, and put you on a bus to Las Vegas. The futures markets are nothing more than a respectable game of craps. Don't you think you're taking enough risk trading bonds?" How would you try to persuade the senior partner to allow you to use futures?
22. In a description of the CBOT 10-year Municipal Note Index futures contract, the following appears: "CBOT municipal note futures correlate closely with portfolios of tax-exempt securities, offering targeted and effective hedges." Why is the correlation important to the success of this futures contract?

CHAPTER
27 INTEREST-RATE OPTIONS

After reading this chapter you will understand:

■ the basic features of interest-rate options contracts

■ why over-the-counter interest-rate options are used by institutional investors

■ what futures options are, their trading mechanics, and the reasons for their popularity

■ the differences between options and futures

■ the basic option positions

■ the factors that affect the value of an option

■ what the intrinsic value and time value of an option are

■ the relationship between the price of a put and a call option

■ the limitations of applying the Black–Scholes option pricing model to options on fixed-income securities

■ how the arbitrage-free binomial model can be used to value options on fixed-income securities

■ how the Black model is used to value an option on an interest rate futures contract

■ measures to estimate the sensitivity of the option price to the factors that determine the price

■ what implied volatility is

■ how to calculate the duration of an option

■ how futures options can be used to hedge

In this chapter we explain the various types of interest-rate options, their applications to money management, and how they are priced.

OPTIONS DEFINED

An **option** is a contract in which the writer of the option grants the buyer of the option the right to purchase from or sell to the writer a designated instrument at a specified price within a specified period of time. The writer, also referred to as the seller, grants this right to the buyer in exchange for a certain sum of money called the **option price** or **option premium**. The price at which the instrument may be bought or sold is called the **strike** or **exercise price**. The date after which an option is void is called the **expiration date**. An **American option** may be exercised at any time up to and including the expiration date. A **European option** may be exercised only on the expiration date.

When an option grants the buyer the right to purchase the designated instrument from the writer, it is called a **call option**. When the option buyer has the right to sell the designated instrument to the writer (seller), the option is called a **put option**. The buyer of any option is said to be **long the option**; the writer (seller) is said to be **short the option**.

The maximum amount that an option buyer can lose in such a transaction is the option price. The maximum profit that the option writer (seller) can realize likewise is the option price. The option buyer has substantial upside return potential, whereas the option writer has substantial downside risk. We will investigate the risk/reward relationship for option positions later in this chapter.

DIFFERENCES BETWEEN AN OPTION AND A FUTURES CONTRACT

Notice that options differ from futures contracts, in that the buyer of an option has the right but not the obligation to perform, whereas the option seller (writer) has the obligation to perform. In the case of a futures contract, both the buyer and the seller are obligated to perform. Also notice that in a futures contract, the buyer does not pay the seller to accept the obligation; in the case of an option, the buyer pays the seller the option price.

Consequently, the risk/reward characteristics of the two contracts are also different. In a futures contract the long position realizes a dollar-for-dollar gain when the price of the futures increases and suffers a dollar-for-dollar loss when the price of the futures decreases. The opposite occurs for the short position. Options do not provide such a symmetric risk/reward relationship. The most that a long may lose is the option price, yet the long retains all the upside potential, although the gain is always reduced by the option price. The maximum profit that the short may realize is the option price, but this position has substantial downside risk.

TYPES OF INTEREST-RATE OPTIONS

Interest-rate options can be written on cash instruments or futures. At one time, there were several exchange-traded option contracts whose underlying instrument was a debt instrument. These contracts are referred to as **options on physicals**. The most liquid exchange-traded option on a fixed-income security at the time of this writing is an option on Treasury bonds traded on the Chicago Board Options Exchange. For reasons to be explained later, options on futures have been far more popular than options on physicals. In recent years, market participants have made increasingly greater use of over-the-counter options on Treasury and mortgage-backed securities.

Certain institutional investors who want to purchase an option on a specific Treasury security or a Ginnie Mae pass-through can do so on an over-the-counter basis.[1] There are government and mortgage-backed securities dealers who make a market in options on specific securities. Over-the-counter (or dealer) options typically are purchased by institutional investors who want to hedge the risk associated with a specific security. For example, a thrift may be interested in hedging its position in a specific mortgage pass-through security. Typically, the maturity of the option coincides with the time period over which the buyer of the option wants to hedge, so the buyer is usually not concerned with the option's liquidity. Besides options on fixed-income securities, there are over-the-counter options on the shape of the yield curve[2] or the yield spread between two securities (such as the spread between mortgage pass-through securities and Treasuries, or between double A corporates and Treasuries).

Exchange-Traded Futures Options

An option on a futures contract, commonly referred to as a **futures option**, gives the buyer the right to buy from or sell to the writer a designated futures contract at a designated price at any time during the life of the option. If the futures option is a call option, the buyer has the right to purchase one designated futures contract at the exercise price. That is, the buyer has the right to acquire a long futures position in the designated futures contract. If the buyer exercises the call option, the writer (seller) acquires a corresponding short position in the futures contract.

A put option on a futures contract grants the buyer the right to sell one designated futures contract to the writer at the exercise price. That is, the option buyer has the right to acquire a short position in the designated futures contract. If the put option is exercised, the writer acquires a corresponding long position in the designated futures contract.

Mechanics of Trading Futures Options

Exercising a Futures Option

As the parties to the futures option will realize a position in a futures contract when the option is exercised, the question is: What will the futures price be? That is, at what price will the long be required to pay for the instrument underlying the futures contract, and at what price will the short be required to sell the instrument underlying the futures contract?

Upon exercise, the futures price for the futures contract will be set equal to the exercise price. The position of the two parties is then immediately marked to market in terms of the then-current futures price. Thus, the futures position of the two parties will be at the prevailing futures price. At the same time, the option buyer will receive from the option seller the economic benefit from exercising. In the case of a call futures option, the option writer must pay the difference between the current futures price and the exercise price to the buyer of the option. In the case of a put futures option, the

---

[1]For a more detailed discussion of over-the-counter options, see Mark Pitts and Frank J. Fabozzi, *Interest Rate Futures and Options* (Chicago: Probus Publishing, 1989), Chapter 2.
[2]For example, Goldman, Sachs offers an option on the slope of the yield curve, which it calls SYCURVE. The option represents the right to buy (in the case of a call option) or sell (in the case of a put option) specific segments of the yield curve.

option writer must pay the option buyer the difference between the exercise price and the current futures price.

For example, suppose that an investor buys a call option on some futures contract in which the exercise price is 85. Assume also that the futures price is 95 and that the buyer exercises the call option. Upon exercise, the call buyer is given a long position in the futures contract at 85 and the call writer is assigned the corresponding short position in the futures contract at 85. The futures positions of the buyer and the writer are immediately marked to market by the exchange. Because the prevailing futures price is 95 and the exercise price is 85, the long futures position (the position of the call buyer) realizes a gain of 10, while the short futures position (the position of the call writer) realizes a loss of 10. The call writer pays the exchange 10 and the call buyer receives from the exchange 10. The call buyer, who now has a long futures position at 95, can either liquidate the futures position at 95 or maintain a long futures position. If the former course of action is taken, the call buyer sells a futures contract at the prevailing futures price of 95. There is no gain or loss from liquidating the position. Overall, the call buyer realizes a gain of 10. The call buyer who elects to hold the long futures position will face the same risk and reward of holding such a position, but still has realized a gain of 10 from the exercise of the call option.

Suppose instead that the futures option is a put rather than a call, and the current futures price is 60 rather than 95. Then if the buyer of this put option exercises it, the buyer would have a short position in the futures contract at 85; the option writer would have a long position in the futures contract at 85. The exchange then marks the position to market at the then-current futures price of 60, resulting in a gain to the put buyer of 25 and a loss to the put writer of the same amount. The put buyer who now has a short futures position at 60 can either liquidate the short futures position by buying a futures contract at the prevailing futures price of 60 or maintain the short futures position. In either case the put buyer realizes a gain of 25 from exercising the put option.

Margin Requirements

There are no margin requirements for the buyer of a futures option after the option price has been paid in full. Because the option price is the maximum amount that the buyer can lose, regardless of how adverse the price movement of the underlying instrument, there is no need for margin.

Because the writer (seller) of an option has agreed to accept all of the risk (and none of the reward) of the position in the underlying instrument, the writer (seller) is required to deposit not only the margin required on the interest rate futures contract position if that is the underlying instrument, but also (with certain exceptions) the option price that is received for writing the option. In addition, as prices adversely affect the writer's position, the writer would be required to deposit variation margin as it is marked to market.

Reasons for the Popularity of Futures Options

There are three reasons why futures options on fixed-income securities have largely supplanted options on physicals as the options vehicle of choice for institutional investors. First, unlike options on fixed-income securities, options on Treasury coupon futures do not require payments for accrued interest to be made. Consequently, when a futures option is exercised, the call buyer and the put writer need not compensate the other party for accrued interest.

Second, futures options are believed to be "cleaner" instruments because of the reduced likelihood of delivery squeezes. Market participants who must deliver an instrument are concerned that at the time of delivery the instrument to be delivered will be in short supply, resulting in a higher price to acquire the instrument. As the deliverable supply of futures contracts is more than adequate for futures options currently traded, there is no concern about a delivery squeeze. Finally, in order to price any option, it is imperative to know at all times the price of the underlying instrument. In the bond market, current prices are not as easily available as price information on the futures contract.

Specifications for the Actively Traded Futures Options

There are options on all of the futures contracts described in Chapter 26. Options on Treasury bond and note futures are traded on the Chicago Board of Trade (CBOT) and options on the Eurodollar CD futures are traded on the International Monetary Market (IMM). All futures options are of the American type. If the option buyer elects to exercise early, he or she must notify the clearing corporation, which then randomly selects a clearing member that must select a short from among its customers.

The CBOT's Treasury bond futures contracts have delivery months of March, June, September, and December. In Chapter 26 we described the delivery process and the choices granted to the short. There are futures options that expire in the next three regular quarterly expiration months. Trading of futures options on Treasury bonds stops in the month prior to the underlying futures contract's delivery month. The day in that month in which the futures options stop trading is the first Friday preceding, by at least five days, the first notice day for the Treasury bond futures contract. The CBOT also lists futures options for the current front month.

In an attempt to compete with the over-the-counter (OTC) option market, the CBOT introduced the **flexible Treasury futures options**. These futures options allow counterparties to customize options within certain limits. Specifically, the strike price, expiration date, and type of exercise (American or European) can be customized subject to CBOT constraints. One key constraint is that the expiration date of a flexible contract cannot exceed that of the longest standard option traded on the CBOT. Unlike an OTC option, where the option buyer is exposed to counterparty risk, a flexible Treasury futures option is guaranteed by the clearing house. The minimum size requirement for the launching of a flexible futures option is 100 contracts.

INTRINSIC VALUE AND TIME VALUE OF AN OPTION

The cost to the buyer of an option is primarily a reflection of the option's intrinsic value and any additional amount over that value. The premium over intrinsic value is often referred to as **time value**.

Intrinsic Value of an Option

The intrinsic value of an option is the economic value of the option if it is exercised immediately. Because the buyer of an option need not exercise the option, and, in fact, will not do so if no economic gain will result from exercising it, the intrinsic value cannot be less than zero.

Call Options

The intrinsic value of a call option on a bond is the difference between the bond price and the strike price. For example, if the strike price for a call option is $100 and the current bond price is $105, the intrinsic value is $5. That is, if the option buyer exercises the option and sells the bond simultaneously, the option buyer would realize $105 from the sale of the bond, which would be covered by acquiring the bond from the option writer for $100, thereby netting a $5 gain.

When a call option has intrinsic value, it is said to be **in-the-money**. Our call option with a strike price of $100 is in-the-money when the price of the underlying bond is greater than $100. When the strike price of a call option exceeds the bond price, the call option is said to be **out-of-the-money** and has no intrinsic value. An option for which the strike price is equal to the current bond price is said to be **at-the-money**. Both at-the-money and out-of-the-money options have an intrinsic value of zero because it is not profitable to exercise the option.

Put Options

For a put option, the intrinsic value is equal to the amount by which the bond price is below the strike price. For example, if the strike price of a put option is $100 and the current bond price is $92, the intrinsic value is $8. That is, the buyer of the put option who exercises the put option and buys the bond simultaneously will net $8 because the bond will be sold to the writer for $100 and purchased in the market for $92.

When the put option has intrinsic value, the option is said to be in-the-money. For our put option with a strike price of $100, the option will be in-the-money when the bond price is less than $100. A put option is out-of-the-money when the current bond price exceeds the strike price. A put option is at-the-money when the strike price is equal to the bond price.

Time Value of an Option

The time value of an option is the amount by which the option price exceeds the intrinsic value. The option buyer hopes that at some time prior to expiration, changes in the market yield will increase the value of the rights conveyed by the option. For this prospect, the option buyer is willing to pay a premium above the intrinsic value. For example, if the price of a call option with a strike price of $100 is $9 when the current bond price is $105, the time value of this option is $4 ($9 minus the intrinsic value of $5). If the current bond price is $90 instead of $105, the time value of this option is $9 because the option has no intrinsic value.

There are two ways in which an option buyer may realize the value of a position taken in the option. First, the investor may exercise the option. In the case of a futures option, by exercising the buyer will be assigned a position in the underlying futures contract at the current futures price and be paid by the writer any difference between the current futures price and the strike price. The investor can sell the futures contract at the current price. For example, for our hypothetical call option with a strike price of $100 and an option price of $9, in which the current futures price is $105, the option buyer can exercise the option. This will produce a long position in the futures contract currently at $105. The call writer will pay the buyer $5 (the difference between the current futures price of $105 and the strike price of $100). By simultaneously selling the underlying futures for $105, the option buyer will realize $5.

The second way of realizing the value of an option position is by selling the call option for $9. Obviously, this is the preferable alternative because the exercise of an option will cause the immediate loss of any time value (in this case, $4).

Whether any option will be exercised prior to the expiration date depends on whether the total proceeds at the expiration date would be greater by holding the option or by exercising and reinvesting any cash proceeds received until the expiration date.

PROFIT AND LOSS PROFILES FOR SIMPLE NAKED OPTION STRATEGIES

To appreciate the opportunities available with interest-rate options, the profit and loss profiles for various option strategies must be understood. We begin with simple strategies in only one option on a bond, which are referred to as **naked option strategies**. That is, no other position is taken in another option or bond. *The profit and loss profiles that we present assume that each option position is held to the expiration date and not exercised earlier.* Also, to simplify the illustrations, we assume that there are no transactions costs to implement the strategies.

The four naked option strategies that we illustrate are (1) long call strategy (buying call options), (2) short call strategy (selling or writing call options), (3) long put strategy (buying put options), and (4) short put strategy (selling or writing put options).

Long Call Strategy (Buying Call Options)

The most straightforward option strategy for participating in an anticipated decrease in interest rates (increase in the price of bonds) is to buy a call option on a debt instrument. This is called a **long call strategy**. To illustrate this strategy, assume that there is a call option on a particular 8% coupon bond with a par value of $100 and 20 years and one month to maturity. The call option expires in one month and the strike price is $100. The option price is $3. Although this option is an option on a cash market security, the principles apply equally to futures options.

Suppose that the current price of the bond is $100 (i.e., the bond is selling at par), which means that the yield on this bond is currently 8%. As the strike price is equal to the current price of the bond, this option is at-the-money. What would the profit or loss be for the investor who purchases this call option and holds it to the expiration date?

The profit and loss from the strategy will depend on the price of the bond at the expiration date. The price, in turn, will depend on the yield on 20-year bonds with an 8% coupon, because in one month the bond will have only 20 years to maturity. Exhibit 27-1 shows the price of a 20-year 8% coupon bond for interest rates ranging from 4% to 12%. Five outcomes are possible:

1. If the price of the bond at the expiration date is less than $100 (which means that the market yield is greater than 8%), the investor would not exercise the option. (Why bother exercising the option and paying the option writer $100 when the same bond can be purchased in the market at a lower price?) In this case the option buyer will lose the entire option price of $3. Notice, however, that this is the maximum loss that the option buyer will realize, no matter how far the price of the bond declines.

EXHIBIT 27-1	Price/Yield Relationship for a 20-year 8% Coupon Bond		
Yield	Price	Yield	Price
4.0	154.71	8.1	99.02
4.2	151.08	8.2	98.05
4.4	147.56	8.3	97.10
4.6	144.15	8.4	96.16
4.8	140.85	8.5	95.23
5.0	137.65	8.6	94.32
5.2	134.56	8.7	93.42
5.4	131.56	8.8	92.53
5.6	128.66	8.9	91.66
5.8	125.84	9.0	90.80
6.0	123.11	9.1	89.95
6.1	121.78	9.2	89.11
6.2	120.47	9.3	88.29
6.3	119.18	9.4	87.48
6.4	117.91	9.5	86.68
6.5	116.66	9.6	85.89
6.6	115.42	9.7	85.11
6.7	114.21	9.8	84.34
6.8	113.01	9.9	83.59
6.9	111.84	10.0	82.84
7.0	110.68	10.2	81.38
7.1	109.54	10.4	79.96
7.2	108.41	10.6	78.58
7.3	107.30	10.8	77.24
7.4	106.21	11.0	75.93
7.5	105.14	11.2	74.66
7.6	104.08	11.4	73.42
7.7	103.04	11.6	72.22
7.8	102.01	11.8	71.05
7.9	101.00	12.0	69.91
8.0	100.00		

2. If the price of the bond is equal to $100 (which means that the market yield is unchanged at 8%), no economic value will result from exercising the option. As in the outcome when the price of the bond is less than $100, the buyer of this call option will lose the entire option price, $3.

3. If the price of the bond is greater than $100 but less than $103 (which means that the market yield is less than 8% but greater than 7.70% — see Exhibit 27-1), the option buyer will exercise the option. By exercising, the option buyer purchases the bond for $100 (the strike price) and can sell it in the market for a higher price. Suppose, for example, that the market yield is 7.8%, so that the price of the

bond is about $102 at the expiration date. The buyer of this call option will realize a $2 gain by exercising the option, offset by the $3 cost of purchasing the call option. Hence $1 is the total loss on this strategy. If the investor fails to exercise the option, the $3 is lost.

4. If the price of the bond at the expiration date is equal to $103 (a market yield of about 7.70%), the investor will exercise the option. In this case, the investor breaks even, realizing a gain of $3 on the bond, which offsets the cost of the option, $3. Although there is no net gain, the price of the option is recouped.

5. If the price of the bond at the expiration date is greater than $103 (a market yield of less than 7.70%), the investor will exercise the option and realize a profit. For example, if the price of the bond is $113 because the market yield has declined from 8% to 6.8%, exercising the option will generate a profit on the bond of $13. Reducing this gain by the cost of the option ($3) means that the investor realizes a net profit of $10 on this strategy.

Exhibit 27-2 shows the profit/loss in tabular form for the buyer of the hypothetical call option, and Exhibit 27-3 portrays it graphically. Although the break-even point and the loss will depend on the option price and the strike price, the shape shown in Exhibit 27-3 will hold for all buyers of call options. That shape indicates that the maximum loss is the option price, yet there is substantial upside potential.

It is worthwhile to compare the profit and loss profile of a call option buyer to a long bond strategy in the same bond. The payoff from the strategy depends on the price of the bond at the expiration date, which, in turn, depends on the market yield at the expiration date. Consider again the five price outcomes given previously:

1. If the price of the bond at the expiration date is less than $100 (market yield rises above 8%), the investor would lose the entire option price of $3. In contrast, a long bond position will have one of three possible outcomes:
   a. If the price of the bond is lower than $100 (market yield greater than 8%) but higher than $97 (market yield less than about 8.3%), the loss on the long bond position will be less than $3.
   b. If the price of the bond is $97 (market yield of about 8.3%), the loss on the long bond position will be $3.
   c. If the price of the bond is lower than $97, the loss on the long bond position will be more than $3. For example, if the price at the expiration date is $80 because the market yield has risen to 10.4%, the long bond position will result in a loss of $20.

2. If the price of the bond is equal to $100 because the market yield is unchanged, the buyer of the call option will realize a loss of $3 (the cost of the option). There will be no gain or loss on the long bond position.

3. If the price of the bond is higher than $100 because the market yield has fallen below 8% but lower than $103 (market yield above 7.70%), the option buyer will realize a loss of less than $3, while the long bond position will realize a profit.

4. If the market yield falls to about 7.70% so that the price of the bond at the expiration date is equal to $103, there will be no loss or gain from buying the call option. The long bond position will produce a gain of $3.

EXHIBIT 27-2   Profit/Loss Profile for a Long Call Strategy

Assumptions:
Call option price: 3
Strike price: 100
Time to expiration: 1 month

At Expiration Date:			At Expiration Date:		
Market Yield	Price of Bond	Net Profit	Market Yield	Price of Bond	Net Profit
4.0	154.71	51.71	8.1	99.02	−3.00
4.2	151.08	48.08	8.2	98.05	−3.00
4.4	147.56	44.56	8.3	97.10	−3.00
4.6	144.15	41.15	8.4	96.16	−3.00
4.8	140.85	37.85	8.5	95.23	−3.00
5.0	137.65	34.65	8.6	94.32	−3.00
5.2	134.56	31.56	8.7	93.42	−3.00
5.4	131.56	28.56	8.8	92.53	−3.00
5.6	128.66	25.66	8.9	91.66	−3.00
5.8	125.84	22.84	9.0	90.80	−3.00
6.0	123.11	20.11	9.1	89.95	−3.00
6.1	121.78	18.78	9.2	89.11	−3.00
6.2	120.47	17.47	9.3	88.29	−3.00
6.3	119.18	16.18	9.4	87.48	−3.00
6.4	117.91	14.91	9.5	86.68	−3.00
6.5	116.66	13.66	9.6	85.89	−3.00
6.6	115.42	12.42	9.7	85.11	−3.00
6.7	114.21	11.21	9.8	84.34	−3.00
6.8	113.01	10.01	9.9	83.59	−3.00
6.9	111.84	8.84	10.0	82.84	−3.00
7.0	110.68	7.68	10.2	81.38	−3.00
7.1	109.54	6.54	10.4	79.96	−3.00
7.2	108.41	5.41	10.6	78.58	−3.00
7.3	107.30	4.30	10.8	77.24	−3.00
7.4	106.21	3.21	11.0	75.93	−3.00
7.5	105.14	2.14	11.2	74.66	−3.00
7.6	104.08	1.08	11.4	73.42	−3.00
7.7	103.04	0.04	11.6	72.22	−3.00
7.8	102.01	−0.99	11.8	71.05	−3.00
7.9	101.00	−2.00	12.0	69.91	−3.00
8.0	100.00	−3.00			

5. If the price of the bond at the expiration date is higher than $103 because the market yield has fallen below 7.70%, both the call option purchase and the long bond position will result in a profit. However, the profit for the buyer of the call option will be $3 less than that on the long bond position. For example, if the

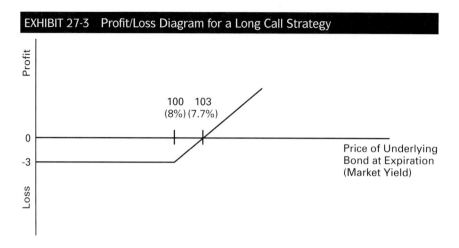

EXHIBIT 27-3   Profit/Loss Diagram for a Long Call Strategy

market yield falls to 6.8% so that the price of the bond is $113, the profit from the long call position is $10 and the profit from the long bond position is $13.

Exhibit 27-4 compares the long call strategy and the long bond strategy. This comparison clearly demonstrates the way in which an option can change the risk/return profile available to investors. An investor who takes a long position in the bond realizes a profit of $1 for every $1 increase in the price of the bond as the market yield falls. However, as the market yield rises, this investor loses dollar for dollar. So if the price decreases by more than $3, this strategy will result in a loss of more than $3. The long call strategy, in contrast, limits the loss to only the option price of $3, but retains the upside potential, which will be $3 less than for the long bond position.

We can use this hypothetical call option to demonstrate the speculative appeal of options. Suppose that an investor has strong expectations that market yields will fall in one month. With an option price of $3, the speculator can purchase 33.33 call options for each $100 invested. Thus, if the market yield declines, the investor realizes the price appreciation associated with 33.33 bonds of $100 par each (or $3,333 par). With the same $100, the investor could buy only one $100 par value bond and realize the appreciation associated with that one bond if the market yield declines. Now, suppose that in one month the market yield declines to 6% so that the price of the bond increases to $123.11. The long call strategy will result in a profit of $670.26 ($23.11 × 33.33 – $100), a return of 670% on the $100 investment in the call options. The long bond strategy results merely in a profit of $23.11, a 23% return on $100.

It is this greater leverage that an option buyer can achieve that attracts investors to options when they wish to speculate on interest-rate movements. It does not come without drawbacks, however. Suppose that the market yield is unchanged at the expiration date so that the price of the bond is $100. The long call strategy will result in the loss of the entire investment of $100, whereas the long bond strategy will produce neither a gain nor a loss.

EXHIBIT 27-4   Comparison of a Long Call Strategy and a Long Bond Strategy

Assumptions:
Current price of bond: 100
Call option price: 3
Strike price: 100
Time to expiration: 1 month

At Expiration Date:		Profit		At Expiration Date:		Profit	
Market Yield	Price of Bond	Long Call	Long Bond	Market Yield	Price of Bond	Long Call	Long Bond
4.0	154.71	51.71	54.71	8.1	99.02	−3.00	−0.98
4.2	151.08	48.08	51.08	8.2	98.05	−3.00	−1.95
4.4	147.56	44.56	47.56	8.3	97.10	−3.00	−2.90
4.6	144.15	41.15	44.15	8.4	96.16	−3.00	−3.84
4.8	140.85	37.85	40.85	8.5	95.23	−3.00	−4.77
5.0	137.65	34.65	37.65	8.6	94.32	−3.00	−5.68
5.2	134.56	31.56	34.56	8.7	93.42	−3.00	−6.58
5.4	131.56	28.56	31.56	8.8	92.53	−3.00	−7.47
5.6	128.66	25.66	28.66	8.9	91.66	−3.00	−8.34
5.8	125.84	22.84	25.84	9.0	90.80	−3.00	−9.20
6.0	123.11	20.11	23.11	9.1	89.95	−3.00	−10.05
6.1	121.78	18.78	21.78	9.2	89.11	−3.00	−10.89
6.2	120.47	17.47	20.47	9.3	88.29	−3.00	−11.71
6.3	119.18	16.18	19.18	9.4	87.48	−3.00	−12.52
6.4	117.91	14.91	17.91	9.5	86.68	−3.00	−13.32
6.5	116.66	13.66	16.66	9.6	85.89	−3.00	−14.11
6.6	115.42	12.42	15.42	9.7	85.11	−3.00	−14.89
6.7	114.21	11.21	14.21	9.8	84.34	−3.00	−15.66
6.8	113.01	10.01	13.01	9.9	83.59	−3.00	−16.41
6.9	111.84	8.84	11.84	10.0	82.84	−3.00	−17.16
7.0	110.68	7.68	10.68	10.2	81.38	−3.00	−18.62
7.1	109.54	6.54	9.54	10.4	79.96	−3.00	−20.04
7.2	108.41	5.41	8.41	10.6	78.58	−3.00	−21.42
7.3	107.30	4.30	7.30	10.8	77.24	−3.00	−22.76
7.4	106.21	3.21	6.21	11.0	75.93	−3.00	−24.07
7.5	105.14	2.14	5.14	11.2	74.66	−3.00	−25.34
7.6	104.08	1.08	4.08	11.4	73.42	−3.00	−26.58
7.7	103.04	0.04	3.04	11.6	72.22	−3.00	−27.78
7.8	102.01	−0.99	2.01	11.8	71.05	−3.00	−28.95
7.9	101.00	−2.00	1.00	12.0	69.91	−3.00	−30.09
8.0	100.00	−3.00	0.00				

Short Call Strategy (Selling or Writing Call Options)

An investor who believes that interest rates will rise or change very little can, if those expectations prove correct, realize income by writing (selling) a call option. This strategy is called a **short call strategy**.

To illustrate this option strategy, we use the same call option we used to demonstrate the long call strategy. The profit and loss profile of the short call strategy (the position of the call option writer) is the mirror image of the profit and loss profile of the long call strategy (the position of the call option buyer). That is, the profit (loss) of the short call position for any given price of the bond at the expiration date is the same as the loss (profit) of the long call position. Consequently, the maximum profit that the short call strategy can produce is the option price. But the maximum loss is limited only by how high the price of the bond can increase (i.e., how low the market yield can fall) by the expiration date, less the option price. Exhibit 27-5 diagrams the profit and loss profile for a short call strategy.

Long Put Strategy (Buying Put Options)

The most straightforward option strategy for benefiting from an expected increase in interest rates is to buy a put option. This strategy is called a long put strategy.

To illustrate this strategy, we'll assume a hypothetical put option for an 8% coupon bond with a par value of $100, 20 years and one month to maturity, and a strike price of $100 that is selling for $2. The current price of the bond is $100 (yield of 8%); hence the put option is at-the-money. The profit or loss for this strategy at the expiration date depends on the market yield at the time. The following outcomes are possible:

1. If the price of the bond is higher than $100 because the market yield has fallen below 8%, the buyer of the put option will not exercise it because exercising would mean selling the bond to the writer for a price that is lower than the

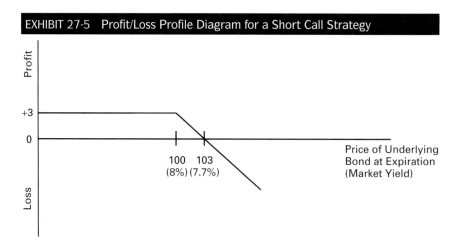

EXHIBIT 27-5   Profit/Loss Profile Diagram for a Short Call Strategy

current market price. Consequently, a loss of $2 (the option price) will result from the long put strategy. Once again, the option price represents the maximum loss to which the buyer of the put option is exposed.

2. If the price of the bond at expiration is equal to $100 because the market yield has remained at 8%, the put will not be exercised, leaving the long put position with a loss equal to the option price of $2.

3. Any price for the bond that is lower than $100 because the market yield has risen above 8% but higher than $98 (market yield of approximately 8.2%) will result in a loss; exercising the put option, however, limits the loss to less than the option price of $2. For example, suppose that the market yield rises to 8.6%, resulting in a price of $99.03 for the bond at the expiration date. By exercising the option, the option buyer will realize a loss of $1.03. This is because the buyer of the put option can sell the bond, purchased in the market for $99.03 to the writer for $100, realizing a gain of $0.97. Deducting the $2 cost of the option results in a loss of $1.03.

4. At a $98 price for the bond (a market yield of roughly 8.2%) at the expiration date, the long put strategy will break even: The investor will realize a gain of $2 by selling the bond to the writer of the option for $100, offsetting the cost of the option ($2).

5. If the market yield rises above 8.2% so that the price of the bond is below $98 at the expiration date, the long put position will realize a profit. For example, if the market yield rises 260 basis points (from 8% to 10.6%), the price of the bond at expiration will be $78.58. The long put strategy will produce a profit of $19.42: a gain of $21.42 on the bond less the $2 option price.

The profit and loss profile for the long put strategy is shown in tabular form in Exhibit 27-6 and in graphic form in Exhibit 27-7. As with all long option positions, the loss is limited to the option price. However, the profit potential is substantial, the theoretical maximum profit being generated if the bond price falls to zero.

Once again, we can see how an option alters the risk/return profile for an investor by comparing it with a position in the bond. In the case of a long put position, it would be compared with a short bond position, because both strategies realize profits if market yields rise (the price falls). Suppose that an investor sells the bond short for $100. The short bond position would produce the following profit or loss as compared with the long put position:

1. If the price of the bond increases above $100 because the market yield declines, the long put option will result in a loss of $2, but the short bond position will realize one of the following:

   a. If the price of the bond is lower than $102 because the market yield has fallen to below 7.80%, there will be a loss of less than $2.

   b. If the price of the bond is equal to $102, the loss will be $2, the same as for the long put strategy.

   c. If the price of the bond is higher than $102, the loss will be more than $2. For example, if the price is $125.84, because market yields declined to 5.8%, the short bond position will realize a loss of $25.84, because the short seller must now pay $125.84, for a bond sold short at $100.

EXHIBIT 27-6   Profit/Loss Profile for a Long Put Strategy

Assumptions:
Put option price: 2
Strike price: 100
Time to expiration: 1 month

Market Yield	Price of Bond	Net Profit	Market Yield	Price of Bond	Net Profit
\multicolumn{3}{c}{At Expiration Date:}			\multicolumn{3}{c}{At Expiration Date:}		
4.0	154.71	−2.00	8.1	99.02	−1.92
4.2	151.08	−2.00	8.2	98.05	−0.05
4.4	147.56	−2.00	8.3	97.10	0.90
4.6	144.15	2.00	8.4	96.16	1.84
4.8	140.85	−2.00	8.5	95.23	2.77
5.0	137.65	−2.00	8.6	94.32	3.68
5.2	134.56	−2.00	8.7	93.42	4.58
5.4	131.56	−2.00	8.8	92.53	5.47
5.6	128.66	−2.00	8.9	91.66	6.34
5.8	125.84	−2.00	9.0	90.80	7.20
6.0	123.11	−2.00	9.1	89.95	8.05
6.1	121.78	−2.00	9.2	89.11	8.89
6.2	120.47	−2.00	9.3	88.29	9.71
6.3	119.18	−2.00	9.4	87.48	10.52
6.4	117.91	−2.00	9.5	86.68	11.32
6.5	116.66	−2.00	9.6	85.89	12.11
6.6	115.42	−2.00	9.7	85.11	12.89
6.7	114.21	−2.00	9.8	84.34	13.66
6.8	113.01	−2.00	9.9	83.59	14.41
6.9	111.84	2.00	10.0	82.84	15.16
7.0	110.68	−2.00	10.2	81.38	16.62
7.1	109.54	−2.00	10.4	79.96	18.04
7.2	108.41	−2.00	10.6	78.58	19.42
7.3	107.30	−2.00	10.8	77.24	20.76
7.4	106.21	−2.00	11.0	75.93	22.07
7.5	105.14	−2.00	11.2	74.66	23.34
7.6	104.08	−2.00	11.4	73.42	24.58
7.7	103.04	−2.00	11.6	72.22	25.78
7.8	102.01	−2.00	11.8	71.05	26.95
7.9	101.00	−2.00	12.0	69.91	28.09
8.0	100.00	−2.00			

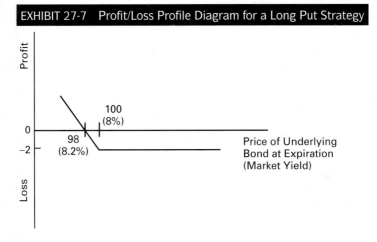

EXHIBIT 27-7   Profit/Loss Profile Diagram for a Long Put Strategy

2. If the price of the bond at expiration is equal to $100 because the market yield is unchanged, the long put strategy will realize a $2 loss, and there will be no profit or loss on the short bond strategy.
3. Any price for the bond that is lower than $100 but higher than $98 (market yield of about 8.2%) will result in a loss of less than $2 for the long put strategy but a profit for the short bond strategy. For example, a price of $99.02 (market yield of 8.1%) will result in a loss of less than $2 for the long put strategy but a profit for the short bond strategy. For example, a price of $99.02 (market yield of 8.1%) at the expiration date will result in a loss of $1.02 for the long put strategy but a profit of $.98 for the short bond strategy.
4. At a $98 price for the bond at the expiration date, the long put strategy will break even, but the short bond strategy will generate a $2 profit.
5. At a price below $98 (market yield greater than 8.2%) both strategies will generate a profit. However, the profit will always be $2 less for the long put strategy.

Exhibit 27-8 is a tabular comparison of the profit and loss profile for the long put and short bond strategies. Whereas the investor who pursues a short bond strategy participates in all the upside potential and faces all the downside risk, the long put strategy allows the investor to limit the downside risk to the option price while still maintaining upside potential. However, the upside potential is less than that for a short put position by an amount equal to the option price.

Short Put Strategy (Selling or Writing Put Options)

The last naked option position that we shall consider is the short put strategy. The **short put strategy** involves the selling (writing) of put options. This strategy is employed if the investor expects interest rates to fall or stay flat so that the price of the bond will increase or stay the same. The profit and loss profile for a short put option is the mirror image of that for the long put option. The maximum loss is limited only by how low the price of the bond can fall by the expiration date less the option price received for writing the option. Exhibit 27-9 graphically depicts this profit and loss profile.

EXHIBIT 27-8   Comparison of a Long Put Strategy and a Short Bond Strategy

Assumptions:
Current price of bond: 100
Put option price: 2
Strike price: 100
Time to expiration: 1 month

At Expiration Date:		Profit		At Expiration Date:		Profit	
Market Yield	Price of Bond	Long Put	Short Bond	Market Yield	Price of Bond	Long Put	Short Bond
4.0	154.71	−2.00	−54.71	8.1	99.02	−1.02	0.98
4.2	151.08	−2.00	−51.08	8.2	98.05	−0.05	1.95
4.4	147.56	−2.00	−47.56	8.3	97.10	0.90	2.90
4.6	144.15	−2.00	−44.15	8.4	96.16	1.84	3.84
4.8	140.85	−2.00	−40.85	8.5	95.23	2.77	4.77
5.0	137.65	−2.00	−37.65	8.6	94.32	3.68	5.68
5.2	134.56	−2.00	−34.56	8.7	93.42	4.58	6.58
5.4	131.56	−2.00	−31.56	8.8	92.53	5.47	7.47
5.6	128.66	−2.00	−28.66	8.9	91.66	6.34	8.34
5.8	125.84	−2.00	−25.84	9.0	90.80	7.20	9.20
6.0	123.11	−2.00	−23.11	9.1	89.95	8.05	10.05
6.1	121.78	−2.00	−21.78	9.2	89.11	8.89	10.89
6.2	120.47	−2.00	−20.47	9.3	88.29	9.71	11.71
6.3	119.18	−2.00	−19.18	9.4	87.48	10.52	12.52
6.4	117.91	−2.00	−17.91	9.5	86.68	11.32	13.32
6.5	116.66	−2.00	−16.66	9.6	85.89	12.11	14.11
6.6	115.42	−2.00	−15.42	9.7	85.11	12.89	14.89
6.7	114.21	−2.00	−14.21	9.8	84.34	13.66	15.66
6.8	113.01	−2.00	−13.01	9.9	83.59	14.41	16.41
6.9	111.84	−2.00	−11.84	10.0	82.84	15.16	17.16
7.0	110.68	−2.00	−10.68	10.2	81.38	16.62	18.62
7.1	109.54	−2.00	−9.54	10.4	79.96	18.04	20.04
7.2	108.41	−2.00	−8.41	10.6	78.58	19.42	21.42
7.3	107.30	−2.00	−7.30	10.8	77.24	20.76	22.76
7.4	106.21	−2.00	−6.21	11.0	75.93	22.07	24.07
7.5	105.14	−2.00	−5.14	11.2	74.66	23.34	25.34
7.6	104.08	−2.00	−4.08	11.4	73.42	24.58	26.58
7.7	103.04	−2.00	−3.04	11.6	72.22	25.78	27.78
7.8	102.01	−2.00	−2.01	11.8	71.05	26.95	28.95
7.9	101.00	−2.00	−1.00	12.0	69.91	28.09	30.09
8.0	100.00	−2.00	0.00				

To summarize, long calls and short puts allow the investor to gain if bond prices rise (interest rates fall). Short calls and long puts allow the investor to gain if bond prices fall (interest rates rise). An investor would want to use each strategy under the following circumstances:

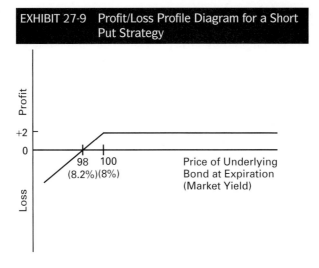

EXHIBIT 27-9   Profit/Loss Profile Diagram for a Short Put Strategy

Circumstance	Strategy
Very bullish	Buy call
Slightly bullish	Write put
Slightly bearish	Write call
Very bearish	Buy put

Considering the Time Value of Money

Our illustrations of the four naked option positions do not reflect the time value of money. Specifically, the buyer of an option must pay the seller the option price at the time the option is purchased. Thus, the buyer must either finance the purchase price of the option or, if the proceeds do not have to be borrowed, lose the interest that could be earned by investing the option price until the expiration of the option. The seller, in contrast, assuming that the option price does not have to be used as margin for the short position, has the opportunity to invest this option price.

The profit profiles of the naked option positions change when the time value of money is taken into consideration. The break-even price for the buyer and the seller of an option will not be the same as in our illustrations. The break-even price for the underlying instrument at the expiration date is higher for the buyer of the option; for the seller, it is lower.

We also ignored the time value of money in comparing the option strategies with positions in the underlying instrument. In this case, we did not consider the fact that when the underlying instrument is a cash market coupon security, coupon payments may be made between the time the option is purchased and the option's expiration date. When these coupon payments are received, they can be reinvested. Thus, reinvestment income must be factored into the analysis of an option position. Also, the effects of financing costs and opportunity costs on the long or short bond positions, respectively, must be factored into the analysis. For the sake of simplicity, however, we shall ignore the time value of money throughout the remainder of this chapter.

PUT–CALL PARITY RELATIONSHIP AND EQUIVALENT POSITIONS

Is there a relationship between the price of a call option and the price of a put option on the same underlying instrument, with the same strike price and the same expiration date? There is. To see this relationship, which is commonly referred to as the **put–call parity relationship**, let's use an example.

Previous illustrations have used a put and a call option on the same underlying instrument (a bond currently with 20 years and one month to maturity), both options having a strike price of $100 and one month to expiration. The price of the underlying bond is assumed to be $100. The call price and put price are assumed to be $3 and $2, respectively. Consider the following strategy:

- Buy the bond at a price of $100.
- Sell a call option at a price of $3.
- Buy a put option at a price of $2.

This strategy therefore involves the following:

- Long the bond.
- Short the call option.
- Long the put option.

Exhibit 27-10 shows the profit and loss profile at the expiration date for this strategy. Notice that no matter what the price of the underlying bond at expiration date, the

---

EXHIBIT 27-10   Profit/Loss Profile for a Strategy Involving a Long Bond Position, Short Call Option Position, and Long Put Option Position

Assumptions:

Current price of bond: 100	Price of put option: 2
Price of call option: 3	Put strike price: 100
Call strike price: 100	Time to expiration: 1 month

At Expiration Date:

Market Yield	Price of Bond	Profit from Long Bond	Price Received for Call	Price Paid for Put	Overall Profit
5.0	137.65	0*	3	−2	1
6.0	123.11	0*	3	−2	1
7.0	110.68	0*	3	−2	1
7.9	101.00	0*	3	−2	1
8.0	100.00	0	3	−2	1
8.1	99.02	0‡	3	−2	1
9.0	90.80	0‡	3	−2	1
10.0	82.84	0‡	3	−2	1
11.0	75.93	0‡	3	−2	1

*If the price of the bond is more than the strike price, the buyer of the call option will exercise the option.
‡If the price of the bond is lower than the strike price, the investor will exercise the put option.

strategy produces a profit of $1. Ignoring the cost of financing the long position and the long put position, this situation cannot exist in an efficient market. The actions of market participants in implementing this strategy to capture the $1 profit will result in one or more of the following consequences, which will tend to eliminate the $1 profit: (1) an increase in the price of the bond, (2) a decrease in the call option price, and/or (3) an increase in the put option price.

In our example, assuming that the bond price does not change, this means that the call price and the put price must be equal. But this is true only when we ignore the time value of money (financing cost, opportunity cost, coupon income, and reinvestment income). Also, in the illustration we did not consider the possibility of early exercise of the options. Thus, we have been considering a put–call parity relationship only for European options. Ignoring the time value of money and considering European options, the outcome from the following position must be one of no arbitrage profits:

$$\text{long the bond} + \text{short call option} + \text{long put option} = 0 \qquad \textbf{(27.1)}$$

In terms of price, it can be shown that there will be no arbitrage profits at any time (not just expiration) if

$$P_{po} = P_{co} + S - P_b \qquad \textbf{(27.2)}$$

where:

P_{po} = price of put option
P_{co} = price of call option
  S = strike price of option
P_b = current price of the underlying bond

and the strike price and expiration date are the same for both options. This relationship is one form of the put–call parity relationship for European options when the time value of money is ignored. It is approximately true for American options. Considering the time value of money, the put–call parity relationship for coupon bonds is

$$P_{po} = P_{co} + \text{PV}(S) + \text{PV}(\text{coupon}) - P_b \qquad \textbf{(27.3)}$$

where:

  PV(S) = present value of the strike price
PV(coupon) = present value of the coupon payments

Equivalent Positions
Working with equation (27.1), we can identify equivalent positions; that is, positions that will provide the same profit profile. For example, subtracting the long put position from both sides of equation (27.1), we have

$$\text{long the bond} + \text{short call option} = -\text{long put option} \qquad \textbf{(27.4)}$$

But the position on the right-hand side of equation (27.4) is the same as a short put position. Therefore,

$$\text{long the bond} + \text{short call option} = \text{short put option} \qquad \textbf{(27.5)}$$

We will see later in this chapter that a covered call position, which is a long bond position plus a short call option position on the same bond, has the same profit profile as a short put option position. This is what equation (27.5) states. Owning callable securities is equivalent to a long bond position plus a short call position. Thus, these securities will have a payoff similar to a short put position. But remember, the equivalent position holds only for European options, and a more precise relationship requires that the time value of money be considered.

Manipulating equation (27.1) gives us the following equivalent positions:

short the bond + short put = short call
long the bond + long put = long call
short the bond + long call = long put
long call + short put = long the bond
long put + short call = short the bond

Thus, an investor can synthetically create any of the positions on the right-hand side of these equations by taking the two positions indicated on the left-hand side.

OPTION PRICE

Six factors will influence the option price:

1. Current price of the underlying instrument
2. Strike price
3. Time to expiration
4. Short-term risk-free interest rate over the life of the option
5. Coupon rate on the bond
6. Expected volatility of yields (or prices) over the life of the option

The impact of each of these factors may depend on whether (1) the option is a call or a put, (2) the option is an American option or a European option, and (3) the underlying instrument is a bond or a futures contract on a bond.[3]

Current Price of the Underlying Instrument

For a call option, as the current price of the underlying instrument increases (decreases), the option price increases (decreases). For a put option, as the current price of the underlying instrument decreases (increases), the option price increases (decreases).

Strike Price

All other factors being constant, the higher the strike price, the lower the price of a call option. For a put option, the opposite is true: The higher the strike price, the higher the price of a put option.

---

[3]For a more detailed discussion of the impact of these factors, see Pitts and Fabozzi, *Interest Rate Futures and Options.*

Time to Expiration

For American options (both puts and calls), all other factors held constant, the longer the time to expiration, the higher the option price. No general statement can be made for European options. The impact of the time to expiration on European options will depend on whether the option is a put or a call.

Short-Term Risk-Free Interest Rate over the Life of the Option

Holding all other factors constant, the price of a call option on a bond will increase as the short-term risk-free interest rate rises. For a put option, the opposite is true: An increase in the short-term risk-free interest rate will decrease the price of a put option. In contrast, for a futures option, the price of both a call and a put option will decrease if the short-term risk-free interest rate rises.[4]

Coupon Rate

For options on bonds, coupons tend to reduce the price of a call option because the coupons make it more attractive to hold the bond than the option. Thus, call options on coupon-bearing bonds will tend to be priced lower than similar call options on non–coupon-bearing bonds. Conversely, coupons tend to increase the price of put options.

Expected Volatility of Yields over the Life of the Option

As the expected volatility of yields over the life of the option increases, the price of the option will also increase. The reason is that the greater the expected volatility, as measured by the standard deviation or variance of yields, the greater the probability that the price of the underlying bond or futures contract will move in the direction that will benefit the option buyer.

MODELS FOR PRICING OPTIONS

Several models have been developed for determining the theoretical value of an option. These models are referred to as option pricing models. There are models for valuing options on bonds and options on bond futures. We discuss these various models here.

Models for Valuing Options on Bonds

First we will discuss models for valuing options on bonds (i.e., options on physicals). In the equity options area, the most popular model is the Black–Scholes option pricing model.[5] This model, however, is limited in pricing options on bonds, as we shall see next. A more appropriate model that takes into account the yield curve builds on the valuation procedure described in Chapter 17, where we introduced a binomial interest-rate tree.

---

[4]Pitts and Fabozzi, *Interest Rate Futures and Options.*
[5]Fischer Black and Myron Scholes, "The Pricing of Corporate Liabilities," *Journal of Political Economy,* May–June 1973, pp. 637–659.

Black–Scholes Option Pricing Model

By imposing certain assumptions (to be discussed later) and using arbitrage arguments, the **Black–Scholes option pricing model** computes the fair (or theoretical) price of a European call option on a non–dividend-paying stock with the following formula:

$$C = SN(d_1) - Xe^{-rt} N(d_2) \qquad \text{(27.6)}$$

where

$$d_1 = \frac{\ln(S/X) + (r + 0.5s^2)t}{s\sqrt{t}} \qquad \text{(27.7)}$$

$$d_2 = d_1 - s\sqrt{t} \qquad \text{(27.8)}$$

where:

$\ln$ = natural logarithm
C = call option price
S = current stock price
X = strike price
r = short-term risk-free interest rate
e = 2.718 (natural antilog of 1)
t = time remaining to the expiration date (measured as a fraction of a year)
s = standard deviation of the stock return
$N(\cdot)$ = cumulative probability density (the value of $N(\cdot)$ is obtained from a normal distribution function that is tabulated in most statistics textbooks)

With the exception of the cash payments, notice that the factors that we said earlier influence the price of an option are included in the formula. Cash payments are not included because the model is for a non–dividend-paying stock.

The option price derived from the Black–Scholes option pricing model is "fair" in the sense that if any other price existed, it would be possible to earn riskless arbitrage profits by taking an offsetting position in the underlying stock. That is, if the price of the call option in the market is higher than that derived from the Black–Scholes option pricing model, an investor could sell the call option and buy a certain number of shares in the underlying stock. If the reverse is true, that is, the market price of the call option is less than the "fair" price derived from the model, the investor could buy the call option and sell short a certain number of shares in the underlying stock. This process of hedging by taking a position in the underlying stock allows the investor to lock in the riskless arbitrage profit. The number of shares necessary to hedge the position changes as the factors that affect the option price change, so the hedged position must be changed constantly.

Computing the Price of a Call Option on a Zero-Coupon Bond

Because the basic Black–Scholes formula as given by equation (27.6) is for a non–cash-paying security, let's apply it to a zero-coupon bond with three years to maturity. Assume the following values:

strike price = $88.00
time remaining to expiration = 2 years
current price = $83.96

$$\text{expected return volatility} = \text{standard deviation} = 10\%$$
$$\text{risk-free rate} = 6\%$$

Note that the current price is $83.96, which is the present value of the maturity value of $100 discounted at 6% (assuming a flat yield curve).

In terms of the values in the formula,

$$S = 83.96$$
$$X = 88.00$$
$$t = 2$$
$$s = 0.10$$
$$r = 0.06$$

Substituting these values into equations (27.7) and (27.8) yields

$$d_1 = \frac{\ln(83.96/88) + [0.06 + 0.5(0.10)^2]2}{0.10\sqrt{2}} = 0.5869$$

$$d_2 = 0.5869 - 0.10\sqrt{2} = 0.4455$$

From a normal distribution table,

$$N(0.5869) = 0.7214 \text{ and } N(0.4455) = 0.6720$$

Then, from equation (27.6),

$$C = 83.96(0.7214) - 88\,[e^{-(0.06)(2)}\,(0.6720)] = \$8.116$$

There is no reason to suspect that this estimated value is unreasonable. However, let's change the problem slightly. Instead of a strike price of $88, let's make the strike price $100.25. Substituting the new strike price into equations (27.7) and (27.8):

$$d_1 = \frac{\ln(83.96/100.25) + [0.06 + 0.5(0.10)^2]2}{0.10\sqrt{2}} = -0.3346$$

$$d_2 = -0.3346 - 0.10\sqrt{2} = -0.4761$$

From a normal distribution table,

$$N(-0.3346) = 0.3689 \text{ and } N(-0.4761) = 0.3170$$

Then, from equation (27.6),

$$C = 83.96(0.3689) - 100.25[e^{-(0.06)(2)}\,(0.3170)] = \$2.79$$

Thus, the Black–Scholes option pricing model tells us that this call option has a fair value of $2.79. Is there any reason to believe that this is unreasonable? Well, consider that this is a call option on a zero-coupon bond that will *never* have a value greater than its maturity value of $100. Consequently, a call option struck at $100.25 must have a value of zero. Yet the Black–Scholes option pricing model tells us that the value is $2.79! In fact, with a higher volatility assumption, the model would give an even greater value for the call option.

Why is the Black–Scholes model off by so much in our previous illustration? The answer lies in its underlying assumptions. There are three assumptions underlying the

Black–Scholes model that limit its use in pricing options on interest-rate instruments. First, the probability distribution for the return assumed by the Black–Scholes option pricing model permits some probability — no matter how small — that the return can take on any positive value. But in the case of a zero-coupon bond, the price cannot take on a value above $100, and therefore the return is capped. In the case of a coupon bond, we know that the price cannot exceed the sum of the coupon payments plus the maturity value. For example, for a five-year 10% coupon bond with a maturity value of $100, the price cannot be greater than $150 (five coupon payments of $10 plus the maturity value of $100). Thus, unlike stock returns, bond prices have a maximum return. The only way that a bond's return can exceed the maximum value is if negative interest rates are permitted. This is not likely to occur, so any probability distribution for prices assumed by an option pricing model that permits bond prices to be higher than the maximum bond value could generate nonsensical option prices. The Black–Scholes model does allow bond prices to exceed the maximum bond value (or, equivalently, allows negative interest rates). That is one of the reasons why we can get a senseless option price for the three-month European call option on the three-year zero-coupon bond.

The second assumption of the Black–Scholes option pricing model is that the short term interest rate is constant over the life of the option. Yet the price of an interest-rate option will change as interest rates change. A change in the short-term interest rate changes the rates along the yield curve. Therefore, to assume that the short-term rate will be constant is inappropriate for interest-rate options. The third assumption is that the variance of prices is constant over the life of the option. Recall from Chapter 4 that as a bond moves closer to maturity its price volatility declines. Therefore, the assumption that price variance is constant over the life of the option is inappropriate.

We have illustrated the problem of using the Black–Scholes model to price interest-rate options; we can also show that the binomial option pricing model based on the price distribution of the underlying bond suffers from the same problems.

Arbitrage-Free Binomial Model

The proper way to value options on interest-rate instruments is to use an arbitrage-free model that takes into account the yield curve. These models can incorporate different volatility assumptions along the yield curve. The most popular model employed by dealer firms is the Black–Derman–Toy model.[6]

We have already developed the basic principles for employing this model. In Chapter 17 we explained how to construct a binomial interest-rate tree such that the tree would be arbitrage free. We used the interest-rate tree to value bonds (both option-free and bonds with embedded options). But the same tree can be used to value a stand-alone European option on a bond.

To illustrate how this is done, let's consider a two-year European call option on a 5.25% three-year Treasury bond with a strike price of 99.25. We will assume that the yield for the on-the-run Treasuries is the one in Chapter 17 and that the volatility assumption is 10% per year. Exhibit 17-13 shows the binomial interest-rate tree along with the value of the Treasury bond at each node. It is a portion of that exhibit we use to value the call option. Specifically, Exhibit 27-11 shows the value of our Treasury

---

[6]Fischer Black, Emanuel Derman, and William Toy, "A One-Factor Model of Interest Rates and Its Application to Treasury Bond Options," *Financial Analysis Journal*, January–February 1990, pp. 24–32.

EXHIBIT 27-11 Valuing a European Call Option Using the Binomial Method

Underlying: 3-year, 5.25% Treasury

Call Option:
expiration: 2 years
strike price: 99.25
current price: 102.075
volatility assumption: 10%

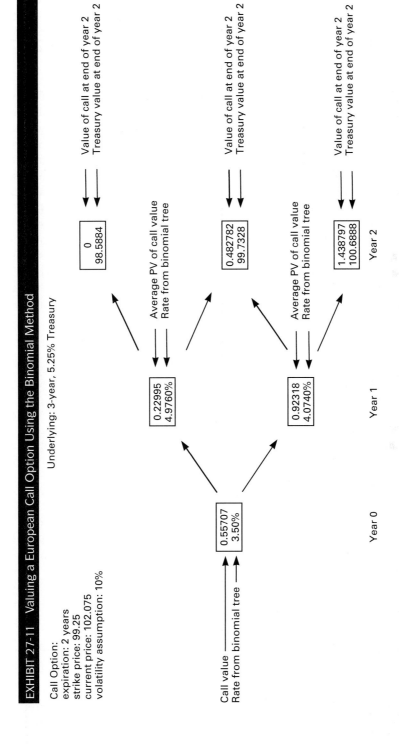

665

bond (excluding coupon interest) at each node at the end of year 2. There are three values shown: 98.5884, 99.7328, and 100.6888. Given these three values, the value of a call option struck at 99.25 can be determined at each node. For example, if in two years the price of this Treasury bond is 98.5884, then because the strike price is 99.25, the value of the call option would be zero. In the other two cases, because the price two years from now is greater than the strike price, the value of the call option is the difference between the price of the bond and 99.25.

Exhibit 27-11 shows the value of the call option two years from now (the option expiration date) for each of the three nodes. Given these values, the binomial interest-rate tree is used to find the present value of the call option. The backward induction procedure is used. The discount rates are those from the binomial interest-rate tree. For years 0 and 1, the discount rate is the second number shown at each node. The first number at each node for year 1 is the average present value found by discounting the call option value of the two nodes to the right using the discount rate at the node. The value of the call option is the first number shown at the root, $0.55707.

The same procedure is used to value a European put option. This is illustrated in Exhibit 27-12 assuming that the put option has two years to expiration and that the strike price is 99.25. The value of the put option two years from now is shown at each of the three nodes in year 2.

To demonstrate that the arbitrage-free binomial model satisfies the put–call parity relationship for European options given by equation (27.3), let's use the values from our illustration. We just found that

$$P_{po} = 0.55707$$
$$P_{co} = 0.15224$$

In Chapter 17 we showed that the theoretical price for the 5.25% three-year option-free bond is 102.075. Therefore,

$$P_b = 102.075$$

Also in Chapter 17, we showed the spot rates for each year. The spot rate for year 2 is 4.01%. Therefore, the present value of the strike price of 99.25 is

$$PV(S) = \frac{99.25}{(1.0401)^2} = 91.7446$$

The present value of the coupon payments are found by discounting the two coupon payments of 5.25 by the spot rates. As just noted, the spot rate for year 2 is 4.01%; the spot rate for year 1 is 3.5%. Therefore,

$$PV(\text{coupon}) = \frac{5.25}{1.035} + \frac{5.25}{(1.0401)^2} = 9.9255$$

The put–call parity relationship as given by equation (27.3) is repeated as follows:

$$P_{po} = P_{co} + PV(S) + PV(\text{coupon}) - P_b$$

Substituting the values into the right-hand side of the relationship, we find that

$$0.55707 + 91.7446 + 9.9255 - 102.075 = 0.15217$$

EXHIBIT 27-12 Valuing a European Put Option Using the Binomial Method

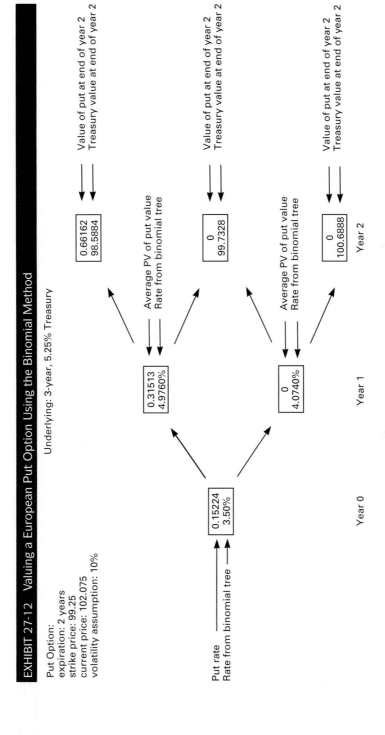

Put Option:
expiration: 2 years
strike price: 99.25
current price: 102.075
volatility assumption: 10%

Underlying: 3-year, 5.25% Treasury

Put rate
Rate from binomial tree

0.15224
3.50%

Average PV of put value
Rate from binomial tree

0.31513
4.9760%

Average PV of put value
Rate from binomial tree

0
4.0740%

Value of put at end of year 2
Treasury value at end of year 2

0.66162
98.5584

Value of put at end of year 2
Treasury value at end of year 2

0
99.7328

Value of put at end of year 2
Treasury value at end of year 2

0
100.6888

Year 0

Year 1

Year 2

The put value that we found is 0.15224. The discrepancy is due simply to rounding error. Therefore, put–call parity holds.

Implied Volatility

Option pricing models provide a theoretical option price depending on the six factors discussed earlier. The only one of these factors that is not known and must be estimated is the expected volatility of yield or price over the life of the option. A popular methodology to assess whether an option is fairly priced is to assume that the option is priced correctly and then, using an option pricing model, estimate the volatility that is implied by that model, given the observed option price and the other five factors that determine the price of an option. The estimated volatility computed in this manner is called the **implied volatility**.

For example, suppose that a money manager using some option pricing model, the current price of the option, and the five other factors that determine the price of an option computes an implied yield volatility of 12%. If the money manager expects that the volatility of yields over the life of the option will be greater than the implied volatility of 12%, the option is considered to be undervalued. In contrast, if the money manager's expected volatility of yields over the life of the option is less than the implied volatility, the option is considered to be overvalued. Although we have focused on the option price, the key to understanding the options market is knowing that trading and investment strategies in this market involve buying and selling volatility. Estimating the implied volatility and comparing it with the trader's or money manager's expectations of future volatility is just another way of evaluating options. If an investor uses expected volatility to compute the fair value of the option, the option will appear cheap or expensive in exactly the same cases.

Models for Valuing Options on Bond Futures

The most commonly used model for futures options was developed by Fischer Black.[7] The model was initially developed for valuing European options on forward contracts. The value of a call and put based on the Black model is:

$$C = e^{-rt}[FN(d_1) - XN(d_2)]$$
$$P = e^{-rt}[XN(-d_2) - FN(-d_1)]$$

where:

$$d_1 = \frac{\ln(F/X) + 0.5s^2t}{s\sqrt{t}}$$

$$d_2 = d_1 - s\sqrt{t}$$

ln = natural logarithm
C = call option price
P = put option price
F = futures price

---

[7]Fischer Black, "The Pricing of Commodity Contracts," *Journal of Financial Economics*, March 1976, pp. 161–179.

X = strike price

r = short-term risk-free interest rate

e = 2.718 (natural antilog of 1)

t = time remaining to the expiration date (measured as a fraction of a year)

s = standard deviation of the return

$N(\cdot)$ = the cumulative probability density. The value for $N(\cdot)$ is obtained from a normal distribution function

There are two problems with this model. First, the Black model does not overcome the problems cited earlier for the Black–Scholes model. Failing to recognize the yield curve means that there will not be a consistency between pricing Treasury futures and options on Treasury futures. Second, the Black model was developed for pricing European options on futures contracts. Treasury futures options, however, are American options.

The second problem can be overcome. The Black model was extended by Barone-Adesi and Whaley to American options on futures contracts.[8] This is the model used by the Chicago Board of Trade to settle the flexible Treasury futures options. However, this model was also developed for equities and is subject to the first problem noted previously. Despite its limitations, the Black model is the most popular option pricing model for options on Treasury futures.

SENSITIVITY OF OPTION PRICE TO CHANGE IN FACTORS

In employing options in an investment strategy, a money manager would like to know how sensitive the price of an option is to a change in any one of the factors that affect its price. Here we look at the sensitivity of a call option's price to changes in the price of the underlying bond, the time to expiration, and expected volatility.

Call Option Price and Price of the Underlying Bond

Exhibit 27-13 shows the theoretical price of a call option based on the price of the underlying bond. The horizontal axis is the price of the underlying bond at any point in time. The vertical axis is the call option price. The shape of the curve representing the theoretical price of a call option, given the price of the underlying bond, would be the same regardless of the actual option pricing model used. In particular, the relationship between the price of the underlying bond and the theoretical call option price is convex. Thus, option prices also exhibit convexity.

The line from the origin to the strike price on the horizontal axis in Exhibit 27-13 is the intrinsic value of the call option when the price of the underlying bond is less than the strike price because the intrinsic value is zero. The 45-degree line extending from the horizontal axis is the intrinsic value of the call option once the price of the underlying bond exceeds the strike price. The reason is that the intrinsic value of the call option will increase by the same dollar amount as the increase in the price of the underlying bond. For example, if the strike price is $100 and the price of the underlying bond increases

---

[8]Giovanni Barone-Adesi and Robert E. Whaley, "Efficient Analytic Approximation of American Option Values," *Journal of Finance*, June 1987, pp. 301–320.

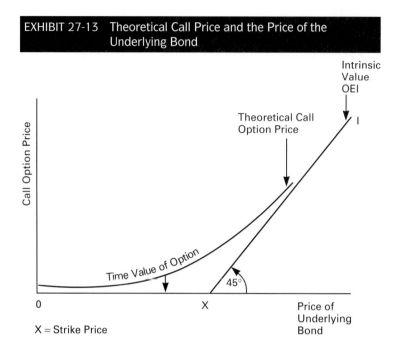

EXHIBIT 27-13   Theoretical Call Price and the Price of the Underlying Bond

from $100 to $101, the intrinsic value will increase by $1. If the price of the bond increases from $101 to $110, the intrinsic value of the option will increase from $1 to $10. Thus, the slope of the line representing the intrinsic value after the strike price is reached is 1.

Because the theoretical call option price is shown by the convex line, the difference between the theoretical call option price and the intrinsic value at any given price for the underlying bond is the time value of the option.

Exhibit 27-14 shows the theoretical call option price but with a tangent line drawn at the price of p^*. The tangent line in the figure can be used to estimate what the new option price will be (and therefore what the change in the option price will be) if the price of the underlying bond changes. Because of the convexity of the relationship between the option price and the price of the underlying bond, the tangent line closely approximates the new option price for a small change in the price of the underlying bond. For large changes, however, the tangent line does not provide as good an approximation of the new option price.

The slope of the tangent line shows how the theoretical call option price will change for small changes in the price of the underlying bond. The slope is popularly referred to as the **delta** of the option. Specifically,

$$\text{delta} = \frac{\text{change in price of call option}}{\text{change in price of underlying bond}}$$

For example, a delta of 0.4 means that a $1 change in the price of the underlying bond will change the price of the call option by approximately $0.40.

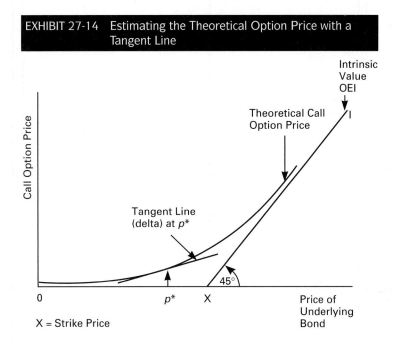

EXHIBIT 27-14   Estimating the Theoretical Option Price with a Tangent Line

Exhibit 27-15 shows the curve of the theoretical call option price with three tangent lines drawn. The steeper the slope of the tangent line, the greater the delta. When an option is deep out of the money (i.e., the price of the underlying bond is substantially below the strike price), the tangent line is nearly flat (see line 1 in Exhibit 27-15). This means that delta is close to zero. To understand why, consider a call option with a strike price of $100 and two months to expiration. If the price of the underlying bond is $20, its price would not increase by much, if anything, should the price of the underlying bond increase by $1, from $20 to $21.

For a call option that is deep in the money, the delta will be close to 1. That is, the call option price will increase almost dollar for dollar with an increase in the price of the underlying bond. In terms of Exhibit 27-15, the slope of the tangent line approaches the slope of the intrinsic value line after the strike price. As we stated earlier, the slope of that line is 1.

Thus, the delta for a call option varies from zero (for call options deep out of the money) to 1 (for call options deep in the money). The delta for a call option at the money is approximately 0.5.

The curvature of the convex relationship can also be approximated. This is the rate of change of delta as the price of the underlying bond changes. The measure is commonly referred to as **gamma** and is defined as follows:

$$\text{gamma} = \frac{\text{change in delta}}{\text{change in price of underlying bond}}$$

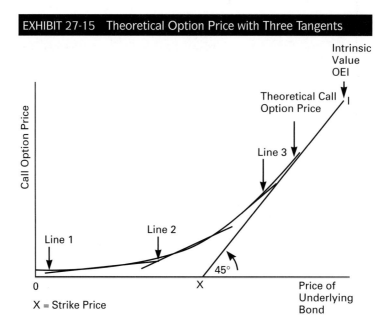

EXHIBIT 27-15   Theoretical Option Price with Three Tangents

Call Option Price and Time to Expiration

All other factors constant, the longer the time to expiration, the greater the option price. Because each day the option moves closer to the expiration date, the time to expiration decreases. The **theta** of an option measures the change in the option price as the time to expiration decreases, or equivalently, it is a measure of **time decay**. Theta is measured as follows:

$$\text{theta} = \frac{\text{change in price of option}}{\text{decrease in time to expiration}}$$

Assuming that the price of the underlying bond does not change (which means that the intrinsic value of the option does not change), theta measures how quickly the time value of the option changes as the option moves towards expiration. Buyers of options prefer a low theta so that the option price does not decline quickly as it moves toward the expiration date. An option writer benefits from an option that has a high theta.

Call Option Price and Expected Interest Rate Volatility

All other factors constant, a change in the expected interest rate volatility will change the option price. The **kappa** of an option measures the dollar price change in the price of the option for a 1% change in the expected price volatility. That is,

$$\text{kappa} = \frac{\text{change in option price}}{\text{1\% change in expected price volatility}}$$

Duration of an Option

The modified duration of an option measures the price sensitivity of the option to changes in interest rates. The modified duration of an option can be shown to be equal to

$$\text{modified duration for an option} = \text{modified duration of underlying instrument} \times$$
$$\text{delta} \times \frac{\text{price of underlying instrument}}{\text{price of option}}$$

As expected, the modified duration of an option depends on the modified duration of the underlying bond. It also depends on the price responsiveness of the option to a change in the underlying instrument, as measured by the option's delta. The leverage created by a position in an option comes from the last ratio in the formula. The higher the price of the underlying instrument relative to the price of the option, the greater the leverage (i.e., the more exposure to interest rates for a given dollar investment).

It is the interaction of all three factors that affects the modified duration of an option. For example, a deep-out-of-the-money option offers higher leverage than a deep-in-the-money option, but the delta of the former is less than that of the latter.

Because the delta of a call option is positive, the modified duration of an interest rate call option will be positive. Thus, when interest rates decline, the value of an interest rate call option will rise. A put option, however, has a delta that is negative. Thus, the modified duration is negative. Consequently, when interest rates rise, the value of a put option rises.

HEDGE STRATEGIES

Hedge strategies involve taking a position in an option and a position in the underlying bond in such a way that changes in the value of one position will offset any unfavorable price (interest rate) movement in the other position. We discuss two popular hedge strategies here: (1) the protective put buying strategy, and (2) the covered call writing strategy. In this section we demonstrate these two strategies using futures options. The exercise is worthwhile because it shows how complicated hedging with futures options is and the key parameters involved in the process. We also compare the outcome of hedging with futures and hedging with futures options.[9]

Hedging Long-Term Bonds with Puts on Futures

Investors often want to hedge their bond positions against a possible increase in interest rates. Buying puts on futures is one of the easiest ways to purchase protection against rising rates. To illustrate this strategy, we can use the same utility bond example that we used in Chapter 26 to demonstrate how to hedge with Treasury bond futures. In that example, an investor held 11 3/4% bonds of 2023 and used futures to lock in a sale price for those bonds on a futures delivery date. Now we want to show how the hedger could have used futures options instead of futures to protect against rising rates.

---

[9]The illustrations in this section are taken from Chapter 10 of Pitts and Fabozzi, *Interest Rate Futures and Options*.

In the example (summarized at the top of Exhibit 27-16) rates were already fairly high; the hedged bonds were selling at a yield of 12.40%, the Treasury 7 5/8% of 2007 (the cheapest to deliver issue at the time) were at 11.50%. For simplicity, we assumed that this yield spread would remain at 90 basis points. In terms of a yield regression, this would be equivalent to a regression in which the beta equals 1.0 and the intercept term is 0.90%.

The hedger must determine the minimum price that she wants to establish for the hedged bonds. In our illustration it is assumed that the minimum price is 87.668. This is equivalent to saying that the hedger wants to establish a strike price for a put option on the hedged bonds of 87.668. But the hedger is not buying a put option on the utility bonds. She is buying a put option on a Treasury bond futures contract. Therefore, the hedger must determine the strike price for a put option on a Treasury bond futures contract that is equivalent to a strike price of 87.668 for the utility bonds.

EXHIBIT 27-16   Hedging a Nondeliverable Bond to a Delivery Date with Puts on Futures

Instrument to be hedged: $11\frac{3}{4}$ % of 4/19/23
Hedge ratio: 1.24
Strike price for puts on futures: 66-0
Target minimum price for hedged bonds: 87.203
Put option price per contract: $375

Actual Sale Price of Hedged Bonds	Futures Price[a]	Value of 124 Put Options[b]	Cost of 124 Put Options	Effective Sale Price[c]
$ 7,600,000	56.511	$1,176,636	$46,500	$ 8,730,136
7,800,000	58.144	974,144	46,500	8,727,644
8,000,000	59.773	772,148	46,500	8,725,648
8,200,000	61.401	570,276	46,500	8,723,776
8,400,000	63.030	368,280	46,500	8,721,780
8,600,000	64.649	167,524	46,500	8,721,024
8,800,000	66.271	0	46,500	8,753,500
9,000,000	67.888	0	46,500	8,953,500
9,200,000	69.497	0	46,500	9,153,500
9,400,000	71.100	0	46,500	9,353,500
9,600,000	72.705	0	46,500	9,553,500
9,800,000	74.299	0	46,500	9,753,500
10,000,000	75.892	0	46,500	9,953,500
10,200,000	77.473	0	46,500	10,153,500
10,400,000	79.052	0	46,500	10,353,500
10,600,000	80.625	0	46,500	10,553,500
10,800,000	82.188	0	46,500	10,753,500
11,000,000	83.746	0	46,500	10,953,500
11,200,000	85.303	0	46,500	11,153,500

[a]These numbers are approximate because futures trade in even 32nds.
[b]From $124 \times \$1,000 \times \text{Max}[(66 - \text{futures price}), 0]$.
[c]Does not include transaction costs or the financing of the options position.

This can be done with the help of Exhibit 27-17. We begin at the top left-hand box of the exhibit. Because the minimum price is 87.668 for the utility bonds, this means that the hedger is attempting to establish a maximum yield of 13.41%. This is found from the relationship between price and yield: Given a price of 87.668 for the utility bond, this is equivalent to a yield of 13.41%. (This gets us to the lower left-hand box in Exhibit 27-17.) From our assumption that the spread between the utility bonds and the cheapest-to-deliver issue is a constant 90 basis points, setting a maximum yield of 13.41% for the utility bond is equivalent to setting a maximum yield of 12.51% for the cheapest-to-deliver issue. (Now we are at the lower box in the middle column of Exhibit 27-17.) Given the yield of 12.51% for the cheapest-to-deliver issue, the minimum price can be determined (the top box in the middle column of the figure). A 12.51% yield for the Treasury 7 5/8% of 2007 (the cheapest-to-deliver issue at the time) is 63.756. The corresponding futures price is found by dividing the price of the cheapest-to-deliver by the conversion factor. This gets us to the box in the right-hand column of Exhibit 27-17. Because the conversion factor is 0.9660, the futures price is about 66 (63.7567 divided by 0.9660). This means that a strike price of 66 for a put option on a Treasury bond futures contract is roughly equivalent to a put option on the utility bonds with a strike price of 87.668.

The foregoing steps are always necessary to obtain the appropriate strike price on a put futures option. The process is not complicated. It involves simply (1) the relationship between price and yield, (2) the assumed relationship between the yield spread between the hedged bonds and the cheapest-to-deliver issue, and (3) the conversion factor for the cheapest-to-deliver issue. As with hedging employing futures illustrated earlier in Chapter 26, the success of the hedging strategy will depend on (1) whether the cheapest-to-deliver issue changes, and (2) the yield spread between the hedged bonds and the cheapest-to-deliver issue.

The hedge ratio is determined using equation (26.12) of Chapter 26 because we will assume a constant yield spread between the security to be hedged and the

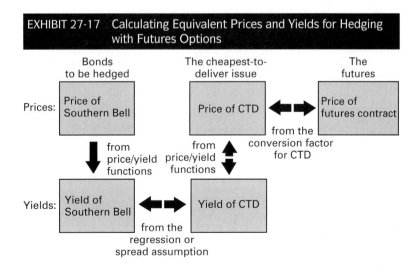

EXHIBIT 27-17 Calculating Equivalent Prices and Yields for Hedging with Futures Options

cheapest-to-deliver issue. For increased accuracy, we calculate the price values of a basis point at the option expiration date (assumed to be June 28, 1985) and at the yields corresponding to the futures strike price of 66 (12.51% for the cheapest-to-deliver issue and 13.41% for the hedged bonds). The respective price values of a basis point are 0.065214 and 0.050969. This results in a hedge ratio of 1.236 for the options hedge, or 1.24 with rounding.

To create a table for the protective put hedge, we can use some of the numbers from Exhibit 26-4 of Chapter 26. Everything will be the same except the last two columns. For the put option hedge we have to insert the value of the 124 futures put options in place of the 124 futures contracts in the next-to-last column. This is easy because the value of each option at expiration is just the strike price of the futures option (66) minus the futures price (or zero if that difference is negative), all multiplied by $1,000. The effective sale price for the hedged bonds is then just the actual market price for the hedged bonds, plus the value of the options at expiration, minus the cost of the options.

Suppose that the price of the put futures option with a strike price of 66 is 24. An option price of 24 means 24/64 of 1% of par value, or $375. With a total of 124 options, the cost of the protection would have been $46,500 (124 × $375, not including financing costs and commissions). This cost, together with the final value of the options, is combined with the actual sale price of the hedged bonds to arrive at the effective sale price for the hedged bonds. These final prices are shown in the last column of Exhibit 27-16. This effective sale price is never less than 87.203. This equals the price of the hedged bonds equivalent to the futures strike price of 66 (i.e., 87.668), minus the cost of the puts (i.e., 0.4650 = 1.24 × 24/64). This minimum effective sale price is something that can be calculated before the hedge is ever initiated. (As prices decline, the effective sale price actually exceeds the projected effective minimum sale price of 87.203 by a small amount. This is due only to rounding and the fact that the hedge ratio is left unaltered, although the relative price values of a basis point that go into the hedge ratio calculation change as yields change.) As prices increase, however, the effective sale price of the hedged bonds increases as well; unlike the futures hedge shown in Exhibit 26-4, the options hedge using puts protects the investor if rates rise but allows the investor to profit if rates fall.

Covered Call Writing with Futures Options

Unlike the protective put strategy, covered call writing is not entered into with the sole purpose of protecting a portfolio against rising rates. The covered call writer, believing that the market will not trade much higher or much lower than its present level, sells out of the money calls against an existing bond portfolio. The sale of the calls brings in premium income that provides partial protection in case rates increase. The premium received does not, of course, provide the kind of protection that a long put position provides, but it does provide some additional income that can be used to offset declining prices. If, on the other hand, rates fall, portfolio appreciation is limited because the short call position constitutes a liability for the seller, and this liability increases as rates go down. Consequently, there is limited upside potential for the covered call writer. Of course, this is not so bad if prices are essentially going nowhere; the added income from the sale of options is obtained without sacrificing any gains.

To see how covered call writing with futures options works for the bond used in the protective put example, we construct a table much as we did before. With futures selling around 71-24 on the hedge initiation date, a sale of a 78 call option on futures might be appropriate. As before, it is assumed that the hedged bond will remain at a 90 basis point spread off the cheapest-to-deliver Treasury bond, the 7 5/8% of 2007. We also assume for simplicity that the price of the 78 calls is 24/64. The number of options contracts sold will be the same, namely 124 contracts for $10 million face value of underlying bonds. Exhibit 27-18 shows the results of the covered call writing strategy given these assumptions.

To calculate the effective sale price of the bonds in the covered call writing strategy, the premium received from the sale of calls is added to the actual sale price of the bonds, and the liability associated with the short call position is subtracted from the actual sale price. The liability associated with each call is the futures price minus the strike price of 78 (or zero if this difference is negative), all multiplied by $1,000. The middle column in the table is just this value multiplied by 124, the number of options sold.

EXHIBIT 27-18 Hedging a Nondeliverable Bond to a Delivery Date with Calls on Futures

Instrument to be hedged: $11\frac{3}{4}$ % of 4/19/23
Hedge ratio: 1.24
Strike price for calls on futures: 78-0
Expected maximum price for hedged bonds: 103.131
Call option price per contract: $375

Actual Sale Price of Hedged Bonds	Futures Price[a]	Liability of 124 Call Options[b]	Premium from 124 Call Options	Effective Sale Price[c]
$ 7,600,000	56.511	0	$46,500	$ 7,646,500
7,800,000	58.144	0	46,500	7,846,500
8,000,000	59.773	0	46,500	8,046,500
8,200,000	61.401	0	46,500	8,246,500
8,400,000	63.030	0	46,500	8,446,500
8,600,000	64.649	0	46,500	8,646,500
8,800,000	66.271	0	46,500	8,846,500
9,000,000	67.888	0	46,500	9,046,500
9,200,000	69.497	0	46,500	9,246,500
9,400,000	71.100	0	46,500	9,446,500
9,600,000	72.705	0	46,500	9,646,500
9,800,000	74.299	0	46,500	9,846,500
10,000,000	75.892	0	46,500	10,046,500
10,200,000	77.473	0	46,500	10,246,500
10,400,000	79.052	130,448	46,500	10,316,052
10,600,000	80.625	325,500	46,500	10,321,000
10,800,000	82.188	519,312	46,500	10,327,188
11,000,000	83.746	712,504	46,500	10,333,996
11,200,000	85.303	905,572	46,500	10,340,928

[a]These numbers are approximate because futures trade in even 32nds.
[b]From $124 \times \$1,000 \times \text{Max}[(\text{futures price} - 76), 0]$.
[c]Does not include transaction costs or the financing of the options position.

Just as the minimum effective sale price could be calculated beforehand for the protective put strategy, the maximum effective sale price can be calculated beforehand for the covered call writing strategy. The maximum effective sale price will be the price of the hedged security corresponding to the strike price of the option sold, plus the premium received. In this case the strike price on the futures call option was 76. A futures price of 76 corresponds to a price of 75.348 (from 76 times the conversion factor), and a corresponding yield of 10.536% for the cheapest-to-deliver bond, the 7 5/8% of 2007. The equivalent yield for the hedged bond is 90 basis points higher, or 11.436%, for a corresponding price of 102.666. Adding on the premium received, 0.465 point, the final maximum effective sale price will be about 103.131. As Exhibit 27-18 shows, if the hedged bond does trade at 90 basis points over the cheapest-to-deliver issue as assumed, the maximum effective sale price for the hedged bond is, in fact, slightly over 103. The discrepancies shown in the table are due to rounding and the fact that the position is not adjusted even though the relative price values of a basis point change as yields change.

Comparing Alternative Strategies

In Chapter 26 and this chapter we reviewed three basic hedging strategies for hedging a bond position: (1) hedging with futures, (2) hedging with out-of-the-money protective puts, and (3) covered call writing with out-of-the-money calls. Similar but opposite strategies exist for those whose risks are that rates will decrease. As might be expected, there is no "best" strategy. Each strategy has advantages and disadvantages, and we never get something for nothing. To get anything of value, something else of value must be forfeited.

To make a choice among strategies, it helps to lay the alternatives side by side. Using the futures and futures options examples from this chapter, Exhibit 27-19 shows the final values of the portfolio for the various alternatives. It is easy to see from Exhibit 27-19 that if one alternative is superior to another alternative at one level of rates, it will be inferior at some other level of rates.

Consequently, we cannot conclude that one strategy is the best strategy. The manager who makes the strategy decision makes a choice among probability distributions, not usually among specific outcomes. Except for the perfect hedge, there is always some range of possible final values of the portfolio. Of course, exactly what that range is, and the probabilities associated with each possible outcome, is a matter of opinion.

SUMMARY

An option grants the buyer of the option the right either to buy (in the case of a call option) or to sell (in the case of a put option) the underlying asset to the seller (writer) of the option at a stated price called the strike (exercise) price by a stated date called the expiration date. The price that the option buyer pays to the writer of the option is called the option price or option premium. An American option allows the option buyer to exercise the option at any time up to and including the expiration date; a European option may be exercised only at the expiration date.

Interest-rate options include options on fixed-income securities and options on interest-rate futures contracts. The latter, more commonly called futures options, are the preferred vehicle for implementing investment strategies. Because of the difficulties of

EXHIBIT 27-19   Alternative Hedging Strategies Compared

Actual Sale Price of Bonds	Effective Sale Price with Futures Hedge	Effective Sale Price with Protective Puts	Effective Sale Price with Covered Calls
$ 7,600,000	$9,272,636	$ 8,730,136	$ 7,646,500
7,800,000	9,270,144	8,727,644	7,846,500
8,000,000	9,268,148	8,725,648	8,046,500
8,200,000	9,266,276	8,723,776	8,246,500
8,400,000	9,264,280	8,721,780	8,446,500
8,600,000	9,263,524	8,721,024	8,646,500
8,800,000	9,262,396	8,753,500	8,846,500
9,000,000	9,261,888	8,953,500	9,046,500
9,200,000	9,262,372	9,153,500	9,246,500
9,400,000	9,263,600	9,353,500	9,446,500
9,600,000	9,264,580	9,553,500	9,646,500
9,800,000	9,266,924	9,753,500	9,846,500
10,000,000	9,269,392	9,953,500	10,046,500
10,200,000	9,273,348	10,153,500	10,246,500
10,400,000	9,277,552	10,353,500	10,316,052
10,600,000	9,282,500	10,553,500	10,321,000
10,800,000	9,288,688	10,753,500	10,327,188
11,000,000	9,295,496	10,953,500	10,333,996
11,200,000	9,302,428	11,153,500	10,340,928

hedging particular bond issues or pass-through securities, many institutions find over-the-counter options more useful; these contracts can be customized to meet specific investment goals.

The buyer of an option cannot realize a loss greater than the option price and has all the upside potential. By contrast, the maximum gain that the writer (seller) of an option can realize is the option price; the writer is exposed to all the downside risk.

The option price consists of two components: the intrinsic value and the time value. The intrinsic value is the economic value of the option if it is exercised immediately (except that if there is no positive economic value that will result from exercising immediately, the intrinsic value is zero). The time value is the amount by which the option price exceeds the intrinsic value. Six factors influence the option price: (1) the current price of the underlying bond, (2) the strike price of the option, (3) the time remaining to the expiration of the option, (4) the expected price volatility of the underlying bond (i.e., expected interest-rate volatility), (5) the short-term risk-free interest rate over the life of the option, and (6) coupon payments.

An option pricing model determines the theoretical or fair value of an option. There are option pricing models for options on bonds (i.e., options on physicals) and options on bond futures. The two models used to value options on bonds are the Black–Scholes option pricing model and the arbitrage-free binomial option pricing model. The limitations of the former when applied to options on bonds are that it fails to incorporate the yield curve in the model and does not recognize that there is a maximum price that a bond can reach. The most common model to value an option on a bond futures contract is the Black model. The two popular strategies using options are protective put buying and covered call writing.

Questions

1. An investor owns a call option on bond X with a strike price of 100. The coupon rate on bond X is 9% and has 10 years to maturity. The call option expires today at a time when bond X is selling to yield 8%. Should the investor exercise the call option?

2. When the buyer of a put option on a futures contract exercises, explain the resulting position for the buyer and the writer.

3. An investor wants to protect against a rise in the market yield on a Treasury bond. Should the investor purchase a put option or a call option to obtain protection?

4. What is the intrinsic value and time value of a call option on bond W given the following information?

   strike price of call option = 97
   current price of bond W = 102
   call option price = 9

5. "There's no real difference between options and futures. Both are hedging tools, and both are derivative products. It's just that with options you have to pay an option premium, whereas futures require no upfront payment except for a 'good faith' margin. I can't understand why anyone would use options." Do you agree with this statement?

6. What arguments would be given by those who feel that the Black–Scholes model does not apply in pricing interest-rate options?

7. Here are some excerpts from an article titled "It's Boom Time for Bond Options as Interest-Rate Hedges Bloom," published in the November 8, 1990, issue of the *Wall Street Journal*:
   a. "The threat of a large interest-rate swing in either direction is driving people to options to hedge their portfolios of long-term Treasury bonds and medium-term Treasury notes," said Steven Northern, who manages fixed-income mutual funds for Massachusetts Financial Services Company in Boston. Why would a large interest rate swing in either direction encourage people to hedge?
   b. "If the market moves against an option purchaser, the option expires worthless, and all the investor has lost is the relatively low purchase price, or 'premium,' of the option." Comment on the accuracy of this statement.
   c. "Futures contracts also can be used to hedge portfolios, but they cost more, and there isn't any limit on the amount of losses they could produce before an investor bails out." Comment on the accuracy of this statement.
   d. "Mr. Northern said Massachusetts Financial has been trading actively in bond and note put options. 'The concept is simple,' he said. 'If you're concerned about interest rates but don't want to alter the nature of what you own in a fixed-income portfolio, you can just buy puts.'" Why might put options be a preferable means of altering the nature of a fixed-income portfolio?

8. What are the differences between an option on a bond and an option on a bond futures contract?

9. What is the motivation for the purchase of an over-the-counter option?

10. Does it make sense for an investor who wants to speculate on interest-rate movements to purchase an over-the-counter option?

11. "I don't understand how money managers can calculate the duration of an interest-rate option. Don't they mean the amount of time remaining to the expiration date?" Respond to this question.

12. a. What factors affect the modified duration of an interest-rate option?
    b. A deep-in-the-money option always provides a higher modified duration for an option than a deep-out-of-the-money option. Comment.

c. The modified duration of all options is positive. Is this statement correct?

13. How is the implied volatility of an option determined?

14. What are the delta and gamma of an option?

15. Explain why the writer of an option would prefer an option with a high theta (all other factors equal).

16. In implementing a protective put buying strategy, explain the trade-off between the cost of the strategy and the strike price selected.

17. Here is an excerpt from an article titled "Dominguez Barry Looks at Covered Calls," appearing in the July 20, 1992, issue of *Derivatives Week*, p. 7:

SBC Dominguez Barry Funds Management in Sydney, with A$5.5 billion under management, is considering writing covered calls on its Australian bond portfolio to take advantage of very high implied volatilities, according to Carl Hanich, portfolio manager. The implied price volatility on at-the-money calls is 9.8%, as high as Hanich can ever remember. . . .

In response to rising volatility, Hanich is thinking about selling calls with a strike of 8.5%, generating premium income. "I'd be happy to lose bonds at 8.5%, given our market's at 8.87% now," he said.

Explain the strategy that Hanich is considering.

18. Determine the price of a European call option on a 6.5% four-year Treasury bond with a strike price of 100.25 and two years to expiration assuming: (1) the arbitrage-free binomial interest-rate tree shown in Exhibit 27-A (based on a 10% volatility assumption), and (2) the price of the Treasury bond two years from now shown at each node.

19. Determine the price of a European put option on a 6.5% four-year Treasury bond with a strike price of 100.25 and two years to expiration assuming the same information as in Exhibit 27-A.

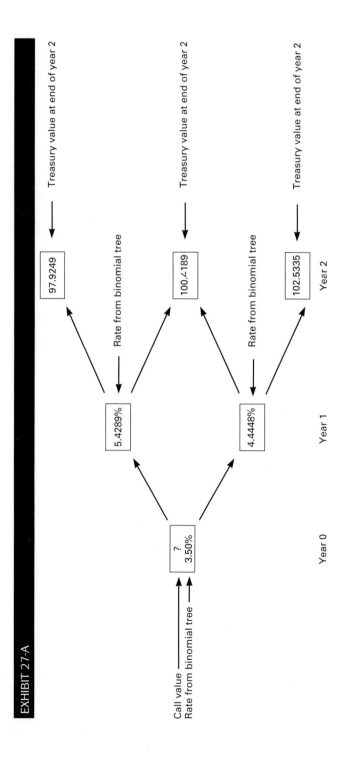

EXHIBIT 27-A

Call value
Rate from binomial tree

?
3.50%

5.4289%

4.4448%

Rate from binomial tree

Rate from binomial tree

97.9249

100.4189

102.5335

Treasury value at end of year 2

Treasury value at end of year 2

Treasury value at end of year 2

Year 0

Year 1

Year 2

28

INTEREST-RATE SWAPS AND AGREEMENTS

After reading this chapter you will understand:

■ what an interest-rate swap is

■ the relationship between an interest-rate swap and forward contracts

■ how interest-rate swap terms are quoted in the market

■ how the swap rate is calculated

■ how the value of a swap is determined

■ the primary determinants of the swap rate

■ how a swap can be used by institutional investors for asset/liability management

■ how a structured note is created using an interest-rate swap

■ what a swaption is and how it can be used by institutional investors

■ what a rate cap and floor are, and how these agreements can be used by institutional investors

■ the relationship between a cap and floor and options

■ how to value caps and floors

■ how an interest-rate collar can be created

In Chapters 26 and 27 we discussed how interest-rate futures and options can be used to control interest-rate risk. There are other contracts useful for controlling such risk that commercial banks and investment banks can customize for their clients. These include (1) interest-rate swaps and options on swaps, and (2) interest-rate caps and floors and options on these agreements. These contracts are relatively new. In this chapter we review each of them and explain how they can be used by institutional investors.

683

INTEREST-RATE SWAPS

In an **interest-rate swap**, two parties (called **counterparties**) agree to exchange periodic interest payments. The dollar amount of the interest payments exchanged is based on a predetermined dollar principal, which is called the **notional principal amount**. The dollar amount that each counterparty pays to the other is the agreed-upon periodic interest rate times the notional principal amount. The only dollars that are exchanged between the parties are the interest payments, not the notional principal amount. In the most common type of swap, one party agrees to pay the other party fixed-interest payments at designated dates for the life of the contract. This party is referred to as the **fixed-rate payer**. The other party, who agrees to make interest rate payments that float with some reference rate, is referred to as the **floating-rate payer**. The frequency with which the interest rate that the floating-rate payer must pay is called the **reset frequency**.

The reference rates that have been used for the floating rate in an interest-rate swap are those on various money market instruments: Treasury bills, the London Interbank Offered Rate, commercial paper, banker's acceptances, certificates of deposit, the federal funds rate, and the prime rate. The most common is the London Interbank Offered Rate (LIBOR). LIBOR is the rate at which prime banks offer to pay on Eurodollar deposits available to other prime banks for a given maturity. Basically, it is viewed as the global cost of bank borrowing. There is not just one rate but a rate for different maturities. For example, there is a one-month LIBOR, three-month LIBOR, and six-month LIBOR.

To illustrate an interest-rate swap, suppose that for the next five years party X agrees to pay party Y 10% per year, while party Y agrees to pay party X six-month LIBOR (the reference rate). Party X is a fixed-rate payer/floating-rate receiver, while party Y is a floating-rate payer/fixed-rate receiver. Assume that the notional principal amount is $50 million and that payments are exchanged every six months for the next five years. This means that every six months, party X (the fixed-rate payer/floating-rate receiver) will pay party Y $2.5 million (10% times $50 million divided by 2). The amount that party Y (the floating-rate payer/fixed-rate receiver) will pay party X will be six-month LIBOR times $50 million divided by 2. If six-month LIBOR is 7%, party Y will pay party X $1.75 million (7% times $50 million divided by 2). Note that we divide by two because one-half year's interest is being paid.

Later we will illustrate how market participants can use an interest-rate swap to alter the cash flow character of assets or liabilities from a fixed-rate basis to a floating-rate basis, or vice versa.

Entering into a Swap and Counterparty Risk

Interest-rate swaps are over-the-counter instruments. This means that they are not traded on an exchange. An institutional investor wishing to enter into a swap transaction can do so through either a securities firm or a commercial bank that transacts in swaps.[1] These entities can do one of the following. First, they can arrange or broker a

---

[1] Don't get confused here about the role of commercial banks. A bank can use a swap in its asset/liability management or a bank can transact (buy and sell) swaps to clients to generate fee income. It is in the later sense that we are discussing the role of a commercial bank in the swap market here.

swap between two parties that want to enter into an interest-rate swap. In this case, the securities firm or commercial bank is acting in a brokerage capacity.

The second way in which a securities firm or commercial bank can get an institutional investor into a swap position is by taking the other side of the swap. This means that the securities firm or the commercial bank is a dealer rather than a broker in the transaction. Acting as a dealer, the securities firm or the commercial bank must hedge its swap position in the same way that it hedges its position in other securities that it holds. Also it means that the dealer (which we refer to as a **swap dealer**) is the counterparty to the transaction. Goldman, Sachs, for example, is a swap dealer. If an institutional investor entered into a swap with Goldman, Sachs, the institutional investor will look to Goldman, Sachs to satisfy the obligations of the swap; similarly, Goldman, Sachs looks to the institutional investor to fulfill its obligations as set forth in the swap. Today, swaps are typically transacted using a swap dealer.

The risks that the two parties take on when they enter into a swap is that the other party will fail to fulfill its obligations as set forth in the swap agreement. That is, each party faces default risk. The default risk in a swap agreement is called **counterparty risk**. In fact, counterparty risk is more general than the default risk for only a swap agreement. In any agreement between two parties that must perform according to the terms of a contract, counterparty risk is the risk that the other party will default. With futures and exchange-traded options, the counterparty risk is the risk that the clearinghouse established to guarantee performance of the contracts will default. Market participants view this risk as small. In contrast, counterparty risk in a swap can be significant.

Because of counterparty risk, not all securities firms and commercial banks can be swap dealers. Several securities firms have actually established subsidiaries that are separately capitalized so that they have a high credit rating, which permits them to enter into swap transactions as a dealer. Thus, it is imperative to keep in mind that any party who enters into a swap is subject to counterparty risk.

Interpreting a Swap Position

There are two ways that a swap position can be interpreted: (1) as a package of forward/futures contracts, and (2) as a package of cash flows from buying and selling cash market instruments.

Package of Forward Contracts

Consider the hypothetical interest-rate swap described earlier to illustrate a swap. Let's look at party X's position. Party X has agreed to pay 10% and receive six-month LIBOR. More specifically, assuming a $50 million notional principal amount, X has agreed to buy a commodity called six-month LIBOR for $2.5 million. This is effectively a six-month forward contract in which X agrees to pay $2.5 million in exchange for delivery of six-month LIBOR. If interest rates increase to 11%, the price of that commodity (six-month LIBOR) is higher, resulting in a gain for the fixed-rate payer, who is effectively long a six-month forward contract on six-month LIBOR. The floating-rate payer is effectively short a six-month forward contract on six-month LIBOR. There is therefore an implicit forward contract corresponding to each exchange date.

Consequently, interest-rate swaps can be viewed as a package of more basic interest-rate control tools, such as forwards. The pricing of an interest-rate swap will then depend on the price of a package of forward contracts with the same settlement dates in which the underlying for the forward contract is the same index.

Although an interest-rate swap may be nothing more than a package of forward contracts, it is not a redundant contract, for several reasons. First, maturities for forward or futures contracts do not extend out as far as those of an interest-rate swap; an interest-rate swap with a term of 15 years or longer can be obtained. Second, an interest-rate swap is a more transactionally efficient instrument. By this we mean that in one transaction an entity can effectively establish a payoff equivalent to a package of forward contracts. The forward contracts would each have to be negotiated separately. Third, the interest-rate swap market has grown in liquidity since its establishment in 1981; interest-rate swaps now provide more liquidity than forward contracts, particularly long-dated (i.e., long-term) forward contracts.

Package of Cash Market Instruments

To understand why a swap can also be interpreted as a package of cash market instruments, consider an investor who enters into the following transaction:

- Buy $50 million par of a five-year floating-rate bond that pays six-month LIBOR every six months.
- Finance the purchase by borrowing $50 million for five years on terms requiring 10% annual interest rate paid every six months.

The cash flows for this transaction are shown in Exhibit 28-1. The second column of the table shows the cash flow from purchasing the five-year floating-rate bond. There is a $50 million cash outlay and then 10 cash inflows. The amount of the cash inflows is uncertain because they depend on future LIBOR. The next column shows the cash flow from borrowing $50 million on a fixed-rate basis. The last column shows the net cash flow from the entire transaction. As the last column indicates, there is no initial cash flow (no cash inflow or cash outlay). In all 10 six-month periods, the net position results in a cash inflow of LIBOR and a cash outlay of $2.5 million. This net position, however, is identical to the position of a fixed-rate payer/floating-rate receiver.

It can be seen from the net cash flow in Exhibit 28-1 that a fixed-rate payer has a cash market position that is equivalent to a long position in a floating-rate bond and a short position in a fixed-rate bond—the short position being the equivalent of borrowing by issuing a fixed-rate bond.

What about the position of a floating-rate payer? It can be easily demonstrated that the position of a floating-rate payer is equivalent to purchasing a fixed-rate bond and financing that purchase at a floating rate, where the floating rate is the reference interest rate for the swap. That is, the position of a floating-rate payer is equivalent to a long position in a fixed-rate bond and a short position in a floating-rate bond.

Terminology, Conventions, and Market Quotes

Here we review some of the terminology used in the swaps market and explain how swaps are quoted. The date that the counterparties commit to the swap is called the **trade date**. The date that the swap begins accruing interest is called the **effective date**, and the date that the swap stops accruing interest is called the **maturity date**.

EXHIBIT 28-1   Cash Flow for the Purchase of a Five-Year Floating-Rate Bond Financed by Borrowing on a Fixed-Rate Basis

Transaction: Purchase for $50 million a five-year floating-rate bond: floating rate = LIBOR, semiannual pay; borrow $50 million for five years: fixed rate = 10%, semiannual payments

| Six-Month Period | Cash Flow (millions of dollars) from: | | |
	Floating-Rate Bond[a]	Borrowing Cost	Net
0	$-\$50$	$+\$50.0$	$\$0$
1	$+ (\text{LIBOR}_1/2) \times 50$	-2.5	$+ (\text{LIBOR}_1/2) \times 50 - 2.5$
2	$+ (\text{LIBOR}_2/2) \times 50$	-2.5	$+ (\text{LIBOR}_2/2) \times 50 - 2.5$
3	$+ (\text{LIBOR}_3/2) \times 50$	-2.5	$+ (\text{LIBOR}_3/2) \times 50 - 2.5$
4	$+ (\text{LIBOR}_4/2) \times 50$	-2.5	$+ (\text{LIBOR}_4/2) \times 50 - 2.5$
5	$+ (\text{LIBOR}_5/2) \times 50$	-2.5	$- (\text{LIBOR}_5/2) \times 50 - 2.5$
6	$+ (\text{LIBOR}_6/2) \times 50$	-2.5	$+ (\text{LIBOR}_6/2) \times 50 - 2.5$
7	$+ (\text{LIBOR}_7/2) \times 50$	-2.5	$+ (\text{LIBOR}_7/2) \times 50 - 2.5$
8	$+ (\text{LIBOR}_8/2) \times 50$	-2.5	$+ (\text{LIBOR}_8/2) \times 50 - 2.5$
9	$+ (\text{LIBOR}_9/2) \times 50$	-2.5	$+ (\text{LIBOR}_9/2) \times 50 - 2.5$
10	$+ (\text{LIBOR}_{10}/2) \times 50 + 50$	-52.5	$+ (\text{LIBOR}_{10}/2) \times 50 - 2.5$

[a]The subscript for LIBOR indicates the six-month LIBOR as per the terms of the floating-rate bond at time t.

Although our illustrations assume that the timing of the cash flows for both the fixed-rate payer and floating-rate payer will be the same, this is rarely the case in a swap. In fact, an agreement may call for the fixed-rate payer to make payments annually but the floating-rate payer to make payments more frequently (semiannually or quarterly). Also, the way in which interest accrues on each leg of the transaction differs because there are several day-count conventions in the fixed-income markets.

The terminology used to describe the position of a party in the swap markets combines cash market jargon and futures jargon, given that a swap position can be interpreted as a position in a package of cash market instruments or a package of futures/forward positions. As we have said, the counterparty to an interest-rate swap is either a fixed-rate payer or floating-rate payer. These positions can be described in the following ways:

Fixed-Rate Payer	Floating-Rate Payer
Pays fixed rate in the swap	Pays floating rate in the swap
Receives floating in the swap	Receives fixed in the swap
Has bought a swap	Has sold a swap
Is long a swap	Is short a swap
Is short the bond market	Is long the bond market

The first two expressions above that describe the position of a fixed-rate payer and floating-rate payer are self-explanatory. To understand why the fixed-rate payer is viewed as short the bond market and the floating-rate payer is viewed as long the bond market, consider what happens when interest rates change. Those who borrow on a fixed-rate basis will benefit if interest rates rise because they have locked in a lower interest rate, but those who have a short bond position will also benefit if interest rates rise. Thus, a fixed-rate payer can be said to be short the bond market. A floating-rate payer benefits if interest rates fall. A long position in a bond also benefits if interest rates fall, so terminology describing a floating-rate payer as long the bond market is not surprising.

Another way to describe the position of the counterparties to a swap is in terms of our discussion of the interpretation of a swap as a package of cash market instruments. That is:

Fixed-rate payer: A position that is exposed to the price sensitivities of a longer-term liability and a floating-rate bond.

Floating-rate payer: A position that is exposed to the price sensitivities of a fixed-rate bond and a floating-rate liability.

The convention that has evolved for quoting swaps levels is that a swap dealer sets the floating rate equal to the index and then quotes the fixed rate that will apply. To illustrate this convention, consider a 10-year swap offered by a dealer to market participants shown in Exhibit 28-2.

The offer price that the dealer would quote the fixed-rate payer would be to pay 8.85% and receive LIBOR "flat" ("flat" meaning with no spread to LIBOR). The bid price that the dealer would quote the floating-rate payer would be to pay LIBOR flat and receive 8.75%. The bid-offer spread is 10 basis points.

The fixed rate is some spread above the Treasury yield curve with the same term to maturity as the swap. In our illustration, suppose that the 10-year Treasury yield is 8.35%. Then the offer price that the dealer would quote to the fixed-rate payer is the 10-year Treasury rate plus 50 basis points versus receiving LIBOR flat. For the floating-rate payer, the bid price quoted would be LIBOR flat versus the 10-year Treasury rate plus 40 basis points. The dealer would quote such a swap as 40–50, meaning that the dealer is willing to enter into a swap to receive LIBOR and pay a fixed rate equal to the 10-year Treasury rate plus 40 basis points, and it would be willing to enter into a swap to pay LIBOR and receive a fixed rate equal to the 10-year Treasury rate plus 50 basis points. The difference between the Treasury rate paid and received is the bid-offer spread.

EXHIBIT 28-2	Meaning of a "40–50" Quote for a 10-Year Swap When Treasuries Yield 8.35% (Bid-Offer Spread of 10 Basis Points)	
	Floating-Rate Payer	Fixed-Rate Payer
Pay	Floating rate of six-month LIBOR	Fixed rate of 8.85%
Receive	Fixed rate of 8.75%	Floating rate of six-month LIBOR

Calculation of the Swap Rate

At the initiation of an interest-rate swap, the counterparties are agreeing to exchange future interest-rate payments, and no upfront payments by either party are made. This means that the swap terms must be such that the present value of the cash flows for the payments to be made by the counterparties must be equal. This is equivalent to saying that the present value of the cash flows of payments to be received by the counterparties must be equal. The equivalence of the cash flows is the principle in calculating the swap rate.

For the fixed-rate side, when a swap rate is determined, the payments of the fixed-rate payer are known. However, the floating-rate payments are not known because they depend on the value of the reference rate at the reset dates. For a LIBOR-based swap, the Eurodollar CD futures contract (discussed in Chapter 26) can be used to establish the forward (or future) rate for three-month LIBOR. Given the cash flow based on the forward rate for three-month LIBOR, the swap rate is the interest rate that will make the present value of the payments on the fixed-rate side equal to the payments on the floating-rate side.

The next question is: What interest rate should be used to discount the payments? As explained in Chapter 5, the appropriate rate to discount any cash flow is the theoretical spot rate. Each cash flow should be discounted at a unique discount rate. Where do we get the theoretical spot rates? Recall from Chapter 5 that spot rates can be obtained from forward rates. It is the same three-month LIBOR forward rates derived from the Eurodollar CD futures contract that can be used to obtain the theoretical spot rates.

We will illustrate the procedure with an example.[2] Consider the following terms for our swap.

- a swap starts today, January 1 of year 1 (swap settlement date)
- the floating-rate payments are made quarterly based on actual/360
- the reference rate is three-month LIBOR
- the notional amount of the swap is $100 million
- the term of the swap is three years

The quarterly floating-rate payments are based on an actual/360-day count convention. This convention means that 360 days are assumed in a year and that in computing the interest for the quarter the actual number of days in the quarter is used. The floating-rate payment is set at the beginning of the quarter but paid at the end of the quarter—that is, the floating-rate payments are made in arrears.

Suppose that today three-month LIBOR is 4.05%. Let's look at what the fixed-rate payer will receive on March 31 of year 1—the date when the first quarterly swap payment is made. There is no uncertainty about what the floating-rate payment will be. In general, the floating-rate payment is determined as follows:

$$\text{notional amount} \times (\text{three-month LIBOR}) \times \frac{\text{no. of days in period}}{360}$$

---

[2]This illustration is taken from Frank J. Fabozzi, *Fixed Income Analysis for the Chartered Financial Analyst Program* (New Hope, PA: Frank J. Fabozzi Associates, 2000), pp. 609–621.

In our illustration, assuming a non-leap year, the number of days from January 1 of year 1 to March 31 of year 1 (the first quarter) is 90. If three-month LIBOR is 4.05%, then the fixed-rate payer will receive a floating-rate payment on March 31 of year 1 equal to

$$\$100,000,000 \times 0.0405 \times \frac{90}{360} = \$1,012,500$$

Now the difficulty is in determining the floating-rate payment after the first quarterly payment. That is, for the three-year swap there will be 12 quarterly floating-rate payments. So, while the first quarterly payment is known, the next 11 are not. However, there is a way to hedge the next 11 floating-rate payments by using a futures contract. Specifically, the futures contract used to hedge the future floating-rate payments in a swap whose reference rate is three-month LIBOR is the Eurodollar CD futures contract. We discussed this contract in Chapter 26, and we will show how these floating-rate payments are computed using this contract.

We begin with the next quarterly payment—from April 1 of year 1 to June 30 of year 1. This quarter has 91 days. The floating-rate payment will be determined by three-month LIBOR on April 1 of year 1 and paid on June 30 of year 1. There is a three-month Eurodollar CD futures contract for settlement on June 30 of year 1. That futures contract provides the rate that can be locked in for three-month LIBOR on April 1 of year 1. For example, if the futures price for the three-month Eurodollar CD futures contract that settles on June 30 of year 1 is 95.85, then as just explained, the three-month Eurodollar futures rate is 4.15%. We will refer to that rate for three-month LIBOR as the forward rate. Therefore, if the fixed-rate payer bought 100 of these three-month Eurodollar CD futures contracts on January 1 of year 1 (the inception of the swap) that settle on June 30 of year 1, then the payment that will be locked in for the quarter (April 1 to June 30 of year 1) is

$$\$100,000,000 \times 0.0415 \times \frac{91}{360} = \$1,049,028$$

(Note that each futures contract is for $1 million and hence 100 contracts have a notional amount of $100 million.) Similarly, the Eurodollar CD futures contract can be used to lock in a floating-rate payment for each of the next 10 quarters. It is important to emphasize that the reference rate at the beginning of period t determines the floating rate that will be paid for the period. However, the floating-rate payment is not made until the end of period t.

Exhibit 28-3 shows this for the three-year swap. Shown in Column (1) is when the quarter begins and in Column (2) when the quarter ends. The payment will be received at the end of the first quarter (March 31 of year 1) and is $1,012,500. That is the known floating-rate payment as explained earlier. It is the only payment that is known. The information used to compute the first payment is in Column (4), which shows the current three-month LIBOR (4.05%). The payment is shown in the last column, Column (8).

Notice that Column (7) numbers the quarters from 1 through 12. Look at the heading for Column (7). It identifies each quarter in terms of the end of the quarter. This is important because we will eventually be discounting the payments (cash flows). We

EXHIBIT 28-3   Floating Cash Flow Based on Initial LIBOR and Eurodollar CD Futures

(1)	(2)	(3)	(4)	(5)	(6)	(7)	(8)
Quarter Starts	Quarter Ends	Number of Days in Quarter	Current 3-Month LIBOR	Euro-dollar Futures Price	Futures Rate	Period = End of Quarter	Floating Cash Flow at End of Quarter
Jan 1 year 1	Mar 31 year 1	90	4.05%			1	1,012,500
Apr 1 year 1	June 30 year 1	91		95.85	4.15%	2	1,049,028
July 1 year 1	Sept 30 year 1	92		95.45	4.55%	3	1,162,778
Oct 1 year 1	Dec 31 year 1	92		95.28	4.72%	4	1,206,222
Jan 1 year 2	Mar 31 year 2	90		95.10	4.90%	5	1,225,000
Apr 1 year 2	June 30 year 2	91		94.97	5.03%	6	1,271,472
July 1 year 2	Sept 30 year 2	92		94.85	5.15%	7	1,316,111
Oct 1 year 2	Dec 31 year 2	92		94.75	5.25%	8	1,341,667
Jan 1 year 3	Mar 31 year 3	90		94.60	5.40%	9	1,350,000
Apr 1 year 3	June 30 year 3	91		94.50	5.50%	10	1,390,278
July 1 year 3	Sept 30 year 3	92		94.35	5.65%	11	1,443,889
Oct 1 year 3	Dec 31 year 3	92		94.24	5.76%	12	1,472,000

must take care to understand when each payment is to be exchanged in order to properly discount. So, the first payment of $1,012,500 will be received at the end of quarter 1. When we refer to the time period for any payment, the reference is to the end of the quarter. So, the fifth payment of $1,225,000 would be identified as the payment for period 5, where period 5 means that it will be exchanged at the end of the fifth quarter.

Now let's turn to the fixed-rate payments. The swap will specify the frequency of settlement for these payments. The frequency need not be the same as the floating-rate payments. For example, in the three-year swap we have been using to illustrate the calculation of the floating-rate payments, the frequency is quarterly. The frequency of the fixed-rate payments could be semiannual rather than quarterly.

In our illustration we will assume that the frequency of settlement is quarterly for the fixed-rate payments, the same as with the floating-rate payments. The day count convention is the same as for the floating-rate payment, actual/360. The equation for determining the dollar amount of the fixed-rate payment for the period is

$$\text{notional amount} \times \text{swap rate} \times \frac{\text{no. of days in period}}{360}$$

It is the same equation as for determining the floating-rate payment except that the swap rate is used instead of the reference rate (three-month LIBOR in our illustration).

For example, suppose that the swap rate is 4.98% and the quarter has 90 days. Then the fixed-rate payment for the quarter is

$$\$100,000,000 \times 0.0498 \times \frac{90}{360} = \$1,245,000$$

Exhibit 28-4 shows the fixed-rate payments based on an assumed swap rate of 4.9875%. (Later we will see how the swap rate is determined.) The first three columns of the exhibit show the same information as in Exhibit 28-3—the beginning and end of the quarter and the number of days in the quarter. Column (4) simply uses the notation for the period. That is, period 1 means the end of the first quarter, period 2 means the end of the second quarter, and so on. Column (5) shows the fixed-rate payments for each period based on a swap rate of 4.9875%.

Given the swap payments, we can demonstrate how to compute the swap rate. At the initiation of an interest-rate swap, the counterparties are agreeing to exchange future payments and no upfront payments by either party are made. This means that the swap terms must be such that the present value of the payments to be made by the counterparties must be at least equal to the present value of the payments that will be received. In fact, to eliminate arbitrage opportunities, the present value of the payments made by a party will be equal to the present value of the payments received by that same party. The equivalence (or no arbitrage) of the present value of the payments is the key principle in calculating the swap rate.

Since we will have to calculate the present value of the payments, let's show how this is done. As explained earlier, we must be careful about how we compute the present value of payments. In particular, we must carefully specify (1) the timing of the payment and (2) the interest rates that should be used to discount the payments. We already addressed the first issue.

In constructing the exhibit for the payments, we indicated that the payments are at the end of the quarter. So, we denoted the timing of the payments with respect to the end of the quarter.

EXHIBIT 28-4 Fixed-Rate Payments Assuming a Swap Rate of 4.9875%				
Quarter Starts	Quarter Ends	Days in Quarter	Period = End of Quarter	Fixed-Rate Payment if Swap Rate Is Assumed to Be 4.9875%
Jan 1 year 1	Mar 31 year 1	90	1	1,246,875
Apr 1 year 1	June 30 year 1	91	2	1,260,729
July 1 year 1	Sept 30 year 1	92	3	1,274,583
Oct 1 year 1	Dec 31 year 1	92	4	1,274,583
Jan 1 year 2	Mar 31 year 2	90	5	1,246,875
Apr 1 year 2	June 30 year 2	91	6	1,260,729
July 1 year 2	Sept 30 year 2	92	7	1,274,583
Oct 1 year 2	Dec 31 year 2	92	8	1,274,583
Jan 1 year 3	Mar 31 year 3	90	9	1,246,875
Apr 1 year 3	June 30 year 3	91	10	1,260,729
July 1 year 3	Sept 30 year 3	92	11	1,274,583
Oct 1 year 3	Dec 31 year 3	92	12	1,274,583

What interest rates should be used for discounting? Every cash flow should be discounted at its own discount rate using a spot rate. So, if we discounted a cash flow of $1 using the spot rate for period t, the present value would be

$$\text{present value of \$1 to be received in } t \text{ period} = \frac{\$1}{(1 + \text{spot rate for period } t)^t}$$

As explained in Chapter 5, forward rates are derived from spot rates so that if we discounted a cash flow using forward rates rather than a spot rate, we would come up with the same value. That is, the present value of $1 to be received in period t, can be rewritten as

$$\text{present value of \$1 to be received in period } t =$$

$$\frac{\$1}{(1 + \text{forward rate for period 1})(1 + \text{forward rate for period 2}) \dots (1 + \text{forward rate for period } t)}$$

We will refer to the present value of $1 to be received in period t as the **forward discount factor**. In our calculations involving swaps, we will compute the forward discount factor for a period using the forward rates. These are the same forward rates that are used to compute the floating-rate payments—those obtained from the Eurodollar CD futures contract. We must make just one more adjustment. We must adjust the forward rates used in the formula for the number of days in the period (i.e., the quarter in our illustrations) in the same way that we made this adjustment to obtain the payments. Specifically, the forward rate for a period, which we will refer to as the **period forward rate**, is computed using the following equation:

$$\text{period forward rate} = \text{annual forward rate} \times \frac{\text{days in period}}{360}$$

For example, look at Exhibit 28-3. The annual forward rate for period 4 is 4.72%. The period forward rate for period 4 is

$$\text{period forward rate} = 4.72\% \times \frac{92}{360} = 1.2062\%$$

Column (5) in Exhibit 28-5 shows the annual forward rate for all 12 periods (reproduced from Exhibit 28-3) and Column (6) shows the period forward rate for all 12 periods. Note that the period forward rate for period 1 is 90/360 of 4.05%, which is 90/360 of the known rate for three-month LIBOR.

Also shown in Exhibit 28-5 is the forward discount factor for all 12 periods. These values are shown in the last column. Let's show how the forward discount factor is computed for periods 1, 2, and 3. For period 1, the forward discount factor is

$$\text{forward discount factor} = \frac{\$1}{1.010125} = 0.9899764$$

EXHIBIT 28-5   Calculating the Forward Discount

(1)	(2)	(3)	(4)	(5)	(6)	(7)
		Number of	Period =		Period	Forward
Quarter	Quarter	Days in	End of	Forward	Forward	Discount
Starts	Ends	Quarter	Quarter	Rate	Rate	Factor
Jan 1 year 1	Mar 31 year 1	90	1	4.05%	1.0125%	0.9899764
Apr 1 year 1	June 30 year 1	91	2	4.15%	1.0490%	0.9796991
July 1 year 1	Sept 30 year 1	92	3	4.55%	1.1628%	0.9684383
Oct 1 year 1	Dec 31 year 1	92	4	4.72%	1.2062%	0.9568960
Jan 1 year 2	Mar 31 year 2	90	5	4.90%	1.2250%	0.9453159
Apr 1 year 2	June 30 year 2	91	6	5.03%	1.2715%	0.9334474
July 1 year 2	Sept 30 year 2	92	7	5.15%	1.3161%	0.9213218
Oct 1 year 2	Dec 31 year 2	92	8	5.25%	1.3417%	0.9091244
Jan 1 year 3	Mar 31 year 3	90	9	5.40%	1.3500%	0.8970147
Apr 1 year 3	June 30 year 3	91	10	5.50%	1.3903%	0.8847147
July 1 ycar 3	Scpt 30 ycar 3	92	11	5.65%	1.4439%	0.8721222
Oct 1 year 3	Dec 31 year 3	92	12	5.76%	1.4720%	0.8594708

For period 2,

$$\text{forward discount factor} = \frac{\$1}{1.010125 \times 1.010490} = 0.9796991$$

For period 3,

$$\text{forward discount factor} = \frac{\$1}{1.010125 \times 1.010490 \times 1.011628} = 0.9684383$$

Given the floating-rate payment for a period and the forward discount factor for the period, the present value of the payment can be computed. For example, from Exhibit 28-3 we see that the floating-rate payment for period 4 is $1,206,222. From Exhibit 28-6, the forward discount factor for period 4 is 0.9568960. Therefore, the present value of the payment is

present value of period 4 payment = $1,206,222 × 0.9568960 = $1,154,229

Exhibit 28-6 shows the present value for each payment. The total present value of the 12 floating-rate payments is $14,052,917. Thus, the present value of the payments that the fixed-rate payer will receive is $14,052,917, and the present value of the payments that the fixed-rate receiver will make is $14,052,917.

The fixed-rate payer will require that the present value of the fixed-rate payments that must be made based on the swap rate not exceed the $14,052,917 to be received from the floating-rate payments. The fixed-rate receiver will require that the present value of the fixed-rate payments received be at least as great as the $14,052,917 that must be paid. This means that both parties will require a present value for the fixed-rate payments to be $14,052,917. If that is the case, the present value of the fixed-rate

EXHIBIT 28-6   Present Value of the Floating-Rate Payments

(1)	(2)	(3)	(4)	(5)	(6)
Quarter Starts	Quarter Ends	Period = End of Quarter	Forward Discount Factor	Floating Cash Flow at End of Quarter	PV of Cash Flow
Jan 1 year 1	Mar 31 year 1	1	0.9899764	1,012,500	1,002,351
Apr 1 year 1	June 30 year 1	2	0.9796991	1,049,028	1,027,732
July 1 year 1	Sept 30 year 1	3	0.9684383	1,162,778	1,126,079
Oct 1 year 1	Dec 31 year 1	4	0.9568960	1,206,222	1,154,229
Jan 1 year 2	Mar 31 year 2	5	0.9453159	1,225,000	1,158,012
Apr 1 year 2	June 30 year 2	6	0.9334474	1,271,472	1,186,852
July 1 year 2	Sept 30 year 2	7	0.9213218	1,316,111	1,212,562
Oct 1 year 2	Dec 31 year 2	8	0.9091244	1,341,667	1,219,742
Jan 1 year 3	Mar 31 year 3	9	0.8970147	1,350,000	1,210,970
Apr 1 year 3	June 30 year 3	10	0.8847147	1,390,278	1,229,999
July 1 year 3	Sept 30 year 3	11	0.8721222	1,443,889	1,259,248
Oct 1 year 3	Dec 31 year 3	12	0.8594708	1,472,000	1,265,141
				Total	14,052,917

payments is equal to the present value of the floating-rate payments and therefore the value of the swap is zero for both parties at the inception of the swap. The interest rates that should be used to compute the present value of the fixed-rate payments are the same interest rates as those used to discount the floating-rate payments.

Beginning with the basic relationship for no arbitrage to exist:

PV of floating-rate payments = PV of fixed-rate payments

The formula for the swap rate is derived as follows. The fixed-rate payment for period t is equal to

$$\text{notional amount} \times \text{swap rate} \times \frac{\text{days in period } t}{360}$$

The present value of the fixed-rate payment for period t is found by multiplying the previous expression by the forward discount factor for period t. That is, the present value of the fixed-rate payment for period t is equal to

$$\text{notional amount} \times \text{swap rate} \times \frac{\text{days in period } t}{360} \times \text{forward discount factor for period } t$$

Summing up the present value of the fixed-rate payment for each period gives the present value of the fixed-rate payments. Letting N be the number of periods in the swap, the present value of the fixed-rate payments can be expressed as

$$\text{swap rate} \times \sum_{t=1}^{N} \text{notional amount} \times \frac{\text{days in period } t}{360} \times \text{forward discount factor for period } t$$

The condition for no arbitrage is that the present value of the fixed-rate payments as given by the preceding expression is equal to the present value of the floating-rate payments. That is,

$$\text{swap rate} \times \sum_{t=1}^{N} \text{notional amount} \times \frac{\text{days in period } t}{360} \times \text{forward discount factor for period } t$$
$$= \text{present value of floating-rate payments}$$

Solving for the swap rate gives

$$\text{swap rate} = \frac{\text{present value of floating-rate payments}}{\sum_{t=1}^{N} \text{notional amount} \times \dfrac{\text{days in period } t}{360} \times \text{forward discount factor for period } t}$$

Note that all the values to compute the swap rate are known.

Let's apply the formula to determine the swap rate for our three-year swap. Exhibit 28-7 shows the calculation of the denominator of the formula. The forward discount factor for each period shown in Column (5) is obtained from Column (4) of Exhibit 28-6. The sum of the last column in Exhibit 28-7 shows that the denominator of the swap rate formula is $281,764,281. We know from Exhibit 28-6 that the present value of the floating-rate payments is $14,052,917. Therefore, the swap rate is

$$\text{swap rate} = \frac{\$14,052,917}{\$281,764,281} = 0.049875 = 4.9875\%$$

EXHIBIT 28-7   Calculating the Denominator for the Swap Rate Formula

(1)	(2)	(3)	(4)	(5)	(6)	(7)
Quarter Starts	Quarter Ends	Number of Days in Quarter	Period = End of Quarter	Forward Discount Factor	Days/360 × Notional	Forward Discount Factor × Days/360
Jan 1 year 1	Mar 31 year 1	90	1	0.98997649	0.25000000	24,749,412
Apr 1 year 1	June 30 year 1	91	2	0.97969917	0.25277778	24,764,618
July 1 year 1	Sept 30 year 1	92	3	0.96843839	0.25555556	24,748,981
Oct 1 year 1	Dec 31 year 1	92	4	0.95689609	0.25555556	24,454,011
Jan 1 year 2	Mar 31 year 2	90	5	0.94531597	0.25000000	23,632,899
Apr 1 year 2	June 30 year 2	91	6	0.93344745	0.25277778	23,595,477
July 1 year 2	Sept 30 year 2	92	7	0.92132183	0.25555556	23,544,891
Oct 1 year 2	Dec 31 year 2	92	8	0.90912441	0.25555556	23,233,179
Jan 1 year 3	Mar 31 year 3	90	9	0.89701471	0.25000000	22,425,368
Apr 1 year 3	June 30 year 3	91	10	0.88471472	0.25277778	22,363,622
July 1 year 3	Sept 30 year 3	92	11	0.87212224	0.25555556	22,287,568
Oct 1 year 3	Dec 31 year 3	92	12	0.85947083	0.25555556	21,964,255
					Total	281,764,281

Given the swap rate, the swap spread can be determined. For example, since this is a three-year swap, the convention is to use the three-year on-the-run Treasury rate as the benchmark. If the yield on that issue is 4.5875%, the swap spread is 40 basis points (4.9875% − 4.5875%).

The calculation of the swap rate for all swaps follows the same principle: equating the present value of the fixed-rate payments to that of the floating-rate payments.

Valuing a Swap

Once the swap transaction is completed, changes in market interest rates will change the payments of the floating-rate side of the swap. The value of an interest rate swap is the difference between the present value of the payments of the two sides of the swap. The three-month LIBOR forward rates from the current Eurodollar CD futures contracts are used to (1) calculate the floating-rate payments and (2) determine the discount factors at which to calculate the present value of the payments.

To illustrate this, consider the three-year swap used to demonstrate how to calculate the swap rate. Suppose that one year later, interest rates change as shown in Columns (4) and (6) in Exhibit 28-8. Column (4) shows the current three-month LIBOR. In Column (5) are the Eurodollar CD futures prices for each period. These rates are used to compute the forward rates in Column (6). Note that the interest rates have increased one year later since the rates in Exhibit 28-8 are greater than those in Exhibit 28-3. As in Exhibit 28-3, the current three-month LIBOR and the forward rates are used to compute the floating-rate payments. These payments are shown in Column (8) of Exhibit 28-8.

In Exhibit 28-9, the forward discount factor is computed for each period. The calculation is the same as in Exhibit 28-5 to obtain the forward discount factor for each period. The forward discount factor for each period is shown in the last column of Exhibit 28-9.

EXHIBIT 28-8   Rates and Floating-Rate Payments One Year Later if Rates Increase

(1)	(2)	(3)	(4)	(5)	(6)	(7)	(8)
Quarter Starts	Quarter Ends	Number of Days in Quarter	Current 3-Month LIBOR	Euro-dollar Futures Price	Futures Rate	Period = End of Quarter	Floating Cash Flow at End of Quarter
Jan 1 year 2	Mar 31 year 2	90	5.25%			1	1,312,500
Apr 1 year 2	June 30 year 2	91		94.27	5.73%	2	1,448,417
July 1 year 2	Sept 30 year 2	92		94.22	5.78%	3	1,477,111
Oct 1 year 2	Dec 31 year 2	92		94.00	6.00%	4	1,533,333
Jan 1 year 3	Mar 31 year 3	90		93.85	6.15%	5	1,537,500
Apr 1 year 3	June 30 year 3	91		93.75	6.25%	6	1,579,861
July 1 year 3	Sept 30 year 3	92		93.54	6.46%	7	1,650,889
Oct 1 year 3	Dec 31 year 3	92		93.25	6.75%	8	1,725,000

EXHIBIT 28-9   Period Forward Rates and Forward Discount Factors One Year Later if Rates Increase

(1)	(2)	(3)	(4)	(5)	(6)	(7)
Quarter Starts	Quarter Ends	Number of Days in Quarter	Period = End of Quarter	Futures Rate	Period Forward Rate	Forward Discount Factor
Jan 1 year 2	Mar 31 year 2	90	1	5.25%	1.3125%	0.98704503
Apr 1 year 2	June 30 year 2	91	2	5.73%	1.4484%	0.97295263
July 1 year 2	Sept 30 year 2	92	3	5.78%	1.4771%	0.95879023
Oct 1 year 2	Dec 31 year 2	92	4	6.00%	1.5333%	0.94431080
Jan 1 year 3	Mar 31 year 3	90	5	6.15%	1.5375%	0.93001186
Apr 1 year 3	June 30 year 3	91	6	6.25%	1.5799%	0.91554749
July 1 year 3	Sept 30 year 3	92	7	6.46%	1.6509%	0.90067829
Oct 1 year 3	Dec 31 year 3	92	8	6.75%	1.7250%	0.88540505

In Exhibit 28-10 the forward discount factor (from Exhibit 28-9) and the floating-rate payments (from Exhibit 28-8) are shown. The fixed-rate payments need not be recomputed. They are the payments shown in Exhibit 28-4 for the swap rate of 4.9875%, and they are reproduced in Exhibit 28-10. Now the two payment streams

EXHIBIT 28-10   Valuing the Swap One Year Later if Rates Increase

(1)	(2)	(3)	(4)	(5)	(6)	(7)
Quarter Starts	Quarter Ends	Forward Discount Factor	Floating Cash Flow at End of Quarter	PV of Floating Cash Flow	Fixed Cash Flow at End of Quarter	PV of Fixed Cash Flow
Jan 1 year 2	Mar 31 year 2	0.98704503	1,312,500	1,295,497	1,246,875	1,230,722
Apr 1 year 2	June 30 year 2	0.97295263	1,448,417	1,409,241	1,260,729	1,226,630
July 1 year 2	Sept 30 year 2	0.95879023	1,477,111	1,416,240	1,274,583	1,222,058
Oct 1 year 2	Dec 31 year 2	0.94431080	1,533,333	1,447,943	1,274,583	1,203,603
Jan 1 year 3	Mar 31 year 3	0.93001186	1,537,500	1,429,893	1,246,875	1,159,609
Apr 1 year 3	June 30 year 3	0.91554749	1,579,861	1,446,438	1,260,729	1,154,257
July 1 year 3	Sept 30 year 3	0.90067829	1,650,889	1,486,920	1,274,583	1,147,990
Oct 1 year 3	Dec 31 year 3	0.88540505	1,725,000	1,527,324	1,274,583	1,128,523
			Total	11,459,496		9,473,392

Summary	Fixed-Rate Payer	Fixed-Rate Receiver
PV of payments received	11,459,496	9,473,392
PV of payments made	9,473,392	11,459,496
Value of swap	1,986,104	−1,986,104

must be discounted using the new forward discount factors. As shown at the bottom of Exhibit 28-10, the two present values are as follows:

Present value of floating-rate payments	$11,459,496
Present value of fixed-rate payments	$ 9,473,392

The two present values are not equal; therefore, for one party the value of the swap increased while for the other party the value of the swap decreased. Let's look at which party gained and which party lost.

The fixed-rate payer will receive the floating-rate payments. These payments have a present value of $11,459,496. The present value of the payments that must be made by the fixed-rate payer is $9,473,392. Thus, the swap has a positive value for the fixed-rate payer equal to the difference in the two present values of $1,986,104. This is the value of the swap to the fixed-rate payer. Notice that when interest rates increase (as they did in the illustration analyzed), the fixed-rate payer benefits because the value of the swap increases.

In contrast, the fixed-rate receiver must make payments with a present value of $11,459,496 but will only receive fixed-rate payments with a present value equal to $9,473,392. Thus, the value of the swap for the fixed-rate receiver is –$1,986,104. The fixed-rate receiver is adversely affected by a rise in interest rates because it results in a decline in the value of a swap.

The same valuation principle applies to more complicated swaps that we describe later in this section.

Duration of a Swap

As with any fixed-income contract, the value of a swap will change as interest rates change. Dollar duration is a measure of the interest-rate sensitivity of a fixed-income contract. From the perspective of the party who pays floating and receives fixed, the interest-rate swap position can be viewed as follows: long a fixed-rate bond + short a floating-rate bond. This means that the dollar duration of an interest-rate swap from the perspective of a floating-rate payer is simply the difference between the dollar duration of the two bond positions that make up the swap; that is,

$$\text{dollar duration of a swap} = \text{dollar duration of a fixed-rate bond}$$
$$- \text{dollar duration of a floating-rate bond}$$

Most of the dollar price sensitivity of a swap due to interest-rate changes will result from the dollar duration of the fixed-rate bond because the dollar duration of the floating-rate bond will be small. The closer the swap is to the date that the coupon rate is reset, the smaller the dollar duration of a floating-rate bond.

Application of a Swap to Asset/Liability Management

So far we have merely described an interest-rate swap and looked at its characteristics. Here we illustrate how they can be used in asset/liability management. Other types of interest-rate swaps have been developed that go beyond the generic or "plain vanilla" swap described, and we describe these later.

An interest-rate swap can be used to alter the cash flow characteristics of an institution's assets so as to provide a better match between assets and liabilities. The two institutions we use for illustration are a commercial bank and a life insurance company.

Suppose that a bank has a portfolio consisting of five-year term commercial loans with a fixed interest rate. The principal value of the portfolio is $50 million, and the interest rate on all the loans in the portfolio is 10%. The loans are interest-only loans; interest is paid semiannually, and the principal is paid at the end of five years. That is, assuming no default on the loans, the cash flow from the loan portfolio is $2.5 million every six months for the next five years and $50 million at the end of five years. To fund its loan portfolio, assume that the bank is relying on the issuance of six-month certificates of deposit. The interest rate that the bank plans to pay on its six-month CDs is six-month LIBOR plus 40 basis points.

The risk that the bank faces is that six-month LIBOR will be 9.6% or greater. To understand why, remember that the bank is earning 10% annually on its commercial loan portfolio. If six-month LIBOR is 9.6%, it will have to pay 9.6% plus 40 basis points, or 10%, to depositors for six-month funds and there will be no spread income. Worse, if six-month LIBOR rises above 9.6%, there will be a loss; that is, the cost of funds will exceed the interest rate earned on the loan portfolio. The bank's objective is to lock in a spread over the cost of its funds.

The other party in the interest-rate-swap illustration is a life insurance company that has committed itself to pay a 9% rate for the next five years on a guaranteed investment contract (GIC) it has issued. The amount of the GIC is $50 million. Suppose that the life insurance company has the opportunity to invest $50 million in what it considers an attractive five-year floating-rate instrument in a private placement transaction. The interest rate on this instrument is six-month LIBOR plus 160 basis points. The coupon rate is set every six months. The risk that the life insurance company faces in this instance is that six-month LIBOR will fall so that the company will not earn enough to realize a spread over the 9% rate that it has guaranteed to the GIC holders. If six-month LIBOR falls to 7.4% or less, no spread income will be generated. To understand why, suppose that six-month LIBOR at the date the floating-rate instrument resets its coupon is 7.4%. Then the coupon rate for the next six months will be 9% (7.4% plus 160 basis points). Because the life insurance company has agreed to pay 9% on the GIC policy, there will be no spread income. Should six-month LIBOR fall below 7.4%, there will be a loss.

We can summarize the asset/liability problems of the bank and the life insurance company as follows.

BANK:

1. Has lent long term and borrowed short term.
2. If six-month LIBOR rises, spread income declines.

LIFE INSURANCE COMPANY:

1. Has lent short term and borrowed long term.
2. If six-month LIBOR falls, spread income declines.

Now let's suppose the market has available a five-year interest-rate swap with a national principal amount of $50 million. The swap terms available to the bank are as follows:

1. Every six months the bank will pay 8.45% (annual rate).
2. Every six months the bank will receive LIBOR.

The swap terms available to the insurance company are as follows:

1. Every six months the life insurance company will pay LIBOR.
2. Every six months the life insurance company will receive 8.40%.

What has this interest-rate contract done for the bank and the life insurance company? Consider first the bank. For every six-month period for the life of the swap agreement, the interest-rate spread will be as follows:

Annual Interest Rate Received:	
From commercial loan portfolio	10.00%
From interest-rate swap	six-month LIBOR
Total	10.00% + six-month LIBOR
Annual Interest Rate Paid:	
To CD depositors	six-month LIBOR
On interest-rate swap	8.45%
Total	8.45% + six-month LIBOR
Outcome:	
To be received	10.00% + six-month LIBOR
To be paid	8.45% + six-month LIBOR
Spread income	1.55% or 1.55 basis points

Thus, whatever happens to six-month LIBOR, the bank locks in a spread of 155 basis points.

Now let's look at the effect of the interest-rate swap on the life insurance company:

Annual Interest Rate Received:	
From floating-rate instrument	1.6% + six-month LIBOR
From interest-rate swap	8.40%
Total	10.00% + six-month LIBOR
Annual Interest Rate Paid:	
To GIC policyholders	9.00%
On interest-rate swap	six-month LIBOR
Total	9.00% + six-month LIBOR
Outcome:	
To be received	10.00% + six-month LIBOR
To be paid	9.00% + six-month LIBOR
Spread income	1.0% or 100 basis points

Regardless of what happens to six-month LIBOR, the life insurance company locks in a spread of 100 basis points.

The interest-rate swap has allowed each party to accomplish its asset/liability objective of locking in a spread.[3] It permits the two financial institutions to alter the cash flow characteristics of their assets: from fixed to floating in the case of the bank, and from floating to fixed in the case of the life insurance company. This type of transaction is referred to as an **asset swap**. Another way the bank and the life insurance company could use the swap market would be to change the cash flow nature of their liabilities. Such a swap is called a **liability swap**.

Of course, there are other ways that two such institutions can accomplish the same objectives. The bank might refuse to make fixed-rate commercial loans. However, if borrowers can find someplace else willing to lend on a fixed-rate basis, the bank has lost these customers. The life insurance company might refuse to purchase a floating-rate instrument. But suppose that the terms on a private-placement instrument offered to the life insurance company were more attractive than those available on a comparable credit-risk floating-rate instrument, and that by using the swap market the life insurance company can earn more than it could by investing directly in a five-year fixed-rate bond. For example, suppose that the life insurance company can invest in a comparable credit risk five-year fixed-rate bond with a yield of 9.8%. Assuming that it commits itself to a GIC with a 9% rate, this would result in spread income of 80 basis points, less than the 100-basis-point spread income it achieves by purchasing the floating-rate instrument and entering into the swap.

Consequently, not only can an interest-rate swap be used to change the risk of a transaction by changing the cash flow characteristics of assets or liabilities, but under certain circumstances, it can also be used to enhance returns. Obviously, this depends on the existence of market imperfections.

Creation of Structured Notes Using Swaps

As explained in Chapter 7, corporations can customize medium-term notes for institutional investors who want to make a market play on interest rate, currency, and/or stock market movements. That is, the coupon rate on the issue will be based on the movements of these financial variables. A corporation can do so in such a way that it can still synthetically fix the coupon rate. This can be accomplished by issuing an MTN and entering into a swap simultaneously. MTNs created in this way are called **structured MTNs**.

The following illustration demonstrates how an interest-rate swap can be used to create a structured note in which the coupon rate floats inversely with LIBOR; that is, an inverse floater. As we explained in Chapter 8, an inverse floater can be created from a fixed-rate security by creating a corresponding floater. By using an interest-rate swap, it is not necessary to create the floater.

To see how this can be done using an interest-rate swap, let's assume the following. The Arbour Corporation wants to issue $100 million of a five-year fixed-rate MTN. The firm's banker indicates that the yield it would have to offer is 6.10%. However, it

---

[3] Whether the size of the spread is adequate is not an issue for us in this illustration.

recommends that the corporation issue an inverse-floating-rate MTN and proposes the following two transactions:

Transaction 1: Issue $100 million of a five-year inverse-floating-rate MTN with a coupon payment that resets every six months based on the following formula: 13% – LIBOR.

Transaction 2: Enter into a five-year interest-rate swap with its banker with a notional principal amount of $100 million in which semiannual payments are exchanged as follows:

Arbour Corporation pays LIBOR.

Arbour Corporation receives 7%.

Notice that Arbour Corporation's MTN is an inverse-floating-rate note because as LIBOR increases, the coupon rate decreases. However, although the MTN may have an inverse floating rate, the combination of the two transactions results in a fixed-rate financing for Arbour Corporation, as follows:

Arbour Corporation Receives:	
From its banker for swap	7%
Arbour Corporation Pays:	
To MTN holders	13% – LIBOR
To its banker for swap	LIBOR
Net payments:	(13% – LIBOR) + LIBOR – 7% = 6%

The advantage of this structured MTN is that the issuer was able to obtain a funding cost of 6% rather than 6.1% if it issued a fixed-rate MTN. By using other types of swaps (equity and currency), any type of coupon rate can be created.

Primary Determinants of Swap Spreads

Earlier we provided two interpretations of a swap: (1) a package of futures/forward contracts, and (2) a package of cash market instruments. The swap spread is determined by the same factors that influence the spread over Treasuries on financial instruments (futures/forward contracts or cash) that produce a similar return or funding profile. As we explain subsequently, the key determinant of the swap spread for swaps with maturities of five years or less is the cost of hedging in the Eurodollar CD futures market. For longer maturity swaps, the key determinant of the swap spread is the credit spreads in the corporate bond market.

Given that a swap is a package of futures/forward contracts, the swap spread can be determined by looking for futures/forward contracts with the same risk/return profile. A Eurodollar CD futures contract is a swap where a fixed dollar payment (i.e., the futures price) is exchanged for three-month LIBOR. There are available Eurodollar CD futures contracts that have maturities every three months for five years. A market participant can synthesize a (synthetic) fixed-rate security or a fixed-rate funding vehicle of up to five years by taking a position in a strip of Eurodollar CD futures contracts (i.e., a position in every three-month Eurodollar CD up to the desired maturity date).

For example, consider a financial institution that has fixed-rate assets and floating-rate liabilities. Both the assets and liabilities have a maturity of three years. The interest rate on the liabilities resets every three months based on three-month LIBOR. This financial institution can hedge this mismatched asset/liability position by buying a three-year strip of Eurodollar CD futures contracts. By doing so, the financial institution is receiving LIBOR over the three-year period and paying a fixed dollar amount (i.e., the futures price). The financial institution is now hedged because the assets are fixed rate, and the strip of long Eurodollar CDs futures synthetically creates a fixed-rate funding arrangement. From the fixed dollar amount over the three years, an effective fixed interest rate that the financial institution pays can be calculated. Alternatively, the financial institution can synthetically create a fixed-rate funding arrangement by entering into a three-year swap in which it pays fixed and receives three-month LIBOR. The financial institution will use the vehicle that gives the lowest cost of hedging the mismatched position. This will drive the synthetic fixed rate in the swap market to that available by hedging in the Eurodollar CD futures market.

For swaps with maturities longer than five years, the spread is determined primarily by the credit spreads in the corporate bond market. Because a swap can be interpreted as a package of long and short positions in a fixed-rate bond and a floating-rate bond, it is the credit spreads in those two market sectors that will be the key determinant of the swap spread. Boundary conditions for swap spreads based on prices for fixed-rate and floating-rate corporate bonds can be determined.[4] Several technical factors, such as the relative supply of fixed-rate and floating-rate corporate bonds and the cost to dealers of hedging their inventory position of swaps, influence where between the boundaries the actual swap spread will be.[5]

Development of the Interest-Rate-Swap Market

The interest-rate swap was developed in late 1981. By 1987, the market had grown to more than $500 billion (in terms of notional principal amount). What is behind this rapid growth? As our asset/liability application earlier demonstrated, an interest-rate swap is a quick way for institutional investors to change the nature of assets and liabilities or to exploit any perceived capital market imperfection. The same applies to borrowers such as corporations, sovereigns, and supranationals.

In fact, the initial motivation for the interest-rate-swap market was borrower exploitation of what were perceived to be "credit arbitrage" opportunities because of differences between the quality spread between lower- and higher-rated credits in the U.S. and Eurodollar bond fixed-rate market and the same spread in these two floating-rate markets. Basically, the argument for swaps was based on a well-known economic principle of comparative advantage in international economics. The argument in the case of swaps is that even though a high credit-rated issuer could borrow at a lower

---

[4]These boundary conditions are derived in the appendix to Ellen Evans and Gioia Parente Bales, "What Drives Interest Rate Swap Spreads?" Chapter 13 in Carl R. Beidleman (ed.), *Interest Rate Swaps* (Homewood, IL: Richard D. Irwin, 1991).
[5]For a discussion of these other factors, see Evans and Bales, "What Drives Interest Rate Swap Spreads?" pp. 293–301.

cost in both the fixed- and floating-rate markets (i.e., have an absolute advantage in both), it will have a comparative advantage relative to a lower credit-rated issuer in one of the markets (and a comparative disadvantage in the other). Under these conditions, each borrower could benefit from issuing securities in the market in which it has a comparative advantage and then swapping obligations for the desired type of financing. The swap market was the vehicle for swapping obligations.

Despite arguments that credit arbitrage opportunities are rare in reasonably efficient international capital markets, and that even if they did exist, they would be eliminated quickly by arbitrage, the number of interest-rate-swap transactions has grown substantially. Another explanation is suggested in a May 1984 contribution sponsored by Citicorp that appeared in *Euromoney*:

> The nature of swaps is that they arbitrage market imperfections. As with any arbitrage opportunity, the more it is exploited, the smaller it becomes. . . .
>
> But some of the causes of market imperfections are unlikely to disappear quickly. For example, insurance companies in many countries are constrained to invest mainly in instruments that are domestic in that country. That requirement will tend to favour domestic issuers artificially, and is unlikely to be changed overnight. And even in the world's most liquid markets there are arbitrage opportunities. They are small and exist only briefly. But they exist nevertheless.[6]

As this opinion demonstrates, as early as 1984 it was argued that the difference in quality spreads in the two markets may be attributable to differences in regulations in two countries. Similarly, differences in tax treatment across countries also create market imperfections that can be exploited using swaps. Thus, swaps can be used for regulatory or tax arbitrage.

Rather than relying exclusively on an arbitrage argument, one study suggests that the swaps market grew because it allowed borrowers to raise a type of financing that was not possible prior to the introduction of interest-rate swaps.[7]

Finally, another argument suggested for the growth of the interest-rate-swap market is the increased volatility of interest rates that has led borrowers and lenders to hedge or manage their exposure. Even though risk/return characteristics can be replicated by a package of forward contracts, interest-rate forward contracts are not as liquid as interest-rate swaps—and entering into or liquidating swap transactions has been facilitated by the standardization of documentation published by the International Swap Dealers Association in early 1987.

Role of the Intermediary

The role of the intermediary in an interest-rate swap sheds some light on the evolution of the market. Intermediaries in these transactions have been commercial banks and investment banks that in the early stages of the market sought out end users of swaps.

---

[6]"Swap Financing Techniques: A Citicorp Guide," Special Sponsored Section, *Euromoney*, May 1984, pp. S1–S7.

[7]Marcelle Arak, Arturo Estrella, Laurie Goodman, and Andrew Silver, "Interest Rate Swaps: An Alternative Explanation," *Financial Management*, Summer 1988, pp. 12–18.

That is, they found in their client bases those entities that needed the swap to accomplish a funding or investing objective, and they matched the two entities. In essence, the intermediary in this type of transaction performed the function of a broker.

The only time that the intermediary would take the opposite side of a swap (i.e., would act as a principal) was to balance out the transaction. For example, if an intermediary had two clients that were willing to do a swap but one wanted the notional principal amount to be $100 million and the other wanted it to be $85 million, the intermediary might become the counterparty to the extent of $15 million. That is, the intermediary would warehouse or take a position as a principal to the transaction to make up the $15 million difference between client objectives. To protect itself against an adverse interest-rate movement, the intermediary would hedge its position.

There is another problem in an interest-rate swap that we have yet to address. The parties to swaps have to be concerned that the other party might default on its obligation. Although a default would not mean any principal was lost because the notional principal amount had not been exchanged, it would mean that the objective for which the swap was entered into would be impaired. As the early transactions involved a higher- and a lower-credit-rated entity, the former would be concerned with the potential for default of the latter. To reduce the risk of default, many early swap transactions required that the lower-credit-rated entity obtain a guarantee from a highly rated commercial bank.

As the frequency and the size of the transactions increased, many intermediaries became comfortable with the transactions and became principals instead of acting as brokers. As long as an intermediary had one entity willing to do a swap, the intermediary was willing to be the counterparty. Consequently, interest-rate swaps became part of an intermediary's inventory of product positions. Advances in quantitative techniques and futures products for hedging complex positions such as swaps made the protection of large inventory positions feasible.

Beyond the Plain Vanilla Swap

Thus far we have described the plain vanilla or generic interest-rate swap. Nongeneric or individualized swaps have evolved as a result of the asset/liability needs of borrowers and lenders. These include swaps where the notional principal changes in a predetermined way over the life of the swap and swaps in which both counterparties pay a floating rate. There are complex swap structures such as options on swaps (called **swaptions**) and swaps where the swap does not begin until some future time (called **forward start swaps**). We discuss all of these swaps next.[8] What is important to appreciate is that these swap structures are not just "bells and whistles" added to the plain vanilla swap to make them more complicated, but features that managers have found that they need to control interest-rate risk.

Varying Notional Principal Amount Swaps

In a generic or plain vanilla swap, the notional principal amount does not vary over the life of the swap. Thus, it is sometimes referred to as a **bullet swap**. In contrast, for amortizing, accreting, and roller coaster swaps, the notional principal amount varies over the life of the swap.

---

[8]See Geoffrey Buetow, Jr., and Frank J. Fabozzi, *Valuation of Interest Rate Swaps and Swaptions* (New Hope, PA: Frank J. Fabozzi Associates, 2001).

An **amortizing swap** is one in which the notional principal amount decreases in a predetermined way over the life of the swap. Such a swap would be used where the principal of the asset that is being hedged with the swap amortizes over time. For example, in our illustration of the asset/liability problem faced by the bank, the commercial loans are assumed to pay interest every six months and repay principal only at the end of the loan term. However, what if the commercial loan is a typical term loan; that is, suppose it is a loan that amortizes. Or, suppose that it is a typical mortgage loan that amortizes. In such circumstances, the outstanding principal for the loans would decline and the bank would need a swap where the notional principal amount amortizes in the same way as the loans.

Less common than the amortizing swap are the accreting swap and the roller coaster swap. An **accreting swap** is one in which the notional principal amount increases in a predetermined way over time. In a **roller coaster swap**, the notional principal amount can rise or fall from period to period.

Basis Swaps and Constant Maturity Swaps

The terms of a generic interest-rate swap call for the exchange of fixed- and floating-rate payments. In a **basis swap**, both parties exchange floating-rate payments based on a different reference rate. As an example, assume a commercial bank has a portfolio of loans in which the lending rate is based on the prime rate, but the bank's cost of funds is based on LIBOR. The risk the bank faces is that the spread between the prime rate and LIBOR will change. This is referred to as **basis risk**. The bank can use a basis swap to make floating-rate payments based on the prime rate (because that is the reference rate that determines how much the bank is receiving on the loans) and receive floating-rate payments based on LIBOR (because that is the reference rate that determines the bank's funding cost).

Another popular swap is to have the floating leg tied to a longer-term rate such as the two-year Treasury note rate rather than a money market rate. One of the parties to the swap would pay the two-year Treasury rate, for example, and the counterparty would pay LIBOR. Such a swap is called a **constant maturity swap**. The reference rate for determining the yield on the constant maturity Treasury in a constant maturity swap is typically the Constant Maturity Treasury (CMT) rate published by the Federal Reserve. Consequently, a constant maturity swap tied to the CMT is called a **Constant Maturity Treasury swap**.

Swaptions

There are options on interest-rate swaps. These swap structures are called **swaptions** and grant the option buyer the right to enter into an interest-rate swap at a future date. The time until expiration of the swap, the term of the swap, and the swap rate are specified. The swap rate is the strike rate for the swaption. The swaption has the American-type exercise provision. That is, the option can be exercised only at the option's expiration date.

There are two types of swaptions—a payer swaption and a receiver swaption. A **payer swaption** entitles the option buyer to enter into an interest-rate swap in which the buyer of the option pays a fixed rate and receives a floating rate. For example, suppose that the strike rate is 7%, the term of the swap is three years, and the swaption expires in two years. Also assume that it is an American-type exercise provision. This means that the buyer of this swaption has the right to enter into a three-year interest-rate swap within the next two years in which the buyer pays 7% (the swap rate, which is equal to the strike rate) and receives the reference rate.

In a **receiver swaption** the buyer of the swaption has the right to enter into an interest-rate swap that requires paying a floating rate and receiving a fixed rate. For example, if the strike rate is 6.25%, the swap term is five years, and the option expires in one year, the buyer of this receiver swaption has the right until the option expires in one year (assuming it is an American-type exercise provision) to enter into a four-year interest-rate swap in which the buyer receives a swap rate of 6.25% (i.e., the strike rate) and pays the reference rate.

How is a swaption used? We can see its usefulness in managing interest-rate risk if we return to the bank–insurance company example. The bank makes the fixed-rate payments in the interest-rate swap (10%) using the interest rate it is earning on the commercial loans (10%). Suppose that the commercial loan borrowers default on their obligations. The bank will then not receive from the commercial loans the 10% to make its swap payments. This problem can be addressed at the outset of the initial swap transaction by the bank entering into a swaption that effectively gives it the right to terminate or cancel the swap. That is, the bank will enter into a receiver swaption—receiving fixed of 10% so as to offset the fixed rate it is obligated to pay under the initial swap. In fact, the borrowers do not have to fail for the swap to have an adverse impact on the bank. Suppose the commercial loans can be prepaid. Then, the bank has a similar problem. For example, suppose rates on commercial loans decline to 7% and the borrowers prepay. Then, the bank would be obligated to make the 10% payments under the terms of the swap. With the proceeds received from the prepayment of the commercial loans, the bank may only be able to invest in similar loans at 7%, for example, a rate that is less than the bank's obligations.

Forward Start Swap

A **forward start swap** is a swap wherein the swap does not begin until some future date that is specified in the swap agreement. Thus, there is a beginning date for the swap at some time in the future and a maturity date for the swap. A forward start swap will also specify the swap rate at which the counterparties agree to exchange payments commencing at the start date.

INTEREST-RATE AGREEMENTS (CAPS AND FLOORS)

An **interest-rate agreement** is an agreement between two parties whereby one party, for an upfront premium, agrees to compensate the other at specific time periods if a designated interest rate, called the **reference rate**, is different from a predetermined level. When one party agrees to pay the other when the reference rate exceeds a predetermined level, the agreement is referred to as an **interest-rate cap** or **ceiling**. The agreement is referred to as an **interest-rate floor** when one party agrees to pay the other when the reference rate falls below a predetermined level. The predetermined interest-rate level is called the **strike rate**.

The terms of an interest-rate agreement include

1. The reference rate
2. The strike rate that sets the ceiling or floor
3. The length of the agreement
4. The frequency of settlement
5. The notional principal amount

Suppose that C buys an interest-rate cap from D with terms as follows:

1. The reference rate is six-month LIBOR
2. The strike rate is 8%
3. The agreement is for seven years
4. Settlement is every six months
5. The notional principal amount is $20 million

Under this agreement, every six months for the next seven years, D will pay C whenever six-month LIBOR exceeds 8%. The payment will equal the dollar value of the difference between six-month LIBOR and 8% times the notional principal amount divided by 2. For example, if six months from now six-month LIBOR is 11%, D will pay C 3% (11% minus 8%) times $20 million divided by 2, or $300,000. If six-month LIBOR is 8% or less, D does not have to pay anything to C.

In the case of an interest-rate floor, assume the same terms as those for the interest-rate cap we just illustrated. In this case, if six-month LIBOR is 11%, C receives nothing from D, but if six-month LIBOR is less than 8%, D compensates C for the difference. For example, if six-month LIBOR is 7%, D will pay C $100,000 (8% minus 7% times $20 million divided by 2).

Interest-rate caps and floors can be combined to create an interest-rate collar. This is done by buying an interest-rate cap and selling an interest-rate floor. Some commercial banks and investment banking firms write options on interest-rate agreements for customers. Options on caps are **captions**; options on floors are called **flotions**.

Risk/Return Characteristics

In an interest-rate agreement, the buyer pays an upfront fee, which represents the maximum amount that the buyer can lose and the maximum amount that the writer of the agreement can gain. The only party that is required to perform is the writer of the interest-rate agreement. The buyer of an interest-rate cap benefits if the underlying interest rate rises above the strike rate because the seller (writer) must compensate the buyer. The buyer of an interest rate floor benefits if the interest rate falls below the strike rate, because the seller (writer) must compensate the buyer.

To better understand interest-rate caps and floors, we can look at them as in essence equivalent to a package of interest-rate options. Because the buyer benefits if the interest rate rises above the strike rate, an interest-rate cap is similar to purchasing a package of call options on an interest rate or purchasing a put option on a bond. The seller of an interest-rate cap has effectively sold a package of call options on an interest rate or sold a package of put options on a bond. The buyer of an interest-rate floor benefits from a decline in the interest rate below the strike rate. Therefore, the buyer of an interest-rate floor has effectively bought a package of put options on an interest rate or a package of call options on a bond from the writer of the option.

Once again, a complex contract can be seen to be a package of basic contracts, or options in the case of interest-rate agreements. Captions and flotions can be viewed as options on a package of options.

Valuing Caps and Floors[9]

The arbitrage-free binomial model described in Chapter 17 can also be used to value a cap and a floor. This is because, as previously explained, a cap and a floor are nothing more than a package or strip of options. More specifically, they are a strip of European options on interest rates. Thus, to value a cap, the value of each period's cap, called a **caplet**, is found and all the caplets are then summed. We refer to this approach to valuing a cap as the **caplet method**. (The same approach can be used to value a floor.) Once the caplet method is demonstrated, we'll show an easier way of valuing a cap.

To illustrate the caplet method, we will use the binomial interest-rate tree used in Chapter 17 to value an interest rate option to value a 5.2%, three-year cap with a notional amount of $10 million. The reference rate is the one-year rates in the binomial tree. The payoff for the cap is annual.

There is one wrinkle having to do with the timing of the payments for a cap and floor that requires a modification of the binomial approach presented to value an interest rate option. This is due to the fact that settlement for the typical cap and floor is paid in arrears. As explained elsewhere, this means that the interest rate paid on a financial instrument with this feature is determined at the beginning of the period but paid at the end of the period (i.e., beginning of the next period). We will use Arabic numbers for dates (i.e., Date 0, Date 1, Date 2, and Date 3) and words for years (i.e., Year One, Year Two, and Year Three) to avoid confusion regarding when a payment is determined and when it is made. Exhibit 28-11 shows the binomial interest rate tree with dates and years.

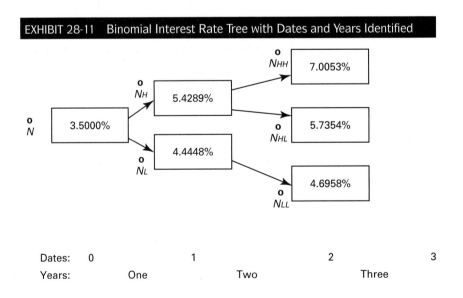

EXHIBIT 28-11   Binomial Interest Rate Tree with Dates and Years Identified

---

[9]The presentation here is based on the framework provided by Professor Donald Smith of Boston University.

Using Exhibit 28-11 we can understand what is meant by payment in arrears. Consider Date 1. There are two interest rates, 4.4448% and 5.4289%. Suppose today, Date 0, that an investor enters into an agreement whereby if a reference rate at Date 1 exceeds 5.2%, the investor will receive at Date 2 the difference between the reference rate and 5.2% multiplied by $10 million; if the reference rate is less than 5.2% nothing is received. This agreement specifies payment in arrears. For example, consider at Date 1 the interest rate (reference rate) of 5.4289%. Then there would be a payoff of

$$(5.4289\% - 5.2000\%) \times \$10,000,000 = \$22,890$$

The payment of $22,890 would be made at Date 2.

With this background, we will first show how to use the caplet method to value the three-year cap.

Caplet Method

Consider first the value of the caplet for Year One, which is shown in Panel a in Exhibit 28-12. At Date 0, the one-year rate is 3.5%. Since it does not exceed the cap rate of 5.2%, the payoff is zero.

We now move on to the Year Two caplet as shown in Panel b in Exhibit 28-12. There are two interest rates at Day 1: 4.4448% and 5.4289%. If the interest rate is 4.4448% on Date 1, there is no payoff because the rate is less than 5.2%. If the interest rate is 5.4289%, there is a payoff as explained earlier. The payoff is $22,890 and will be made at Date 2.

The payoff at Date 2 is either $0 or $22,890. These values have to be discounted back to Date 0. The discounting requires first discounting back to Date 1 and then discounting back to Date 0. At each date, the present values are averaged because of the assumption that both payoffs are equally likely.

What discount rate should be used? The discount rate that should be used is the one at the node at the date where the interest rate is to be discounted back to. For example, the payoff of $22,890 at Date 2 should be discounted at 5.4289% to get the present value at Date 1. The present value is $21,711 (= $22,890/1.054289) and is shown at the node in Panel b. Obviously, the present value of the $0 payoff is $0. The average of these two present values at Date 1 is $10,855.5.

The present value at Date 1 is then discounted back to Date 0 by using 3.5%. The present value is $10,488.41 (= $10,855.5/1.035). The rounded value of $10,488 is shown at Date 0.

Panel c of Exhibit 28-12 shows the valuation of the Year Three caplet. There are three interest rates shown at Date 2: 4.6958%, 5.7354%, and 7.0053%. There is no payoff if the interest rate at Date 2 is 4.6958%. For the other two interest rates, the payoff is:

$$(5.7354\% - 5.2000\%) \times \$10,000,000 = \$53,540$$
$$(7.0053\% - 5.2000\%) \times \$10,000,000 = \$180,530$$

These payoffs are shown at Date 3 because they are paid in arrears. The present value of these two payoffs on Date 2 to be received at Date 3 is:

$$\$53,540/1.057354 = \$50,636$$
$$\$180,530/1.070053 = \$168,711$$

These present values are shown at Date 2.

EXHIBIT 28-12   Value a Cap Using the Caplet Method

a. Value of the Year One Caplet at 5.20%

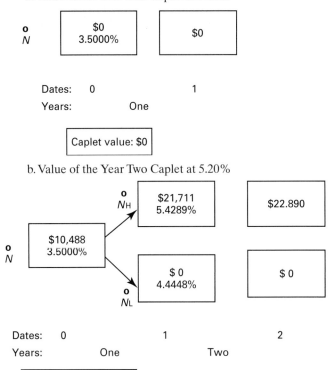

Dates: 0   1

Years: One

Caplet value: $0

b. Value of the Year Two Caplet at 5.20%

	o N$_H$	$21,711 5.4289%		$22.890
o N	$10,488 3.5000%			
	o N$_L$	$ 0 4.4448%		$ 0

Dates: 0   1   2

Years: One   Two

Caplet value: $10,488

c. Value of the Year Three Caplet at 5.20%

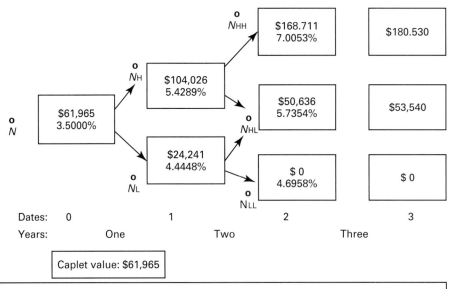

Dates: 0   1   2   3

Years: One   Two   Three

Caplet value: $61,965

Value of cap = $0 + $10,488 + $61,965 = $72,453

Moving backwards to Date 1, we have to average the two values at Date 2 and discount back at the corresponding interest rate. For the lower interest rate at Date 1, 4.4448%, the average value at Date 2 is $25,318 = ($0 + $50,636). The present value at Date 1 is therefore $24,240.56 (= $25,318/1.044448). The rounded value is shown at the node at Date 1. Similarly, the average value for the higher interest rate, 5.4289%, is the average of $50,636 and $168,711, which is $109,673.5. The present value at Date 1, discounting back $109,673.5 at 5.4289%, is $104,026.

The final step is to discount back to Date 0 the values of the two payoffs at Date 1. The average of the two payoffs at Date 1 is $64,134. Discounting at 3.5% gives the value of the Year Three caplet of $61,964.73. The rounded value of $61,965 is shown in Panel c.

The value of the three-year interest rate cap is then the sum of the three caplets; That is, value of cap = value of Year One caplet + value of Year Two caplet + value of Year Three caplet. In our illustration

Value of Year One caplet:	$ 0
Value of Year Two caplet:	$10,488
Value of Year Three caplet:	$61,965
Three-year interest rate cap:	$72,453

Using a Single Binomial Tree to Value a Cap

The valuation of a cap can be done by using a single binomial tree. The procedure is easier only in the sense that the number of times discounting is required is reduced.

The method is shown in Exhibit 28-13. The three values at Date 2 are obtained by simply computing the payoff at Date 3 and discounting back to Date 2. These are the values shown for Date 2 in Panel c of Exhibit 28-12.

Let's look at the higher node at Date 1 (interest rate of 5.4289%). The top number, $104,026, is the present value of the two Date 2 values that branch out from that node. It is computed in the same way as in Panel c in Exhibit 28-12. The number below it, $21,711, is the payoff of the Year Two caplet on Date 1 as calculated in Exhibit 28-12. The third number down at the top node at Date 1 in Exhibit 28-13, which is in bold, is the sum of the top two values above it. It is this value that is then used in the backward induction. The same procedure is used to get the values shown in the boxes at the lower node at Date 1.

Given the values at the two nodes at Date 1, the bolded values are averaged to obtain $74,989 [= ($125,737 + $24,241)/2]. Discounting this value at 3.5% gives $72,453. This is the same value obtained from using the caplet approach.

Valuing a Floor

An interest rate floor can be valued using the two approaches just illustrated for valuing a cap except that there is a payoff when the interest rate is less than the strike rate. In the case of a floor, the value for the floor for any year is called a **floorlet**. The sum of the floorlets is the value of the floor. Alternatively, a floor can be valued using a single binomial tree.

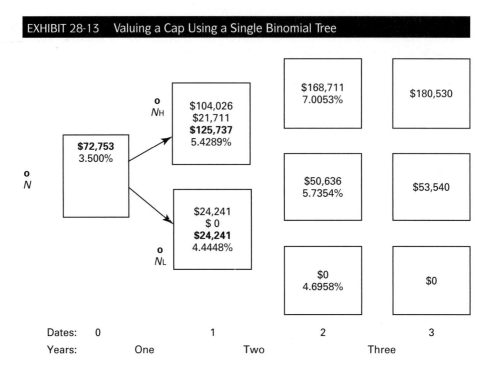

EXHIBIT 28-13   Valuing a Cap Using a Single Binomial Tree

Dates: 0   1   2   3

Years: One   Two   Three

Applications

To see how interest-rate agreements can be used for asset/liability management, con-sider the problems faced by the commercial bank and the life insurance company we discussed in demonstrating the use of an interest-rate swap.[10] Recall that the bank's objective is to lock in an interest-rate spread over its cost of funds. Yet because it bor-rows short term, its cost of funds is uncertain. The bank may be able to purchase a cap, however, so that the cap rate plus the cost of purchasing the cap is less than the rate it is earning on its fixed-rate commercial loans. If short-term rates decline, the bank does not benefit from the cap, but its cost of funds declines. The cap, therefore, allows the bank to impose a ceiling on its cost of funds while retaining the opportunity to benefit from a decline in rates.

The bank can reduce the cost of purchasing the cap by selling a floor. In this case the bank agrees to pay the buyer of the floor if the reference rate falls below the strike rate. The bank receives a fee for selling the floor, but it has sold off its opportunity to benefit from a decline in rates below the strike rate. By buying a cap and selling a floor, the bank has created a predetermined range for its cost of funds (i.e., a collar).

Recall the problem of the life insurance company that guarantees a 9% rate on a GIC for the next five years and is considering the purchase of an attractive floating-rate instrument in a private placement transaction. The risk that the company faces is

---

[10]For additional applications in the insurance industry, see David F. Babbel, Peter Bouyoucos, and Robert Stricker, "Capping the Interest Rate Risk in Insurance Products," Chapter 21 in Frank J. Fabozzi (ed.), *Fixed Income Portfolio Strategies* (Chicago: Probus Publishing, 1989).

that interest rates will fall so that it will not earn enough to realize the 9% guaranteed rate plus a spread. The life insurance company may be able to purchase a floor to set a lower bound on its investment return, yet retain the opportunity to benefit should rates increase. To reduce the cost of purchasing the floor, the life insurance company can sell an interest-rate cap. By doing so, however, it gives up the opportunity of benefiting from an increase in six-month LIBOR above the strike rate of the interest-rate cap.

SUMMARY

An interest-rate swap is an agreement specifying that the parties exchange interest payments at designated times. In a typical swap, one party will make fixed-rate payments, and the other will make floating-rate payments, with payments based on the notional principal amount. Participants in financial markets use interest-rate swaps to alter the cash flow characteristics of their assets or liabilities, or to capitalize on perceived capital market inefficiencies.

A swap position can be interpreted as either a package of forward/futures contracts or a package of cash flows from buying and selling cash market instruments. The swap rate is determined by finding the rate that will make the present value of the cash flow of both sides of the swap equal. The value of an existing swap is equal to the difference in the present value of the two payments. The interest-rate sensitivity or duration of a swap from the perspective of a floating-rate payer is just the difference between the duration of the fixed-rate bond and duration of the floating-rate bond that compose the swap. Most of the interest-rate sensitivity of a swap will result from the duration of the fixed-rate bond since the duration of the floating-rate bond will be small.

Nongeneric swaps include swaps where the notional amount changes in a predetermined way over the life of the swap (amortizing, accreting, and roller coaster swaps) and swaps in which both counterparties pay a floating rate (basis swaps and Constant Maturity Treasury swaps). There are complex swap structures, such as options on swaps (swaptions) and swaps where the swap does not begin until some future time (forward start swaps).

An interest-rate agreement allows one party for an upfront premium the right to receive compensation from the writer of the agreement if a designated interest rate is different from a predetermined level. An interest-rate cap calls for one party to receive a payment if a designated interest rate is above the strike rate. An interest-rate floor lets one party receive a payment if a designated interest rate is below the strike rate. An interest-rate cap can be used to establish a ceiling on the cost of funding; an interest-rate floor can be used to establish a floor return. Buying a cap and selling a floor creates a collar. A cap and a floor can be valued using the binomial model.

Questions

1. Consider an interest-rate swap with these features: maturity is five years, notional principal is $100 million, payments occur every six months, the fixed-rate payer pays a rate of 9.05% and receives LIBOR, while the floating-rate payer pays LIBOR and receives 9%. Now suppose that at a payment date, LIBOR is at 6.5%. What is each party's payment and receipt at that date?

2. Suppose that a dealer quotes these terms on a five-year swap: fixed-rate payer to pay

9.5% for LIBOR and floating-rate payer to pay LIBOR for 9.2%.

   a. What is the dealer's bid-ask spread?

   b. How would the dealer quote the terms by reference to the yield on five-year Treasury notes?

3. Give two interpretations of an interest-rate swap.

4. In determining the cash flow for the floating-rate side of a LIBOR swap, explain how the cash flow is determined.

5. How is the swap rate calculated?

6. How is the value of a swap determined?

7. What factors affect the swap rate?

8. Describe the role of an intermediary in a swap.

9. What types of transactions occur in the secondary market for an interest-rate swap?

10. Suppose that a life insurance company has issued a three-year GIC with a fixed rate of 10%. Under what circumstances might it be feasible for the life insurance company to invest the funds in a floating-rate security and enter into a three-year interest-rate swap in which it pays a floating rate and receives a fixed rate?

11. The following excerpt is taken from an article titled "IRS Rule to Open Swaps to Pension Funds," which appeared in the November 18, 1991, issue of *BondWeek*, pp. 1–2:

A proposed Internal Revenue Service rule that gives tax-free status to income earned on swaps by pension funds and other tax-exempt institutions is expected to spur pension fund use of these products, say swap and pension fund professionals. . . .

UBS Asset Management has received permission from most of its pension fund clients to use interest rate and currency swaps in its fixed-income portfolios and is awaiting the IRS regulation before stepping into the market, says Kenneth Choie, v.p. and head of research and product development. . . . "The IRS' proposed rule is great news for pension fund managers," as the use of swaps can enhance returns and lower transaction costs, Choie says. . . .

While some pension funds are exploring the swap market, pension fund consultants underscore that the funds' entrance into the market is likely to be slow. Counterparty risk has been a more formidable obstacle than the ambiguity of the tax status of income from interest-rate and currency swaps, says Paul Burik, director of research at Ennis, Knupp & Associates, a pension fund consulting firm.

[Note that the rule referred to above has been adopted.]

   a. In the article, Choie indicates that one "possible application that UBS is considering is to switch between fixed- and floating-rate income streams without incurring the transaction costs of trading chunks of securities." Explain how an interest-rate swap can be used for this application.

   b. What is counterparty risk?

   c. How can counterparty risk be reduced?

12. A portfolio manager buys a swaption with a strike rate of 6.5% that entitles the portfolio manager to enter into an interest-rate swap to pay a fixed rate and receive a floating rate. The term of the swaption is five years.

   a. Is this swaption a payer swaption or a receiver swaption? Explain.

   b. What does the strike rate of 6.5% mean?

13. The manager of a savings and loan association is considering the use of a swap as part of its asset/liability strategy. The swap would be used to convert the payments of its portfolio of fixed-rate residential mortgage loans into a floating payment.

   a. What is the risk with using a plain vanilla or generic interest-rate swap?

   b. Why might a manager consider using an interest-rate swap in which the notional principal amount declines over time?

   c. Why might a manager consider buying a swaption?

14. Consider the following interest-rate swap:

- the swap starts today, January 1 of year 1
- the floating-rate payments are made quarterly based on actual/360
- the reference rate is three-month LIBOR

- the notional amount of the swap is $40 million
- the term of the swap is three years

a. Suppose that today three-month LIBOR is 5.7%. What will the fixed-rate payer for this interest rate swap receive on March 31 of year 1 (assuming that year 1 is not a leap year)?

b. Assume the Eurodollar CD futures price for the next seven quarters is as follows:

Quarter Starts	Quarter Ends	No. of Days in Quarter	Euro-dollar CD Futures Price
April 1 year 1	June 30 year 1	91	94.10
July 1 year 1	Sept 30 year 1	92	94.00
Oct 1 year 1	Dec 31 year 1	92	93.70
Jan 1 year 2	Mar 31 year 1	90	93.60
April 1 year 2	June 30 year 2	91	93.50
July 1 year 2	Sept 30 year 2	92	93.20
Oct 1 year 2	Dec 31 year 2	92	93.00

Compute the forward rate for each quarter and the floating-rate payment at the end of each quarter.

c. What is the floating-rate payment at the end of each quarter for this interest-rate swap?

15. a. Assume that the swap rate for an interest-rate swap is 7% and that the fixed-rate swap payments are made quarterly on an actual/360 basis. If the notional amount of a two-year swap is $20 million, what is the fixed-rate payment at the end of each quarter assuming the following number of days in each quarter?

Period Quarter	Days in Quarter
1	92
2	92
3	90
4	91
5	92
6	92
7	90
8	91

b. Assume that the swap in question a requires payments semiannually rather than quarterly. What is the semiannual fixed-rate payment?

c. Suppose that the notional amount for the two-year swap is not the same in both years. Suppose instead that in year 1 the notional amount is $20 million, but in year 2 the notional amount is $12 million. What is the fixed-rate payment every six months?

16. Given the current three-month LIBOR and the Eurodollar CD futures prices shown in the table below, compute the forward rate and the forward discount factor for each period.

Period	Days in Quarter	3-Month LIBOR	Current Eurodollar CD Futures Price
1	90	5.90%	
2	91		93.90
3	92		93.70
4	92		93.45
5	90		93.20
6	91		93.15

17. a. Suppose that at the inception of a five-year interest-rate swap in which the reference rate is three-month LIBOR, the present value of the floating-rate payments is $16,555,000. The fixed-rate payments are assumed to be semiannual. Assume also that the following is computed for the fixed-rate payments (using the notation in the chapter):

$$\sum_{t=1}^{10} \text{notional amount} \times \text{swap rate} \times \frac{\text{days in period } t}{360} \times \text{forward discount factor for period } t = \$236,500,000$$

What is the swap rate for this swap?

b. Suppose that the five-year yield from the on-the-run Treasury yield curve is 6.4%. What is the swap spread?

18. An interest-rate swap had an original maturity of five years. Today, the swap has two years to maturity. The present value of the fixed-rate payments for the remainder of the term of the swap is $910,000. The

present value of the floating-rate payments for the remainder of the swap is $710,000.

a. What is the value of this swap from the perspective of the fixed-rate payer?

b. What is the value of this swap from the perspective of the fixed-rate receiver?

19. Suppose that a savings and loan association buys an interest-rate cap that has these terms: The reference rate is the six-month Treasury bill rate; the cap will last for five years; payment is semiannual; the strike rate is 5.5%; and the notional amount is $10 million. Suppose further that at the end of a six-month period, the six-month Treasury bill rate is 6.1%.

a. What is the amount of the payment that the savings and loan association will receive?

b. What would the seller of this cap pay if the six-month Treasury rate were 5.45% instead of 6.1%?

20. What is the relationship between an interest-rate agreement and an option on an interest rate?

21. How can an interest-rate collar be created?

22. Value a three-year interest rate floor with a $10 million notional amount and a floor rate of 4.8% using the binomial interest-rate tree shown in Exhibit 28-11

CHAPTER

29 | CREDIT DERIVATIVES*

After reading this chapter you will understand:

- what a credit derivative is

- the different types of credit risk

- what an asset swap is

- what a credit default swap is and how a credit event can be defined

- the difference between a single-name credit default swap and a basket default swap

- what a credit default index is

- what a total return swap is and the types of risk faced in such a swap

- the different types of credit options

- what a credit forward is

- securities that are created using credit derivatives: synthetic collateralized debt obligations and credit-linked notes

Interest-rate derivatives such as Treasury futures contracts, Treasury options, interest-rate swaps, caps, and floors can be used to control interest-rate risk with respect to changes in the level of interest rates. However, there are also changes in the credit spread that must be controlled by the portfolio manager when investing in non-Treasury securities. What has developed in the over-the-counter or dealer market are derivative instruments that provide protection against credit risk. These products are referred to as **credit derivatives**.

Credit derivatives are used by bond portfolio managers in the normal course of activities to more efficiently control the credit risk of a portfolio and

---

*As in the fifth edition, some parts of this chapter draw from Mark J. P. Anson and Frank J. Fabozzi, "Credit Derivatives for Bond Portfolio Management," in Frank J. Fabozzi (ed.), *Fixed Income Readings for the Chartered Financial Analyst Program: Second Edition* (New Hope, PA: Frank J. Fabozzi Associates, 2003).

to more efficiently transact than by transacting in the cash market. For example, credit derivatives allow a mechanism for portfolio managers to more efficiently short a credit-risky security than by shorting in the cash market, which is often-times difficult to do. For traders and hedge fund managers, credit derivatives provide a means for leveraging an exposure in the credit market.

There are five types of credit derivatives: asset swaps, total return swaps, credit default swaps, credit spread options, and credit spread forwards. There are also credit derivatives embedded in some bonds; the two most prominent being synthetic collateralized debt obligations and credit-linked notes. Bonds with embedded credit derivatives are referred to as **structured credit products**. In this chapter these relatively new derivatives and structured credit products are explained.

TYPES OF CREDIT RISK

An investor who lends funds by purchasing a bond issue is exposed to three types of credit risk: (1) default risk, (2) credit spread risk, and (3) downgrade risk.

Traditionally, credit risk is defined as the risk that the issuer will fail to satisfy the terms of the obligation with respect to the timely payment of interest and repayment of the amount borrowed. This form of credit risk is called **default risk**. If a default does occur, this does not mean the investor loses the entire amount invested because the investor can expect to recover a portion of the investment.

Even in the absence of default, an investor is concerned that the market value of a bond will decline and/or the price performance of that bond will be worse than that of other bonds against which the investor is compared. The price performance of a non-Treasury bond issue and its return that the investor will realize by holding that issue over some time period will depend on how the credit spread changes. If the credit spread increases, the market price of the bond issue will decline (assuming Treasury rates have not changed). The risk that an issuer's debt obligation will perform poorly relative to other bonds due to an increase in the credit spread is called **credit spread risk**.

While there are investors who seek to allocate funds among different sectors of the bond market to capitalize on anticipated changes in credit spreads, an investor investigating the credit quality of an individual issue is concerned with the prospects of the credit spread increasing for that particular issue. Market participants gauge the default risk of an issue by looking at the credit ratings assigned to issues by the rating agencies—Moody's Investors Service, Inc.; Standard & Poor's Corporation; and Fitch Ratings. Once a credit rating is assigned to a debt obligation, a rating agency monitors the credit quality of the issuer and can reassign a different credit rating. An improvement in the credit quality of an issue or issuer is rewarded with a better credit rating, referred to as an **upgrade**; a deterioration in the credit rating of an issue or issuer is penalized by the assignment of an inferior credit rating, referred to as a **downgrade**. An unanticipated downgrading of an issue or issuer increases the credit spread and results in a decline in the price of the issue or the issuer's bonds. This risk is referred to as **downgrade risk** and is closely related to credit spread risk.

CATEGORIZATION OF CREDIT DERIVATIVES

There are several ways to characterize credit derivatives. One such categorization is shown in Exhibit 29-1. As we shall see, some of the derivatives described in the exhibit are not true credit derivatives in that they do not provide protection against credit risk. Rather, they provide protection against both interest rate risk and credit spread risk. This applies to asset swaps and total return swaps. Credit default products provide protection against credit events. We will define what is meant by credit events shortly.

ISDA DOCUMENTATION

Prior to 1998, the development of the credit derivatives market was hindered by the lack of standardization of legal documentation. Every trade (i.e., the buying and selling of a credit derivative contract) had to be customized. In 1998, the International Swap and Derivatives Association (ISDA) developed a standard contract that could be used by parties to trades of a credit derivatives contract. While the documentation is primarily designed for credit default swaps and total return swaps, the contract form is sufficiently flexible so that it can be used for the other credit derivatives described in this chapter.

Reference Entity and Reference Obligation

The documentation will identify the reference entity and the reference obligation. The **reference entity** is the issuer of the debt instrument and hence also referred to as the **reference issuer**. It could be a corporation or a sovereign government. The **reference obligation**, also referred to as the **reference asset**, is the particular debt issue for which the credit protection is being sought. For example, a reference entity could be Ford Motor Credit Company. The reference obligation would be a specific Ford Motor Credit Company bond issue.

EXHIBIT 29-1   Categorization of Credit Derivatives

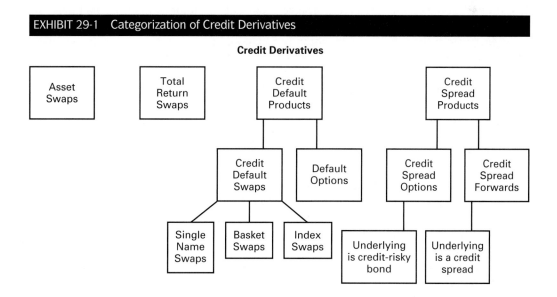

Credit Events

Credit default products have a payout that is contingent upon a **credit event** occurring. The ISDA provides definitions of what credit events are. The *1999 ISDA Credit Derivatives Definitions* (referred to as the "1999 Definitions") provides a list of eight credit events: (1) bankruptcy, (2) credit event upon merger, (3) cross acceleration, (4) cross default, (5) downgrade, (6) failure to pay, (7) repudiation/moratorium, and (8) restructuring. These eight events attempt to capture every type of situation that could cause the credit quality of the reference entity to deteriorate, or cause the value of the reference obligation to decline.

Bankruptcy is defined as a variety of acts that are associated with bankruptcy or insolvency laws. **Failure to pay** results when a reference entity fails to make one or more required payments when due. When a reference entity breaches a covenant, it has defaulted on its obligation.

When a default occurs, the obligation becomes due and payable prior to the scheduled due date had the reference entity not defaulted. This is referred to as an **obligation acceleration**. A reference entity may disaffirm or challenge the validity of its obligation. This is a credit event that is covered by **repudiation/moratorium**.

The most controversial credit event that may be included in a credit default product is restructuring of an obligation. A **restructuring** occurs when the terms of the obligation are altered so as to make the new terms less attractive to the debt holder than the original terms. The terms that can be changed would typically include, but are not limited to, one or more of the following: (1) a reduction in the interest rate, (2) a reduction in the principal, (3) a rescheduling of the principal repayment schedule (e.g., lengthening the maturity of the obligation) or postponement of an interest payment, or (4) a change in the level of seniority of the obligation in the reference entity's debt structure.

The reason why restructuring is so controversial is a protection buyer benefits from the inclusion of restructuring as a credit event and feels that eliminating restructuring as a credit event will erode its credit protection. The protection seller, in contrast, would prefer not to include restructuring since even routine modifications of obligations that occur in lending arrangements would trigger a payout to the protection buyer. Moreover, if the reference obligation is a loan and the protection buyer is the lender, there is a dual benefit for the protection buyer to restructure a loan. The first benefit is that the protection buyer receives a payment from the protection seller. Second, the accommodating restructuring fosters a relationship between the lender (who is the protection buyer) and its customer (the corporate entity that is the obligor of the reference obligation).

Because of this problem, the *Restructuring Supplement to the 1999 ISDA Credit Derivatives Definitions* (the "Supplement Definition") issued in April 2001 provided a modified definition for restructuring. There is a provision for the limitation on reference obligations in connection with restructuring of loans made by the protection buyer to the borrower that is the obligor of the reference obligation. This provision requires the following in order to qualify for a restructuring: (1) there must be four or more holders of the reference obligation and (2) there must be a consent to the restructuring of the reference obligation by a supermajority (66 2/3%). In addition, the supplement limits the maturity of reference obligations that are physically deliverable when restructuring results in a payout triggered by the protection buyer.

As the credit derivatives market developed, market participants learned a great deal about how to better define credit events, particularly with the record level of high-yield corporate bond default rates in 2002, and the sovereign defaults, particularly the experience with the 2001–2002 Argentina debt crisis. In January 2003, the ISDA published its revised credit events definitions in the *2003 ISDA Credit Derivative Definitions* (referred to as the "2003 Definitions"). The revised definitions reflected amendments to several of the definitions for credit events set forth in the 1999 Definitions. Specifically, there were amendments for bankruptcy, repudiation, and restructuring.

The major change was to restructuring, whereby the ISDA allows parties to a given trade to select from among the following four definitions: (1) no restructuring; (2) "full" or "old" restructuring, which is based on the 1998 Definitions; (3) "modified restructuring," which is based on the Supplement Definition; and (4) "modified modified restructuring." The last choice is new and was included to address issues that arose in the European market.

The ISDA's confirmation form for credit derivative transactions, "Exhibit A to 2003 ISDA Credit Derivatives Definitions," sets forth the terms and conditions for the transaction. The definitions for a credit event are in check box format.

ASSET SWAPS

As explained in the previous chapter, an investor can use an interest-rate swap to change the cash flow nature of a bond owned to the desired cash flow characteristics — fixed to floating or floating to fixed. When an investor owns an asset and converts its cash flow characteristics, the investor is said to have created an asset swap. A common asset swap is for an investor to buy a credit-risky bond with a fixed rate and convert it to a floating rate. If the issuer of the bond defaults on the issue, the investor must continue to make payments to the counterparty of the interest-rate swap (i.e., the swap dealer) and is therefore still exposed to the credit risk of the issuer.

Let's now illustrate a basic asset swap. Suppose that an investor purchases $10 million par value of a 7.85%, five-year bond of a BBB-rated utility company at par value. The coupon payments are semiannual. At the same time, the investor enters into a five-year interest-rate swap with a dealer where the investor is the fixed-rate payer and the payments are made semiannually. Suppose that the swap rate is 7.00% and the investor receives six-month LIBOR.

Let's look at the cash flow for the investor every six months for the next five years:

Received from utility bonds:	7.85%
– Payment to dealer on swap:	7.00%
+ Payment from dealer on swap:	6-month LIBOR
Net received by investor:	0.85% + 6-month LIBOR

Thus, regardless of how interest rates change, if the utility issuer does not default on the issue, the investor earns 85 basis points over six-month LIBOR. Effectively, the investor has converted a fixed-rate BBB five-year bond into a five-year floating-rate bond with a spread over six-month LIBOR. Thus, the investor has created a synthetic floating-rate bond. The purpose of an asset swap is to do precisely that: create a synthetic credit-risky floating-rate security.

While in our description of an asset swap the investor bought the credit-risky bond and entered into an interest-rate swap with a dealer, an asset swap typically combines the sale of a credit-risky bond owned to a counterparty at par and with no interest accrued, with an interest-rate swap. This type of asset swap structure or package is referred to as a **par asset swap**. If there is a default by the issuer of the credit-risky bonds, the asset swap transaction is terminated and the defaulted bonds are returned to the investor plus or minus any mark-to-market on the asset swap transaction. Hence the investor is still exposed to the issuer's credit risk.

The coupon on the bond in the par asset swap is paid in return for LIBOR, plus a spread if necessary. This spread is the **asset swap spread** and is the price of the asset swap. In effect the asset swap allows investors that pay LIBOR-based funding to receive the asset swap spread. This spread is a function of the credit risk of the underlying credit-risky bond.

To illustrate this asset swap structure, suppose that in our previous illustration the swap rate prevailing in the market is 7.30% rather than 7.00%. The investor owns the utility bonds and sells them to a dealer at par with no accrued interest. The asset swap agreement between the dealer and the investor is as follows:

- the term is five years
- the investor agrees to pay the dealer semiannually 7.30%
- the dealer agrees to pay the investor every six months six-month LIBOR plus an asset swap spread of 30 basis points

Let's look at the cash flow for the investor every six months for the next five years for this asset swap structure:

Received from utility bonds:	7.85%
– Payment to dealer on swap:	7.30%
+ Payment from dealer on swap:	6-month LIBOR + 30 basis points
Net received by investor:	0.85% + 6-month LIBOR

In our first illustration of an asset swap, the investor is creating a synthetic floater without a dealer. The investor owns the bonds. The only involvement of the dealer is as a counterparty to the interest-rate swap. In the second structure, the dealer is the counterparty to the asset swap structure and the dealer owns the underlying credit-risky bonds. If there is a default, the dealer returns the bonds to the investor.

There are variations of the basic asset swap structure to remove unwanted non-credit structural features of the underlying credit-risky bond. The simplest example of an asset swap variation to remove an unwanted non-credit structural feature is when the bond is callable. If the bond is callable, then the future cash flows of the bond are uncertain because the issue can be called. Moreover, the issue is likely to be called if interest rates decline below the bond's coupon rate.

This problem can be handled in the case where the investor buys the bond and enters into an interest-rate swap. The tenor of the interest-rate swap would still be for the term of the bond. However, the investor would also enter into a swaption in which he or she has the right to effectively terminate the swap from the time of the first call date for the bond to the maturity date of the bond. In the swaption, since the investor is paying fixed and receiving floating, the swaption must be one in which the investor receives fixed and pays floating. Specifically, the investor will enter into a receive fixed swaption.

As we will see in this chapter, credit derivatives allow investors to manage the credit risk exposure of their portfolios or asset holdings by providing protection against a deterioration in credit quality of the borrowing entity. While an asset swap is not a true credit derivative, it is closely associated with the credit derivatives market because it explicitly sets out the price of credit as a spread over LIBOR. It allows the acquiring of credit risk while minimizing interest-rate risk but it does not allow an investor to transfer credit risk. It is because of this shortcoming of an asset swap that the other types of credit derivative instruments and structured products discussed in this chapter were created.

TOTAL RETURN SWAPS

A **total return swap** in the fixed-income market is a swap in which one party makes periodic floating-rate payments to a counterparty in exchange for the total return realized on a reference obligation or a basket of reference obligations. A total return payment includes all cash flows that flow from the reference obligations as well as the capital appreciation or depreciation of those reference obligations. When the reference obligation is a bond market index, the swap is referred to as a **total return index swap**.

The party that agrees to make the floating payments and receive the total return is referred to as the **total return receiver**; the party that agrees to receive the floating payments and pay the total return is referred to as the **total return payer**.

Notice that in a total return swap, the total return receiver is exposed to both credit risk and interest-rate risk. For example, the credit risk spread can decline (resulting in a favorable price movement for the reference obligation), but this gain can be offset by a rise in the level of interest rates.

A portfolio manager typically uses a total return swap to increase exposure to a reference obligation, in contrast to a credit default swap, which is described later, that is used to hedge a credit exposure. A total return swap transfers all of the economic exposure of a reference obligation or reference obligations to the total return receiver. In return for receiving this exposure, the total return receiver pays a floating or fixed rate to the total return payer.

As an example of a total return swap, consider a portfolio manager who believes that the fortunes of Izzobaf Corporation will improve over the next year, and that the company's credit spread relative to U.S. Treasury securities will decline. The company has issued a 10-year bond at par with a coupon rate of 9% and therefore the yield is 9%. Suppose that at the time of issuance the 10-year Treasury yield is 6.2%. This means that the credit spread is 280 basis points, and the portfolio manager believes it will decrease over the year to less than 280 basis points.

The portfolio manager can express this view by entering into a total return swap that matures in one year as a total return receiver with the reference obligation being the 10-year, 9% Izzobaf Corporate bond issue. For simplicity, assume that the swap calls for an exchange of payments semiannually. Suppose the terms of the swap are that the total return receiver pays the six-month Treasury rate plus 160 basis points in order to receive the total return on the reference obligation. The notional amount for the contract is $10 million.

Suppose that over the one year, the following occurs:

- the six-month Treasury rate is 4.8% initially
- the six-month Treasury rate for computing the second semiannual payment is 5.4%
- at the end of one year the 9-year Treasury rate is 7.6%
- at the end of one year the credit spread for the reference obligation is 180 basis points

First let's look at the payments that must be made by the portfolio manager. The first swap payment made by the portfolio manager is 3.2% (4.8% plus 160 basis points divided by 2) multiplied by the $10 million notional amount. The second swap payment made is 3.5% (5.4% plus 160 basis points divided by 2) multiplied by the $10 million notional amount. Thus,

First swap payment: $10 million × 3.2% =	$320,000
Second swap payment: $10 million × 3.5% =	$350,000
Total payments =	$670,000

The payments that will be received by the portfolio manager are the coupon payments plus the change in the value of the reference obligation. There will be two coupon payments. Since the coupon rate is 9%, the amount received for the coupon payments is $900,000.

Finally, the change in the value of the reference obligation must be determined. At the end of one year, the reference obligation has a maturity of 9 years. Since the 9-year Treasury rate is assumed to be 7.6% and the credit spread is assumed to decline from 280 basis points to 180 basis points, the reference obligation will sell to yield 9.4%. The price of a 9%, nine-year bond selling to yield 9.4% is 97.61. Since the par value is $10 million, the price is $9,761,000. The capital loss is therefore $239,000. The payment to the total return receiver is then

Coupon payment =	$900,000
Capital loss =	$239,000
Swap payment =	$661,000

Netting the swap payment made and the swap payment received, the portfolio manager must make a payment of $9,000.

Notice that even though the portfolio manager's expectations were realized (i.e., a decline in the credit spread), the portfolio manager had to make a net outlay. This illustration highlights one of the disadvantages of a total return swap: The return to the investor is dependent on both credit risk (declining or increasing credit spreads) and market risk (declining or increasing market rates). Two types of market interest-rate risk can affect the price of a fixed-income asset. Credit-independent market risk is the risk that the general level of interest rates will change over the term of the swap. This type of risk has nothing to do with the credit deterioration of the reference obligation. Credit-dependent market interest-rate risk is the risk that the discount rate applied to the value of an asset will change based on either perceived or actual default risk.

In the illustration, the reference obligation was adversely affected by market interest-rate risk, but positively rewarded for accepting credit-dependent market interest-rate risk. To remedy this problem, a total return receiver can customize the total return swap transaction. For example, the portfolio manager could negotiate to receive the coupon income on the reference obligation plus any change in value due to changes in the credit spread. Now the portfolio manager has expressed a view exclusively on credit risk; credit-independent market risk does not affect the swap value. In this case, in addition to the coupon income, the portfolio manager would receive the difference between the present value of the reference obligation at a current spread of 280 basis points and the present value of the reference obligation at a credit spread of 180 basis points.

Benefits of Total Return Swaps

There are several benefits in using a total return swap as opposed to purchasing reference obligations themselves. First, the total return receiver does not have to finance the purchase of the reference assets. Instead, it pays a fee to the total return payer in return for receiving the total return on the reference obligations.

Second, the total return receiver can achieve the same economic exposure to a diversified basket of assets in one swap transaction that would otherwise take several cash market transactions to achieve. In this way a total return swap is a much more efficient means for transacting than the cash market.

Finally, an investor who wants to short the corporate bond will find it difficult to do so in the corporate bond market. An investor can do so efficiently by using a total return swap. In this case the investor will use a total return swap in which it is a total return payer and will receive a floating payment.

CREDIT DEFAULT SWAPS[1]

By far, the most popular type of credit derivative is the **credit default swap**. It is categorized as one of two credit default products (see Exhibit 29-1). Not only is this form of credit derivative the most commonly used stand-alone product, but it is also used extensively in structured credit products, such as synthetic collateralized debt obligations, which will be discussed later. A credit default swap is probably the simplest form of credit risk transference among all credit derivatives. Because of the popularity of credit default swaps, the other type of credit default product—the credit default option—is rarely used. Hence, we will not discuss that product here.

Credit default swaps are used to shift credit exposure to a credit protection seller. Their primary purpose is to hedge the credit exposure to a particular asset or issuer. In

---

[1]For a further discussion of credit default swaps, see Chapter 3 in Mark J. P. Anson, Frank J. Fabozzi, Moorad Choudhry, and Ren-Raw Chen, *Credit Derivatives: Instruments, Applications, and Pricing* (Hoboken, NJ: John Wiley & Sons, 2003).

this sense, credit default swaps operate much like a standby letter of credit or insurance policy. In contrast, a total return swap allows an investor to increase exposure to a reference obligation.

A credit default swap in which there is one reference obligation is called a **single-name credit default swap**. When the reference obligation is a basket or portfolio of obligations (e.g., 10 high-yield corporate bond of 10 different issuers), it is referred to as a **basket credit default swap**. In a **credit default swap index** there are multiple issuers as in a basket credit default swap. However, unlike a basket credit default swap, there is a standardized basket of reference entities.

In a credit default swap, the protection buyer pays a fee to the protection seller in return for the right to receive a payment conditional upon the occurrence of a credit event by the reference obligation or the reference entity. Should a credit event occur, the protection seller must make a payment.

The interdealer market has evolved to where single-name credit default swaps for corporate and sovereign reference entities are standardized. While trades between dealers have been standardized, there are occasional trades in the interdealer market where there is a customized agreement. For portfolio managers seeking credit protection, dealers are willing to create customized products. The tenor, or length of time of a credit default swap, is typically five years. Portfolio managers can have a dealer create a tenor equal to the maturity of the reference obligation or have it constructed for a shorter time period to match the manager's investment horizon.

Credit default swaps can be settled in cash or physically. Physical delivery means that if a credit event as defined by the documentation occurs, the reference obligation is delivered by the protection buyer to the protection seller in exchange for a cash payment. Because physical delivery does not rely upon obtaining market prices for the reference obligation in determining the amount of the payment in a single-name credit default swap, this method of delivery is more efficient.

The payment by the credit protection seller if a credit event occurs may be a predetermined fixed amount or it may be determined by the decline in value of the reference obligation. The standard single-name credit default swap when the reference entity is a corporate bond or a sovereign bond is fixed based on a notional amount. When the cash payment is based on the amount of asset value deterioration, this amount is typically determined by a poll of several dealers. If no credit event has occurred by the maturity of the swap, both sides terminate the swap agreement and no further obligations are incurred.

The methods used to determine the amount of the payment obligated of the protection seller under the swap agreement can vary greatly. For instance, a credit default swap can specify at the contract date the exact amount of payment that will be made by the protection seller should a credit event occur. Conversely, the credit default swap can be structured so that the amount of the swap payment by the seller is determined after the credit event. Under these circumstances, the amount payable by the protection seller is determined based upon the observed prices of similar debt obligations of the reference entity in the market. Finally, the swap can be documented much like a credit put option (discussed later) where the amount to be paid by the protection seller is an established strike price less the current market value of the reference obligation.

In a typical credit default swap, the protection buyer pays for the protection premium over several settlement dates rather than upfront. A standard credit default swap specifies quarterly payments.

Single-Name Credit Default Swap

Let's illustrate the mechanics of a single-name credit default swap. Assume that the reference entity or reference name is XYX Corporation and the underlying is $10 million par value of XYZ bonds. The $10 million is the notional amount of the contract. The swap premium—the payment made by the protection buyer to the protection seller—is 200 basis points.

The standard contract for a single-name credit default swap calls for a quarterly payment of the swap premium. The quarterly payment is determined using one of the day count conventions in the bond market. The day count convention used for credit default swaps is actual/360, the same convention as used in the interest-rate swap market. A day convention of actual/360 means that to determine the payment in a quarter, the actual number of days in the quarter are used and 360 days are assumed for the year. Consequently, the swap premium payment for a quarter is

$$\text{quarterly swap premium payment} =$$
$$\text{notional amount} \times \text{swap rate (in decimal)} \times \frac{\text{actual no. of days in quarter}}{360}$$

For example, assume a hypothetical credit default swap where the notional amount is $10 million and there are 92 actual days in a quarter. Since the swap premium is 200 basis points (0.02), the quarterly swap premium payment made by the protection buyer would be

$$\$10,000,000 \times 0.02 \times \frac{92}{360} = \$51,111.11$$

In the absence of a credit event, the protection buyer will make a quarterly swap premium payment over the life of the swap. If a credit event occurs, two things happen. First, there are no further payments of the swap premium by the protection buyer to the protection seller. Second, a **termination value** is determined for the swap. The procedure for computing the termination value depends on the settlement terms provided for by the swap. This will be either physical settlement or cash settlement. The market practice for settlement for single-name credit default swaps is physical delivery.

With **physical settlement** the protection buyer delivers a specified amount of the face value of bonds of the reference entity to the protection seller. The protection seller pays the protection buyer the face value of the bonds. Since all reference entities that are the subject of credit default swaps have many issues outstanding, there will be a number of alternative issues of the reference entity that the protection buyer can deliver to the protection seller. These issues are known as **deliverable obligations**. The swap documentation will set forth the characteristics necessary for an issue to qualify as a deliverable obligation. Recall that for Treasury bond and note futures contracts the short has the choice of which Treasury issue to deliver that the exchange specifies as acceptable for delivery. The short will select the cheapest-to-deliver issue, and the choice granted to the short is effectively an embedded option. The same is true for physical settlement for a single-name credit default swap. From the list of deliverable obligations, the protection buyer will select for delivery to the protection seller the cheapest-to-deliver issue.

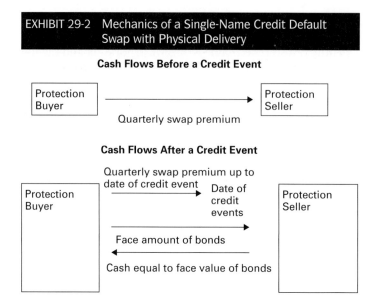

EXHIBIT 29-2   Mechanics of a Single-Name Credit Default Swap with Physical Delivery

Cash Flows Before a Credit Event

Protection Buyer → Quarterly swap premium → Protection Seller

Cash Flows After a Credit Event

Quarterly swap premium up to date of credit event

Protection Buyer → Date of credit events → Protection Seller

Face amount of bonds →

Cash equal to face value of bonds ←

Exhibit 29-2 shows the mechanics of a single-name credit default swap. The cash flows are shown before and after a credit event. It is assumed in the exhibit that there is physical settlement.

Single-name credit default swaps can be used in the following ways by portfolio managers:

- The liquidity of the swap market compared to the corporate bond market makes it more efficient to obtain exposure to a reference entity by taking a position in the swap market rather than in the cash market. To obtain exposure to a reference entity, a portfolio manager would sell protection and thereby receive the swap premium.
- Conditions in the corporate bond market may be such that it is difficult for a portfolio manager to sell the current holding of a corporate bond of an issuer for which he has a credit concern. Rather than selling the current holding, the portfolio can buy protection in the swap market.
- If a portfolio manager expects that an issuer will have difficulties in the future and wants to take a position based on that expectation, it will short the bond of that issuer. However, shorting bonds in the corporate bond market is difficult. The equivalent position can be obtained by entering into a swap as the protection buyer.
- For a portfolio manager seeking a leveraged position in a corporate bond, this can be done in the swap market. The economic position of a protection buyer is equivalent to a leveraged position in a corporate bond.

Basket Credit Default Swaps

With a basket credit default swap, or simply basket default swaps, when a payout must be made must be specified. For example, if a basket credit default swap has 10 reference obligations, does a credit event for just one of the 10 reference obligations result in the triggering of a payment by the protection seller? It depends. Basket default swaps can be structured in different ways.

The simplest case is that if any of the reference obligations default, there is a payout and then termination of the swap. This type of swap is referred to as a **first-to-default basket swap**. Similarly, if a payout is triggered only after two reference obligations default, the swap is referred to as a **second-to-default basket swap**. In general, if it takes k reference obligations to trigger a payout, the swap is referred to as a k-**to-default basket swap**.

Unlike a single-name credit default swap, the preferred settlement term for a basket default swap is cash settlement. With **cash settlement**, the termination value is equal to the difference between the nominal amount of the reference obligation for which a credit event has occurred and its market value at the time of the credit event. The termination value is then the amount of the payment made by the protection seller to the protection buyer. No bonds are delivered by the protection buyer to the protection seller. The documentation for the basket default swap will set forth how the market value at the time of the credit event is determined.

As explained later in this chapter, basket default swaps are typically used in synthetic collateralized debt obligations.

Credit Default Swap Index

In a **credit default swap index**, the credit risk of a standardized basket of reference entities is transferred between the protection buyer and protection seller. As of year-end 2005, the only standardized indexes are those compiled and managed by Dow Jones. For the corporate bond indexes, there are separate indexes for investment grade and high-grade names. The most actively traded contract as of year-end 2005 is the one based on the North American Investment Grade Index (denoted by DJ.CDX.NA.IG). As the name suggests, the reference entities in this index are those with an investment-grade rating. The index includes 125 corporate names in North America. The index is an equally weighted index. That is, each corporate name (i.e., reference entity) comprising the index has a weight of 0.8%. The index is updated semi-annually by Dow Jones.

The mechanics of a credit default swap index are slightly different from that of a single-name credit default swap. As with a single-name credit default swap, a swap premium is paid. However, if a credit event occurs, the swap premium payment ceases in the case of a single-name credit default swap. In contrast, for a credit default swap index, the swap payment continues to be made by the protection buyer. However, the amount of the quarterly swap premium payment is reduced. This is because the notional amount is reduced as result of a credit event for a reference entity.

For example, suppose that a portfolio manager is the protection buyer for a DJ.CDX.NA.IG and the notional amount is $200 million. Using the formula below for computing the quarterly swap premium payment, the payment before a credit event occurs would be

$$\$200,000,000 \times \text{swap rate (in decimal)} \times \frac{\text{actual no. of days in quarter}}{360}$$

After a credit event occurs for one reference entity, the notional amount declines from $200 million to $199,840,000. The reduction is equal to 99.2% of the $200 million because each reference entity for the DJ.CDX.NA.IG is 0.8%. Thus, the revised quarterly swap premium payment until the maturity date or until another credit event occurs for one of the other 124 reference entities is

$$\$199,840,000 \times \text{swap rate (in decimal)} \times \frac{\text{actual no. of days in quarter}}{360}$$

As of this writing, the settlement term for a credit default swap index is physical settlement. However, the market is considering moving to cash settlement. The reason is because of the cost of delivering an odd lot of the bonds of the reference entity in the case of a credit event. For example, in our hypothetical credit default swap index if there is a credit event, the protection buyer would have to deliver to the protection seller bonds of the reference entity with a face value of $160,000. Neither the protection buyer nor the protection seller would like to deal with such a small position.

Exhibit 29-3 shows the cash flow for a generic credit default index swap after a credit event for one reference entity.

Because a credit default swap index, such as the DJ.CDX.NA.IG, provides exposure to a diversified basket of credits, it can be used by a portfolio manager to help adjust a portfolio's exposure to the credit sector of a bond market index. By entering into a credit default swap index as the protection seller, a portfolio manager increases exposure to the credit sector. Exposure to the credit sector is reduced by a portfolio manager being the protection buyer.

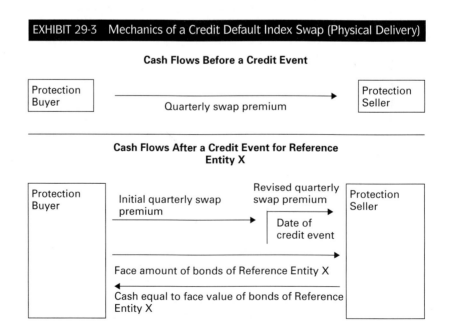

EXHIBIT 29-3   Mechanics of a Credit Default Index Swap (Physical Delivery)

Cash Flows Before a Credit Event

Protection Buyer → Quarterly swap premium → Protection Seller

Cash Flows After a Credit Event for Reference Entity X

Protection Buyer — Initial quarterly swap premium — Revised quarterly swap premium — Date of credit event — Protection Seller

Face amount of bonds of Reference Entity X

Cash equal to face value of bonds of Reference Entity X

CREDIT SPREAD OPTIONS

A credit spread option is an option whose value/payoff depends on the change in credit spread for a reference obligation. It is critical in discussing credit spread options to define what the underlying is. The underlying can be either

1. a reference obligation, which is a credit-risky bond with a fixed credit spread, or
2. the level of the credit spread for a reference obligation

Underlying Is a Reference Obligation with a Fixed Credit Spread

When the underlying is a reference obligation with a fixed credit spread, then a credit spread option is defined as follows:

> **Credit spread put option:** An option that grants the option buyer the right, but not the obligation, to sell a reference obligation at a price that is determined by a strike credit spread over a referenced benchmark.

> **Credit spread call option:** An option that grants the option buyer the right, but not the obligation, to buy a reference obligation at a price that is determined by a strike credit spread over a referenced benchmark.

A credit spread option can have any exercise style: European (exercisable only at the expiration date), American (exercisable at any time prior to and including the exercise date), or Bermuda (exercisable only on specified dates).

The price for the reference obligation (i.e., the credit-risky bond) is determined by specifying a strike credit spread over the referenced benchmark, typically a default-free government security. For example, suppose that the reference obligation is an 8% 10-year bond selling to yield 8%. The price of this bond is 100. Suppose further that the referenced benchmark is a same-maturity U.S. Treasury bond that is selling to yield 6%. Then the current credit spread is 200 basis points. Assume that a strike credit spread of 300 basis points is specified and that the option expires in six months. At the end of six months, suppose that the 9.5-year Treasury rate is 6.5%. Since the strike credit spread is 300 basis points, then the yield used to compute the strike price for the reference obligation is 9.5% (the Treasury rate of 6.5% plus the strike credit spread of 300 basis points). The price of a 9.5-year 8% coupon bond selling to yield 9.5% is $90.75 per $100 par value.

The payoff at the expiration date would then depend on the market price for the reference obligation. For example, suppose that at the end of six months, the reference obligation is trading at 82.59. This is a yield of 11% and therefore a credit spread of 450 basis points over the 9.5-year Treasury yield of 6.5%. For a credit spread put option, the buyer can sell the reference obligation selling at 82.59 for the strike price of 90.75. The payoff from exercising is 8.16. This payoff is reduced by the cost of the option. For a credit spread call option, the buyer will not exercise the option and will allow it to expire worthless. There is a loss equal to the cost of the option.

There is one problem with using a credit spread option in which the underlying is a reference obligation with a fixed credit spread. The payoff is dependent upon the value of the reference obligation's price, which is affected by both the change in the level of the interest rates (as measured by the referenced benchmark) and the change in the credit spread. For example, suppose in our illustration that the 9.5-year Treasury rate at the exercise date is 4.5% (instead of 6.5%) and the credit spread increases to 450 basis points. This means that the reference obligation is trading at 9% (4.5% plus 450 basis points). Since it is an 8% coupon bond with 9.5 years to maturity selling at 9%, the price is 93.70. In this case, the credit spread put option would have a payoff of zero because the price of the reference obligation is 93.70, and the strike price is 90.74. Thus, there was no protection against credit spread risk because interest rates for the referenced benchmark fell enough to offset the increase in the credit spread.

Notice the following payoff before taking into account the option cost when the underlying for the credit spread option is the reference obligation with a fixed credit spread:

Type of Option	Positive Payoff if at Expiration
Put	credit spread at expiration > strike credit spread
Call	credit spread at expiration < strike credit spread

Consequently, to protect against credit spread risk, an investor can buy a credit spread *put* option where the underlying is a reference obligation with a fixed credit spread.

Underlying Is a Credit Spread on a Reference Obligation

When the underlying for a credit spread option is the credit spread for a reference obligation over a referenced benchmark, then the payoff of a call and a put option are as follows:

Credit spread call option:
payoff =
   (credit spread at exercise − strike credit spread) × notional amount × risk factor

Credit spread put option:
payoff =
   (strike credit spread − credit spread at exercise) × notional amount × risk factor

The strike credit spread (in decimal form) is fixed at the outset of the option. The credit spread at exercise (in decimal form) is the credit spread over a referenced benchmark at the exercise date.

The risk factor is equal to

risk factor = 10,000 × percentage price change for 1-basis-point change in rates for the
                reference obligation

By including the risk factor, this form of credit spread option overcomes the problem we identified with the credit spread option in which the underlying is a reference obligation: The payoff depends on both changes in the level of interest rates (the yield on the referenced benchmark) and the credit spread. Instead, it is only dependent upon the change in the credit spread. Therefore, fluctuations in the level of the referenced benchmark's interest rate will not affect the value of these credit spread options.

Notice that when the underlying for the credit spread option is the credit spread for a reference obligation over a referenced benchmark, a credit spread *call* option is used to protect against an increase in the credit spread. In contrast, when the underlying for the credit spread option is the reference obligation, a credit spread *put* option is used to protect against an increase in the credit spread.

To illustrate the payoff, suppose that the current credit spread for a credit spread call option is 300 basis points, and the investor wants to protect against a spread widening to more than 350 basis points. Accordingly, suppose that a strike credit spread of 350 basis points is selected. Assuming that the risk factor is 5 and the notional amount is $10 million, then the payoff for this option is

$$\text{payoff} = (\text{credit spread at exercise} - 0.035) \times \$10,000,000 \times 5$$

If at the exercise date the credit spread is 450 basis points, then the payoff is

$$\text{payoff} = (0.045 - 0.035) \times \$10,000,000 \times 5 = \$500,000$$

The profit realized from this option is $500,000 less the cost of the option.

CREDIT SPREAD FORWARDS

A **credit spread forward** requires an exchange of payments at the settlement date based on a credit spread. As with a credit spread option, the underlying can be the value of the reference obligation or the credit spread. The payoff depends on the credit spread at the settlement date of the contract. The payoff is positive (i.e., the party receives cash) if the credit spread moves in favor of the party at the settlement date. The party makes a payment if the credit spread moves against the party at the settlement date.

For example, suppose that a manager has a view that the credit spread will increase (i.e., widen) to more than the current 250 basis points in one year for a reference obligation. Then the payoff function for this credit spread forward contract would be

$$(\text{credit spread at settlement date} - 250) \times \text{notional amount} \times \text{risk factor}$$

Assuming that the notional amount is $10 million and the risk factor is 5, and the credit spread at the settlement date is 350 basis points, then the amount that will be received by the portfolio manager is

$$(0.035 - 0.025) \times \$10,000,000 \times 5 = \$500,000$$

Instead, suppose that the credit spread at the settlement date decreased to 190 basis points. The portfolio manager would then have to pay out $300,000 as shown below:

$$(0.019 - 0.025) \times \$10,000,000 \times 5 = -\$300,000$$

In general, if a portfolio manager takes a position in a credit spread forward contract to benefit from an increase in the credit spread, then the payoff would be as follows:

$$(\text{credit spread at settlement date} - \text{credit spread in contract})$$
$$\times \text{notional amount} \times \text{risk factor}$$

For a portfolio manager taking a position that the credit spread will decrease, the payoff is

$$(\text{credit spread in contract} - \text{credit spread at settlement date})$$
$$\times \text{notional amount} \times \text{risk factor}$$

STRUCTURED CREDIT PRODUCTS

Credit derivatives are used to create debt instruments with structures whose payoffs are linked to, or derived from, the credit characteristics of a basket of reference obligations. These products are called **structured credit products**. The two most common structures employing credit derivatives are synthetic collateralized debt obligations and credit-linked notes.

Synthetic Collateralized Debt Obligations[2]

In Chapter 15, collateralized debt obligations are explained. A collateralized debt obligation (CDO) is backed by a diversified pool of one or more types of debt obligations (e.g., U.S. domestic investment-grade corporate bonds, high-yield corporate bonds, emerging market bonds, bank loans, asset-backed securities, and residential and commercial mortgage-backed securities). The funds to purchase the collateral assets are obtained from the issuance of bonds. There is a collateral manager responsible for managing the collateral of assets.

A CDO is classified as a **cash CDO** or a **synthetic CDO**. The adjective *cash* means that the collateral manager purchases cash market instruments. A synthetic CDO is so named because the collateral manager does not actually own the pool of assets on which it has the credit risk exposure. Stated differently, a synthetic CDO absorbs the credit risk, but not the legal ownership, of the reference obligations. A credit default swap allows institutions to transfer the credit risk, but not the legal ownership, of the reference obligations it may own.

Synthetic CDO deals now dominate the CDO market.[3] As explained in Chapter 15, a CDO can be arbitrage motivated (i.e., "arbitrage CDOs") or balance sheet motivated (i.e., "balance sheet CDO"). Today, synthetic arbitrage deals dominate the market.

A synthetic CDO works as follows. There are liabilities issued as with a cash CDO. The proceeds received from the bonds sold are invested by the collateral manager in assets with low risk. At the same time, the collateral manager enters into a credit default swap with a counterparty. In the swap, the collateral manager will provide credit protection (i.e., the collateral manager is the protection seller) for a basket of reference obligations that have credit risk exposure. Because it is selling credit protection, the collateral manager will receive the credit default swap premium.

On the other side of the credit default swap is a protection buyer who will be paying the swap premium to the collateral manager. This entity will be a financial institution seeking to shed the credit risk of assets that it owns and that are the reference obligations for the credit default swap.

If a credit event does not occur, the return realized by the collateral manager that will be available to meet the payment to the CDO bondholders is the return on the collateral consisting of low-risk assets plus the credit default swap premium. If a credit event occurs that requires a payout, the collateral manager must make a payment to the protection buyer. This reduces the return available to meet the payments to the CDO bondholders.

---

[2]For a comprehensive discussion of synthetic CDOs along with several case studies, see Chapter 6 of Anson, Fabozzi, Choudhry, and Chen, *Credit Derivatives: Instruments, Applications, and Pricing.*
[3]The reasons for this are explained in Laurie S. Goodman and Frank J. Fabozzi, *Collateralized Debt Obligations: Structures & Analysis* (Hoboken, NJ: John Wiley & Sons, 2002), Chapter 9.

There are now standard synthetic CDO tranches that can be purchased by investors based on a standardized reference portfolio, the most common being the Dow Jones North American Investment Grade Index. Each tranche is denoted by two percentages. The first percentage is a the subordination level. Once the realized losses exceed the subordination level, the investor in that tranche realizes a loss. The second percentage is the upper limit on the credit loss with the loss expressed as a percentage of the size of the underlying reference portfolio. For example, for the standard synthetic CDO in which the underlying is the Dow Jones North American Investment Grade Index, standard tranches are an equity tranche 0%–3%, followed by a junior mezzanine 3%–7%, a 7%–10% senior mezzanine, a 10%–15% senior, and a 15%–30% super senior tranche. For example, consider the 7%–10% senior mezzanine tranche. An investor in this tranche will only realize a principal loss if there are a sufficient number of defaults for the losses to exceed the subordination of 7% over the life of the tranche.

Credit-Linked Notes[4]

A **credit-linked note** (CLN) is a security issued by an investment banking firm or another issuer (typically a special-purpose vehicle), which has credit risk to a second issuer (called the reference issuer), and the return is linked to the credit performance of the reference issuer. Embedded in a CLN is a credit derivative, typically a credit default swap.

A CLN can be quite complicated, so we will focus on the basic structure only. The issuer of a CLN is the credit protection buyer; the investor in the CLN is the credit protection seller. The basic CLN is just like a standard bond: It has a coupon rate (fixed or floating), maturity date, and a maturity value. However, in contrast to a standard bond, the maturity value depends on the performance of the reference issuer. Specifically, if a credit event occurs with respect to the reference issuer then (1) the bond is paid off and (2) the maturity value is adjusted down. How the adjustment is made is described in the prospectus. The compensation for the investor accepting the credit risk of the reference issuer is an enhanced coupon payment.

Typically, CLNs have a maturity of anywhere from three months to several years, with one to three years being the most likely term of credit exposure. The short maturity of CLNs reflects the desire of investors to take a credit view for such a time period.

SUMMARY

Interest-rate derivatives can be used to control interest-rate risk with respect to changes in the level of interest rates. Credit derivatives can be used to control the credit risk of a security or a portfolio or to increase exposure. Credit risk includes three types of risk: (1) the risk that the issuer will default (default risk), (2) the risk that the credit spread will increase (credit spread risk), and (3) the risk that an issue will be downgraded (downgrade risk).

Credit derivatives include asset swaps, total return swaps, credit default products (credit default swaps and default options), and credit spread products (credit spread options and credit spread forwards). For credit derivatives where a payment depends

---

[4]For a comprehensive discussion of CLNs, see Chapter 6 in Anson, Fabozzi, Choudhry, and Chen, *Credit Derivatives: Instruments, Applications, and Pricing.*

on a credit event occurring, the ISDA defines potential credit events. The most controversial credit event is restructuring.

An asset swap structured by a dealer firm involves an investor selling a fixed-rate credit-risky bond to the dealer firm and receiving floating-rate payments. While market participants refer to an asset swap as a credit derivative, it fails to provide protection against a credit event.

In a total return swap, one party (the total return receiver) makes periodic floating rate payments to a counterparty (the total return payer) in exchange for the total return realized on a reference obligation or a basket of reference obligations. The total return receiver is exposed to both credit risk and interest-rate risk.

By far, the most dominant type of credit derivative is the credit default swap wherein the protection buyer makes a payment of the swap premium to the protection seller; however, the protection buyer receives a payment from the protection seller only if a credit event occurs. There are single-name credit default swaps, basket credit default swaps, and credit default index swaps.

There are two types of credit spread options—an option written on a reference obligation where the strike price for the reference obligation is computed based on a specified credit spread—and an option written on a credit spread. For the former credit spread option, the investor is exposed to interest-rate risk as well as credit risk. For the latter, interest-rate risk is controlled for by including a risk factor that takes into account the sensitivity of a bond to interest-rate changes in the payoff function.

For a credit spread forward contract, the underlying can be either a reference obligation (with the contracted value at settlement specified in terms of a specified credit spread) or a credit spread. The payoff depends on the credit spread at the settlement date of the contract. One party receives cash if the credit spread moves in favor of the party at the settlement date but makes a payment if the credit spread moves against the party at the settlement date.

Credit derivatives are used to create debt instruments with structures whose payoffs are linked to, or derived from, the credit characteristics of a basket of reference obligations. These products are called structured credit products, with synthetic collateralized debt obligations and credit-linked notes the two most prominent examples.

In a synthetic CDO, the CDO collateral manager does not actually own the pool of assets on which it has the credit risk exposure. The collateral manager is the protection seller in a credit default swap and receives the swap premium. The proceeds received from the issuance of the CDO are used by the collateral manager to buy low-risk assets. If a credit event does not occur, funds available to meet the payments to the CDO bondholders are the return on the collateral consisting of low-risk assets plus the credit default swap premium. If a credit event occurs that requires a payout, the collateral manager must make a payment to the protection buyer, thereby reducing funds available to meet the obligation to the CDO bondholders. Standard synthetic CDO tranches are traded.

A credit-linked note is a security whose return is linked to the credit performance of some reference issuer who is not the issuer of the CLN. In a basic CLN structure, the maturity value is adjusted based on credit performance if the reference issuer experiences a credit event. The investor is compensated with an enhanced coupon rate for accepting the credit risk of the reference issuer.

Questions

1. Why is a portfolio manager concerned with more than default risk when assessing a portfolio's credit exposure?
2. Rating transition tables published periodically by rating agencies indicate the percentage of issues with a specific rating change over some specified time period (e.g., one year). How can a rating transition table be used by a portfolio manager to assess downgrade risk?
3. What is meant by
   a. a reference entity?
   b. a reference obligation?
4. What authoritative source is used for defining a "credit event"?
5. Why is "restructuring" the most controversial credit event?
6. a. What is an asset swap?
   b. Is an asset swap a true credit derivative?
7. Explain how a total return swap can be used by a portfolio manager to increase credit exposure to several issuers of corporate bonds.
8. Explain how a total return swap can be used by a portfolio manager to effectively short corporate bonds.
9. Why is the total return receiver in a total return swap exposed to more than just credit risk?
10. Marsha Brady is a fixed-income portfolio manager. After reviewing a research report issued by a major brokerage firm on Worldwide Global Communications Corporation in which it is suggested that within one year the firm's credit fundamentals will strengthen such that the market will demand a lower credit spread, she decides that she wants to take a credit view on that issue. Next week, Worldwide Global Communications Corporation will be coming to market with a 15-year senior bond issue at par with a coupon rate of 12%, offering a spread of 600 basis points over the 15-year Treasury issue.
    Rather than purchase the bonds, Ms. Brady prefers to express her view on the company's credit risk by entering into a total return swap that matures in one year with the reference obligation being the

senior bonds that will be issued by Worldwide Global Communications Corporation. The total return swap calls for an exchange of payments semiannually with the total return receiver paying the six-month Treasury rate plus 350 basis points. The notional amount for the contract is $10 million.

Suppose that over the one year, the following occurs:

- the six-month Treasury rate is 6% initially
- the six-month Treasury rate for computing the second semiannual payment is 7%
- at the end of one year the 14-year Treasury rate is 8%
- at the end of one year the credit spread for the reference obligation is 400 basis points

a. Would Brady enter the total return swap as the total return receiver or total return payer? Explain why.
b. What is the 15-year Treasury rate at the time the bonds are issued?
c. If at the end of the year the 14-year Treasury rate is 8% and the credit spread declines to 400 basis points, what will be the price of the reference obligation?
d. What is the cash flow paid for the year to the total return receiver assuming that the issuer makes the coupon payments?
e. What are the payments that will be made by the total return receiver?
f. What is the net payment made by the total return receiver?
11. Why does a credit default swap have an option-type payoff?
12. a. What is a basket default swap?
    b. When does the protection seller have to make a payment to the protection buyer in a basket default swap?
13. For a credit default swap with the following terms, indicate the quarterly premium payment.

Swap Premium	Notional Amount	Days in Quarter	Quarterly Premium Payment
a. 600 bps	$15,000,000	90	
b. 450 bps	$ 8,000,000	91	
c. 720 bps	$15,000,000	92	

14. Comment on the following statement: "Restructuring is included in credit default swaps and therefore the reduction in a reference obligation's interest rate will result in the triggering of a payout. This exposes the protection seller to substantial risk."

15. All other factors constant, for a given reference obligation and a given scheduled term, explain whether a credit default swap using full or old restructuring or modified restructuring would be more expensive.

16. a. For a single-name credit default swap, what is the difference between physical settlement and cash settlement?
    b. In physical settlement, why is there a cheapest-to-deliver issue?

17. How do the cash flows for a credit default index swap differ from that of a single-name credit default swap?

18. a. Explain how a single-name credit default swap can be used by a portfolio manager who wants to short a reference entity.
    b. Explain how a single-name credit default swap can be used by a portfolio manager who is having difficulty acquiring the bonds of a particular corporation in the cash market.

19. How are credit default index swaps used by portfolio managers?

20. Why is a risk factor used in determining the payoff for an option on a credit spread?

21. What is the advantage of a credit spread option where the underlying is a credit spread over a credit spread option where the underlying is a credit-risky bond whose strike price is established by a specified credit spread?

22. The manager of a bond portfolio enters into a European credit spread call option for Company W based on the credit spread widening from its current level of 320 basis points. Suppose that the strike credit spread for the option is 320 basis points and the notional amount is $20 million. Suppose also that the risk factor for this issue is 4.
    a. If at the expiration date of this option the credit spread for this issue of Company W is 400 basis points, what is the dollar amount of the payoff?
    b. If at the expiration date of this option the credit spread for this issue of Company W is 200 basis points, what is the dollar amount of the payoff?

23. The senior and junior portfolio managers of a mutual fund are discussing the use of credit spread options to control the exposure of a position in the fund. The senior portfolio manager believes that a credit spread put option should be employed. The junior portfolio manager believes that a credit spread call option should be used. Which portfolio manager is correct?

24. A portfolio manager has a view that the credit spread for the bonds of Zen.com will increase (i.e., widen) to more than the current 450 basis points in one year. How can the manager use a credit spread forward contract to capitalize on this view?

25. The following questions relate to synthetic collateralized debt obligations.
    a. What type of credit derivative is used in a synthetic CDO?
    b. Is the collateral manager a credit protection buyer or credit protection seller?
    c. In what types of assets does the collateral manager invest?
    d. What happens if a credit event occurs and how does this impact the ability to pay the CDO bondholders?

26. a. In a basic credit-linked note, how does the maturity value differ compared to a standard bond structure?
    b. What is the maturity date of a credit-linked note?

Index

A

Ability to pay, analysis of, 446–447
Absolute prepayment speed, 343
Absolute priority
    rule, 182–183
    upholding (*See* Securities and
        Exchange commission)
Absolute rate change, 55
Absolute yield change, 55
ABSs. *See* Asset-backed
    securities
Accelerated distribution
    percentage, 334
Accelerated redemption,
    399–400
Accelerated sinking fund
    provision, 161
Accounting. *See also* Book value
        accounting; Generally
        Accepted Accounting
        Principles
    method (*See* Market)
    surplus, 565–566
Accounting surplus, 565
Accreting swap, 707
Accrual bonds, 279–282
Accrual tranche, 279–280
Accrued interest (AI), 144–145
    corporate bonds, 161–162
    pricing, 31
Active bond portfolio management
        strategies, 512, 519,
        522–539, 585–586
    interest rate futures, 630–637
Active return, 515
Active risk, 515
Active strategies
    contrast (*See* tracking error)
    immunization strategies,
        combination, 585–586
    portfolio management,
        522–539
Actual tracking error, 518
Actual/actual day count
        convention, 145

Ad hoc auction system, 216
ADB (Asian Development
        Bank), 208
Adjustable-rate HELs, 344
Adjustable-rate mortgage
        (ARM), 232–233
    credit risk, 238–239
Affirmative covenants, 444
After-tax yield, 99
Agency pass-through securities,
        245–246
Agency securities. *See* Federal
        agency securities
AI. *See* accrued interest
Airport revenue bonds, 190
Aït-Sahalia, Y., 370
Akoury, Ravi, 556
All-in cost of funds, 175
Allocation
    bond, 636–637
    stocks, 636–637
Alt-A loans, 236
Alt-B loan, 236
Alternative return measures,
        593–599
Alternative (substitute)
        investments
    pricing bonds, 20
Altman, Edward I., 165, 169,
        170, 495
AMBAC Indemnity Corporation
        (AMBAC),
        192, 332
American option, 641. *See also*
        Futures contracts
American-type exercise
        provision, 733
Amortization
    bond features, 5
Amortization
    period, 337
    schedule, 5, 230, 231
Amortization schedule, 230
Amortized cost method, 565
Amortizing securities, 5, 43
Amortizing swap, 707

Analysis of covenants,
        444–446
Anheuser-Busch Companies, Inc.,
        159–160
Annualizing
    returns, 599
    yields, 37–38
Annuities
    due, 19
    factor, 232
    future value (*See* ordinary
        annuity)
    present value, 19 (*See also*
        ordinary annuity)
Anson, Mark J.P., 498, 507, 719,
        727, 736–737
Appropriation-backed
        obligations, 188–189
Arak, Marcelle, 705
Arbitrage
    collateralized debt obligations,
        350–353
    instruments/processes, 10
    model, basis (*See* theoretical
        futures price)
Arbitrage-free binomial model,
        664–668
Arbitrage-free models,
        366–368
Arbitrageurs, 440
Argentina debt crisis, 723
Arithmetic average of
        LIBOR/LIBID
        (LIMEAN), 212
Arithmetic average rate of return,
        595–596
ARM. *See* adjustable-rate
        mortgage
Arnott, Robert, 637
Asia, 219–220, 221
Asian Development Bank
        (ADB), 208
Asquith, Paul, 170
Asset allocation strategies,
        536–539
Asset-backed commercial
        paper, 178

741

Asset-backed securities (ABSs), 2, 328–329
  collateral type and securitization structure, 337–338
  creation, 329–337
  credit risks, 338–341
  transaction structure, 331
  types, 341–342
Asset/liability management
  interest-rate agreements, 714–715
  interest-rate swap, application of, 699–702
  principles, 561–566
Assets
  collateral, 349
  nonamortizing, 337
  selecting, 514
  swap, 702
    spread, 724
  type classification, 357
At-the-money options, 645
Attribution analysis, 600–605. *See also* Performance process, requirements
Auctions
  process, 335–336
  single-price, 141
  systems, 173
  U.S. Treasury securities, 135–142
Australia, 209
Austria, 209
Auto loan-backed securities, 342–343
Available funds cap, 344
Available-for-sale account, 565
Average life, 267. *See also* simulated average life; weighted average life

B

Babbel, David F., 423, 714
Backshall, Tim, 495–496
Backward-looking tracking error, 518
Bailey, Jeffrey V., 601
Baird, Douglas G., 183
Balance sheet transaction, 350
Balance test, 335
Bales, Gioia Parente, 704
Balloon maturity, 161
  provisions, 307
Balloon mortgage, 233–234
Balloon risk, 314–315. *See also* Commercial MBS
Banc of America Commercial Mortgage Series 2001-1, 308–315, 317, 319–322, 323
Bank discount basis, 142
Bank of International Settlements classification system, 10

Bank-backed municipal bonds, 192
Bankruptcy, 722
  code, 494
  corporate debt, 182–184
  recovery process, 504
Banks
  interest-rate swap program, 700–701
  investment objectives, setting, 511
  lines of credit, 454
BANs (bond anticipation notes), 195
Barbell portfolio, 577
  key rate durations, 90
  performance, 531–532
  yield curve strategy, 529
Barbell strategy, 527, 528
Barclays Capital, 217
Barone-Adesi, Giovanni, 669
Bartter, Brit J., 441
Base interest rate, 95
  relationship (*See* spot rates)
Basis, 632
  price, 203
  price value, 62–63
  risk, 632, 707
  swaps, 707
Basket credit default swap, 728, 730–731
Battery Park City Authority, 201
BDT (Black-Derman-Troy) model, 368
Bear Stearns
  cash-out refinancing, 260–263
  housing turnover model, 258–260
Bebchuk, L.A., 183
Beers, David T., 218–219
Beidleman, Carl R. (ed), 704
Belgium, 209
Benchmark
  expectations strategies, 522–523
  interest rate, 95
  portfolios, 514, 600–601
Benchmark bills, 149
Benchmark bonds, 149
Benchmark instruments, 366
Benchmark notes, 149
Bencivenga, Joseph C., 170
Bendt, Douglas L., 238
Bermuda-type exercise provision, 733
Beta, 636. *See also* yield
BEY (bond-equivalent yield), 39, 265–266
Bhattacharya, Anand K., 234
Bhattacharya, Mihir, 433, 434, 442
Bhojraj, Sanjeev, 452
Bid on LIBOR (LIBID), 212
Bid-to-cover ratio, 139

Bierwag, G.O., 581
BIG (Broad Investment-Grade Bond Index) (SSB), 516, 603
Bills. *See* U.S. Treasury bills
Binomial interest-rate tree, 389, 393–397
Binomial model, 389. *See also* arbitrage-free binomial model
Black, Fischer, 367, 368, 441, 496–497, 501, 661–668
Black-Derman-Troy (BDT) model, 368
Black-Karasinski model, 367–368
Black-Scholes option pricing model, 441, 661–668
Black-Scholes-Merton (BSM) model, 497–500
Blume, Marshall E., 170
BMA (Bond Market Association), 258
Bobls. *See* Bundesobligationen
Bond anticipation notes (BANs), 195
Bond Buyer, 202
Bond equivalent yield, 143
Bond futures, 668–669
Bond indentures, 156
Bond insurance, 332
Bond Market Association (BMA), 258
Bond performance. *See also* high-yield bonds
  attribution analysis, 600–605
  measurement/evaluation, 592–599
Bond portfolio
  management (*See* Active bond portfolio management strategies)
  managers, 440
Bond value, 443
Bond yields
  to call, 40–42
  cash flow and reinvestment risk, 49
  cash flow yield, 43
  changes, calculating, 54–55
  current, 38
  to maturity, 95
  to maturity and reinvestment risk, 47–48
  portfolio, internal rate of return for, 43–44
  promised, 49
  spread measures for floating-rate securities, 44–46
  yield to maturity, 38–40
  yield to put, 42–43
  yield to worst, 43

Bond-equivalent yield (BEY), 39, 265–266. *See also* spot rates
Bonds, 157
 allocation, 636–637
 amortization features, 5
 collateralized mortgage obligations (CMOs), 279–282, 294–295, 297
 coupon rate, 3–5
 covered, 221
 embedded options, 386–387
 embedded options, 5–6
 features, overview, 3–6
 issuer, type, 3
 market
  financial innovations, 10–11
  secondary, 9–10
 maturity, 3
 pricing, 20–27
  accrued interest, 31
  complications, 28–29
  floating rate, 29
  inverse-floating-rate securities, 29–30
  quotes, 31
 principal, 3–5
 ratings, 217–220
 sectors, 536–539
 selectivity effect, 605
 swaps, 54
 with warrants, 213
 yield, term of, 3
Book value accounting, 565
Bootstrapping, 103–105, 108, 109
Borrowers
 credit risk to underlying, 236–237
 credit worthiness, 239–240
 multiple, 316
 single, 315
Bouyoucos, Peter, 714
Brace, Alan, 368
Brady, Nicholas, 222
Brady bonds, 221–222
Brauer, Jane Sachar, 222
Brennan, Michael, 368, 442
Brenner, Robin J., 370
Bridge financing, 177
Briys, Eric, 501
Broad Investment-Grade (BIG) Bond Index (SSB), 516, 603
Broad-based market index, 553–554
Brown & Williamson, 194
BSM (Black-Scholes-Merton) model, 497–500
BTANs (Tresor a Taux Fixe et a interet Annuel), 215
BTPs (Buoni del Tresoro Poliennali), 215

Bucyrus-Erie Company, 400
Budgetary flexibility, 218
Buetow, Geoffrey Jr., 706
Buetow, Gerald W., 367
Bulldog bonds, 207
Bullet bonds, 161
Bullet portfolio, 577
 key rate durations, 90
 performance, 531–532
 yield curve strategy, 529
Bullet strategy, 527, 528
Bullet swap, 706
Bulow, J.I., 184
Bundesobligationen (Bobls), 214
Bunds, 214
Buoni del Tresoro Poliennali (BTPs), 215
Burik, Paul, 716
Burnout effect, 261
Business risk analysis, 447–450
Butterfly shift, 524–526
Buy hedge, 633
Buy-and-hold strategy. *See* commercial paper

C

Calendar auction, 216
Calibration, 502
Call date, 335
Call feature, 5
Call option, 641, 645
 bond yields, 40–42
 buying, 646–651
 convertible bonds, 441
 price, 669–672
 risks, 7
 value, 399
Call price, 40
Call protection, 306–307
Call provisions, 158–161
Call risk, 439, 578
Call schedule, 40
Call writing, futures option (usage). *See* covered call writing
Callable benchmark notes, 149
Callable bonds
 corporate, valuing, 398
 price-yield relationship, 384–385
 valuation, 383–384
Callable reference notes, 149
Callable securities, spread, 534
Canada, 209, 210
Capital, working, 446, 456
Capital Groups Committee, 497
Caplet method, 710, 711–713
Caps, 29, 399–400. *See also* interest-rate agreements
 available funds cap, 344
 collared floors, 29

Captions, 709
Carleton, Willard, 88, 110
Carlson, Steven J., 299
Carry, 627
Cash CDO, 736
 structures, 350
Cash flow ratio, 454
Cash flow yield, 249, 265–267
 bond yields, 43
 static method, 408–416
Cash flow-matched portfolios, 513
Cash flows
 bond yields, 49
 characteristics (*See* mortgage pass-through securities)
 collateralized debt obligations, 353–356
 collateralized mortgage obligations (CMOs), 277–279, 281
 corporate bond credit analysis, 454–455
 discretionary, 455
 liquidity, 563
 matching, 582–584
 monthly cash flow construction, 252–256
 one future, calculating yield on investment with only one, 37
 simulation generating, 418–419
 tests, 446
 tranches, 281
 unknown, bond price and, 28
 waterfall, 333
 yield, 249, 265–267
 yield curve, 101
Cash management bills, 135
Cash market
 coupon security, 110
 instruments, 686
Cash reserves, 247
Cash settle, 433
Cash settlement contract, 610
Cash-and-carry trade, 623
Cash-out refinancing, 260–262
 mortgage-backed securities, 257
Caterpillar Financial Asset Trust 1997, 336–337
Cavanaugh, Marie, 218–219
CBOs. *See* collateralized bond obligations
CBOT. *See* Chicago Board of Trade; Chicago Board of Trade (CBOT)
CD equivalent yield, 143
CDOs. *See* collateralized debt obligations
CDR (conditional default rate), 322–323
CDs. *See* certificates of deposit
Cedel, 223

Cell approach. *see* indexing
Cell approach, indexing, 555–556
Certificates of deposit (CDs), 143.
    See also Eurodollar CD
    futures
Certificati di Tresoro a Zero
    Coupon (CTZs), 215
CEV model (constant elasticity of
    variance model), 365–366
CFA Institute, 593–599
Chambers, Donald, 88
Champion Home Equity Loan
    Trust, 344
Chan, K.C., 370
Chang, S. Esther, 234
Chapter 11 bankruptcy, 494
Charge-offs, 342
Cheapest-to-deliver issue
    (CTD), 634
Chen, Ren-Raw, 498, 507, 727,
    736–737
Cheng, Da, 307
Cheung, Rayner, 170
Cheyette, Oren, 370, 371–372
Chicago Board of Trade (CBOT)
    interest-rate options, 641, 644
    Municipal Note Index futures
        contract, 639
    swap futures contracts,
        621–622
    Treasury bond futures, 616
Choudhry, Moorad, 498, 507,
    727, 736–737
    (ed), 211
Christensen, Peter C., 579, 588
Christopherson, Jon, 600
Chrysler Financial, 174, 179
CIR (Cox-Ingersoll-Ross)
    specification, 366
Clean price, 31
Clearinghouse, 610–611
Client-to-dealer systems, 173
CLNs (credit-linked notes), 737
CLOs. *See* collateralized loan
    obligations
CMBS. *See* commercial MBS
CMBS (commercial MBS),
    304–305, 307–308
CMOs. *See* collateralized mortgage
    obligation; collateralized
    mortgage obligations
CMT (Constant Maturity
    Treasury), 707
CoCo bonds, 433
COFI (Eleventh Federal Home
    Loan Bank Board District
    Cost of Funds Index), 232
Collared floors/caps, 212
Collateral, 29, 157, 349
    analysis of, 316–318, 446
    assets, 349
    general, 545

hot, 545
overcollateralization tests, 355,
    357–358
percent of collateral call, 335
rolling stock, 157–158
Standard & Poor's Corporation,
    355
Collateral assets, 349
Collateral manager, 349
Collateral trust bonds, 157
Collateralized bond obligations
    (CBOs), 349
Collateralized debt obligations
    (CDOs), 348
    arbitrage, 350–353
    cash flow transaction, 353–356
    early termination, 353
    market value transactions,
        356–358
    structure, 349–350
    synthetic, 358–359
Collateralized loan obligations
    (CLOs), 349
Collateralized mortgage obligations
    (CMOs), 274–300
    bonds, 279–282, 294–295, 297
    credit risk, 297
    notional interest-only (IO)
        class, 295
    residual, 295
    strips, 298–300
    structure, 274–275
    tax considerations, 297–298
    tranches
        floating-rate, 282–284
        horizon price for, 428
        planned amortization class,
            284–294
        sequential-pay, 275–280
College and university revenue
    bonds, 190
Combination matching, 584
Commercial banks, 684
    mortgage pass-through
        securities, 268
Commercial MBS (CMBS),
    304–305, 307–308
    deals, types, 315–316
    loans, 305–307
Commercial mortgage sector,
    2–3
Commercial paper, 177–181
    credit ratings, 179
    default risk, 179
    directly placed versus
        dealer-placed, 179–181
    issuers, 178–179
    secondary market, 181
    Tier 1 and Tier 2, 181
    VRDO hybrid, 196
    yields, 181
Commissions, 612

Committee for Performance
    Standards of the
    Association for
    Investment Management
    and Research. *See* CFA
    Institute
Committees, board, 451
Companion bonds, 285
Comparable risk, 20
Competitive bid, 136. *See also* non-
    competitive bid
Competitive transition charge
    (CTC), 344–345
Compound interest bond, 194
Concentration risk, 338–339
Conditional default rate (CDR),
    322–323
Conditional prepayment rate
    (CPR), 249
Conduits, 227, 330–331
    deals, 316
Conforming balance limit, 235–236
Conforming mortgage, 227
Conseco Finance, 340–341
Consolidated debt obligations, 151
Constant elasticity of variance
    model (CEV model),
    365–366
Constant Maturity Treasury
    (CMT), 707
Constant-OAS total return, 428
Consumer price index (CPI), 216
Contingent convertible
    bonds, 433
Contingent immunization, 579–581
Continuous-time stochastic
    process, 363
Contract rate
    interest rate futures, 609–610
    weighted average contract rate
        (WAC), 261
Contraction risk, 268
Conventional, nonconforming
    loan, 235
Conventional mortgage, 226
Conventional pass-through
    securities, 246
Conversion factors, 617
Conversion parity price, 435
Conversion ratio, 433
Conversion value, 434
Convertible bonds, 6, 213
    analysis, 441–442
    arbitrageurs, 440
    contingent, 433
    current income versus stocks,
        436–437
    downside risk, 437–438
    investment
        characteristics, 438
        pros and cons, 438–440
    investors, types of, 440

market conversion price, 435–436
minimum value, 434–435
provisions, 432–434
Convertibles, 198
Convex price-yield relationship, 59
Convexity
approximating, 84–86
bias, 122
cost of, 530
measures, 75–79
percentage price change, 79–80
properties of, 82–83
value of, 81–82
Cook, Karen, 331
Cooper, Adrian, 307
Cooper, Ian, 110
Copula, 504
Corcoran, Patrick, 324–325
Cornell, Bradford, 170
Corporate bond credit analysis, 454–455
Corporate bonds, 156–173
accrued interest, 161–162
call provisions, 158–161
callable, valuing, 398
credit analysis, 444–447
credit analysis and equity analysis, 456–457
default rates, 164, 165
defaults, 723
Eurobond covenants, 211
event risk, 164–167
head recovery ratings, 170–171
high-yield sector, 167–168, 168–170
issues, features, 156–161
medium-term note (MTN), 174–177
private-placement market, 173
ratings, 162–164
risk analysis
business risk, 447–450
corporate governance risk, 450–453
financial risk, 453–456
secondary market, 171–173
Corporate debt, 182–184
Corporate governance risk, 450–453
Corporate scandals, 508
Corporate sector, 2
Corporation, liquidation, 182
Cost of carry, 627
Cost of convexity, 530
Counterparty risk, 612, 684–685
Coupon, 4
due in less than six months, setting prices when, 28
leverage, 283
reset formula, 4, 167–168
risk, 521
securities, 110

step-up and step-down bonds, 213
stripping, 146 (*See also* U.S. Treasury coupons)
Coupon rate, 4, 661
Bonds, 3–5
required yield and price, relationship among, 24–26
Covered call writing, 676–678
futures options, 676–678
Cox, John C., 118, 119, 366, 441, 501
Cox-Ingersoll-Ross (CIR) specification, 366
CPI (consumer price index), 216
CPI-U (U.S. City Average All Items Consumer Price Index for All Urban Consumers), 129
Cpmarket.com, 180
CPR (conditional prepayment rate), 249
Crabbe, Leland E., 176, 177, 536–538
Credit
analysis, 162, 444–447, 456–457
credit-risk-transferring instruments, 10
default swap, 359
default swap index, 728, 731–732
enhancement, 246–248, 332–335
events, 722–723
ratings, 7, 179
scores, 240
Credit derivatives, 719–720
asset swaps, 723–725
categorization, 720
credit default swaps, 727–732
credit spread forwards, 735
credit spread options, 733–735
ISDA documentation, 721–723
structured credit products, 736–737
total return swaps, 725–727
Credit risk
asset-backed securities, 338–341
collateralized mortgage obligations, 297
Federal National Mortgage Association (Fannie Mae), 236
GSE, 152–153
instruments, 10
investing in mortgages, 236–240
modeling, 493–496
incomplete information, 507–508
KMV model, 501–502
municipal securities ratings, 199–200
reduced-form, 504–507
municipal bond insurance, 192
repo transactions, 543–544
target yield, 578

types, 720
yield and, 7–8
Credit spread, 8, 533–534
forwards, 735
options, 733–735
risk, 8, 720
U.S. Treasury securities, 98
Credit worthiness
issuer, perceived, 98
mortgage credit risk, 239–240
Credit-generating instruments, 10
Credit-linked notes (CLNs), 737
Creditor rights, 182–184
Credit-supported commercial paper, 178, 179
Cross, Graham H., 221
Cross hedging, 632
Cross-collateralization feature, 315
Cross-default clauses, 211
Cross-default feature, 315
Cross-matching systems, 173
CTC (competitive transition charge), 344–345
CTD (cheapest-to-deliver) issue, 634
CTZs (Certificati di Tresoro a Zero Coupon), 215
Culbertson, J.M., 120
Currency
appreciated, 209
default frequency, 217
risk, 8
warrant, 213
Current income, 436–437
Current issue, 142
Current LTV, 237–238
Current ratio, 456
Curtailment, 258
CUSIP number, 146–147
Custodial fees, 551

D

Das, Sanjiv, 507
Dattatreya, Ravi E., 529
De Varenne, Francois, 501
Deal step-down provisions, 334–335
Dealer-placed commercial paper, 181
Dealer-placed paper, contrast, 179–181
Debenture bonds, 158
Debt
incurrence test, 446
issuers, 98
net assets to total, 455–456
obligations
consolidated debt obligations, 151

Debt (*Contd.*)
  public credit enhancement
      programs, 189
  warrant, 213
Debt service reserve fund, 189
Debtor in possession, 182
Debt-to-service coverage ratio
      (DSC ratio), 305
Dedicated revenue bonds,
      193–194
Dedication, 513
Default
  bonds, 31
  frequency, non-U.S. bonds, 217
  intensity, 505
  interest rate, 307
  loss of coupon, 170
  loss of principal, 170
  loss rate, 170
  probability, 495
  rating, 7
  risk, 7, 400, 720
      commercial paper, 179
  time, 504, 506
Defeasance, 306
Defensive equity portfolio, 440
Deferred coupon structures, 167
Deferred-coupon bonds, 4–5
Deferred-interest bonds, 4, 167
Delinquencies, 342
Delinquency test, 335
Deliverable bond is not known,
      628–629
Deliverable options, 729
Delivery date, 610
Delivery date, unknown, 629
Delivery options, 619
Della Sala, F. Jim, 331
Delta, 670
Dempster, Michael A.H. (ed), 369
Denmark, 209
Denominator, swap rate
      formula, 696
Depew, David, 639
Depreciated currency, 209
Derivative contracts, 609
Derivative securities, 196–198
Derman, Emanuel, 368, 664
Determinants, repo rate, 544–545
Deterministic models, 584
Dialynas, Chris P., 440
Directly placed paper, dealer-placed
      paper (contrast), 179–181
Dirty price, 31
Discount, 26
Discount margin, 44–46
Discount notes, GSE, 149–152
Discount rate, 17
  all cash flows, 29
Discounted value, 17
Discounting, 17
Discretionary cash flow, 455

Distribution
  non-U.S. government bonds,
      215–216
  path values, Monte Carlo
      simulation, 421–422
Diversity score, 354–355
Documentation loans, 239
Dollar, 210
  bloc, 209
  bond, 203
  convexity measure, 76, 529
  price change, approximating,
      70–71
  price volatility, 62
  value of an 01, 62
Dollar duration
  volatility, 70
  weighting, 534–535
Dollar return
  interest-on-interest, 47
  potential sources, 46–49
Dollar roll, 543–544
Dollar-weighted rate of return,
      597–599
Domestic bond market, 207
Dothan, L. Uri, 366
Dothan specification, 366
Double-barreled, 188
Dow Jones, 731
Down-and-out barrier option, 501
Downgrade, 720
  rating agency, 8
  risk, 720
Drift term, 364–365
Drop-lock bonds, 212
DSC ratio (debt-to-service
      coverage ratio), 305
Dual-currency bonds, 212, 223–224
Duffie, Darrell, 504, 506–507, 508
Duffie-Singleton model, 504,
      506–507
Dunlevy, John N., 315
Duration
  approximating, 84–86
  effective, 83, 401–403, 413–415
  of inverse floater, 85–86
  key rate, 88–90
  leveraged portfolio, 540–541
  not as measure of time, 83–84
  option, 673
  percentage price change, 79–80
  properties, 68–69
  risk, 443
  swap, 699
  vectors, 88
  volatility, 63–71
  yield curve reshaping, 87–88
  yield curve shifts, 528
Dutch style auction system,
      141, 216
Dybvig, Philip, 369
Dynkin, Lev, 519

E

Early amortization provision, 341
Early termination, 353
Eastern Europe, 221
Eastman Kodak, 161
ECNs (Electronic Communication
      networks), 9
Economic growth prospects, 218
Economic surplus, 564–565
EDF (expected default
      frequency), 495, 501–502
Effective collar, 289, 290–293
Effective convexity, 401–403, 416
Effective date, 686
Effective duration, 401–403,
      413–415, 423
Electronic bond trading, 172–173
Electronic Communication
      networks (ECNs), 9
Eleventh Federal Home Loan
      Bank Board District
      Cost of Funds Index
      (COFI), 232
Embedded options, 5–6, 378
Emerging markets, 221–222
EMU (European Monetary
      Union), 214
Enhanced indexing, 513
Ennis, Knupp & Associates, 716
Equifax, 240
Equilibrium models, 368–369
Equity managers seeking
      income, 440
Equity warrant, 213
Equity-generating instruments, 10
Equivalent positions, 658–660
Equivalent positions, interest-rate
      options, 659–660
Equivalent taxable yield, 99
Ervolini, Michael, 325
Escrowed-to-maturity bonds, 193
Esser, Stephen F., 456–457
Estrella, Arturo, 705
Euro reference notes, 149
Euro straights, 212
Euro zone market bloc, 209
Eurobond market, 208, 210–214
      covenants, 211
Euroclear, 223
Eurodollar bonds, 210
Eurodollar CD futures, 615–616,
      644, 703–704
European bloc, 209
European Investment Bank,
      223–224
European Monetary Union
      (EMU), 214
European option, 641
European-type exercise
      provision, 733
Euroyen bonds, 210

Eurozone's Harmonised Index of Consumer Prices (HICP), 216
Evans, Ellen, 704
Event risk, 164–167
Ex ante tracking error, 518
Exceptional Dental Equipment, Inc., 329–337
Excess spread, 333
Excess spread accounts, 248
Exchange rate, 209
Exchangeable bonds, 6, 433
Exchange-rate risk, 8
Exercise price, 641
Exercising futures option, 642–643
Expectations strategies, 522–523
Expectations theories, 116
Expected default frequency (EDF), 495, 501–502
Expected incremental return, 537
Expected liquidity of an issue, 100
Experian, 240
Expiration date, 641
Ex-post tracking error, 518
Extendable reset, 167–168
Extension risk, 268, 307
External bond market, 208
External credit enhancements, 247
External liquidity, 219
External tail, 315

F

Fabozzi, Frank J., 38, 44, 86, 103, 117, 128, 149, 158, 170, 172, 183, 184, 199, 208, 234, 238, 248, 254, 274, 307, 315, 341, 367, 387, 407, 417, 424, 449, 495, 496, 498, 506, 507, 529, 533, 579, 588, 601, 622, 633, 637, 642, 660, 673, 689, 706, 719, 727, 736–737
 (ed), 86, 121, 149, 162, 164, 166, 176, 182, 200, 210, 211, 299, 331, 422, 433, 437, 442, 497, 519, 556, 558, 600
Fabozzi, T. Dessa, 584
Face value. See principal
FACO (Farm Credit Financial Assistance Corporation), 152
Failure to pay, 722
Fair, Isaacs, & Company, 240
Fair market credit spread, 496
Fama, Eugene F., 115
Fannie Mae. See Federal National Mortgage Association
Fannie Mae Subordinated Benchmark Notes, 149
Farm Credit Financial Assistance Corporation (FACO), 152

FASB 115 Financial Accounting Standards Board Statements, 512, 565–566
Fed fund rate, 616
Federal agency securities, 147–153
Federal Agricultural Mortgage Corporation, 149, 151
Federal Farm Credit Bank System (FFCBS), 149, 151–152
Federal Farm Credit Banks Funding Corporation (FFCBFC), 151
Federal Farmers Administration (FmHA), 226, 228
Federal funds, 616
Federal funds rate, 616
Federal Home Loan Bank System (FHLBanks), 149, 151
Federal Home Loan Mortgage Corporation (Freddie Mac), 149, 150–151, 227, 234
 conforming balance limit, 235–236
 credit risk to underlying borrowers, 236–237
 LTV, 259
 secondary market trading pool, 269
Federal Housing Administration (FHA), 226, 228
 prepayment benchmark, 249, 266
Federal National Mortgage Association (Fannie Mae), 149, 150, 227, 234
 agency pass-through securities, 245–246
 conforming balance limit, 235–236
 credit risk to underlying borrowers, 236
 LTV, 259
 stripped mortgage-backed securities (MBSs), 298
Federal Reserve Bank of New York, 178
Federal Reserve Banks, 616
Federal Savings and Loan Insurance Corporation (FSLIC), 152
Federally related institutions, 147–149
Feldstein, Sylvan G., 199
 (ed), 200
FFCBFC (Federal Farm Credit Banks Funding Corporation), 151
FFCBS (Federal Farm Credit Bank System), 149, 151–152

FGIC (Financial Guaranty Insurance Company), 192, 332
FHA. See Federal Housing Administration
FHLBanks (Federal Home Loan Bank System), 149, 151
FICO (Financing Corporation), 152
FICO scores, 240
Financeability of an issue, 100
Financial Guaranty Insurance Company (FGIC), 192, 332
Financial risk, 453–456
Financial Security Assurance, Inc. (FSA), 192, 332
Financial statements, 565
Financing Insurance Corporation (FICO), 152
Financing rate, 625, 628
Finland, 209
Finnerty, John D., 400
FIPS (foreign interest payment bonds), 223
First-to-default basket swap, 731
Fiscal flexibility, 218
FitchRatings
 business risk analysis, 447, 448
 commercial paper ratings, 180
 corporate bond rating, 162
 credit rating, 7, 720
 credit risk modeling, 503
 head recovery ratings, 170–171
 mortgage credit risk, 237
Fixed charge coverage ratio, 454
Fixed credit spread, 733–734
Fixed income floor, 443
Fixed-principal Treasury securities, 128
Fixed-rate, 338
Fixed-rate payer, 684
Flanagan, Christopher, 262
Flat bonds, 31
Flattening of the yield curve, 525
Fleming, Michael J., 121
Flexible Treasury futures options, 644
Floaters, HEL, 344
Floating rate securities, 29–30
Floating rate-bonds, 4
Floating-rate assets, 338
Floating-rate notes, 212
Floating-rate payer, 684
Floating-rate securities, 196–198
 spread measures for, 44–46
Floating-rate tranches, 282–284
Floor, 29. See also interest-rate agreements
 on floating-rate notes, 399–400
 valuing, 713–714

Floorlet, 713–714
Florida Power & Light case, 160–161
Flotions, 709
FmHA (Federal Farmers Administration), 226, 228
Fong, H. Gifford, 495, 575, 577, 579, 581, 601
Ford Motor Credit company, 174, 179, 721
Foreclosure rate, 237
Foreign bond market, 207
Foreign currency-denominated debt, 217
Foreign exchange risk, 209
Foreign interest payment bonds (FIPS), 223
Foreign risk and returns, 209–210
Forex-linked bonds, 223
Forward contract, 612, 685–686
futures, 612
Forward discount factor, 693
Forward rates
as a hedgeable rate, 115–116
U.S. Treasury securities, 112–116
Forward start swap, 706, 708
Forward-looking tracking error, 518
Fractional recovery model, 507
France, 209
government-issued bonds, 215
inflation-indexed bonds, 216
Franks, Julian R., 183
Freddie Mac. *See* Federal Home Loan Mortgage Corporation
Freddie Mac Subs, 152
Free operating cash flow, 455
FSA Financial Security Assurance, Inc., 192, 332
FSLIC (Federal Savings and Loan Insurance Corporation), 152
Full price, 31
Fully amortizing, 231
Fully modified pass-throughs, 245–246
Funding strategies, 561, 584–586
Funds from operations, 455
Fusion conduit deals, 316
Future value
of money, 14
ordinary annuity, 15–16
Futures
forward contracts versus, 612
leveraging, 613
options, covered call writing, 676–678
price, 610
trading, 610–612

Futures contracts
pricing, 623–627
risk and return, 613

G

GAAP. *See* Generally Accepted Accounting Principles
Galdi, Philip H., 109, 556
Gamma, 671
GANs (grant anticipation notes), 195
GARCH (Generalized Autoregressive Conditional Heteroscedasticity), 370
Gatarek, Dariusz, 368
Gay, Gerald D., 629
GDP (gross domestic product) growth, 449
GE Capital (General Electric Capital Corporation), 180
General collateral, 545
General Electric Capital Corporation (GE Capital), 180
General Electric Company, 180
General government debt burden, 218
General Motors Acceptance Corporation (GMAC), 174, 179, 316
General names, 203
General obligation bonds, 99, 202–203
General obligation debt, 188
Generalized Autoregressive Conditional Heteroscedasticity (GARCH), 370
Generally Accepted Accounting Principles (GAAP)
accounting surplus, 565
convertible bonds, 433
financial risk, assessing, 453
institutional investor statements, 512
Geographical distribution of properties, 318
Geometric rate of return, 596–597
Germany, 209
government-issued bonds, 214, 215
mortgage-bond market (Pfandbriefe), 221–222
Geske, Robert, 500–501
GIC (Guaranteed Investment Contract), 562, 588–589, 700
Giesecke, Kay, 495–496, 508
Gifford Fong Associates, 582, 585, 601–605

Ginnie Mae. *See* Government National Mortgage Association
Global bond, 208
GMAC Commercial Mortgage Corporation, 316
GMAC (General Motors Acceptance Corporation), 174, 179, 316
Gold PC, 246
Goldberg, Lisa, 495–496, 508
Goldman, Sachs, 198, 642, 685
Goldstein, Sylvan G., 190
Goodman, Laurie, 705
Governing law, 211
Government National Mortgage Association (Ginnie Mae), 149
agency pass-through securities, 245–246
conforming balance limit, 236
credit risk to underlying borrowers, 236
options, purchasing, 642
secondary market trading pool, 269
U.S. Treasury securities yield spread, 267
Government-sponsored enterprises (GSE), 149–152
Grant anticipation notes (GANs), 195
Great Depression, 370
Greece, 209
Green, K., 170
Gross domestic product (GDP) growth, 449
Gross portfolio yield, 342
Gross weighted average coupon (GWAC), 337
Grow, Brian D., 338
GSE (government-sponsored enterprises), 149–152
Guaranteed bonds, 158
Guaranteed final maturity bonds, 294
Guaranteed Investment Contract (GIC), 562, 588–589, 700
GWAC (gross weighted average coupon), 337

H

Haig, Harold, 325
Haircut, 543–544
Haldeman, Robert G., 495
Hard put, 433
Harjes, Richard H., 370
Harmonised Index of Consumer Prices (HICP), 216
Hawthorne, Fran, 557
Head recovery ratings, 170–171

Heath, David, 368
Heath-Jarrow-Morton (HJM) model, 368
Heaven and hell bonds, 223
Hedge ratio, 633–636
Hedgeable rates, 116
Hedging
  interest rate futures, 632–636
  interest-rate options with puts on futures, 673–676
  strategies, 673–679
  swaps, 177
HEL (home equity loan), 343–345
  floaters, 344
Held-to-maturity account, 565
Hemler, Michael J., 629
Hess, Arleigh P., Jr., 160
HIC (hold-in-custody repo), 544
Hicks, John R., 119
High grade, 162
High quality, 162
High yield, 138
High yield (junk bond) sector, 4–5
High-LTV loans, 236
High-yield bonds, 162, 163, 164
  corporate, 167–170
  leveraged buyout, 4–5
  original-issue high-yield bonds, 167
  performance, 168–170
Hiller, Randall S., 584
Historical returns, shifts in the yield curve and, 524–525
Historical volatility, 372–374
HJM (Heath-Jarrow-Morton model), 368
Ho, Thomas S.Y., 88, 367
Hold-in-custody repo (HIC repo), 544
Ho-Lee model, 367
Holland, 209
Home appreciation index (HPI), 259
Home equity loan (HEL), 343–345
  floaters, 344
Home Keeper Mortgage, 235
Horizon
  analysis, 54
  matching, 513, 584
  price (See collateralized mortgage obligations)
Horovitz, David S., 424
Hospital revenue bonds, 190
Hot collateral, 545
Hotels, 321–322
Housing turnover, 257, 258–260
Housing-backed securities, 345
Howe, Jane Tripp, 162, 182, 183
HPI (home appreciation index), 259
Huang, Jason, 307
Huang, Jay, 501
Huang, Ming, 501

Hull, John, 367
Hull-White model, 372
Hybrid and special bond securities, 191–194
Hybrid ARM, 233
Hyman, Jay, 519
Hypotheken Pfandbriefe, 221

I

ICON (Index Currency Option Notes), 223
Ilmanen, Antii, 120–122
Imai, Kenji, 495
IMM (International Monetary Market), 614, 644
Immunization, 513. See also contingent immunization; multiperiod immunization; portfolio
  active strategies, combining, 585–586
  liabilities, 581–584
  risk, 575–577
  single liability, satisfying, 566–581
Immunized portfolio
  construction, 566–581
  rebalancing, 574–575
Implied repo rate, 619
Implied volatility, 372
Incentive hypothesis, 183
Income
  current, 436–437
  distribution, 353–354
  economic structure, 218
  reinvestment, 6–7, 46
Indenture, 3
Index Currency Option Notes (ICON), 223
Indexing, 550
  broad-based market indexes and specialized market indexes, 553–554
  enhanced, 557–558
  logistical problems in implementing, 556–557
  methods, 554–556
  objective of and motivation for, 551–552
  plus, 513
  selection factors, 552–553
  tracking error, 554
Indonesia, 220
Industrial properties, 321
Industry trends, analysis of, 447–448
Inflation risk, 8
Inflation-adjusted principal, 129
Inflation-indexed bonds
  consumer price index (CPI), 216
  non-U.S., 216–217
INFLOS, 198

Ingersoll, E. Jr., 366
Ingersoll, Jonathan, 442
Ingersoll, Jonathan Jr., 118, 119
Initial margin, 611
Initial PAC
  bands, 287
  collars, 287
Institutional investor statements, 512
Insurance agencies
  mortgage pass-through securities, 247
  municipal bond insurance, 192
Insurance companies
  convertible bonds, 440
  mortgage, 228–229
  mortgage pass-through securities, 268
  surety bond, 179
Insured bonds, 191–192
Insurer call, 336
Intensity-based models, 505
Inter-American Development Bank, 208
Interdealer brokers, 142
Interdealer systems, 173
Interest, taxability of, 98–100
Interest coverage tests, 356, 453–454
Interest rate
  base, 95
  cap, 708
  ceiling, 708
  determinants of the shape of, 116–119
  expectations strategies, 522–523
  floor, 708
  lattice, 389–391
  liquidity theory, 119–120
  model, 389
  models, 362–366
    arbitrage-free, 366–368
    equilibrium, 368–369
    selecting, 371–372
  negative, 370–371
  nonparallel changes, bond portfolio's responsiveness to, 86–89
  risk, controlling, 630–631
  risk-free, 504
  risks, 6
  term structure, 101–122
  volatility, 372–375, 389–393, 426–427
  volatility of rates, 369–370
Interest rate futures
  bond portfolio management applications, 630–637
  contracts, 609–610
  Eurodollar CD, 615–616
  federal funds, 616
  options versus, 641

Interest rate futures (*Contd.*)
  pricing and arbitrage, 622–629
  swap, 621–622
  10-year municipal notes, 621
  Treasury bill, 613–615
  Treasury bond, 616–619
  U.S. Treasury notes, 620–621
Interest-on-interest component, 46
Interest-only hybrid ARM, 233
Interest-only (IO)
  notional, 295–296
  securities, 298–300
  tranches, 295
Interest-rate agreements, 708–715
  asset-liability management
    applications, 714–715
  risk/return characteristics,
    709–710
Interest-rate derivative
  instruments, 541
Interest-rate options, 640–641
  Chicago Board of Trade
    (CBOT), 641, 644
  equivalent positions, 659–660
  hedging with puts on futures,
    673–676
  intrinsic value and time value,
    644–646
  long call strategy, 646–651
  long put strategy, 652–655
  price, 660–661
  pricing models, 661–669
  put-call parity relationship and
    equivalent positions,
    658–660
  short call strategy, 652
  types, 641–644
Interest-rate paths, 418–419
  present value, calculating,
    419–421
  residential mortgage-backed
    securities (RMBS), 423
Interest-rate risk, 240
Interest-rate swaps, 684–708
  intermediary, 705–706
  London interbank offered rate
    (LIBOR), 684
  market development, 704–706
  rate calculation, 689–697
Interim cash flows, 627
Intermarket sector spread, 96
Intermarket spread swaps, 533
Intermediary, role of, 705–706
Internal bond market, 207
Internal credit enhancements,
  247–248
Internal rate of return (IRR), 597
  on any investment, 35–38
  bond yields, 43–44
Internal Revenue Service, 716
  municipal securities, 200–201
Internal tail, 315

International Bank for
  Reconstruction and
  Development. *See* World
  Bank
International bond market, 208
International bonds, 206–207
  classification, 207–209
  Eurobond market, 210–214
  foreign risk and returns,
    209–210
  governments, 214–220
  inflation-indexed, 216–217
  Pfandbriefe market, 221–222
  regulatory agencies, 208
International Monetary Market
  (IMM), 614, 644
International Swap and
  Derivatives Association
  (ISDA), 622, 721–723
International Swap Dealers
  Association, 705
Internet browser-based portal
  for commercial paper
  transactions, 180
In-the-money options, 645
Intramarket sector spread, 98
Intrinsic value, 644–645. *See also*
  options
Inverse floating-rate securities
  (inverse floaters),
  4, 29–30, 283
  duration, 85–86
Inverse-floating-rate bond,
  4, 196–198
Inverted yield curve, 116
Investment companies, 511
Investment management process,
  511–514
Investment notes, 149
Investment objectives, setting, 511
Investment policy, establishing,
  511–512
Investment-grade bonds, 162, 163,
  164
Invoice price, 618
Involuntary bankruptcy, 182
IO. *See* interest-only
IRR (internal rate of return), 597
Irrevocable line of credit, 192
ISDA (International Swap and
  Derivatives Association),
  622, 721–723
Issuer
  ability to pay, analysis of,
    446–447
  bonds, 3
  commercial paper, 178–179
  credit worthiness, perceived, 98
  types of, 96–98
Issuer-specific risk, 521
Issue-specific risk, 521
Italy, 209, 215

Ito process, 365
Izzobaf Corporation, 725–726

J

Jackson, Thomas H., 183
Jacob, David, 307
Japan, 207, 370
Jarrow, Robert, 368, 504, 506
Jarrow-Turnbull model, 504,
  506, 507
Jeffrey, Andrew, 368
Jegadeesh, Narasimgan (ed), 121
Jensen, Michael, 184, 450
J.J. Kenny index, 198
Johnson, Herbert, 500
Jones, Frank J., 172, 525
Jumbo loans, 227, 236, 263
Jumbo Pfandbriefe, 221
Junk bonds, 162, 163, 164
  extendable reset, 167–168

K

Kalotay, Andrew, 367, 387, 399
Kalotay-Williams-Fabozzi (KWF)
  model, 367–368
Kamakura Corporation, 496
Kane, Alex, 629
Kao, Duen-Li, 325
Kappa, 672
Karasinski, Piotr, 367
Karolyi, G.A., 370
Kaufman, George K., 575, 581
Kegler, George P., 149
Kipnis, Gregory, 637
Klaffy, Thomas E., 87
KMV credit risk model, 501–502
Knecht, Luke, 437
Kopprasch, Robert W., 422, 424
Kritzman, Mark, 600
Kroner, Kenneth F., 370
K-to-default basket swap, 731
KWF (Kalotay-Williams-Fabozzi)
  model, 367–368

L

Ladder strategy, 90, 527, 528
Lando, David, 506, 508
Latin America, 221–222
Latter of percent or date call, 335
LBO. *See* leveraged buyout
Leach, William R., 86
Lear Corp., 450, 453, 459–488
LEDUR (long-end duration),
  87–88
Lee, Sang, 367
Legal issues, asset-backed
  securities, 340–341
Lehman Brothers, 95, 198

Lehman Brothers Aggregate Bond Index, 515–516, 518–522
Lehman Brothers U.S. Aggregate Bond Index, 553–554
Leibowitz, Martin L., 579
Letter of credit, 179, 192, 247
Level of subordination, 333
Level-payment fixed-rate mortgage, 229–232
Leverage
　financeability of an issue, 100
　futures, 613
　portfolio management, 539–545
　ratio, 454
Leveraged buyout (LBO)
　event risk, 164–167
　high-yield bond sector, 4–5
Leveraged portfolio, 540–541
Levered portfolio, 539
Levin, Alexander, 370, 371–372
Levine, Robert, 444
Liabilities
　classification, 561–563
　funding strategies, 561, 584–586
　immunization
　　for multiple, 581–584
　　for single, 566–581
　swap, 702
LIBID (bid on LIBOR), 212
LIBOR. See London interbank offered rate
Life insurance company
　interest-rate swap program, 700, 701–702
　investment objectives, setting, 511
LIFFE (London International Financial Futures Exchange), 622
LIMEAN (Arithmetic average of LIBOR/LIBID), 212
Limited tax general obligation debt, 188
Lines of credit, 454
Linkers, 216–217
Liquid yield option note (LYON), 443
Liquidation, 182
　absolute priority rule, 182–183
　futures position, 610
　value of assets, 455–456
Liquidity, 563
　government-sponsored enterprises (GSE), 149
　risk, 240
　risks, 8–9
　theory, 116, 119–120
　U.S. Treasury securities, 128
Liquidity-generating innovations, 10

Litterman, Robert, 210, 525
Loan-to-value (LTV), 227, 228, 237–238, 259
　ratio, 305
LOC (letter of credit), 179, 192
Local currency return, 209
Local expectations theory, 119
Local general credits, 203
Lockout
　period, 234–235, 337
　structure, 293
LoFasto, Anthony, 588
Lognormal random walk, 390
London exchange, 210
London interbank offered rate (LIBOR), 4, 212, 343
　asset swaps, 723–725
　Eurodollar CDs, 615–616
　interest-rate agreements, 709
　interest-rate swaps, 684
London International Financial Futures Exchange (LIFFE), 622
Long futures, 610
Long hedge, 633
Long position, 610
Long put
　option, 641
　strategy, 652–655
Long-end duration (LEDUR), 87–88
Longstaff, Francis, 100, 368, 370, 501
Long-term bonds, 3, 49, 101
　hedging with puts on futures, 673–676
Lorillard, settlement, 194
Lower of cost, 565
LTV (loan-to-value), 227, 228, 237–238, 259
　ratio, 305
LTV Steel Company, 340–341
Lu, Shenglin, 109
Lucas et al v. Florida Power & Light Company, 160–161
Lutz, F., 118
Luxembourg, 209
Luxembourg exchange, 210
Lynch, J. Hank, 208
LYON (liquid yield option note), 443

M

Ma, Y.Y., 87
MAC (New York State Municipal Assistance Corporation of the City of New York Bonds), 194
Macaulay, Frederck, 64–68
Macaulay duration, 64–68, 574
Maintenance margin, 611
Maintenance test, 446

Makabe, Takashi, 183
Make-whole premium provision, 159
Make-whole redemption price, 159
Management
　expectations, 522
　restrictions, 354–355
　strategies (See active bond portfolio management strategies)
Manaster, Steven, 629
Mann, Steven V., 44
Manufactured housing-backed securities, 345
Manville Corporation, 179
Manzi, James M., 307
Marcus, Alan, 629
Margin, 543–544
　buying, 541
　discount, 44–46
　initial, 611
　maintenance, 611
　repo, 543–544
　requirements, 611–612, 643
　of safety, 454
　variation, 611
Market
　consensus, 522
　conversion price, 435–436
　general obligation bonds, 202–203
　implied rating, 502
　method, 565
　risk, 6
　sectors, 96
　segmentation theory, 116, 120
　value accounting method, 565
　value transactions, 353, 356–358
Marketability risk, 8–9
Market-broadening instruments, 10
Marking a position for market/marking a market, 8–9
Markowitz, Harry M., 551
Martellini, Lionel (ed), 496, 497, 533
Master servicer, 316
Matador bonds, 207
Material assets, prohibition on sale of, 211
Maturity
　bond yields, 38–40, 95
　bonds, 3
　date, 686
　risk, 47–48
　sectors, 101
　spread, 101
　structure of debt, 454
　term to, 100–101
Maturity value. See principal
MBIA (Municipal Bond Insurance Corporation), 332

MBS. *See* mortgage-backed securities
McCowin, Mike, 437
McCulloch, J. Huston, 110
M.D.C. Mortgage Funding Corporation CMO Series 0, 284–294
Mean-reverting square root model, 366
Meckling, William, 183, 450
Medium grade, 162
Medium-term notes (MTNs), 149, 174
  primary market, 175–176
  structured, 176–177
Megliola, Michael, 325
Menn, Christian, 506
Merrill Lynch, 109, 174, 198, 443
Merrill Lynch Domestic Market Index, 553
Merton, Robert, 497
Miller, Merton H., 183
Minimum value convertible bonds, 434–435
Mithal, Sanjay, 100
Mobile home properties, 320
Modeling risk, 400, 426
Modified duration, 65, 413
Modified pass-throughs, 246
Modigliani, Franco, 120
Monetary flexibility, 218
Money, future value of, 14
Money, time value of, 13–20, 657
Money market equivalent yield, 143
Monte Carlo simulation method, 417–427
Monthly cash flow construction, 252–256
Monthly mortgage payment, 231–232
Monthly mortgage payment, determining, 231–232
Monthly payment rate (MPR), 342
Monthly prepayment, 250
Monthly standard deviation formula, 374
Moody's Investors Service
  asset type classification, 357
  business risk analysis, 447, 448, 449
  commercial paper ratings, 180
  corporate bond ratings, 162–164
  corporate governance risk analysis, 452–453
  credit rating, 7, 720
  credit risk modeling, 503
    KMV model, 501–502
    mortgage credit risk, 237
    municipal securities ratings, 199–200
  non-U.S. bond ratings, 217
  financial risk analysis, 453

Moral obligation bonds, 188
Morel, Raymond, 338
Mortgage pass-through securities, 245–246
  cash flow, 244, 248–256, 263–265
  credit enhancement, 246–248
  dollar roll, 543
  prepayment risk and asset-liability management, 267–269
  secondary market, 269–270
  WAC and WAM, 244–245
Mortgage Pfandbriefe, 221
Mortgage-backed securities (MBS), 246
  prepayment models, 256–263
  prepayment risk, 521
  pricing bonds and, 28
  sector risk, 521
  volatility risk, 521
Mortgage-bond market, German (Pfandbriefe), 221–222
Mortgages
  credit risk, 238–239
  insurers, 228–229
  originators, 226–227
  refinancing rates, 419
  secondary market, 227
  servicers, 227–228
  strips, 298
Morton, Andrew J., 368
Mossavar-Rahmani, Sharmin, 551
Most distant futures contract, 610
MPR (monthly payment rate), 342
MSCI Barra, 370
MTNs. *See* medium-term notes
Mullins, David W. Jr., 170
Multi-borrower deals, 316
Multidealer systems, 173
Multi-factor risk models, 518
Multifamily properties, 319
Multifamily revenue bonds, 190
Multiperiod immunization, 581–582
Multi-property deals, 315
Municipal Bond Insurance Corporation (MBIA), 332
Municipal Bond Investors Assurance Corporation (MBIA Corp.), 192
Municipal bonds
  derivative securities, 196
  insurance, 192
  market, 202–203
  primary market, 202–203
  tax exemption, 98–99
  taxable, 203–204
  yields, 201–202
Municipal derivative securities, 196–198

Municipal money market products, 195–196
Municipal multiplier, 194
Municipal Note Index futures contract, 639
Municipal notes, 195
  10-year, 621
  10-year index futures contract, 621
Municipal sector, 2
Municipal securities, 187
  credit risk, 199–200
  hybrid and special bond securities, 191–194
  redemption features, 194
  revenue bonds, 189–191
  risks, 200–201
  special investment features, 194–195
  tax-backed debt, 188–189
Municipal strip obligations, 198
Munves, David, 211
Musiela, Marcek, 368
Muth, Christopher, 262
Mutual funds, 511

N

Naked option strategies
  profit/loss profiles, 646–657
  time value of money, 657
Nammacher, Scott A., 170
Narayann, Paul, 495
NASDAQ, 9–10
National Association of Securities Dealers (NASD), 171–172
National bond market, 207
National Century Financial Enterprises (NCFE), 340
National Cost of Funds Index, 232, 233
NCFE (National Century Financial Enterprises), 340
Nearby futures contract, 610
Negative carry, 627
Negative convexity, 267–268, 385, 414
Negative covenants, 444
Negative pledges, 211
Negative yield, 370
Neis, Eric, 100
Net assets, 455–456
Net financing cost, 627
Net operating income (NOI), 305
Net portfolio yield, 342
Netherlands, the, 207
New York State Municipal Assistance Corporation of the City of New York Bonds (MAC), 194

New Zealand, 209
1996 Series A Querty Income
        Debt Securities (QIDS),
        148
No-arbitrage models, 366
Nodes, 390
    bond value, 443
    value, determining, 392–393
NOI (net operating income), 305
Nominal rate. *See* coupon rate
Nonamortizing assets, 337
Nonamortizing securities, 5
Noncallable bonds, 160
Noncompetitive bid, 135
Nonconforming mortgage, 227
Non-euro zone market bloc, 209
Noninvestment-grade bonds,
        162, 163, 164
Nonparallel changes, bond
        portfolio's responsiveness
        to interest rates, 86–89
Nonparallel shift in the yield
        curve, 524
Nonrecourse loans, 305
Nonrefundable bonds, 160
Nonresidential property, 226
Non-term structure risk factors, 520
Non-U.S. bonds, 206–207
    classification, 207–209
    Eurobond market, 210–214
    foreign risk and returns,
        209–210
    governments, 214–220
    inflation-indexed, 216–217
    Pfandbriefe market, 221–222
    regulatory agencies, 208
Normal model, 366
Normal portfolio, 514, 600
Normal (positive) yield curve, 116
North American Investment
        Grade index, 731
Norway, 209
Note rate, 229
Notes, 157
Notional amount, 295
Notional IOs, 295–296
Notional principal amount, 684
    swaps, 706–707
Nozari, Ardavan, 87

O

OAS (option-adjusted spread),
        400–401, 423–424
OATS (Obligation Assimilable du
        Tresor), 215
Objectives, setting investment, 511
Obligation acceleration, 722
Obligation Assimilable du Tresor
        (OATS), 215
Observation period, tracking error
        measurement, 516–518

Occupancy status, mortgage credit
        risk, 239
OECD (Organisation of
        Economic Cooperation
        and Development), 451
Ofentliche Pfandbriefe, 221
Off-budget and contingent
        liabilities, 218
Office property risks, 321
Official statement, 203
Offshore bond market, 208
Off-the-run issues, 142
One-factor models, 363
On-the-run issues, 104–108, 142
Opening position, 610
Operating cash flow, 455
Operating leases, 454
Operation and maintenance
        fund, 189
Optimization approach to
        indexing, 556
Option cost, 399
    residential mortgage-backed
        securities (RMBS),
        422–423
Option-adjusted duration, 402
Option-adjusted spread (OAS),
        400–401, 423–424
    Monte Carlo simulation, 422
    prepayments, 426
Optionality risk, 521
Option-free bonds, 388
    price volatility characteristics,
        60–62
    price-yield relationship, 59–60
    valuation, 397–398
Options
    convertible bonds analysis,
        441–442
    currency bonds, 212
    inclusion of, 98
    on physicals, 641
    premium, 641
    price, 641
        sensitivity to change,
        669–673
Ordinary annuity, future value,
        15–16
Organisation of Economic
        Cooperation and
        Development (OECD),
        451
Original LTV, 237
Original-issue high-yield bonds,
        167
Originator, loan, 330
Out-of-the-money, 645
Overcollateralization, 248
    tests, 355, 357–358
Overnight repo, 541
Over-the-counter (OTC), 9–10,
        644

P

PAC. *See* planned amortization
        class
Packer, Frank, 220
Par asset swap, 724
Par call, yield to first, 41
Par coupon curve, 104
Par value. *See* principal
Par value test, 355
Parallel shift, yield curve,
        524, 530
Parker, Phillip D., 587
PARRS (Putable Automatic
        Rate Reset Securities)
        bonds, 148
PARS (periodic auction reset
        securities), 198
Partial strips, municipal bonds, 198
Participation certificate (PC), 246
Passive strategies, 512, 519
Pass-through securities. *See also*
        mortgage pass-through
        securities
    agency, 245–246
Pass-through structure, 274, 285
Pasternack, Brent, 165, 169
Patel, Sandeep A., 170
Path dependent, 417
Paths, interest rate, 418–421, 423
Pay, ability to, 446–447
Payer swaption, 707
Payment factor, 232
Payment-in-kind (PIK) bonds,
        4–5, 167
Payments frequency, present
        value, 19–20
Payment-to-income (PTI), 227, 228
Pay-through structure, 274
PC (participation certificate), 246
Pennsylvania Housing
        Authority, 198
Pension fund
    mortgage pass-through
        securities, 268
    normal portfolios, 601
Percent of bonds clean-up call,
        335
Percent of collateral call, 335
Percent of tranche clean-up call, 335
Percentage price change
    approximating, 69–70
    approximating with duration
        and convexity measures,
        79–80
Percentage yield change, 55
Perfect hedge, 632
Performance
    attribution analysis, 600–605
    attribution analysis model,
        601–605

Performance (*Contd.*)
  high-yield bonds, 168–170
  indicators for properties
    CMBS, 318
  indicators of potential, 305–306
  measuring and evaluating, 514
Period forward rate, 693
Periodic auction reset securities
    (PARS), 198
Perpetual issue, 212
Personal property, as security,
    157–158
Pfandbriefe, 221–222
Philip Morris, 194
Phillips, Joshua, 324–325
Phoa, Wesley, 497
Physical settle, 433
Physical settlement, 729
Pieces and strips, 198
PIK (payment-in-kind) bonds,
    4–5, 167
Pitts, Mark, 622, 633, 642, 660, 673
Planned amortization class (PAC)
  bonds, 285
    greater prepayment protection,
        providing, 293–294
    tranches, 284–294
    window, 290
Pliska, Stanley (ed), 369
PO (principal-only)
  bond class, 295
  collateralized CMOs, 300
Points, mortgage, 226
Poisson process, 505–506
Policy effect, 605
Political risk, 218
Pollack, Irving M. (ed), 200, 579
Portfolio
  dedicating, 582
  insurance strategies, 513
  internal rate of return for, 43–44
  management
    active strategies, 522–539
    interest rate futures, 630–637
    leverage, 539–545
    strategies, 510–511
    tracking error, 514–522
    yield spreads, 53–535
Portugal, 209
Positive carry, 627
Positive yield curve, 116
Post, Mitchell A., 179, 180
PPMs (prepayment penalty
    mortgages), 234–235
Predicted tracking error, 518
Preferred habitat theory, 116, 120
Prefinancing cash flow, 455
Premium, 26, 562
Prepayment, 43
  auto loan-backed securities,
    342–343
  lockout, 306

mortgage pass-through
    securities, cash flow of,
    248–256, 248–263
  option-adjusted spread
    (OAS), 426
  penalty points, 306
  protection and distribution of
    prepayment premiums,
    312–314
  risk, 240–241
  risk and asset-liability
    management, 267–269
  sensitivity measures, residential
    mortgage-backed
    securities, 416
Prepayment penalty mortgages
    (PPMs), 234–235
Prerefunded municipal bonds, 193
Present value, 17–18
  of an ordinary annuity, 19,
    231–232
  calculating for scenario interest-
    rate path, 419–421
  of floating-rate payments, 695
  payments frequency, 19–20
  of a series of future values, 18
Pressman, Aaron, 198
Pretax interest coverage ratio, 453
Priaulet, Philippe, 533
  (ed), 496, 497
Price
  change, yield value, 63
  interest-rate options, 660–661
  quotes for Treasury bills,
    142–143
  relative, 502
  risks, 118
  and time if interest rates
    unchanged, 26, 27
Price compression, 383
Price convexity, 73–83
Price volatility characteristics,
    60–62
Price-risk-transferring
    innovations, 10
Price-yield relationship, 24
  callable bond, 384–385
  Option-free bonds, 59–60
Pricing
  accrued interest, 31
  alternative (substitute)
    investments, 20
  Bonds, 20–27
  futures contracts, 623–627
  quotes, 31
  theoretical spot rate curve,
    111–112
  yield curve, caution against
    using, 101–103
Prime, 162
Prime loans, 237
Principal

bonds, 3–5
  cash flow, 354
  pay-down window, 279
  strips, 146
Principal loss test, 335
Principal-only (PO)
  bond class, 295
  securities, 298–300
Private mortgage insurance, 228
Private sector external debt
    burden, 219
Probability of default, 495
Profit/loss profiles. *See* naked
    option strategies
Property release provisions, 315
Property types
  CMBS, 318
  mortgage credit risk, 239
Proportional volatility model,
    366
Prospectus prepayment curve,
    344
Protected call, 433
PSA. *See* Public Securities
    Association
PTI (payment-to-income),
    227, 228
Public credit enhancement
    programs, 189
Public Debt Act of 1942, 135
Public Pfandbriefe, 221
Public power revenue bonds, 191
Public sector external debt
    burden, 219
Public Securities Association
    (PSA)
  housing turnover, 258
  prepayment benchmark, 249,
    250–254
  secondary mortgage-backed
    securities market, 270,
    408–410, 413
  standard default assumption
    (SDA) benchmark,
    264–265
Puerto Rico Telephone Agency,
    198
Purchasing-power risk, 8
Pure expectations theory,
    116–119
Put options, 399–400, 641, 645
  buying, 652–655
  hedging interest-rate options,
    673–676
Put provision, 5
Putable Automatic Rate Reset
    Securities (PARRS)
    bonds, 148
Putable bonds, 386
Put-call parity relationship and
    equivalent positions
  interest-rate options, 658–660

Q

QIDS (1996 Series A Querty Income Debt Securities), 148
Quality, 428
    option, 619
    risk, 521
    spreads, 202
Quality tests, 354–355
Quoted margin, 44
Quotes
    pricing, 31
    for Treasury bills, 142–143
    Treasury coupon securities, 144–145

R

Rachev, Svetlozar T., 506
Railway companies, 157–158
Ramirez, Frank, 407
Ramp-up period, 353
Ramsey, Chuck, 238, 248, 274, 407
RANs (revenue anticipation notes), 195
Rapid amortization process, 341
Rate anticipation swaps, 523
Rate duration, 88
Rate reduction bonds, 344–345
Rate/term refinancing
    component, 261–262
    mortgage-backed securities, 257
Rating agency
    listed, 7
    mortgage credit risk, 237
    upgrade and downgrade, 8
Rating transition matrix, 162–164
Ravano, Emanuele, 214
R&D (research and development) expenditures, 449
Real Estate Mortgage Investment Conduit (REMIC), 297–298
Real property as security, 157–158
Rebalancing immunized portfolio, 574–575
Receivables, 342
Receiver swaption, 708
Recessions, 202
Reconstitution, bond, 147
Recontracting process hypothesis, 183
Recovery rate process, 504
Recovery ratings, 170–171
Reddington, F.M., 64, 566–567
Redemption features, municipal securities, 194
Redemption value. See principal
Reduced-form models, 504–507
Reference assets, 359, 721
Reference bills, 149

Reference bonds, 149
Reference entity, 721
Reference issuer, 721
Reference notes, 149
Reference obligation, 721
    credit spread, 734–735
Reference option, fixed credit spread, 733–734
Reference rates, 44, 232–233, 708
Reference set, 366
Refinancing ratio, 257
Refunded bonds, 192–193
Refunding, 160–161
    yield to, 41
Regular calendar auction/Dutch style auction system, 216
Regular or general redemption prices, 160
Regulatory agencies, non-U.S. bonds, 208
Regulatory surplus, 566
Reinvestment income, 6–7, 46
Reinvestment period, 353
Reinvestment risk, 6–7, 47–48, 49, 118
Reitano, Robert, 88, 582
Relative prices, 502
Relative yield spread, 96
Rembrandt bonds, 207
REMIC (Real Estate Mortgage Investment Conduit), 297–298
Rendleman, Richard J., 441
Renewal and replacement fund, 189
Reorganization, 182
Repo margin, 543–544
Repo rate, 541
Republic of Italy, 208
Repudiation/moratorium, 722
Repurchase agreement, 100
Required rating percentages, 355
Research and development (R&D) expenditures, 449
Reserve cash-and-carry trade, 624
Reserve funds, 247
Reserve maintenance fund, 189
Reset frequency, 684
Residential mortgage loans, 225–226
    alternative instruments, 229–235
    nonconforming, 235–236
    participants, 226–229
    risks, 236–241
Residential mortgage sector, 2–3
Residential mortgage-backed securities (RMBS)
    analysis
        Monte Carlo simulation method, 417–427
        static cash flow yield method, 408–416
        total return, 427–428
    CMBS versus, 307–308

option cost, 422–423
    static cash flow yield method, 408–416
Residual interest bonds (RIBs), 198
Residual interest tax-exempt securities (RITES), 198
Resolution Trust Corporation (RTC), 152
Resource recovery revenue bonds, 191
Restrictive covenants, 190, 444
Restructuring, 722
Retail properties, 320
Return. See also internal rate of return (IRR)
    active, 515
    alternative measures, 593–599
    annualizing, 599
    arithmetic average rate of, 595–596
    constant-OAS total, 428
    dollar
        interest-on-interest, 47
        potential sources, 46–49
    dollar-weighted rate of, 597–599
    expected incremental, 537
    foreign risk and, 209–210
    futures contracts, 613
    geometric rate, 596–597
    historical, shifts in the yield curve and, 524–525
    interest-rate agreements, 709–710
    international, 209–210
    local currency, 209
    payer, 725
    portfolio, internal rate of return for, 43–44
    residential mortgage-backed securities (RMBS), 427–428
    safety net, 579
    subperiod, 595
    time-weighted rate of, 596–597
    total, 49–54, 427–428, 605
    total potential, 528–533
    total return index swap, 725
    total swaps, 725–727
Return-to-maturity expectations interpretation, 119
Revenue anticipation notes (RANs), 195
Revenue bonds, 99, 189–191
Reverse inquiry, 177
Reverse mortgages, 235
Reverse repurchase agreement, 541–543
Revese repo, 541
Revolving line of credit, 192
Revolving period, 337, 353
Revolving structure, 337
RIBs (residual interest bonds), 198

Richard, Scott F., 417, 424
Rich/Cheap methodology, 489–492
Risk
　call, 7
　counterparty, 612
　credit, 7–8
　exchange-rate, 8
　immunization, 575–577
　inflation, 8
　interest rate, controlling, 630–631
　interest-rate, 6
　interest-rate agreements, 709–710
　leverage, 540
　liquidity or marketability, 8–9
　municipal securities, 200–201
　portfolio management
　　strategies, 519–521
　premium, 96–101
　price, 118
　reinvestment, 118
　reinvestment income or
　　reinvestment risk, 6–7
　residential mortgage loans,
　　236–241
　risk risk, 9
　tracking error, minimizing, 556
　volatility, 9
Risk analysis
　business risk, 447–450
　corporate governance risk,
　　450–453
　financial risk, 453–456
Risk risk, 9
Risk-free interest rate, 504
Risk-management instruments, 10
RiskMetric Group's
　　CreditGrades, 501
Ritchie, John C. Jr., 440
RITES (residual interest tax-
　　exempt securities), 198
R.J. Reynolds, 194
RJR Nabisco, 164, 167
RMBS. See residential mortgage-
　　backed securities
Roever, W. Alexander, 331
Roller coaster swap, 707
Rolling over short-term paper, 178
Rolling stock collateral, 157–158
Rollover risk, commercial paper,
　　178
Rosenberg, Michael R., 210
Ross, Stephen A., 10, 118, 119,
　　366, 441
RTC (Resolution Trust
　　Corporation), 152
Rubinstein, Mark, 10, 441

S

Safety cushion, 579
Safety net return, 579

Sallie Mae (Student Loan Marketing
　　Association), 149
Salomon Brothers, 87
Salomon Smith Barney BIG
　　Index, 516, 553, 603
Samuelson, Paul A., 64
Samurai bonds, 207
Sanders, Anthony B., 370
SAVRS (selection auction variable-
　　rate securities), 198
SBC Dominguez Barry Funds
　　Management, 682
Schaack, Christian, 584
Schedule, amortization, 230
Scheinkman, Jose, 525
Scholes, Myron, 441, 495–496,
　　661–668
Schultz, Glenn, 262
Schwartz, Eduardo, 368, 442, 501
S-curve for prepayments, 261
SDA (standard default assumption)
　　benchmark, 264–265
SDEs (stochastic differential
　　equations), 363
Seaport revenue bonds, 191
Sears, Timothy D., 299
Seasonality effect, 260
SEC. See Securities and Exchange
　　Commission
Secondary market, 9–10
　mortgages, 227
　municipal bonds, 203
Secondary marketing profit, 226
Second-to-default basket swap, 731
Sector risk, 520
Sector/quality effect, 605
Securities Act of 1933, 178
Securities and Exchange
　　Commission (SEC)
　corporate governance, 451
　federally related institutions,
　　148
　medium-term notes (MTNs), 174
　Rule 144A (privately placed
　　securities), 148
Securitized, 227
Security, 157–158
　Eurobonds, 211
　individual selection strategies,
　　535–536
　nonamortizing, 5
　personal property, 157–158
SEDUR (short-end duration),
　　87–88
Seix, Christina, 556
Selection auction variable-rate
　　securities (SAVRS), 198
Selection factors, indexing,
　　552–553
Self-liquidating structure, 337
Self-storage properties, 322
Sell hedge, 632–633

Sengupta, Partha, 452
Senior home owners, reverse
　　mortgages, 235
Senior interest, 333
Senior percentage, 333
Senior prepayment percentage, 334
Senior/subordinate structure, 248,
　　333–334
Sensitivity measures, prepayment,
　　416
Separate Trading of Registered
　　Interest and Principal of
　　Securities (STRIPS), 146
Sequential-pay tranches, 275
Serial bonds, 157
Serial correlation, 372
Serial maturity structure, 194
Series of PAC bonds, creating,
　　287–290
Servicer, commercial MBS, 316
Servicing fee, 228, 231
Settlement, 610
Settlement date, 145
Shapiro, Arnold, 110
Sharpe, William F., 441, 551
Shifting interest mechanism,
　　333–334
Shifting interest structure, 248
Shifts in the yield curve, 524–525
Shimko, David C., 501
Short call strategy, 652
Short futures, 610
Short hedge, 632–633
Short position, 610
Short put strategy, 655–657
Short term bonds, 101
Short the option, 641
Short-end duration (SEDUR),
　　87–88
Short-term bonds, 3
Short-term GSE discount notes,
　　149–152
Short-term interest rate, 628
Short-term risk-free interest rate
　　over the life of the
　　option, 661
Shoven, J.B., 184
Silver, Andrew, 338, 705
Simple annual interest rate, 37
Simulated average life, Monte
　　Carlo simulation, 422
Single binomial tree, 713
Single borrower deals, 315
Single liability, satisfying, 566–581
Single-dealer systems, 173
Single-family mortgage revenue
　　bonds, 190
Single-monthly mortality rate
　　(SMM), 249–250
Single-name credit default swap,
　　728, 729–730

Single-price auctions, 141
Singleton, Kenneth, 504, 506–507
Sinking fund, 189
Sinking fund provision, 161–162
Six-month forward rates and spot
    rates, 115
SLGS (state and local government
    series), 121
Smith, Donald, 710
SMM (single-monthly mortality)
    rate, 249–250
SMRT (stabilized mortgage reduc-
    tion term) bonds, 284–285
Snook, Randy, 164, 166
Sochacki, James, 367
Soft put, 433
South Korea, 220
Southern Bell, 633–635
Sovereignty
    bond ratings, 217–220
    defaults, 723
S&P 500, 514
Spain, 207, 209
Special collateral, 545
Special purpose vehicle (SPV),
    330, 331–332
Special redemption prices, 160
Special servicer, 316
Speed, 249
Speed of adjustment, 365
Spot rates, 103, 112
    curve, 103
Spread, 8
    banking, 561
    interest-rate swaps, 703–704
    for life, 44
    measures for floating-rate
        securities, 44–46
    static, 378–383
        residential mortgage-backed
            securities (RBMS),
            411–413
    volatility, 71–72
SPV (special purpose vehicle),
    330, 331–332
Square-root model, 366
Srinivasan, V.S., 258–264
Stabilized mortgage reduction term
    (SMRT) bonds, 284–285
Standard & Poor's Corporation
    business risk analysis, 447,
        448, 450
    collateral, 355
    commercial paper ratings, 180
    corporate bond rating, 162
    corporate governance risk
        analysis, 452
    credit rating, 7, 720
    emerging markets, 221
    financial risk analysis, 454–455
    head recovery ratings, 170–171,
        172

mortgage credit risk, 237
municipal securities ratings,
    199–200
non-U.S. bond ratings, 217, 219
Standard default assumption (SDA)
    benchmark, 264–265
Standard deviation, volatility and,
    391–392
State and local government series
    (SLGS), 121
State and local government taxes,
    99–100
State of Illinois Chicago School
    Finance Authority
    Bonds, 194
State of New York's Urban
    Development
    Corporation, 199
Static cash flow yield method,
    408–416
Static spread, 378–383
    residential mortgage-backed
        securities (RBMS),
        411–413
Steepening of the yield curve, 525
Step-down provisions, 334–335
Step-up bonds, 4, 167, 198
Steward, Christopher B., 208
Stochastic default models, 505
Stochastic differential equations
    (SDEs), 363
Stochastic models, 584
Stochastic programming, 585
Stock allocation, 636–637
Stockholders' influence on the
    reorganization plan
    hypothesis, 183
Stonberg, William, 165, 169
Stop-out yield, 138
Straight value, 434
Stranded asset bonds, 345
Stranded cost bonds, 345
Strategic bargaining process
    hypothesis, 183–184
Stratified sampling approach to
    indexing, 555–556
Stress testing structures, CMBS,
    318–325
Stricker, Robert, 714
Strike, 641
    price, 660
    rate, 708
Stripped mortgage-backed
    securities (MBSs), 298
Strips
    collateralized mortgage
        obligations (CMOs),
        298–300
    coupon, 146
    municipal obligations, 198
    principal, 146

U.S. Treasury securities,
    110–111
STRIPS (Separate Trading of
    Registered Interest and
    Principal of Securities),
    146
Structural models, 497
Structural risks, 339
Structured bonds, 193–194
Structured credit products, 720
    credit derivatives, 736–737
Structured IO, 295
Structured MTNs, 702–703
Structured notes, 177
    creation using swaps, 702–703
Structured portfolio strategies, 513
Structured/asset-backed bonds,
    193–194
Student loan revenue bonds, 191
Subordinate interest, 333
Subordinated benchmark
    notes, 149
Subordinated securities, 151
Subordination
    Eurobonds, 211
    level of, 333
Subperiod return, 595
Subprime, 236
Sub-servicer, 316
Substitute investments, 20
Substitution swap, 536
Sudo, Toshihide, 183
Support bonds, 285, 297
Supranational, 210–211
Surety bond, 179, 332
    insurance company, 179
Surplus
    accounting, 565–566
    fund, 189
    management, 563–566
Sutch, Richard, 120
Swap dealer, 685
Swaps
    futures contracts, 621–622
    hedging, 177
    MTNs, 177
    option, 619
    position, interpreting,
        685–686
    rate calculation, 689–697
Swaptions, 706, 707–708
Sweden, 209
Symmetric cash matching, 584
Synthetic CDO structures, 350
Synthetic collateralized debt
    obligations (CDO),
    736–737
Synthetic collateralized debt
    obligations (CDOs),
    358–359
Synthetic securities, 631–632
Systematic risk factors, 519–520

T

TAC (targeted amortization class) bond, 294
Takeover risk, convertible bonds, 440
TANs (tax anticipation notes), 195
Tap system, 216
Target term trusts, 511
Target yield, 578
Targeted amortization class (TAC) bond, 294
Tax anticipation notes (TANs), 195
Tax considerations, 297–298
Tax exemption, 98–99
  commercial paper, 195
  sector, 2
Tax Reform Act of 1986, 297–298
Tax risk, 200
Taxable municipal bonds, 203–204
Tax-backed debt, 188–189
Taxes
  interest, 98–100
  stripped Treasury securities, 147
  U.S. Treasury securities, 99
Tax-exempt sector, 2
Taylor series, 75
Teaser rate, 233
Tejima, Naohiko, 501
Tennessee Valley Authority, 148–149
Term bonds, 157
Term maturity structure, 194
Term repo, 541
Term structure, interest rates, 101–122
Term structure of interest rate, 103
Term structure risk factors, 520
Termination value, 729
Thailand, 220
Theoretical futures price, 625–627
Theoretical spot rate curve, 103
  pricing, 111–112
  U.S. Treasury securities, 103–112
Theoretical value, 421
Theta, 672
Third-party providers, 339–340
32nds, 144
Threshold media effect, 262
Thrifts
  investment objectives, setting, 511
  mortgage pass-through securities, 268
Tier 1 and Tier 2 commercial paper, 181
Tierney, David E., 601
Time
  decay, 672
  to expiration, 661
  price if interest rates unchanged, 26, 27

Time value of money, 13–20, 644, 645–646
  naked option positions, 657
Time-weighted rate of return, 596–597
Timing option, 619
TIPS (Treasury inflation protection securities), 128–134
Tobacco company settlement, 194
Toevs, Alden, 575, 581
Toll road and gas tax revenue bonds, 191
Tong, Tom, 584
Torous, Walter N., 183
Total return, 49–54, 427–428, 605
  horizon analysis, 54
  index swap, 725
  payer, 725
  potential, 528–533
  receiver, 725
Toy, William, 368, 664
TRACE (Trade Reporting and Compliance Engine), 171–172
Tracking error, 521–522
  indexing, 554
  portfolios, 514–522
Trade date, 145, 686
Trade Reporting and Compliance Engine (TRACE), 171–172
Trading
  account, 565
  blocs, world bond market, 208–209
  futures, 610–612
Traditional Pfandbriefe, 221
Traditional spread analysis, drawbacks of yield, 378
Tranches, 196–198, 275–279, 349–350, 409–413
  horizon price, 428
Transaction costs, 554
Transaction structure, 331
Transaction type, 239
Transactions cost, 605
Transunion, 240
Treasury inflation protection securities (TIPS), 128–134
Treasury notes, bonds, bills. See U.S. Treasury
Tresor a Taux Fixe et a interet Annuel (BTANs), 215
Trigger, 355–356
Trinomial models, 389
Tri-party repo, 544
Troubled city bailout bonds, 194
Trust indenture, 190
Trustee event trigger, 340
Tuckman, Bruce (ed), 121
Tufano, Peter, 507
Turnbull, Stuart, 504, 506

Two-sided prepayment protection, 285
Tzucker, Robert, 217

U

Undated issue, 212
Underlying instrument, price of, 660
Underwriting standards, 330
United Kingdom, 207, 209, 211
  inflation-indexed bonds, 216
Unlevered portfolio, 539
Unlimited tax general obligation debt, 188
Unprotected call, 433
Upgrade, 8, 720
Upgrade and downgrade rating agency, 8
Upper medium grade, 162
U.S. bonds
  Eurodollar versus, 213–214
  market
    sectors, 2–3
  world position, 209
U.S. City Average All Items Consumer Price Index for All Urban Consumers (CPI-U), 129
U.S. dollar, 210
U.S. Treasury bills, 128
  interest rate futures, 613–615
U.S. Treasury bonds, 128
  futures, 616
U.S. Treasury coupons, 110
U.S. Treasury notes, 128
  futures, 620–621
U.S. Treasury sector, 2
U.S. Treasury securities, 127–145
  auction process, 135–142
  coupon securities and bills, 110
  coupon strips, 110–111
  credit spread, 98
  defeasance, 306
  forward rate as a hedgeable rate, 115–116
  forward rates, 112–116
  high-yield bond spreads, 169
  negative yield, 370
  on-the-run issues and selected off-the-run issues, 108, 110
  on-the-run Treasury issues, 104–108
  options, purchasing, 642, 644
  secondary market, 142–145
  six-month forward rates and spot rates, 115
  spot rates and the base interest rate, 112
  static spread, 378–383

stripped, 146–147
target yield, 578
tax status, 99
theoretical spot rate curve,
    103–112
yield curve strategies, 523–533
yield spread
    mortgage-backed securities,
        266–267
yields, 95
U.S. Treasury spot rate curve,
    88–89

V

VA (Veterans Administration),
    226, 228
    prepayment rate, 266
VADM (very accurately
    determined maturity),
    294–295
Valuation
    callable bonds, 383–384
    model, 387–400
    swap, 697–699
Van Deventer, Donald R., 495,
    496, 501
The Vanguard Group, 552, 557
Variable-rate demand obligations
    (VRDOs), 195, 196
Variance reduction, 423
Variation margin, 611
Vasicek, Oldrich A., 110, 366, 575,
    577, 581
Vasicek specification, 366
Vector analysis, 408–409
Very accurately determined
    maturity (VADM),
    294–295
Veterans Administration (VA),
    226, 228
    prepayment rate, 266
Vijayarghavan, N.R., 164, 166
Villarroya, Antonio, 214–215
Volatility, 633
    contribution to portfolio
        duration, 72
    dollar duration, 70
    duration, 63–71
    expected, 661
    implied, 668
    interest rates, 369–370,
        372–375
    portfolio duration, 72–73
    price value of a basis point,
        62–63
    risks, 9
    spread duration, 71–72
    standard deviation, 391–392
    term, 364
        dynamics, specifying,
            365–366

yield value of a price change, 63
Volpert, Kenneth, 552, 557–558
Volume, U.S. Treasury securities,
    128
Voluntary bankruptcy, 182
VRDOs (variable-rate demand
    obligations), 195, 196

W

WAC (weighted average contract
    rate), 261
WAC (weighted-average coupon)
    rate, 244–245
Wachovia Securities, 459–462
WALA (weighted average loan
    age), 261–262
Wall Street Journal, 161
Walt Disney Corporation, 174
WAM (weighted average
    maturity), 337
WAM (weighted-average
    maturity), 244–245
Wang, Paul C., 234
WARF (weighted-average rating
    factor), 355
Warner, Jerome B., 183
Washington Public Power Supply
    System (WPPSS), 199
Water revenue bonds, 191
Waterfall, 333
Weekly standard deviation
    formula, 372
Weighted average contract rate
    (WAC), 261
Weighted average life, 5
Weighted average loan age
    (WALA), 261–262
Weighted average maturity
    (WAM), 337
Weighted-average coupon rate
    (WAC), 244–245
Weighted-average maturity
    (WAM), 244–245
Weighted-average rating factor
    (WARF), 355
Weiss, Lawrence A., 183
Westhoff, Dale, 258–264
Whaley, Robert E., 669
When-issued market, 142
White, Alan, 367
Wi market, 142
Wild card option, 619
Williams, George O., 367, 387,
    399
Wilson, Richard S., 158
Winn, Willis J., 160
Wolff, Eric D., 170
Working capital, 456
Working capital maintenance
    provisions, 446
World Bank, 208

WPPSS (Washington Public Power
    Supply System), 199
Wrap, 332
Wruck, Karen Hooper, 183
Wu, Wei, 519

Y

Yankee bonds, 207
Yen-dominated bonds, 207
Yield
    annualizing, 37–38
    appropriate, bond pricing
        and, 28
    bonds, term of, 3
    calculation (*See* Bond yields)
    cash flow, 249, 265–267
    commercial paper, 181
    computing on any investment,
        35–38
    credit risk and, 7–8
    decrease, percentage price
        change and, 79–80
    enhancing with synthetic
        securities, 631–632
    expected volatility over life of
        option, 661
    maintenance charge, commercial
        MBS, 306–307
    to maturity, price volatility, 62
    price convexity, 73–83
    target, 578
    traditional spread analysis,
        drawbacks of, 378
    U.S. Treasury securities, 95
    U.S. versus Eurodollar bonds,
        213–214
Yield beta, 636
Yield curve, 101
    cash flow, 101
    influences on, 120–122
    reshaping duration, 87
    strategies, 523–533
Yield spreads
    municipal bonds, 201–202
    portfolio management strate-
        gies, 53–535
    residential mortgage-backed
        securities (RBMS),
        410–411
Yield to call, 41, 383
Yield to first call, 41
Yield to first par call, 41
Yield to next call, 41
Yield to put, 42–43
Yield to refunding, 41
Yield to worst, 383
    bond yields, 43
Yield value, 63
Yield-maintenance premium
    provision, 159

Z

Z bond, 280
Zenios, Stavros A., 423
Zero-coupon bonds, 4,
   500–501

call option price, computing,
   662–664
immunization, 577–578
pricing, 24
Zero-coupon Treasury securities,
   146

Zero-volatility OAS, 412
Zero-volatility spread, 379–380
Zhou, Chunsheng, 501
Zhu, Yu, 442, 584
Zurak, Mark, 637
Zurich exchange, 210